Lecture Notes in Computer Science   10678

Commenced Publication in 1973
Founding and Former Series Editors:
Gerhard Goos, Juris Hartmanis, and Jan van Leeuwen

Yael Kalai · Leonid Reyzin (Eds.)

Theory of Cryptography

15th International Conference, TCC 2017
Baltimore, MD, USA, November 12–15, 2017
Proceedings, Part II

 Springer

Editors
Yael Kalai
Microsoft Research New England
Cambridge, MA
USA

Leonid Reyzin
Boston University
Boston, MA
USA

ISSN 0302-9743 ISSN 1611-3349 (electronic)
Lecture Notes in Computer Science
ISBN 978-3-319-70502-6 ISBN 978-3-319-70503-3 (eBook)
https://doi.org/10.1007/978-3-319-70503-3

Library of Congress Control Number: 2017957860

LNCS Sublibrary: SL4 – Security and Cryptology

Printed on acid-free paper

This Springer imprint is published by Springer Nature
The registered company is Springer International Publishing AG
The registered company address is: Gewerbestrasse 11, 6330 Cham, Switzerland

Preface

The 15th Theory of Cryptography Conference (TCC 2017) was held during November 12–15, 2017, at Johns Hopkins University in Baltimore, Maryland. It was sponsored by the International Association for Cryptographic Research (IACR). The general chair of the conference was Abhishek Jain. We would like to thank him for his great work in organizing the conference.

The conference received 150 submissions, of which the Program Committee (PC) selected 51 for presentation (with three pairs of papers sharing a single presentation slot per pair). Each submission was reviewed by at least three PC members, often more. The 33 PC members (including PC chairs) were helped by 170 external reviewers, who were consulted when appropriate. These proceedings consist of the revised version of the 51 accepted papers. The revisions were not reviewed, and the authors bear full responsibility for the content of their papers.

As in previous years, we used Shai Halevi's excellent web-review software, and are extremely grateful to him for writing, maintaining, and adding features to it, and for providing fast and reliable technical support whenever we had any questions. Based on the experience from previous years, we made extensive use of the interaction feature supported by the review software, where PC members may directly and anonymously interact with authors. This was used to clarify specific technical issues that arose during reviews and discussions, such as suspected bugs or suggested simplifications. We felt this approach helped us prevent potential misunderstandings and improved the quality of the review process.

This was the fourth time TCC presented the Test of Time Award to an outstanding paper that was published at TCC at least eight years ago, making a significant contribution to the theory of cryptography, preferably with influence also in other areas of cryptography, theory, and beyond. This year the Test of Time Award Committee selected the following paper, presented at TCC 2006: "Efficient Collision-Resistant Hashing from Worst-Case Assumptions on Cyclic Lattices," by Chris Peikert and Alon Rosen, "for advancing the use of hard algebraic lattice problems in cryptography, paving the way for major theoretical and practical advances." The authors delivered an invited talk at TCC 2017.

The conference also featured an invited talk by Cynthia Dwork.

We are greatly indebted to many people and organizations who were involved in making TCC 2017 a success. First of all, a big thanks to the most important contributors: all the authors who submitted fantastic papers to the conference. Next, we would like to thank the PC members for their hard work, dedication, and diligence in reviewing and selecting the papers. We are also thankful to the external reviewers for their volunteered hard work and investment in reviewing papers and answering questions, often under time pressure. We thank Stefano Tessaro for organizing the Program Committee meeting. For running the conference itself, we are very grateful to the general chair, Abhishek Jain, and the people who helped him, including Anton

Dahbura, Revelie Niles, Jessica Finkelstein, Arka Rai Choudhuri, Nils Fleishhacker, Aarushi Goel, and Zhengzhong Jin. For help with these proceedings, we thank Anna Kramer, Alfred Hofmann, Abier El-Saeidi, Reegin Jeeba Dhason, and their staff at Springer. We appreciate the sponsorship from the IACR, the Department of Computer Science and the Information Security Institute at Johns Hopkins University, Microsoft Research, IBM, and Google. Finally, we are thankful to the TCC Steering Committee as well as the entire thriving and vibrant TCC community.

November 2017   Yael Kalai
                                                        Leonid Reyzin

TCC 2017

Theory of Cryptography Conference

Baltimore, Maryland, USA
November 12–15, 2017

Sponsored by the *International Association for Cryptologic Research.*

General Chair

Abhishek Jain   Johns Hopkins University, USA

Program Committee

Benny Applebaum   Tel Aviv University, Israel
Elette Boyle   IDC Herzliya, Israel
Nir Bitansky   MIT, USA and Tel Aviv University, Israel
Zvika Brakerski   Weizmann Institute of Science, Israel
Ran Canetti   Boston University, USA and Tel Aviv University,
                                Israel
Alessandro Chiesa   University of California, Berkeley, USA
Kai-Min Chung   Academia Sinica, Taiwan
Dana Dachman-Soled   University of Maryland, USA
Stefan Dziembowski   University of Warsaw, Poland
Serge Fehr   CWI Amsterdam, The Netherlands
Ben Fuller   University of Connecticut, USA
Divya Gupta   Microsoft Research India, USA
Carmit Hazay   Bar-Ilan University, Israel
Yael Kalai (Co-chair)   Microsoft Research New England, USA
Anja Lehmann   IBM Research Zurich, Switzerland
Benoît Libert   CNRS and ENS de Lyon, France
Pratyay Mukherjee   Visa Research, USA
Omer Paneth   MIT, USA
Rafael Pass   Cornell University, USA
Krzysztof Pietrzak   IST Austria
Mariana Raykova   Yale University, USA
Leonid Reyzin (Co-chair)   Boston University, USA
Guy Rothblum   Weizmann Institute of Science, Israel
Ron Rothblum   MIT, USA
Amit Sahai   University of California, Los Angeles, USA
Elaine Shi   Cornell University, USA
Stefano Tessaro   University of California, Santa Barbara, USA
Salil Vadhan   Harvard University, USA

Daniel Wichs	Northeastern University, USA
Hoeteck Wee	CNRS and ENS, France
Yu Yu	Shanghai Jiao Tong University, China
Mark L. Zhandry	Princeton University, USA
Hong-Sheng Zhou	Virginia Commonwealth University, USA

TCC Steering Committee

Mihir Bellare	University of California, San Diego, USA
Ivan Damgård	Aarhus University, Denmark
Shai Halevi (Chair)	IBM Research, USA
Russell Impagliazzo	University of California, San Diego, USA
Tal Malkin	Columbia University, USA
Ueli Maurer	ETH, Switzerland
Moni Naor	Weizmann Institute of Science, Israel

Additional Reviewers

Divesh Aggarwal
Hamidreza Amini
Prabhanjan Ananth
Gilad Asharov
Saikrishna
Badrinarayanan
Marshall Ball
Boaz Barak
Carsten Baum
Amos Beimel
Fabrice Benhamouda
Itay Berman
Jeremiah Blocki
Adam Bouland
Mark Bun
Angelo De Caro
Ignacio Cascudo
Nishanth Chandran
Binyi Chen
Yen-Tsung Chen
Yi-Hsiu Chen
Yilei Chen
Ran Cohen
Geoffroy Couteau
Akshay Degwekar
Nico Döttling

Manu Drijvers
Leo Ducas
Yfke Dulek
Tuyet Duong
Frédéric Dupuis
Naomi Ephraim
Leo Fan
Pooya Farshim
Sebastian Faust
Rex Fernando
Marc Fischlin
Tore Kasper Frederiksen
Tommaso Gagliardoni
Romain Gay
Peter Gaži
Ran Gelles
Marios Georgiou
Satrajit Ghosh
Irene Giacomelli
Huijing Gong
Junqing Gong
Rishab Goyal
Vipul Goyal
Jens Groth
Chun Guo
Siyao Guo

Tom Gur
Shai Halevi
Shuai Han
Ethan Heilman
Justin Holmgren
Kristina Hostáková
I-Hung Hsu
Ziyuan Hu
Yan Huang
Yin-Hsun Huang
Pavel Hubáček
Shih-Han Hung
Yuval Ishai
Tibor Jager
Aayush Jain
Abhishek Jain
Stanislaw Jarecki
Chethan Kamath
Yuan Kang
Bhavana Kanukurthi
Tomasz Kazana
Dakshita Khurana
Sam Kim
Susumu Kiyoshima
Ilan Komargodski
Swastik Kopparty

Venkata Koppula
Pravesh Kothari
Luke Kowalczyk
Mukul Kulkarni
Ashutosh Kumar
Alptekin Küpçü
Eyal Kushilevitz
Kim Laine
Tancrède Lepoint
Zengpeng Li
Jyun-Jie Liao
Han-Hsuan Lin
Huijia Rachel Lin
Wei-Kai Lin
Feng-Hao Liu
Qipeng Liu
Yamin Liu
Xianhui Lu
Lin Lyu
Vadim Lyubashevsky
Fermi Ma
Mohammad Mahmoody
Hemanta K. Maji
Daniel Malinowski
Alex Malozemoff
Antonio Marcedone
Daniel Masny
Peihan Miao
Daniele Micciancio
Pratyush Mishra
Payman Mohassel
Tal Moran

Andrew Morgan
Kirill Morozov
Fabrice Mouhartem
Tamalika Mukherjee
Gregory Neven
Hai H. Nguyen
Adam O'Neill
Claudio Orlandi
Alain Passelègue
Valerio Pastro
Alice Pellet-Mary
Thomas Peters
Benny Pinkas
Oxana Poburinnaya
Antigoni Polychroniadou
Manoj Prabhakaran
Baodong Qin
Willy Quach
Somindu C. Ramanna
Peter Rasmussen
Ling Ren
Silas Richelson
Peter Byerley Rindal
Aviad Rubinstein
Alexander Russell
Alessandra Scafuro
Christian Schaffner
Peter Scholl
Adam Sealfon
Maciej Skórski
Pratik Soni
Akshayaram Srinivasan

Damien Stehlé
Ron Steinfeld
Noah
Stephens-Davidowitz
Björn Tackmann
Qiang Tang
Aishwarya
Thiruvengadam
Eran Tromer
Dominique Unruh
Vinod Vaikuntanathan
Margarita Vald
Eduardo Soria Vazquez
Muthuramakrishnan
    Venkitasubramaniam
Daniele Venturi
Frederik Vercauteren
Damien Vergnaud
Emanuele Viola
Satyanarayana Vusirikala
Wen Weiqiang
Mor Weiss
David Wu
Keita Xagawa
Haiyang Xue
Sophia Yakoubov
Avishay Yanay
Arkady Yerukhimovich
Karol Żebrowski
Bingsheng Zhang
Cong Zhang
Giorgos Zirdelis

Sponsors

Platinum Sponsors:

- Department of Computer Science, Johns Hopkins University
- Johns Hopkins University Information Security Institute

Gold Sponsors:

- Microsoft Research
- IBM

Silver Sponsor:

- Google

Contents – Part II

Database Privacy

Assumptions

Contents – Part I

Encryption

Moderately Hard Functions

Blockchains

Multiparty Computation

Garbled Circuits and Oblivious RAM

Actively Secure Garbled Circuits with Constant Communication Overhead in the Plain Model

Carmit Hazay[1]([⊠]), Yuval Ishai[2],
and Muthuramakrishnan Venkitasubramaniam[3]

[1] Bar-Ilan University, Ramat Gan, Israel
carmit.hazay@biu.ac.il
[2] Technion and UCLA, Haifa, Israel
yuvali@cs.technion.ac.il
[3] University of Rochester, Rochester, USA
muthuv@cs.rochester.edu

Abstract. We consider the problem of constant-round secure two-party computation in the presence of active (malicious) adversaries. We present the first protocol that has only a *constant* multiplicative communication overhead compared to Yao's protocol for passive adversaries and can be implemented in the *plain model* by only making a black-box use of (parallel) oblivious transfer and a pseudo-random generator. This improves over the polylogarithmic overhead of the previous best protocol. A similar result could previously be obtained only in an amortized setting, using preprocessing, or by assuming bit-oblivious-transfer as an ideal primitive that has a constant cost.

We present two variants of this result, one which is aimed at minimizing the number of oblivious transfers and another which is aimed at optimizing concrete efficiency. Our protocols are based on a novel combination of previous techniques together with a new efficient protocol to certify that pairs of strings transmitted via oblivious transfer satisfy a global relation. The communication complexity of the second variant of our protocol can beat the best previous protocols even for realistic values of the circuit size and the security parameter. This variant is particularly attractive in the offline-online setting, where the online cost is dominated by a single evaluation of an authenticated garbled circuit, and can also be made non-interactive using the Fiat-Shamir heuristic.

1 Introduction

Secure two-party computation allows two parties to perform a distributed computation while protecting to the extent possible the secrecy of the inputs and the correctness of the outputs. The most practical approach to *constant-round* secure two-party computation is Yao's garbling paradigm [49]. It is convenient to describe Yao's protocol for the case of computing deterministic two-party functionalities, described by Boolean circuits, that deliver output to only one party. (The general case can be easily reduced to this case.) We will refer to the party who gets an output as the *receiver* and to the other party as the *sender*.

Y. Kalai and L. Reyzin (Eds.): TCC 2017, Part II, LNCS 10678, pp. 3–39, 2017.
https://doi.org/10.1007/978-3-319-70503-3_1

The protocol proceeds by having the sender randomly generate an encoded version of the circuit, referred to as a *garbled circuit,* together with pairs of *input keys,* a pair for each input bit. It sends the garbled circuit to the receiver along with the input keys corresponding to the sender's inputs, and allows the receiver to select its own input keys using oblivious transfer (OT). From the garbled circuit and the selected input keys, the receiver can compute the output.

This simple version of Yao's protocol is only secure in the presence of passive (semi-honest) corruptions, since it allows a malicious sender to freely manipulate the honest receiver's output by sending a badly formed garbled circuit. Nevertheless, being the simplest protocol of its type, it serves as a benchmark for the efficiency of secure two-party computation. Given a length-doubling pseudo-random generator[1] (PRG) $G : \{0,1\}^\kappa \to \{0,1\}^{2\kappa}$, this protocol can be used to evaluate a Boolean circuit C using $O(\kappa|C|)$ bits of communication, $O(|C|)$ PRG invocations, and n OTs on pairs of κ-bit strings, where n is the length of the receiver's input. Obtaining security in the presence of active (malicious) adversaries is much more challenging. To rule out practically inefficient solutions that rely on general zero-knowledge proofs [13] or alternatively require public-key operations for every gate in the circuit [12,28], it is useful to restrict the attention to protocols that make a *black-box* use of a PRG, as well as a constant-round parallel oblivious transfer (OT) protocol. The latter is in a sense necessary, since parallel OT is an instance of secure computation. It is convenient to abstract away from the use of an actual OT sub-protocol by casting protocols in the *OT-hybrid* model, where the parties can invoke an ideal OT oracle. This is justified by the fact that the cost of implementing the OTs is typically not an efficiency bottleneck.[2] In the following, we will refer to a protocol that only makes a black-box use of a PRG (or a stronger "symmetric" primitive)[3] and OT (either a parallel OT protocol or an ideal OT oracle) as a *black-box protocol.* Yao's passively secure protocol is black-box in this sense.

Lindell and Pinkas [35] (following [39]) presented the first constant-round black-box protocol that achieves simulation-based security against active adversaries. Their protocol replaces expensive (and non-black-box) zero-knowledge proofs by an ad-hoc use of a "cut-and-choose" technique. Since then, a large body of works attempted to improve the efficiency of such protocols both

---

[1] Garbled circuits are often described and implemented using a pseudo-random function (PRF) $F : \{0,1\}^\kappa \times \{0,1\}^\kappa \to \{0,1\}^\kappa$ instead of a length doubling PRG G. Since G can be implemented via two calls to F but the converse direction is not known, formulating positive (asymptotic) results in terms of the number of PRG calls makes them stronger.

[2] The number of OTs used by such protocols is typically smaller than the circuit size. Moreover, the cost of a large number of OTs can be amortized via efficient OT extension [17,29].

[3] It is sometimes helpful to replace the PRG by a stronger symmetric primitive, such as symmetric encryption, a correlation-robust hash function [17], or even a random oracle. While the main question we consider was open even when the use of such stronger symmetric primitives is allowed, our main asymptotic results only require a PRG.

asymptotically and concretely (see, e.g., [19,42,47,48] and references therein). The main goal of the present work is to minimize the asymptotic communication complexity of this type of protocols.

In protocols that rely on the "cut-and-choose" technique, the sender sends $O(s)$ independent copies of the garbled circuit, for some statistical parameter s, following which a subset chosen by the receiver is opened to demonstrate correctness. The parameters in this approach have been sharpened, and the best protocols can achieve sender simulation error of 2^{-s} using only s copies [15,34]. However, the multiplicative communication overhead[4] in all these protocols over Yao's protocol is at least s, and similarly the cryptographic cost involves at least $\Omega(s)$ PRG calls per gate, compared to $O(1)$ in Yao's protocol. Using a different technique (see Sect. 1.2), the asymptotic communication overhead has been improved to $\mathsf{polylog}(s)$ [19,20], at the cost of relying on heavy "non-cryptographic" machinery (that includes linear-time encodable error-correcting codes and routing networks) and poor concrete efficiency.

Towards minimizing the overhead of security in the presence of active adversaries, another line of works analyzed the *amortized* setting, where multiple evaluations of the same circuit are conducted by the two parties [16,38,42,44]. In this setting, a recent work of Nielsen and Orlandi [42] shows how to protect Yao's protocol against active adversaries with only a constant (amortized) multiplicative communication overhead. Besides relying on a collision-resistant hash-function (or even private information retrieval schemes for functions with large inputs), the main caveat is that this approach only applies in the case of multiple circuit evaluations, and moreover the number of evaluations must be bigger than the size of the circuit.

Finally, a recent work of Wang et al. [48] obtains an actively secure version of Yao's protocol that can be instantiated to have constant communication overhead in the OT-hybrid model. Unfortunately, this protocol requires $\Omega(\kappa)$ separate *bit-OT* invocations for each gate of the circuit. As a result, its black-box implementation in the plain model has $\tilde{\Omega}(\kappa)$ communication overhead over Yao's protocol.[5] A similar overhead applies to the computational cost in the plain model. We note that even in the bit-OT hybrid, the constant-overhead variant

---

[4] Following the common convention in the secure computation literature, the multiplicative overhead considers the typical case where the circuit is (polynomially) bigger than the input length and the security parameter, and ignores low-order additive terms that are asymptotically dominated by the circuit size when the circuit size is a sufficiently large polynomial in the other parameters. Concretely, when we say that the asymptotic multiplicative overhead is $c(s)$, we mean that the communication complexity can be bounded by $c(s) \cdot O(\kappa|C|) + |C|^\epsilon \cdot \mathsf{poly}(n, s, \kappa)$ for every constant $\epsilon > 0$.

[5] There are no known protocols for realizing many instances of bit-OT in the plain model with less than $\tilde{\Omega}(\kappa)$ bits per instance, except via a heavy use of public-key cryptography for each OT instance [5,23] or polynomial-stretch local PRGs [22]. This is true even for passively secure bit-OT, even in the random oracle model, and even when using the best known OT extension techniques [17,32].

of [48] inherits from [7,25] the use of heavy tools such as algebraic geometric codes, and has poor concrete efficiency.

To conclude, prior to the present work there was no constant-round actively secure protocol that makes a black-box use of oblivious transfer and symmetric primitives and has a constant communication overhead over Yao's protocol in plain model. This state of affairs leaves the following question open:

> *What is the best achievable communication overhead of constant-round "black-box" actively secure two-party protocols* in the plain model *compared to Yao's passively secure protocol? In particular, is constant multiplicative overhead achievable?*

As discussed above, it will be convenient to consider this question in the OT-hybrid model. To ensure relevance to the plain model we will only consider a "κ-bit string-OT" hybrid, where each ideal OT is used to transfer a string whose length is at least κ (a computational security parameter) and the communication cost also includes the communication with the OT oracle.

As a secondary goal, we will also be interested in minimizing the *computational overhead*. The computational cost of Yao's protocol is dominated by a constant number of PRG calls per gate.

1.1   Our Results

Our main result is an affirmative answer to the question of actively secure garbled circuits with constant communication overhead. This is captured by the following theorem.

Theorem 1.1 (Informal). *Let κ denote a computational security parameter, s a statistical security parameter, and n the length of the shorter input. Then, for any constant $\epsilon > 0$, there exists an actively secure constant-round two-party protocol Π_C for evaluating a Boolean circuit C with the following efficiency features (ignoring lower order additive terms):*

- *It uses $O(\kappa \cdot |C|)$ bits of communication;*
- *It makes $O(|C|)$ black-box calls to a length-doubling PRG of seed length κ;*
- *It makes $n + O(s \cdot |C|^\epsilon)$ calls to κ-bit string OT oracle, or alternatively $(n + |C|^\epsilon) \cdot \mathsf{poly}(\kappa)$ calls to any (parallel, constant-round) bit-OT protocol in the plain model, assuming explicit constant-degree polynomially unbalanced unique-neighbor expanders.[6]*

Concrete Efficiency. The above result is focused on optimizing the asymptotic communication complexity while using a small number of OTs. We also present

---

[6] This assumption is needed for the existence of polynomial-stretch local s-wise PRGs. It is a mild assumption (arguably more so than standard cryptographic assumptions) that can be instantiated heuristically (see, e.g., [2,22,40]). One can dispense with this assumption by allowing $O(|C|)$ OTs of κ-bit strings, or using a stronger symmetric primitive such as a correlation-robust hash function.

a second variant of the main result which is geared towards concrete efficiency. In this variant we do not attempt to minimize the number of string OTs, but only attempt to minimize the complexity in the κ-bit string-OT hybrid. Efficient OT extension techniques [17,29] can be used to get a similar complexity in the plain model. An additional advantage of the second variant is that it avoids the heavy machinery of linear-time encodable error-correcting codes and AG codes that are used in the first variant. Eliminating the use of AG codes makes the protocol realizable with polylogarithmic *computational* overhead compared to Yao's protocol (as opposed to $\Omega(s)$ computational overhead in the first variant, which is incurred by applying the encoding of an AG code on a message of length $\Omega(s)$).

Optimizing our second variant, we get better concrete communication complexity than the best previous protocols. For instance, for computational security $\kappa = 128$ and statistical security $s = 40$ and sufficiently large circuits, our multiplicative communication overhead is roughly 7 (compared to 40 in optimized cut-and-choose and roughly 10 in [48]). Similarly to [48], our technique is compatible with the standard Free XOR garbled circuit optimization [33], but not with the "half-gate" optimization from [50]. Thus, for a fair comparison with the best passively secure cut-and-choose based protocols in the random oracle model, our overhead should be multiplied by 2. We leave the question of combining our technique with half-gate optimizations for future work.

For the case of evaluating a single AES circuit, the communication complexity of our optimized protocol is 3.39 MB, roughly half of that of [48]. Our concrete efficiency advantages are even bigger when choosing bigger values of s. This is needed for the non-interactive setting discussed below. See Sect. 6.2 (and also Sect. 1.3) for a detailed concrete analysis of this variant of our construction and comparison with the concrete efficiency of other recent protocols.

We note that, similarly to the protocol from [48], the second variant of our protocol is particularly attractive in the offline-online setting. In this setting, the overhead of handling active adversaries is mainly restricted to an input-independent offline phase, where the concrete cost of the online phase is comparable to the passively secure variant. Moreover, the amount of data the receiver needs to store following the offline phase is comparable to a single garbled circuit. This should be contrasted with (single-instance) cut-and-choose based protocols, where only roughly half of the factor-s multiplicative communication overhead can be moved to an offline phase [38].

Another useful feature of our protocol is that, following a function-independent preprocessing, it can be made *non-interactive* in the sense of [20] by using the Fiat-Shamir heuristic. In the non-interactive variant, the receiver can post an "encryption" of its input and go offline, allowing the sender to evaluate a circuit C on the inputs by sending a single message to the receiver. The protocol from [48] cannot be made non-interactive in this sense.

1.2 Our Techniques

At a high level, our results combine the following main techniques. First, to break the cut-and-choose barrier we apply an authenticated variant of the garbled circuit construction, as was previously done in [20,48]. To eliminate selective failure attacks by a malicious sender, we apply the multiparty circuit garbling technique of Beaver, Micali, and Rogaway (BMR) [3], which was used for a similar purpose in the two-party protocols of [37,48]. Finally, we crucially rely on a new "certified oblivious transfer" protocol to prove in zero-knowledge that pairs of strings transmitted via OT satisfy a global relation, providing a more efficient alternative to a similar protocol from [20].

We now give a more detailed account of our techniques. Our starting point is the work of Ishai, Kushilevitz, Ostrovsky, Prabhakaran, and Sahai [20] (IKOPS), which obtained a "non-interactive" black-box protocol with polylogarithmic communication overhead. More concretely, the IKOPS protocol only makes use of parallel OTs and a single additional message from the sender to the receiver, and its communication complexity is $\mathsf{polylog}(s) \cdot \kappa$ bits per gate. On a high-level, the IKOPS protocol for a functionality circuit $\mathcal{F}$ can be broken into the following three non-interactive reductions.

1. **Reducing $\mathcal{F}$ to an NC^0 functionality $\widehat{\mathcal{F}}$.** The first step is to securely reduce the computation of $\mathcal{F}$ to a single invocation of a related NC^0 functionality $\widehat{\mathcal{F}}$ whose output length is $O(\kappa \cdot |\mathcal{F}|)$. The functionality $\widehat{\mathcal{F}}$ takes from the sender a pair of keys for each wire and the purported PRG outputs on these keys. It also takes from the receiver a secret key that is used to authenticate the information provided by the sender. Note that $\widehat{\mathcal{F}}$ is non-cryptographic and cannot check that the given PRG outputs are consistent with the inputs. However, the authentication ensures that the output of $\widehat{\mathcal{F}}$ obtained by the receiver commits the sender to unique values. If the receiver detects an inconsistency with the authentication information during the garbled circuit evaluation, it aborts. The protocol for $\mathcal{F}$ only invokes $\widehat{\mathcal{F}}$ once, and only makes a black-box use of the given PRG. In fact, two variants of this reduction are suggested in [20]: one where $\widehat{\mathcal{F}}$ authenticates every PRG output provided by the sender, and one where only the color bits are authenticated.
2. **Reducing $\widehat{\mathcal{F}}$ to certified OT.** The second step is an information-theoretic protocol for $\widehat{\mathcal{F}}$ using an ideal *certified oblivious transfer* (COT) oracle, namely a parallel OT oracle in which the receiver is assured that the pairs of transmitted strings (which also include strings it does not receive) satisfy some global predicate. Such a protocol is obtained in two steps: (1) Start with a non-interactive protocol for $\widehat{\mathcal{F}}$ using a standard parallel OT oracle, where the protocol is only secure in the presence of a passive sender and an active receiver. (This is equivalent to an information-theoretic projective garbling scheme [4] or decomposable randomized encoding [22] for $\widehat{\mathcal{F}}$.) (2) Use the COT oracle to enforce honest behavior of the sender.
3. **Reducing certified OT to parallel OT.** The third step is an information-theoretic protocol for COT using parallel OTs. This step is implemented using

a variant of the "MPC-in-the-head" approach of [21], using a virtual MPC protocol in which each transmitted OT string is received by a different party, and an honest majority of servers is used to guarantee global consistency. The COT protocol is inherently susceptible to a benign form of input-dependent selective failure attacks, but these can be eliminated at a relatively low cost by using a local randomization technique [20,31,35].

The main instance of the IKOPS protocol is based on the first variant of $\widehat{\mathcal{F}}$, which authenticates the PRG outputs. This protocol has a polylog(s) communication overhead that comes from two sources. First, the implementation of $\mathcal{F}$ given $\widehat{\mathcal{F}}$ (Step 1 above) is subject to selective failure attacks by a malicious sender. These attacks make the receiver abort if some *disjunctive* predicate of the wire values is satisfied. (The second variant of $\widehat{\mathcal{F}}$ from [20] is subject to more complex selective failure predicates, and hence is not used for the main result.) Such a disjunctive selective failure is eliminated in [19,20] by using leakage-resilient circuits, which incur a polylogarithmic overhead. We eliminate this overhead by defining an alternative NC^0 functionality $\widehat{\mathcal{F}}$ that introduces a BMR-style randomization of the wire labels (as done in [37,48], but using the first variant of $\widehat{\mathcal{F}}$ from [20]). This requires $\widehat{\mathcal{F}}$ to take $O(|C|)$ random bits from the receiver, which results in the protocol using $O(|C|)$ OTs of $O(\kappa)$-bit strings. To reduce the number of OTs, we use a local s-wise PRG [40] to make the receiver's input to $\widehat{\mathcal{F}}$ small while still ensuring that the probability of the receiver detecting failure is essentially independent of its secret input. We note that the reduction in the number of OTs is essential in order to get a protocol with constant communication overhead in *the plain model* by using only a (parallel) bit-OT protocol and a PRG in a black box way.

Another source of polylogarithmic overhead in [20] comes from the COT construction, which relies on perfectly secure honest-majority MPC protocols. The best known protocols of this type have a polylogarithmic communication overhead [9]. Our approach for reducing this overhead is to obtain an interactive variant of COT that can rely on any *statistically secure* honest-majority MPC protocol, and in particular on ones with constant communication overhead [7,8,26]. Our new COT protocol extends in a natural way the recent MPC-based zero-knowledge protocol from [1].

The first variant of our protocol uses the above COT protocol for a consistency predicate defined by Boolean circuits. As in [20], these boolean circuits employ information-theoretic MACs based on linear-time encodable codes [46]. To compute such a predicate with constant communication overhead, we rely on statistical honest-majority MPC based on algebraic geometric codes [7,21]. This results in poor concrete efficiency and $\Omega(s)$ computational overhead.

The second variant of our protocol eliminates the above heavy machinery and obtains good concrete efficiency by making the following two changes: (1) using the second variant of the NC^0 functionality $\widehat{\mathcal{F}}$ for Step 1; (2) applying COT for a predicate defined by an *arithmetic* circuit over a field of size $2^{O(s)}$. The latter change allows us to use simpler honest-majority MPC protocols for *arithmetic* circuits over large fields. Such protocols are simpler than their Boolean analogues and have better concrete efficiency (see [26], Appendix C, and [1]). Another advantage is polylogarithmic computational overhead. A disadvantage of this approach is that the corresponding functionality $\widehat{\mathcal{F}}$ does not allow us to use an s-wise PRG for reducing the number of OTs. As a result, the protocol requires $O(|C|)$ OTs of $O(\kappa)$-bit strings.

1.3   Comparison with Wang et al. [48]

The recent results of [48] are the most relevant to our work. Like the second variant of our protocol, the protocol from [48] uses a combination of: (1) an "authenticated garbled circuit functionality" which is similar to the second variant from [20] that only authenticates the color bits, and (2) a BMR-style randomization to defeat selective failure attacks. (In contrast, the first variant of our protocol that we use to get our main asymptotic results relies on the first variant of the functionality from [20] that authenticates the entire PRG outputs, since in this variant the selective failure predicate is simple.) The main difference between the second variant of our protocol and the protocol from [48] is in how the NC^0 functionality $\widehat{\mathcal{F}}$ is securely realized against active adversaries. While the work of [48] uses a "GMW-style" interactive protocol for realizing $\widehat{\mathcal{F}}$, we rely on the non-interactive COT-based approach of IKOPS [20].

In slightly more detail, the protocol of [48] for evaluating $\widehat{\mathcal{F}}$ first creates a large number of authenticated "AND triples" using a variant of the "TinyOT" protocol [41]. Then, using the AND triples, the parties securely compute $\widehat{\mathcal{F}}$. This protocol, which follows an optimized cut-and-choose approach, has $\Omega(s/\log|C|)$ communication overhead. Alternatively, [48] also propose using a protocol from [25] to make the communication overhead constant, but this only holds in the bit-OT hybrid model that cannot be instantiated in the plain model in our black-box model and leads to prohibitive concrete overhead. In contrast, our protocols realize $\widehat{\mathcal{F}}$ using a passively secure non-interactive protocol in the κ-bit OT-hybrid, and apply an improved implementation of COT to achieve security against active adversaries with constant communication overhead. The good concrete efficiency of the second variant of our protocol is inherited from a careful implementation of the passively secure protocol for $\widehat{\mathcal{F}}$ and a sublinear-communication implementation of COT (Table 1).

Table 1. Total concrete communication cost of computing a single instance of AES circuit with $\kappa = 128$ and $s = 40$. The data about [43,48] was obtained from [48].

Protocol	Total comm.
[43]	15.12 MB
[48]	6.29 MB
This work	3.39 MB

2   Preliminaries

We assume functions to be represented by a Boolean circuit C (with AND, OR, XOR gates of fan-in 2 and NOT gates), and denote the size of C by $|C|$. By default we define the size to include the total number of gates, excluding NOT gates but including input gates. In the context of protocols that employ the FreeXOR garbled circuit optimization [33], the size does not include XOR gates.

We use a standard notion of secure two-party computation in the standalone model, in the presence of static, adaptive corruptions. See Appendix A for details.

2.1   Local s-Wise PRGs

An s-wise pseudorandom generator (PRG) $G_{sPRG} : \{0,1\}^\delta \mapsto \{0,1\}^n$ satisfies the property that for a random r the bits in $G_{sPRG}(r)$ are s-wise independent, in the sense that their projection to any s coordinates is a uniformly random s-bit string. Standard constructions of such PRGs exist based on random $(s-1)$-degree polynomials in a finite field. In our work, we will require s-wise PRGs that additionally have the property of being computed by an NC^0 circuit, namely ones where every output bit depends on a constant number of input bits. Such "local" s-wise PRGs can be based on unique-neighbor bipartite expander graphs [40].

In more detail, consider a bipartite expander graph with left degree d, such that any subset of $v \leq s$ vertices on the left has at least $\frac{3}{4}vd$ neighbors on the right. Then we associate every left vertex with an output bit and every right vertex with an input bit. An s-wise PRG can now be obtained setting an output bit as the XOR of its neighbors. If we further assume that the bipartite graph has constant-degree d for the left vertices, we obtain an s-wise PRG that can be computed by an NC^0 circuit.

Some of our results require an s-wise PRGs with polynomial stretch. Concretely, for every $0 < \epsilon < 1$ we need an explicit NC^0 construction of an s-wise PRG G_{sPRG} from $\delta = O(n^\epsilon + s)$ to n bits. (In fact, $\delta = O(n^\epsilon) + s^{O(1)}$ would suffice for obtaining slightly weaker but qualitatively similar results.) Expander graphs with the corresponding parameters are known to exist, and in fact a random graphs has the required expansion property with high probability (cf. [19], Theorem 2). While no provable explicit constructions are known, assuming the existence of such an explicit construction (e.g., by using the binary expansion of π) can be viewed as a mild assumption compared to standard cryptographic assumptions. Some of our results rely such an assumption, which is necessary for the existence of explicit polynomial-stretch local PRGs. See, e.g.,[2,22] for further discussion.

2.2   Message Authentication Codes

Simple MAC for a Single Bit. Our first construction for message space $\{0,1\}$ is a trivial MAC that picks two random strings $\{\sigma_0, \sigma_1\}$ as the key and assigns σ_b as the MAC for bit $b \in \{0,1\}$.

Low-Depth MAC for Strings. We consider a second MAC that will allow for a sender to authenticate a κ-bit string via a secure computation of an NC^0 function to a receiver holding the MAC key. It is easy to see that if the MAC itself is computable in NC^0 then it can only have a constant soundness error. To overcome this barrier, we follow the approach of [20,22] where the message to be authenticated is first locally encoded. Since the NC^0 computation cannot compute the encoding, we will require from the sender to provide the encoding to the NC^0 functionality along with a proof, where both the MAC computation given the encoding and the proof verification are done in NC^0. We will additionally require that the encoding procedure be efficient, since the proof verification circuit size grows with the encoding circuit size. By relying on Spielman's codes [46], we obtain an asymptotically optimal code that can be encoded by linear-size circuits. More formally, such codes imply that there exist constants $\ell_{lin}, \ell_{out}, \ell_{key}$ such that for every length κ, there exists an explicit linear-size circuit $Enc_{lin} : \{0,1\}^\kappa \to \{0,1\}^{\ell_{lin}\kappa}$ and an NC^0 function family $\{MAC_{SK} : \{0,1\}^{\ell_{lin}\kappa} \to \{0,1\}^{\ell_{out}\kappa}\}_{SK\in\{0,1\}^{\ell_{key}\kappa}}$ such that $MAC_{SK}(Enc_{lin}(\sigma))$ is a $2^{-\kappa}$ information-theoretically secure MAC.

Special-Hiding Information-Theoretic MAC. For our concretely efficient protocol, we will employ another simple information theoretic MAC. We formalize the security requirement next and then present a construction.

Definition 2.1 (Special-hiding IT-MAC). *Let $\mathbb{F}$ be a finite field. We say that a family of functions $\mathcal{H} = \{H : \mathbb{F}^\ell \times \mathbb{F} \to \mathbb{F}\}$ is ϵ-secure special-hiding if the following two properties hold:*

Privacy. *For every $x, x' \in \mathbb{F}^\ell$ and $H \in \mathcal{H}$, the distributions $H(x;r)$ and $H(x';r)$ are identical for a random $r \in \mathbb{F}$.*

Unforgeability. *For any x, r, x', r' such that $(x,r) \neq (x',r')$, we have:* $\Pr[H \leftarrow \mathcal{H} : H(x;r) = H(x',r')] \leq \epsilon.$

Proposition 2.1. *Let $\ell \in \mathbb{N}$. Define the family $\mathcal{H} = \{H_w\}_{w\in\mathcal{I}}$ where the index set $\mathcal{I}$ includes all vectors $(k_0, \ldots, k_\ell)$ such that $\sum_{i=0}^\ell k_i \neq 0$ and the hash function is defined as*

$$H_{(k_0,\ldots,k_\ell)}((x_1,\ldots,x_\ell),r) = \sum_{i=0}^\ell k_i \cdot (r + x_i)$$

where x_0 is set to 0. Then $\mathcal{H}$ is a $\frac{1}{|\mathbb{F}|}$-secure special-hiding IT-MAC.

3   Framework for Actively Secure Garbled Circuits

In this section we present a general framework for designing an actively secure two-party computation protocol for a functionality $\mathcal{F}$ given its Boolean circuit representation. It is based on (and can capture) the approach of [20], but incorporates several additional ideas. The framework consists of the following steps:

Step 1: Reduce $\mathcal{F}$ to a local $\widehat{\mathcal{F}}$. In this step, given a circuit for $\mathcal{F}$ and a (computational) security parameter κ, we obtain an NC^0 functionality $\widehat{\mathcal{F}}$ and a two-party protocol Π_1 that securely realizes $\mathcal{F}$ in the $\widehat{\mathcal{F}}$-hybrid model with active security. In Sect. 4 we describe two implementations of this step that combine Yao-style garbling with BMR-style randomization. The protocol Π_1 will have the feature of invoking $\widehat{\mathcal{F}}$ just once and making only a black-box use of a PRG. Our first implementation of this step is used for our main asymptotic result and the second for our concretely efficient protocol.

Step 2: Reduce $\widehat{\mathcal{F}}$ to COT. In this step, we obtain an actively secure protocol Π_2 for $\widehat{\mathcal{F}}$ where the parties have access to an augmented OT functionality we refer to as *certified oblivious transfer* (COT). The COT functionality $\mathcal{F}_{\mathrm{COT}}$ in its core performs the parallel OT functionality but additionally assures the receiver that the pairs of strings transmitted satisfy a global consistency predicate. This step is implemented via two intermediate steps:

1. Start with a perfectly secure non-interactive protocol $\Pi_{1.5}$ for $\widehat{\mathcal{F}}$ using a standard parallel OT oracle, where security should only hold in the presence of a passive sender and an active receiver. Such protocols were referred to in [20] as NISC/OT protocols, and can be based on any decomposable randomized encoding for $\widehat{\mathcal{F}}$ [18,22] (which can also be viewed as a perfectly secure projective garbling scheme [4,49] or a private simultaneous messages protocol [10] with 1-bit inputs). We exploit the simplicity of $\widehat{\mathcal{F}}$ to get an efficient realization of this step via the standard reduction from $\binom{n}{1}$-OT to $\binom{2}{1}$-OT [6].
2. Compile $\Pi_{1.5}$ into a protocol Π_2 in the $\mathcal{F}_{\mathrm{COT}}$-hybrid where the sender and receiver rely on the COT oracle to perform the parallel OTs prescribed by $\Pi_{1.5}$ while assuring the receiver that the sender's inputs to the parallel OT oracle were constructed correctly according to $\Pi_{1.5}$. To make the COT predicate simpler, we allow it to be non-deterministic: the predicate depends on an additional NP-witness provided by the sender. The receiver accepts the selected strings if the witness used by an honest sender is valid, and rejects (except with negligible probability) if there is no valid witness that satisfies the global consistency predicate.

Step 3: Reduce COT to commit-and-prove and parallel-OT. We obtain a constant-round protocol Π_3 for the COT functionality in a hybrid model where the parties have access to a commit-and-prove (C&P) oracle and a parallel-OT oracle. Loosely speaking, the C&P functionality is a *reactive* functionality that proceeds in two phases. In the first phase, the sender commits to an input, and in the second phase it proves that this input satisfies some NP relation chosen by the receiver.

Our implementation of COT in this step deviates from the approach of [20] which relies on an information theoretic MPC protocol to simultaneously perform both the computations of the parallel OT and the "certification." We decouple the two by relying on the parallel OT and the C&P functionalities individually in separate steps, which leads to an efficiency improvement over the COT implementation of [20].

Step 4: Reduce commit-and-prove to parallel-OT. Finally, we use a protocol Π_4 to reduce the C&P functionality to parallel-OT via an MPC-in-the-head approach [21]. Prior works [24,27] have shown how to realize C&P with sublinear communication using PCPs and CRHFs. We provide a leaner alternative construction that realizes the C&P functionality in the parallel-OT hybrid with constant communication overhead.[7] This construction is a variant of the recent sublinear zero-knowledge protocol from [1].

Input-dependent failures. A (standard) issue (also present in [20]) that we have to address is that Step 2 will only achieve a slightly relaxed notion of security where an active adversary corrupting the COT sender can cause an input-dependent abort for the receiver.[8] More precisely, a corrupted sender can induce a disjunctive predicate (such as $x_3 \vee x_5 \vee \overline{x_7}$) on the receiver's input bits that if satisfied, will make the receiver abort. We refer to this as an input-value disjunction (IVD) attack and the resulting abort as IVD-abort. The IVD attack on Step 2 results in the final protocol (obtained by composing all 4 steps) realizing a relaxed functionality that allows for similar IVD attacks on $\mathcal{F}$ (and *only* such attacks). We address this issue as in [20] by precompiling $\mathcal{F}$ into another functionality $\mathcal{F}_{\mathrm{IVD}}$ such that securely realizing $\mathcal{F}$ reduces to securely realizing $\mathcal{F}_{\mathrm{IVD}}$ up to IVD attacks. Finally, for our concretely efficient protocol we will rely on efficient variants of this reduction from [35,45] that increase the length of the receiver's input by a constant (≤ 4) factor and adds only XOR gates in $\mathcal{F}_{\mathrm{IVD}}$ which can be handled efficiently via the Free XOR optimization [33]. An alternative implementation of $\mathcal{F}_{\mathrm{IVD}}$ that increases the input length by only a sublinear amount is given in [20].

4   Secure 2PC in NC⁰-Hybrid

In this section, we provide our compilation from an arbitrary 2PC functionality $\mathcal{F}$ to a NC⁰ functionality $\widehat{\mathcal{F}}$ and a protocol Π_1 that securely realizes $\mathcal{F}$ in the $\widehat{\mathcal{F}}$-hybrid. We provide two such compilations which will be variants of analogous constructions in [20]. Previous two-party protocols essentially have a sender who creates and delivers a garbling to a receiver. In contrast, we modify the constructions in [20] to incorporate additional randomization from the receiver inspired by the BMR approach [3].

Overview. On a high-level, the BMR protocol proceeds in two phases: (1) First, in an offline phase, the parties jointly compute a garbling of the circuit they wish to evaluate on their inputs, and (2) in an online phase, the parties share keys corresponding to their inputs and shares of the garbled circuit and output a translation table. Each party then individually reconstructs the garbled circuit,

---

[7] We remark that our protocol can be instantiated using ideal commitments (or even one-way functions in the plain model), but we present a version based on OT as our end goal is to design an efficient secure protocol which anyway requires OT.

[8] For example, it can modify an honest sender's strategy by setting some of the OT inputs to $\perp$, which will cause the receiver to abort for those values as inputs.

evaluates the garbled circuit using the input keys and then obtains the result of the computation. When instantiated in the two-party setting, the BMR protocol differs from the standard Yao's protocol [49] in that the garbling is constructed jointly by both parties as opposed to just by one party in [49].

In slight more detail and restricting our discussion to the two-party setting, both parties provide two keys for every wire in the circuit so that the keys for the output wires of each gate are encrypted in each garbled row under both keys associated with the input wires of this gate. A key difference between the BMR and the Yao protocol is that the association of the keys with the actual values remain hidden from both parties as both of them contribute shares (or masks) that are combined to decide the association. This allows both parties to evaluate the garbled circuit while maintaining privacy. One can model the offline phase as a actively secure computation of a "garbling" functionality where parties provide keys and masks for each wire. However, unless we assume some strong form of a PRG (i.e. PRGs that can be computed by a constant-depth circuits), the computation in the offline phase will not be a constant-depth circuit.

An important optimization considered in [37], observes that if the parties provide both the keys and PRG values under these keys as inputs in the offline phase, then the garbling can be computed via an NC^0 circuit over the inputs. However, such a functionality cannot guarantee the correctness of the PRG values provided by corrupted parties. Nevertheless, [37] show that to achieve security against active adversaries in the overall protocol, it suffices to securely compute the NC^0 functionality with active security. In other words, [37] demonstrate that bad PRG values provided by corrupted parties do not affect the correctness or privacy in the overall protocol. The key idea here is that a bad PRG value can at most trigger an abort when the particular wire associated with the PRG value assumes some particular value in the computation. However, since the associations of keys to values are randomized by both parties, the event of such an abort will be independent of the true value associated with that wire. Using an induction argument, it is possible to establish an invariant that if the evaluation does not abort due to a bad PRG value then the computation will be correct because the protocol guarantees correctness of the NC^0 computation. Combining the invariant with the key idea implies that the event of an abort is independent of the actual honest parties' inputs (as opposed to just the particular intermediate wire value) thereby guaranteeing privacy. Finally, [37] demonstrate that if the evaluation path in the garbled circuit never hits a bad PRG value, then the computation will be correct.

The IKOPS protocol [20], on the other hand, is an extension of the standard Yao protocol where the garbling is computed by a sender and the keys are delivered to a receiver via an OT protocol. As previously observed [35, 36], it must be ensured that an active sender does not create a bad garbled circuit. In the IKOPS protocol, the authors show how to restrict the effects of such an attack by introducing two variants of functionalities. In the first variant, the NC^0 functionality authenticates the PRG values that are input by the sender, whereas in the second variant only the color bits (or point-and-permute bits) are authenticated. The high-level idea is that the authentication information makes the sender commit to parts of the garbling and restricts the space of attacks that can be carried out by the sender. Nevertheless, in both these variants, the sender may still cause the receiver to abort depending on its input or the actual wire values. To make the abort independent of the receiver's input, the IKOPS protocol incurs a $\mathsf{polylog}(\kappa)$ factor overhead as it precompiles the functionality $\mathcal{F}$ to be immune to such attacks. Consequently, the resulting final protocol has a $\mathsf{polylog}(\kappa)$ communication complexity overhead over the standard passively secure Yao protocol.

Our new approach combines the benefits of the BMR protocol with the IKOPS variants to achieve a protocol that achieves communication efficiency with a constant overhead over the semi-honest Yao protocol. On a high-level, we will continue to have a sender that provides the keys and PRG values to the garbling functionality as in the IKOPS protocol, but will randomize the association of keys to values following the BMR approach.

4.1 Variant 1: Authenticating PRG Values

In our first variant the functionality authenticates the PRG values submitted by the sender for creating the garbling. Following [20], the functionality will receive as input from the sender, for every garbled gate, keys and the PRG evaluations under these keys and from the receiver it receives as input a MAC key SK that is used to authenticate the PRG evaluations. The high-level idea here is to require the receiver to verify whether the PRG values obtained during the evaluation of the garbled circuit are consistent with authentication information received from the functionality and letting it abort if the authentication fails. We deviate from [20] by including additional randomization in the form of random bits supplied by the receiver to randomize the association of key and values for each wire.

Formally, we establish the following Lemma.

Lemma 4.1 (AuthPRG Compiler). *There exists a compiler* AuthPRG *that given* κ *(PRG seed length),* s *(statistical security parameter) and a two-party functionality* $\mathcal{F}(x, y)$*, expressed by a circuit* C*, outputs another two-party functionality* $\widehat{\mathcal{F}}$ *and protocol* Π_1 *that securely realizes* $\mathcal{F}$ *in the* $\widehat{\mathcal{F}}$*-hybrid with the following features:*

- $\widehat{\mathcal{F}}$ *is represented by an* NC^0 *circuit of size* $O(|C|\kappa)$*. The receiver's inputs to* $\widehat{\mathcal{F}}$ *include its original input* y *to* $\mathcal{F}$ *and a string of length* $O(|C| + \kappa)$ *that it will choose uniformly at random.*
- Π_1 *makes a single invocation to the* $\widehat{\mathcal{F}}$ *oracle.*
- Π_1 *makes* $O(|C|)$ *black-box calls to a length-doubling PRG:* $G_{\mathrm{PRG}} : \{0,1\}^\kappa \to \{0,1\}^{2\kappa}$*.*

Proof. We begin with a description of the compiled functionality $\widehat{\mathcal{F}} = \mathcal{F}_{\mathrm{AuthPRG}}$ and then continue with our protocol description. If $s > \kappa$ then the compiler sets $s = \kappa$. This is because we require our simulation error to be only bounded by $2^{-s} + \nu(\kappa)$ for some negligible function $\nu(\cdot)$.

The $\mathbf{NC}^0$ Functionality $\widehat{\mathcal{F}} = \mathcal{F}_{\mathbf{AuthPRG}}$. In more details, in this variant the $\mathbf{NC}^0$ functionality $\mathcal{F}_{\mathrm{AuthPRG}}$ computes a BMR-style garbling for the functionality $\mathcal{F}$ that is expressed by a set of wires W and a set of gates G, where only the sender provides the keys and PRG values to be used for this generation. Namely, the functionality obtains the parties' respective inputs (x, y) to the function $\mathcal{F}$ and shares for masking $\{\lambda_w\}_{w \in W}$, as well as the PRG evaluations from the sender and the authenticated information from the receiver, and creates the garbling for all gates $g \in G$; the complete details can be found in Fig. 1.

Protocol 1 (Protocol Π_1). *The parties's common input is a Boolean circuit C, expressed by a set of wires W and a set of gates G.*

Parameters: *Let s be the statistical security parameter and κ be the computational security parameter. Let $\mathrm{G}_{\mathrm{PRG}} : \{0,1\}^\kappa \to \{0,1\}^{2\kappa}$ be a PRG and let $(\mathsf{ECC}, \mathsf{MAC})$ be a $2^{-\kappa}$ secure MAC-scheme (cf. Sect. 2.2) where $\mathsf{ECC} = \{\mathsf{Enc}_{\mathsf{lin}} : \{0,1\}^\kappa \to \{0,1\}^{\ell_{\mathsf{lin}}\kappa}\}$ and $\mathsf{MAC} = \{\mathsf{MAC}_{\mathrm{SK}} : \{0,1\}^{\ell_{\mathsf{lin}}\kappa} \to \{0,1\}^{\ell_{\mathsf{out}}\kappa}\}_{\mathrm{SK} \in \{0,1\}^{\ell_{\mathsf{key}}\kappa}}$.*

Convention for expressing PRG values. *The number of random bits that we need to extract from each key (acting as a seed to the PRG) depends on the number of gates the wire associated with the key occurs as an input. In standard garbling, if a wire occurs as input in T gates, then each key associated with the wire will be used in $2T$ rows and in each row we will require κ (output key) $+\ell_{\mathsf{out}}$ (authentication information) $+1$ (point-and-permute bit) bits. In order to describe our protocol succinctly we will employ a PRF-type definition: $F_k(g, r)$ will represent a unique portion of $\kappa + \ell_{\mathsf{out}} + 1$ bits in the output of $\mathrm{G}_{\mathrm{PRG}}(k)$ that is used for gate g in row r.*

- **Input:** *The sender is given input x and the receiver is given input y. Both parties are given the security parameters $1^\kappa, 1^s$ and the description of a Boolean circuit C.*
- **The sender's input to $\mathcal{F}_{\mathrm{AuthPRG}}$:**
  - *Input x.*
  - *For every wire $w \in W$, keys k_w^0, k_w^1 sampled uniformly at random from $\{0,1\}^\kappa$ and a mask bit $\lambda_w^S \leftarrow \{0,1\}$ sampled uniformly at random.*
  - *For every gate $g \in G$, input wire $w \in W$, point-and-permute bit b and a row r, a tag $\tau_{w,b,S}^{g,r}$ (that will be used to generate the MAC tag for the PRG value computed based on the key k_w^b).*
  - *For every gate $g \in G$, with input wires a and b, the PRG values, $F_{k_a^0}(g, 0)$, $F_{k_a^0}(g, 1), F_{k_a^1}(g, 0), F_{k_a^1}(g, 1), F_{k_b^0}(g, 0), F_{k_b^0}(g, 1), F_{k_b^1}(g, 0), F_{k_b^1}(g, 1)$.*
- **The receiver's input to $\mathcal{F}_{\mathrm{AuthPRG}}$:**
  - *Input y.*
  - *A random seed β to an s-wise PRG $\mathrm{G}_{\mathrm{sPRG}} : \{0,1\}^\kappa \mapsto \{0,1\}^t$.*
  - *A MAC key $\mathrm{SK} \in \{0,1\}^{\gamma_2\kappa}$.*
- **The receiver's outcome from $\mathcal{F}_{\mathrm{AuthPRG}}$:**
  - *$\{(R_g^{00}, R_g^{01}, R_g^{10}, R_g^{11})\}_{g \in G}$.*
  - *$k_w \| z_w$ for every input wire w.*
  - *The masked MAC for every PRG value, namely, $\tau_{w,b,R}^{g,r}$.*
  - *λ_w for every output wire.*

Functionality $\mathcal{F}_{\text{AuthPRG}}$

Let C represent the circuit that computes the functionality $\mathcal{F}$ and comprises of a set of wires W and a set of gates G.

The sender's inputs to the functionality are:
- Input x.
- For every wire $w \in W$ (excluding output wires), keys $k_w^0, k_w^1 \leftarrow \{0,1\}^\kappa$ and mask λ_w^S.
- For every gate $g \in G$ with input wires a and b, the PRG values, $F_{a,0}^{g,0}, F_{a,0}^{g,1}, F_{a,1}^{g,0}, F_{a,1}^{g,1}, F_{b,0}^{g,0}, F_{b,0}^{g,1}, F_{b,1}^{g,0}, F_{b,1}^{g,1}$ and their encodings under Enc_{lin}, $EF_{a,0}^{g,0}, EF_{a,0}^{g,1}, EF_{a,1}^{g,0}, EF_{a,1}^{g,1}, EF_{b,0}^{g,0}, EF_{b,0}^{g,1}, EF_{b,1}^{g,0}, EF_{b,1}^{g,1}$
- For every gate g, input wire w, $b, r \in \{0,1\}$, a tag $\tau_{w,b,S}^{g,r}$ (that will be used to generate the MAC tag for the PRG value computed based on the key k_w^b).

The receiver's inputs to the functionality are:
- Input y.
- A random seed β to an s-wise PRG $G_{\text{sPRG}} : \{0,1\}^\kappa \mapsto \{0,1\}^t$.
- A MAC key $\text{SK} \in \{0,1\}^{\ell_{\text{key}}\kappa}$.

The functionality performs the following computations:

1. Compute the combined masks for every wire $w \in W$ as $\lambda_w = \lambda_w^S \oplus \lambda_w^R$, where λ_w^R is computed by choosing the wth bit in $G_{\text{sPRG}}(\beta)$.

2. For every gate $g \in G$ with input wires a and b and output wire c, compute the garbled table as follows:

$$R_g^{00} = F_{a,0}^{g,0} \oplus F_{b,0}^{g,0} \oplus (k_c^0 \| 0) \oplus \left((\lambda_a \lambda_b \oplus \lambda_c)(k_c^1 \| 1 \oplus k_c^0 \| 0) \right)$$

$$R_g^{01} = F_{a,0}^{g,1} \oplus F_{b,1}^{g,0} \oplus (k_c^0 \| 0) \oplus \left((\lambda_a \oplus \lambda_a \lambda_b \oplus \lambda_c)(k_c^1 \| 1 \oplus k_c^0 \| 0) \right)$$

$$R_g^{10} = F_{a,1}^{g,0} \oplus F_{b,0}^{g,1} \oplus (k_c^0 \| 0) \oplus \left((\lambda_b \oplus \lambda_a \lambda_b \oplus \lambda_c)(k_c^1 \| 1 \oplus k_c^0 \| 0) \right)$$

$$R_g^{11} = F_{a,1}^{g,1} \oplus F_{b,1}^{g,1} \oplus (k_c^0 \| 0) \oplus \left((1 \oplus \lambda_a \oplus \lambda_b \oplus \lambda_a \lambda_b \oplus \lambda_c)(k_c^1 \| 1 \oplus k_c^0 \| 0) \right)$$

3. Send the receiver Rec the following values:
   - $\{(R_g^{00}, R_g^{01}, R_g^{10}, R_g^{11})\}_{g \in G}$.
   - $(k_w^0 \| 0) \oplus \left((\lambda_w \oplus x_i) \wedge (k_w^1 \| 1 \oplus k_w^0 \| 0) \right)$ for every pair (w, i) where the input wire w carries the ith bit of x.
   - $(k_w^0 \| 0) \oplus \left((\lambda_w \oplus y_i) \wedge (k_w^1 \| 1 \oplus k_w^0 \| 0) \right)$ for every pair (w, i) where the input wire w carries the ith bit of y.
   - The masked MAC for every PRG value, namely, $\tau_{w,b,R}^{g,r} = \tau_{w,b,S}^{g,r} \oplus \text{MAC}_{\text{SK}}(EF_{w,b}^{g,r})$.
   - λ_w for every output wire.

Fig. 1. The offline functionality $\mathcal{F}_{\text{AuthPRG}}$.

- *In addition, the sender encrypts the mask used to mask the MAC values and sends it to the receiver. Namely, it sends the ciphertext $c_{w,b}^{g,r} = \mathsf{Enc}_{k_w^b}(\tau_{w,b,S}^{g,r}) = F_{k_w^b}(g\|(2+r)) \oplus \tau_{w,b,S}^{g,r}$.*

- **Concluding the output.** *The receiver then proceeds to evaluate the garbled circuit as follows: Let the gates be arranged in some topological order. We will maintain the invariant that if the receiver has not aborted when it processes some gate g with input wires a and b, then it possess keys k_a and k_b and colors Λ_a and Λ_b.*

  Base case: *For each input wire $w \in W$, the receiver obtains $k_w\|z_w$, where the key is k_w and the color Λ_w is set to z_w.*

  Induction step: *Consider an arbitrary gate $g \in G$ in the topological sequence with input wires a and b and output wire c. By our induction hypothesis, if the receiver has not yet aborted then it has keys k_a, k_b and colors Λ_a and Λ_b. Then the receiver first checks the correctness of the PRG values as follows:*

  - *For $\alpha \in \{0,1\}$, compute $\tau_{a,\Lambda_a,S}^{g,\alpha} = \mathsf{Dec}_{k_a}(c_{a,\Lambda_a}^{g,\alpha}) = c_{a,\Lambda_a}^{g,\alpha} \oplus F_{k_a}(g\|(2+\alpha))$ and check if it equals*

  $$\tau_{a,\Lambda_a,R}^{g,\alpha} \oplus \mathsf{MAC}_{SK}(F_{k_a}(g,\alpha)).$$

  If the checks fail, it aborts. Otherwise, it computes

  $$k_c\|\Lambda_c = R_g^{\Lambda_a \Lambda_b} \oplus F_{k_a}(g,\Lambda_a) \oplus F_{k_b}(g,\Lambda_b).$$

  Finally, if the receiver has not aborted, it possesses the colors Λ_w for every output wire $w \in W$. It then outputs $\Lambda_w \oplus \lambda_w$ as the output on wire w for every output wire.

Next, we provide another variant of our first compiler where we further reduce the number of random bits input by the receiver to $\widehat{\mathcal{F}}$. This will be important in our compilation as the number of bits input by the receiver to $\widehat{\mathcal{F}}$ will directly correspond to the number of calls made in the final protocol to the parallel OT functionality.

Lemma 4.2 (AuthPRG2 Compiler). *Suppose there exist explicit s-wise PRGs in NC^0 with $O(s)$ seed size and an arbitrary polynomial stretch. Then there exists a compiler AuthPRG2 that, given κ (PRG seed), s (statistical parameter), ϵ (statistical PRG parameter) and a two-party functionality $\mathcal{F}(x,y)$ expressed by a circuit C, outputs another two-party functionality $\widehat{\mathcal{F}}$ and protocol Π_1 that securely realizes $\mathcal{F}$ in the $\widehat{\mathcal{F}}$-hybrid with the following features:*

- *$\widehat{\mathcal{F}}$ is represented by an NC^0 circuit of size $O(|C|\kappa)$. The receiver's inputs to $\widehat{\mathcal{F}}$ include its original input y to $\mathcal{F}$ and a string of length $O(|C|^\epsilon + s)$ that it chooses uniformly at random.*
- *Π_1 makes a single call to the $\widehat{\mathcal{F}}$ oracle.*
- *Π_1 makes $O(|C|)$ black-box calls to a length-doubling PRG: $\mathsf{G}_{\mathrm{PRG}} : \{0,1\}^\kappa \to \{0,1\}^{2\kappa}$.*

Moreover, any active corruption of the sender induces a disjunctive predicate P on the random bits r input by the receiver to $\widehat{\mathcal{F}}$ such that the receiver aborts whenever P on the receiver's input is satisfied.

4.2   Variant 2: Authenticating Color Bits

In the second variant, the parties submit their inputs to an NC^0 functionality that computes the garbled circuit. In this variant the color bits are encrypted within each garbled row in an authenticated manner using an information-theoretic MAC, where the MAC secret-key is chosen by the receiver. In contrast to the protocol described in Sect. 4.1, the number of OTs in this protocol will be proportional to the circuit's size since the abort predicate cannot be viewed as a disjunctive function any longer. On the other hand, the main advantage of this variant will be that the NP relation between the OT inputs of the sender and the sender's inputs and randomness can be expressed by a constant-degree arithmetic circuit over a large field. As we rely on an MPC protocol to boost the security of the passive protocol to the active case by certifying that the OT inputs of the sender satisfy the NP relation, we can rely on efficient MPC protocols for arithmetic circuits over large fields. In the full version we prove the following Lemma.

Lemma 4.3 (AuthCol Compiler). *There exists a compiler* AuthCol *that, given κ (PRG seed length), s (statistical parameter) and a two-party deterministic functionality $\mathcal{F}(x, y)$ expressed by a circuit* C, *outputs another two-party functionality $\widehat{\mathcal{F}}$ and protocol Π_1 that securely realizes $\mathcal{F}$ in the $\widehat{\mathcal{F}}$-hybrid with the following features:*

- *$\widehat{\mathcal{F}}$ is represented by an NC^0 circuit of size $O(|\mathsf{C}| \cdot (\kappa + s))$. The receiver's inputs to $\widehat{\mathcal{F}}$ include its original input y to $\mathcal{F}$ and a string of length $W + 2s$ that it will chosen uniformly at random where $W = |\mathsf{C}|$ is the number of distinct[9] wires in the circuit.*
- *Π_1 makes a single call to the $\widehat{\mathcal{F}}$ oracle.*
- *Π_1 makes $O(|\mathsf{C}|)$ black-box calls to a length-doubling PRG: $\mathsf{G}_{\mathrm{PRG}} : \{0, 1\}^\kappa \to \{0, 1\}^{2\kappa}$.*

The NC^0 Functionality $\widehat{\mathcal{F}} = \mathcal{F}_{\mathbf{AuthCol}}$. In this variant the NC^0 functionality $\mathcal{F}_{\mathrm{AuthCol}}$ computes a BMR-style garbling for some function $\mathcal{F}$ that is expressed by a set of wires W and a set of garbled gates G, where only the sender provides the keys and PRG values to be used for this generation. The main difference over the NC^0 functionality from Sect. 4.1 is that in this case the functionality authenticates the color bits instead of the PRG values submitted by the sender, where authentication is computed based on the receiver's secret-key for an information theoretic MAC (see Sect. 2.2). More concretely, the functionality obtains the parties' inputs (x, y) to the function $\mathcal{F}$ and masking $\{\lambda_w\}_{w \in W}$, as well as

---

[9] Wires as part of a fan out from a gate are considered the same wire.

Functionality $\mathcal{F}_{\text{AuthCol}}$

The functionality runs with parties S, R and an adversary $\mathcal{S}$. The parties' joint input is a Boolean circuit C, expressed by a set of wires W and a set of garbled gates G.

The sender's inputs to the functionality are:
- Input x.
- For every wire $w \in W$, keys $k_w^0, k_w^1 \leftarrow \{0,1\}^\kappa$ and a mask λ_w^S.
- For every gate $g \in G$ with input wires a and b, the PRG values $F_{a,0}^{g,0}, F_{a,0}^{g,1}, F_{a,1}^{g,0}, F_{a,1}^{g,1}, F_{b,0}^{g,0}, F_{b,0}^{g,1}, F_{b,1}^{g,0}, F_{b,1}^{g,1}$.

The receiver's inputs to the functionality are:
- Input y.
- For every wire $w \in W$, a mask λ_w^R.
- Two strings $\sigma_0, \sigma_1 \leftarrow \{0,1\}^s$.

The functionality performs the following computations:

1. Compute the combined masks for every wire $w \in W$ as $\lambda_w = \lambda_w^S \oplus \lambda_w^R$.

2. For every gate $g \in G$, compute the garbled table as follows:

$$R_g^{00} = F_{a,0}^{g,0} \oplus F_{b,0}^{g,0} \oplus (k_c^0 || \sigma_0) \oplus \Big((\lambda_a \lambda_b \oplus \lambda_c)(k_c^1 || \sigma_1 \oplus k_c^0 || \sigma_0) \Big)$$

$$R_g^{01} = F_{a,0}^{g,1} \oplus F_{b,1}^{g,0} \oplus (k_c^0 || \sigma_0) \oplus \Big((\lambda_a \oplus \lambda_a \lambda_b \oplus \lambda_c)(k_c^1 || \sigma_1 \oplus k_c^0 || \sigma_0) \Big)$$

$$R_g^{10} = F_{a,1}^{g,0} \oplus F_{b,0}^{g,1} \oplus (k_c^0 || \sigma_0) \oplus \Big((\lambda_b \oplus \lambda_a \lambda_b \oplus \lambda_c)(k_c^1 || \sigma_1 \oplus k_c^0 || \sigma_0) \Big)$$

$$R_g^{11} = F_{a,1}^{g,1} \oplus F_{b,1}^{g,1} \oplus (k_c^0 || \sigma_0) \oplus \Big((1 \oplus \lambda_a \oplus \lambda_b \oplus \lambda_a \lambda_b \oplus \lambda_c)(k_c^1 || \sigma_1 \oplus k_c^0 || \sigma_0) \Big)$$

3. Send the receiver R the following values:
   - $\{(R_g^{00}, R_g^{01}, R_g^{10}, R_g^{11})\}_{g \in G}$.
   - $(k_w^0 || \sigma_0) \oplus \Big((\lambda_w \oplus x_i) \wedge (k_w^1 || \sigma_1 \oplus k_w^0 || \sigma_0) \Big)$ for every pair (w,i) where input wire w carries the ith bit of x.
   - $(k_w^0 || \sigma_0) \oplus \Big((\lambda_w \oplus y_i) \wedge (k_w^1 || \sigma_1 \oplus k_w^0 || \sigma_0) \Big)$ for every pair (w,i) where input wire w carries the ith bit of y.
   - λ_w for every output wire.

Fig. 2. The offline functionality $\mathcal{F}_{\text{AuthCol}}$.

the PRG evaluations from the sender, and the authenticated information from the receiver, and creates the garbling for all gates $g \in G$; the complete details can be found in Fig. 2.

Protocol 2 (Protocol Π_1). *The parties' common input is a Boolean circuit C, expressed by a set of wires W and a set of gates G. Let s be the statistical security parameter and κ be the computational security parameter. Let $G_{\text{PRG}} : \{0,1\}^\kappa \to \{0,1\}^{2\kappa}$ be a PRG and let $\{\text{MAC}_{\text{SK}} : \{0,1\} \to \{0,1\}^s\}_{\text{SK} \in \{0,1\}^{2s}}$ be an information theoretically secure MAC computable in NC^0.*

– **Input:** *The sender is given input x and the receiver is given input y. Both parties are given the security parameters $1^\kappa, 1^s$ and the description of a Boolean circuit C.*

– **The sender's input to $\mathcal{F}_{\text{AuthCol}}$:**
   - *Input x.*
   - *For every wire $w \in W$, keys k_w^0, k_w^1 sampled uniformly at random from $\{0,1\}^\kappa$, and mask bit $\lambda_w^S \leftarrow \{0,1\}$ sampled uniformly at random.*
   - *For every gate $g \in G$, with input wires a and b, PRG values, $F_{k_a^0}(g,0)$, $F_{k_a^0}(g,1), F_{k_a^1}(g,0), F_{k_a^1}(g,1), F_{k_b^0}(g,0), F_{k_b^0}(g,1), F_{k_b^1}(g,0), F_{k_b^1}(g,1)$.*

– **The receiver's input to $\mathcal{F}_{\text{AuthCol}}$:**
   - *Input y.*
   - *for every $w \in W$, a random mask bit $\lambda_w^R \leftarrow \{0,1\}$.*
   - *Two strings $\sigma_0, \sigma_1 \leftarrow \{0,1\}^s$ chosen uniformly at random.*

– **The receiver's outcome from $\mathcal{F}_{\text{AuthCol}}$:**
   - *$\{(R_g^{00}, R_g^{01}, R_g^{10}, R_g^{11})\}_{g \in G}$.*
   - *$k_w || z_w$ for every input wire w.*
   - *A mask λ_w for every output wire.*

– **Concluding the output.** *The receiver then proceeds to evaluate the garbled circuit as follows: Let the gates be arranged in topological order. We will maintain the invariant that if the receiver has not aborted when it processes some gate g with input wires a and b, then it possess keys k_a and k_b and color bits Λ_a and Λ_b.*

   Base case: *For each input wire $w \in W$, the receiver holds an input key k_w and a color Λ_w that is set to 0 if $z_w = \sigma_0$, and set to 1 if $z_w = \sigma_1$. In case the receiver does not have these values in the correct format, it aborts.*

   Induction step: *Consider an arbitrary gate $g \in G$ in the topological sequence with input wires a and b and output wire c. By our induction hypothesis, if the receiver has not yet aborted then it has keys k_a, k_b and color bits Λ_a and Λ_b. Then the receiver computes*

$$k_c || z_c = R_g^{\Lambda_a \Lambda_b} \oplus F_{k_a}(g, \Lambda_a) \oplus F_{k_b}(g, \Lambda_b).$$

   If $z_c \notin \{\sigma_0, \sigma_1\}$, the receiver aborts. Otherwise it sets the color Λ_c such that $z_c = \sigma_{\Lambda_c}$.

Finally, if the receiver has not aborted, it possesses the colors Λ_w for every output wire $w \in W$. It then outputs $\Lambda_w \oplus \lambda_w$ as the output on wire w for every output wire.

Claim 4.4 *Let $\mathcal{F}$ a two-party functionality as above and assume that F is a PRG. Then Protocol 2 securely computes $\mathcal{F}$ in the $\mathcal{F}_{\text{AuthCol}}$-hybrid.*

We can modify all our variants to incorporate (by now standard) optimization of Free XOR [33]. Implicit in this optimization is a mechanism that restricts the space of keys sampled for the wires.

5 Realizing $\mathcal{F}_{\text{COT}}$ in the Presence of IVD Attacks

In this section, we design our protocol that securely realizes the COT functionality (cf. Fig. 3) with security in the presence of active adversaries up to IVD-abort. On a high-level, we combine the MPC-in-the-head approach of [21] to "certify" the inputs to the OT executions. A similar approach was taken in the work of [20]. However, our approach significantly deviates from the previous approaches in the following way:

- In the [20] approach, the receiver obtains the output of the individual OTs by obtaining the view of the corresponding receivers in the MPC network. In our approach, the sender and receiver first engage in the OT protocol as in a normal OT execution and later a "zero-knowledge" proof for the correctness of the values, that are transferred via the OT protocol, is provided. The main savings of our approach is in the communication complexity. In the [20] approach, the view of the receivers contain redundant information from each of the servers and we avoid this redundancy.

Functionality $\mathcal{F}_{\text{COT-IVD}}$

Functionality $\mathcal{F}_{\text{COT-IVD}}$ communicates with sender S and receiver R, and adversary $\mathcal{S}$ and is parameterized by an NP relation $\mathcal{R}(\cdot, \cdot)$ and integers m, n, κ.

1. Upon receiving input $(P, \{(s_1^0, s_1^1)\}_{j \in [m]}, w)$ from S where $s_j^b \in \{0,1\}^\kappa$ and $w \in \{0,1\}^{\text{poly}(n,\kappa)}$ it checks if the predicate P is a disjunction of literals and records $(P, \bar{s}, w)$ if it is a disjunction where $\bar{s} = \{(s_1^0, s_1^1)\}_{j \in [m]}$.
2. Upon receiving $(u_1, \ldots, u_m)$ from R where $u_j \in \{0,1\}$, record $(\bar{u})$ where $\bar{u} = (u_1, \ldots, u_m))$. If there is no record from the sender the functionality waits until it receives a message from S. If there is a record $(\bar{s}, w)$ then it sends $(\{s_j^{u_j}\}_{j \in [m]}, \mathcal{R}(\bar{s}, w))$ to R only if $P(\bar{u}) \neq 1$ and $\bot$ if $P(\bar{u}) = 1$.

Fig. 3. The certified oblivious transfer functionality with IVD.

We will describe our protocol Π_3 in the $(\mathcal{F}_{\text{OT}}, \mathcal{F}_{\text{CnP}})$-hybrid where $\mathcal{F}_{\text{OT}}$ is the parallel OT functionality and $\mathcal{F}_{\text{CnP}}$ is a slight variant of the standard commit-and-prove functionality that allows a sender to first commit to a witness w and then, given a function H from the receiver and an image y from the sender, delivers the output of the predicate $H(w) = y$; see Fig. 4 for the formal description.

Beside employing functionalities $\mathcal{F}_{\text{OT}}$ and $\mathcal{F}_{\text{CnP}}$, our protocol uses a special-hiding information theoretic MAC that preserves the properties of privacy and unforgeability in a way that enforces the sender to properly commit to its inputs; see Definition 2.1 for more details. More formally,

---

Functionality $\mathcal{F}_{\mathrm{CnP}}$

Functionality $\mathcal{F}_{\mathrm{CnP}}$ communicates with sender S and receiver R, and adversary $\mathcal{S}$ and is parameterized by an NP relation $\mathcal{R}(\cdot, \cdot)$ and integers n, κ.

Commit phase. Upon receiving input (z, w) from S where $z = \{(s_j^b, r_j^b)\}_{j \in [m], b \in \{0,1\}}$ and $w \in \{0, 1\}^{\mathrm{poly}(n,\kappa)}$, record this message.

Prove phase. Upon receiving H from R, forward H to S. Upon receiving y from S, check if there exists a record (z, w) that it received from S. Ignore if no such record exists. Otherwise, send 1 to R only if $H(z) = y$ and $\mathcal{R}(\bar{\mathbf{s}}, w) = 1$ where $\bar{\mathbf{s}} = \{(s_1^0, s_1^1)\}_{j \in [m]}$. Return 0 otherwise.

Fig. 4. The commit-and-prove functionality.

Protocol 3 (Protocol Π_3 for realizing functionality $\mathcal{F}_{\mathrm{COT-IVD}}$).

- **Inputs:** *The sender S_{COT}'s input is $\{(s_j^0, s_j^1)\}_{j \in [m]}$ and a witness w with respect to some NP relation $\mathcal{R}$, and the receiver R_{COT}'s input is $b_1, \ldots, b_m$.*
- **The protocol:**
  1. $S_{\mathrm{COT}} \overset{\mathcal{F}_{\mathrm{OT}}}{\longleftrightarrow} R_{\mathrm{COT}}$: *The parties engage in m oblivious transfers in parallel using $\mathcal{F}_{\mathrm{OT}}$ where S_{COT} uses $((s_j^0, r_j^0), (s_j^1, r_j^1))$ and R_{COT} uses b_j, as their respective inputs in the jth ($j \in [m]$) oblivious transfer execution, where r_j^b is a sufficiently long string. (Looking ahead, this string will serve as the randomness for some MAC function H.)*
  2. $S_{\mathrm{COT}} \overset{\mathcal{F}_{\mathrm{CnP}}}{\longleftrightarrow} R_{\mathrm{COT}}$: *The sender commits to the witness $(\{(s_j^b, r_j^b)\}_{j \in [m]}, b \in \{0,1\}, w)$ by sending it to the $\mathcal{F}_{\mathrm{CnP}}$ functionality.*
  3. $S_{\mathrm{COT}} \leftarrow R_{\mathrm{COT}}$: *The receiver chooses a random MAC key $H \leftarrow \mathcal{H}$ and sends it to the sender via functionality $\mathcal{F}_{\mathrm{CnP}}$.*
  4. $S_{\mathrm{COT}} \rightarrow R_{\mathrm{COT}}$: *The sender sends the MAC of every string, namely it sends $\{H(s_j^b; r_j^b)\}_{j \in [m], b \in \{0,1\}}$ to R_{COT}. If the MACed value transmitted for $(s_j^{u_j}, r_j^{u_j})$ does not match $H(s_j^{u_j}; r_j^{u_j})$ for some $j \in [m]$, then R_{COT} rejects.*
  5. $S_{\mathrm{COT}} \overset{\mathcal{F}_{\mathrm{CnP}}}{\longleftrightarrow} R_{\mathrm{COT}}$: *The sender and receiver interact via the $\mathcal{F}_{\mathrm{CnP}}$ functionality where S_{COT} submits $\{H(s_j^b; r_j^b)\}_{j \in [m], b \in \{0,1\}}$ and R_{COT} submits H. $\mathcal{F}_{\mathrm{CnP}}$ checks if H was computed correctly on every pair (s_j^b, r_j^b) committed to before as part of the witness and if $\mathcal{R}(\{(s_j^0, s_j^1)\}_{j \in [m]}, w)$. If both these checks pass, it delivers 1 to R_{COT} and otherwise 0.*

Since we can only realize a relaxed functionality $\mathcal{F}_{\mathrm{COT-IVD}}$ that allows IVD attacks, we need to understand how the attack propagates into the protocol for $\mathcal{F}$ (the original functionality that the parties want to compute) in the $\mathcal{F}_{\mathrm{COT}}$-hybrid. The key point is that the receiver's inputs to $\mathcal{F}_{\mathrm{COT}}$ in the latter protocol consist of either actual inputs y for $\mathcal{F}$ or independently random bits (for the BMR masking and MAC keys). Thus, any disjunctive predicate on the receiver's inputs to $\mathcal{F}_{\text{COT}}$ can be emulated by a (randomized) disjunctive predicate on the receiver's inputs y to $\mathcal{F}$.

Theorem 5.1. *Let $\mathcal{H}$ be a family of special-hiding MAC according to Definition 2.1 for κ-bit strings. Then Protocol 3 securely computes $\mathcal{F}_{\text{COT-IVD}}$ in the $(\mathcal{F}_{\text{OT}}, \mathcal{F}_{\text{CnP}})$-hybrid.*

6 Putting it Together

In this section we instantiate our framework for two-party computation by instantiating the computation of our two NC^0 functionalities and the information-theoretic MPC protocols and obtain different efficiency guarantees, both in the asymptotic and concrete regimes. We use the following convention:

- We use κ and s for the computational and statistical security parameter respectively.
- We use n to denote the input lengths of the parties and m to denote the output length of the function $\mathcal{F}$ that the parties want to securely compute.

Both of our variants will have constant overhead communication complexity over the passively secure Yao protocol. The second uses a large number of OTs but has better concrete efficiency.

6.1 Variant 1: Asymptotically Optimal Construction

The first variant incurs communication complexity of $O(|C|\kappa)$ bits in the κ-bit string OT oracle. We first provide a basic result for this variant that will employ $O(|C|)$ calls to κ-bit string OT oracle. Next, by relying on an information-theoretic PRG, we will be able to reduce the number of calls to $n + O(s \cdot |C|^\epsilon)$ for an arbitrary constant $\epsilon > 0$. Such information-theoretic PRGs exist assuming explicit constant-degree unbalanced unique-neighbor expanders.

The basic result we obtain in this variant is the following theorem.

Theorem 6.1. *There exists a protocol compiler that given κ (PRG seed length), s (statistical security parameter), and a two-party deterministic functionality $\mathcal{F}$ expressed as a Boolean circuit $C : \{0,1\}^n \times \{0,1\}^n \to \{0,1\}^m$, outputs a protocol Π_C that securely realizes $\mathcal{F}$ in the κ-bit string OT hybrid, namely using ideal calls to κ-bit string OT. The protocol Π_C has the following efficiency features:*

- *It makes $O(|C|) + \text{poly}(\log(|C|), s)$ black-box calls to a PRG $\text{G}_{\text{PRG}} : \{0,1\}^\kappa \to \{0,1\}^{2\kappa}$.*
- *It makes $O(|C| + s)$ calls to κ-bit string OT oracle.*
- *It communicates $O(\kappa \cdot |C|) + \text{poly}(\log(|C|), \log \kappa, s)$ bits.*

Remark 6.1. Recall that we require the distinguishing advantage to be bounded by $2^{-s} + \nu(\kappa)$ for some negligible function $\nu(\cdot)$. We state our asymptotic result with s as a parameter as we would like to make the distinction between protocols that achieve 2^{-s} error versus negligible in s error. Furthermore, it allows us to compare our protocols with prior works that achieve the same simulation error. We remark that we can assume $s < \kappa$ without loss of generality as we require the distinguishing error to be bounded by a negligible function in κ and if s is bigger than κ, we can let $s = \kappa$.

Proof of Theorem 6.1. We follow the framework described in Sect. 3.

1. Following an approach based on [35], we first transform the original functionality $\mathcal{F}$ into a new functionality $\mathcal{F}_{\text{IVD}}$ that will resist input-dependent attack.
   - The circuit size of $\widehat{\mathcal{F}}_{\text{IVD}}$ is $O(\kappa \cdot |C| + \kappa \cdot s)$ for any circuit C that computes the original functionality $\mathcal{F}$.
   - The receiver's input length in $\widehat{\mathcal{F}}_{\text{IVD}}$ is $O(|C|) + O(\max(n, s)) = O(|C| + s)$.
2. We next consider an information-theoretic protocol Π_2 that realizes $\widehat{\mathcal{F}}_{\text{IVD}}$ in the $\mathcal{F}_{\text{COT-IVD}}$-hybrid (where functionality $\mathcal{F}_{\text{COT-IVD}}$ is defined in Sect. 5). Such a protocol is obtained in two steps: (1) First, we take a non-interactive protocol $\Pi_{1.5}$ for $\widehat{\mathcal{F}}_{\text{IVD}}$ using a standard parallel OT oracle, where this protocol only needs to be secure in the presence of a passive sender and an active receiver. (which can also be viewed as a perfectly secure projective garbling scheme [4,49] or a private simultaneous messages protocol [10] with 1-bit inputs. See next variant for more details.) (2) We then use the $\mathcal{F}_{\text{COT-IVD}}$ oracle to enforce honest behavior of the sender up to IVD attacks.

   This protocol Π_2 has the following features:
   - The receiver's input size is $O(|C| + s)$.
   - The sender's algorithm makes $O(|C| + s)$ black-box calls to a length-doubling PRG $G_{\text{PRG}} : \{0,1\}^\kappa \to \{0,1\}^{2\kappa}$.
   - The total length of the sender's OT inputs across all OTs is $O(\kappa \cdot |C| + \kappa \cdot s)$.

   We remark that we only track the number of OTs and the sum total of the lengths of the sender OT inputs as we can rely on a standard transformation that takes n_{OT} parallel OTs where the sum of OT input lengths is ℓ_{OT} and compile it to n_{OT} parallel OTs with κ-bit inputs that will require the sender to make $\lceil \frac{\ell_{\text{OT}}}{\kappa} \rceil$ calls to the underlying length doubling PRG G_{PRG} and send one additional message to the receiver of length ℓ_{OT}. This transformation simply requires the sender to use κ-bit keys sampled independent from a semantically-secure encryption scheme as the OT sender inputs and send encryptions of the corresponding inputs with that key.
3. We replace the oracle call to the $\mathcal{F}_{\text{COT-IVD}}$ in Π_2 by replacing it with the protocol Π_3 from Sect. 5 in the $(\mathcal{F}_{\text{OT}}, \mathcal{F}_{\text{CnP}})$-hybrid. Then we replace the oracle call to $\mathcal{F}_{\text{CnP}}$ with our protocol Π_4 where we instantiate our MPC protocol using a variant of the protocol from [8] further used in [21]. The resulting protocol is in the $\mathcal{F}_{\text{OT}}$-hybrid and realizes $\mathcal{F}_{\text{COT-IVD}}$ against active adversaries. The communication complexity of the protocol can be computed as follows:

(a) The sender and receiver first engage in parallel OTs where they execute only the oblivious-transfer part of the COT protocol. This involves $O(|C| + s)$ inputs from the receiver and the sum total of the lengths of the sender's OT inputs across all OTs is $O(\kappa \cdot |C| + \kappa \cdot s)$.

(b) The sender transmits a MAC of length s corresponding to each OT input. There are totally $O(|C| + s)$ strings transmitted via 1-out-of-2 OTs. Therefore, sending the MACs will require the sender to transmit $2 \cdot s \cdot O(|C| + s) = O(s \cdot |C| + s^2)$ bits.

(c) The NP-relation associated with $\mathcal{F}_{\mathrm{CnP}}$ is of size $O(\kappa \cdot C + \kappa \cdot s) + O(s \cdot |C| + s^2) = O(\kappa \cdot C) + \kappa \cdot \mathsf{poly}(s)$. We can conclude the communication complexity of the protocol realizing $\mathcal{F}_{\mathrm{CnP}}$ to be $O(\kappa \cdot C) + \mathsf{poly}(\log|C|, \log\kappa, s)$ and involves $O(|C|) + \mathsf{poly}(\log|C|, s)$ calls to the PRG.

This compilation has the following efficiency features:

- The protocol makes $O(|C|) + \mathsf{poly}(\log|C|, s)$ black-box calls to a length-doubling PRG $\mathrm{G}_{\mathrm{PRG}} : \{0,1\}^\kappa \to \{0,1\}^{2\kappa}$.
- The protocol involves $O(\kappa \cdot |C|) + \mathsf{poly}(\log|C|, \log\kappa, s)$ bits of communication.
- The protocol incurs $O(|C| + s)$ calls to $O(\kappa)$-bit string OTs.

This concludes the proof of Theorem 6.1.

Based on Theorem 6.1, we obtain the first construction of actively secure 2PC protocol that achieves constant overhead communication complexity over Yao's passively secure protocol in a model where all parties have black-box access to any protocol realizing the OT oracle. In contrast, prior works based on the cut-and-choose paradigm induce a multiplicative overhead of $\Omega(s)$.

Next, we improve our construction from Theorem 6.1 to one that requires fewer calls to the OT oracle to something that is sublinear in the circuit size. This is obtained by replacing the compilation from $\mathcal{F}_{\mathrm{IVD}}$ to $\widehat{\mathcal{F}}_{\mathrm{IVD}}$ in Step 2 using Lemma 4.2. This compilation results in $\widehat{\mathcal{F}}_{\mathrm{IVD}}$ where the receiver's input length is $n + O(s \cdot |C|^\epsilon)$ assuming s-wise PRGs. Then we observe that the number of calls made to the OT in our final protocol is equal to the receiver's input length to $\widehat{\mathcal{F}}_{\mathrm{IVD}}$. We thus get the following corollary.

Corollary 6.2. *Suppose there exist explicit s-wise PRGs in NC^0 with $O(s)$ seed size and an arbitrary polynomial stretch. Then, for every $\epsilon > 0$, there exists a protocol compiler that, given (κ, s) and a functionality $\mathcal{F}$ expressed as a Boolean circuit $C : \{0,1\}^n \times \{0,1\}^n \to \{0,1\}^m$, outputs a protocol Π_C that securely realizes $\mathcal{F}$ in the κ-bit string OT hybrid with the following efficiency features:*

- *It makes $O(|C|) + \mathsf{poly}(\log(|C|), s)$ black-box calls to a length-doubling PRG $\mathrm{G}_{\mathrm{PRG}} : \{0,1\}^\kappa \to \{0,1\}^{2\kappa}$.*
- *It makes $n + O(s \cdot |C|^\epsilon)$ calls to a κ-bit string OT oracle.*
- *It communicates $O(\kappa \cdot |C|) + \mathsf{poly}(\log(|C|), \log\kappa, s)$ bits.*

Remark 6.2. As discussed in Footnote 6 and Sect. 2.1, the combinatorial assumption about explicit s-wise PRGs is a seemingly mild assumption that was already used in other contexts.

This corollary provides the first black-box protocol that simultaneously achieves asymptotically constant overhead communication complexity over Yao's passively secure protocol and requires sublinear (in circuit size) number of calls to a OT protocol. In contrast, prior works have either obtained constant overhead (e.g., [48], albeit in the bit-OT hybrid model) or a small number of calls to the OT oracle-(e.g., protocols based on cut-and-choose).

6.2   Variant 2: Concretely Efficient Variant

Our second variant will also achieve a communication complexity of $O(\kappa \cdot |C|)$ bits and employ $O(|C|)$ calls to a κ-bit string OT oracle. We will identity the precise constant in the overhead. In this variant we will be able to incorporate the FreeXOR optimization.

More precisely, we have the following theorem:

Theorem 6.3. *There exists a protocol compiler that, given κ (PRG seed length), s (statistical security parameter) and a functionality $\mathcal{F}(x, y)$ expressed as a circuit $C : \{0, 1\}^n \times \{0, 1\}^n \to \{0, 1\}^m$, outputs a protocol Π_C which securely realizes $\mathcal{F}$ in the κ-bit string OT-hybrid with the following features:*

- *The protocol makes $|C| + 2 \cdot s + \max(4 \cdot n, 8 \cdot s)$ calls to κ-bit string OT.*
- *The protocol communicates (in bits)*

$$(16 \cdot \kappa + 26 \cdot s) \cdot |C| + 2 \cdot s \cdot (|C| + 2 \cdot s + \max(4 \cdot n, 8 \cdot s))$$
$$+ 8 \cdot s^{1.5} \cdot \sqrt{|C| \cdot (55 \cdot \lceil \kappa/s \rceil + 6 \cdot \kappa + 73)}.$$

Proof of Theorem 6.3. The compilation takes as input a circuit C and security parameter κ and proceeds by following the same approach as in our first variant with the exception that we use our transformation in the $\mathcal{F}_{\text{AuthCol}}$-hybrid as described in Sect. 4.2 and the MPC protocol instantiated above. More precisely,

1. We transform the original functionality $\mathcal{F}$ into $\mathcal{F}_{\text{IVD}}$ that is resistant to IVD attacks just as in the previous compilation. In our initial computation in this section, we ignore the additive overhead that is incurred as a result of this transformation. At the end of the section, we provide bounds for the additive terms. The circuit size of $\mathcal{F}_{\text{IVD}}$ will therefore be $|C|$ and the recipe input $|C| + n + 2s$.

2. Next, we compile $\mathcal{F}_{\text{IVD}}$ to $\widehat{\mathcal{F}}_{\text{IVD}}$ using $\mathcal{F}_{\text{AuthCol}}$-hybrid as described in Sect. 4.2. The NC^0 functionality $\widehat{\mathcal{F}}_{\text{IVD}}$ has the following features:

   - The receiver's input size is $|C| + 2 \cdot s + \max(4 \cdot n, 8 \cdot s)$ where $\max(4 \cdot n, 8 \cdot s)$ is the length of the encoding of the receiver's input following [35].
   - The output length of the NC^0 functionality is $4 \cdot |C| \cdot (\kappa + s)$. Note that $\widehat{\mathcal{F}}_{\text{IVD}}$ includes an additional n^2 XOR gates compared to $\mathcal{F}_{\text{IVD}}$. These are required to decode the receiver's input before the computation begins. We will not include these gates in our circuit size as we can rely on the FreeXOR optimization.

We will compute the precise size in the next step.

3. We next consider an information-theoretic protocol Π that realizes $\widehat{\mathcal{F}}_{\mathrm{IVD}}$ in the $\mathcal{F}_{\mathrm{COT-IVD}}$-hybrid. As before, this proceeds in two steps: (1) Take a non-interactive protocol for $\widehat{\mathcal{F}}$ using a parallel OT oracle, where the protocol only needs to be secure in the presence of a passive sender and an active receiver. (2) Use the $\mathcal{F}_{\mathrm{COT-IVD}}$ oracle to enforce honest behavior of the sender up to IVD attacks.

First, we compute the communication complexity of the passive protocol that realizes the NC^0 functionality in (1). Note that the computation of $\widehat{\mathcal{F}}_{\mathrm{IVD}}$ involves a computation with constant locality, in fact, at most 4 locality on the receiver's inputs. We recall from [6] that there is a NISC protocol in the 1-out-of-2^d OT-hybrid to compute any function with locality d. This incurs a communication cost of $2^{d+1} - 2$ bits. Following this construction naively results in a total communication complexity of $2^{4+1} - 2 = 30$ per output bit for total of $30 \cdot 4 \cdot (\kappa + s) \cdot |C|$ bits for computing $\widehat{\mathcal{F}}_{\mathrm{IVD}}$.

We tighten the analysis in two ways:

- First, we observe that each bit in the output of the NC^0 functionality we are computing can be expressed as a sum of monomials. This means we can break the monomials into different sections where the locality of each section is small. Then, we compute each section using the standard approach prescribed above. Additionaly, to ensure privacy we will have to mask the outputs each section with shares of 0.
- Certain monomials (or sum of monomials) appear in multiple expression (for e.g., the four garbled rows share monomials as we describe below) and we can compute the shared monomials only once.

The general formula for computing the garbled row (r_1, r_2) in gate g with input wires a, b and output wire c is given by

$$F_{k_a^{r_1}}(g, r_1, r_1) \oplus F_{k_b^{r_2}}(g, r_1, r_2) \oplus [(\lambda_a^R \oplus \lambda_a^S \oplus r_1) \wedge (\lambda_b^R \oplus \lambda_b^S \oplus r_2) \oplus \lambda_c^R \oplus \lambda_c^A] \wedge (k_c^0 \oplus k_c^1)$$

Next, we consider the following monomials and explain how the first κ bits of the four rows of a garbled gate can be computed from them.

$$M_1 = [(\lambda_a^R \wedge \lambda_b^R) \oplus (\lambda_a^R \wedge \lambda_b^S) \oplus (\lambda_a^S \wedge \lambda_b^R) \oplus \lambda_c^A] \wedge (k_c^0 \oplus k_c^1) \oplus R_1$$
$$M_2 = [\lambda_a^R \wedge (k_c^0 \oplus k_c^1)] \oplus R_2$$
$$M_3 = [\lambda_b^R \wedge (k_c^0 \oplus k_c^1)] \oplus R_3$$
$$M_4 = [\lambda_c^R \wedge (k_c^0 \oplus k_c^1)] \oplus R_3$$

We will also have the sender send the receiver the following four strings (ciphertexts): For $r_1, r_2 \in \{0, 1\}$

$$c_{g, r_1, r_2} = F_{k_a^{r_1}}(g, r_1, r_1, 0) \oplus F_{k_b^{r_2}}(g, r_1, r_2, 0) \oplus R_1 \oplus (r_1 \wedge R_2) \oplus (r_2 \wedge R_3) \oplus R_4$$

In the evaluation, if the receiver obtains $k_a^{r_1}$ and $k_b^{r_2}$, then it can obtain key for the c wire by computing

$$c_{g, r_1, r_2} \oplus M_1 \oplus (r_1 \wedge M_2) \oplus (r_2 \wedge M_3) \oplus M_4$$

By our preceding calculations, M_1 is a monomial over two variable λ_a^R, λ_b^R from the receiver and can be computed with overhead 6 per bit of the key. The other three monomials involve only one variable from the receiver and can be computed with overhead 2. Overall the communication of transmitting this will be $6 \cdot \kappa + (2 + 2 + 2) \cdot \kappa$ as part of the oblivious-transfer and $4 \cdot |C| \cdot \kappa$ bits in the clear.

The next s bits which will encrypt the color bits can be computed analogously, where each of the terms above will additionally involve a multiplicand $\sigma_0 \oplus \sigma_1$ from the receiver. Following a similar analysis the number of bits transmitted will be $14 \cdot s + (6 + 6 + 6) \cdot s$ bits as part of the oblivious transfer and $4 \cdot |C| \cdot s$ bits in the clear. We can improve this further because we can compress the sender's input to the OT when it is communicating strings that are long and chosen uniformly random. For example, in the OTs involving each bit of $\sigma_0 \oplus \sigma_1$ as receiver's input, the sender's input length is $O(|C|)$. This can be reduced to sending a PRG seed of length κ and the receiver expanding it to $O(|C|)$ bits. This reduces the cost to

$$2 \cdot \kappa \cdot s + 10 \cdot s + (4 + 4 + 4) \cdot s = 2 \cdot \kappa \cdot s + 22 \cdot s$$

Looking ahead, in our final protocol we will employ protocol Π directly as a sub-protocol. We will need two measures of complexity from this protocol. First, we need the communication complexity which we compute by calculating the receiver's input size (which translates to number of parallel OT invocations) and the sums of the lengths of the sender's inputs in all the parallel OT. Second, we estimate the size of the global predicate defined by the NISC/OT protocol which will dictate the complexity of our commit-and-prove protocol in the next step.

Following the calculations described above, we can conclude that this protocol incurs the following costs:

- The receiver's input size is $|C| + 2s + \max(4 \cdot n, 8 \cdot s)$.
- The sum total of the sender OT inputs is $(12 \cdot \kappa + 22 \cdot s) \cdot |C| + 2 \cdot \kappa \cdot s$ bits.
- The length of the sender's message is $4 \cdot (\kappa + s) \cdot |C|$.
- The global predicate that will be the NP relation used in the $\mathcal{F}_{\text{COT-IVD}}$ oracle can be expressed as an arithmetic circuit over the $\mathbb{GF}(2^s)$ field. We will only count the number of multiplication gates, as addition will be free. Recall that the global predicate is required to enforce honest behavior of the sender in Π. Given the sender inputs to the parallel OT, we compute the size of the global predicate as follows:

  Input size to NP relation. The witness to the NP statement includes (1) the strings for the OT, the sum of the lengths of inputs of which are $(12 \cdot \kappa + 22 \cdot s) \cdot |C| + 2 \cdot \kappa \cdot s$, (2) The PRF values which totals to $4 \cdot |C| \cdot (\kappa + s)$, and (3) for each wire w, $\lambda_w^R, k_w^0, k_w^1$ that sums up $|C| + 2|C| \cdot \kappa$.

  Key part of the output. Consider one of the garbled rows for a gate g with input wires a, b and output wire c. For very possible assignment

(a_1, a_2, a_3) of $\lambda_a^R, \lambda_b^R, \lambda_c^R$ the first κ bits of a garbled row can be expressed as

$$F_{\mathsf{prg}}^a + F_{\mathsf{prg}}^b + k_c^0 + f_{g,row}^{a_1,a_2,a_3}(\lambda_a^S, \lambda_b^S, \lambda_c^S) \cdot (k_c^1 - k_c^0)$$

where $F_{\mathsf{prg}}^a, F_{\mathsf{prg}}^b, \lambda_a^S, \lambda_b^S, \lambda_c^S, k_c^0, k_c^1$ will be include in the witness for the predicate. The function $f_{g,row}^{a_1,a_2,a_3}$ can further be expressed as

$$c_1 \cdot \lambda_a^S \cdot \lambda_b^S + c_2 \cdot \lambda_a^S + c_3 \cdot \lambda_b^S + c_4 \cdot \lambda_c^S + c_5$$

for some coefficient c_1 through c_5 that will depend on the particular assignment for $\lambda_a^R, \lambda_b^R, \lambda_c^R$.

Each garbled row can also be computed from the sender's OT inputs (again included in the witness) using only addition operations (this is exactly the computation of the receiver once it receivers the OT outputs). The predicate will check that the garbled row computed the two ways are equal.

We only include the number of multiplication operations in our circuit size. It suffices to compute the product of each of $\lambda_a^S \cdot \lambda_b^S, \lambda_a^S, \lambda_b^S, \lambda_c^S$ with $(k_c^1 - k_c^0)$ to compute all of $f_{g,row}^{a_1 a_2 a_3}$ (where $a_1, a_2, a_3 \in \{0,1\}$ and $row \in \{1, 2, 3, 4\}$). Since we first split k_c^0, k_c^1 into chunks of s bits, there will be $\lceil \frac{\kappa}{s} \rceil$ chunks and for each garbled row, the predicate will include $5 \cdot \lceil \frac{\kappa}{s} \rceil$ multiplications per gate.

MAC part of the output. Again, for every combination of λ_w^R values, we compute the MAC part in two ways and check if they are equal. However, we will not do this check for every garbled row, we will do this for every column of the matrix where the MAC part of the garbled rows across all gates are stacked up. Furthermore, as we describe below, it will incur no additional multiplication gates.

As before, for very possible assignment (a_1, a_2, a_3) of $\lambda_a^R, \lambda_b^R, \lambda_c^R$ corresponding to a gate, the last s bits (i.e. the MAC part) of a garbled row can be expressed as

$$F_{\mathsf{prg}}^a + F_{\mathsf{prg}}^b + \sigma_0 + f_{g,row}^{a_1,a_2,a_3}(\lambda_a^S, \lambda_b^S, \lambda_c^S) \cdot (\sigma_1 - \sigma_0).$$

First, we observe that σ_0 and σ_1 are provided by the receiver. We consider the computation of each bit of this string. For every position, i, if the i^t bit of σ_0 and $\sigma_1 - \sigma_0$ are b_1 and b_2 respectively, the result will be $v_{g,row}^{b_1 b_2}$, where

$$v_{g,row}^{b_1 b_2} = F_{\mathsf{prg}}^a + F_{\mathsf{prg}}^b + b_1 + f_{g,row}^{a_1,a_2,a_3}(\lambda_a^S, \lambda_b^S, \lambda_c^S) \cdot b_2.$$

Since $f_{g,row}^{a_1,a_2,a_3}$ was already computed in the previous part, the values $v_{g,row}^{b_1 b_2}$ can be achieved with no additional multiplication gates. We further note that $v_{g,row}^{b_1 b_2}$ is independent of the position in the MAC part.

Again, we can compute $v_{g,row}^{b_1 b_2}$ using the sender OT input strings by using only an addition operation for each position in the MAC part. We can check for every position if this value matches the computation above from the witness. There is no additional cost for this part.

Binary constraints. The λ_w^S values need to be sampled from $\{0, 1\}$ and since we are operating in $\mathbb{GF}(2^s)$ we need enforce this constraint. This will require a single multiplication[10] per wire for a total of $|C|$ multiplications. However, it will not affect the communication length and only the computations that need to performed.

Combining the above, we have a total of $|C| \cdot 5 \cdot \lceil \frac{\kappa}{s} \rceil$ multiplications.

4. As in our previous compilation, we replace the oracle call to $\mathcal{F}_{\mathrm{COT-IVD}}$ in Π with the protocol Π_3 from Sect. 5 in the $(\mathcal{F}_{\mathrm{OT}}, \mathcal{F}_{\mathrm{CnP}})$-hybrid. We then replace the oracle call to $\mathcal{F}_{\mathrm{CnP}}$ with our protocol Π_4 in the $\mathcal{F}_{\mathrm{OT}}$-hybrid where we instantiate our MPC protocol using [1]. The resulting protocol realizes $\mathcal{F}_{\mathrm{COT-IVD}}$ against static corruptions by active adversaries. This communication complexity of the protocol can be computed as follows:

   (a) The sender communicates $(12 \cdot \kappa + 22 \cdot s) \cdot |C| + 2 \cdot \kappa \cdot s$ bits to the OT functionality and $4 \cdot (\kappa + s) \cdot |C|$ bits in a direct message to the receiver in the first step of the protocol as part of the passively secure protocol for realizing the $\widehat{\mathcal{F}}_{\mathrm{IVD}}$ functionality.

   (b) Transmitting a MAC for each OT input. We transmit a MAC value of length s for each OT string independent of its length. There are $2 \cdot (|C| + 2 \cdot s + \max(4 \cdot n, 8 \cdot s))$ strings transmitted via OTs. Therefore, sending the MACs will require the sender to transmit $2 \cdot s \cdot (|C| + 2 \cdot s + \max(4 \cdot n, 8 \cdot s))$ bits.

   (c) The commit-and-prove protocol. The communication complexity of this protocol can be bounded by $8 \cdot s^{1.5} \cdot \sqrt{I + 3 \cdot M}$ bits, where M represents the number of field multiplications over $\mathbb{GF}(2^s)$ involved in the computation of the NP-relation and I denotes the any additional witness bits (involved only in additions). Our NP-relation can be expressed as an arithmetic circuit over $\mathbb{GF}(2^s)$, including the global predicate from the previous step and an additional check to ensure that the MACs are correct. From the previous step we know that the first part requires $5 \cdot |C| \cdot \lceil \frac{\kappa}{s} \rceil$ multiplications for verifying the OT inputs whereas the second part, verifying the MACs requires one multiplication per s bits of the OT sender inputs. This results in $\lceil \Gamma/s \rceil$ multiplications where Γ is the total length of OT sender inputs. From the previous step, we know $\Gamma = (12 \cdot \kappa + 22 \cdot s) \cdot |C| + 2 \cdot \kappa \cdot s$. In addition, as part of the witness, the PRF values that are used only for additions need to be included this sums up to $4 \cdot |C| \cdot (\kappa + s)$. For an arithmetic circuit C we denote by $|C|$ the number of multiplication gates. Our proof length is given by

$$8 \cdot s^{1.5} \cdot \sqrt{4 \cdot |C| \cdot (\kappa + s) + 3 \cdot |C| \cdot (5 \cdot \lceil \kappa/s \rceil + 12 \lceil \kappa/s \rceil + 22 + 2 \cdot \kappa \cdot s)}$$
$$= 8 \cdot s^{1.5} \cdot \sqrt{|C| \cdot (55 \cdot \lceil \kappa/s \rceil + 6 \cdot \kappa + 73)}$$

---

[10] We express this as $x^2 - x = 0$.

Finally, the overall communication complexity of the protocol in the κ-bit string OT-hybrid for circuits with more than 5000 AND gates is

$$\underbrace{(12 \cdot \kappa + 22 \cdot s) \cdot |C| + 4 \cdot (\kappa + s) \cdot |C|}_{\text{passive NISC/OT communication}} + \underbrace{2 \cdot s \cdot (|C| + 2 \cdot s + \max(4 \cdot n, 8 \cdot s))}_{\text{MAC for every OT input}}$$
$$\underbrace{+ 8 \cdot s^{1.5} \cdot \sqrt{|C| \cdot (55 \cdot \lceil \kappa/s \rceil + 6 \cdot \kappa + 73)}}_{\text{CnP protocol}}.$$

In Table 2, we provide estimate communication cost incurred by our protocol. We set $\kappa = 128$ and $s = 40$ and 80. The communication cost for the OT invocations were computed assuming an implementation based on the actively secure OT extension protocol of [29] and can be bounded by $3 \cdot (\#OT) \cdot \kappa$. Furthermore, to accommodate arbitrary length strings for the sender's inputs the communication cost of OT is computed on κ'-bit strings from the sender, where $\kappa' = 128$ in practice, and longer strings are handled by transferring random keys and encrypting the bigger strings via the keys.

Computational efficiency. In contrast to the concrete communication complexity, which is implementation independent, the concrete computation cost is sensitive to many implementation details. Although we have not implemented our protocol, we believe that it can be reasonably fast. The parties engage in $O(|C|)$ instances of parallel OT execution which can be implemented efficiently via OT-extensions [17,30]. Reconstructing the garbled circuit from the output of the parallel OTs relies only on simple bitwise XOR operation on bit strings. The computationally intensive part of the COT protocol is sharing several blocks of secrets via packed secret-sharing and evaluating polynomials by both the sender and the receiver. Since we instantiate our packed-secret sharing scheme over a large finite field, this can be done efficiently via Fast Fourier Transforms. An implementation of a similar FFT-based protocol is provided in [1]. Furthermore, the communication complexity of the COT protocol is significantly smaller than the overall communication (as can be seen in the calculations above). This allows trading a slight increase in the communication cost for more significant improvements in computational cost by using a larger number of FFTs on shorter blocks.

Non-interactive variant. With function independent preprocessing for generating random OTs between the sender and the receiver, we can make our protocol non-interactive in the sense of [20], namely implement the protocol with one message from the receiver to the sender, followed by one message from the sender to the receiver. At a high-level, this is done by executing the passively secure information theoretic "Yao-style" protocol, followed by our commit and prove protocol. By OT preprocessing we can make the passively secure NISC/OT protocol a two-message protocol in the online phase. Our commit and prove protocol is public coin and can be made non-interactive via a standard Fiat-Shamir transform [11]. However, in the non-interactive case, the statistical security parameter s becomes a computational parameter, since a malicious sender can just try sampling 2^s instances of its message until finding one that would lead the receiver to accept a badly formed transcript. It is therefore needed in this case

Table 2. We give our total estimated communication cost of our concretely efficient variant where $\kappa = 128$ and $s = 40$ and 80. We also provide our overhead over the passively secure Yao protocol (with FreeXOR but no half-gate optimization).

Circuit size	Comm. (MB) ($s = 40$)	Overhead ($s = 40$)	Comm. (MB) ($s = 80$)	Overhead ($s = 80$)
1024	0.71	11.33	1.07	17.16
2048	1.19	9.49	1.89	15.09
4096	2.12	8.46	3.16	12.65
6800 (AES)	3.39	8.16	4.80	11.56
8192	3.94	7.88	5.63	11.27
16384	7.53	7.53	10.46	10.46
32768	14.64	7.32	19.96	9.98
65536	28.76	7.19	38.74	9.69
131072	56.86	7.11	75.99	9.50
262144	112.85	7.05	150.05	9.38
524288	224.54	7.02	297.55	9.30
1048576	447.52	6.99	591.66	9.24
2097152	892.90	6.98	1178.65	9.21
4194304	1782.85	6.96	2350.87	9.18

6800 is the size of the AES circuit excluding XOR gates.

to use a larger value of s, say $s = 80$. A useful feature of non-interactive protocols is that the sender can use the same encrypted receiver input for multiple evaluations.[11]

Offline-online variant. Our protocol is particularly attractive in the offline-online setting. In an offline preprocessing phase, before the inputs are known, the sender and the receiver can run the entire protocol except for the oblivious transfers that depend on the receiver's input. Following this offline interaction, the receiver verifies that the information obtained from the sender is consistent, and can then "compress" this information into a single authenticated garbled circuit whose size is comparable to a standard garbled circuit. In an online phase, once the inputs are known, the receiver uses a small number of OTs to obtain the input keys, and performs garbled circuit evaluation and verification whose total cost is comparable to a single garbled circuit evaluation.

Acknowledgements. We thank Peter Rindal, Mike Rosulek and Xiao Wang, for helpful discussions and the anonymous TCC reviewers for helpful comments.

The first author was supported by the European Research Council under the ERC consolidators grant agreement n. 615172 (HIPS), and by the BIU Center for Research in Applied Cryptography and Cyber Security in conjunction with the Israel

---

[11] As discussed in [20], the multiple evaluation setting is subject to selective failure attacks when the sender can learn the receiver's output in each evaluation.

National Cyber Bureau in the Prime Minister's Office. The second author was supported by a DARPA/ARL SAFEWARE award, DARPA Brandeis program under Contract N66001-15-C-4065, NSF Frontier Award 1413955, NSF grants 1619348, 1228984, 1136174, and 1065276, ERC grant 742754, NSF-BSF grant 2015782, ISF grant 1709/14, BSF grant 2012378, a Xerox Faculty Research Award, a Google Faculty Research Award, an equipment grant from Intel, and an Okawa Foundation Research Grant. This material is based upon work supported by the Defense Advanced Research Projects Agency through the ARL under Contract W911NF-15-C-0205. The views expressed are those of the authors and do not reflect the official policy or position of Google, the Department of Defense, the National Science Foundation, or the U.S. Government. The third author was supported by Google Faculty Research Grant and NSF Awards CNS-1526377 and CNS-1618884.

A   Secure Two-Party Computation

We use a standard standalone definition of secure two-party computation protocols. In this work, we only consider static corruptions, i.e. the adversary needs to decide which party it corrupts before the execution begins. Following [14], we use two security parameters in our definition. We denote by κ a computational security parameter and by s a statistical security parameter that captures a statistical error of up to 2^{-s}. We assume $s \leq \kappa$. We let $\mathcal{F}$ be a two-party functionality that maps a pair of inputs of equal length to a pair of outputs. Without loss of generality, our protocols only deliver output to one party (the receiver), which can be viewed as a special case in which the other party's output is fixed.

Let $\Pi = \langle P_0, P_1 \rangle$ denote a two-party protocol, where each party is given an input (x for P_0 and y for P_1) and security parameters 1^s and 1^κ. We allow honest parties to be PPT in the entire input length (this is needed to ensure correctness when no party is corrupted) but bound adversaries to time $\mathsf{poly}(\kappa)$ (this effectively means that we only require security when the input length is bounded by *some* polynomial in κ). We denote by $\mathbf{REAL}_{\Pi,\mathcal{A}(z),P_i}(x,y,\kappa,s)$ the output of the honest party P_i and the adversary $\mathcal{A}$ controlling P_{1-i} in the real execution of Π, where z is the auxiliary input, x is P_0's initial input, y is P_1's initial input, κ is the computational security parameter and s is the statistical security parameter. We denote by $\mathbf{IDEAL}_{\mathcal{F},\mathcal{S}(z),P_i}(x,y,\kappa,s)$ the output of the honest party P_i and the simulator $\mathcal{S}$ in the ideal model where $\mathcal{F}$ is computed by a trusted party. In some of our protocols the parties have access to ideal model implementation of certain cryptographic primitives such as ideal oblivious-transfer ($\mathcal{F}_{\mathrm{OT}}$) and we will denote such an execution by $\mathbf{REAL}^{\mathcal{F}_{\mathrm{OT}}}_{\Pi,\mathcal{A}(z),P_i}(x,y,\kappa,s)$.

Definition A.1. *A protocol* $\Pi = \langle P_0, P_1 \rangle$ *is said to securely compute a functionality* $\mathcal{F}$ *in the presence of active adversaries if the parties always have the correct output* $\mathcal{F}(x,y)$ *when neither party is corrupted, and moreover the following security requirement holds. For any probabilistic* $\mathsf{poly}(\kappa)$-*time adversary* $\mathcal{A}$ *controlling* P_i *(for* $i \in \{0,1\}$*) in the real model, there exists a probabilistic* $\mathsf{poly}(\kappa)$-*time adversary (simulator)* $\mathcal{S}$ *controlling* P_i *in the ideal model, such that* *for every non-uniform* $\mathsf{poly}(\kappa)$-*time distinguisher $\mathcal{D}$ there exists a negligible function* $\nu(\cdot)$ *such that the following ensembles are distinguished by $\mathcal{D}$ with at most* $\nu(\kappa) + 2^{-s}$ *advantage:*

- $\{\mathbf{REAL}_{\Pi,\mathcal{A}(z),P_i}(x,y,\kappa,s)\}_{\kappa\in\mathbb{N},s\in\mathbb{N},x,y,z\in\{0,1\}^*}$
- $\{\mathbf{IDEAL}_{\mathcal{F},\mathcal{S}(z),P_i}(x,y,\kappa,s)\}_{\kappa\in\mathbb{N},s\in\mathbb{N},x,y,z\in\{0,1\}^*}$

Secure circuit evaluation. The above definition considers $\mathcal{F}$ to be an infinite functionality, taking inputs of an arbitrary length. However, our protocols (similarly to other protocols from the literature) are formulated for a finite functionality $\mathcal{F} : \{0,1\}^n \times \{0,1\}^n \rightarrow \{0,1\}^m$ described by a Boolean circuit C. Such protocols are formally captured by a polynomial-time *protocol compiler* that, given security parameters $1^\kappa, 1^s$ and a circuit C, outputs a pair of circuits (P_0, P_1) that implement the next message function of the two parties in the protocol (possibly using oracle calls to a cryptographic primitive or an ideal functionality oracle). While the correctness requirement (when no party is corrupted) holds for any choice of $\kappa, s,$ C, the security requirement only considers adversaries that run in time $\mathsf{poly}(\kappa)$. That is, we require indistinguishability (in the sense of Definition A.1) between

- $\{\mathbf{REAL}_{\Pi,\mathcal{A}(z),P_i}(C,x,y,\kappa,s)\}_{\kappa\in\mathbb{N},s\in\mathbb{N},C\in\mathcal{C},x,y,z\in\{0,1\}^*}$
- $\{\mathbf{IDEAL}_{\mathcal{F},\mathcal{S}(z),P_i}(C,x,y,\kappa,s)\}_{\kappa\in\mathbb{N},s\in\mathbb{N},C\in\mathcal{C},x,y,z\in\{0,1\}^*}$

where $\mathcal{C}$ is the class of boolean circuits that take two bit-strings as inputs and output two bit-strings, x,y are of lengths corresponding to the inputs of C, $\mathcal{F}$ is the functionality computed by C, and the next message functions of the parties P_0, P_1 is as specified by the protocol compiler on inputs $1^\kappa, 1^s,$ C.

References

1. Ames, S., Hazay, C., Ishai, Y., Venkitasubramaniam, M.: Ligero: lightweight sublinear arguments without a trusted setup. In: Proceedings of the ACM CCS 2017 (2017, to appear)
2. Applebaum, B., Damgård, I., Ishai, Y., Nielsen, M., Zichron, L.: Secure arithmetic computation with constant computational overhead. In: Katz, J., Shacham, H. (eds.) CRYPTO 2017. LNCS, vol. 10401, pp. 223–254. Springer, Cham (2017). doi:10.1007/978-3-319-63688-7_8
3. Beaver, D., Micali, S., Rogaway, P.: The round complexity of secure protocols (extended abstract). In: STOC, pp. 503–513 (1990)
4. Bellare, M., Hoang, V.T., Rogaway, P.: Foundations of garbled circuits. In: CCS, pp. 784–796 (2012)
5. Boyle, E., Gilboa, N., Ishai, Y.: Group-based secure computation: optimizing rounds, communication, and computation. In: Coron, J.-S., Nielsen, J.B. (eds.) EUROCRYPT 2017. LNCS, vol. 10211, pp. 163–193. Springer, Cham (2017). doi:10.1007/978-3-319-56614-6_6
6. Brassard, G., Crepeau, C., Robert, J.-M.: All-or-nothing disclosure of secrets. In: Odlyzko, A.M. (ed.) CRYPTO 1986. LNCS, vol. 263, pp. 234–238. Springer, Heidelberg (1987). doi:10.1007/3-540-47721-7_17

7. Chen, H., Cramer, R.: Algebraic geometric secret sharing schemes and secure multi-party computations over small fields. In: Dwork, C. (ed.) CRYPTO 2006. LNCS, vol. 4117, pp. 521–536. Springer, Heidelberg (2006). doi:10.1007/11818175_31

8. Damgård, I., Ishai, Y.: Scalable secure multiparty computation. In: Dwork, C. (ed.) CRYPTO 2006. LNCS, vol. 4117, pp. 501–520. Springer, Heidelberg (2006). doi:10.1007/11818175_30

9. Damgård, I., Ishai, Y., Krøigaard, M.: Perfectly secure multiparty computation and the computational overhead of cryptography. In: Gilbert, H. (ed.) EUROCRYPT 2010. LNCS, vol. 6110, pp. 445–465. Springer, Heidelberg (2010). doi:10.1007/978-3-642-13190-5_23

10. Feige, U., Kilian, J., Naor, M.: A minimal model for secure computation (extended abstract). In: STOC, pp. 554–563 (1994)

11. Fiat, A., Shamir, A.: How to prove yourself: practical solutions to identification and signature problems. In: Odlyzko, A.M. (ed.) CRYPTO 1986. LNCS, vol. 263, pp. 186–194. Springer, Heidelberg (1987). doi:10.1007/3-540-47721-7_12

12. Gentry, C.: Fully homomorphic encryption using ideal lattices. In: STOC, pp. 169–178 (2009)

13. Goldreich, O., Micali, S., Wigderson, A.: How to play any mental game or a completeness theorem for protocols with honest majority. In: STOC, pp. 218–229 (1987)

14. Hazay, C., Lindell, Y.: Efficient Secure Two-Party Protocols - Techniques and Constructions. Information Security and Cryptography. Springer, Heidelberg (2010)

15. Huang, Y., Katz, J., Evans, D.: Efficient secure two-party computation using symmetric cut-and-choose. In: Canetti, R., Garay, J.A. (eds.) CRYPTO 2013. LNCS, vol. 8043, pp. 18–35. Springer, Heidelberg (2013). doi:10.1007/978-3-642-40084-1_2

16. Huang, Y., Katz, J., Kolesnikov, V., Kumaresan, R., Malozemoff, A.J.: Amortizing garbled circuits. In: Garay, J.A., Gennaro, R. (eds.) CRYPTO 2014. LNCS, vol. 8617, pp. 458–475. Springer, Heidelberg (2014). doi:10.1007/978-3-662-44381-1_26

17. Ishai, Y., Kilian, J., Nissim, K., Petrank, E.: Extending oblivious transfers efficiently. In: Boneh, D. (ed.) CRYPTO 2003. LNCS, vol. 2729, pp. 145–161. Springer, Heidelberg (2003). doi:10.1007/978-3-540-45146-4_9

18. Ishai, Y., Kushilevitz, E.: Perfect constant-round secure computation via perfect randomizing polynomials. In: Widmayer, P., Eidenbenz, S., Triguero, F., Morales, R., Conejo, R., Hennessy, M. (eds.) ICALP 2002. LNCS, vol. 2380, pp. 244–256. Springer, Heidelberg (2002). doi:10.1007/3-540-45465-9_22

19. Ishai, Y., Kushilevitz, E., Li, X., Ostrovsky, R., Prabhakaran, M., Sahai, A., Zuckerman, D.: Robust pseudorandom generators. In: Fomin, F.V., Freivalds, R., Kwiatkowska, M., Peleg, D. (eds.) ICALP 2013. LNCS, vol. 7965, pp. 576–588. Springer, Heidelberg (2013). doi:10.1007/978-3-642-39206-1_49

20. Ishai, Y., Kushilevitz, E., Ostrovsky, R., Prabhakaran, M., Sahai, A.: Efficient non-interactive secure computation. In: Paterson, K.G. (ed.) EUROCRYPT 2011. LNCS, vol. 6632, pp. 406–425. Springer, Heidelberg (2011). doi:10.1007/978-3-642-20465-4_23

21. Ishai, Y., Kushilevitz, E., Ostrovsky, R., Sahai, A.: Zero-knowledge from secure multiparty computation. In: STOC, pp. 21–30 (2007)

22. Ishai, Y., Kushilevitz, E., Ostrovsky, R., Sahai, A.: Cryptography with constant computational overhead. In: STOC, pp. 433–442 (2008)

23. Ishai, Y., Kushilevitz, E., Ostrovsky, R., Sahai, A.: Zero-knowledge proofs from secure multiparty computation. SIAM J. Comput. **39**(3), 1121–1152 (2009)

24. Ishai, Y., Mahmoody, M., Sahai, A.: On efficient zero-knowledge PCPs. In: Cramer, R. (ed.) TCC 2012. LNCS, vol. 7194, pp. 151–168. Springer, Heidelberg (2012). doi:10.1007/978-3-642-28914-9_9

25. Ishai, Y., Prabhakaran, M., Sahai, A.: Founding cryptography on oblivious transfer – efficiently. In: Wagner, D. (ed.) CRYPTO 2008. LNCS, vol. 5157, pp. 572–591. Springer, Heidelberg (2008). doi:10.1007/978-3-540-85174-5_32

26. Ishai, Y., Prabhakaran, M., Sahai, A.: Secure arithmetic computation with no honest majority. In: Reingold, O. (ed.) TCC 2009. LNCS, vol. 5444, pp. 294–314. Springer, Heidelberg (2009). doi:10.1007/978-3-642-00457-5_18

27. Ishai, Y., Weiss, M.: Probabilistically checkable proofs of proximity with zero-knowledge. In: Lindell, Y. (ed.) TCC 2014. LNCS, vol. 8349, pp. 121–145. Springer, Heidelberg (2014). doi:10.1007/978-3-642-54242-8_6

28. Jarecki, S., Shmatikov, V.: Efficient two-party secure computation on committed inputs. In: Naor, M. (ed.) EUROCRYPT 2007. LNCS, vol. 4515, pp. 97–114. Springer, Heidelberg (2007). doi:10.1007/978-3-540-72540-4_6

29. Keller, M., Orsini, E., Scholl, P.: Actively secure OT extension with optimal overhead. In: Gennaro, R., Robshaw, M. (eds.) CRYPTO 2015. LNCS, vol. 9215, pp. 724–741. Springer, Heidelberg (2015). doi:10.1007/978-3-662-47989-6_35

30. Keller, M., Orsini, E., Scholl, P.: MASCOT: faster malicious arithmetic secure computation with oblivious transfer. IACR Cryptology ePrint Archive 2016:505 (2016)

31. Kilian, J.: Founding cryptography on oblivious transfer. In: STOC, pp. 20–31 (1988)

32. Kolesnikov, V., Kumaresan, R.: Improved OT extension for transferring short secrets. IACR Cryptology ePrint Archive 2013:491 (2013)

33. Kolesnikov, V., Schneider, T.: Improved garbled circuit: free XOR gates and applications. In: Aceto, L., Damgård, I., Goldberg, L.A., Halldórsson, M.M., Ingólfsdóttir, A., Walukiewicz, I. (eds.) ICALP 2008. LNCS, vol. 5126, pp. 486–498. Springer, Heidelberg (2008). doi:10.1007/978-3-540-70583-3_40

34. Lindell, Y.: Fast cut-and-choose-based protocols for malicious and covert adversaries. J. Cryptol. 29(2), 456–490 (2016)

35. Lindell, Y., Pinkas, B.: An efficient protocol for secure two-party computation in the presence of malicious adversaries. In: Naor, M. (ed.) EUROCRYPT 2007. LNCS, vol. 4515, pp. 52–78. Springer, Heidelberg (2007). doi:10.1007/978-3-540-72540-4_4

36. Lindell, Y., Pinkas, B.: Secure two-party computation via cut-and-choose oblivious transfer. J. Cryptol. 25(4), 680–722 (2012)

37. Lindell, Y., Pinkas, B., Smart, N.P., Yanai, A.: Efficient constant round multiparty computation combining BMR and SPDZ. In: Gennaro, R., Robshaw, M. (eds.) CRYPTO 2015. LNCS, vol. 9216, pp. 319–338. Springer, Heidelberg (2015). doi:10.1007/978-3-662-48000-7_16

38. Lindell, Y., Riva, B.: Cut-and-choose yao-based secure computation in the online/offline and batch settings. In: Garay, J.A., Gennaro, R. (eds.) CRYPTO 2014. LNCS, vol. 8617, pp. 476–494. Springer, Heidelberg (2014). doi:10.1007/978-3-662-44381-1_27

39. Mohassel, P., Franklin, M.: Efficiency tradeoffs for malicious two-party computation. In: Yung, M., Dodis, Y., Kiayias, A., Malkin, T. (eds.) PKC 2006. LNCS, vol. 3958, pp. 458–473. Springer, Heidelberg (2006). doi:10.1007/11745853_30

40. Mossel, E., Shpilka, A., Trevisan, L.: On e-Biased generators in NC0. In: FOCS, pp. 136–145 (2003)

41. Nielsen, J.B., Nordholt, P.S., Orlandi, C., Burra, S.S.: A new approach to practical active-secure two-party computation. In: Safavi-Naini, R., Canetti, R. (eds.) CRYPTO 2012. LNCS, vol. 7417, pp. 681–700. Springer, Heidelberg (2012). doi:10.1007/978-3-642-32009-5_40

42. Nielsen, J.B., Orlandi, C.: Cross and clean: amortized garbled circuits with constant overhead. In: Hirt, M., Smith, A. (eds.) TCC 2016. LNCS, vol. 9985, pp. 582–603. Springer, Heidelberg (2016). doi:10.1007/978-3-662-53641-4_22

43. Nielsen, J.B., Schneider, T., Trifiletti, R.: Constant round maliciously secure 2PC with function-independent preprocessing using LEGO. In: 24th Annual Network and Distributed System Security Symposium (NDSS 2017). The Internet Society, 26 February–1 March 2017

44. Rindal, P., Rosulek, M.: Faster malicious 2-party secure computation with online/offline dual execution. In: 25th USENIX Security Symposium, USENIX Security 16, Austin, TX, USA, 10–12 August 2016, pp. 297–314 (2016)

45. Shelat, A., Shen, C.-H.: Fast two-party secure computation with minimal assumptions. In: CCS, pp. 523–534 (2013)

46. Spielman, D.A.: Linear-time encodable and decodable error-correcting codes. In: STOC, pp. 388–397 (1995)

47. Wang, X., Malozemoff, A.J., Katz, J.: Faster secure two-party computation in the single-execution setting. In: Coron, J.-S., Nielsen, J.B. (eds.) EUROCRYPT 2017. LNCS, vol. 10212, pp. 399–424. Springer, Cham (2017). doi:10.1007/978-3-319-56617-7_14

48. Wang, X., Ranellucci, S., Katz, J.: Authenticated garbling and efficient maliciously secure multi-party computation. In: Proceedings of the ACM CCS, (2017, to appear). Full version: Cryptology ePrint Archive, Report 2017/030

49. Yao, A.C.-C.: How to generate and exchange secrets (extended abstract). In: FOCS, pp. 162–167 (1986)

50. Zahur, S., Rosulek, M., Evans, D.: Two halves make a whole. In: Oswald, E., Fischlin, M. (eds.) EUROCRYPT 2015. LNCS, vol. 9057, pp. 220–250. Springer, Heidelberg (2015). doi:10.1007/978-3-662-46803-6_8

Adaptively Indistinguishable Garbled Circuits

Zahra Jafargholi[1][✉], Alessandra Scafuro[2], and Daniel Wichs[3]

[1] Aarhus University, Aarhus, Denmark
zahra@cs.au.dk
[2] North Carolina State University, Raleigh, USA
ascafur@ncsu.edu
[3] Northeastern University, Boston, USA
wichs@ccs.neu.edu

Abstract. A garbling scheme is used to garble a circuit C and an input x in a way that reveals the output $C(x)$ but hides everything else. An adaptively secure scheme allows the adversary to specify the input x after seeing the garbled circuit. Applebaum et al. (CRYPTO '13) showed that in any garbling scheme with adaptive simulation-based security, the size of the garbled input must exceed the output size of the circuit. Here we show how to circumvent this lower bound and achieve significantly better efficiency under the minimal assumption that one-way functions exist by relaxing the security notion from simulation-based to indistinguishability-based.

We rely on the recent work of Hemenway et al. (CRYPTO '16) which constructed an adaptive simulation-based garbling scheme under one-way functions. The size of the garbled input in their scheme is as large as the *output size* of the circuit plus a certain *pebble complexity* of the circuit, where the latter is (e.g.,) bounded by the space complexity of the computation. By building on top of their construction and adapting their proof technique, we show how to remove the output size dependence in their result when considering indistinguishability-based security.

As an application of the above result, we get a symmetric-key functional encryption based on one-way functions, with indistinguishability-based security where the adversary can obtain an unbounded number of function secret keys and then adaptively a single challenge ciphertext. The size of the ciphertext only depends on the maximal pebble complexity of each of the functions but not on the number of functions or their circuit size.

1 Introduction

Garbled Circuits. A *garbling scheme* [Yao82, Yao86] can be used to garble a circuit C and an input x to derive a garbled circuit $\widetilde{C}$ and a garbled input $\tilde{x}$. It's possible to evaluate $\widetilde{C}$ on $\tilde{x}$ and get the correct output $C(x)$. However,

Z. Jafargholi—Supported by the European Research Council (ERC) under the European Unions' Horizon 2020 research and innovation programme under grant agreement No. 669255 (MPCPRO).

D. Wichs—Supported by NSF grants CNS-1314722, CNS-1413964.

© International Association for Cryptologic Research 2017
Y. Kalai and L. Reyzin (Eds.): TCC 2017, Part II, LNCS 10678, pp. 40–71, 2017.
https://doi.org/10.1007/978-3-319-70503-3_2

the garbled values $\widetilde{C}, \tilde{x}$ should not reveal anything else beyond this. In many applications, the garbled circuit $\widetilde{C}$ can be computed in an *off-line* pre-processing phase before the input is known and therefore we are not overly concerned with the efficiency of this procedure. On the other hand, once the input x becomes available in the *on-line* phase, creating the garbled input $\tilde{x}$ should be extremely efficient. Therefore, the main efficiency measure that we consider here is the *on-line complexity* of a garbling scheme, which is the time it takes to garble an input x, and hence also a bound on the size of $\tilde{x}$.

Security of Garbled Circuits. There are several natural notions of garbled circuit security that one can consider.

Firstly, we can consider either *selective* or *adaptive* security. For selective security, we consider a scenario where the adversary chooses the circuit C and the input x first and only then gets the garbled versions $\widetilde{C}, \tilde{x}$. For adaptive security, we consider a scenario where the adversary first gets the garbled circuit $\widetilde{C}$ and can then adaptively chooses the input x to be garbled. Adaptive security is the natural notion in the on-line/off-line setting where we envision the garbled circuit to be created first in an earlier stage before the input is selected.

Secondly, we can consider either *simulation-based* or *indistinguishability-based* definitions of security. In the simulation-based setting, we require that the garbled circuit and the garbled input can be simulated given only the output of the computation and the topology of the circuit. In the indistinguishability-based setting, we require that the adversary cannot distinguish between a garbling of C_0, x_0 or C_1, x_1 as long as $C_0(x_0) = C_1(x_1)$ and C_0, C_1 have the same topology.

Prior Work. Yao's construction of garbled circuits under one-way functions already achieves essentially optimal on-line complexity, where the time to garble an input x and the size of $\tilde{x}$ are only linear in the input size $|x|$, independent of the circuit size.[1] However, it was only shown to satisfy *selective* simulation-based security [LP09].

Recently, the work of Hemenway et al. [HJO+16] showed how to modify Yao's construction and get *adaptive* simulation-based security under one-way functions. The on-line complexity of their scheme depends linearly on a certain "*pebble complexity*" t of the circuit, its *input size* n and *output size* m. Furthermore, they showed that the pebble complexity t is upper bounded by the circuit width which is in turn bounded by the space complexity of the computation. The work of [JW16] also shows that even Yao's original garbled circuit construction already achieves adaptive simulation-based security via reduction with a 2^t security loss as long as the mapping between output labels and the bits they represent is only given in the garbled input.

In both of the above works, the online complexity is always at least as large as the output size m. The work of Applebaum et al. [AIKW13] (see also [HW15])

---

[1] More precisely, in Yao's garbled circuits, the garbled input is of size $|x| \cdot \mathsf{poly}(\lambda)$ where λ is the security parameter. The work of Applebaum et al. [AIKW13] shows how to reduce this to $|x| + \mathsf{poly}(\lambda)$ assuming stronger assumptions such as DDH, RSA or LWE.

gives a lower bound showing that this is inherent for adaptive simulation-secure garbled circuits.

Our Results. In this work, we show how to construct adaptively secure garbling schemes based on one-way functions, where the on-line complexity of our scheme can be smaller than the output size of the circuit. This necessarily requires us to give up on simulation-based security and instead we achieve indistinguishability-based security. In more detail, we propose a new garbling scheme which builds on top of the ideas of [HJO+16] but essentially removes the output size dependence in their construction, making the on-line complexity only linear in the pebble complexity t and the input size n, but independent of the output size m.

As an application of the above result, we consider the scenario where we garble a circuit C which consists of many disjoint boolean sub-circuits $C_1, \ldots, C_\ell$ which all take the same input x but do not share any other wires/gates except for the input wires. In that case, although the output size of C is ℓ (which we think of as large) the pebble complexity of C is just $t = \max\{t_i\}$ where t_i denote the pebble complexities of the individual circuits C_i, and therefore is independent of the number of circuits ℓ. We can also think of the above as allowing us to construct an adaptively indistinguishable private-key functional encryption (FE) scheme by thinking of the garbled versions of the circuits C_i as function secret keys and the garbled input as a ciphertext. The size of the ciphertext is linear in the size of the input x and the maximal pebble complexity of the individual functions, which we can bound by their space complexity, but is independent of the number of function secret keys ℓ or even their circuit size.

Finally it bears mentioning that an adaptively indistinguishable scheme is also adaptively secure under the simulation-based security definition for any efficiently invertible function.[2] Therefore for this class of functions our construction provides a *simulation-based adaptively secure* garbling scheme with online complexity independent of the output size.

1.1   Our Techniques

Before we can explain our techniques, we first review Yao's garbled circuit construction, the issue with adaptive security and the technique of [HJO+16]. The discussion below is adapted from [HJO+16].

Yao's Scheme. First, let's start by recalling Yao's garbled circuits. For each wire w in the circuit, we pick two keys k_w^0, k_w^1 for a symmetric-key encryption scheme. For each gate in the circuit computing a function $g : \{0,1\}^2 \rightarrow \{0,1\}$ and having input wires a, b and output wire c we create a *garbled gate* consisting of 4 randomly ordered ciphertexts created as:

$$
\begin{aligned}
c_{0,0} &= \mathsf{Enc}_{k_a^0}(\mathsf{Enc}_{k_b^0}(k_c^{g(0,0)})) & c_{1,0} &= \mathsf{Enc}_{k_a^1}(\mathsf{Enc}_{k_b^0}(k_c^{g(1,0)})), \\
c_{0,1} &= \mathsf{Enc}_{k_a^0}(\mathsf{Enc}_{k_b^1}(k_c^{g(0,1)})) & c_{1,1} &= \mathsf{Enc}_{k_a^1}(\mathsf{Enc}_{k_b^1}(k_c^{g(1,1)}))
\end{aligned}
\tag{1}
$$

---

[2] More generally, any function f for which, given any image element y it is possible to efficiently find a canonical pre-image x.

where (Enc, Dec) is a CPA-secure encryption scheme. The garbled circuit $\widetilde{C}$ consists of all of the gabled gates, along with an *output map*

$$\{k_w^0 \to 0, k_w^1 \to 1\}$$

which maps the keys to the bits they represent for each output wire w. To garble an n-bit value $x = x_1 x_2 \cdots x_n$, the garbled input $\tilde{x}$ consists of the keys $k_{w_i}^{x_i}$ for the n input wires w_i.

To evaluate the garbled circuit on the garbled input, it's possible to decrypt exactly one ciphertext in each garbled gate and get the key $k_w^{v(w)}$ corresponding to the bit $v(w)$ going over the wire w during the computation $C(x)$. Once the keys for the output wires are computed, it's possible to recover actual output bits by looking them up in the output map.

To prove the selective simulation-based security of Yao's scheme, we have a simulator that gets the output $y = y_1 y_2 \cdots y_m = C(x)$ and must produce $\widetilde{C}, \tilde{x}$. The simulator picks random keys k_1^0, k_w^1 for each wire w just like the real scheme, but it creates the garbled gates as follows:

$$
\begin{aligned}
c_{0,0} &= \mathsf{Enc}_{k_a^0}(\mathsf{Enc}_{k_b^0}(k_c^0)) \quad c_{1,0} = \mathsf{Enc}_{k_a^1}(\mathsf{Enc}_{k_b^0}(k_c^0)), \\
c_{0,1} &= \mathsf{Enc}_{k_a^0}(\mathsf{Enc}_{k_b^1}(k_c^0)) \quad c_{1,1} = \mathsf{Enc}_{k_a^1}(\mathsf{Enc}_{k_b^1}(k_c^0))
\end{aligned}
\tag{2}
$$

where all four ciphertext encrypt the same key k_c^0. It then sets the output map as $\{k_w^0 \to y_w, k_w^1 \to 1 - y_w\}$ by "programming it" so that the key k_w^0 corresponds to the correct output bit y_w for each output wire w. This defines the simulated garbled circuit $\widetilde{C}$. To create the simulated garbled input $\tilde{x}$ the simulator simply gives out the keys k_w^0 for each input wire w. Note that, when evaluating the simulated garbled circuit on the simulated garbled input, the adversary only sees the keys k_w^0 for every wire w.

Proof of Security and Issues with Adaptivity. There are two main issues with proving adaptive security of Yao's construction.

The first issue is that, in the simulation-based security setting, the simulator now cannot "program" the output map since it is given as part of the garbled circuit before the output $y_1, \ldots, y_m$ is defined. This can be fixed by modifying the construction and moving the output map from the garbled circuit to the garbled input, at the cost of raising the on-line complexity to depend on the output size. In the simulation-based setting we know this to be inherent, but one could hope to avoid this in the indistinguishability-based setting.

The second and more serious issue is the sequence of hybrids used to prove security. At a high level, the selective proof proceeds via a series of carefully defined hybrid games that switch the distribution of one garbled gate at a time, starting with the input level and proceeding up the circuit level by level. In addition to the two modes of creating garbled gates defined above, we also define an additional mode where the garbled gate is set to:

$$
\begin{aligned}
c_{0,0} &= \mathsf{Enc}_{k_a^0}(\mathsf{Enc}_{k_b^0}(k_c^{v(c)})) \quad c_{1,0} = \mathsf{Enc}_{k_a^1}(\mathsf{Enc}_{k_b^0}(k_c^{v(c)})), \\
c_{0,1} &= \mathsf{Enc}_{k_a^0}(\mathsf{Enc}_{k_b^1}(k_c^{v(c)})) \quad c_{1,1} = \mathsf{Enc}_{k_a^1}(\mathsf{Enc}_{k_b^1}(k_c^{v(c)}))
\end{aligned}
\tag{3}
$$

where $v(c)$ is the correct *value* of the bit going over the wire c during the computation of $C(x)$. Let us give names to the three modes for creating garbled gates that we defined above: (1) is called RealGate mode, (2) is called SimGate mode, and (3) is called InputDepSimGate mode, since the way that it is defined depends adaptively on the choice of the input x. The proof of selective security of Yao's garbled circuits proceeds in a sequence of hybrids where the way we garble a gate goes from RealGate mode to InputDepSimGate mode to SimGate mode in some carefully chosen order. The problem with adapting this technique to the adaptive setting is that the InputDepSimGate mode is not (even syntactically) well defined; in this mode the way that we garble the gate depends on the value that the output wire takes on during the computation $C(x)$ but in the adaptive setting the input x is not yet defined when we create the garbled circuit.

The Technique of [HJO+16]. Essentially, the work of [HJO+16] proves adaptive security by leveraging two ideas.

Firstly, they encrypt the entire Yao garbled circuit under an additional layer of encryption using a special "somewhere equivocal encryption scheme", and give the decryption key as part of the garbled input. Such a scheme can be used to create a simulated ciphertext given only some but not all of the plaintext blocks (think of the unknown blocks as "holes") and later create a secret key that decrypts all the known blocks correctly but "plugs the holes" with arbitrarily specified values. The size of the secret key only depends on the number of holes and not the entire size of the plaintext. By leveraging this type of encryption, they can define hybrid games where some of the gates are in InputDepSimGate mode (which is not well defined when the circuit is created) by putting "holes" in place of all such gates when creating the garbled circuit and then coming up with a decryption key that opens the holes to the correct value when creating the garbled input (at which point InputDepSimGate is well defined).

Secondly, the above idea requires the number of holes (and therefore the size of the garbled input) to scale with the number of gates in InputDepSimGate mode in any hybrid. Therefore, to get a non-trivial result, we need a sequence of hybrids that minimizes the number of gates in InputDepSimGate mode at any point in time. Recall that we start with all gates in RealGate mode and want to end with all gates in SimGate mode. We are allowed to make the following changes:

- We can change a gate from RealGate to InputDepSimGate (and back) as long as its predecessors are in InputDepSimGate mode (or it is at the input level). This is because, in this case, only one of the keys for each input wire appears in the game.
- We can change a gate from InputDepSimGate to SimGate (and back) as long as all of its successors are in SimGate mode (or it is at the output level). This is because the two keys associated with the output wire are used interchangeably in the game.

The work of [HJO+16] connects the above with a *pebbling game* over the circuit, where the goal is to change all the gates from RealGate to SimGate subject to the above rules while minimizing the number of gates in InputDepSimGate mode at any point in time: this latter number is defined to be the *pebble complexity* of the circuit. For example, they show that the pebble complexity of a circuit is bounded by its *width* which in turn corresponds to the space complexity of the computation. The size of the garbled input in their scheme is the maximum of the pebble complexity of the circuit and the input/output size.

Our Construction and Proof Technique. One could hope to get rid of output dependence in the construction of [HJO+16] by simply sending the output map (the mapping between the keys of the output wires and the bits they represent) with the garbled circuit rather than with the garbled input. Although we know that such a construction cannot achieve adaptive simulation security, one could conjecture it to achieve adaptive indistinguishability security. Unfortunately, we do not know how to prove such a construction secure. Essentially, the issue is that the only reason we can change output gates from InputDepSimGate to SimGate in the proof of [HJO+16] is that we can "program" the output map after the actual output of the computation is known; if the output map is sent with the garbled circuit this is no longer possible. Instead, we come up with a modified construction which we are able to prove secure.

Our new garbling construction leverages that of [HJO+16] and proceeds as follows. To garble a circuit C we use the scheme of [HJO+16] and garble two copies of C completely independently: we call the resulting garbled circuits C_L, C_R. These are just Yao garbled circuits (without an output map) encrypted under an additional layer of somewhere equivocal encryption. We choose one of the two garbled circuits at random to be the "active" one: active $\leftarrow \{L, R\}$. Then we merge the two garbled circuits by creating a layer of garbled "selection gates" (s-gates): for each output bit $i \in [m]$ we create an s-gate that takes the i'th output wire from both garbled circuits, and outputs the value on the wire coming from the active circuit (the output of the garbled s-gate is a bit in the clear rather than a wire key). The garbled circuit consists of $\widetilde{C} = (C_L, C_R, \widetilde{\mathsf{sgate}})$. To garbled an input x we use the scheme of [HJO+16] to garble two copies of it for the left and right garbled circuit. The evaluation procedure does the natural thing by evaluating both C_L, C_R respectively, and using the output wire keys on the garbled s-gates to recover the output bits in the clear. Ideas similar to the use of two circuits along with a selection layer have appeared in prior works, e.g., [PST14].

To prove security, we consider an adversary that chooses C_0, C_1, gets a garbled version of C_b, then adaptively chooses x_0, x_1 such that $C_0(x_0) = C_1(x_1)$, and gets a garbled version of x_b. We want to show that the adversary cannot distinguish between $b = 0$ and $b = 1$. We show security via the following sequence of hybrids.

1. We start with the security game where the challenge bit is $b = 0$. In this case, both C_L, C_R garble C_0 and both garbled inputs correspond to x_0. Let active $\in \{L, R\}$ be the identity of the active circuit. We use the notation $C_{\mathsf{active}}, C_{\mathsf{passive}}$ to denote the active and passive garbled circuits respectively.
2. We change the passive garbled circuit C_{passive} and the garbled input for it to be simulated. This change essentially follows the proof of [HJO+16]. In

particular, we rely on the fact that the keys associated with the bits 0 and 1 for the output wires of $C_{passive}$ are used symmetrically by the s-gates (since the s-gates are ignoring the output of the passive circuit) and therefore we can safely change the garbled output gates of $C_{passive}$ from InputDepSimGate to SimGate.

3. We change the passive garbled circuit $C_{passive}$ and the garbled input for it from being simulated to being a garbling of C_1, x_1. This follows from the same argument as the previous step.

4. We now modify the s-gates one-by-one to output the value of the passive circuit instead of the active circuit. This is the most delicate part of the proof. It essentially follows via a sequence of steps where, for each output $i \in [m]$, we use the proof strategy of [HJO+16] to change the i'th output gate of both $C_{active}, C_{passive}$ to be in InputDepSimGate mode. This means that these garbled gates aren't really created until the on-line phase when the garbled input is given out. Furthermore, when they are created in the on-line phase, each of these garbled gates only contains one key for the output wire corresponding to the correct bit going over that wire during the computation (either both corresponding to 0 or both to 1 since $C_0(x_0) = C_1(x_1)$). This allows us to change the encrypted value in 2 out 4 of the ciphertexts in the garbled s-gate so as to switch it from outputting the value of the active circuit to the one of the passive circuit.

5. We now repeat steps 2 and 3 for C_{active} to switch it from a garbling C_0, x_0, to simulated, to a garbling of C_1, x_1. Finally, we are left with the original security game with the challenge bit $b = 1$.

The above steps – except for step 4 – rely on the adaptive security of the underlying garbling scheme in a blackbox manner. It remains an open problem whether it is possible to show a more general transformation from garbled circuits with adaptive security (and maybe other natural properties) to garbled circuits with indistinguishability based adaptive security and online complexity independent of the output size.

2   Preliminaries

General Notation. For a positive integer n, we define the set $[n] := \{1, \ldots, n\}$. We use the notation $x \leftarrow X$ for the process of sampling a value x according to the distribution X. For a vector $\overline{m} = (m_1, m_2, \cdots, m_n)$, and a subset $P \subset [n]$, we use $(m_i)_{i \in P}$ to denote a vector containing only the values m_i in positions $i \in P$ and $\perp$ symbols in all other positions. We use $(m_i)_{i \notin P}$ as shorthand for $(m_i)_{i \in [n] \setminus P}$.

Circuit Notation. A boolean circuit C consists of gates $\mathsf{gate}_1, \ldots, \mathsf{gate}_q$ and wires $w_1, w_2, \ldots, w_p$. A gate is defined by the tuple $\mathsf{gate}_i = (g, w_a, w_b, w_c)$ where $g : \{0,1\}^2 \rightarrow \{0,1\}$ is the function computed by the gate, w_a, w_b are the incoming wires, and w_c is the outgoing wire. Although each gate has a unique outgoing wire w_c, this wire can be used as an incoming wire to several different gates and therefore this models a circuit with fan-in 2 and unbounded fan-out. We let q denote the number of gates in the circuit, n denotes the number of input wires and m denote the number of output wires. The total number of wires is $p = n + q$ (since each wire can either be input wire or an outgoing wire of some gate). For convenience, we denote the n input wires by $\text{in}_1, \ldots, \text{in}_n$ and the m output wires by $\text{out}_1, \ldots, \text{out}_m$. For $x \in \{0,1\}^n$ we write $C(x)$ to denote the output of evaluating the circuit C on input x.

Definition 1. *Two distributions X and Y are (T, ε)-indistinguishable, denote $\mathbf{D}_T [X, Y] = \varepsilon$ if for any probabilistic algorithm $\mathcal{A}$, running in time T,*

$$|\Pr[\mathcal{A}(X) = 1] - \Pr[\mathcal{A}(Y) = 1]| \leq \varepsilon.$$

For two games GAME *and* GAME' *we say they are $(T(\lambda), \varepsilon(\lambda))$- indistinguishable, $\mathbf{D}_{T(\lambda)}[\text{GAME}, \text{GAME}'] = \varepsilon(\lambda)$, if for any adversary $\mathcal{A}$ running in time $T(\lambda)$,*

$$|\Pr[\text{GAME}_{\mathcal{A}} = 1] - \Pr[\text{GAME}'_{\mathcal{A}} = 1]| \leq \varepsilon(\lambda).$$

Let games GAME(λ) *and* GAME'(λ) *be parametrized by the security parameter λ. If for any polynomial function $T(\lambda)$, there exists a negligible function $\varepsilon(\lambda)$, such that for all λ, $\mathbf{D}_{T(\lambda)}[\text{GAME}(\lambda), \text{GAME}'(\lambda)] \leq \varepsilon(\lambda)$, we say the two games are computationally indistinguishable and denote this by* GAME$(\lambda) \overset{\text{comp}}{\approx}$ GAME'(λ).

We say C is leveled, if each gate has an associated level and any gate at level l has incoming wires only from gates at level $l - 1$ and outgoing wires only to gates at level $l + 1$. We let the *depth d* denote the number of levels and the *width w* denote the maximum number of gates in any level.

A circuit C is fully specified by a list of gate tuples $\text{gate}_i = (g, w_a, w_b, w_c)$. We use $\varPhi(C)$ to refer to the topology of a circuit - which indicates how gates are connected, without specifying the function implement by each gate. In other words, $\varPhi(C)$ is the list of *sanitized gate tuples* $\widehat{\text{gate}}_i = (\bot, w_a, w_b, w_c)$ where the function g that the gate implements is removed from the tuple.

3   Definitions

The bulk of this section defining what garbled circuits are and presenting Yao's construction, is taken verbatim from [HJO+16]. We now give a formal definition of a garbling scheme. There are many variants of such definitions in the literature, and we refer the reader to [BHR12] for a comprehensive treatment.

Definition 2. *A Garbling Scheme is a tuple of PPT algorithms* GC = (GCircuit, GInput, Eval) *such that:*

- $(\widetilde{C}, k) \overset{\$}{\leftarrow}$ GCircuit$(1^\lambda, C)$: *takes as input a security parameter λ, a circuit $C : \{0,1\}^n \to \{0,1\}^m$, and outputs the garbled circuit $\widetilde{C}$, and key k.*
- $\tilde{x} \leftarrow$ GInput(k, x): *takes as input, $x \in \{0,1\}^n$, and key k and outputs $\tilde{x}$.*
- $y =$ Eval$(\widetilde{C}, \tilde{x})$: *given a garbled circuit $\widetilde{C}$ and a garbled input $\tilde{x}$ output $y \in \{0,1\}^m$.*

Correctness. *There is a negligible function ν such that for any $\lambda \in \mathbb{N}$, any circuit C and input x it holds that $\Pr[C(x) = \mathsf{Eval}(\widetilde{C}, \tilde{x})] = 1 - \nu(\lambda)$, where $(\widetilde{C}, k) \leftarrow \mathsf{GCircuit}(1^\lambda, C)$, $\tilde{x} \leftarrow \mathsf{GInput}(k, x)$.*

Adaptive Security (Based on Simulation). *There exists a PPT simulator $\mathsf{Sim} = (\mathsf{SimC}, \mathsf{SimIn})$ such that, for any PPT adversary $\mathcal{A}$, there exists a negligible function ε such that:*

$$\Pr[\mathsf{Exp}^{\mathsf{adaptive}}_{\mathcal{A}, \mathsf{GC}, \mathsf{Sim}}(\lambda, 0) = 1] - \Pr[\mathsf{Exp}^{\mathsf{adaptive}}_{\mathcal{A}, \mathsf{GC}, \mathsf{Sim}}(\lambda, 1) = 1] \leq \varepsilon(\lambda)$$

where the experiment $\mathsf{Exp}^{\mathsf{adaptive}}_{\mathcal{A}, \mathsf{GC}, \mathsf{Sim}}(\lambda, b)$ is defined as follows:

1. *The adversary $\mathcal{A}$ specifies C and gets $\widetilde{C}$ where $\widetilde{C}$ is created as follows:*
   - *if $b = 0$: $(\widetilde{C}, k) \leftarrow \mathsf{GCircuit}(1^\lambda, C)$,*
   - *if $b = 1$: $(\widetilde{C}, \mathsf{state}) \leftarrow \mathsf{SimC}(1^\lambda, \Phi(C))$.*
2. *The adversary $\mathcal{A}$ specifies x and gets $\tilde{x}$ created as follows:*
   - *if $b = 0$, $\tilde{x} \leftarrow \mathsf{GInput}(k, x)$,*
   - *if $b = 1$, $\tilde{x} \leftarrow \mathsf{SimIn}(C(x), \mathsf{state})$.*
3. *Finally, the adversary outputs a bit b', which is the output of the experiment.*

*In other words, we say GC is **adaptively secure** if*

$$\mathbf{D}_{T(\lambda)}\left[\mathsf{Exp}^{\mathsf{adaptive}}_{\mathsf{GC}, \mathsf{Sim}}(\lambda, 0), \mathsf{Exp}^{\mathsf{adaptive}}_{\mathsf{GC}, \mathsf{Sim}}(\lambda, 1)\right] = \varepsilon(\lambda).$$

Adaptive Security (Based on Indistinguishability). *For any PPT adversary $\mathcal{A}$, there exists a negligible function ε such that:*

$$\Pr[\mathsf{Exp}^{\mathsf{adaptive}}_{\mathcal{A}, \mathsf{GC}, \mathsf{Ind}}(\lambda, 0) = 1] - \Pr[\mathsf{Exp}^{\mathsf{adaptive}}_{\mathcal{A}, \mathsf{GC}, \mathsf{Ind}}(\lambda, 1) = 1] \leq \varepsilon(\lambda)$$

where the experiment $\mathsf{Exp}^{\mathsf{adaptive}}_{\mathcal{A}, \Pi, \mathsf{Ind}}(\lambda, b)$ is defined as follows:

1. *$\mathcal{A}$ specifies two circuits C_0, C_1 of the same topology, and gets back $\widetilde{C}_b \leftarrow \mathsf{GCircuit}(1^\lambda, C_b)$.*
2. *$\mathcal{A}$ specifies x_0, x_1 such that $C_0(x_0) = C_1(x_1)$ and gets $\tilde{x}_b \leftarrow \mathsf{GInput}(k, x_b)$.*
3. *Finally, the adversary outputs a bit b', which is the output of the experiment.*

*In other words, we say GC is **adaptively indistinguishable** if*

$$\mathbf{D}_{T(\lambda)}\left[\mathsf{Exp}^{\mathsf{adaptive}}_{\mathsf{GC}, \mathsf{Ind}}(\lambda, 0), \mathsf{Exp}^{\mathsf{adaptive}}_{\mathsf{GC}, \mathsf{Ind}}(\lambda, 1)\right] = \varepsilon(\lambda).$$

On-line Complexity. The time it takes to garble an input x, (i.e., time complexity of $\mathsf{GInput}(\cdot, \cdot)$) is the *on-line complexity* of the scheme. Clearly the on-line complexity of the scheme gives a bound on the size of the garbled input $\tilde{x}$. Ideally, the on-line complexity should be much smaller than the circuit size $|C|$.

Projective Scheme. We say a garbling scheme is *projective* if each bit of the garbled input $\tilde{x}$ only depends on one bit of the actual input x. In other words, each bit of the input, is garbled independently of other bits of the input.

Projective schemes are essential for two-party computation where the garbled input is transmitted using an oblivious transfer (OT) protocol. Our constructions will be projective.

Hiding Topology. A garbling scheme that satisfies the above security definition may reveal the topology of the circuit C. However, there is a way to transform any such garbling scheme into one that hides everything, including the topology of the circuit, without a significant asymptotic efficiency loss. More precisely, we rely on the fact that there is a function $\mathsf{HideTopo}(\cdot)$ that takes a circuit C as input and outputs a functionally equivalent circuit C', such that for any two circuits C_1, C_2 of equal size, if $C_1' = \mathsf{HideTopo}(C_1)$ and $C_2' = \mathsf{HideTopo}(C_2)$, then $\Phi(C_1') = \Phi(C_2')$. An easy way to construct such function $\mathsf{HideTopo}$ is by setting C' to be a universal circuit, with a hard-coded description of the actual circuit C. Therefore, to get a topology-hiding garbling scheme, we can simply use a topology-revealing scheme but instead of garbling the circuit C directly, we garble the circuit $\mathsf{HideTopo}(C)$.

4   Construction of [HJO+16]

In our construction (presented in the following section), we will use the construction of [HJO+16], as a building block. Furthermore we will need the details of this construction in order to proceed with the proof of security of our construction. Therefore in this section we present the construction of [HJO+16] which consists of two simple steps: (1) garble the circuit using Yao's garbling scheme; (2) hide the garbled circuit (without the output tables) under an **outer** layer of encryption instantiated with a *somewhere-equivocal* encryption scheme. In the on-line phase, the garbled input consists of Yao's garbled input plus the output tables. Next we provide the formal description of the scheme of [HJO+16] which contains the details of Yao's garbling scheme.

Let C be a leveled boolean circuit with fan-in 2 and unbounded fan-out, with inputs size n, output size m, depth d and width w. Let q denote the number of gates in C. Recall that wires are uniquely identified with labels $w_1, w_2, \ldots, w_p$, and a circuit C is specified by a list of gate tuples $\mathsf{gate} = (g, w_a, w_b, w_c)$. The topology of the circuit $\Phi(C)$ consists of the sanitized gate tuples $\widehat{\mathsf{gate}}_i = (\bot, w_a, w_b, w_c)$. For simplicity, we implicitly assume that $\Phi(C)$ is public and known to the circuit evaluator without explicitly including it as part of the garbled circuit $\widetilde{C}$. To simplify the description of our construction, we first describe the procedure for garbling a single gate, that we denote by $\mathsf{GarbleGate}$.

Let $\Gamma = (\mathsf{Gen}, \mathsf{Enc}, \mathsf{Dec})$ be a CPA-secure symmetric-key encryption scheme satisfying the special correctness property defined in Appendix A. $\mathsf{GarbleGate}$ is defined as follows.

- $\widetilde{g} \leftarrow \mathsf{GarbleGate}(g, \{k_a^\sigma, k_b^\sigma, k_c^\sigma\}_{\sigma \in \{0,1\}})$: This function computes 4 ciphertexts $c_{\sigma_0, \sigma_1} : \sigma_0, \sigma_1 \in \{0, 1\}$ as defined below and outputs them in a random order as $\widetilde{g} = [c_1, c_2, c_3, c_4]$.

$$c_{0,0} \leftarrow \mathsf{Enc}_{k_a^0}(\mathsf{Enc}_{k_b^0}(k_c^{g(0,0)}))c_{0,1} \leftarrow \mathsf{Enc}_{k_a^0}(\mathsf{Enc}_{k_b^1}(k_c^{g(0,1)}))$$
$$c_{1,0} \leftarrow \mathsf{Enc}_{k_a^1}(\mathsf{Enc}_{k_b^0}(k_c^{g(1,0)}))c_{1,1} \leftarrow \mathsf{Enc}_{k_a^1}(\mathsf{Enc}_{k_b^0}(k_c^{g(1,1)}))$$

Let $\Pi = (\mathsf{seKeyGen}, \mathsf{seEnc}, \mathsf{seDec}, \mathsf{SimEnc}, \mathsf{SimKey})$ be a somewhere-equivocal symmetric-encryption scheme as defined in Appendix B. Recall that in this primitive the plaintext is a vector of n blocks, each of which has s bits. In this construction the following parameters are used: the vector size $n = q$ is the number of gates and the block size $s = |\tilde{g}|$ is the size of a single garbled gate. The equivocation parameter t is defined by the strategy used in the security proof and will be specified later. The garbling scheme is formally described in Fig. 1.

GCircuit$(1^\lambda, C)$

1. Garble Circuit: //Yao's scheme
   - (Wires) $k_{w_i}^\sigma \leftarrow \mathsf{Gen}(1^\lambda)$ for $i \in [p]$, $\sigma \in \{0,1\}$.
     (Input wires) $K = (k_{\mathsf{in}_i}^0, k_{\mathsf{in}_i}^1)_{i \in [n]}$.
   - (Gates) For $\mathsf{gate}_i = (g, w_a, w_b, w_c)$ in C:
     $\tilde{g}_i \leftarrow \mathsf{GarbleGate}\left(g, \{k_{w_a}^\sigma, k_{w_b}^\sigma, k_{w_c}^\sigma\}_{\sigma \in \{0,1\}}\right)$.
   - (Output tables) For $j \in [m]$: $\tilde{d}_j := \left[\left(k_{\mathsf{out}_j}^0 \rightarrow 0\right), \left(k_{\mathsf{out}_j}^1 \rightarrow 1\right)\right]$.
2. Outer Encryption: key $\xleftarrow{\$} \mathsf{seKeyGen}(1^\lambda)$, $\tilde{C} \leftarrow \mathsf{seEnc}(\mathsf{key}, (\tilde{g}_1, \ldots, \tilde{g}_q))$.
3. **Output** $\tilde{C}$, $k = \left(K, \mathsf{key}, (\tilde{d}_j)_{j \in [m]}\right)$.

GInput(x, k)

1. (Select input keys) $K^x = \left(k_{\mathsf{in}_1}^{x_1}, \ldots, k_{\mathsf{in}_n}^{x_n}\right)$.
2. **Output** $\tilde{x} = \left(K^x, \mathsf{key}, (\tilde{d}_j)_{j \in [m]}\right)$.

Fig. 1. Adaptively secure garbling scheme: GCircuit and GInput functions. See Fig. 2 for function Eval.

4.1 Adaptive Simulator

The adaptive security simulator for [HJO+16] is essentially the same as the selective security simulator for Yao's scheme (as in [LP09]), with the only difference that the output table is sent in the on-line phase, and is computed adaptively to map to the correct output. Note that the garbled circuit simulator does not rely on the simulation properties of the somewhere equivocal encryption scheme - these are only used in the proof of indistinguishability.

More specifically, the adaptive simulator (SimC, SimIn) works as follows. In the off-line phase, SimC computes the garbled gates using procedure GarbleSimGate, that generates 4 ciphertexts that encrypt the same output key.

$\text{Eval}(\widetilde{C}, \tilde{x})$

1. Parse $\tilde{x} = (K, \mathsf{key}, (\widetilde{d}_j)_{j \in [m]})$.
2. Decrypt Outer Encryption: $(\widetilde{g}_i)_{i \in q} \leftarrow \mathsf{seDec}(\mathsf{key}, \widetilde{C})$.
3. Evaluate Circuit:
   - Parse $K = (k_{\mathsf{in}_1}, \ldots, k_{\mathsf{in}_n})$.
   - For each level $j = 1, \ldots, d$, and each $\widehat{\mathsf{gate}}_i = (\bot, w_a, w_b, w_c)$ at level j:
     • Let $\widetilde{g}_i = [c_1, c_2, c_3, c_4]$; for $\delta \in [4]$, let $k'_{w_c} \leftarrow \mathsf{Dec}_{k_{w_a}}(\mathsf{Dec}_{k_{w_b}}(c_\delta))$
     • If $k'_{w_c} \neq \bot$ then set $k_{w_c} := k'_{w_c}$.
4. Decrypt output: For $j \in [m]$,
   - parse $\widetilde{d}_j = \left[(k^0_{\mathsf{out}_j} \to 0), (k^1_{\mathsf{out}_j} \to 1) \right]$, Set $y_j = b$ iff $k_{\mathsf{out}_j} = k^b_{\mathsf{out}_j}$.
5. **Output** $y_1, \ldots, y_m$.

Fig. 2. Adaptively secure garbling scheme: Eval function.

More precisely,

- GarbleSimGate($\{k^\sigma_{w_a}, k^\sigma_{w_b}\}_{\sigma \in \{0,1\}}, k'_{w_c}$) takes both keys for input wires w_a, w_b and a single key for the output wire w_c, that we denote by k'_{w_c}. It then output $\widetilde{g}_c = [c_1, c_2, c_3, c_4]$ where the ciphertexts, arranged in random order, are computed as follows.
$c_{0,0} \leftarrow \mathsf{Enc}_{k^0_a}(\mathsf{Enc}_{k^0_b}(k'_c)) c_{1,0} \leftarrow \mathsf{Enc}_{k^1_a}(\mathsf{Enc}_{k^0_b}(k'_c))$
$c_{0,1} \leftarrow \mathsf{Enc}_{k^0_a}(\mathsf{Enc}_{k^1_b}(k'_c)) c_{1,1} \leftarrow \mathsf{Enc}_{k^1_a}(\mathsf{Enc}_{k^0_b}(k'_c))$

The simulator invokes GarbleSimGate on input $k'_c = k^0_c$. It then encrypts the garbled gates so obtained by using the honest procedure for the somewhere equivocal encryption.

In the on-line phase, SimIn, on input $y = C(x)$ adaptively computes the output tables so that the evaluator obtains the correct output. This is easily achieved by associating each bit of the output, y_j, to the only key encrypted in the output gate g_{out_j}, which is $k^0_{\mathsf{out}_j}$. For the input keys, SimIn just sends keys $k^0_{\mathsf{in}_i}$ for each $i \in [n]$. The detailed definition of (SimC, SimIn) is provided in Fig. 3.

5 Our Construction

Let $\mathsf{cGC} = (\mathsf{cGCircuit}, \mathsf{cGInput}, \mathsf{cEval})$ be the adaptive garbling scheme of [HJO+16], with simulator $\mathsf{cSim} = (\mathsf{cSimC}, \mathsf{cSimIn})$. In this section we construct a new garbling scheme, using cGC as a building block. See Fig. 5 for a formal description of our construction. The new garbling scheme creates two copies of the garbled circuit (called $\mathsf{C_L}, \mathsf{C_R}$). It chooses one at random to be the "active" one (active $= R$ or active $= L$). Then for each output bit $i \in [m]$, it creates a selection gate that takes the output wire i from both garbled circuits, and

---

Simulator

$\underline{\mathsf{SimC}(1^\lambda, \Phi(C))}$

– (Wires) $k_{w_i}^\sigma \leftarrow \mathsf{Gen}(1^\lambda)$ for $i \in [p]$, $\sigma \in \{0,1\}$.
– (Garbled gates) For each gate $\widetilde{\mathsf{gate}}_i = (\bot, w_a, w_b, w_c)$ in $\Phi(C)$:
   $\widetilde{g}_i \leftarrow \mathsf{GarbleSimGate}\,(\{k_{w_a}^\sigma, k_{w_b}^\sigma\}_{\sigma \in \{0,1\}}, k_{w_c}^0)$.
– (Outer Encryption): key $\overset{\$}{\leftarrow} \mathsf{seKeyGen}(1^\lambda)$, $\widetilde{C} \leftarrow \mathsf{seEnc}(\mathsf{key}, \widetilde{g}_1, \ldots, \widetilde{g}_q)$.
– **Output** $\widetilde{C}$, state $= (\{k_{w_i}^\sigma\}, \mathsf{key})$.

$\underline{\mathsf{SimIn}(y, \mathsf{state})}$

– Generate output table: $\widetilde{sd}_j \leftarrow [(k_{\mathsf{out}_j}^{y_j} \to 0), (k_{\mathsf{out}_j}^{1-y_j} \to 1)]_{j \in [m]}$. // ensures $k_{\mathsf{out}_j}^0 \to y_j$
– **Output** $\widetilde{x} = ((k_{\mathsf{in}_i}^0)_{i \in [n]}, \mathsf{key}, (\widetilde{sd}_j)_{j \in [m]})$.

Fig. 3. Simulator for adaptive security.

selects the value on the wire coming from the active circuit. We call these selection gates, s-gates, to distinguish them from the output gates of the two original garbled circuits. Let ℓ^b and r^b be the output wires of $\mathsf{C_L}$ and $\mathsf{C_R}$, then s-gate (for each output bit) is defined as in Fig. 4.

sgate$_R$	sgate$_L$
$\mathsf{Enc}_{\ell^0}(\mathsf{Enc}_{r^1}(1))$	$\mathsf{Enc}_{\ell^0}(\mathsf{Enc}_{r^1}(0))$
$\mathsf{Enc}_{\ell^0}(\mathsf{Enc}_{r^0}(0))$	$\mathsf{Enc}_{\ell^0}(\mathsf{Enc}_{r^0}(0))$
$\mathsf{Enc}_{\ell_1}(\mathsf{Enc}_{r^1}(1))$	$\mathsf{Enc}_{\ell^1}(\mathsf{Enc}_{r^1}(1))$
$\mathsf{Enc}_{\ell^1}(\mathsf{Enc}_{r^0}(0))$	$\mathsf{Enc}_{\ell^1}(\mathsf{Enc}_{r^0}(1))$

Fig. 4. s-gates. sgate$_L$(sgate$_R$) outputs the value associated with the wire coming form $\mathsf{C_L}, (\mathsf{C_R})$.

Note that $\mathsf{C_{active}}$ and $\mathsf{C_{passive}}$ are encrypted Yao garbled circuits. But the output wires and the output map are not encrypted and are part of the key k which is an output of $\mathsf{cGCircuit}(\cdot, \cdot)$.

6 Hybrid Games

Overview. We need to prove that $\mathrm{GAME}_0 = \mathsf{Exp}_{\mathcal{A},\mathsf{NGC},\mathsf{Ind}}^{\mathsf{adaptive}}(\lambda, 0)$ and $\mathrm{GAME}_1 = \mathsf{Exp}_{\mathcal{A},\mathsf{NGC},\mathsf{Ind}}^{\mathsf{adaptive}}(\lambda, 1)$ are indistinguishable. Namely, we need to show a strategy to move from GAME_0, where $(\mathsf{C_{passive}}, \mathsf{C_{active}})$ are both garbling of C_0 and $(x_{\mathsf{active}},$

N Garbling Scheme

$\text{NGCircuit}(1^\lambda, C)$.

1. active $\leftarrow \{L, R\}$. If active $= L$ then passive $= R$ else passive $= L$.
2. $(C_L, k_L) \leftarrow \text{cGCircuit}(1^\lambda, C)$ and
   $(C_R, k_R) \leftarrow \text{cGCircuit}(1^\lambda, C)$
3. Parse k_α into $\left(K_\alpha, \text{key}_\alpha, (\widetilde{cd}_{\alpha,i})_{i \in [m]}\right)$ for $\alpha \in \{L, R\}$
4. For $i \in [m]$ let sgate_i computed as $\text{sgate}_{\text{active}}$ (Figure 4) with the ith
   output wire of C_R and C_L as input. Let $\widetilde{\text{sgate}} = (\text{sgate}_1, \ldots, \text{sgate}_m)$
5. $\widetilde{C} := \left(C_L, C_R, \widetilde{\text{sgate}}\right)$.
6. $k_L := (K_L, \text{key}_L)$, $k_R := (K_R, \text{key}_R)$, $k := (k_L, k_R)$.
7. Output $\widetilde{C}, k$.

$\text{NGInput}(x, k)$

1. (select keys) $K_L^x = \text{SelGInput}(x, K_L)$.
2. (select keys) $K_R^x = \text{SelGInput}(x, K_R)$.
3. $\tilde{x}_L = (K_L^x, \text{key}_L)$, $\tilde{x}_R = (K_R^x, \text{key}_R)$
4. Output $\tilde{x} = (\tilde{x}_L, \tilde{x}_R)$

$\text{NEval}(\widetilde{C}, \tilde{x})$

1. $\{w_{\alpha,i}\}_{i \in [m]} := \text{cEval}(C_\alpha, \tilde{x}_\alpha)$, for $\alpha \in \{L, R\}$
2. Parse $\text{sgate}_1, \ldots, \text{sgate}_m \leftarrow \widetilde{\text{sgate}}$.
3. Use keys $\{w_{\alpha,i}\}_{i \in [m]}$ to evaluate gates $\text{sgate}_1, \ldots, \text{sgate}_m$ and obtain y.
4. Output y.

Fig. 5. New garbling scheme

x_{passive}) are garblings of x_0; to GAME$_1$ where $(C_{\text{passive}}, C_{\text{active}})$ are garbling of C_1
and $(x_{\text{active}}, x_{\text{passive}})$ are garblings of x_1.

At high-level, the proof strategy is the following: starting from GAME$_0$, (1)
first we change $C_{\text{passive}}, x_{\text{passive}}$ to be the garbling of C_1, x_1, (2) then we change
the selection gates so that they select outputs from C_{passive}, (3) finally we change
$C_{\text{active}}, x_{\text{active}}$ to be the garbling of C_1, x_1.

For step (1) and (3), we switch from garbling C_0, x_0 to garbling C_1, x_1 by
using simulated circuits, namely first we change C_{passive} into a simulated circuit,
and then we switch it into a real garbling of C_1. Indistinguishability of this
steps follows directly from the adaptive simulation-based security of the underlying garbling scheme in a black-box manner (we discuss this next in Sect. 6.1).
Changing the selection gates (Step 2) instead requires a surgical proof, where we
selective simulate one *output gate* of $C_{\text{passive}}, C_{\text{active}}$ at the time, and this enable us
to change (switch) the content of the selection gates, from selecting the output
of C_{passive} instead of C_{active} (or viceversa). Following the language of [HJO+16],

this means that we need to place black pebbles on the output gates of circuits $C_{\mathsf{passive}}, C_{\mathsf{active}}$. We discuss this in details in Lemma 3.

6.1 Hybrid Games Template

The hybrid games are parameterized by the distributions of $C_{\mathsf{active}}, C_{\mathsf{passive}}$, their respective inputs $x_{\mathsf{active}}, x_{\mathsf{passive}}$ and a flag $\alpha \in \{\mathsf{active}, \mathsf{passive}\}$ denoting the fact that s-gates are selecting the output of C_α

For example the original GAME_b is described as:

- $\mathrm{GAME}_0 = \left((\mathsf{cGCircuit}(1^\lambda, C_0), x_0), (\mathsf{cGCircuit}(1^\lambda, C_0), x_0) \right), \mathsf{active}$
- $\mathrm{GAME}_1 = \left((\mathsf{cGCircuit}(1^\lambda, C_1), x_1), (\mathsf{cGCircuit}(1^\lambda, C_1), x_1) \right), \mathsf{active}$

Note that when the active and passive garbled circuit distributions are the same, it does not make a difference whether $\alpha = \mathsf{active}$ or $\alpha = \mathsf{passive}$. However in our hybrid argument we will sometimes set $\alpha = \mathsf{passive}$ when these distributions are different. We use $\mathsf{cSimC}(1^\lambda, \Phi(C))$ to denote a simulated circuit. Since the simulated garbling of any circuit only depends on its topology and not the function it computes, the output of the simulation has the same distribution for C_0 and C_1, thus for simplicity we write $\mathsf{cSimC}(1^\lambda, \Phi(C))$.

Using this template we define 4 new hybrid games: HybA through HybD. See Fig. 6. The changes in these hybrids follow a two-step simulate and switch approach. In HybA the passive circuit is simulated. Note that the garbled input to a simulated circuit is created independent of the input, therefore its distribution does not change whether it's x_0 that is garbled or x_1. In HybB the passive circuit is switched from simulation to real garbling of C_1. Now with both active and passive circuits outputing the same value $y = C_0(x_0) = C_1(x_1)$, we go to the next hybrid. In HybC we change the content of the s-gates to output the passive circuit. Then we turn the active circuit into a garbling of C_1 with input x_1, by first simulating it (HybD) and then changing it to a garbling of C_1 with input x_1 (GAME_1). The transitions from GAME_0 to HybA then to HybB are identical to the ones going from GAME_1 to HybD and then to HybC. Thus we only prove it once for $\mathrm{GAME}_0 \overset{\mathsf{comp}}{\approx} \mathsf{HybA} \overset{\mathsf{comp}}{\approx} \mathsf{HybB}$.

Hybrids	GAME_0	HybA	HybB
$C_{\mathsf{active}}, x_{\mathsf{active}}$	$\mathsf{cGCircuit}(1^\lambda, C_0), x_0$	$\mathsf{cGCircuit}(1^\lambda, C_0), x_0$	$\mathsf{cGCircuit}(1^\lambda, C_0), x_0$
$C_{\mathsf{passive}}, x_{\mathsf{passive}}$	$\mathsf{cGCircuit}(1^\lambda, C_0), x_0$	$\mathsf{cSimC}(1^\lambda, \Phi(C)), x_1$	$\mathsf{cGCircuit}(1^\lambda, C_1), x_1$
sgate outputs	active	active	active
Hybrids	HybC	HybD	GAME_1
$C_{\mathsf{active}}, x_{\mathsf{active}}$	$\mathsf{cGCircuit}(1^\lambda, C_0), x_0$	$\mathsf{cSimC}(1^\lambda, \Phi(C)), x_1$	$\mathsf{cGCircuit}(1^\lambda, C_1), x_1$
$C_{\mathsf{passive}}, x_{\mathsf{passive}}$	$\mathsf{cGCircuit}(1^\lambda, C_1), x_1$	$\mathsf{cGCircuit}(1^\lambda, C_1), x_1$	$\mathsf{cGCircuit}(1^\lambda, C_1), x_1$
sgate outputs	passive	passive	passive

Fig. 6. Hybrids.

From GAME_0 **to HybA.** To prove this, we are going to need a special property that is enjoyed by the garbling scheme cGC. We define the special property below.

Definition 3 (Output-key Security). *We say that an adaptively simulation-secure garbling scheme is* output-key *secure if it is adaptively secure even when the output keys (e.g., $\{w_{\alpha,i}\}_{i \in [m]}$) –without the output mapping– are sent together with the garbled circuit $\widetilde{C}$.*

Proposition 1. *Under the same assumptions as [HJO+16], the garbling scheme cGC is adaptively secure and output-key secure.*

[Proof Sketch]. Intuitively this is true because throughout the proof of security for cGC we rely on the CPA security of the encryption scheme used to garble the gates, to prove the adversary does not learn the content of any gates, before getting the garbled input, and even after seeing the garbled input he can only decipher one ciphertext from each garbled gate. During these reductions, we can even let the adversary choose the keys encrypted in a garbled output gate (as in the game for the CPA security, the adversary can choose any message to be encrypted). Furthermore the output keys are not used as an encryption key somewhere else in the same garbled circuit, therefore revealing the output key does not jeopardize the adaptive security of cGC.

Now that we have defined the property above, we can prove the following Lemma.

Lemma 1. *If cGC is adaptively secure and output-key secure, then GAME_0 and* HybA *are computationally indistinguishable.*

Proof. If a PPT adversary $\mathcal{A}$ distinguishes GAME_0 and HybA with advantage ε, we construct adversary $\mathcal{B}$ that breaks the adaptive security of cGC with the same advantage ε. $\mathcal{B}$ will receive C_0, C_1 from $\mathcal{A}$, and sends C_0 to its challenger, and gets back $\widetilde{C}^*$, which is $(\widetilde{C}^*, k) \leftarrow \text{cGCircuit}(1^\lambda, C_0)$ if $b = 0$ and $(\widetilde{C}^*, \text{state}) \leftarrow \text{cSimC}(1^\lambda, \Phi(C))$ if $b = 1$. $\mathcal{B}$ then sets $(\mathsf{C}_{\text{active}}, k_0) \leftarrow \text{cGCircuit}(1^\lambda, C_0)$ and $\mathsf{C}_{\text{passive}} = \widetilde{C}^*$. Next, $\mathcal{B}$ creates the s-gates so that they would reveal the output of $\mathsf{C}_{\text{active}}$. Note that $\mathcal{B}$ does not need the output map of $\widetilde{C}^*$ to create s-gates, it only needs the keys encrypted in the output level gates of $\widetilde{C}^*$. Which we assume are given as part of the garbled circuit, without jeopardizing the security of cGC (due to output-key security). Finally $\mathcal{B}$ sends $\widetilde{C} = \left(\mathsf{C}_\mathsf{L}, \mathsf{C}_\mathsf{R}, \widetilde{\text{sgate}}\right)$ to $\mathcal{A}$ and gets back x_0, x_1. $\mathcal{B}$ sends x_0 to the challenger and gets back $\tilde{x}^*$ which is $\tilde{x}^* \leftarrow \text{cGInput}(x_0, k)$ if $b = 0$ and $\tilde{x}^* \leftarrow \text{SimIn}(C_0(x_0), \text{state})$ if $b = 1$. The reduction will set $\tilde{x}_{\text{active}} \leftarrow \text{cGInput}(x_0, k_{\text{active}})$, $\tilde{x}_{\text{passive}} = \tilde{x}^*$ and sends $(\tilde{x}_L, \tilde{x}_R)$ to $\mathcal{A}$ and outputs $\mathcal{A}$'s final output, b'. Note, since SimIn does not even take in the input x_1 or x_0, it only gets the output of the computation in order to create the appropriate output map. And in this application, the output wires are treated the same way, regardless of whether they are mapped to 0 or 1, it doesn't matter which input is garbled by the simulator (Fig. 7).

Reduction $\mathcal{B}$

1. Receive C_0, C_1 from $\mathcal{A}$.
2. active $\leftarrow \{L, R\}$. If active $= L$ then passive $= R$ else passive $= L$.
3. Send C_0 to the challenger and get back $\widetilde{C}^*$.
4. Follow the steps for creating $\mathsf{NGCircuit}(1^\lambda, C_0)$ with one exception; use $\widetilde{C}^*$ as $\mathsf{C_{passive}}$.
5. Send $\widetilde{C} := \left(\mathsf{C_L}, \mathsf{C_R}, \widetilde{\mathsf{sgate}}\right)$ to $\mathcal{A}$ and receive x_0, x_1
6. Send x_0 to the challenger and get back $\tilde{x}^*$.
7. (select keys) $K^{x_0} = \mathsf{SelGInput}(x_0, K_{\mathsf{active}})$.
8. $\tilde{x}_{\mathsf{active}} = (K^{x_0}, \mathsf{key}_{\mathsf{active}}), \tilde{x}_{\mathsf{passive}} = \tilde{x}^*$
9. Send $\tilde{x} = (\tilde{x}_L, \tilde{x}_R)$ to $\mathcal{A}$ and receive b' from $\mathcal{A}$
10. Output b'

Fig. 7. Reduction of Lemma 1

Lemma 2. *If* cGC *is adaptively secure and output-key secure, then* HybA *and* HybB *are computationally indistinguishable.*

Proof. It follows from a similar reduction to the one used in the proof of Lemma 1, with the difference that C_1, x_1 are sent to the challenger instead of C_0, x_0.

Lemmas 1 and 2 prove that:

$$\mathrm{GAME}_0 \overset{comp}{\approx} \mathsf{HybA} \overset{comp}{\approx} \mathsf{HybB} \text{ and } \mathsf{HybC} \overset{comp}{\approx} \mathsf{HybD} \overset{comp}{\approx} \mathrm{GAME}_1.$$

From HybB to HybC. Recall the distribution of hybrid HybB and HybC

– $\mathsf{HybB} = \left(\left(\mathsf{cGCircuit}(1^\lambda, C_0), x_0\right), \left(\mathsf{cGCircuit}(1^\lambda, C_1), x_1\right)\right), \mathsf{active})$
– $\mathsf{HybC} = \left(\left(\mathsf{cGCircuit}(1^\lambda, C_0), x_0\right), \left(\mathsf{cGCircuit}(1^\lambda, C_1), x_1\right)\right), \mathsf{passive})$

The difference between these two hybrids is only in the s-gates: instead of selecting the output from $\mathsf{C_{active}}$ (in HybB), now s-gates will select the output from $\mathsf{C_{passive}}$ (in HybC). Recall the description of s-gate in Fig. 4. Changing the s-gates from active to passive entails changing 2 of the encryptions. In order to argue that these changes are indistinguishable, we must rely on the CPA security of the encryption. However the keys used to create these ciphertexts are not *independent*, since they are used in the garbling of the output gates of $\mathsf{C_L}$ and $\mathsf{C_R}$. Therefore, if we want to change even one encryption, we need to *remove* those keys from the correspondent gates in $\mathsf{C_L}$ and $\mathsf{C_R}$. In other words, those two gates need to be *simulated*. Now, in order to change one gate at the time from real to simulated, we need to leverage the details of the proof provided in [HJO+16].

Proof Strategy in [HJO+16]. We now give an overview of the proof strategy of [HJO+16]; we rely on specific components of the strategy in our proof. For more details see Appendix C. In [HJO+16] hybrid games are parametrized by a *circuit configuration*, that is, a vector indicating the way the gates are garbled. There are three modes for how each gate can be garbled: RealGate, InputDepSimGate, SimGate. There are also *rules* that allow one to indistinguishably move from one configuration to another. These configurations/rules are summarized via a pebbling game where we associate RealGate mode to a gate *not having a pebble on it*, InputDepSimGate mode is associated with a gate having a *black pebble*, and SimGate mode is associated with a gate having a *grey pebble*. The indistinguishability *rules* are then translated to rules for the pebbling game:

Pebbling Rule A. We can place or remove a black pebble on a gate as long as both predecessors of that gate have black pebbles on them (or the gate is an input gate).

Pebbling Rule B. We can replace a black pebble with a grey pebble on a gate as long as all successors of that gate have black or grey pebbles on them (or the gate is an output gate).

We can follow the same rules for the two garbled circuits C_{active}, $C_{passive}$ with one major difference: we cannot replace a black pebble with a grey pebble on the output gates (this part relied on the fact that the output map, which specified the correspondence between wire keys at the output level and the bits they correspond to, was only sent in the on-line phase; in our case this correspondence is needed to create the s-gates in the off-line phase, at least for the active circuit). We rely on one more property (*): if a gate has an output wire w which is associated with keys k_w^0, k_w^1 and we garble the gate in InputDepSimGate mode then we only use one key (k_w^b where b is the bit that the wire takes on during the computation $C(x)$) when creating this garbled gate in the on-line phase.

Let us define $C[\gamma, t]$ to be the class of circuits C such that we can place a black pebble on any single output gate of C in γ pebbling steps and using at most t black pebbles at each step. For the following lemma, theorem and corollaries, assume:

1. The adversary selects $C_0, C_1 \in C[\gamma, t]$.
2. $\Pi = $ (seKeyGen, seEnc, seDec, SimEnc, SimKey) is a somewhere equivocal encryption scheme with equivocation parameter t.
3. $\Gamma = $ (Gen, Enc, Dec) is an encryption scheme secure under *chosen double encryption*.

Lemma 3. HybB *and* HybC *are computationally indistinguishable.*

Proof. Let m be the output size of the circuits C_0, C_1 selected by the adversary. For $i = 1, \ldots, m$, we rely on the following sequence of sub-hybrids:

1. Via a sequence of sub-sub-hybrids, change the configurations of both C_{active} and $C_{passive}$ so that the i'th output gate is in InputDepSimGate mode (has a black pebble on it). This follows using the same argument as in [HJO+16].

2. Change the i'th s-gate from $\mathsf{sgate}_{\mathsf{active}}$ to $\mathsf{sgate}_{\mathsf{passive}}$ (see Fig. 4). This change relies on property (*) and the CPA-security of the encryption scheme $\varGamma$ used to garble the gates. In particular, this change requires changing the contents of the ciphertexts $\mathsf{Enc}_{\ell^0}(\mathsf{Enc}_{r^1}(?))$ and $\mathsf{Enc}_{\ell_1}(\mathsf{Enc}_{r^0}(?))$ in s-gate. However, since $C_0(x_0) = C_1(x_1)$ by property (*) the only keys that are used as plaintexts in other garbled gates in this hybrid are either (ℓ^0, r^1) or (ℓ^1, r^0). In either case, we can rely on encryption security to change the contents of the above two ciphertexts.
3. Via a sequence of sub-sub-hybrids, change the configurations of both C_{active} and C_{passive} back so that all gates are in $\mathsf{RealGate}$ mode (no pebbles). This is the same as step 1 in reverse.

From Lemmas 1, 2, 3, it follows that GAME_0 and GAME_1 are computationally indistinguishable which proves our main result, summarized in the following theorem.

Theorem 1. *Assuming the existence of one-way functions, NGC is adaptively indistinguishable with online complexity $(n + t)\mathsf{poly}(\lambda)$ for all circuits in $\mathcal{C}[\mathsf{poly}(\lambda), t]$.*

Using the pebbling strategies from [HJO+16] summarized in Appendix D we get the following bounds.

Lemma 4. *Any circuit C of depth d, width w, with input size n and output size m, is in the class $\mathcal{C}[\gamma, t]$ with either of the following two settings of γ, t:*

○ $\gamma = 2^{(2d+1)}m$ *steps using $t = 2d$ black pebbles.*
○ $\gamma = 4|C|$ *steps using $t = 2w$ black pebbles.*

Plugging the above lemma into Theorem 1 we get the following corollary.

Corollary 1. *Assuming the existence of one-way functions, NGC is adaptively indistinguishable with online complexity $n \cdot \mathsf{poly}(\lambda)$ for all circuits with either linear width $w = O(n)$ or logarithmic depth $d = O(\log n)$.*

Note that any computation which can be performed in linear space can be represented by a circuit with linear width. Therefore the above covers all linear space computations.

7   Application: Private-Key Adaptively Secure Functional Encryption

Overview. Our new garbling scheme can be used to implement a private-key functional encryption [SW05,BSW11] based on one-way functions, with indistinguishability based security where the adversary can obtain an unbounded number of function secret keys and then adaptively a single challenge ciphertext (the formal definition is provided in Sect. 7.1).

In our scheme (described in Fig. 8), the functional keys are garbled circuits computed according to (a slightly modified version of) NGCircuit, and the ciphertext for a message m corresponds to the garbling of the input m. Since a single garbled input should be used to evaluate multiple garbled circuits, we slightly tweak the construction of our garbling scheme so to allow an initial state that is used upon each invocation of the garbling function. We explain this modification in greater length in Sect. 7.2.

7.1 Definition

A private-key functional encryption scheme Π, over a message space $\mathcal{M} = \{\mathcal{M}_\lambda\}_\lambda$ and a circuit space $\mathcal{C} = \{\mathcal{C}_\lambda\}_\lambda$ is a tuple of PPT algorithms (Π.FE.Setup, Π.FE.KeyGen, Π.FE.Enc, FE.Dec) defined as follows:

- Π.FE.Setup(1^λ): The setup algorithm takes as input the unary representation of the security parameter, and outputs a secret key MSK.
- Π.FE.KeyGen(MSK, C): The key-generation algorithm takes as input a secret key MSK and a circuit $C \in \mathcal{C}_\lambda$ and outputs a functional key sk_C.
- Π.FE.Enc(MSK, m): The encryption algorithm takes as input a secret key MSK and a message $m \in \mathcal{M}_\lambda$ and outputs a ciphertext CT.
- Π.FE.Dec(sk_C, CT) The decryption algorithm takes as input a functional key sk_C and a ciphertext CT, and outputs $m \in \mathcal{M}_\lambda \cup \{\bot\}$.

The correctness property requires that there exists a negligible function $negl(\cdot)$ such that for all sufficiently large $\lambda \in N$, for every message $m \in \mathcal{M}_\lambda$, and for every circuit $C \in \mathcal{C}_\lambda$ it holds that:

$$Pr[\text{FE.Dec}(\Pi.\text{FE.KeyGen}(\text{MSK}, C), \text{FE.Enc}(\text{MSK}, m)) = C(m)] \geq 1 - negl(\lambda)$$

where MSK = FE.Setup(1^λ) and the probability is taken over the random choices of all algorithms.

Many Functions Single Message Adaptive Security. For any PPT adversary $\mathcal{A}$, there exists a negligible function ε such that:

$$Pr[\text{Exp}_{\mathcal{A},\Pi,\text{Ind}}^{\text{Private}-\text{FE}}(\lambda, 0) = 1] - Pr[\text{Exp}_{\mathcal{A},\Pi,\text{Ind}}^{\text{Private}-\text{FE}}(\lambda, 1) = 1] \leq \varepsilon(\lambda)$$

where the experiment $\text{Exp}_{\mathcal{A},\text{Ind}}^{\text{Private}-\text{FE}}(\lambda, b)$ is defined as follows:

1. **Query.** The adversary $\mathcal{A}$ specifies circuits $C^1, C^2, \ldots$. It then obtain functional keys $sk_1, sk_2, \ldots$ which are created as follow:
   - Run MSK = Π.FE.Setup(1^λ).
   - Let q be the number of queries. $\forall i \in [q]$, $sk_i = \Pi$.FE.KeyGen(MSK, C^i).
2. **Challenge.** The adversary $\mathcal{A}$ specifies messages m_0, m_1, such that for all $i \in [q]$, $C^i(m_0) = C^i(m_1)$ and obtains CT, which is created as follows:
   - CT = Π.FE.Enc(MSK, m_b)
3. **Output.** Finally, the adversary outputs a bit b', which is the output of the experiment.

7.2 Construction

Our private-key functional encryption scheme is depicted in Fig. 8. The FE.Setup algorithm generates the keys that need to be shared by all garbled circuits. Such keys are: (1) the keys for the input wires (i.e., K_L, K_R) (2) the keys for the outer somewhere-equivocal encryption seEnc (i.e., $\mathsf{key}_L, \mathsf{key}_R$). The FE.Setup also sets the flag active.

The FE.KeyGen algorithm generates a garbled circuit according to procedure NGCircuit* which is a slight modification of NGCircuit (shown in Fig. 4) that enables to use a single garbled input to evaluate many garbled circuits generated at different times. The modifications are: (1) instead of running procedure GCircuit$(1^\lambda, C)$ (described in Fig. 1) – which would select fresh keys for the input wires and for the outer encryption – it runs a slightly modified procedure GCircuit*$(1^\lambda, C, Input\ keys)$ which takes such keys as an external input; (2) the encryption algorithm seEnc used in GCircuit, is also slightly modified so that it allows blocks to be encrypted in a streaming fashion (that is, instead of having a one-time encryption of n blocks, we allow for many encryptions, where the total number of encrypted blocks is overall $\leq N$ where N is an upperbound (e.g., 2^λ)). In Appendix B we discuss why this modification (that we call seEnc*) follows naturally from the implementation of seEnc provided in [HJO+16].

The FE.Enc algorithm takes in input a message m and simply runs the procedure GInput$(m, Input\ keys)$ to select the keys for m. The ciphertext then consists of the keys for the garbled inputs, and the keys for the outer encryption $\mathsf{key}_R, \mathsf{key}_L$. Note that the size of the ciphertext depends on the length of the input and the length of the keys $\mathsf{key}_R, \mathsf{key}_L$ for somewhere-equivocal encryption. Finally the decryption algorithm simply consists of the evaluation of the garbled circuits.

7.3 Security Proof

In this section we show that protocol in Fig. 8 is a private-key functional encryption scheme that is adaptively secure for many function queries and a single message query (according to Sect. 7.1).

Let GAME_0, be the experiment $\mathsf{Exp}^{\mathsf{Private-FE}}_{\mathcal{A},\Pi,\mathsf{Ind}}(\lambda, 0)$ where the adversary receives encryption of m_0, and let GAME_1 be the experiment $\mathsf{Exp}^{\mathsf{Private-FE}}_{\mathcal{A},\Pi,\mathsf{Ind}}(\lambda, 1)$. The proof of security consists of a sequence of hybrid games from GAME_0 to GAME_1, and each hybrid is computational indistinguishable. We now argue that this sequence of hybrids follows exactly the hybrids provided in the proof of Theorem 1.

Recall that in the security experiment $\mathsf{Exp}^{\mathsf{Private-FE}}_{\mathcal{A},\Pi,\mathsf{Ind}}(\lambda, b)$, $\mathcal{A}$ sends all function queries $C^1, C^2, \ldots, C^q$ at the beginning in one-shot. Concretely, by instantiating the experiment with Π, when $\mathcal{A}$ sends functional queries $C^1, C^2, \ldots, C^q$, she obtains:

Functional Keys: $([\mathsf{C_L}^1, \mathsf{C_R}^1, \mathsf{SG}^1], \ldots, [\mathsf{C_L}^q, \mathsf{C_R}^q, \mathsf{SG}^q])$
where SG^j is the selection circuit $\widetilde{\mathsf{sgate}}$ associated to $\mathsf{C_L}^j, \mathsf{C_R}^j$.

Private-Key Functional Encryption Π.FE.Setup(λ).

1. Select active garbled circuit.
   active $\leftarrow \{L, R\}$. If active $= L$ then passive $= R$ else passive $= L$.

2. Select keys for input wires:
   (left circuits) $K_L = \left(k_{\mathsf{in}_i}^{0,\mathsf{a}}, k_{\mathsf{in}_i}^{1,\mathsf{a}} \right)_{i \in [n]}$,

   (rigth circuits) $K_R = \left(k_{\mathsf{in}_i}^{0,\mathsf{p}}, k_{\mathsf{in}_i}^{1,\mathsf{p}} \right)_{i \in [n]}$.

   with $k_{w_i}^{\sigma,\alpha} \leftarrow \mathsf{Gen}(\lambda)$ for $i \in [n]$, $\sigma \in \{0,1\}$, $\alpha \in \{L, R\}$.

3. Select keys for outer encryption:
   (left/right circuits) $\mathsf{key}_L, \mathsf{key}_R$; where $\mathsf{key}_\alpha \xleftarrow{\$} \mathsf{seKeyGen}(\lambda)$, $\alpha \in \{L, R\}$.

4. **Output** MSK $:= \{K_L, \mathsf{key}_L, K_R, \mathsf{key}_R, \mathsf{active}\}$.

Π.FE.KeyGen(MSK, C).	Π.FE.Enc(MSK, m).
1. $\widetilde{C} := \mathsf{NGCircuit}^\star(C, \mathsf{MSK})$ 2. Ouput $sk_C = \widetilde{C}_b$.	1. $\tilde{x} = \mathsf{NGInput}(m, \mathsf{MSK})$. 2. Output $\mathsf{CT} = \tilde{x} = (K_L^x, \mathsf{key}_L, K_R^x, \mathsf{key}_R)$
FE.Dec(sk_C, CT).	
1. Output $m = \mathsf{NEval}\,(sk_C, \mathsf{CT})$.	

Fig. 8. Private-key FE

In the challenge phase, $\mathcal{A}$ receives the garbling of message m_b. Specifically:
Ciphertext: $\tilde{x} = (K_L, \mathsf{key}_L, K_R, \mathsf{key}_R)$.

Now, note that, because the functional keys (i.e., the garbled circuits) are sent all at once, and they will be evaluated with the same garbled input $\tilde{x}$, we can conceptually think of $C^1, C^2, \ldots, C^q$ as disjoint sub-circuits (which have no wires in common) of one big circuit $\mathbb{C}$. Let us define $\mathbb{C} = [C^1, C^2, \ldots, C^q]$.

Next, we observe that the garbling function $\mathsf{NGCircuit}^\star$ is such that garbling circuits $(C^1, C^2, \ldots, C^q)$ one at the time will generate a garbled circuit which is equivalent to the one obtained by garbling $\mathbb{C}$ as a single circuit. To see why, note that the garbling function $\mathsf{NGCircuit}^\star$ operates by encrypting one gate at the time, and only connected gates have correlated keys. As $(C^1, C^2, \ldots, C^q)$ are disjoint, they are encrypted separately regardless of whether they are presented as a single circuit $\mathbb{C}$ or as many independent circuits. Therefore, we can group the view of adversary as follows:

$$\tilde{\mathbb{C}}_L = (\mathsf{C_L}^1, \ldots, \mathsf{C_L}^q)$$
$$\tilde{\mathbb{C}}_R = (\mathsf{C_R}^1, \ldots, \mathsf{C_R}^q)$$
$$\mathbb{S}_L = (\mathsf{SG}^1, \ldots, \mathsf{SG}^q)$$
$$\tilde{x} = (K_L, \mathsf{key}_L, K_R, \mathsf{key}_R).$$

Finally, recall that the flag active is set once and for all in FE.Setup (Fig. 8) That is, either $L =$ active and $R =$ passive, or viceversa. Therefore, we can further represent the view of the adversary as follows:

$$\tilde{\mathbb{C}}_{\text{active}}, \tilde{x}_{\text{active}}$$
$$\tilde{\mathbb{C}}_{\text{passive}}, \tilde{x}_{\text{passive}}$$
$$\mathbb{S}$$

This view fits the template of high-level hybrids shown in Fig. 6. The exact same arguments then follow to show that GAME_0 and GAME_1 are indistinguishable. In GAME_b, $\tilde{x}_{\text{active}}$ and $\tilde{x}_{\text{passive}}$ are both garbling of m_b.

Following the same template, the proof strategy is to move from GAME_0, where $\tilde{x}_{\text{active}}$ and $\tilde{x}_{\text{passive}}$ are garbling of m_0, to intermediate games where $\tilde{x}_{\text{passive}}$ is a garbling of m_1 and finally change $\tilde{x}_{\text{active}}$ into garbling of m_1 and thus reaching GAME_1.

Theorem 2. *Assuming the existence of one-way functions, Π is a many functions single message adaptive secure private-key functional encryption, for all circuits in $\mathcal{C}\,[\text{poly}(\lambda), t]$, with ciphertext size $(n + t)\text{poly}(\lambda)$, where n is the length of the plaintext.*

Proof. It follows from the proof of Theorem 2 applied to the circuit $\mathbb{C}$ defined above.

7.4   Extensions

We leave as an extension to consider a *full adaptive* security definition for functional encryption where the adversary can choose the functional queries adaptively [ABSV15]. Concretely, this means that the adversary can choose functions adaptively based on the garbled circuits received so far.

To prove security of our construction in this setting, one needs to prove that the underlying garbling scheme (NGCircuit*, NGInput, NEval) satisfies a stronger adaptivity property that we call *many-time* adaptive security. That is, in the security experiment the adversary is allowed to adaptively ask for many garbled circuits and then choose an single input to evaluate all of them.

Showing that (NGCircuit*, NGInput, NEval) achieves this stronger property amounts to show that the underlying new somewhere-equivocal encryption scheme (Definition 6) achieves a stronger security property where the adversary can choose the plaintexts adaptively on the ciphertexts received so far.

A   Symmetric-Key Encryption with Special Correctness [LP09]

In our construction of the garbling scheme, we use a symmetric-key encryption scheme $\Gamma = (\text{Gen}, \text{Enc}, \text{Dec})$ which satisfies the standard definition of CPA security and an additional *special correctness* property below (this is a simplified and sufficient variant of the property described in from [LP09]). We need this property to ensure the correctness of our garbled circuit construction.

Definition 4 (Special Correctness). *A CPA-secure symmetric-key encryption $\Gamma = (\mathsf{Gen}, \mathsf{Enc}, \mathsf{Dec})$ satisfies special correctness if there is some negligible function ε such that for any message m we have:*

$$\Pr[\mathsf{Dec}_{k_2}(\mathsf{Enc}_{k_1}(m)) \neq \perp \; : \; k_1, k_2 \leftarrow \mathsf{Gen}(1^\lambda)] \leq \varepsilon(\lambda).$$

Construction. Let $F = \{f_k\}$ be a family of pseudorandom functions where $f_k : \{0,1\}^\lambda \rightarrow \{0,1\}^{\lambda+s}$, for $k \in \{0,1\}^\lambda$ and s is a parameter denoting the message length. Define $\mathsf{Enc}_k(m) = (r, f_k(r) \oplus m0^\lambda)$ where $m \in \{0,1\}^s$, $r \overset{\$}{\leftarrow} \{0,1\}^\lambda$ and $m0^\lambda$ denotes the concatenation of m with a string of 0s of length λ. Define $\mathsf{Dec}_k(c)$ which parses $c = (r, z)$, computes $w = z \oplus f_k(r)$ and if the last λ bits of w are 0's it outputs the first s bits of w, else it outputs $\perp$.

It's easy to see that this scheme is CPA secure and that it satisfies the special correctness property.

Double Encryption Encryption Security. For convenience, we define a notion of double encryption security, following [LP09]. This notion is implied by standard CPA security but is more convenient to use in our security proof of garbled circuit security.

Definition 5 (Double-encryption security). *An encryption scheme $\Gamma = (\mathsf{Gen}, \mathsf{Enc}, \mathsf{Dec})$*

– *is $(T(\lambda), \varepsilon(\lambda))$-secure under chosen double encryption if*

$$\mathbf{D}_{T(\lambda)} \left[\mathsf{Exp}^{\mathsf{double}}(\lambda, 0), \mathsf{Exp}^{\mathsf{double}}(\lambda, 1) \right] = \varepsilon(\lambda).$$

– *is secure under chosen double encryption if*

$$\mathsf{Exp}^{\mathsf{double}}(\lambda, 0) \overset{\mathsf{comp}}{\approx} \mathsf{Exp}^{\mathsf{double}}(\lambda, 1).$$

– *is sub-exponentially secure if*

$$\exists \, \nu > 0, \forall \, T(\lambda) \in \mathsf{poly}(\lambda) \quad \mathbf{D}_{T(\lambda)} \left[\mathsf{Exp}^{\mathsf{double}}(\lambda, 1), \mathsf{Exp}^{\mathsf{double}}(\lambda, 0) \right] \leq \varepsilon(\lambda) = 1/2^{\lambda^\nu}.$$

where the experiment $\mathsf{Exp}_\mathcal{A}^{\mathsf{double}}$ is defined as follows.

Experiment $\mathsf{Exp}_\mathcal{A}^{\mathsf{double}}(\lambda, b)$

1. *The adversary $\mathcal{A}$ on input 1^λ outputs two keys k_a and k_b of length λ and two triples of messages (x_0, y_0, z_0) and (x_1, y_1, z_1) where all messages are of the same length.*
2. *Two keys $k_a', k_b' \overset{\$}{\leftarrow} \mathsf{Gen}(1^\lambda)$ are chosen.*
3. *$\mathcal{A}^{\mathsf{Enc}_{k_a'}(\cdot), \mathsf{Enc}_{k_b'}(\cdot)}$ is given the challenge ciphertexts $c_x \leftarrow \mathsf{Enc}_{k_a}(\mathsf{Enc}_{k_b'}(x_b))$, $c_y \leftarrow \mathsf{Enc}_{k_a'}(\mathsf{Enc}_{k_b}(y_b))$, $c_z \leftarrow \mathsf{Enc}_{k_a'}(\mathsf{Enc}_{k_b'}(z_b))$ as well as **oracle access** to $\mathsf{Enc}_{k_a'}(\cdot)$ and $\mathsf{Enc}_{k_b'}(\cdot)$.*
4. *$\mathcal{A}$ outputs b' which is the output of the experiment.*

The following lemma is essentially immediate - see [LP09] for a formal proof.

Lemma 5. *If $(\mathsf{Gen}, \mathsf{Enc}, \mathsf{Dec})$ is CPA-secure then it is secure under chosen double encryption with the same security parameter.*

B   Somewhere Equivocal Symmetric-Key Encryption [HJO+16]

Definition 6. *A somewhere equivocal encryption scheme with block-length s, message-length n (in blocks), and equivocation-parameter t (all polynomials in the security parameter) is a tuple of probabilistic polynomial algorithms $\Pi =$ (seKeyGen, seEnc, seDec, SimEnc, SimKey) such that:*

- *The key generation algorithm seKeyGen takes as input the security parameter 1^λ and outputs a key:* key $\leftarrow$ seKeyGen(1^λ).
- *The encryption algorithm seEnc takes as input a vector of n messages $\overline{m} = m_1, \ldots, m_n$, with $m_i \in \{0,1\}^s$, and a key* key, *and outputs ciphertext* $\overline{c} \leftarrow$ seEnc(key, $\overline{m}$).
- *The decryption algorithm seDec takes as input ciphertext $\overline{c}$ and a key* key *and outputs a vector of messages $\overline{m} = m_1, \ldots, m_n$. Namely, $\overline{m} \leftarrow$* seDec(key, $\overline{c}$).
- *The simulated encryption algorithm SimEnc takes as input a set of indexes $I \subset [n]$, such that $|I| \leq t$, and a vector of $n-|I|$ messages $(m_i)_{i \notin I}$ and outputs ciphertext $\overline{c}$, and a state* state*. Namely,* (state, $\overline{c}$) $\leftarrow$ SimEnc$((m_i)_{i \notin I}, I)$.
- *The simulated key algorithm SimKey, takes as input the variable* state *and messages $(m_i)_{i \in I}$ and outputs a key* key′*. Namely,* key′ $\leftarrow$ SimKey(state, $(m_i)_{i \in I}$).

and satisfies the following properties:

Correctness. *For every* key $\leftarrow$ seKeyGen(1^λ), *for every $\overline{m} \in \{0,1\}^{s \times n}$ it holds that:*

$$\text{seDec(key, (seEnc(key, } \overline{m}))) = \overline{m}$$

Simulation with No Holes. *We require that the distribution of $(\overline{c}, \text{key})$ computed via $(\overline{c}, \text{state}) \leftarrow$ SimEnc$(\overline{m}, \emptyset)$ and* key $\leftarrow$ SimKey(state, $\emptyset$) *to be identical to* key $\leftarrow$ seKeyGen(1^λ) *and $\overline{c} \leftarrow$* seEnc(key, $\overline{m}$). *In other words, simulation when there are no holes (i.e., $I = \emptyset$) is identical to honest key generation and encryption.*

Security. *For any PPT adversary $\mathcal{A}$, there exists a negligible function $\nu = \nu(\lambda)$ such that:*

$$\Pr[\text{Exp}_{\mathcal{A},\Pi}^{\text{simenc}}(1^\lambda, 0) = 1] - \Pr[\text{Exp}_{\mathcal{A},\Pi}^{\text{simenc}}(1^\lambda, 1) = 1] \leq \nu(\lambda)$$

where the experiment $\text{Exp}_{\mathcal{A},\Pi}^{\text{simenc}}$ is defined as follows:

Experiment $\text{Exp}_{\mathcal{A},\Pi}^{\text{simenc}}(1^\lambda, b)$

1. *The adversary $\mathcal{A}$ on input 1^λ outputs a set $I \subseteq [n]$ s.t. $|I| < t$, vector $(m_i)_{i \notin I}$, and a challenge index $j \in [n] \setminus I$. Let $I' = I \cup j$.*
2.   – *If $b = 0$, compute $\overline{c}$ as follows:* (state, $\overline{c}$) $\leftarrow$ SimEnc$((m_i)_{i \notin I}, I)$.
  – *If $b = 1$, compute $\overline{c}$ as follows:* (state, $\overline{c}$) $\leftarrow$ SimEnc$((m_i)_{i \notin I'}, I')$.
3. *Send $\overline{c}$ to the adversary $\mathcal{A}$.*

4. *The adversary $\mathcal{A}$ outputs the set of remaining messages $(m_i)_{i \in I}$.*
   - *If $b = 0$, compute* key *as follows:* key $\leftarrow$ SimKey(state, $(m_i)_{i \in I}$).
   - *If $b = 1$, compute* key *as follows:* key $\leftarrow$ SimKey(state, $(m_i)_{i \in I'}$).
5. *Send* key *to the adversary $\mathcal{A}$.*
6. *$\mathcal{A}$ outputs b' which is the output of the experiment.*

In [HJO+16], a somewhere equivocal encryption is constructed from one-way functions, proving the following theorem.

Theorem 3. *Assuming the existence of one-way functions, there exists a somewhere equivocal encryption scheme for any polynomial message-length n, block-length s, and equivocation parameter t, having key size $t \cdot s \cdot \text{poly}(\lambda)$ and ciphertext of size $n \cdot s$ bits.*

Extension. Such construction naturally extends to a modified encryption algorithm seEnc*, that instead of taking in input the entire vector $\overline{m} = m_1, \ldots, m_n$, it takes in input a few blocks that arrive in a streaming fashion. Namely, seEnc* takes as input an upperbound N, a vector of $j \geq 1$ messages $\overline{m} = m_1, \ldots, m_j$, and a key key and it outputs j encryptions, while keeping a counter on the number of encryptions computed so far. The messages are encrypted as long as the counter is less than the upper bound N.

To see why the implementation provided in [HJO+16] also supports the modified version seEnc*, note that their encryption is performed by xoring the output of a special pseudo-random function (PRF) with the plaintext. To encrypt n blocks, one evaluates the PRF on inputs $1, 2, \ldots, n$ and then xor the result with the blocks. Naturally, one can encrypt any number of blocks at different times. The construction will still work provided that the algorithm is stateful and remembers the last index on which the PRF has been evaluated on (so that the same PRF evaluation is not used twice).

Concering security, for our application it suffices that seEnc* satisfies the same "non-adaptive" definition of security as in experiment Exp^{simenc} where the adversary needs to commit to the *entire* vector $(m_i)_{i \notin I}$ in advance.

C Hybrid Games of [HJO+16]

Gate/Circuit Configuration. We start by defining a *gate configuration*. A gate configuration is a pair (outer mode, garbling mode) indicating the way a gate is computed. The outer encryption mode can be {EquivEnc, BindEnc} depending on whether the outer encryption contains a "hole" in place of that gate or whether it is binding on that gate. The garbling mode can be {RealGate, SimGate, InputDepSimGate} which corresponds to the distributions outlined in Fig. 9. We stress that, if the garbling mode of a gate is InputDepSimGate then we require that the outer encryption mode is EquivEnc. This means that there are 5 valid gate configurations for each gate.

A *circuit configuration* simply consists of the gate configuration for each gate in the circuit. More specifically, we represent a circuit configuration by a tuple $(I, (\text{mode}_i)_{i \in [q]})$ where

RealGate	SimGate	InputDepSimGate
$c_{0,0} \leftarrow \mathsf{Enc}_{k_a^0}(\mathsf{Enc}_{k_b^0}(k_c^{g(0,0)}))$	$c_{0,0} \leftarrow \mathsf{Enc}_{k_a^0}(\mathsf{Enc}_{k_b^0}(k_c^0))$	$c_{0,0} \leftarrow \mathsf{Enc}_{k_a^0}(\mathsf{Enc}_{k_b^0}(k_c^{v(c)}))$
$c_{0,1} \leftarrow \mathsf{Enc}_{k_a^0}(\mathsf{Enc}_{k_b^1}(k_c^{g(0,1)}))$	$c_{0,1} \leftarrow \mathsf{Enc}_{k_a^0}(\mathsf{Enc}_{k_b^1}(k_c^0))$	$c_{0,1} \leftarrow \mathsf{Enc}_{k_a^0}(\mathsf{Enc}_{k_b^1}(k_c^{v(c)}))$
$c_{1,0} \leftarrow \mathsf{Enc}_{k_a^1}(\mathsf{Enc}_{k_b^0}(k_c^{g(1,0)}))$	$c_{1,0} \leftarrow \mathsf{Enc}_{k_a^1}(\mathsf{Enc}_{k_b^0}(k_c^0))$	$c_{1,0} \leftarrow \mathsf{Enc}_{k_a^1}(\mathsf{Enc}_{k_b^0}(k_c^{v(c)}))$
$c_{1,1} \leftarrow \mathsf{Enc}_{k_a^1}(\mathsf{Enc}_{k_b^1}(k_c^{g(1,1)}))$	$c_{1,1} \leftarrow \mathsf{Enc}_{k_a^1}(\mathsf{Enc}_{k_b^1}(k_c^0))$	$c_{1,1} \leftarrow \mathsf{Enc}_{k_a^1}(\mathsf{Enc}_{k_b^1}(k_c^{v(c)}))$

Fig. 9. Garbling Gate modes: RealGate (left), SimGate (center), InputDepSimGate (right). The value $v(c)$ depends on the input x and corresponds to the bit going over the wire c in the computation $C(x)$.

- Set $I \subseteq [q]$ contains the indices of the gates i whose outer mode is EquivEnc.
- The value $\mathsf{mode}_i \in \{\mathsf{RealGate}, \mathsf{SimGate}, \mathsf{InputDepSimGate}\}$ describes the garbling mode of gate i.

A *valid circuit configuration* is one where all indexes i such that $\mathsf{mode}_i = \mathsf{InputDepSimGate}$ satisfy $i \in I$.

The Hybrid Game $\mathsf{Hyb}(I, (\mathsf{mode}_i)_{i \in [q]})$. Every valid circuit configuration $I, (\mathsf{mode}_i)_{i \in [q]}$ defines a hybrid game $\mathsf{Hyb}(I, (\mathsf{mode}_i)_{i \in [q]})$ as specified formally Fig. 10 and described informally below. The hybrid game consists of two procedures: GCircuit$'$ for creating the garbled circuit $\widetilde{C}$ and GInput$'$ for creating the garbled input $\tilde{x}$ respectively. The garbled circuit is created by picking random keys $k_{w_j}^\sigma$ for each wire w_j. For each gate i, such that $\mathsf{mode}_i \in \{\mathsf{RealGate}, \mathsf{SimGate}\}$ it creates a garbled gate $\widetilde{g}_i$ using the corresponding distribution as described in Fig. 9. The garbled circuit $\widetilde{C}$ is then created by simulating the outer encryption using the values $\widetilde{g}_i$ in locations $i \notin I$ and "holes" in the locations I. The garbled input is created by first sampling the garbled gates $\widetilde{g}_i$ for each i such that $\mathsf{mode}_i = \mathsf{InputDepSimGate}$ using the corresponding distribution in Fig. 9 and using knowledge of the input x. Then the decryption key key is simulated by plugging in the holes in locations I with the correctly sampled garbled gates $\widetilde{g}_i$. There is some subtlety about how the input labels $K[i]$ and the output label maps $\widetilde{d}_j$ are created when computing $\tilde{x}$:

- If all of the gates having in_i as an input wire are in SimGate mode, then $K[i] := k_{\mathsf{in}_i}^0$ else $K[i] := k_{\mathsf{in}_i}^{x_i}$.
- If the unique gate having out_j as an output wire is in SimGate mode, then we give the simulated output map $\widetilde{d}_j := [(k_{\mathsf{out}_j}^{y_j} \to 0), (k_{\mathsf{out}_j}^{1-y_j} \to 1)]$ else the real one $\widetilde{d}_j := [(k_{\mathsf{out}_j}^0 \to 0), (k_{\mathsf{out}_j}^1 \to 1)]$.

Real game and Simulated Game. By definition of adaptively secure garbled circuits (Definition 2), the real game $\mathsf{Exp}_{\mathcal{A},\mathsf{GC},\mathsf{Sim}}^{\mathsf{adaptive}}(1^\lambda, 0)$ is equivalent to $\mathsf{Hyb}(I = \emptyset, (\mathsf{mode}_i = \mathsf{RealGate})_{i \in [q]})$ and the simulated game $\mathsf{Exp}_{\mathcal{A},\mathsf{GC},\mathsf{Sim}}^{\mathsf{adaptive}}(1^\lambda, 1)$

Game $\mathsf{Hyb}(I, (\mathsf{mode}_i)_{i \in [q]})$

<u>Garble Circuit C:</u>

– Garble Gates
(Wires) $k_{w_i}^{\sigma} \leftarrow \mathsf{Gen}(1^{\lambda})$ for $i \in [p]$, $\sigma \in \{0,1\}$.
(Gates) For each $\mathsf{gate}_i = (g, w_a, w_b, w_c)$ in C.

  – If $\mathsf{mode}_i = \mathsf{RealGate}$: run $\widetilde{g}_i \leftarrow \mathsf{GarbleGate}(g, \{k_{w_a}^{\sigma}, k_{w_b}^{\sigma}, k_{w_c}^{\sigma}\}_{\sigma \in \{0,1\}})$.
  – if $\mathsf{mode}_i = \mathsf{SimGate}$: run $\widetilde{g}_i \leftarrow \mathsf{GarbleSimGate}(\{k_{w_a}^{\sigma}, k_{w_b}^{\sigma}\}_{\sigma \in \{0,1\}}, k_{w_c}^0)$.

– Outer Encryption.

  1. $(\mathsf{state}, \widetilde{C}) \leftarrow \mathsf{SimEnc}((\widetilde{g}_i)_{i \notin I}, I)$.
  2. Output $\widetilde{C}$.

<u>Garble Input x:</u>

(Compute adaptive gates)
For each $i \in I$ s.t. $\mathsf{mode}_i = \mathsf{InputDepSimGate}$:

  Let $\mathsf{gate}_i = (g_i, w_a, w_b, w_c)$, and let $v(c)$
  be the bit on the wire w_c during the computation $C(x)$.
  Set $\widetilde{g}_i \leftarrow \mathsf{GarbleSimGate}((k_{w_a}^{\sigma}, k_{w_b}^{\sigma})_{\sigma \in \{0,1\}}, k_{w_c}^{v(c)})$.

(Decryption key) $\mathsf{key}' \leftarrow \mathsf{SimKey}(\mathsf{state}, (\widetilde{g}_i)_{i \in I})$
(Output tables) Let $y = C(x)$. For $j = 1, \ldots, m$:
Let i be the index of the gate with output wire out_j.

  – If $\mathsf{mode}_i \neq \mathsf{SimGate}$, set $\widetilde{d}_j := [(k_{\mathsf{out}_j}^0 \to 0), (k_{\mathsf{out}_j}^1 \to 1)]$,
  – else, set $\widetilde{d}_j := [(k_{\mathsf{out}_j}^{y_j} \to 0), (k_{\mathsf{out}_j}^{1-y_j} \to 1)]$.

(Select input keys) For $j = 1, \ldots, n$:

  – If all gates i having in_j as an input wire satisfy $\mathsf{mode}_i = \mathsf{SimGate}$, then
    set $K[i] := k_{\mathsf{in}_i}^0$,
  – else set $K[i] := k_{\mathsf{in}_i}^{x_i}$.

Output $\widetilde{x} := (K, \mathsf{key}', \{\widetilde{d}_j\}_{j \in [m]})$.

Fig. 10. The hybrid game.

is equivalent to $\mathsf{Hyb}(I = \emptyset, (\mathsf{mode}_i = \mathsf{SimGate})_{i \in [q]})$. Therefore, the main aim is to show that these hybrids are indistinguishable.[3]

C.1   Rules for Indistinguishable Hybrids

Next, we provide rules that allow us to move from one configuration to another and prove that the corresponding hybrid games are indistinguishable. We define three rules that allow us to do this. We define $\mathsf{mode} \overset{\text{def}}{=} (\mathsf{mode}_i)_{i \in [q]}$.

---

[3] Note that, the games $\mathsf{Hyb}(\cdots)$ use the simulated encryption and key generation procedures of the somewhere equivocal encryption, while the games $\mathsf{Exp}_{A,\mathsf{GC},\mathsf{Sim}}^{\mathsf{adaptive}}(1^{\lambda}, b)$ only use the real key generation and encryption procedures. However, by definition, these are equivalent when $I = \emptyset$ (no "holes").

Indistinguishability Rule 1: Changing the Outer Encryption Mode
BindEnc $\leftrightarrow$ EquivEnc. This rule allows to change the outer encryption of a single gate. It says that one can move from a valid circuit configuration (I, mode) to a circuit configuration (I', mode) where $I' = I \cup j$. Thus one more gate is now computed equivocally (and vice versa).

Lemma 6. *Let (I, mode) be any valid circuit configuration, let $j \in [q] \setminus I$ and let $I' = I \cup j$. Then $\mathsf{Hyb}(I, \mathsf{mode}) \overset{comp}{\approx} \mathsf{Hyb}(I', \mathsf{mode})$ are computationally indistinguishable as long as $\Pi = (\mathsf{seKeyGen}, \mathsf{seEnc}, \mathsf{seDec}, \mathsf{SimEnc}, \mathsf{SimKey})$ is a somewhere equivocal encryption scheme with equivocation parameter t such that $|I'| \le t$.*

Definition 7 *(Predecessor/Successor/Sibling Gates* [HJO+16]*).* *Given a circuit C and a gate $j \in [q]$ of the form $\mathsf{gate}_j = (g, w_a, w_b, w_c)$ with incoming wires w_a, w_b and outgoing wire w_c:*

- *We define the predecessors of j, denoted by $\mathsf{Pred}(j)$, to be the set of gates whose outgoing wires are either w_a or w_b. If w_a, w_b are input wires then $\mathsf{Pred}(j) = \emptyset$, else $|\mathsf{Pred}(j)| = 2$.*
- *We define the successors of j, denoted by $\mathsf{Succ}(j)$ to be the set of gates that contain w_c as an incoming wire. If w_c is an output wires then $\mathsf{Succ}(j) = \emptyset$.*
- *We define the siblings of j, denoted by $\mathsf{Siblings}(j)$ to be the set of gates that contain either w_a or w_b as an incoming wire.*

Indistinguishability Rule 2. Changing the Garbling Mode RealGate $\leftrightarrow$ InputDepSimGate. This rule allows us to change the mode of a gate j from RealGate to InputDepSimGate as long as $j \in I$ and that $\mathsf{gate}_j = (g, w_a, w_b, w_c)$ has incoming wires w_a, w_b that are either input wires or are the outgoing wires of some predecessor gates both of which are in InputDepSimGate mode.

Lemma 7. *Let $(I, \mathsf{mode} = (\mathsf{mode}_i)_{i \in [q]})$ be a valid circuit configuration and let $j \in I$ be an index such that $\mathsf{mode}_j = \mathsf{RealGate}$ and for all $i \in \mathsf{Pred}(j)$: $\mathsf{mode}_i = \mathsf{InputDepSimGate}$. Let $\mathsf{mode}' = (\mathsf{mode}'_i)_{i \in [q]}$ be defined by $\mathsf{mode}'_i = \mathsf{mode}_i$ for all $i \ne j$ and $\mathsf{mode}'_j = \mathsf{InputDepSimGate}$. Then the games $\mathsf{Hyb}(I, \mathsf{mode}) \overset{comp}{\approx} \mathsf{Hyb}(I, \mathsf{mode}')$ are computationally indistinguishable as long as $\Gamma = (\mathsf{Gen}, \mathsf{Enc}, \mathsf{Dec})$ is an encryption scheme secure under chosen double encryption.*

Indistinguishability Rule 3. Changing the Garbling Mode:
InputDepSimGate $\leftrightarrow$ SimGate. This rule allows us to change the mode of a gate j from InputDepSimGate to SimGate under the condition that all successor gates $i \in \mathsf{Succ}(j)$ satisfy that $\mathsf{mode}_i \in \{\mathsf{InputDepSimGate}, \mathsf{SimGate}\}$.

Lemma 8. *Let $(I, \mathsf{mode} = (\mathsf{mode}_i)_{i \in [q]})$ be a valid circuit configuration and let $j \in I$ be an index such that $\mathsf{mode}_j = \mathsf{InputDepSimGate}$ and for all $i \in \mathsf{Succ}(j)$ we have $\mathsf{mode}_i \in \{\mathsf{SimGate}, \mathsf{InputDepSimGate}\}$. Let $\mathsf{mode}' = (\mathsf{mode}'_i)_{i \in [q]}$ be defined by $\mathsf{mode}'_i = \mathsf{mode}_i$ for all $i \ne j$ and $\mathsf{mode}'_j = \mathsf{SimGate}$. Then the games $\mathsf{Hyb}(I, \mathsf{mode}) \equiv \mathsf{Hyb}(I, \mathsf{mode}')$ are identically distributed.*

C.2   Pebbling and Sequences of Hybrid Games

In the last section we defined hybrid games parameterized by a configuration (I, mode). We also gave 3 rules, which describe ways that allow us to indistinguishably move from one configuration to another. Now our goal is to use the given rules so as to define a *sequence of indistinguishable hybrid games* that takes us from the *real game* $\text{Hyb}(I = \emptyset, (\text{mode}_i = \text{RealGate})_{i \in [q]})$ to the simulation $\text{Hyb}(I = \emptyset, (\text{mode}_i = \text{SimGate})_{i \in [q]})$.

Pebbling Game. We show that the problem of finding such sequences of hybrid games can be captured by a certain type of *pebbling game* on the circuit C. Each gate can either have *no pebble*, a *black pebble*, or *a gray pebble* on it (this will correspond to RealGate, InputDepSimGate and SimGate modes respectively). Initially, the circuit starts out with no pebbles on any gate. The game consist of the following possible moves:

Rule A. We can place or remove a black pebble on a gate as long as both predecessors of that gate have black pebbles (or the gate is an input gate).

Rule B. We can replace a black pebble with a gray one, only if successors of that gate have black or gray pebbles on them (or the gate is an output gate).

A *pebbling* of a circuit C is a sequence of γ moves that follow rules A and B and that end up with a gray pebble on every gate. We say that a pebbling uses t black pebbles if this is the maximal number of black pebbles on the circuit at any point in time during the game.

From Pebbling to Sequence of Hybrids. In next theorem we prove that any pebbling of a circuit C results in a sequence of hybrids that shows indistinguishability of the real and simulated games. The number of hybrids is proportional to the number of moves in the pebbling and the equivocation parameter is proportional to the number of black pebbles it uses.

Theorem 4. *Assume that there is a pebbling of the circuit C in γ moves. Then there is a sequence of $2 \cdot \gamma + 1$ hybrid games, starting with the real game $\text{Hyb}(I = \emptyset, (\text{mode}_i = \text{RealGate})_{i \in [q]})$ and ending with the simulated game $\text{Hyb}(I = \emptyset, (\text{mode}_i = \text{SimGate})_{i \in [q]})$ such that any two adjacent hybrid games in the sequence are indistinguishable by rules 1,2 or 3 from the previous section. Furthermore if pebbling uses t^* black pebbles then every hybrid $\text{Hyb}(I, \text{mode})$ in the sequence satisfies $|I| \leq t^*$. In particular, indistinguishability holds as long as the equivocation parameter is at least t^*.*

D   Pebbling Strategies [HJO+16]

In this section we give two pebbling strategies for arbitrary circuit with width w, depth d, and q gates. The first strategy uses $O(q)$ moves and $O(w)$ black pebbles. The second strategy uses $O(q2^d)$ moves and $O(d)$ black pebbles.

Strategy 1. To pebble the circuit proceed as follows:

Pebble(C):
1. Put a black pebble on each gate at the input level (level 1).
2. For $i = 1$ to $d - 1$, repeat:
   (a) Put a black pebble on each gate at level $i + 1$.
   (b) For each gate at level i, replace the black pebble with a gray pebble.
   (c) $i \leftarrow i + 1$.
3. For each gate at level d, replace the black pebble with a gray pebble.

This strategy uses $\gamma = 2q$ moves and $t^* = 2w$ black pebbles.

Strategy 2. This is a recursive strategy defined as follows.

– Pebble(C):
For each gate i in C starting with the gates at the top level moving to the bottom level:
   1. RecPutBlack(C, i)
   2. Replace the black pebble on gate i with a gray pebble.
– RecPutBlack(C, i): // Let LeftPred(C, i) and RightPred(C, i) be the two predecessors of gate i in C.
   1. If gate i is an input gate, put a black pebble on i and **return**.
   2. Run RecPutBlack(C, LeftPred(C, i)), RecPutBlack(C, RightPred(C, i)).
   3. Put a black pebble on gate i.
   4. Run RecRemoveBlack(C, LeftPred(C, i)) and
      RecRemoveBlack(C, RightPred(C, i)).
– RecRemoveBlack(C, i): This is the same as RecPutBlack, except that instead of putting a black pebble on gate i, in steps 1 and 3, we remove it.

The above gives us a strategy to pebble any circuit with at most $\gamma = q4^d$ moves and $t = 2d$ black pebbles.

References

[ABSV15] Ananth, P., Brakerski, Z., Segev, G., Vaikuntanathan, V.: From selective to adaptive security in functional encryption. In: Gennaro, R., Robshaw, M. (eds.) CRYPTO 2015. LNCS, vol. 9216, pp. 657–677. Springer, Heidelberg (2015). doi:10.1007/978-3-662-48000-7_32

[AIKW13] Applebaum, B., Ishai, Y., Kushilevitz, E., Waters, B.: Encoding functions with constant online rate or how to compress garbled circuits keys. In: Canetti, R., Garay, J.A. (eds.) CRYPTO 2013. LNCS, vol. 8043, pp. 166–184. Springer, Heidelberg (2013). doi:10.1007/978-3-642-40084-1_10

[BHR12] Bellare, M., Hoang, V.T., Rogaway, P.: Foundations of garbled circuits. In: Yu, T., Danezis, G., Gligor, V.D. (eds.), 19th Conference on Computer and Communications Security, ACM CCS 2012, Raleigh, NC, USA, 16–18 October 2012, pp. 784–796. ACM Press (2012)

[BSW11] Boneh, D., Sahai, A., Waters, B.: Functional encryption: definitions and challenges. In: Ishai, Y. (ed.) TCC 2011. LNCS, vol. 6597, pp. 253–273. Springer, Heidelberg (2011). doi:10.1007/978-3-642-19571-6_16

[HJO+16] Hemenway, B., Jafargholi, Z., Ostrovsky, R., Scafuro, A., Wichs, D.: Adaptively secure garbled circuits from one-way functions. In: Robshaw, M., Katz, J. (eds.) CRYPTO 2016. LNCS, vol. 9816, pp. 149–178. Springer, Heidelberg (2016). doi:10.1007/978-3-662-53015-3_6

[HW15] Hubacek, P., Wichs, D.: On the communication complexity of secure function evaluation with long output. In: Roughgarden, T. (ed.) 6th Innovations in Theoretical Computer Science, ITCS 2015, Rehovot, Israel, 11–13 January 2015, pp. 163–172. Association for Computing Machinery (2015)

[JW16] Jafargholi, Z., Wichs, D.: Adaptive security of Yao's garbled circuits. In: Hirt, M., Smith, A. (eds.) TCC 2016. LNCS, vol. 9985, pp. 433–458. Springer, Heidelberg (2016). doi:10.1007/978-3-662-53641-4_17

[LP09] Lindell, Y., Pinkas, B.: A proof of security of Yao's protocol for two-party computation. J. Cryptol. **22**(2), 161–188 (2009)

[PST14] Pass, R., Seth, K., Telang, S.: Indistinguishability obfuscation from semantically-secure multilinear encodings. In: Garay, J.A., Gennaro, R. (eds.) CRYPTO 2014. LNCS, vol. 8616, pp. 500–517. Springer, Heidelberg (2014). doi:10.1007/978-3-662-44371-2_28

[SW05] Sahai, A., Waters, B.: Fuzzy identity-based encryption. In: Cramer, R. (ed.) EUROCRYPT 2005. LNCS, vol. 3494, pp. 457–473. Springer, Heidelberg (2005). doi:10.1007/11426639_27

[Yao82] Yao, A.C.: Protocols for secure computations (extended abstract). In: 23rd Annual Symposium on Foundations of Computer Science, Chicago, Illinois, 3–5 November 1982, pp. 160–164. IEEE Computer Society Press (1982)

[Yao86] Yao, A.C.: How to generate and exchange secrets (extended abstract). In: 27th Annual Symposium on Foundations of Computer Science, Toronto, Ontario, Canada, 27–29 October 1986, pp. 162–167. IEEE Computer Society Press (1986)

Circuit OPRAM: Unifying Statistically and Computationally Secure ORAMs and OPRAMs

T.-H. Hubert Chan[1(✉)] and Elaine Shi[2]

[1] The University of Hong Kong, Pokfulam, Hong Kong
hubert@cs.hku.hk
[2] Cornell University, Ithaca, USA

Abstract. An Oblivious Parallel RAM (OPRAM) provides a general method to simulate any Parallel RAM (PRAM) program, such that the resulting memory access patterns leak nothing about secret inputs. OPRAM was originally proposed by Boyle et al. as the natural parallel counterpart of Oblivious RAM (ORAM), which was shown to have broad applications, e.g., in cloud outsourcing, secure processor design, and secure multi-party computation. Since parallelism is common in modern computing architectures such as multi-core processors or cluster computing, OPRAM is naturally a powerful and desirable building block as much as its sequential counterpart ORAM is.

Although earlier works have shown how to construct OPRAM schemes with polylogarithmic simulation overhead, in comparison with best known sequential ORAM constructions, all existing OPRAM schemes are (poly-)logarithmic factors more expensive. In this paper, we present a new framework in which we construct both statistically secure and computationally secure OPRAM schemes whose asymptotical performance matches the best known ORAM schemes in each setting. Since an OPRAM scheme with simulation overhead χ directly implies an ORAM scheme with simulation overhead χ, our result can be regarded as providing a unifying framework in which we can subsume all known results on statistically and computationally secure ORAMs and OPRAMs alike. Particularly for the case of OPRAMs, we also improve the state-of-the-art scheme by superlogarithmic factors.

To achieve the aforementioned results requires us to combine a variety of techniques involving (1) efficient parallel oblivious algorithm design; and (2) designing tight randomized algorithms and proving measure concentration bounds about the rather involved stochastic process induced by the OPRAM algorithm.

Keywords: Oblivious parallel RAM · Oblivious RAM · Statistical and computational security

1 Introduction

Oblivious RAM (ORAM), initially proposed by Goldreich and Ostrovsky [17,18], is a powerful primitive that allows oblivious accesses to sensitive data, such that

---

Online eprint version [6] of this paper: https://eprint.iacr.org/2016/1084.

© International Association for Cryptologic Research 2017
Y. Kalai and L. Reyzin (Eds.): TCC 2017, Part II, LNCS 10678, pp. 72–107, 2017.
https://doi.org/10.1007/978-3-319-70503-3_3

access patterns during the computation reveal no secret information. Since its original proposal [18], ORAM has been shown to be promising in various application settings including secure processors [11,13,14,25,30], cloud outsourced storage [19,32,33,40] and secure multi-party computation [15,16,20,22,24,37].

Although ORAM is broadly useful, it is inherently sequential and does not support parallelism. On the other hand, parallelism is universal in modern architectures such as cloud platforms and multi-core processors. Motivated by this apparent discrepancy, in a recent seminal work [3], Boyle et al. extended the ORAM notion to the parallel setting. Specifically, they defined Oblivious Parallel RAM (OPRAM), and demonstrated that any PRAM program can be simulated obliviously while incurring roughly $O(\log^4 N)$ blowup in running time when consuming the same number of CPUs as the PRAM where N is the total memory size. The result by Boyle et al. [3] was later improved by Chen et al. [7], who showed a logarithmic factor improvement, attaining $O(\log^3 N)$ overhead.

However, we still know of no OPRAM algorithm whose performance can "match" the state-of-the-art sequential counterparts [23,35,36]. In particular, in the sequential setting, it is known that computationally secure ORAMs can be constructed with $O(\frac{\log^2 N}{\log \log N})$ simulation overhead [23], and statistically secure ORAMs can be achieved with $O(\log^2 N)$ simulation overhead [36] — these results apply when assuming $O(1)$ blocks of CPU private cache, and they hold for general block sizes, as long as the block is large enough to store its own address. Thus in comparison, state-of-the-art OPRAM schemes are at least a logarithmic factor slower. We thus ask the question:

Can we construct an OPRAM scheme whose asymptotical performance matches the best known sequential counterpart?

Our paper answers this question in the affirmative. To this end, we construct the Circuit OPRAM framework — under this framework we demonstrate both statistically and computationally secure ORAMs whose performance matches the best known ORAM schemes in these respective settings. Our main results are summarized in the following informal theorems.

Theorem 1 (Informal: statistically secure OPRAM). *There exists a statistically secure OPRAM scheme that achieves $O(\log^2 N)$ simulation overhead for general block sizes and $O(1)$ blocks of CPU cache.*

Theorem 2 (Informal: computationally secure OPRAM). *There exists a computationally secure OPRAM scheme that achieves $O(\frac{\log^2 N}{\log \log N})$ simulation overhead for general block sizes and $O(1)$ blocks of CPU cache.*

In both the above theorems, an OPRAM simulation overhead of χ means the following: suppose that the original PRAM consumes m CPUs and computes a program in T time; then we can compile the PRAM into an OPRAM also consuming m CPUs, but completes in $\chi \cdot T$ time[1]. Since an OPRAM scheme with

---

[1] Thus, by classical metrics of the parallel algorithms literature, an OPRAM scheme with χ *simulation overhead* incurs a *total work* blowup and a *parallel runtime* blowup of both χ in comparison with the original PRAM.

χ simulation overhead immediately implies an ORAM scheme with χ simulation overhead[2] to — in some sense, our work provides a unifying framework under which we subsume all known results for statistically secure and computationally secure ORAMs and OPRAMs — and specifically for the case of OPRAM, we improve best known results by at least a logarithmic factor.

For generality, we describe our construction in a way that supports the case of varying number of CPUs, i.e., when the underlying PRAM consumes a different number of CPUs in different PRAM steps — this is a desirable property phrased in the original OPRAM work by Boyle et al. [3], although the subsequent work by Chen et al. [7] fails to achieve it.

Last but not the least, we show that when the block size is sufficiently large, our framework implies an OPRAM scheme with $O(\log N)$ simulation overhead (when m is not too small) — also matching the best-known sequential ORAM result for large block sizes [36].

1.1   Technical Highlights

Obtaining an OPRAM as tight as its sequential counterpart turns out to be rather non-trivial. Part of the technical sophistication stems from the fact that we did not find any generic method that can blackbox-compile an efficient ORAM to an OPRAM scheme with matching overhead. As a result, our construction requires opening up and building atop the Circuit ORAM scheme [36] (which is a state-of-the-art ORAM scheme among others) in a *non-blackbox* manner[3].

We follow the paradigm for constructing OPRAM schemes proposed by Boyle et al. [3] and Chen et al. [7]. On a high level, we leverage a tree-based ORAM scheme [31,36] but truncate the tree at a level with m nodes, thus creating m disjoint subtrees. At this point, a simple approach that is taken by earlier works [7] is to have a single CPU in charge of each subtree. When a batch of m memory requests come in, each request will want to fetch data from a random subtree. By a simple balls-and-bins argument, while each subtree receives only $O(1)$ requests in expectation, the most unlucky sub-tree will need to serve super-logarithmically many requests (to obtain a negligible failure probability). Thus the naive approach is to have each subtree's CPU serve these super-logarithmically many requests sequentially. After fetching the m blocks, the OPRAM data structure must be maintained by remapping every fetched block to a random new subtree. Again, although each subtree gets assigned $O(1)$ remapped blocks in expectation during this maintain stage, the most unlucky subtree can obtain super-logarithmically many blocks. For obliviousness, it is important that we hide from the adversary to which subtree each block gets remapped. Unfortunately this also means that we cannot disclose how many remapped blocks are received by each subtree — and thus previous works [7]

---

[2] In other words, when $m = 1$ our scheme essentially is the same as Circuit ORAM. Thus our work can also be viewed as a strict generalization of Circuit ORAM.

[3] We did not build atop the Path ORAM [35] scheme since Path ORAM achieves the same simulation overhead as Circuit ORAM [36] but consuming super-logarithmic CPU cache rather than $O(1)$.

adopt the simple approach of padding: even when a subtree may receive only 1 remapped block, it still must perform dummy operations to pretend that it receives superlogarithmically many blocks.

Thus, a primary reason that causes existing constructions [3,7] to be inefficient is the *discrepancy between the average-case contention and the worst-case contention associated with a subtree.* In the above description, this discrepancy reflects in both the request phase and the maintain phase. In both phases, each subtree receives $O(1)$ requests or blocks in expectation, but the worst-case can be superlogarithmic (assuming negligible failure probability).

Thus the core of the question is how to avoid the blowup resulting from the aforementioned average-case and worst-case discrepancy. We would like our scheme to incur a cost that reflects the average-case contention, not the worst-case. To achieve this, we need different techniques for the online request and offline maintain phases respectively:

- For the request phase, it does not violate obliviousness to disclose how many requests are received by each subtree, and thus the nature of the problem is how to design an efficient parallel oblivious algorithm to serve all m requests in parallel with m CPUs, and avoid any subtree's CPU having to process superlogarithmically many requests sequentially. As we will show in later sections, the core of the problem is how to design an efficient and oblivious parallel removal algorithm (referred to "simultaneous removal" in later sections) that removes fetched blocks from the tree-paths — this is challenging since several CPUs may read paths that overlap with one another, leading to possible write contention.
- In the maintain phase, on the contrary, it would violate obliviousness to disclose how many remapped blocks are received by each subtree. Earlier schemes achieve this by pretending to reroute superlogarithmically many blocks to every subtree, thus always incurring the worst-case cost. Our idea is to redesign the underlying stochastic process to avoid this padding-related loss. To this end, we introduce a new technique called "lazy eviction"[4], where we do not route remapped blocks to their new subtrees immediately — instead, with every operation, each subtree has a budget for receiving only a constant number of remapped blocks; and the overflowing blocks that do not have a chance to be rerouted to their assigned subtrees will remain in a "pool" data structure whose size we shall bound with measure concentration techniques.

When we put these techniques together, we obtain on OPRAM scheme that induces a stochastic process that is somewhat involved to reason about. Analyzing this OPRAM-induced stochastic process and proving measure concentration results (e.g., bounds on pool and stash sizes) are non-trivial challenges that we have to overcome in this paper. Although we build on top of the Circuit ORAM scheme in a non-blackbox manner, we wish to maximally reuse the (somewhat involved) measure concentration results proven in the Circuit ORAM work [36]

---

[4] Techniques similar in spirit has appeared in earlier ORAM [34] and OPRAM works [7].

(albeit in a non-blackbox manner). Thus, when we design our Circuit OPRAM algorithm, we take care to ensure that the resulting randomized process is *stochastically dominated* by that of the underlying Circuit ORAM algorithm (in terms of overflows) — to this end, our algorithm tries to "imitate" the stochastic behavior of Circuit ORAM in several places, e.g., in selecting which remapped block gets priority to be rerouted back to its subtree. A rather technical part of our proof is to show that the resulting OPRAM scheme is indeed stochastically dominated by Circuit ORAM in terms of overflows.

1.2 Related Work

Closely related and independent works. Subsequent to our online technical report, Nayak and Katz [26] also released a technical report that claimed seemingly similar results. We stress that *our construction is a* $\log N \cdot$ poly $\log \log N$ *factor more efficient than the work by Nayak and Katz* — despite their paper's title claiming to achieve $O(\log^2 N)$ overhead, their $O(\log^2 N)$ overhead did not account for the inter-CPU communication which is $O(\log^3 N$poly $\log \log N)$ in their scheme assuming $O(1)$ CPU cache — more specifically, Nayak and Katz's scheme does not improve the inter-CPU communication in comparison with Chen et al. [7] (whereas we improve by a super-logarithmic factor); but they adopt a variant of our simultaneous removal algorithm to improve the CPU-memory communication of Chen et al. [7].

In our paper, we adopt a more general and cleaner model than earlier and concurrent OPRAM works [3,7,26], in that we assume that all inter-CPU communication is routed through memory too. In this way, we use a single metric called simulation overhead to characterize both CPU-memory cost and inter-CPU communication. Using our metric, an OPRAM scheme with simulation overhead χ means that both the CPU-memory cost and the inter-CPU communication have at most χ blowup in comparison with the original PRAM.

Below we review the line of works on constructing ORAMs and OPRAMs.

Oblivious RAM (ORAM). Oblivious RAM (ORAM) was initially proposed by Goldreich and Ostrovsky [17,18] who showed that any RAM program can be simulated obliviously incurring only $O(\alpha \log^3 N)$ runtime blowup, while achieving a security failure probability that is negligible in N. Numerous subsequent works [10,19,23,28,29,31,35,36,36–40] improved Goldreich and Ostrovsky's seminal result in different application settings including cloud outsourcing, secure processor, and secure multi-party computation.

Most of these schemes follow one of two frameworks: the hierarchical framework, originally proposed by Goldreich and Ostrovsky [17,18], or the tree-based framework proposed by Shi et al. [31]. To date, some of the (asymptotically) best schemes include the following: (1) Kushilevitz et al. [23] showed a *computationally secure* ORAM scheme with $O(\log^2 N/ \log \log N)$ runtime blowup for general block sizes; and (2) Wang et al. construct Circuit ORAM [36], a *statistically secure* ORAM that achieves $O(\alpha \log^2 N)$ runtime blowup for general block sizes[5] and $O(\alpha \log N)$ runtime blowup for large enough blocks. At the time of the writing, we are not aware of any approach that transforms a state-of-the-art hierarchical ORAM such as Kushilevitz et al. [23] into an OPRAM scheme with matching simulation overhead — even if this could be done, it still would not be clear how to match the best known ORAM results for the statistical security setting. Our work henceforth builds on top of the tree-based ORAM framework, and specifically, Circuit ORAM [36].

On the lower bound side, Goldreich and Ostrovsky [17, 18] demonstrated that any ORAM scheme (with constant CPU cache) must incur at least $\Omega(\log N)$ runtime blowup. This well-known lower bound was recently shown to be tight (under certain parameter ranges) by the authors of Circuit ORAM [36], who showed a matching upper bound for sufficiently large block sizes. Goldreich and Ostrovsky's lower bound applies to OPRAM too since by our definition of simulation overhead, an OPRAM scheme with χ simulation overhead implies an ORAM scheme with χ simulation overhead. We note that while the Goldreich and Ostrovsky lower bound is quite general, it models each block as being opaque — recently, an elegant result by Boyle and Naor [4] discussed the possibility of proving a lower bound without this restriction. Specifically, they showed that proving a lower bound without the block opaqueness restriction is as hard as showing a superlinear lower bound on the sizes of certain sorting circuits. Further, the Goldreich-Ostrovsky lower bound is also known not to hold when the memory (i.e., ORAM server) is capable of performing computation [2, 10] — in this paper, we focus on the classical ORAM/OPRAM setting where the memory does not perform any computation besides storing and fetching data at the request of the CPU.

Oblivious Parallel RAM (OPRAM). Given that many modern computing architectures support parallelism, it is natural to extend ORAM to the parallel setting. As mentioned earlier, Boyle et al. [3] were the first to formulate the OPRAM problem, and they constructed an elegant scheme that achieves $O(\alpha \log^4 N)$ blowup both in terms of total work and parallel runtime. Their result was later improved by Chen et al. [7] who were able to achieve $O(\alpha \log^3 N)$ blowup both in terms of total work and parallel runtime under $O(\log^2 N)$ blocks of CPU cache. These results can easily be recast to the $O(1)$ CPU cache setting by applying a standard trick that leverages oblivious sorting to perform eviction [36, 37]. We note that Chen et al. [7] actually considered *CPU-memory communication* and *inter-CPU communication* as two separate metrics, and their scheme achieves $O(\alpha \log^2 N \log \log N)$ CPU-memory communication blowup, but $O(\alpha \log^3 N)$ inter-CPU communication blowup. In this paper, we consider the more general

---

[5] The term α is related to the ORAM's failure probability. For the failure probability to be negligible we can set α to be any super-constant function. Note that in this paper, the new OPRAM techniques we introduce allow us to remove the super-constant factor α and thus we achieve $O(\log^2 N)$ overhead for general block sizes. Therefore, strictly speaking, we improve the best-known results for statistical security [36] by a super-constant factor. For sufficiently large block sizes, we achieve $O(\alpha \log N)$ simulation overhead, matching the sequential counterpart Circuit ORAM.

PRAM model where all inter-CPU communication is implemented through CPU-memory communication. In this case, the two metrics coalesce into one (i.e., the maximum of the two).

Besides OPRAM schemes in the standard setting, Dachman-Soled et al. [9] considered a variation of the problem (which they refer to as "Oblivious Network RAM") where each memory bank is assumed to be oblivious within itself, and the adversary can only observe which bank a request goes to. Additionally, Nayak et al. [27] show that for parallel computing models that are more restrictive than the generic PRAM (e.g., the popular GraphLab and MapReduce models), there exist efficient parallel oblivious algorithms that asymptotically outperform known generic OPRAM. Some of the algorithmic techniques employed by Nayak et al. [27] are similar in nature to those of Boyle et al. [3].

Subsequent work. In subsequent work, Chan et al. [5] consider a new model for OPRAM, where the OPRAM has access to more CPUs than the original PRAM. In that model, they characterize an OPRAM's overhead using two metrics, *total work blowup* and *parallel runtime blowup* (the latter metric also referred to as depth blowup). Chan et al. show that any OPRAM scheme that treats block contents as opaque must incur at least $\Omega(\log m)$ depth blowup where m is the number of CPUs of the original PRAM. Further, they devise non-trivial algorithmic techniques that improves the depth of Circuit OPRAM (while preserving total work) by recruiting the help of logarithmically many more CPUs. Further, Chan et al. [5] show that their algorithm's depth is tight in the parameter m when the block size is sufficiently large.

2   Informal Overview of Our Results

In this section, we take several intermediate steps to design a basic Circuit OPRAM construction. Specifically, we start out by reviewing the high-level idea introduced earlier by Chen et al. [7]. Then, we point out why their scheme suffers from an extra logarithmic blowup in performance in comparison with the best known sequential algorithm. Having made these observations, we describe our new techniques to avoid this blowup. For simplicity, in this section, we focus on describing the basic, statistically secure Circuit OPRAM algorithm with a fixed number of CPUs denoted m. In later formal sections, we will describe the full scheme supporting the case of varying m, and additional techniques that allow us to shave another $\log \log N$ factor by leveraging a PRF to compress the storage of the random position maps. Like in earlier ORAM/OPRAM works [17–19,31,35,36], we will assume that the number of blocks N is also the security parameter.

2.1   Background: Circuit ORAM

We review tree-based ORAMs [8,31,35,36] originally proposed by Shi et al. [31]. We specifically focus on describing the Circuit ORAM algorithm [36] which we build upon.

We assume that memory is divided into atomic units called blocks. We first focus on describing the *non-recursive version*, in which the CPU stores in its local cache a *position map* henceforth denoted as posmap that stores the position for every block.

Data structures. The memory is organized in the form of a binary tree, where every tree node is a *bucket* with a capacity of $O(1)$ blocks. Buckets hold blocks, where each block is either dummy or real. Throughout the paper, we use the notation N to denote the total number of blocks. Without loss of generality, we assume that $N = 2^L$ is a power of two. The ORAM binary tree thus has height L.

Besides the buckets, there is also a *stash* in memory that holds overflowing blocks. The stash is of size $O(\alpha \log N)$, where $\alpha = \omega(1)$ is a parameter related to the failure probability. Just like buckets, the stash may contain both real and dummy blocks. Henceforth, for convenience, we will often *treat the stash as part of the root bucket.*

Main path invariant. The main invariant of tree-based ORAMs is that every block is assigned to the path from the root to a randomly chosen leaf node. Hence, the path for each block is indicated by the *leaf identifier* or the *position identifier*, which is stored in the aforementioned position map posmap. A block with virtual address i must reside on the path indicated by posmap[i].

Operations. We describe the procedures for reading or writing a block at virtual address i.

- *Read and remove.* To read a block at virtual address i, the CPU looks up its assigned path indicated by posmap[i], and reads this entire path. If the requested block is found at some location on the path, the CPU writes a dummy block back into the location. Otherwise, the CPU simply writes the original block back. In both cases, the block written back is re-encrypted such that the adversary cannot observe which block is removed.
- *Remap.* Once a block at virtual address i is fetched, it is immediately assigned to a new path. To do this, a fresh random path identifier is chosen and posmap[i] is modified accordingly. The block fetched is then written to the last location in the stash (the last location is guaranteed to be empty except with negligible probability at the end of each access). If this is a write operation, the block's contents may be updated prior to writing it back to the stash.
- *Evict.* Two paths (particularly, one to the left of the root and one to the right of the root) are chosen for eviction according to an appropriate data independent criterion. Specifically, for the remainder of the paper, we will assume that the paths are chosen based on the deterministic reverse lexicographical order algorithm adopted in earlier works [15,36], the choice of eviction path is non-essential to the understanding of the algorithm (but matters to the stochastic analysis).

  For each path chosen (that includes the stash), the CPU performs an eviction procedure along this path. On a high level, eviction is a maintenance operation that aims to move blocks along tree paths towards the leaves — and importantly, in a way that respects the aforementioned path invariant. The purpose of eviction is to avoid overflow at any bucket.

Specifically in Circuit ORAM, this eviction operation involves making two metadata scans of the eviction path followed by a single data block scan [36].

A useful property of Circuit ORAM's eviction algorithm. For the majority of this paper, the reader need not know the details of the eviction algorithm. However, we point out a useful observation regarding Circuit ORAM's eviction algorithm.

Fact 1 (Circuit ORAM eviction). *Suppose Circuit ORAM's eviction algorithm is run once on some path denoted* path$[0..L]$, *where by convention we use* path$[0]$ *to denote the root (together with the stash) and* path$[L]$ *is the leaf in the path. Then, for every height $i \in \{1, \ldots, L\}$, it holds that at most one block moves from* path$[0..i-1]$ *to* path$[i..L]$. *Further, if a block did move from* path$[0..i-1]$ *to* path$[i..L]$, *then it must be the block that can be evicted the deepest along the eviction path (and if more than one such block exists, an arbitrary choice could be made).*

Jumping ahead, we stress that Fact 1 is why later we can evict exactly 1 block to each subtree — in comparison, had we built on top of Path ORAM, we would not be able to achieve the same.

Recursion. So far, we have assumed that the CPU can store the entire position map posmap in its local cache. This assumption can be removed using a standard recursion technique [31]. Specifically, instead of storing the position map in the CPU's cache, we store it in a smaller ORAM in memory — and we repeat this process until the position map is of constant size.

As long as each block can store at least two position identifiers, each level of the recursion will reduce the size of the ORAM by a constant factor. Therefore, there are at most $O(\log N)$ levels of recursion. Several tree-based ORAM schemes also describe additional tricks in parametrizing the recursion for larger block sizes [35, 36]. We will not describe these tricks in detail here, but later in the full version [6] we will recast these tricks in our OPRAM context and describe further optimizations for large block sizes.

Circuit ORAM performance. For general block sizes, Circuit ORAM achieves $O(\alpha \log N)$ blowup (in terms of bandwidth and the number of accesses) in the non-recursive version, and $O(\alpha \log^2 N)$ blowup across all levels of recursion. The CPU needs to hold only $O(1)$ blocks at any point in time.

2.2   Warmup: The CLT OPRAM Scheme

We outline the elegant approach by Chen et al. [7] which achieves $O(\log^3 N)$ simulation overhead. Although Chen et al. [7]'s construction builds on top of Path ORAM [35], we describe a (slightly improved) variant of their scheme [7] that builds atop Circuit ORAM instead, but in a way that captures the core ideas of Chen et al. [7].

Suppose we start with Circuit ORAM [36], a state-of-the-art tree-based ORAM. Circuit ORAM is sequential, i.e., supports only one access at a time — but we now would like to support m simultaneous accesses. Without loss of generality, we assume that $m \leq N$ throughout the paper. In our informal overview, we often assume that m is not too small for convenience (more precisely we assume that $m > \omega(\log \log N)$ for our informal description), and we deal with the case of small m in later technical sections.

Challenge for parallel accesses: write conflicts. A strawman idea for constructing OPRAM is to have m CPUs perform m ORAM access operations simultaneously. Reads are easy to handle, since the m CPUs can read m paths simultaneously. The difficulty is due to write conflicts, which arise from the need for m CPUs to (1) each remove a block from its bucket if it is the requested one; and (2) to perform eviction after the reads. In particular, observe that the paths accessed by the m CPUs overlap, and therefore it may be possible that two or more CPUs will be writing the same location at the same time. It is obvious that if such write conflicts are resolved arbitrarily where an arbitrary CPU wins, we will not be able to maintain even correctness.

Subtree partitioning to reduce write contention. Chen et al.'s core idea is to remove buckets from smaller heights of the Circuit ORAM tree, and start at a height with m buckets. In this way, we can view the Circuit ORAM tree as m disjoint subtrees — write contentions can only occur inside each subtree but not across different subtrees.

Now since there are m CPUs in the original PRAM, each batch contains m memory access requests — without loss of generality, we will assume that all of these m requests are distinct — had it not been the case, it is easy to apply the conflict resolution algorithm of Boyle et al. [3] to suppress duplicates, and then rely on oblivious routing to route fetched results back to all m requesting CPUs.

Each of these m requests will look for its block in a random subtree independently. By the Chernoff bound, each subtree receives $O(\alpha \log N)$ requests with all but $\mathsf{negl}(N)$ probability where $\alpha = \omega(1)$ is any super-constant function. Chen et al.'s algorithm proceeds as follows, where performance metrics are *without recursion*.

1. *Fetch.* A designated CPU per subtree performs the read phase of these $O(\alpha \log N)$ requests *sequentially*, which involves reading up to $O(\alpha \log N)$ paths in the tree. Since each path is $O(\log N)$ in length, this incurs $O(\alpha \log^2 N)$ parallel steps.
2. *Route.* Obliviously route the fetch results to the requesting CPUs. This incurs $O(\log m)$ parallel steps with m CPUs.
3. *Remap.* Assign each fetched block to a random new subtree and a random leaf within that subtree. Similarly, each subtree receives $\mu = O(\alpha \log N)$ blocks with all but $\mathsf{negl}(N)$ probability. Now, adopt an oblivious routing procedure to route exactly μ blocks back to each subtree, such that each tree receives blocks destined for itself together with padded dummy blocks. This incurs $O(\alpha \log m \log N)$ parallel steps with m CPUs.

4. *Evict.* Each subtree CPU *sequentially* performs $\mu = O(\alpha \log N)$ evictions for its own subtree. This incurs $O(\alpha \log^2 N)$ parallel steps with m CPUs.

Note that to make the above scheme work, Chen et al. [7] must assume that each subtree CPU additionally stores an $O(\alpha \log N)$-sized stash that holds all overflowing blocks that are destined for the particular subtree — we will get rid of this CPU cache, such that each CPU only needs $O(1)$ blocks of transient storage and does not need any permanent storage.

Recursive version. The above performance metrics assumed that all CPUs get to store, read, and update a shared position map for free. To remove this assumption, we can employ the standard recursion technique of the tree-based ORAM framework [31] to store this position map. We stress that when applying recursion, we must perform conflict resolution at each recursion level to ensure that all non-dummy requests have distinct addresses at each recursion level. The position identifiers fetched at a position map level will be obliviously routed to the fetch CPUs at the next recursion level.

Assuming that each block has size at least $\Omega(\log N)$ bits, there can be up to $\log N$ levels of recursion. Therefore, Chen et al.'s OPRAM scheme incurs $O(\alpha \log^3 N)$ simulation overhead using the same number of CPUs as the original PRAM.

2.3   Our Construction: Intuition

Why the CLT OPRAM is inefficient. First, we need to observe why the CLT OPRAM [7] is inefficient. There are two fundamental reasons why the CLT OPRAM scheme suffers from an extra $\log N$ factor in overhead.

1. During the fetch phase, a single CPU per subtree acts sequentially to fetch all requests that belong to the subtree. Although on average, each subtree receives $O(1)$ requests, in the worst case a subtree may receive up to $\alpha \log N$ requests (to obtain $\mathsf{negl}(N)$ security failure). Since serving each request involves reading a tree path of $\log N$ in length and then removing the block fetched from the path, serving all $\alpha \log N$ requests sequentially with a single CPU would then require $O(\alpha \log^2 N)$ time — over all $O(\log N)$ recursion levels, the blowup would then be $O(\alpha \log^3 N)$.
2. Similarly, during the eviction phase, a single CPU is in charge of performing all evictions a subtree receives. Although on average, each subtree receives $O(1)$ evictions, in the worst case a subtree may receive up to $\alpha \log N$ evictions (to obtain $\mathsf{negl}(N)$ security failure). Similarly, to serve all $\alpha \log N$ evictions with a single CPU would require $O(\alpha \log^2 N)$ time — and after recursion, the blowup would be $O(\alpha \log^3 N)$.

Therefore, the crux is how to improve the efficiency of the above two steps. To this end, we need to introduce a few new ideas described below.

Simultaneous removal. Reading data from the m subtrees can be split into two steps: (1) reading m paths to search for the m blocks requested; and (2) removing the m fetched blocks. Reading m paths can be parallelized trivially by having m CPUs each read a path — note that it is safe to reveal how many requests go to each subtree. Therefore, the crux is how to in parallel remove the m fetched blocks from the respective tree paths. The challenge here is that the tree paths may intersect — recall that each subtree may receive up to $\alpha \log N$ requests in the worst-case, and therefore the simultaneous removal algorithm must handle potential write conflicts.

We detail our new simultaneous removal algorithm in Sect. 7.1.

Lazy eviction. The eviction stage is more tricky. Unlike the fetch phase where it is safe to reveal which requests go to which subtrees, here it must be kept secret from the adversary how many evictions each subtree receives. At first sight, it would seem like it is necessary to pad the number of evictions per subtree to $\alpha \log N$ to hide the actual number of evictions each subtree receives.

Our idea is to perform eviction lazily. We perform only a single (possibly dummy) eviction per subtree for each batch of m requests — for technical reasons we will have $2m$ subtrees in total instead of m subtrees, since this makes evictions on average faster than the rate of access. In particular, if there exists one or more blocks wanting to be evicted to a subtree, a real eviction takes place; otherwise, a dummy eviction takes place for the corresponding subtree.

Obviously, such lazy eviction would mean that some elements will be left over and cannot be evicted back into the subtrees. Therefore, we introduce a new data structure called a *pool* to store the leftover blocks that fail to be evicted. Later, we will prove that the pool size is upper bounded by $O(m + \alpha \log N)$ except with $\mathsf{negl}(N)$ probability.

Due to the introduction of the pool, when a batch of requests come, we will need to serve these requests not only from the subtrees, but also from the pool as well — serving requests from the pool can be done in parallel through a standard building block called oblivious routing [3].

Selection of eviction candidates and pool occupancy. Recall that during the eviction stage, we would like to perform a single eviction per subtree. This would require an oblivious algorithm to select eviction candidates from the pool and route these candidates to the respective subtrees. Intuitively, if multiple blocks in the pool are destined for a given subtree, we should select one that has a maximum chance of being evicted, since this can hopefully give us a tight bound on the leftover blocks in the pool. As a result, suppose that a certain path denoted path is being evicted for a certain subtree, we will select a block in the pool that is *deepest* with respect to path for this subtree — as defined in the Circuit ORAM [36] work, this means that this block can legally reside in a deepest height (i.e., closest to the leaf) in path.

It turns out that using this eviction candidate selection strategy, we can view the union of the subtrees and the pool logically as a big Circuit ORAM tree — where the subtrees represent heights $\log_2(2m)$ or higher; and the pool represents smaller heights below $\log_2(2m)$ as well as the stash of Circuit ORAM. At this moment, it would seem like bounding on the pool occupancy would directly translate to bounding blocks remaining in the smaller heights of Circuit

ORAM — although there is one additional subtlety: in Circuit ORAM, we perform one access followed by one eviction, whereas here we perform a batch of m accesses followed by a batch of m evictions. To handle this difference, we prove a stochastic domination result, showing that such *batched* eviction can only reduce the number of blocks in height $\log_2(2m)$ or smaller than non-batched — in this way, we can reuse Circuit ORAM's stochastic analysis for bounding the pool size.

2.4 Putting it Altogether

Putting the above ideas together would expose a few more subtleties. We give a high-level overview of our basic construction below.

A pool and 2m subtrees: reduce write contention by partitioning. Following the approach of Chen et al. [7], we reduce write contention by partitioning the Circuit ORAM into $2m$ subtrees[6]. However, on top of Chen et al. [7], we additionally introduce the notion of a pool, a data structure that we will utilize to amortize evictions across time.

We restructure a standard Circuit ORAM tree in the following manner. First, we consider a height with $2m$ buckets, which gives us $2m$ disjoint subtrees. All buckets from smaller heights, including the Circuit ORAM's stash, contain at most $O(m + \alpha \log N)$ blocks — we will simply store these $O(m + \alpha \log N)$ blocks in an unstructured fashion in memory, henceforth referred to as a *pool*.

Fetch. Given a batch of m memory requests, henceforth without loss of generality, we assume that the m requests are for distinct addresses. This is because we can adopt the conflict resolution algorithm by Boyle et al. [3] to suppress duplicates, and after data has been fetched, rely on oblivious routing to send fetched data to all request CPUs.

Now, we look up the requested blocks in two places, both the pool and the subtrees:

- *Subtree lookup:* Suppose that the position labels of the m requests have been retrieved (we will later show how to achieve this through a standard recursion technique) — this defines m random paths in the $2m$ subtrees. We can now have m fetch CPUs each read a path to look for a desired block. All fetched blocks are merged into the central pool. Notice that at this moment, the pool size has grown by a constant factor, but later in a cleanup step, we will compress the pool back to its original size. Also, at this moment, we have not removed the requested blocks from the subtrees yet, and we will remove them later in the maintain phase.
- *Pool lookup:* At this moment, all requested blocks must be in the pool. Assuming that m is not too small, we can now rely on oblivious routing to route blocks back to each requesting CPU — and this can be completed in $O(\log N)$ parallel steps with m CPUs. We will treat the case of small m separately later in the paper.

---

[6] Although we choose $2m$ for concreteness, any $c \cdot m$ for a constant $c > 1$ would work.

Maintain. In the maintain phase, we must (1) remove all blocks fetched from the paths read; and (2) perform eviction on each subtree.

- *Efficient simultaneous removals.* After reading each subtree, we need to remove up to $\mu := O(\alpha \log N)$ blocks that are fetched. Such removal operations can lead to write contention when done in parallel: since the paths read by different CPUs overlap, up to $\mu := O(\alpha \log N)$ CPUs may try to write to the same location in the subtree.

  Therefore, we propose a new oblivious parallel algorithm for efficient simultaneous removal. Our algorithm allows removal of the m fetched blocks across all trees in $O(\log N)$ time using m CPUs. We defer the detailed description of this simultaneous removal algorithm to Sect. 7.

- *Selection of eviction candidates and pool-to-subtree routing.* At this moment, we will select exactly one eviction candidate from the pool for each subtree. If there exists one or more blocks in the pool to be evicted to a certain subtree, then the *deepest* block with respect to the current eviction path will be chosen (as mentioned later, eviction paths are chosen using a standard deterministic order lexicographical ordering mechanism [15, 36]). Otherwise, a dummy block will be chosen for this subtree. Roughly speaking, using the above criterion as a preference rule, we can rely on oblivious routing to route the selected eviction candidate from the pool to each subtree. This can be accomplished in $O(\log N)$ parallel steps with m CPUs assuming that m is not too small — we defer the treatment of small m to later parts of the paper. The details of this algorithm will be spelled out in the full version [6].

- *Eviction.* We then perform eviction over one tree path for every subtree where the eviction path is selected using the standard deterministic lexicographically order algorithm — since the details of eviction path selection are non-essential to the understanding of our Circuit OPRAM, we refer the reader to earlier works for a detailed exposition [15, 36]. At the end of this step, each subtree will output an eviction leftover block: the leftover block is dummy if the chosen eviction candidate was successfully evicted into the subtree (or if the eviction candidate was dummy to start with); otherwise the leftover block is the original eviction candidate. All these eviction leftovers will be merged back into the central pool.

- *Pool cleanup.* Notice that in the process of serving a batch of requests, the pool size has grown — however, blocks that have entered the pool may be dummy. In particular, we shall prove that the pool's occupancy will never exceed $c \cdot m + \alpha \log N$ for an appropriate constant c except with negl(N) probability. Therefore, at the end of the maintain phase, we must compress the pool back to $c \cdot m + \alpha \log N$. Such compression can easily be achieved through oblivious sorting in $O(\log N)$ parallel steps with m CPUs, assuming that m is not too small. We defer the special treatment of small m to later parts of the paper.

Recursion and performance. So far, we have assumed that a position map can be stored and accessed by the CPUs for free. We can remove this assumption through a standard recursion technique [3,31]. Note that we need to perform conflict resolution at all levels of recursion, and perform oblivious routing to route the fetched position identifiers to the fetch CPUs at the next recursion level. When we count all $O(\log N)$ recursion levels, the above basic construction achieves $O(\log^2 N)$ blowup when m is not too small — we defer the special-case treatment of small m to later parts of the paper.

2.5 Extensions

Improve performance asymptotically with PRFs. In the full version [6], we will describe additional techniques that allow us to improve the OPRAM's blowup to $O(\frac{\log^2 N}{\log \log N})$ assuming the usage of a pseudo-random function (PRF) — of course, the resulting scheme would then only have computational security rather than statistical security. To this end, we rely on an elegant technique first proposed by Fletcher et al. [12] that effectively "compresses" position labels by relying on a PRF to compute the blocks' leaf identifiers from "compressed counters". Fletcher et al.'s technique was designed for tree-based ORAMs — as we show later in the paper, we need to make some adaptations to their algorithm to make it work with OPRAMs.

Varying number of CPUs. Our overview earlier assumes that the original PRAM always has the same number of CPUs in every time step, i.e., all batches of memory requests have the same size. We can further extend our scheme for the case when the number of PRAM CPUs varies over time. Below we briefly describe the idea while leaving details to Sect. 7. Without loss of generality, henceforth we assume that in every time step, the number of requests in a batch m is always a power of 2 — if not, we can simply round it to the nearest power of 2 incurring only $O(1)$ penalty in performance.

Suppose that the OPRAM scheme currently maintains $2\widehat{m}$ subtrees, but the incoming batch has $m > \widehat{m}$ number of requests. In this case, we will immediately adjust the number of subtrees to $2m$. This can be done simply by merging more heights of the tree into the pool.

The more difficult case is when the incoming batch contains less than $m < \widehat{m}$ requests. In this case, we need to decrease the number of subtrees. In the extreme case when m drops from $\sqrt{N}$ to 1, it will be too expensive to reconstruct up to $\Theta(\log N)$ heights of the ORAM tree.

Instead, we argue in Sect. 3.2 that without loss of generality, we may assume that if m decreases, it may only decrease by a factor of 2. Hence, every time we just need to halve the number of subtrees — and to achieve this we only need to reconstruct one extra height of the big ORAM tree, which can be achieved through oblivious sorting in $O(\log \widehat{m})$ parallel steps with $O(\widehat{m})$ CPUs.

Results for large block sizes. Finally, we note that when the block size is N^ϵ for any constant $0 < \epsilon < 1$, Circuit OPRAM achieves $O(\log N)$ simulation overhead when $m \geq \alpha \log \log N$. In light of Goldreich and Ostrovsky's $\Omega(\log N)$ lower bound [17,18], Circuit OPRAM is therefore asymptotically optimal under large block sizes.

2.6 Paper Organization

The remainder of the paper will formally present the ideas described in this section and describe additional results including

1. How to support the case when the number of CPUs varies over time (Sects. 5, 6, 7, and details in [6]);
2. Algorithmic details for the case of small m (Sects. 5, 6, 7, and details in [6]);
3. Additional techniques to improve the overhead of the scheme by a $\log \log N$ factor assuming the existence of PRFs and achieving computational (rather than statistical) security in full version [6];
4. Detailed proofs (in full version [6]) where the security proof is somewhat straightforward but the most technically involved part is to prove that Circuit OPRAM's stochastic process is dominated by that of Circuit ORAM such that we can leverage Circuit ORAM's stochastic analysis [36] for bounding the pool and stash sizes of Circuit OPRAM; and
5. Interpretations of our results under larger block sizes and other relevant metrics in full version [6].

3 Preliminaries

3.1 Parallel Random-Access Machines

A *parallel random-access machine* (PRAM) consists of a set of CPUs and a shared memory denoted mem indexed by the address space $[N] := \{1, 2, \ldots, N\}$. In this paper, we refer to each memory word also as a *block*, and we use B to denote the bit-length of each block.

We support a more general PRAM model where the number of CPUs in each time step may vary. Specifically, in each step $t \in [T]$, we use m_t to denote the number of CPUs. In each step, each CPU executes a next instruction circuit denoted Π, updates its CPU state; and further, CPUs interact with memory through request instructions $\boldsymbol{I}^{(t)} := (I_i^{(t)} : i \in [m_t])$. Specifically, at time step t, CPU i's instruction is of the form $I_i^{(t)} := (\mathsf{op}, \mathsf{addr}, \mathsf{data})$, where the operation is $\mathsf{op} \in \{\mathsf{read}, \mathsf{write}\}$ performed on the virtual memory block with address addr and block value $\mathsf{data} \in \{0, 1\}^B \cup \{\bot\}$. If $\mathsf{op} = \mathsf{read}$, then we have $\mathsf{data} = \bot$ and the CPU issuing the instruction should receive the content of block mem[addr] at the initial state of step t. If $\mathsf{op} = \mathsf{write}$, then we have $\mathsf{data} \neq \bot$; in this case, the CPU still receives the initial state of mem[addr] in this step, and at the end of step t, the content of virtual memory mem[addr] should be updated to data.

Write conflict resolution. By definition, multiple read operations can be executed concurrently with other operations even if they visit the same address. However, if multiple concurrent write operations visit the same address, a conflict resolution rule will be necessary for our PRAM be well-defined. In this paper, we assume the following just like earlier OPRAM works [3, 7]:

- The original PRAM supports concurrent reads and concurrent writes (CRCW) with an arbitrary, parametrizable rule for write conflict resolution. In other words, there exists some priority rule to determine which write operation takes effect if there are multiple concurrent writes in some time step t.
- The compiled, oblivious PRAM (defined below) is a "concurrent read, exclusive write" PRAM (CREW). In other words, the design of our OPRAM construction must ensure that there are no concurrent writes at any time.

We note that a CRCW-PRAM with a parametrizable conflict resolution rule is among the most powerful CRCW-PRAM model, whereas CREW is a much weaker model. Our results are stronger if we allow the underlying PRAM to be more powerful but the our compiled OPRAM uses a weaker PRAM model. For a detailed explanation on how stronger PRAM models can emulate weaker ones, we refer the reader to the work by Hagerup [21].

CPU-to-CPU communication. In the remainder of the paper, we sometimes describe our algorithms using CPU-to-CPU communication. For our OPRAM algorithm to be oblivious, the inter-CPU communication pattern must be oblivious too. We stress that such inter-CPU communication can be emulated using shared memory reads and writes. Therefore, when we express our performance metrics, we assume that all inter-CPU communication is implemented with shared memory reads and writes. In this sense, our performance metrics already account for any inter-CPU communication, and there is no need to have separate metrics that characterize inter-CPU communication. In contrast, Chen et al. [7] defines separate metrics for inter-CPU communication.

Additional assumptions and notations. Henceforth, we assume that each CPU can only store $O(1)$ memory blocks. Further, we assume for simplicity that the runtime of the PRAM, and the number of CPUs activated in each time step are *fixed* a priori and *publicly known* parameters. Therefore, we can consider a PRAM to be a tuple

$$\mathsf{PRAM} := (\Pi, N, T, \ (m_t : t \in [T])),$$

where Π denotes the next instruction circuit, N denotes the total memory size (in terms of number of blocks), T denotes the PRAM's total runtime, and m_t denotes the number of CPUs to be activated in each time step $t \in [T]$. Henceforth, we refer to the vector $(m_1, \ldots, m_T)$ as the PRAM's *activation schedule* as defined by Boyle et al. [3].

Without loss of generality, we assume that $N \geq m_t$ for all t. Otherwise, if some $m_t > N$, we can adopt a trivial parallel oblivious algorithm (through a combination of conflict resolution and oblivious multicast) to serve the batch of m_t requests in $O(\log m_t)$ parallel time with m_t CPUs.

3.2   Oblivious Parallel Random-Access Machines

Randomized PRAM. A *randomized PRAM* is a special PRAM where the CPUs are allowed to generate private, random numbers. For simplicity, we assume that a randomized PRAM has a priori known, deterministic runtime, and that the CPU activation pattern in each time step is also fixed a priori and publicly known.

Statistical and computational indistinguishability. Given two ensembles of distributions $\{X_N\}$ and $\{Y_N\}$ (parameterized with N), we use the notation $\{X_N\} \stackrel{\epsilon(N)}{\equiv} \{Y_N\}$ to mean that for any (possibly computationally unbounded) adversary $\mathcal{A}$,

$$\left| \Pr[\mathcal{A}(x) = 1 \,|\, x \stackrel{\$}{\leftarrow} X_N] - \Pr[\mathcal{A}(y) = 1 \,|\, y \stackrel{\$}{\leftarrow} Y_N] \right| \le \epsilon(N).$$

We use the notation $\{X_N\} \stackrel{\epsilon(N)}{\equiv_c} \{Y_N\}$ to mean that for any non-uniform p.p.t. adversary $\mathcal{A}$,

$$\left| \Pr[\mathcal{A}(1^N, x) = 1 \,|\, x \stackrel{\$}{\leftarrow} X_N] - \Pr[\mathcal{A}(1^N, y) = 1 \,|\, y \stackrel{\$}{\leftarrow} Y_N] \right| \le \epsilon(N).$$

Oblivious PRAM (OPRAM). A randomized PRAM parametrized with total memory size N is said to be *statistically oblivious*, iff there exists a negligible function $\epsilon(\cdot)$ such that for any inputs $x_0, x_1 \in \{0, 1\}^*$,

$$\mathsf{Addresses}(\mathsf{PRAM}, x_0) \stackrel{\epsilon(N)}{\equiv} \mathsf{Addresses}(\mathsf{PRAM}, x_1),$$

where $\mathsf{Addresses}(\mathsf{PRAM}, x)$ denotes the joint distribution of memory accesses made by PRAM upon input x. More specifically, for each time step $t \in [T]$, $\mathsf{Addresses}(\mathsf{PRAM}, x)$ includes the memory addresses requested by the set of active CPUs S_t in time step t along with their CPU identifiers, as well as whether each memory request is a read or write operation.

Similarly, a randomized PRAM parametrized with total memory size N is said to be *computationally oblivious*, iff there exists a negligible function $\epsilon(\cdot)$ such that for any inputs $x_0, x_1 \in \{0, 1\}^*$,

$$\mathsf{Addresses}(\mathsf{PRAM}, x_0) \stackrel{\epsilon(N)}{\equiv_c} \mathsf{Addresses}(\mathsf{PRAM}, x_1)$$

Note the only difference from statistical security is that here the access patterns only need to be indistinguishable to computationally bounded adversaries. Henceforth we often use the notation OPRAM to denote a PRAM that satisfies obliviousness.

In this paper, following the convention of most existing ORAM and OPRAM works [17,18,23,35,36], we will require that the security failure probability be negligible in the N, i.e., the PRAM's total memory size.

Oblivious simulation and performance measures. We say that a given OPRAM *simulates* a PRAM if for every input $x \in \{0, 1\}^*$, $\Pr[\mathsf{OPRAM}(x) = \mathsf{PRAM}(x)] = 1$ where the probability is taken over the randomness consumed by the OPRAM — in other words, we require that the OPRAM and PRAM output the same outcome on any input x.

Like in prior works on OPRAM [3,7], in this paper, we consider *activation-preserving* oblivious simulation of PRAM. Specifically, let $(m_1, \ldots, m_T)$ be the original PRAM's activation schedule, we require that the corresponding OPRAM's activation schedule to be

$$(m_1)_{i=1}^{\chi}, (m_2)_{i=1}^{\chi}, \ldots, (m_T)_{i=1}^{\chi},$$

where χ is said to be the OPRAM's *simulation overhead* (also referred to as *blowup*). In other words, henceforth in the paper, we will simulate the i-th step of the PRAM using m_i CPUs — the same number as the original PRAM. Without loss of generality, we will often assume $O(m_i)$ CPUs are available, since we can always use one CPU to simulate $O(1)$ CPUs with only constant blowup. As a special case, when the number of CPUs is fixed for the PRAM, i.e., $m_i = m$ for any $i \in [T]$, an oblivious simulation overhead of χ means that the OPRAM needs to run in $\chi \cdot T$ steps consuming m CPUs (same as the original PRAM) where T is the runtime of the original PRAM.

An oblivious simulation overhead of χ also implies the OPRAM's CPU-to-memory bandwidth overhead is a factor of χ more than the original PRAM. Since our model simulates all inter-CPU communication with memory-to-CPU communication, an OPRAM with simulation overhead χ under our model immediately implies that the inter-CPU communication is bounded by χ too. In this sense, our metrics are stronger than those adopted in earlier work [7] which treated CPU-to-memory communication and inter-CPU communication separately — this makes our upper bound results more general.

Assumption on varying number of CPUs. Without loss of generality, henceforth in the paper we may assume that in the original PRAM, the number of CPUs in adjacent steps can increase arbitrarily, but may only decrease by a factor of 2. In other words, we may assume that for any $i \in [T-1]$, $m_{i+1} \geq \frac{m_i}{2}$. This assumption is without loss of generality, since it is not hard to see that *any PRAM where the number of CPUs can vary arbitrarily can be simulated by a PRAM where the number of CPUs can decrease by at most $\frac{1}{2}$ in adjacent steps — and such simulation preserves the PRAM's total work and parallel runtime asymptotically.* Such a simulation is straightforward: if the original PRAM consumes more CPUs than the simulated PRAM in the next step, then the simulated PRAM immediately increases the number of CPUs to a matching number. If the original PRAM's consumes fewer CPUs than the simulated PRAM in the next step, the simulated PRAM decreases its CPUs by at most a factor of 2 each time (and if there are more CPUs in the simulation than needed by the PRAM, the additional CPUs simply idle and perform dummy work).

4   Building Blocks

We now describe some standard or new building blocks that we use.

Oblivious sort. Parallel oblivious sort solves the following problem. The input is an array denoted arr containing n elements and a total ordering over all elements.

The output is a sorted array arr' that is constructed obliviously. Parallel oblivious sorting can be achieved in a straightforward way through sorting networks [1], by using $O(n)$ CPUs and consuming $O(n \log n)$ total work and $O(\log n)$ parallel steps.

Oblivious conflict resolution. Oblivious conflict resolution solves the following problem: given a list of memory requests of the form In $:=$ $\{(\mathsf{op}_i, \mathsf{addr}_i, \mathsf{data}_i)\}_{i \in [m]}$, output a new list of requests denoted Out also of length m, such that the following holds:

- Every non-dummy entry in Out appears in In;
- Every address addr that appears in In appears exactly once in Out. Further, if multiple entries in In have the address addr, the following priority rule is applied to select an entry: (1) writes are preferred over reads; and (2) if there are multiple writes, a parametrizable function priority is used to select an entry.

We will use the standard parallel oblivious conflict resolution algorithm described by Boyle et al. [3], which can accomplish the above in $O(m \log m)$ total work and $O(\log m)$ parallel steps. More specifically, Boyle et al.'s conflict resolution algorithm relies on a constant number of oblivious sorts and oblivious aggregation.

Oblivious aggregation for a sorted array. Given an array Inp $:= \{(k_i, v_i)\}_{i \in [n]}$ of (key, value) pairs sorted in increasing order of the keys, we call all elements with the same key a *group*. We say that index $i \in [n]$ is a *representative* of its group if it is the leftmost element of its group. Let Aggr be a commutative and associative aggregation function and we assume that its output range can be described by $O(1)$ number of blocks. The goal of oblivious aggregation is to output the following array:

$$\mathsf{Outp}_i := \begin{cases} \mathsf{Aggr}\left(\{v \,:\, (k, v) \in \mathsf{Inp} \text{ and } k = k_i\}\right), & \text{if } i \text{ is a representative;} \\ \bot, & \text{o.w.} \end{cases}$$

Boyle et al. [3] and Nayak et al. [27] show that oblivious aggregation for a sorted array of length n can be accomplished in $O(\log n)$ parallel time consuming n CPUs.

When the input array has a maximum group size of k, we show that oblivious aggregation can be accomplished in $O(\log k)$ parallel steps consuming $O(\frac{n}{\log k})$ CPUs. We defer the detailed description of the algorithm to the full version [6].

Oblivious routing. Oblivious routing solves the following problem. Suppose n source CPUs each holds a data block with a distinct key (or a dummy block). Further, n destination CPUs each holds a key and requests a data block identified by its key. An oblivious routing algorithm routes the requested data block to the destination CPU in an oblivious manner. Boyle et al. [3] showed that through a combination of oblivious sorts and oblivious aggregation, oblivious routing can be achieved in $O(n \log n)$ total work and $O(\log n)$ parallel runtime.

In this paper, we sometimes also need a variant of the oblivious routing algorithm, a source CPU gets informed in the end whether its block is successfully routed to one or more destination CPUs. We elaborate how to modify Boyle et al. [3]'s oblivious routing building block to accomplish this.

Oblivious bin packing. Oblivious bin packing is the following primitive. We are given B bins each of capacity Z, and an input array of possibly dummy elements where each real element is tagged with a destined bin number and priority value. We wish to maximally pack each bin with elements destined for the bin — if there are more than Z elements destined for a bin, the Z elements with the highest priority should be chosen. Let n be the size of the input array, In the end, the algorithm outputs an array of size $B \cdot Z$ denoting the packed bins and an array of size n denoting the remaining elements — both padded with dummies.

Let $\widehat{n} := \max(n, B \cdot Z)$. We devise an algorithm for performing such oblivious bin packing in $O(\log \widehat{n})$ parallel steps consuming $\widehat{n}$ CPUs. The details of this algorithm and a more formal definition of oblivious bin packing are deferred to the full version [6].

5 Our Basic OPRAM Construction

We now describe our basic OPRAM construction.

5.1 Notations

Addresses in each recursion level. Recall that we reviewed the Circuit ORAM construction earlier. Here we define some notations for expressing recursion levels, including given each logical memory request, which metadata blocks to fetch from each recursion level.

In the presentation below, we assume that each position map block can store the position labels of γ blocks at the next recursion level, i.e., the *branching factor* is denoted by γ. Given a logical address addr of a data block, we say that its level-d prefix (denoted addr$^{\langle d \rangle}$) is the d most significant characters of addr when expressed in base-γ format. Specifically, a block at address addr$^{\langle d \rangle}$ in recursion level d will store the position labels for the γ blocks at addresses $\{(\text{addr}^{\langle d \rangle}||j) : j \in [\gamma]\}$ in recursion level $d + 1$; we say that the level-$(d + 1)$ address (addr$^{\langle d \rangle}||j)$ is the jth child of the level-d address addr$^{\langle d \rangle}$. For the special case $\gamma = 2$, we sometimes refer to the level-$(d + 1)$ addresses (addr$^{\langle d \rangle}||0)$ and (addr$^{\langle d \rangle}||1)$ as the *left child* and the *right child* respectively of the level-d address addr$^{\langle d \rangle}$.

Example 1. We give an example for $\gamma = 2$, i.e., when each position map block can store exactly two position labels. Imagine that one of the memory requests among the batch of m requests asks for the logical address $(0101100)_2$ in binary format. For this request,

- A fetch CPU at recursion level 0 will look for the level-0 address $(0*)$, and the fetched block will contain the position labels for the level-1 addresses $(00*)$ and $(01*)$; and a corresponding fetch CPU at recursion level 1 will receive the position label for the level-1 address $(01*)$.
- A fetch CPU at recursion level 1 will look for the level-1 address $(01*)$, and the fetched block will contain the position labels for the level-2 addresses $(010*)$ and $(011*)$; and a corresponding fetch CPU at the next recursion level is to receive the position label for $(010*)$;
- This goes on until the final recursion level is reached. Except for the final recursion level which stores actual data blocks, all other recursion levels store position map blocks.

Here we focused on what happens for fetching one logical address $(0101100)_2$ — but keep in mind that there are m such addresses in a batch and thus the above process is repeated m times in parallel.

Notations for varying number of CPUs. For simplicity, below we use m (omitting the subscript t) to denote the number of CPUs of the present PRAM step; we use the notation $\widehat{m}$ to denote the number of CPUs in the previous PRAM step. Without loss of generality, we also assume that both m and $\widehat{m}$ are powers of 2, since if not, we can always round it to the nearest power of 2 while incurring only a constant factor blowup. Recall that due to our bounded change assumption on the number of CPUs, we may also assume without loss of generality that $m \geq \frac{\widehat{m}}{2}$. Therefore, if $m < \widehat{m}$ it must be the case that $m := \frac{\widehat{m}}{2}$.

Our OPRAM scheme will try to maintain the following invariant: at the end of a PRAM step with m CPUs, the OPRAM data structure will have exactly $2m$ disjoint subtrees. Henceforth, we assume that at the beginning of the PRAM step we are concerned about, there are exactly $2\widehat{m}$ disjoint subtrees since $\widehat{m}$ denotes the number of CPUs in the previous PRAM step.

Parameter α. Throughout the description, we use $\alpha = \omega(1)$ to denote an appropriately small super constant function in N such that the failure probability is at most $\frac{1}{N^{\Theta(\alpha)}}$, i.e., negligible in N.

5.2 Data Structures

Subtrees and overflowing pool. For each of the recursion levels, we maintain a binary tree structure as in Circuit ORAM [36]. We refer the reader to Sect. 2.1 for a review of the Circuit ORAM algorithm. However, instead of having a complete tree, our OPRAM scheme truncates the tree at height $\ell := \log_2(2m)$ containing $2m$ buckets. In this way, we can view the tree data structure as $2m$ disjoint subtrees.

In the Circuit ORAM algorithm, all buckets with heights smaller than ℓ contain at most $O(m + \alpha \log N)$ blocks. In our OPRAM scheme, these blocks are treated as overflowing blocks, and they are held in an overflowing data structure called a *pool* as described below.

Position map. As in Circuit ORAM (see Sect. 2.1), each address addr is associated with a random path in one of the subtrees, and the path is identified by a leaf node. We use a position map posmap[addr] to store the position identifier for address addr.

Our main *path invariant* states that a block with address addr must reside on the path to the leaf posmap[addr] in one of the subtrees, or reside in the overflowing pool. When block addr is accessed (via read or write), its position posmap[addr] will be updated to a new leaf chosen uniformly and independently at random. As in previous works [31,35,36], the position map is stored in a smaller OPRAM recursively. We use the notation pos-OPRAMs to denote all recursion levels for storing the position map, and we use data-OPRAM to denote the top recursion level for storing data blocks.

5.3 Overview of One Simulated PRAM Step

To serve each batch of memory requests, a set of CPUs interact with memory in two synchronized phases: in the *fetch* phase, the request CPUs receive the contents of the requested blocks; in the second *maintain* phase, the CPUs collaborate to maintain the data structure to be ready for the next PRAM step. The description below can be regarded as an expanded version of Sect. 2.4. In particular, we now spell out what happens if m_t varies over time. Further, it turns out that for OPRAM, the recursion is somewhat more complicated than ORAM, we also spell out all the details of the recursion — this choice is made also partly in anticipation of the additional computational security techniques described later in the full version [6] where it is somewhat important to not treat the recursion as a blackbox like most earlier tree-based ORAM/OPRAM works [3,7,8,35,36]. Our algorithm below employs several subroutines the details of which will be expanded in Sects. 6 and 7 respectively.

Fetch phase. The fetch phase has an array of m addresses as input denoted $(\mathsf{addr}_1, \ldots, \mathsf{addr}_m)$. Recall that at the beginning of the fetch phase, each recursion level has $2\widehat{m}$ disjoint subtrees, where $\widehat{m}$ is the number of active CPUs in the previous PRAM step.

(i) *Preparation: all recursion levels in parallel.* For all recursion levels $d :=$ $0, 1, \ldots, D$ in parallel, perform the following:
   – *Generate level-d prefix addresses.* Write down the level-d prefixes of all m requests addresses $(\mathsf{addr}_1, \ldots, \mathsf{addr}_m)$. Clearly, this step can be accomplished in $O(1)$ parallel step with m CPUs.
   – *Conflict resolution.* Given a list of m possibly dummy level-d addresses denoted $(\mathsf{addr}_1^{\langle d \rangle}, \ldots, \mathsf{addr}_m^{\langle d \rangle})$, we run an instance of the oblivious conflict resolution algorithm to suppress duplicate requests (and pad the resulting array with dummies). This step can be accomplished in $O(\log m)$ parallel steps with m CPUs.
   – *Discover which children addresses are needed by the next recursion level.* Let $\mathsf{Addr}^{\langle d \rangle} := \{\mathsf{addr}_i^{\langle d \rangle}\}_{i \in [m]}$ denote the list of level-d addresses after conflict resolution. Each of these m level-d addresses has γ children addresses

in the next recursion level. By jointly examining $\mathsf{Addr}^{\langle d \rangle}$ and $\mathsf{Addr}^{\langle d+1 \rangle}$, recursion level d learns for each non-dummy $\mathsf{addr}_i^{\langle d \rangle} \in \mathsf{Addr}^{\langle d \rangle}$, which of its children are needed for the next recursion level (see Sect. 6.1 for details of this subroutine). At the end of this step, each of the m level-d addresses receives a bit vector containing γ bits, indicating whether each child address is needed by the next recursion level. As mentioned in Sect. 6.1, this can be accomplished through $O(1)$ number of oblivious sorts. Therefore, it takes m CPUs $O(\log m)$ steps to complete.

- *Choose fresh position labels for the next recursion level.* For any child that is needed, recursion level d chooses a new position label for the next recursion level. For recursion level d, the result of this step is a new position array

$$\{\mathsf{addr}_i^{\langle d \rangle}, (\mathsf{npos}_j : j \in [\gamma])\}_{i \in [m]}$$

where npos_j is a fresh random label in level $d+1$ if $\mathsf{addr}_i^{\langle d \rangle} \| j$ is needed in the next recursion level, otherwise $\mathsf{npos}_j := \bot$. Later in our algorithm, each recursion level d will inform the next recursion level $d+1$ of the chosen new position labels.

This step can be accomplished in $O(\gamma)$ steps with m CPUs — for our statistically secure OPRAM scheme, we shall assume $\gamma = O(1)$.

- *Pool lookup.* We have m CPUs each of which now seeks to fetch the level-d block at address $\mathsf{addr}^{\langle d \rangle}$. The m CPUs first tries to fetch the desired blocks inside the central pool; and at the end, the fetched blocks will be marked as dummy in the pool.

If $m \geq \alpha \log \log N$, then we rely on an instance of the oblivious routing algorithm, such that each of these m CPUs will attempt to receive the desired block from the pool. If $m < \alpha \log \log N$, oblivious routing is too expensive, instead we invoke a special-case algorithm for small m to accomplish this in $O(\alpha \log N)$ steps with m CPUs.

We defer the details of the algorithm to Sect. 6.

(ii) *Fetch: level by level.* Now, for each recursion level, m CPUs will each look for a block in one of the subtrees. This step must be performed sequentially one recursion level at a time since each recursion level must receive the position labels from the previous level before looking for blocks in the subtrees.

For each recursion level $d = 0, 1, \ldots, D$ in sequential order, we perform the following:

- *Receive position labels from previous recursion level.* Unless $d = 0$ in which case the position labels can be fetched in $O(1)$ parallel step, each of the m level-d addresses will receive a pair of position labels from the previous recursion level denoted $(\mathsf{pos}, \mathsf{npos})$, where pos represents the tree path to look for the desired block, and npos denotes a freshly chosen label to be assigned to the block after the fetch is complete. This can be accomplished through an instance of oblivious routing consuming $O(\log m)$ parallel steps with m CPUs.

- *Subtree lookup.* Now, each of the m CPUs receives an instruction of the form $(\mathsf{addr}^{\langle d \rangle}, \mathsf{pos})$ that could be possibly dummy. Each CPU will now read a tree path leading to the leaf node numbered pos, in search of the block with logical address $\mathsf{addr}^{\langle d \rangle}$ (but without removing the block). If found, the CPU will remember the location where the block is found — and this information will later be useful for the simultaneous removal step that is part of the maintain phase. If a CPU receives a dummy instruction, it simply scans through a randomly chosen path in a random subtree.

  At this moment, each of the m CPUs has fetched the desired block either from the pool or the tree path (or the CPU has fetched dummy if it received a dummy instruction to start with). The fetched position labels (as well as the new position labels chosen for the next recursion level) are ready to be routed to the next recursion level.

(iii) *Oblivious multicast: once per batch of requests.* Finally, when the data-OPRAM has fetched all requested blocks, we rely on a standard oblivious routing algorithm (see Sect. 4) to route the resulting blocks to the request CPUs. This step takes $O(\log m)$ parallel time with m CPUs.

Remark 1. Note that in the above exposition, we made explicit which steps can be parallelized across recursion levels and which steps must be performed sequentially across recursion levels — in particular, the level-to-level position label routing must be performed sequentially across recursion levels since the next recursion level must receive the position labels before learning which tree paths to traverse. Although this distinction may not be very useful in this paper, it will turn out to be important in a companion paper by Chan et al. [5], where the authors further parallelize the level-to-level routing algorithm. In particular, Chan et al. [5] introduce a new and better notion of an OPRAM's "depth" by assuming that the OPRAM can consume more CPUs than the original PRAM. In this case, they show that an OPRAM's depth can be made asymptotically smaller by further parallelizing Circuit OPRAM's level-to-level routing algorithm.

Maintain phase. All of the following steps are performed in parallel across all recursion levels $d = 0, 1, \ldots, D$:

(i) *Simultaneous removal of fetched blocks from subtrees.* After each of the m CPUs fetches its desired block from m tree paths, they perform a simultaneous removal procedure to remove the fetched blocks from the tree paths. This step can be accomplished in $O(\log N)$ parallel steps using m CPUs. We defer a detailed description of this new simultaneous removal subroutine in Sect. 7.1.

(ii) *Passing updated blocks to the pool.* Each CPU updates the contents of the fetched block — if the block belongs to a position map level, the block's content should now store the new position labels (for the·next recursion level) chosen earlier in the preparation phase. Further, each block will be tagged with a new position label that indicates where the block can now reside in the current recursion level — this position label was received earlier from the previous recursion level during the fetch phase (recall that each recursion level chooses position labels for the next recursion level). The updated blocks are merged into the pool. The pool temporarily increases its capacity to hold these extra blocks, but the extra memory will be released at the end of the maintain phase during a cleanup operation.

(iii) *Increasing the number of subtrees if necessary.* At this moment, if $m > \widehat{m}$, i.e., if the number of CPUs has increased since the last PRAM step, then we increase the number of subtrees to $2m$, and merge all smaller heights of the tree into the pool. If the number of CPUs has decreased (by a factor of 2) since the last PRAM step, we will handle this case later.

(iv) *Selection of eviction candidates.* Following the deterministic, reverse-lexicographical order eviction strategy of Circuit ORAM [36], we choose the next $2m$ eviction paths (pretending that all subtrees are part of the same big ORAM tree). The $2m$ eviction paths will go through $2m$ subtrees henceforth referred to as *evicting subtrees*. If m has decreased (by a factor of 2) since the last PRAM step, then not all subtrees are evicting subtrees. We devise an eviction candidate selection algorithm that will output one (possibly dummy) block to evict for each evicting subtree, as well as the remainder of the pool (with these selected blocks removed). The block selected for each evicting subtree is based on the *deepest* criterion with respect to the current eviction path. When $m \geq \alpha \log \log N$, we rely on oblivious sorting to accomplish this in $O(\log N)$ parallel steps with m CPUs. When $m < \alpha \log \log N$, oblivious sorting will be too expensive, so we rely on a different algorithm to accomplish this step in $O(\alpha \log N)$ parallel steps with m CPUs. We defer a detailed description of the algorithm to Sect. 7.2.

(v) *Eviction into subtrees.* In parallel, for each evicting subtree, the eviction algorithm of Circuit ORAM [36] is performed for the candidate block the subtree has received. The straightforward strategy takes $O(\log N)$ parallel steps consuming m CPUs.

After the eviction algorithm completes, if the candidate block fails to be evicted into the subtree, it will be returned to the pool; otherwise if the candidate block successfully evicts into the subtree, a dummy block is returned to the pool.

(vi) *Decreasing the number of subtrees if necessary.* If $m < \widehat{m}$, this means that the number of CPUs has decreased since the previous PRAM step. Also note that in this case, by assumption, it must be the case that $m = \frac{\widehat{m}}{2}$. At this moment, we will halve the number of subtrees by reconstructing one more height of the big Circuit ORAM tree containing $2m$ buckets. Let Z be the bucket size of the ORAM tree. To reconstruct a height of size $2m$, we must reconstruct $2m$ buckets each of size Z. This can be achieved by repeating the eviction candidate selection algorithm Z number of times (see Sect. 7.3 for details).

(vii) *Cleanup.* Finally, since the pool size has grown in the above process, we perform a compression procedure to remove dummy blocks and compress the pool back to $c \cdot m + \alpha \log N$ size. Probabilistic analysis (in full version [6]) shows that the pool occupancy is bounded by $c \cdot m + \alpha \log N$ except with negl(N) probability, and thus ensures that no real blocks are lost during this reconstruction with all but negligible probability.

Again, if $m \geq \alpha \log \log N$, this can be accomplished through a simple oblivious sort procedure in $O(\log N)$ steps with m CPUs. Else if $m < \alpha \log \log N$, we devise a different procedure to perform the pool cleanup that completes in $O(\alpha \log N)$ parallel steps consuming m CPUs.

6   Details of the Fetch Phase

The outline of the fetch phase was described in Sect. 5. Almost all steps are self-explanatory as described in Sect. 5, and it remains to spell out only a couple subroutines of the preparation stage.

6.1   Discovering Which Children Addresses are Needed

Recall that during the preparation stage, for each recursion level, each conflict resolved address wants to learn which of its γ child addresses are needed by the next recursion level. Henceforth we assume that $\gamma = O(\log N)$.

We can accomplish this task using the following algorithm. We use $\mathsf{Addr}^{\langle d \rangle}$ to denote an array of size m that contain the conflict resolved (possibly dummy) addresses for recursion level d.

For each recursion level $d = 0, 1, \ldots, D - 1$ in parallel:

- Let X be the concatenation of $\mathsf{Addr}^{\langle d \rangle}$ and $\mathsf{Addr}^{\langle d+1 \rangle}$ where each element additionally carries a tag denoting whether it comes from $\mathsf{Addr}^{\langle d \rangle}$ or $\mathsf{Addr}^{\langle d+1 \rangle}$.
- Oblivious sort X such that the addresses from $\mathsf{Addr}^{\langle d \rangle}$ always appear immediately before its up to γ children addresses that come from $\mathsf{Addr}^{\langle d+1 \rangle}$ — henceforth we say that these addresses share the same key. Let the resulting array be X'.
- Invoke an instance of the oblivious aggregation algorithm, such that each address in X' that comes from $\mathsf{Addr}^{\langle d \rangle}$ receives a (compacted) bit vector indicating whether each of its γ children is needed in the next recursion level. Notice that as long as $\gamma := O(\log N)$, the resulting bit vector can be packed in a single block.
- For each element of the resulting array in parallel, if the element comes from $\mathsf{Addr}^{\langle d+1 \rangle}$, mark it as dummy. Let the resulting array be denoted Y.
- Obliviously sort the resulting array Y such that all dummy elements are pushed to the end. Output $Y[1 : m]$.

Clearly, the above algorithm can be completed in $O(\log m)$ steps with m CPUs.

6.2 Fetching and Removing Blocks from the Pool

Recall that another step of the preparation stage is to look for desired blocks from the pool and then remove any fetched block from the pool (by marking it as dummy). To achieve this, we consider two cases — and recall that the pool size is upper bounded by $O(m + \alpha \log N)$ except with negligible probability (due to our probabilistic analysis in the full version [6]).

- **Case 1:** $m \geq \alpha \log \log N$. In this case, we simply invoke an instance of the oblivious routing algorithm (particularly, the variant that removes routed elements from the source array) to accomplish this. This step can be completed in $O(\log N)$ parallel steps consuming m CPUs for an appropriately small super-constant $\alpha = \omega(1)$.
- **Case 2:** $m < \alpha \log \log N$. In this case, oblivious sorting would be too expensive. Therefore, we instead adopt the following algorithm. Recall that in this case, the pool size is dominated by $O(\alpha \log N)$.
  - First, each of the m CPUs perform a linear scan of the pool to look for its desired block.
  - Next, all m CPUs perform a a pipelined linear scan of the pool. During the linear scan, each CPU marks its fetched block (if any) as dummy. To ensure no write conflicts, we require that CPU number i starts its scan in the i-th step, i.e., in a pipelined fashion.

  Clearly, the above algorithm can be accomplished in $O(m + \alpha \log N)$ parallel steps consuming m CPUs.

6.3 Performance of the Fetch Phase

Taking into account the cost of all steps of the fetch phase, we have the following lemma.

Lemma 1 (Performance of the fetch phase). *Suppose that the block size $B = \Omega(\log N)$. Then, to serve the batch of m requests, the fetch phase, over all $O(\log N)$ levels of recursion, completes in $O(\log^2 N)$ parallel steps with m CPUs when $m \geq \alpha \log \log N$; and in $O(\alpha \log^2 N)$ parallel steps when $m < \alpha \log \log N$.*

7 Details of the Maintain Phase

An overview of the maintain phase was provided in Sect. 5.3. It remains to spell out the details of various subroutines needed by the maintain phase.

7.1 Simultaneous Removal of Fetched Blocks from Subtrees

Problem definition. Suppose that there are m fetch paths for each batch of m memory requests. Simultaneous removal provides the following abstraction:

- *Inputs:* Each of m CPUs has a tuple of the form (pathid_i, s_i) or $\perp$. More specifically, $\perp$ denotes nothing to remove, or else

- pathid$_i$ denotes the leaf identifier of a random tree path containing $O(\log N)$ slots. In particular, a tree path contains $O(\log N)$ heights and each height contains $O(1)$ slots; and
- s_i denotes a slot in the tree path to remove a block from;

Note that each tree path is random such that each disjoint subtree may receive at most $\alpha \log N$ tree paths. Although the m paths, we are guaranteed that all the non-dummy inputs of the m CPUs must correspond to distinct slots, i.e., no two CPUs want to remove from the same slot.

- *Outputs:* Each of the m CPUs outputs an array of length $O(\log N)$, denoting for each slot on its path: (1) whether the CPU is the representative CPU; and (2) if so, whether the block in the slot needs removal. The outputs should maintain the following invariants: every slot on the m input paths has exactly one representative, and if some CPU wanted to remove the block in the slot, then the representative is informed of the removal instruction.

Note that given the above output, each CPU simply carry out the instruction for every physical slot it is representative for:

- if the instruction is to remove, the CPU reads the block and writes dummy back;
- if the instruction is not to remove, the CPU reads the block and writes the same block back;
- if the CPU is not a representative for this physical slot, do nothing for this slot.

Simultaneous removal algorithm. We describe our simultaneous removal algorithm below. We note that since all the fetch paths are already observable by the adversary, it is okay for us to employ a non-oblivious propagation algorithm.

- *Sorting fetch paths.* All m CPUs write down their input tuple, forming an array of size m. We now obliviously sort this array by their fetch path such that the leftmost fetch path appears first, where the other of the fetch paths are determined by the leaves they intersect. This step takes $O(m \log m)$ total work and $O(\log m)$ parallel steps.
- *Table creation.* In parallel, fill out a table Q where each row corresponds to a slot in the tree, and each column corresponds to a fetch path (in sorted order from left to right). Specifically, $Q[\ell][i] = 1$ if the i-CPU wants to remove the block in slot ℓ on its fetch path; else $Q[\ell][i] = 0$. It is not hard to see that this step can be completed in $O(1)$ parallel steps with $m \log N$ CPUs.

Notice that since the m fetch paths may overlap, table Q may contain entries that correspond to the same physical slot. However, since the fetch paths were sorted from left to right, all entries corresponding to the same physical slot must appear in consecutive locations in the same row. Further, it is not hard to see that except with negligible probability, at most $\alpha \log N$ entries in Q correspond to the same physical slot (since each disjoint subtree receives at most $\alpha \log N$ fetch paths except with negligible probability).

Henceforth we say that $Q[\ell][i]$ is a *representative* if $Q[\ell][i]$ is the first occurrence of a physical slot in the row $Q[\ell]$.

– *Oblivious aggregation.* Now, for each row of the table Q, invoke an instance of the oblivious aggregation algorithm (for bounded-size groups) such that the representative of each group learns the OR of all entries belonging to the group. As mentioned above, since the group size is bounded by $\alpha \log N$, we can complete such oblivious aggregation in $O(\log \log N)$ parallel steps with $\frac{m}{\log \log N}$ CPUs, or alternatively, in $O(\log N)$ steps with $\frac{m}{\log N}$ CPUs. Therefore, over all rows of the table Q, this step completes in $O(\log N)$ parallel steps with m CPUs.

7.2   Evictions

Recall that in the sequential Circuit ORAM [36], whenever a fetched (and possibly updated) block is added to the root, two path evictions must be performed. The goal of Circuit OPRAM is to simulate the stochastic process of Circuit ORAM. However, since Circuit OPRAM does not maintain the tree structure for lower heights of the tree, we only need to partially simulate Circuit ORAM's stochastic process for the $O(m)$ disjoint subtrees that Circuit OPRAM does maintain. Our algorithms described below make use of certain non-blackbox properties of the Circuit ORAM algorithm [36]. In our description below, we will point out these crucial properties as the need arises, without re-explaining the entire Circuit ORAM construction [36].

Select $2m$ distinct eviction paths in $2m$ distinct subtrees. At this point, a batch of m requests have been made, and m possibly dummy blocks have been fetched, possibly update, and merged into the pool. As mentioned earlier, we now consider the pool as a flattened data structure containing all the smaller levels of the big Circuit ORAM tree as well as the stash. To simulate Circuit ORAM's stochastic process, at this point we must perform $2m$ evictions on $2m$ distinct paths. We leverage Circuit ORAM's deterministic, reverse-lexicographical order for determining the next $2m$ eviction paths. The specifics of the eviction path selection criterion is not important here, and the reader only needs to be aware that this selection criterion is fixed a priori and data independent. For more details on eviction path selection, we refer the reader to Circuit ORAM [36].

Fact 2. *Observe that at this point, the number of disjoint subtrees is at least $2m$. Due to Circuit ORAM's eviction path selection criterion, all $2m$ eviction paths will not only be distinct, but also correspond to distinct subtrees — henceforth we refer to these subtrees as evicting subtrees. For the special case when m stays the same over time, all $2m$ subtrees are evicting subtrees, and exactly one path is evicted in each subtree.*

Select $2m$ eviction candidates. We will now leverage a special property of the Circuit ORAM's eviction algorithm described earlier by Fact 1 such that we perform a "partial eviction" only on the subtrees maintained by our Circuit OPRAM. Recall that Fact 1 says the following:

- For Circuit ORAM's eviction algorithm, at most one block passes from path$[: i]$ to path$[i + 1 :]$ for each height i on the eviction path denoted path. In this case we also say that the block passes through the boundary between height i and height $i + 1$.
- Moreover, if a block does pass through the boundary between height i and height $i + 1$, it must be the block that is *deepest* with respect to the eviction path, where *deepest* is a criterion defined by Circuit ORAM [36]. Intuitively, a block is deeper if it can reside in a bucket on the eviction path with higher height. The reader can refer to Circuit ORAM [36] for details.

Therefore, we only need to elect one candidate block from the pool for each of the $2m$ eviction paths on which we would like to perform eviction. We describe an algorithm for performing such selection based on two different cases:

- **Case 1: when** $m > \alpha \log \log N$. We devise an algorithm based on a constant number of oblivious sorts. Since the pool contains $O(m + \alpha \log N)$ blocks, this algorithm completes in $O(\log N)$ parallel steps with m CPUs.
  (a) In the beginning, each block in the pool is tagged with the block's position identifier. Now, for each block in the pool in parallel, compute and tag the block with the additional metadata (treeid, priority) which will later be used as a sort key:
    • treeid denotes the block's destined subtree if the destined subtree is an evicting subtree, otherwise treeid $:= \perp$. All dummy blocks have treeid $:= \perp$.
    • priority denotes the block's eviction priority within the subtree. The block's priority value can be computed based on the block's position identifier and the current eviction path (in the subtree identified by treeid), a higher priority is assigned to blocks that can be reside deeper (i.e., closer to leaf) along the eviction path. The definition of *deep* is the same as in Circuit ORAM [36].
  (b) Now, invoke an instance of the oblivious bin-packing algorithm, where each evicting subtree can be regarded as a bin of capacity 1, and all the blocks are balls tagged with its destination bin. We wish to place one ball into each bin — if multiple balls are eligible for a bin, we prefer to place the ball with a higher priority value. The output of the algorithm is one (possibly dummy) eviction candidate for each evicting subtree, as well as the remainder of the pool minus those chosen blocks.
- **Case 2: when** $m \leq \alpha \log \log N$. In this case, the pool contains $\Theta(\alpha \log N)$ blocks, and performing oblivious sort will cause a total work of $\Omega(\log N \log \log N)$, which is too expensive if m is small. Instead, we perform the following, which can be accomplished in $O(\alpha \log N)$ parallel steps with $2m$ CPUs — below we describe the algorithm assuming $2m$ CPUs, but clearly the algorithm also works with m CPUs since we can always have each CPU simulate $O(1)$ CPUs.
  (a) Assign one CPU for each of the $2m$ eviction paths. Each CPU linearly scans through the pool and selects the deepest element with respect to

the eviction path. If no element is eligible for the current eviction path, a dummy element is selected. Clearly, this incurs $O(\alpha \log N)$ parallel steps. This step outputs an array of $2m$ elements selected for eviction for each of the $2m$ eviction paths. The rest of the algorithm will output the remainder of the pool.

(b) In $O(\alpha \log N + m)$ parallel steps, the $2m$ CPUs make a "pipelined linear scan", where CPU i starts its linear scan in the i-th step (note that this avoids write conflicts). When each CPU is making a linear scan, if the (real) block is what the CPU has selected for eviction, replace it with dummy; otherwise, write the original block back.

(c) Output the resulting pool.

Evictions. At this point, each of the $2m$ eviction paths has received one candidate block (which can be dummy). Hence, these $2m$ evictions can be carried out in parallel, each according to the (sequential) eviction algorithm of Circuit ORAM [36]. More specifically, we first expand the capacity of each eviction path by adding a bucket at the beginning of the path that holds the eviction candidate selected earlier; we call this the *smallest bucket* on the path. We then run Circuit ORAM's (sequential) eviction algorithm on each of these $2m$ (expanded) paths in parallel.

At the end, the block in the smallest bucket on each eviction path is returned to the pool. Note that if the eviction candidate has been successfully evicted into the path, then the smallest block on the path would be dummy, and thus a dummy block is returned to the pool. Doing this according to Circuit ORAM's eviction algorithm [36] takes $O(\log N)$ parallel runtime with $2m$ CPUs.

In a final cleanup step described later, we suppress a subset of the dummy blocks in the pool such that the pool size will not keep growing.

7.3   Data Structure Cleanup

Adjusting the number of subtrees. If $\widehat{m} > m$, i.e., the number of CPUs has decreased (by a factor of 2 according to our assumption) since the last PRAM step, we will halve the number of subtrees. This means that we must reconstruct one more height of the big Circuit ORAM tree.

Let $Z = O(1)$ be the bucket size of the ORAM tree. To reconstruct a height of size $2m$, we must reconstruct $\widehat{m}$ buckets each of size Z. To achieve this, we invoke an instance of the oblivious bin packing algorithm, where we wish to pack $2m$ buckets each of capacity Z. If a block can legally reside in a bucket by Circuit ORAM's path invariant, it is deemed eligible for a bucket. If more than Z blocks are eligible for a bucket, we break ties arbitrarily. Such oblivious bin packing can be completed in $O(\log m)$ parallel steps with m CPUs.

Although the reconstructed height of the big ORAM tree may contain different blocks from the scenario had we maintained the whole tree from the start, in the full version [6], we will show that the difference is in our favor in the sense that it will not make the pool occupancy larger.

Compress the pool. During the simulation of this PRAM step, the pool size has enlarged by at most $O(m)$. We now compress the pool size by removing a subset of the dummy blocks. There are two cases — recall also that the pool size is bounded by $O(m + \alpha \log N)$ except with negligible probability which we shall formally prove in the full version [6]:

- **Case 1:** $m \geq \alpha \log \log N$. In this case, we can perform such compression through a simple oblivious sort operation that move all dummy blocks to the end of the array representing the pool, and then truncating the array retaining only the first $c \cdot m + \alpha \log N$ blocks for an appropriate constant c. This can be completed in $O(\log N)$ parallel steps with m CPUs.
- **Case 2:** $m < \alpha \log \log N$. In this case, oblivious sorting would be too expensive. Instead, we perform compression by conducting a pipelined, partial bubble sort. Let $s = O(m + \alpha \log N)$ be the current pool size, and suppose that we need to compress the array back to $s' := s - O(m)$ blocks. Recall that a normal bubble sort of s elements would make s bubbling passes over the array, where after the i-th pass, the largest i elements are at the end. Here we make only $O(m)$ bubbling passes where each CPU is in charge of $O(1)$ passes. The passes are performed in a pipelined fashion to avoid write conflicts. At the end of this partial bubble sort, the last $s - s'$ blocks of the array may be removed.
  This is completed in $O(m + \alpha \log N)$ parallel steps with m CPUs.

7.4   Performance of the Maintain Phase

Accounting for the cost of all of the above steps, we can easily derive the following lemma for the performance of the maintain phase.

Lemma 2 (Performance of the maintain phase). *Suppose that the block size $B = \Omega(\log N)$. Then, to serve the batch of m requests, the maintain phase, over all $O(\log N)$ levels of recursion, completes in $O(\log^2 N)$ parallel steps with m CPUs when $m \geq \alpha \log \log N$; and in $O(\alpha \log^2 N)$ parallel steps when $m < \alpha \log \log N$.*

Deferred Materials

In the interest of space, we defer to our full online version [6] the following addtional contents: (1) detailed proofs, (2) further optimizations for small m, (3) how to reduce a $\log \log$ factor relying on PRFs and achieving computational security, and (4) extensions for large block sizes and non-uniform block sizes.

Acknowledgments. We are extremely grateful to Rafael Pass without whose insights and support this work would not have been possible. We are grateful to Joshua Gancher for helpful discussions in an earlier phase of the project, and to Kai-Min Chung for many supportive conversations. We thank Ling Ren for (re)explaining the position map compression trick to us and Kartik Nayak for very helpful comments on a draft of the paper. This work is supported in part by NSF grants CNS-1314857, CNS-1514261,

CNS-1544613, CNS-1561209, CNS-1601879, CNS-1617676, an Office of Naval Research Young Investigator Program Award, a DARPA Safeware grant (subcontract under IBM), a Packard Fellowship, a Sloan Fellowship, Google Faculty Research Awards, a VMWare Research Award, and a Baidu Research Award.

References

1. Ajtai, M., Komlós, J., Szemerédi, E.: An O(n log n) sorting network. In: Proceedings of the Fifteenth Annual ACM Symposium on Theory of Computing, STOC 1983, pp. 1–9. ACM, New York (1983)

2. Apon, D., Katz, J., Shi, E., Thiruvengadam, A.: Verifiable oblivious storage. In: Krawczyk, H. (ed.) PKC 2014. LNCS, vol. 8383, pp. 131–148. Springer, Heidelberg (2014). doi:10.1007/978-3-642-54631-0_8

3. Boyle, E., Chung, K.-M., Pass, R.: Oblivious parallel RAM and applications. In: Kushilevitz, E., Malkin, T. (eds.) TCC 2016. LNCS, vol. 9563, pp. 175–204. Springer, Heidelberg (2016). doi:10.1007/978-3-662-49099-0_7

4. Boyle, E., Naor, M.: Is there an oblivious RAM lower bound? In: Proceedings of the 2016 ACM Conference on Innovations in Theoretical Computer Science, Cambridge, MA, USA, 14–16 January 2016, pp. 357–368 (2016)

5. Hubert Chan, T.-H., Chung, K.-M., Shi, E.: On the depth of oblivious parallel ORAM (2017, manuscript)

6. Hubert Chan, T.-H., Shi, E.: Circuit OPRAM: unifying statistically and computationally secure ORAMs and OPRAMs (2016). Online full version of the present paper https://eprint.iacr.org/2016/1084

7. Chen, B., Lin, H., Tessaro, S.: Oblivious parallel RAM: improved efficiency and generic constructions. In: Kushilevitz, E., Malkin, T. (eds.) TCC 2016. LNCS, vol. 9563, pp. 205–234. Springer, Heidelberg (2016). doi:10.1007/978-3-662-49099-0_8

8. Chung, K.-M., Liu, Z., Pass, R.: Statistically-secure ORAM with $\tilde{O}(\log^2 n)$ overhead. In: Sarkar, P., Iwata, T. (eds.) ASIACRYPT 2014. LNCS, vol. 8874, pp. 62–81. Springer, Heidelberg (2014). doi:10.1007/978-3-662-45608-8_4

9. Dachman-Soled, D., Liu, C., Papamanthou, C., Shi, E., Vishkin, U.: Oblivious network RAM and leveraging parallelism to achieve obliviousness. In: Iwata, T., Cheon, J.H. (eds.) ASIACRYPT 2015. LNCS, vol. 9452, pp. 337–359. Springer, Heidelberg (2015). doi:10.1007/978-3-662-48797-6_15

10. Devadas, S., van Dijk, M., Fletcher, C.W., Ren, L., Shi, E., Wichs, D.: Onion ORAM: a constant bandwidth blowup oblivious RAM. In: Kushilevitz, E., Malkin, T. (eds.) TCC 2016. LNCS, vol. 9563, pp. 145–174. Springer, Heidelberg (2016). doi:10.1007/978-3-662-49099-0_6

11. Fletcher, C.W., van Dijk, M., Devadas, S.: A secure processor architecture for encrypted computation on untrusted programs. In: STC (2012)

12. Fletcher, C.W., Ren, L., Kwon, A., van Dijk, M., Devadas, S.: Freecursive ORAM [nearly] free recursion and integrity verification for position-based oblivious RAM. In: ASPLOS (2015)

13. Fletcher, C.W., Ren, L., Kwon, A., van Dijk, M., Stefanov, E., Devadas, S.: RAW Path ORAM: a low-latency, low-area hardware ORAM controller with integrity verification. IACR Cryptology ePrint Archive 2014:431 (2014)

14. Fletcher, C.W., Ren, L., Yu, X., van Dijk, M., Khan, O., Devadas, S.: Suppressing the oblivious RAM timing channel while making information leakage and program efficiency trade-offs. In: HPCA, pp. 213–224 (2014)

15. Gentry, C., Goldman, K.A., Halevi, S., Julta, C., Raykova, M., Wichs, D.: Optimizing ORAM and using it efficiently for secure computation. In: De Cristofaro, E., Wright, M. (eds.) PETS 2013. LNCS, vol. 7981, pp. 1–18. Springer, Heidelberg (2013). doi:10.1007/978-3-642-39077-7_1

16. Gentry, C., Halevi, S., Jutla, C., Raykova, M.: Private database access with he-over-ORAM architecture. Cryptology ePrint Archive, Report 2014/345 (2014). http:// eprint.iacr.org/

17. Goldreich, O.: Towards a theory of software protection and simulation by oblivious RAMs. In: STOC (1987)

18. Goldreich, O., Ostrovsky, R.: Software protection and simulation on oblivious RAMs. J. ACM **43**, 431–473 (1996). Please check and confirm if the inserted volume id and page range are correct for Ref. [18]

19. Goodrich, M.T., Mitzenmacher, M.: Privacy-preserving access of outsourced data via oblivious RAM simulation. In: Aceto, L., Henzinger, M., Sgall, J. (eds.) ICALP 2011. LNCS, vol. 6756, pp. 576–587. Springer, Heidelberg (2011). doi:10.1007/ 978-3-642-22012-8_46

20. Gordon, S.D., Katz, J., Kolesnikov, V., Krell, F., Malkin, T., Raykova, M., Vahlis, Y.: Secure two-party computation in sublinear (amortized) time. In: CCS (2012)

21. Hagerup, T.: Fast and optimal simulations between CRCW PRAMs. In: Finkel, A., Jantzen, M. (eds.) STACS 1992. LNCS, vol. 577, pp. 45–56. Springer, Heidelberg (1992). doi:10.1007/3-540-55210-3_172

22. Keller, M., Scholl, P.: Efficient, oblivious data structures for MPC. In: Sarkar, P., Iwata, T. (eds.) ASIACRYPT 2014. LNCS, vol. 8874, pp. 506–525. Springer, Heidelberg (2014). doi:10.1007/978-3-662-45608-8_27

23. Kushilevitz, E., Lu, S., Ostrovsky, R.: On the (in)security of hash-based oblivious RAM and a new balancing scheme. In: SODA (2012)

24. Liu, C., Huang, Y., Shi, E., Katz, J., Hicks, M.: Automating efficient RAM-model secure computation. In: S & P, May 2014

25. Maas, M., Love, E., Stefanov, E., Tiwari, M., Shi, E., Asanovic, K., Kubiatowicz, J., Song, D.: Phantom: practical oblivious computation in a secure processor. In: CCS (2013)

26. Nayak, K., Katz, J.: An oblivious parallel ram with $o(\log^2 n)$ parallel runtime blowup. Cryptology ePrint Archive, Report 2016/1141 (2016). http://eprint.iacr. org/2016/1141

27. Nayak, K., Wang, X.S., Ioannidis, S., Weinsberg, U., Taft, N., Shi, E.: GraphSC: parallel secure computation made easy. In: IEEE S & P (2015)

28. Pinkas, B., Reinman, T.: Oblivious RAM revisited. In: Rabin, T. (ed.) CRYPTO 2010. LNCS, vol. 6223, pp. 502–519. Springer, Heidelberg (2010). doi:10.1007/ 978-3-642-14623-7_27

29. Ren, L., Fletcher, C.W., Kwon, A., Stefanov, E., Shi, E., van Dijk, M., Devadas, S.: Constants count: practical improvements to oblivious RAM. In: 24th USENIX Security Symposium (USENIX Security 15), pp. 415–430. USENIX Association, Washington, D.C. (2015)

30. Ren, L., Yu, X., Fletcher, C.W., van Dijk, M., Devadas, S.: Design space exploration and optimization of path oblivious RAM in secure processors. In: ISCA, pp. 571– 582 (2013)

31. Shi, E., Hubert Chan, T.-H., Stefanov, E., Li, M.: Oblivious RAM with $O((\log N)^3)$ worst-case cost. In: Lee, D.H., Wang, X. (eds.) ASIACRYPT 2011. LNCS, vol. 7073, pp. 197–214. Springer, Heidelberg (2011). doi:10.1007/978-3-642-25385-0_11

32. Stefanov, E., Shi, E.: Multi-cloud oblivious storage. In: ACM Conference on Computer and Communications Security (CCS) (2013)

33. Stefanov, E., Shi, E.: Oblivistore: high performance oblivious cloud storage. In: IEEE Symposium on Security and Privacy (S & P) (2013)

34. Stefanov, E., Shi, E., Song, D.: Towards practical oblivious RAM. In: Network and Distributed System Security Symposium (NDSS) (2012)

35. Stefanov, E., van Dijk, M., Shi, E., Fletcher, C., Ren, L., Yu, X., Devadas, S.: Path ORAM - an extremely simple oblivious ram protocol. In: CCS (2013)

36. Wang, X.S., Hubert Chan, T.-H., Shi, E., Circuit, O.: On tightness of the Goldreich-Ostrovsky lower bound. In: ACM CCS (2015)

37. Wang, X.S., Huang, Y., Hubert Chan, T.-H., Shelat, A., Shi, E.: SCORAM: oblivious RAM for Secure Computation. In: CCS (2014)

38. Williams, P., Sion, R.: Usable PIR. In: Network and Distributed System Security Symposium (NDSS) (2008)

39. Williams, P., Sion, R.: Round-optimal access privacy on outsourced storage. In: ACM Conference on Computer and Communication Security (CCS) (2012)

40. Williams, P., Sion, R., Carbunar, B.: Building castles out of mud: practical access pattern privacy and correctness on untrusted storage. In: CCS, pp. 139–148 (2008)

Zero-Knowledge and Non-Malleability

Resettably-Sound Resettable Zero Knowledge in Constant Rounds

Wutichai Chongchitmate[1]([⊠]), Rafail Ostrovsky[1], and Ivan Visconti[2]

[1] University of California, Los Angeles, CA, USA
{wutichai,rafail}@cs.ucla.edu
[2] Università di Salerno, Fisciano, Italy
visconti@unisa.it

Abstract. In FOCS 2001 Barak et al. conjectured the existence of zero-knowledge arguments that remain secure against resetting provers and resetting verifiers. The conjecture was proven true by Deng et al. in FOCS 2009 under various complexity assumptions and requiring a polynomial number of rounds. Later on in FOCS 2013 Chung et al. improved the assumptions requiring one-way functions only but still with a polynomial number of rounds.

In this work we show a *constant-round* resettably-sound resettable zero-knowledge argument system, therefore improving the round complexity from polynomial to constant. We obtain this result through the following steps.

1. We show an explicit transform from any ℓ-round concurrent zero-knowledge argument system into an $O(\ell)$-round resettable zero-knowledge argument system. The transform is based on techniques proposed by Barak et al. in FOCS 2001 and by Deng et al. in FOCS 2009. Then, we make use of a recent breakthrough presented by Chung et al. in CRYPTO 2015 that solved the longstanding open question of constructing a constant-round concurrent zero-knowledge argument system from plausible polynomial-time hardness assumptions. Starting with their construction Γ we obtain a constant-round resettable zero-knowledge argument system Λ.

2. We then show that by carefully embedding Λ inside Γ (i.e., essentially by playing a modification of the construction of Chung et al. against the construction of Chung et al.) we obtain the first constant-round resettably-sound concurrent zero-knowledge argument system Δ.

3. Finally, we apply a transformation due to Deng et al. to Δ obtaining a resettably-sound resettable zero-knowledge argument system Π, the main result of this work.

While our round-preserving transform for resettable zero knowledge requires one-way functions only, both Λ, Δ and Π extend the work of Chung et al. and as such they rely on the same assumptions (i.e., families of collision-resistant hash functions, one-way permutations and indistinguishability obfuscation for $\mathcal{P}/\texttt{poly}$, with slightly super-polynomial security).

© International Association for Cryptologic Research 2017
Y. Kalai and L. Reyzin (Eds.): TCC 2017, Part II, LNCS 10678, pp. 111–138, 2017.
https://doi.org/10.1007/978-3-319-70503-3_4

1   Introduction

Private randomness is essential for many cryptographic tasks, including zero-knowledge (ZK) proofs [24]. A natural question regards the possibility of having ZK proofs in applications where the computing machine is stateless and not equipped with a continuous source of randomness.

Resettable zero knowledge. The above question was put forth by Canetti et al. [8]. In particular, they considered a cheating verifier that mounts a *reset attack*, where provers are forced to execute the protocol multiple times possibly on the same inputs and random tapes, and without the ability to maintain states between executions. These attacks include the case of stateless provers, as well as provers implemented by devices that can physically be restored to their original states (e.g., through cloning, battery replacement).

More specifically, in [8], Canetti et al. introduced the notion of *resettable zero knowledge (rZK)*, in which the zero-knowledge property is required to hold even against cheating verifiers that can reset the provers to the initial states therefore forcing them to play again with the same randomnesses. This notion is closely related to *concurrent zero knowledge (cZK)* proposed earlier by Dwork et al. [19] where a cheating verifier can engage in multiple possibly interleaving concurrent executions (called *sessions*) of the protocol. rZK is at least as hard to achieve as cZK since a resetting cheating verifier through specific reset strategies can emulate interleaving concurrent executions. In [21] Garg et al. showed that resettable *statistical* zero knowledge is possible for several interesting languages.

Round complexity of cZK and rZK. Constant-round cZK under plausible hardness assumptions has been a long-standing challenging open question that received a positive answer in the work of Chung et al. [11] by means of indistinguishability obfuscation ($i\mathcal{O}$) [11]. Instead the situation for rZK is worse. Canetti et al. in [8] constructed rZK proofs in the *standard model* relying on standard cryptographic assumptions but with polynomial round complexity[1].

The round complexity was then improved to poly-logarithmic in [29]. The state of affair leaves the following open problem.

Open Problem 1: *is there a construction for rZK with sub-logarithmic rounds?*

Resettably-sound zero knowledge. Barak et al. [3] considered the natural opposite setting, called *resettably-sound zero knowledge (rsZK)* arguments, where soundness is required to hold even against cheating provers that can reset the verifiers forcing them to re-use the same random tapes. The standard zero-knowledge property remains untouched. They showed a constant-round construction assuming collision-resistant hash functions. The recent work of [12] reached optimal round complexity and assumptions (i.e., 4 rounds and one-way functions).

---

[1] In addition they proposed a mild setup assumption based on bare public keys showing that it is sufficient for constant-round resettable zero knowledge. Follow up work optimized round complexity and complexity assumptions for rZK with bare public keys [16,17,31,34,35].

The simultaneous resettability conjecture. Barak et al. in [3] conjectured the existence of a zero-knowledge argument that is secure simultaneously against resetting verifiers and against resetting provers: a resettably-sound resettable zero-knowledge argument system. The conjecture was proven true by Deng et al. [15] that presented a construction with a polynomial number of rounds and assuming collision-resistant hash functions and trapdoor permutations. The computational assumptions have been improved to one-way functions [4,5,13,14,33], while the barrier of the polynomial round complexity has remained untouched so far.

Open Problem 2: *is there a construction for resettably-sound rZK with sub-polynomial rounds?*

We stress that by relaxing the security against resetting verifiers from zero knowledge to witness indistinguishability, then constant-round simultaneous resettability is possible. Indeed just 1 or 2 rounds (i.e., ZAPs) are needed to obtain proofs, and a larger constant number of rounds is sufficient to obtain arguments of knowledge [9].

1.1   Our Results

In this paper, we answer the above questions positively. In the main result we construct a *constant-round* simultaneous resettable zero-knowledge argument for $\mathcal{NP}$. Our result requires the existence of families of collision-resistant hash functions, one-way permutations and indistinguishability obfuscation ($i\mathcal{O}$) for $\mathcal{P}/\texttt{poly}$ (with slightly super-polynomial security). These assumptions are the same as the ones in [11] that showed a constant-round concurrent zero-knowledge argument for $\mathcal{NP}$. Our result makes uses of the protocol of [11] twice in some nested way. More precisely, the first time we use the protocol of [11] Γ is to obtain a constant-round rZK argument Λ. Then we start again with Γ and we modify it by using Λ (that is a modification of Γ) as subprotocol in the opposite direction (i.e., the verifier will prove something to the prover). Therefore we roughly use the protocol of [11] against the protocol of [11] which is somehow intriguing. This nested use of the protocol of [11] allows us to obtain a constant-round resettably-sound concurrent zero-knowledge argument Δ. We can then apply a compiler due to [15] to Δ therefore obtaining our main argument system Π that is secure simultaneously against resetting provers and resetting verifiers needing only a constant number of rounds.

We now give our formal theorems that specify the precise complexity assumptions.

Theorem 1. *Assuming the existence of one-way functions, than any ℓ-round concurrent zero-knowledge argument system can be transformed in a $\mathcal{O}(\ell)$-round resettable zero-knowledge argument system.*

Theorem 2. *Assuming the existence of collision-resistant hash functions, one-way permutations and indistinguishability obfuscation for $\mathcal{P}/\texttt{poly}$ (with slightly super-polynomial security), there exists a constant-round resettably-sound resettable zero-knowledge argument system for $\mathcal{NP}$.*

1.2 Main Tools and Our New Techniques

Our constructions rely on new ideas as well as a combined use of several techniques used in previous results on concurrent, resettable and resettably-sound zero knowledge. We start by briefly describing the important tools that we use along with our new techniques for our constructions.

Barak's non-black-block protocol. The starting point is Barak's non-black-box zero-knowledge argument for $\mathcal{NP}$ [1] that works as follows. The prover P sends a commitment $c \in \{0,1\}^n$ of 0 to the verifier V. The verifier V then sends a uniformly generated random string $r \in \{0,1\}^{2n}$. Finally, the prover gives a witness-indistinguishable universal argument (WIUA) that $x \in L$ or there exists $\sigma \in \{0,1\}^n$ such that c is a commitment of a program M such that $M(\sigma) = r^2$. The soundness follows from the binding of the commitment scheme and the soundness of the WIUA as any program M committed by the cheating prover does not have r in its support with overwhelming probability. For the zero-knowledge property, the simulator uses the code of the adversary. Indeed it commits to a program M corresponding to the code of V^*, the cheating verifier. Let σ be the commitment. We have that $M(\sigma) = r$ and σ is short compared to r.

Chung et al.'s constant-round cZK argument. In [11], Chung et al. construct a constant-round cZK argument by using unique $\mathcal{P}$-certificate systems [10] with delegatable CRS generation and $i\mathcal{O}$. Informally, a $\mathcal{P}$-certificate system allows an efficient prover to convince a verifier of the validity of any deterministic polynomial-time computation $M(x) = y$ using a certificate of fixed (polynomial) length, independent of the size and the running time of M. The verifier can also verify the certificate in fixed (polynomial) time, independent of the running time of M. In a $\mathcal{P}$-certificate system with delegatable CRS generation, the certificate is generated using a common reference string (CRS) that can be computed by using resources delegated by the verifier. More specifically, in this $\mathcal{P}$-certificate system, the $\mathcal{P}$-certificate verifier generates public and private parameters, PP and κ, and sends PP to the $\mathcal{P}$-certificate prover. The $\mathcal{P}$-certificate prover uses the public parameter PP and the statement $q = (M, x, y)$ to deterministically compute a short digest d, whose length is independent of the length of q, and sends it to the $\mathcal{P}$-certificate verifier. The $\mathcal{P}$-certificate verifier then computes the CRS from d and κ. Finally, the $\mathcal{P}$-certificate prover computes the certificate from the CRS and q. The $\mathcal{P}$-certificate system is unique if there exists at most one accepted certificate for any statement and CRS.

The argument of [11] proceeds similarly to Barak's argument with the following modifications. In the last step, instead of requiring the prover P to prove

---

[2] Since the size of M may not be known in advance, the commitment is to the hash of the program M using a hash function h sampled from a family of collision-resistant hash functions chosen in the beginning of the protocol by the verifier. The soundness is also based on the collision resistance of h.

that $x \in L$ or there exists σ such that c is a commitment to a program M such that $M(\sigma) = r$, the prover provides a special-sound witness-indistinguishability proof that $x \in L$ or there exists a $\mathcal{P}$-certificate π which certifies that $M(\sigma) = r$ for some short string σ. Additionally, P also commits and gives a WIUA proving that either $x \in L$ or there exists a $\mathcal{P}$-certificate for the statement $q = (M, \sigma, r)$ before receiving the public parameter PP from V. Note that since the honest prover of the protocol in [11] has a witness for $x \in L$, it can just ignore CRS, d and q, and simply commit to zeroes. In order to allow the zero-knowledge simulator (note that an honest prover will just use the witness for $x \in L$) to compute the CRS from d and κ, the verifier sends an obfuscated program with κ embedded inside, that allows the simulator to compute CRS from d committed earlier. Finally, V also provides a zero-knowledge argument that the obfuscated program is computed correctly.

The simulator does not know a witness for $x \in L$ but is instead able to commit to the code of the adversary. More formally, the simulator is divided in two parts: S_1, which takes a $\mathcal{P}$-certificates π_i in the i-th round as an input, and interacts with the verifier V^*, and S_2 which, in the i-th round provides $\mathcal{P}$-certificates certifying that S_1 on input $(1, \pi_1), \ldots, (i - 1, \pi_{i-1})$ outputs m_i. Instead of committing to a program M, using the verifier V^*'s code, such that $M(\sigma) = r$ for some short string σ, the simulator $S = (S_1, S_2)$ commits to a program $\widetilde{S}_1$. The program, on input $(1^n, j, s)$, runs an interaction between S_1 and V^* for j rounds using s as a seed to generate pseudorandom coins while having an access to the oracle $\mathcal{O}_{V_{cert}}$ which provides $\mathcal{P}$-certificates. This prevents the nesting of concurrent sessions which may result in the blow-up in the running time as the expensive part of S consists in generating the $\mathcal{P}$-certificates. The simulator of the protocol in [11] can therefore succeed in the special-sound witness-indistinguishability proof for the statement $x \in L$ or there exists a $\mathcal{P}$-certificate π which certifies that $\widetilde{S}_1^{\mathcal{O}_{V_{cert}}}(1^n, j, s) = r$ for some short string $(1^n, j, s)$ using the output from the oracle as a witness.

Deng, Goyal and Sahai's transformation. In [15,25], Deng et al. construct a hybrid resettably-sound and relaxed concurrent zero-knowledge argument Π_{DGS}. Then they apply a series of transformations to achieve simultaneous resettability.

Relaxed concurrent zero knowledge allows verifiers to interact in multiple sessions with independent provers. However, the zero-knowledge property only guarantees for "relaxed" concurrent verifiers whose random coins are fixed in the beginning of each session, independently of sessions that start after that session. Note that any concurrent zero-knowledge argument/proof is also relaxed concurrent zero-knowledge as any relaxed concurrent verifier is also a concurrent verifier.

Hybrid resettable soundness means that the verifier can be separated into two parts, V_1 and V_2. V_1 directly interacts with P, may relay some messages between P and V_2, and can be reset by a cheating prover. V_2 only interacts with V_1, cannot be reset by a cheating prover, and is responsible to decide whether to "accept" or "reject" the argument. Moreover, for each *determining message* (the first message V_2 receives in the protocol), P cannot find two different messages that P can convince V_1 to pass to V_2 in each round. We refer to [25] for a precise definition. Note that any resettably-sound argument is also hybrid resettably sound by letting V_1 behave as V except that instead of accepting the argument, it sends a message to V_2, and V_2 always accepts the argument when it receives a message from V_1.

The transformation of Deng et al. uses ZAPs and one-way functions to achieve simultaneous resettability and only increases the round complexity by a constant factor. However, the round complexity of Π_{DGS} is polynomial [15]. Thus, their simultaneously resettable argument system also requires polynomial rounds.

Inapplicability of the transformation of [15] to the construction of Chung et al. [11]. Intuitively, one may try to apply the transformation of [15] to the constant-round concurrent zero-knowledge argument in [11] to get simultaneous resettability. However, in order for the result of the transformation to be simultaneously resettable, it is required that the starting protocol be relaxed concurrent zero-knowledge and hybrid resettably sound. While the protocol in [11] is concurrent zero-knowledge, which implies that it is relaxed concurrent zero-knowledge, we argue that if the (non-resettable) ZK argument (proving that the obfuscated program is computed correctly) is not zero-knowledge against *resetting* verifiers, then the protocol can not be proved hybrid resettably sound. Two reasons follow below.

1. Suppose in the extreme case that there exists an adversarial resetting prover for the argument of [11] that runs a resetting adversary $\mathcal{A}_{ZK}$ in the (non-resetting) zero-knowledge subprotocol in which the honest verifier proves that the obfuscated program is computed correctly. Remember that the zero-knowledge subprotocol could also be an argument of knowledge admitting a black-box (rewinding) extractor. By managing to run $\mathcal{A}_{ZK}$, the adversarial resetting prover could succeed in extracting some relevant information (e.g., the secret parameter for $\mathcal{P}$-certificate CRS generation, that is used in the (non-resettable) ZK argument proven by the verifier to prover to guarantee the correctness of the obfuscated program). However, according to the definition of hybrid resettable soundness, we need to consider two separate parts of the verifier $V = (V_1, V_2)$. One out of V_1 and V_2 will run as prover of the ZK argument proving that the obfuscated program is generated correctly. If the (non-resettable) ZK argument is played by V_1 (as a prover), which can be reset, the malicious prover of the protocol in [11] can run $\mathcal{A}_{ZK}$ to learn some relevant information (.e.g, the secret parameter), and this can potentially be used to generate a certificate for a false statement. On the other hand, if the (non-resettable) ZK argument is played by V_2 (as a prover) then since the messages of the verifier of this argument are not fixed by a determining message in the protocol of [11], we have that V_2 can receive two different messages for the same determining message, and thus, even in this case, the protocol is not hybrid resettably sound.
2. The $\mathcal{P}$-certificate generation in the protocol of [11] cannot be transformed into a resettably-sound protocol using the techniques of [3]. This is because

the $\mathcal{P}$-certificate system is not public coin. Recall that the proof of resettable soundness in [3] uses the reduction to the non-resettable case by starting (by contradiction) with a (successful) resetting prover. If we repeat here the same reduction, we have that the non-resetting prover runs all but one session by simulating the verifier itself. Of course this requires to generate legit verifier messages under reset attacks. When trying to send the legit verifier messages, the non-resetting prover may send the obfuscated program of the real verifier of the reduction to the resetting prover, and the resetting prover may reset to the step after which it receives the public parameter for the $\mathcal{P}$-certificate. In that case, the non-resetting prover will not be able to generate a new obfuscated program as specified in the protocol without knowing the secret parameter.

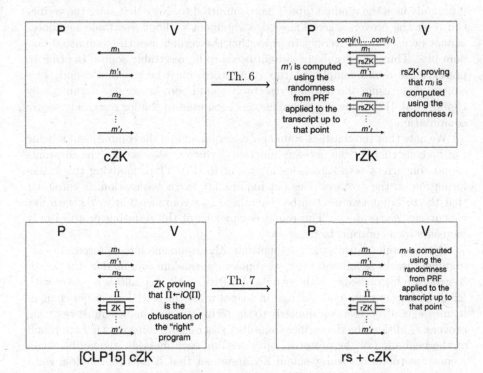

Fig. 1. Our transformations of zero-knowledge argument systems

1.3 Our Approach

In order to get a constant-round resettably-sound concurrent zero-knowledge argument system, we consider the protocol from [11] which is constant round and concurrent zero knowledge, but not resettably sound. As discussed above, there are two main problems that separate the protocol of [11] from resettable soundness: the non-resettable ZK argument for $i\mathcal{O}$ and the delegatable CRS generation of the $\mathcal{P}$-certificate system, which cannot be generated without knowing the secret parameter generated in the earlier step.

Solving the first problem. We resolve the first problem by constructing a constant-round resettable ZK argument from the concurrent ZK argument of [11]. This transformation is implicit in some previous works on the topic [3,15]. We explicitly present it here for completion (Fig. 1).

Unlike the concurrent verifier, the resetting verifier can exploit the reuse of the random tape during the resetting attack by sending different messages in order to extract additional information from the prover. We prevent such behavior by requiring (1) the verifier to commit to its random tape using a statistically binding commitment scheme and (2) to provide a zero-knowledge argument that it actually uses the random tape it has committed to. Note that since the verifier can reset the prover, a zero-knowledge argument without resettable soundness cannot be used by the verifier to prove that the verifier uses the committed random bits. Thus, the argument system needs to be resettably sound. In order to preserve the round complexity, this subprotocol must be constant round. This can be done using the 4-round resettably-sound zero-knowledge argument by Chung et al. [12]. A similar technique has been used in [26] for resettably-secure computation.

We note that the constant-round rsZK argument and the commitment scheme can be constructed from one-way functions, which is assumed for the constant-round concurrent zero-knowledge argument in [11]. Thus, applying this transformation on the protocol does not require any extra assumption. It turns out that the technique we use can be generalized to a compiler that works with *any* concurrent ZK protocol. The round complexity of the resulting protocol only increases by a constant factor.

Our compiler turning any concurrent ZK argument into a resettable ZK argument works as follows. First, we replace the random coin used by the prover to generate his messages with outputs of a PRF. This step allows a prover with fixed random tape to send different messages when the resetting verifier changes its messages after resetting similarly to the technique used in [3] against resetting provers. Additionally, the verifier commits to its random coins used in each round at the beginning of the protocol. After sending each message, the verifier gives a constant-round resettably-sound ZK argument that it uses the random coins committed in the first round. This modification ensures that the verifier follows the protocol in every session.

Solving the second problem. In order to solve the second problem, we observe that while the protocol of [11] is not public-coin, it is "almost public-coin". By almost public-coin, we mean that, beside the ZK argument which is replaced by rZK argument above, there is only one message from the verifier that cannot be generated independently as public-coin, but depends on a hidden randomness. Thus, we modify the technique in [3] to resolve the problem in two steps as follows (Fig. 1).

First, we consider a modified version of the protocol of [11], in which we can prove its (non-resettable) soundness. In this protocol, the round in which the message from V cannot be generated with uniformly random coins is repeated m times, where $m = \texttt{poly}(n)$ is the upper bound on the running time of a cheating prover P^*. More specifically, after receiving the public parameter for $\mathcal{P}$-certificate, the prover for the modified protocol P_S repeatedly commits to and proves the validity of the digest d of his statement while the verifier V_S repeatedly replies with the obfuscated program verifying the committed value and output the CRS for the $\mathcal{P}$-certificate. P_S then chooses which commitment and obfuscated program pair P_S will use to complete the protocol. Because of the security of the $i\mathcal{O}$, P_S does not learn the secret parameter for the $\mathcal{P}$-certificate even after m repetitions. Thus, the resulting protocol is still sound.

Then we reduce the resettable soundness of the final protocol to the non-resettable soundness of the above protocol with polynomial reduction in success probability as follows. Given a resetting prover P^*, we construct a non-resetting prover P_S^* by internally simulating P^* interaction with a verifier V, and randomly choosing which of the m repetitions will lead to accepting transcript. For other repetitions, P_S^* will generate the parameters for $\mathcal{P}$-certificate itself to get around the non-public-coin situation. In the case that P_S^* guesses the accepting transcript correctly, which occurs with probability $1/m$, it will convince the verifier V_S with the accepting transcript from the simulation.

1.4   Open Questions

Unlike the above compiler from concurrent ZK to resettable ZK, our construction for resettably sound resettable zero knowledge uses in a non-black-box way the protocol of [11].

Our work leaves open the natural questions of producing a generic round-preserving transform from cZK to rZK, and of obtaining constant-round resettably sound resettable zero knowledge under more standard complexity assumptions.

2   Definitions

A polynomial-time relation R is a relation for which it is possible to verify in time polynomial in $|x|$ whether $R(x, w) = 1$. Let us consider an $\mathcal{NP}$-language L and denote by R_L the corresponding polynomial-time relation such that $x \in L$ if and only if there exists w such that $R_L(x, w) = 1$. We will call such a w a *valid witness for $x \in L$*. Let λ denote the security parameter. A *negligible* function $\nu(\lambda)$ is a non-negative function such that for any constant $c < 0$ and for all sufficiently large λ, $\nu(\lambda) < \lambda^c$. We will denote by $\Pr_r[X]$ the probability of an event X over coins r, and $\Pr[X]$ when r is not specified. The abbreviation "PPT" stands for probabilistic polynomial time. For a randomized algorithm A, let $A(x; r)$ denote running A on an input x with random coins r. If r is chosen uniformly at random with an output y, we denote $y \leftarrow A(x)$. For a pair of interactive Turing machines

(P, V), let $\langle P, V \rangle(x)$ denotes V's output after interacting with P upon common input x. We say V accepts if $\langle P, V \rangle(x) = 1$ and rejects if $\langle P, V \rangle(x) = 0$. We denote by $\mathtt{view}_{V(x,z)}^{P(w)}$ the view (i.e., its private coins and the received messages) of V during an interaction with $P(w)$ on common input x and auxiliary input z. We will use the standard notion of computational indistinguishability [23].

We now give definitions for interactive proof/argument systems with all variants that are useful in this work.

Definition 1 (interactive proofs [24]). *An interactive proof system for the language L, is a pair of interactive Turing machines (P, V) running on common input x such that:*

- *Efficiency: P and V are PPT.*
- *Completeness: For every $\lambda \in \mathbb{N}$ and for every pair (x, w) such that $R_L(x, w) = 1$,*

$$\Pr[\langle P(w), V \rangle(1^\lambda, x) = 1] = 1.$$

- *Soundness[3]: There exists a negligible function $\nu(\cdot)$ such that for every pair of interactive Turing machines (P_1^*, P_2^*)*

$$\Pr[(x, z) \leftarrow P_1^*(1^\lambda) : x \notin L \wedge \langle P_2^*, V \rangle(1^\lambda, x) = 1] < \nu(\lambda).$$

In the above definition we can relax the soundness requirement by considering P^* as PPT. In this case, we say that (P, V) is an *interactive argument system* [7].

Definition 2 (zero-knowledge arguments [24]). *Let (P, V) be an interactive argument system for a language L. We say that (P, V) is zero knowledge (ZK) if, for any probabilistic polynomial-time adversary V^*, there exists a probabilistic polynomial-time algorithm S_{V^*} such for all auxiliary inputs z and all pairs $(x, w) \in R_L$ the ensembles $\{\mathtt{view}_{V^*(x,z)}^{P(w)}\}$ and $\{S_{V^*}(x, z)\}$ are computationally indistinguishable.*

Suppose (P, V) is used as a sub-protocol of another interactive protocol (A^1, A^2) where A^1 runs P and A^2 runs V. We call a Turing machine A_α^1 a *residual prover* if A_α^1 runs A^1 on inputs $\alpha = (\alpha_1, \dots, \alpha_\ell)$ from A^2 up to and including the ℓth round when A^1 invokes P. A *residual verifier* A_α^2 is defined similarly by switching A^1 and A^2. Note that the residual prover is invoked when simulating V (for soundness) while the residual verifier is invoked when simulating P (for zero-knowledge).

Definition 3 (resetting adversary [8]). *Let (P, V) be an interactive proof or argument system for a language L, $t = \mathtt{poly}(\lambda)$, $\bar{x} = x_1, \dots, x_t$ be a sequence of common inputs and $\bar{w} = w_1, \dots, w_t$ the corresponding witnesses (i.e., $(x_i, w_i) \in R_L$) for $i = 1, \dots, t$. Let $r_1, \dots, r_t$ be independent random tapes. We say that*

---

[3] This version of soundness given by [11] is slightly different from standard version with one Turing machine P^*. Separating them makes the proof cleaner while it is still equivalent to the standard version.

a PPT V^* is a resetting verifier if it concurrently interacts with an unbounded number of independent copies of P by choosing for each interaction the value i so that the common input will be $x_i \in \bar{x}$, and the prover will use witness w_i, and choosing j so that the prover will use r_j as randomness, with $i, j \in \{1, \ldots, t\}$. The scheduling or the messages to be sent in the different interactions with P are freely decided by V^*. Moreover we say that the transcript of such interactions consists of the common inputs $\bar{x}$ and the sequence of prover and verifier messages exchanged during the interactions. We refer to $\mathrm{view}_{V^*(\bar{x},z)}^{P(\bar{w})}$ as the random variable describing the content of the random tape of V^* and the transcript of the interactions between P and V^*, where z is an auxiliary input received by V^*.

Definition 4 (resettable zero knowledge [8]). *Let (P, V) be an interactive argument system for a language L. We say that (P, V) is resettable zero knowledge (rZK) if, for any PPT resetting verifier V^* there exists a expected probabilistic polynomial-time algorithm S_{V^*} such that the for all pairs $(\bar{x}, \bar{w}) \in R_L$ the ensembles $\{\mathrm{view}_{V^*(\bar{x},z)}^{P(\bar{w})}\}$ and $\{S_{V^*}(\bar{x}, z)\}$ are computationally indistinguishable.*

The definition of concurrent zero knowledge can be seen as a relaxation of the one of resettable zero knowledge. The adversarial concurrent verifier has the same power of the resetting verifier except it can not ask the prover to run multiple sessions with the same randomness.

Definition 5 (concurrent adversary). *Let (P, V) be an interactive proof or argument system for a language L, $t = \mathrm{poly}(\lambda)$, $\bar{x} = x_1, \ldots, x_t$ be a sequence of common inputs and $\bar{w} = w_1, \ldots, w_t$ the corresponding witnesses (i.e., $(x_i, w_i) \in R_L$) for $i = 1, \ldots, t$. We say that a PPT V^* is a concurrent verifier if it concurrently interacts with an unbounded number of independent copies of P by choosing for each interaction the value i so that the common input will be $x_i \in \bar{x}$, and the prover will use witness w_i. Each copy of P runs with independent randomness. The scheduling or the messages to be sent in the different interactions with P are freely decided by V^*. Moreover we say that the transcript of such interactions consist of the common inputs $\bar{x}$ and the sequence of prover and verifier messages exchanged during the interactions. We refer to $\mathrm{view}_{V^*(\bar{x},z)}^{P(\bar{w})}$ as the random variable describing the content of the random tape of V^* and the transcript of the interactions between P and V^*, where z is an auxiliary input received by V^*.*

Definition 6 (concurrent zero knowledge [19]). *Let (P, V) be an interactive argument system for a language L. We say that (P, V) is concurrent zero knowledge (cZK) if, for any PPT concurrent verifier V^* there exists a probabilistic polynomial-time algorithm S_{V^*} such that the for all pairs $(\bar{x}, \bar{w}) \in R_L$ the ensembles $\{\mathrm{view}_{V^*(\bar{x},z)}^{P(\bar{w})}\}$ and $\{S_{V^*}(\bar{x}, z)\}$ are computationally indistinguishable.*

Definition 7 (witness indistinguishability [20]). *Let L be a language in $\mathcal{NP}$ and R_L be the corresponding relation. An interactive argument (P, V) for L is* witness indistinguishable *(WI)* *if for every verifier* V^*, *every pair* (w_0, w_1) *such that* $(x, w_0) \in R_L$ *and* $(x, w_1) \in R_L$ *and every auxiliary input* z, *the following ensembles are computationally indistinguishable:*

$$\{\text{view}_{V^*(x,z)}^{P(w_0)}\} \quad and \quad \{\text{view}_{V^*(x,z)}^{P(w_1)}\}.$$

Definition 8 (resettable WI [8]**).** *Let* L *be a language in* $\mathcal{NP}$ *and* R_L *be the corresponding relation. An interactive argument* (P, V) *for* L *is resettable witness indistinguishable (rWI) if for every PPT resetting verifier* V^* *every* $t = \text{poly}(\lambda)$, *and every pair* $(\bar{w}^0 = (w_1^0, \ldots, w_t^0), \bar{w}^1 = (w_1^1, \ldots, w_t^1))$ *such that* $(x_i, w_i^0) \in R_L$ *and* $(x_i, w_i^1) \in R_L$ *for* $i = 1, \ldots, t$, *and any auxiliary input* z, *the following ensembles are computationally indistinguishable:*

$$\{\text{view}_{V^*(\bar{x},z)}^{P(\bar{w}^0)}\} \quad and \quad \{\text{view}_{V^*(\bar{x},z)}^{P(\bar{w}^1)}\}.$$

In [18], a construction of 2-round resettable witness-indistinguishable proof based on NIZK proofs has been shown, and then in [27], a non-interactive resettable witness-indistinguishable proof has been shown by relying on specific number-theoretic assumptions, and from $i\mathcal{O}$ [6].

Let us recall the definition of resettable soundness due to [3].

Definition 9 (resettably-sound arguments [3]**).** *A resetting attack of a cheating prover* P^* *on a resettable verifier* V *is defined by the following two-step random process, indexed by a security parameter* λ.

1. *Uniformly select and fix* $t = \text{poly}(\lambda)$ *random-tapes, denoted* $r_1, \ldots, r_t$, *for* V, *resulting in deterministic strategies* $V^{(j)}(x) = V_{x, r_j}$ *defined by* $V_{x, r_j}(\alpha) = V(x, r_j, \alpha)$,[4] *where* $x \in \{0, 1\}^\lambda$ *and* $j \in [t]$. *Each* $V^{(j)}(x)$ *is called an incarnation of* V.
2. *On input* 1^λ, *machine* P^* *is allowed to initiate* $\text{poly}(\lambda)$-*many interactions with the* $V^{(j)}(x)$'s. *The activity of* P^* *proceeds in rounds. In each round* P^* *chooses* $x \in \{0, 1\}^\lambda$ *and* $j \in [t]$, *thus defining* $V^{(j)}(x)$, *and conducts a complete session with it.*

Let (P, V) *be an interactive argument for a language* L. *We say that* (P, V) *is a* resettably-sound argument *for* L *if the following condition holds:*

– Resettable-soundness: *For every polynomial-size resetting attack, the probability that in some session the corresponding* $V^{(j)}(x)$ *has accepted and* $x \notin L$ *is negligible.*

Definition 10 (commitment scheme). *Given a security parameter* 1^λ, *a commitment scheme* com *is a two-phase protocol between two PPT interactive algorithms, a sender* S *and a receiver* R. *In the commitment phase* S *on input*

---

[4] Here, $V(x, r, \alpha)$ denotes the message sent by the strategy V on common input x, random-tape r, after seeing the message-sequence α.

a message m interacts with R to produce a commitment c = com(m). In the decommitment phase, S sends to R a decommitment information d such that R accepts m as the decommitment of c.

Formally, we say that com is a perfectly binding commitment scheme if the following properties hold:

Correctness:
- *Commitment phase. Let c = com(m) be the commitment of the message m given as output of an execution of com where S runs on input a message m. Let d be the private output of S in this phase.*
- *Decommitment phase[5]. R on input m and d accepts m as decommitment of c.*

Statistical (resp. Computational) Hiding [30]: *for any adversary (resp. PPT adversary) $\mathcal{A}$ and a randomly chosen bit $b \in \{0, 1\}$, consider the following hiding experiment $\mathsf{ExpHiding}^b_{\mathcal{A},\mathsf{com}}(\lambda)$:*
- *Upon input 1^λ, the adversary $\mathcal{A}$ outputs a pair of messages m_0, m_1 that are of the same length.*
- *S on input the message m_b interacts with $\mathcal{A}$ to produce a commitment of m_b.*
- *$\mathcal{A}$ outputs a bit b' and this is the output of the experiment.*

For any adversary (resp. PPT adversary) $\mathcal{A}$, there exist a negligible function ν, s.t.:

$$\left| \Pr[\mathsf{ExpHiding}^0_{\mathcal{A},\mathsf{com}}(\lambda) = 1] - \Pr[\mathsf{ExpHiding}^1_{\mathcal{A},\mathsf{com}}(\lambda) = 1] \right| < \nu(\lambda).$$

Statistical (resp. Computational) Binding: *for every commitment com generated during the commitment phase by a possibly malicious unbounded (resp. malicious PPT) sender S^* there exists a negligible function ν such that S^*, with probability at most $\nu(\lambda)$, outputs two decommitments (m_0, d_0) and (m_1, d_1), with $m_0 \neq m_1$, such that R accepts both decommitments.*
We also say that a commitment scheme is perfectly binding iff $\nu(\lambda) = 0$.

In this paper, we consider non-interactive perfectly binding computationally hiding commitment schemes, which can be constructed from one-to-one one-way functions [22]. Two-message statistically binding commitment schemes can be obtained from one-way functions [28,32].

Definition 11 (pseudorandom function (PRF)). *A family of functions $\{f_s\}_{s \in \{0,1\}^*}$ is called* pseudorandom *if for all adversarial PPT machines $\mathcal{A}$, for every positive polynomial $p()$, and sufficiently large $\lambda \in \mathbb{N}$, it holds that*

$$|\Pr[\mathcal{A}^{f_s}(1^\lambda) = 1] - \Pr[\mathcal{A}^F(1^\lambda) = 1]| \leq \frac{1}{p(\lambda)}.$$

where $|s| = n$ and F denotes a truly random function.

---

[5] In this paper we consider a non-interactive decommitment phase only.

Definition 12 (indistinguishability obfuscation). *A uniform machine iO is an* indistinguishability obfuscator *for a class of deterministic circuits $\{C_\lambda\}_{\lambda \in \mathbb{N}}$ if it satisfies the following:*

- *Correctness: For all security parameter $\lambda \in \mathbb{N}$, for all $C \in C_\lambda$, for all input x,*

$$\Pr[\Lambda \leftarrow iO(1^\lambda, C) : \Lambda(x) = C(x)] = 1.$$

- *Security: For every non-uniform PPT sampleable distribution $\mathcal{D}$ and adversary $\mathcal{A}$, there exists a negligible function ν such that for sufficiently large $\lambda \in \mathbb{N}$, if*

$$\Pr[(C_1, C_2, z) \leftarrow \mathcal{D} : \forall x, C_1(x) = C_2(x)] > 1 - \nu(\lambda),$$

then
$$\begin{aligned}&\Pr[(C_1, C_2, z) \leftarrow \mathcal{D} : \mathcal{A}(iO(1^\lambda, C_1), z) = 1] \\ &- \Pr[(C_1, C_2, z) \leftarrow \mathcal{D} : \mathcal{A}(iO(1^\lambda, C_2), z) = 1]\end{aligned} \leq \nu(\lambda).$$

We say an iO is super-polynomially secure *if there is a super-polynomial function T such that the above condition holds for all adversary $\mathcal{A}$ running in time at most $T(\lambda)$.*

Let $R_U = \{((M, x, t), w) : M$ accepts (x, w) in t steps$\}$, $S_U = \{(M, x, t) : \exists w, ((M, x, t), w) \in R_U\}$ and $R_U(M, x, t) = \{w : ((M, x, t), w) \in R_U\}$. Let $T_M(x, w)$ denote the number of steps made by M on input (x, w).

Definition 13 (universal argument [2]). *A pair of interactive Turing machines (P, V) is called a* universal argument system *if it satisfies the following properties:*

- *Efficient verification: There exists a polynomial p such that for any $y = (M, x, t)$, the total time spent by the (probabilistic) verifier V, on common input y, is at most $p(|y|)$. In particular, all messages exchanged in the protocol have length smaller than $p(|y|)$.*
- *Completeness via a relatively efficient prover: For every $((M, x, t), w) \in R_U$,*

$$\Pr[\langle P(w), V \rangle(M, x, t) = 1] = 1.$$

Furthermore, there exists a polynomial q such that for every $((M, x, t), w) \in R_U$, the total time spent by $P(w)$, on common input (M, x, t), is at most $q(|M| + T_M(x, w)) \leq q(|M| + t)$.
- *Computational soundness: For every polynomial-size circuit family $\{\widetilde{P}_n\}_{n \in \mathbb{N}}$, and every $(M, x, t) \in \{0, 1\}^n \setminus S_U$, there exists a negligible function ν such that*

$$\Pr[\langle \widetilde{P}_n, V \rangle(M, x, t) = 1] < \nu(n).$$

- *Weak proof-of-knowledge property: For every positive polynomial p there exists a positive polynomial p' and a probabilistic polynomial-time oracle machine E such that the following holds: for every polynomial-size circuit* family $\{\widetilde{P}_n\}_{n \in \mathbb{N}}$, and every sufficiently long $y = (M, x, t) \in \{0, 1\}^*$, if $\Pr[\langle \widetilde{P}_n, V \rangle(y) = 1] > 1/p(|y|)$, then

$$\Pr_r[\exists w = w_1 \ldots w_t \in R_U(y), \forall i \in [t], E_r^{\widetilde{P}_n}(y, i) = w_i] > 1/p'(|y|)$$

where $E_r^{\widetilde{P}_n}$ denotes the function defined by fixing the random-tape of E to r and providing it with oracle access to $\widetilde{P}_n$.

By abusing the notation, we let E be the oracle machine, running in time $\mathsf{poly}(n) \cdot t$, that extracts the whole witness. We call E a *global proof-of-knowledge extractor*. Note that E is not necessarily polynomial time.

Definition 14 (witness-indistinguishable universal argument [2]). *A universal argument system, (P, V), is called* witness-indistinguishable (WIUA) *if, for every polynomial p, every polynomial-size circuit family $\{V_n^*\}_{n \in \mathbb{N}}$, and every three sequences $\langle y_n = (M_n, x_n, t_n) \rangle_{n \in \mathbb{N}}$, $\langle w_n^1 \rangle_{n \in \mathbb{N}}$ and $\langle w_n^2 \rangle_{n \in \mathbb{N}}$ such that $|y_n| = n$, $t_n \leq p(|x_n|)$ and $(y_n, w_n^1), (y_n, w_n^2) \in R_U$, the probability ensembles $\{\langle P(w_n^1), V_n^* \rangle(y_n)\}_{n \in \mathbb{N}}$ and $\{\langle P(w_n^2), V_n^* \rangle(y_n)\}_{n \in \mathbb{N}}$ are computationally indistinguishable.*

Theorem 3 [2]. *Assuming the existence of families of collision-resistant hash functions, there exists a 4-round public-coin WIUA.*

Definition 15 (special-sound witness-indistinguishable proof [11]). *A 4-round public-coin interactive proof for the language $L \in \mathcal{NP}$ with witness relation R_L is* special-sound *with respect to R_L, if for any two transcripts $(\delta, \alpha, \beta, \gamma)$ and $(\delta', \alpha', \beta', \gamma')$ such that the initial two messages, (δ, α) and (δ', α'), are the same but the challenges β and β' are different, there is a deterministic procedure to extract the witness from the two transcripts and runs in polynomial time. Special-sound proofs with witness-indistinguishability (WISSP) for languages in $\mathcal{NP}$ can be based on one-way functions.*

Definition 16 (ZAP [25]). *ZAPs are two round public coin witness indistinguishable proofs introduced by Dwork and Naor [18]. ZAPs further have the special property that the first message (sent by the prover) can be reused for multiple proofs. As noted in [3], any ZAP system already has the property of resettable soundness. Furthermore, resettable witness indistinguishability property can be obtained by applying the transformation in [8]. We refer to the resulting system as an rZAP system having the property of resettable soundness as well as resettable witness indistinguishability.*

2.1 $\mathcal{P}$-Certificate with Delegatable CRS Generation

For $c \in \mathbb{N}$, let $L_c = \{(M, x, y) : M(x) = y \text{ within } |x|^c \text{ steps}\}$. Let $T_M(x)$ denote the number of steps made by M on input x.

Definition 17 ($\mathcal{P}$-certificate system [11]). *A tuple of PPT algorithms $(\mathsf{Gen}, \mathsf{P_{cert}}, \mathsf{V_{cert}})$ is a $\mathcal{P}$-certificate system in the CRS model if there exist polynomials l_{CRS} and l_π such that for $c, \lambda \in \mathbb{N}$ and $q = (M, x, y) \in L_c$.*

- *CRS Generation: $CRS \leftarrow \mathsf{Gen}(1^\lambda, c)$, where Gen runs in time $\mathtt{poly}(\lambda)$. The length of CRS is bounded by $l_{CRS}(\lambda)$.*
- *Proof Generation: $\pi \leftarrow \mathsf{P_{cert}}(1^\lambda, c, CRS, q)$, where $\mathsf{P_{cert}}$ runs in time $\mathtt{poly}(\lambda, |x|, T_M(x))$ with $T_M(x) \leq |x|^c$. The length of π is bounded by $l_\pi(\lambda)$.*
- *Proof Verification: $b = \mathsf{V_{cert}}(1^\lambda, c, CRS, q, \pi)$, where $\mathsf{V_{cert}}$ runs in time $\mathtt{poly}(\lambda, |q|)$.*

Completeness: For every $c, d, \lambda \in \mathbb{N}$ and $q = (M, x, y) \in L_c$ such that $|q| \leq \lambda^d$,

$$\Pr[CRS \leftarrow \mathsf{Gen}(1^\lambda, c), \pi \leftarrow \mathsf{P_{cert}}(1^\lambda, c, CRS, q) : \mathsf{V_{cert}}(1^\lambda, c, CRS, q, \pi) = 1] = 1.$$

Strong soundness: There exists a super-polynomial function $T(\lambda) = \lambda^{\omega(1)}$ and a super-constant function $C(\lambda) = \omega(1)$ such that for every probabilistic algorithm P^* with running time bounded by $T(\lambda)$, there exists a negligible function ν such that for every $\lambda \in \mathbb{N}$ and $c \leq C(\lambda)$,

$$\Pr \begin{bmatrix} (q, st) \leftarrow P^*(1^\lambda, c), \\ CRS \leftarrow \mathsf{Gen}(1^\lambda, c), & : \mathsf{V_{cert}}(1^\lambda, c, CRS, q, \pi) = 1 \wedge q \notin L_c \\ \pi \leftarrow P^*(st, CRS) \end{bmatrix} \leq \nu(\lambda).$$

A $\mathcal{P}$-certificate system is two-message *if the generation of the CRS Gen also depends on the statement q, i.e. $CRS \leftarrow \mathsf{Gen}(1^\lambda, c, q)$. The two-message $\mathcal{P}$-certificate system can be considered an interactive protocol as follows: the prover sends q to the verifier; the verifier replies with $CRS \leftarrow \mathsf{Gen}(1^\lambda, c, q)$; the prover sends $\pi \leftarrow \mathsf{P_{cert}}(1^\lambda, c, CRS, q)$; the verifier accepts if $\mathsf{V_{cert}}(1^\lambda, c, CRS, q, \pi) = 1$.*

A two-message $\mathcal{P}$-certificate system has a simple verification *procedure if the verification algorithm $\mathsf{V_{cert}}$ only depends on the security parameter 1^λ, the CRS and the proof π, i.e. it is independent of the statement q and the language index c. In this case, we denote the verification by $\mathsf{V_{cert}}(1^\lambda, CRS, \pi)$.*

A $\mathcal{P}$-certificate system is unique *if for every $\lambda, c \in \mathbb{N}$, $CRS, q \in \{0,1\}^*$, there exists at most one $\pi \in \{0,1\}^*$ such that $\mathsf{V_{cert}}(1^\lambda, c, CRS, q, \pi) = 1$.*

Note that the uniqueness of a $\mathcal{P}$-certificate holds even against invalid CRS.

Definition 18 (delegatable CRS generation [11]). *A two-message $\mathcal{P}$-certificate $(\mathsf{Gen}, \mathsf{P_{cert}}, \mathsf{V_{cert}})$ has* delegatable CRS generation *if Gen consists of three subroutines: SetUp, PreGen and CRSGen, and there exist polynomials l_d and l_{CRS} satisfying the following properties:*

- *Parameters Generation: $(PP, K) \leftarrow \mathsf{SetUp}(1^\lambda, c)$, where SetUp is probabilistic and runs in time $\mathtt{poly}(\lambda)$. PP is a public parameter and K is a secret parameter.*
- *Statement Processing: $d = \mathsf{PreGen}(PP, q)$, where PreGen is deterministic and runs in time $\mathtt{poly}(\lambda, |q|)$ and the length of d is bounded by $l_d(\lambda)$ independent of $|q|$.*
- *CRS Generation: $\kappa \leftarrow \mathsf{CRSGen}(PP, K, d)$, where CRSGen is probabilistic and runs in time $\mathtt{poly}(\lambda)$ and the length of κ is bounded by $l_{CRS}(\lambda)$.*

Gen *outputs $CRS = (PP, \kappa)$.*

Theorem 4 [11]. *Assuming the existence of an indistinguishability obfuscation for $\mathcal{P}/poly$ and an injective one-way function (that are super-polynomially secure), there exists a (super-polynomially secure) two-message $\mathcal{P}$-certificate system with (strong) soundness, uniqueness and delegatable CRS generation.*

3   Constant-Round Resettable Zero Knowledge

In [11], Chung et al. construct a constant-round concurrent ZK argument assuming the existence of families of collision-resistant hash functions, one-way permutations, and indistinguishability obfuscators for $\mathcal{P}/\text{poly}$ (with slightly super-polynomial security). We present it here as follows:

Let com be a non-interactive perfectly binding computationally hiding commitment scheme. As mentioned in [11], the protocol can be modified to work with a 2-message statistically binding commitment scheme based on one-way functions [28,32]. Let $\{\mathcal{H}_n\}_{n\in\mathbb{N}}$ be a family of collision-resistant hash functions. Let (Gen, $\mathsf{P_{cert}}$, $\mathsf{V_{cert}}$) be a two-message $\mathcal{P}$-certificate system with strong soundness, uniqueness and delegatable CRS generation where Gen consists of subroutines (SetUp, PreGen, CRSGen). Let $D = D(n)$ be a super-constant function such that $D(n) \leq C(n)$ for $C(\cdot)$ in Definition 17. Let (P_{UA}, V_{UA}) be a constant-round public-coin WIUA. Let (P_{SS}, V_{SS}) be a constant-round public-coin WISSP. Let (P_{ZK}, V_{ZK}) be a constant-round ZK argument.

Let $\Pi_{n,c_3,PP,K,\rho_{\mathsf{CRSGen}}}$ and $\Pi'_{n,c_3,\kappa}$ be programs defined as follows:

$\Pi_{n,c_3,PP,K,\rho_{\mathsf{CRSGen}}}$: on input (d,ρ)

1. If $c_3 \neq \mathsf{com}(d;\rho)$, output $\bot$.
2. Output $\mathsf{CRSGen}(PP,K,d;\rho_{\mathsf{CRSGen}})$.

$\Pi'_{n,c_3,\kappa}$: on input (d,ρ)

1. If $c_3 \neq \mathsf{com}(d;\rho)$, output $\bot$.
2. Output κ.

Let $\mathcal{O}^n_{\mathsf{V_{cert}}}$ be a (deterministic) $\mathcal{P}$-certificate oracle which, on input CRS, outputs a (unique) π such that $\mathsf{V_{cert}}(1^n, CRS, \pi) = 1$.

Let Emu_n be a deterministic polynomial-time machine which, on input (S, y, σ), emulates the execution of the deterministic oracle machine S on input y with access to the oracle $\mathcal{O}^n_{\mathsf{V_{cert}}}$. Emu_n simulates $\mathcal{O}^n_{\mathsf{V_{cert}}}$ by, on input CRS_i in the ith call from S, checking if π_i in $\sigma = (\pi_1, \pi_2, \ldots)$ satisfies $\mathsf{V_{cert}}(1^n, CRS_i, \pi) = 1$. If so, it returns π_i to S, and halts otherwise.

Constant-Round Concurrent Zero-Knowledge Argument Γ [11]

The prover P and the verifier V on common input 1^n and x, and private input w for P:

1. V sends $h \leftarrow \mathcal{H}_n$ to P.
2. P sends $c_1 = \text{com}(0; \rho_1)$ to V.
3. V sends $r \leftarrow \{0, 1\}^{4n}$ to P.
4. P sends $c_2 = \text{com}(0; \rho_2)$ to V.
5. P and V run (P_{UA}, V_{UA}) for the following statement: either $x \in L$ or there exists $S, j \in [m], s \in \{0, 1\}^n, \sigma, \rho_1, \rho_2$ such that
   - $c_1 = \text{com}(h(S); \rho_1)$ and
   - $c_2 = \text{com}(h(q); \rho_2)$ where $q = (\text{Emu}_n, (S, (1^n, j, s), \sigma), r)$.

   V rejects if V_{UA} rejects.
6. V runs $(PP, K) \leftarrow \text{SetUp}(1^n, D)$ and sends PP to P.
7. P sends $c_3 = \text{com}(0; \rho_3)$ to V.
8. P and V run (P_{UA}, V_{UA}) so that P proves to V that either $x \in L$ or there exists q, ρ_2, ρ_3 such that $c_2 = \text{com}(h(q); \rho_2)$ and $c_3 = \text{com}(d; \rho_3)$ where $d = \text{PreGen}(PP, q)$. V rejects if V_{UA} rejects.
9. V computes $\widehat{\Pi} \leftarrow i\mathcal{O}(\Pi_{n, c_3, PP, K, \rho_{\text{CRSGen}}})$ and sends $\widehat{\Pi}$ to P.
10. V and P run (P_{ZK}, V_{ZK}) so that V proves to P that there exist K, $\rho_{\text{SetUp}}, \rho_{\text{CRSGen}}, \rho_{i\mathcal{O}}$ such that
    - $(PP, K) = \text{SetUp}(1^n, D; \rho_{\text{SetUp}})$ and
    - $\widehat{\Pi} = i\mathcal{O}(\Pi_{n, c_3, PP, K, \rho_{\text{CRSGen}}}; \rho_{i\mathcal{O}})$.

    P aborts if V_{ZK} rejects.
11. P sends $c_4 = com(0; \rho_4)$ to V.
12. P and V run (P_{SS}, V_{SS}) so that P proves to V that either $x \in L$ or there exists d, ρ_3, ρ_4 such that $c_3 = com(d; \rho_3)$ and $c_4 = \text{com}(CRS; \rho_4)$ where $CRS = (PP, \widehat{\Pi}(d, \rho_3))$. V rejects if V_{SS} rejects.
13. P and V run (P_{SS}, V_{SS}) so that P proves to V that either $x \in L$ or there exists CRS, ρ_4 and P-certificate π such that $c_4 = \text{com}(CRS; \rho_4)$ and $V_{\text{cert}}(CRS, \pi) = accept$. V accepts if V_{SS} accepts. Otherwise, V rejects.

Theorem 5 [11]. *Assuming the existence of families of collision-resistant hash functions, one-way permutations, and indistinguishability obfuscators for P/poly that are super-polynomially secure, there exists a constant-round concurrent zero-knowledge argument for $\mathcal{NP}$.*

3.1 From Concurrent ZK to Resettable ZK

Let $\Gamma = (P_\Gamma, V_\Gamma)$ be an ℓ-round concurrent ZK argument. We construct a $\mathcal{O}(\ell)$-round resettable ZK argument Λ as follows:

Let com be a non-interactive perfectly binding computationally hiding commitment scheme. Let (P_{rsZK}, V_{rsZK}) be a constant-round resettably-sound ZK argument with the simulator Sim_{rsZK}.

Constant-Round Resettable Zero-Knowledge Argument Λ

The prover P and the verifier V on common input 1^n and x, and private input w for P:

1. V sending $m_0 = (\mathsf{com}(r_1), \ldots, \mathsf{com}(r_\ell))$ to P.
2. P chooses a random seed s for a pseudorandom function $f_s : \{0,1\}^* \to \{0,1\}^{l(n)}$ where $l(n)$ is the upper bound on the size of random bits P_Γ needs in each round of Γ.
3. P and V run Γ with the following modifications:
   - For each message m_i that V_Γ sends in the ith round of Γ, V and P run (P_{rsZK}, V_{rsZK}) so that V proves to P that m_i is computed using random bits r_i committed in m_0 in the first round.
   - For each message m_i' that P_Γ sends in the ith round of Γ, P applies f_s to the transcript so far and uses the output as random bits to compute m_i'.

3.2 Proofs

Lemma 1. Λ *is a resettable ZK argument system.*

Proof. First, we consider the protocol Λ_F where we replace a pseudorandom function f_s by a truly random function $F : \{0,1\}^* \to \{0,1\}^{l(n)}$. We argue that Λ_F is indistinguishable from Λ by the reduction to the security of pseudorandom function as follows. We construct an adversary $\mathcal{A}_{PRF}$ having access to an oracle computing either f_s or F such that $\mathcal{A}_{PRF}$ runs Λ (or Λ_F) with the following modification: for each message m_i' sent by an honest P, $\mathcal{A}_{PRF}$ asks the oracle using the transcript of the protocol up to that point as input; it then uses the oracle output as the random bits to compute m_i'. Finally, $\mathcal{A}_{PRF}$ runs and outputs the output of the distinguisher on the view of the protocol. Since $\mathcal{A}_{PRF}$ runs the honest P from the beginning to the end, it has access to private parameters of P, and thus is able to finish the protocol. Thus, any non-uniform polynomial-size verifiers must behave in the same way except with negligible probability.

Let V_{RES}^* be a resetting verifier in Λ_F. We construct a concurrent verifier V_{CONC}^* such that for any P_{CONC} there exists P_{RES} such that $\{\mathsf{view}_{V_{RES}^*}^{P_{RES}}\}$ and $\{\mathsf{view}_{V_{CONC}^*}^{P_{CONC}}\}$ are computationally indistinguishable as follows: V_{CONC}^* runs V_{RES}^* internally and delivers messages between V_{RES}^* and P_{CONC} while recording the first message (commitments) of V_{RES}^* and every message of P_{CONC}.

Whenever V_{RES}^* resets P_{RES} and sends the first message, V_{CONC}^* checks if it has been sent before. If so, V_{CONC}^* resends the appropriate responses or continues the session if necessary. Otherwise, V_{CONC}^* starts a new session of P_{CONC}. The randomness used in this new session is indistinguishable from the randomness P_{RES} used by applying F to the new transcript (as m_0 is different).

Claim. For a fixed seed s and m_0, for each $i \in [\ell]$, V_r^* cannot find two different messages m_i, m_i' in the ith round such that it can make P_{RES} accepting the ith resettably-sound ZK argument except with negligible probability.

Proof. Let the first round message $m_0 = (c_1, \ldots, c_\ell)$. Assume for contradiction that there exists $i \in [\ell]$ such that V_r^* can find $m_i \neq m_i'$ and the corresponding resettably-sound ZK argument that P_{RES} accepts with non-negligible probability. In such case, by the resettable soundness of the ZK argument, m_i and m_i' are both computed correctly with respect to the protocol Λ_F using the randomness committed in c_i. In other words, there exists a deterministic polynomial-time function μ_i such that m_i and m_i' have the form $m_i = \mu_i(r_i)$ with $c_i = \text{com}(r_i)$ and $m_i' = \mu_i(r_i')$ with $c_i = \text{com}(r_i')$, for some $r_i \neq r_i'$. However, this implies $\text{com}(r_i) = \text{com}(r_i')$, which contradicts the perfectly binding of com.   □

Thus, the transcript of the whole session depends only on s and m_0. Therefore, $\{\text{view}_{V_{RES}^*}^{P_{RES}}\}$ and $\{\text{view}_{V_{CONC}^*}^{P_{CONC}}\}$ are computationally indistinguishable.   □

Lemma 2. Λ *is sound.*

Proof. Suppose there exists a cheating prover P_{RES}^* that can prove a false theorem $x \notin L$ with non-negligible probability. Consider the following hybrid experiments:

Exp_0: Run $\langle P_{RES}^*, V_{RES} \rangle (1^n, x)$.

Let $\text{Exp}_{1,0}$ be the same as Exp_0, and for $i = 1, \ldots, \ell$,

$\text{Exp}_{1,i}$: Similar to $\text{Exp}_{1,i-1}$ except that the execution of $P_{rsZK}(r_i)$ following the message m_i is replaced by the execution of $\text{Sim}_{rsZK}^{P_{RES,i}^*}$ where $P_{RES,i}^*$ is the residual rsZK verifier (note that P_{RES}^* runs V_{rsZK}) who has received $m_0, \ldots, m_i$ as inputs. Assume for contradiction that there exists a distinguisher D for $\text{Exp}_{1,i}$ and $\text{Exp}_{1,i-1}$. We construct a distinguisher D' for the (standard) zero-knowledge property of (P_{rsZK}, V_{rsZK}) as follows. First, we generate $r_1, \ldots, r_{i-1}, r_{i+1}, \ldots, r_\ell$ uniformly and let $\tilde{c}_i = \text{com}(0)$. Then we produce the transcript for P_{RES}^* as in Λ except that we use $\tilde{c}_i$ instead of $c_i = \text{com}(r_i)$. By the computational hiding of com, P_{RES}^* cannot distinguish $\tilde{c}_i$ from c_i. Given either $\{\text{view}_{V_{rsZK}}^{P_{rsZK}}\}$ where V_{rsZK} is run by $P_{RES,i}^*$ or $\text{Sim}_{rsZK}^{P_{RES,i}^*}$, we generate the rest of the transcript for protocol Λ using r_j generated earlier. Finally, D' runs D on the entire transcript. In either case, the transcript is computationally indistinguishable to either $\text{Exp}_{1,i}$ or $\text{Exp}_{1,i-1}$. Thus, D' can break the zero-knowledge property of (P_{rsZK}, V_{rsZK}), which is a contradiction. Hence, $\text{Exp}_{1,i}$ and $\text{Exp}_{1,i-1}$ are indistinguishable.

Let $\text{Exp}_{2,0}$ be the same as $\text{Exp}_{1,\ell}$, and for $i = 1, \ldots, \ell$,

$\text{Exp}_{2,i}$: Similar to $\text{Exp}_{2,i-1}$ except that $\mathsf{com}(r_i)$ in the first message m_0 is replaced by $\mathsf{com}(0)$. Consider the following reduction to the computational hiding property of com: $\mathcal{A}_{\mathsf{com}}$ sends r_i and 0 to S_{com}; it passes the commitment from S_{com} as the ith commitment in m_0 of $\text{Exp}_{2,i-1}$ (or $\text{Exp}_{2,i}$); $\mathcal{A}_{\mathsf{com}}$ can complete the experiment as it does not need to know which message it commits using Sim_{rsZK}; $\mathcal{A}_{\mathsf{com}}$ outputs the output of the experiment. The computational hiding property implies that $\text{Exp}_{2,i}$ and $\text{Exp}_{2,i-1}$ are indistinguishable.

Now we construct a cheating prover P^*_{CONC} for Γ by running $\text{Exp}_{2,\ell}$ internally as follows: P^*_{CONC} sends $\mathsf{com}(0)$ to P^*_{RES}; P^*_c passes every messages from P^*_{RES} to V_{CONC}; P^*_{CONC} passes every message from V_{CONC} to P^*_{RES} then runs Sim_{rsZK} while P^*_{RES} runs V_{rsZK}. Thus, P^*_{CONC} can prove a false theorem $x \notin L$ with non-negligible probability, which contradicts the soundness of Γ. $\square$

Theorem 6. *Assuming one-way functions, there exists a compiler transforming an ℓ-round concurrent zero-knowledge argument to a $\mathcal{O}(\ell)$-round resettable zero-knowledge argument.*

Proof. The resettable zero knowledge and soundness are proved in Lemmas 1 and 2, respectively. The completeness follows from the completeness of Γ by inspection. For each round of Γ, P and V has to run additional $\mathcal{O}(1)$ rounds for resettably-sound ZK protocol that V uses the committed random bits, and 1 extra round in the beginning. Thus, the round complexity is $\mathcal{O}(\ell)$. $\square$

Corollary 1. *Assuming the existence of families of collision-resistant hash functions, one-way permutations, and indistinguishability obfuscators for $\mathcal{P}/\mathsf{poly}$ that are super-polynomially secure, there exists a constant-round resettable zero-knowledge argument for $\mathcal{NP}$.*

Proof. We instantiate Λ by letting Γ be the constant-round concurrent zero-knowledge argument system of [11]. Perfectly binding com can be constructed from one-way permutations. A constant-round resettably-sound ZK argument can be constructed from one-way functions [12]. $\square$

4   Concurrent ZK with Resettable Soundness

In this section, we construct a constant-round resettably-sound concurrent ZK argument based on the constant-round cZK argument in [11]. We make use of our constant-round rZK argument from the previous section (Corollary 1), the technique used in [3] to add resettable soundness to a public-coin protocol, and our new techniques to deal with non-public coin nature of the cZK protocol in [11].

4.1   Construction

Let Γ be the constant-round concurrent ZK argument from [11] described in Sect. 3. We construct a constant-round concurrent ZK argument with resettable soundness Δ as follows:

Let (P_{rZK}, V_{rZK}) be a constant-round resettable ZK argument with the simulator Sim_{rZK}. The verifier V chooses a random seed s for a pseudorandom function $f_s : \{0,1\}^* \to \{0,1\}^{l(n)}$, where $l(n)$ is the upper bound on the size of random bits V need in each round of Γ. Then P and V run Γ with the following modifications. In Step 10, instead of running a ZK argument (P_{ZK}, V_{ZK}), V and P run the resettable ZK argument (P_{rZK}, V_{rZK}). Additionally, for each message m that V sends in Γ, V uses the output of f_s applying to the transcript from the protocol up to this point as random bits to compute m.

4.2   Proofs

Before we prove that the protocol above is a concurrent ZK argument with resettable soundness, we consider another modification, Γ', of the protocol Γ in [11]. First, P and V repeat Steps 7–9 for t times with V using the same ρ_{CRSGen} for some $t = \mathtt{poly}(n)$. Let Steps $7j$–$9j$ denoted jth repeat of Steps 7–9. Secondly, we remove the zero-knowledge proof in Step 10, and replace it with "P chooses $i \in [t]$ and sends i to V", and then P and V follows the rest of the protocol ignoring Steps $7j$–$9j$ for $j \neq i$.

Lemma 3. Γ' *is a sound interactive argument.*

Proof. We strictly follow the proof of soundness of Γ in [11] with a modification necessary for the repetition of Steps 7–9. Assume for contradiction that there is a non-uniform deterministic polynomial-time prover P^* and a positive polynomial p such that for infinitely many $n \in \mathbb{N}$, P^* can convince V to accept $x \notin L$ with non-negligible probability $1/p(n)$. Let E be the global proof-of-knowledge extractor of the WIUA (P_{UA}, V_{UA}), and E' be the knowledge extractor of the WISSP (P_{SS}, V_{SS}). We define the experiment Exp which runs $\langle P^*, V \rangle (1^n, x)$ with the following addition:

- In Step 5, let $P^*_{\mathsf{prefix}_1}$ be the residual WIUA prover who has received $\mathsf{prefix}_1 = (h, r)$ in Steps 1 and 3. Run $w_1 \leftarrow E_{s_1}^{P^*_{\mathsf{prefix}_1}}$, where s_1 is uniform randomness. If E fails, halt and output $\bot$.
- In Step 7j, for $j = 1, \ldots, t$, let $P^*_{\mathsf{prefix}_{2,j}}$ be the residual WIUA prover who has received $\mathsf{prefix}_{2,j}$ consisting of h, r, WIUA messages, PP and $\widehat{\Pi}_k$ in Steps 1, 3, 5, $8k$ and $9k$ for $k = 1, \ldots, j-1$. Run $w_{2,j} \leftarrow E_{s_{2,j}}^{P^*_{\mathsf{prefix}_{2,j}}}$, where $s_{2,j}$ is uniform randomness. If E fails, halt and output $\bot$.
- In Step 12, let $P^*_{\mathsf{prefix}_3}$ be the residual WISSP prover who has received prefix_3 consisting of h, r, WIUA messages, PP and $\widehat{\Pi}_j$ in Steps 1, 3, 5, 6, $8j$ and $9j$ for $j = 1, \ldots, t$. Run $w_3 \leftarrow E'^{P^*_{\mathsf{prefix}_3}}_{s_3}$, where s_3 is uniform randomness. If E' fails, halt and output $\bot$.
- In Step 13, let $P^*_{\mathsf{prefix}_4}$ be the residual WISSP prover who has received prefix_4 consisting of prefix_3 and WISSP messages in Step 12. Run $w_4 \leftarrow E'^{P^*_{\mathsf{prefix}_4}}_{s_4}$, where s_4 is uniform randomness. If E' fails, halt and output $\bot$.

  – If V rejects, output $\bot$. Otherwise,
- Parse $w_1 = (S, j, s, \sigma, \rho_1, \rho_2)$. If w_1 does not have this form, output $\bot$.
- Let $q = (\mathsf{Emu}_n, (S, (1^n, j, s), \sigma), r)$. For $j = 1, \ldots, t$, if $w_{2,j} \neq (q, \rho_{2,j}, \rho_{3,j})$ for some $\rho_{2,j}, \rho_{3,j}$, output $\bot$.
- Let $d = \mathsf{PreGen}(PP, q)$. If $w_3 \neq (d, \rho_{3,i}, \rho_4)$ for some ρ_4 where $i \in [t]$ is chosen by P^* in Step 10, output $\bot$.
- Let $CRS = (PP, \widehat{\Pi}(d, \rho_{3,i}))$. If $w_4 \neq (CRS, \rho_4, \pi)$ for some π, output $\bot$.

  – output (S, q, r).

By the weak proof-of-knowledge property of WIUA and special soundness of WISSP, when P^* convinces V to accept $x \notin L$, the extractors E and E' succeed in extracting the witnesses described above (instead of the actual witness of the theorem) with non-negligible probability $1/p'(n)$. By perfectly binding property of com and collision-resistance of $\mathcal{H}$, the consistency check in the last step will pass except with negligible probability $\nu(n)$. In this case, except with negligible probability, $c_{3,j}$ sent in Step $7j$ is $\mathsf{com}(d; \rho_{3,j})$ for the same $d = \mathsf{PreGen}(PP, q)$ for all $j = 1, \ldots, t$. Otherwise, we can construct a cheating WIUA prover that commits to $c' = \mathsf{com}(d'; \rho')$ with $d' \neq \mathsf{PreGen}(PP, q)$ with non-negligible probability by randomly pick $j \in [t]$ and commit to $c' = c_{3,j}$. This breaks the soundness of WIUA. So, the only output of $\widehat{\Pi}_j$ is $\mathsf{CRSGen}(PP, K, d, \rho_{\mathsf{CRSGen}}) = \kappa$ for all $j = 1, \ldots, m$ except with negligible probability $\nu'(n)$. Thus, the probability that Exp does not output $\bot$ and every $\widehat{\Pi}_j$ output the same κ is $1/p'(n) - \nu(n) - \nu'(n)$ which is non-negligible. We call this event Good.

Now consider a series of experiments Exp'_j for $j \in [t]$ defined as follows: $\mathsf{Exp}'_0 = \mathsf{Exp}$, and Exp'_j differs from Exp'_{j-1} in Step $9j$ where we replace $\widehat{\Pi}_j \leftarrow i\mathcal{O}(\Pi_{n, c_{3,j}, PP, K, \rho_{\mathsf{CRSGen}}})$ with $\widehat{\Pi}'_j \leftarrow i\mathcal{O}(\Pi'_{n, c_{3,j}, \kappa})$ where $\kappa = \mathsf{CRSGen}(PP, K, d; \rho_{\mathsf{CRSGen}})$. When Good occurs, by perfectly binding property of com, $\Pi'_{n, c_{3,j}, \kappa}$ and $\Pi_{n, c_{3,j}, PP, K, \rho_{\mathsf{CRSGen}}}$ are functionally equivalent except with negligible probability. In this case, Exp'_{j-1} and Exp'_j are indistinguishable by the reduction to $i\mathcal{O}$ as follows: $\mathcal{D}_{i\mathcal{O}}$ runs Exp'_{j-1} (or Exp'_j) up to Step $8j$ and outputs $\Pi'_{n, c_{3,j}, \kappa}$ and $\Pi_{n, c_{3,j}, PP, K, \rho_{\mathsf{CRSGen}}}$ and the state of the experiment z; up to receiving obfuscated program $\widehat{\Pi}$ and z, $\mathcal{A}_{i\mathcal{O}}$ sends $\widehat{\Pi}$ to P^*, continues the experiment until the end, and outputs the output of the experiment. Thus, Exp'_{j-1} and Exp'_j are indistinguishable by the security of $i\mathcal{O}$. Hence, by hybrid argument, the probability of Good event is non-negligible in Exp'_j for $j = 1, \ldots, t$. Let $\mathsf{Exp}' = \mathsf{Exp}'_t$.

Now suppose that Good and q is false occurs with non-negligible probability. Then we construct $P^*_{\mathcal{P}\mathsf{cert}}$ that breaks the strong soundness of the $\mathcal{P}$-certificate system as follows: $P^*_{\mathcal{P}\mathsf{cert}}$ runs Exp' up to Step 5 where it extracts q from w_1. Up on receiving $CRS = (PP, \kappa)$ where $(PP, K) \leftarrow \mathsf{SetUp}(1^n, D)$ and $\kappa \leftarrow \mathsf{CRSGen}(PP, K, \mathsf{PreGen}(PP, q))$, it continues Exp' using PP and κ and output π extracted from w_4. If Good occurs, by the soundness of WISSP, $P^*_{\mathcal{P}\mathsf{cert}}$ succeeds and $\mathsf{V}_{\mathsf{cert}}(CRS, \pi) = 1$ except with negligible probability. Thus, $P^*_{\mathcal{P}\mathsf{cert}}$ contradicts the strong soundness of the $\mathcal{P}$-certificate system. Hence, Good and q is true occurs with non-negligible probability. We call this event Good$'$. By averaging argument, there exists h such that Good$'|h$ occurs with non-negligible probability.

Finally, consider Exp'' where Exp' is run twice with this h but with the second execution replacing r in Step 3 by an independent random string r'. With non-negligible probability, both executions succeed and output (S, q, r) and (S', q', r'). Since c_1 must be the same in both executions, $S = S'$ except with negligible probability by perfectly binding property of com and collision-resistance of $\mathcal{H}$. Since $q = (\mathsf{Emu}_n, (S, (1^n, j, s), \sigma), r)$ and $q' = (\mathsf{Emu}_n, (S, (1^n, j', s'), \sigma'), r')$ are true, we have $S^{\mathcal{O}^n_{\mathsf{Vcert}}}(1^n, j, s) = r$ and $S^{\mathcal{O}^n_{\mathsf{Vcert}}}(1^n, j', s') = r'$. We have that $|(1^n, j, s)| < 3n < 4n = |r|$ and $|(1^n, j', s')| < |r'|$. However, the deterministic machine $S^{\mathcal{O}^n_{\mathsf{Vcert}}}$ predicts independent r and r' with non-negligible probability. This is information theoretically impossible as there are at most 2^{3n} possible outputs for $S^{\mathcal{O}^n_{\mathsf{Vcert}}}$. Thus, we reach a contradiction.

As in the proof of soundness of Γ in [11], the WIUA global proof-of-knowledge extractor E runs in super-polynomial time as a part of the witness q is of super-polynomial size. Thus, the collision-resistant hash functions $\mathcal{H}$, the commitment scheme com and indistinguishability obfuscators $i\mathcal{O}$ need to be super-polynomially secure.   □

Now we can prove the main theorem of this section.

Theorem 7. Δ is a concurrent ZK argument with resettable soundness.

Proof. Since the rZK argument (P_{rZK}, V_{rZK}) is also a ZK argument and we only further modify an honest verifier V, the concurrent zero-knowledge of Δ follows directly from the concurrent zero-knowledge property of Γ. Now we consider the protocol Δ_F where we replace a pseudorandom function f_s by a truly random function $F : \{0,1\}^* \to \{0,1\}^{l(n)}$. We argue that Δ_F is indistinguishable from Δ by the reduction to the security of pseudorandom function as follows. Fix $x \notin L$ and P^*_{RES} that convinces a resettable verifier V_{RES} to accept $x \notin L$ with probability ϵ through protocol Δ_F. We construct an adversary $\mathcal{A}_{PRF}$ having access to an oracle computing either f_s or F such that $\mathcal{A}_{PRF}$ runs Δ (or Δ_F) with the following modification: for each message m sent by an honest V_{RES}, $\mathcal{A}_{PRF}$ asks the oracle using the transcript of the protocol up to that point as input; it then uses the oracle output as the random bits to compute m. $\mathcal{A}_{PRF}$ outputs the output of V. Since $\mathcal{A}_{PRF}$ runs the honest V_{RES} from the beginning to the end, it has access to private parameter K that V generates in Step 6, and thus is able to compute the obfuscated program and rZK messages in Steps 9 and 10. Thus, any non-uniform polynomial-size provers must behave in the same way except with negligible probability. Hence, the completeness follows from the completeness of Γ.

We now show the resettable soundness of the protocol. Assume for contradiction that there is a non-uniform polynomial-time resetting prover P^*_{RES} that convinces a resettable verifier V_{RES} to accept $x \notin L$ with probability ϵ through protocol Δ_F. We construct a polynomial-time (standard) prover P^*_S, emulating P^*_{RES}, that convinces a (standard) verifier V_S to accept the same $x \notin L$ through protocol Γ' repeating Steps 7–9 for t times, where $t = \mathsf{poly}(n)$ is the total number of messages sent by P^*_{RES}. Let c be the number of (prover) rounds in Δ.

The cheating prover P_S^* proceeds as follows. First it uniformly selects $i_1, \ldots, i_c \in \{1, \ldots, t\}$. It invokes P_{RES}^* while emulating V_{RES}. In the jth round of Δ_F, P_S^* answers a message from P_{RES}^* according to the following cases:

- If the prefix of the current session transcript is identical to a corresponding prefix of a previous session, then P_{CONC}^* answers by using the same answer it has given in the previous session.
- Otherwise, P_S^* either forwards the message to V_S and then forwards the reply it receives, or generates the reply itself according to the following conditions:
  - If the message is c_3 or WIUA in Steps $7j$–$8j$, P_S^* repeats its decision whether to forward the message in Step 6. In other words, if P_S^* forwards the message in Step 6, it will forward this message. If it generates the reply in Step 6 itself, it will generate the reply for this message as well. This is because it can only generate an answer in Step $9i$ if it has generated the answer in Step 6 of the same transcript (instead of passing to V_S).
  - If the message is $i \in [t]$ in Step 10, P_S^* does not forward the message, but instead runs the simulator Sim_{rZK} with P_{RES}^* corresponding to obfuscated program in Step $9i$.
  - If the index of the current message from P_{RES}^* does not equal to i_j selected previously, P_S^* generates a reply message using a uniformly selected random bits.
  - Otherwise, P_S^* forwards the current message to V_S and sends P_{RES}^* a reply it receives from V_S.
  In each case, P_{CONC}^* records the messages from both sides for later use.

By the resettable zero-knowledge of (P_{rZK}, V_{rZK}), the probability of P_{RES}^* proving a false theorem $x \notin L$ only changes negligibly by running Sim_{rZK} instead of P_{rZK}. By the property of truly random function, the view of P_{RES}^* is identical to the distribution that P_{RES}^* sees when interacting with an honest V_{RES}. If the chosen $i_1, \ldots, i_c$ equal the indices of the messages that correspond to the c messages sent in a session in which P_{RES}^* convinces V_{RES} to accept $x \notin L$, then P_S^* will also convince V_S to accept $x \notin L$ by our construction of V_{RES}. Thus, the probability of V_S accepting $x \notin L$ is at least $\epsilon/t^c - \nu(n)$ for some negligible function ν. This probability is non-negligible. Therefore, it contradicts Lemma 3. $\qquad\square$

Let $\Lambda = (P_{rZK}, V_{rZK})$ be the constant-round resettable ZK protocol obtained in Corollary 1, we get the following corollary.

Corollary 2. *Assuming the existence of families of collision-resistant hash functions, one-way permutations, and indistinguishability obfuscators for $\mathsf{P}/poly$ that are super-polynomially secure, there exists a constant-round resettably-sound concurrent zero-knowledge argument for $\mathcal{NP}$.*

5 Simultaneous Resettable ZK

To obtain our main theorem, we apply a combination of the transformations in Theorem 4 and 5 in Sect. 6, and Theorem 6 and 7 in Appendix C of [25] to our protocol in Sect. 4 to obtain simultaneous resettability.

More specifically, we combine three transformations in [25]:

- from resettably-sound (relaxed) concurrent zero-knowledge argument to hybrid-sound hybrid-resettable zero-knowledge argument;
- from hybrid-sound zero-knowledge argument to resettably-sound zero-knowledge argument while maintaining (hybrid) resettability;
- from hybrid-resettable zero-knowledge argument to resettable zero-knowledge argument while maintaining (hybrid) resettable soundness.

We refer to Sect. 1 for an informal discussion and [25] for formal definitions of relaxed concurrent zero-knowledge, hybrid resettability and hybrid soundness.

Theorem 8 (implied from [25]). *Assuming the existence of ZAPs (i.e., 2-round resettably-sound resettable witness-indistinguishable proof systems) and family of pseudorandom functions, there exists a transformation from an ℓ-round resettably-sound concurrent zero-knowledge argument to a $\mathcal{O}(\ell)$-round resettably-sound resettable zero-knowledge argument.*

Applying the transformations to the protocol Δ in Corollary 2 results in the following theorem. Note that ZAPs can be constructed from $i\mathcal{O}$ and one-way functions [6], which can then be transformed to have resettable soundness and resettable witness indistinguishability. Furthermore, only the first transformation is based on ZAPs while all of them assume pseudorandom functions.

Theorem 9. *Assuming the existence of families of collision-resistant hash functions, one-way permutations, and indistinguishability obfuscators for $\mathcal{P}/\text{poly}$ that are super-polynomially secure, there exists a constant-round resettably-sound resettable zero-knowledge argument for $\mathcal{NP}$.*

Acknowledgments. Research supported in part by "GNCS - INdAM", EU COST Action IC1306, NSF grants 1065276, 1118126, 1136174 and 1619348, DARPA, US-Israel BSF grant 2008411 and 2012366, OKAWA Foundation Research Award, IBM Faculty Research Award, Xerox Faculty Research Award, B. John Garrick Foundation Award, Teradata Research Award, and Lockheed-Martin Corporation Research Award. This material is based upon work supported in part by DARPA Safeware program. The views expressed are those of the authors and do not reflect the official policy or position of the Department of Defense or the U.S. Government. The work of the 3rd author has been done in part while visiting UCLA.

References

1. Barak, B.: How to go beyond the black-box simulation barrier. In: FOCS 2001, pp. 106–115 (2001)
2. Barak, B., Goldreich, O.: Universal arguments and their applications. SIAM J. Comput. **38**(5), 1661–1694 (2008)
3. Barak, B., Goldreich, O., Goldwasser, S., Lindell, Y.: Resettably-sound zero-knowledge and its applications. In: FOCS 2002, pp. 116–125 (2001)
4. Bitansky, N., Paneth, O.: On the impossibility of approximate obfuscation and applications to resettable cryptography. In: STOC 2013 (2013)

5. Bitansky, N., Paneth, O.: On non-black-box simulation and the impossibility of approximate obfuscation. SIAM J. Comput. **44**(5), 1325–1383 (2015)
6. Bitansky, N., Paneth, O.: ZAPs and non-interactive witness indistinguishability from indistinguishability obfuscation. In: Dodis, Y., Nielsen, J.B. (eds.) TCC 2015. LNCS, vol. 9015, pp. 401–427. Springer, Heidelberg (2015). doi:10.1007/978-3-662-46497-7_16
7. Brassard, G., Chaum, D., Crépeau, C.: Minimum disclosure proofs of knowledge. J. Comput. Syst. Sci. **37**(2), 156–189 (1988)
8. Canetti, R., Goldreich, O., Goldwasser, S., Micali, S.: Resettable zero-knowledge (extended abstract). In: STOC 2000, pp. 235–244 (2000)
9. Cho, C., Ostrovsky, R., Scafuro, A., Visconti, I.: Simultaneously resettable arguments of knowledge. In: Cramer, R. (ed.) TCC 2012. LNCS, vol. 7194, pp. 530–547. Springer, Heidelberg (2012). doi:10.1007/978-3-642-28914-9_30
10. Chung, K.M., Lin, H., Pass, R.: Constant-round concurrent zero knowledge from p-certificates. In: FOCS 2013, pp. 50–59. IEEE (2013)
11. Chung, K.-M., Lin, H., Pass, R.: Constant-round concurrent zero-knowledge from indistinguishability obfuscation. In: Gennaro, R., Robshaw, M. (eds.) CRYPTO 2015. LNCS, vol. 9215, pp. 287–307. Springer, Heidelberg (2015). doi:10.1007/978-3-662-47989-6_14
12. Chung, K.-M., Ostrovsky, R., Pass, R., Venkitasubramaniam, M., Visconti, I.: 4-round resettably-sound zero knowledge. In: Lindell, Y. (ed.) TCC 2014. LNCS, vol. 8349, pp. 192–216. Springer, Heidelberg (2014). doi:10.1007/978-3-642-54242-8_9
13. Chung, K.M., Ostrovsky, R., Pass, R., Visconti, I.: Simultaneous resettability from one-way functions. In: FOCS 2013, pp. 60–69. IEEE (2013)
14. Chung, K.M., Pass, R., Seth, K.: Non-black-box simulation from one-way functions and applications to resettable security. In: STOC 2013. ACM (2013)
15. Deng, Y., Goyal, V., Sahai, A.: Resolving the simultaneous resettability conjecture and a new non-black-box simulation strategy. In: FOCS 2009, pp. 251–260. IEEE (2009)
16. Deng, Y., Lin, D.: Instance-dependent verifiable random functions and their application to simultaneous resettability. In: Naor, M. (ed.) EUROCRYPT 2007. LNCS, vol. 4515, pp. 148–168. Springer, Heidelberg (2007). doi:10.1007/978-3-540-72540-4_9
17. Di Crescenzo, G., Persiano, G., Visconti, I.: Constant-round resettable zero knowledge with concurrent soundness in the bare public-key model. In: Franklin, M. (ed.) CRYPTO 2004. LNCS, vol. 3152, pp. 237–253. Springer, Heidelberg (2004). doi:10.1007/978-3-540-28628-8_15
18. Dwork, C., Naor, M.: Zaps and their applications. In: FOCS 2000, pp. 283–293. IEEE (2000)
19. Dwork, C., Naor, M., Sahai, A.: Concurrent zero-knowledge. In: STOC 1998, pp. 409–418. ACM (1998)
20. Feige, U., Shamir, A.: Witness indistinguishable and witness hiding protocols. In: STOC 1990, pp. 416–426 (1990)
21. Garg, S., Ostrovsky, R., Visconti, I., Wadia, A.: Resettable statistical zero knowledge. In: Cramer, R. (ed.) TCC 2012. LNCS, vol. 7194, pp. 494–511. Springer, Heidelberg (2012). doi:10.1007/978-3-642-28914-9_28
22. Goldreich, O.: Foundations of Cryptography - Basic Tools. Cambridge University Press, Cambridge (2001)
23. Goldwasser, S., Micali, S.: Probabilistic encryption. J. Comput. Syst. Sci. **28**(2), 270–299 (1984)

24. Goldwasser, S., Micali, S., Rackoff, C.: The knowledge complexity of interactive proof-systems. In: STOC 1985, pp. 291–304. ACM (1985)
25. Goyal, V., Sahai, A.: Resolving the simultaneous resettability conjecture and a new non-black-box simulation strategy. IACR Cryptology ePrint Archive 2008/545 (2008)
26. Goyal, V., Sahai, A.: Resettably secure computation. In: Joux, A. (ed.) EURO-CRYPT 2009. LNCS, vol. 5479, pp. 54–71. Springer, Heidelberg (2009). doi:10.1007/978-3-642-01001-9_3
27. Groth, J., Ostrovsky, R., Sahai, A.: Non-interactive zaps and new techniques for NIZK. In: Dwork, C. (ed.) CRYPTO 2006. LNCS, vol. 4117, pp. 97–111. Springer, Heidelberg (2006). doi:10.1007/11818175_6
28. Håstad, J., Impagliazzo, R., Levin, L., Luby, M.: A pseudorandom generator from any one-way function. SIAM J. Comput. **28**, 12–24 (1999)
29. Kilian, J., Petrank, E.: Concurrent and resettable zero-knowledge in poly-loalgorithm rounds. In: STOC 2001, pp. 560–569 (2001)
30. Lindell, Y.: Foundations of cryptography 89-856 (2010). http://u.cs.biu.ac.il/lindell/89-856/complete-89-856.pdf
31. Micali, S., Reyzin, L.: Soundness in the public-key model. In: Kilian, J. (ed.) CRYPTO 2001. LNCS, vol. 2139, pp. 542–565. Springer, Heidelberg (2001). doi:10.1007/3-540-44647-8_32
32. Naor, M.: Bit commitment using pseudorandomness. J. Cryptol. **4**(2), 151–158 (1991)
33. Ostrovsky, R., Visconti, I.: Simultaneous resettability from collision resistance. In: Electronic Colloquium on Computational Complexity (ECCC), vol. 19, p. 164 (2012)
34. Scafuro, A., Visconti, I.: On round-optimal zero knowledge in the bare public-key model. In: Pointcheval, D., Johansson, T. (eds.) EUROCRYPT 2012. LNCS, vol. 7237, pp. 153–171. Springer, Heidelberg (2012). doi:10.1007/978-3-642-29011-4_11
35. Yung, M., Zhao, Y.: Generic and practical resettable zero-knowledge in the bare public-key model. In: Naor, M. (ed.) EUROCRYPT 2007. LNCS, vol. 4515, pp. 129–147. Springer, Heidelberg (2007). doi:10.1007/978-3-540-72540-4_8

Round Optimal Concurrent Non-malleability from Polynomial Hardness

Dakshita Khurana[✉]

Department of Computer Science, UCLA, Los Angeles, USA
dakshita@cs.ucla.edu

Abstract. Non-malleable commitments are a central cryptographic primitive that guarantee security against man-in-the-middle adversaries, and their exact round complexity has been a subject of great interest. Pass (TCC 2013, CC 2016) proved that non-malleable commitments with respect to commitment are impossible to construct in less than three rounds, via black-box reductions to polynomial hardness assumptions. Obtaining a matching positive result has remained an open problem so far.

While three-round constructions of non-malleable commitments have been achieved, beginning with the work of Goyal, Pandey and Richelson (STOC 2016), current constructions require super-polynomial assumptions.

In this work, we settle the question of whether three-round non-malleable commitments can be based on polynomial hardness assumptions. We give constructions based on polynomial hardness of ZAPs, as well as one out of DDH/QR/N^{th} residuosity. Our protocols also satisfy concurrent non-malleability.

1 Introduction

Non-malleable commitments are a fundamental primitive in cryptography, that help prevent man-in-the-middle attacks. A man-in-the-middle (MIM) adversary participates simultaneously in multiple protocol executions, using information obtained in one execution to breach security of the other execution. To counter such adversaries, the notion of non-malleable commitments was introduced in a seminal work of Dolev et al. [7]. From their inception, non-malleable commitments have been instrumental to building various several important

The full version of this paper is available at http://eprint.iacr.org/2017/734.

Research supported in part by the UCLA Dissertation Year Fellowship 2017–18. Research also supported in part from a DARPA/ARL SAFEWARE award, NSF Frontier Award 1413955, NSF grants 1619348, 1228984, 1136174, and 1065276, BSF grant 2012378. This material is based upon work supported by the Defense Advanced Research Projects Agency through the ARL under Contract W911NF-15-C-0205. The views expressed are those of the authors and do not reflect the official policy or position of the Department of Defense, the National Science Foundation, or the U.S. Government.

Y. Kalai and L. Reyzin (Eds.): TCC 2017, Part II, LNCS 10678, pp. 139–171, 2017.
https://doi.org/10.1007/978-3-319-70503-3_5

non-malleable protocols, including but not limited to non-malleable proof systems and round-efficient constructions of secure multi-party computation.

A commitment scheme is a protocol between a committer $\mathcal{C}$ and receiver $\mathcal{R}$, where the committer has an input message m. Both parties engage in an interactive probabilistic commitment protocol, and the receiver's view at the end of this phase is denoted by $\mathsf{com}(m)$. Later in a opening phase, the committer and receiver interact again to generate a transcript, that allows the receiver to verify whether the message m was actually committed to, during the commit phase. A cryptographic commitment must be binding, that is, with high probability over the randomness of the experiment, no probabilistic polynomial time committer can claim to have used a different message $m' \neq m$ in the commit phase. In short, the commitment cannot be later opened to any message $m' \neq m$. A commitment must also be hiding, that is, for any pair of messages (m, m'), the distributions $\mathsf{com}(m)$ and $\mathsf{com}(m')$ should be computationally indistinguishable. Very roughly, a commitment scheme is *non-malleable* if for every message m, no MIM adversary, intercepting a commitment protocol $\mathsf{com}(m)$ and modifying every message sent during this protocol arbitrarily, is able to efficiently *generate* a commitment to a message $\tilde{m}$ related to the original message m.

Round Complexity. The study of the round complexity of non-malleable commitments has been the subject of a vast body of research over the past 25 years. The original construction of non-malleable commitments of [7] was conceptually simple, but it required logarithmically many rounds. Subsequently, Barak [2], Pass [20], and Pass and Rosen [22] constructed constant-round protocols relying on non-black box techniques. Pass and Wee [23], Wee [24], Goyal [9], Lin and Pass [17] and Goyal et al. [11] then gave several round-optimized constant-round black-box constructions of non-malleable commitments based on various sub-exponential or polynomial hardness assumptions.

More recently, there has been noteworthy progress in understanding the exact amount of interaction necessary for non-malleable commitments. Pass [21] showed an impossibility for constructing non-malleable commitments using 2 rounds of communication or less, via a black-box reduction to any "standard" polynomial intractability assumption. Goyal et al. [13] constructed four round non-malleable commitments in the standard model based on the existence of one-way functions. Even more recently, Goyal et al. [12] constructed three round non-malleable commitments (matching the lower bound of [21]) using quasi-polynomially hard injective one-way functions, by exploiting properties of non-malleable codes. Ciampi et al. [5] showed how to bootstrap the result of [12] to obtain concurrent non-malleable commitments in three rounds assuming sub-exponential one-way functions. In fact, in the sub-exponential hardness regime, Khurana and Sahai [16] and concurrently Lin et al. [18] showed how to achieve two-round non-malleable commitments from DDH and from time-lock puzzles, respectively. Subsequently, [1] used these to obtain various concurrently secure protocols in two or three rounds. All these works use complexity leveraging and therefore must inherently rely on super-polynomial hardness. This state of affairs begs the following fundamental question:

"Can we construct round optimal non-malleable commitments from polynomial assumptions?"

We answer this question in the affirmative, by giving an explicit construction of three-round non-malleable commitments, based on polynomial hardness of any one out of the Decisional Diffie-Hellman, Quadratic Residuosity or N^{th} residuosity assumptions. We additionally assume ZAPs, which can be built from trapdoor permutations [8], the decisional linear assumption on bilinear maps [14] or indistinguishability obfuscation together with one-way functions [4]. Our construction additionally satisfies concurrent (many-many) non-malleability.

Informal Theorem 1. *Assuming polynomial DDH or QR or N^{th}-residuosity, and ZAPs, there exist three-round concurrent non-malleable commitments.*

Related Work. Goyal et al. [10] recently constructed two-round non-malleable commitments with respect to opening, secure against synchronizing adversaries, from polynomial hardness of injective one-way functions. Their result is incomparable to ours because they achieve a weaker notion of security (non-malleability with respect to opening), in two rounds, but against only synchronizing adversaries.

2   Technical Overview

We now describe the key technical roadblocks that arise in constructing non-malleable commitments from polynomial hardness, and illustrate how we overcome these hurdles.

As we already explained, proving non-malleability requires arguing that the value committed by a man-in-the-middle adversary remain independent of the value committed by an honest committer. This seems to inherently require extraction (as also implicit in [21]): a reduction must successfully extract the value committed by the MIM and use this value to contradict an assumption. However, current constructions of non-malleable commitments in three rounds based on polynomial assumptions [12] suffer from a problem known as over-extraction. That is, they admit extractors which suffer from the following undesirable issue: the extractor may sometimes extract a valid value from the MIM even though the MIM committed to an invalid value. Non-malleable commitments built using such extractors suffer from "selective abort": a man-in-the-middle can choose to commit to invalid values depending upon the value in the honest commitment, and an over-extracting reduction may never even be able to detect such attacks.

Non-synchronizing adversaries. Let us begin by considering a *non-synchronizing* man-in-the-middle (MIM) adversary that interacts with an honest committer C

in a left session, then tries to maul this message and commit to a related message when interacting with an honest receiver $\mathcal{R}$ in a different (right) session. By non-synchronizing, we mean that this MIM completes the entire left execution before beginning the right session. Known protocols for achieving weaker notions of non-malleability from polynomial hardness (these include the three-round sub-protocol without the ZK argument from [13] which we will denote by Π, and the basic three-round protocol from [12] which we will denote by Π') do not achieve non-malleability with respect to commitment, even in this restricted setting[1].

On the other hand, *any* extractable commitment is non-malleable in this restricted setting of non-synchronizing adversaries. The reason is simple: Suppose a non-synchronizing MIM managed to successfully maul the honest commitment. For a fixed transcript of the honest commitment, a reduction can rewind the MIM and use the extractor of the commitment scheme to extract the value committed by the MIM. If this value is related to the value within the honest commitment, this can directly be used to contradict hiding of the honestly generated commitment.

The main technical goal of this paper is to find a way to bootstrap the basic schemes Π, Π' to obtain non-malleability against general synchronizing and non-synchronizing adversaries, while only relying on polynomial hardness.

Barrier I: Over-Extraction. A natural starting point, then, is to add extractability to the schemes Π, Π', by using some variant of an AoK of committed values, and within three rounds.

We cannot rely on witness indistinguishable (WI) arguments of knowledge, since arguing hiding of the scheme would require allowing a committer to commit to *two* witnesses to invoke WI security. Moreover, all existing constructions of WI arguments with black-box proofs, involve a parallel repetition of constant-soundness arguments. Now, a malicious committer could commit to two different witnesses: and use one witness in some parallel executions of the WI argument, and a different witness in some others. In this situation, even though the commitment may be invalid, one cannot guarantee that an extractor will detect the invalidity of the commitment, and over-extraction is possible. This is a known problem with 3 round protocols based on one-one one-way functions.

On the other hand, very recently, new protocols have been constructed in situations unrelated to non-malleability, that do not suffer from over-extraction [15]. Assuming polynomial hardness of DDH or Quadratic Residuosity or N^{th} residuosity, [15] demonstrated how to achieve arguments of knowledge in three rounds, that do not over-extract and have a "weak" ZK property[2].

However, the protocols of [15] guarantee privacy only when proving statements that are chosen from a distribution, by a prover, exclusively in the third round. On the other hand, both schemes Π, Π', and in fact most general

---

[1] The basic protocol from [12] however, does achieve non-malleability against synchronous adversaries.

[2] Very roughly, this means that for every (malicious) PPT verifier and distinguisher $\mathcal{D}$, there exists a distinguisher-dependent simulator $\mathsf{Sim}_{\mathcal{D}}$, that can generate a simulated proof.

non-malleable commitment schemes follow a commit-challenge-response structure, where cryptography is necessarily used in the first round. Thus, the statement being proved is already fully/partially decided in the first round, which are incompatible withthe kind of statements that [15] allows proofs for. Thus ideally, we would either like to inject non-malleability into the scheme of [15], or we would like to give an argument of knowledge of the message committed in the first round of Π, Π', that doesn't overextract. The protocols of [15] are unlikely to directly help us achieve these objectives, because of their restriction to proving messages generated in the third round. However, before describing how we solve this problem, we describe another technical barrier.

Barrier II: Composing Non-Malleability with Extraction. Many state-of-the-art protocols for non-malleable commitments admit black-box proofs of security. Naturally then, security reductions for these protocols must rely on rewinding the adversary in order to prove non-malleability. This makes these protocols notoriously hard to compose with other primitives that rely on rewinding. More specifically, it is necessary to ensure that the knowledge extractor for the extractable commitment does not interfere with the rewinding strategies used in the proof of non-malleability, and vice-versa.

A relatively straightforward technique to get around this difficulty, used in [9, 11, 13, 17] is to arrange the protocol such that the non-malleable component and the argument of knowledge appear in completely different rounds and do not overlap. A more challenging method that does not add rounds, that is also used in prior work [13], is to use "bounded-rewinding-secure" WIAoK's while making careful changes to the non-malleable commitment scheme.

Our Solution: First Attempt. Our first technical idea is to turn the problem of incompatibility between non-malleability and arguments of knowledge on its head, and try to use the same commitments to both argue non-malleability and perform knowledge-extraction. In other words, the only extractable primitive that we rely on will be a non-malleable commitment scheme. This is explained in more detail below.

In the following, we will rely on non-malleable commitments with a weak extraction property. Very roughly, we will require the existence of a probabilistic "over"-extractor $\mathcal{E}$ parameterized by error ϵ (we will usually think of ϵ as being inverse-polynomial). We will require given a PPT (synchronizing) man-in-the-middle adversary and a transcript of an execution between the MIM and honest committer, $\mathcal{E}$ "extracts" a value v such that if the value committed by the MIM in the transcript is valid, then it equals v except with probability ϵ. Furthermore, the extractor $\mathcal{E}$ *does not* rewind the honest execution. As noted in [9,12], this already guarantees a flavor of non-malleability: since it is possible to extract the value from the MIM while maintaining hiding of the honest commitment. The weak extraction property is satisfied, even in the one-many setting (where the MIM participates in multiple right executions) by the protocol Π. In the one-one setting, this property is satisfied by Π'.

We note that a non-malleable commitment satisfying the weak extraction property is not an extractable commitment (and in particular, need not be non-malleable with respect to commitment), because $\mathcal{E}$ is allowed to output a valid value even when the MIM committed to an incorrect/invalid value in the transcript. Thus, a MIM may cheat for example, by generating a commitment to an invalid value when the honest commitment is to 0, and to a valid value when the honest commitment is to 1: and the extractor $\mathcal{E}$ may fail to observe the difference. On the other hand, in order to achieve non-malleability with respect to commitment, we will have to solve this problem and know when incorrectly extracted a valid value even though the MIM committed to an invalid value.

Now in order to gain confidence in the correctness of the value we extract, our scheme will have the committer generate two non-malleable commitments in parallel, and give a WI argument that one of the two was correctly constructed. This argument will satisfy a specific type of security under rewinding, and can be constructed based on ZAPs and DDH in three rounds via [15]. For the purposes of this overview, even though we don't actually require a non-interactive proof, assume that we use a non-interactive witness indistinguishable proof, NIWI [3, 14]. Let ϕ_1 denote the protocol that results from committing to the message twice using the non-malleable commitment scheme Π, and giving a NIWI proof that one of the two was correctly computed.

This partial solution still leaves scope for over-extraction: how can we be sure that the extractor does not output any valid value even when a malicious committer could be committing to two different values within the non-malleable commitments and using both witnesses for the WI?

Second Attempt. Since protocol ϕ_1 also suffers from over-extraction, it may seem like we made no progress at all. However, note that the same protocol can be easily modified to a WIAoK (witness indistinguishable argument of knowledge): by committing to a *witness* twice using Π and proving via NIWI that one of the two non-malleable commitments is a valid commitment to a witness. Let us call the resulting protocol ϕ_2. At a high level, the protocol ϕ_2 has the following properties:

- **Knowledge Extraction.** ϕ_2 is an argument of knowledge (which suffers from over-extraction).
- **Non-malleability.** Weak non-malleability of Π implies a limited form of non-malleability of the protocol ϕ_2.

Third Attempt. In order to prevent over-extraction, we will need to force any prover that generates a proof according to ϕ_2 to use a *unique* witness in ϕ_2. We will now try to rely on three round "weak" zero-knowledge arguments of [15], which are secure when used to prove cryptographic statements chosen by the prover in the last round. These arguments also retain a limited type of security under rewinding, which will help ensure that rewinding for extraction from the non-malleable commitment does not interfere with simulation security.

Assume again, for the purposes of this overview, that these arguments satisfy the standard notion of simulation for zero-knowledge, except that the statement to be proved, must be chosen in the last round. Let us denote them by wzk.

We will now use wzk to set up a trapdoor for ϕ_2. This trapdoor will include a statistically binding commitment c_1 using a non-interactive statistically binding commitment scheme com, and a wzk argument that c_1 was generated correctly as a commitment to 1. The trapdoor statement will be that c_1 is a commitment to 0. This trapdoor statement will serve as the 'other' witness for ϕ_2.

Given these building blocks, our actual commitment scheme ϕ will have the following structure:

- **Trapdoor:** The committer will generate commitment c_1 to 1, via com in the third round. In parallel, the committer will prove via wzk, that c_1 was correctly generated as a commitment to 1.
- **Actual Commitment:** The committer will also generate commitment c to input message m, via com, only in the third round. In parallel the committer will also run scheme ϕ_2, proving that either c was correctly generated, or that c_1 was generated as a commitment to 0.

Note that the protocol ϕ_2 as described is not delayed-input: the non-malleable commitment Π requires an input (that is, the witness) in the first round, whereas the witness for the statement is only decided in the third round. However, suffices to use one-time pads to get this delayed-input property from ϕ_2, by using the two non-malleable commitments within ϕ_2 to commit to random values r_1, r_2 and then sending in the last round, the messages $r_1 \oplus w, r_2 \oplus w$.

A simple (informal) description that captures the essence of our final protocol, ϕ, is in Fig. 1. The scheme ϕ is opened up into its components: two non-malleable commitments and a WI argument. This scheme can be shown to be computationally hiding by the privacy properties of ϕ, wzk and com.

Extraction. We first argue that the scheme in Fig. 1 is an extractable commitment. We already discussed that there exists a knowledge extractor for ϕ_2 that extracts at least one out of γ_1, γ_2: which can then be used to extract the randomness r via z_1, z_2. All we need to argue is that this extractor does not over-extract. However, soundness of wzk already forces a computational committer to set c_1 as a commitment to 1, which means that there remains only one randomness (the randomness used for committing to m), that the committer can use in order to generate z_1 or z_2 in the WI. Extractability of this scheme is already enough to guarantee security against non-synchronizing adversaries, even if such adversaries simultaneously participate in several parallel executions.

Non-malleability. Now, we need to argue that the resulting scheme is concurrent non-malleable with respect to commitment, when instantiated with Π from [13], or is non-malleable with respect to commitment when instantiated with Π' from [12]. Since Π helps us obtain a more general result, we restrict the rest of this overview to only consider the scheme Π.

At a very high level, the system ϕ_2 behaves like a non-malleable witness indistinguishable argument of knowledge. Like we already discussed, only relying on the witness indistinguishability of ϕ_2 gives rise to issues such as over-extraction. It is here that the weak zero-knowledge argument helps: soundness of the weak ZK argument ensures that any PPT MIM adversary interacting with the honest committer, can generate c_1 as a commitment to 0 with only negligible probability. Thus, such a MIM is "forced" to use as witness, the actual randomness used

Inputs: Committer C has input a message $m \in \{0,1\}^n$, receiver R has no input.

1. – C samples $\gamma_1, \gamma_2 \xleftarrow{\$} \{0,1\}^n$.
    – Next, C sends the first message of wzk to R.
    – Finally, C sends the first message of $\Pi(\gamma_1), \Pi(\gamma_2)$.
2. – R sends the second message of wzk to C.
    – R sends the second message for both executions of Π.
3. – C computes and sends $c_1 = \text{com}(1; r)$ for $r \xleftarrow{\$} \{0,1\}^n$.
    – C sends the third message of wzk to R, proving that c_1 commits to 1.
    – C computes and sends $c = \text{com}(m; r')$ for $r' \xleftarrow{\$} \{0,1\}^n$.
    – C sends the third message of $\Pi(\gamma_1), \Pi(\gamma_2)$.
    – C sends $z_1 = (\gamma_1 \oplus r'), z_2 = (\gamma_2 \oplus r')$ to R.
    – C uses $(c, m, r', \gamma_1, z_1)$ as witness to prove using the WI that :
      - c is a valid commitment to some message m with randomness r', and $\Pi(\gamma_1)$ is a valid non-malleable commitment to γ_1 and $z_1 = \gamma_1 \oplus r'$, OR
      - c is a valid commitment to some message m with randomness r', and $\Pi(\gamma_2)$ is a valid non-malleable commitment to γ_2 and $z_2 = \gamma_2 \oplus r'$, OR
      - c_1 is a valid commitment to 0 with randomness r, and $\Pi(\gamma_1)$ is a valid non-malleable commitment to γ_1 and $z_1 = \gamma_1 \oplus r$, OR
      - c_1 is a valid commitment to 0 with randomness r, and $\Pi(\gamma_2)$ is a valid non-malleable commitment to γ_2 and $z_2 = \gamma_2 \oplus r$

Fig. 1. A simplified description of the final non-malleable commitment scheme ϕ

to generate a commitment to his value, and will therefore will never commit to an invalid value.

However, while formally arguing non-malleability, some subtle technical issues arise that require careful analysis. For instance, the distinguisher-dependent simulation strategy of weak ZK if used naively, only guarantees that the view of the distinguisher remains indistinguishable under simulation. However, while arguing non-malleability, it is imperative to ensure that not just the view, but the joint distribution of the *view and the value committed* by the MIM remains indistinguishable under simulation. It is here that the over-extraction property of Π helps: in hybrids where we must argue non-malleability while also performing distinguisher-dependent simulation, we will use the extractor that is guaranteed by the weak non-malleability of Π, to extract the value committed by the MIM *without* having to rewind the left non-malleable commitment. This helps us guarantee that the joint distribution of the view and values committed by the MIM remains indistinguishable under simulation.

Our actual protocol is formalized in Sect. 4 and is identical to the protocol described above, except the following modification: For technical reasons, in our actual protocol, instead of masking the randomness r' with γ, we mask it with $\text{PRF}(\gamma, \alpha)$ for randomly chosen α. The committer must also send α to the receiver. This is for similar reasons as [15]: the simulator for wzk sends *many* third protocol messages for the same fixed transcript of the first two messages, and we require security to hold even in this setting.

On Rewinding Techniques in the Proof. The weak ZK protocol of [15] that we use in this work, relies on the simulator rewinding the distinguisher. Because of this, our actual proof of security relies on two sequential rewindings within a three round protocol: one which rewinds to the end of the first round, and helps extract values committed in the MIM executions, and the second that rewinds to the end of the second round, in order to simulate the argument with respect to a distinguisher. This requires careful indistinguishability arguments that take such sequential rewindings into account, and can also be found in Sect. 4. We believe that the careful use of two sets of rewindings within a three-round protocol is another novel contribution of this work, and may be of independent interest.

In Sect. 3, we recall preliminaries and definitions, and in Sect. 4, we describe our construction and provide a proof of non-malleability.

3   Preliminaries

We first recall some preliminaries that will be useful in our constructions.

3.1   Proofs and Arguments

Definition 1 (Delayed-Input Distributional ϵ-Weak Zero Knowledge) [15]. *An interactive argument (P, V) for a language L is said to be* delayed-input distributional ϵ-weak zero knowledge *if for every efficiently samplable distribution $(\mathcal{X}_n, \mathcal{W}_n)$ on R_L, i.e., $\mathsf{Supp}(\mathcal{X}_n, \mathcal{W}_n) = \{(x, w) : x \in L \cap \{0,1\}^n, w \in R_L(x)\}$, every non-adaptive PPT verifier V^*, every $z \in \{0,1\}^*$, every PPT distinguisher $\mathcal{D}$, and every $\epsilon = 1/\mathsf{poly}(n)$, there exists a simulator $\mathcal{S}$ that runs in time $\mathsf{poly}(n, \epsilon)$ such that:*

$$\left| \Pr_{(x,w) \leftarrow (\mathcal{X}_n, \mathcal{W}_n)} \left[\mathcal{D}(x, z, \mathsf{view}_{V^*}[\langle P, V^*(z)\rangle(x, w)] = 1 \right] \right.$$

$$\left. - \Pr_{(x,w) \leftarrow (\mathcal{X}_n, \mathcal{W}_n)} \left[\mathcal{D}(x, z, \mathcal{S}^{V^*, \mathcal{D}}(x, z)) = 1 \right] \right| \leq \epsilon(n),$$

where the probability is over the random choices of (x, w) as well as the random coins of the parties.

Definition 2 (Weak Resettable Delayed-Input Distributional ϵ-Weak Zero Knowledge) [15]. *A three round delayed-input interactive argument (P, V) for a language L is said to be* weak resettable distributional weak zero-knowledge, *if for every efficiently samplable distribution $(\mathcal{X}_n, \mathcal{W}_n)$ on R_L, i.e., $\mathsf{Supp}(\mathcal{X}_n, \mathcal{W}_n) = \{(x, w) : x \in L \cap \{0,1\}^n, w \in R_L(x)\}$, every non-adaptive PPT verifier V^*, every $z \in \{0,1\}^*$, every PPT distinguisher $\mathcal{D}$, and every*

$\epsilon = 1/\mathsf{poly}(n)$, *there exists a simulator* $\mathcal{S}$ *that runs in time* $\mathsf{poly}(n, \epsilon)$ *and generates a simulated proof for instance* $x \xleftarrow{\$} \mathcal{X}_n$, *such that over the randomness of sampling* $(x, w) \leftarrow (\mathcal{X}_n, \mathcal{W}_n)$, $\Pr[b' = b] \leq \frac{1}{2} + \epsilon(n) + \mathsf{negl}(n)$ *in the following experiment, where the challenger* C *plays the role of the prover:*

- *At the beginning,* (C, V^*) *receive the size of the instance,* V^* *receives auxiliary input* z, *and they execute the first 2 rounds. Let us denote these messages by* τ_1, τ_2.
- *Next,* (C, V^*) *run* $\mathsf{poly}(n)$ *executions, with the same fixed first message* τ_1, *but different second messages chosen potentially maliciously by* V^*. *In each execution,* C *picks a fresh sample* $(x, w) \leftarrow (\mathcal{X}_n, \mathcal{W}_n)$, *and generates a proof for it according to honest verifier strategy.*
- *Next,* C *samples bit* $b \xleftarrow{\$} \{0, 1\}$ *and if* $b = 0$, *for* $(x, w) \xleftarrow{\$} (\mathcal{X}_n, \mathcal{W}_n)$ *it generates an honest proof with first two messages* τ_1, τ_2, *else if* $b = 1$, *for* $x \xleftarrow{\$} \mathcal{X}_n$ *it generates a simulated proof with first two messages* τ_1, τ_2 *using simulator* $\mathcal{S}$ *that has oracle access to* $V^*, \mathcal{D}$.
- *Finally,* V^* *sends its view to a distinguisher* $\mathcal{D}$ *that outputs* b.

Imported Theorem 1 [15]. *Assuming* $DDH/QR/N^{th}$ *residuosity, along with ZAPs, there exist three-message arguments that satisfy delayed-input weak resettable distributional* ϵ-*weak zero knowledge/strong WI. In our protocols, we will always use weak zero-knowledge/strong witness-indistinguishable arguments in the "delayed-input" setting, that is, to prove statements that are chosen by the prover only in the third round of the execution.*

Definition 3 (Resettable Reusable WI Argument). *We say that a two-message delayed-input interactive argument* (P, V) *for a language* L *is resettable reusable witness indistinguisable, if for every PPT verifier* V^*, *every* $z \in \{0, 1\}^*$, $\Pr[b = b'] \leq \frac{1}{2} + \mathsf{negl}(n)$ *in the following experiment, where we denote the first round message function by* $m_1 = \mathsf{wi}_1(r_1)$ *and the second round message function by* $\mathsf{wi}_2(x, w, m_1, r_2)$.

The challenger samples $b \xleftarrow{\$} \{0, 1\}$. V^* *(with auxiliary input* z) *specifies* $(m_1^1, x^1, w_1^1, w_2^1)$ *where* w_1^1, w_2^1 *are (not necessarily distinct) witnesses for* x^1. V^* *then obtains second round message* $\mathsf{wi}_2(x^1, w_b^1, m_1^1, r)$ *generated with uniform randomness* r. *Next, the adversary specifies arbitrary* $(m_1^2, x^2, w_1^2, w_2^2)$, *and obtains second round message* $\mathsf{wi}_2(x^2, w_b^2, m_1^2, r)$. *This continues* $m(n) = \mathsf{poly}(n)$ *times for a-priori unbounded* m, *and finally* V^* *outputs* b.

Remark 1. Note that ZAPs (more generally, any two-message WI) can be modified to obtain resettable reusable WI, by having the prover apply a PRF on the verifier message and the instance to compute randomness for the proof. This allows to argue, via a hybrid argument, that fresh randomness can be used for each proof, and therefore perform a hybrid argument so that each proof remains WI. In our construction, we will use resettable reusable ZAPs.

3.2 Non-malleable Commitments

Throughout this paper, we will use n to denote the security parameter, and $\mathsf{negl}(n)$ to denote any function that is asymptotically smaller than $\frac{1}{\mathsf{poly}(n)}$ for any polynomial $\mathsf{poly}(\cdot)$. We will use PPT to describe a probabilistic polynomial time machine. We will also use the words "rounds" and "messages" interchangeably.

We follow the definition of non-malleable commitments introduced by Pass and Rosen [22] and further refined by Lin et al. [19] and Goyal [9] (which in turn build on the original definition of [7]). In the real interaction, there is a man-in-the-middle adversary MIM interacting with a committer $\mathcal{C}$ (where $\mathcal{C}$ commits to value v) in the left session, and interacting with receiver $\mathcal{R}$ in the right session. Prior to the interaction, the value v is given to C as local input. MIM receives an auxiliary input z, which might contain a-priori information about v. Let $\mathsf{MIM}_{\langle C,R\rangle}(\mathsf{value}, z)$ denote a random variable that describes the value $\widetilde{\mathsf{val}}$ committed by the MIM in the right session, jointly with the view of the MIM in the full experiment. In the simulated experiment, a simulator $\mathcal{S}$ directly interacts with $\mathcal{R}$. Let $\mathsf{Sim}_{\langle C,R\rangle}(1^n, z)$ denote the random variable describing the value $\widetilde{\mathsf{val}}$ committed to by $\mathcal{S}$ and the output view of $\mathcal{S}$. If the tags in the left and right interaction are equal, the value $\widetilde{\mathsf{val}}$ committed in the right interaction, is defined to be $\perp$ in both experiments.

Definition 4 (Non-malleable Commitments w.r.t. Commitment). *A commitment scheme $\langle C, R\rangle$ is said to be non-malleable if for every PPT* MIM, *there exists an expected PPT simulator $\mathcal{S}$ such that the following ensembles are computationally indistinguishable:*

$$\{\mathsf{MIM}_{\langle C,R\rangle}(\mathsf{value}, z)\}_{n\in\mathbb{N}, v\in\{0,1\}^n, z\in\{0,1\}^*} \ and \ \{\mathsf{Sim}_{\langle C,R\rangle}(1^n, z)\}_{n\in\mathbb{N}, v\in\{0,1\}^n, z\in\{0,1\}^*}$$

The setting of concurrent non-malleability considers an adversary that participates in multiple sessions with an honest committer, acting as receiver. The adversary simultaneously participates in multiple sessions with an honest receiver, acting as committer. In the left sessions, the MIM interacts with honest committer(s) obtaining commitments to values $m_1, m_2, \ldots m_{\mathsf{poly}(n)}$ (say, from distribution val using tags $t_1, t_2, t_{\mathsf{poly}(n)}$ of its choice. In the right session, $\mathcal{A}$ interacts with $\mathcal{R}$ attempting to commit to a sequence of related values $\tilde{m}_1, \ldots \tilde{m}_{\mathsf{poly}(n)}$ again using identities $\tilde{t}_1, \ldots \tilde{t}_{\mathsf{poly}(n)}$. If any of the right commitments are invalid, or undefined, their value is set to $\perp$. For any i such that $\tilde{t}_i = t_j$ for some j, set $\tilde{m}_i$ (the value committed using that tag) to $\perp$. Let $\mathsf{MIM}_{\langle C,R\rangle}(\mathsf{value}, z)$ denote a random variable that describes the values $\widetilde{\mathsf{val}}$ committed by the MIM in the right sessions, jointly with the view of the MIM in the full experiment, when the value is the joint distribution of values committed in the left sessions. In a simulated execution, there is an expected polynomial time simulator that interacts with the MIM and generates a distribution Sim consisting of the views and values committed by the MIM. Then, the definitions of concurrent non-malleable commitment scheme w.r.t. commitment, replacement and opening are defined as above.

Definition 5 (Concurrent Non-malleable Commitments w.r.t. Commitment). *A commitment scheme $\langle C, R \rangle$ is said to be concurrently non-malleable if for every PPT MIM, there exists an expected PPT simulator S such that the ensembles* real *and* sim *defined above are indistinguishable.*

Definition 6 (One-Many Weak Non-malleable Commitments against Synchronizing Adversaries). *A statistically binding commitment scheme $\langle C, R \rangle$ is said to be one-many weak non-malleable against synchronizing adversaries, if there exists a probabilistic "over"-extractor $\mathcal{E}$ parameterized by ϵ, that given a PPT synchronizing MIM which participates in one left session and $p = \mathsf{poly}(n)$ right sessions, and given only the transcript of a main-thread interaction τ where the MIM interacts with an honest committer and honest receiver, together with oracle access to the MIM, outputs a set of values $v_1, v_2, \ldots v_p$ in time $\mathsf{poly}(n, \frac{1}{\epsilon})$. These values are such that:*

- *For any $j \in [p]$, if the jth commitment in τ is a commitment to a valid message m_j, then $v_j = m_j$ over the randomness of the extractor and the transcript, except with probability $\frac{\epsilon}{p}$.*
- *For any $j \in [p]$, if the jth commitment in τ is a commitment to some invalid message (which we will denote by $\perp$), then v_j need not necessarily be $\perp$.*

Remark 2. By the union bound, the values output by the extractor are correct for *all* p sessions in which the MIM committed to valid messages in the transcript τ, except with probability ϵ.

This formalization helps us to abstract out the exact properties satisfied by existing three-round schemes based on polynomial assumptions, which we can rely on for our bootstrapping protocol. We note that this is an alternative way of formalizing the requirement of "security against non-aborting adversaries" from [6]. When invoking the security of non-malleable commitments in our proof, the adversary will always be forced (via appropriate proofs) to not generate a commitment to $\perp$, except with negligible probability.

Instantiating one-many weak non-malleable commitments. The three-round subprotocol in the non-malleable commitment scheme from [13] (their basic construction without the zero-knowledge argument of knowledge), based on injective one-way functions, is a one-many weak non-malleable commitment according to Definition 6. On the other hand, the basic protocol of [12] based on injective one-way functions, that is only secure against synchronous adversaries, is a one-one weak non-malleable commitment scheme against synchronizing adversaries according to Definition 6.

4   Non-malleable Commitments w.r.t. Commitment

In this section, we describe a round-preserving way to transform one-many weak non-malleable commitments against synchronous adversaries, to (one-many) non-malleable commitments with respect to commitment. Our construction of three round non-malleable commitments is described in Fig. 2.

Let $\varPi^i = (\mathsf{nmc}_1^i, \mathsf{nmc}_2^i, \mathsf{nmc}_3^i)$ for $i \in \{1, 2\}$ denote the three messages of, two independent instances (indexed by i) of a weak non-malleable commitment.
Let $\mathsf{wi} = (\mathsf{wi}_1, \mathsf{wi}_2)$ denote a delayed-input reusable resettable WI argument.
Let $\mathsf{wzk} = (\mathsf{wzk}_1, \mathsf{wzk}_2, \mathsf{wzk}_3)$ denote the three messages of a delayed-input weak resettable weak distributional ZK.
Let $\mathsf{PRF}(K, r)$ denote a pseudorandom function evaluated on key K, input r.
Let $\mathsf{com}(\cdot)$ denote a non-interactive, statistically binding commitment scheme.

Tag: Let the tag be $\mathsf{tag} \in [n]$, and n denote the security parameter.
Committer Input: A message $m \in \{0, 1\}^p$, along with tag tag.

1. **Committer Message:** Sample independent randomness $r_1, r_2, \gamma_1, \gamma_2$, and send $\mathsf{nmc}_1^1(\gamma_1, r_1, \mathsf{tag}), \mathsf{nmc}_1^2(\gamma_2, r_2, \mathsf{tag})$ together with wzk_1.
2. **Receiver Message:** Send the second message for both non-malleable commitments $(\mathsf{nmc}_2^1, \mathsf{nmc}_2^2)$ for tag, to the prover together with $\mathsf{wi}_1, \mathsf{wzk}_2$.
3. **Committer Message:** Sample $r \xleftarrow{\$} \{0, 1\}^*$ and send $c = \mathsf{com}(m; r)$ to $\mathcal{R}$.
   Additionally, sample $\widehat{r} \xleftarrow{\$} \{0, 1\}$ and send $c_1 = \mathsf{com}(1; \widehat{r})$. Along with c_1, send wzk_3 proving that $\exists \widehat{r}$ such that $c_1 = \mathsf{com}(1; \widehat{r})$.
   Send $\mathsf{nmc}_3^1(\gamma_1, r_1, \mathsf{tag})$ and $\mathsf{nmc}_3^2(\gamma_2, r_2, \mathsf{tag})$ to $\mathcal{R}$.
   Finally, sample $\{\alpha_1, \alpha_2\} \xleftarrow{\$} \{0, 1\}^{2n}$ and send $\delta_1 = \mathsf{PRF}(\gamma_1, \alpha_1) \oplus r$ and $\delta_2 = \mathsf{PRF}(\gamma_2, \alpha_2) \oplus r$. Send wi_2 proving (using witness $\varPi^1$) that:
     - Either $\varPi^1$ is a valid non-malleable commitment to some γ_1 with randomness r_1 AND $r = \mathsf{PRF}(\gamma_1, \alpha_1) \oplus \delta_1$ such that $(c = \mathsf{com}(m; r)$ OR $c_1 = \mathsf{com}(0; r))$
     - Or, $\varPi^2$ is a valid non-malleable commitment to some γ_2 with randomness r_2 AND $r = \mathsf{PRF}(\gamma_2, \alpha_2) \oplus \delta_2$ such that $(c = \mathsf{com}(m; r)$ OR $c_1 = \mathsf{com}(0; r))$
4. **Decommitment:** The committer reveals the message m and randomness r. The verifier accepts iff c is a commitment to m using randomness r.

Fig. 2. Non-malleable commitment scheme ϕ

4.1 Proof of Security

We begin by proving that the scheme is statistically binding and computationally hiding. We note that computational hiding is in fact, implied by non-malleability: therefore as a warm up, we sketch the proof of hiding via a sequence of hybrid experiments without giving formal reductions. In Theorem 1, we prove formally that not only is the view of a receiver indistinguishable between these hybrids, in fact, the joint distribution of the view *and values committed* by a MIM interacting with an honest committer remains indistinguishable between these hybrids.

Lemma 1. *The protocol in Fig. 2 is a statistically binding, computationally hiding, commitment scheme.*

Proof (Sketch). The statistical binding property follows directly from statistical hiding property of the underlying commitment scheme com($\cdot$).

The computational hiding property follows from the hiding of com and nmc, the weak zero-knowledge property of wzk, and the witness indistinguishability of wi. Here, we sketch a proof of computational hiding. Note that computational hiding is implied by non-malleability, therefore the proof of Theorem 1 can also be treated as a formal proof of hiding of the commitment scheme ϕ. Let $\langle \mathcal{C}_\phi(m; r), \mathcal{R} \rangle$ denote an execution where the committer uses input message m and randomness R. We prove that the view of any malicious receiver $\mathcal{R}^*$, that is, $\text{view}_{\mathcal{R}^*}\langle \mathcal{C}_\phi(m_0; r), \mathcal{R}^* \rangle \approx_c \text{view}_{\mathcal{R}^*}\langle \mathcal{C}_\phi(m_1; r), \mathcal{R}^* \rangle$ for all m_0, m_1, via the following sequence of hybrid experiments:

Hybrid_{m_0}: This hybrid corresponds to an interaction of $\mathcal{C}$ and $\mathcal{R}^*$ where $\mathcal{C}$ uses input message m_0, that is, the output is $\text{view}_{\mathcal{R}^*}\langle \mathcal{C}_\phi(m_0; r), \mathcal{R}^* \rangle$.

Hybrid_1: In this hybrid, the challenger behaves identically to Hybrid_{m_0}, except that it generates nmc^2 as a non-malleable commitment to a different randomness γ_2' than the (uniform) randomness γ_2 used to compute δ_2. This hybrid is indistinguishable from Hybrid_0 because of the hiding of Π.

$\text{Hybrid}_{2,\mathcal{D}}$: In this hybrid, the challenger behaves identically to Hybrid_1, except that it outputs the transcript of an execution where the wzk argument is simulated[3]. The challenger uses the simulation strategy of the weak zero-knowledge argument wzk, which executes the last message of the protocol multiple times, and learns the wzk challenge based on the distinguisher's output. However, the challenger continues to commit to m_0 while generating a simulated wzk argument. By the simulation security of wzk, for any distinguisher $\mathcal{D}$ and any inverse polynomial ϵ, there exists a polynomial time distinguisher-dependent simulator/challenger such that $\text{Hybrid}_{2,\mathcal{D}}$ is ϵ-indistinguishable from Hybrid_1.

$\text{Hybrid}_{3,\mathcal{D}}$: In this hybrid, the challenger behaves identically to $\text{Hybrid}_{2,\mathcal{D}}$, except that it sets $c_1 = \text{com}(0; \widehat{r})$ for some randomness $\widehat{r}$, in the main thread. Note that this is possible because the challenger is generating a simulated proof in the output transcript. This hybrid is indistinguishable from $\text{Hybrid}_{2,\mathcal{D}}$ by the computational hiding property of com.

$\text{Hybrid}_{4,\mathcal{D}}$: In this hybrid, the challenger behaves identically to $\text{Hybrid}_{3,\mathcal{D}}$ except that in the output transcript, it sets $\delta_2 = \text{PRF}(\gamma_2, \alpha_2) \oplus \widehat{r}$ where $\widehat{r}$ is the randomness used to generate $c_1 = \text{com}(0; \widehat{r})$. Note that the committer is committing to a different value γ_2' in the protocol Π^2, thus the key γ_2 does not appear anywhere in the rest of the protocol. Therefore, this hybrid is indistinguishable from $\text{Hybrid}_{3,\mathcal{D}}$ by the security of the PRF.

$\text{Hybrid}_{5,\mathcal{D}}$: In this hybrid, the challenger behaves identically to $\text{Hybrid}_{4,\mathcal{D}}$ except that in all transcripts, it sets nmc^2 as a non-malleable commitment to the same

---

[3] Note that in all hybrid experiments, we will actually use the extended simulation strategy of the weak ZK argument wzk as described in [15]– that is used for strong witness indistinguishability, and where the simulator takes into account both messages m_0 and m_1 during simulation.

randomness γ_2' that is used to compute δ_2. This hybrid essentially "reverts" the cheating performed in Hybrid_1. Indistinguishability of this hybrid follows because of the hiding of Π^2.

Note that the transcript output by the challenger in this experiment is such that Π^1 is a valid non-malleable commitment to γ_1 with randomness r_1 AND $r = \mathsf{PRF}(\gamma_1, \alpha_1) \oplus \delta_1$ such that $c = \mathsf{com}(m; r)$. Additionally, Π^2 is a valid non-malleable commitment to γ_2 with randomness r_2 AND $\widehat{r} = \mathsf{PRF}(\gamma_2, \alpha_2) \oplus \delta_2$ such that $c_1 = \mathsf{com}(0; \widehat{r})$.

$\mathsf{Hybrid}_{6,\mathcal{D}}$: In this hybrid, the challenger behaves the same was as $\mathsf{Hybrid}_{5,\mathcal{D}}$, except that it uses the second witness, (r_2, γ_2), to generate the argument wi in the output transcript. This hybrid is indistinguishable from $\mathsf{Hybrid}_{5,\mathcal{D}}$ by the reusable witness-indistinguishability of wi, that is, witness indistinguishability in the setting where multiple proofs are provided for different statements, using the same first two messages transcript.

$\mathsf{Hybrid}_{7,\mathcal{D}}$: In this hybrid, the challenger behaves the same way as $\mathsf{Hybrid}_{6,\mathcal{D}}$, except that it uses the second witness, r_2, γ_2, to generate the arguments wi all the "lookahead executions" of the simulation strategy, as well as in the output transcript. That is, in every message that the challenger ever sends, it uses the second witness instead of the first. This hybrid is indistinguishable from $\mathsf{Hybrid}_{6,\mathcal{D}}$ by the reusable witness-indistinguishability of wi.

$\mathsf{Hybrid}_{8,\mathcal{D}}$: In this hybrid, the challenger behaves the same way as $\mathsf{Hybrid}_{7,\mathcal{D}}$, except that in all transcripts, it sets nmc^1 as a non-malleable commitment to a *different* randomness γ_1' than the one used to compute δ_1. The view of a malicious receiver in this hybrid is indistinguishable from $\mathsf{Hybrid}_{7,\mathcal{D}}$ by the hiding of the non-malleable commitment Π^1.

$\mathsf{Hybrid}_{9,\mathcal{D}}$: In this hybrid, the challenger behaves the same way as $\mathsf{Hybrid}_{8,\mathcal{D}}$, except that in the output transcript, it sets $\delta_1 \xleftarrow{\$} \{0,1\}^*$, instead of setting $\delta_1 = \mathsf{PRF}(\gamma_1, \alpha_1) \oplus r$. Note that the committer is committing to a different value γ_1' in the protocol Π^1, thus the key γ_1 does not appear in the rest of the protocol. Therefore, this hybrid is indistinguishable from $\mathsf{Hybrid}_{8,\mathcal{D}}$ by PRF security.

$\mathsf{Hybrid}_{10,\mathcal{D}}$: In this hybrid, the challenger behaves the same way as $\mathsf{Hybrid}_{10,\mathcal{D}}$ except that it replaces $\mathsf{com}(m_0; r)$ with $\mathsf{com}(m_1; r)$ in the output transcript. Note that at this point, r is not used anywhere else in the protocol, and hence the commitment can be obtained externally. This hybrid is indistinguishable from $\mathsf{Hybrid}_{9,\mathcal{D}}$ by computational hiding of the non-interactive commitment.

At this point, we have successfully indistinguishably switched to an experiment where the commitment is generated to message m_1 instead of m_0 in the main transcript output by the challenger. Computational hiding follows by repeating the above hybrids in reverse order, until in Hybrid_{m_1}, the challenger generates an honest commitment to message m_1. This completes the proof of hiding, and we now prove that the scheme ϕ is an extractable commitment.

Lemma 2. *There exists a PPT extractor $\mathcal{E}$ that given oracle access to any committer $\mathcal{C}^*$, and a valid commitment transcript τ generated by $\mathcal{C}^*$ participating in* *an execution of ϕ with an honest receiver $\mathcal{R}$, outputs the value committed by C^* in τ, with probability $1 - \mathsf{negl}(n)$ over the randomness of $\mathcal{R}$ and $\mathcal{E}$.*

Proof. For any accepting commitment transcript generated by a committer, with probability $1 - \mathsf{negl}(n)$, because of adaptive soundness of wi, the ith extractable commitment is generated as a valid extractable commitment to randomness r_i, such that $\mathsf{PRF}(r_i, a_i) \oplus x_i$ yields a valid witness for wi, for some $i \in \{1, 2\}$. Furthermore, by soundness of wzk, c_1 is a commitment to 1, and by statistical binding of com, c_1 cannot be a commitment to 0. Thus, the only possible valid witness in wi, with overwhelming probability, must necessarily be a witness for c, which is the actual commitment to the message.

We now argue that this witness can be extracted by a polynomial time extractor. This follows roughly because of the (over)-extraction property of Π and the soundness of wi, similar to [15]. Specifically, we consider a committer that generates an accepting transcript with probability $\frac{1}{\mathsf{poly}(n)}$. Then, within $n \cdot \mathsf{poly}(n)$ rewindings, such a committer generates an expected n accepting transcripts. Moreover, with overwhelming probability at least $\sqrt{n}$ of the accepting transcripts (in the lookahead threads) generate a valid commitment using scheme Π for the same index i as the main thread. This allows for extraction of randomness r from the over-extracting commitment Π^i. Next, the extractor checks the extracted value r against c to ensure that r is the correct randomness that was used to compute c. Note that this scheme does not suffer from over-extraction, since by the soundness of wzk and wi, a malicious committer is always forced to use the unique witness corresponding to the commitment c. Furthermore, an extractor can extract with error at most ϵ by running in time $\mathsf{poly}(1/\epsilon)$.

Next, we directly prove concurrent non-malleability of the resulting scheme when instantiated with the basic protocol Π from [13]. The scheme can also be instantiated with the protocol from [12], to yield one-one non-malleability.

Theorem 1. *The protocol ϕ in Fig. 2, when instantiated with the one-many weak non-malleable commitment Π from [13], is a concurrent non-malleable commitment with respect to commitment according to Definition 5.*

Proof. We first note that it suffices to argue non-malleability against one-many adversaries, that participate in one left session and polynomial right sessions. By [19], security against such adversaries already implies concurrent non-malleability. Suppose the MIM opens $p = \mathsf{poly}(n)$ sessions on the right.

The proof of non-malleability against non-synchronizing adversaries, that complete the left session before opening right sessions, follows directly because ϕ is an extractable commitment, by Lemma 2. In other words, given a non-synchronizing MIM adversary, there exists a reduction that runs an extractor to extract the value committed by the MIM from the right execution(s) by rewinding the adversary, and uses the view jointly with the values extracted from such a malleating adversary to directly break hiding of the commitment in the left execution. Because of the non-synchronizing scheduling, the reduction can rewind the MIM's commitment and run the extractor of Lemma 2 without rewinding the honest commitment at all. This leads to a contradiction, ruling out the existence of any PPT MIM adversary that successfully mauls the honest commitment.

It remains to argue non-malleability in the fully synchronizing setting (these arguments directly combine to argue security against adversaries that are synchronizing in some executions and non-synchronizing in others). We do this via a sequence of hybrid experiments, relying on the non-malleability of Π, along with various properties of other primitives used in the protocol. These hybrids are all parameterized by an inverse polynomial error parameter ϵ, and sometimes require the challenger to run in time $\mathsf{poly}(n, \frac{1}{\epsilon})$. Later, we will set ϵ to be significantly smaller than the advantage of any distinguisher between $\mathsf{MIM}_{\langle C,R\rangle}(V_1, z)$ and $\mathsf{MIM}_{\langle C,R\rangle}(V_2, z)$ (but ϵ will still be some inverse polynomial $\frac{1}{\mathsf{poly}(\cdot)}$), thereby proving the lemma. We will use $\tilde{a}$ to denote message a sent in the right execution, and a message a sent during the left execution will just be denoted by a.

Overview of Hybrid Experiments. Before describing the hybrid arguments in detail, we provide an overview. The sequence of experiments follows the same pattern as the proof of hiding, except that we now argue about the joint distribution of the view and values committed by the MIM. Whenever the challenger rewinds and generates lookahead threads to learn γ or to simulate the weak ZK, the challenger always generates multiple lookahead threads where half commit to value V_1 and half to V_2 (this is possible since the message is decided in the last round), and combines information extracted using both V_1, V_2, like [15].

In the following hybrids, the challenger will never generate simulated wzk proofs in any rewinding execution. The wzk proof will be carefully simulated only in the main transcript (in some of the hybrids). Thus, by soundness of the wi, the MIM will always commit to the witness for the commitment, by correctly generating a non-malleable commitment to at least one of the γ values, in any rewinding execution. Therefore, a rewinding extractor will correctly extract at least one γ value committed by the MIM, with high probability. Furthermore, when relying on the extractor of the non-malleable commitment scheme, we will again generate a transcript for the extractor that does not contain any simulated proofs – therefore, this extractor is guaranteed to correctly extract at least one of the γ values committed by the MIM.

Hybrid_{V_1}: The output of the first experiment, Hybrid_{V_1} corresponds to the joint distribution of the view and values committed by the MIM on input an honest commitment to value V_1.

Hybrid_1: In the first hybrid, the challenger changes the left execution by first sampling (γ_2, γ'_2) independently and uniformly at random. The value committed using the second non-malleable commitment Π^2 is γ'_2, while the third message $\delta_2 = \mathsf{PRF}(\gamma_2, \alpha_2) \oplus r$ is computed honestly using a different γ_2. At this point, we invoke soundness of the wi and wzk to argue that the MIM must commit to at least one valid $\tilde{\gamma}_i^1$ or $\tilde{\gamma}_i^2$ in the main execution, for every $i \in [p(n)]$. Therefore, we can invoke the extractor for Π^2, to extract the joint distribution of the values committed by the man-in-the-middle (MIM) in all right executions.

By the property of the non-malleable commitment, when the MIM commits to a valid value in the main execution, such an extractor will successfully extract at least one of the committed values $\widetilde{\gamma}_i^1$ or $\widetilde{\gamma}_i^2$ from the ith right interaction, for all $i \in [p(n)]$. Because of soundness of wi and wzk, this extracted value will directly help recover the message committed by the MIM in this interaction. Since this extractor operates *without* rewinding the left execution, if the joint distribution of the view and values changes from Hybrid_0 to Hybrid_1, we obtain a contradiction to the hiding of Π.

Hybrid_2: In the next hybrid, the challenger modifies the left execution by generating an output view where the left execution contains a simulated weak ZK argument. When applied naively, the simulation guarantee is that the view of the MIM remains indistinguishable when provided a transcript with a simulated proof. However, there are no guarantees about the MIM's committed values.

In order to ensure that the joint distribution of committed values remains indistinguishable, we modify the input to the distinguisher-dependent simulator. That is, we modify the experiment so that, the challenger first rewinds the MIM and extracts the joint distribution of values $\widetilde{\gamma}$ committed by the MIM. Here, we rely on the fact that Π is stand-alone extractable (with over-extraction). Note that once extracted, these $\widetilde{\gamma}$'s can be used to extract the messages committed by the MIM in any transcript with the same fixed first two messages, with overwhelming probability. The only situation in which the $\widetilde{\gamma}_i^b$ extracted for some execution i does not help recover the message committed by the MIM from transcript τ with the same fixed first message, is if the MIM uses a different witness $\widetilde{\gamma}_i^{1-b}$ in τ and uses $\widetilde{\gamma}_i^b$ in all the rewinding executions. However, this event occurs only with probability at most $\mathsf{negl}(n)$.

Upon extracting these values, with the same fixed first message, the challenger begins running the simulation strategy of weak ZK to output a main transcript with a simulated proof. That is, the challenger uses the $\widetilde{\gamma}$'s to extract the joint distribution of the values committed by the MIM from any right execution, and runs the distinguisher-dependent simulator on a distinguisher that obtains the joint distribution of the view output by the MIM, together with these extracted values. Now, by the guarantee of distinguisher-dependent simulation, we have that the joint distribution remains indistinguishable between Hybrid_1 and Hybrid_2. In our actual reduction, we require a special type of weak resettable security of the weak ZK. Additional details are in the formal proof.

Hybrid_3: In the next hybrid, the output transcript generated in the left execution, consists of a commitment $c_1 = \mathsf{com}(0; \widehat{r})$ with uniform randomness $\widehat{r}$, instead of c_1 being a commitment to 1. This is allowed because the weak ZK proof is being simulated by this point. The joint distribution of the view and values committed do not change in this hybrid, because c_1 is non-interactive, and thus can be replaced in the main transcript, while rewinding the MIM and extracting the joint distribution of the values committed by the MIM in all right executions.

Hybrid_4: In this next hybrid, the challenger sets $\delta_2 = \mathsf{PRF}(\gamma_2, \alpha_2) \oplus \widehat{r}$ (instead of $\mathsf{PRF}(\gamma_2, \alpha_2) \oplus r$), where $\widehat{r}$ is the randomness used to generate c_1. Since the

PRF key γ_2 does not appear elsewhere in the protocol, the joint distribution of the view and values committed do not change in this hybrid. This is δ_2 can be replaced in the main transcript, while rewinding the MIM and extracting the joint distribution of the values committed by the MIM in all right executions.

Hybrid$_5$: In this next hybrid, the challenger changes the non-malleable commitment Π^2 to commit to the same randomness γ_2, that is used to compute δ_2 in all threads (instead of committing to a different γ_2'). In order to argue indistinguishability of the view and committed values, we now rely on the non-malleability of Π^2. The challenger runs the extractor for Π^2 on a transcript that contains honestly generated wzk proofs: again by soundness, at least one of the $\widetilde{\gamma}$ values committed by the MIM in every execution is a valid commitment in the main thread. Thus, the extractor outputs this value. Next, the challenger uses this extracted value to recover the joint distribution of messages from transcripts generated by the MIM. This helps the challenger generate an output transcript with a simulated wzk proof, such that the joint distribution of the view of the MIM and values committed remains indistinguishable.

Note that in this experiment, even though the left execution is rewound to generate lookahead threads for distinguisher-dependent simulation, this rewinding happens after the first two rounds have been fixed. Thus, the *non-malleable commitment* used in the left execution is never rewound, and can be obtained externally. If the joint distribution of view and values output by the extractor for Π changes in this hybrid, then this contradicts hiding of Π. The argument of indistinguishability again requires a specific ordering to generate the lookahead threads for extracting the MIM's committed values, and the lookahead threads for simulation. Additional details can be found in the formal proof.

Hybrid$_6$, Hybrid$_7$: By the end of these hybrids, the challenger will behave the same way as Hybrid$_5$, except that it will use the second witness γ_2 in all executions (in the main as well as lookahead threads). For the main thread, for which the witness is switched in Hybrid$_6$, the challenger will use witness $\gamma_2, \widehat{r}, \delta_2, c_1$ to compute the wi. In the rewinding threads, for which the witness is switched in Hybrid$_7$, the challenger will use witness γ_2, r, δ_2, c. The joint distribution of the view and value extracted remains indistinguishable because of the reusable resettable security of wi allows for switching the witness even when multiple proofs are given in the main as well as rewinding executions.

Hybrid$_8$: In this hybrid, the challenger sets Π^1 as a non-malleable commitment to a different independently uniform randomness γ_1', than the randomness γ that is used to compute δ_1 in all executions. The joint distribution of view and values committed by the MIM remains indistinguishable by the non-malleability of Π. The proof follows in a similar manner as of the indistinguishability of Hybrid$_5$.

Hybrid$_9$: In this hybrid, the challenger behaves similar to the previous hybrid except setting δ_1 to uniformly at random, only in the output transcript. Since the key γ_1 no longer appears elsewhere in the protocol, indistinguishability of the view and committed values follows by security of the PRF.

$Hybrid_{10}$: In this hybrid, the challenger behaves similar to the previous hybrid, except in the output transcript, it sets c as a commitment to value V_2 instead of to value V_1. This is allowed because the randomness used to compute c in the output transcript is not used elsewhere in the protocol. Indistinguishability of the view and values committed by the MIM in this execution, follows by hiding of the non-interactive commitment c.

At this point, the main transcript consists of a commitment to V_2 instead of to V_1, while the lookahead transcripts are generated using both V_1 and V_2. Now, following the same sequence of hybrids in reverse order, we get to a hybrid experiment where the challenger generates an honest commitment to V_2 in the left execution. Thus, the joint distribution of the view and values committed by the MIM remains indistinguishable between when the left commitment is to V_1, versus to V_2, which is the guarantee required by the definition of non-malleability.

Hybrid Experiments. We now formally describe the hybrid arguments that we use to prove non-malleability.

$Hybrid_{V_1}$: This hybrid corresponds to an interaction of the challenger and the MIM where the challenger uses input message V_1 in the honest interaction. Let $MIM_{\langle C,R \rangle}(V_1, z)$ denote the joint distribution of the view and values committed by the MIM in this interaction.

$Hybrid_1$: In this hybrid, the challenger behaves identically to $Hybrid_{V_1}$, except that it generates Π^2 as a non-malleable commitment to a different randomness γ_2' chosen uniformly and independently at at random, from the randomness γ_2 that was used to compute δ_2. Let $MIM_{\langle C,R \rangle}(value, z)_{Hybrid_1}$ denote the joint distribution of the view and values committed by the MIM in this interaction, in all the right sessions.

Lemma 3. *For any PPT distinguisher $\mathcal{D}$ with auxiliary information z,*
$$|\Pr[\mathcal{D}(z, MIM_{\langle C,R \rangle}(V_1, z)) = 1] - \Pr[\mathcal{D}(z, MIM_{\langle C,R \rangle}(value, z)_{Hybrid_1}) = 1]| \leq \epsilon + \mathsf{negl}(n).$$

Proof. The proof of this lemma follows via a reduction to the weak non-malleability of the scheme Π. More specifically, given a distinguisher $\mathcal{D}$ that distinguishes $MIM_{\langle C,R \rangle}(value, z)_{Hybrid_1}$ and $MIM_{\langle C,R \rangle}(V_1, z)$, we construct an adversary $\mathcal{A}^{\mathcal{D}}$ against the weak one-many non-malleability of Π according to Definition 6.

The adversary $\mathcal{A}$ participates in the experiment exactly as $Hybrid_{V_1}$, except that it samples $\gamma_2, \gamma_2' \xleftarrow{\$} \{0,1\}^*$ and submits these to an external challenger. It obtains externally, the messages of Π^2, which are either a non-malleable commitment to γ_2 or to γ_2'. It complete the third message of the protocol using γ_2 to compute δ_2.

By the weak non-malleability of Π, there exists an extractor that runs in time $\mathsf{poly}(\frac{1}{\epsilon})$ and extracts the values committed by the MIM in all the non-malleable commitments for all $j \in [p]$, *without* rewinding the honest execution. Further, this extractor has the property that it only extracts an incorrect value if the

MIM is committing to $\perp$ in the main thread in the honest execution, except with error ϵ.

However, in both Hybrid_{V_1} and Hybrid_1, by the soundness of wi, the adversary is guaranteed to generate at least one out of the two non-malleable commitments (to $\tilde{\gamma}_1$ or $\tilde{\gamma}_2$) from each session, correctly in any execution, except with probability $\mathsf{negl}(n)$. Moreover, by soundness of wzk, the extracted value from at least one of the non-malleable commitments generated by the MIM in each session, will correspond to a witness for the commitment c, and therefore directly help recover the value committed by the MIM in each right session.

$\mathcal{A}$ then samples a random main thread execution, and then just runs this extractor to extract the values $\{\tilde{\gamma}_i^1, \tilde{\gamma}_i^2\}_{i \in [n]}$ committed by the MIM, and by soundness of wi and wzk, at least one is correctly extracted. Depending upon whether the challenge non-malleable commitment is to γ_2 or γ_2', the joint distribution of the view and value extracted by $\mathcal{A}$ corresponds to either $\mathsf{MIM}_{\langle C,R \rangle}(V_1, z)$ or $\mathsf{MIM}_{\langle C,R \rangle}(\mathsf{value}, z)_{\mathsf{Hybrid}_1}$.

Therefore, if the joint distribution of the view and the values committed by the MIM changes by more than ϵ between these executions, it can be used to contradict the one-many weak non-malleability of Π. Thus, if

$$| \Pr[\mathcal{D}(z, \mathsf{MIM}_{\langle C,R \rangle}(V_1, z)) = 1] - \Pr[\mathcal{D}(z, \mathsf{MIM}_{\langle C,R \rangle}(\mathsf{value}, z)_{\mathsf{Hybrid}_1}) = 1]| \geq \epsilon + \frac{1}{\mathsf{poly}}(n),$$

$$\text{then, } |\Pr[\mathcal{A}^{\mathcal{D}} = 1 | \gamma'] - \Pr[\mathcal{A}^{\mathcal{D}} = 1 | \gamma]| \geq \frac{1}{\mathsf{poly}}(n).$$

This gives a contradiction, thus the distributions are indistinguishable upto ϵ error.

We note that in Hybrid_1, soundness of the wi and wzk arguments in the left as well as right interactions is still maintained, thus a rewinding extractor always successfully extracts the value committed by the MIM.

$\mathsf{Hybrid}_{2,\mathcal{D}}$: In this hybrid, the challenger behaves similarly to Hybrid_1, except that it outputs the transcript of an execution where the distinguisher-dependent weak zero-knowledge protocol wzk is simulated as follows. For simplicity of exposition, we add some clearly demarcated analysis to the description of the experiment.

1. Run the execution until the MIM sends the first message for the right execution. With fixed first messages, ϕ_1 and $\tilde{\phi}_1^j$ for $j \in [p]$, run the rest of the protocol as follows.
2. Send second messages $\tilde{\phi}_2^j$ for the right interactions, and wait for the MIM's response ϕ_2. These will correspond to the first and second messages for the main transcript.
3. With first two messages fixed as above, generate a lookahead thread as follows: send the third message on behalf of the honest party, computed as a commitment to V_1 honestly as in Hybrid_1 (this is later also repeated for V_2). Let $\{\tilde{\gamma}_1^j, \tilde{\gamma}_2^j\}_{j \in [p]}$ denote the joint distribution of values committed by the MIM in this execution. If the MIM produced an invalid transcript, abort. Otherwise, continue.

4. With the same fixed first messages, ϕ_1 and $\widetilde{\phi}_1^j$ for $j \in [p]$, rewind the MIM $(1/\epsilon^2)$ times sending various second round challenge messages to the MIM on behalf of honest receiver. When the MIM sends a challenge for the left (honest) execution, complete the transcript as an honest commitment to V_1 (this is later also repeated for V_2), and wait for the MIM's response.

   Use these rewinding executions to extract the value committed in at least one (or both) of the non-malleable commitments $\{\widehat{\gamma}_1^j, \widehat{\gamma}_2^j\}_{j \in [p]}$ provided by the MIM adversary, for each session.

   Analysis. Whenever the MIM completes a right execution (that is, it does not generate any invalid messages), by soundness of the WI and the weak ZK argument, we have that with probability at least $1 - \mathsf{negl}(n)$, at least one of the non-malleable commitments were generated correctly in each execution. Thus, by the same argument as used in the Lemma 3, with overwhelming probability, the extractor runs in time $\mathsf{poly}(\frac{1}{\epsilon^2})$ and correctly extracts at least one of the values committed by the MIM using the non-malleable commitment in all executions, except with error at most ϵ^2.

5. Repeat Steps 3 and 4, $\frac{1}{\epsilon^4}$ times for both V_1 and V_2, and compute the union of extracted values (by checking whenever a value was correctly extracted). For each right session $j \in [p]$, denote the values extracted by the challenger by $\widetilde{\gamma}_1^j, \widetilde{\gamma}_2^j$.

   Analysis. At the end of this step, at least one value must be correctly extracted for every right session, except with total failure probability at most ϵ^2. Moreover, if for any right execution the extractor successfully extracted only *one* value, then by a Markov argument, the MIM will continue to use the same value as witness for the wi in all lookahead executions that we will create for distinguisher-dependent simulation, except with probability at most ϵ^2 (otherwise, if the MIM used a different value as witness for the wi, then that value would also be extracted with significant probability). Therefore, $\{\widetilde{\gamma}_1^j, \widetilde{\gamma}_2^j\}_{j \in [p]}$ can be used to recover the value committed by the MIM from any transcript generated by the MIM with fixed first two messages $\phi_1, \widetilde{\phi}_1^j, \phi_2, \widetilde{\phi}_2^j$, except with failure probability ϵ^2.[4]

6. After completing the previous step, with the first message transcript fixed, go back and again fix first two messages $\phi_1, \widetilde{\phi}_1^j, \widetilde{\phi}_2^j, \phi_2$. These will now remain fixed for the rest of the experiment. Since these same first two round messages were in fact fixed at the start of the protocol, by the weak resettable weak ZK property of wzk, the simulation security of wzk holds with respect to the partial transcript $(\phi_1, \phi_2, \widetilde{\phi}_1^j, \widetilde{\phi}_2^j)$.

   In particular, weak resettable security implies that indistinguishability between real and simulated view must hold even against a distinguisher that performed the rewindings in the previous step and obtained $\{\widetilde{\gamma}_1^j, \widetilde{\gamma}_2^j\}_{j \in [p]}$. Note that these values $\{\widetilde{\gamma}_1^j, \widetilde{\gamma}_2^j\}_{j \in [p]}$ can now be used to extract the message committed in the string c by the MIM from any transcript generated by the MIM with fixed first two messages, except with error at most $\epsilon^2 + \mathsf{negl}(n)$.

---

[4] Please refer to the full version for exact calculations and additional details.

7. Next, run the distinguisher-dependent simulation strategy S of the weak zero-knowledge argument, with error ϵ^2, on the distinguisher D' constructed as follows. D' is given the view of the MIM, together with auxiliary information $\{\widetilde{\gamma}_1^j, \widetilde{\gamma}_2^j\}_{j \in [p]}$. On input the view of the MIM, it uses this information to extract the value committed by the MIM from all its executions. It then runs the distinguisher D on the joint distribution of the view and the extracted values and mirrors the output of D.

Recall, that the distinguisher-dependent simulation strategy S of [15] generates several different third messages (corresponding to the same fixed messages $(\phi_1, \phi_2, \widetilde{\phi}_1^j, \widetilde{\phi}_2^j)$), while sampling fresh α_1, α_2 each time. Also note that the output transcript still contains a commitment to V_1, and is infact identical to Hybrid$_1$ except that it contains a simulated wzk argument.

Let $\text{MIM}_{\langle C,R \rangle}(\text{value}, z)_{\text{Hybrid}_{2,D}}$ denote the joint distribution of the view and value committed by the MIM when interacting with an honest committer in this hybrid.

Lemma 4. *For any PPT distinguisher D with auxiliary information z, $|\Pr[D(z, \text{MIM}_{\langle C,R \rangle}(\text{value}, z)_{\text{Hybrid}_{2,D}}) = 1] - \Pr[D(z, \text{MIM}_{\langle C,R \rangle}(\text{value}, z)_{\text{Hybrid}_1}) = 1]| \leq \epsilon + \text{negl}(n)$.*

Proof. This claim follows by the weak resettable security of distinguisher-dependent simulation: since $\text{MIM}_{\langle C,R \rangle}(\text{value}, z)_{\text{Hybrid}_{2,D}}$ is the result of executing distinguisher-dependent simulation against distinguisher D', which itself runs the distinguisher D on $\text{MIM}_{\langle C,R \rangle}(\text{value}, z)_{\text{Hybrid}_1}$. Note that the weak resettable security experiment for distinguisher-dependent simulation allows the adversary to obtain, in addition to a real/simulated main transcript, several "lookahead" transcripts, where all lookahead transcripts contain honestly generated proofs, that may all use the same first message of the argument.

In other words, we consider a reduction that first fixes the first two messages of the honest and MIM execution corresponding to the main thread. Next, it generates multiple lookahead threads, as allowed by the security experiment of weak resettable wzk, using these threads to extract the values $\{\widetilde{\gamma}_1^j, \widetilde{\gamma}_2^j\}_{j \in [p]}$ committed by the MIM. In all these lookahead threads, the challenger generates all messages on its own according to Hybrid$_1$, except that it obtains the honestly generated wzk proofs for these threads externally from a challenger for weak resettable weak ZK.

Finally, the challenger flips a bit b, and if $b = 0$, it outputs an honestly generated weak ZK argument for the main transcript. On the other hand, if $b = 1$, it outputs a simulated argument (with error at most ϵ), while simulating the output of distinguisher D on input the view and values extracted from the MIM. The reduction obtains this proof from the challenger and uses it to complete the main transcript. Because of correctness of extracted values argued in the analysis above, we note that if $b = 0$, the experiment corresponds to running D on $\text{MIM}_{\langle C,R \rangle}(\text{value}, z)_{\text{Hybrid}_{1,D}}$ and if $b = 1$, the experiment corresponds to running the distinguisher D on $\text{MIM}_{\langle C,R \rangle}(\text{value}, z)_{\text{Hybrid}_{2,D}}$. Thus, if

$|\Pr[\mathcal{D}(z, \mathsf{MIM}_{\langle C,R \rangle}(\mathsf{value}, z)_{\mathsf{Hybrid}_{2,\mathcal{D}}}) = 1] - \Pr[\mathcal{D}(z, \mathsf{MIM}_{\langle C,R \rangle}(\mathsf{value}, z)_{\mathsf{Hybrid}_1}) = 1]| > \epsilon + \mathsf{negl}(n)$, this gives a distinguisher against the weak resettable simulation security of the weak ZK argument according to Definition 2, which is a contradiction.

$\mathsf{Hybrid}_{3,\mathcal{D}}$: In this hybrid, the challenger behaves identically to $\mathsf{Hybrid}_{2,\mathcal{D}}$, except that it sets $c_1 = \mathsf{com}(0; \widehat{r})$ by picking uniform randomness $\widehat{r}$, in the main transcript (instead of generating c_1 as a commitment to 1). Note that this is possible because the challenger is generating a simulated proof in the output transcript, for the fact that c_1 is a commitment to 1. Let $\mathsf{MIM}_{\langle C,R \rangle}(\mathsf{value}, z)_{\mathsf{Hybrid}_{3,\mathcal{D}}}$ denote the joint distribution of the view and values committed by the MIM when interacting with the challenger in this hybrid.

Lemma 5. *For any PPT distinguisher $\mathcal{D}$ with auxiliary information z,* $|\Pr[\mathcal{D}(z, \mathsf{MIM}_{\langle C,R \rangle}(\mathsf{value}, z)_{\mathsf{Hybrid}_{2,\mathcal{D}}}) = 1] - \Pr[\mathcal{D}(z, \mathsf{MIM}_{\langle C,R \rangle}(\mathsf{value}, z)_{\mathsf{Hybrid}_{3,\mathcal{D}}}) = 1]| \leq \mathsf{negl}(n)$.

Proof. This hybrid is indistinguishable from Hybrid_2 by the computational hiding property of the non-interactive commitment scheme com. More formally, consider a reduction $\mathcal{R}$ that behaves identically to $\mathsf{Hybrid}_{2,\mathcal{D}}$, first extracting $\{\widetilde{\gamma}_1^j, \widetilde{\gamma}_2^j\}_{j \in [p]}$. Next, it obtains the commitment c_1 (only for the main thread and not for any of the rewinding executions), externally, as either a commitment to 0 or a commitment to 1, and uses this to complete the main transcript. It then uses the extracted values $\{\widetilde{\gamma}_1^j, \widetilde{\gamma}_2^j\}_{j \in [p]}$ to recover the values committed by the MIM in the main transcript. It outputs the joint distribution of the transcript and the values committed by the MIM to distinguisher $\mathcal{D}$. Then given a distinguisher $\mathcal{D}$ where: $|\Pr[\mathcal{D}(z, \mathsf{MIM}_{\langle C,R \rangle}(\mathsf{value}, z)_{\mathsf{Hybrid}_{2,\mathcal{D}}}) = 1] - \Pr[\mathcal{D}(z, \mathsf{MIM}_{\langle C,R \rangle}(\mathsf{value}, z)_{\mathsf{Hybrid}_{3,\mathcal{D}}}) = 1]| \geq \frac{1}{\mathsf{poly}(n)}$, the reduction mirrors the output of this distinguisher such that:

$$|\Pr[\mathcal{R} = 1 | c_1 = \mathsf{com}(1; r)] - \Pr[\mathcal{R} = 1 | c_1 = \mathsf{com}(0; r)]| \geq \frac{1}{\mathsf{poly}(n)}$$

This is a contradiction to the hiding of com.

$\mathsf{Hybrid}_{4,\mathcal{D}}$: In this hybrid, the challenger behaves identically to $\mathsf{Hybrid}_{3,\mathcal{D}}$ except that in the output transcript, it sets $\delta_2 = \mathsf{PRF}(\gamma_2, \alpha_2) \oplus \widehat{r}$ where $\widehat{r}$ is the randomness used to generate $c_1 = \mathsf{com}(0; \widehat{r})$. Note that the committer is using PRF key γ_2' in the protocol Π^2, thus the key γ_2 does not appear anywhere else in the rest of the protocol.

Let $\mathsf{MIM}_{\langle C,R \rangle}(\mathsf{value}, z)_{\mathsf{Hybrid}_{4,\mathcal{D}}}$ denote the joint distribution of the view and value committed by the MIM when interacting with an honest committer in this hybrid.

Lemma 6. *For any PPT distinguisher $\mathcal{D}$ with auxiliary information z,* $|\Pr[\mathcal{D}(z, \mathsf{MIM}_{\langle C,R \rangle}(\mathsf{value}, z)_{\mathsf{Hybrid}_{4,\mathcal{D}}}) = 1] - \Pr[\mathcal{D}(z, \mathsf{MIM}_{\langle C,R \rangle}(\mathsf{value}, z)_{\mathsf{Hybrid}_{3,\mathcal{D}}}) = 1]| \leq \mathsf{negl}(n)$.

Proof. This hybrid is indistinguishable from $\mathsf{Hybrid}_{3,\mathcal{D}}$ by the security of the PRF. More formally, consider a reduction $\mathcal{R}$ that behaves identically to $\mathsf{Hybrid}_{3,\mathcal{D}}$ except that for all lookahead (recall that the distinguisher is rewound several times) threads, it samples fresh α_2 each time and obtains $\mathsf{PRF}(\gamma_2, \alpha_2) \oplus \widehat{r}$ externally from a PRF challenger.

Then, *for the main thread* it obtains the value δ_2 externally as either $\mathsf{PRF}(\gamma_2, \alpha_2) \oplus \widehat{r}$, or $\mathsf{PRF}(\gamma_2, \alpha_2) \oplus r$, where r is the randomness used generate commitment c in the left execution, and $\widehat{r}$ is the randomness used to generate commitment c_1. It uses the externally obtained δ_2 to complete the main transcript. It then uses the extracted values $\{\widetilde{\gamma}_1^j, \widetilde{\gamma}_2^j\}_{j \in [p]}$ to obtain the values committed by the MIM in the main transcript. It outputs the joint distribution of the transcript and the values committed by the MIM to distinguisher $\mathcal{D}$.

Given a distinguisher $\mathcal{D}$ where $|\Pr[\mathcal{D}(z, \mathsf{MIM}_{\langle C,R \rangle}(\mathsf{value}, z)_{\mathsf{Hybrid}_{4,\mathcal{D}}}) = 1] - \Pr[\mathcal{D}(z, \mathsf{MIM}_{\langle C,R \rangle}(\mathsf{value}, z)_{\mathsf{Hybrid}_{3,\mathcal{D}}}) = 1]| \geq \frac{1}{\mathsf{poly}(n)}$, the reduction can mirror the output of this distinguisher to directly contradict the security of the PRF.

$\mathsf{Hybrid}_{5,\mathcal{D}}$: In this hybrid, the challenger behaves identically to $\mathsf{Hybrid}_{4,\mathcal{D}}$ except that it sets Π^2 as a non-malleable commitment to the same randomness γ_2 that is used to compute δ_2, for all executions.

This hybrid essentially "reverts" the changes performed in Hybrid_1. Note that the challenger in this hybrid, first extracts the values committed via the non-malleable commitments provided by the MIM, and then rewinds the *distinguisher* multiple times – however, the first two messages of the protocol are fixed at the time of rewinding the distinguisher. In particular, for fixed nmc_1^2 and nmc_2^2, the challenger gives the same response nmc_3^2 for all the third messages it generates while/before simulating wzk argument.

Since the main thread transcript output in this hybrid consists of a simulated proof, indistinguishability of this hybrid is the most interesting to argue. We prove that it follows by the weak non-malleability of Π^2. It is important, for the proof of non-malleability to go through, that the witness used by the prover in the proof of WI in this hybrid, is always the randomness used to compute Π^1 and never the randomness used to compute Π^2 – because the messages of Π^2 will be obtained externally. Moreover, recall that the proof of non-malleability of the weak non-malleable commitment scheme Π requires a simulator-extractor to "cheat" in the scheme Π^2 in rewinding executions.

Note that the challenger in this hybrid, fixes the first two rounds for the output transcript. Then, with the same fixed first round, it attempts to extract the values $(\widetilde{\gamma}_1^j, \widetilde{\gamma}_2^j)$ committed by the MIM in the non-malleable commitments in all right sessions. After extraction, it rewinds the *distinguisher* multiple times – at this point the first two messages of the protocol are again the first two rounds that were fixed prior to extraction. Note that the transcript output by the challenger in this experiment is such that Π^1 is a valid non-malleable commitment to γ_1 with randomness r_1 AND $r = \mathsf{PRF}(\gamma_1, \alpha_1) \oplus \delta_1$ such that $c = \mathsf{com}(m; r)$ (and this is the witness used in wi). Additionally, Π^2 is also a valid non-malleable commitment to γ_2 with randomness r_2 AND $\widehat{r} = \mathsf{PRF}(\gamma_2, \alpha_2) \oplus \delta_2$ such that $c_1 = \mathsf{com}(0; \widehat{r})$. However, the witness used in wi is always Π^1.

Let $\mathsf{MIM}_{\langle C,R \rangle}(\mathsf{value}, z)_{\mathsf{Hybrid}_{5,\mathcal{D}}}$ denote the joint distribution of the view and value committed by the MIM when interacting with an honest committer in this hybrid.

Lemma 7. *For any PPT distinguisher $\mathcal{D}$ with auxiliary information z, $| \Pr[\mathcal{D}(z,$ $\mathsf{MIM}_{\langle C,R \rangle}(\mathsf{value}, z)_{\mathsf{Hybrid}_{5,\mathcal{D}}}) = 1] - \Pr[\mathcal{D}(z, \mathsf{MIM}_{\langle C,R \rangle}(\mathsf{value}, z)_{\mathsf{Hybrid}_{4,\mathcal{D}}}) = 1]| \leq$ $3\epsilon + \mathsf{negl}(n)$.*

Proof. Recall that the challenger strategy in both $\mathsf{Hybrid}_{5,\mathcal{D}}$ and $\mathsf{Hybrid}_{4,\mathcal{D}}$ is as follows: The challenger first generates and fixes the first two messages of the main transcript $\phi_1, \widetilde{\phi}_1^j, \widetilde{\phi}_2^j, \phi_2$. It then rewinds the MIM multiple times with the same fixed first message but different second round messages, to extract $\widetilde{\gamma}_1^j, \widetilde{\gamma}_2^j$ for all $j \in [n]$. Finally, it runs the distinguisher-dependent simulation strategy with partial transcript $\phi_1, \widetilde{\phi}_1^j, \widetilde{\phi}_2^j, \phi_2$ to output a main transcript with a simulated proof.

The main difference between $\mathsf{Hybrid}_{4,\mathcal{D}}$ and $\mathsf{Hybrid}_{5,\mathcal{D}}$ is that the committer commits to γ_2' using Π^2 in $\mathsf{Hybrid}_{4,\mathcal{D}}$, and uses a different γ_2 for the rest of the protocol, whereas in $\mathsf{Hybrid}_{5,\mathcal{D}}$, $\gamma_2' = \gamma_2$. However, both hybrids involve the challenger rewinding the MIM (and consequently rewinding the left session) several times in order to extract $\widetilde{\gamma}_1^j, \widetilde{\gamma}_2^j$ for $j \in [n]$. In this rewinding situation, invoking weak one-malleability of Π^2 requires care.

Our first observation is that by the weak non-malleability of Π, there exists an extractor that runs in time $\mathsf{poly}(\frac{1}{\epsilon})$ and extracts the values committed by the MIM in all the non-malleable commitments for all $j \in [p]$, *without rewinding the left execution*. The reduction to one-many weak non-malleability of Π uses this extractor and proceeds as follows:

1. The reduction begins by fixing the first two messages in the left and right executions in the main thread. For these messages, it obtains an externally generated non-malleable commitment to either $\gamma_2' = \gamma_2$ or γ_2' chosen uniformly at random independent of γ_2. The former corresponds to $\mathsf{Hybrid}_{5,\mathcal{D}}$ and the latter to $\mathsf{Hybrid}_{4,\mathcal{D}}$.

   Instead of rewinding the MIM providing honestly generated transcripts in the left interaction as is done in $\mathsf{Hybrid}_{5,\mathcal{D}}$ and $\mathsf{Hybrid}_{4,\mathcal{D}}$, we will now consider two sub-hybrids, $\mathsf{Hybrid}_{4,a,\mathcal{D}}$ and $\mathsf{Hybrid}_{5,a,\mathcal{D}}$ where the reduction uses the extractor $\mathcal{E}$ for the non-malleable commitment to extract the values committed by the MIM without rewinding the left interaction. We will show that the view and values extracted from these sub-hybrids will remain identical to the view and value extracted via rewinding in $\mathsf{Hybrid}_{4,\mathcal{D}}$ and $\mathsf{Hybrid}_{5,\mathcal{D}}$, respectively. This will essentially follow because of correctness of extractor $\mathcal{E}$, and because of soundness of wi and wzk in the interactions from which extraction occurs. We will also directly give a reduction proving that the joint distribution of the views and values extracted must be indistinguishable between these sub-hybrids.

2. Recall that $\mathcal{E}$ extracts the values committed by the MIM in a main transcript, without rewinding the messages sent in the non-malleable commitment in the left interaction (the extractor $\mathcal{E}$ may still rewind the MIM, only in all such rewindings it will not need to rewind the left non-malleable commitment, indeed it will suffice to generate "fake" third round messages for the non-malleable commitment to γ_2 – please refer to [13] for details on the extraction procedure). It is important to note that the wzk simulation strategy requires that the MIM's committed values be extracted first, therefore we cannot generate a simulated wzk argument without first extracting all values $\widetilde{\gamma}_1^j, \widetilde{\gamma}_2^j$ committed by the MIM.

3. Thus, in sub-hybrids $\mathsf{Hybrid}_{i,a,\mathcal{D}}$ for $i \in \{4,5\}$, the challenger just runs extractor $\mathcal{E}$ to extract the values $\{\widetilde{\gamma}_1^j, \widetilde{\gamma}_2^j\}_{j \in [n]}$, instead of rewinding the left execution. $\mathcal{E}$ extracts the value committed in a main transcript without rewinding the left execution. Thus, first the challenger generates a special main transcript for the extractor $\mathcal{E}$ as follows. It generates $\phi_1, \widetilde{\phi}_1^j, \widetilde{\phi}_2^j, \phi_2$ the same way as $\mathsf{Hybrid}_{4,\mathcal{D}}$, and then completes the third message by generating an honest commitment to V_1 (also repeated with V_2), that is, giving an honestly generated wzk argument and using γ_1 as witness for the wi[5]. It waits for the MIM to generate the third messages for the right executions, and now feeds the transcript of the interaction to $\mathcal{E}$ (if the MIM aborts, the challenger just repeats again with the same fixed first two messages, $\mathsf{poly}(1/\epsilon)$ times). Whenever $\mathcal{E}$ requests to rewind the MIM, the challenger rewinds the MIM, except that it obtains the messages for the left commitment Π^2 in all rewinding executions from $\mathcal{E}$. Further, recall that $\mathcal{E}$ has the property that it only extracts an incorrect value when the MIM is committing to $\bot$ in the honest execution, except with error ϵ, however, this is not true except with probability $1 - \mathsf{negl}(n)$, by soundness of wi and wzk. The MIM waits for $\mathcal{E}$ to output the extracted values $\{\widetilde{\gamma}_1^j, \widetilde{\gamma}_2^j\}$. Next, the MIM repeats this again (ϵ^4 times, with same fixed first two messages, waiting for the extractor to output (potentially different) extracted values. Finally the challenger uses the union of these extracted values to complete the rest of the experiment according to $\mathsf{Hybrid}_{4,\mathcal{D}}$.

Claim. The joint distribution of the views and values committed by the MIM remain indistinguishable (with error at most $\epsilon + \mathsf{negl}(n)$) between $\mathsf{Hybrid}_{i,\mathcal{D}}$ and $\mathsf{Hybrid}_{i,a,\mathcal{D}}$ for $i \in \{4,5\}$.

Proof. Note that the special main transcript provided to $\mathcal{E}$ to facilitate extraction in the sub-hybrids, is distributed identically to the transcripts provided in the lookahead executions for extraction in $\mathsf{Hybrid}_{4,\mathcal{D}}$ and $\mathsf{Hybrid}_{5,\mathcal{D}}$. Additionally, in all these executions, the challenger always provides honestly generated proofs, thus the soundness of wi and wzk provided by the MIM is guaranteed in all these executions. Therefore, the adversary is guaranteed to generate at least one out of the two non-malleable commitments from each session correctly in any non-aborting execution, except with probability $\mathsf{negl}(n)$.

---

[5] Note that the actual transcript that is output by the experiment must contain a simulated wzk argument: the transcript with the honest wzk argument is only generated to facilitate extraction.

Moreover, by soundness of wzk, the extracted value from at least one of the non-malleable commitments generated by the MIM in the jth session, will correspond to a witness for the commitment to $\widetilde{\gamma}_j^1$ or $\widetilde{\gamma}_j^2$, directly allowing to recover the message committed by the MIM in each non-aborting right session (if only one $\widetilde{\gamma}_j$ was extracted, w.h.p. the MIM continues to use the same witness). By correctness of extraction from $\mathcal{E}$ and because of soundness of wi and wzk in all rewinding executions as well as the special main execution, the joint distribution of views and value extracted via rewinding in $\mathsf{Hybrid}_{i,\mathcal{D}}$ is ϵ-indistinguishable from the distribution when $\mathcal{A}$ extracts using $\mathcal{E}$ in $\mathsf{Hybrid}_{i,a,\mathcal{D}}$ for $i \in \{4, 5\}$.

4. Next, keeping the first two messages of the transcript τ fixed, the challenger outputs a main transcript with a simulated weak ZK argument, where the simulation strategy runs on the distinguisher that obtains input the view of the MIM as well as the value extracted in the previous step, in a similar manner to $\mathsf{Hybrid}_{4,\mathcal{D}}$.

If the joint distribution of the view and values committed by the MIM between $\mathsf{Hybrid}_{4,a,\mathcal{D}}$ and $\mathsf{Hybrid}_{5,a,\mathcal{D}}$ are more than ϵ-distinguishable, there exists a reduction to the hiding of the non-malleable commitment Π^2, which obtains the messages of Π^2 externally to generate the first two round messages. In response to the MIM's challenge for the left execution, it obtains the third message of Π^2 externally, and uses it to generate the special main transcript for $\mathcal{E}$. Next, it runs the extractor $\mathcal{E}$, which does not need to rewind Π^2 in the left execution. Once it obtains $\{\widetilde{\gamma}_j^1, \widetilde{\gamma}_j^2\}_{j \in [p]}$ from $\mathcal{E}$, it proceeds to run the distinguisher-dependent simulation strategy. In this step, since the first two messages for the main transcript have already been fixed, the challenger can use the same third message Π_2^3 that it obtained externally, to complete the second non-malleable commitment in the left execution, in all third messages it generates in order to simulate the wzk argument by rewinding the distinguisher.

Therefore, if the joint distribution of the view and the values committed by the MIM changes by more than ϵ between $\mathsf{Hybrid}_{4,a,\mathcal{D}}$ and $\mathsf{Hybrid}_{5,a,\mathcal{D}}$, it can be used directly to contradict the hiding of Π^2. That is, if $|\Pr[\mathcal{D}(z, \mathsf{MIM}_{\langle C,R \rangle}(\text{value}, z)_{\mathsf{Hybrid}_{5,a,\mathcal{D}}}) = 1] - \Pr[\mathcal{D}(z, \mathsf{MIM}_{\langle C,R \rangle}(\text{value}, z)_{\mathsf{Hybrid}_{4,a,\mathcal{D}}}) = 1]| \geq \epsilon + \frac{1}{\mathsf{poly}}(n)$,

$$\text{then, } |\Pr[\mathcal{A}^{\mathcal{D}} = 1 | \gamma_2 = \gamma_2'] - \Pr[\mathcal{A}^{\mathcal{D}} = 1 | \gamma_2 \neq \gamma_2']| \geq \frac{1}{\mathsf{poly}}(n).$$

This gives a contradiction, thus the distributions $\mathsf{Hybrid}_{4,\mathcal{D}}$ and $\mathsf{Hybrid}_{5,\mathcal{D}}$ are indistinguishable upto at most 3ϵ-error.

$\mathsf{Hybrid}_{6,\mathcal{D}}$: In this hybrid, the challenger behaves the same way as $\mathsf{Hybrid}_{5,\mathcal{D}}$, except that it uses the second witness, r_2, γ_2, to generate the witness-indistinguishable argument wi in the output transcript.

Lemma 8. *For any PPT distinguisher $\mathcal{D}$ with auxiliary information z,*
$|\Pr[\mathcal{D}(z, \mathrm{MIM}_{\langle C,R \rangle}(\text{value}, z)_{\mathrm{Hybrid}_{6,\mathcal{D}}}) = 1] - \Pr[\mathcal{D}(z, \mathrm{MIM}_{\langle C,R \rangle}(\text{value}, z)_{\mathrm{Hybrid}_{5,\mathcal{D}}})$
$= 1]| \leq \epsilon + \mathsf{negl}(n).$

Proof. The proof of this lemma relies on the reusable resettable witness indistinguishability of wi.

The reduction $\mathcal{R}$ samples all messages for the experiment according to $\mathrm{Hybrid}_{5,D}$, except that it obtains WI proofs for all lookahead (rewinding) executions externally from the challenger, by providing the first witness to the challenger. In this experiment, note that some executions rewind the MIM to the end of the first round, thus proofs for these executions are provided with respect to new verifier messages generated by the MIM. Some other executions (corresponding to weak ZK simulation strategy) rewind the MIM to the end of the second round: thus different statements are proved in these executions, corresponding to the same verifier message from the MIM, that is fixed before the end of the second round. Thus, this experiment exactly corresponds to the security game of resettable reusable WI.

For the main/output transcript generated during distinguisher-dependent simulation, $\mathcal{R}$ samples all messages except the WI proof according to $\mathrm{Hybrid}_{5,D}$. Note that the statement being proved in this transcript has two valid witnesses, $w_1 = (r_1, \gamma_1$ randomness r and commitment $c)$ and $w_2 = (r_2, \gamma_2$, randomness $\hat{r}$ and commitment $c_1)$, which are sampled by the reduction $\mathcal{R}$. $\mathcal{R}$ forwards the verifier message wi_1 to the challenger, together with both witnesses, and obtains wi_2 that is generated using either witness w_1 or w_2. The reduction uses this externally generated proof to complete the experiment. If w_1 was used, the experiment is identical to $\mathrm{Hybrid}_{5,D}$, otherwise it is identical to $\mathrm{Hybrid}_{6,D}$.

Note that in the experiment, $\mathcal{R}$ behaves according to $\mathrm{Hybrid}_{5,\mathcal{D}}$ or $\mathrm{Hybrid}_{6,\mathcal{D}}$: that is, it first extracts $\{\tilde{\gamma}_1^j, \tilde{\gamma}_2^j\}_{j \in [p]}$. It then uses the extracted values $\{\tilde{\gamma}_1^j, \tilde{\gamma}_2^j\}_{j \in [p]}$ to obtain the values committed by the MIM in the main transcript. It outputs the joint distribution of the transcript and the values committed by the MIM to distinguisher $\mathcal{D}$. Given a distinguisher $\mathcal{D}$ where $|\Pr[\mathcal{D}(z,$ $\mathrm{MIM}_{\langle C,R \rangle}(\text{value}, z)_{\mathrm{Hybrid}_{6,\mathcal{D}}}) = 1] - \Pr[\mathcal{D}(z, \mathrm{MIM}_{\langle C,R \rangle}(\text{value}, z)_{\mathrm{Hybrid}_{5,\mathcal{D}}}) = 1]| \geq \frac{1}{\mathsf{poly}(n)}$, the reduction mirrors the output of this distinguisher to directly contradict the security of wi. Thus, the joint distribution in this hybrid is indistinguishable from $\mathrm{Hybrid}_{5,\mathcal{D}}$ by the resettable reusable witness-indistinguishability of wi.

$\mathrm{Hybrid}_{7,\mathcal{D}}$: In this hybrid, the challenger behaves the same way as $\mathrm{Hybrid}_{6,\mathcal{D}}$, except that it uses the second witness, r_2, γ_2, to generate the witness-indistinguishable arguments wi in all the lookahead executions. That is, in every message sent by the challenger, it uses the second witness instead of the first. This hybrid is indistinguishable from $\mathrm{Hybrid}_{6,\mathcal{D}}$ by the resettable reusable witness-indistinguishability of wi.

Lemma 9. *For any PPT distinguisher $\mathcal{D}$ with auxiliary information z, $|\Pr[\mathcal{D}(z,$ $\mathsf{MIM}_{\langle C,R\rangle}(\text{value}, z)_{\mathsf{Hybrid}_{7,\mathcal{D}}}) = 1] - \Pr[\mathcal{D}(z, \mathsf{MIM}_{\langle C,R\rangle}(\text{value}, z)_{\mathsf{Hybrid}_{6,\mathcal{D}}}) = 1]| \leq$ $\mathsf{negl}(n)$.*

Proof. The proof of this lemma follows similarly to that of Lemma 8, by relying on the resettable reusable witness-indistinguishability of wi. In this experiment, note that some executions rewind the MIM to the end of the first round, thus proofs for these executions are provided with respect to new verifier messages generated by the MIM. Some other executions (corresponding to weak ZK simulation strategy) rewind the MIM to the end of the second round: thus different statements are proved in these executions, corresponding to the same verifier message from the MIM, that is fixed before the end of the second round. This experiment exactly corresponds to the security game of resettable reusable WI.

That is, the reduction obtains WI proofs externally from the challenger by providing both witnesses $w_1 = (r_1, \gamma_1$, randomness r and commitment c) and $w_2 = (r_2, \gamma_2$, randomness r and commitment c). The challenger sends proofs that are all generated either using witness w_1 or all using witness w_2. The reduction completes the rest of the protocol according to $\mathsf{Hybrid}_{6,\mathcal{D}}$, except using the externally generated proofs in the left execution. If the challenger used witness w_1, the game corresponds to $\mathsf{Hybrid}_{6,\mathcal{D}}$ otherwise it corresponds to $\mathsf{Hybrid}_{7,\mathcal{D}}$.

Note that in the experiment, R behaves according to $\mathsf{Hybrid}_{6,\mathcal{D}}$ or $\mathsf{Hybrid}_{7,\mathcal{D}}$: that is, it first extracts $\{\widetilde{\gamma}_1^j, \widetilde{\gamma}_2^j\}_{j \in [p]}$. It then uses the extracted values $\{\widetilde{\gamma}_1^j, \widetilde{\gamma}_2^j\}_{j \in [p]}$ to obtain the values committed by the MIM in the main transcript. It outputs the joint distribution of the transcript and the values committed by the MIM to distinguisher $\mathcal{D}$. Given a distinguisher $\mathcal{D}$ where $|\Pr[\mathcal{D}(z,$ $\mathsf{MIM}_{\langle C,R\rangle}(\text{value}, z)_{\mathsf{Hybrid}_{7,\mathcal{D}}}) = 1] - \Pr[\mathcal{D}(z, \mathsf{MIM}_{\langle C,R\rangle}(\text{value}, z)_{\mathsf{Hybrid}_{6,\mathcal{D}}}) = 1]| \geq \frac{1}{\mathsf{poly}(n)}$, the reduction mirrors the output of this distinguisher to directly contradict the resettable reusable security of wi.

We note that the changes made in $\mathsf{Hybrid}_{7,\mathcal{D}}$ and $\mathsf{Hybrid}_{6,\mathcal{D}}$ can be collapsed into a single hybrid experiment relying on resettable reusable security of WI, however we keep them separate for additional clarity – since the witness used in the main transcript refers to Π^2 and the randomness for $c_1 = \mathsf{com}(0; \widehat{r})$ while the witness used in the lookahead transcripts refer to Π^2 and the randomness for $c = \mathsf{com}(V_1; r)$. At this point, the value γ_1 committed using the first non-malleable commitment Π^1 is not used as a witness in any of the WI proofs.

$\mathsf{Hybrid}_{8,\mathcal{D}}$: In this hybrid, the challenger behaves the same way as $\mathsf{Hybrid}_{7,\mathcal{D}}$, except that in all transcripts, it sets Π^1 as a non-malleable commitment to *a different* randomness γ_1' than the one used to compute δ_1.

Lemma 10. *For any PPT distinguisher $\mathcal{D}$ with auxiliary information z, $|\Pr[\mathcal{D}$ $(z, \mathsf{MIM}_{\langle C,R\rangle}(\text{value}, z)_{\mathsf{Hybrid}_{8,\mathcal{D}}}) = 1] - \Pr[\mathcal{D}(z, \mathsf{MIM}_{\langle C,R\rangle}(\text{value}, z)_{\mathsf{Hybrid}_{7,\mathcal{D}}}) = 1]| \leq$ $\epsilon + \mathsf{negl}(n)$.*

Proof. The proof of this lemma is exactly the same as that of Lemma 7. The joint distribution of the view and value committed by a malicious receiver in $\mathsf{Hybrid}_{8,\mathcal{D}}$ is ϵ-indistinguishable from $\mathsf{Hybrid}_{7,\mathcal{D}}$ by the non-malleability of the commitment Π^1.

$\mathsf{Hybrid}_{9,\mathcal{D}}$: In this hybrid, the challenger behaves the same way as $\mathsf{Hybrid}_{8,\mathcal{D}}$, except that in the output transcript, it sets $\delta_1 \xleftarrow{\$} \{0,1\}^*$, instead of setting $\delta_1 = \mathsf{PRF}(\gamma_1, \alpha_1) \oplus r$. Note that the committer is using PRF key γ_1' in the protocol Π^1, thus the key γ_1 does not appear in the rest of the protocol.

Lemma 11. *For any PPT distinguisher $\mathcal{D}$ with auxiliary information z, $| \Pr[\mathcal{D}(z, \mathsf{MIM}_{\langle C,R \rangle}(\text{value}, z)_{\mathsf{Hybrid}_{9,\mathcal{D}}}) = 1] - \Pr[\mathcal{D}(z, \mathsf{MIM}_{\langle C,R \rangle}(\text{value}, z)_{\mathsf{Hybrid}_{8,\mathcal{D}}}) = 1]| \leq$ $\mathsf{negl}(n)$.*

Proof. The proof of this lemma is the same as that of Lemma 6, by relying on the security of the PRF.

$\mathsf{Hybrid}_{10,\mathcal{D}}$: In this hybrid, the challenger behaves the same way as $\mathsf{Hybrid}_{9,\mathcal{D}}$ except that it replaces $c = \mathsf{com}(V_1; r)$ with $c = \mathsf{com}(V_2; r)$ in the output transcript. Note that in this transcript, the randomness r is not used elsewhere in the protocol.

Lemma 12. *For any PPT distinguisher $\mathcal{D}$ with auxiliary information z, $| \Pr[\mathcal{D}(z, \mathsf{MIM}_{\langle C,R \rangle}(\text{value}, z)_{\mathsf{Hybrid}_{10,\mathcal{D}}}) = 1] - \Pr[\mathcal{D}(z, \mathsf{MIM}_{\langle C,R \rangle}(\text{value}, z)_{\mathsf{Hybrid}_{9,\mathcal{D}}}) = 1]| \leq \mathsf{negl}(n)$.*

Proof. This hybrid is indistinguishable from $\mathsf{Hybrid}_{9,\mathcal{D}}$ because of computational hiding of the non-interactive commitment scheme com. More formally, consider a reduction $\mathcal{R}$ that behaves identical to $\mathsf{Hybrid}_{9,\mathcal{D}}$ except that it obtains the commitment c (only for the main thread and not for any of the lookahead threads), externally, as either a commitment to V_1 or a commitment to V_2. This is allowed because by the end of $\mathsf{Hybrid}_{9,\mathcal{D}}$, the randomness used to generate this commitment is not used anywhere else in the protocol.

Note that in the experiment, the reduction it first extracts $\{\widetilde{\gamma}_1^j, \widetilde{\gamma}_2^j\}_{j \in [p]}$. It then uses the extracted values $\{\widetilde{\gamma}_1^j, \widetilde{\gamma}_2^j\}_{j \in [p]}$ to obtain the values committed by the MIM in the main transcript. It outputs the joint distribution of the transcript and the values committed by the MIM to distinguisher $\mathcal{D}$. Then given distinguisher $\mathcal{D}$ where $| \Pr[\mathcal{D}(z, \mathsf{MIM}_{\langle C,R \rangle}(\text{value}, z)_{\mathsf{Hybrid}_{9,\mathcal{D}}}) = 1] - \Pr[\mathcal{D}(z, \mathsf{MIM}_{\langle C,R \rangle}(\text{value}, z)_{\mathsf{Hybrid}_{10,\mathcal{D}}}) = 1]| \geq \frac{1}{\mathsf{poly}(n)}$, The reduction mirrors the output of this distinguisher such that:

$$| \Pr[\mathcal{R} = 1 | c = \mathsf{com}(V_1; r)] - \Pr[\mathcal{R} = 1 | c = \mathsf{com}(V_2; r)]| \geq \frac{1}{\mathsf{poly}(n)}$$

This is a contradiction to the hiding of com.

At this point, we have successfully switched (with distinguishing advantage at most $\Theta(\epsilon) + \mathsf{negl}(n)$) to an experiment where the commitment is generated to message V_2 instead of V_1 in the transcript output by the challenger. However, note that the wzk argument is still being simulated in this hybrid. Also note that throughout these hybrids, lookahead threads for extraction will be generated according to both values V_1 and V_2. Non-malleability follows by repeating the above hybrids in reverse order, until in Hybrid_{V_2}, the challenger generates an honest commitment to message V_2m and. setting $n\epsilon$ to be less than the distinguishing advantage of the given distinguisher $\mathcal{D}$ to arrive at a contradiction. By invoking [19], this completes the proof of concurrent non-malleability.

Acknowledgements. We are extremely grateful to Vipul Goyal for helpful discussions about the properties of the protocol in [13], Yael Kalai for several useful discussions regarding [15] and Amit Sahai for very valuable feedback about this writeup. We also thank the anonymous reviewers of TCC 2017 for their useful comments.

References

1. Badrinarayanan, S., Goyal, V., Jain, A., Khurana, D., Sahai, A.: Round optimal concurrent MPC via strong simulation. IACR Cryptology ePrint Archive 2017, 597 (2017). http://eprint.iacr.org/2017/597
2. Barak, B.: Constant-round coin-tossing with a man in the middle or realizing the shared random string model. In: FOCS 2002, pp. 345–355 (2002)
3. Barak, B., Ong, S.J., Vadhan, S.P.: Derandomization in cryptography. SIAM J. Comput. **37**(2), 380–400 (2007). http://dx.doi.org/10.1137/050641958
4. Bitansky, N., Paneth, O.: ZAPs and non-interactive witness indistinguishability from indistinguishability obfuscation. In: Dodis, Y., Nielsen, J.B. (eds.) TCC 2015. LNCS, vol. 9015, pp. 401–427. Springer, Heidelberg (2015). doi:10.1007/978-3-662-46497-7_16
5. Ciampi, M., Ostrovsky, R., Siniscalchi, L., Visconti, I.: Concurrent non-malleable commitments (and more) in 3 rounds. In: Robshaw, M., Katz, J. (eds.) CRYPTO 2016. LNCS, vol. 9816, pp. 270–299. Springer, Heidelberg (2016). doi:10.1007/978-3-662-53015-3_10
6. Ciampi, M., Ostrovsky, R., Siniscalchi, L., Visconti, I.: Four-round concurrent non-malleable commitments from one-way functions. In: Katz, J., Shacham, H. (eds.) CRYPTO 2017. LNCS, vol. 10402, pp. 127–157. Springer, Cham (2017). doi:10.1007/978-3-319-63715-0_5
7. Dolev, D., Dwork, C., Naor, M.: Non-malleable cryptography (extended abstract). In: STOC 1991 (1991)
8. Dwork, C., Naor, M.: Zaps and their applications. SIAM J. Comput. **36**(6), 1513–1543 (2007). https://doi.org/10.1137/S0097539703426817
9. Goyal, V.: Constant round non-malleable protocols using one-way functions. In: STOC 2011, pp. 695–704. ACM (2011)
10. Goyal, V., Khurana, D., Sahai, A.: Breaking the three round barrier for non-malleable commitments. In: FOCS (2016)
11. Goyal, V., Lee, C.K., Ostrovsky, R., Visconti, I.: Constructing non-malleable commitments: a black-box approach. In: FOCS (2012)
12. Goyal, V., Pandey, O., Richelson, S.: Textbook non-malleable commitments. In: Wichs, D., Mansour, Y. (eds.) Proceedings of the 48th Annual ACM SIGACT Symposium on Theory of Computing, STOC 2016, Cambridge, MA, USA, 18–21 June 2016, pp. 1128–1141. ACM (2016)

13. Goyal, V., Richelson, S., Rosen, A., Vald, M.: An algebraic approach to non-malleability. In: FOCS 2014, pp. 41–50 (2014)
14. Groth, J., Ostrovsky, R., Sahai, A.: New techniques for noninteractive zero-knowledge. J. ACM **59**(3), 11:1–11:35 (2012). http://doi.acm.org/10.1145/22203 57.2220358
15. Jain, A., Kalai, Y.T., Khurana, D., Rothblum, R.: Distinguisher-dependent simulation in two rounds and its applications. In: Katz, J., Shacham, H. (eds.) CRYPTO 2017. LNCS, vol. 10402, pp. 158–189. Springer, Cham (2017). doi:10.1007/978-3-319-63715-0_6
16. Khurana, D., Sahai, A.: How to achieve non-malleability in one or two rounds. Electronic Colloquium on Computational Complexity (ECCC) 24, Report no. 100 (2017). https://eccc.weizmann.ac.il/report/2017/100
17. Lin, H., Pass, R.: Constant-round non-malleable commitments from any one-way function. In: STOC 2011, pp. 705–714 (2011)
18. Lin, H., Pass, R., Soni, P.: Two-round and non-interactive concurrent non-malleable commitments from time-lock puzzles. Cryptology ePrint Archive, Report 2017/273 (2017). http://eprint.iacr.org/2017/273
19. Lin, H., Pass, R., Venkitasubramaniam, M.: Concurrent non-malleable commitments from any one-way function. In: Canetti, R. (ed.) TCC 2008. LNCS, vol. 4948, pp. 571–588. Springer, Heidelberg (2008). doi:10.1007/978-3-540-78524-8_31
20. Pass, R.: Bounded-concurrent secure multi-party computation with a dishonest majority. In: Proceedings of the 36th Annual ACM Symposium on Theory of Computing, STOC 2004, pp. 232–241 (2004)
21. Pass, R.: Unprovable security of perfect NIZK and non-interactive non-malleable commitments. In: Sahai, A. (ed.) TCC 2013. LNCS, vol. 7785, pp. 334–354. Springer, Heidelberg (2013). doi:10.1007/978-3-642-36594-2_19
22. Pass, R., Rosen, A.: New and improved constructions of non-malleable cryptographic protocols. In: STOC 2005, pp. 533–542 (2005)
23. Pass, R., Wee, H.: Black-box constructions of two-party protocols from one-way functions. In: Reingold, O. (ed.) TCC 2009. LNCS, vol. 5444, pp. 403–418. Springer, Heidelberg (2009). doi:10.1007/978-3-642-00457-5_24
24. Wee, H.: Black-box, round-efficient secure computation via non-malleability amplification. In: Proceedings of the 51th Annual IEEE Symposium on Foundations of Computer Science, pp. 531–540 (2010)

Zero Knowledge Protocols from Succinct Constraint Detection

Eli Ben-Sasson[1], Alessandro Chiesa[2]([⊠]), Michael A. Forbes[3],
Ariel Gabizon[4], Michael Riabzev[1], and Nicholas Spooner[2]

[1] Technion, Haifa, Israel
{eli,mriabzev}@cs.technion.ac.il
[2] UC Berkeley, Berkeley, USA
alexch@berkeley.edu, spooner@eecs.berkeley.edu
[3] University of Illinois Urbana-Champaign, Champaign, USA
miforbes@illinois.edu
[4] ZcashCo, Haifa, Israel
ariel@z.cash

Abstract. We study the problem of constructing proof systems that achieve both soundness and zero knowledge unconditionally (without relying on intractability assumptions). Known techniques for this goal are primarily *combinatorial*, despite the fact that constructions of interactive proofs (IPs) and probabilistically checkable proofs (PCPs) heavily rely on *algebraic* techniques to achieve their properties.

We present simple and natural modifications of well-known 'algebraic' IP and PCP protocols that achieve unconditional (perfect) zero knowledge in recently introduced models, overcoming limitations of known techniques.

- We modify the PCP of Ben-Sasson and Sudan [BS08] to obtain zero knowledge for **NEXP** in the model of Interactive Oracle Proofs [BCS16,RRR16], where the verifier, in each round, receives a PCP from the prover.
- We modify the IP of Lund et al. [LFKN92] to obtain zero knowledge for #**P** in the model of Interactive PCPs [KR08], where the verifier first receives a PCP from the prover and then interacts with him.

The simulators in our zero knowledge protocols rely on solving a problem that lies at the intersection of coding theory, linear algebra, and computational complexity, which we call the *succinct constraint detection* problem, and consists of detecting dual constraints with polynomial support size for codes of exponential block length. Our two results rely on solutions to this problem for fundamental classes of linear codes:

- An algorithm to detect constraints for Reed–Muller codes of exponential length. This algorithm exploits the Raz–Shpilka [RS05] deterministic polynomial identity testing algorithm, and shows, to our knowledge, a first connection of algebraic complexity theory with zero knowledge.

M.A. Forbes—Work conducted while at Stanford.
A. Gabizon—Work conducted while at Technion.
N. Spooner—Work conducted while at the University of Toronto.

Y. Kalai and L. Reyzin (Eds.): TCC 2017, Part II, LNCS 10678, pp. 172–206, 2017.
https://doi.org/10.1007/978-3-319-70503-3_6

- An algorithm to de tect constraints for PCPs of Proximity of Reed–
Solomon codes [BS08] of exponential degree. This algorithm exploits
the recursive structure of the PCPs of Proximity to show that small-
support constraints are "locally" spanned by a small number of
small-support constraints.

Keywords: Probabilistically checkable proofs · Interactive proofs ·
Sumcheck · Zero knowledge · Polynomial identity testing

1   Introduction

The study of interactive proofs (IPs) [BM88, GMR89] that unconditionally
achieve zero knowledge [GMR89] has led to a rich theory, with connections
well beyond zero knowledge. For example, the class of languages with statistical zero knowledge IPs, which we denote by **SZK-IP**, has complete problems
that make no reference to either zero knowledge or interaction [SV03, GV99] and
is closed under complement [Oka00, Vad99]. Despite the fact that all **PSPACE**
languages have IPs [Sha92], **SZK-IP** is contained in **AM ∩ coAM**, and thus **NP**
is not in **SZK-IP** unless the polynomial hierarchy collapses [BHZ87]; one consequence is that Graph Non-Isomorphism is unlikely to be NP-complete. Moreover, constructing **SZK-IP** for a language is equivalent to constructing instance-
dependent commitments for the language [IOS97, OV08], and has connections
to other fundamental information-theoretic notions like randomized encodings
[AR16, VV15] and secret-sharing schemes [VV15].

Unconditional zero knowledge in other models behaves very differently. Ben-
Or et al. [BGKW88] introduced the model of multi-prover interactive proofs
(MIPs) and showed that *all* such proofs can be made zero knowledge unconditionally. The analogous statement for IPs is equivalent to the existence of
one-way functions, as shown by [GMR89, IY87, BGG+88] in one direction and
by [Ost91, OW93] in the other (unless **BPP = PSPACE**, in which case the
statement is trivial). Subsequent works not only established that all **NEXP**
languages have MIPs [BFL91], but also led to formulating probabilistically checkable proofs (PCPs) and proving the celebrated PCP Theorem [FRS88, BFLS91,
FGL+96, AS98, ALM+98], as well as constructing statistical zero knowledge
PCPs [KPT97] and applying them to black-box cryptography [IMS12, IMSX15].

The theory of zero knowledge for these types of proofs, however, is not as
rich as in the case of IPs. Most notably, known techniques to achieve zero knowledge MIPs or PCPs are limited, and come with caveats. Zero knowledge MIPs
are obtained via complex generic transformations [BGKW88], assume the full
power of the PCP Theorem [DFK+92], or support only languages in **NP** [LS95].
Zero knowledge PCPs are obtained via a construction that incurs polynomial
blowups in proof length and requires the honest verifier to adaptively query the
PCP [KPT97]. Alternative approaches are not known, despite attempts to find
them. For example, [IWY16] apply PCPs to leakage-resilient circuits, obtaining
PCPs for **NP** that do have a non-adaptive honest verifier but are only witness
indistinguishable.

Even basic questions such as "are there zero-knowledge PCPs of quasilinear-size?" or "are there zero-knowledge PCPs with non-adaptive honest verifiers?" have remained frustratingly hard to answer, despite the fact the answers to these questions are well understood when removing the requirement of zero knowledge. This state of affairs begs the question of whether a richer theory about zero knowledge MIPs and PCPs could be established.

The current situation is that known techniques to achieve zero knowledge MIPs and PCPs are combinatorial, namely they make black-box use of an underlying MIP or PCP, despite the fact that most MIP and PCP constructions have a rich algebraic structure arising from the use of error correcting codes based on evaluations of low-degree polynomials. This separation is certainly an attractive feature, and perhaps even unsurprising: while error-correcting codes are designed to help recover information, zero knowledge proofs are designed to hide it.

Yet, a recent work by Ben-Sasson et al. [BCGV16] brings together linear error correcting codes and zero knowledge using an algebraic technique that we refer to as 'masking'. The paper introduces a "2-round PCP" for **NP** that unconditionally achieves zero knowledge and, nevertheless, has both quasilinear size and a non-adaptive honest verifier. Their work can be viewed not only as partial progress towards some of the open questions above, but also as studying the power of zero knowledge for a natural extension of PCPs ("multi-round PCPs" as discussed below) with its own motivations and applications [BCS16, RRR16,BCG+17].

The motivation of this work is to understand the power of algebraic tools, such as linear error correcting codes, for achieving zero knowledge unconditionally (without relying on intractability assumptions).

1.1   Results

We present new protocols that unconditionally achieve soundness and zero knowledge in recently suggested models that combine features of PCPs and IPs [KR08,BCS16,RRR16]. Our protocols consist of simple and natural modifications to well-known constructions: the PCP of Ben-Sasson and Sudan [BS08] and the IP for polynomial summation of Lund et al. [LFKN92]. By leveraging the linear codes used in these constructions, we reduce the problem of achieving zero knowledge to solving exponentially-large instances of a new linear-algebraic problem that we call *constraint detection*, which we believe to be of independent interest. We design efficient algorithms for solving this problem for notable linear code families, along the way exploiting connections to algebraic complexity theory and local views of linear codes. We now elaborate on the above by discussing each of our results.

Zero knowledge for non-deterministic exponential time. Two recent works [BCS16,RRR16] independently introduce and study the notion of an *interactive oracle proof* (IOP), which can be viewed as a "multi-round PCP". Informally, an IOP is an IP modified so that, whenever the prover sends to the verifier a message, the verifier does not have to read the message in full but may probabilistically query it. Namely, in every round, the verifier sends the prover a message, and the prover replies with a PCP. IOPs enjoy better efficiency compared to PCPs [BCG+17], and have applications to constructing argument systems [BCS16] and IPs [RRR16].

The aforementioned work of [BCGV16] makes a simple modification to the PCP of Ben-Sasson and Sudan [BS08] and obtains a 2-round IOP for **NP** that is perfect zero knowledge, and yet has quasilinear size and a non-adaptive honest verifier. Our first result consists of extending this prior work to all languages in **NEXP**, positively answering an open question raised there. We do so by constructing, for each time T and query bound b, a suitable IOP for **NTIME**(T) that is zero knowledge against query bound b; the result for **NEXP** follows by setting b to be super-polynomial.

The foregoing notion of zero knowledge for IOPs directly extends that for PCPs, and requires showing the existence of an algorithm that simulates the view of any (malicious and adaptive) verifier interacting with the honest prover and making at most b queries across all oracles; here, 'view' consists of the answers to queries across all oracles.[1]

Theorem 1 (informal). *For every time bound T and query bound b, the complexity class **NTIME**(T) has 2-round Interactive Oracle Proofs that are perfect zero knowledge against b queries, and where the proof length is $\tilde{O}(T + b)$ and the (honest verifier's) query complexity is* $\mathrm{polylog}(T + b)$.

The prior work of [BCGV16] was "stuck" at **NP** because their simulator runs in $\mathrm{poly}(T + b)$ time so that T, b must be polynomially-bounded. In contrast, we achieve all of **NEXP** by constructing, for essentially the same simple 2-round IOP, a simulator that runs in time $\mathrm{poly}(\tilde{q} + \log T + \log b)$, where $\tilde{q}$ is the *actual* number of queries made by the malicious verifier. This is an *exponential* improvement in simulation efficiency, and we obtain it by conceptualizing and solving a linear-algebraic problem about Reed–Solomon codes, and their proximity proofs, as discussed in Sect. 1.1.

In sum, our theorem gives new tradeoffs compared to [KPT97]'s result, which gives statistical zero knowledge PCPs for **NTIME**(T) with proof length $\mathrm{poly}(T, b)$ and an adaptive honest verifier. We obtain perfect zero knowledge for **NTIME**(T), with quasilinear proof length and a non-adaptive honest verifier, at the price of "2 rounds of PCPs".

Zero knowledge for counting problems. Kalai and Raz [KR08] introduce and study the notion of *interactive PCPs* (IPCPs), which "sits in between" IPs and IOPs: the prover first sends the verifier a PCP, and then the prover and verifier engage in a standard IP. IPCPs also enjoy better efficiency compared to PCPs or IPs alone [KR08].

---

[1] More precisely, while in a zero knowledge IP or MIP one is required to simulate the entire transcript of interaction (with one or multiple provers), in a zero knowledge IOP or PCP one is merely required to simulate answers to the oracle queries but not the entire oracle.

We show how a natural and simple modification of the sumcheck protocol of Lund et al. [LFKN92] achieves perfect zero knowledge in the IPCP model, even with a non-adaptive honest verifier. By running this protocol on the usual arithmetization of the counting problem associated to 3SAT, we obtain our second result, which is IPCPs for $\#\mathbf{P}$ that are *perfect zero knowledge against unbounded queries*. This means that there exists a polynomial-time algorithm that simulates the view of any (malicious and adaptive) verifier making any polynomial number of queries to the PCP oracle. Here, 'view' consists of answers to oracle queries and the transcript of interaction with the prover. (In particular, this notion of zero knowledge is a 'hybrid' of corresponding notions for PCPs and IPs.)

Theorem 2 (informal). *The complexity class $\#\mathbf{P}$ has Interactive PCPs that are perfect zero knowledge against unbounded queries. The PCP proof length is exponential, and the communication complexity of the interaction and the (honest verifier's) query complexity are polynomial.*

Our construction relies on a random self-reducibility property of the sumcheck protocol (see Sect. 2.2 for a summary) and its completeness and soundness properties are straightforward to establish. As in our previous result, the "magic" lies in the construction of the simulator, which must solve the same type of exponentially-large linear-algebraic problem, except that this time it is about Reed–Muller codes rather than Reed–Solomon codes. The algorithm that we give to solve this task relies on connections to the problem of polynomial identity testing in the area of algebraic complexity theory, as we discuss further below.

Goyal et al. [GIMS10] also study zero knowledge for IPCPs, and show how to obtain IPCPs for $\mathbf{NP}$ that (i) are statistical zero knowledge against unbounded queries, and yet (ii) each location of the (necessarily) super-polynomial size PCP is polynomial-time computable given the NP witness. They further prove that these two properties are not attainable by zero knowledge PCPs. Their construction consists of replacing the commitment scheme in the zero knowledge IP for 3-colorability of [GMW91] with an information-theoretic analogue in the IPCP model. Our Theorem 2 also achieves zero knowledge against unbounded queries, but targets the complexity class $\#\mathbf{P}$ (rather than $\mathbf{NP}$), for which there is no clear analogue of property (ii) above.

Information-theoretic commitments also underlie the construction of zero knowledge PCPs [KPT97]. One could apply the [KPT97] result for $\mathbf{NEXP}$ to obtain zero knowledge PCPs (thus also IPCPs) for $\#\mathbf{P}$, but this is an indirect and complex route (in particular, it relies on the PCP Theorem) that, moreover, yields an adaptive honest verifier. Our direct construction is simple and natural, and also yields a non-adaptive honest verifier.

We now discuss the common algebraic structure that allowed us to obtain both of the above results. We believe that further progress in understanding these types of algebraic techniques will lead to further progress in understanding the power of unconditional zero knowledge for IOPs and IPCPs, and perhaps also for MIPs and PCPs.

Succinct constraint detection for Reed–Muller and Reed–Solomon codes. The constructions underlying both of our theorems achieve zero knowledge by applying a simple modification to well-known protocols: the PCP of Ben-Sasson and Sudan [BS08] underlies our result for **NEXP** and the sumcheck protocol of Lund et al. [LFKN92] underlies our result for #**P**.

In both of these protocols the verifier has access (either via a polynomial-size representation or via a PCP oracle) to an exponentially-large word that allegedly belongs to a certain linear code, and the prover 'leaks' hard-to-compute information in the process of convincing the verifier that this word belongs to the linear code. We achieve zero knowledge via a modification that we call *masking*: the prover sends to the verifier a PCP containing a random codeword in this code, and then convinces the verifier that the *sum* of these two (the original codeword and this random codeword) is close to the linear code.[2] Intuitively, zero knowledge comes from the fact that the prover now argues about a random shift of the original word.

However, this idea raises a problem: how does the simulator 'sample' an exponentially-large random codeword in order to answer the verifier's queries to the PCP? Solving this problem crucially relies on solving a problem that lies at the intersection of coding theory, linear algebra, and computational complexity, which we call the *constraint detection problem*. We informally introduce it and state our results about it, and defer to Sect. 2.2 a more detailed discussion of its connection to zero knowledge.

Detecting constraints in codes. Constraint detection is the problem of determining which linear relations hold across all codewords of a linear code $C \subseteq \mathbb{F}^D$, when considering only a given subdomain $I \subseteq D$ of the code rather than all of the domain D. This problem can always be solved in time that is polynomial in $|D|$ (via Gaussian elimination); however, if there is an algorithm that solves this problem in time that is *polynomial in the subdomain's size* $|I|$, rather than the domain's size $|D|$, then we say that the code has *succinct* constraint detection; in particular, the domain could have *exponential* size and the algorithm would still run in polynomial time.

Definition 1 (informal). *We say that a linear code $C \subseteq \mathbb{F}^D$ has **succinct constraint detection** if there exists an algorithm that, given a subset $I \subseteq D$, runs in time $\mathrm{poly}(\log |\mathbb{F}| + \log |D| + |I|)$ and outputs $z \in \mathbb{F}^I$ such that $\sum_{i \in I} z(i)w(i) = 0$ for all $w \in C$, or "no" if no such z exists. (In particular, $|D|$ may be exponential.)*

We further discuss the problem of constraint detection in Sect. 2.1, and provide a formal treatment of it in Sect. 4.1. Beyond this introduction, we shall use (and achieve) a stronger definition of constraint detection: the algorithm is required to output a basis for the space of dual codewords in $C^\perp$ whose support lies in the subdomain I, i.e., a basis for the space $\{z \in D^I : \forall w \in C, \sum_{i \in I} z(i)w(i) = 0\}$.

---

[2] This is reminiscent of the use of a random secret share of 0 to achieve privacy in information-theoretic multi-party protocols [BGW88].

Note that in our discussion of succinct constraint detection we do not leverage the distance property of the code C, but we do leverage it in our eventual applications.

Our zero knowledge simulators' strategy includes sampling a "random PCP": a random codeword w in a linear code C with exponentially large domain size $|D|$ (see Sect. 2.2 for more on this). Explicitly sampling w requires time $\Omega(|D|)$, and so is inefficient. But a verifier makes only polynomially-many queries to w, so the simulator has to only simulate w when restricted to polynomial-size sets $I \subseteq D$, leaving open the possibility of doing so in time $\mathrm{poly}(|I|)$. Achieving such a simulation time is an instance of (efficiently and perfectly) "implementing a huge random object" [GGN10] via a *stateful* algorithm [BW04]. We observe that if C has succinct constraint detection then this sampling problem for C has a solution: the simulator maintains the set $\{(i, a_i)\}_{i \in I}$ of past query-answer pairs; then, on a new verifier query $j \in D$, the simulator uses constraint detection to determine if w_j is linearly dependent on w_I, and answers accordingly (such linear dependencies characterize the required probability distribution, see Lemma 1).

Overall, our paper thus provides an application (namely, obtaining zero knowledge simulators) where the problem of efficient implementation of huge random objects arises naturally.

We now state our results about succinct constraint detection.

(1) Reed–Muller codes, and their partial sums. We prove that the family of linear codes comprised of evaluations of low-degree multivariate polynomials, along with their partial sums, has succinct constraint detection. This family is closely related to the *sumcheck protocol* [LFKN92], and indeed we use this result to obtain a PZK analogue of the sumcheck protocol (see Sect. 2.2), which yields Theorem 2 (see Sect. 2.3).

Recall that the family of Reed–Muller codes, denoted RM, is indexed by tuples $\mathfrak{n} = (\mathbb{F}, m, d)$, where $\mathbb{F}$ is a finite field and m, d are positive integers, and the $\mathfrak{n}$-th code consists of codewords $w \colon \mathbb{F}^m \to \mathbb{F}$ that are the evaluation of an m-variate polynomial Q of individual degree less than d over $\mathbb{F}$. We denote by ΣRM the family that extends RM with evaluations of all partial sums over certain subcubes of a hypercube:

Definition 2 (informal). *We denote by ΣRM the linear code family that is indexed by tuples $\mathfrak{n} = (\mathbb{F}, m, d, H)$, where H is a subset of $\mathbb{F}$, and where the $\mathfrak{n}$-th code consists of codewords $(w_0, \ldots, w_m)$ such that there exists an m-variate polynomial Q of individual degree less than d over $\mathbb{F}$ for which $w_i \colon \mathbb{F}^{m-i} \to \mathbb{F}$ is the evaluation of the i-th partial sum of Q over H, i.e., $w_i(\boldsymbol{\alpha}) = \sum_{\boldsymbol{\gamma} \in H^i} Q(\boldsymbol{\alpha}, \boldsymbol{\gamma})$ for every $\boldsymbol{\alpha} \in \mathbb{F}^{m-i}$.*

The domain size for codes in ΣRM is $\Omega(|\mathbb{F}|^m)$, but our detector's running time is exponentially smaller.

Theorem 3 (informal statement of Theorem 5). *The family ΣRM has succinct constraint detection: there is a detector algorithm for ΣRM that runs in time $\mathrm{poly}(\log |\mathbb{F}| + m + d + |H| + |I|)$.*

We provide intuition for the theorem's proof in Sect. 2.1 and provide the proof's details in Sect. 4.2; the proof leverages tools from algebraic complexity theory. (Our proof also shows that the family RM, which is a restriction of ΣRM, has succinct constraint detection.) Our theorem implies perfect and stateful implementation of a random low-degree multivariate polynomial and its partial sums over any hypercube; our proof extends an algorithm of [BW04], which solves this problem in the case of parity queries to boolean functions on subcubes of the boolean hypercube.

(2) Reed–Solomon codes, and their PCPPs. Second, we prove that the family of linear codes comprised of evaluations of low-degree univariate polynomials concatenated with corresponding BS proximity proofs [BS08] has succinct constraint detection. This family is closely related to quasilinear-size PCPs for **NEXP** [BS08], and indeed we use this result to obtain PZK proximity proofs for this family (see Sect. 2.2), from which we derive Theorem 1 (see Sect. 2.3).

Definition 3 (informal). *We denote by* BS-RS *the linear code family indexed by tuples* $\mathfrak{n} = (\mathbb{F}, L, d)$, *where* $\mathbb{F}$ *is an extension field of* $\mathbb{F}_2$, L *is a linear subspace in* $\mathbb{F}$, *and* d *is a positive integer; the* $\mathfrak{n}$-*th code consists of evaluations on* L *of univariate polynomials* Q *of degree less than* d, *concatenated with corresponding* [BS08] *proximity proofs.*

The domain size for codes in BS-RS is $\Omega(|L|)$, but our detector's running time is exponentially smaller.

Theorem 4 (informal statement of Theorem 6). *The family* BS-RS *has succinct constraint detection: there is a detector algorithm for* BS-RS *that runs in time* $\mathrm{poly}(\log|\mathbb{F}| + \dim(L) + |I|)$.

We provide intuition for the theorem's proof in Sect. 2.1 and provide the proof's details in Sect. 4.3; the proof leverages combinatorial properties of the recursive construction of BS proximity proofs.

2 Techniques

We informally discuss intuition behind our algorithms for detecting constraints (Sect. 2.1), their connection to zero knowledge (Sect. 2.2), and how we derive our results about #**P** and **NEXP** (Sect. 2.3). Throughout, we provide pointers to the technical sections that contain further details.

2.1 Detecting Constraints for Exponentially-Large Codes

As informally introduced in Sect. 1.1, the *constraint detection problem* corresponding to a linear code family $\mathscr{C} = \{C_{\mathfrak{n}}\}_{\mathfrak{n}}$ with domain $D(\cdot)$ and alphabet $\mathbb{F}(\cdot)$ is the following: given an index $\mathfrak{n} \in \{0,1\}^*$ and subset $I \subseteq D(\mathfrak{n})$, output a basis for the space $\{z \in D(\mathfrak{n})^I : \forall w \in C_{\mathfrak{n}}, \sum_{i \in I} z(i)w(i) = 0\}$. In other words, for a given subdomain I, we wish to determine all linear relations that hold for codewords in $C_\mathfrak{n}$ restricted to the subdomain I.

If a generating matrix for $C_\mathfrak{n}$ can be found in polynomial time, this problem can be solved in $\mathrm{poly}(|\mathfrak{n}| + |D(\mathfrak{n})|)$ time via Gaussian elimination (such an approach was implicitly taken by [BCGV16] to construct a perfect zero knowledge simulator for an IOP for **NP**). However, in our setting $|D(\mathfrak{n})|$ is *exponential* in $|\mathfrak{n}|$, so the straightforward solution is inefficient. With this in mind, we say that $\mathscr{C}$ has *succinct constraint detection* if there exists an algorithm that solves its constraint detection problem in $\mathrm{poly}(|\mathfrak{n}| + |I|)$ time, even if $|D(\mathfrak{n})|$ is exponential in $|\mathfrak{n}|$.

The formal definition of succinct constraint detection is in Sect. 4.1. In the rest of this section we provide intuition for two of our theorems: succinct constraint detection for the family ΣRM and for the family BS-RS. As will become evident, the techniques that we use to prove the two theorems differ significantly. Perhaps this is because the two codes are quite different: ΣRM has a simple and well-understood algebraic structure, whereas BS-RS is constructed recursively using proof composition.

From algebraic complexity to detecting constraints for Reed–Muller codes and their partial sums. The purpose of this section is to provide intuition about the proof of Theorem 3, which states that the family ΣRM has succinct constraint detection. (Formal definitions, statements, and proofs are in Sect. 4.2.) We thus outline how to construct an algorithm that detects constraints for the family of linear codes comprised of evaluations of low-degree multivariate polynomials, along with their partial sums. Our construction generalizes the proof of [BW04], which solves the special case of parity queries to boolean functions on subcubes of the boolean hypercube by reducing this problem to a probabilistic identity testing problem that is solvable via an algorithm of [RS05].

Below, we temporarily ignore the partial sums, and focus on constructing an algorithm that detects constraints for the family of Reed–Muller codes RM, and at the end of the section we indicate how we can also handle partial sums.

Step 1: phrase as linear algebra problem. Consider a codeword $w\colon \mathbb{F}^m \to \mathbb{F}$ that is the evaluation of an m-variate polynomial Q of individual degree less than d over $\mathbb{F}$. Note that, for every $\boldsymbol{\alpha} \in \mathbb{F}^m$, $w(\boldsymbol{\alpha})$ equals the inner product of Q's coefficients with the vector $\phi_{\boldsymbol{\alpha}}$ that consists of the evaluation of all d^m monomials at $\boldsymbol{\alpha}$. One can argue that constraint detection for RM is equivalent to finding the nullspace of $\{\phi_{\boldsymbol{\alpha}}\}_{\boldsymbol{\alpha}\in I}$. However, "writing out" this $|I| \times d^m$ matrix and performing Gaussian elimination is too expensive, so we must solve this linear algebra problem *succinctly*.

Step 2: encode vectors as coefficients of polynomials. While each vector $\phi_{\boldsymbol{\alpha}}$ is long, it has a succinct description; in fact, we can construct an m-variate polynomial $\Phi_{\boldsymbol{\alpha}}$ whose coefficients (after expansion) are the entries of $\phi_{\boldsymbol{\alpha}}$, but has an arithmetic circuit of only size $O(md)$: namely, $\Phi_{\boldsymbol{\alpha}}(\boldsymbol{X}) := \prod_{i=1}^{m}(1 + \alpha_i X_i + \alpha_i^2 X_i^2 + \cdots + \alpha_i^{d-1} X_i^{d-1})$. Computing the nullspace of $\{\Phi_{\boldsymbol{\alpha}}\}_{\boldsymbol{\alpha}\in I}$ is thus equivalent to computing the nullspace of $\{\phi_{\boldsymbol{\alpha}}\}_{\boldsymbol{\alpha}\in I}$.

Step 3: computing the nullspace. Computing the nullspace of a set of polynomials is a problem in algebraic complexity theory, and is essentially equivalent to the Polynomial Identity Testing (PIT) problem, and so we leverage tools from that area.[3] While there are simple randomized algorithms to solve this problem (see for example [Kay10, Lemma 8] and [BW04]), these algorithms, due to a nonzero probability of error, suffice to achieve statistical zero knowledge but do not suffice to achieve perfect zero knowledge. To obtain perfect zero knowledge, we need a solution that has *no probability of error*. Derandomizing PIT for arbitrary algebraic circuits seems to be beyond current techniques (as it implies circuit lower bounds [KI04]), but derandomizations are currently known for some restricted circuit classes. The polynomials that we consider are special: they fall in the well-studied class of "sum of products of univariates", and for this case we can invoke the deterministic algorithm of [RS05] (see also [Kay10]). (It is interesting that derandomization techniques are ultimately used to obtain a qualitative improvement for an inherently probabilistic task, i.e., perfect sampling of verifier views.)

The above provides an outline for how to detect constraints for RM. The extension to ΣRM, which also includes partial sums, is achieved by considering a more general form of vectors ϕ_{α} as well as corresponding polynomials Φ_{α}. These polynomials also have the special form required for our derandomization. See Sect. 4.2 for details.

From recursive code covers to detecting constraints for Reed–Solomon codes and their PCPPs. The purpose of this section is to provide intuition about the proof of Theorem 4, which states that the family BS-RS has succinct constraint detection. (Formal definitions, statements, and proofs are in Sect. 4.3.) We thus outline how to construct an algorithm that detects constraints for the family of linear codes comprised of evaluations of low-degree univariate polynomials concatenated with corresponding BS proximity proofs [BS08].

Our construction leverages the recursive structure of BS proximity proofs: we identify key combinatorial properties of the recursion that enable "local" constraint detection. To define and argue these properties, we introduce two notions that play a central role throughout the proof:

A *(local) view* of a linear code $C \subseteq \mathbb{F}^D$ is a pair $(\tilde{D}, \tilde{C})$ such that $\tilde{D} \subseteq D$ and $\tilde{C} = C|_{\tilde{D}} \subseteq \mathbb{F}^{\tilde{D}}$.

A *cover* of C is a set of local views $S = \{(\tilde{D}_j, \tilde{C}_j)\}_j$ of C such that $D = \cup_j \tilde{D}_j$.

Combinatorial properties of the recursive step. Given a finite field $\mathbb{F}$, domain $D \subseteq \mathbb{F}$, and degree d, let $C := \text{RS}[\mathbb{F}, D, d]$ be the Reed–Solomon code

---

[3] PIT is the following problem: given a polynomial f expressed as an algebraic circuit, is f identically zero? This problem has well-known randomized algorithms [Zip79, Sch80], but deterministic algorithms for all circuits seem to be beyond current techniques [KI04]. PIT is a central problem in algebraic complexity theory, and suffices for solving a number of other algebraic problems. We refer the reader to [SY10] for a survey.

consisting of evaluations on D of univariate polynomials of degree less than d over $\mathbb{F}$; for concreteness, say that the domain size is $|D| = 2^n$ and the degree is $d = |D|/2 = 2^{n-1}$.

The first level of [BS08]'s recursion appends to each codeword $f \in C$ an auxiliary function $\pi_1(f) \colon D' \to \mathbb{F}$ with domain D' disjoint from D. Moreover, the mapping from f to $\pi_1(f)$ is linear over $\mathbb{F}$, so the set $C^1 := \{f\|\pi_1(f)\}_{f \in C}$, where $f\|\pi_1(f) \colon D \cup D' \to \mathbb{F}$ is the function that agrees with f on D and with $\pi_1(f)$ on D', is a linear code over $\mathbb{F}$. The code C^1 is the "first-level" code of a BS proximity proof for f.

The code C^1 has a naturally defined cover $S^1 = \{(\tilde{D}_j, \tilde{C}_j)\}_j$ such that each $\tilde{C}_j$ is a Reed–Solomon code $\mathrm{RS}[\mathbb{F}, \tilde{D}_j, d_j]$ with $2d_j \le |\tilde{D}_j| = O(\sqrt{d})$, that is, with rate $1/2$ and block length $O(\sqrt{d})$. We prove several combinatorial properties of this cover:

- S^1 *is* 1 *-intersecting.* For all distinct j, j' in J, $|\tilde{D}_j \cap \tilde{D}_{j'}| \le 1$ (namely, the subdomains are almost disjoint).
- S^1 *is* $O(\sqrt{d})$*-local.* Every partial assignment to $O(\sqrt{d})$ domains $\tilde{D}_j$ in the cover that is *locally consistent* with the cover can be extended to a *globally consistent* assignment, i.e., to a codeword of C^1. That is, there exists $\kappa = O(\sqrt{d})$ such that every partial assignment $h \colon \cup_{\ell=1}^{\kappa} \tilde{D}_{j_\ell} \to \mathbb{F}$ with $h|_{\tilde{D}_{j_\ell}} \in \tilde{C}_{j_\ell}$ (for each ℓ) equals the restriction to the subdomain $\cup_{\ell=1}^{\kappa} \tilde{D}_{j_\ell}$ of some codeword $f\|\pi_1(f)$ in C^1.
- S^1 *is* $O(\sqrt{d})$*-independent.* The ability to extend locally-consistent assignments to "globally-consistent" codewords of C^1 holds in a stronger sense: even when the aforementioned partial assignment h is extended *arbitrarily* to κ additional point-value pairs, this new partial assignment still equals the restriction of some codeword $f\|\pi_1(f)$ in C^1.

The locality property alone already suffices to imply that, given a subdomain $I \subseteq D \cup D'$ of size $|I| < \sqrt{d}$, we can solve the constraint detection problem on I by considering only those constraints that appear in views that intersect I. But C has exponential block length so a "quadratic speedup" does not yet imply succinct constraint detection. To obtain it, we also leverage the intersection and independence properties to reduce "locality" as follows.

Further recursive steps. So far we have only considered the first recursive step of a BS proximity proof; we show how to obtain covers with smaller locality (and thereby detect constraints with more efficiency) by considering additional recursive steps. Each code $\tilde{C}_j$ in the cover S^1 of C^1 is a Reed–Solomon code $\mathrm{RS}[\mathbb{F}, \tilde{D}_j, d_j]$ with $|\tilde{D}_j|, d_j = O(\sqrt{d})$, and the next recursive step appends to each codeword in $\tilde{C}_j$ a corresponding auxiliary function, yielding a new code C^2. In turn, C^2 has a cover S^2, and another recursive step yields a new code C^3, which has its own cover S^3, and so on. The crucial technical observation is that the intersection and independence properties, which hold recursively, enable us to deduce that C^i is 1-intersecting, $O(\sqrt[2^i]{d})$-local, and $O(\sqrt[2^i]{d})$-independent; in particular, for $r = \log \log d + O(1)$, S^r is 1-intersecting, $O(1)$-local, $O(1)$-independent.

Then, recalling that detecting constraints for local codes requires only the views in the cover that intersect I, our constraint detector works by choosing $i \in \{1, \ldots, r\}$ such that the cover S^i is $\text{poly}(|I|)$-local, finding in this cover a $\text{poly}(|I|)$-size set of $\text{poly}(|I|)$-size views that intersect I, and computing in $\text{poly}(|I|)$ time a basis for the dual of each of these views — thereby proving Theorem 4.

Remark 1. For the sake of those familiar with BS-RS we remark that the domain D' is the carefully chosen subset of $\mathbb{F} \times \mathbb{F}$ designated by that construction, the code C^1 is the code that evaluates bivariate polynomials of degree $O(\sqrt{d})$ on $D \cup D'$ (along the way mapping $D \subseteq \mathbb{F}$ to a subset of $\mathbb{F} \times \mathbb{F}$), the subdomains $\tilde{D}_j$ are the axis-parallel "rows" and "columns" used in that recursive construction, and the codes $\tilde{C}_j$ are Reed–Solomon codes of block length $O(\sqrt{d})$. The $O(\sqrt{d})$-locality and independence follow from basic properties of bivariate Reed–Muller codes; see the full version for more details.

Remark 2. It is interesting to compare the above result with *linear lower bounds on query complexity* for testing proximity to random low density parity check (LDPC) codes [BHR05, BGK+10]. Those results are proved by obtaining a basis for the dual code such that every small-support constraint is spanned by a small subset of that basis. The same can be observed to hold for BS-RS, even though this latter code is locally testable with *polylogarithmic query complexity* [BS08, Theorem 2.13]. The difference between the two cases is due to the fact that, for a random LDPC code, an assignment that satisfies all but a single basis-constraint is (with high probability) far from the code, whereas the recursive and 1-intersecting structure of BS-RS implies the existence of words that satisfy all but a single basis constraint, yet are negligibly close to being a codeword.

2.2 From Constraint Detection to Zero Knowledge via Masking

We provide intuition about the connection between constraint detection and zero knowledge (Sect. 2.2), and how we leverage this connection to achieve two intermediate results: (i) protocol that is zero knowledge in the Interactive PCP model (Sect. 2.2); and (ii) proximity proofs for Reed–Solomon codes that are zero knowledge in the Interactive Oracle Proof model (Sect. 2.2).

Local simulation of random codewords. Suppose that the prover and verifier both have oracle access to a codeword $w \in C$, for some linear code $C \subseteq \mathbb{F}^D$ with exponential-size domain D, and that they need to engage in some protocol that involves w. During the protocol, the prover may leak information about w that is hard to compute (e.g., requires exponentially-many queries to w), and so would violate zero knowledge (as we see below, this is the case for protocols such as sumcheck).

Rather than directly invoking the protocol, the prover first sends to the verifier a random codeword $r \in C$ (as an oracle since r has exponential size) and the verifier replies with a random field element $\rho \in \mathbb{F}$; then the prover and verifier invoke the protocol on the new codeword $w' := \rho w + r \in C$ rather than w.

Intuitively, running the protocol on w' now does not leak information about w, because w' is random in C (up to resolvable technicalities). This *random self-reducibility* makes sense for only some protocols, e.g., those where completeness is preserved for any choice of ρ and soundness is broken for only a small fraction of ρ; but this will indeed be the case for the settings described below.

The aforementioned *masking* technique was used by [BCGV16] for codes with polynomial-size domains, but we use it for codes with exponential-size domains, which requires exponentially more efficient simulation techniques. Indeed, to prove (perfect) zero knowledge, a simulator must be able to reproduce, exactly, the view obtained by any malicious verifier that queries entries of w', a uniformly random codeword in C; however, it is too expensive for the simulator to explicitly sample a random codeword and answer the verifier's queries according to it. Instead, the simulator must sample the "local view" that the verifier sees while querying w' at a *small* number of locations $I \subseteq D$.

But simulating local views of the form $w'|_I$ is reducible to detecting *constraints*, i.e., codewords in the dual code $C^\perp$ whose support is contained in I. Indeed, if no word in $C^\perp$ has support contained in I then $w'|_I$ is uniformly random; otherwise, each additional linearly independent constraint of $C^\perp$ with support contained in I further reduces the entropy of $w'|_I$ in a well-understood manner. (See Lemma 1 for a formal statement.) In sum, succinct constraint detection enables us to "implement" [GGN10,BW04] random codewords of C despite C having exponential size.

Note that in the above discussion we implicitly assumed that the set I is known in advance, i.e., that the verifier chooses its queries in advance. This, of course, need not be the case: a verifier may adaptively make queries based on answers to previous queries and, hence, the set I need not be known a priori. This turns out to not be a problem because, given a constraint detector, it is straightforward to compute the conditional distribution of the view $w'|_I$ given $w'|_J$ for a subset J of I. This is expressed precisely in Lemma 1.

We now discuss two concrete protocols for which the aforementioned random self-reducibility applies, and for which we also have constructed suitably-efficient constraint detectors.

Zero knowledge sumchecks. The celebrated sumcheck protocol [LFKN92] is *not* zero knowledge. In the sumcheck protocol, the prover and verifier have oracle access to a low-degree m-variate polynomial F over a field $\mathbb{F}$, and the prover wants to convince the verifier that $\sum_{\alpha \in H^m} F(\alpha) = 0$ for a given subset H of $\mathbb{F}$. During the protocol, the prover communicates partial sums of F, which are #**P**-hard to compute and, as such, violate zero knowledge.

We now explain how to use random self-reducibility to make the sumcheck protocol *(perfect) zero knowledge*, at the cost of moving from the Interactive Proof model to the Interactive PCP model.

IPCP sumcheck. Consider the following tweak to the classical sumcheck protocol: rather than invoking sumcheck on F directly, the prover first sends to the verifier (the evaluation of) a random low-degree polynomial R as an oracle; then, the prover sends the value $z := \sum_{\alpha \in H^m} R(\alpha)$ and the verifier replies with a random field element ρ; finally, the two invoke sumcheck on the claim "$\sum_{\alpha \in H^m} Q(\alpha) = z$" where $Q := \rho F + R$.

Completeness is clear because if $\sum_{\alpha \in H^m} F(\alpha) = 0$ and $\sum_{\alpha \in H^m} R(\alpha) = z$ then $\sum_{\alpha \in H^m} (\rho F + R)(\alpha) = z$; soundness is also clear because if $\sum_{\alpha \in H^m} F(\alpha) \neq 0$ then $\sum_{\alpha \in H^m} (\rho F + R)(\alpha) \neq z$ with high probability over ρ, regardless of the choice of R. (For simplicity, we ignore the fact that the verifier also needs to test that R has low degree.) We are thus left to show (perfect) zero knowledge, which turns out to be a much less straightforward argument.

The simulator. Before we explain how to argue zero knowledge, we first clarify what we mean by it: since the verifier has oracle access to F we cannot hope to 'hide' it; nevertheless, we can hope to argue that the verifier, by participating in the protocol, does not learn anything about F beyond what the verifier can directly learn by querying F (and the fact that F sums to zero on H^m). What we shall achieve is the following: an algorithm that simulates the verifier's view by making as many queries to F as the *total* number of verifier queries to either F or R.[4]

On the surface, zero knowledge seems easy to argue, because $\rho F + R$ seems random among low-degree m-variate polynomials. More precisely, consider the simulator that samples a random low-degree polynomial Q and uses it instead of $\rho F + R$ and answers the verifier queries as follows: (a) whenever the verifier queries $F(\alpha)$, respond by querying $F(\alpha)$ and returning the true value; (b) whenever the verifier queries $R(\alpha)$, respond by querying $F(\alpha)$ and returning $Q(\alpha) - \rho F(\alpha)$. Observe that the number of queries to F made by the simulator equals the number of (mutually) distinct queries to F and R made by the verifier, as desired.

However, the above reasoning, while compelling, is insufficient. First, $\rho F + R$ is *not* random because a malicious verifier can choose ρ depending on queries to R. Second, even if $\rho F + R$ were random (e.g., the verifier does not query R before choosing ρ), the simulator must run in polynomial time, both producing correctly-distributed 'partial sums' of $\rho F + R$ and answering queries to R, but sampling Q alone requires exponential time. In this high level discussion we ignore the first problem (which nonetheless has to be tackled), and focus on the second.

At this point it should be clear from the discussion in Sect. 2.2 that the simulator does not have to sample Q explicitly, but only has to perfectly simulate local views of it by leveraging the fact that it can keep state across queries. And doing so requires solving the succinct constraint detection problem for a suitable code C. In this case, it suffices to consider the code $C = \Sigma \mathrm{RM}$, and our Theorem 3 guarantees the required constraint detector.

We refer the reader to the full version for further details.

---

[4] A subsequent work [CFS17] shows how to bootstrap this IPCP sumcheck protocol into a more complex one that has a stronger zero knowledge guarantee: the simulator can sample the verifier's view by making as many queries to F as the number of verifier queries (plus one). Nevertheless, the weaker zero knowledge guarantee that we achieve suffices for our purposes.

Zero knowledge proximity proofs for Reed–Solomon. Testing proximity of a codeword w to a given linear code C can be aided by a *proximity proof* [DR04,BGH+06], which is an auxiliary oracle π that facilitates testing (e.g., C is not locally testable). For example, testing proximity to the Reed–Solomon code, a crucial step towards achieving short PCPs, is aided via suitable proximity proofs [BS08].

From the perspective of zero knowledge, however, a proximity proof can be 'dangerous': a few locations of π can in principle leak a lot of information about the codeword w, and a malicious verifier could potentially learn a lot about w with only a few queries to w and π. The notion of zero knowledge for proximity proofs requires that this cannot happen: it requires the existence of an algorithm that simulates the verifier's view by making as many queries to w as the *total* number of verifier queries to either w or π [IW14]; intuitively, this means that any bit of the proximity proof π reveals no more information than one bit of w.

We demonstrate again the use of random self-reducibility and show a general transformation that, under certain conditions, maps a PCP of proximity (P, V) for a code C to a corresponding 2-round Interactive Oracle Proof of Proximity (IOPP) for C that is *(perfect) zero knowledge*.

IOP of proximity for C. Consider the following IOP of Proximity: the prover and verifier have oracle access to a codeword w, and the prover wants to convince the verifier that w is close to C; the prover first sends to the verifier a random codeword r in C, and the verifier replies with a random field element ρ; the prover then sends the proximity proof $\pi' := P(w')$ that attests that $w' := \rho w + r$ is close to C. Note that this is a 2-round IOP of Proximity for C, because completeness follows from the fact that C is linear, while soundness follows because if w is far from C, then so is $\rho w + r$ for every r with high probability over ρ. But is the zero knowledge property satisfied?

The simulator. Without going into details, analogously to Sect. 2.1, a simulator must be able to sample local views for random codewords from the code $L := \{ w \| P(w) \}_{w \in C}$, so the simulator's efficiency reduces to the efficiency of constraint detection for L. We indeed prove that if L has succinct constraint detection then the simulator works out. See the full version for further details.

The case of Reed–Solomon. The above machinery allows us to derive a zero knowledge IOP of Proximity for Reed–Solomon codes, thanks to our Theorem 4, which states that the family of linear codes comprised of evaluations of low-degree univariate polynomials concatenated with corresponding BS proximity proofs [BS08] has succinct constraint detection; see the full version for details. This is one of the building blocks of our construction of zero knowledge IOPs for **NEXP**, as described below in Sect. 2.3.

2.3   Achieving Zero Knowledge Beyond NP

We outline how to derive our results about zero knowledge for #**P** and **NEXP**.

Zero knowledge for counting problems. We provide intuition for the proof of Theorem 2, which states that the complexity class #**P** has Interactive PCPs that are perfect zero knowledge.

We first recall the classical (non zero knowledge) Interactive Proof for #**P** [LFKN92]. The language $\mathscr{L}_{\#3\text{SAT}}$, which consists of pairs (ϕ, N) where ϕ is a 3-CNF boolean formula and N is the number of satisfying assignments of ϕ, is #**P**-complete, and thus it suffices to construct an IP for it. The IP for $\mathscr{L}_{\#3\text{SAT}}$ works as follows: the prover and verifier both *arithmetize* ϕ to obtain a low-degree multivariate polynomial p_ϕ and invoke the (non zero knowledge) sumcheck protocol on the claim "$\sum_{\alpha \in \{0,1\}^n} p_\phi(\alpha) = N$", where arithmetic is over a large-enough prime field.

Returning to our goal, we obtain a perfect zero knowledge Interactive PCP by simply replacing the (non zero knowledge) IP sumcheck mentioned above with our perfect zero knowledge IPCP sumcheck, described in Sect. 2.2. In the full version we provide further details, including proving that the zero knowledge guarantees of our sumcheck protocol suffice for this case.

Zero knowledge for nondeterministic time. We provide intuition for the proof of Theorem 1, which implies that the complexity class **NEXP** has Interactive Oracle Proofs that are perfect zero knowledge. Very informally, the proof consists of combining two building blocks: (i) [BCGV16]'s reduction from **NEXP** to *randomizable* linear algebraic constraint satisfaction problems, and (ii) our construction of perfect zero knowledge IOPs of Proximity for Reed–Solomon codes, described in Sect. 2.2. Besides extending [BCGV16]'s result from **NP** to **NEXP**, our proof provides a conceptual simplification over [BCGV16] by clarifying how the above two building blocks work together towards the final result. We now discuss this.

Starting point: [BS08]. Many PCP constructions consist of two steps: (1) arithmetize the statement at hand (in our case, membership of an instance in some **NEXP**-complete language) by reducing it to a "PCP-friendly" problem that looks like a *linear-algebraic* constraint satisfaction problem (LACSP); (2) design a tester that probabilistically checks witnesses for this LACSP. In this paper, as in [BCGV16], we take [BS08]'s PCPs for **NEXP** as a starting point, where the first step reduces **NEXP** to a "univariate" LACSP whose witnesses are codewords in a Reed–Solomon code of exponential degree that satisfy certain properties, and whose second step relies on suitable *proximity proofs* [DR04, BGH+06] for that code. Thus, overall, the PCP consists of two oracles, one being the LACSP witness and the other being the corresponding BS proximity proof, and it is not hard to see that such a PCP is *not* zero knowledge, because both the LACSP witness and its proximity proof reveal hard-to-compute information.

Step 1: sanitize the proximity proof. We first address the problem that the BS proximity proof "leaks", by simply replacing it with our own perfect zero knowledge analogue. Namely, we replace it with our perfect zero knowledge 2-round IOP of Proximity for Reed–Solomon codes, described in Sect. 2.2. This modification ensures that there exists an algorithm that perfectly simulates the verifier's view by making as many queries to the LACSP witness as the *total* number of verifier queries to *either the LACSP witness or other oracles used to facilitate proximity testing*. At this point we have obtained a perfect zero knowledge 2-round IOP of Proximity for **NEXP** (analogous to the notion of a zero knowledge PCP of Proximity [IW14]); this part is where, previously, [BCGV16] were restricted to **NP** because their simulator only handled Reed–Solomon codes with *polynomial* degree while our simulator is efficient even for such codes with *exponential* degree. But we are not done yet: to obtain our goal, we also need to address the problem that the LACSP witness itself "leaks" when the verifier queries it, which we discuss next.

Step 2: sanitize the witness. Intuitively, we need to inject randomness in the reduction from **NEXP** to LACSP because the prover ultimately sends an LACSP witness to the verifier as an oracle, which the verifier can query. This is precisely what [BCGV16]'s reduction from **NEXP** to *randomizable* LACSPs enables, and we thus use their reduction to complete our proof. Informally, given an a-priori query bound b on the verifier's queries, the reduction outputs a witness w with the property that one can efficiently sample *another* witness w' whose entries are b-wise independent. We can then simply use the IOP of Proximity from the previous step on this randomized witness. Moreover, since the efficiency of the verifier is polylogarithmic in b, we can set b to be super-polynomial (e.g., exponential) to preserve zero knowledge against any polynomial number of verifier queries.

The above discussion is only a sketch and we refer the reader to the full version for further details. One aspect that we did not discuss is that an LACSP witness actually consists of two sub-witnesses, where one is a "local" deterministic function of the other, which makes arguing zero knowledge somewhat more delicate.

2.4 Roadmap

Our results are structured as in the table below. For details, see the full version.

§4.2 **Theorem 3/5** detecting constraints for ΣRM	§4.3 **Theorem 4/6** detecting constraints for BS-RS
↓	↓
PZK IPCP for sumcheck	PZK IOP of Proximity for RS codes
↓	↓
Theorem 2 PZK IPCP for #P	**Theorem 1** PZK IOP for **NEXP**

3 Definitions

3.1 Basic Notations

Functions, distributions, fields. We use $f \colon D \to R$ to denote a function with domain D and range R; given a subset $\tilde{D}$ of D, we use $f|_{\tilde{D}}$ to denote the restriction of f to $\tilde{D}$. Given a distribution $\mathcal{D}$, we write $x \leftarrow \mathcal{D}$ to denote that x is sampled according to $\mathcal{D}$. We denote by $\mathbb{F}$ a finite field and by $\mathbb{F}_q$ the field of size q; we say $\mathbb{F}$ is a *binary field* if its characteristic is 2. Arithmetic operations over $\mathbb{F}_q$ cost polylog q but we shall consider these to have unit cost (and inspection shows that accounting for their actual polylogarithmic cost does not change any of the stated results).

Distances. A distance measure is a function $\Delta \colon \Sigma^n \times \Sigma^n \to [0,1]$ such that for all $x,y,z \in \Sigma^n$: (i) $\Delta(x,x) = 0$, (ii) $\Delta(x,y) = \Delta(y,x)$, and (iii) $\Delta(x,y) \leq \Delta(x,z) + \Delta(z,y)$. We extend Δ to distances to sets: given $x \in \Sigma^n$ and $S \subseteq \Sigma^n$, we define $\Delta(x,S) := \min_{y \in S} \Delta(x,y)$ (or 1 if S is empty). We say that a string x is ϵ-close to another string y if $\Delta(x,y) \leq \epsilon$, and ϵ-far from y if $\Delta(x,y) > \epsilon$; similar terminology applies for a string x and a set S. Unless noted otherwise, we use the *relative Hamming distance* over alphabet Σ (typically implicit): $\Delta(x,y) := |\{i : x_i \neq y_i\}|/n$.

Languages and relations. We denote by $\mathscr{R}$ a (binary ordered) relation consisting of pairs (x, w), where x is the *instance* and w is the *witness*. We denote by $\mathrm{Lan}(\mathscr{R})$ the language corresponding to $\mathscr{R}$, and by $\mathscr{R}|_{\mathsf{x}}$ the set of witnesses in $\mathscr{R}$ for x (if $\mathsf{x} \notin \mathrm{Lan}(\mathscr{R})$ then $\mathscr{R}|_{\mathsf{x}} := \emptyset$). As always, we assume that $|\mathsf{w}|$ is bounded by some computable function of $n := |\mathsf{x}|$; in fact, we are mainly interested in relations arising from nondeterministic languages: $\mathscr{R} \in \mathbf{NTIME}(T)$ if there exists a $T(n)$-time machine M such that $M(\mathsf{x}, \mathsf{w})$ outputs 1 if and only if $(\mathsf{x}, \mathsf{w}) \in \mathscr{R}$. Throughout, we assume that $T(n) \geq n$. We say that $\mathscr{R}$ has relative distance $\delta_{\mathscr{R}} \colon \mathbb{N} \to [0,1]$ if $\delta_{\mathscr{R}}(n)$ is the minimum relative distance among witnesses in $\mathscr{R}|_{\mathsf{x}}$ for all x of size n. Throughout, we assume that $\delta_{\mathscr{R}}$ is a constant.

Polynomials. We denote by $\mathbb{F}[X_1, \ldots, X_m]$ the ring of polynomials in m variables over $\mathbb{F}$. Given a polynomial P in $\mathbb{F}[X_1, \ldots, X_m]$, $\deg_{X_i} P[X_i]$ is the degree of P in the variable X_i. We denote by $\mathbb{F}^{<d}[X_1, \ldots, X_m]$ the subspace consisting of $P \in \mathbb{F}[X_1, \ldots, X_m]$ with $\deg_{X_i} P[X_i] < d$ for every $i \in \{1, \ldots, m\}$.

Random shifts. We later use a folklore claim about distance preservation for random shifts in linear spaces.

Claim. Let n be in $\mathbb{N}$, $\mathbb{F}$ a finite field, S an $\mathbb{F}$-linear space in $\mathbb{F}^n$, and $x, y \in \mathbb{F}^n$. If x is ϵ-far from S, then $\alpha x + y$ is $\epsilon/2$-far from S, with probability $1 - |\mathbb{F}|^{-1}$ over a random $\alpha \in \mathbb{F}$. (Distances are relative Hamming distances.)

3.2   Single-Prover Proof Systems

We use two types of proof systems that combine aspects of interactive proofs [Bab85, GMR89] and probabilistically checkable proofs [BFLS91, AS98, ALM+98]: **interactive PCPs** (IPCPs) [KR08] and **interactive oracle proofs** (IOPs) [BCS16, RRR16]. We first describe IPCPs (Sect. 3.2) and then IOPs (Sect. 3.2), which generalize the former.

Interactive probabilistically checkable proofs. An **IPCP** [KR08] is a PCP followed by an IP. Namely, the prover P and verifier V interact as follows: P sends to V a probabilistically checkable proof π; afterwards, P and V^π engage in an interactive proof. Thus, V may read a few bits of π but must read subsequent messages from P in full. An *IPCP system* for a relation $\mathscr{R}$ is thus a pair (P, V), where P, V are probabilistic interactive algorithms working as described, that satisfies naturally-defined notions of perfect completeness and soundness with a given error $\varepsilon(\cdot)$; see [KR08] for details.

We say that an IPCP has k rounds if this "PCP round" is followed by a $(k-1)$-round interactive proof. (That is, we count the PCP round towards round complexity, unlike [KR08].) Beyond round complexity, we also measure how many bits the prover sends and how many the verifier reads: the *proof length* l is the length of π in bits plus the number of bits in all subsequent prover messages; the *query complexity* q is the number of bits of π read by the verifier plus the number of bits in all subsequent prover messages (since the verifier must read all of those bits).

In this work, we do not count the number of bits in the verifier messages, nor the number of random bits used by the verifier; both are bounded from above by the verifier's running time, which we do consider. Overall, we say that a relation $\mathscr{R}$ belongs to the complexity class **IPCP**$[k, l, q, \varepsilon, tp, tv]$ if there is an IPCP system for $\mathscr{R}$ in which: (1)the number of rounds is at most $k(n)$; (2) the proof length is at most $l(n)$; (3) the query complexity is at most $q(n)$; (4) the soundness error is $\varepsilon(n)$; (5) the prover algorithm runs in time $tp(n)$; (6) the verifier algorithm runs in time $tv(n)$.

Interactive oracle proofs. An **IOP** [BCS16, RRR16] is a "multi-round PCP". That is, an IOP generalizes an interactive proof as follows: whenever the prover sends to the verifier a message, the verifier does not have to read the message in full but may probabilistically query it. In more detail, a k-round IOP comprises k rounds of interaction. In the i-th round of interaction: the verifier sends a message m_i to the prover; then the prover replies with a message π_i to the verifier, which the verifier can query in this and later rounds (via oracle queries). After the k rounds of interaction, the verifier either accepts or rejects.

An *IOP system* for a relation $\mathscr{R}$ with soundness error ε is thus a pair (P, V), where P, V are probabilistic interactive algorithms working as described, that satisfies the following properties. (See [BCS16] for more details.)

Completeness: For every instance-witness pair (x, w) in the relation $\mathscr{R}$, $\Pr[\langle P(x, w), V(x) \rangle = 1] = 1$.

Soundness: For every instance x not in $\mathscr{R}$'s language and unbounded malicious prover $\tilde{P}$, $\Pr[\langle \tilde{P}, V(x) \rangle = 1] \leq \varepsilon(n)$.

Beyond round complexity, we also measure how many bits the prover sends and how many the verifier reads: the *proof length* l is the total number of bits in all of the prover's messages, and the *query complexity* q is the total number of bits read by the verifier across all of the prover's messages. Considering all of these parameters, we say that a relation $\mathscr{R}$ belongs to the complexity class **IOP**$[k, l, q, \varepsilon, tp, tv]$ if there is an IOP system for $\mathscr{R}$ in which: (1) the number of rounds is at most $k(n)$; (2) the proof length is at most $l(n)$; (3) the query complexity is at most $q(n)$; (4) the soundness error is $\varepsilon(n)$; (5) the prover algorithm runs in time $tp(n)$; (6) the verifier algorithm runs in time $tv(n)$.

IOP vs. IPCP. An IPCP (see Sect. 3.2) is a special case of an IOP because an IPCP verifier must read in full all of the prover's messages except the first one (while an IOP verifier may query any part of any prover message). The above complexity measures are consistent with those defined for IPCPs.

Restrictions and extensions. The definitions below are about IOPs, but IPCPs inherit all of these definitions because they are a special case of IOP.

Adaptivity of queries. An IOP system is *non-adaptive* if the verifier queries are non-adaptive, i.e., the queried locations depend only on the verifier's inputs.

Public coins. An IOP system is *public coin* if each verifier message m_i is chosen uniformly and independently at random, and all of the verifier queries happen after receiving the last prover message.

Proximity. An *IOP of proximity* extends the definition of an IOP in the same way that a PCP of proximity extends that of a PCP [DR04, BGH+06]. An *IOPP system* for a relation $\mathscr{R}$ with soundness error ε and proximity parameter δ is a pair (P, V) that satisfies the following properties.

Completeness: For every instance-witness pair (x, w) in the relation $\mathscr{R}$,
$\Pr[\langle P(x, w), V^w(x) \rangle = 1] = 1$.
Soundness: For every instance-witness pair (x, w) with $\Delta(w, \mathscr{R}|_x) \geq \delta(n)$ and unbounded malicious prover $\tilde{P}$, $\Pr[\langle \tilde{P}, V^w(x) \rangle = 1] \leq \varepsilon(n)$.

Similarly to above, a relation $\mathscr{R}$ belongs to the complexity class **IOPP**$[k, l, q, \varepsilon, \delta, tp, tv]$ if there is an IOPP system for $\mathscr{R}$ with the corresponding parameters. Following [IW14], we call an IOPP *exact* if $\delta(n) = 0$.

Promise relations. A *promise relation* is a relation-language pair $(\mathscr{R}^{\text{YES}}, \mathscr{L}^{\text{NO}})$ with $\mathrm{Lan}(\mathscr{R}^{\text{YES}}) \cap \mathscr{L}^{\text{NO}} = \emptyset$. An IOP for a promise relation is the same as an IOP for the (standard) relation $\mathscr{R}^{\text{YES}}$, except that soundness need only hold for $x \in \mathscr{L}^{\text{NO}}$. An IOPP for a promise relation is the same as an IOPP for the (standard) relation $\mathscr{R}^{\text{YES}}$, except that soundness need only hold for $x \in \mathrm{Lan}(\mathscr{R}^{\text{YES}}) \cup \mathscr{L}^{\text{NO}}$.

Prior constructions. In this paper we give new IPCP and IOP constructions that achieve perfect zero knowledge for various settings. Below we summarize known constructions in these two models.

IPCPs. Prior work obtains IPCPs with proof length that depends on the witness size rather than computation size [KR08, GKR08], and IPCPs with statistical zero knowledge [GIMS10] (see Sect. 3.3 for more details).

IOPs. Prior work obtains IOPs with perfect zero knowledge for **NP** [BCGV16], IOPs with small proof length and query complexity [BCG+17], and an amortization theorem for "unambiguous" IOPs [RRR16]. Also, [BCS16] show how to compile public-coin IOPs into non-interactive arguments in the random oracle model.

3.3   Zero Knowledge

We define the notion of zero knowledge for IOPs and IPCPs achieved by our constructions: *unconditional (perfect) zero knowledge via straightline simulators.*

This notion is quite strong not only because it unconditionally guarantees simulation of the verifier's view but also because straightline simulation implies desirable properties such as composability. We now provide some context and then give formal definitions.

At a high level, zero knowledge requires that the verifier's view can be efficiently simulated without the prover. Converting the informal statement into a mathematical one involves many choices, including choosing which verifier class to consider (e.g., the honest verifier? all polynomial-time verifiers?), the quality of the simulation (e.g., is it identically distributed to the view? statistically close to it? computationally close to it?), the simulator's dependence on the verifier (e.g., is it non-uniform? or is the simulator universal?), and others. The definitions below consider two variants: perfect simulation via universal simulators against either unbounded-query or bounded-query verifiers.

Moreover, in the case of universal simulators, one distinguishes between a non-blackbox use of the verifier, which means that the simulator takes the verifier's code as input, and a blackbox use of it, which means that the simulator only accesses the verifier via a restricted interface; we consider this latter case. Different models of proof systems call for different interfaces, which grant carefully-chosen "extra powers" to the simulator (in comparison to the prover) so to ensure that efficiency of the simulation does not imply the ability to efficiently decide the language. For example: in ZK IPs, the simulator may rewind the verifier; in ZK PCPs, the simulator may adaptively answer oracle queries. In ZK IPCPs and ZK IOPs (our setting), the natural definition would allow a blackbox simulator to rewind the verifier *and also* to adaptively answer oracle queries. The definitions below, however, consider only simulators that are straightline [FS89, DS98], that is they do not rewind the verifier, because our constructions achieve this stronger notion.

We are now ready to define the notion of unconditional (perfect) zero knowledge via straightline simulators. We first discuss the notion for IOPs, then for IOPs of proximity, and finally for IPCPs.

ZK for IOPs. We define zero knowledge (via straightline simulators) for IOPs. We begin by defining the view of an IOP verifier.

Definition 4. *Let A, B be algorithms and x, y strings. We denote by View $\langle B(y), A(x) \rangle$ the **view** of $A(x)$ in an interactive oracle protocol with $B(y)$, i.e., the random variable $(x, r, a_1, \ldots, a_n)$ where x is A's input, r is A's randomness, and $a_1, \ldots, a_n$ are the answers to A's queries into B's messages.*

Straightline simulators in the context of IPs were used in [FS89], and later defined in [DS98]. The definition below considers this notion in the context of IOPs, where the simulator also has to answer oracle queries by the verifier. Note that since we consider the notion of unconditional (perfect) zero knowledge, the definition of straightline simulation needs to allow the efficient simulator to work even with inefficient verifiers [GIMS10].

Definition 5. *We say that an algorithm B has* **straightline access** *to another algorithm A if B interacts with A, without rewinding, by exchanging messages with A and also answering any oracle queries along the way. We denote by B^A the concatenation of A's random tape and B's output. (Since A's random tape could be super-polynomially large, B cannot sample it for A and then output it; instead, we restrict B to not see it, and we prepend it to B's output.)*

Recall that an algorithm A is b-query if, on input x, it makes at most $\mathsf{b}(|\mathsf{x}|)$ queries to any oracles it has access to. We are now ready to define zero knowledge IOPs.

Definition 6. *An IOP system (P, V) for a relation $\mathscr{R}$ is perfect zero knowledge (via straightline simulators)* against unbounded queries *(resp.,* against query bound b) *if there exists a simulator algorithm S such that for every algorithm (resp., b-query algorithm) $\tilde{V}$ and instance-witness pair $(\mathsf{x}, \mathsf{w}) \in \mathscr{R}$, $S^{\tilde{V}}(\mathsf{x})$ and View $\langle P(\mathsf{x}, \mathsf{w}), \tilde{V}(\mathsf{x}) \rangle$ are identically distributed. Moreover, S must run in time $\mathrm{poly}(|\mathsf{x}| + \mathsf{q}_{\tilde{V}}(|\mathsf{x}|))$, where $\mathsf{q}_{\tilde{V}}(\cdot)$ is $\tilde{V}$'s query complexity.*

For zero knowledge against arbitrary polynomial-time adversaries, it suffices for b to be superpolynomial. Note that S's running time need not be polynomial in b (in our constructions it is polylogarithmic in b); rather its running time may be polynomial in the input size $|\mathsf{x}|$ and the *actual* number of queries $\tilde{V}$ makes (as a random variable).

We say that a relation $\mathscr{R}$ belongs to the complexity class **PZK-IOP**[k, l, $\mathsf{q}, \varepsilon, \mathsf{tp}, \mathsf{tv}, \mathsf{b}$] if there is an IOP system for $\mathscr{R}$, with the corresponding parameters, that is perfect zero knowledge with query bound b; also, it belongs to the complexity class **PZK-IOP**[$\mathsf{k}, \mathsf{l}, \mathsf{q}, \varepsilon, \mathsf{tp}, \mathsf{tv}, *$] if the same is true with unbounded queries.

ZK for IOPs of proximity. We define zero knowledge (via straightline simulators) for IOPs of proximity. It is a straightforward extension of the corresponding notion for PCPs of proximity, introduced in [IW14].

Definition 7. *An IOPP system (P, V) for a relation $\mathscr{R}$ is perfect zero knowledge (via straightline simulators)* against unbounded queries *(resp.,* against query bound b) *if there exists a simulator algorithm S such that for every algorithm (resp., b-query algorithm) $\tilde{V}$ and instance-witness pair $(\mathsf{x}, \mathsf{w}) \in \mathscr{R}$, the following two random variables are identically distributed:*

$$\left(S^{\tilde{V}, \mathsf{w}}(\mathsf{x}) , q_S \right) \quad \text{and} \quad \left(\text{View} \langle P(\mathsf{x}, \mathsf{w}), \tilde{V}^{\mathsf{w}}(\mathsf{x}) \rangle , q_{\tilde{V}} \right),$$

where q_S is the number of queries to w made by S, and $q_{\tilde{V}}$ is the number of queries to w or to prover messages made by $\tilde{V}$. Moreover, S must run in time $\mathrm{poly}(|\mathsf{x}| + \mathsf{q}_{\tilde{V}}(|\mathsf{x}|))$, where $\mathsf{q}_{\tilde{V}}(\cdot)$ is $\tilde{V}$'s query complexity.

We say that a relation $\mathscr{R}$ belongs to the complexity class **PZK-IOPP**[k, l, $\mathsf{q}, \varepsilon, \delta, \mathsf{tp}, \mathsf{tv}, \mathsf{b}$] if there is an IOPP system for $\mathscr{R}$, with the corresponding parameters, that is perfect zero knowledge with query bound b; also, it belongs to the complexity class **PZK-IOPP**$[k, l, q, \varepsilon, \delta, tp, tv, *]$ if the same is true with unbounded queries.

Remark 3. Analogously to [IW14], our definition of zero knowledge for IOPs of proximity requires that the number of queries to w by S equals the total number of queries (to w or prover messages) by $\tilde{V}$. Stronger notions are possible: "the number of queries to w by S equals the number of queries to w by $\tilde{V}$"; or, even more, "S and $\tilde{V}$ read the same locations of w". The definition above is sufficient for the applications of IOPs of proximity that we consider.

ZK for IPCPs. The definition of perfect zero knowledge (via straightline simulators) for IPCPs follows directly from Definition 6 in Sect. 3.3 because IPCPs are a special case of IOPs. Ditto for IPCPs of proximity, whose perfect zero knowledge definition follows directly from Definition 7 in Sect. 3.3. (For comparison, [GIMS10] define statistical zero knowledge IPCPs, also with straightline simulators.)

3.4   Codes

An error correcting code C is a set of functions $w \colon D \to \Sigma$, where D, Σ are finite sets known as the domain and alphabet; we write $C \subseteq \Sigma^D$. The message length of C is $k := \log_{|\Sigma|} |C|$, its block length is $\ell := |D|$, its rate is $\rho := k/\ell$, its (minimum) distance is $d := \min\{\Delta(w, z) \ : \ w, z \in C, w \neq z\}$ when Δ is the (absolute) Hamming distance, and its (minimum) relative distance is $\tau := d/\ell$. At times we write $k(C), \ell(C), \rho(C), d(C), \tau(C)$ to make the code under consideration explicit. All the codes we consider are linear codes, discussed next.

Linearity. A code C is *linear* if Σ is a finite field and C is a Σ-linear space in Σ^D. The dual code of C is the set $C^\perp$ of functions $z \colon D \to \Sigma$ such that, for all $w \colon D \to \Sigma$, $\langle z, w \rangle := \sum_{i \in D} z(i)w(i) = 0$. We denote by $\dim(C)$ the dimension of C; it holds that $\dim(C) + \dim(C^\perp) = \ell$ and $\dim(C) = k$ (dimension equals message length).

Code families. A code family $\mathscr{C} = \{C_\mathfrak{n}\}_{\mathfrak{n} \in \{0,1\}^*}$ has domain $D(\cdot)$ and alphabet $\mathbb{F}(\cdot)$ if each code $C_\mathfrak{n}$ has domain $D(\mathfrak{n})$ and alphabet $\mathbb{F}(\mathfrak{n})$. Similarly, $\mathscr{C}$ has message length $k(\cdot)$, block length $\ell(\cdot)$, rate $\rho(\cdot)$, distance $d(\cdot)$, and relative distance $\tau(\cdot)$ if each code $C_\mathfrak{n}$ has message length $k(\mathfrak{n})$, block length $\ell(\mathfrak{n})$, rate $\rho(\mathfrak{n})$, distance $d(\mathfrak{n})$, and relative distance $\tau(\mathfrak{n})$. We also define $\rho(\mathscr{C}) := \inf_{\mathfrak{n} \in \mathbb{N}} \rho(\mathfrak{n})$ and $\tau(\mathscr{C}) := \inf_{\mathfrak{n} \in \mathbb{N}} \tau(\mathfrak{n})$.

Reed–Solomon codes. The Reed–Solomon (RS) code is the code consisting of evaluations of *univariate* low-degree polynomials: given a field $\mathbb{F}$, subset S of $\mathbb{F}$, and positive integer d with $d \leq |S|$, we denote by $\mathrm{RS}[\mathbb{F}, S, d]$ the linear code consisting of evaluations $w \colon S \to \mathbb{F}$ over S of polynomials in $\mathbb{F}^{<d}[X]$. The code's message length is $k = d$, block length is $\ell = |S|$, rate is $\rho = \frac{d}{|S|}$, and relative distance is $\tau = 1 - \frac{d-1}{|S|}$.

Reed–Muller codes. The Reed–Muller (RM) code is the code consisting of evaluations of *multivariate* low-degree polynomials: given a field $\mathbb{F}$, subset S of $\mathbb{F}$, and positive integers m, d with $d \leq |S|$, we denote by $\mathrm{RM}[\mathbb{F}, S, m, d]$ the linear code consisting of evaluations $w \colon S^m \to \mathbb{F}$ over S^m of polynomials in $\mathbb{F}^{<d}[X_1, \ldots, X_m]$ (i.e., we bound individual degrees rather than their sum). The code's message length is $k = d^m$, block length is $\ell = |S|^m$, rate is $\rho = (\frac{d}{|S|})^m$, and relative distance is $\tau = (1 - \frac{d-1}{|S|})^m$.

4 Succinct Constraint Detection

We introduce the notion of *succinct constraint detection* for linear codes. This notion plays a crucial role in constructing perfect zero knowledge simulators for super-polynomial complexity classes (such as #**P** and **NEXP**), but we believe that this naturally-defined notion is also of independent interest. Given a linear code $C \subseteq \mathbb{F}^D$ we refer to its dual code $C^\perp \subseteq \mathbb{F}^D$ as the *constraint space* of C. The *constraint detection problem* corresponding to a family of linear codes $\mathscr{C} = \{C_\mathfrak{n}\}_\mathfrak{n}$ with domain $D(\cdot)$ and alphabet $\mathbb{F}(\cdot)$ is the following:

> Given an index $\mathfrak{n}$ and subset $I \subseteq D(\mathfrak{n})$, output a basis for
> $\{z \in D(\mathfrak{n})^I : \forall w \in C_\mathfrak{n}, \sum_{i \in I} z(i)w(i) = 0\}$.[5]

If $|D(\mathfrak{n})|$ is polynomial in $|\mathfrak{n}|$ and a generating matrix for $C_\mathfrak{n}$ can be found in polynomial time, this problem can be solved in $\mathrm{poly}(|\mathfrak{n}| + |I|)$ time via Gaussian elimination; such an approach was implicitly taken by [BCGV16] to construct a perfect zero knowledge simulator for an IOP for **NP**. However, in our setting, $|D(\mathfrak{n})|$ is *exponential* in $|\mathfrak{n}|$ and $|I|$, and the aforementioned generic solution requires exponential time. With this in mind, we say $\mathscr{C}$ has *succinct constraint detection* if there exists an algorithm that solves the constraint detection problem in $\mathrm{poly}(|\mathfrak{n}| + |I|)$ time when $|D(\mathfrak{n})|$ is *exponential* in $|\mathfrak{n}|$. After defining succinct constraint detection in Sect. 4.1, we proceed as follows.

- In Sect. 4.2, we construct a succinct constraint detector for the family of linear codes comprised of evaluations of partial sums of low-degree polynomials. The construction of the detector exploits derandomization techniques from algebraic complexity theory. We leverage this result to construct a perfect zero knowledge simulator for an IPCP for #**P**; see the full version for details.
- In Sect. 4.3, we construct a succinct constraint detector for the family of evaluations of univariate polynomials concatenated with corresponding BS proximity proofs [BS08]. The construction of the detector exploits the recursive structure of these proximity proofs. We leverage this result to construct a perfect zero knowledge simulator for an IOP for **NEXP**; this simulator can

---

[5] In fact, the following weaker definition suffices for the applications in our paper: *given an index $\mathfrak{n}$ and subset $I \subseteq D(\mathfrak{n})$, output $z \in \mathbb{F}(\mathfrak{n})^I$ such that $\sum_{i \in I} z(i)w(i) = 0$ for all $w \in C_\mathfrak{n}$, or 'independent' if no such z exists*. We achieve the stronger definition, which is also easier to work with.

be interpreted as an analogue of [BCGV16]'s simulator that runs *exponentially faster* and thus enables us to "scale up" from **NP** to **NEXP**; see the full version for details.

Throughout this section we assume familiarity with terminology and notation about codes, introduced in Sect. 3.4. We assume for simplicity that $|\mathfrak{n}|$, the number of bits used to represent $\mathfrak{n}$, is at least $\log D(\mathfrak{n}) + \log \mathbb{F}(\mathfrak{n})$; if this does not hold, then one can replace $|\mathfrak{n}|$ with $|\mathfrak{n}| + \log D(\mathfrak{n}) + \log \mathbb{F}(\mathfrak{n})$ throughout the section.

Remark 4 (sparse representation). In this section we make statements about vectors v in $\mathbb{F}^D$ where the cardinality of the domain D may be super-polynomial. When such statements are computational in nature, we assume that v is not represented as a list of $|D|$ field elements (which requires $\Omega(|D| \log |\mathbb{F}|)$ bits) but, instead, assume that v is represented as a list of the elements in $\mathrm{supp}(v)$ (and each element comes with its index in D); this *sparse* representation only requires $\Omega(|\mathrm{supp}(v)| \cdot (\log |D| + \log |\mathbb{F}|))$ bits.

4.1 Definition of Succinct Constraint Detection

Formally define the notion of a *constraint detector*, and the notion of *succinct constraint detection*.

Definition 8. *Let $\mathscr{C} = \{C_{\mathfrak{n}}\}_{\mathfrak{n}}$ be a linear code family with domain $D(\cdot)$ and alphabet $\mathbb{F}(\cdot)$. A **constraint detector** for $\mathscr{C}$ is an algorithm that, on input an index $\mathfrak{n}$ and subset $I \subseteq D(\mathfrak{n})$, outputs a basis for the space*

$$\left\{ z \in D(\mathfrak{n})^I : \forall w \in C_{\mathfrak{n}}, \sum_{i \in I} z(i)w(i) \right\}.$$

*We say that $\mathscr{C}$ has $T(\cdot, \cdot)$ -**time constraint detection** if there exists a detector for $\mathscr{C}$ running in time $T(\mathfrak{n}, \ell)$; we also say that $\mathscr{C}$ has **succinct constraint detection** if it has $\mathrm{poly}(|\mathfrak{n}| + \ell)$-time constraint detection.*

A constraint detector induces a corresponding probabilistic algorithm for 'simulating' answers to queries to a random codeword; this is captured by the following lemma, the proof of which is in the full version. We shall use such probabilistic algorithms in the construction of perfect zero knowledge simulators.

Lemma 1. *Let $\mathscr{C} = \{C_{\mathfrak{n}}\}_{\mathfrak{n}}$ be a linear code family with domain $D(\cdot)$ and alphabet $\mathbb{F}(\cdot)$ that has $T(\cdot, \cdot)$-time constraint detection. Then there exists a probabilistic algorithm $\mathcal{A}$ such that, for every index $\mathfrak{n}$, set of pairs $S = \{(\alpha_1, \beta_1), \dots, (\alpha_\ell, \beta_\ell)\} \subseteq D(\mathfrak{n}) \times \mathbb{F}(\mathfrak{n})$, and pair $(\alpha, \beta) \in D(\mathfrak{n}) \times \mathbb{F}(\mathfrak{n})$,*

$$\Pr\left[\mathcal{A}(\mathfrak{n}, S, \alpha) = \beta \right] = \Pr_{w \leftarrow C_{\mathfrak{n}}} \left[w(\alpha) = \beta \, \middle| \, \begin{matrix} w(\alpha_1) = \beta_1 \\ \vdots \\ w(\alpha_\ell) = \beta_\ell \end{matrix} \right].$$

Moreover $\mathcal{A}$ runs in time $T(\mathfrak{n}, \ell) + \mathrm{poly}(\log |\mathbb{F}(\mathfrak{n})| + \ell)$.

For the purposes of *constructing* a constraint detector, the sufficient condition given in Lemma 2 below is sometimes easier to work with. To state it we need to introduce two ways of restricting a code, and explain how these restrictions interact with taking duals; the interplay between these is delicate (see Remark 5).

Definition 9. *Given a linear code $C \subseteq \mathbb{F}^D$ and a subset $I \subseteq D$, we denote by (i) $C_{\subseteq I}$ the set consisting of the codewords $w \in C$ for which $\mathrm{supp}(w) \subseteq I$, and (ii) $C|_I$ the restriction to I of codewords $w \in C$.*

Note that $C_{\subseteq I}$ and $C|_I$ are *different* notions. Consider for example the 1-dimensional linear code $C = \{00, 11\}$ in $\mathbb{F}_2^{\{1,2\}}$ and the subset $I = \{1\}$: it holds that $C_{\subseteq I} = \{00\}$ and $C|_I = \{0, 1\}$. In particular, codewords in $C_{\subseteq I}$ are defined over D, while codewords in $C|_I$ are defined over I. Nevertheless, throughout this section, we sometimes compare vectors defined over different domains, with the implicit understanding that the comparison is conducted over the union of the relevant domains, by filling in zeros in the vectors' undefined coordinates. For example, we may write $C_{\subseteq I} \subseteq C|_I$ to mean that $\{00\} \subseteq \{00, 10\}$ (the set obtained from $\{0, 1\}$ after filling in the relevant zeros).

Claim. Let C be a linear code with domain D and alphabet $\mathbb{F}$. For every $I \subseteq D$,

$$(C|_I)^{\perp} = (C^{\perp})_{\subseteq I},$$

that is,

$$\left\{ z \in D(\mathfrak{n})^I : \forall w \in C_\mathfrak{n}, \sum_{i \in I} z(i)w(i) \right\} = \left\{ z \in C_\mathfrak{n}^{\perp} : \mathrm{supp}(z) \subseteq I \right\}.$$

Proof. For the containment $(C^{\perp})_{\subseteq I} \subseteq (C|_I)^{\perp}$: if $z \in C^{\perp}$ and $\mathrm{supp}(z) \subseteq I$ then z lies in the dual of $C|_I$ because it suffices to consider the subdomain I for determining duality. For the reverse containment $(C^{\perp})_{\subseteq I} \supseteq (C|_I)^{\perp}$: if $z \in (C|_I)^{\perp}$ then $\mathrm{supp}(z) \subseteq I$ (by definition) so that $\langle z, w \rangle = \langle z, w|_I \rangle$ for every $w \in C$, and the latter inner product equals 0 because z is in the dual of $C|_I$; in sum z is dual to (all codewords in) C and its support is contained in I, so z belongs to $(C^{\perp})_{\subseteq I}$, as claimed.

Observe that Claim 4.1 tells us the constraint detection is equivalent to determining a basis of $(C_\mathfrak{n}|_I)^{\perp} = (C_\mathfrak{n}^{\perp})_{\subseteq I}$. The following lemma asserts that if, given a subset $I \subseteq D$, we can find a set of constraints W in $C^{\perp}$ that spans $(C^{\perp})_{\subseteq I}$ then we can solve the constraint detection problem for C; see the full version for a proof.

Lemma 2. *Let $\mathscr{C} = \{C_\mathfrak{n}\}_\mathfrak{n}$ be a linear code family with domain $D(\cdot)$ and alphabet $\mathbb{F}(\cdot)$. If there exists an algorithm that, on input an index $\mathfrak{n}$ and subset $I \subseteq D(\mathfrak{n})$, outputs in $\mathrm{poly}(|\mathfrak{n}| + |I|)$ time a subset $W \subseteq \mathbb{F}(\mathfrak{n})^{D(\mathfrak{n})}$ (in sparse representation) with $(C_\mathfrak{n}^{\perp})_{\subseteq I} \subseteq \mathrm{span}(W) \subseteq C_\mathfrak{n}^{\perp}$, then $\mathscr{C}$ has succinct constraint detection.*

Remark 5. The following operations do *not* commute: (i) expanding the domain via zero padding (for the purpose of comparing vectors over different domains), and (ii)taking the dual of the code. Consider for example the code $C = \{0\} \subseteq \mathbb{F}_2^{\{1\}}$: its dual code is $C^\perp = \{0,1\}$ and, when expanded to $\mathbb{F}_2^{\{1,2\}}$, the dual code is expanded to $\{(0,0),(1,0)\}$; yet, when C is expanded to $\mathbb{F}_2^{\{1,2\}}$ it produces the code $\{(0,0)\}$ and its dual code is $\{(0,0),(1,0),(0,1),(1,1)\}$. To resolve ambiguities (when asserting an equality as in Claim 4.1), we adopt the convention that expansion is done *always last* (namely, as late as possible without having to compare vectors over different domains).

4.2   Partial Sums of Low-Degree Polynomials

We show that evaluations of partial sums of low-degree polynomials have succinct constraint detection (see Definition 8). In the following, $\mathbb{F}$ is a finite field, m, d are positive integers, and H is a subset of $\mathbb{F}$; also, $\mathbb{F}^{<d}[X_1,\ldots,X_m]$ denotes the subspace of $\mathbb{F}[X_1,\ldots,X_m]$ consisting of those polynomials with individual degrees less than d. Moreover, given $Q \in \mathbb{F}^{<d}[X_1,\ldots,X_m]$ and $\boldsymbol{\alpha} \in \mathbb{F}^{\leq m}$ (vectors over $\mathbb{F}$ of length at most m), we define $Q(\boldsymbol{\alpha}) := \sum_{\boldsymbol{\gamma} \in H^{m-|\alpha|}} Q(\boldsymbol{\alpha},\boldsymbol{\gamma})$, i.e., the answer to a query that specifies only a suffix of the variables is the sum of the values obtained by letting the remaining variables range over H. We begin by defining the code that we study, which extends the Reed–Muller code (see Sect. 3.4) with partial sums.

Definition 10. *We denote by* $\Sigma\mathrm{RM}[\mathbb{F}, m, d, H]$ *the linear code that comprises evaluations of partial sums of polynomials in* $\mathbb{F}^{<d}[X_1,\ldots,X_m]$; *more precisely,* $\Sigma\mathrm{RM}[\mathbb{F}, m, d, H] := \{w_Q\}_{Q \in \mathbb{F}^{<d}[X_1,\ldots,X_m]}$ *where* $w_Q \colon \mathbb{F}^{\leq m} \to \mathbb{F}$ *is the function defined by* $w_Q(\boldsymbol{\alpha}) := \sum_{\boldsymbol{\gamma} \in H^{m-|\alpha|}} Q(\boldsymbol{\alpha},\boldsymbol{\gamma})$ *for each* $\boldsymbol{\alpha} \in \mathbb{F}^{\leq m}$.[6] *We denote by* $\Sigma\mathrm{RM}$ *the linear code family indexed by tuples* $\mathfrak{n} = (\mathbb{F}, m, d, H)$ *and where the* $\mathfrak{n}$-*th code equals* $\Sigma\mathrm{RM}[\mathbb{F}, m, d, H]$. *(We represent indices* $\mathfrak{n}$ *so to ensure that* $|\mathfrak{n}| = \Theta(\log|\mathbb{F}| + m + d + |H|)$.*)*

We prove that the linear code family $\Sigma\mathrm{RM}$ has succinct constraint detection:

Theorem 5 (formal statement of 3). $\Sigma\mathrm{RM}$ *has* $\mathrm{poly}(\log|\mathbb{F}| + m + d + |H| + \ell)$-*time constraint detection.*

Combined with Lemma 1, the theorem above implies that there exists a probabilistic polynomial-time algorithm for answering queries to a codeword sampled at random from $\Sigma\mathrm{RM}$, as captured by the following corollary.

---

[6] Note that $\Sigma\mathrm{RM}[\mathbb{F}, m, d, H]$ is indeed linear: for every $w_{Q_1}, w_{Q_2} \in \Sigma\mathrm{RM}[\mathbb{F}, m, d, H]$, $a_1, a_2 \in \mathbb{F}$, and $\boldsymbol{\alpha} \in \mathbb{F}^{\leq m}$, it holds that $a_1 w_{Q_1}(\boldsymbol{\alpha}) + a_2 w_{Q_2}(\boldsymbol{\alpha}) = a_1 \sum_{\boldsymbol{\gamma} \in H^{m-|\alpha|}} Q_1(\boldsymbol{\alpha},\boldsymbol{\gamma}) + a_2 \sum_{\boldsymbol{\gamma} \in H^{m-|\alpha|}} Q_2(\boldsymbol{\alpha},\boldsymbol{\gamma}) = \sum_{\boldsymbol{\gamma} \in H^{m-|\alpha|}} (a_1 Q_1 + a_2 Q_2)(\boldsymbol{\alpha},\boldsymbol{\gamma}) = w_{a_1 Q_1 + a_2 Q_2}(\boldsymbol{\alpha})$. But $w_{a_1 Q_1 + a_2 Q_2} \in \Sigma\mathrm{RM}[\mathbb{F}, m, d, H]$, since $\mathbb{F}^{<d}[X_1,\ldots,X_m]$ is a linear space.

Corollary 1. *There exists a probabilistic algorithm $\mathcal{A}$ such that, for every finite field $\mathbb{F}$, positive integers m, d, subset H of $\mathbb{F}$, subset $S = \{(\alpha_1, \beta_1), \ldots, (\alpha_\ell, \beta_\ell)\} \subseteq \mathbb{F}^{\leq m} \times \mathbb{F}$, and $(\alpha, \beta) \in \mathbb{F}^{\leq m} \times \mathbb{F}$,*

$$\Pr\left[\mathcal{A}(\mathbb{F}, m, d, H, S, \alpha) = \beta\right] = \Pr_{R \leftarrow \mathbb{F}^{<d}[X_1, \ldots, X_m]}\left[R(\alpha) = \beta \left|\begin{array}{c} R(\alpha_1) = \beta_1 \\ \vdots \\ R(\alpha_\ell) = \beta_\ell \end{array}\right.\right].$$

Moreover $\mathcal{A}$ runs in time $\mathrm{poly}(\log|\mathbb{F}| + m + d + |H| + \ell)$.

We sketch the proof of Theorem 5, for the simpler case where the code is $\mathrm{RM}[\mathbb{F}, m, d, H]$ (i.e., without partial sums). We can view a polynomial $Q \in \mathbb{F}^{<d}[X_1, \ldots, X_m]$ as a vector over the monomial basis, with an entry for each possible monomial $X_1^{i_1} \ldots X_m^{i_m}$ (with $0 \leq i_1, \ldots, i_m < d$) containing the corresponding coefficient. The evaluation of Q at a point $\boldsymbol{\alpha} \in \mathbb{F}^m$ then equals the inner product of this vector with the vector $\phi_{\boldsymbol{\alpha}}$, in the same basis, whose entry for $X_1^{i_1} \ldots X_m^{i_m}$ is equal to $\alpha_1^{i_1} \ldots \alpha_m^{i_m}$. Given $\boldsymbol{\alpha}_1, \ldots, \boldsymbol{\alpha}_\ell$, we could use Gaussian elimination on $\phi_{\boldsymbol{\alpha}_1}, \ldots, \phi_{\boldsymbol{\alpha}_\ell}$ to check for linear dependencies, which would be equivalent to constraint detection for $\mathrm{RM}[\mathbb{F}, m, d, H]$.

However, we cannot afford to explicitly write down $\phi_{\boldsymbol{\alpha}}$, because it has d^m entries. Nevertheless, we can still implicitly check for linear dependencies, and we do so by reducing the problem, by building on and extending ideas of [BW04], to computing the nullspace of a certain set of polynomials, which can be solved via an algorithm of [RS05] (see also [Kay10]). The idea is to encode the entries of these vectors via a succinct description: a polynomial $\Phi_{\boldsymbol{\alpha}}$ whose coefficients (after expansion) are the entries of $\phi_{\boldsymbol{\alpha}}$. In our setting this polynomial has the particularly natural form:

$$\Phi_{\boldsymbol{\alpha}}(\boldsymbol{X}) := \prod_{i=1}^{m}(1 + \alpha_i X_i + \alpha_i^2 X_i^2 + \cdots + \alpha_i^{d-1} X_i^{d-1});$$

note that the coefficient of each monomial equals its corresponding entry in $\phi_{\boldsymbol{\alpha}}$. Given this representation we can use standard polynomial identity testing techniques to find linear dependencies between these polynomials, which corresponds to linear dependencies between the original vectors. Crucially, we cannot afford any mistake, even with exponentially small probability, when looking for linear dependencies for otherwise we would not achieve perfect simulation; this is why the techniques we leverage rely on derandomization. We now proceed with the full proof.

Proof (Proof of Theorem 5). We first introduce some notation. Define $[< d] := \{0, \ldots, d-1\}$. For vectors $\boldsymbol{\alpha} \in \mathbb{F}^m$ and $\boldsymbol{a} \in [< d]^m$, we define $\boldsymbol{\alpha}^{\boldsymbol{a}} := \prod_{i=1}^{m} \alpha_i^{a_i}$; similarly, for variables $\boldsymbol{X} = (X_1, \ldots, X_m)$, we define $\boldsymbol{X}^{\boldsymbol{a}} := \prod_{i=1}^{m} X_i^{a_i}$.

We identify $\Sigma\mathrm{RM}[\mathbb{F}, m, d, H]$ with $\mathbb{F}^{[<d]^m}$; a codeword w_Q then corresponds to a vector $\boldsymbol{Q}$ whose $\boldsymbol{a}$-th entry is the coefficient of the monomial $\boldsymbol{X}^{\boldsymbol{a}}$ in Q. For $\boldsymbol{\alpha} \in \mathbb{F}^{\le m}$, let

$$\phi_{\boldsymbol{\alpha}} := \left(\boldsymbol{\alpha}^{\boldsymbol{a}} \sum_{\gamma \in H^{m-|\boldsymbol{\alpha}|}} \gamma^{\boldsymbol{b}} \right)_{\boldsymbol{a} \in [<d]^{|\boldsymbol{\alpha}|}, \, \boldsymbol{b} \in [<d]^{m-|\boldsymbol{\alpha}|}}.$$

We can also view $\phi_{\boldsymbol{\alpha}}$ as a vector in $\mathbb{F}^{[<d]^m}$ by merging the indices, so that, for all $\boldsymbol{\alpha} \in \mathbb{F}^{\le m}$ and $w_Q \in \Sigma\mathrm{RM}[\mathbb{F}, m, d, H]$,

$$w_Q(\boldsymbol{\alpha}) = \sum_{\gamma \in H^{m-|\boldsymbol{\alpha}|}} Q(\boldsymbol{\alpha}, \gamma) = \sum_{\gamma \in H^{m-|\boldsymbol{\alpha}|}} \sum_{\boldsymbol{a} \in [<d]^{|\boldsymbol{\alpha}|}} \sum_{\boldsymbol{b} \in [<d]^{m-|\boldsymbol{\alpha}|}} \boldsymbol{Q}_{\boldsymbol{a},\boldsymbol{b}} \cdot \boldsymbol{\alpha}^{\boldsymbol{a}} \gamma^{\boldsymbol{b}}$$

$$= \sum_{\boldsymbol{a} \in [<d]^{|\boldsymbol{\alpha}|}} \sum_{\boldsymbol{b} \in [<d]^{m-|\boldsymbol{\alpha}|}} \boldsymbol{Q}_{\boldsymbol{a},\boldsymbol{b}} \cdot \boldsymbol{\alpha}^{\boldsymbol{a}} \sum_{\gamma \in H^{m-|\boldsymbol{\alpha}|}} \gamma^{\boldsymbol{b}} = \langle \boldsymbol{Q}, \phi_{\boldsymbol{\alpha}} \rangle.$$

Hence for every $\boldsymbol{\alpha}_1, \ldots, \boldsymbol{\alpha}_\ell, \boldsymbol{\alpha} \in \mathbb{F}^{\le m}$ and $a_1, \ldots, a_\ell \in \mathbb{F}$, the following statements are equivalent (i)$w(\boldsymbol{\alpha}) = \sum_{i=1}^{\ell} a_i w(\boldsymbol{\alpha}_i)$ for all $w \in \Sigma\mathrm{RM}[\mathbb{F}, m, d, H]$; (ii)$\langle \boldsymbol{f}, \phi_{\boldsymbol{\alpha}} \rangle = \sum_{i=1}^{\ell} a_i \langle \boldsymbol{f}, \phi_{\boldsymbol{\alpha}_i} \rangle$ for all $\boldsymbol{f} \in \mathbb{F}^{[<d]^m}$ (iii)$\phi_{\boldsymbol{\alpha}} = \sum_{i=1}^{\ell} a_i \phi_{\boldsymbol{\alpha}_i}$. We deduce that constraint detection for $\Sigma\mathrm{RM}[\mathbb{F}, m, d, H]$ is equivalent to the problem of finding $a_1, \ldots, a_\ell \in \mathbb{F}$ such that $\phi_{\boldsymbol{\alpha}} = \sum_{i=1}^{\ell} a_i \phi_{\boldsymbol{\alpha}_i}$, or returning 'independent' if no such $a_1, \ldots, a_\ell$ exist.

However, the dimension of the latter vectors is d^m, which may be much larger than $\mathrm{poly}(\log |\mathbb{F}| + m + d + |H| + \ell)$, and so we cannot afford to "explicitly" solve the $\ell \times d^m$ linear system. Instead, we "succinctly" solve it, by taking advantage of the special structure of the vectors, as we now describe. For $\boldsymbol{\alpha} \in \mathbb{F}^m$, define the polynomial

$$\varPhi_{\boldsymbol{\alpha}}(\boldsymbol{X}) := \prod_{i=1}^{m} (1 + \alpha_i X_i + \alpha_i^2 X_i^2 + \cdots + \alpha_i^{d-1} X_i^{d-1}).$$

Note that, while the above polynomial is computable via a small arithmetic circuit, its coefficients (once expanded over the monomial basis) correspond to the entries of the vector $\phi_{\boldsymbol{\alpha}}$. More generally, for $\boldsymbol{\alpha} \in \mathbb{F}^{\le m}$, we define the polynomial

$$\varPhi_{\boldsymbol{\alpha}}(\boldsymbol{X}) := \left(\prod_{i=1}^{|\boldsymbol{\alpha}|} (1 + \alpha_i X_i + \cdots + \alpha_i^{d-1} X_i^{d-1}) \right)$$
$$\left(\prod_{i=1}^{m-|\boldsymbol{\alpha}|} \sum_{\gamma \in H} (1 + \gamma X_{i+|\boldsymbol{\alpha}|} + \cdots + \gamma^{d-1} X_{i+|\boldsymbol{\alpha}|}^{d-1}) \right).$$

Note that Φ_α is a product of univariate polynomials. To see that the above does indeed represent ϕ_α, we rearrange the expression as follows:

$$\Phi_\alpha(\boldsymbol{X}) = \left(\prod_{i=1}^{|\alpha|} (1 + \alpha_i X_i + \cdots + \alpha_i^{d-1} X_i^{d-1}) \right)$$
$$\left(\sum_{\gamma \in H^{m-|\alpha|}} \prod_{i=1}^{m-|\alpha|} (1 + \gamma_i X_{i+|\alpha|} + \cdots + \gamma_i^{d-1} X_{i+|\alpha|}^{d-1}) \right)$$
$$= \Phi_\alpha(X_1, \ldots, X_{|\alpha|}) \left(\sum_{\gamma \in H^{m-|\alpha|}} \Phi_\gamma(X_{|\alpha|+1}, \ldots, X_m) \right);$$

indeed, the coefficient of $\boldsymbol{X}^{a,b}$ for $\boldsymbol{a} \in [< d]^{|\alpha|}$ and $\boldsymbol{b} \in [< d]^{m-|\alpha|}$ is $\alpha^a \sum_{\gamma \in H^{m-|\alpha|}} \gamma^b$, as required.

Thus, to determine whether $\phi_\alpha \in \mathrm{span}(\phi_{\alpha_1}, \ldots, \phi_{\alpha_\ell})$, it suffices to determine whether $\Phi_\alpha \in \mathrm{span}(\Phi_{\alpha_1}, \ldots, \Phi_{\alpha_\ell})$. In fact, the linear dependencies are in correspondence: for $a_1, \ldots, a_\ell \in \mathbb{F}$, $\phi_\alpha = \sum_{i=1}^\ell a_i \phi_{\alpha_i}$ if and only if $\Phi_\alpha = \sum_{i=1}^\ell a_i \Phi_{\alpha_i}$. Crucially, each Φ_{α_i} is not only in $\mathbb{F}^{<d}[X_1, \ldots, X_m]$ but is a product of m univariate polynomials each represented via an $\mathbb{F}$-arithmetic circuit of size $\mathrm{poly}(|H|+d)$. We leverage this special structure and solve the above problem by relying on an algorithm of [RS05] that computes the nullspace for such polynomials (see also [Kay10]), as captured by the lemma below;[7] for completeness, we provide an elementary proof of the lema in the full version.

Lemma 3. *There exists a deterministic algorithm $\mathcal{D}$ such that, on input a vector of m-variate polynomials $\boldsymbol{Q} = (Q_1, \ldots, Q_\ell)$ over $\mathbb{F}$ where each polynomial has the form $Q_k(\boldsymbol{X}) = \prod_{i=1}^m Q_{k,i}(X_i)$ and each $Q_{k,i}$ is univariate of degree less than d with $d \leq |\mathbb{F}|$ and represented via an $\mathbb{F}$-arithmetic circuit of size s, outputs a basis for the linear space $\boldsymbol{Q}^\perp := \{(a_1, \ldots, a_\ell) \in \mathbb{F}^\ell : \sum_{k=1}^\ell a_k Q_k \equiv 0\}$. Moreover, $\mathcal{D}$ runs in $\mathrm{poly}(\log |\mathbb{F}| + m + d + s + \ell)$ time.*

The above lemma immediately provides a way to construct a constraint detector for $\Sigma\mathrm{RM}$: given as input an index $\mathfrak{n} = (\mathbb{F}, m, d, H)$ and a subset $I \subseteq D(\mathfrak{n})$, we construct the arithmetic circuit Φ_α for each $\alpha \in I$, and then run the algorithm $\mathcal{D}$ on vector of circuits $(\Phi_\alpha)_{\alpha \in I}$, and directly output $\mathcal{D}$'s result. The lemma follows.

4.3   Univariate Polynomials with BS Proximity Proofs

We show that evaluations of univariate polynomials concatenated with corresponding BS proximity proofs [BS08] have succinct constraint detection (see

---

[7] One could use polynomial identity testing to solve the above problem in probabilistic polynomial time; see [Kay10, Lemma 8]. However, due to a nonzero probability of error, this suffices only to achieve statistical zero knowledge, but *does not suffice to achieve perfect zero knowledge.*

Definition 8). Recall that the Reed–Solomon code (see Sect. 3.4) is not locally testable, but one can test proximity to it with the aid of the quasilinear-size proximity proofs of Ben-Sasson and Sudan [BS08]. These latter apply when low-degree univariate polynomials are evaluated over *linear spaces*, so from now on we restrict our attention to Reed–Solomon codes of this form. More precisely, we consider Reed–Solomon codes $RS[\mathbb{F}, L, d]$ where $\mathbb{F}$ is an extension field of a base field $\mathbb{K}$, L is a $\mathbb{K}$-linear subspace in $\mathbb{F}$, and $d = |L| \cdot |\mathbb{K}|^{-\mu}$ for some $\mu \in \mathbb{N}^+$. We then denote by $BS\text{-}RS[\mathbb{K}, \mathbb{F}, L, \mu, k]$ the code obtained by concatenating codewords in $RS[\mathbb{F}, L, |L| \cdot |\mathbb{K}|^{-\mu}]$ with corresponding BS proximity proofs whose recursion terminates at "base dimension" $k \in \{1, \ldots, \dim(L)\}$ (for a formal definition of these, see the full version); typically $\mathbb{K}, \mu, k$ are fixed to certain constants (e.g., [BS08] fixes them to $\mathbb{F}_2, 3, 1$, respectively) but below we state the cost of constraint detection in full generality. The linear code family BS-RS is indexed by tuples $\mathfrak{n} = (\mathbb{K}, \mathbb{F}, L, \mu, k)$ and the $\mathfrak{n}$-th code is $BS\text{-}RS[\mathbb{K}, \mathbb{F}, L, \mu, k]$, and our result about BS-RS is the following:

Theorem 6 (formal statement of 4). BS-RS *has* $\text{poly}(\log |\mathbb{F}| + \dim(L) + |\mathbb{K}|^{\mu} + \ell)$-*time constraint detection.*

The proof of the above theorem is technically involved, and we refer the reader to the full version for details.

The role of code covers. We are interested in succinct constraint detection: solving the constraint detection problem for certain code families with exponentially-large domains (such as BS-RS). We now build some intuition about how code covers can, in some cases, facilitate this.

Consider the simple case where the code $C \subseteq \mathbb{F}^D$ is a direct sum of many small codes: there exists $S = \{(\tilde{D}_j, \tilde{C}_j)\}_j$ such that $D = \cup_j \tilde{D}_j$ and $C = \oplus_j \tilde{C}_j$ where, for each j, $\tilde{C}_j$ is a linear code in $\mathbb{F}^{\tilde{D}_j}$ and the subdomain $\tilde{D}_j$ is small and disjoint from other subdomains. The detection problem for this case can be solved efficiently: use the generic approach of Gaussian elimination independently on each subdomain $\tilde{D}_j$.

Next consider a more general case where the subdomains are not necessarily disjoint: there exists $S = \{(\tilde{D}_j, \tilde{C}_j)\}_j$ as above but we do not require that the $\tilde{D}_j$ form a partition of D; we say that each $(\tilde{D}_j, \tilde{C}_j)$ is a *local view* of C because $\tilde{D}_j \subseteq D$ and $\tilde{C}_j = C|_{\tilde{D}_j}$, and we say that S is a *code cover* of C. Now suppose that for each j there exists an efficient constraint detector for $\tilde{C}_j$ (which is defined on $\tilde{D}_j$); in this case, the detection problem can be solved efficiently at least for those subsets I that are contained in $\tilde{D}_j$ for some j. Generalizing further, we see that we can efficiently solve constraint detection for a code C if there is a cover $S = \{(\tilde{D}_j, \tilde{C}_j)\}_j$ such that, given a subset $I \subseteq D$, (i) I is contained in some subdomain $\tilde{D}_j$, and (ii) constraint detection for $\tilde{C}_j$ can be solved efficiently.

We build on the above ideas to derive analogous statements for recursive code covers, which arise naturally in the case of BS-RS. But note that recursive constructions are common in the PCP literature, and we believe that our cover-based techniques are of independent interest as, e.g., they are applicable to *other* PCPs, including [BFLS91, AS98].

Acknowledgments. Work of E. Ben-Sasson, A. Gabizon, and M. Riabzev was supported by the Israel Science Foundation (grant 1501/14). Work of A. Chiesa and N. Spooner was partially supported in part by the UC Berkeley Center for Long-Term Cybersecurity. Work of M. A. Forbes was supported by the NSF, including NSF CCF-1617580, and the DARPA Safeware program; it was also partially completed when the author was at Princeton University, supported by the Princeton Center for Theoretical Computer Science.

References

[ALM+98] Arora, S., Lund, C., Motwani, R., Sudan, M., Szegedy, M.: Proof verification, the hardness of approximation problems. J. ACM **45**(3), 501–555 (1998). Preliminary version in FOCS 1992

[AR16] Applebaum, B., Raykov, P.: On the relationship between statistical zero-knowledge and statistical randomized encodings. In: Robshaw, M., Katz, J. (eds.) CRYPTO 2016. LNCS, vol. 9816, pp. 449–477. Springer, Heidelberg (2016). doi:10.1007/978-3-662-53015-3_16

[AS98] Arora, S., Safra, S.: Probabilistic checking of proofs: a new characterization of NP. J. ACM **45**(1), 70–122 (1998). Preliminary version in FOCS 1992

[Bab85] Babai, L.: Trading group theory for randomness. In: Proceedings of the 17th Annual ACM Symposium on Theory of Computing, STOC 1985, pp. 421–429 (1985)

[BCG+17] Ben-Sasson, E., Chiesa, A., Gabizon, A., Riabzev, M., Spooner, N.: Interactive oracle proofs with constant rate and query complexity. In: Proceedings of the 44th International Colloquium on Automata, Languages and Programming, ICALP 2017, pp. 40:1–40:15 (2017)

[BCGV16] Ben-Sasson, E., Chiesa, A., Gabizon, A., Virza, M.: Quasi-linear size zero knowledge from linear-algebraic PCPs. In: Kushilevitz, E., Malkin, T. (eds.) TCC 2016. LNCS, vol. 9563, pp. 33–64. Springer, Heidelberg (2016). doi:10.1007/978-3-662-49099-0_2

[BCS16] Ben-Sasson, E., Chiesa, A., Spooner, N.: Interactive oracle proofs. In: Hirt, M., Smith, A. (eds.) TCC 2016. LNCS, vol. 9986, pp. 31–60. Springer, Heidelberg (2016). doi:10.1007/978-3-662-53644-5_2

[BFL91] Babai, L., Fortnow, L., Lund, C.: Non-deterministic exponential time has two-prover interactive protocols. Comput. Complexity **1**, 3–40 (1991). Preliminary version appeared in FOCS 1990

[BFLS91] Babai, L., Fortnow, L., Levin, L.A., Szegedy, M.: Checking computations in polylogarithmic time. In: Proceedings of the 23rd Annual ACM Symposium on Theory of Computing, STOC 1991, pp. 21–32 (1991)

[BGG+88] Ben-Or, M., Goldreich, O., Goldwasser, S., Håstad, J., Kilian, J., Micali, S., Rogaway, P.: Everything provable is provable in zero-knowledge. In: Goldwasser, S. (ed.) CRYPTO 1988. LNCS, vol. 403, pp. 37–56. Springer, New York (1990). doi:10.1007/0-387-34799-2_4

[BGH+06] Ben-Sasson, E., Goldreich, O., Harsha, P., Sudan, M., Vadhan, S.P.: Robust PCPs of proximity, shorter PCPs, and applications to coding. SIAM J. Comput. **36**(4), 889–974 (2006)

[BGK+10] Ben-Sasson, E., Guruswami, V., Kaufman, T., Sudan, M., Viderman, M.: Locally testable codes require redundant testers. SIAM J. Comput. **39**(7), 3230–3247 (2010)

[BGKW88] Ben-Or, M., Goldwasser, S., Kilian, J., Wigderson, A.: Multi-prover inter-active proofs: how to remove intractability assumptions. In: Proceedings of the 20th Annual ACM Symposium on Theory of Computing, STOC 1988, pp. 113–131 (1988)

[BGW88] Ben-Or, M., Goldwasser, S., Wigderson, A.: Completeness theorems for non-cryptographic fault-tolerant distributed computation. In: Proceedings of the 20th Annual ACM Symposium on Theory of Computing, STOC 1988, pp. 1–10 (1988)

[BHR05] Ben-Sasson, E., Harsha, P., Raskhodnikova, S.: Some 3CNF properties are hard to test. SIAM J. Comput. **35**(1), 1–21 (2005)

[BHZ87] Boppana, R.B., Håstad, J., Zachos, S.: Does co-NP have short interactive proofs? Inf. Process. Lett. **25**(2), 127–132 (1987)

[BM88] Babai, L., Moran, S.: Arthur-merlin games: a randomized proof system, and a hierarchy of complexity classes. J. Comput. Syst. Sci. **36**(2), 254–276 (1988)

[BS08] Ben-Sasson, E., Sudan, M.: Short PCPs with polylog query complexity. SIAM J. Comput. **38**(2), 551–607 (2008). Preliminary version appeared in STOC 2005

[BW04] Bogdanov, A., Wee, H.: A stateful implementation of a random function supporting parity queries over hypercubes. In: Jansen, K., Khanna, S., Rolim, J.D.P., Ron, D. (eds.) APPROX/RANDOM -2004. LNCS, vol. 3122, pp. 298–309. Springer, Heidelberg (2004). doi:10.1007/978-3-540-27821-4_27

[CFS17] Chiesa, A., Forbes, M.A., Spooner, N.: A zero knowledge sumcheck and its applications. Cryptology ePrint Archive, Report 2017/305 (2017)

[DFK+92] Dwork, C., Feige, U., Kilian, J., Naor, M., Safra, M.: Low communication 2-prover zero-knowledge proofs for NP. In: Brickell, E.F. (ed.) CRYPTO 1992. LNCS, vol. 740, pp. 215–227. Springer, Heidelberg (1993). doi:10.1007/3-540-48071-4_15

[DR04] Dinur, I., Reingold, O.: Assignment testers: towards a combinatorial proof of the PCP theorem. In: Proceedings of the 45th Annual IEEE Symposium on Foundations of Computer Science, FOCS 2004, pp. 155–164 (2004)

[DS98] Dwork, C., Sahai, A.: Concurrent zero-knowledge: reducing the need for timing constraints. In: Krawczyk, H. (ed.) CRYPTO 1998. LNCS, vol. 1462, pp. 442–457. Springer, Heidelberg (1998). doi:10.1007/BFb0055746

[FGL+96] Feige, U., Goldwasser, S., Lovász, L., Safra, S., Szegedy, M.: Interactive proofs, the hardness of approximating cliques. J. ACM **43**(2), 268–292 (1996). Preliminary version in FOCS 1991

[FRS88] Fortnow, L., Rompel, J., Sipser, M.: On the power of multi-prover inter-active protocols. In: Theoretical Computer Science, pp. 156–161 (1988)

[FS89] Feige, U., Shamir, A.: Zero knowledge proofs of knowledge in two rounds. In: Brassard, G. (ed.) CRYPTO 1989. LNCS, vol. 435, pp. 526–544. Springer, New York (1990). doi:10.1007/0-387-34805-0_46

[GGN10] Goldreich, O., Goldwasser, S., Nussboim, A.: On the implementation of huge random objects. SIAM J. Comput. **39**(7), 2761–2822 (2010). Preliminary version appeared in FOCS 2003

[GIMS10] Goyal, V., Ishai, Y., Mahmoody, M., Sahai, A.: Interactive locking, zero-knowledge PCPs, and unconditional cryptography. In: Rabin, T. (ed.) CRYPTO 2010. LNCS, vol. 6223, pp. 173–190. Springer, Heidelberg (2010). doi:10.1007/978-3-642-14623-7_10

[GKR08] Goldwasser, S., Kalai, Y.T., Rothblum, G.N.: Delegating computation: interactive proofs for Muggles. In: Proceedings of the 40th Annual ACM Symposium on Theory of Computing, STOC 2008, pp. 113–122 (2008)

[GMR89] Goldwasser, S., Micali, S., Rackoff, C.: The knowledge complexity of interactive proof systems. SIAM J. Comput. 18(1), 186–208 (1989). Preliminary version appeared in STOC 1985

[GMW91] Goldreich, O., Micali, S., Wigderson, A.: Proofs that yield nothing but their validity or all languages in NP have zero-knowledge proof systems. J. ACM 38(3), 691–729 (1991). Preliminary version appeared in FOCS 1986

[GV99] Goldreich, O., Vadhan, S.P.: Comparing entropies in statistical zero knowledge with applications to the structure of SZK. In: Proceedings of the 14th Annual IEEE Conference on Computational Complexity, CCC 1999, p. 54 (1999)

[IMS12] Ishai, Y., Mahmoody, M., Sahai, A.: On efficient zero-knowledge PCPs. In: Cramer, R. (ed.) TCC 2012. LNCS, vol. 7194, pp. 151–168. Springer, Heidelberg (2012). doi:10.1007/978-3-642-28914-9_9

[IMSX15] Ishai, Y., Mahmoody, M., Sahai, A., Xiao, D.: On zero-knowledge PCPs: limitations, simplifications, and applications (2015). http://www.cs.virginia.edu/~mohammad/files/papers/ZKPCPs-Full.pdf

[IOS97] Itoh, T., Ohta, Y., Shizuya, H.: A language-dependent cryptographic primitive. J. Cryptol. 10(1), 37–50 (1997)

[IW14] Ishai, Y., Weiss, M.: Probabilistically checkable proofs of proximity with zero-knowledge. In: Lindell, Y. (ed.) TCC 2014. LNCS, vol. 8349, pp. 121–145. Springer, Heidelberg (2014). doi:10.1007/978-3-642-54242-8_6

[IWY16] Ishai, Y., Weiss, M., Yang, G.: Making the best of a leaky situation: zero-knowledge PCPs from leakage-resilient circuits. In: Kushilevitz, E., Malkin, T. (eds.) TCC 2016. LNCS, vol. 9563, pp. 3–32. Springer, Heidelberg (2016). doi:10.1007/978-3-662-49099-0_1

[IY87] Impagliazzo, R., Yung, M.: Direct minimum-knowledge computations (extended abstract). In: Pomerance, C. (ed.) CRYPTO 1987. LNCS, vol. 293, pp. 40–51. Springer, Heidelberg (1988). doi:10.1007/3-540-48184-2_4

[Kay10] Kayal, N.: Algorithms for arithmetic circuits (2010). ECCC TR10-073

[KI04] Kabanets, V., Impagliazzo, R.: Derandomizing polynomial identity tests means proving circuit lower bounds. Comput. Complexity 13(1–2), 1–46 (2004)

[KPT97] Kilian, J., Petrank, E., Tardos, G.: Probabilistically checkable proofs with zero knowledge. In: Proceedings of the 29th Annual ACM Symposium on Theory of Computing, STOC 1997, pp. 496–505 (1997)

[KR08] Kalai, Y.T., Raz, R.: Interactive PCP. In: Aceto, L., Damgård, I., Goldberg, L.A., Halldórsson, M.M., Ingólfsdóttir, A., Walukiewicz, I. (eds.) ICALP 2008. LNCS, vol. 5126, pp. 536–547. Springer, Heidelberg (2008). doi:10.1007/978-3-540-70583-3_44

[LFKN92] Lund, C., Fortnow, L., Karloff, H.J., Nisan, N.: Algebraic methods for interactive proof systems. J. ACM 39(4), 859–868 (1992)

[LS95] Lapidot, D., Shamir, A.: A one-round, two-prover, zero-knowledge protocol for NP. Combinatorica 15(2), 204–214 (1995)

[Oka00] Okamoto, T.: On relationships between statistical zero-knowledge proofs. J. Comput. Syst. Sci. 60(1), 47–108 (2000)

[Ost91] Ostrovsky, R.: One-way functions, hard on average problems, and statistical zero-knowledge proofs. In: Proceedings of the 6th Annual Structure in Complexity Theory Conference, CoCo 1991, pp. 133–138 (1991)

[OV08]   Ong, S.J., Vadhan, S.: An equivalence between zero knowledge and commitments. In: Canetti, R. (ed.) TCC 2008. LNCS, vol. 4948, pp. 482–500. Springer, Heidelberg (2008). doi:10.1007/978-3-540-78524-8_27

[OW93]   Ostrovsky, R., Wigderson, A.: One-way functions are essential for nontrivial zero-knowledge. In: Proceedings of the 2nd Israel Symposium on Theory of Computing Systems, ISTCS 1993, pp. 3–17 (1993)

[RRR16] Reingold, O., Rothblum, R., Rothblum, G.: Constant-round interactive proofs for delegating computation. In: Proceedings of the 48th ACM Symposium on the Theory of Computing, STOC 2016, pp. 49–62 (2016)

[RS05]   Raz, R., Shpilka, A.: Deterministic polynomial identity testing in noncommutative models. Comput. Complexity **14**(1), 1–19 (2005). Preliminary version appeared in CCC 2004

[Sch80] Schwartz, J.T.: Fast probabilistic algorithms for verification of polynomial identities. J. ACM **27**(4), 701–717 (1980)

[Sha92] Shamir, A.: IP = PSPACE. J. ACM **39**(4), 869–877 (1992)

[SV03]   Sahai, A., Vadhan, S.P.: A complete problem for statistical zero knowledge. J. ACM **50**(2), 196–249 (2003)

[SY10]   Shpilka, A., Yehudayoff, A.: Arithmetic circuits: a survey of recent results and open questions. Found. Trends Theoret. Comput. Sci. **5**(3–4), 207–388 (2010)

[Vad99] Vadhan, S.P.: A Study of statistical zero-knowledge proofs. Ph.D. thesis, MIT, August 1999

[VV15]   Vaikuntanathan, V., Vasudevan, P.N.: Secret sharing and statistical zero knowledge. In: Iwata, T., Cheon, J.H. (eds.) ASIACRYPT 2015. LNCS, vol. 9452, pp. 656–680. Springer, Heidelberg (2015). doi:10.1007/978-3-662-48797-6_27

[Zip79] Zippel, R.: Probabilistic algorithms for sparse polynomials. In: Ng, E.W. (ed.) Symbolic and Algebraic Computation. LNCS, vol. 72, pp. 216–226. Springer, Heidelberg (1979). doi:10.1007/3-540-09519-5_73

Leakage and Tampering

How to Construct a Leakage-Resilient (Stateless) Trusted Party

Daniel Genkin[1,2], Yuval Ishai[3,4], and Mor Weiss[5(✉)]

[1] University of Pennsylvania, Philadelphia, USA
danielg3@cis.upenn.edu
[2] University of Maryland, College Park, USA
[3] Technion, Haifa, Israel
yuvali@cs.technion.ac.il
[4] UCLA, Los Angeles, USA
[5] Northeastern University, Boston, USA
m.weiss@northeastern.onmicrosoft.com

Abstract. Trusted parties and devices are commonly used in the real world to securely perform computations on secret inputs. However, their security can often be compromised by side-channel attacks in which the adversary obtains partial leakage on intermediate computation values. This gives rise to the following natural question: *To what extent can one protect the trusted party against leakage?*

Our goal is to design a hardware device T that allows $m \geq 1$ parties to securely evaluate a function $f(x_1, \ldots, x_m)$ of their inputs by feeding T with encoded inputs that are obtained using local secret randomness. Security should hold even in the presence of an active adversary that can corrupt a subset of parties and obtain restricted leakage on the internal computations in T.

We design hardware devices T in this setting both for zero-knowledge proofs and for general multi-party computations. Our constructions can unconditionally resist either AC^0 leakage or a strong form of "only computation leaks" (OCL) leakage that captures realistic side-channel attacks, providing different tradeoffs between efficiency and security.

Keywords: Leakage-resilience · Secure multiparty computation · Algebraic manipulation detection · AMD Circuits.

1 Introduction

There is a long and successful line of work on protecting general computations against partial information leakage. Originating from the works on general secure multiparty computation (MPC) [4,11,22,37], the question has been "scaled down" to the domain of protecting circuits against local probing attacks [26] and then extended to different types of global information leakage [7–10,13,15,16,23–25,28,31,32,34].

© International Association for Cryptologic Research 2017
Y. Kalai and L. Reyzin (Eds.): TCC 2017, Part II, LNCS 10678, pp. 209–244, 2017.
https://doi.org/10.1007/978-3-319-70503-3_7

Most of the works along this line consider the challenging goal of protecting computations against *continual leakage*. In a general instance of this problem, a desired ideal functionality is specified by a *stateful* circuit C, which maps the current input and state to the current output and the next state. The input and output are considered to be public whereas the state is secret. The goal is to securely realize the functionality C by a leakage-resilient randomized circuit $\hat{C}$. The circuit $\hat{C}$ is initialized with some randomized encoding $\hat{s}$ of an initial secret state s. The computation can then proceed in a virtually unlimited number of rounds, where in each round $\hat{C}$ receives an input, produces an output, and replaces the old encoding of the secret state by a fresh encoding of a new state.

The correctness goal is to ensure that $\hat{C}[\hat{s}]$ has the same input-output functionality as $C[s]$. The security goal is defined with respect to a class $\mathcal{L}$ of *leakage functions* ℓ, where each function ℓ returns some partial information on the values of the internal wires of $\hat{C}$. The adversary may adaptively choose a different function $\ell \in \mathcal{L}$ in each round. The security goal is to ensure that whatever the adversary learns by interacting with $\hat{C}[\hat{s}]$ and by additionally observing the leakage, it can simulate by interacting with $C[s]$ without obtaining any leakage.

While general solutions to the above problem are known for broad classes of leakage functions $\mathcal{L}$, they leave much to be desired. Some rely on leak-free hardware components [15,16,23,28,32]. Others make a heavy use of public-key cryptography [7,10,23,25,28] or even indistinguishability obfuscation [25]. Other issues include the need for internal fresh randomness in each round, big computational overhead that grows super-linearly with the amount of tolerable leakage, complex and subtle analysis, and poor concrete parameters. All of the above works suffer from at least some of these limitations.

In this work we take a step back, and study a simpler *stateless* variant of the problem, where both C and $\hat{C}$ are stateless circuits. The goal is to replace an ideal computation of $C(x)$ by a functionally equivalent but leakage-resilient computation $\hat{C}(\hat{x})$. Here x is a secret input which is randomly encoded into an encoded input $\hat{x}$ to protect it against leakage. Solutions for the above continuous leakage model can be easily specialized to the stateless model by considering a single round where the input is used as the initial secret state. This stateless variant of the problem has been considered before [25,26,32], but mainly as an intermediate step and not as an end goal.

Our work is motivated by the observation that this simpler setting, which is relevant to many real-world scenarios, does not only offer an opportunity to get around the limitations of previous solutions, but also poses new challenges that were not addressed before. For instance, can correctness be guaranteed even when the input encoding $\hat{x}$ is invalid, in the sense that the output corresponds to *some* valid input x? Can the solutions be extended to the case where the encoded inputs for $\hat{C}$ are contributed by several, mutually distrusting, parties? To further motivate these questions, we put them in the context of natural applications.

Protecting a trusted party. We consider the goal of protecting (stateless) trusted parties against leakage. Trusted Parties (TPs) are commonly used to perform computations that involve secret inputs. They are already widely deployed in payment terminals and access control readers, and will be even more so in future Trusted Platform Modules. TPs have several advantages over distributed protocols for secure multiparty computation (MPC) [4,11,22,37]. First, they avoid the expensive interaction typically required by MPC protocols. Second, they are very light-weight and allow the computational complexity of the other (untrusted) parties to be independent of the complexity of the computation being performed. Finally, TPs may offer *unconditional* security against *computationally unbounded* adversaries.

An important special case which is a major focus of this work is that of a hardware implementation of zero-knowledge (ZK) proofs, a fundamental primitive for identification and a useful building block for cryptographic protocol design. Informally, a ZK hardware takes a statement and witness from a prover, and outputs the verified statement, or rej, to a verifier. While there are efficient ZK protocols without hardware (including non-interactive zero-knowledge protocols (NIZKs) [21,35], or succinct non-interactive arguments of knowledge (SNARKs) [5]), such protocols do not (and cannot) have the last two features of TP-based solutions.

A primary concern when using trusted hardware are so-called "side-channel" attacks which allow the adversary to obtain leakage on the internal computations of the device (e.g., through measuring its running time [30], power consumption [29], or the electromagnetic radiation it emits [33]). Such attacks were shown to have devastating effects on security. As discussed above, a large body of works attempted to incorporate the information obtained through such leakage into the security model, and develop schemes that are provably secure in these models. More specifically, these works have focused on designing leakage-resilient circuit compilers (LRCCs) that, informally, compile any circuit C into its leakage-resilient version $\hat{C}$, where $\hat{C}$ withstands side-channel attacks in the sense that these reveal nothing about the (properly encoded) input $\hat{x}$. However, all of the schemes obtained in these works suffer from some of the limitations discussed above. In particular, none considers the questions of invalid encodings provided by malicious parties or combining encoded inputs that originate from mutually distrusting parties. These questions arise naturally in the context of ZK and in other contexts where TPs are used.

1.1 Our Contribution

Our main goal is to study the feasibility and efficiency of protecting TPs against general classes of leakage, without leak-free hardware or trusted setup. Eliminating the leak-free hardware unconditionally [24], or under computational assumptions [13,34] has been a major research goal. However, in contrast to earlier works, we consider here the easier case of realizing a *stateless* TP in the presence of *one-time* leakage.

We model the TP as a leaky (but otherwise trusted) hardware device T that is used by $m \geq 1$ parties to execute a multiparty computation task. More specifically, in this setting each party locally encodes its input and feeds the encoded input into the device, that evaluates a boolean (or arithmetic) circuit on the encoded inputs, and returns the output. This computation should preserve the secrecy of the inputs, as well as the correctness of the output, in the presence of a computationally-unbounded adversary that corrupts a subset of the parties, and additionally obtains leakage on the internals of the device. (Notice that the secrecy requirement necessitates some encoding of the inputs, otherwise we cannot protect even against a probing attack on a single bit.)

We note that the stateless hardware should be reusable on an arbitrary number of different inputs. Thus, we cannot take previous leakage-secure computation protocols that employ correlated randomness (such as the ones from [15,16]) and embed this randomness into the hardware. Indeed, we consider the internals of the hardware as being public, since any secret internal embedded values can be leaked over multiple invocations.

The model has several different variants, depending on whether the adversary is passive (i.e., only sees the inputs of corrupted parties and obtains leakage on the internals of the TP) or active (namely, it may also cause corrupted parties to provide the TP with ill-formed "encoded" inputs that may not correspond to any inputs for the original computation); whether there is a single party providing input to the TP (as in the ZK example described below) or multiple parties; whether the TP is deterministic or randomized (namely, has randomness gates that generate uniformly-random bits); and finally, whether the output of the TP is encoded or not (in the latter, one cannot protect the privacy of the output even when the adversary only obtains leakage on the internals of the TP *without* corrupting any parties, whereas in the former the outputs will remain private in this case). We focus on the variant with an active adversary, and a randomized TP with encoded outputs. We consider both the single-party and multi-party setting. In the ZK setting, we also construct deterministic TPs (at the expense of somewhat increasing the complexity of the prover and verifier).

The leakage model. We consider an extended version of the "only computation leaks" (OCL) model of Micali and Reyzin [31], also known as "OCL+" [6]. Informally, in this context, the wires of the circuit $\hat{C}$ are partitioned into a "left component" $\hat{C}_L$ and a "right component" $\hat{C}_R$. Leakage functions correspond to bounded-communication 2-party protocols between $\hat{C}_L, \hat{C}_R$, where the output of the leakage function is the transcript of the protocol when the views of $\hat{C}_L, \hat{C}_R$ consist of the internal values of the wires of these two "components". Following the terminology of Goyal et al. [25], we refer to this model as *bounded communication leakage (BCL)*. The model is formalized in the next definition.

Definition 1 (*t*-BCL [25]). *Let $t \in \mathbb{N}$ be a leakage bound parameter. We say that a deterministic 2-party protocol is t-bounded if its communication complexity is at most t. Given a t-bounded protocol Π, we define the t-bounded-communication leakage (t-BCL) function f_Π associated with Π, that given the views of the two parties, outputs the transcript of Π. The class $\mathcal{L}_{\mathrm{BCL}}^t$ consists of all t-BCL functions f_Π associated with t-bounded protocols Π, namely:*
$$\mathcal{L}_{\mathrm{BCL}}^t = \{f_\Pi \ : \ \Pi \ is \ t - bounded\}.$$

We say that a size-s circuit $\hat{C}$ is t-BCL resilient if there exists a partition $\mathcal{P} = \{s_1, s_2\}$ of the wires of $\hat{C}$, such that the circuit resists any t-BCL function f_Π for a protocol Π that respects the partition $\mathcal{P}$.

We note that BCL is broad enough to capture several realistic leakage attacks such as the sum of all circuit wires over the integers, as well as linear functions over the wires of the circuit. This captures several realistic attacks on hardware devices, where a single electromagnetic probe measures involuntary leakage which can be approximated by a linear function of the wires of the circuit.

1.2 Our Results

We construct TPs for both ZK proofs, and general MPC, which simultaneously achieve many of the desired features described above: they resist a wide class of leakage functions (BCL), without using any leak-free components, and are quite appealing from the perspective of asymptotic efficiency, since the complexity of the parties is *independent* of the size of the computation. Our constructions combine ideas and results from previous works on leakage-resilient circuits, with several new ideas, as discussed in Sect. 1.3.

TPs for ZK. In the context of ZK, the hardware device enables the verification of NP-statements of the form "$(x, w) \in \mathcal{R}$" for an NP-relation $\mathcal{R}$. That is, the prover provides (x, w) as input to the device, which computes the function $f(x, w) = (x, \mathcal{R}(x, w))$. Since the device is leaky, the prover is unwilling to provide its secret witness w to the device "in the clear". Instead, the prover prepares in advance a "leak-free" encoding $\hat{w}$ of w, which it stores on a small isolated device (such as a smartcard or USB drive). It then provides $(x, \hat{w})$ as input to the leaky device (e.g., by plugging in his smartcard) which outputs the public verification outcome. We say that the hardware device is an $\mathcal{L}$-secure ZK circuit if it resists leakage from $\mathcal{L}$ with negligible error. We construct $\mathcal{L}_{\mathrm{BCL}}^t$-secure ZK circuits for NP:

Theorem 1 (Leakage-secure ZK circuit). *For any leakage bound $t \in \mathbb{N}$, statistical security parameter $\sigma \in \mathbb{N}$, and length parameter $n \in \mathbb{N}$, any NP-relation $\mathcal{R} = \mathcal{R}(x, w)$ with verification circuit of size s, depth d, and n inputs has an $\mathcal{L}_{\mathrm{BCL}}^t$-secure ZK circuit $C_{\mathcal{R}}$ that outputs the outcome of verification, where $\mathcal{L}_{\mathrm{BCL}}^t$ is the family of all t-BCL functions. Moreover, to prove that $(x, w) \in \mathcal{R}$, the prover runs in time $\mathsf{poly}(t, \sigma, n, |w|)$, and $|C_{\mathcal{R}}| = \widetilde{O}(s + d(t + \sigma + n)) + \mathsf{poly}(t, \sigma, n)$.*

We also construct a variant of the ZK circuit that allows one to "trade" efficiency of the prover and verifier with the randomness used by the ZK circuit:

Theorem 2 (Deterministic leakage-secure ZK circuit). *For any leakage bound $t \in \mathbb{N}$, statistical security parameter $\sigma \in \mathbb{N}$, and length parameter $n \in \mathbb{N}$, any NP-relation $\mathcal{R} = \mathcal{R}(x, w)$ with verification circuit of size s, depth d, and n inputs has a deterministic $\mathcal{L}_{\mathrm{BCL}}^t$-secure ZK circuit $C_{\mathcal{R}}$. Moreover, $|C_{\mathcal{R}}| = \widetilde{O}(s + d(t + \sigma + n)) + \mathsf{poly}(t, \sigma, n)$, to prove that $(x, w) \in \mathcal{R}$, the prover runs in time $\widetilde{O}(s + d(t + \sigma + n)) + \mathsf{poly}(t, \sigma, n, |w|)$, and the verifier runs in time $\mathsf{poly}(t, \sigma, n)$.*

General MPC. We consider hardware devices that allow the evaluation of general functions in both the single-party setting, and the multiparty setting with $m \geq 2$. More specifically, we construct m-*party LRCCs* that given a circuit C that takes inputs from m parties, output a circuit $\hat{C}$ that operates on encoded inputs and outputs. Informally, we say the m-party LRCC is $(\mathcal{L}, \epsilon)$-secure if the evaluation of $\hat{C}$ guarantees (except with probability ϵ) privacy of the honest parties' inputs, and correctness of the output, in the presence of an adversary that may actively corrupt a strict subset of parties, and obtain leakage from $\mathcal{L}$ on the internals of the device. We construct m-party LRCCs that are secure against t-BCL:

Theorem 3 (Leakage-secure m-party LRCC). *For any leakage bound $t \in \mathbb{N}$, statistical security parameter $\sigma \in \mathbb{N}$, input and output length parameters $n, k \in \mathbb{N}$, and size and depth parameters $s, d \in \mathbb{N}$, any m-party function $f : (\{0,1\}^n)^m \rightarrow \{0,1\}^k$ computable by a circuit of size s and depth d has an m-party $(\mathcal{L}^t_{\text{BCL}}, \epsilon)$-secure LRCC, where $\mathcal{L}^t_{\text{BCL}}$ is the family of all t-BCL functions, and $\epsilon = \mathsf{negl}(\sigma)$. Moreover, the leakage-secure circuit has size $\tilde{O}(s + d(t + \sigma \log m)) + m \cdot \mathsf{poly}(t, \sigma, \log m, k)$, its input encodings can be computed in time $\tilde{O}(n) + \mathsf{poly}(t, \sigma, \log m, k)$, and its outputs can be decoded in time $\tilde{O}(m \cdot k(t + \sigma \log m + k))$.*

1.3 Our Techniques

1.3.1 Leakage-Resilient Zero-Knowledge

Recall that the leaky ZK device allows a prover P to prove claims of the form "$(x, w) \in \mathcal{R}$" for some NP-relation $\mathcal{R}$. We model the device as a stateless boolean (or more generally, arithmetic) circuit C. Though C cannot be assumed to withstand leakage, using an LRCC it can be transformed into a leakage-resilient circuit $\hat{C}$. Informally, an LRCC is associated with a function class $\mathcal{L}$ (the *leakage class*), a (randomized) input encoding scheme E, and a (deterministic) output decoder $\mathsf{Dec}_{\mathsf{Out}}$. The LRCC compiles a circuit C into a (public) circuit $\hat{C}$ that emulates C over encoded inputs and outputs. $\hat{C}$ resists leakage from $\mathcal{L}$ in the sense that for any input z for C, and any $\ell \in \mathcal{L}$, the output of ℓ on the wire values of $\hat{C}$, when evaluated on $\mathsf{E}(z)$, can be efficiently simulated given only the description of C.

Our starting point in constructing leakage-resilient ZK hardware is the recent result of Goyal et al. [25], who use MPC protocols to protect computation against BCL leakage. More specifically, they design information-theoretically secure protocols in the OT-hybrid model that allow a user, aided by a pair of "honest-but-curious" servers, to compute a function of her input while preserving the privacy of the input and output even under BCL leakage on the internals of the servers. We observe that when these server programs are implemented as circuits (in particular, the OT calls are implemented by constant-sized sub-circuits), this construction gives an LRCC that resists BCL leakage.

In the context of designing leakage-resilient TPs, the main advantage of this construction over previous information-theoretically secure LRCCs that resist similar leakage classes [15,16,32] is that [25] *does not use any leak-free components*. More specifically, these LRCCs use the leak-free components (or leak-free preprocessing in [23]) to generate "masks", which are structured random bits that are used to mask the internal computations in $\hat{C}$, thus guaranteeing leakage-resilience.

These leak-free components could be eliminated if the parties include the masks as part of their input encoding. However, this raises three issues. First, in some constructions (e.g. [15,16,32]) the number of masks is proportional to the size of $\hat{C}$, so the running time of the parties would not be independent of the computation size (which defeats the purpose of delegating most of the computation to the TP). Second, in the multi-party setting, it is not clear how to combine the masks provided by different parties into a single set of masks to be used in $\hat{C}$, such that these masks are *unknown to each one of the parties*, which is crucial for the leakage-resilience property to hold. (We show in [36] how to do so for the LRCC of [16] which resists AC^0 leakage, but this construction has the efficiency shortcomings mentioned above.) Finally, even with a single party, these constructions totally break when the party provides "ill-formed" masks (namely, masks that do not have the required structure), since correctness is guaranteed *only when the masks have the required structure*. This is not only a theoretical concern, but rather an *actual* one. To see why, consider the ZK setting. If the prover provides the masks to the device then it *has a way* of choosing (ill-formed) masks that flip the output gate, thus causing the device to accept false NP statements. Alternative "solutions" also fail: the device cannot verify that the masks provided by the prover are well-formed, since the aforementioned constructions *crucially* rely on the fact that the leakage-resilience simulator can use ill-formed masks; and the verifier cannot provide the masks, since leakage-resilience relies on the leakage function not knowing the masks.

Though using the LRCC of [25] eliminates all these issues, it has one shortcoming: its leakage-resilience simulator is *inefficient*. In the context of ZK hardware, this gives *witness-indistinguishability*, namely the guarantee that a malicious verifier that can leak on the internals of the ZK hardware cannot distinguish between executions on the same statement x with different witnesses w, w'. This falls short of our desired security guarantee that leakage reveals *no* information about the witness. (In particular, notice that if a statement x has only one witness then witness-indistinguishability provides no security.) We note that this weaker security guarantee is inherent to the construction of [25].

To achieve efficient simulation, we leverage the fact that the construction of [25] operates over encodings that resist BCL leakage. We observe that one can obtain simulation-based security if the encodings at the output of $\hat{C}$ are decoded using a circuit $\hat{C}_{\mathsf{Dec}}$ that "tolerates" BCL leakage, in the sense that such leakage on its *entire* wire values can be simulated given only (related) BCL leakage on the inputs and outputs of the circuit [7]. Indeed, the simulator can evaluate $\hat{C}$ on an *arbitrary* (*non*-satisfying) "witness" (thus generating the entire wire values of $\hat{C}$, and in particular allowing the simulator to compute any leakage on them), and then simulate leakage on the internals of $\hat{C}_{\mathsf{Dec}}$ by computing (related) leakage on its inputs (namely, the outputs of $\hat{C}$) and output (which is $(x,1)$). Since the outputs of $\hat{C}$ resist BCL leakage, this is indistinguishable from the leakage on the internal wires of $\hat{C}, \hat{C}_{\mathsf{Dec}}$ when $\hat{C}$ is evaluated on an actual witness. We note that the decoding circuit $\hat{C}_{\mathsf{Dec}}$ can be constructed using the LRCC of [15], which by a recent result of Bitansky et al. [8] is leakage-tolerant against BCL leakage.

Though this construction achieves efficient simulation, it is no longer sound. Indeed, soundness crucially relies on the fact that $\hat{C}_{\mathsf{Dec}}$ emulates C_{Dec} (which decodes the output of $\hat{C}$). Recall that in current LRCC constructions that offer information-theoretic security against wide leakage classes (e.g., [15,16,32]), the correctness of the computation crucially relies on the fact that the masks (which are provided as part of the input encoding) have the "correct" structure. Consequently, by providing $\hat{C}_{\mathsf{Dec}}$ with *ill-formed* masks, a malicious prover P^* can *arbitrarily* modify the functionality emulated by $\hat{C}_{\mathsf{Dec}}$, and in particular, may flip the output of $\hat{C}_{\mathsf{Dec}}$, causing the device to accept $x \notin L_{\mathcal{R}}$.[1] Recall that the device cannot verify that the masks are well-formed, since this would violate leakage-resilience.

To overcome this, we observe that when $\hat{C}_{\mathsf{Dec}}$ is generated using the LRCC of Dziembowski and Faust [15], the effect of ill-formed masks on the computation in $\hat{C}_{\mathsf{Dec}}$ is equivalent to adding a vector of fixed (but possibly different) field elements to the wires of C_{Dec}. Such attacks are called "additive attacks", and one can use *AMD circuits* [17–19] to protect against them. Informally, AMD circuits are randomized circuits that offer the best possible security under additive attacks, in the sense that the effect of every additive attack that may apply to all internal wires of the circuit can be simulated by an ideal attack that applies only to its inputs and outputs.

Thus, by replacing C_{Dec} with an AMD circuit C'_{Dec} before applying the LRCC, the effect of ill-formed encoded inputs is further restricted to an additive attack on the inputs and output of C_{Dec}. Finally, to protect the inputs and outputs of C'_{Dec} from additive attacks, we use the AMD code of [12]. (We note that encoding the inputs and outputs of C'_{Dec} using AMD codes is inherent to any AMD-based construction, otherwise a malicious prover P^* can use ill-formed encoded inputs to $\hat{C}'_{\mathsf{Dec}}$ to flip the output.) As we show in Sect. 4, the resultant construction satisfies the properties of Theorem 1. To obtain the *deterministic* circuit of Theorem 2, we have the prover provide (as part of its input encoding) the randomness used by the $\hat{C}$ component (which was generated using the LRCC of [25]), and the verifier provides the randomness used by the AMD circuit in $\hat{C}_{\mathsf{Dec}}$. (We note that the prover cannot provide this randomness, since the security of AMD circuits crucially relies on their randomness being *independent* of the additive attack. Therefore, if the prover provides the randomness for the AMD circuit, a malicious prover may correlate the randomness used by the AMD circuit with the additive attack, rendering the AMD circuit useless.)

---

[1] We note that "ill-formed" encodings do not pose a problem for *stateful* circuits (intuitively, the compiled circuit can use the secret state to overcome the influence of ill-formed masks). However, we are interested in *stateless* circuits.

1.3.2   General Leakage-Resilient Computation

Recall that the setting consists of $m \geq 1$ parties that utilize a leaky, but otherwise trusted, device to compute a joint function of their inputs; while protecting the privacy of the inputs, and the correctness of the output, against an active adversary that corrupts a subset of the parties, and may also obtain leakage on the internals of the device. More specifically, we construct m-party LRCCs that given a (boolean or arithmetic) circuit C with m inputs, output a circuit $\hat{C}$ that operates on encoded inputs and outputs. (Recall that encoded outputs are needed to guarantee privacy against adversaries that do not corrupt any parties.) As in other LRCCs, the circuit compiler is associated with an input encoder Enc, and an output decoder Dec (used to encode the inputs to, and the output of, $\hat{C}$, respectively).

The multiparty setting introduces an additional complication which did not arise in the ZK setting. Recall that the leakage-resilience property of $\hat{C}$ crucially relies on the fact that its internal computations are randomized using masks which are *unknown to the leakage function*. As already discussed in Sect. 1.3.1, to avoid the need for leak-free hardware we let the participating parties provide these masks. Consequently, the adversary (who also chooses the leakage function) knows the identity of the masks provided by all corrupted parties. We note that this issue occurs *even in the passive setting*, in which parties are guaranteed to honestly encode their inputs. This raises the following question: *how can we preserve the leakage-resilience property when the leakage function "knows" a subset of the masks?*

Our solution is to first replace the circuit C with a circuit C' that computes an *m-out-of-m additive secret sharing* of the output of C. We then construct the leakage-resilient version $\hat{C}'$ of C' using the LRCC of [25], which outputs encodings of the secret shares which C' computes. Then, each encoding is refreshed in a leakage-resilient manner. (This is similar to using a leakage-resilient version of the decoder in the ZK setting of Sect. 1.3.1.) More specifically, let C_{refresh} be a circuit that given an encoding of some value v outputs a fresh encoding of v. Similar to the construction of ZK circuits in Sect. 1.3.1, we replace C_{refresh} with an AMD circuit C'_{refresh} that emulates C_{refresh} but operates on AMD encodings. Finally, we compile C'_{refresh} using the LRCC of [15] into a leakage-resilient circuit $\hat{C}'_{\mathsf{refresh}}$, which (as discussed in Sect. 1.3.1) has the additional feature that ill-formed masks are detected. We use m copies of $\hat{C}'_{\mathsf{refresh}}$ to refresh the m secret shares, where the i'th copy is associated with the i'th party, who provides (as part of its input encoding) the masks needed for the computation of the i'th copy. Finally, the decoder Dec decodes the secret shares, and uses them to reconstruct the output.

Having the leakage-resilience circuit generate (encodings of) *secret-shares* of the output, instead of (an encoding of) the output itself guarantees leakage-resilience even when the adversary corrupts parties and learns the masks which they provide for the computation. At a very high level, this holds because even if the adversary learns (through the leakage, and knowledge of the masks) the *entire wire values* of the copies of $\hat{C}'_{\mathsf{refresh}}$ associated with corrupted parties, these only reveal information about the *secret shares* which these copies operate on. Therefore, the secrecy of the secret-sharing scheme guarantees that no information is revealed about the *actual* output, or inputs, of the computation. Thus, we obtain Theorem 3. (The analysis is in fact much more complex, see Sect. 6 for the construction and its analysis.)

1.4   Open Problems

Our work leaves several interesting open problems for further research. One is that of making the TP deterministic, while minimizing the complexity of the parties. Currently, we can make the TP deterministic, but only at the expense of making the parties work as hard as the entire original computation. A natural approach is via derandomization of the LRCC of [25]. Another research direction is to obtain a better understanding of the leakage classes that can be handled in this model, and extend the results to the setting of continuous leakage with stateful circuits. Another question is that of improving the asymptotic and concrete efficiency of our constructions, by providing better underlying LRCCs, or better analysis of existing ones. These questions are interesting even in the simple setting of a single semi-honest party.

1.5   Related Work

Originating from [26], MPC techniques are commonly used as a defense against side-channel attacks (see [2,3] and references therein). However, except for the works of [14,26] (discussed below) these techniques either rely on cryptographic assumptions [13,25], or on structured randomness which is generated by leak-free hardware, and is used to mask the internal computations [6,8,15,16,23]. To eliminate the leak-free hardware, the parties can provide the structured randomness as part of their input encoding. However, since the correctness of the computation crucially relies on the randomness having the "correct" structure, this allows corrupted parties to arbitrarily modify the functionality computed by the circuit, by providing randomness that does not have the required structure.

The only exception to the above are the works of [14,26], that provide provable information-theoretic security guarantees (without relying on structured randomness) against probing attacks, and some natural types of "noisy" leakage, but fail to protect against other simple types of realistic attacks, such as the sum of a subset of wires over the integers. (For example, when an AND gate is implemented using the LRCC of [26], the sum of a subset of wires in the resultant circuit allows an adversary to distinguish between the case in which both inputs are 0, and the case in which one of them is 1.)

2   Preliminaries

Let $\mathbb{F}$ be a finite field, and Σ be a finite alphabet (i.e., a set of symbols). For a function f over Σ^n, we use $\mathsf{supp}(f)$ to denote the image of f, namely

$\mathsf{supp}(f) = \{f(x) : x \in \Sigma^n\}$. For an NP-relation $\mathcal{R} = \mathcal{R}(x, w)$, we denote $L_\mathcal{R} = \{x : \exists w, (x, w) \in \mathcal{R}\}$. Vectors will be denoted by boldface letters (e.g., $\mathbf{a}$). If $\mathcal{D}$ is a distribution then $X \leftarrow \mathcal{D}$, or $X \in_R \mathcal{D}$, denotes sampling X according to the distribution $\mathcal{D}$. Given two distributions X, Y, $\mathsf{SD}(X, Y)$ denotes the statistical distance between X and Y. For a natural n, $\mathsf{negl}(n)$ denotes a function that is negligible in n. For a function family $\mathcal{L}$, we sometimes use the term "leakage family $\mathcal{L}$", or "leakage class $\mathcal{L}$". In the following, n usually denotes the input length, k usually denotes the output length, d, s denote depth and size, respectively (e.g., of circuits, as defined below), and m is used to denote the number of parties.

Circuits. We consider boolean circuits C over the set $X = \{x_1, \cdots, x_n\}$ of variables. C is a directed acyclic graph whose vertices are called *gates* and whose edges are called *wires*. The wires of C are labeled with functions over X. Every gate in C of in-degree 0 has out-degree 1 and is either labeled by a variable from X and referred to as an *input gate*; or is labeled by a constant $\alpha \in \{0, 1\}$ and referred to as a const_α *gate*. Following [16], all other gates are labeled by one of the operations $\wedge, \vee, \neg, \oplus$, where $\wedge, \vee, \oplus$ vertices have fan-in 2 and fan-out 1; and $\neg$ has fan-in and fan-out 1. We write $C : \{0, 1\}^n \to \{0, 1\}^k$ to indicate that C is a boolean circuit with n inputs and k outputs. The *size* of a circuit C, denoted $|C|$, is the number of wires in C, together with input and output gates.

We also consider arithmetic circuits C over a finite field $\mathbb{F}$ and the set X. Similarly to the boolean case, C has input and constant gates, and all other gates are labeled by one of the following functions $+, -, \times$ which are the addition, subtraction, and multiplication operations of the field. We write $C : \mathbb{F}^n \to \mathbb{F}^k$ to indicate that C is an arithmetic circuit over $\mathbb{F}$ with n inputs and k outputs. Notice that boolean circuits can be viewed as arithmetic circuits over the binary field in a natural way. Therefore, we sometimes describe boolean circuits using the operations $+, -, \times$ instead of $\oplus, \neg, \wedge, \vee$.

Additive Attacks. Following the terminology of [17], an additive attack $\mathbf{A}$ affects the evaluation of a circuit C as follows. For every wire connecting gates a and b in C, a value specified by the attack $\mathbf{A}$ is added to the output of a and then the derived value is used for the computation of b. Similarly, for every output gate, a value specified by $\mathbf{A}$ is added to the value of this output. Note that an additive attack on C is a fixed vector of (possibly different) field elements which is independent from the inputs and internal values of C. We denote the evaluation of C under additive attack $\mathbf{A}$ by $C^{\mathbf{A}}$.

At a high level, an additively-secure implementation of a function f is a circuit which evaluates f, and guarantees the "best" possible security against additive attacks, in the sense that any additive attack on it is equivalent (up to a small statistical distance) to an additive attack on the inputs and outputs of f. Formally,

Definition 2 (Additively-secure implementation [18]). *Let $\epsilon > 0$. A randomized circuit $C : \mathbb{F}^n \to \mathbb{F}^k$ is an ϵ-additively-secure implementation of a function $f : \mathbb{F}^n \to \mathbb{F}^k$ if the following holds.*

- **Completeness.** For every $x \in \mathbb{F}^n$, $\Pr[C(x) = f(x)] = 1$.
- **Additive-attack security.** For any additive attack $\mathbf{A}$ there exist $\mathbf{a}^{\text{in}} \in \mathbb{F}^n$, and a distribution $\mathcal{A}^{\text{Out}}$ over $\mathbb{F}^k$, such that for every $\mathbf{x} \in \mathbb{F}^n$, $\mathsf{SD}(C^{\mathbf{A}}(\mathbf{x}), f(\mathbf{x} + \mathbf{a}^{\text{in}}) + \mathcal{A}^{\text{out}}) \leq \epsilon$.

We also consider the notion of an additively-secure circuit compiler, which is a single PPT algorithm that compiles a given circuit C into its additively-secure implementation.

Definition 3 (Additively-secure circuit compiler). Let $n \in \mathbb{N}$ be an input length parameter, $k \in \mathbb{N}$ be an output length parameter, and $\epsilon(n) : \mathbb{N} \to \mathbb{R}^+$. Let Comp be a PPT algorithm that on input a circuit $C : \mathbb{F}^n \to \mathbb{F}^k$, outputs a circuit $\hat{C}$. Comp is an $\epsilon(n)$-additively-secure circuit compiler over $\mathbb{F}$ if for every circuit $C : \mathbb{F}^n \to \mathbb{F}^k$ that computes a function f_C, $\hat{C}$ is an $\epsilon(n)$-additively-secure implementation of f_C.

We will need the following theorem.

Theorem 4 [19]. Let n be an input length parameter, and $\epsilon(n) : \mathbb{N} \to \mathbb{R}^+$ be a statistical error function. Then there exists an $\epsilon(n)$-additively-secure circuit compiler Comp over $\mathbb{F}_2$. Moreover, on input a depth-d boolean circuit $C : \{0,1\}^n \to \{0,1\}^k$, Comp outputs a circuit $\hat{C}$ such that $|\hat{C}| = |C| \cdot \text{polylog}\left(|C|, \log \frac{1}{\epsilon(n)}\right) + \text{poly}\left(n, k, d, \log \frac{1}{\epsilon(n)}\right)$. Furthermore, there exists a PPT algorithm Alg that on input C, $\epsilon(n)$, and an additive attack $\mathcal{A}$, outputs a vector $\mathbf{a}^{\text{in}} \in \{0,1\}^n$, and a distribution $\mathcal{A}^{\text{out}}$ over $\{0,1\}^k$, such that for any $\mathbf{x} \in \{0,1\}^n$ it holds that $\mathsf{SD}(\hat{C}^{\mathcal{A}}(\mathbf{x}), C(\mathbf{x} + \mathbf{a}^{\text{in}}) + \mathcal{A}^{\text{out}}) \leq \epsilon(n)$.

Encoding schemes. An encoding scheme E over alphabet Σ is a pair (Enc, Dec) of algorithms, where the *encoding algorithm* Enc is a PPT algorithm that given a message $x \in \Sigma^n$ outputs an encoding $\hat{x} \in \Sigma^{\hat{n}}$ for some $\hat{n} = \hat{n}(n)$; and the *decoding algorithm* Dec is a deterministic algorithm, that given an $\hat{x}$ of length $\hat{n}$ in the image of Enc, outputs an $x \in \Sigma^n$. Moreover, $\Pr[\mathsf{Dec}(\mathsf{Enc}(x)) = x] = 1$ for every $x \in \Sigma^n$. It would sometimes be convenient to explicitly describe the randomness used by Enc, in which case we think of Enc as a deterministic function $\mathsf{Enc}(x; r)$ of its input x, and random input r. Following [27], we say that a vector $\mathbf{v} \in \Sigma^{\hat{n}(n)}$ is *well-formed* if $\mathbf{v} \in \mathsf{Enc}(0^n)$.

Parameterized encoding schemes. We consider encoding schemes in which the encoding and decoding algorithms are given an additional input 1^t, which is used as a security parameter. Concretely, the encoding length depends also on t (and not only on n), i.e., $\hat{n} = \hat{n}(n, t)$, and for every t the resultant scheme is an encoding scheme (in particular, for every $x \in \Sigma^n$ and every $t \in \mathbb{N}$, $\Pr[\mathsf{Dec}(\mathsf{Enc}(x, 1^t), 1^t) = x] = 1$). We call such schemes *parameterized*. For $n, t \in \mathbb{N}$, a vector $\mathbf{v} \in \Sigma^{\hat{n}(n,t)}$ is *well-formed* if $\mathbf{v} \in \mathsf{Enc}(0^n, 1^t)$. Furthermore, we sometimes consider encoding schemes that take *a pair* of security parameters $1^t, 1^{t_{\text{ln}}}$. (t_{ln} is used in cases when the encoding scheme employs an "internal" encoding scheme, and is used in the internal scheme.) In such cases, the encoding length depends on n, t, t_{In}, and the resultant scheme should be an encoding scheme for every $t, t_{\mathsf{In}} \in \mathbb{N}$. We will usually omit the term "parameterized", and use "encoding scheme" to describe both *parameterized and non-parameterized* encoding schemes.

Next, we define leakage-indistinguishable encoding schemes.

Definition 4 (Leakage-indistinguishability of functions and encodings, [27]). *Let D, D' be finite sets, $\mathcal{L}_D = \{\ell : D \to D'\}$ be a family of leakage functions, and $\epsilon > 0$. We say that two distributions X, Y over D are $(\mathcal{L}_D, \epsilon)$-leakage-indistinguishable, if for any function $\ell \in \mathcal{L}_D$, $\mathsf{SD}\left(\ell\left(X\right), \ell\left(Y\right)\right) \leq \epsilon$. In case $\mathcal{L}_D$ consists of functions over a union of domains, we say that X, Y over D are $(\mathcal{L}_D, \epsilon)$-leakage-indistinguishable if $\mathsf{SD}\left(\ell\left(X\right), \ell\left(Y\right)\right) \leq \epsilon$ for every function $\ell \in \mathcal{L}$ with domain D.*

Let $\mathcal{L}$ be a family of leakage functions. We say that a randomized function $f : \Sigma^n \to \Sigma^m$ is $(\mathcal{L}, \epsilon)$-leakage-indistinguishable if for every $x, y \in \Sigma^n$, the distributions $f\left(x\right), f\left(y\right)$ are $(\mathcal{L}, \epsilon)$-leakage-indistinguishable. We say that an encoding scheme $\mathsf{E} = (\mathsf{Enc}, \mathsf{Dec})$ is $(\mathcal{L}, \epsilon)$-leakage-indistinguishable if for every large enough $t \in \mathbb{N}$, $\mathsf{Enc}\left(\cdot, 1^t\right)$ is $(\mathcal{L}, \epsilon)$-leakage indistinguishable.

Algebraic Manipulation Detection (AMD) Encoding Schemes. Informally, an AMD encoding scheme is an encoding scheme which guarantees that additive attacks on codewords are detected by the decoder (except with small probability), where the decoder outputs (in addition to the decoded output) also a flag indicating whether an additive attack was detected. Formally,

Definition 5 (AMD encoding scheme, [12,18]). *Let $\mathbb{F}$ be a finite field, $n \in \mathbb{N}$ be an input length parameter, $t \in \mathbb{N}$ be a security parameter, and $\epsilon\left(n, t\right) : \mathbb{N} \times \mathbb{N} \to \mathbb{R}^+$. An $(n, t, \epsilon\left(n, t\right))$-algebraic manipulation detection (AMD) encoding scheme $(\mathsf{Enc}, \mathsf{Dec})$ over $\mathbb{F}$ is an encoding scheme with the following guarantees.*

- *Perfect completeness. For every $\mathbf{x} \in \mathbb{F}^n$, $\Pr\left[\mathsf{Dec}\left(\mathsf{Enc}\left(\mathbf{x}, 1^t\right), 1^t\right) = (0, \mathbf{x})\right] = 1.$*
- *Additive soundness. For every $0^{\hat{n}(n,t)} \neq \mathbf{a} \in \mathbb{F}^{\hat{n}(n,t)}$, and every $\mathbf{x} \in \mathbb{F}^n$, $\Pr\left[\mathsf{Dec}\left(\mathsf{Enc}\left(\mathbf{x}, 1^t\right) + \mathbf{a}, 1^t\right) \notin \mathsf{ERR}\right] \leq \epsilon\left(n, t\right)$ where $\mathsf{ERR} = (\mathbb{F} \setminus \{0\}) \times \mathbb{F}^n$, and the probability is over the randomness of Enc.*

We will use the following theorem from the full version of [18].

Theorem 5 (AMD encoding scheme, [18]). *Let $\mathbb{F}$ be a finite field, and $n, t \in \mathbb{N}$. Then there exists an $\left(n, t, |\mathbb{F}|^{-t}\right)$-AMD encoding scheme $(\mathsf{Enc}, \mathsf{Dec})$ with encodings of length $\hat{n}\left(n, t\right) = O\left(n + t\right)$. Moreover, encoding and decoding of length-n inputs with parameter t can be performed by circuits of size $O\left(n + t\right)$.*

2.1 Leakage-Resilient Circuit Compilers (LRCCs)

In this section we define the notion of a leakage-resilient circuit compiler. This notion, and its variants defined in later sections, will be extensively used in this work.

Definition 6 (Circuit compiler with abort). *We say that a triplet* $(\mathsf{Comp}, \mathsf{E}, \mathsf{Dec_{Out}})$ *is a circuit compiler with abort if:*

- $\mathsf{E} = (\mathsf{Enc}, \mathsf{Dec})$ *is an encoding scheme, where* Enc *on input* $x \in \mathbb{F}^n$, *and* $1^t, 1^{t_{\mathsf{In}}}$, *outputs a vector* $\hat{x}$ *of length* $\hat{n}$ *for some* $\hat{n} = \hat{n}(n, t, t_{\mathsf{In}})$.
- Comp *is a polynomial-time algorithm that given an arithmetic circuit* C *over* $\mathbb{F}$, *and* 1^t, *outputs an arithmetic circuit* $\hat{C}$.
- $\mathsf{Dec_{Out}}$ *is a deterministic decoding algorithm associated with a length function* $\hat{n}_{\mathsf{Out}} : \mathbb{N} \to \mathbb{N}$ *that on input* $\hat{x} \in \mathbb{F}^{\hat{n}_{\mathsf{Out}}(n)}$ *outputs* $(f, x) \in \mathbb{F} \times \mathbb{F}^n$.

We require that $(\mathsf{Comp}, \mathsf{E}, \mathsf{Dec_{Out}})$ *satisfy the following* correctness with abort *property: there exists a negligible function* $\epsilon(t) = \mathsf{negl}(t)$ *such that for any arithmetic circuit* C, *and input* x *for* C, $\Pr\left[\mathsf{Dec_{Out}}\left(\hat{C}(\hat{x})\right) = (0, C(x))\right] \geq 1 - \epsilon(t)$, *where* $\hat{x} \leftarrow \mathsf{Enc}\left(x, 1^t, 1^{|C|}\right)$.

Informally, a circuit compiler is *leakage resilient* for a class $\mathcal{L}$ of functions if for every "not too large" circuit C, and every input x for C, the wire values of the compiled circuit $\hat{C}$, when evaluated on a random encoding $\hat{x}$ of x, can be simulated given only the description of C; and functions in $\mathcal{L}$ cannot distinguish between the actual and simulated wire values.

Notation 6. For a Circuit C, a function $\ell : \mathbb{F}^{|C|} \to \mathbb{F}^m$ for some natural m, and an input x for C, $[C, x]$ denotes the wire values of C when evaluated on x, and $\ell[C, x]$ denotes the output of ℓ on $[C, x]$.

Definition 7 (LRCC). *Let* $t \in \mathbb{N}$ *be a security parameter, and* $\mathbb{F}$ *be a finite field. For a function class* $\mathcal{L}$, $\epsilon(t) : \mathbb{N} \to \mathbb{R}^+$, *and a size function* $\mathsf{S}(n) : \mathbb{N} \to \mathbb{N}$, *we say that* $(\mathsf{Comp}, \mathsf{E}, \mathsf{Dec_{Out}})$ *is an* $(\mathcal{L}, \epsilon(t), \mathsf{S}(n))$-LRCC *if there exists a PPT algorithm* Sim *such that the following holds. For all sufficiently large* t, *every arithmetic circuit* C *over* $\mathbb{F}$ *of input length* n *and size at most* $\mathsf{S}(n)$, *every* $\ell \in \mathcal{L}$ *of input length* $|\hat{C}|$, *and every* $x \in \mathbb{F}^n$, *we have* $\mathsf{SD}\left(\ell[\mathsf{Sim}(C, 1^t)], \ell\left[\hat{C}, \hat{x}\right]\right) \leq \epsilon(t)$, *where* $\hat{x} \leftarrow \mathsf{Enc}\left(x, 1^t, 1^{|C|}\right)$.

If the above holds with an inefficient *simulator* Sim, *then we say that* $(\mathsf{Comp}, \mathsf{E})$ *is an* $(\mathcal{L}, \epsilon(t), \mathsf{S}(n))$-relaxed LRCC.

2.2   Gadget-Based Leakage-Resilient Circuit Compilers

In this section we describe gadget-based LRCCs [15,16,26], which are the basis of all our constructions. We choose to describe the operation of these compilers over a finite field $\mathbb{F}$, but the description naturally adjusts to the boolean case as well. At a high level, given a circuit C, a gadget-based LRCC replaces every wire in C with a bundle of wires, which carry an encoding of the wire value, and every gate with a sub-circuit that emulates the operation of the gate on encoded inputs. More specifically:

Gadgets. A bundle is a sequence of field elements, encoding a field element according to some encoding scheme E; and a gadget is a circuit which operates on bundles and emulates the operation of the corresponding gate in C.

A gadget has both standard inputs, that represent the wires in the original circuit, and masking inputs (so-called "masks"), that are used to achieve privacy. More formally, a gadget emulates a specific boolean or arithmetic operation on the standard inputs, and outputs a bundle encoding the correct output. Every gadget G is associated with a set M_G of "well-formed" masking input bundles (e.g., in the LRCC of [16], M_G consists of sets of 0-encodings). For every standard input x, on input a bundle $\mathbf{x}$ encoding x, and *any* masking input bundles $\mathsf{m} \in M_G$, the output of the gadget G should be consistent with the operation on x. For example, if G computes multiplication, then for every standard input $x = (x_1, x_2)$, for every bundle encoding $\mathbf{x} = (\mathbf{x}_1, \mathbf{x}_2)$ of x according to E, and for every masking input bundles $\mathsf{m} \in M_G$, $G(\mathbf{x}, \mathsf{m})$ is a bundle encoding $x_1 \times x_2$ according to E. Because the encoding schemes we use have the property that the encoding function is onto its range, we may think of the masking input bundles m as encoding some set mask of values. The internal computations in the gadget will remain private as long as its masking input bundles are a uniformly random encoding of mask, *regardless* of the actual value of mask.

Gadget-based LRCCs. In our constructions, the compiled circuit $\hat{C}$ is obtained from a circuit C by replacing every wire with a bundle, and every gate with the corresponding gadget. Recall that the gadgets also have masking inputs (which in previous works [15,16] were generated by leak-free hardware). These are provided as part of the encoded input of $\hat{C}$, in the following way. $\mathsf{E} = (\mathsf{Enc}, \mathsf{Dec})$ uses an "inner" encoding scheme $\mathsf{E}^{\mathsf{In}} = (\mathsf{Enc}^{\mathsf{In}}, \mathsf{Dec}^{\mathsf{In}})$, where Enc uses $\mathsf{Enc}^{\mathsf{In}}$ to encode the inputs of C, concatenated with $0^{t_{\mathsf{In}}}$ for a "sufficiently large" t_{In} (these 0-encodings will be the masking inputs of the gadgets, that are used to achieve privacy); and Dec uses $\mathsf{Dec}^{\mathsf{In}}$ to decode its input, and discards the last t_{In} symbols.

3   LRCCs Used in this Work

In this section we review the various LRCC constructions used in this work.

3.1   The LRCC of [25]

We use a slight modification of the LRCC of Goyal et al. [25], which we describe in this section. Their construction uses *small-bias* encodings over $\mathbb{F}_2$, namely encodings for which linear distinguishers obtain only a small distinguishing advantage between encodings of 0 and 1. Formally:

Definition 8 (Small-bias encoding schemes). *Let $\epsilon \in (0, 1)$, and $(\mathsf{Enc}, \mathsf{Dec})$ be an encoding scheme over $\mathbb{F}_2$ with encodings of length $\hat{n}$. We say that $(\mathsf{Enc}, \mathsf{Dec})$ is ϵ-biased if for every $x \in \mathbb{F}_2$, and every $\emptyset \neq S \subseteq [\hat{n}]$, $|\Pr[P_S(\mathsf{Enc}(x)) = 1] - \Pr[P_S(\mathsf{Enc}(x)) = 0]| \leq \epsilon$, where $P_S(z) = \oplus_{i \in S} z_i$, and the probability is over the randomness of Enc.*

At a high level, given a circuit C (which, without loss of generality, contains only NAND gates), its leakage-resilient version is constructed in three steps: first, C is compiled into a *parity resilient* circuit $C_\oplus$, which emulates the operation of C on small-bias encodings of its inputs, and resists leakage from the class of all parity function (namely, all functions that output the parity of a subset of wires). $C_\oplus$ is constructed using a single constant-size gadget $\mathcal{G}$ that operates over the small-bias encoding. Second, a GMW-style 2-party protocol π is constructed, which emulates $C_\oplus$ (gate-by-gate) on additive secret shares of the input, and outputs additive secret shares of the output. π uses an oracle to the functionality computed by the gadget $\mathcal{G}$. In the final step, each oracle call to $\mathcal{G}$ is replaced with a constant number of OT calls, and the resultant 2-party protocol is converted into a boolean circuit, in which the OT calls are implemented using a constant number of gates.[2] The resultant circuit C' operates on encoded inputs, and returns encoded outputs. More specifically, the encoding scheme first encodes each input bit using the small-bias encoding, then additively secret shares these encodings into two shares.

The reason we need to modify the compiler is the small-bias encoding it uses. The LRCC can use *any* small-bias encoding, and [25] construct a robust gadget $\mathcal{G}$, that can emulate *any* constant-sized boolean function, over inputs and outputs encoded according to *any* constant-sized small-bias encoding (the inputs and outputs may actually be encoded using different encoding schemes). However, the specific encoding used in [25] is insufficient for our needs. More specifically, we need an encoding scheme $\Big($Enc $: \{0,1\} \times \{0,1\}^c \to \{0,1\}^{c'}$,

Dec $: \{0,1\}^{c'} \to \{0,1\}^2\Big)$ (for some natural constants c, c')[3] satisfying the following two properties for some constant $\epsilon > 0$.

- **Property (1):** (Enc, Dec) is ϵ-biased, and $|\mathsf{supp}\,(\mathsf{Enc}\,(0;\cdot))| = |\mathsf{supp}\,(\mathsf{Enc}\,(1;\cdot))|$.
- **Property (2):** For every $\mathbf{0} \neq \mathbf{A} \in \{0,1\}^{c'}$, and every $b \in \{0,1\}$, $\Pr_{r\in_R\{0,1\}^c}$ $[\mathsf{Enc}\,(b;r) \oplus \mathbf{A} \in \mathsf{supp}\,(\mathsf{Enc}\,(1 \oplus b;\cdot))] \leq \epsilon$.

The first property is needed for the leakage-resilience property of the LRCC of [25]. The second property implies that with constant probability, additive attacks on encodings are "harmless", in the sense that they either do not change the encoded value, or result in an invalid encoding. The reason that the second property is needed will become clear in Sect. 4.1.

Since the encoding scheme used in [25] does not possess property (2), we replace it with an encoding that does.[4] As noted in [25], a probabilistic argument implies that for a large enough constant c, and $c' = 2c$, most encoding

---

[2] We note that the conversion from protocol to circuit is not explicitly described in [25].

[3] Dec returns a pair of bits of which one is a flag indicating whether decoding failed. This is necessary since for $c' > c + 1$, not all possible inputs to Dec are valid encoding.

[4] To improve efficiency of our construction by a factor of 2, one could use the encoding of [25] (in which $c' = c + 1$) throughout the circuit, and only use our new encoding for the outputs of the circuit. However, to simplify the construction we choose to use the same encoding throughout the circuit.

schemes with a 1:1 Enc satisfy property (1). A similar argument shows that most encoding schemes posses property (2). Therefore, there exists an encoding scheme $\left(\mathsf{Enc}^{\oplus} : \{0,1\} \times \{0,1\}^c \to \{0,1\}^{2c}, \mathsf{Dec}^{\oplus} : \{0,1\}^{2c} \to \{0,1\}^2\right)$ with both properties. (Moreover, one can find an explicit description of this scheme, since c is constant.) Since $\mathcal{G}$ is a generic gadget, that can be used to emulate any function over any encoding, we can replace the encoding scheme of [25] with $\left(\mathsf{Enc}^{\oplus}, \mathsf{Dec}^{\oplus}\right)$.

We are now ready to define the encoding used by the LRCC of [25].

Construction 1. *The encoding scheme* $\left(\mathsf{Enc}^{\mathrm{GIMSS}}, \mathsf{Dec}^{\mathrm{GIMSS}}\right)$ *over* $\mathbb{F}_2$ *is defined as follows:*

- *for every* $x \in \mathbb{F}_2$, $\mathsf{Enc}^{\mathrm{GIMSS}}(x, 1^t)$:
  - *Generates* $x^1, \cdots, x^t \leftarrow \mathsf{Enc}^{\oplus}(x)$.
  - *Picks* $\boldsymbol{x}^L, \boldsymbol{x}^R \in \mathbb{F}_2^{2ct}$ *uniformly at random subject to the constraint that* $\boldsymbol{x}^L \oplus \boldsymbol{x}^R = (x^1, \cdots, x^t)$.
- $\mathsf{Dec}^{\mathrm{GIMSS}} : \mathbb{F}_2^{2ct} \times \mathbb{F}_2^{2ct} \to \mathbb{F}_2^2$, *on input* $\left(\boldsymbol{x}^L, \boldsymbol{x}^R\right)$ *operates as follows:*
  - *Computes* $\boldsymbol{x} = \boldsymbol{x}^L \oplus \boldsymbol{x}^R$, *and denotes* $\boldsymbol{x} = (x^1, \cdots, x^t)$. *(Intuitively,* $\boldsymbol{x}^L, \boldsymbol{x}^R$ *are interpreted as random secret shares of* $\boldsymbol{x}$, *and* $\boldsymbol{x}$ *consists of* t *copies of encodings, according to* $\mathsf{Enc}^{\oplus}$, *of a bit* b.)
  - *For every* $1 \leq i \leq t$, *let* $(f_i, x_i) = \mathsf{Dec}^{\oplus}(x^i)$. *(This step decodes each of the* t *copies of* b.)
  - *If there exist* $1 \leq i_1, i_2 \leq t$ *such that* $f_{i_1} \neq 0$, *or* $x_{i_1} \neq x_{i_2}$, *then sets* $f = 1$. *Otherwise, sets* $f = 0$. *(This step checks that all copies of* b *are consistent, and that no flag is set, otherwise the decoder sets a flag* f.)
  - *Outputs* (f, x^1).

We will need the fact that every additive attack on encodings generated by Construction 1 is either "harmless" (in the sense that it does not change the encoded value), or causes a decoding failure. This is formalized in the next lemma.

Lemma 1. *Let* $t \in \mathbb{N}$ *be a security parameter. Then for every* $\boldsymbol{0} \neq \mathbf{A} \in \mathbb{F}_2^{4ct}$, *and for every* $x \in \mathbb{F}_2$,

$$\Pr\left[\mathsf{Dec}^{\mathrm{GIMSS}}\left(\mathsf{Enc}^{\mathrm{GIMSS}}(x, 1^t) + \mathbf{A}\right) \notin \{(0, x), \mathsf{ERR}\}\right] = \mathsf{negl}(t).$$

Proof. Let $\boldsymbol{0} \neq \mathbf{A} = \left(\mathbf{A}^L, \mathbf{A}^R\right) \in \mathbb{F}_2^{2ct} \times \mathbb{F}_2^{2ct}$, and let $\left(\mathbf{x}^L, \mathbf{x}^R\right) \leftarrow \mathsf{Enc}^{\mathrm{GIMSS}}(x, 1^t)$. Then on input $\left(\mathbf{y}^L, \mathbf{y}^R\right) = \left(\mathbf{x}^L, \mathbf{x}^R\right) + \left(\mathbf{A}^L, \mathbf{A}^R\right)$, the decoder $\mathsf{Dec}^{\mathrm{GIMSS}}$ first computes

$$\mathbf{x}' = \left(x^{1\prime}, \cdots, x^{t\prime}\right) = \mathbf{y}^L \oplus \mathbf{y}^R = \mathbf{x}^L \oplus \mathbf{x}^R \oplus \mathbf{A}^L \oplus \mathbf{A}^R$$

and then for every $1 \leq i \leq t$, computes $(f_i, x_i') \leftarrow \mathsf{Dec}^{\oplus}(x^i, 1^t)$. We consider two possible cases.

First, if $\mathbf{A}^L \oplus \mathbf{A}^R = \mathbf{0}$, then $\mathbf{x}' = \mathbf{x}^L \oplus \mathbf{x}^R$, namely the additive attack cancels out, and so the output of $\mathsf{Dec}^{\mathrm{GIMSS}}$ would be $(0, x)$ (with probability 1) by the correctness of the scheme.

Second, assume that $\mathbf{A}^L \oplus \mathbf{A}^R \neq \mathbf{0}$ and $\mathsf{Dec}^{\mathrm{GIMSS}}(\mathbf{x} \oplus \mathbf{A}, 1^t) \neq (0, x)$. We show that in this case $\mathsf{Dec}^{\mathrm{GIMSS}}$ outputs ERR except with negligible probability. Recall that $\mathsf{Enc}^{\oplus}$ has the property that for every $\mathbf{0} \neq \mathbf{A}'$, and every $z \in \mathbb{F}$, $\Pr\left[\mathsf{Enc}^{\oplus}(z) \oplus \mathbf{A}' \in \mathsf{supp}\left(\mathsf{Enc}^{\oplus}(\bar{z})\right)\right] \leq \epsilon$ for some constant $\epsilon \in (0, 1)$, where the probability is over the randomness used by $\mathsf{Enc}^{\oplus}$ to generate the encoding. Consequently, for every $1 \leq i \leq t$, $\Pr\left[\mathsf{Dec}^{\oplus}\left(x^{i\prime}\right) = (0, \bar{x})\right] \leq \epsilon$. Since $\mathsf{Dec}^{\mathrm{GIMSS}}$ outputs $(0, \bar{x})$ only if all $x^{i\prime}$ decoded to $\bar{x}$, and each of these t copies was generated using fresh, independent randomness in $\mathsf{Enc}^{\oplus}$, this happens only with probability $\epsilon^t = \mathsf{negl}(t)$.

The final modification we need is in the gadget $\mathcal{G}$. Notice that unlike the semi-honest setting considered in [25], in our setting *the parties* provide the inputs to the leakage-resilient circuit, where a malicious party may provide inputs that are *not* properly encoded, and therefore do not correspond to *any* input for the original circuit. (We note that the inputs are the only encodings that may be invalid, since $\mathcal{G}$ is guaranteed to always output valid encodings.) To guarantee correctness of the computation even in this case, the encoded inputs should induce inputs to the original circuit. Therefore, we have $\mathcal{G}$ interpret invalid encodings as encoding the all-zeros string. More specifically, given encodings $\hat{x}, \hat{y}$, $\mathcal{G}$ operates as follows: decodes $\hat{x}, \hat{y}$ to obtain x, y, where if decoding failed then x, y are set to the all-zero strings; computes $z = \mathrm{NAND}(x, y)$; and outputs a fresh encoding of z.

Combining the aforementioned modifications, we have the following.

Construction 2 (LRCC, [25]). *Let* $c \in \mathbb{N}$ *and* $\epsilon \in (0, 1)$ *be constants,* $t, t_{\mathsf{In}} \in \mathbb{N}$ *be security parameters, and* $n \in \mathbb{N}$ *be an input length parameter. Let* $\left(\mathsf{Enc}^{\oplus} : \mathbb{F}_2 \times \mathbb{F}_2^c \to \mathbb{F}_2^{2c}, \mathsf{Dec}^{\oplus} : \mathbb{F}_2^{2c} \to \mathbb{F}_2\right)$ *be an encoding scheme satisfying properties (1) and (2) described above. (We also use* $\mathsf{Enc}^{\oplus}, \mathsf{Dec}^{\oplus}$ *to denote the natural extension of encoding and decoding to bit strings, where every bit is encoded or decoded separately.) The relaxed LRCC with abort* $\left(\mathsf{Comp}^{\mathrm{GIMSS}}, \mathsf{E}_{\mathsf{In}}^{\mathrm{GIMSS}}, \mathsf{Dec}_{\mathsf{Out}}^{\mathrm{GIMSS}}\right)$ *is defined as follows.*

- *The input encoding scheme* $\mathsf{E}_{\mathsf{In}}^{\mathrm{GIMSS}} = \left(\mathsf{Enc}_{\mathsf{In}}^{\mathrm{GIMSS}}, \mathsf{Dec}_{\mathsf{In}}^{\mathrm{GIMSS}}\right)$ *is defined as follows:*
  - *for every* $x \in \mathbb{F}_2$, $\mathsf{Enc}_{\mathsf{In}}^{\mathrm{GIMSS}}(x, 1^{t_{\mathsf{In}}}) = (\boldsymbol{x}^L, \boldsymbol{x}^R, r)$ *where* $\boldsymbol{x}^L, \boldsymbol{x}^R$ *are a random additive secret sharing of* $\mathsf{Enc}^{\oplus}(x)$, *and* $r \in_R \bar{\mathbb{F}}_2^{t_{\mathsf{In}}}$.
  - $\mathsf{Dec}_{\mathsf{In}}^{\mathrm{GIMSS}}\left(\left(\left(\boldsymbol{x}^L, \boldsymbol{x}^R\right), r\right), 1^{t_{\mathsf{In}}}\right)$ *computes* $(f, x) = \mathsf{Dec}^{\oplus}\left(\boldsymbol{x}^L + \boldsymbol{x}^R\right)$, *and outputs* x.
- *The output decoding algorithm* $\mathsf{Dec}_{\mathsf{Out}}^{\mathrm{GIMSS}} : \mathbb{F}_2^{n \cdot t \cdot 2c} \times \mathbb{F}_2^{n \cdot t \cdot 2c} \to \mathbb{F}_2^{n+1}$, *on input* $\left(\boldsymbol{x}^L, \boldsymbol{x}^R\right) = \left(\left(\boldsymbol{x}_1^L, \cdots, \boldsymbol{x}_n^L\right), \left(\boldsymbol{x}_1^R, \cdots, \boldsymbol{x}_n^R\right)\right)$ *operates as follows:*
  - *For every* $1 \leq i \leq n$, *computes* $(f_i, x_i) = \mathsf{Dec}^{\mathrm{GIMSS}}\left(\left(\boldsymbol{x}_i^L, \boldsymbol{x}_i^R\right), 1^t\right)$ *(where* $\mathsf{Dec}^{\mathrm{GIMSS}}$ *is the decoder from Construction 1).*
  - *If there exist* $1 \leq i \leq n$ *such that* $f_i \neq 0$, *outputs* $(1, 0^n)$. *Otherwise, outputs* $(f, x_1, \cdots, x_n)$.

- Let $r \in \mathbb{N}$ denote the number of random inputs used by each gadget $\mathcal{G}$. Then $\mathsf{Comp}^{\mathrm{GIMSS}}$, on input 1^t and a circuit $C : \mathbb{F}^n \to \mathbb{F}^k$ containing s NAND gates, outputs a circuit $C^{\mathrm{GIMSS}} : \mathbb{F}_2^{4c \cdot n} \times \mathbb{F}_2^{r(s+t \cdot k)} \to \mathbb{F}_2^{4c \cdot k \cdot t}$ generated as follows:
  - Let $C' : \mathbb{F}_2^{2c \cdot n} \times \mathbb{F}_2^{r \cdot s} \to \mathbb{F}_2^{2c \cdot k}$ denote the circuit in which every gate of C is replaced with the gadget $\mathcal{G}$ of [25] that emulates a NAND gate over encodings generated by $\mathsf{Enc}^\oplus$. The random inputs used by the gadgets in C' are taken from the second input to C' (each random input is used only once).
  - Let $C'' : \mathbb{F}_2^{2c \cdot n} \times \mathbb{F}_2^{r(s+t \cdot k)} \to \mathbb{F}_2^{2c \cdot k \cdot t}$ denote the circuit obtained from C' by adding after each output gadget of C' (namely each gadget whose output is an output of C') t gadgets $\mathcal{G}$ emulating the identity function. As in C', the random inputs used by the gadgets in C'' are taken from the second input to C''. (This step encodes each output bit using the repetition code.)[5]
  - Let π denote a 2-party GMW-style protocol in the OT-hybrid model which emulates C'' gadget-by-gadget on inputs encoded according to $\mathsf{Enc}^{\mathrm{GIMSS}}$ (i.e., on additive shares of encodings according to $\mathsf{Enc}^\oplus$). Then C^{GIMSS} is the circuit obtained from π by implementing the programs of the parties as a circuit, where each OT call with inputs $(x_0, x_1), b$ is implemented using the following constant-sized circuit: $\mathsf{OT}((x_0, x_1), b) = (x_0 \wedge \bar{b}) \oplus (x_1 \wedge b)$. (The wires of this circuit are divided between the parties as follows: the input wires x_0, x_1 are assigned to the OT sender; whereas the wires corresponding to $b, \bar{b}$, the outputs of the $\wedge$ gates, and the output of the $\oplus$ gate, are assigned to the OT receiver.[6])

Goyal et al. [25] show that Construction 2 resists BCL (Definition 1):

Theorem 7 (Implicit in [25]). *For every leakage-bound $t \in \mathbb{N}$, input and output lengths $n, k \in \mathbb{N}$, and size bound $s \in \mathbb{N}$, there exists an $(\mathcal{L}_{\mathrm{BCL}}^t, 2^{-t}, s)$-relaxed LRCC with abort, where $\mathcal{L}_{\mathrm{BCL}}^t$ is the family of all t-BCL functions. Moreover, on input a size-s, depth d circuit $C : \{0,1\}^n \to \{0,1\}^k$, the leakage-resilient circuit C^{GIMSS} has size $\widetilde{O}(s + td + t^2)$, the input encoder $\mathsf{Enc}_{\mathrm{In}}^{\mathrm{GIMSS}}$ can be implemented by a circuit of size $\widetilde{O}(n+t)$, and the output decoder $\mathsf{Dec}_{\mathrm{Out}}^{\mathrm{GIMSS}}$ can be implemented by a circuit of size $\widetilde{O}(t^2 + tk)$.[7]*

---

[5] This step, which we add to the LRCC of [25], is used to reduce the decoding error when the LRCC is used to construct leakage-secure ZK circuits in Sect. 4.1. We note that this modification preserves the parity-resilience property since it is equivalent to duplicating each output of C t times before transforming it into C'.

[6] Notice that this division of the wires preserves the leakage-resilience guarantee of [25]. Indeed, in [25] the view of the OT sender contains the input wires x_0, x_1, whereas the view of the OT receiver contains the input wire b and the output of the OT (i.e., the output of the $\oplus$ gate). Notice that $\bar{b}$ and the outputs of the $\wedge$ gates are computable from b and the OT output, so the view of the OT receiver contains exactly the same information in [25] and in our implementation of their protocol.

[7] The output decoder in the original construction of [25] has size $\widetilde{O}(t + k)$, the decoder of Construction 2 is larger due to the modified encoding we use, which replaces each encoded output bit with t copies.

3.2   The Leakage-Tolerant Circuit-Compiler of [15]

In this section we describe the Leakage-Tolerant Circuit-Compiler (LTCC) obtained from [15] through the transformation of [8]. Informally, the LRCC of Dziembowski and Faust [15], denoted DF-LRCC, is a gadget-based LRCC which uses the inner-product encoding scheme that encodes a value x as a pair of vectors whose inner-product is x:

Definition 9 (Inner product encoding scheme). *Let $\mathbb{F}$ be a finite field, and $n \in \mathbb{N}$ be an input length parameter. The* inner product encoding scheme $\mathsf{E_{IP}} = (\mathsf{Enc_{IP}}, \mathsf{Dec_{IP}})$ *over $\mathbb{F}$ is a parameterized encoding scheme defined as follows:*

- *For every input $x = (x_1, \cdots, x_n) \in \mathbb{F}^n$, and security parameter $t \in \mathbb{N}$, $\mathsf{Enc_{IP}}(x, 1^t) = \left((\boldsymbol{y}_1^L, \boldsymbol{y}_1^R), \cdots, (\boldsymbol{y}_n^L, \boldsymbol{y}_n^R)\right)$, where for every $1 \le i \le n$, $\boldsymbol{y}_i^L, \boldsymbol{y}_i^R$ are random in $(\mathbb{F} \setminus \{0\})^t$ subject to the constraint that $\langle \boldsymbol{y}_i^L, \boldsymbol{y}_i^R \rangle = x_i$.*
- *For every $t \in \mathbb{N}$, and every $\left((\boldsymbol{y}_1^L, \boldsymbol{y}_1^R), \cdots, (\boldsymbol{y}_n^L, \boldsymbol{y}_n^R)\right) \in \mathbb{F}^{2nt}$, $\mathsf{Dec_{IP}}\left((\boldsymbol{y}_1^L, \boldsymbol{y}_1^R), \cdots, (\boldsymbol{y}_n^L, \boldsymbol{y}_n^R)\right) = (\langle \boldsymbol{y}_1^L, \boldsymbol{y}_1^R \rangle, \cdots, \langle \boldsymbol{y}_n^L, \boldsymbol{y}_n^R \rangle)$.*

More specifically, the DF-LRCC is an LRCC variant in which the compiled circuit takes un-encoded inputs, as well as masking inputs that are used in the gadgets. The construction uses 4 gadgets: a refresh gadget which emulates the identity function, and is used to generate fresh encodings of the wires; a *generalized-multiplication* gadget which emulates the function $f_c(x, y) = c - x \times y$, for a constant $c \in \mathbb{F}$; a *multiplication by a constant* gadget that emulates the function $f_c(x) = c \times x$, for a constant $c \in \mathbb{F}$; and an *addition by a constant* gadget that emulates the function $f_c(x) = c + x$, for a constant $c \in \mathbb{F}$. (The field operations $\times, +, -$ can be implemented using a constant number of these gadgets.) For completeness, these gadgets are described in Appendix A. We will only need the following property of these gadgets: the effect of evaluating a gadget with ill-formed masking inputs is equivalent to an additive attack on the gate that the gadget emulates (this is formalized in Lemma 3).

As explained in Sect. 1.3.1, we use a leakage-tolerant variant of the DF-LRCC. Roughly speaking, a leakage-tolerant circuit operates on un-encoded inputs and outputs (the input encoding function simply returns the inputs, concatenated with masking inputs), where any leakage on the computation can be simulated by related leakage *on the inputs and outputs alone*. (Leakage on the inputs and outputs is unavoidable since these are provided to the circuit "in the clear".) Formally,

Definition 10 (LTCC (for BCL)). *Let $t, \epsilon(t), \mathsf{S}(n)$ be as in Definition 7, let $n, k \in \mathbb{N}$ be input and output length parameters (respectively), and let $\mathcal{L}_{\mathrm{BCL}}^t$ be the family of t-BCL functions. We say that a pair $(\mathsf{Comp}, \mathsf{E})$ is an $(\mathcal{L}_{\mathrm{BCL}}^t, \epsilon(t), \mathsf{S}(n))$-leakage-tolerant circuit-compiler (LTCC) if $\mathsf{Comp}, \mathsf{E}$ have the syntax of Definition 6, and satisfy the following properties for some negligible function $\epsilon(t) = \mathsf{negl}(t)$:*

- **Correctness.** *For any arithmetic circuit C, and input x for C, $\Pr\left[\hat{C}(\hat{x}) = C(x)\right] \ge 1 - \epsilon(t)$, where $\hat{x} \leftarrow \mathsf{Enc}(x, 1^t, 1^{|C|})$.*

– *(Oblivious) leakage-tolerance. There exists a partition $\mathcal{P} = ((n_1, n_2), (k_1, k_2))$ of input and output lengths, and a PPT algorithm* Sim *such that the following holds for all sufficiently large $t \in \mathbb{N}$, all $n, k \in \mathbb{N}$, every arithmetic circuit $C : \mathbb{F}^n \to \mathbb{F}^k$ of size at most* S (n), *and every $\ell \in \mathcal{L}_{\mathrm{BCL}}^t$ of input length $\cdot |\hat{C}|$.* Sim *is given C, and outputs a view translation circuit $\mathcal{T} = (\mathcal{T}_1, \mathcal{T}_2)$ such that for every $(x_1, x_2) \in \mathbb{F}^{n_1} \times \mathbb{F}^{n_2}$,*

$$\mathsf{SD}\left(\ell\left(\mathcal{T}_1\left(x_1, C\left(x_1, x_2\right)_1\right), \mathcal{T}_2\left(x_2, C\left(x_1, x_2\right)_2\right)\right), \ell\left[\hat{C}, (\hat{x}_1, \hat{x}_2)\right] \right) \leq \epsilon\left(t\right)$$

where $C\left(x_1, x_2\right) = \left(C\left(x_1, x_2\right)_1, C\left(x_1, x_2\right)_2\right) \in \mathbb{F}^{k_1} \times \mathbb{F}^{k_2}$.

We use a recent result of Bitansky et al. [8], that show a general transformation from LRCCs with a strong simulation guarantee against OCL, to LTCCs. Recently, Dachman-Soled et al. [13] observed that the DF-LRCC has this strong simulation property, namely the transformation can be applied directly to the DF-LRCC.[8] The final LTCC will use the following circuit $C^{\mathrm{LR-DF}}$:

Definition 11. *Let $t \in \mathbb{N}$ be a security parameter, and let $r = r\left(t\right)$ denote the maximal length of masking inputs used by a gadget of Construction 6. For an arithmetic circuit $C : \mathbb{F}^n \to \mathbb{F}^k$ containing $+$ and $\times$ gates, defined the circuit $C^{\mathrm{LR-DF}} : \mathbb{F}^{n+r(t)\cdot(n+|C|)} \to \mathbb{F}^k$ as follows:*

– *The input $(x = (x_1, \cdots, x_n), \boldsymbol{m}) \in \mathbb{F}^n \times \left(\mathsf{supp}\left(\mathsf{Enc}_{\mathrm{DF}}^{\mathsf{In}}\left(0, 1^t\right)\right)\right)^{|C|+n}$ of $C^{\mathrm{LR-DF}}$ is interpreted as an input x for C, and a collection $\boldsymbol{m}$ of masking inputs for gadgets.*
– *Every gate of C is replaced with the corresponding gadget (as defined in Construction 6), and gadgets corresponding to output gates are followed by decoding sub-circuits (computing the decoding algorithm $\mathsf{Dec}_{\mathsf{IP}}$ of the inner product encoding of Definition 9). The masking inputs used in the gadgets are taken from $\boldsymbol{m}$ (every masking input in $\boldsymbol{m}$ is used at most once).*
– *Following each input gate x_i, an encoding sub-circuit (with some fixed, arbitrary randomness hard-wired into it) is added, computing the inner-product encoding of x_i.*
– *A refresh gadget is added following every encoding sub-circuit, where the masking inputs used in the gadgets are taken from $\boldsymbol{m}$.*

We now describe the LTCC of [15]. To simplify the notations and constructions, we define the LTCC only for circuits operating on pairs of inputs.

Construction 3 (LTCC, [15] and [8]). *Let $t, t_{\mathsf{In}} \in \mathbb{N}$, and $n \in \mathbb{N}$ be an input length parameter. Let $\mathsf{S} : \mathbb{N}^4 \to \mathbb{N}$ be a length function whose value is set below. The LTCC $\left(\mathsf{Comp}^{\mathrm{DF}}, \mathsf{E}^{\mathrm{DF}}\right)$ is defined as follows:*

---

[8] We note that though Bitansky et al. [8] construct leakage-tolerant circuits based on the DF-LRCC, since they are interested in obtaining UC-security against continuous leakage, they use a more complex variant of the LRCC. We prefer to use the DF-LRCC directly, since it suffices for our needs, and gives a much simpler construction.

– $\mathsf{E}^{\mathrm{DF}} = \left(\mathsf{Enc}^{\mathrm{DF}}, \mathsf{Dec}^{\mathrm{DF}}\right)$, *where:*

  • *For every* $x \in \mathbb{F}^n$, $\mathsf{Enc}^{\mathrm{DF}}\left(x, 1^t, 1^{t_{\mathrm{ln}}}\right) = \left(x, \left(\mathsf{Enc}^{\mathrm{In}}_{\mathrm{DF}}\left(0, 1^t\right)\right)^{2t_{\mathrm{ln}}}\right)$, *where*
    $\left(\mathsf{Enc}^{\mathrm{In}}_{\mathrm{DF}}\left(0, 1^t\right)\right)^k$ *denotes* k *random and independent evaluations of*
    $\mathsf{Enc}^{\mathrm{In}}_{\mathrm{DF}}\left(0, 1^t\right)$.
  • $\mathsf{Dec}^{\mathrm{DF}}\left((x, \boldsymbol{m}), 1^t, 1^{t_{\mathrm{ln}}}\right) = x$.
– $\mathsf{Comp}^{\mathrm{DF}}$, *on input an arithmetic circuit* $C : \mathbb{F}^{n_L} \times \mathbb{F}^{n_R} \to \mathbb{F}^k$, *outputs the*
  circuit $C^{\mathrm{DF}} : \mathbb{F}^{2n_R + n_L + \mathsf{S}(t, n_L, n_R, |C|)} \to \mathbb{F}^k$ *constructed as follows:*
  • *Construct a circuit* $C_1 : \mathbb{F}^{n_R} \times \mathbb{F}^{n_R} \to \mathbb{F}^{n_R}$ *that evaluates the function*
    $f_1(x, y) = x + y$. *Denote* $s_1 = |C_1|$, *and let* C_1' *be the circuit obtained from*
    C_1 *by the transformation of Definition 11. (Notice that if* y *is uniformly*
    random then C_1' *outputs a one-time pad encryption of* x.*)*
  • *Construct the circuit* $C_2 : \mathbb{F}^{n_L + n_R} \times \mathbb{F}^{n_R} \to \mathbb{F}^k$ *such that* $C_2((z, c), y) =$
    $C(c + y, z)$. *Denote* $s_2 = |C_2|$, *and let* C_2' *be the circuit obtained from* C_2
    by the transformation of Definition 11. (Notice that if c *is a one-time pad*
    encryption of some value x *with pad* y, *then* C_2' *emulates* C *on* x *and* z.*)*
  • *Let* $r = r(t)$ *denote the total length of masking inputs used by a gadget of*
    Construction 6. Then $\mathsf{S} = \mathsf{S}(t, n_L, n_R, |C|) = r(t) \cdot (s_1 + s_2 + n_L + 4n_R)$.
    (Notice that S *is the number of masking inputs used in* C_1' *and* C_2'.*)*
  • $C^{\mathrm{DF}}(x, y, z) = C_2'(z, (C_1'(x, y)), y)$. *(Intuitively,* C^{DF} *first uses* C_1' *to*
    encrypt x *with pad* y, *and then evaluates* C_2' *on the encryption output by*
    C_1', z *and pad* y.*)*

We note that the correctness error of the LTCC of Theorem 3.2 might be abused by malicious parties (e.g., a malicious ZK prover in Sect. 4.1, or malicious parties in Sect. 6) to violate the correctness of the computation, which we overcome by checking whether a correctness error occurred, as described in the following remark.

Remark 1 (Dealing with gadget failures). We will actually use a modified version of Construction 3, in which C^{DF} also computes an error flag, indicating whether the computation failed in one of its gadget (i.e., failed in *all* t *copies of the gadget*, see Remark 3). More specifically, each of the two parties implementing the gadget computes *in the clear* a flag indicating whether its encoding of the output is a valid encoding (i.e., all entries are non-zero), and each party locally combines the flags it generated for all the gadgets. This additional computation is needed since malicious parties (e.g., a malicious prover in the leakage-secure ZK circuit of Construction 4) may *not* choose the masking inputs at random, and might generate them in a "smart" way which will *always* cause gadgets to fail.

We note that thought these flags are generated in the clear, they do not violate the leakage-tolerance property of Construction 3. The reason is these flags are generated locally (by each of the parties), and so could be generated by the leakage function from the simulated wire values which the LT simulator (of Definition 10) generates. This observation gives a reduction from any t-BCL function on the modified circuit to a t-BCL function on the *original* circuit, and so when using Construction 3 as a building block, we will implicitly disregard these additional wires (remembering that any leakage on the modified circuit *with* the flags can be generated by related leakage on the original circuit). Finally, we note that in an honest execution the flag is set only with negligible probability (and so the fact that the flag is computed in the clear does not violate leakage-resilience).

Remark 2. To combine Construction 3 with Construction 2, we assume that Construction 3 is implemented using a boolean circuit (implementing group operations via operations over $\mathbb{F}_2$) that operates over a standard basis.

Dziembowski and Faust (Corollary 2 in the full version of [15]) show that the DF-LRCC resists OCL leakage, which by the result of [8] implies the existence of an LTCC against such leakage. Combined with Lemma 2 below (which shows a relation between OCL and BCL), we have the following:

Theorem 8 ([15] and [8], and Lemma 2). *Let $t \in \mathbb{N}$ be a leakage bound, and $n, k \in \mathbb{N}$ be input and output length parameters. Then for every polynomial $p(t)$ there exist a finite field $\mathbb{F}$ of size $\Omega(t)$, and a negligible function $\epsilon(t) = \mathsf{negl}(t)$ for which there exists an $\left(\mathcal{L}_{\mathrm{BCL}}^{\tilde{t}}, \epsilon(t), p(t) \right)$-LTCC, where $\tilde{t} = 0.16t \log_2 |\mathbb{F}| - 1 - \log_2 |\mathbb{F}|$, and $\mathcal{L}_{\mathrm{BCL}}^{T}$ is the family of all $\tilde{t}$-BCL functions.*

Theorem 8 relies on the next lemma (whose proof appears in Appendix A) which states that security against so-called "only computation leaks" (OCL) implies security against BCL. (One can also show that $2t$-BCL implies resilience against t-OCL.) Recall that in the context of OCL, the wires of the leakage-resilient circuit $\widehat{C}$ are divided according to some partition $\mathcal{P}$, into two "parts" $\widehat{C}_L, \widehat{C}_R$. The input encodings of $\widehat{C}$ are also divided into two parts, e.g., an encoding $\widehat{x}$ is divided into $\widehat{x}_L$ (which is the input of $\widehat{C}_L$) and $\widehat{x}_R$ (which constitutes the input to $\widehat{C}_R$) The adversary can (adaptively) pick functions $f_1^L, \cdots, f_{n_L}^L$, and $f_1^R, \cdots, f_{n_R}^R$ for some $n_L, n_R \in \mathbb{N}$, where the combined output lengths of $f_1^L, \cdots, f_{n_L}^L$ (and $f_1^R, \cdots, f_{n_R}^R$) is at most t. In the execution of $\widehat{C}$ on $\widehat{x}$, the adversary is given $f_i^L \left[\widehat{C}_L, \widehat{x}_L \right], 1 \leq i \leq n_L$ and $f_i^R \left[\widehat{C}_R, \widehat{x}_R \right], 1 \leq i \leq n_R$, and chooses the next leakage functions based on previous leakage. The output of the leakage is taken to be the combined outputs of all leakage functions $f_1^L, \cdots, f_{n_L}^L, f_1^R, \cdots, f_{n_R}^R$. We say that a circuit is $(\mathcal{L}_{\mathrm{OCL}}^t, \epsilon)$-leakage-resilient with relation to the partition $\mathcal{P} = \left(\widehat{C}_L, \widehat{C}_R \right)$, if the real-world output of the OCL functions can be efficiently simulated (given only the description of the circuit, and its outputs if $\widehat{C}$ computes the outputs in the clear), and the statistical distance between the actual and simulated wire values is at most ϵ. (We refer the reader to, e.g., [15] for a more formal definition of OCL.) We note that we allow the adversary to leak on the two components of the computation in an arbitrary order, a notion which is sometimes referred to as "OCL+".

Lemma 2 (OCL+-resilience implies BCL-resilience). *Let $\epsilon \in (0,1)$ be an error bound, $t \in \mathbb{N}$ be a leakage bound, and C be a boolean circuit. If C is $(\mathcal{L}_{OCL}^t, \epsilon)$-leakage-resilient with relation to partition $\mathcal{P}$, then C is also $(\mathcal{L}, \epsilon)$-leakage-resilient for the family $\mathcal{L}$ of all t-BCL functions with relation to the same partition $\mathcal{P}$.*

The following property of Construction 3 will be used to guarantee correctness of our constructions in the presence of malicious parties (see Appendix A for the proof).

Lemma 3 (Ill-formed masking inputs correspond to additive attacks). *Let $S : \mathbb{N}^4 \to \mathbb{N}$ be the length function from Definition 11. Then Construction 3 has the following property. For every circuit $C : \mathbb{F}^{n_L} \times \mathbb{F}^{n_R} \to \mathbb{F}^k$, every security parameter $t \in \mathbb{N}$, and every $\mathsf{m} \in \mathbb{F}^{S(t,n_L,n_R,|C|)}$, there exists an additive attack $\mathcal{A}_\mathsf{m}$ on C such that for every $x \in \mathbb{F}^{n_L + n_R}$, and every $\hat{x} = (x, \mathsf{m})$ it holds that $C^{DF}(\hat{x}) = C^{\mathcal{A}_\mathsf{m}}(x)$. Moreover, there exists a PPT algorithm Alg such that $\mathsf{Alg}(\mathsf{m}) = \mathcal{A}_\mathsf{m}$.*

4   Leakage-Secure Zero-Knowledge

In this section we describe our leakage-secure zero-knowledge circuits. At a high level, an $\mathcal{L}$-secure ZK circuit for a family $\mathcal{L}$ of functions is a randomized algorithm Gen that given an error parameter ϵ, and an input length n, outputs a randomized *prover input encoder* Enc_P, and a circuit T. T takes an input from a *prover* P, and returns output to a *verifier* V, and is used by P to convince V that $x \in L_\mathcal{R}$. T guarantees soundness, and zero-knowledge even when V obtains leakage from $\mathcal{L}$ on the internals of T.

Definition 12 ($\mathcal{L}$-secure ZK circuit). *Let $\mathcal{R} = \mathcal{R}(x, w)$ be an NP-relation, $\mathcal{L}$ be a family of functions, and $\epsilon > 0$ be an error parameter. We say that Gen is an $\mathcal{L}$-secure zero-knowledge (ZK) circuit if the following holds.*

- *Syntax. Gen is a deterministic algorithm that has input $\epsilon, 1^n$, runs in time $\mathrm{poly}(n, \log(1/\epsilon))$, and outputs (Enc_P, T) defined as follows. Enc_P is a randomized circuit that on input (x, w) such that $|x| = n$ (x is the input, and w is the witness) outputs the prover input y for T; and T is a randomized circuit that takes input y and returns $z \in \{0, 1\}^{n+1}$.*
- *Correctness. For every $\epsilon > 0$, every $n \in \mathbb{N}$ and every $(x, w) \in \mathcal{R}$ such that $|x| = n$, $\Pr[T(\mathsf{Enc}_P(x, w)) = (x, 1)] \geq 1 - \epsilon$, where $(\mathsf{Enc}_P, T) \leftarrow \mathsf{Gen}(\epsilon, 1^n)$, and the probability is over the randomness used by Enc_P, T.*
- *Soundness. For every (possibly malicious, possibly unbounded) prover P^*, every $\epsilon > 0$, every $n \in \mathbb{N}$, and any $x \notin L_\mathcal{R}$ such that $|x| = n$, $\Pr[T(P^*(x)) = (x, 1)] \leq \epsilon$, where $(\mathsf{Enc}_P, T) \leftarrow \mathsf{Gen}(\epsilon, 1^n)$, and the probability is over the randomness used by P^*, T.*
- *$\mathcal{L}$-Zero-knowledge. For $(x, w) \in \mathcal{R}$ we define the following experiments.*

- For a (possibly malicious, possibly unbounded) verifier V^*, define the experiment $\mathsf{Real}_{V^*,\mathsf{Gen}}(x,w,\epsilon)$ where V^* has input x,ϵ, and chooses a leakage function $\ell \in \mathcal{L}$, and $\mathsf{Real}_{V^*,\mathsf{Gen}}(x,w,\epsilon) = (T(\mathsf{Enc}_P(x,w)),\ell[T,\mathsf{Enc}_P(x,w)])$, where $(\mathsf{Enc}_P,T) \leftarrow \mathsf{Gen}(\epsilon,1^n)$, and $[T,y]$ denotes the wires of T when evaluated on y.
- For a simulator algorithm Sim that has input x,ϵ, and one-time oracle access to ℓ, the experiment $\mathsf{Ideal}_{\mathsf{Sim},\mathcal{R}}(x,w,\epsilon)$ is defined as follows: $\mathsf{Ideal}_{\mathsf{Sim},\mathcal{R}}(x,w,\epsilon) = \mathsf{Sim}^\ell(\epsilon,x)$, where $\mathsf{Sim}^\ell(\epsilon,x)$ is the output of Sim, given one-time oracle access to ℓ.

We say that Gen has $\mathcal{L}$-zero-knowledge ($\mathcal{L}$-ZK) if for every (possibly malicious, possibly unbounded) verifier V^* there exists a simulator Sim such that for every $\epsilon > 0$, every $n \in \mathbb{N}$, and every $(x,w) \in \mathcal{R}$ such that $|x| = n$, $\mathsf{SD}(\mathsf{Real}_{V^*,\mathsf{Gen}}(x,w,\epsilon),\mathsf{Ideal}_{\mathsf{Sim},\mathcal{R}}(x,w,\epsilon)) \leq \epsilon$.

4.1   The Leakage-Secure ZK Circuit

We now construct the leakage-secure ZK circuit by combining the LRCC $\left(\mathsf{Comp}^{\mathrm{GIMSS}}, \mathsf{E}^{\mathrm{GIMSS}}_{\mathsf{Inp}}, \mathsf{Dec}^{\mathrm{GIMSS}}_{\mathsf{Out}}\right)$ of Theorem 7 with the LTCC $\left(\mathsf{Comp}^{\mathrm{DF}}, \mathsf{E}^{\mathrm{DF}}\right)$ of Theorem 8.

At a high level, we compile the verification circuit $C_\mathcal{R}$ of an NP-relation $\mathcal{R}$ using $\mathsf{Comp}^{\mathrm{GIMSS}}$, where the prover provides the encoded input and witness for the compiled circuit $\hat{C}_\mathcal{R}$. $\hat{C}_\mathcal{R}$ has encoded outputs, and only guarantees that BCL leakage cannot distinguish between the executions on two different witnesses. To achieve full-fledged ZK, we use $\mathsf{Comp}^{\mathrm{DF}}$ to decode the outputs of $\hat{C}_\mathcal{R}$. Recall that circuits compiled with $\mathsf{Comp}^{\mathrm{DF}}$ have masking inputs, and moreover, their leakage-tolerance property crucially relies on the fact that the masks are *unknown to the leakage function*. Therefore, these masking inputs must be provided by the prover as part of the input encoding (which is generated using Enc_P). However, since the correctness of the computation is guaranteed *only when the masking inputs are well-formed*, a malicious prover P^* can violate soundness by providing ill-formed masking inputs (which were *not* drawn according to the "right" distribution), and thus modify the computed functionality, and potentially cause the circuit to accept $x \notin L_\mathcal{R}$. As discussed in Sect. 3.2, the effect of ill-formed masking inputs corresponds to applying an additive attack on the original decoding circuit, so we can protect against such attacks by first replacing the decoding circuit with an AMD circuit.

Construction 4 (Leakage-secure ZK circuit). *Let $n \in \mathbb{N}$ be an input length parameter, $t \in \mathbb{N}$ be a security parameter, and $c \in \mathbb{N}$ be a constant. Let $\mathcal{R} = \mathcal{R}(x,w)$ be an NP-relation, with verification circuit $C_\mathcal{R}$ of size $s = |C_\mathcal{R}|$. The leakage-secure ZK circuit uses the following building blocks (where any field operations are implemented via bit operations).*

- *The LRCC $\left(\mathsf{Comp}^{\mathrm{GIMSS}}, \mathsf{E}^{\mathrm{GIMSS}}_{\mathsf{In}} = \left(\mathsf{Enc}^{\mathrm{GIMSS}}_{\mathsf{In}}, \mathsf{Dec}^{\mathrm{GIMSS}}_{\mathsf{In}}\right), \mathsf{Dec}^{\mathrm{GIMSS}}_{\mathsf{Out}}\right)$ of Theorem 7 (Construction 2), and its underlying small-bias encoding scheme $\left(\mathsf{Enc}^\oplus : \mathbb{F}_2 \times \mathbb{F}_2^c \to \mathbb{F}_2^{2c}, \mathsf{Dec}^\oplus : \mathbb{F}_2^{2c} \to \mathbb{F}_2^2\right)$.*

- The LTCC $\left(\mathsf{Comp}^{\mathrm{DF}}, \mathsf{E}^{\mathrm{DF}}\right)$ of Theorem 8 (Construction 3) over a field $\mathbb{F} = \Omega(t)$, and its underlying encoding scheme $\mathsf{E}_{\mathrm{DF}}^{\mathsf{In}} = \left(\mathsf{Enc}_{\mathrm{DF}}^{\mathsf{In}}, \mathsf{Dec}_{\mathrm{DF}}^{\mathsf{In}}\right)$.
- The additively-secure circuit compiler $\mathsf{Comp}^{\mathsf{add}}$ of Theorem 4.
- The AMD encoding scheme $\left(\mathsf{Enc}^{\mathsf{amd}}, \mathsf{Dec}^{\mathsf{amd}}\right)$ of Theorem 5, with encodings of length $\hat{n}^{\mathsf{amd}}(n, t)$.

On input $1^n, 1^t$, Gen outputs (Enc_P, T) defined as follows.

- For every input $x \in \{0,1\}^n$, and witness w, $\mathsf{Enc}_P(x, w) = (\mathsf{Enc}_{\mathrm{GIMSS}}((x, w), 1^t), \mathsf{Enc}_{\mathrm{DF}}^{\mathsf{In}}(0^{s'}, 1^t))$ for a parameter s' whose value is set below.
- Let n_w be a bound on the maximal witness length for inputs of length n. T is obtained by concatenating the decoding component T'' to the verification component C'' (namely, applying T'' to the outputs of C'') which are defined next.

  1. **The verification component C''.** Define $C' : \mathbb{F}_2^{n+n_w} \to \mathbb{F}_2^{n+1}$ as $C'(x, w) = (x, C_\mathcal{R}(x, w))$. Let C_2' denote the circuit that emulates C', but replaces each output bit with (the bit string representation of) the bit as an element of $\mathbb{F}$. Then $C'' = \mathsf{Comp}^{\mathrm{GIMSS}}(C_2')$.

  2. **The decoding component.**
     - Construct the circuit $C^{\mathsf{amd}} : \mathbb{F}^{2c \cdot t \cdot (n+1)} \to \mathbb{F}^{\hat{n}^{\mathsf{amd}}(n+1, t)}$ that operates as follows:
       * Decodes its input using $\mathsf{Dec}_{\mathrm{Out}}^{\mathrm{GIMSS}}$ to obtain the output (f, x, z).
       * If $f = 1$, $x \notin \{0,1\}^n$, or $z \neq 1$, then C^{amd} sets $z' = 0$. Otherwise, it sets $z' = 1$.
       * Generates $e \leftarrow \mathsf{Enc}^{\mathsf{amd}}((x, z'), 1^t)$, and outputs e.
     - Generate $\widehat{C}^{\mathsf{amd}} = \mathsf{Comp}^{\mathsf{add}}(C^{\mathsf{amd}})$.
     - Generate $T' = \mathsf{Comp}^{\mathrm{DF}}(\widehat{C}^{\mathsf{amd}})$. Let s' denote the number of masking inputs used in T'.
     - Construct the circuit T'' that on input y, operates as follows:
       * Computes $(f_L, f_R, e) = T'(y)$. (Recall that f_L, f_R are flags indicating whether a gadget of T' has failed.)
       * Computes $(f, x, z) = \mathsf{Dec}^{\mathsf{amd}}(e, 1^t)$, where $f, z \in \mathbb{F}$ and $x \in \mathbb{F}^n$. If $f = f_L = f_R = 0$, $x \in \{0,1\}^n$, and $z = 1$ then T' outputs $(x, 1)$. Otherwise, it outputs 0^{n+1}.

We show in the full version [20] that Construction 4 is a leakage-secure ZK circuit, proving Theorems 1 and 2 (for Theorem 1, we have the prover provide the masking inputs used for the computation in C''', while the verifier provides the randomness used in T'').

5   Multiparty LRCCs: Definition

In this section we define the notion of multiparty LRCCs, a generalization of leakage-secure ZK circuits to evaluation of general functions with $m \geq 1$ parties. We first formalize the notion of secure computation with a single piece of trusted (but leaky) hardware device, where security with abort holds in the presence of adversaries that corrupt a subset of parties, and obtain leakage (from a pre-defined leakage class) on the internals of the device. This raises the following points.

1. The output should include a flag signaling whether there was an abort.
2. Leakage on the wires of the device should reveal nothing about the internal computations, or the inputs of the honest parties, other than what can be computed from the output. This necessitates randomized computation.
3. The inputs should be encoded, otherwise leakage on the input wires may reveal information that cannot be computed from the outputs. This should be contrasted with the ZK setting, in which x is assumed to be public, and so when all parties are honest the output is $(x, 1)$ and can therefore be computed in the clear.

To guarantee that an adversary that only obtains leakage on the internals of the device (but does not corrupt any parties) learns nothing about the inputs or internal computations, the outputs must be encoded. Therefore, the device, which is implemented as a circuit, is associated with an input encoding algorithm Enc, and an output decoding algorithm Dec. The above discussion is formalized in the next definition.

Definition 13 (Secure function implementation). *Let* $m \in \mathbb{N}$, $f : (\{0,1\}^n)^m \to \{0,1\}^k$ *be an m-argument function,* $\mathcal{L}$ *be a family of leakage functions, and* $\epsilon > 0$. *We say that* (Enc, C, Dec) *is an m-party* $(\mathcal{L}, \epsilon)$-*secure implementation of* f *if it satisfies the following requirements.*

- **Syntax:**
  - Enc : $\{0,1\}^n \to \{0,1\}^{\hat{n}}$ *is a randomized function, called the input encoder.*
  - $C : (\{0,1\}^{\hat{n}})^m \to \{0,1\}^{\hat{k}}$ *is a randomized circuit.*
  - Dec : $\{0,1\}^{\hat{k}} \to \{0,1\}^{k+1}$ *is a deterministic function called the output decoder.*
- **Correctness.** *For every* $x_1, \cdots, x_m \in \{0,1\}^n$,

$$\Pr\left[\mathsf{Dec}\left(C\left(\mathsf{Enc}\left(x_1\right), \cdots, \mathsf{Enc}\left(x_m\right)\right)\right) = (0, f\left(x_1, \cdots, x_m\right))\right] \geq 1 - \epsilon.$$

- **Security.** *For every adversary* $\mathcal{A}$ *there exists a simulator* Sim *such that for every input* $(x_1, \cdots, x_m) \in (\{0,1\}^n)^m$, *and every leakage function* $\ell \in \mathcal{L}$, SD (Real, Ideal) $\leq \epsilon$, *where* Real, Ideal *are defined as follows.*
  Real:
  - $\mathcal{A}$ *picks a set* $\mathsf{B} \subset [m]$ *of corrupted parties, and (possibly ill-formed) encoded inputs* $x'_i \in \{0,1\}^{\hat{n}}$ *for every* $i \in \mathsf{B}$.
  - *For every uncorrupted party* $j \notin \mathsf{B}$, *let* $x'_j = \mathsf{Enc}(x_j)$.
  - *If* $\mathsf{B} \neq \emptyset$ *then* $z = (C(x'_1, \cdots, x'_m), \mathsf{Dec}(C(x'_1, \cdots, x'_m)))$, *otherwise* z *is empty. (Intuitively,* z *represents the information* $\mathcal{A}$ *has about the output of* C. *If* $\mathsf{B} = \emptyset$ *then* $\mathcal{A}$ *learns nothing.)*
  - Real $= \left(\mathsf{B}, \{x'_i\}_{i \in \mathsf{B}}, \ell\left[C, (x'_1, \cdots, x'_m)\right], z\right)$.

Ideal:

- Sim *picks a set* $B \subset [m]$ *of corrupted parties and receives their inputs* $\{x_i\}_{i \in B}$. Sim *then chooses effective inputs* $w_i \in \{0,1\}^n$ *for every* $i \in B$, *and if* $B \neq \emptyset$ *obtains* $f(w_1 \cdots, w_m)$, *where* $w_j = x_j$ *for every* $j \notin B$.
- Sim *chooses* $b \in \{0,1\}$. *(Intuitively, b indicates whether to abort the computation.)*
- *If* $B \neq \emptyset$ *and* $b = 0$, *set* $y = (0, f(w_1, \cdots, w_m))$, *if* $B \neq \emptyset$ *and* $b = 1$, *set* $y = (1, 0^k)$, *and if* $B = \emptyset$ *then* y *is empty.*
- *Let* $(W, \{x_i'\}_{i \in B})$ *denote the output of* Sim, *where* W *contains a bit for each wire of* C, *and* $x_i' \in \{0,1\}^{\hat{n}}$ *for every* $i \in B$. *Denote the restriction of* W *to the output wires by* W_{Out}.
- *If* $B \neq \emptyset$, *let* $z = (W_{\mathsf{Out}}, y)$. *Otherwise, z is empty.*
- Ideal $= (B, \{x_i'\}_{i \in B}, \ell(W), z)$.

We say that (Enc, C, Dec) *is a* passive-secure *implementation of* f *if the security property holds with the following modifications: (1) $\mathcal{A}$ does not choose x_i', $i \in B$, and instead, $x_i' \leftarrow$ Enc (x_i) for every $i \in B$; and (2)* Sim *always chooses $b = 0$.*

We now define an m-party LRCC which, informally, is an asymptotic version of Definition 13.

Definition 14 (m-party circuit). *Let* $m \in \mathbb{N}$. *We say that a boolean circuit* C *is an m-party circuit if its input can be partitioned into m equal-length strings, i.e., $C : (\{0,1\}^n)^m \to \{0,1\}^k$ for some $n, k \in \mathbb{N}$.*

Definition 15 (Multiparty LRCCs and passive-secure multiparty LRCCs). *Let* $m \in \mathbb{N}$, $\mathcal{L}$ *be a family of leakage functions,* $\mathsf{S}(n)$ *be a size function, and* $\epsilon(n) : \mathbb{N} \to \mathbb{R}^+$. *Let* Comp *be a PPT algorithm that on input m, and an m-party circuit $C : (\{0,1\}^n)^m \to \{0,1\}^k$, outputs a circuit $\hat{C}$.*

We say that (Enc, Comp, Dec) *is an m-party $(\mathcal{L}, \epsilon(n), \mathsf{S}(n))$-leakage-resilient circuit compiler (m-party LRCC, or multiparty LRCC) if there exists a PPT simulator* Sim *such that for all sufficiently large n's, and every m-party circuit $C : (\{0,1\}^n)^m \to \{0,1\}^k$ of size at most $\mathsf{S}(n)$ that computes a function f_C,* $(\text{Enc}, \hat{C}, \text{Dec})$ *is an $(\mathcal{L}, \epsilon(n))$-secure implementation of f_C, where the security property holds with simulator* Sim *that is given the description of C, and has black-box access to the adversary. We say that* (Enc, Comp, Dec) *is a passively-secure m-party $(\mathcal{L}, \epsilon(n), \mathsf{S}(n))$-LRCC if* $(\text{Enc}, \hat{C}, \text{Dec})$ *is an $(\mathcal{L}, \epsilon(n))$-passively-secure implementation of f_C, where security holds with simulator* Sim.

Remark 1. *Definitions 13–15 naturally extend to the arithmetic setting in which C is an arithmetic circuit over a finite field $\mathbb{F}$. When discussing the arithmetic setting, we explicitly state the field over which we are working (e.g., we use "multiparty LRCC over $\mathbb{F}$" to denote that the multiparty LRCC is in the arithmetic setting with field $\mathbb{F}$).*

6   A Multiparty LRCC

In this section we construct a multiparty LRCC that withstands active adversaries. The high-level idea of the construction is as follows. Given an m-party protocol C, we first replace it with a circuit C^{share} that emulates C but outputs a secret-sharing of the outputs, then compile C^{share} using the LRCC of [25]. We then refresh each of the shares using a circuit C_{Dec}. However, to guarantee leakage-resilience, and correctness of the computation in the presence of actively-corrupted parties, we first replace the circuit C_{Dec} with its additively-secure version C'_{Dec}, then compile C'_{Dec} using the LTCC of [15] to obtain a leakage-tolerant circuit $\widehat{C}'_{\text{Dec}}$. We use m copies of $\widehat{C}'_{\text{Dec}}$, where the i'th copy refreshes the i'th secret share, using masking inputs provided by the i'th party. Each party provides, as its input encoding to the device, both a leakage-resilient encoding of its input, and the masking inputs needed for the computation in $\widehat{C}_{\text{Dec}}$. The output decoder decodes each of the secret shares, and reconstructs the output from the shares (unless it detects that one of the parties provided ill-formed masking inputs, in which case the computation aborts). This is formalized in the next construction.

Construction 5 (Multiparty LRCC). *Let $m \in \mathbb{N}$ denote the number of parties, $t \in \mathbb{N}$ be a security parameter, $n \in \mathbb{N}$ be an input length parameter, $k \in \mathbb{N}$ be an output length parameter, and $c \in \mathbb{N}$ be a constant. The m-party LRCC uses the following building blocks:*

- *The LRCC $\left(\text{Comp}^{\text{GIMSS}}, \text{E}^{\text{GIMSS}}_{\text{In}} = \left(\text{Enc}^{\text{GIMSS}}_{\text{In}}, \text{Dec}^{\text{GIMSS}}_{\text{In}}\right), \text{Dec}^{\text{GIMSS}}_{\text{Out}}\right)$ of Theorem 7 (Construction 2), where the outputs of the leakage-resilient circuit are encoded by the encoding scheme $\left(\text{Enc}_{\text{GIMSS}} : \mathbb{F}_2 \to \mathbb{F}^{4ct}_2, \text{Dec}_{\text{GIMSS}} : \mathbb{F}^{4ct}_2 \to \mathbb{F}^2_2\right)$.*

- *The LTCC $\left(\text{Comp}^{\text{DF}}, \text{E}^{\text{DF}}\right)$ of Theorem 8 (Construction 3) over a field $\mathbb{F} = \Omega(t)$, and its underlying encoding scheme $\text{E}^{\text{In}}_{\text{DF}} = \left(\text{Enc}^{\text{In}}_{\text{DF}}, \text{Dec}^{\text{In}}_{\text{DF}}\right)$ that outputs encodings of length $\hat{n}^{\text{DF}}(n, t)$.*

- *The additively-secure circuit compiler Comp^{add} of Theorem 4.*

The m-party LRCC $(\text{Enc}, \text{Comp}, \text{Dec})$ is defined as follows.

- *For every $n, t, t_{\text{In}} \in \mathbb{N}$ and every $x \in \mathbb{F}^n$, $\text{Enc}\left(x, 1^t, 1^{t_{\text{In}}}\right) = \left(\text{Enc}^{\text{GIMSS}}_{\text{In}}\left(x, 1^t, 1^{t_{\text{In}}}\right), \text{Enc}^{\text{DF}}_{\text{In}}\left(0^{t_{\text{In}}}, 1^t\right)\right)$.*

- *For every $y = \left(\left(f^1_L, f^1_R, y^1\right), \cdots, \left(f^m_L, f^m_R, y^m\right)\right) \in \left(F^{2+2tc(k+1)}\right)^m$, $\text{Dec}\left(y, 1^t\right)$ computes $\left(f_i, z^i\right) = \text{Dec}^{\text{Out}}_{\text{GIMSS}}\left(y^i, 1^t\right)$. If $f^i_L = f^i_R = f_i = 0$ for all $1 \le i \le m$ then Dec outputs $\left(0, \sum^m_{i=1} z^i\right)$, otherwise it outputs $\left(1, 0^k\right)$. (Intuitively, each triplet $\left(f^i_L, f^i_R, y^i\right)$ consists of a pair of flags output by the LTCC, indicating whether the computation in one of its gadgets failed; and an encoding of a flag, concatenated with an additive secret share of the output.)*

- *Comp on input $m \in \mathbb{N}$, and an m-party circuit $C : \left(\mathbb{F}^n\right)^m \to \mathbb{F}^k$:*

  1. Constructs the circuit $C^{\text{share}} : \left(\mathbb{F}^n\right)^m \to \mathbb{F}^{mk}$ that operates as follows:

- *Evaluates C on inputs $x_1, \cdots, x_m$ to obtain the output $y = C(x_1, \cdots, x_m)$.*
- *Generates $y_1, \cdots, y_{m-1} \in_R \mathbb{F}^k$, and sets $y_m = y \oplus \sum_{i=1}^{m-1} y_i$. ($y_1, \cdots, y_m$ are random additive secret shares of y.)*
- *For every $1 \leq i \leq m$, generates y_i' by replacing each bit of y_i with (the bit string representation of) the bit as an element of $\mathbb{F}$.*
- *Outputs $(y_1', \cdots, y_m')$.*

2. *Computes $C' = \mathsf{Comp}^{\mathrm{GIMSS}}(C^{\mathsf{share}})$.*
3. *Construct the circuit $C^{\mathsf{Dec}} : \mathbb{F}^{4ct(k+1)} \to \mathbb{F}^{4ct(k+1)}$ that operates as follows:*
   - *Decodes its input using $\mathsf{Dec}_{\mathsf{Out}}^{\mathrm{GIMSS}}$ to obtain a flag $f \in \mathbb{F}_2$ and output $z \in \mathbb{F}^k$.*
   - *If $f = 1$, sets $z' = 0^k$, otherwise $z' = z$.*
   - *Generates $e \leftarrow \mathsf{Enc}_{\mathrm{GIMSS}}((f, z'), 1^t)$, and outputs e.*
4. *Generate $\widehat{C}^{\mathsf{amd}} = \mathsf{Comp}^{\mathsf{add}}(C^{\mathsf{Dec}})$.*
5. *Generate $C'' = \mathsf{Comp}^{\mathrm{DF}}(\widehat{C}^{\mathsf{amd}})$.*
6. *Outputs the circuit $\widehat{C}$ obtained by concatenating a copy of C'' to each of the m outputs of C'. (We note that the i'th copy of C'' takes its masking inputs from the encoding of the i'th input to $\widehat{C}$.)*

The next theorem (whose proof appears in the full version [20]) states that Construction 5 is a multiparty LRCC.

Theorem 9 (Multiparty LRCC). *Let $n, k \in \mathbb{N}$ be input and output length parameters, $\mathbf{S}(n) : \mathbb{N} \to \mathbb{N}$ be a size function, $\epsilon(n), \epsilon'(n) : \mathbb{N} \to (0, 1)$ be error functions, $t \in \mathbb{N}$ be a leakage bound, let $c \in \mathbb{N}$ be a constant, and let $\mathsf{m} \in \mathbb{N}$ denote the number of parties. Let $\mathcal{L}$ denote the family of all t-BCL functions. If:*

- *$\left(\mathsf{Comp}^{\mathrm{GIMSS}}, \mathsf{Enc}_{\mathsf{In}}^{\mathrm{GIMSS}}, \mathsf{Dec}_{\mathsf{Out}}^{\mathrm{GIMSS}}\right)$ is an $(\mathcal{L}, \epsilon, \mathbf{S}(n) + 2m)$-relaxed LRCC with abort, where for security parameter t, $\mathsf{Dec}_{\mathsf{Out}}^{\mathrm{GIMSS}}, \mathsf{Enc}_{\mathrm{GIMSS}}$ can be evaluated using circuits of size $s^{\mathrm{GIMSS}}(t)$,*
- *$\mathsf{Comp}^{\mathsf{add}}$ is an $\epsilon'(n)$-additively-secure circuit compiler over $\mathbb{F}$, where there exist: (1) $B : \mathbb{N} \to \mathbb{N}$ such that for any circuit C, $\mathsf{Comp}^{\mathsf{add}}(C)$ has size at most $B(|C|)$; and (2) a PPT algorithm Alg' that given an additive attack $\mathcal{A}$ outputs the ideal attack $\left(\mathsf{a}^{\mathsf{in}}, \mathcal{A}^{\mathsf{Out}}\right)$ (whose existence follows from the additive-attack security property of Definition 3), and*
- *$\left(\mathsf{Comp}^{\mathrm{DF}}, \mathsf{E}^{\mathrm{DF}}\right)$ is an $\left(\mathcal{L}, \epsilon, B\left(2s^{\mathrm{GIMSS}}(t) + ck\right)\right)$-LTCC.*

Then Construction 5 is an m-party $(\mathcal{L}, (2m+1)\epsilon(n) + \epsilon'(n) + \mathsf{negl}(t), \mathbf{S}(n))$-LRCC.

Moreover, if on input a circuit of size s, $\mathsf{Comp}^{\mathrm{GIMSS}}, \mathsf{Comp}^{\mathrm{DF}}$ output circuits of size $\widehat{s}^{\mathrm{GIMSS}}(s)$, and $s^{\mathrm{DF}}(s)$, respectively, then on input a circuit C of size s, the compiler of Construction 5 outputs a circuit $\widehat{C}$ of size $\widehat{s}^{\mathrm{GIMSS}}(s + 2m) + s^{\mathrm{DF}}\left(B\left(2s^{\mathrm{GIMSS}}(t) + ck\right)\right)$.

In the full version, we use Theorem 9 to prove Theorem 3. We also provide a (somewhat) more efficient MPCC construction for passive corruptions.

Acknowledgments. This work was supported in part by the 2017–2018 Rothschild Postdoctoral Fellowship; by the Warren Center for Network and Data Sciences; by the financial assistance award 70NANB15H328 from the U.S. Department of Commerce, National Institute of Standards and Technology; and by the Defense Advanced Research Project Agency (DARPA) under Contract #FA8650-16-C-7622. The second author was supported in part by NSF-BSF grant 2015782, BSF grant 2012366, ISF grant 1709/14, ERC grant 742754, DARPA/ARL SAFEWARE award, NSF Frontier Award 1413955, NSF grants 1619348, 1228984, 1136174, and 1065276, a Xerox Faculty Research Award, a Google Faculty Research Award, an equipment grant from Intel, and an Okawa Foundation Research Grant. This material is based upon work supported by the DARPA through the ARL under Contract W911NF-15-C-0205. The views expressed are those of the authors and do not reflect the official policy or position of the DoD, the NSF, or the U.S. Government. This work was supported in part by NSF grants CNS-1314722, CNS-1413964.

A   Gadgets for the LRCC of [15]

In this section we describe the gadgets used in the LRCC of [15], and prove Lemmas 2 and 3.

Construction 6 (Gadgets for an LRCC, [15]). *Let $\mathbb{F}$ be a finite field, and $E_{\mathsf{IP}} = (\mathsf{Enc}_{\mathsf{IP}}, \mathsf{Dec}_{\mathsf{IP}})$ denote the inner product encoding over $\mathbb{F}$ of Definition 9. Each gadget consists of a* left component C^L, *and a* right component C^R *that are connected to each other. We use the term "X is sent from component Y to component Z" to denote that the value X computed in component Y is the input to some sub-computation performed in component Z.*

1. **Refresh gadget:**[9] *inputs* $(a^L, a^R) \in \mathsf{Enc}_{\mathsf{IP}}(a, 1^{t^2})$ *for* $a \in \mathbb{F}$, *and masking inputs* $((r^{L,1}, r^{L,2}), (r^{R,1}, r^{R,2})) \in \mathsf{Enc}_{\mathsf{DF}}^{\mathsf{In}}(0, 1^{t^2})$; *outputs* $(a^{L\prime}, a^{R\prime}) \in \mathsf{Enc}_{\mathsf{IP}}(a, 1^{t^2})$.
    - (a) C^L *generates* $b \in \mathbb{F}^{t^2}$ *such that* $b_i = (a_i^L)^{-1} \times r_i^{L,1}$ *for every* $1 \le i \le t^2$, *and sends* b *to* C^R.
    - (b) C^R *computes* $c \in \mathbb{F}^{t^2}$ *such that* $c_i = b_i \times r_i^{R,1}$ *for every* $1 \le i \le t^2$.
    - (c) C^R *computes* $a^{R\prime} = a^R + c$.
    - (d) C^R *generates* $d \in \mathbb{F}^{t^2}$ *such that* $d_i = (a_i^{R\prime})^{-1} \times r_i^{R,2}$ *for every* $1 \le i \le t^2$, *and sends* d *to* C^L.
    - (e) C^L *computes* $e \in \mathbb{F}^{t^2}$ *such that* $e_i = d_i \times r_i^{L,2}$ *for every* $1 \le i \le t^2$.
    - (f) C^L *computes* $a^{L\prime} = a^L + e$.
2. **Multiplication by constant gadget:** *inputs constant* $c \in \mathbb{F} \setminus \{0\}$, *and* $(a^L, a^R) \in \mathsf{Enc}_{\mathsf{IP}}(a, 1^t)$ *for* $a \in \mathbb{F}$; *output* $(b^L, b^R) \in \mathsf{Enc}_{\mathsf{IP}}(c \times a, 1^t)$.
    - (a) C^L *computes* $b_i^L = c \times a_i^L$ *for every* $1 \le i \le t$.
    - (b) C^R *sets* $b^R = a^R$.

---

[9] This refresh gadget is a simpler construction than the original gadget of [15], due to [1].

3. **Addition by constant gadget:** inputs constant $c \in \mathbb{F}$, and $\left(a^L, a^R\right) \in$ $\mathsf{Enc}_{\mathsf{IP}}\left(a, 1^t\right)$ for $a \in \mathbb{F}$; output $\left(b^L, b^R\right) \in \mathsf{Enc}_{\mathsf{IP}}\left(c + a, 1^t\right)$.
   (a) C^L sets $b^L = a^L$, and sends a_1^L to C^R.
   (b) C^R sets $b^R = a^R + \left(\left(a_1^L\right)^{-1} \times c, 0, \cdots, 0\right)$.

4. **Generalized multiplication gadget:** inputs a constant $c \in \mathbb{F}$, $\left(a^L, a^R\right) \in \mathsf{Enc}_{\mathsf{IP}}\left(a, 1^t\right), \left(b^L, b^R\right) \in \mathsf{Enc}_{\mathsf{IP}}\left(b, 1^t\right)$ for $a, b \in \mathbb{F}$, and masking inputs $\left(\left(r^{L,1}, r^{L,2}\right), \left(r^{R,1}, r^{R,2}\right)\right) \in \mathsf{Enc}_{\mathsf{DF}}^{\mathsf{In}}\left(0, 1^t\right)$; output $\left(c^L, c^R\right) \in \mathsf{Enc}_{\mathsf{IP}}\left(c - a \times b, 1^t\right)$.

   (a) C^L generates a $t \times t$ Matrix $\boldsymbol{L} = \boldsymbol{a}^L \left(\boldsymbol{b}^L\right)^T = \left(a_i^L \times b_j^L\right)_{i,j \in [t]}$. We interpret L as a length-t^2 vector.

   (b) C^R enerates a $t \times t$ Matrix $\boldsymbol{R} = \boldsymbol{a}^R \left(\boldsymbol{b}^R\right)^T = \left(a_i^R \times b_j^R\right)_{i,j \in [t]}$. We interpret R as a length-t^2 vector.

   (c) C^L, C^R evaluate the Refresh gadget with inputs $\boldsymbol{L}, \boldsymbol{R}$, and masking inputs $\left(\left(r^{L,1}, r^{L,2}\right), \left(r^{R,1}, r^{R,2}\right)\right)$, to obtain $\boldsymbol{L}', \boldsymbol{R}'$ (which are length-t^2 vectors).
   (d) C^L sends $L_1', L_{t+1}', \cdots L_{t^2}'$ to C^R.
   (e) C^R computes $d = \langle \left(L_{t+1}', \cdots L_{t^2}'\right), \left(R_{t+1}', \cdots, R_{t^2}'\right)\rangle$.
   (f) C^R computes $c^R = -\left(R_1', \cdots, R_t'\right) + \left(\left(L_1'\right)^{-1}\left(c - d\right), 0, \cdots, 0\right)$.
   (g) C^L computes $c^L = \left(L_1', \cdots, L_t'\right)$.

Remark 3 (Amplifying correctness). The execution in each gadget can fail (if the generated encodings are not valid inner-product encodings). However, [15] show that for $|\mathbb{F}| = \Omega\left(t\right)$, if each computation step is implemented using t copies of the corresponding gadget (and the output of the computation step is set to the output of the first gadget whose output is valid), then each computation step succeeds except with $\mathsf{negl}\left(t\right)$ probability. In what follows, we implicitly assume that each computation step is implemented using this amplification technique over t gadgets.

We now prove Lemmas 2 and 3.

Proof (of Lemma 2 (sketch)). Let ℓ be a t-BCL function that corresponds to a two party protocol Π, defined in relation to partition $\mathcal{P}$. Let $\mathsf{NextMsg}_L, \mathsf{NextMsg}_R$ be the next-message functions defining the messages the parties send, given their current view, and assume without loss of generality that the left party sends the first message in the protocol. Let $(\widehat{x}_L, \widehat{x}_R)$ be the input on which $\widehat{C}$ is evaluated, and denote $\mathcal{W}_L = \left[\widehat{C}_L, \widehat{x}_L\right]$, and $\mathcal{W}_R = \left[\widehat{C}_R, \widehat{x}_R\right]$.

To generate the transcript of Π, the adversary operates as follows. First, it picks $f_1^L\left(z\right) = \mathsf{NextMsg}_L\left(z\right)$. Then, given $f_1^L\left(\mathcal{W}_L\right)$, which is the first message that the left party sends in Π, it picks f_1^R to be the function which $\mathsf{NextMsg}_R$ computes, conditioned on the event that $f_1^L\left(\mathcal{W}_L\right)$ was the first message which the right party received, and sends f_1^R, to be evaluated on $\mathcal{W}_R$. The adversary continues in this way until all messages of Π have been computed. Since Π is

t-bounded, then in particular each of the two participating parties sends at most t bits, namely the leakage functions we have defined leak at most t bits on each of $\mathcal{W}_L, \mathcal{W}_R$. Therefore, the t-OCL resilience of C guarantees that the leakage can be efficiently simulated, up to statistical distance ϵ.

Proof (of Lemma 3). We analyze the effect of ill-formed masking inputs m in the gadgets of Construction 6, and show that they correspond to applying an additive attack on the underlying gate.

- **Refresh gadget.** Denote $m = \langle \mathbf{r}^{L,1}, \mathbf{r}^{R,1} \rangle + \langle \mathbf{r}^{L,2}, \mathbf{r}^{R,2} \rangle$ (which, if the masking inputs are ill-formed, may not be 0). Then the output of the gadget encodes the value $\langle \mathbf{a}^{L\prime}, \mathbf{a}^{R\prime} \rangle$. We analyze this value. $\langle \mathbf{a}^{L\prime}, \mathbf{a}^{R\prime} \rangle = \sum_{i=1}^{t^2} a_i^{L\prime}, a_i^{r\prime}$ which, by the definition of $\mathbf{a}^{L\prime}, \mathbf{a}^{L\prime}$ is equal to

$$\sum_{i=1}^{t^2} \left(a_i^L + e_i \right) \left(a_i^R + c_i \right) = \sum_{i=1}^{t^2} a_i^L a_i^R + \sum_{i=1}^{t^2} e_i \left(a_i^R + c_i \right) + \sum_{i=1}^{t^2} a_i^L c_i$$

$$= a + \sum_{i=1}^{t^2} e_i a_i^{R\prime} + \sum_{i=1}^{t^2} a_i^L c_i$$

which, by the definition of $\mathbf{c}, \mathbf{e}$, is equal to

$$a + \sum_{i=1}^{t^2} \left(a_i^{R\prime} \right)^{-1} r_i^{R,2} r_i^{L,2} a_i^{R\prime} + \sum_{i=1}^{t^2} a_i^L \left(a_i^{L,1} \right)^{-1} r_i^{L,1} r_i^{R,1} = a + \langle \mathbf{r}^{L,1}, \mathbf{r}^{R,1} \rangle + \langle \mathbf{r}^{L,2}, \mathbf{r}^{R,2} \rangle$$

which is equal to $a + m$. Moreover, notice that m can be efficiently computed from $\mathbf{r}^{L,1}, \mathbf{r}^{R,1}, \mathbf{r}^{L,2}, \mathbf{r}^{R,2}$ by computing $\langle \mathbf{r}^{L,1}, \mathbf{r}^{R,1} \rangle + \langle \mathbf{r}^{L,2}, \mathbf{r}^{R,2} \rangle$.

- **Generalized multiplication gadget.** Denote $m = \langle \mathbf{r}^{L,1}, \mathbf{r}^{R,1} \rangle + \langle \mathbf{r}^{L,2}, \mathbf{r}^{R,2} \rangle$. The output of the gadget encodes the value $\langle \mathbf{c}^L, \mathbf{c}^R \rangle = \sum_{i=1}^{t} c_i^L c_i^R$ which, by the definition of $\mathbf{c}^L, \mathbf{c}^R$, is equal to

$$L_1' \left(-R_1' + \left(L_1' \right)^{-1} (c - d) \right) + \sum_{i=2}^{t} L_i' \cdot \left(-R_i' \right) = c - \sum_{i=1}^{t} L_i' R_i' - d = c - \sum_{i=1}^{t^2} L_i' R_i' - m$$

which is equal to $c - a \times b - m$ (the rightmost equality follows from the analysis of the refresh gadget).

- **Multiplication and addition by constant gadgets.** Notice that these gadget do not use any masking inputs, and so the computation in these gadgets is always correct (corresponds to computation under the all-zeros attack).

References

1. Andrychowicz, M.: Efficient refreshing protocol for leakage-resilient storage based on the inner-product extractor. arXiv preprint arXiv:1209.4820 (2012)
2. Andrychowicz, M., Dziembowski, S., Faust, S.: Circuit compilers with $O(1/\log(n))$ leakage rate. In: Fischlin, M., Coron, J.-S. (eds.) EUROCRYPT 2016. LNCS, vol. 9666, pp. 586–615. Springer, Heidelberg (2016). doi:10.1007/978-3-662-49896-5_21

3. Battistello, A., Coron, J.-S., Prouff, E., Zeitoun, R.: Horizontal side-channel attacks and countermeasures on the ISW masking scheme. In: Gierlichs, B., Poschmann, A.Y. (eds.) CHES 2016. LNCS, vol. 9813, pp. 23–39. Springer, Heidelberg (2016). doi:10.1007/978-3-662-53140-2_2

4. Ben-Or, M., Goldwasser, S., Wigderson, A.: Completeness theorems for non-cryptographic fault-tolerant distributed computation (extended abstract). In: STOC 1988, pp. 1–10. ACM (1988)

5. Bitansky, N., Canetti, R., Chiesa, A., Tromer, E.: From extractable collision resistance to succinct non-interactive arguments of knowledge, and back again. In: ITCS 2012, pp. 326–349 (2012)

6. Bitansky, N., Canetti, R., Goldwasser, S., Halevi, S., Kalai, Y.T., Rothblum, G.N.: Program obfuscation with leaky hardware. In: Lee, D.H., Wang, X. (eds.) ASI-ACRYPT 2011. LNCS, vol. 7073, pp. 722–739. Springer, Heidelberg (2011). doi:10.1007/978-3-642-25385-0_39

7. Bitansky, N., Canetti, R., Halevi, S.: Leakage-tolerant interactive protocols. In: Cramer, R. (ed.) TCC 2012. LNCS, vol. 7194, pp. 266–284. Springer, Heidelberg (2012). doi:10.1007/978-3-642-28914-9_15

8. Bitansky, N., Dachman-Soled, D., Lin, H.: Leakage-tolerant computation with input-independent preprocessing. In: Garay, J.A., Gennaro, R. (eds.) CRYPTO 2014. LNCS, vol. 8617, pp. 146–163. Springer, Heidelberg (2014). doi:10.1007/978-3-662-44381-1_9

9. Boyle, E., Garg, S., Jain, A., Kalai, Y.T., Sahai, A.: Secure computation against adaptive auxiliary information. In: Canetti, R., Garay, J.A. (eds.) CRYPTO 2013. LNCS, vol. 8042, pp. 316–334. Springer, Heidelberg (2013). doi:10.1007/978-3-642-40041-4_18

10. Boyle, E., Goldwasser, S., Jain, A., Kalai, Y.T.: Multiparty computation secure against continual memory leakage. In: STOC 2012, pp. 1235–1254 (2012)

11. Chaum, D., Crépeau, C., Damgård, I.: Multiparty unconditionally secure protocols (extended abstract). In: FOCS 1988, pp. 11–19 (1988)

12. Cramer, R., Dodis, Y., Fehr, S., Padró, C., Wichs, D.: Detection of algebraic manipulation with applications to robust secret sharing and fuzzy extractors. In: Smart, N. (ed.) EUROCRYPT 2008. LNCS, vol. 4965, pp. 471–488. Springer, Heidelberg (2008). doi:10.1007/978-3-540-78967-3_27

13. Dachman-Soled, D., Liu, F.-H., Zhou, H.-S.: Leakage-resilient circuits revisited – optimal number of computing components without leak-free hardware. In: Oswald, E., Fischlin, M. (eds.) EUROCRYPT 2015. LNCS, vol. 9057, pp. 131–158. Springer, Heidelberg (2015). doi:10.1007/978-3-662-46803-6_5

14. Duc, A., Dziembowski, S., Faust; S.: Unifying leakage models: from probing attacks to noisy leakage. In: Nguyen, P.Q., Oswald, E. (eds.) EUROCRYPT 2014. LNCS, vol. 8441, pp. 423–440. Springer, Heidelberg (2014). doi:10.1007/978-3-642-55220-5_24

15. Dziembowski, S., Faust, S.: Leakage-resilient circuits without computational assumptions. In: Cramer, R. (ed.) TCC 2012. LNCS, vol. 7194, pp. 230–247. Springer, Heidelberg (2012). doi:10.1007/978-3-642-28914-9_13

16. Faust, S., Rabin, T., Reyzin, L., Tromer, E., Vaikuntanathan, V.: Protecting circuits from leakage: the computationally-bounded and noisy cases. In: Gilbert, H. (ed.) EUROCRYPT 2010. LNCS, vol. 6110, pp. 135–156. Springer, Heidelberg (2010). doi:10.1007/978-3-642-13190-5_7

17. Genkin, D., Ishai, Y., Polychroniadou, A.: Efficient multi-party computation: from passive to active security via secure SIMD circuits. In: Gennaro, R., Robshaw, M. (eds.) CRYPTO 2015. LNCS, vol. 9216, pp. 721–741. Springer, Heidelberg (2015). doi:10.1007/978-3-662-48000-7_35

18. Genkin, D., Ishai, Y., Prabhakaran, M., Sahai, A., Tromer, E.: Circuits resilient to additive attacks with applications to secure computation. In: STOC 2014, pp. 495–504 (2014)

19. Genkin, D., Ishai, Y., Weiss, M.: Binary AMD circuits from secure multiparty computation. In: Hirt, M., Smith, A. (eds.) TCC 2016. LNCS, vol. 9985, pp. 336–366. Springer, Heidelberg (2016). doi:10.1007/978-3-662-53641-4_14

20. Genkin, D., Ishai, Y., Weiss, M.: How to construct a leakage-resilient (stateless) trusted party. IACR Cryptology ePrint Archive (2017). http://eprint.iacr.org/2017/926

21. Goldreich, O.: The Foundations of Cryptography - Volume 1, Basic Techniques. Cambridge University Press, Cambridge (2001)

22. Goldreich, O., Micali, S., Wigderson, A.: How to play any mental game or a completeness theorem for protocols with honest majority. In: STOC 1987, pp. 218–229. ACM (1987)

23. Goldwasser, S., Rothblum, G.N.: Securing computation against continuous leakage. In: Rabin, T. (ed.) CRYPTO 2010. LNCS, vol. 6223, pp. 59–79. Springer, Heidelberg (2010). doi:10.1007/978-3-642-14623-7_4

24. Goldwasser, S., Rothblum, G.N.: How to compute in the presence of leakage. In: FOCS 2012, pp. 31–40 (2012)

25. Goyal, V., Ishai, Y., Maji, H.K., Sahai, A., Sherstov, A.A.: Bounded-communication leakage resilience via parity-resilient circuits. In: FOCS 2016, pp. 1–10 (2016)

26. Ishai, Y., Sahai, A., Wagner, D.: Private circuits: securing hardware against probing attacks. In: Boneh, D. (ed.) CRYPTO 2003. LNCS, vol. 2729, pp. 463–481. Springer, Heidelberg (2003). doi:10.1007/978-3-540-45146-4_27

27. Ishai, Y., Weiss, M., Yang, G.: Making the best of a leaky situation: zero-knowledge PCPs from leakage-resilient circuits. In: Kushilevitz, E., Malkin, T. (eds.) TCC 2016. LNCS, vol. 9563, pp. 3–32. Springer, Heidelberg (2016). doi:10.1007/978-3-662-49099-0_1

28. Juma, A., Vahlis, Y.: Protecting cryptographic keys against continual leakage. In: Rabin, T. (ed.) CRYPTO 2010. LNCS, vol. 6223, pp. 41–58. Springer, Heidelberg (2010). doi:10.1007/978-3-642-14623-7_3

29. Kocher, P., Jaffe, J., Jun, B.: Differential power analysis. In: Wiener, M. (ed.) CRYPTO 1999. LNCS, vol. 1666, pp. 388–397. Springer, Heidelberg (1999). doi:10.1007/3-540-48405-1_25

30. Kocher, P.C.: Timing attacks on implementations of Diffie-Hellman, RSA, DSS, and other systems. In: Koblitz, N. (ed.) CRYPTO 1996. LNCS, vol. 1109, pp. 104–113. Springer, Heidelberg (1996). doi:10.1007/3-540-68697-5_9

31. Micali, S., Reyzin, L.: Physically observable cryptography. In: Naor, M. (ed.) TCC 2004. LNCS, vol. 2951, pp. 278–296. Springer, Heidelberg (2004). doi:10.1007/978-3-540-24638-1_16

32. Miles, E., Viola, E.: Shielding circuits with groups. In: STOC 2013, pp. 251–260 (2013)

33. Quisquater, J.-J., Samyde, D.: Electromagnetic analysis (EMA): measures and counter-measures for smart cards. In: Attali, I., Jensen, T. (eds.) E-smart 2001. LNCS, vol. 2140, pp. 200–210. Springer, Heidelberg (2001). doi:10.1007/3-540-45418-7_17

34. Rothblum, G.N.: How to compute under $\mathcal{AC}^0$ leakage without secure hardware. In: Safavi-Naini, R., Canetti, R. (eds.) CRYPTO 2012. LNCS, vol. 7417, pp. 552–569. Springer, Heidelberg (2012). doi:10.1007/978-3-642-32009-5_32
35. Santis, A., Micali, S., Persiano, G.: Non-interactive zero-knowledge proof systems. In: Pomerance, C. (ed.) CRYPTO 1987. LNCS, vol. 293, pp. 52–72. Springer, Heidelberg (1988). doi:10.1007/3-540-48184-2_5
36. Weiss, M.: Secure computation and probabilistic checking. Ph.D. thesis (2016)
37. Yao, A.C.-C.: How to generate and exchange secrets (extended abstract). In: FOCS 1986, pp. 162–167 (1986)

Blockwise p-Tampering Attacks on Cryptographic Primitives, Extractors, and Learners

Saeed Mahloujifar[✉] and Mohammad Mahmoody

University of Virginia, Charlottesville, USA
{saeed,mohammad}@virginia.edu

Abstract. Austrin et al. [1] studied the notion of bitwise p-tampering attacks over randomized algorithms in which an efficient 'virus' gets to control each bit of the randomness with independent probability p in an online way. The work of [1] showed how to break certain 'privacy primitives' (e.g., encryption, commitments, etc.) through bitwise p-tampering, by giving a bitwise p-tampering *biasing* attack for increasing the average $\mathbb{E}[f(U_n)]$ of any efficient function $f\colon \{0,1\}^n \mapsto [-1,+1]$ by $\Omega(p \cdot \mathrm{Var}[f(U_n)])$.

In this work, we revisit and extend the bitwise tampering model of [1] to *blockwise* setting, where blocks of randomness becomes tamperable with independent probability p. Our main result is an efficient blockwise p-tampering attack to bias the average $\mathbb{E}[f(\overline{X})]$ of any efficient function f mapping arbitrary $\overline{X}$ to $[-1,+1]$ by $\Omega(p \cdot \mathrm{Var}[f(\overline{X})])$ *regardless* of how $\overline{X}$ is partitioned into individually tamperable blocks $\overline{X} = (X_1, \dots, X_n)$. Relying on previous works of [1,19,36], our main biasing attack immediately implies efficient attacks against the privacy primitives as well as seedless multi-source extractors, in a model where the attacker gets to tamper with each block (or source) of the randomness with independent probability p. Further, we show how to increase the classification error of deterministic learners in the so called 'targeted poisoning' attack model under Valiant's adversarial noise. In this model, an attacker has a 'target' test data d in mind and wishes to increase the error of classifying d while she gets to tamper with each training example with independent probability p an in an online way.

1 Introduction

In this work, we study *tampering* attacks that efficiently manipulate the *randomness* of randomized algorithms with adversarial goals in mind. Tampering attacks could naturally be studied in the context of cryptographic algorithms that (wish to) access perfectly uniform and untampered randomness for sake of

S. Mahloujifar—Supported by University of Virginia's SEAS Research Innovation Award.

M. Mahmoody—Supported by NSF CAREER award CCF-1350939, and University of Virginia's SEAS Research Innovation Award.

Y. Kalai and L. Reyzin (Eds.): TCC 2017, Part II, LNCS 10678, pp. 245–279, 2017.
https://doi.org/10.1007/978-3-319-70503-3_8

achieving security. However, the scope of such attacks goes beyond the context of cryptography and could be studied more broadly for any class of algorithms that depend on some form of untampered random input and try to achieve specific goals (e.g., learning algorithms using untampered training data to generate a hypothesis). Here, we are interested in understanding the power and limitations of such tampering attacks over the randomness, when the adversary can tamper with, or even control, $\approx p$ fraction of the randomness.[1]

The most relevant to our study here is the work of Austrin et al. [1] that introduced the notion of *bitwise p-tampering* attacks on the randomness of cryptographic primitives. In this model, the adversary generates an efficient 'virus' who gets into the 'infected' device, can read everything, but is limited in what it can alter. As the stream of bits of randomness $R = (r_1, \ldots, r_n)$ is being generated, for every bit r_i, the p-tampering virus gets to change r_i with independent probability p (i.e., with probability $(1-p)$ the bit remains unchanged). p-tampering attacks are online, so the virus does not know the future incoming bits, but it can base its decisions based on the history of the (potentially tampered) bits. The work of [1] proved that bitwise p-tampering attacks can always increase the average of efficient bounded functions $f \colon \{0,1\}^n \mapsto [-1,+1]$ by $\Omega(p \cdot \mathrm{Var}[f(U_n)])$ where $\mathrm{Var}[f(U_n)]$ is the variance of $f(U_n)$.

Austrin et al. [1] showed how to break a variety of 'privacy' cryptographic primitives (e.g., public-key and private key encryption, zero knowledge, commitments, etc.) that have 'indistinguishability-based' security games using their main efficient bitwise p-tampering biasing attack. In such cryptographic attacks, the *code* of the p-tampering virus is generated by an outside adversary who only knows the public information (e.g. public key). Previously, Dodis et al. [19] had shown that for the same cryptographic primitives, there are high-min-entropy Santha-Vazirani sources of randomness [39] that make them insecure. Thus, the work of [1] was a strengthening of the results of [19] showing how to generate such 'bad' SV sources through efficient p-tampering attacks. The p-tampering attacks of [1], and in particular their core attack for biasing the output of balanced bounded functions, crucially depend on the fact that the attacker can tamper with *every single bit* of the randomness *independently* with probability p. However, randomness is usually generated in blocks rather than bits [4,16,21,28], e.g., during the boot time [30], and is also made available to the algorithms requesting them in blocks. Thus, it is indeed natural to consider tampering attackers who sometimes get to change an incoming *block* of randomness.

Blockwise p-tampering attacks. In this work, we revisit the bitwise p-tampering model of [1] and extend it to a setting where the tampering could happen over blocks. Suppose A is an algorithm taking $\overline{X} = (X_1 \times \cdots \times X_n)$ as input where $\overline{X}$ is a distribution consisting of n blocks and the i'th block is independently sampled from the distribution X_i. For example, A could be a cryptograhpic algorithm in which X_i is the i'th block of *uniform* randomness given to A. Or A could also be a learning algorithm given n i.i.d training examples. Roughly speaking, a

---

[1] Note that if the adversary can control all the randomness, we are effectively back to what we can do in the deterministic setting.

blockwise p-tampering attack on (the randomness of) A is an algorithm Tam work-ing as follows. Suppose we sample the blocks $x_i \leftarrow X_i$ one by one. Then the i'th block x_i becomes 'tamperable' with independent probability p for each i, and it remains intact with probability $1 - p$. In case x_i becomes tamperable, then Tam could substitute x_i with another value x'_i in the support set[2] of X_i in an online way. Namely, when Tam gets the chance to tamper with x_i it could decide on a new block x'_i based on the knowledge of previous (tampered) blocks. The tamper-ing algorithm Tam could also depend on (and thus know everything about) the algorithm A including all of its inputs selected so far, but it cannot write anything except when it is given the chance to tamper with a block of randomness.

Different p-tampering attackers could pursue different goals. For example, as it was done in the bitwise setting of [1], a p-tampering attack might aim to 'signal out' a secret information (e.g., the plain-text). Another example is when Tam wants to increase the classification error of the hypothesis output by a learner A where each block $x_i = (d, t)$ consists of a labeled example sampled from the same distribution.

We also note that, though called primarily a tampering attack, p-tampering attacks are not blind tampering attackers and naturally rely on the knowledge of the previous random bits before deciding on the tampering of the next bit/block, although such knowledge is only given to the tampering virus, and e.g., not the external adversary generating the code of the virus. That is a reason why the proven power of p-tampering attacks in this work is not in contradiction with known *positive* results such as [18, 24, 26, 32] that guarantee tamper resilience.

1.1 Our Results

Our main result is a generalization of the biasing attack of [1] to the blockwise setting. We first describe this result, and then we will describe some of the applications of this biasing attack.

Theorem 1 (Informally stated). *Let $\overline{X} = (X_1 \times \cdots \times X_n)$ be a product distribution where each of X_i's is efficiently samplable. For any efficient function $f\colon \mathrm{Supp}(\overline{X}) \mapsto [-1, +1]$ there is an efficient blockwise p-tampering attack that increases the average of f over a sampled input by at least $\Omega(p) \cdot \mathrm{Var}[f(\overline{X})]$.*

See Theorem 4 for a formalization. Similarly to [1], we also prove a variant of Theorem 1 for the special case of Boolean functions, but with better parame-ters (see Theorem 5). However, some of the applications of this biasing lemma (e.g., for attacking cryptographic primitives, or attacking learning algorithms with non-Boolean cost/loss functions) we need to use the non-Boolean attack of Theorem 1.

Our main biasing p-tampering attack on bounded functions even applies to the settings where $\overline{X}$ is *not* a product distribution. In that case, we assume

---

[2] We only allow the tampering algorithm to produce something in the support set. A more general definition allows the tampering algorithm to make choices out of the support set, however, our restriction only makes our attacks stronger.

that $\overline{X}$ is sampled in a 'stateful' way, and that the next block X_i is sampled conditioned on adversary's choices of blocks. This extension allows our model to include previous special models of p-tampering attacks against random walks on graphs [3].

We also prove some applications for our main biasing attack that rely on the *blockwise* nature of it. In addition to obtaining attacks against the security of cryptographic primitives as well as multi-source randomness extractors through blockwise p-tampering, we also demonstrate applications beyond cryptography. In particular, by relying on the power of biasing attacks over *non-uniform* distributions, we show how to attack and increase the error of *learning* algorithms that output classifiers, through an attack that injects a p fraction of adversarial data in an online way. In what follows we briefly discuss each of these applications.

Attacks on Randomness of Cryptographic Primitives. As mentioned, the bitwise p-tampering attack of [1] for biasing functions was at the core of their attacks breaking the security of cryptographic primitives by tampering with their randomness. By using our biasing attack of Theorem 1 we immediately obtain blockwise attacks against the same primitives. This time, our attacks work *regardless* of how randomness is packed into blocks, and is also 'robust' in the sense that the attack succeeds even if the tampering probabilities $p_1, p_2, \ldots$ are *not* equal so long as $p \leq p_i$ for all i.[3]

Corollary 1 (Informal). *Let $\mathcal{P}$ be one of the following primitives. CPA secure public-key or private-key encryption, efficient-prover zero-knowledge proofs for **NP**, commitment schemes, or two party computation where only one party gets the output. Then there is an efficient blockwise p-tampering attack that breaks the security of $\mathcal{P}$ with advantage $\Omega(p)$. In particular, the attack succeeds even if the length of the tampered randomness blocks are* unknown *a priori and only become clear during the attack.*

The above theorem could be obtained by plugging in our biasing attack of Theorem 1 into the proofs of [1].

Achieving security against blockwise p-tampering? In addition to presenting the power of bitwise p-tampering attacks, the work of [1] also showed how to achieve secure protocols against bitwise p-tampering attacks for 'forging-based' primitives such as signatures for $p = 1/\mathrm{poly}(\kappa)$ where κ is the security parameter. For the same primitives, when we move to the blockwise setting, whether or not achieving positive (secure) results is possible *depends* on the block sizes of the tampering attack. For example, if the *whole* randomness of the key generation algorithm of a signature scheme becomes tamperable as a single

---

[3] In fact, we observe that the bitwise p-tampering attack of [1] is also robust, but proving robustness becomes more challenging for our blockwise p-tampering attack. Moreover, we believe robustness is an important feature for cryptographic attacks and so worth to be studied explicitly, as some attacks, e.g., the reduction from bitwise to blockwise p-tampering (Please see the full version for the proof.), are not necessarily robust.

block (with probability $p \geq 1/\mathrm{poly}(\kappa)$) the adversary can choose an insecure key. On the other hand, if all the blocks are of constant size (or even of size $o(\lg \kappa)$) similar arguments to those in [1] could be used to make 'forging-based' primitives secure for any $p \leq \kappa^{-\Omega(1)}$.

Efficient Attacks for Biasing Extractors. Our blockwise p-tampering attacks for biasing functions are natural tools for 'biasing attacks' against (seedless) randomness extractors from block sources.

Biasing Multi-source Seedless Extractors. We can directly use our p-tampering attacks against *any* specific, multi-source, seedless randomness extractors [12,39,43]. Namely, suppose f is an efficient seedless extractor who takes n blocks of randomness $(x_1, \ldots, x_n) \leftarrow (X_1 \times \cdots \times X_n)$ where the distribution X_i belongs to a class of randomness source. Then, for any choice of samplable $\overline{X} = (X_1, \ldots, X_n)$, Theorem 5 gives an efficient p-tampering attacker who could transform the distribution $\overline{X}$ into $\overline{Y}$ such that $|\mathbb{E}[f(\overline{Y})]| \geq \Omega(p)$. Note that the interesting aspect of $\overline{Y}$ is that it is identical to $\overline{X}$ in ($\approx 1 - p$) fraction of the blocks. In particular, as we will see, our attacker of Theorem 1 has the property that upon tampering with each block, all it does is to either leave as is or 'resample' it once.

The second application of our p-tampering attacks against extractors is different in the sense that instead of attacking extractors when unbiased extraction is possible, it gives an alternative algorithmic proof for a known impossibility result [6,19,22,36] regarding block Santha-Vazirani sources [39]. Below, by $U_i^j = U_i \times \cdots \times U_i$ we refer to j blocks each consisting of i uniform bits.

Impossibility of Randomness Extraction from SV Sources. The celebrated work of Santha and Vazirani [39] proved a strong negative result about deterministic randomness extraction from sources with high min-entropy. An SV source (see Definition 7) is a joint distribution $(X_1, \ldots, X_n)$ over $\{0,1\}^n$ with the guarantee that every bit is δ-close to uniform even if we condition on all the previous bits. In particular, [39] proved that for any deterministic (supposedly extractor) function $f \colon \{0,1\}^n \mapsto \{+1, -1\}$, there is always an δ-SV source $\overline{X} = (X_1, \ldots, X_n)$ such that $|\mathbb{E}[f(\overline{X})]| \geq \Omega(\delta)$. The work of Reingold et al. [36] gave an elegant simple proof for this result using the so called 'half-space' sources, and this idea found its way into the work of Dodis et al. [19] where they generalized the result of [39] to *block* sources [13]. A (ℓ, k)-block SV source is a sequence of blocks of length ℓ bits such that each block has min-entropy at least k conditioned on previous blocks (see Definition 8).

Even though p-tampering attacks do *not* generate block-SV sources with 'high' min-entropy in general, we show that the *specific* p-tampering attacker of our Theorem 1 does indeed generate an $(\ell, \ell - p)$ block-SV source. As a result, we get an alternative proof for the impossibility of deterministic extraction from block-SV sources, but this time through *efficient* p-tampering attacks.[4] In particular, we prove the following.

---

[4] Note that this is indeed a stronger condition than just getting a samplable source. See Remark 1.

Theorem 2 (Efficient p-tampering attacks over block SV sources). *Let the function $f: \{0,1\}^{\ell \cdot n} \mapsto \{+1,-1\}$ be a 'candidate' efficient deterministic extractor for $(\ell, \ell - p)$ block SV sources. Then there is an efficient p-tampering attack that generates a $(\ell, \ell - p)$ block SV source for which the average of f becomes $\Omega(p)$.*

Our main contribution in Theorem 2 is the efficiency of its p-tampering attacker, as without that condition one can prove Theorem 2 using a *computationally unbounded* p-tampering attacker and the proof implicit in [19,36] and explicit in [6,22] for the case of block SV sources. In fact, we prove a more general result than Theorem 2 by proving the impossibility of efficient bit bit extractors from yet another generalization of SV sources, called mutual max-divergence [23] (MMD) sources (see Definition 6).

Attacking Learners. In this work, we also use our blockwise p-tampering attack in the context of "adversarial" machine learning [5,35] where an adversary aims to increase the error of a learning algorithms for a specific test data that is known to him. In what follows, the reader might find the review of the standard terminology at the beginning of Sect. 4.2 useful.

Targeted poisoning attacks against learners. Poisoning attacks (a.k.a causative attacks) [2,40,44] model attacks against learning systems in which the adversary manipulates the training data $\overline{x} = (x_1, \ldots, x_n)$, where x_i is the i'th *labeled* training example, in order to increase the error of the learning algorithm. Poisoning attacks could model scenarios where the tampering happens *over time* [37,38] e.g., because the learning algorithm is "retrained" daily or weekly using potentially tamperable data. *Targeted* (poisoning) attacks [40] refer to the setting where the adversary *knows* a specific test data $\mathcal{X}$ over which the hypothesis will be tested, and she probably has some interest in increasing the error of the hypothesis over that particular test set $\mathcal{X}$. For simplicity of discussion, below we assume that $\mathcal{X} = \{(d,t)\}$ where t is the label of d and the adversary's goal is to make the learning algorithm output a wrong label for d.

A very natural model for how the poisoning attacks occur was defined by Valiant [42]. In this model, a training oracle $O_X(.)$ for a distribution X (from which the training sequence $\overline{x} = (x_1, \ldots, x_n)$ will be sampled) would be manipulated by an adversary as follows. Whenever the training algorithm queries this oracle, with probability $1 - p$ the answer is generated from the original oracle O_X and with probability p a stateful adversary A gets control over the oracle and answers with an arbitrary pair (d,t). Many subsequent work (e.g., [10,31]) studied how to make learners secure against such noise but *not* in the targeted setting.

Valiant's model vs p-tampering. Valiant's adversarial model for the training oracle is indeed very similar to our blockwise p-tampering model except for the fact that in the Valiant's model, the adversary is allowed to use wrong labels (i.e., $x_i = (d,t)$ where t is *not* the correct label for d). However, as we discussed above, our p-tampering attackers are not allowed to go out of the 'support set' of the distribution (see Definition 18). In this work, we prove the following attack against deterministic learners of classifiers (see Theorem 8 for a formalization). One subtle difference between the models is that in Valiant's model, the adversary knows everything about the *current* state of the learner, while in our model, the adversary knows the history of the blocks. For all of our attacks, all adversary needs is to 'continue' the computation done by the learner, and knowing the current state (as in Valiant's model) allows us to do so, even if the previous blocks are unknown. Therefore, all of our p-tampering attacks indeed apply in Valiant's model.

Theorem 3 (Informal–Targeted poisoning attacks against classifiers).
Let L be a deterministic learning algorithm L that takes a sequence $\overline{x} = (x_1, \ldots, x_n)$ of i.i.d samples from the same distribution X, where $x_i = (d_i, \ell_i)$ and ℓ_i is the label of d_i. Suppose, without tampering, the probability of L making a mistake on test example d is δ over the choice of $x_1, \ldots, x_n \leftarrow X$. Then there exists a p-tampering attack over the training sequence $(x_1, \ldots, x_n)$ that increases the error for classifying d to $\delta' \geq \delta + \Omega_\delta(p)$. Moreover, if X is efficiently samplable, the attack is efficient as well.

Note that the above attacker is a p-tampering one, meaning it never goes out of the support set of the distribution. In other words, our attacker does *not* use any wrong labels in its adversarial samples! Therefore, our attacks are 'defensible' in the sense that what they produce is always a possible legitimate outcome of the honest sampling, so it could not be *proved* in court that the data is not generated honestly! Previous work on poisoning attacks (e.g., [2,40,44]) has studied attacks against *specific* learners, while our result can be applied to *any* learner.

Comparison with the distribution-independent setting of [10,31]. Previous works of Kearns and Li [31] and Bshouty et al. [10] have already proved impossibility of PAC learning in Valiant's model of adversarial noise. In addition to using wrong label in their attacks (which is not allowed in the p-tampering model) there is also another distinction between their model and our p-tampering poisoning attacks. The attacks of [10,31] are proved in the *distribution-independent* setting, and their negative results heavily rely on the *existence* of some initial distribution that is not PAC learnable under adversarial noise. Our attacks, on the other hand, apply even to the *distribution-specific* setting, where the adversary has no control over the initial distribution, and it can always turn that distribution against the learner.

1.2 Ideas Behind Our Blockwise p-Tampering Biasing Attack

In this subsection we describe some of the ideas behind the proof of our Theorem 1.

Reduction to bitwise tampering? Our first observation is that blockwise $\widetilde{p}$-tampering over *uniformly* distribute blocks $U_{s_1} \times \ldots U_{s_n}$ could be reduced to p-tampering over $N = \sum_i s_i$ many uniform bits, as long as $1 - \widetilde{p} \leq (1 - p)^{s_i}$

for every s_i. The idea is that if $1 - \widetilde{p} \le (1 - p)^{s_i}$, then the probability of the whole block U_{s_i} getting tampered with in the blockwise model is at least the probability that *at least* one of the bits are tampered with in the bitwise model. Therefore, a blockwise attacker can 'emulate' the bitwise attacker internally. See the full version for a formalization of this argument.)

However, this reduction is imperfect in three aspects. (1) Firstly, to use this reduction we will need to use $p \approx \widetilde{p}/s$ where s is the maximum length of any block. Therefore, we cannot gain any bias more than $1/s$ which, in particular, would be at most $o(1)$ for non-constant block sizes $s = \omega(1)$. This prevents us from getting applications (e.g., attacks against extractors) that require large $\Omega(1)$ bias. (2) Secondly, this reduction only works for blocks that are originally distributed as uniform bits (i.e., U_s), and so it cannot be applied to general non-uniform distributions, which is indeed the setting of our p-tampering attacks against learners. (3) Finally, this reduction does not preserve robustness as the $\widetilde{p}$-tampering algorithm would need to know the *exact* probabilities under which the tampering happens, while in our applications of blockwise tampering to cryptographic primitives robustness we aim for robust attacks that do not depend on this exact knowledge. Because of all this, in this work we aim for a direct attack analyzed in the blockwise regime.

The work of [1] used a so called 'mild-greedy' attack for biasing real-valued bounded function in a bitwise p-tampering attack. Roughly speaking, this attack works as follows. When the tampering happens, the tampering algorithm first picks a random bits b_i'. Then, using a random continuation $b_{i+1}', \ldots, b_n'$ it interprets $s = f(b_1, \ldots, b_{i-1}, b_i', \ldots)$ as how good the choice of b_i' is. Then, using a biased coin based on s, the tampering algorithm either keeps b_i' or it flips it to $1 - b_i'$. This attack, unfortunately, is tailored of the bitwise setting, as flipping a block is not natural (or even well defined).

Our new one rejection sampling attack. In this work propose a new attack for the blockwise setting that is inspired by the mild-greedy attack of [1]. Our attack is not exactly a 'generalization' of the mild-greedy attack to the blockwise setting, as even for the case of uniform blocks of one bit, it still differs from the mild-greedy attack, but it is nonetheless inspired by the one-greedy attack and its analysis also uses ideas from the analysis of mild-greedy attack [1]. We call our tampering attack *one rejection sampling*, denoted by ORSam, and it works as follows: given previously chosen blocks $(y_1, \ldots, y_{i-1})$ for $\overline{X}$ (some of which might be the tampered blocks) the tampering algorithm ORSam first samples $(y_i' \leftarrow X_i, \ldots, y_n' \leftarrow X_n)$ 'in its head', then gets $s = f(y_1, \ldots, y_{i-1}, y_i', \ldots, y_n')$, and outputs:

$$\begin{cases} \text{Case 1: with probability } \frac{1+s}{2} : \text{ keep } y_i' \\ \text{Case 2: with probability } \frac{1-s}{2} : \text{ use a fresh sample } y_i'' \leftarrow X_i. \end{cases}$$

Why does one-rejection sampling work? The main challenge is to show that the simple one-rejection sampling attack described above actually achieves bias proportional to the variance. In order to relate the bias to the variance of the function, we first need to define two notations. For every prefix $x_{\leq i} = x_1, \ldots, x_i$ let $\hat{f}[x_{\leq i}] = \mathbb{E}[f(\overline{X})|X_1 = x_1, \ldots, X_i = x_i]$ to be the average of function f w.r.t to distribution $\overline{X}$ conditioned on that prefix. Also let $g[x_{\leq i}] = \hat{f}[x_{\leq i}] - \hat{f}[x_{\leq i-1}]$ be the change in average of f (i.e., $\hat{f}$) when we go from $x_{\leq i-1}$ to $x_{\leq i}$. A straightforward calculation shows that

$$\mathrm{Var}[f(\overline{X})] = \mathop{\mathbb{E}}_{(x_1, \ldots, x_n) \leftarrow \overline{X}} \left[\sum_{i \in [n]} g[x_{\leq i}]^2 \right] = \sum_{i \in [n]} \mathop{\mathbb{E}}_{x_{\leq i} \leftarrow (X_1, \ldots, X_i)} \left[g[x_{\leq i}]^2 \right]. \quad (1)$$

That is simply because the sequence $(\hat{f}[x_{\leq 0}], \ldots, \hat{f}[x_{\leq n}])$ forms a martingale. Suppose $\overline{Y} = (Y_1, \ldots, Y_n)$ is the new distribution after the p-tampering happens over $\overline{X}$. Equation (1) suggests the following natural idea for lower bounding the amount of "global gain" that is achieved for increasing the average $d = \mathbb{E}[f(\overline{Y})] - \mathbb{E}[f(\overline{X})]$ under the attack's generated distribution by relating it to the variance $\mathrm{Var}[f(\overline{X})]$. In particular, it would suffice to lower bound the "local gains" for average of f when we apply our *one rejection sampling* with probability p for a particular block i, by relating it the term $\mathbb{E}_{(x_1, \ldots, x_n) \leftarrow \overline{X}}[g[x_{\leq i}]^2]$ (for the same fixed i). Direct calculation shows that the 'local gain' obtained by our one-rejection sampling attack for any prefix $x_{\leq i}$ is *exactly* $\frac{p}{2} \cdot \mathbb{E}_{x_{i+1} \leftarrow X_{i+1}}[g[x_{\leq i}, x_{i+1}]^2]$.

Unfortunately, a subtle point prevents us from using the above argument, because as soon tampering happens, we *deviate* from the original distribution $\overline{X}$, and the 'prefixes' of the blocks come from a new distribution $\overline{Y}$ rather than $\overline{X}$, so we cannot directly use to Eq. (1) to lower bound the local gains by relating them to $\mathrm{Var}[f(\overline{X})]$. Nonetheless, it can be shown that a variant of Eq. (1) still holds in which, roughly speaking, $\mathrm{Var}[f(\overline{Y})]$ substitutes $\mathrm{Var}[f(\overline{X})]$. Therefore, it would be sufficient to lower bound $\mathrm{Var}[f(\overline{Y})]$ based on $\mathrm{Var}[f(\overline{X})]$. For this goal, we employ similar ideas to those of [1] to show by induction over i that at any moment during the attack *either* the average *or* the variance of $\hat{f}[x_{\leq i}]$ under the *new* tampered distribution $\overline{Y}$ is large enough. See Sect. 5 for more details.

1.3 Further Related Work and Models

Since the work of Boneh et al. [9] it is known that even *random* tampering with computation of certain protocols could lead to devastating attacks. The work of Gennaro et al. [26] initiated a formal study of algorithmic tamper resilience. Along this direction, non-malleable codes, introduced by Dziembowski et al. [25], become a central tool for preventing tampering attacks on the internal state of an algorithm. More recently, Chandran et al. [11] studied non-malleable codes in the *blockwise* tampering model that bears similariteis to our model in this work, though our goals are completely different. Finally, Bellare et al. [7] initiated the study of *algorithm substitution* attacks where a powerful attacker can adversarially substitute components of the algorithm.

Coin-tossing. At a high level, our blockwise tampering attacks, specially for biasing Boolean functions, have some conceptual similarities to attacks against coin-tossing protocols [8,15,17,29,34]. Indeed, both types of attacks aim at biasing a final bit by 'substituting' some 'blocks'. In our setting, the block is the next sampled chunk of randomness, and for coin tossing blocks are maliciously chosen messages to the other party! However, the pattern of tampering in such attacks is one out of two complementing sets (referring to each party's turns), while in our setting each block becomes tamperable with an independent probability p.

Tampering with 'bounded budget'. The works of [15,27,33] studied the power of related tampering attacks in the blockwise setting where the goal of the adversary is indeed to bias the output of a function. However, in these papers, while the adversary has a 'limited budged' of how many times to tamper, it *can choose* when to tamper with a block, while, in our model the adversary will have no control on about $1 - p$ fraction of the blocks, and he does not get to choose which blocks will be so. The work of Dodis [20] studies a 'mixture' of both models where the adversary has a bounded budged that she can use upon choice, but she also gets to tamper 'randomly' otherwise.

2   Preliminaries

Logarithms are denoted by $\lg(\cdot)$ and, unless specified otherwise, they are in base 2. By $a, b \in \mathcal{D}$ we mean that $a \in \mathcal{D}$ and $b \in \mathcal{D}$. For a string $x \in \{0,1\}^*$, by $|x| = n$ we denote that $x \in \{0,1\}^n$. For a randomized algorithm S, we only explicitly represent its input and do not represent its randomness and by $y \leftarrow S(x)$ we denote the process of running $S(x)$ using fresh randomness and getting y as output.

Notation on distributions and random variables. Unless specified otherwise, all of the random variables and distributions in this work are discrete and finite. We use uppercase letters to denote random variables and distributions (e.g., X). For real valued random variable X, by $\mathbb{E}[X]$ and $\mathrm{Var}[X]$, we mean (in order) the expected value and variance of X. We usually use the same letter to refer to distributions and random variables sampled from them. By $\mathrm{Supp}(X) = \{x \mid \Pr[X = x] > 0\}$ we denote the support set of X. The process of sampling x from X is denoted by $x \leftarrow X$ and $X \equiv Y$ is used to show that X and Y are distributed identically.

By U_m we denote the random variable uniformly distributed over $\{0,1\}^m$. By (X, Y) we denote random variables X, Y that are distributed jointly. By $(X \times Y)$ we mean (X, Y) where X and Y are independently sampled from their marginal distribution. For joint random variables (X, Y) and for any $y \leftarrow Y$, by $(X \mid y)$ we denote the distribution of X conditioned on $Y = y$. By using a random variable like X in an expected value (or probability) we mean that the expected value (or the probability) is also over X (e.g., $\mathbb{E}[f(X)] = \mathbb{E}_{x \leftarrow X}[f(x)]$ and $\Pr[f(X) = 1] = \Pr_{x \leftarrow X}[f(x) = 1]$). We also use the tradition that the multiple appearances of the same random variable X in the same phrase refer to identical samples (e.g., it always holds that $\Pr[X = X] = 1$). For a random variable D, we also use $D(x)$ to denote $\Pr[D = x]$.

Definition 1 (Bit extraction). *Let $\mathcal{X}$ be a set of distributions over a domain $\mathcal{D}$. We call a function $f\colon \mathcal{D} \mapsto \{+1, -1\}$ an ε-extractor for $\mathcal{X}$ (sources) if for every $X \in \mathcal{X}$ it holds that $|\mathbb{E}[f(X)]| \le \varepsilon$.*

Definition 2. $\mathrm{H}_\infty(X) = \min_{x \in \mathrm{Supp}(X)} \lg(1/p(x))$ *is the* min-entropy *of X.*

Definition 3 (Span of distributions). *Let $\mathcal{X} = \{X_1, \ldots, X_k\}$ be a set of distributions over the same domain. For $\alpha_1 + \cdots + \alpha_k = 1$, by $X = \sum_{i \in [k]} \alpha_i X_i$ we refer to the distribution X such that $\Pr[X = a] = X(a) = \sum_i \alpha_i X_i(a)$. Namely, X can be sampled by the following process: first sample $i \in [k]$ with probability α_i, then sample $x \leftarrow X_i$ and output x. The* span *of distributions in $\mathcal{X}$ is defined to be the set of all convex combinations of distributions in $\mathcal{X}$: $\mathrm{Span}(\mathcal{X}) = \{X = \sum_{i \in [k]} \alpha_i X_i \mid \sum_{i \in [k]} \alpha_i = 1\}$.*

Lemma 1 (Hoeffding's inequality). *Suppose $A_1, \ldots, A_n$ are i.i.d random variables distributed over $[-1, +1]$ with expected value $\mathbb{E}[A_i] = \mu$, and let $A = \mathbb{E}_{i \leftarrow [n]}[A_i]$ be their average. Then, for all $\varepsilon \ge 0$ we have $\Pr\left[\|A - \mu\| \ge \varepsilon\right] \le e^{-n \cdot \varepsilon^2 / 2}$.*

2.1 Distance Measures

Definition 4 (Statistical distance). *The* statistical distance *(a.k.a. total variation distance) between random variables X, Y is defined as*

$$D_{\mathrm{SD}}(X, Y) = \max_{E \subseteq \mathrm{Supp}(X)} \Pr[X \in E] - \Pr[Y \in E].$$

The following lemma gives a well known characterization of the statistical distance.

Lemma 2 (Characterizing statistical distance). *It holds that $D_{\mathrm{SD}}(X, Y) \le p$ iff there are distributions Z, X', Y' such that $X = (1 - p)Z + pX'$ and $Y = (1 - p)Z + pY'$. In particular, if $Y = (1 - p)X + pZ$ then we have $D_{\mathrm{SD}}(X, Y) \le p$ because it always holds that $X = (1 - p)X + pX$.*

Definition 5 (KL-divergence). *The* Kullback-Leibler (KL) divergence *from distribution Q to distribution P is defined as follows: $D_{\mathrm{KL}}(P\|Q) = \mathbb{E}_{a \leftarrow P} \lg(P(a)/Q(a))$ if $\mathrm{Supp}(P) \subseteq \mathrm{Supp}(Q)$, and $D_{\mathrm{KL}}(P\|Q) = \infty$ if $\mathrm{Supp}(P) \not\subseteq \mathrm{Supp}(Q)$.*

Definition 6 (Max-divergence[23]). *The* max-divergence *from Q to P is defined as follows: $D_\infty(P\|Q) = \max_{a \in \mathrm{Supp}(P)} \lg(P(a)/Q(a))$ if $\mathrm{Supp}(P) \subseteq \mathrm{Supp}(Q)$, and if $\mathrm{Supp}(P) \not\subseteq \mathrm{Supp}(Q)$, then $D_\infty(P\|Q) = \infty$.*

The work of [23] defined the notion of max-divergence using e as the base for logarithm, but in this work we use a variation of it using base 2, which is the same up to a multiplicative constant factor $\lg e$. The following lemma lists some of the basic properties of max-divergence (see Definition 6).

Lemma 3 (Properties of max-divergence). *Let X, Y be distributions and $p < 1$.*

1. *The following conditions are equivalent.*
    (a) $D_\infty(X\|Y) \le \lg(1/(1-p))$.
    (b) *For all $a \in \mathrm{Supp}(X)$ it holds that $\Pr[X = a] \cdot (1-p) \le \Pr[Y = a]$.*
    (c) *There exists some random variable Z such that $Y = (1-p)X + pZ$. Namely, Y can be sampled as: with probability $1-p$ sample from X and with probability p sample from Z.*
2. *For $\mathrm{Supp}(Y) \subseteq \{0,1\}^m$, $\mathrm{H}_\infty(Y) \ge k$ iff $D_\infty(Y\|U_m) \le m - k$.*
3. *If $D_\infty(X\|Y) \le r$ and $D_\infty(Y\|X) \le r$, then $D_{\mathsf{KL}}(X\|Y) \le r(2^r - 1)$.*

Proof (Proof Sketch). Here we only sketch the proofs as they are straightforward. The equivalence of Parts 1a and 1b directly follows from the definition of max-divergence, so here we only show the equivalence of Parts 1b and 1c. Assuming Part 1c we have

$$\Pr[X = a] \cdot (1-p) \le \Pr[X = a] \cdot (1-p) + \Pr[Z = a] \cdot p = \Pr[Y = a]$$

which implies Part 1b. Assuming Part 1b, we define the distribution Z over $\mathrm{Supp}(Y)$ as follows: $Z(a) = (Y(a) - (1-p) \cdot X(a))/p$. It is easy to see that $Z(a) \ge 0$ and that $\sum_a Z(a) = 1$, so Z indeed defines a distribution. Moreover, we have

$$X(a) \cdot (1-p) + Z(a) \cdot p = X(a) \cdot (1-p) + (Y(a) - X(a) \cdot (1-p)) = \Pr[Y = a]$$

which implies that $Y = (1-p)X + pZ$, proving Part 1c.

Part 2 directly follows from the definitions of min-entropy and max-divergence.

Part 3 follows from the same proof give in [23] but using the logarithm base 2 istead of e in the definition of max-divergence. □

2.2   Santha-Vazirani Sources and Their Generalizations

Definition 7 (SV sources [39]). *A joint distribution $\overline{X} = (X_1, \ldots, X_n)$ where $X_i \in \{0,1\}$ for all $i \in [n]$ is a δ-Santha-Vazirani (δ-SV) source with bias at most $\delta \in [0,1]$, if for all $i \in [n]$ and all $x_1, \ldots, x_i \in \{0,1\}$ it holds that $(1-\delta)/2 \le \Pr[X_i = x_i \mid X_1 = x_1, \ldots, X_{i-1} = x_{i-1}] \le (1+\delta)/2$.*

The following definition is a close variant of Block SV Sources defined in [13] where we allow the blocks to have different lengths and specify the amount of *loss* in the min-entropy (compared to the uniform distributing) in each block.

Definition 8 (Block SV Sources [13]). *Suppose $\overline{X} = (X_1, \ldots, X_n)$ is a joint distribution where $X_i \in \{0,1\}^\ell$ for all $i \in [n]$. We call $\overline{X}$ a (ℓ, k)-block SV source if for all $i \in [n]$ and all possible $(x_1, \ldots, x_{i-1}) \leftarrow (X_1, \ldots, X_{i-1})$ it hold that $\mathrm{H}_\infty(X_i \mid x_1, \ldots, x_{i-1}) \ge k$.*

It is easy to see that a δ-SV source is a $(1, 1 - \gamma)$-block-SV source for $\gamma = \lg(1 + \delta) \leq \delta$. The following definition by Beigi et al. [6] generalizes both of the above definitions of SV and Block-SV sources.

Definition 9 (Generalized SV Sources [6]). *Let $\mathcal{D}$ be a set of distributions (dices) over alphabet C. A distribution $\overline{X} = (X_1, \ldots, X_n)$ over C^n is a Generalized SV source w.r.t $\mathcal{D}$ if for all $i \in [n]$ and $x_1, \ldots, x_{i-1} \in C$ there exists $S \in \mathrm{Span}(\mathcal{D})$ such that for all $x_i \in C$ it holds that*

$$\Pr[X_i = x_i \mid X_1 = x_1, \ldots, X_{i-1} = x_{i-1}] = \Pr[S = x_i].$$

3 Blockwise p-Tampering: Definitions and Main Results

In this section, we will describe our results formally.

Notation on sequences of random variables. By D^n we denote the product distribution $D \times \cdots \times D$ (n times). Using this notation, by U_m^n we mean a sequence of n blocks each distributed independently like U_m. Thus, although both of U_m^n and U_n^m are eventually $m \cdot n$ random bits, one is divided into n blocks and one is divided into m blocks. For a vector $x = (x_1, \ldots, x_n)$ we let $x_{\leq i} = (x_1, \ldots, x_i)$, $x_{<i} = (x_1, \ldots, x_{i-1})$.

Definition 10 (Valid prefixes and conditional sampling). *Let $\overline{X} = (X_1, \ldots, X_n)$ be a joint distribution. We call $x_{\leq i} = (x_1, \ldots, x_i)$ a valid prefix for $\overline{X}$ if there are $x_{i+1}, \ldots, x_n$ such that $(x_1, \ldots, x_n) \in \mathrm{Supp}(\overline{X})$ (i.e., $x_{\leq i} \in \mathrm{Supp}(X_{\leq i})$). We use $\mathrm{ValPref}(\overline{X})$ to denote the set of all valid prefixes of $\overline{X}$ (including the empty string $x_{\leq 0}$). For a valid prefix $y_{\leq i} \in \mathrm{ValPref}(\overline{X})$, by $(X_i \mid y_{\leq i-1})$ we denote the conditional distribution $(X_i \mid X_1 = y_1, \ldots, X_{i-1} = y_{i-1})$.*

Definition 11 (Online-samplable sequences of random variables). *We call a randomized algorithm $S(\cdot)$ an online sampler for a joint distribution. Let $\overline{X} = (X_1, \ldots, X_n)$ if for every valid prefix $x_{\leq i-1} \in \mathrm{ValPref}(\overline{X})$, it holds that $S(x_{\leq i-1})$ outputs according to $(X_i \mid x_{\leq i-1})$. If $\overline{X} = \overline{X}^{(n)}$ is a vector from a family of vectors indexed by n, we let $N = N(n)$ be the total length of the representation of $\overline{X}$ (i.e., $(X_1, \ldots, X_n) \in \{0,1\}^N$) and assume that n could be derived from $N(n)$. In that case, an online sampler $S(\cdot)$ for $\overline{X}^{(n)}$ takes also N as input and it holds that $S(1^N, x_{\leq i-1}) \equiv (X_i \mid x_{\leq i-1})$. We call $\overline{X} = \overline{X}^{(n)}$ efficiently online samplable if there exists an online sampler S for $\overline{X}$ that runs in polynomial time (i.e. $\mathrm{poly}(N)$). When n is clear from the context we might simply drop 1^N and simply write $S(x_{\leq i-1})$.*

Definition 12 (Tampering algorithms for sequences of random variables). *Let $\overline{X} = (X_1, \ldots, X_n)$ be an arbitrary joint distribution. We call a (potentially randomized and even computationally unbounded) algorithm Tam an (online) tampering algorithm for $\overline{X}$ if given any valid prefix $x_{\leq i-1} \in \mathrm{ValPref}(\overline{X})$, $\mathsf{Tam}(x_{\leq i-1})$ always outputs x_i such that $x_{\leq i} \in \mathrm{ValPref}(\overline{X})$.*

If $\overline{X} = \overline{X}^{(n)}$ is a vector from a family of vectors indexed by n, we call Tam an efficient *tampering algorithm for* $\overline{X}$ if it runs in time $\text{poly}(N)$ where $N = N(n)$ is the total bit length of the vector $\overline{X}$ (i.e., $(X_1, \ldots, X_n) \in \{0,1\}^N$).

Note that in Definition 12, we only allow the tampering algorithm to produce something in the support set of the joint distribution.

The following definition defines a notation for representing the "chances" that might be given to a tampering algorithm to tamper with the joint distribution $\overline{X} = (X_1, \ldots, X_n)$. We need this generalization to formally define the robustness of p-tampering attack when p changes during the attack.

Definition 13 (Probability trees over sequences of random variables). Let $\overline{X} = (X_1, \ldots, X_n)$ be an arbitrary joint distribution. We call a function $\rho \colon \text{ValPref}(\overline{X}) \mapsto [0,1]$ a *probability tree over* $\overline{X}$. For $0 \le p \le q \le 1$, we call $\rho[\cdot]$ a $[p,q]$-*probability tree over* $\overline{X}$ if $\rho(x_{\le i}) \in [p,q]$ for all $x_{\le i} \in \text{ValPref}(\overline{X})$. We call $\rho[\cdot]$ the p-*probability tree over* $\overline{X}$ if $\rho[x_{\le i}] = p$ for all $x_{\le i} \in \text{ValPref}(\overline{X})$.

Now we define the outcome of an actual "tampering game" in which a tampering algorithm gets to tamper with a joint distribution $\overline{X} = (X_1, \ldots, X_n)$ according to some probability tree defined over $\overline{X}$.

Definition 14 (ρ-tampering variations of distributions). Let $\overline{X} = (X_1, \ldots, X_n)$ be an arbitrary joint distribution, and let $\rho[\cdot]$ be a probability tree over $\overline{X}$. We say that a tampering algorithm Tam for $\overline{X}$ generates $\overline{Y}$ from $\overline{X}$ through a ρ-tampering attack if $\overline{Y} = (Y_1, \ldots, Y_n)$ is inductively sampled as follows. Given any valid prefix $y_{\le i-1} \in \text{ValPref}(\overline{Y})$ we will sample Y_i through the following process:

- with probability $1 - \rho[y_{\le i-1}]$, sample Y_i from $(X_i \mid X_{\le i-1} = y_{\le i-1})$, and
- with probability $\rho[y_{\le i-1}]$, sample $Y_i \leftarrow \text{Tam}(y_{\le i-1})$.

Equivalently, using Definition 3, for all $y_{\le i-1} \in \text{ValPref}(\overline{Y})$ *we have* $(Y_i \mid y_{\le i-1}) = (1 - \rho[y_{\le i-1}]) \cdot (X_i \mid X_{\le i-1} = y_{\le i-1}) + \rho[y_{\le i-1}] \cdot \text{Tam}(y_{\le i-1})$. *In this case, we also call* $\overline{Y}$ *a* ρ-*tampering variation of* $\overline{X}$. *In case* ρ *is the constant function* p, *we call* $\overline{Y}$ *a* p-*tampering variation of* $\overline{X}$ *and we say that* Tam *generates* $\overline{Y}$ *from* $\overline{X}$ *through a* p-*tampering attack.*

Note that even in cases where we end up sampling Y_i from the "untampered" distribution of X_i (which happens with probability at least $1 - \rho[x_{\le i-1}]$) we still sample from X_i conditioned on the *possibly tampered* prefix $(y_1, \ldots, y_i)$. In other words, the result of the tampering algorithm determines, in case it happens, will completely substitute the tampered block and the sampling will continue as if the history of the blocks were from the untampered sequence $X_1, \ldots, X_i$. For the special case that X_i's are independent distributions (e.g., when $\overline{X}$ is uniform distribution over some set Σ^n) we will not need to do this.

Prefixes remain valid. Note that because in Definition 14 the algorithm Tam is a (valid) tampering algorithm for $\overline{X}$, all the resulting prefixes will remain valid for $\overline{X}$ and we will have $\mathrm{ValPref}(\overline{Y}) \subseteq \mathrm{ValPref}(\overline{X})$. In fact, we get $\mathrm{ValPref}(\overline{Y}) = \mathrm{ValPref}(\overline{X})$ if $\rho[x_{\leq i}] < 1$ for all $x_{\leq i} \in \mathrm{ValPref}(\overline{X})$. A more general definition of tampering algorithms (compared to Definition 12) could use a larger support set $\mathcal{Z}$ where $\mathrm{ValPref}(\overline{X}) \subset \mathcal{Z}$ and only require the tampering algorithm to produce prefixes in $\mathcal{Z}$. However, since our main contributions in this paper is to give attacks, by restricting our model to require the attackers to remain in $\mathrm{ValPref}(\overline{X})$ only makes our results stronger.

Remark 1 (Efficient tampering vs. efficient sampling). Note that an *efficient tampering* refers only to when the algorithm Tam is polynomial time, and it can apply even to settings where $\overline{X}$ and its variation generated by Tam are *not* efficiently samplable. On the other hand, using the standard terminology, $\overline{X}$ is efficiently samplable if one can efficiently sample *all* of the blocks of $\overline{X}$ *simultaneously*. Of course, if $\overline{X}$ is efficiently *online* samplable and if Tam is also an efficient tampering for $\overline{X}$, then the variation $\overline{Y}$ of $\overline{X}$ produced by tampering attack Tam will also be trivially efficiently online-samplable, but we emphasize that this is a specific way of getting an efficient sampler for $\overline{Y}$, and so the efficiency of our tampering attacks shall not be confused with mere efficient samplability of the final distribution $\overline{Y}$.

Remark 2 (An alternative definition). An alternative variant of Definition 14 could 'strengthen' the tampering algorithm Tam who, now, receives the 'original' sample x_i before substituting it with something else. Namely, we would first sample $x_i \leftarrow (X_i \mid y_{\leq i-1})$, and then with probability $1 - p$ we let $y_i = x_i$ and with probability p we let $y_i = \mathsf{Tam}(y_{\leq i-1}, x_i)$. This definition is natural for scenarios in which the adversary gets to see the first initial sample and then might decide to change or not change it. However, as long as either (1) tampering is allowed to be inefficient or (2) $\overline{X}$ is efficiently online samplable, the power of tampering attacks under this alternative definition is the same as those under Definition 14. To see why, first note that $\mathsf{Tam}(y_{\leq i-1}, x_i)$ can always ignore the extra input x_i. In the other direction, suppose Tam' is a tampering algorithm under the alternative definition and suppose a tampering algorithm $\mathsf{Tam}(y_{\leq i-1})$ is only given $y_{\leq i-1}$. If Tam can obtain a sample $x_i' \leftarrow (X_i \mid y_{\leq i-1})$, then it could also emulate $\mathsf{Tam}'(y_{\leq i-1}, x_i')$. Interestingly, although x_i and x_i' might be different samples, this emulation of $\mathsf{Tam}'(y_{\leq i-1}, x_i')$ by Tam leads to the same final distribution.

Now we define what it means for a tampering adversary to successfully bias the output of a function, while being robust to changes in probabilities.

Definition 15 (Robust p-tampering attacks for biasing real functions).
Let $\overline{X} = (X_1, \ldots, X_n)$ be a joint distribution, $f \colon \mathrm{Supp}(\overline{X}) \mapsto \mathbb{R}$ a real function and Tam a tampering algorithm for $\overline{X}$.

- *For a probability tree ρ over $\overline{X}$, we say that Tam is a ρ-tampering attack biasing $f(\overline{X})$ by at least δ, if Tam generates $\overline{Y}$ from $\overline{X}$ through a ρ-tampering attack and $\mathbb{E}[f(\overline{Y})] \geq \mathbb{E}[f(\overline{X})] + \delta$.*

- *For $p \in [0,1]$, we say that* Tam *is a p-tampering attack biasing $f(\overline{X})$ by at least δ, if* Tam *a ρ-tampering attack biasing $f(\overline{X})$ by at least δ for the constant probability tree $\rho[x_{\leq i}] = p$.*
- *We say that* Tam *is a robust p-tampering attack biasing $f(\overline{X})$ by at least δ, if for every $[p,1]$-probability tree ρ over $\overline{X}$ it holds that* Tam *is a ρ-tampering attack biasing $f(\overline{X})$ by at least δ.*

3.1   Main Results: Blockwise p-Tampering of Bounded Functions

Now, we are ready our main results that are about biasing real functions through *efficient* blockwise p-tampering attacks. We will then describe our results about the computationally unbounded setting where the tampering algorithm Tam is not necessarily polynomial time. Our main motivation for studying the computationally unbounded setting is to understand the *limitations* of what amount of bias could be achieved. We will then describe the applications of our results for attacking candidate randomness extractors (over multiple sources or variations of SV sources) through p tampering attacks.

Theorem 4 (Efficient blockwise p-tampering of bounded real functions). *Let $\overline{X} = (X_1, \ldots, X_n)$ be a joint distribution, $f \colon \mathrm{Supp}(\overline{X}) \mapsto [-1, +1]$ be a real-output function defined over $\mathrm{Supp}(\overline{X})$. Then there is a tampering algorithm* Tam *for $\overline{X}$ such that:*

1. **(Bias)** Tam *is a robust p-tampering attack biasing $f(\overline{X})$ by at least $\frac{p}{3+4p} \cdot \mathrm{Var}[f(\overline{X})]$. Furthermore, if the function $f \colon \mathrm{Supp}(\overline{X}) \mapsto \{-1, +1\}$ is Boolean, then the bias is at least $\frac{p}{2+2p} \cdot \mathrm{Var}[f(\overline{X})]$.*
2. **(Efficiency)** *Moreover,* Tam *could be implemented efficiently given oracle access to any online sampler $S(\cdot)$ for $\overline{X}$ and $f(\cdot)$. In particular, given only two samples $y_i^1, y_i^2 \leftarrow S(y_{\leq i-1})$,* Tam$(y_{\leq i-1})$ *chooses between y_i^1, y_i^2 by making use of a biased coin that only depends on $\hat{f}[y_{\leq i-1}, y_i^1]$. Such biased coin could be sampled efficiently using further calls to $S(\cdot)$ and one call to $f(\cdot)$.*

See Sect. 5 (in particular Sect. 5.1) for the full proof of Theorem 4.

Theorem 4 above extends the previous result of [1] from bitwise to blockwise p-tampering. We also get bias $\Omega(p)$ though with worse constants. Also, for the case of Boolean functions, we again extend the previous result of [1] from bitwise p-tampering to blockwise p-tampering.

Importance of the efficiency features of the attacker in Theorem 4. As we will see in Theorem 5 below, we can get better biasing bounds for the Boolean case than $p \cdot \mathrm{Var}[f(\overline{X})]/4$, however, the reason that we pointed this out in Theorem 4 was that result comes along with the efficiency feature specified in Theorem 4 (and this is not the case in our Theorem 5 below). As mentioned, the attacker of Theorem 4 only needs *two honestly* generated samples $\{y_i^1, y_i^2\}$ for the next tampered block X_i and chooses one of them. Interestingly, this means that if the tampering algorithm is actually given an 'initial true value' x_i for block X_i (e.g., the honestly generated randomness to be used in a randomized algorithm) then the tampering algorithm could basically just either keep x_i or substitute it with another fresh sample from X_i. This is a natural attack strategy when the adversary can "reset" the sampling procedure for the block X_i.

Biasing Martingales. An interesting special case of Theorem 4 is when the joint distribution $\overline{X} = (X_1, \ldots, X_n)$ is a martingale (i.e., $X_i \in \mathbb{R}$ and $\mathbb{E}[X_i \mid x_{\leq i-1}] = x_{i-1}$) and $f(\overline{X}) = X_n \in [-1, +1]$. In this case, it holds that $\hat{f}[x_{\leq i}] = x_i$, and so our attacker of Theorem 4 becomes extremely simple: given any two samples $y_i^1, y_i^2 \leftarrow (X_i \mid y_{\leq i-1})$, $\mathsf{Tam}(y_{\leq i-1})$ chooses $y_i = y_i^1$ with a probability that only depends on y_i^1 and chooses $y_i = y_i^2$ otherwise. Note that *no* further calls to the online sampler nor $f(\cdot)$ is needed! Moreover, this simple attack not only biases the final value $X_n = f(\overline{X})$ but it does bias *every* other X_i as well. The reason is that if we define $f_i(X_{\leq i}) = X_i \in [-1, +1]$, then the attacker's algorithm would be identical for biasing $f_i(\cdot)$ compared to biasing $f_n(\cdot) = f(\cdot)$. Therefore, our attack generates a p-tampering variation $\overline{Y}$ of $\overline{X}$ that *simultaneously* achieves bias $Y_i \geq X_i + (p/7) \cdot \mathrm{Var}[X_i]$ for *every* block $i \in [n]$. Moreover, the p-tampering is efficient if the martingale is online samplable.

Tampering with only a part of randomness. The specific way that the attacker of Theorem 4 chooses between the two samples $\{y_i^1, y_i^2\}$ for block X_i allows us to generalize the attack to settings where the tamping happens only over *part* of the randomness and some subsequent randomness R is also used for computing f. As we will see, this corollary would also be useful for attacking randomized learners through the so called 'targeted poisoning' attacks.

Corollary 2 (Biasing bounded 'randomized' functions). *Let $\overline{X} = (X_1, \ldots, X_n)$ be a joint distribution, R another distribution, and $f \colon \mathrm{Supp}(\overline{X} \times R) \mapsto [-1, +1]$. For any fixed $x \leftarrow \overline{X}$, let $g(x) = \mathbb{E}_{r \leftarrow R}[f(x, r)] \in [-1, +1]$. Then there is a tampering algorithm Tam for $\overline{X}$ (not receiving R) such that:*

1. **(Bias)** Tam *is a robust p-tampering attack biasing $g(\overline{X})$ by $\geq \frac{p}{3+4p} \cdot \mathrm{Var}[g(\overline{X})]$.*
2. **(Efficiency)** Tam *could be implemented efficiently given oracle access to any online sampler $S(\cdot)$ for $\overline{X}$ and $f(\cdot, \cdot)$. In particular, $\mathsf{Tam}(y_{\leq i-1})$ again chooses between two samples $y_i^1, y_i^2 \leftarrow S(y_{\leq i-1})$ using further calls to $S(\cdot)$ and one call to $f(\cdot, \cdot)$ and one sample from R.*

Proof (Proof of Corollary 2 using Theorem 4). To derive Corollary 2 from Theorem 4 we apply Theorem 4 directly to the function $g(x) = \mathbb{E}f(x, R)$, and we rely on the properties specified in the efficiency part of Theorem 4 to derive the efficiency of the new attacker. All we need is to provide a sample from the distribution Z (for choosing between $y_i^1, y_i^2 \leftarrow S(y_{\leq i-1})$) when we try to bias g. In order to do so, we can first sample $x \leftarrow (\overline{X} \mid y_{\leq i-1}, y_i^1)$ using $S(\cdot)$, and then output $Z \leftarrow f(x, R)$ using one sample $r \leftarrow R$. By the linearity of expectation, even though we did not really compute $g(x)$, this way of sampling Z using only one $r \leftarrow R$ has the needed properties for the (average) function g as well.

The following theorem gives a better biasing bound for the important special case of Boolean functions. On the down side, the attacker will be less efficient and asks more queries to the online sampler $S(\cdot)$.[5]

Theorem 5 (Biasing Attacks on Boolean functions). *Let $\overline{X} = (X_1, \ldots, X_n)$ be a joint distribution, $f \colon \mathrm{Supp}(\overline{X}) \mapsto \{+1, -1\}$ a Boolean function defined over $\mathrm{Supp}(\overline{X})$, and $\mu = \mathbb{E}[f(\overline{X})]$. Suppose S is a sampler for $\overline{X}$ and let N be an upper bound on the total binary length of $\overline{X} = (X_1, \ldots, X_n) \in \{0,1\}^N$, and $\varepsilon < 1$ be an input parameter. Then there is a tampering algorithm* Tam *for $\overline{X}$ that:*

1. **(Bias)** Tam *is a robust p-tampering attack biasing $f(\overline{X})$ by $\geq \frac{p(1-\mu^2)}{2-p(1-\mu)} - \frac{\varepsilon}{1+\mu}$.[6]*
2. **(Efficiency)** *Moreover,* Tam *could be implemented in time* $\mathrm{poly}(N/\varepsilon)$ *given oracle access to any online sampler $S(\cdot)$ for $\overline{X}$ and $f(\cdot)$. Thus, if $\varepsilon \geq 1/\mathrm{poly}(N)$, $\overline{X}$ is efficiently online samplable, and f is efficient, then* Tam *would be efficient as well.*

We prove our Theorem 5 using ideas from the attack of [1] also for the Boolean case. In a nutshell, we follow the same 'greedy' approach, but the analysis of the attack in the blockwise setting becomes more challenging and we can no longer get the same bias of $+p$ in the balanced case. Indeed, achieving the bias of $+p$ for balanced functions in the blockwise setting is *not* possible in general! For full proof of Theorem 5 please see the full version.

Remark 3 (Robustness vs. p-obliviousness). Note that in both Theorems 5 and 4 the attackers are robust in the sense that they work simultaneously for all $[p, 1]$ probability trees (i.e., they only rely on the lower-bound p for the probability of the tampering to happen for each block). However, this feature of the attacker should not be confused with another aspect of our attackers that they are *p-oblivious*, meaning the tampering algorithm Tam does not rely on knowing p either. Putting these two together, it means that the attackers of Theorems 4 and 5 could be "generated" independently of the probability tree ρ under which the tampering to the randomness will eventually happen, and yet the quality of obtained bias only depend on the minimum over all the probabilities under which the blocks become tamperable.

---

[5] The sample complexity measure is an important factor in some of the applications of our biasing attacks. For example, to attack the soundness of learning algorithms through targeted poisoning attacks, the sample complexity of the attacker translates into how much 'fresh' data is needed to substitute the original training examples when the tampering happens.

[6] The analysis of the greedy attack of [1] shows that the amount of bias is at least $p \cdot (1 - |\mu|)$. Our bound depends on $1 - \mu^2$ instead of $1 - |\mu|$. The reason behind this is that we use a better approximation of the probabilities for the output to be -1 or $+1$.

Computationally Unbounded p-Tampering. One might wonder what are the 'potential' and 'limitations' of the power of blockwise p-tampering attacks. Even though our focus in this work is on the computationally bounded setting, we also study the power and limitations of computationally unbounded p-tampering attacks. Showing the power of attackers in the unbounded model might eventually shed light into how to get better efficient attackers as well, and proving limitations in this model imply strong limits for efficient tampering algorithms as well. In Full version of this paper we show that the better biasing bound of Theorem 5 could be obtained for bounded real functions as well, but this comes with an inefficient p-tampering, and achieving this bound efficiently remains as an open question. Perhaps surprisingly, we also show that there are balanced functions over block sources where the best bias by (even inefficient) p-tampering attacks is smaller than $0.7p$. This comes in contrast with the bitwise p-tampering model where p is the optimal possible bias in general. See Full version for more details.

4 Applications of p-Tampering Biasing Attacks

In this subsection we describe some of the applications of our main results on blockwise p-tampering of bounded functions in several different contexts.

4.1 Efficient p-Tampering Attacks on Extractors

Rather than proving Theorem 2, here we prove a more general result by defining yet another generalization of SV sources based on the notion of max-divergence [23] (see Definition 6) which is tightly related to p-tampering variations. Intuitively, we will show that $\overline{X}$ is an (ℓ, γ) block SV source if the uniform distribution U_ℓ^n is a p-tampering variation of $\overline{X}$ for $p \approx \gamma$. We will then show that our p-tampering attacker of Theorem 4 produces $\overline{Y}$ such that $\overline{X}$ itself is a $O(p)$-tampering variation of $\overline{Y}$! We first define the following generalization of block-SV sources based on max-divergence.

Definition 16 (MD and MMD Sources). *Let $\overline{X} = (X_1, \ldots, X_n)$ be a joint distribution. For real number $r \geq 0$, we call a joint distribution $\overline{Y} = (Y_1, \ldots, Y_n)$ an $(\overline{X}, r)$-max-divergence (MD) source if $\operatorname{Supp}(\overline{Y}) = \operatorname{Supp}(\overline{X})$ and for all $i \in [n], x_{<i} \in \operatorname{ValPref}(\overline{X})$ the max-divergence $D_\infty((X_i \mid x_{<i}) \| (Y_i \mid x_{<i}))$ is at most r. We call $\overline{Y}$ an $(\overline{X}, r)$ mutual MD (MMD) source if in addition $\overline{X}$ is an $(\overline{Y}, r)$ MD source as well.*

Remark 4 (Sources based on other distance measures). The above definition uses max-divergence in order to limit how 'far' the source $\overline{Y}$ can be from the 'central' random process $\overline{X} = (X_1, \ldots, X_n)$. Alternative definitions could be obtained by using other distance metrics and measures. For example, we can also define $(\overline{X}, r)$ KL sources to include all distributions $\overline{Y}$ such that $D_{\mathsf{KL}}((X_i \mid x_{<i}) \| (Y_i \mid x_{<i})) \leq r$. A result of [23] (see Part 3 of Lemma 3) shows that any $(\overline{X}, r)$ *mutual* MD source is also a $(\overline{X}, r')$ KL-source for $r' = r(2^r - 1)$ which is $r' \leq r^2$ for any $r \leq 1$.

The following claim shows that MD sources and p-tampering variations are tightly related. The proof directly follows from definitions of MD sources and p-variations.

Claim 1 (MD sources vs. tampering variations). $\overline{Y} = (Y_1, \ldots, Y_n)$ *is an* $(\overline{X}, r)$-*MD source iff it is a p-tampering variation of* $\overline{X}$ *for* $p = 1 - 2^{-r}$.

The following claim shows that MD sources are also related to SV block sources (in the 'reverse' direction), and its proof directly follows from the definition of MD sources and Part 2 of Lemma 3.

Claim 2 (MD sources vs. block SV sources). *For a joint distribution* $\overline{X} = (X_1, \ldots, X_n)$, U_ℓ^n *is an* $(\overline{X}, r)$-*MD source iff* $\overline{X}$ *is an* $(\ell, \ell - r)$ *block SV source. In particular, if* $\overline{X}$ *is an* $(U_\ell^n, \ell - r)$-*MMD source, then it is also an* $(\ell, \ell - r)$-*block SV source.*

Theorem 2 follows from Claim 2 above and the following general result about the impossibility of deterministic extraction from MMD sources.

Theorem 6 (Impossibility of extractors from MMD sources). *Let* $\overline{X} = (X_1, \ldots, X_n)$ *be a joint distribution with an efficient online sampler, and let* $f \colon \mathrm{Supp}(\overline{X}) \mapsto \{+1, -1\}$ *be an efficient Boolean function. Then, there is a p-tampering variation* $\overline{Y}$ *of* $\overline{X}$ *where:*

1. $\overline{Y}$ *is an* $(\overline{X}, p)$ *MMD source.*
2. $|\mathbb{E}[f(\overline{Y})]| \geq \Omega(p)$.
3. $\overline{Y}$ *is generated by an* efficient *tampering algorithm* Tam.

The first two items in Theorem 6 imply that f cannot be an extractor for $(\overline{X}, p)$ MMD sources for *any* $\overline{X} = (X_1, \ldots, X_n)$. Moreover, one can show that the source $\overline{Y}$ is also a $(\overline{X}, p^2)$ KL source because it is a $(\overline{X}, p)$ *mutual* MD source (see Remark 4).

Efficiency of the attacker. The last condition shows that the p-tampering attack against such f (as a candidate extractor) could be implemented by an *efficient p-tampering attacker*. We emphasize that the efficiency condition again is crucial here. In fact, if we change the statement of Theorem 6 by (1) restricting $\overline{X} = (Z \times \cdots \times Z)$ to iid distributions and more importantly (2) allowing Tam to be computationally unbounded, then we can derive this weaker version of Theorem 6 from the recent impossibility result of [6] for generalized SV sources as follows. Beigi et al. [6] showed that bit extraction with $o(1)$ bias from generalized SV sources (Definition 9) is impossible if (1) all the distributions $D \in \mathcal{D}$ available to the adversary have full support over the alphabet set C and that (2) the span of distributions $\mathcal{D}$ (see Definition 3) has full dimension $|C|$. To apply their result to MMD sources, we observe that (1) the distribution of Y_i where $\overline{Y} = (Y_1, \ldots, Y_n)$ is an $(\overline{X}, r)$ MMD source has full support (i.e., $\mathrm{Supp}(Z) = C$) and that (2) conditioned on any $y_{\leq i-1}$, the set of all possible distributions for Y_i forms a polytope with *full* rank $|\mathrm{Supp}(Z)|$.

Proof (Proof of Theorem 6). To prove Theorem 6 we use Theorem 4 and rely on some specific properties of the p-tampering attacker there. Even though the function f is Boolean, for some minor technical reasons, we will actually use the p-tampering attacker of Theorem 4 for *real* output functions. In the following we will show that this attacker has the properties listed in Theorem 6.

First note that without loss of generality, we can assume that $\mathbb{E}[f(\overline{X})] \geq 0$ (as otherwise we can work with $-f$ and bias it towards $+1$). In that case, the second and third properties of Theorem 6 follow from the main properties of Tam as stated in Theorem 4. However, for getting the first property (that it gives us an MMD source) we need to get into the actual attack's description from the proof of Theorem 4 given in Subsect. 5.1, which we also describe here. This attacker Tam (for the *real* output case) is based on one-rejection sampling (of Construction 1) modified as follows. Whenever the tampering algorithm is given the chance to tamper with a new block (which happens with probability p), the attacker itself tosses a coin and decides *not* to tamper with the block with probability 0.5, and otherwise will actually run the one-rejection sampling of Construction 1. Thus, during the execution of the p-tampering attack, tampering actually happens with probability $p/2$.

As described above, the tampering happens with probability $p/2$, so by Claim 1, it holds that $\overline{Y}$ is an $(\overline{X}, r)$ MD source for $r \leq \lg(1/(1 - p/2)) \leq p$ (by $p \in [0,1]$). On the other hand, the one-rejection sampling is actually used only with probability $p/2$. Therefore, for every possible $y_{\leq i}$, if we let $\alpha = \Pr[X_i = y_i \mid y_{\leq i-1}]$, then it holds that $\Pr[Y_i = y_i \mid y_{\leq i-1}] \leq (1 - p/2) \cdot \alpha + (p/2) \cdot (2\alpha) \leq (1 + p/2) \cdot \alpha$, because, either no tampering happens with probability $1 - p/2$ and even if it happens, because the tampering algorithm only uses two samples for the tampered block, by a union bound, the probability of sampling y_i in this case is at most 2α, which means that $\overline{X}$ is an $(\overline{Y}, r)$ MD source for $r \leq \lg(1 + p/2) \leq p$ (by $p \in [0,1]$).

Putting things together, it holds that $\overline{Y}$ is indeed an $(\overline{X}, p)$ MMD source.

4.2 Targeted Poisoning Attacks on Learners

Terminology. Let $\mathcal{D}$ be the domain containing all the objects of interest in a learning problem, and let $\mathcal{C}$ be a class of *concept* functions mapping objects in $\mathcal{D}$ to a set of labels $\mathcal{T}$. A labeled example from the set $\mathcal{D}$ for a concept function $c \in \mathcal{C}$ is a pair $x = (d, c(d))$ where $d \in \mathcal{D}$. We use $\mathcal{P}_c = \{(d, c(d)) \mid d \in \mathcal{D}\}$ to denote all the labeled examples from $\mathcal{D}$. The goal of a learning algorithm L is to produce a *hypothesis* $h \in \mathcal{H}$ after receiving a sequence $x = (x_1, \ldots, x_n)$ of labeled examples that we call the training sequence, such that h can predict the label of a given input from $\mathcal{D}$. The examples in the training sequence are usually sampled independently from a distribution X over $\mathcal{P}_c$ through an oracle $O_X(.)$ that we call the *training oracle*. A subset $\mathcal{X} \subseteq \mathcal{P}_c$ is a *test set* if we use it to evaluate the performance of the hypothesis h.

Definition 17 (Cost and average cost). *A cost function* $\mathsf{cost} : \mathcal{H} \times 2^{\mathcal{P}_c} \to [0,1]$ *captures the quality of a hypothesis, and the lower the value of* $\mathsf{cost}(h, \mathcal{X})$, *the better h is performing on the examples in* $\mathcal{X}$. *We define the average cost function for a learning algorithm L and a test set* $\mathcal{X}$ *according to a specific training oracle as follows:*

$$\overline{\text{cost}}_L^O(\mathcal{X}) = \underset{\substack{x_1,\ldots,x_n \leftarrow O \\ h \leftarrow L(x_1,\ldots,x_n)}}{\mathbb{E}} [\text{cost}(h,\mathcal{X})]$$

For example the cost functions might be the fraction of examples in $\mathcal{X}$ that h generate a wrong label for. The test set itself can consist of only one point, or it might be very large to model the scenario where sampling an example from $\mathcal{X}$ is equivalent to sampling from X.[7]

Definition 18 (p-tampering training oracles). *Let* O_X *be the training oracle for a distribution* X. *A p-tampering oracle* $\widehat{O}_X^p$ *works as follows. Whenever the training algorithm queries this oracle, with probability* $1 - p$ *the answer is generated from the original oracle* O_X *and with probability p a stateful adversary gets the control over the oracle and answers with an arbitrary pair* (d,t) *such that* $(d,t) \in \mathcal{P}_c$. *We call* $\widehat{O}_X^p$ *efficient, if the pair* (d,t) *is generated using an efficient p-tampering algorithm that takes as input* 1^N, *where N is the total length of the training sequence x, and all the previous samples in the training sequence.*

We can use our Theorem 4 to increase the average cost of even randomized learners where the cost could also be a real number. In the following theorem we do exactly that. However, the quality of this attack depends on the variance of the learner's success probability (as defined in Theorem 7). Thus, a provable randomized remedy against our attacks need, as the first step, to bound the variance parameter defined in Theorem 7.

Theorem 7 (Power of targeted poisoning attack against real cost functions). *Let* $\mathcal{C}$ *be a concept class defined over domain* $\mathcal{D}$. *Also let L be a (potentially randomized) learning algorithm for* $\mathcal{C}$ *which takes a sequence of labeled examples* $x = (x_1,\ldots,x_n)$ *that are sampled using an efficient training oracle* O_X *and outputs a hypothesis* $h \in \mathcal{H}$. *For any such learning algorithm L that tries to learn a concept* $c \in \mathcal{C}$, *any* $p \in [0,1]$, *any test set* $\mathcal{X}$ *and any cost function* $\text{cost} : \mathcal{H} \times 2^{\mathcal{P}_c} \rightarrow [0,1]$ *there exists a p-tampering training oracle* $\widehat{O}_X^p$ *such that if we sample x using* $\widehat{O}_X^p$ *instead of* O_X *the average cost increases as follows:*

$$\overline{\text{cost}}_L^{\widehat{O}_X^p}(\mathcal{X}) \geq \overline{\text{cost}}_L^{O_X}(\mathcal{X}) + \Omega(p \cdot \sigma^2)$$

where

$$\sigma^2 = \text{Var}_{x_1,\ldots,x_n \leftarrow O_X} \left[\underset{h \leftarrow L(x_1,\ldots,x_n)}{\mathbb{E}} [\text{cost}(h,\mathcal{X})] \right].$$

---

[7] In case the test data comes from X itself (i.e., $\mathcal{X} \equiv X$), the average cost becomes tightly related to PAC learnability [41]. In particular, if we define cost to be one whenever the hypothesis h generates a wrong label, then any (ε, δ)-PAC learner has average cost at most $\varepsilon + \delta$. Conversely, if the average cost is at most γ, then by an averaging argument we get a $(\sqrt{\gamma}, \sqrt{\gamma})$-PAC learner.

Moreover, if L is efficient, X is efficiently samplable, and $\mathsf{cost}(\cdot)$ is efficiently computable, then the corresponding p-tampering attack is efficient as well.

Proof. Assume L uses its own randomness $r \leftarrow R$ in addition to $(x_1, \ldots, x_n)$ and outputs a hypothesis h. For a fixed test set $\mathcal{X}$, we define a function $f : \mathcal{C}_p^n \times \mathrm{Supp}(R) \to [-1, +1]$ as follows:

$$f(x_1, \ldots, x_n, r) = 2 \cdot \mathsf{cost}(L(x_1, \ldots, x_n, r), \mathcal{X}) - 1.$$

The output of the cost function is between 0 and 1, so the output of f is between -1 and $+1$. Now by using our biasing attacks over *part* of the randomness of randomized functions (i.e., Corollary 2) there exists a p-tampering variation $\overline{Y}$ of X^n, generated through an efficient tampering attack, that biases f as follows:

$$\widehat{\mu} = \mathop{\mathbb{E}}_{\substack{x_1, \ldots, x_n \leftarrow \overline{Y} \\ r \leftarrow R}} [f(x_1, \ldots, x_n, r)] > \mu + \frac{p}{7} \cdot v$$

$$\text{where} \quad \mu = \mathop{\mathbb{E}}_{\substack{x_1, \ldots, x_n \leftarrow X^n \\ r \leftarrow R}} [f(x_1, \ldots, x_n, r)]$$

$$\text{and} \quad v = \mathrm{Var}_{x_1, \ldots, x_n \leftarrow X^n} \left[\mathbb{E}_{r \leftarrow R}[f(x_1, \ldots, x_n, r)] \right].$$

Since $\overline{Y}$ is a p-tampering variation of X^n generated by an efficient tampering attack, there is an efficient p-tampering training oracle $\widehat{O}_X^p$ that generates $\overline{Y}$. By the linearity of expectation, we have $\widehat{\mu} = 2 \cdot \overline{\mathsf{cost}}_L^{\widehat{O}_X^p}(\mathcal{X}) - 1$, $\mu = 2 \cdot \overline{\mathsf{cost}}_L^{O_X^p}(\mathcal{X}) - 1$. In addition, it holds that $v = 4 \cdot \sigma^2$, so by replacing $\widehat{\mu}$, μ and v we get

$$\overline{\mathsf{cost}}_L^{\widehat{O}_X^p}(\mathcal{X}) \geq \overline{\mathsf{cost}}_L^{O_X^p}(\mathcal{X}) + \frac{2p}{7} \cdot \sigma^2.$$

This bound of the above theorem could be indeed very weak as it depends on the variance of the cost of the generated hypothesis. In particular, the change could be $o(1)$. As we will see, for the special case of Boolean cost functions (e.g., classification) we can increase the error arbitrarily close to one.

Theorem 8. (Power of targeted poisoning attacks against classifiers). *Let $\mathcal{C}$ be a concept class defined over domain $\mathcal{D}$. Also let L be a deterministic, learning algorithm for $\mathcal{C}$ which takes a sequence of labeled examples $x = (x_1, \ldots, x_n)$ that are sampled using an efficient training oracle O_X and outputs a hypothesis $h \in \mathcal{H}$. For any such learning algorithm L that tries to learn a concept $c \in \mathcal{C}$, any $p \in [0, 1]$, any test set $\mathcal{X}$ and any cost function $\mathsf{cost} : \mathcal{H} \times 2^{\mathcal{P}_c} \to \{0, 1\}$ there exist a p-tampering training oracle $\widehat{O}_X^p$ such that if we sample x using $\widehat{O}_X^p$ instead of O_X, the average cost increases as:*

$$\overline{\mathsf{cost}}_L^{\widehat{O}_X^p}(\mathcal{X}) \geq \delta + \frac{p(\delta - \delta^2)}{1 - p(1 - \delta)} \quad \text{where} \quad \delta = \overline{\mathsf{cost}}_L^{O_X}(\mathcal{X}).$$

Moreover, if L and $\mathsf{cost}(\cdot)$ are efficient and X is efficiently samplable, then for any $\varepsilon > 0$ our p-tampering training oracle can be implemented in time $\mathrm{poly}(\frac{n}{\varepsilon \cdot \delta})$ and achieve $\overline{\mathsf{cost}}_L^{\widehat{O}_X^p}(\mathcal{X}) \geq \delta + \frac{p(\delta - \delta^2)}{1 - p(1 - \delta)} - \varepsilon.$

The proof of Theorem 8 is based on Theorem 5.

Proof (Proof of Theorem 8). We define a function $f : \mathcal{C}_p^n \to [-1, +1]$ as follows:

$$f(x_1, \ldots, x_n) = 2 \cdot \text{cost}(L(x_1, \ldots, x_n), \mathcal{X}) - 1.$$

Now using Theorem 5, there exist a p-tampering variation $\overline{Y}$ of X^n that biases f as follows:

$$\widehat{\mu} = \mathop{\mathbb{E}}_{x_1, \ldots, x_n \leftarrow \overline{Y}} \geq \mu + \frac{p \cdot (1 - \mu^2)}{2 - p(1 - \mu)} \quad \text{where} \quad \mu = \mathop{\mathbb{E}}_{x_1, \ldots, x_n \leftarrow X^n} [f(x_1, \ldots, x_n)].$$

Since $\overline{Y}$ is a p-tampering variation of X^n, there is an p-tampering training oracle $\widehat{O}_X^p$ that generates $\overline{Y}$. With a simple calculation we have $\widehat{\mu} = 2 \cdot \overline{\text{cost}}_L^{\widehat{O}_X^p}(\mathcal{X}) - 1$ and $\mu = 2 \cdot \delta - 1$. By replacing $\widehat{\mu}$ and μ we get

$$\overline{\text{cost}}_L^{\widehat{O}_X^p}(\mathcal{X}) \geq \delta + \frac{p \cdot (\delta - \delta^2)}{1 - p \cdot (1 - \delta)}.$$

The efficient version of our attack also directly follows from the efficient version of Theorem 5.

A natural Boolean cost function can be defined as

$$\text{cost}(h, \mathcal{X}) = \begin{cases} 0 & \text{if } h(d) = t \text{ for all } (d, t) \in \mathcal{X} \\ 1 & \text{otherwise} \end{cases}$$

where the cost function outputs 0 if the hypothesis is correct on all the examples in the test set. A special interesting case is where X' contains a single element $t \leftarrow X$ sampled from X itself, but the adversary knows this test example and hopes to increase the error of classifying t.

Corollary 3 (Doubling the error). *For every deterministic learning algorithm L that outputs a hypothesis h by taking a sequence of n labeled examples generated by an oracle O_X and for every Boolean cost function $\text{cost} \colon \mathcal{H} \times 2^{\mathcal{P}_c} \to \{0, 1\}$, there exist a p-tampering training oracle $\widehat{O}_X^p$, using $p = \frac{1}{2(1-\delta)}$, such that doubles the average cost $\delta = \overline{\text{cost}}_L^{O_X}(\mathcal{X})$ into 2δ. (I.e., for small error δ, we can double it by using $p \approx 1/2$.)*

5 Efficient p-Tampering Attacks Biasing Bounded Functions

In this section we will formally prove Theorems 4. As described in Sect. 1.2, some of the ideas (and even notation) that we use here goes back to the original work of Austrin et al. [1] and here we show how to extend these arguments to the blockwise setting and overcome challenges that emerge.

Before doing so, we need to define some useful notation for the notions that naturally come up in our proofs. We will also make some basic observations about these quantities before proving our main theorems.

Definition 19 (Functions $\hat{f}, g, \mathcal{G}, \mathcal{A}, \mathcal{Q}$). *Suppose $f \colon \mathrm{Supp}(\overline{X}) \mapsto \mathbb{R}$ is defined over a joint distribution $\overline{X} = (X_1, \ldots, X_n)$, $i \in [n]$, and $x_{\leq i} \in \mathrm{ValPref}(\overline{X})$ is a valid prefix for $\overline{X}$. Then we define the following with respect to $f, \overline{X}, x_{\leq i}$.*

- *$f_{x_{\leq i}}(\cdot)$ is a function defined as $f_{x_{\leq i}}(x_{\geq i+1}) = f(x)$ where $x = (x_{\leq i}, x_{\geq i+1})$.*
- *$\hat{f}[x_{\leq i}] = \mathbb{E}_{x_{\geq i+1} \leftarrow (X_{\geq i+1} | x_{\leq i})} [f_{x_{\leq i}}(x_{\geq i+1})]$. We also use $\mu = \hat{f}[\varnothing]$ to denote $\hat{f}[x_{\leq 0}] = \mathbb{E}[f(\overline{X})]$.*
- *We define the gain of the "node" $x_{\leq i}$ (compared to its parent $x_{\leq i-1}$) as $g[x_{\leq i}] = \hat{f}[x_{\leq i}] - \hat{f}[x_{\leq i-1}]$. This defines the change in $\hat{f}[x_{\leq i}]$ after moving to the i'th block.*
- *For every $x_{\leq i-1}$ and every distribution Z that could depend on $x_{\leq i-1}$ (e.g., Z is the output of a randomized algorithm that takes $x_{\leq i-1}$ as input) and $\mathrm{Supp}(Z \mid x_{\leq i-1}) \subseteq \mathrm{Supp}(X_i \mid x_{\leq i-1})$ we define:*
  - *The average of the gain over the "children" of node $x_{\leq i-1}$ under distribution $(Z \mid x_{\leq i-1})$:*

$$\mathcal{G}_Z[x_{\leq i-1}] = \mathop{\mathbb{E}}_{x_i \leftarrow (Z | x_{\leq i-1})} [g[x_{\leq i}]].$$

  - *The average of the squares of the gains:*

$$\mathcal{Q}_Z[x_{\leq i-1}] = \mathop{\mathbb{E}}_{x_i \leftarrow (Z | x_{\leq i-1})} \left[g[x_{\leq i}]^2 \right].$$

Notation. Throughout the following sections, whenever we define $\overline{X}$ and f, then we will use all the notations defined in Definition 19 with respect to f and $\overline{X}$ even if there are other distributions like $\overline{Y}$ defined.

The following lemma directly follows from the definition of μ and $g[x_{\leq i}]$.

Proposition 1. *For every $x \in \mathrm{Supp}(\overline{X})$, $f(x) = \mu + \sum_{i \in [n]} g[x_{\leq i}]$.*

The following two intuitive propositions also follow from the definition of $\mathcal{G}_{X_i}[x_{\leq i-1}]$ (See the full version for the proofs.).

Proposition 2. *For every valid prefix $x_{\leq i-1} \in \mathrm{ValPref}(\overline{X})$, we have $\mathcal{G}_{X_i}[x_{\leq i-1}] = 0$.*

Proposition 3. *Let $f \colon \mathrm{Supp}(\overline{X}) \mapsto \mathbb{R}$ be any real-output function. Then for any distribution $\overline{Y}$ such that $\mathrm{Supp}(\overline{Y}) \subseteq \mathrm{Supp}(\overline{X})$ it holds that $\mathbb{E}[f(\overline{Y})] - \mathbb{E}[f(\overline{X})] = \sum_{i \in [n]} \mathbb{E}_{Y_{\leq i-1}} [\mathcal{G}_{Y_i}[Y_{\leq i-1}]]$.*

The above proposition holds for any distribution $\overline{Y}$ as long as $\mathrm{Supp}(\overline{Y}) \subseteq \mathrm{Supp}(\overline{X})$, but the following is just about ρ-tampering variations.

Proposition 4. *For any probability tree ρ over $\overline{X}$, and any ρ-tampering variation $\overline{Y}$ of $\overline{X}$ generated by a (possibly randomized) tampering algorithm Tam, and for any $y_{\leq i-1} \in \mathrm{ValPref}(\overline{X})$, it holds that $\mathcal{G}_{Y_i}[y_{\leq i-1}] = \rho[y_{\leq i-1}] \cdot \mathcal{G}_{\mathsf{Tam}}[y_{\leq i-1}]$.*

Proof. The proof simply follows from the definition of ρ-tampering variations. When we sample from the distribution $(Y_i \mid \overline{Y}_{\leq i-1} = y_{\leq i})$, by definition, with probability $1 - \rho[y_{\leq i-1}]$ we will be sampling Y_i from $(X_i \mid X_{\leq i-1} = y_{\leq i-1})$ which by Proposition 2 leads to gaining $\mathcal{G}_{X_i}[y_{\leq i-1}] = 0$, and with probability $\rho[y_{\leq i-1}]$ we will be sampling Y_i from $\mathsf{Tam}(y_{\leq i-1})$ which leads to gaining $\mathcal{G}_{\mathsf{Tam}}[y_{\leq i-1}]$. Putting together, this implies an average gain of $\rho[y_{\leq i-1}] \cdot \mathcal{G}_{\mathsf{Tam}}[y_{\leq i-1}]$.

5.1   Biasing Real-Output Functions: Proving Theorem 4

In this Section we will prove our Theorem 4.

Construction 1. *Let* $\overline{X} = (X_1, \ldots, X_n)$ *be the joint distribution and* $f \colon \mathrm{Supp}(\overline{X}) \mapsto [-1, +1]$. *The one rejection sampling tampering algorithm* ORSam *works as follows. Given the valid prefix* $y_{\leq i-1} \in \mathrm{ValPref}(\overline{X})$, *the tampering algorithm would sample* $y_{\geq i} \leftarrow (X_{\geq i} \mid y_{\leq i-1})$ *by multiple invocations of the online sampler* S. *Then it computes* $s = f(y_1, \ldots, y_n)$ *and output from the following random variable.*

$$
T = \begin{cases} \text{Case 1: with probability} \frac{1+s}{2} \text{output} y_i. \\ \text{Case 2: with probability} \frac{1-s}{2} \text{output a fresh sample} y_i' \leftarrow S(y_{\leq i-1}). \end{cases}
$$

Claim 3. *For every* $f : \mathrm{Supp}(\overline{X}) \to [-1, +1]$ *and every* $[p, q]$-*probability tree* ρ *over* $\overline{X}$, *the tampering algorithm* ORSam *of construction 1 generates a* ρ-*tampering variation* $\overline{Y}$ *of* $\overline{X}$ *such that* $\mathbb{E}[f(\overline{Y})] \geq \mathbb{E}[f(\overline{X})] + \frac{p \cdot (1-q)}{2 + 2p - 2q - pq} \cdot$ $\mathrm{Var}[f(\overline{X})]$, *and if* $f : \mathrm{Supp}(\overline{X}) \to \{+1, -1\}$ *is Boolean, then* $\mathbb{E}[f(\overline{Y})] \geq \mathbb{E}[f(\overline{X})] + \frac{p}{2+2p} \cdot \mathrm{Var}[f(\overline{X})]$.

We first prove Theorem 4 using Claim 3, and then we will prove Claim 3

Proof (Proof of Theorem 4). We need to show that there is an attack that can bias f by $\Omega(p)$. For the Boolean case the proof follows directly from the statement of Claim 3. For the case of real-output functions we use an attacker that with probability 0.5 uses uses a fresh sample, and with probability 0.5 it runs the one-rejection sampling attack of Construction 1. This algorithm gives a ρ-tampering variation $\overline{Y}$ of $\overline{X}$ such that $\forall y_{\leq i} \in \mathrm{ValPref}(\overline{X}), \frac{p}{2} \leq \rho[y_{\leq i}] \leq \frac{1}{2}$ so using Claim 3 we have:

$$
\mathbb{E}[f(\overline{Y})] - \mathbb{E}[f(\overline{X})] \geq \frac{p/4}{1 + 3p/4} \mathrm{Var}[f(\overline{X})] = \frac{p}{4 + 3p} \mathrm{Var}[f(\overline{X})].
$$

In the rest of this section we will first prove three lemmas and then will use them to prove Claim 3. All along we use $\overline{Y}$ to denote the ρ-tampering variation of $\overline{X}$ generated by one rejection sampling algorithm ORSam of Construction 1.

Claim 4. *Let* $T \equiv \mathsf{ORSam}(y_{\leq i-1})$ *be a random variable defined over the randomness of* ORSam *running on a valid prefix* $y_{\leq i-1} \in \mathrm{ValPref}(\overline{X})$. *The probability distribution of this random variable is:*

$$
\Pr[T = y_i] = \left(1 + \frac{g[y_{\leq i}]}{2}\right) \cdot \Pr[X_i = y_i \mid y_{\leq i-1}].
$$

Proof. We have two cases in the attack. We first compute the probability of Case 1.

$$\Pr[\text{Case } 1 \wedge T = y_i] = \underset{y_{>i} \leftarrow (X_{>i}|y_{\leq i-1})}{\mathbb{E}} \left[\frac{1 + f(y)}{2} \right] \cdot \Pr[X_i = y_i \mid y_{\leq i-1}]$$

$$= \left(\frac{1 + \hat{f}[y_{\leq i}]}{2} \right) \cdot \Pr[X_i = y_i \mid y_{\leq i-1}].$$

On the other hand, the probability of Case 2 is

$$\Pr[\text{Case } 2 \wedge T = y_i] = \Pr[T = y_i \mid \text{Case } 2] \cdot \Pr[\text{Case } 2]$$

$$= \Pr[X_i = y_i \mid y_{\leq i-1}] \cdot \underset{y_{>i-1} \leftarrow (X_{>i-1}|y_{\leq i-1})}{\mathbb{E}} \left[\frac{1 - f(y)}{2} \right]$$

$$= \Pr[X_i = y_i \mid y_{\leq i-1}] \cdot \left(\frac{1 - \hat{f}[y_{\leq i-1}]}{2} \right).$$

Thus, we have

$$\Pr[T = y_i] = \Pr[\text{Case } 1 \wedge T = y_i] + \Pr[\text{Case } 2 \wedge T = y_i]$$

$$= \left(\frac{1 + \hat{f}[y_{\leq i}]}{2} \right) \cdot \Pr[X_i = y_i \mid y_{\leq i-1}]$$

$$+ \Pr[X_i = y_i \mid y_{\leq i-1}] \cdot \left(\frac{1 - \hat{f}[y_{\leq i-1}]}{2} \right)$$

$$= \left(1 + \frac{g[y_{\leq i}]}{2} \right) \cdot \Pr[X_i = y_i \mid y_{\leq i-1}].$$

Corollary 4. *For any $y_{\leq i} \in \mathrm{ValPref}(\overline{X})$, it holds that*

$$\Pr[Y_i = y_i \mid y_{\leq i-1}] = \left(1 + \frac{\rho[y_{\leq i-1}] \cdot g[y_{\leq i}]}{2} \right) \cdot \Pr[X_i = y_i \mid y_{\leq i-1}].$$

Proof. By definition of $\overline{Y}$ we have

$$\Pr[Y_i = y_i \mid y_{\leq i-1}] = (1 - \rho[y_{\leq i-1}]) \cdot \Pr[X_i = y_i \mid y_{\leq i-1}]$$
$$+ \rho[y_{\leq i-1}] \cdot \Pr[y_i = \mathrm{ORSam}(y_{\leq i-1})]$$
$$(\text{by Claim } 4) \quad = (1 - \rho[y_{\leq i-1}] + \rho[y_{\leq i-1}] \cdot (1 + \frac{g[y_{\leq i}]}{2})) \Pr[X_i = y_i \mid y_{\leq i-1}]$$
$$= \left(1 + \frac{\rho[y_{\leq i-1}] \cdot g[y_{\leq i}]}{2} \right) \cdot \Pr[X_i = y_i \mid y_{\leq i-1}].$$

Lemma 1. *Let $\overline{X} = (X_1, \ldots, X_n)$. For every function $f \colon \mathrm{Supp}(\overline{X}) \to [-1, +1]$ and every $[p, 1]$-probability tree ρ over $\overline{X}$, if $\overline{Y}$ is the ρ-tampering variation of* *distribution* $\overline{X}$ *generated by tampering algorithm* ORSam *of construction 1, and if* $\mu = \mathbb{E}[f(\overline{X})]$, *then it holds that*

$$\mathbb{E}[f(\overline{Y})] \geq \mu + \frac{p}{2(1+p)} \cdot \left(\mathbb{E}[f(\overline{Y})^2] - \mu^2\right).$$

Before proving the above lemma, we will need to prove several other claims.

Claim 5 (One rejection sampling's local gains). *For any* $y_{\leq i} \in$ ValPref$(\overline{X})$, *it holds that*

$$\mathcal{G}_{\mathsf{ORSam}}[y_{\leq i-1}] = \mathcal{Q}_{X_i}[y_{\leq i-1}]/2.$$

Proof. First note that $\mathcal{G}_{\mathsf{ORSam}}[y_{\leq i-1}] = \sum_{y_i} \Pr[y_i = \mathsf{ORSam}(y_{\leq i})] \cdot g[y_{\leq i}]$. By Claim 4 we get

$$\mathcal{G}_{\mathsf{ORSam}}[y_{\leq i-1}] = \sum_{y_i} \Pr[X_i = y_i \mid y_{\leq i-1}] \cdot \left(1 + \frac{g[y_{\leq i}]}{2}\right) \cdot g[y_{\leq i}]$$

$$= \sum_{y_i} \Pr[X_i = y_i \mid y_{\leq i-1}] \cdot g[y_{\leq i}] + \sum_{y_i} \Pr[X_i = y_i \mid y_{\leq i-1}] \cdot \frac{g[y_{\leq i}]^2}{2}$$

$$= \mathcal{G}_{X_i}[y_{\leq i-1}] + \frac{\mathcal{Q}_{X_i}[y_{\leq i-1}]}{2}.$$

By Proposition 2 we also know that $\mathcal{G}_{X_i}[y_{\leq i-1}] = 0$, so $\mathcal{G}_{\mathsf{ORSam}}[y_{\leq i-1}] = \mathcal{Q}_{X_i}[y_{\leq i-1}]/2$.

Corollary 5. *For any* $y_{\leq i-1} \in$ ValPref$(\overline{X})$, *it holds that* $\mathcal{G}_{Y_i}[y_{\leq i-1}] = \frac{\rho[y_{\leq i-1}]}{2} \cdot \mathcal{Q}_{X_i}[y_{\leq i-1}]$.

Proof.

$$\mathcal{G}_{Y_i}[y_{\leq i-1}] = \sum_{y_i} \Pr[y_i = Y_i \mid y_{\leq i-1}] \cdot g[y_{\leq i}]$$

$$= \sum_{y_i} \left((1 - \rho[y_{\leq i-1}]) \cdot \Pr[y_i = X_i \mid y_{\leq i-1}]\right) \cdot g[y_{\leq i}]$$

$$+ \sum_{y_i} \left(\rho[y_{\leq i-1}] \cdot \Pr\left[y_i = \mathsf{ORSam}(y_{\leq i-1})\right]\right) \cdot g[y_{\leq i}]$$

$$= (1 - \rho[y_{\leq i-1}]) \cdot \mathcal{G}_{X_i}[y_{\leq i-1}] + \rho[y_{\leq i-1}] \cdot \mathcal{G}_{\mathsf{ORSam}}[y_{\leq i-1}]$$

(by Proposition 2) $\quad = \rho[y_{\leq i-1}] \cdot \mathcal{G}_{\mathsf{ORSam}}[y_{\leq i-1}]$

(by Claim 5) $\quad = \frac{\rho[y_{\leq i-1}]}{2} \cdot \mathcal{Q}_{X_i}[y_{\leq i-1}].$

Corollary 6. $\mathbb{E}_{\overline{Y}}[f(\overline{Y})] = \mu + \sum_{i=1}^{n} \mathbb{E}_{Y_{\leq i-1}}\left[\frac{\rho[Y_{\leq i-1}]}{2} \cdot \mathcal{Q}_{X_i}[Y_{\leq i-1}]\right].$

Proof. Using Claim 3, we have $\mathbb{E}_{\overline{Y}}[f(\overline{Y})] = \mu + \sum_{i=1}^{n} \mathbb{E}_{Y_{\leq i-1}}[\mathcal{G}_{Y_i}[Y_{\leq i-1}]]$. By also using Corollary 5 we obtain $\mathbb{E}_{\overline{Y}}[f(\overline{Y})] = \mu + \sum_{i=1}^{n} \mathbb{E}_{Y_{\leq i-1}}\left[\frac{\rho[Y_{\leq i-1}]}{2} \cdot \mathcal{Q}_{X_i}[Y_{\leq i-1}]\right].$

Claim 6. *For every $x \in \text{Supp}(\overline{X})$, it holds that*

$$f(x)^2 = \mu^2 + \sum_{i=1}^{n} \left(g[x_{\leq i}]^2 + 2\hat{f}[x_{\leq i-1}] \cdot g[x_{\leq i}] \right).$$

Proof. By squaring the equation in Proposition 1 we get

$$f(x)^2 = \mu^2 + \sum_{i=1}^{n} g[x_{\leq i}]^2 + 2 \sum_{i=1}^{n} g[x_{\leq i}] \cdot (\mu + \sum_{j=1}^{i-1} .g[x_{\leq j}])$$

By the definition of $g[x_{\leq j}]$ it holds that $\hat{f}[x_{\leq i-1}] = \mu + \sum_{j=1}^{i-1} g[x_{\leq j}]$. So we get

$$f(x)^2 = \mu^2 + \sum_{i=1}^{n} \left(g[x_{\leq i}]^2 + 2\hat{f}[x_{\leq i-1}] \cdot g[x_{\leq i}] \right).$$

You can find the proof of the following two claims in the full version of this paper.

Claim 7. *For any $y_{\leq i-1} \in \text{ValPref}(\overline{X})$, it holds that*

$$\mathcal{Q}_{Y_i}[y_{\leq i-1}] = \mathcal{Q}_{X_i}[y_{\leq i-1}] + \underset{X_i | y_{\leq i-1}}{\mathbb{E}} \left[\frac{\rho[y_{\leq i-1}]}{2} \cdot g[(y_{\leq i-1}, X_i)]^3 \right].$$

Claim 8. *For any $y_{\leq i-1} \in \text{ValPref}(\overline{X})$, it holds that*

$$\hat{f}[y_{\leq i-1}] \cdot \mathcal{Q}_{X_i}[y_{\leq i-1}] + \underset{X_i | y_{\leq i-1}}{\mathbb{E}} \left[g[(y_{\leq i-1}, X_i)]^3 \right] \leq \mathcal{Q}_{X_i}[y_{\leq i-1}].$$

Claim 9. *For any $[p, 1]$-probability tree ρ over $\overline{X}$ it holds that*

$$\mathbb{E}[f(\overline{Y})^2] \leq \mu^2 + \frac{1+p}{p} \cdot \sum_{i=1}^{n} \underset{Y_{\leq i-1}}{\mathbb{E}} \left[\rho[Y_{\leq i-1}] \mathcal{Q}_{X_i}[Y_{\leq i-1}] \right].$$

Proof. Using Claim 6 we have

$$\underset{\overline{Y}}{\mathbb{E}}[f(\overline{Y})^2] - \mu^2 = \sum_{i=1}^{n} \underset{\overline{Y}}{\mathbb{E}} \left[g[Y_{\leq i}]^2 + 2\hat{f}[Y_{\leq i-1}] \cdot g[Y_{\leq i}] \right]$$

$$= \sum_{i=1}^{n} \underset{Y_{\leq i-1}}{\mathbb{E}} [\underset{Y_i | Y_{\leq i-1}}{\mathbb{E}} [g[Y_{\leq i}]^2]] + 2\sum_{i=1}^{n} \underset{Y_{\leq i-1}}{\mathbb{E}} [\hat{f}[Y_{\leq i-1}] \cdot \underset{Y_i | Y_{\leq i-1}}{\mathbb{E}} [g[Y_{\leq i}]]]$$

$$= \sum_{i=1}^{n} \underset{Y_{\leq i-1}}{\mathbb{E}} [\mathcal{Q}_{Y_i}[Y_{\leq i-1}]] + 2 \sum_{i=1}^{n} \underset{Y_{\leq i-1}}{\mathbb{E}} [\hat{f}[Y_{\leq i-1}] \cdot \mathcal{G}_{Y_i}[\overline{Y}_{\leq i-1}]]$$

$$\text{(by Claim 7)} \quad = \sum_{i=1}^{n} \underset{Y_{\leq i-1}}{\mathbb{E}} \left[\mathcal{Q}_{X_i}[Y_{\leq i-1}] + \frac{\rho[Y_{\leq i-1}]}{2} \underset{X_i | Y_{\leq i-1}}{\mathbb{E}} [g[(Y_{\leq i-1}, X_i)]^3] \right]$$

$$+ \sum_{i=1}^{n} \mathop{\mathbb{E}}_{Y_{\leq i-1}} \left[2\hat{f}[Y_{\leq i-1}] \cdot \mathcal{G}_{Y_i}[Y_{\leq i-1}] \right]$$

(by Corollary 5) $$= \sum_{i=1}^{n} \mathop{\mathbb{E}}_{Y_{\leq i-1}} \left[\mathcal{Q}_{X_i}[Y_{\leq i-1}] + \frac{\rho[Y_{\leq i-1}]}{2} \mathop{\mathbb{E}}_{X_i | Y_{\leq i-1}} [g[(Y_{\leq i-1}, X_i)]^3] \right]$$

$$+ \sum_{i=1}^{n} \mathop{\mathbb{E}}_{Y_{\leq i-1}} \left[\rho[Y_{\leq i-1}] \hat{f}[Y_{\leq i-1}] \mathcal{Q}_{X_i}[Y_{\leq i-1}] \right]$$

(by Claim 8) $$\leq \sum_{i=1}^{n} \mathop{\mathbb{E}}_{Y_{\leq i-1}} \left[\mathcal{Q}_{X_i}[Y_{\leq i-1}] + \frac{\rho[Y_{\leq i-1}]}{2} \cdot \mathcal{Q}_{X_i}[Y_{\leq i-1}] \right]$$

$$+ \sum_{i=1}^{n} \mathop{\mathbb{E}}_{Y_{\leq i-1}} \left[\frac{\rho[Y_{\leq i-1}]}{2} \cdot \hat{f}[Y_{\leq i-1}] \cdot \mathcal{Q}_{X_i}[Y_{\leq i-1}] \right]$$

(by $\hat{f}[Y_{\leq i-1}] \leq 1$) $$\leq \sum_{i=1}^{n} \mathop{\mathbb{E}}_{Y_{\leq i-1}} [(1 + \rho[Y_{\leq i-1}]) \cdot \mathcal{Q}_{X_i}[Y_{\leq i-1}]]$$

(by $\rho[Y_{\leq i-1}] \geq p$) $$\leq \left(\frac{1}{p} + 1 \right) \cdot \sum_{i=1}^{n} \mathop{\mathbb{E}}_{Y_{\leq i-1}} [\rho[Y_{\leq i-1}] \cdot \mathcal{Q}_{X_i}[Y_{\leq i-1}]].$$

Now we will prove Lemma 1.

Proof (Proof of Lemma 1). Using Claim 9 we have

$$\sum_{i=1}^{n} \mathop{\mathbb{E}}_{Y_{\leq i-1}} [\rho[Y_{\leq i-1}] \mathcal{Q}_{X_i}[Y_{\leq i-1}]] \geq \frac{p}{1+p} \cdot (\mathop{\mathbb{E}}_{\overline{Y}}[f(\overline{Y})^2] - \mu^2)$$

By also applying Corollary 6 we get $\mathbb{E}[f(\overline{Y})] \geq \mu + \frac{p}{2(1+p)} \cdot (\mathbb{E}[f(\overline{Y})^2] - \mu^2)$.

Lemma 2. *For every function* $f \colon \overline{X} \to [-1, +1]$ *and every* $[0, q]$*-probability tree* ρ *over* $\overline{X}$, *if* $\overline{Y}$ *is the* ρ*-tampering variation of distribution* $\overline{X}$ *generated by tampering algorithm* ORSam *of construction 1 it holds that*

$$\mathop{\mathbb{E}}_{\overline{Y}}[f(\overline{Y})] + \frac{1-q}{q} \cdot \mathop{\mathbb{E}}_{\overline{Y}}[f(\overline{Y})^2] + \frac{1-q}{2q} \cdot \mathop{\mathbb{E}}_{\overline{Y}}[f(\overline{Y})^2]^2 \geq \mathbb{E}[f(\overline{X})] + \frac{1-q}{q} \mathbb{E}[f(\overline{X})^2]$$

$$+ \frac{1-q}{2q} \cdot \mathbb{E}[f(\overline{X})^2]^2.$$

Before proving Lemma 2 we need to define a few useful functions.

Definition 20 (Functions $t, r, \hat{t}$ **and the potential function).** *Let* $t \colon \mathrm{Supp}(\overline{X}) \to [0, 1]$ *be the square of* f, *namely for every* $y \in \mathrm{Supp}(\overline{X}), t(y) = f(y)^2$. *We also define* $\hat{t}$ *the same way we defined* $\hat{f}$ *in Definition 19. Namely, for every valid prefix* $x_{\leq i} \in \mathrm{ValPref}(\overline{X})$ *we have* $\hat{t}[x_{\leq i}] = \mathbb{E}_{x_{\geq i+1} \leftarrow (X_{\geq i+1} | x_{\leq i})}[t_{x_{\leq i}}(x_{\geq i+1})]$. *Also for every valid prefix* $y_{\leq i}$ *for* $\overline{X}$ *let* r *be defined as* $r[y_{\leq i}] = \hat{t}[y_{\leq i}] - \hat{t}[y_{\leq i-1}]$ *and for every* $i \in [n]$ *and every valid prefix* $y_{\leq i} \in \mathrm{ValPref}(\overline{X})$ *let the potential function* Φ *be defined as follows:* $\Phi(y_{\leq i}) = \hat{f}[y_{\leq i}] + \frac{1-q}{q} \cdot \hat{t}[y_{\leq i}] + \frac{1-q}{2q} \cdot (\hat{t}[y_{\leq i}])^2$.

Proposition 5. *If $y_{\leq i} \in \text{ValPref}(\overline{X})$, then $\mathbb{E}_{y_i \leftarrow (X_i | y_{\leq i-1})}[r[y_{\leq i}]] = 0$.*

Proof. The proof is identical to the proof of Proposition 2.

Claim 10 (Potential function does not decrease). $\mathbb{E}[\Phi(Y_{\leq i})] \geq \mathbb{E}[\Phi(Y_{\leq i-1})]$.

Proof. Please see the full version for the proof.

Now, Lemma 2 immediately follows from Claim 10.

Proof (Proof of Lemma 2). Using Claim 10 together with a simple induction we get

$$\mathbb{E}[\Phi(Y_{\leq n})] \geq \mathbb{E}[\Phi(Y_{\leq 0})]$$

which means

$$\mathbb{E}[f(\overline{Y})] + \frac{1-q}{q} \cdot \mathbb{E}[f(\overline{Y})^2] + \frac{1-q}{2q} \cdot \mathbb{E}[f(\overline{Y})^2]^2 \geq \mathbb{E}[f(\overline{X})] + \frac{1-q}{q}\mathbb{E}[f(\overline{X})^2]$$
$$+ \frac{1-q}{2q} \cdot \mathbb{E}[f(\overline{X})^2]^2.$$

Finally, we prove Claim 3.

Proof (Proof of Claim 3). Let $\alpha = \mathbb{E}[f(\overline{X})^2] - \mathbb{E}[f(\overline{Y})^2]$ and $\text{Var}[f(\overline{X})] = \mathbb{E}[f(\overline{X})^2] - \mathbb{E}[f(\overline{X})]^2$. Using Lemma 1 we have

$$\mathbb{E}[f(\overline{Y})] \geq \mathbb{E}[f(\overline{X})] + \frac{p}{2(1+p)} \cdot (\text{Var}[f(\overline{X})] - \alpha). \tag{2}$$

If $\alpha < 0$, using this inequality we have the following. (We assume $q < 1$ otherwise the inequality below holds trivially).

$$\mathbb{E}[f(\overline{Y})] \geq \mathbb{E}[f(\overline{X})] + \frac{p}{2(1+p)} \cdot \text{Var}[f(\overline{X})]$$

$$\geq \mathbb{E}[f(\overline{X})] + \frac{p(1-q)}{2(1+p)(1-q)} \cdot \text{Var}[f(\overline{X})]$$

$$\geq \mathbb{E}[f(\overline{X})] + \frac{p(1-q)}{2+2 \cdot p - 2 \cdot q - p \cdot q} \cdot \text{Var}[f(\overline{X})].$$

So we can assume $\alpha \geq 0$, in which case by also using Lemma 2 we get

$$\mathbb{E}[f(\overline{Y})] - \mathbb{E}[f(\overline{X})] \geq \frac{(1-q)}{q} \cdot (\mathbb{E}[f(\overline{X})^2] - \mathbb{E}[f(\overline{Y})^2]) + \frac{(1-q)}{2q}(\mathbb{E}[f(\overline{X})^2]^2$$

$$-\mathbb{E}[f(\overline{Y})^2]^2) \, (\text{By } \alpha \geq 0) \geq \frac{(1-q)}{q} \cdot (\mathbb{E}[f(\overline{X})^2] - \mathbb{E}[f(\overline{Y})^2]) = \frac{\alpha \cdot (1-q)}{q}. \tag{3}$$

By combining the Inequalities 2 and 3 we get

$$\mathbb{E}[f(\overline{Y})] - \mathbb{E}[f(\overline{X})] \geq \max\left(\frac{p}{2(1+p)} \cdot (\text{Var}[f(\overline{X})] - \alpha), \frac{\alpha \cdot (1-q)}{q} \right)$$

$$\geq \frac{p(1-q)}{2+2 \cdot p - 2 \cdot q - p \cdot q} \text{Var}[f(\overline{X})].$$

where the minimum is achieved when at $\frac{p\cdot(\text{Var}[f(\overline{X})]-\alpha)}{2(1+p)} = \frac{\alpha\cdot(1-q)}{q}$ at $\alpha = \frac{\text{Var}[f(\overline{X})]\cdot p\cdot q}{2p+2-pq-2q}$.

Remark 5. Austrin et al. [1] analyzed their mild greedy attack using a different potential function defined as follows:

$$\Phi(y_{\leq i}) = \hat{f}[y_{\leq i}] + \frac{1}{2}\cdot\hat{t}[y_{\leq i}] + \frac{1}{4}\cdot(\hat{t}[y_{\leq i}])^2.$$

Using this potential function they show that the amount of bias for mild greedy is at least $\frac{p}{1+4p}\cdot\text{Var}[f(\overline{X})]$. Using our p-dependent potential function

$$\Phi(y_{\leq i}) = \hat{f}[y_{\leq i}] + \frac{1}{2p}\cdot\hat{t}[y_{\leq i}] + \frac{1}{4p}\cdot(\hat{t}[y_{\leq i}])^2$$

one can get a slightly better bound (mainly for small p) of $\frac{p}{1+2p+2p^2}\cdot\text{Var}[f(/\overline{X})]$.

6   Open Questions

We conclude by describing some open questions and interesting directions for future research.

Power of k-sampling attacks for small k. A natural yet more general class of attacks that include k-resetting attacks at special case is the class of $k+1$ sampling attacks in which the tampering algorithm first gets $k+1$ samples from the distribution of the i'th tampered block and then it chooses one of these samples (perhaps by calls to the online sampler and the function f). Our ℓ-greedy algorithm is indeed an ℓ sampling attack but to get good bias, it needs to use many $\ell = \text{poly}(n/\varepsilon)$ samples. What is the power of ℓ-sampling attacks in general, when ℓ is small, e.g. constant?

Power of 'very' efficient viruses. What is the power of tampering attacks whose computational resources is not sufficient for sampling the next block or even computing f? Such tampering algorithms are natural for cryptographic attacks where computing f is heavy and the virus might prefer to use very limited resources not to be detected by the system. Our efficient tampering attacks of Theorems 4 and 5 both need to run the online sampler as well as the function f. It remains an interesting future direction to study the power of limited tampering attacks whose decisions are more 'local' and cannot be based on sampling the blocks from the original distribution or computing f.

We conjecture that such efficient viruses that cannot depend on f or the distribution $\overline{X}$ are not powerful to achieve constant bias $\Omega(p)$. However, it is interesting to find out what is the *minimum* number of calls needed to f or the sampler for getting bias $\Omega(p)$.

Biasing up vs. biasing either way. Our Theorems 4 and 5 always bias the function towards $+1$. Inspired by models of attacks against coin-tossing protocols

[8,14,15,17,29,34] one can ask the following questions. What is the power of p-tampering biasing attacks whose goal is to *either* bias the average of the function up *or* bias it down? Some of the applications of our biasing attacks (e.g., against learners) need to bias the function always in a fixed direction to increase the 'error', but other attacks (e.g., against extractors) could achieve their goal by biasing the function in either direction.

Acknowledgement. We thank Dimitrios Diochnos, Yevgeniy Dodis, and Yanjun Qi for useful discussions.

References

1. Austrin, P., Chung, K.-M., Mahmoody, M., Pass, R., Seth, K.: On the impossibility of cryptography with tamperable randomness. In: Garay, J.A., Gennaro, R. (eds.) CRYPTO 2014. LNCS, vol. 8616, pp. 462–479. Springer, Heidelberg (2014). doi:10.1007/978-3-662-44371-2_26
2. Awasthi, P., Balcan, M.F., Long, P.M.: The power of localization for efficiently learning linear separators with noise. In: Proceedings of the 46th Annual ACM Symposium on Theory of Computing, pp. 449–458. ACM (2014)
3. Azar, Y., Broder, A.Z., Karlin, A.R., Linial, N., Phillips, S.: Biased random walks. In: Proceedings of the Twenty-Fourth Annual ACM Symposium on Theory of Computing, pp. 1–9. ACM (1992)
4. Barak, B., Halevi, S.: A model and architecture for pseudo-random generation with applications to/dev/random. In: Proceedings of the 12th ACM Conference on Computer and Communications Security, pp. 203–212. ACM (2005)
5. Barreno, M., Nelson, B., Joseph, A.D., Tygar, J.D.: The security of machine learning. Mach. Learn. **81**(2), 121–148 (2010)
6. Beigi, S., Etesami, O., Gohari, A.: Deterministic randomness extraction from generalized and distributed santha-vazirani sources. SIAM J. Comput. **46**(1), 1–36 (2017)
7. Bellare, M., Paterson, K.G., Rogaway, P.: Security of symmetric encryption against mass surveillance. In: Garay, J.A., Gennaro, R. (eds.) CRYPTO 2014. LNCS, vol. 8616, pp. 1–19. Springer, Heidelberg (2014). doi:10.1007/978-3-662-44371-2_1
8. Berman, I., Haitner, I., Tentes, A.: Coin flipping of any constant bias implies one-way functions. In: Proceedings of the 46th Annual ACM Symposium on Theory of Computing, pp. 398–407. ACM (2014)
9. Boneh, D., DeMillo, R.A., Lipton, R.J.: On the importance of checking cryptographic protocols for faults. In: Fumy, W. (ed.) EUROCRYPT 1997. LNCS, vol. 1233, pp. 37–51. Springer, Heidelberg (1997). doi:10.1007/3-540-69053-0_4
10. Bshouty, N.H., Eiron, N., Kushilevitz, E.: PAC learning with nasty noise. Theor. Comput. Sci. **288**(2), 255–275 (2002)
11. Chandran, N., Goyal, V., Mukherjee, P., Pandey, O., Upadhyay, J.: Block-wise non-malleable codes. In: LIPIcs-Leibniz International Proceedings in Informatics, vol. 55. Schloss Dagstuhl-Leibniz-Zentrum fuer Informatik (2016)
12. Chor, B., Goldreich, O.: Unbiased bits from sources of weak randomness and probabilistic communication complexity. In: Proceedings of 26th FOCS, pp. 429–442. IEEE (1985)
13. Chor, B., Goldreich, O.: Unbiased bits from sources of weak randomness and probabilistic communication complexity. SIAM J. Comput. **17**(2), 230–261 (1988)

14. Cleve, R.: Limits on the security of coin flips when half the processors are faulty. In: Proceedings of the Eighteenth Annual ACM Symposium on Theory of Computing, pp. 364–369. ACM (1986)
15. Cleve, R., Impagliazzo, R.: Martingales, collective coin flipping and discrete control processes. In other words 1, 5 (1993)
16. Corrigan-Gibbs, H., Jana, S.: Recommendations for randomness in the operating system, or how to keep evil children out of your pool and other random facts. In: HotOS (2015)
17. Dachman-Soled, D., Lindell, Y., Mahmoody, M., Malkin, T.: On the black-box complexity of optimally-fair coin tossing. In: Ishai, Y. (ed.) TCC 2011. LNCS, vol. 6597, pp. 450–467. Springer, Heidelberg (2011). doi:10.1007/978-3-642-19571-6_27
18. Damgård, I., Faust, S., Mukherjee, P., Venturi, D.: Tamper resilient cryptography without self-destruct. Cryptology ePrint Archive, Report 2013/124 (2013). http://eprint.iacr.org/2013/124
19. Dodis, Y., Ong, S.J., Prabhakaran, M., Sahai, A.: On the (im)possibility of cryptography with imperfect randomness. In: FOCS: IEEE Symposium on Foundations of Computer Science (FOCS) (2004)
20. Dodis, Y.: New imperfect random source with applications to coin-flipping. In: Orejas, F., Spirakis, P.G., van Leeuwen, J. (eds.) ICALP 2001. LNCS, vol. 2076, pp. 297–309. Springer, Heidelberg (2001). doi:10.1007/3-540-48224-5_25
21. Dodis, Y., Pointcheval, D., Ruhault, S., Vergniaud, D., Wichs, D.: Security analysis of pseudo-random number generators with input:/dev/random is not robust. In: Proceedings of the 2013 ACM SIGSAC Conference on Computer & Communications Security, pp. 647–658. ACM (2013)
22. Dodis, Y., Yao, Y.: Privacy with imperfect randomness. In: Gennaro, R., Robshaw, M. (eds.) CRYPTO 2015. LNCS, vol. 9216, pp. 463–482. Springer, Heidelberg (2015). doi:10.1007/978-3-662-48000-7_23
23. Dwork, C., Rothblum, G.N., Vadhan, S.: Boosting and differential privacy. In: 2010 51st Annual IEEE Symposium on Foundations of Computer Science (FOCS), pp. 51–60. IEEE (2010)
24. Dziembowski, S., Faust, S., Standaert, F.-X.: Private circuits III: hardware Trojan-resilience via testing amplification. In: Weippl, E.R., Katzenbeisser, S., Kruegel, C., Myers, A.C., Halevi, S. (eds.) 23rd Conference on Computer and Communications Security, ACM CCS 2016, pp. 142–153. ACM Press, Vienna (2016)
25. Dziembowski, S., Pietrzak, K., Wichs, D.: Non-malleable codes. In: Yao, A.C.-C. (ed.) ICS, pp. 434–452. Tsinghua University Press (2010)
26. Gennaro, R., Lysyanskaya, A., Malkin, T., Micali, S., Rabin, T.: Algorithmic tamper-proof (ATP) security: theoretical foundations for security against hardware tampering. In: Naor, M. (ed.) TCC 2004. LNCS, vol. 2951, pp. 258–277. Springer, Heidelberg (2004). doi:10.1007/978-3-540-24638-1_15
27. Goldwasser, S., Kalai, Y.T., Park, S.: Adaptively secure coin-flipping, revisited. In: Halldórsson, M.M., Iwama, K., Kobayashi, N., Speckmann, B. (eds.) ICALP 2015. LNCS, vol. 9135, pp. 663–674. Springer, Heidelberg (2015). doi:10.1007/978-3-662-47666-6_53
28. Gutterman, Z., Pinkas, B., Reinman, T.: Analysis of the Linux random number generator. In: 2006 IEEE Symposium on Security and Privacy, p. 15. IEEE (2006)
29. Haitner, I., Omri, E.: Coin flipping with constant bias implies one-way functions. SIAM J. Comput. 43(2), 389–409 (2014)
30. Heninger, N., Durumeric, Z., Wustrow, E., Halderman, J.A.: Mining your Ps and Qs: detection of widespread weak keys in network devices. In: USENIX Security Symposium, vol. 8 (2012)

31. Kearns, M., Li, M.: Learning in the presence of malicious errors. SIAM J. Comput. **22**(4), 807–837 (1993)
32. Kiayias, A., Tselekounis, Y.: Tamper resilient circuits: the adversary at the gates. In: Sako, K., Sarkar, P. (eds.) ASIACRYPT 2013. LNCS, vol. 8270, pp. 161–180. Springer, Heidelberg (2013). doi:10.1007/978-3-642-42045-0_9
33. Lichtenstein, D., Linial, N., Saks, M.: Some extremal problems arising from discrete control processes. Combinatorica **9**(3), 269–287 (1989)
34. Maji, H.K., Prabhakaran, M., Sahai, A.: On the computational complexity of coin flipping. In: 2010 51st Annual IEEE Symposium on Foundations of Computer Science (FOCS), pp. 613–622. IEEE (2010)
35. Papernot, N., McDaniel, P., Sinha, A., Wellman, M.: Towards the science of security and privacy in machine learning. arXiv preprint arXiv:1611.03814 (2016)
36. Reingold, O., Vadhan, S., Wigderson, A.: A note on extracting randomness from santha-vazirani sources. Unpublished manuscript (2004)
37. Rubinstein, B.I.P., Nelson, B., Huang, L., Joseph, A.D., Lau, S.-H., Rao, S., Taft, N., Tygar, J.D.: Antidote: understanding and defending against poisoning of anomaly detectors. In: Proceedings of the 9th ACM SIGCOMM Conference on Internet Measurement Conference, pp. 1–14. ACM (2009)
38. Rubinstein, B.I.P., Nelson, B., Huang, L., Joseph, A.D., Lau, S.-H., Rao, S., Taft, N., Tygar, J.D.: Stealthy poisoning attacks on PCA-based anomaly detectors. ACM SIGMETRICS Perform. Eval. Rev. **37**(2), 73–74 (2009)
39. Santha, M., Vazirani, U.V.: Generating quasi-random sequences from semi-random sources. J. Comput. Syst. Sci. **33**(1), 75–87 (1986)
40. Shen, S., Tople, S., Saxena, P.: A uror: defending against poisoning attacks in collaborative deep learning systems. In: Proceedings of the 32nd Annual Conference on Computer Security Applications, pp. 508–519. ACM (2016)
41. Valiant, L.G.: A theory of the learnable. Commun. ACM **27**(11), 1134–1142 (1984)
42. Valiant, L.G.: Learning disjunction of conjunctions. In: IJCAI, pp. 560–566 (1985)
43. Von Neumann, J.: 13. various techniques used in connection with random digits. Appl. Math Ser **12**, 36–38 (1951)
44. Xiao, H., Biggio, B., Brown, G., Fumera, G., Eckert, C., Roli, F.: Is feature selection secure against training data poisoning? In: ICML, pp. 1689–1698 (2015)

Delegation

On Zero-Testable Homomorphic Encryption and Publicly Verifiable Non-interactive Arguments

Omer Paneth[1]([⊠]) and Guy N. Rothblum[2]

[1] MIT, Cambridge, USA
omerpa@gmail.com
[2] Weizmann Institute of Science, Rehovot, Israel

Abstract. We define and study *zero-testable homomorphic encryption* (ZTHE) – a *semantically secure*, somewhat homomorphic encryption scheme equipped with a *weak zero test* that can identify *trivial zeros*. These are ciphertexts that result from homomorphically evaluating an arithmetic circuit computing the zero polynomial over the integers. This is a relaxation of the (strong) zero test provided by the notion of graded encodings, which identifies all encodings of zero.

We show that ZTHE can suffice for powerful applications. Based on any ZTHE scheme that satisfies the additional properties of correctness on adversarial ciphertexts and multi-key homomorphism, we construct publicly verifiable non-interactive arguments for delegating computation. Such arguments were previously constructed from indistinguishability obfuscation or based on so-called knowledge assumptions. The arguments we construct are adaptively sound, based on an efficiently falsifiable assumption, and only make black-box use of the underlying cryptographic primitives.

We also show that a ZTHE scheme that is sufficient for our application can be constructed based on an efficiently-falsifiable assumption over so-called "clean" graded encodings.

1 Introduction

Recent breakthroughs in the study of fully homomorphic encryption [Gen09] and program obfuscation [GGH+13b] have revolutionized the foundations of cryptography. Fully homomorphic encryption (FHE) allows arbitrary polynomial-time computations to be performed "homomorphically" on encrypted data, while

---

This work subsumes an earlier report posted on the Cryptology ePrint Archive [PR14]. The current version features new results and addresses correctness issues with the earlier report.

O. Paneth—Research supported in part by NSF Grants CNS-1350619, CNS-1414119 and CNS-1413920, by the Defense Advanced Research Projects Agency (DARPA) and the U.S. Army Research Office under contracts W911NF-15-C-0226 and W911NF-15-C-0236 and by Simons Investigator Award Agreement Dated 6-5-12.

© International Association for Cryptologic Research 2017
Y. Kalai and L. Reyzin (Eds.): TCC 2017, Part II, LNCS 10678, pp. 283–315, 2017.
https://doi.org/10.1007/978-3-319-70503-3_9

ensuring that semantic security is maintained and *nothing* about the data can be learned. While this powerful security guarantee enables important applications, other scenarios require more fine-grained control: allowing some information about the data to be exposed, while other information remains hidden. Multilinear maps [BS02] and graded encodings [GGH13a] are basic building blocks that have proven to be incredibly useful in such scenarios. Intuitively, a graded encoding scheme is a *somewhat homomorphic encryption*, supporting homomorphic evaluation of low-degree algebraic computations, with an additional capability: an efficient *zero test* procedure that publicly identifies encodings of zero. Graded encodings cannot be semantically secure: the zero test procedure leaks *partial information* on the encoded elements. Nevertheless, other information can remain hidden (in particular, inverting the encoding might still be hard). This balance between functionality and security makes the notion of graded encoding incredibly useful for computing on encrypted data, with applications such as indistinguishability obfuscation and functional encryption [GGH+13b, GGHZ16].

While homomorphic encryption can by based on the Learning with Errors assumption [BV11, GSW13], the situation for graded encodings is less clear. Analyzing the security of existing candidates and designing new ones are central challenges [GGH13a, CLT15, GGH15, CHL+15, HJ16, MSZ16, GMM+16].

Zero-testable homomorphic encryption. In this work we define and study a new relaxation of graded encodings that we call zero-testable (somewhat) homomorphic encryption (ZTHE). A ZTHE is a semantically secure somewhat homomorphic encryption scheme equipped with a *weak zero test* that can only identify *trivial zeros*. These are ciphertexts that result from homomorphically evaluating an arithmetic circuit computing the zero polynomial over $\mathbb{Z}$. The weak zero test should accept such trivial zeros, but reject ciphertexts that encrypt non-zero values.

Importantly, an efficient weak zero test poses no contradiction to semantic security, since it does not allow to distinguish between encryptions of two different values. Given a ciphertext c it is possible to homomorphically evaluate a circuit P on c and test if the result is a trivial zero. However, this does not give any information on the value encrypted in c, since the zero test only required to pass if P vanishes on *all* values. Intuitively, the zero test is giving information on the evaluated computation P rather then on the ciphertext c. Indeed, semantic security implies that if P only vanishes on some values, then even if the evaluated ciphertext encrypts zero it will not pass the weak zero test (except with negligible probability). Otherwise, the zero test would have revealed information on the original encrypted evaluation point.

From ZTHE to delegation. The main technical result in this work demonstrates that ZTHE can suffice for powerful applications. Based on any ZTHE scheme that satisfies the additional properties of correctness on adversarial ciphertexts and multi-key homomorphism (we elaborate on these additional properties below), we construct *publicly verifiable non-interactive arguments for delegating computation*. Such arguments were previously constructed from indistinguishability obfuscation or based on so-called knowledge assumptions. Our construction follows a new approach and has important properties, such as adaptive soundness, reduction to an efficiently falsifiable assumption, and black-box use of the underlying cryptographic primitives. We note that the additional properties we assume (adversarial correctness and multi-key homomorphism) make ZTHE incomparable to "vanilla" graded encodings: the weak zero test assumption is more relaxed than the strong zero test of graded encodings schemes, but we require a stronger correctness property (namely correctness on adversarially generated ciphertexts).

ZTHE Candidate. We study the feasibility of constructing ZTHE. First, we observe that several existing somewhat homomorphic encryption schemes [Gen09, vDGHV10] admit a simple weak zero test. These schemes, however, do not satisfy the additional properties required for our non-interactive arguments. We construct ZTHE that is sufficient for our application based on an efficiently-falsifiable assumption over graded encodings with strong properties such as adversarial correctness. Our construction cannot be instantiated based on the existing graded encoding candidates (so-called "clean" graded encodings [Zim15, LV16] do guarantee these stronger properties). We leave the question of ZTHE instantiations as an important open problem and hope it will lead to new and improved deletion protocols based on weaker assumptions, as well as other applications.

Organization. In the rest of this introduction we elaborate on our results and techniques. Section 1.1 gives background on non-interactive arguments and discusses our main technical result, a construction of non-interactive arguments from ZTHE. In Sect. 1.2 we present our results in more detail. The construction of non-interactive arguments from ZTHE is described in Sect. 1.3. The construction of ZTHE from graded encodings is described in Sect. 1.4.

1.1 Non-interactive Arguments

Background. The power of efficiently verifiable proof systems is a foundational issue in the study of computation. A central goal is constructing proof systems that can be used by a powerful prover to convince a weak verifier of the correctness of a complex computational statement, usually framed as proving membership of an input x in a language $\mathcal{L}$. Beyond its foundational importance in the theory of computation, this question has real-world applications, such as *delegating computation*. In this setting, a powerful server (playing the role of the prover) can run a complex computation for a much weaker client (playing the role of the verifier), and provide a proof of the output's correctness.

A similar question was raised by Babai, Lund, Fortnow and Szegedy [BFLS91] in the PCP setting. Kilian [Kil92] and Micali [Mic94] gave the first candidate scheme for delegating computation. The question re-emerged in the theoretical literature in the work of Goldwasser, Kalai and Rothblum [GKR08], and became the focus of a rich body of research spanning theory and systems. See the recent survey by Walfish and Blumberg [WB13].

A "holy grail" for delegating computations is *fully non-interactive proofs*, comprised of a single message sent from the prover to the verifier with unconditional soundness, as in classic NP or Merlin-Arthur proofs. Unfortunately, there are serious barriers to constructing such proofs for delegating general deterministic computations (in particular, they imply Merlin-Arthur speedups for deterministic computations). Thus, a body of research has focused on computationally sound proofs in the common reference string model, where:

1. Soundness is only required to hold against *efficient* cheating provers. Computationally sound proof systems are commonly called *argument systems*.
2. There is a (public) *common reference string* (CRS), generated in advance by a trusted authority (or the verifier herself). This CRS can be used (repeatedly) by different parties to verify proofs. The prover and the verifier both have access to the CRS, but neither has access to the secret coins used to generate the CRS.

We focus on non-interactive argument systems for polynomial-time computations, where the verifier should be super-efficient (nearly-linear in the input length), and the honest prover should run in polynomial time. Non-interactive arguments are especially attractive for delegating computation, as any untrusted server can simply use the CRS to generate proofs and send them off (noninteractively and asynchronously), to be verified at the clients' convenience. We refer to such a system as a *publicly verifiable non-interactive argument for delegating computation*. For the remainder of this work, we use the term *non-interactive argument* as shorthand.

Prior works on non-interactive arguments. In his seminal work, Micali [Mic94] gave the first construction of non-interactive arguments in the random oracle model. However, instantiating random oracle model constructions in a provably secure way is notoriously difficult, and often impossible [CGH04, GW11]. A rich body of research has aimed to construct non-interactive arguments in the plain model led to a variety of beautiful constructions based on strong cryptographic assumptions.

One line of works based non-interactive arguments on non-falsifiable[1] *knowledge assumptions* such as the *knowledge of exponent assumption* in bilinear groups [Gro10, Lip12, DFH12, GGPR13, BCI+13, BCCT13]. A recent sequence of works [SW14, BGL+15, CHJV14, KLW14] show how to base non-interactive arguments on *indistinguishability obfuscation* (IO). Based on standard assumptions such as somewhat-homomorphic encryption or private information retrieval schemes, the works of [KRR13, KRR14, BHK16] achieve the weaker notion of *designated-verifier arguments*. These are two-message arguments where, in the first message, the verifier samples the CRS and sends it to the prover. The secret coins used to sample the CRS are required to verify the proof sent in the second message.

---

[1] A "falsifiable" assumption [Nao03] is one that can be efficiently refuted. Falsifiability is a basic "litmus test" for cryptographic assumptions.

This work. Our main technical result is a construction of non-interactive arguments from any ZTHE with the additional properties mentioned above (see Sect. 1.2). Our construction follows a different approach from previous works and leverages ideas and techniques that were previously used only in the context of designated-verifier arguments [KRR14,BHK16], such as efficient probabilistically checkable proofs and no-signaling soundness. As a result, our non-interactive arguments have some notable advantages compared to previous works:

- **Efficiently falsifiable assumptions.** Our arguments are based on the semantic security of the underlying ZTHE - an efficiently falsifiable assumption. Moreover, in our candidate construction of ZTHE from graded encodings, we further base semantic security of the ZTHE on a simple and efficiently falsifiable assumption on the graded encodings. Taken together, we can base soundness of the argument system on a falsifiable assumption on graded encodings.

  In contrast, the constructions of publicly verifiable non-interactive argument are based on assumptions that are not efficiently falsifiable. IO was recently constructed from simpler primitives such as multi-linear maps or functional encryption. However, these construction involve a sub-exponential security loss. While many applications of IO can be based directly on polynomially secure functional encryption, currently non-interactive arguments still require the full power of IO. For more information on this line of work, see [GPSZ17] and references therein.

  We note that for any particular non-interactive argument candidate, the assumption that the candidate is secure is efficiently falsifiable. Therefore, our focus will be on falsifiable assumptions that are elementary and natural compared to the tautological assumption that the candidate is secure.

- **Adaptive soundness.** The soundness of our non-interactive arguments is adaptive: it holds even when the statement proven is chosen as a function of the CRS. Adaptive soundness is required in many applications, and it is especially important in settings where the CRS is set "once and for all".

  We note that any sound argument can be turned into an adaptively sound one via "complexity leveraging". However, this reduction incurs an exponential loss in security, and therefore cannot be based on efficiently falsifiable assumptions.

- **Black-box construction.** In contrast to all previous construction of non-interactive arguments, our construction makes only black-box use of the underlying cryptographic primitives.[2] Understanding the feasibility and limitation of black-box constructions in cryptography is the subject of a rich body of work motivated both by theoretical interest as well as efficiency considerations.

---

[2] One exception is instantiating Micali's random oracle construction with a cryptographic hash function. However, beyond assuming this construction is secure, we do not know how to reduce its security to a simpler assumption.

1.2   Our Results in More Details

In this section we present our results in more details. We start by describing the basic notion of zero testable homomorphic encryption and the additional properties we consider.

Zero-testable homomorphic encryption. A homomorphic encryption is a semantically secure public key encryption equipped with a public evaluation algorithm that adds, subtracts and multiplies values homomorphically "under the encryption". We focus on somewhat homomorphic encryption that only supports homomorphic evaluation of polynomial-size arithmetic circuits of logarithmic degree. That is, of degree $c \cdot \log \lambda$ for any constant c, where λ is the security parameter. We require that ciphertexts are succinct: their size is bounded by some fixed polynomial in λ that is independent of c.

A zero-testable somewhat homomorphic encryption (ZTHE) has an additional zero test procedure that takes a ciphertext and tests if it is a trivial zero. In more detail, we consider the homomorphic evaluation of a circuit P over freshly encrypted ciphertexts $c_1, \ldots, c_n$, resulting in the evaluated ciphertext c. If the polynomial computed by P is identically zero over $\mathbb{Z}$, then we require that c passes the zero test. We also require that a ciphertext c' that decrypts to a non-zero value does not pass the zero-test. If c decrypts to zero, but it is not a trivial zero, we make no requirement on the outcome of the zero test. However, as discussed above, it follows from the semantic security of the encryption that such a ciphertext should not pass the zero test. Moreover, we note that even if P vanishes on all boolean inputs, but it is not identically zero as a polynomial over $\mathbb{Z}$, we still expect the zero test to fail. Otherwise, the zero test can be used to efficiently decide the satisfiability of P.

We further study the following additional properties of ZTHE, which we use in our construction of non-interactive arguments:

Multi-key evaluation. In multi-key homomorphic encryption, introduced by López-Alt et al. [LTV12], homomorphic computation can be executed over ciphertexts encrypted under different keys. To ensure semantic security, decrypting the result requires all secret keys. We use ZTHE for three keys. That is, it is possible to homomorphically compute over ciphertexts encrypted under at most three different keys, and to run a weak zero test on the result. Importantly, a system can generate ciphertext under an unbounded number of keys and any three of them can be combined in a homomorphic computation. The encryption may also use shared public parameters to generate all keys.

Correctness for adversarially generated ciphertexts. We require that an efficient adversary, given the public key, cannot generate a pair of ciphertexts that result in an evaluation error. A pair of ciphertexts c_1, c_2 cause an evaluation error if computing a homomorphic operation $\star$ over c_1, c_2 and decrypting the evaluated ciphertext c give a different result than decrypting c_1 and c_2 and computing $\star$ on the decrypted values. If c_1 and c_2 are generated honestly, this follows from the standard correctness guarantee of the encryption. However, we require correctness even when the ciphertext are not generated honestly. Note that the zero test is only required to accept honest ciphertexts that are trivially zero. However, even a malformed ciphertext that decrypts to a non-zero value should make the zero test reject.

In known constructions of somewhat homomorphic encryption, there exist invalid ciphertexts that do not represent an encryption of any value. To account for such candidates, we allow the decryption algorithm to fail. If c_1 or c_2 are invalid (fail to decrypt) we require that the evaluated ciphertext c is invalid as well. If both c_1 and c_2 are valid, we require that c is either invalid or it decrypts to the correct value.

Theorem 1.1 (Informal). *Assuming a 3-key zero-testable somewhat homomorphic encryption scheme with correctness for adversarially-generated ciphertexts, there exists an adaptively-secure publicly-verifiable non-interactive argument for delegating all polynomial time computations. The non-interactive argument uses the encryption scheme as a black box.*

Instantiations: discussion. We observe that existing constructions of somewhat homomorphic encryption, such as the ones in [Gen09, vDGHV10], already support zero testing: simply test if the ciphertext is zero in the ring of ciphertexts. More generally, in any encryption scheme where ciphertexts are elements of some ring, and the homomorphic operations on ciphertext identify with the ciphertext-ring operations, every trivial zero is represented by the zero of the ciphertext ring. While these construction satisfy the weak zero test requirement, they do not seem to support the additional properties stated above.

Following the observations in [LTV12, GHV10, HRSV11], any homomorphic encryption scheme that supports homomorphic computations of sufficiently large degree can be generically modified to satisfy both multi-key evaluation for a constant number of keys and correctness for adversarially generated ciphertexts. This transformation, however, may not preserve the weak zero test property. Roughly speaking, the generic transformation is based on the idea of bootstrapping [Gen09], where the evaluated circuit is modified to include the decryption circuit of the scheme itself. Now, even if we evaluate a circuit computing the zero polynomial, the modified circuit, which now runs the scheme's decryption circuit, will not be identically zero.

We show that ZTHE satisfying both additional properties can be constructed from graded encodings with additional properties described below.

Graded encoding. A graded encoding is an encoding scheme for elements of a ring. We consider a symmetric graded encoding that supports homomorphic computations of bounded degree Δ. The encoding scheme also features a (strong) zero test that identifies encodings of zero (even non-trivial ones). In Sect. 1.4 we describe the interface of a graded encoding scheme in more detail.

We consider graded encodings that satisfy a simple and natural decisional assumption.

Assumption 1.2 (Informal). *Given encoded coefficients $\alpha_0, \ldots, \alpha_\Delta$ of a random degree Δ polynomial, it is hard to distinguish an encoding of a root from an encoding of a random element.*

Intuitively, this problem should be hard since testing if the given encoding is a root requires a homomorphic computation of degree $\Delta + 1$.

To reduce the semantic security of the ZTHE to the above assumption on the graded encoding, we need the graded encodings to support a re-randomization operation. Intuitively, re-randomizing an encoding results in a new encoding of the same value that is otherwise independent of the original encodings. As in many other applications of graded encoding (for example [GLSW15]), the re-randomization operation is only needed in the reduction and not in the construction. We note that it is possible to avoid the use of randomization, but this requires making a more complicated and less natural (though still efficiently falsifiable) hardness assumption.

Correctness for adversarially generated encodings. In order to construct a ZTHE scheme with correctness for adversarially generated ciphertexts we need to require that the graded encoding themselves have correctness for adversarially generated ciphertexts. This is a non-standard requirement for graded encoding schemes, and it is not required in other applications such as obfuscation (where all encodings are generated by an honest party).

The correctness requirement for adversarially generated encodings is somewhat stronger than in the context of encryption. We require that it is hard to find a pair of valid encodings such that a homomorphic operation on them results in an invalid encoding. In order to support "noisy" candidates, where such an evaluation error always occurs after a large enough number of homomorphic evaluations, we also consider a relaxed requirement. Intuitively, it should be possible to publicly test that the level of noise in an adversarially generated encoding is low. If we determine that an encoding has low noise, it should support a large number of homomorphic operation without an error.

Theorem 1.3 (Informal). *Assuming a graded encoding scheme satisfying Assumption 1.2, there exists a $O(1)$-key zero-testable somewhat homomorphic encryption scheme. Moreover, if the graded encoding scheme is correct for adversarially generated encodings, then the encryption scheme is correct for adversarially generated ciphertexts.*

Instantiations: discussion. The existing constructions of graded encodings [GGH13a, CLT15, GGH15] that support re-randomization do not satisfy our hardness assumption [GGH13a, CHL+15, HJ16]. We don't know if in existing constructions of graded encodings it is possible to publicly test for low noise level. One potential strategy to implement such a test would be to combine the re-randomization and zero test operations. We note that so-called "clean" graded encoding schemes (see for example [Zim15, LV16]), where every element has a unique encoding, trivially satisfy correctness for adversarially generated encodings, and support re-randomization.

1.3 Non-interactive Arguments from Zero-Testable Homomorphic Encryption

Our construction is based on ideas developed in the context of designated-verifier arguments.

Designated-verifier arguments. Aiello *et al.* [ABOR00] suggested the following approach to constructing designated verifier arguments: The prover computes a probabilistically checkable proof (PCP) for the statement. The verifier's message contains PCP queries, encrypted using an FHE scheme, where each query is encrypted under a different key. The prover computes the PCP answers homomorphically, and the verifier decrypts and verifies the answers. The hope was that since a cheating prover couldn't tailor its answer to one query depending on other queries's values, the argument would inherit the PCP's soundness. Dwork *et al.* [DLN+04, DNR16] showed obstacles to proving this construction's soundness. Nonetheless, Kalai, Raz and Rothblum [KRR14] proved that when the underlying PCP satisfies a strong notion of soundness called *no-signaling* soundness, the suggested arguments are in fact sound.

Leaking information on queries: a failed attempt. A naive attempt to turn the above designated-verifier protocol into a publicly verifiable non-interactive argument would be to place the verifier's encrypted queries in the CRS, and provide some leakage on encrypted queries that allows verifying the evaluated answers, but (somehow) does not compromise the soundness of the protocol. We argue, however, that any such leakage must (inherently) compromise soundness. A cheating prover can begin with an accepting PCP proof, changing it into a rejecting proof one symbol at a time. By observing which of the intermediate proofs makes the verifier reject, the prover can recover the encrypted queries and break soundness.

Our approach: intuition. Our protocol follows the blueprint described above: the CRS contains encrypted queries, and the prover homomorphically evaluates the PCP and sends the evaluated queries as the proof. However, to make the proof publicly verifiable we *do not leak any information about the encrypted queries or their answers*. The main idea is to encrypt the queries with a ZTHE. By executing a sequence of homomorphic evaluations and zero tests on the evaluated ciphertexts in the proof, the verifier *learns information about the PCP proof computed by the prover*, which is sufficient to verify its validity.

Next we elaborate on this idea. We start by giving some background on the PCP system we use.

The BFLS PCP. The PCP of Babai et al. [BFLS91] proves that a given computation accepts its input. The tableau of the computation is translated into a multi-variate low-degree polynomial P_0 and the PCP proof contains all the evaluations of P_0 over some finite field. Testing the validity of the tableau is reduced to testing that P_0 is indeed a low-degree polynomial and that it vanishes on all *boolean* inputs. The proof that P_0 vanishes on all boolean inputs is based on the well-known sum-check protocol. The sum-check proof contains auxiliary polynomials $P_1, \ldots, P_m$ and the verifier tests that these polynomials satisfy some local low-degree relations of the form $R(P_i, P_{i+1}) \equiv 0$. These tests are carried out by probing the polynomials on a small number of random inputs and testing that the relations are satisfied.

A sketch of our protocol. As described above, the CRS contains encryptions $c_1, \ldots, c_m$ that specify queries to the PCP. Each triplet c_j, c_k, c_ℓ specifies an evaluation point for the polynomials $P_1, \ldots, P_m$. For every such triplet, and for every polynomial P_i, the proof contains the homomorphically evaluated answer $d_i = P_i(c_j, c_k, c_\ell)$. To verify the relation $R(P_i, P_{i+1}) \equiv 0$, the verifier homomorphically evaluates $R(d_i, d_{i+1})$ and tests that the evaluation results in a trivial zero. Since the different queries are encrypted under different keys, we use a *multi-key* homomorphic encryption scheme. While the CRS contains encryptions under m different keys, the verifier only computes homomorphically on three keys at a time, therefore we only need 3-key homomorphism.

The proof strategy. Intuitively, if the prover is cheating and $R(P_i, P_{i+1}) \not\equiv 0$ it follows from sematic security that the verifier's zero test fails. Alas, this intuition is fundamentally flawed. A cheating prover may not derive its answers by homomorphically evaluating the low degree polynomials $P_1, \ldots, P_m$, or any other polynomial for that matter. Our actual proof strategy is inspired by that of Kalai, Raz and Rothblum [KRR14] and consists of the following steps.

1. Since the encryption is semantically secure, the prover's answers are *no-signaling*, meaning that the decrypted answer to one query gives no information on the other queries values.
2. In the BFLS PCP, it is possible to reconstruct any small subset of entries L of the computation's tableau based on PCP values in some small set of locations $q(L)$. We show that our proof satisfies the following local soundness guarantee: if the verifier's encrypted queries include the locations $q(L)$ and if the verifier accepts the prover's encrypted answers then the reconstructed subset of the tableau is *locally consistent*. That is, it obeys the computation's local constrains. To show that this is the case even when the prover sends malformed answers we use the fact that the encryption scheme is correct for *adversarially generated ciphertext*.
3. By the semantic security of encrypted queries, and by the fact that the protocol is publicly verifiable, we deduce that if the verifier accepts the answers to *any* queries encrypted in the CRS (say the all-0 queries), it would also accept the answers to the to queries $q(L)$, for *every* subset L.
4. It follows that we can turn any convincing prover in our protocol into an algorithm that samples local assignments for any subset L of the computation's tableau that are guaranteed to be *both no-signaling and locally consistent*.
5. Based on the *augmented circuit technique* of [KRR14], we show how to use such a *local-assignment generator* to reconstruct a complete and valid tableau.

We note that our soundness proof is significantly simpler than that of [KRR14]. In particular we only use a striped down version of the BFLS PCP without any low-degree tests, and we do not argue that this PCP has no-signaling soundness. Intuitively, what enables this simplification is that in the publicly-verifiable setting we can move from local consistency for one subset to local consistency on all subsets using semantic security (see Step 3 above) and without using global properties of the PCP.

Proving *adaptive* soundness presents additional challenges. To argue adaptive soundness, we use ideas inspired by the recent work of Brakerski et al. [BHK16], who constructed an adaptively sound arguments in the designated-verifier setting. Roughly, they show how to reconstruct a tableau from any local-assignment generator that can chose the statement adaptively as a function of the subset L.

On the notion of local-assignment generator. The augmented circuit technique as well as the technique of reconstructing the computation's tableau by reading subsets that are no-signaling and locally-consistent originates from the analysis of [KRR14]. The notion of local-assignment generator and the generic transformation from a local-assignment generator to global soundness first appeared in an earlier version of this work [PR14]. Since then the local-assignment generator abstraction played a key role in achieving stronger designated-verifier arguments for RAM computations [KP16] and Batch-NP computations [BHK16], as well as in achieving adaptive soundness [BHK16]. In the current version of this work we use the adaptive local-assignment generator of [BHK16].

1.4   Zero-Testable Homomorphic Encryption from Graded Encodings

We start by describing the interface of a graded encoding scheme in more details. The scheme has public parameters that define a ring R and a maximal degree Δ. The scheme encodes elements in R and supports homomorphic computations up to degree Δ. Every encoding has a level. Freshly generated encodings are of level 1 and level-δ encodings are the result of a degree-δ homomorphic computation. We also refer to the elements of R as level-0 encoding. Following the standard formulation of graded encodings, we do not assume that the ring R is public. Instead, there is a public interface for sampling random level-0 encodings and evaluating the ring operations. We also assume that the public parameters include encodings of the constants 0 and 1 in every level.

The graded encoding supports a (strong) zero test that can publicly identify encodings of zero in any level. It also supports a re-randomization operation that, given an encoding, generates a new random encoding of the same element. For example, re-randomizing an encoding can be used to hide the homomorphic computation that generated it.

The ZTHE scheme. We construct multi-key ZTHE from graded encoding as follows. The scheme's public parameters are the parameters of a graded encoding scheme with degree bound Δ. The secret key is a random ring element $t \in R$ and the corresponding public key is a level-1 encoding of t.

An encryption c of a message $m \in \{0,1\}$ is given by a random degree-Δ univariate polynomial P such that $P(t) = m$. The ciphertext c consists of level-1 encodings of the $\Delta+1$ coefficients $\alpha_0,\ldots,\alpha_\Delta$ of P. The semantic security of this encryption follows from Assumption 1.2 that states that even given the public key encoding of t, the encodings in c are indistinguishable from encodings of random elements, independent of m.

Encryption. We need to sample such an encryption using only the public parameters and the public key encoding of t. A naive approach would be to sample all the coefficients of P except for the free coefficient α_0 randomly and then homomorphically compute an encoding of α_0. However, this would result in an encoding in level Δ instead of level 1. Instead we can sample all the coefficients of P as linear functions of t. We sample random ring elements $r_1,\ldots,r_\Delta$ and homomorphically compute encodings of the coefficients

$$\alpha_0 = m - r_1 \cdot t, \quad \ldots \quad, \alpha_i = r_i - r_{i+1}\cdot t, \quad \ldots \quad, \alpha_\Delta = r_\Delta.$$

Note that $\alpha_0,\ldots,\alpha_\Delta$ are indeed random subject to $\sum \alpha_i \cdot t^i = m$. Finally, we re-randomize the encoded coefficient to hide the process in which they where sampled (which depends on m).

We note that the re-randomization operation is only used during encryption. In our non-interactive argument the ZTHE encryption procedure is only used to generate the CRS and in the security proof. As noted above, we could avoid the use of re-randomization at the cost of making a more complicated assumption on the graded encoding that implies the CPA security of our encryption scheme in the secret key setting.

Same-Key homomorphic evaluation. Let c_1 and c_2 be ciphertexts encrypting messages m_1 and m_2 respectively under the same secret key t. Let P_1 and P_2 be the polynomials encoded by c_1 and c_2, where

$$P_1(t) = m_1, \quad P_2(t) = m_2.$$

To evaluate a homomorphic operation $\star \in \{+, -, \times\}$ we homomorphically compute the encoded coefficients of the polynomial $P_1 \star P_2$. Correctness follows since

$$(P_1 \star P_2)(t) = P_1(t) \star P_1(t) = m_1 \star m_2.$$

For addition and subtraction, the homomorphic computation of the new coefficients is a linear operation (over the input coefficients), and the degree of the resulting polynomial is the maximal degree of the two input polynomials. For multiplication, we homomorphically compute a convolution of the input coefficients, and the degree of the resulting polynomial is the sum of the degrees of the input polynomials. Thus, the evaluation of a degree-δ homomorphic computation yields coefficients that are encoded in level-δ of the graded encoding scheme, and the resulting (univariate) polynomial has degree $(\delta \cdot \Delta)$. It follows that the encryption supports degree-Δ homomorphic computations, before the level of encoded coefficient exceeds the degree bound.

Multi-key homomorphic evaluation. To compute a homomorphic operation $\star$ over ciphertexts c_1, c_2 encrypted under different secret keys t_1, t_2, we homomorphically compute the coefficients of the *bivariate* polynomial $P(x, y) \equiv P_1(x) \star P_2(y)$, where P_1 and P_2 are the polynomials encoded by c_1 and c_2 respectively. In general, a homomorphic computation involving ciphertexts under d different keys will result in a ciphertext encoding a d-variate polynomial. Since the number of coefficients grows exponentially with d, we only support homomorphic computation involving a constant number of keys.

Decryption. To decrypt a ciphertext c, we homomorphically evaluate the polynomial P it encodes on the secret key t. Since the secret key is a level-0 encoding, this homomorphic evaluation does not exceed the degree bound Δ. We then use the graded encoding zero test to compare the evaluated encoding to an encoding of 0 or of 1. If none of the tests succeed decryption fails.

Note that in homomorphic evaluation, the algebraic operation on the plaintexts are evaluated over the ring R. However, since our decryption only obtains *an encoding of* the plaintext, we can only decrypt messages in $\{0, 1\}$ (or more generally, messages taken from a small plaintext space). This is analogous to the behaviour of the additively-homomorphic ElGamal encryption and other schemes [BGN05]. Such decryption is sufficient for our application, where we evaluate arithmetic circuits (over $\mathbb{Z}$) whose outputs are expected to be boolean.

Zero Test. A ciphertext c that results from a homomorphic evaluation of a polynomial that is identically zero always encodes a polynomial $P \equiv 0$. We can test this by using the zero test procedure of the graded encoding, testing that all the encoded coefficient of P are zero. It is also the case that a ciphertext that passes the zero test must encode a polynomial $P \equiv 0$ and therefore it must decrypt to zero.

Correctness for adversarially generated ciphertexts. If the graded encoding scheme is correct even on adversarially generated encodings, we inherit this strong correctness guarantee also for the ciphertext. Note, however, that even a ciphertext that consists of valid encodings may encode a polynomial P such that $P(t) \notin \{0, 1\}$, and therefore fail to decrypt. To deal with this case, we consider an alternative decryption algorithm that is inefficient and can decrypt any value in R. The correctness requirement for adversarially generated ciphertexts is therefore defined with respect to this inefficient decryption procedure. The weaker correctness requirement suffices for proving the computational soundness of the non-interactive argument, even though it considers an inefficient decryption algorithm: once the correctness requirement is guaranteed, the remainder of the soundness proof is information theoretic.

1.5   Organization

The definition of non-interactive arguments and other preliminaries are given in Sect. 2. In Sect. 3 we define the notion of ZTHE and the additional properties we use. Section 4 describes the construction of non-interactive argument from ZTHE. The analysis of the non-interactive argument and the construction of ZTHE from graded encodings appear in the full version of this work.

2   Preliminaries

For a sequence $\mathbf{x} = (x_1, \ldots, x_n)$, we denote by $\mathbf{x}_{-i}$ the sequence with the i-th elements removed

$$\mathbf{x}_{-i} = (x_1, \ldots, x_{i-1}, x_{i+1}, x_n).$$

For a pair of sequences $\mathbf{x} = (x_1, \ldots, x_n)$ and $\mathbf{y} = (y_1, \ldots, y_{n'})$ we denote by $\mathbf{x} \mid \mathbf{y}$ the concatenated sequence

$$\mathbf{x} \mid \mathbf{y} = (x_1, \ldots, x_n, y_1, \ldots, y_{n'}).$$

2.1   Arithmetic Circuits

We consider arithmetic circuits with binary addition, subtraction and multiplication gates. We only allow use of the constants $\{0, 1\}$.

Degree. For an arithmetic circuit C, the degree (resp. total degree) of C is the individual (resp. total) degree of the formal polynomial computed by C. A degree-1 circuit is said to be multi-linear.

Equivalence. An arithmetic circuit C is said to be identically zero (denoted by $C \equiv 0$) if the formal polynomial computed by C is identically zero over $\mathbb{Z}$. Two arithmetic circuits C_1, C_2 are said to be equivalent (denoted by $C_1 \equiv C_2$) if $C_1 - C_2 \equiv 0$.

Computing boolean functions. An arithmetic circuit C is said to compute a boolean function f if C agrees with f when evaluated over $\mathbb{Z}$. That is, if f takes n inputs, then for every $x \in \{0, 1\}^n$ we have that $f(x) = C(x)$ when C is evaluated over $\mathbb{Z}$.

Fact 2.1. *Let C_1 and C_2 be arithmetic circuits with n inputs wires computing boolean functions f_1 and f_2 respectively.*

1. *The circuit $1 - C_1$ computes the boolean function $1 - f_1$.*
2. *The circuit $C_1 \cdot C_2$ computes the boolean function $f_1 \cdot f_2$.*
3. *If for every $x \in \{0, 1\}^n$, at most one of the values $C_1(x)$ and $C_2(x)$ is nonzero, then the circuit $C_1 + C_2$ computes the boolean function $f_1 + f_2$.*

Circuit restrictions. Let C be an arithmetic circuit with n inputs wires and individual degree δ. For $i \in [n]$ let $C|_{i,0}, \ldots, C|_{i,\delta}$ be the arithmetic circuits with $n - 1$ inputs wires and individual degree δ such that

$$C(x_1, \ldots, x_n) \equiv \sum_{j \in [0, \delta]} C|_{i,j}(x_1, \ldots, x_{i-1}, x_{i+1}, \ldots, x_n) \cdot x_i^j. \tag{1}$$

For $j > \delta$ let $C|_{i,j}$ denote the identically 0 circuit.

Fact 2.2. *There is an procedure that given an arithmetic circuit C with n inputs wires and individual degree δ and given an index $i \in [n]$ computes $C|_{i,0}, \ldots, C|_{i,\delta}$ in time $\mathrm{poly}(|C|, \delta)$.*

2.2 Multi-linear Extension

A multi-linear extension of a boolean function f is a multi-linear arithmetic circuit C computing f. Next we describe a multi-linear extension circuit of an arbitrary boolean function f.

Let β_n be the multi-linear arithmetic circuit with $2n$ inputs computing the boolean identity function. That is, for every $\mathbf{x}, \mathbf{y} \in \{0,1\}^n$, $\beta_n(\mathbf{x}, \mathbf{y}) = 1$ if and only if $\mathbf{x} = \mathbf{y}$. The arithmetic circuit β_n is given by the expression

$$\beta_n(x_1, \ldots, x_n, y_1, \ldots, y_n) = \prod_{i \in [n]} x_i y_i + (1 - x_i)(1 - y_i). \tag{2}$$

We sometimes omit the subscript n when it is clear from the context.

The multi-linear extension of a boolean function f with n inputs is given by the arithmetic circuit

$$C(\mathbf{x}) = \sum_{\mathbf{y} \in \{0,1\}^n} \beta_n(\mathbf{x}, \mathbf{y}) \cdot f(\mathbf{y}). \tag{3}$$

Since for every $\mathbf{x} \in \{0,1\}^n$ there exist only one value of $\mathbf{y} \in \{0,1\}^n$ such that $\beta_n(\mathbf{x}, \mathbf{y}) \neq 0$, it follows by Fact 2.1 that C computes the boolean function f.

2.3 Publicly-Verifiable Non-interactive Arguments

In this section we define publicly verifiable non-interactive arguments.

Let $\mathcal{U}$ be the universal language such that $(x, \mathsf{T}) \in \mathcal{U}$ for $x = (M, y)$ if and only if the Turing machine M accepts the input y within at most T steps.

Syntax. A publicly verifiable non-interactive argument scheme for the universal language $\mathcal{U}$ consists of PPT algorithms $(\mathsf{Del.Gen}, \mathsf{Del.P}, \mathsf{Del.V})$ with the following syntax.

$\mathsf{Del.Gen}$: Given the security parameter 1^λ, outputs a common reference string CRS.

$\mathsf{Del.P}$: Given the common reference string, a time bound 1^T in unary representation and an instance $x \in \{0,1\}^*$, outputs a proof Π.

$\mathsf{Del.V}$: Given the common reference string, a time bound T in binary representation, an instance $x \in \{0,1\}^*$ and a proof Π, outputs a bit.

Definition 2.1. *A publicly verifiable non-interactive argument scheme* $(\mathsf{Del.Gen}, \mathsf{Del.P}, \mathsf{Del.V})$ *for the universal language* $\mathcal{U}$ *satisfies the following requirements*

Completeness: *For every* $\lambda \in \mathbb{N}$ *and every* $(x, \mathsf{T}) \in \mathcal{U}$

$$Pr\left[\mathsf{Del.V}(\mathsf{CRS}, \mathsf{T}, x, \Pi) = 1 \;\middle|\; \begin{array}{l} \mathsf{CRS} \leftarrow \mathsf{Del.Gen}(1^\lambda) \\ \Pi \leftarrow \mathsf{Del.P}(\mathsf{CRS}, 1^\mathsf{T}, x) \end{array}\right] = 1.$$

Efficiency: *In the above (honest) experiment the size of the proof Π is* poly$(\lambda, \log \mathsf{T})$. *The running time of* Del.V *is* $|x| \cdot$ poly$(|\mathsf{CRS}|, |\Pi|, \log \mathsf{T})$.

Adaptive Soundness: *For every polynomial* T *and for every poly-size cheating prover* P^* *there exists a negligible function* μ *such that for every* $\lambda \in \mathbb{N}$

$$Pr \left[\begin{matrix} (x^*, \mathsf{T}(\lambda)) \notin \mathcal{U} \\ \mathsf{Del.V}(\mathsf{CRS}, \mathsf{T}, x^*, \Pi^*) = 1 \end{matrix} \middle| \begin{matrix} \mathsf{CRS} \leftarrow \mathsf{Del.Gen}(1^\lambda) \\ (x^*, \Pi^*) \leftarrow \mathsf{P}^*(\mathsf{CRS}) \end{matrix} \right] \leq \mu(\lambda),$$

3   Zero-Testable Homomorphic Encryption

In this section we define the notion of zero-testable homomorphic encryption. We also define a multi-key variant [LTV12].

3.1   Homomorphic Encryption

We start by recalling the notion of homomorphic encryption.

Syntax. A homomorphic encryption scheme consists of PPT algorithms

$$(\mathsf{HE.KeyGen}, \mathsf{HE.Enc}, \mathsf{HE.Dec}, \mathsf{HE.Eval})$$

with the following syntax.

HE.KeyGen: Given the security parameter 1^λ, outputs a secret key sk, a public key pk and a description of a ring R.

HE.Enc: Given the public key pk and a message $m \in \{0, 1\}$, outputs a ciphertext c.

HE.Dec: Given the secret key sk and a ciphertext c, outputs a ring element $\alpha \in R$ or a special symbol $\bot$.

HE.Eval: Given e public key pk, an operation $\star \in \{+, -, \times\}$, and a pair of ciphertexts c_1, c_2, outputs a ciphertext c or a special symbol $\bot$.

Evaluating circuits. Some formulations of homomorphic encryption only consider an evaluation algorithm for circuits and not individual gates. By explicitly requiring that the evaluation is performed gate by gate, we ensure correctness for a "multi-hop" evaluation [GHV10] where ciphertexts that result from a homomorphic computation support further homomorphic operations.

Homomorphic evaluation of an arithmetic circuit C is implemented by iteratively applying the basic evaluation algorithm HE.Eval for every gate in C. This process is described formally below.

We only consider arithmetic circuits containing constants from $\{0, 1\}$, which can be evaluated over any ring. When evaluating a gate that takes a constant $b \in \{0, 1\}$ we do not generate a fresh random encryption of b. Instead, we assume that the public key includes ciphertexts $\hat{0}$ and $\hat{1}$ of 0 and 1 respectively. This evaluation strategy guarantees that all occurrences of a constant in C are replaced with the same ciphertext. This will be crucial later when we introduce the notion of zero-testable homomorphic encryption.

For an arithmetic circuit C, and ciphertexts $(c_1, \ldots, c_n)$ encrypted under public key pk we denote by $\langle C(c_1, \ldots, c_n) \rangle$ the evaluated ciphertext c computed as follows.

- If C is the constant 0 then $c = \hat{0}$.
- If C is the constant 1 then $c = \hat{1}$.
- If C is the i-th input wire then $c = c_i$.
- If C is of the form $C = C_1 \star C_2$ then

$$c = \mathsf{HE.Eval}\left(\mathsf{pk}, \star, \left(\langle C_1(c_1, \ldots, c_n) \rangle, \langle C_2(c_1, \ldots, c_n) \rangle\right)\right).$$

Definition 3.1 (Homomorphic Encryption). *Let* $\mathcal{C} = \{\mathcal{C}_\lambda\}_{\lambda \in \mathbb{N}}$ *be an ensemble of circuits. A homomorphic encryption scheme* (HE.KeyGen, HE.Enc, HE.Dec, HE.Eval) *for* $\mathcal{C}$ *satisfies the following requirements.*

Correctness: *For every* $\lambda \in \mathbb{N}$, *every* $C \in \mathcal{C}_\lambda$ *with* n *inputs wires, and every* $m_1, \ldots, m_n \in \{0, 1\}$

$$Pr\left[C(m_1, \ldots, m_n) = \alpha \;\middle|\; \begin{array}{l} (\mathsf{sk}, \mathsf{pk}, R) \leftarrow \mathsf{HE.KeyGen}(1^\lambda) \\ \forall i \in [n] : c_i \leftarrow \mathsf{HE.Enc}(\mathsf{pk}, m_i) \\ c \leftarrow \langle C(c_1, \ldots, c_n) \rangle \\ \alpha \leftarrow \mathsf{HE.Dec}(\mathsf{sk}, c) \end{array} \right] = 1,$$

where C is evaluated over R.

Compactness: *There exists a polynomial L such that in the above honest experiment* $|c| \leq L(\lambda)$ *(independently of $|C|$).*

Semantic Security: *For every poly-size adversary* Adv *there exists a negligible function μ such that for every* $\lambda \in \mathbb{N}$

$$Pr\left[m = m' \;\middle|\; \begin{array}{l} m \leftarrow \{0, 1\} \\ (\mathsf{sk}, \mathsf{pk}, R) \leftarrow \mathsf{HE.KeyGen}(1^\lambda) \\ c \leftarrow \mathsf{HE.Enc}(\mathsf{pk}, m) \\ m' \leftarrow \mathsf{Adv}(\mathsf{pk}, c) \end{array} \right] \leq \frac{1}{2} + \mu(\lambda).$$

Definition 3.2 (Somewhat Homomorphic Encryption). *For* $B, \Delta \in \mathbb{N}$ *let* $\mathcal{C}_{B,\Delta}$ *be the set of arithmetic circuits of size at most B and total degree at most Δ. Let* $B = B(\lambda), \Delta = \Delta(\lambda)$ *be polynomially bounded functions. A homomorphic encryption scheme is* (B, Δ)-*somewhat homomorphic if it satisfies Definition 3.1 for the circuit ensemble* $\{\mathcal{C}_{B(\lambda),\Delta(\lambda)}\}_{\lambda \in \mathbb{N}}$. *A scheme is* Δ-*somewhat homomorphic if it is* (B, Δ)-*somewhat homomorphic for every polynomial B.*

3.2 Correctness for Adversarial Ciphertexts

We formulate an additional correctness requirement that considers evaluation of adversatively generated ciphertexts. Informally, we require that an efficient adversary cannot generate a pair of ciphertexts that cause en evaluation error. A homomorphic evaluation $\langle c_1 \star c_2 \rangle$ is erroneous if the following two experiments have different outputs

1. Homomorphically evaluate $\langle c_1 \star c_2 \rangle$ and output the decryption of the evaluated ciphertext.
2. Decrypt c_1, c_s. If one of the ciphertexts fails to decrypt (decryption output $\perp$), then output $\perp$. Otherwise output the evaluation of $\star$ on the decrypted elements.

Many existing homomorphic encryption candidates only support a polynomially bounded number of homomorphic operations before the noise in the ciphertexts becomes too large and causes an evaluation error. Therefore, in such candidates, ciphertexts that cause en evaluation error are easy to generate. To support candidate of this nature we allow the output of the first experiment above to be $\perp$ even if the output of the second experiment is different than $\perp$.

Correctness for Adversarial Ciphertexts: For every poly-size adversary Adv there exists a negligible function μ such that for every $\lambda \in \mathbb{N}$ and for every operation $\star \in \{+, -, \times\}$

$$\Pr \left[\alpha \notin \{\alpha_1 \star \alpha_2, \perp\} \;\middle|\; \begin{array}{l} (\mathsf{sk}, \mathsf{pk}, R) \leftarrow \mathsf{HE.KeyGen}(1^\lambda) \\ c_1, c_2 \leftarrow \mathsf{Adv}(\mathsf{pk}) \\ c \leftarrow \mathsf{HE.Eval}(\mathsf{pk}, \star, (c_1, c_2)) \\ \forall i \in \{1, 2\} : \alpha_i \leftarrow \mathsf{HE.Dec}(\mathsf{sk}, c_i) \\ \alpha \leftarrow \mathsf{HE.Dec}(\mathsf{sk}, c) \end{array} \right] \leq \mu(\lambda),$$

where in the probability above, if $\alpha_1, \alpha_2 \in R$, the expression $\alpha_1 \star \alpha_2$ is evaluated over R. If either $\alpha_1 = \perp$ or $\alpha_1 = \perp$ then $\alpha_1 \star \alpha_2 = \perp$.

3.3 Zero Test

A zero test for a homomorphic encryption scheme is a PPT algorithm HE.ZT that can identify trivial encryptions of 0. These are ciphertexts that result from homomorphically evaluating an arithmetic circuit that is identically zero. We additionally require that the zero test never incorrectly identifies encryptions of non-zero values. This holds even for adversatively generated ciphertexts.

Given the public key pk and a ciphertext c, the zero test HE.ZT outputs a bit. The zero test satisfies the following requirements.

Zero-Test Completeness: For every $\lambda \in \mathbb{N}$, every $C \in \mathcal{C}_\lambda$ with n inputs wires such that C is identically zero, and every $m_1, \ldots, m_n \in \{0, 1\}$

$$\Pr \left[\mathsf{HE.ZT}(\mathsf{pk}, c) = 1 \;\middle|\; \begin{array}{l} (\mathsf{sk}, \mathsf{pk}, R) \leftarrow \mathsf{HE.KeyGen}(1^\lambda) \\ \forall i \in [n] : c_i \leftarrow \mathsf{HE.Enc}(\mathsf{pk}, m_i) \\ c \leftarrow \langle C(c_1, \ldots, c_n) \rangle \end{array} \right] = 1.$$

Zero-Test Soundness: For every poly-size adversary Adv there exists a negligible function μ such that for every $\lambda \in \mathbb{N}$

$$\Pr \left[\begin{array}{l} \mathsf{HE.ZT}(\mathsf{pk}, c) = 1 \\ \alpha \neq 0 \end{array} \;\middle|\; \begin{array}{l} (\mathsf{sk}, \mathsf{pk}, R) \leftarrow \mathsf{HE.KeyGen}(1^\lambda) \\ c \leftarrow \mathsf{Adv}(\mathsf{pk}) \\ \alpha \leftarrow \mathsf{HE.Dec}(\mathsf{sk}, c) \end{array} \right] \leq \mu(\lambda).$$

3.4 Weak Decryption

We define a relaxation of homomorphic encryption where

- The decryption procedure HE.Dec is not required to be PPT.
- Instead we require that there exists a weak decryption procedure HE.WeakDec which is PPT but does not decrypt messages outside $\{0, 1\}$.
- The weak decryption result should be consistent with the inefficient decryption result even for adversarially generated ciphertexts.

The encryption scheme we construct from graded encodings will only satisfy this relaxation which is sufficient for our application.

Given the secret key sk and a ciphertext c, the weak decryption procedure HE.WeakDec outputs a message $m \in \{0, 1\}$ or a special symbol $\bot$. The weak decryption procedure satisfies the following requirement.

Weak Decryption: For every poly-size adversary Adv there exists a negligible function μ such that for every $\lambda \in \mathbb{N}$

$$\Pr\left[m \neq \alpha' \;\middle|\; \begin{array}{l} (\mathsf{sk}, \mathsf{pk}, R) \leftarrow \mathsf{HE.KeyGen}(1^\lambda) \\ c \leftarrow \mathsf{Adv}(\mathsf{pk}) \\ \alpha \leftarrow \mathsf{HE.Dec}(\mathsf{sk}, c) \\ m \leftarrow \mathsf{HE.WeakDec}(\mathsf{sk}, c) \end{array}\right] \leq \mu(\lambda),$$

where in the above probability, $\alpha' = \alpha$ if $\alpha \in \{0, 1\}$ and $\alpha' = \bot$ otherwise.

3.5 Multi-key Zero-Testable Homomorphic Encryption

In this section we define a multi-key variant of homomorphic encryption that also satisfies the other requirements defined above. In multi-key homomorphic encryption, introduced by López-Alt et al. [LTV12] homomorphic computation can be executed over ciphertexts encrypted under d different keys. To ensure semantic security, decrypting the result requires all secret keys. Importantly, a system can generate ciphertext under an unbounded number of keys and any d of them can be combined in a homomorphic computation. We assume that the number of different keys d is constant. We also allow for common public parameters used to generate all keys.

Syntax. A d-key zero-testable homomorphic encryption scheme consists of PPT algorithms

(MHE.ParamGen, MHE.KeyGen, MHE.Enc, MHE.WeakDec, MHE.Eval, MHE.ZT)

and an unbounded algorithm MHE.Dec with the following syntax.

MHE.ParamGen: Given the security parameter 1^λ, outputs public parameters pp and a description of a ring R.

MHE.KeyGen: Given the public parameters pp, outputs a secret key sk and a public key pk.

MHE.Enc: Given public parameters pp, a public key pk and a message $m \in \{0,1\}$, outputs a ciphertext c.

MHE.Dec: Given public parameters pp, d secret keys $\mathsf{sk}_1, \ldots, \mathsf{sk}_d$ and a ciphertext c, outputs a ring element $\alpha \in R$ or a special symbol $\perp$.

MHE.WeakDec: Given public parameters pp, d secret keys $\mathsf{sk}_1, \ldots, \mathsf{sk}_d$ and a ciphertext c, outputs a message $m \in \{0,1\}$ or a special symbol $\perp$.

MHE.Eval: Given public parameters pp, a pair of public keys $\mathsf{pk}_1, \mathsf{pk}_2$, an operation $\star \in \{+, -, \times\}$ and a pair c_1, c_2, outputs a ciphertext c or a special symbol $\perp$.

MHE.ZT: Given public parameters pp, d public keys $\mathsf{pk}_1, \ldots, \mathsf{pk}_d$ and a ciphertext c, outputs a bit.

Remark 3.1 (Superfluous keys). The decryption and zero test algorithms take d keys, even if the input ciphertext results from a computation involving less keys. We assume without loss of generality that adding superfluous keys does not affect the procedures functionality.

Definition 3.3 (Multi-key Zero-Testable Homomorphic Encryption).
Let $\mathcal{C} = \{\mathcal{C}_\lambda\}_{\lambda \in \mathbb{N}}$ be an ensemble of circuits. A d-key zero-testable homomorphic encryption scheme

$$\text{(MHE.ParamGen, MHE.KeyGen, MHE.Enc, MHE.Dec, MHE.WeakDec,}$$

$$\text{MHE.Eval, MHE.ZT)}$$

for $\mathcal{C}$ satisfies the following requirements.

Correctness: *There exists a negligible function μ such that for every $\lambda \in \mathbb{N}$, every $C \in \mathcal{C}_\lambda$ with n inputs wires, every $m_1, \ldots, m_n \in \{0,1\}$ and every indices $j_1, \ldots, j_n \in [d]$*

$$Pr\left[C(m_1, \ldots, m_n) = \alpha \;\middle|\; \begin{array}{l} (\mathsf{pp}, R) \leftarrow \mathsf{MHE.ParamGen}(1^\lambda) \\ \forall j \in [d] : (\mathsf{pk}_j, \mathsf{sk}_j) \leftarrow \mathsf{MHE.KeyGen}(\mathsf{pp}) \\ \forall i \in [n] : c_i \leftarrow \mathsf{MHE.Enc}(\mathsf{pp}, \mathsf{pk}_{j_i}, m_i) \\ c \leftarrow \langle C(c_1, \ldots, c_n) \rangle \\ \alpha \leftarrow \mathsf{MHE.Dec}(\mathsf{pp}, (\mathsf{sk}_1, \ldots, \mathsf{sk}_d), c) \end{array} \right] \geq 1 - \mu(\lambda),$$

where C is evaluated over R.

Compactness: *There exists a polynomial L (that may depend on d) such that in the above honest experiment $|c| \leq L(\lambda)$ (independently of $|C|$).*

Correctness for Adversarial Ciphertexts: *For every poly-size adversary Adv there exists a negligible function μ such that for every $\lambda \in \mathbb{N}$ and for every operation $\star \in \{+, -, \times\}$*

$$Pr\left[\alpha \notin \{\alpha_1 \star \alpha_2, \perp\} \;\middle|\; \begin{array}{l} (\mathsf{pp}, R) \leftarrow \mathsf{MHE.ParamGen}(1^\lambda) \\ \forall j \in [d] : (\mathsf{pk}_j, \mathsf{sk}_j) \leftarrow \mathsf{MHE.KeyGen}(\mathsf{pp}) \\ c_1, c_2 \leftarrow \mathsf{Adv}(\mathsf{pp}, \mathsf{pk}_1, \ldots, \mathsf{pk}_d) \\ c \leftarrow \mathsf{MHE.Eval}(\mathsf{pp}, (\mathsf{pk}_1, \ldots, \mathsf{pk}_d), \star, (c_1, c_2)) \\ \forall i \in \{1, 2\} : \alpha_i \leftarrow \mathsf{MHE.Dec}(\mathsf{pp}, (\mathsf{sk}_1, \ldots, \mathsf{sk}_d), c_i) \\ \alpha \leftarrow \mathsf{MHE.Dec}(\mathsf{pp}, (\mathsf{sk}_1, \ldots, \mathsf{sk}_d), c) \end{array} \right] \leq \mu(\lambda),$$

where in the probability above, if $\alpha_1, \alpha_2 \in R$, the expression $\alpha_1 \star \alpha_2$ is evaluated over R. If either $\alpha_1 = \perp$ or $\alpha_1 = \perp$ then $\alpha_1 \star \alpha_2 = \perp$.

Zero Test Completeness: *There exists a negligible function μ such that for every $\lambda \in \mathbb{N}$, every $C \in \mathcal{C}_\lambda$ with n inputs wires that is identically zero, every $m_1, \ldots, m_n \in \{0, 1\}$, and every indices $j_1, \ldots, j_n \in [d]$*

$$Pr\left[b = 1 \middle| \begin{array}{l} (\mathsf{pp}, R) \leftarrow \mathsf{MHE.ParamGen}(1^\lambda) \\ \forall j \in [d] : (\mathsf{pk}_j, \mathsf{sk}_j) \leftarrow \mathsf{MHE.KeyGen}(\mathsf{pp}) \\ \forall i \in [n] : c_i \leftarrow \mathsf{MHE.Enc}(\mathsf{pp}, \mathsf{pk}_{j_i}, m_i) \\ c \leftarrow \langle C(c_1, \ldots, c_n) \rangle \\ b \leftarrow \mathsf{MHE.ZT}(\mathsf{pp}, (\mathsf{pk}_1, \ldots, \mathsf{pk}_d), c) \end{array} \right] \geq 1 - \mu(\lambda).$$

Zero-Test Soundness: *For every poly-size adversary Adv there exists a negligible function μ such that for every $\lambda \in \mathbb{N}$*

$$Pr\left[\begin{array}{l} b = 1 \\ \alpha \neq 0 \end{array} \middle| \begin{array}{l} (\mathsf{pp}, R) \leftarrow \mathsf{MHE.ParamGen}(1^\lambda) \\ \forall j \in [d] : (\mathsf{pk}_j, \mathsf{sk}_j) \leftarrow \mathsf{MHE.KeyGen}(\mathsf{pp}) \\ c \leftarrow \mathsf{Adv}(\mathsf{pp}, \mathsf{pk}_1, \ldots, \mathsf{pk}_d) \\ \alpha \leftarrow \mathsf{MHE.Dec}(\mathsf{pp}, (\mathsf{sk}_1, \ldots, \mathsf{sk}_d), c) \\ b \leftarrow \mathsf{MHE.ZT}(\mathsf{pp}, (\mathsf{pk}_1, \ldots, \mathsf{pk}_d), c) \end{array} \right] \leq \mu(\lambda).$$

Weak Decryption: *For every poly-size adversary Adv there exists a negligible function μ such that for every $\lambda \in \mathbb{N}$*

$$Pr\left[m \neq \alpha' \middle| \begin{array}{l} (\mathsf{pp}, R) \leftarrow \mathsf{MHE.ParamGen}(1^\lambda) \\ \forall j \in [d] : (\mathsf{pk}_j, \mathsf{sk}_j) \leftarrow \mathsf{MHE.KeyGen}(\mathsf{pp}) \\ c \leftarrow \mathsf{Adv}(\mathsf{pp}, \mathsf{pk}_1, \ldots, \mathsf{pk}_d) \\ \alpha \leftarrow \mathsf{MHE.Dec}(\mathsf{pp}, (\mathsf{sk}_1, \ldots, \mathsf{sk}_d), c) \\ m \leftarrow \mathsf{MHE.WeakDec}(\mathsf{pp}, (\mathsf{sk}_1, \ldots, \mathsf{sk}_d), c) \end{array} \right] \geq 1 - \mu(\lambda),$$

where in the above probability, $\alpha' = \alpha$ if $\alpha \in \{0, 1\}$ and $\alpha' = \perp$ otherwise.

Semantic Security: *For every poly-size adversary Adv there exists a negligible function μ such that for every $\lambda \in \mathbb{N}$*

$$Pr\left[m = m' \middle| \begin{array}{l} m \leftarrow \{0, 1\} \\ (\mathsf{pp}, R) \leftarrow \mathsf{MHE.ParamGen}(1^\lambda) \\ (\mathsf{sk}, \mathsf{pk}) \leftarrow \mathsf{MHE.KeyGen}(1^\lambda) \\ c \leftarrow \mathsf{MHE.Enc}(\mathsf{pp}, \mathsf{pk}, m) \\ m' \leftarrow \mathsf{Adv}(\mathsf{pk}, c) \end{array} \right] \leq \frac{1}{2} + \mu(\lambda).$$

4 A Non-interactive Argument

This section describes our publicly-verifiable non-interactive arguments. We start with an overview of the construction.

4.1 Overview

We construct a non-interactive argument system for the universal language $\mathcal{U}$. Given an instance $x = (M, y) \in \{0, 1\}^n$ and a time bound T the verifier wants to ascertain that $(x, \mathsf{T}) \in \mathcal{U}$, that is, that the Turing machine M accepts the input y within T steps. The protocol should be *adaptively sound*: even an adaptive cheating prover, who first sees the CRS and then picks an instance $(x, \mathsf{T}) \notin \mathcal{U}$ adaptively, should not be able to generate am accepting proof.

In the protocol, the prover and verifier translate the instance (x, T) into a 3CNF formula φ over $\mathrm{poly}(n, \mathsf{T})$ variables, which is satisfiable if and only if $(x, \mathsf{T}) \in \mathcal{U}$. φ has a "short" implicit description via an arithmetic circuit Φ of small size and degree that, given the labels of three literals, determines whether their disjunction is a clause in φ. Note that given φ, the formula Φ and the original instance (x, T) can be efficiently reconstructed. More over, if $(x, \mathsf{T}) \in \mathcal{U}$, a satisfying assignment for φ can be efficiently computed. With this formula in mind, the argument system has two main ingredients:

Ingredient 1: the core protocol. The first ingredient is a publicly-verifiable non-interactive "core protocol". The prover in the core protocol is presented with a CRS, a circuit Φ describing a 3CNF φ (as above), and a satisfying assignment σ to φ. It generates a proof Π that will convince the verifier that the 3CNF described by Φ is satisfiable.

The core protocol has a relaxed soundness property: it is *not* guaranteed that an adaptive cheating prover P^* cannot generate a circuit Φ describing an unsatisfiable 3CNF together with a proof Π^* that makes the verifier accept. Rather, the soundness guarantee is that any adaptive cheating prover for the core protocol can be used to derive a *no-signalling adaptive local assignment generator* Assign. The adaptive assignment generator Assign is a randomized algorithm that gets as input a small set S of variables, and outputs a pair (Φ, σ), where $\sigma : S \to \{0, 1\}$ is a local assignment to the variables in S. The algorithm Assign satisfies the following properties:

1. **No-signalling.** Given a set S of variables, Assign outputs a pair (Φ, σ). Intuitively, the joint distribution of Φ and the values assigned to any subset of the variables in S are independent of the other variables in S. More precisely, for every two sets of variables S_1, S_2 both containing a subset T, the distributions obtained by executing Assign on S_1 and on S_2 to obtain (Φ, σ), and then restricting σ to the variables in T, are computationally indistinguishable.
2. **Adaptive local soundness.** We consider an execution of the cheating prover P^* in the core protocol that generates a pair (Φ, Π^*). Additively, for every small subset S of variables, we consider an execution of Assign on the set S that generates a pair (Φ', σ'). We require that Φ' is indistinguishable from Φ, and moreover, if the proof Π^* is accepting, then the assignment σ' is *locally-consistent* with the 3CNF φ' described by Φ'. We say that the assignment $\sigma' : S \to \{0, 1\}$ is locally-consistent with φ' if σ' satisfies all clauses of φ' that are comprised entirely of variables in S.
   In particular, we have that if P^* has a noticeable probability of generating a pair (Φ, Π^*) such that Φ describes an unsatisfiable 3CNF, but the verifier accepts Π^*. Then for every small subset S of variables, running Assign on the set S has a noticeable probability of producing a pair (Φ', σ') where Φ' describes an unsatisfiable 3CNF φ', but σ is a locally-consistent with Φ'.

Some remarks are in order. First, we note that the relaxed soundness property has a flavor of "knowledge extraction": while we do not claim that any cheating prover for the core protocol must "know" a satisfying assignment to the 3CNF (indeed, the 3CNF might not be satisfiable, in which case no such assignment exists), a cheating prover *can* be used to generate "locally consistent" assignments on any set of variables. This extraction property is slightly more involved because it is concerned with *adaptive* cheating provers: the 3CNF is not fixed in advance. Rather, an adaptive cheating prover for the core protocol can be used to adaptively generate, given a set S of variables, an unsatisfiable 3CNF together with a locally-consistent assignment for those variables in S. The distribution of 3CNFs generated by the core protocol cheating prover (together with the bit indicating whether the verifier accepts the jointly-generated proof) is computationally indistinguishable from the distribution of 3CNFs generated by the assignment generator (together with the bit indicating whether the jointly-generated assignment is locally satisfiable). We note further that the no-signalling property implies that for any two sets S and S', the distributions of the circuit Φ generated by Assign are themselves computationally indistinguishable.

While the core protocol's soundness guarantee is robust to adaptive provers, it is weak in the sense that it only guarantees *local* consistency of the assignment generator. Even for a fixed 3CNF (let alone for an adaptively-generated one) the existence of no-signalling locally-consistent assignments does not imply that the 3CNF is satisfiable! As in prior works, we provide a "circuit-augmentation" procedure that encodes a Turing Machine computation as a 3CNF with a particular structure. The existence of a (no-signalling) locally-consistent assignment generator for the augmented 3CNF guarantees that the Turing Machine accepts its input. Here too, we need to take care to handle adaptive adversaries. This is the second main ingredient of our delegation protocol.

Ingredient 2: adaptive augmented circuit. To build an adaptively-sound delegation protocol we need an adaptive variant of the *augmented circuit construction* from [KRR14]. We describe this as a circuit-augmentation algorithm that transforms an instance (x, T) for $\mathcal{U}$ into an arithmetic circuit Φ of small size and degree, which describes a 3CNF φ. The 3CNF φ should be satisfiable if and only if $(x, \mathsf{T}) \in \mathcal{U}$. This property alone, of course, is not sufficient, since the core protocol does not prove the 3CNF's global satisfiability. Prior work showed a transformation where if $(x, \mathsf{T}) \notin \mathcal{U}$, then it is not possible to generate even locally-consistent assignments in a no-signalling manner. Since we want an adaptively-sound delegation protocol, we need an even stronger property: let Assign be a no-signalling adaptive assignment generator as above. We assume that Assign generates the circuit Φ by applying the adaptive circuit-augmentation procedure to an instance (x, T). Then for some small set S^* of variables the probability that $(x, \mathsf{T}) \notin \mathcal{U}$ but Assign generates a locally-consistent assignment for S^* is negligible. The transformation and its proof are based on [KRR14, PR14, BHK16].

There is a (slight) gap between the soundness we consider in the augmented-circuit transformation and in the core protocol: the core protocol is simply concerned with 3CNFs described by small circuits. The augmented-circuit transformation, on the other hand, considers (and relies on) the procedure used to derive these 3CNFs from a computation described by a Turing Machine. This gap makes the presentation of the core protocol considerably simpler and more modular (in particular, there is no need to consider Turing Machines in the core protocol). We bridge the gap by noting that the augmentation procedure Aug is easy to invert: given a circuit Φ, it is easy to recover the instance (x, T) from which it was derived (or to output $\perp$ if Φ is not an output of Aug). This allows us to argue that for two computationally indistinguishable distributions on Φ, if the first distribution is over outputs of Aug, then the second must be over such outputs too (except with negligible probability). Moreover, given a circuit Φ produced by Aug, we can determine whether it describes a satisfiable 3CNF by recovering the original instance for $\mathcal{U}$ and testing (in polynomial time) whether the Turing Machine accepts or rejects.

Putting it together. To derive a delegation protocol, we use the core protocol's CRS. Given an instance (x, T), the prover and verifier both use the augmented-circuit transformation to derive Φ and execute the core protocol on Φ. A prover P^* that cheats with noticeable probability can be used to derive a no-signalling adaptive local assignment generator Assign*. By the core protocol's soundness we conclude that for every set S of variables, with noticeable probability Assign* generates pairs (Φ, σ) where Φ describes an unsatisfiable 3CNF, but σ is locally consistent. Moreover, Φ is derived by running the augmented circuit construction on an instance $(x, \mathsf{T}) \notin \mathcal{U}$ (this is true for the execution of the core protocol, by computational indistinguishability it holds also for the outputs of Assign*). However, the the augmented circuit construction guarantees that no such assignment generator exists, leading to a contradiction.

Organization. We define adaptive no-signalling local assignment generators in Sect. 4.2. The core protocol is given in Sect. 4.3. The properties of the augmented-circuit transformation are discussed in Sect. 4.4. The analysis of the core protocol, the augmented-circuit transformation, and the full delegation protocol appear in the full version of this work.

4.2   Adaptive No-Signaling Local-Assignment Generator

Before stating the properties of the core protocol, we introduce some notation and formalize the notion of an adaptive no-signaling local-assignment generator.

Succinct formula representation $\mathcal{I}_\varphi$. Let φ be a 3CNF boolean formula with variables $\alpha_1, \ldots, \alpha_B$. Let $B = 2^m$ and identify the indices in $[B]$ with strings in $\{0, 1\}^m$. We define a boolean *indicator function* $\mathcal{I}_\varphi : \{0, 1\}^{3m+3} \to \{0, 1\}$ of φ as follows. For every indices $\mathbf{u}_1, \mathbf{u}_2, \mathbf{u}_3 \in \{0, 1\}^m$ and for every bits $b_1, b_2, b_3 \in \{0, 1\}^3$, we have that

$$\mathcal{I}_\varphi(\mathbf{u}_1, \mathbf{u}_2, \mathbf{u}_3, b_1, b_2, b_3) = 1,$$

if and only if φ contains the clause:

$$(\alpha_{\mathbf{u}_1} = b_1) \vee (\alpha_{\mathbf{u}_2} = b_2) \vee (\alpha_{\mathbf{u}_3} = b_3).$$

The locally consistency verifier V_{local}. We denote by V_{local} the verification algorithm for local assignments to φ. The algorithm is given as input

- An arithmetic circuit Φ computing a boolean function with $3m + 3$ inputs (we think of Φ as computing the indicator function $\mathcal{I}_\varphi$ for some formula φ).
- A partial assignments $\sigma : S \to \{0, 1\}$ for a set $S \subseteq \{0, 1\}^m$.

$V_{local}(\Phi, \sigma)$ accepts if an only if the assignment σ is locally consistent with the formula described by Φ. That is, for every $\mathbf{u}_1, \mathbf{u}_2, \mathbf{u}_3 \in S$ and every $b_1, b_2, b_3 \in \{0, 1\}$

$$\Phi(\mathbf{u}_1, \mathbf{u}_2, \mathbf{u}_3, b_1, b_2, b_3) = 1 \quad \Rightarrow \quad (\sigma(\mathbf{u}_1) = b_1) \vee (\sigma(\mathbf{u}_2) = b_2) \vee (\sigma(\mathbf{u}_3) = b_3).$$

Adaptive local-assignment generator. Let $Q = Q(\lambda), B = B(\lambda)$ be functions and let $B = 2^m$. An adaptive Q-local-assignment generator Assign for B-variate formulas is a probabilistic algorithm with the following syntax: given the the security parameter 1^λ and a set of indices $S \subseteq \{0, 1\}^m$ of size at most Q, Assign outputs

- An arithmetic circuit Φ computing a boolean function with $3m + 3$ inputs.
- A partial assignment $\sigma : S \to \{0, 1\}$.

We define a no-signaling adaptive local-assignment generator

Definition 4.1 (No-Signaling Adaptive Local-Assignment Generator).
A Q-local-assignment generator Assign for $B = 2^m$-variate formulas is (computationally) no-signalling if for every polynomial-size distinguisher D there exists a negligible function μ such that for every $\lambda \in \mathbb{N}$ and every subsets $S \subseteq S' \subseteq \{0, 1\}^m$ of size at most Q

$$\left| \Pr_{(\Phi, \sigma) \leftarrow \mathsf{Assign}(1^\lambda, S)} [D(\Phi, \sigma(S)) = 1] - \Pr_{(\Phi, \sigma') \leftarrow \mathsf{Assign}(1^\lambda, S')} [D(\Phi, \sigma'(S)) = 1] \right|$$

$$\leq \mu(\lambda).$$

4.3 The Core Protocol

In this section we describe the syntax and the properties of the core delegation protocol. The protocol itself is given in Sect. 4.3.

Syntax. Let $\Delta = \Delta(\lambda)$ be a polynomially bounded function. The core protocol with degree bound Δ consists of PPT algorithms (Core.Gen, Core.P, Core.V) with the following syntax. Let φ be a B-variate 3CNF boolean formula where $B = 2^m$ and let Φ be an arithmetic circuit of total degree $\delta \leq \Delta$ computing the function $\mathcal{I}_\varphi$.

Core.Gen: Given the security parameter 1^λ and a locality parameter 1^Q outputs a common reference string CRS.

Core.P: Given the common reference string CRS, the circuit Φ and an assignment $\sigma : \{0,1\}^m \to \{0,1\}$, outputs a proof Π.

Core.V: Given the common reference string CRS, the circuit Φ and the proof Π outputs a bit.

The protocol satisfies the following requirements.

Completeness. For every security parameter $\lambda \in \mathbb{N}$, every 3CNF boolean formula φ with B variables, every satisfying assignment σ, every arithmetic circuit Φ of individual degree $\delta \leq \Delta$ computing the function $\mathcal{I}_\varphi$, and every locality parameter $Q \in [B]$

$$\Pr\left[\text{Core.V}(\text{CRS}, \Phi, \Pi) = 1 \; \middle| \; \begin{array}{l} \text{CRS} \leftarrow \text{Core.Gen}(1^\lambda, 1^Q) \\ \Pi \leftarrow \text{Core.P}(\text{CRS}, \Phi, \sigma) \end{array}\right] = 1.$$

Efficiency. There exists a polynomial L such that in the above honest experiment $|\Pi| \leq L(\lambda) \cdot Q \cdot \delta$ where δ is the individual degree of the circuit Φ. Additionally the verifier's running time is bounded by $L(|\text{CRS}|) \cdot (|\Phi| + |\Pi|)$.

No-Signaling adaptive local soundness. For every polynomially bounded functions $Q = Q(\lambda), B = B(\lambda)$ there exists an algorithm Assign such that for every poly-size cheating prover P^* the following holds

- Assign^{P^*} is a no-signaling adaptive Q-local-assignment generator for B-variate formulas.
- For every polynomial-size distinguisher D there exists a negligible function μ such that for every $\lambda \in \mathbb{N}$, letting $B = 2^m$, for every set of indices $S \subseteq \{0,1\}^m$ of size at most Q

$$\left| \Pr\left[D(\Phi, b) = 1 \; \middle| \; \begin{array}{l} \text{CRS} \leftarrow \text{Core.Gen}(1^\lambda, 1^Q) \\ (\Phi, \Pi^*) \leftarrow P^*(\text{CRS}) \\ b \leftarrow \text{Core.V}(\text{CRS}, \Phi, \Pi^*) \end{array}\right] \right.$$
$$\left. - \Pr\left[D(\Phi, b) = 1 \; \middle| \; \begin{array}{l} (\Phi, \sigma) \leftarrow \text{Assign}^{P^*}(1^\lambda, S) \\ b \leftarrow \text{V}_{\text{local}}(\Phi, \sigma) \end{array}\right] \right| \leq \mu(\lambda).$$

Construction. Let $\Delta = \Delta(\lambda)$ be the function bounding the total degree of the circuit Φ. The core protocol makes use of a 3-key zero-testable 2Δ-somewhat homomorphic encryption scheme

$$(\text{MHE.ParamGen}, \text{MHE.KeyGen}, \text{MHE.Enc}, \text{MHE.Dec}, \text{MHE.WeakDec},$$

$$\text{MHE.Eval}, \text{MHE.ZT}).$$

The CRS generator. The CRS generation algorithm Core.Gen is given as input the security parameter 1^λ and a locality parameter 1^Q. It outputs a common reference string CRS as follows.

1. Sample public parameters for the encryption scheme

$$(\mathsf{pp}, R) \leftarrow \mathsf{MHE.ParamGen}(1^\lambda).$$

2. For every $q \in [Q]$, generate a key pair

$$(\mathsf{sk}^q, \mathsf{pk}^q) \leftarrow \mathsf{MHE.KeyGen}(\mathsf{pp}),$$

and λ encryptions of 0

$$\{c_i^q \leftarrow \mathsf{MHE.Enc}(\mathsf{pp}, \mathsf{pk}^q, 0)\}_{i \in [\lambda]}.$$

3. Output a reference string containing the public parameters and all the public keys and ciphers

$$\mathsf{CRS} = \left(\mathsf{pp}, \{\mathsf{pk}^q, (c_1^q, \ldots, c_\lambda^q)\}_{q \in [Q]}\right).$$

The prover. The prover algorithm $\mathsf{Core.P}$ is given as input

– The common reference string

$$\mathsf{CRS} = \left(\mathsf{pp}, \{\mathsf{pk}^q, (c_1^q, \ldots, c_\lambda^q)\}_{q \in [Q]}\right).$$

– An (individual) degree δ arithmetic circuit Φ computing a boolean function with $3m + 3$ inputs.
– An assignment $\sigma : \{0, 1\}^m \to \{0, 1\}$.

We start by introducing some notation.

1. For every query $q \in [Q]$, let $\mathbf{c}^q = (c_1^q, \ldots, c_m^q)$. We refer to the ciphertext vector $\mathbf{c}^q$ as an encryption of the q-th CRS index (in an honestly generated CRS the index value is always 0^m).
2. Let Σ be a multi-linear extension of σ (See Sect. 2.2).
3. For every triplet of bits $\mathbf{b} = (b_1, b_2, b_3) \in \{0, 1\}^3$ let $P_0^{\mathbf{b}}$ be the degree $\delta + 1$ arithmetic circuit taking $3m$ inputs

$$P_0^{\mathbf{b}}(\mathbf{x}_1, \mathbf{x}_2, \mathbf{x}_3) = \Phi(\mathbf{x}_1, \mathbf{x}_2, \mathbf{x}_3, \mathbf{b}) \cdot \prod_{k \in [3]} (1 - \beta(b_k, \Sigma(\mathbf{x}_k))). \qquad (4)$$

(See Sect. 2.2 for the definition of the circuit β.)

4. For every $i \in [3m]$, let $P_i^{\mathbf{b}}$ be the linearization of the first i variables of the circuit $P_0^{\mathbf{b}}$. That is, $P_i^{\mathbf{b}}$ is the following arithmetic circuit taking $3m$ inputs which is multilinear in its first i variables, and of degree at most $\delta + 1$ in its other variables.

$$P_i^{\mathbf{b}}(x_1, \ldots, x_{3m}) = \sum_{y_1, \ldots y_i \in \{0,1\}} \beta(y_1, \ldots y_i, x_1, \ldots x_i) \cdot P_0^{\mathbf{b}}(y_1, \ldots, y_i, x_{i+1}, \ldots, x_{3m}).$$

$$(5)$$

$\mathsf{Core.P}$ outputs a proof Π as follows.

1. For every $q \in [Q]$ obtain an encryption of the assignment Σ evaluated on the q-th CRS index. That is, homomorphically obtain the ciphertext $d^q = \langle \Sigma(\mathbf{c}^q) \rangle$.

2. For every triplet of bits $\mathbf{b} \in \{0,1\}^3$, triplet of queries $\mathbf{q} = (q_1, q_2, q_3) \in [Q]^3$, and $i \in [3m]$ obtain the encrypted coefficients of the circuit $P_{i-1}^{\mathbf{b}}$ evaluated on the CRS indices $\mathbf{q}$ and restricted to its i-th input variable (see Sect. 2.1). Since the individual degree of $P_{i-1}^{\mathbf{b}}$ is at most $\delta + 1$, the restricted polynomial will have at most $\delta + 2$ coefficients. That is, homomorphically obtain the sequence of $\delta + 2$ ciphertexts $\mathbf{e}_{i-1}^{\mathbf{q},\mathbf{b}}$

$$\mathbf{e}_{i-1}^{\mathbf{q},\mathbf{b}} = \left(\left\langle P_{i-1}^{\mathbf{b}} \big|_{i,j} \left((\mathbf{c}^{q_1} \mid \mathbf{c}^{q_2} \mid \mathbf{c}^{q_3})_{-i} \right) \right\rangle \right)_{j \in [0, \delta+1]}.$$

3. Output a proof Π that contains all the ciphertexts

$$\Pi = \left(\{d^q\}_{q \in [Q]}, \quad \left\{ \mathbf{e}_{i-1}^{\mathbf{q},\mathbf{b}} \right\}_{\mathbf{b} \in \{0,1\}^3, \mathbf{q} \in [Q]^3, i \in [3m]} \right).$$

The verifier. The verifier algorithm Core.V is given as input

– The common reference string

$$\mathsf{CRS} = \left(\mathsf{pp}, \{\mathsf{pk}^q, (c_1^q, \ldots, c_\lambda^q)\}_{q \in [Q]} \right).$$

– A degree δ arithmetic circuit Φ computing a boolean function with $3m + 3$ inputs.
– An proof

$$\Pi = \left(\{d^q\}_{q \in [Q]}, \quad \left\{ \mathbf{e}_{i-1}^{\mathbf{q},\mathbf{b}} \right\}_{\mathbf{b} \in \{0,1\}^3, \mathbf{q} \in [Q]^3, i \in [3m]} \right).$$

Core.V performs the following tests for every triplet of bits $\mathbf{b} = (b_1, b_2, b_3) \in \{0,1\}^3$ and triplet of queries $\mathbf{q} = (q_1, q_2, q_3) \in [Q]^3$. Core.V accepts only if all tests pass.

First, Core.V homomorphically evaluates the following ciphertexts

– Let $\tilde{P}^{\mathbf{b}}$ be the following arithmetic circuit taking $3m + 3$ inputs

$$\tilde{P}^{\mathbf{b}}(\mathbf{x}_1, \mathbf{x}_2, \mathbf{x}_3, y_1, y_3, y_3) = \Phi(\mathbf{x}_1, \mathbf{x}_2, \mathbf{x}_3, \mathbf{b}) \cdot \prod_{k \in [3]} (1 - \beta(b_k, y_k)). \qquad (6)$$

Evaluate the ciphertext

$$f_0' = \left\langle \tilde{P}^{\mathbf{b}} \left(\mathbf{c}^{q_1}, \mathbf{c}^{q_2}, \mathbf{c}^{q_3}, d^{q_1}, d^{q_2}, d^{q_3} \right) \right\rangle.$$

– Let F be the following arithmetic circuit taking $\delta + 3$ inputs

$$F(x, y_0, \ldots, y_{\delta+1}) = \sum_{j \in [0, \delta+1]} y_j \cdot x^j. \qquad (7)$$

For $i \in [3m]$, evaluate the ciphertext f_{i-1} that encrypts the evaluation of the univariate polynomial with encrypted coefficient $\mathbf{e}_{i-1}^{\mathbf{q},\mathbf{b}}$ on the i-th input bit of the concatenated CRS indices $\mathbf{q}$. Recall that $\mathbf{e}_{i-1}^{\mathbf{q},\mathbf{b}}$ are supposedly the encrypted coefficients of the circuit $P_{i-1}^{\mathbf{b}}$ evaluated on the CRS indices $\mathbf{q}$ and restricted to its i-th input variable. Therefore, f_{i-1} is suppose to encrypt the evaluation of $P_{i-1}^{\mathbf{b}}$ on the CRS indices $\mathbf{q}$.

$$f_{i-1} = \left\langle F\left((\mathbf{c}^{q_1} \mid \mathbf{c}^{q_2} \mid \mathbf{c}^{q_3})_i \, , \mathbf{e}_{i-1}^{\mathbf{q},\mathbf{b}} \right) \right\rangle.$$

- Let F' be the following arithmetic circuit taking $\delta + 3$ inputs

$$F'(x, y_0, \ldots, y_{\delta+1}) = \sum_{z \in \{0,1\}} \beta(z, x) \cdot F(z, y_0, \ldots, y_{\delta+1}).$$

For $i \in [3m]$, evaluate the ciphertext f_i' that encrypts the linearization of the univariate polynomial with encrypted coefficient $\mathbf{e}_{i-1}^{\mathbf{q},\mathbf{b}}$ evaluated on the on the i-th input bit of the concatenated CRS indices $\mathbf{q}$. Therefore, f_{i-1} is suppose to encrypt the evaluation of the circuit $P_{i-1}^{\mathbf{b}}$ with its i-th variable linearized on the CRS indices $\mathbf{q}$.

$$f_i' = \left\langle F'\left((\mathbf{c}^{q_1} \mid \mathbf{c}^{q_2} \mid \mathbf{c}^{q_3})_i \, , \mathbf{e}_{i-1}^{\mathbf{q},\mathbf{b}} \right) \right\rangle.$$

- Let $f_{3m} = \hat{0}$.
  For every $i \in [0, 3m]$, Core.V tests that

$$\mathsf{MHE.ZT}\left(\mathsf{pp}, (\mathsf{pk}^{q_1}, \mathsf{pk}^{q_2}, \mathsf{pk}^{q_3}) , \langle f_i - f_i' \rangle \right) = 1.$$

4.4 The Augmented Circuit

Syntax. Let $\mathcal{U}$ be the universal language (see Sect. 2.3). The augmented-circuit transformation consists of deterministic polynomial time algorithms $(\mathsf{Aug}, \mathsf{Aug}^{-1}, \mathsf{Trans})$ with the following syntax.

Aug: the circuit-augmentation procedure takes as input an instance $x = (M, y)$ and a time bound T for $\mathcal{U}$. It outputs an arithmetic circuit Φ computing the indicator function $\mathcal{I}_\varphi$ of the "augmented formula" φ (see Sect. 4.2)). We say that Φ *represents* φ.

Aug^{-1}: the inversion procedure takes as input an arithmetic circuit Φ. It either outputs (x, T) or fails and outputs $\perp$.

Trans: the assignment generation procedure takes as input an instance x and a time bound T for $\mathcal{U}$. It outputs an assignment σ for φ.

These procedures satisfy the following properties:

Efficiency. For $x \in \{0,1\}^n$

- $\mathsf{Aug}(x, \mathsf{T})$ runs in time $n \cdot \mathrm{polylog}(\mathsf{T})$ and outputs an arithmetic circuit Φ such that

- Φ is of size $n \cdot \mathrm{polylog}(\mathsf{T})$.
- Φ is of total degree $\delta = \delta(n, \mathsf{T}) = \mathrm{polylog}(n, \mathsf{T})$.
- Φ represents a formula φ on $B = B(n, \mathsf{T}) = \mathrm{poly}(n, \mathsf{T})$ variables.
- $\mathsf{Aug}(x, \mathsf{T})$ and $\mathsf{Aug}^{-1}(\Phi)$ run in time $n \cdot \mathrm{polylog}(\mathsf{T})$.
- $\mathsf{Trans}(x, \mathsf{T})$ runs in time $\mathrm{poly}(n, \mathsf{T})$.

Inversion. For every $(x, \mathsf{T}) \in \{0, 1\}^*$

$$\mathsf{Aug}^{-1}(\mathsf{Aug}(x, \mathsf{T})) = (x, \mathsf{T}).$$

Completeness. For every $(x, \mathsf{T}) \in \mathcal{U}$, $\mathsf{Trans}(x, \mathsf{T})$ outputs a satisfying assignment σ for the formula φ represented by the output of $\mathsf{Aug}(x, \mathsf{T})$.

Soundness. At a high level, the soundness guarantees that there does not exist an adaptive no-signalling local-assignment generator (see Sect. 4.2) that for *every* small set of indices S generates a circuit $\Phi = \mathsf{Aug}(x, \mathsf{T})$, such that $(x, \mathsf{T}) \notin \mathcal{U}$, together with partial assignment $\sigma : S \to \{0, 1\}$ that is locally consistent with the formula represented by Φ.

Lemma 4.1 (Augmented Circuit Soundness). *There exists a function* $Q = \mathrm{polylog}(\lambda)$ *such that for every polynomially bounded function* $B = B(\lambda)$, *and every polynomial-time no-signaling Q-local-assignment generator* Assign *for B-variate formulas there exists a negligible function* μ *such that for every* $\lambda \in \mathbb{N}$, *letting* $B = 2^m$, *there exists a set* $S^* \subseteq \{0, 1\}^m$ *of size at most* Q *such that*

$$Pr\left[\begin{matrix} \mathsf{Aug}^{-1}(\Phi) \notin \mathcal{U} \cup \{\perp\} \\ \mathsf{V}_{\mathsf{local}}(\Phi, \sigma) = 1 \end{matrix} \;\middle|\; (\Phi, \sigma) \leftarrow \mathsf{Assign}(1^\lambda, S^*) \right] \leq \mu(\lambda).$$

Acknowledgements. We thank Zvika Brakerski, Yael Kalai, Ron Rothblum and Nir Bitansky for many helpful and illuminating conversations.

References

[ABOR00] Aiello, W., Bhatt, S., Ostrovsky, R., Rajagopalan, S.R.: Fast verification of any remote procedure call: short witness-indistinguishable one-round proofs for NP. In: Montanari, U., Rolim, J.D.P., Welzl, E. (eds.) ICALP 2000. LNCS, vol. 1853, pp. 463–474. Springer, Heidelberg (2000). doi:10.1007/3-540-45022-X_39

[BCCT13] Bitansky, N., Canetti, R., Chiesa, A., Tromer, E.: Recursive composition and bootstrapping for SNARKS and proof-carrying data. In: STOC, pp. 111–120 (2013)

[BCI+13] Bitansky, N., Chiesa, A., Ishai, Y., Paneth, O., Ostrovsky, R.: Succinct non-interactive arguments via linear interactive proofs. In: Sahai, A. (ed.) TCC 2013. LNCS, vol. 7785, pp. 315–333. Springer, Heidelberg (2013). doi:10.1007/978-3-642-36594-2_18

[BFLS91] Babai, L., Fortnow, L., Levin, L.A., Szegedy, M.: Checking computations in polylogarithmic time. In: Proceedings of the 23rd Annual ACM Symposium on Theory of Computing, 5–8 May 1991, New Orleans, Louisiana, USA, pp. 21–31 (1991)

[BGL+15] Bitansky, N., Garg, S., Lin, H., Pass, R., Telang, S.: Succinct random-ized encodings and their applications. In: Proceedings of the Forty-Seventh Annual ACM on Symposium on Theory of Computing, STOC 2015, Portland, OR, USA, 14–17 June 2015, pp. 439–448 (2015)

[BGN05] Boneh, D., Goh, E.-J., Nissim, K.: Evaluating 2-DNF formulas on cipher-texts. In: Kilian, J. (ed.) TCC 2005. LNCS, vol. 3378, pp. 325–341. Springer, Heidelberg (2005). doi:10.1007/978-3-540-30576-7_18

[BHK16] Brakerski, Z., Holmgren, J., Kalai, Y.T.: Non-interactive RAM and batch NP delegation from any PIR. IACR Cryptology ePrint Archive, 2016:459 (2016)

[BS02] Boneh, D., Silverberg, A.: Applications of multilinear forms to cryptogra-phy. IACR Cryptology ePrint Archive, 2002:80 (2002)

[BV11] Brakerski, Z., Vaikuntanathan, V.: Efficient fully homomorphic encryption from (standard) LWE. IACR Cryptology ePrint Archive, 2011:344 (2011)

[CGH04] Canetti, R., Goldreich, O., Halevi, S.: The random oracle methodology, revisited. J. ACM 51(4), 557–594 (2004)

[CHJV14] Canetti, R., Holmgren, J., Jain, A., Vaikuntanathan, V.: Indistinguishabil-ity obfuscation of iterated circuits and ram programs. Cryptology ePrint Archive, Report 2014/769 (2014). http://eprint.iacr.org/

[CHL+15] Cheon, J.H., Han, K., Lee, C., Ryu, H., Stehlé, D.: Cryptanalysis of the multilinear map over the integers. In: Oswald, E., Fischlin, M. (eds.) EURO-CRYPT 2015. LNCS, vol. 9056, pp. 3–12. Springer, Heidelberg (2015). doi:10.1007/978-3-662-46800-5_1

[CLT15] Coron, J.-S., Lepoint, T., Tibouchi, M.: New multilinear maps over the integers. In: Gennaro, R., Robshaw, M. (eds.) CRYPTO 2015. LNCS, vol. 9215, pp. 267–286. Springer, Heidelberg (2015). doi:10.1007/978-3-662-47989-6_13

[DFH12] Damgård, I., Faust, S., Hazay, C.: Secure two-party computation with low communication. In: Cramer, R. (ed.) TCC 2012. LNCS, vol. 7194, pp. 54–74. Springer, Heidelberg (2012). doi:10.1007/978-3-642-28914-9_4

[DLN+04] Dwork, C., Langberg, M., Naor, M., Nissim, K., Reingold, O.: Succinct proofs for NP and spooky interactions (2004, unpublished manuscript). http://www.cs.bgu.ac.il/~kobbi/papers/spooky_sub_crypto.pdf

[DNR16] Dwork, C., Naor, M., Rothblum, G.N.: Spooky interaction and its discon-tents: compilers for succinct two-message argument systems. In: Robshaw, M., Katz, J. (eds.) CRYPTO 2016. LNCS, vol. 9816, pp. 123–145. Springer, Heidelberg (2016). doi:10.1007/978-3-662-53015-3_5

[Gen09] Gentry, C.: Fully homomorphic encryption using ideal lattices. In: Proceed-ings of the 41st Annual ACM Symposium on Theory of Computing, STOC 2009, Bethesda, MD, USA, 31 May–2 June 2009, pp. 169–178 (2009)

[GGH13a] Garg, S., Gentry, C., Halevi, S.: Candidate multilinear maps from ideal lattices. In: Johansson, T., Nguyen, P.Q. (eds.) EUROCRYPT 2013. LNCS, vol. 7881, pp. 1–17. Springer, Heidelberg (2013). doi:10.1007/978-3-642-38348-9_1

[GGH+13b] Garg, S., Gentry, C., Halevi, S., Raykova, M., Sahai, A., Waters, B.: Candidate indistinguishability obfuscation and functional encryption for all circuits. In: FOCS (2013)

[GGH15] Gentry, C., Gorbunov, S., Halevi, S.: Graph-induced multilinear maps from lattices. In: Dodis, Y., Nielsen, J.B. (eds.) TCC 2015. LNCS, vol. 9015, pp. 498–527. Springer, Heidelberg (2015). doi:10.1007/978-3-662-46497-7_20

[GGHZ16] Garg, S., Gentry, C., Halevi, S., Zhandry, M.: Functional encryption without obfuscation. In: Kushilevitz, E., Malkin, T. (eds.) TCC 2016. LNCS, vol. 9563, pp. 480–511. Springer, Heidelberg (2016). doi:10.1007/978-3-662-49099-0_18

[GGPR13] Gennaro, R., Gentry, C., Parno, B., Raykova, M.: Quadratic span programs and succinct NIZKs without PCPs. In: Johansson, T., Nguyen, P.Q. (eds.) EUROCRYPT 2013. LNCS, vol. 7881, pp. 626–645. Springer, Heidelberg (2013). doi:10.1007/978-3-642-38348-9_37

[GHV10] Gentry, C., Halevi, S., Vaikuntanathan, V.: i-hop homomorphic encryption and rerandomizable yao circuits. In: Rabin, T. (ed.) CRYPTO 2010. LNCS, vol. 6223, pp. 155–172. Springer, Heidelberg (2010). doi:10.1007/978-3-642-14623-7_9

[GKR08] Goldwasser, S., Kalai, Y.T., Rothblum, G.N.: Delegating computation: interactive proofs for muggles. In: Proceedings of the 40th Annual ACM Symposium on Theory of Computing, Victoria, British Columbia, Canada, 17–20 May 2008, pp. 113–122 (2008)

[GLSW15] Gentry, C., Lewko, A.B., Sahai, A., Waters, B.: Indistinguishability obfuscation from the multilinear subgroup elimination assumption. In: IEEE 56th Annual Symposium on Foundations of Computer Science, FOCS 2015, Berkeley, CA, USA, 17–20 October 2015, pp. 151–170 (2015)

[GMM+16] Garg, S., Miles, E., Mukherjee, P., Sahai, A., Srinivasan, A., Zhandry, M.: Secure obfuscation in a weak multilinear map model. In: Hirt, M., Smith, A. (eds.) TCC 2016. LNCS, vol. 9986, pp. 241–268. Springer, Heidelberg (2016). doi:10.1007/978-3-662-53644-5_10

[GPSZ17] Garg, S., Pandey, O., Srinivasan, A., Zhandry, M.: Breaking the subexponential barrier in obfustopia. In: Coron, J.-S., Nielsen, J.B. (eds.) EUROCRYPT 2017. LNCS, vol. 10212, pp. 156–181. Springer, Cham (2017). doi:10.1007/978-3-319-56617-7_6

[Gro10] Groth, J.: Short pairing-based non-interactive zero-knowledge arguments. In: Abe, M. (ed.) ASIACRYPT 2010. LNCS, vol. 6477, pp. 321–340. Springer, Heidelberg (2010). doi:10.1007/978-3-642-17373-8_19

[GSW13] Gentry, C., Sahai, A., Waters, B.: Homomorphic encryption from learning with errors: conceptually-simpler, asymptotically-faster, attribute-based. In: Canetti, R., Garay, J.A. (eds.) CRYPTO 2013. LNCS, vol. 8042, pp. 75–92. Springer, Heidelberg (2013). doi:10.1007/978-3-642-40041-4_5

[GW11] Gentry, C., Wichs, D.: Separating succinct non-interactive arguments from all falsifiable assumptions. In: Proceedings of the 43rd Annual ACM Symposium on Theory of Computing, pp. 99–108 (2011)

[HJ16] Hu, Y., Jia, H.: Cryptanalysis of GGH map. In: Fischlin, M., Coron, J.-S. (eds.) EUROCRYPT 2016. LNCS, vol. 9665, pp. 537–565. Springer, Heidelberg (2016). doi:10.1007/978-3-662-49890-3_21

[HRSV11] Hohenberger, S., Rothblum, G.N., Shelat, A., Vaikuntanathan, V.: Securely obfuscating re-encryption. J. Cryptol. 24(4), 694–719 (2011)

[Kil92] Kilian, J.: A note on efficient zero-knowledge proofs and arguments. In: Proceedings of the 24th Annual ACM Symposium on Theory of Computing, pp. 723–732 (1992)

[KLW14] Koppula, V., Lewko, A.B., Waters, B.: Indistinguishability obfuscation for turing machines with unbounded memory. Cryptology ePrint Archive, Report 2014/925 (2014). http://eprint.iacr.org/

[KP16] Kalai, Y., Paneth, O.: Delegating RAM computations. In: Hirt, M., Smith, A. (eds.) TCC 2016. LNCS, vol. 9986, pp. 91–118. Springer, Heidelberg (2016). doi:10.1007/978-3-662-53644-5_4

[KRR13] Kalai, Y.T., Raz, R., Rothblum, R.D.: Delegation for bounded space. In: STOC, pp. 565–574 (2013)

[KRR14] Kalai, Y.T., Raz, R., Rothblum, R.D.: How to delegate computations: the power of no-signaling proofs. In: Symposium on Theory of Computing, STOC 2014, New York, NY, USA, 31 May–03 June 2014, pp. 485–494 (2014)

[Lip12] Lipmaa, H.: Progression-free sets and sublinear pairing-based non-interactive zero-knowledge arguments. In: Cramer, R. (ed.) TCC 2012. LNCS, vol. 7194, pp. 169–189. Springer, Heidelberg (2012). doi:10.1007/978-3-642-28914-9_10

[LTV12] López-Alt, A., Tromer, E., Vaikuntanathan, V.: On-the-fly multiparty computation on the cloud via multikey fully homomorphic encryption. In: Proceedings of the 44th Symposium on Theory of Computing Conference, STOC 2012, New York, NY, USA, 19–22 May 2012, pp. 1219–1234 (2012)

[LV16] Lin, H., Vaikuntanathan, V.: Indistinguishability obfuscation from DDH-like assumptions on constant-degree graded encodings. In: IEEE 57th Annual Symposium on Foundations of Computer Science, FOCS 2016, 9–11 October 2016, Hyatt Regency, New Brunswick, New Jersey, USA, pp. 11–20 (2016)

[Mic94] Micali, S.: CS proofs (extended abstracts). In: 35th Annual Symposium on Foundations of Computer Science, Santa Fe, New Mexico, USA, 20–22 November 1994, pp. 436–453 (1994)

[MSZ16] Miles, E., Sahai, A., Zhandry, M.: Annihilation attacks for multilinear maps: cryptanalysis of indistinguishability obfuscation over GGH13. In: Robshaw, M., Katz, J. (eds.) CRYPTO 2016. LNCS, vol. 9815, pp. 629–658. Springer, Heidelberg (2016). doi:10.1007/978-3-662-53008-5_22

[Nao03] Naor, M.: On cryptographic assumptions and challenges. In: Boneh, D. (ed.) CRYPTO 2003. LNCS, vol. 2729, pp. 96–109. Springer, Heidelberg (2003). doi:10.1007/978-3-540-45146-4_6

[PR14] Paneth, O., Rothblum, G.N.: Publicly verifiable non-interactive arguments for delegating computation. Cryptology ePrint Archive, Report 2014/981 (2014). http://eprint.iacr.org/2014/981

[SW14] Sahai, A., Waters, B.: How to use indistinguishability obfuscation: deniable encryption, and more. In: STOC (2014)

[vDGHV10] van Dijk, M., Gentry, C., Halevi, S., Vaikuntanathan, V.: Fully homomorphic encryption over the integers. In: Gilbert, H. (ed.) EUROCRYPT 2010. LNCS, vol. 6110, pp. 24–43. Springer, Heidelberg (2010). doi:10.1007/978-3-642-13190-5_2

[WB13] Walfish, M., Blumberg, A.J.: Verifying computations without reexecuting them: from theoretical possibility to near-practicality. Electronic Colloquium on Computational Complexity (ECCC), 20:165 (2013)

[Zim15] Zimmerman, J.: How to obfuscate programs directly. In: Oswald, E., Fischlin, M. (eds.) EUROCRYPT 2015. LNCS, vol. 9057, pp. 439–467. Springer, Heidelberg (2015). doi:10.1007/978-3-662-46803-6_15

Non-Malleable Codes

Inception Makes Non-malleable Codes Stronger

Divesh Aggarwal[1]([✉]), Tomasz Kazana[2], and Maciej Obremski[3]

[1] National University of Singapore, Singapore, Singapore
divesh.aggarwal@gmail.com
[2] University of Warsaw, Warsaw, Poland
[3] Aarhus University, Aarhus, Denmark

Abstract. Non-malleable codes (NMCs), introduced by Dziembowski et al. [DPW10], provide a useful message integrity guarantee in situations where traditional error-correction (and even error-detection) is impossible; for example, when the attacker can completely overwrite the encoded message. NMCs have emerged as a fundamental object at the intersection of coding theory and cryptography.

A large body of the recent work has focused on various constructions of non-malleable codes in the split-state model. Many variants of NMCs have been introduced in the literature i.e. strong NMCs, super strong NMCs and continuous NMCs. Perhaps the most useful notion among these is that of continuous non-malleable codes, that allows for continuous tampering by the adversary.

In this paper we give the first efficient, information-theoretic secure construction of continuous non-malleable codes in the split-state model. Enroute to our main result, we obtain constructions for almost all possible notions of non-malleable codes that have been considered in the split-state model, and for which such a construction is possible. Our result is obtained by a series of black-box reductions starting from the non-malleable codes from [ADL14].

One of the main technical ingredient of our result is a new concept that we call *inception coding*. We believe it may be of independent interest. Also our construction is used as a building block for non-persistent (resettable) continuous non-malleable codes in constant split-state model in [DNO16].

1 Introduction

Non-malleable Codes. Non-malleable codes (NMCs), introduced by Dziembowski, Pietrzak and Wichs [DPW10], provide a useful message integrity

This work is supported by:
The Singapore Ministry of Education and the National Research Foundation, also through the Tier 3 Grant Random numbers from quantum processes MOE2012-T3-1-009;
Polish National Science Centre (NCN) SONATA GRANT UMO-2014/13/D/ST6/03252; and
European research Council (ERC) under the European Unions's Horizon 2020 research and innovation programme (grant agreement No. 669255).

Y. Kalai and L. Reyzin (Eds.): TCC 2017, Part II, LNCS 10678, pp. 319–343, 2017.
https://doi.org/10.1007/978-3-319-70503-3_10

guarantee in situations where traditional error-correction (and even error-detection) is impossible; for example, when the attacker can completely over-write the encoded message. NMCs have emerged as a fundamental object at the intersection of coding theory and cryptography.

Informally, given a tampering family $\mathcal{F}$, an NMC (Enc, Dec) against $\mathcal{F}$ encodes a given message m into a codeword $c \leftarrow \mathsf{Enc}(m)$ in a way that, if the adversary modifies c to $c' = f(c)$ for some $f \in \mathcal{F}$, then the message $m' = \mathsf{Dec}(c')$ is either the original message m, or a completely "unrelated value". As has been shown by the recent progress [DPW10, LL12, DKO13, ADL14, FMVW14, FMNV14, CG14a, CG14b, CZ14, Agg15, ADKO15b, ADKO15a, CGL15, AGM+15b, AGM+15a, AAnHKM+16, Li16] NMCs aim to handle a much larger class of tampering functions $\mathcal{F}$ than traditional error-correcting or error-detecting codes, at the expense of potentially allowing the attacker to replace a given message m by an unrelated message m'. NMCs are useful in situations where changing m to an unrelated m' is not useful for the attacker (for example, when m is the secret key for a signature scheme.)

(Super) Strong Non-malleable Codes. A stronger notion of non-malleability, called *strong non-malleable codes*, was also considered in [DPW10] in which, whenever the codeword c is modified to $c' = f(c) \neq c$, the decoded message $m' = \mathsf{Dec}(c')$ is independent of m. This is in contrast to the plain notion of non-malleability where some modification of the codeword c could still result in $m' = m$. Indeed, this is the case in some of the previous constructions of non-malleable codes like [ADL14, ADKO15a]. For the purpose of conveniently defining continuous non-malleable codes, an even stronger notion called *super-strong non-malleable codes* has been considered in the literature [FMNV14, JW15]. Informally speaking, in this notion, if $c' \neq c$ is a valid codeword, then c' must be independent of c.

An intermediate notion can also be considered where if $m' = \mathsf{Dec}(c') \notin \{m, \bot\}$, then c' must be independent of c. To be consistent with other notions of non-malleable codes, we call these *super non-malleable codes*.

Continuous Non-malleable Codes. It is clearly realistically possible that the attacker repeatedly tampers with the device and observes the outputs. As mentioned in [JW15], non-malleable codes can provide protection against these kind of attacks if the device is allowed to freshly re-encode its state after each invocation to make sure that the tampering is applied to a fresh codeword at each step. After each execution the entire content of the memory is erased. While such perfect erasures may be feasible in some settings, they are rather problematic in the presence of tampering. Due to this reason, Faust et al. [FMNV14] introduced an even stronger notion of non-malleable codes called continuous non-malleable codes where security is achieved against continuous tampering of a single code-word *without* re-encoding. Jafargholi and Wichs [JW15] considered four variants of continuous non-malleable codes depending on

- Whether tampering is *persistent* in the sense that the tampering is always applied to the current version of the tampered codeword, and all previous versions of the codeword are lost. The alternative definition considers non-persistent tampering where the tampering always occurs on the original codeword.

- Whether tampering to an invalid codeword (i.e., when the decoder outputs $\perp$) causes a *"self-destruct"* and the experiment stops and the attacker cannot gain any additional information, or alternatively whether the attacker can always continue to tamper and gain information.

Split-State Model. Although any kind of non-malleable codes do not exist if the family of "tampering functions" $\mathcal{F}$ is completely unrestricted,[1] they are known to exist for many large classes of tampering families $\mathcal{F}$. One such natural family is the family of tampering functions in the so called *t-split-state* model. In this model, the codeword is "split" into $t > 1$ states $c = (c_1, \ldots, c_t)$; a tampering function f is viewed as a list of t functions $(f_1, \ldots, f_t)$ where each function f_i tampers with corresponding component c_i of the codeword independently: i.e., the tampered codeword is $c' = (f_1(c_1), \ldots, f_t(c_t))$.

This family is interesting since it seems naturally useful in applications, especially when t is low and the shares $y_1, \ldots, y_t$ are stored in different parts of memory, or by different parties. Not surprisingly, the setting of $t = 2$ appears the most useful (but also the most challenging from the technical point of view), so it received the most attention so far [DPW10, LL12, DKO13, ADL14, FMNV14, CG14a, CG14b, CZ14, CGL15, ADKO15b, ADKO15a, Li16] and is also the focus of our work.

While some of the above mentioned results achieve security against computationally bounded adversaries, we focus on security in the information-theoretic setting, i.e., security against unbounded adversaries. The known results in the information-theoretic setting can be summarized as follows. Firstly [DPW10] showed the existence of (strong) non-malleable codes, and this result was improved by [CG14a] who showed that the optimal rate of these codes is $1/2$. Faust et al. [FMNV14] showed the impossibility of continuous non-malleable codes against non-persistent split-state tampering. Later [JW15] showed that continuous non-malleable codes exist in the split-state model if the tampering is persistent.

There have been a series of recent results culminating in constructions of efficient non-malleable codes in the split-state model [DKO13, ADL14, CZ14, CGL15, ADKO15a, Li16]. However, there is no known efficient construction in the continuous setting. Since the work of [FMNV14] rules out the possibility of such a construction for the case of non-persistent tampering, the best one can hope for is an efficient construction for the case of persistent tampering in the split-state model.

Our Results and Techniques. This brings us to the main result of the paper which is the following.

---

[1] In particular, $\mathcal{F}$ should not include "re-encoding functions" $f(c) = \mathsf{Enc}(f'(\mathsf{Dec}(c)))$ for any non-trivial function f', as $m' = \mathsf{Dec}(f(\mathsf{Enc}(m))) = f'(m)$ is obviously related to m.

Theorem 1. *For any k, there exists an efficient (in k) information-theoretically secure persistent continuous $2^{-k^{\Omega(1)}}$-non-malleable code with self-destruct in the split-state model that encodes k-bit messages to $\mathsf{poly}(k)$-bit codewords.*

Enroute to Theorem 1, we obtain efficient constructions of almost all possible notions of non-malleable codes in the split-state model for which such a construction is possible.

While it might be argued that the most interesting case of continuous non-malleable codes is that of non-persistent tampering, it was shown to be impossible in the 2-split state model in [FMNV14]. In a recent work, it has been shown that our persistent continuous non-malleable codes can in fact be used to obtain an efficient construction of non-persistent continuous non-malleable codes in the constant split-state model [DNO16].

The construction is obtained in a series of steps. We first show a reduction (Theorem 2 in Sect. 4) that any scheme in the split-state model that is a super-strong non-malleable code is also a persistent continuous non-malleable code with self-destruct in the split-state model. The key idea behind this reduction is the observation by Jafargholi and Wichs [JW15] that for the case of persistent continuous non-malleable codes with self-destruct, without loss of generality, we can assume that the experiment stops at the first instance (say at step I) when there is a non-trivial tampering. This is because if the tampered codeword decodes to $\bot$ then the experiment stops because of the self-destruct property, and if it does not decode to $\bot$, then the adversary learns the entire codeword and can simulate the remaining tampering experiment himself. Thus, the main ingredient of this reduction is showing that for any non-malleable code in the split-state model, the random variable I combined with first non-same tampering experiment output does not reveal the encoded message.

Our main technical reduction (Theorem 3 in Sect. 5) is one that shows that any coding scheme that is super non-malleable in the split-state model can be converted into a scheme that is super-strong non-malleable in the split-state model. To do that we develop a new technique we called *inception coding*. The key difference between a super non-malleable code and a super-strong non-malleable code is that in the former, the adversary is assumed to not gain any useful information if he tampers with and changes the codeword but the tampered codeword still decodes to the same message while in the latter, the adversary in this case gets to see the entire tampered codeword. Our inception coding essentially forces all these non-trivial tampered codewords (that originally decoded to the correct message) to decode to $\bot$. In our reduction, given a super non-malleable code $(\mathsf{Enc}, \mathsf{Dec})$, we modify the encoding procedure to sacrifice a small suffix of the message (it will not carry any message related information anymore) to replace it with validity checks for each of the states that detect whether these states have been tampered with. The message m is encoded as $\mathsf{Enc}(m, \mathsf{check}_x, \mathsf{check}_y) = (X, Y)$ subject to the condition that $\mathsf{Verify}(\mathsf{check}_x; X) = \mathsf{Verify}(\mathsf{check}_y; Y) = \mathrm{OK}$. This ensures that in the case when tampered codeword decodes correctly, the validity check can detect the tampering and output $\bot$. In order to use the super non-malleability of $(\mathsf{Enc}, \mathsf{Dec})$

to conclude super-strong non-malleability of the modified encoding scheme, we need to do rejection sampling to ensure that the codeword is valid with respect to the modified encoding algorithm. This blows up the error by a factor of about 2^{2t} where t is the length of each validity check, and so we require that $2^{2t} \ll 1/\varepsilon$, where ε is the error parameter for (Enc, Dec). We obtain a construction of the check function in Definition 8 using the well-studied Reed-Solomon error-correcting codes. In order to reduce the output length of this construction, we define a composition theorem on validity check functions, and show in Lemma 7 that using this composition theorem repeatedly, we can progressively make the length of the validity check shorter.

Finally, to complete the proof, we show (in Theorem 5 in Sect. 6) that the coding scheme from [ADL14], which was shown to be a non-malleable code in the split-state model, is also super non-malleable. This proof was surprisingly involved, since we need to argue that for any two tampered codewords c'_1, c'_2 of two distinct messages, if they do not decode to $\bot$ or the original messages, respectively, then the two tampered codewords are indistinguishable. This required a careful re-analysis of the various cases in [ADL14], in particular those where their tampering experiment does not output same or $\bot$. Fortunately, this happens only when one of the two tampered parts $f(L)$ or $g(R)$ loses a lot of information about the two parts L and R of the original codeword, and since the construction of [ADL14] is based on the inner product function, which is a strong 2-source extractor, one can conclude that the tampered codeword $(f(L), g(R))$ is independent of the $\langle L, R \rangle$ and hence of the original message.

Background. The notion of non-malleability was introduced by Dolev et al. [DDN00], and has found many applications in cryptography. Traditionally, non-malleability is defined in the computational setting, but recently non-malleability has been successfully defined and applied in the information-theoretic setting (generally resulting in somewhat simpler and cleaner definitions than their computational counter-parts). For example, in addition to non-malleable codes studied in this work, the work of Dodis and Wichs [DW09] defined the notion of non-malleable extractors as a tool for building round-efficient privacy amplification protocols.

Finally, the study of non-malleable codes falls into a much larger cryptographic framework of providing counter-measures against various classes of tampering attacks. This work was pioneered by the early works of [ISW03, GLM+03, IPSW06], and has since led to many subsequent models. We do not list all such tampering models, but we refer to [KKS11, LL12] for an excellent discussion of various such models.

Other Related Work. In addition to the works mentioned above, non-malleable codes have been studied in various tampering models in several recent results. For tampering functions of size $2^{\mathsf{poly}(n)}$, rate-1 codes (with efficient encoding and decoding) exist, and can be obtained efficiently with overwhelming probability [FMVW14].

Cheraghchi and Guruswami [CG14b] gave a rate 1 non-malleable code against the class of bitwise-tampering functions, where each bit of the codewords is tampered independently. Recently, Agrawal et al. [AGM+15b, AGM+15a] improved this result by giving a explicit rate-1 code against a stronger class of tampering functions, which in addition to tampering with each bit of the codeword independently, can also permute the bits of the resulting codeword after tampering, was achieved in [AGM+15b, AGM+15a].

In the "split state" setting, an encoding scheme was proposed in [CKM11]. For the case of only two states, an explicit non-malleable code for encoding one-bit message was proposed by [DKO13]. This was improved by Aggarwal et al. [ADL14] to a scheme that encodes larger messages but with rate $1/\mathrm{poly}(k)$ where k is the length of the message. This was further improved to obtain a constant-rate non-malleable code in [CZ14, ADKO15a].

Another related result by Aggarwal et al. [ADKO15b] obtained efficient construction, of non-malleable codes in a model where the adversary, in addition to performing split-state tampering, is also allowed some limited interaction between the two states.

Coretti et al. [CMTV15, CDTV16] have obtained constructions of information-theoretically secure continuous non-malleable codes in the bit-wise independent tampering model and have used this construct a non-malleable encryption scheme.

In the computational setting, there has been a sequence of works constructing non-malleable codes and its variants [LL12, FMNV14]. Chandran et al. [CGM+15] also rely on the computational setting in defining their new notion of *blockwise non-malleable codes*. Blockwise non-malleable codes are a generalization of the split-state model (and the recent lookahead model of [ADKO15a]) where the adversary tampers with one state at a time.

2   Preliminaries

For a set S, we let U_S denote the uniform distribution over S. For an integer $m \in \mathbb{N}$, we let U_m denote the uniform distribution over $\{0,1\}^m$, the bit-strings of length m. For a distribution or random variable X we write $x \leftarrow X$ to denote the operation of sampling a random x according to X. For a set S, we write $s \leftarrow S$ as shorthand for $s \leftarrow U_S$.

The Hamming distance between two strings $(a_1, \ldots, a_m)$, $(b_1, \ldots, b_m) \in \{0,1\}^m$ is the number of $i \in [m]$ such that $a_i \neq b_i$. We denote it as

$$\mathsf{Ham}((a_1, \ldots, a_m) \, ; \, (b_1, \ldots, b_m)) \, .$$

Entropy and Statistical Distance. The *min-entropy* of a random variable X is defined as $\mathbf{H}_\infty(X) \stackrel{\mathrm{def}}{=} -\log(\max_x \Pr[X = x])$. We say that X is an (n,k)-*source* if $X \in \{0,1\}^n$ and $\mathbf{H}_\infty(X) \geq k$. For $X \in \{0,1\}^n$, we define the *entropy rate* of X to be $\mathbf{H}_\infty(X)/n$. We also define *average (aka conditional) min-entropy* of a random variable X conditioned on another random variable Z as

$$\widetilde{\mathbf{H}}_\infty(X|Z) \stackrel{\mathrm{def}}{=} -\log \left(\mathbb{E}_{z \leftarrow Z} \left[\max_x \Pr[X = x | Z = z] \right] \right)$$

$$= -\log \left(\mathbb{E}_{z \leftarrow Z} \left[2^{-\mathbf{H}_\infty(X|Z=z)} \right] \right) \, .$$

where $\mathbb{E}_{z \leftarrow Z}$ denotes the expected value over $z \leftarrow Z$. We have the following lemma.

Lemma 1 [DORS08]. *Let (X, W) be some joint distribution. Then,*

- *For any $s > 0$, $\Pr_{w \leftarrow W}[\mathbf{H}_\infty(X|W = w) \geq \widetilde{\mathbf{H}}_\infty(X|W) - s] \geq 1 - 2^{-s}$.*
- *If Z has at most 2^ℓ possible values, then $\widetilde{\mathbf{H}}_\infty(X|(W, Z)) \geq \widetilde{\mathbf{H}}_\infty(X|W) - \ell$.*

The *statistical distance* between two random variables W and Z distributed over some set S is

$$\Delta(W, Z) := \max_{T \subseteq S} |W(T) - Z(T)| = \frac{1}{2} \sum_{s \in S} |W(s) - Z(s)|.$$

Note that $\Delta(W, Z) = \max_D(\Pr[D(W) = 1] - \Pr[D(Z) = 1])$, where D is a probabilistic function. We say W is ε-close to Z, denoted $W \approx_\varepsilon Z$, if $\Delta(W, Z) \leq \varepsilon$. We write $\Delta(W, Z|Y)$ as shorthand for $\Delta((W, Y), (Z, Y))$, and note that $\Delta(W, Z|Y) = \mathbb{E}_{y \leftarrow Y} \Delta(W|Y = y, Z|Y = y)$.

Reed-Solomon Codes. In Sect. 5 we will use standard Reed-Solomon error-correcting codes. The following is a folklore result about Reed-Solomon codes. See, for example [RU08].

Lemma 2. *Let $n = 2^\ell$ for some positive integer ℓ, and let $q > 0$ be an integer. There exist a function $RS : \{0, 1\}^n \to \{0, 1\}^{n + q \log n}$[2] such that:*

- *Hamming distance between any two elements of the image of RS is at least $q + 1$,*
- *For any $x \in \{0, 1\}^n$ there exist a unique sequence of bits $u \in \{0, 1\}^{q \log n}$ such that $x \| u$ is an element of the image of RS;*
- *For every $u \in \{0, 1\}^{q \log n}$ the set of all $x \in \{0, 1\}^n$ such that $x \| u$ is an element of the image of RS is affine subspace of $\{0, 1\}^n$.*

3   Various Definitions of Non-malleable Codes

Definition 1. *A coding scheme in the split-state model consists of two functions: a randomized encoding function $\mathsf{Enc} : \{0, 1\}^k \mapsto \{0, 1\}^n \times \{0, 1\}^n$, and a deterministic decoding function $\mathsf{Dec} : \{0, 1\}^n \times \{0, 1\}^n \mapsto \{0, 1\}^k \cup \{\bot\}$ such that, for each $m \in \mathcal{M}$, $\Pr(\mathsf{Dec}(\mathsf{Enc}(m)) = m) = 1$ (over the randomness of the encoding algorithm). Additionally, we say that the coding scheme is almost uniform if for any m, any constant $c > 1/2$ and large enough n, and any $\mathcal{L}, \mathcal{R} \subseteq \{0, 1\}^n$, such that $|\mathcal{L}| \geq 2^{cn}$, and $|\mathcal{R}| \geq 2^{cn}$ we have that*

$$\frac{|\mathcal{L}| \times |\mathcal{R}|}{2^{2n+1}} \leq \Pr(\mathsf{Enc}(m) \in \mathcal{L} \times \mathcal{R}) \leq \frac{|\mathcal{L}| \times |\mathcal{R}|}{2^{2n-1}},$$

where the probability is taken over the randomness of the encoding algorithm.

---

[2] The elements of the image of RS are called valid codewords for RS.

We now define non-malleable codes.

Definition 2 (Non-malleable Code from [DPW10]). *Let* $(\mathsf{Enc} : \mathcal{M} \to \mathcal{X} \times \mathcal{X}, \mathsf{Dec} : \mathcal{X} \times \mathcal{X} \to \mathcal{M} \cup \{\bot\})$ *be an encoding scheme. For* $f, g : \mathcal{X} \to \mathcal{X}$ *and for any* $m \in \mathcal{M}$ *define the experiment* $\mathsf{DPWTamp}_m^{f,g}$ *as:*

$$\mathsf{DPWTamp}_m^{f,g} = \left\{ \begin{array}{c} (X, Y) \leftarrow \mathsf{Enc}(m), \\ X' := f(X), Y' := g(Y) \\ m' := \mathsf{Dec}(X', Y') \\ output: m' \end{array} \right\}$$

We say that an encoding scheme $(\mathsf{Enc}, \mathsf{Dec})$ *is* ε*-DPW-non-malleable in split-state model if for every functions* $f, g : \mathcal{X} \to \mathcal{X}$ *there exists distribution* $D^{f,g}$ *on* $\mathcal{M} \cup \{\mathsf{same}, \bot\}$ *such that for every* $m \in \mathcal{M}$ *we have*

$$\mathsf{DPWTamp}_m^{f,g} \approx_\varepsilon \left\{ \begin{array}{c} d \leftarrow D^{f,g} \\ if\ d = \mathsf{same}\ then\ output\ m \\ otherwise\ output\ d. \end{array} \right\}$$

We will consider the following alternative definition of non-malleable code, which will be a smoother transition to the subsequent definitions in this section. We show the equivalence of this definition to Definition 2 (originally formulated in [DPW10]) in Appendix A.

Definition 3 (Non-malleable Code). *We say that an encoding scheme* $(\mathsf{Enc} : \mathcal{M} \to \mathcal{X} \times \mathcal{X}, \mathsf{Dec} : \mathcal{X} \times \mathcal{X} \to \mathcal{M} \cup \{\bot\})$ *is* ε*-non-malleable in split-state model if for every functions* $f, g : \mathcal{X} \to \mathcal{X}$ *there exists family of distributions* $\{D_{x,y}^{f,g}\}_{x,y \in \mathcal{X}}$ *each on* $\{0,1\}$ *such that for every* $m_0, m_1 \in \mathcal{M}$

$$\mathsf{Tamp}_{m_0}^{f,g} \approx_\varepsilon \mathsf{Tamp}_{m_1}^{f,g}$$

where

$$\mathsf{Tamp}_m^{f,g} = \left\{ \begin{array}{c} (X, Y) \leftarrow \mathsf{Enc}(m), \\ output\ \mathsf{same}\ if\ \mathsf{Dec}(X, Y) = \mathsf{Dec}(f(X), g(Y)) \wedge D_{X,Y}^{f,g} = 0 \\ else\ output: \mathsf{Dec}(f(X), g(Y)) \end{array} \right\}$$

Some results in the literature like [FMNV14, JW15] have considered a notion of super-strong non-malleable codes. We introduce the following intermediate notion of super non-malleable codes.

Definition 4 (Super Non-malleable Code). *We say that an encoding scheme* $(\mathsf{Enc} : \mathcal{M} \to \mathcal{X} \times \mathcal{X}, \mathsf{Dec} : \mathcal{X} \times \mathcal{X} \to \mathcal{M} \cup \{\bot\})$ *is* ε*-super non-malleable in split-state model if for every functions* $f, g : \mathcal{X} \to \mathcal{X}$ *there exists family of distributions* $\{D_{x,y}^{f,g}\}_{x,y \in \mathcal{X}}$ *each on* $\{0,1\}$ *such that for every* $m_0, m_1 \in \mathcal{M}$

$$\mathsf{SupTamp}_{m_0}^{f,g} \approx_\varepsilon \mathsf{SupTamp}_{m_1}^{f,g}$$

where $\mathsf{SupTamp}_m^{f,g} =$

$$\left\{ \begin{array}{c} (X,Y) \leftarrow \mathsf{Enc}(m), \\ output\ \textbf{same}\ if\ \mathsf{Dec}(X,Y) = \mathsf{Dec}(f(X),g(Y)) \wedge D_{X,Y}^{f,g} = 0 \\ else\ if\ \mathsf{Dec}(f(X),g(Y)) = \bot\ output\ \bot \\ else\ output{:}\ (f(X),g(Y)) \end{array} \right\}$$

Definition 5 (Super Strong Non-malleable Code). *We say that an encoding scheme* $(\mathsf{Enc} : \mathcal{M} \to \mathcal{X} \times \mathcal{X}, \mathsf{Dec} : \mathcal{X} \times \mathcal{X} \to \mathcal{M} \cup \{\bot\})$ *is* ε-*super strong non-malleable in split-state model if for every functions* $f, g : \mathcal{X} \to \mathcal{X}$ *and for every* $m_0, m_1 \in \mathcal{M}$

$$\mathsf{SupStrTamp}_{m_0}^{f,g} \approx_\varepsilon \mathsf{SupStrTamp}_{m_1}^{f,g}$$

where

$$\mathsf{SupStrTamp}_m^{f,g} = \left\{ \begin{array}{c} (X,Y) \leftarrow \mathsf{Enc}(m), \\ output\ \textbf{same}\ if\ (X,Y) = (f(X),g(Y)) \\ else\ if\ \mathsf{Dec}(f(X),g(Y)) = \bot\ output\ \bot \\ else\ output{:}\ (f(X),g(Y)) \end{array} \right\}$$

Definition 6 (Continuous Non-malleable Code). [JW15] *define four types of continuous non-malleable codes based on two flags:* $\mathsf{sd} \in \{0,1\}$ *(self-destruct) and* $\mathsf{prs} \in \{0,1\}$ *(persistent). We say that an encoding scheme* $(\mathsf{Enc} : \mathcal{M} \to \mathcal{X} \times \mathcal{X}, \mathsf{Dec} : \mathcal{X} \times \mathcal{X} \to \mathcal{M} \cup \{\bot\})$ *is* $(\mathsf{T}, \varepsilon)$-*continuous* [sd, prs] *non-malleable in split-state model if for every Adversary* $\mathcal{A}$ *and for every* $m_0, m_1 \in \mathcal{M}$

$$\mathsf{ConTamper}_{\mathcal{A},\mathsf{T},m_0} \approx_\varepsilon \mathsf{ConTamper}_{\mathcal{A},\mathsf{T},m_1}$$

where $\mathsf{ConTamper}_{\mathcal{A},\mathsf{T},m} =$

$$\left\{ \begin{array}{l} (X,Y) \leftarrow \mathsf{Enc}(m), \\ f_0, g_0 \equiv \mathsf{id}, \\ \textbf{Repeat}\quad i = 1, 2, ..., \mathsf{T} \\ \quad \mathcal{A}\ chooses\ functions\ f_i', g_i' \\ \quad \textbf{if}\ \mathsf{prs} = 1\ \textbf{then}\ f_i = f_i' \circ f_{i-1},\ g_i = g_i' \circ g_{i-1} \\ \quad \textbf{else}\ f_i = f_i',\ g_i = g_i' \\ \quad \textbf{if}\ (f_i(X), g_i(Y)) = (X,Y)\ \textbf{then}\ output\ \textbf{same} \\ \quad \textbf{else} \\ \quad\quad \textbf{if}\ \mathsf{Dec}(f_i(X), g_i(Y)) = \bot\ \textbf{then}\ output\ \bot \textbf{if}\ \mathsf{sd} = 1\ \textbf{then}\ experiment\ stops \\ \quad\quad \textbf{else}\ output\ (f_i(X), g_i(Y))\ \textbf{if}\ \mathsf{prs} = 1\ \textbf{then}\ experiment\ stops \end{array} \right\}$$

Remark 1. In the case of persistent tampering, the above definition by [JW15] assumes that the tampering experiment stops if there is a non-trivial tampering that does not decode to $\bot$ since in this case the adversary learns the entire tampered codeword, and can simulate the remaining tampering experiment himself.

Remark 2. [FMNV14] show that non-persistent continuous non-malleable codes are impossible to construct in 2-split state model.

Remark 3. In any model allowing bitwise tampering, in particular the 2-split state model, it is not difficult to conclude that the *non-self-destruct* property is impossible to achieve even in the case of persistent tampering if the space of messages contains at least 3 elements. To see this, notice that one can tamper the codeword $c = (c_1, c_2, c_3, \ldots)$ to obtain $c'_1 = (0, c_2, \ldots)$. The adversary then obtains the output of the tampering experiment which is same if and only if $c_1 = 0$. Thus the adversary learns $c_1^\star = c_1$ and continues the tampering experiment with $(c_1^\star, 0, c_3, \ldots)$ (note that this tampering is persistent). Thus, the adversary can continue learn the codeword one bit at a time, thereby learning the entire codeword in N steps where N is the length of the codeword. Such an argument has been used previously for proving impossibility results. See for instance the work of Gennaro et al. [GLM+03].

4   From Super Strong NMCs to Continuous NMCs

In this section we will prove the following statement:

Theorem 2. *If* (Enc, Dec) *is an ε-super strong non-malleable code in the split-state model then* (Enc, Dec) *is a $(T, (2T + 1)\varepsilon)-continuous$ $[1, 1]$ non-malleable code in the split-state model.*

For proving Theorem 2, we will need the following lemmata. The following result states that any non-malleable code in the 2-split state model is a good 2-out-of-2 secret sharing scheme.

Lemma 3 ([ADKO15b, Lemma 6.1]). *Let* Dec $: \mathcal{X} \times \mathcal{X} \rightarrow \mathcal{M}$, *and* Enc $: \mathcal{M} \rightarrow \mathcal{X} \times \mathcal{X}$ *be an $\varepsilon-non-malleable$ code in the split state model for some $\varepsilon < \frac{1}{2}$. For any pair of messages $m_0, m_1 \in \mathcal{M}$, let $(X_1^0, X_2^0) \leftarrow$ Enc(m_0), and let $(X_1^1, X_2^1) \leftarrow$ Enc(m_1). Then $\Delta(X_1^0 ; X_1^1) \leq 2\varepsilon$.*

The following result states that given a non-malleable code (Enc, Dec) in the split-state model, for any sets A, B, and any message m, the probability that Enc(m) falls in the set $A \times B$ is almost independent of the choice of the message m.

Lemma 4. *Let $k \geq 3$, and let $\varepsilon < 1/20$. Let* Enc $: \{0,1\}^k \rightarrow \{0,1\}^n \times \{0,1\}^n$, Dec $: \{0,1\}^n \times \{0,1\}^n \rightarrow \{0,1\}^k$ *be an $\varepsilon-non-malleable$ code in the split state model. For every sets $A, B \subset \{0,1\}^n$ and every messages $m_0, m_1 \in \{0,1\}^k$.*

$$| \Pr(\mathsf{Enc}(m_0) \in A \times B) - \Pr(\mathsf{Enc}(m_1) \in A \times B)| \leq \varepsilon.$$

Proof. We claim that there exist $x, y, z, w \in \{0,1\}^n$ such that $m_0, m_1, \mathsf{Dec}(x, w)$, $\mathsf{Dec}(z, w)$, and $\mathsf{Dec}(z, y)$ are all different from $\mathsf{Dec}(x, y)$. Before proving this claim, we show why this implies the given result. Consider the tampering functions f, g such that $f(c) = x$ if $c \in A$, and $f(c) = z$, otherwise, and $g(c) = y$ if $c \in B$, and $g(c) = w$, otherwise. Thus, for $b = 0, 1$, $\mathsf{Tamp}_{m_b}^{f,g} = \mathsf{Dec}(x, y)$ if and only if $\mathsf{Enc}(m_b) \in A \times B$. The result then follows from the ε-non-malleability of (Enc, Dec).

Now, to prove the claim, we will use the probabilistic method. Let U be uniform in $\{0,1\}^k$, and let $X,Y \leftarrow \mathsf{Enc}(U)$. Furthermore, let $W,Z \in \{0,1\}^n$ be uniform and independent of X,Y,U. We claim that X,Y,Z,W satisfy the required property with non-zero probability.

It is easy to see that the probability that $\mathsf{Dec}(X,Y) = U$ is either of m_0 or m_1 is at most $2/2^k$. Also, by Lemma 3, we have that except with probability 2ε, X is independent of U. Also, W is independent of U. Thus, the probability that $\mathsf{Dec}(X,W) = U$ is at most $2\varepsilon + 1/2^k$. Similarly, the probability that $\mathsf{Dec}(Z,Y) = U$ is at most $2\varepsilon + 1/2^k$. Finally, W,Z are independent of U, and so the probability that $\mathsf{Dec}(Z,W) = U$ is at most $\frac{1}{2^k}$.

Thus, by union bound, the probability that X,Y,Z,W do not satisfy the condition of the claim is at most $\frac{5}{2^k} + 4\varepsilon \leq \frac{5}{8} + 4\varepsilon < 1$.   □

Before proving Theorem 2, let us fix some notation. Let $\mathcal{A}^*$ be any adversary described in Definition 6. Let $(I)_m$ denote the index of a round when *same* is not output in the experiment $\mathsf{ConTamper}_{\mathcal{A}^*,\mathsf{T},m}$ and (f_i, g_i) (for $i = 1, \ldots, T$) denote pairs of functions chosen by $\mathcal{A}^*$ (of course we can assume that they are always the same because the choice for the next round does not depend on (X,Y)).

Proof (of Theorem 2). We will show that

$$\Delta([(I)_{m_0}, f_{I_{m_0}}(X_0), g_{I_{m_0}}(Y_0)] \; ; \; [I_{m_1}, f_{I_{m_1}}(X_1), g_{I_{m_1}}(Y_1)]) \leq (2T+1)\varepsilon. \quad (4.1)$$

The desired result will follow from the observation that $\mathsf{ConTamper}_{\mathcal{A}^*,\mathsf{T},m_b}$ for $b = 0,1$ depends only on $(I)_{m_b}$, $f_{(I)_{m_b}}(X_b)$, and $g_{(I)_{m_b}}(Y_b)$.

In order to simplify the proof, we make use of the following fact about statistical distance: The statistical distance between two random variables Z_0 and Z_1 is at most δ if and only if for any computationally unbounded algorithm that is given as input a sample distributed as Z_b, for a uniformly random bit b, the probability that the algorithm can guess the bit b is at most $1/2 + \delta/2$.

Thus, we wish to bound the probability of guessing the bit b, given $I, f_I(X), g_I(Y)$, where I, X, Y are shorthand for I_{m_b}, X_b, Y_b.

We can partition the codeword space $\{0,1\}^n \times \{0,1\}^n$ into $(2T+1)$ sets: $(A_1^i \times B_1^i), (A_2^i \times B_2^i)$ for $1 \leq i \leq T$, and the set $C \times D$, where

$$A_1^i = \{X \subset \{0,1\}^n | f_j(X) = X, \text{ for all } j < i \text{ and } f_i(X) \neq X\},$$
$$B_1^i = \{Y \subset \{0,1\}^n | g_j(Y) = Y, \text{ for all } j < i\},$$

$$A_2^i = \{X \subset \{0,1\}^n | f_j(X) = X, \text{ for all } j \leq i\},$$
$$B_2^i = \{Y \subset \{0,1\}^n | g_j(Y) = Y, \text{ for all } j < i \text{ and } g_i(Y) \neq Y\},$$

$$C = \{X \subset \{0,1\}^n | f_j(X) = X, \text{ for all } j \leq T\},$$
$$D = \{Y \subset \{0,1\}^n | g_j(Y) = Y, \text{ for all } j \leq T\}.$$

Note that if $(X,Y) \in A_j^i \times B_j^i$ for $j = 1,2$, and $i \in [T]$, then $I = i$, and if $(X,Y) \in C \times D$, then $I = T+1$. Also $f_I(X), g_I(Y)$ are empty strings if $I = T+1$.

We call these partitions $P_1, ..., P_{2T+1}$.

Now suppose there is an adversary $\mathcal{A}$ that guesses the bit b with probability greater than $1/2 + (2T+1)\varepsilon/2$ given $I, f_I(X), g_I(Y)$. Let us say that $\mathcal{A}$ wins if $\mathcal{A}$ guesses the bit b correctly. Then

$$1/2 + (2T+1)\varepsilon/2 < \Pr[\mathcal{A} \text{ wins}]$$

$$= \sum_{r=1}^{2T+1} \Pr[\mathcal{A} \text{ wins} \mid (X,Y) \in P_r] \cdot \Pr[(X,Y) \in P_r]$$

$$= 1/2 + \sum_{r=1}^{2T+1} (\Pr[\mathcal{A} \text{ wins} \mid (X,Y) \in P_r] - 1/2) \cdot \Pr[(X,Y) \in P_r].$$

Thus, there exists some r such that:

$$(\Pr[\mathcal{A} \text{ wins} \mid (X,Y) \in P_r] - 1/2) \cdot \Pr[(X,Y) \in P_r] > \varepsilon/2. \tag{4.2}$$

We now show that this contradicts the fact that $(\mathsf{Enc}, \mathsf{Dec})$ is $\varepsilon-$ super strong non-malleable in the split state model.

Case 1: $P_r = A_1^i \times B_1^i$ for some $i \in [T]$.
Define the tampering function (f, g) as:

$$f(x) := \begin{cases} f_i(x) \text{ if } x \in A_1^i \\ u, \text{ otherwise.} \end{cases}$$

where u is some element not in $f_i(A_1^i)$.

$$g(y) := \begin{cases} g_i(y) \text{ if } y \in B_1^i \\ v, \text{ otherwise.} \end{cases}$$

where v is some element not in $g_i(B_1^i)$.

Then define an adversary $\mathcal{A}^*$ that given the tampering experiment of a random message m_b, outputs a fresh uniform random bit if it sees any of $(u, y), (x, v), \mathsf{same}$, or $\bot$, and calls $\mathcal{A}$ with input i, and the output of the tampering experiment otherwise. The success probability of $\mathcal{A}^*$ in guessing bit b is $\Pr[\mathcal{A} \text{ wins} \mid (X,Y) \in P_r] \cdot \Pr[(X,Y) \in P_r] + \frac{1}{2} \cdot (1 - \Pr[(X,Y) \in P_r])$, which is greater than $\frac{1}{2} \cdot \Pr[(X,Y) \in P_r] + \frac{\varepsilon}{2} + \frac{1}{2} \cdot (1 - \Pr[(X,Y) \in P_r]) = 1/2 + \varepsilon/2$ using Eq. 4.2.

This contradicts the assumption that $(\mathsf{Enc}, \mathsf{Dec})$ is $\varepsilon-$ super strong non-malleable in the split state model.

Case 2: $P_r = A_2^i \times B_2^i$ for some $i \in [T]$.
This case is similar to *Case 1*.

Case 3: $P_r = C \times D$.
In this case, the only information that $\mathcal{A}$ has is that $I = T + 1$, which is equivalent to saying that $(X,Y) \in C \times D$. Then let p_b be $\Pr((X_b, Y_b) \in C \times D)$ for $b = 0, 1$. By Lemma 4, we have that $|p_0 - p_1| \le \varepsilon$. Without loss of generality,

let $p_0 = p_1 + \varepsilon'$ for some $\varepsilon' \in [0, \varepsilon]$. Then given $(X_b, Y_b) \in C \times D$, the adversary has higher chance of winning if the adversary outputs 0.

Thus, $\Pr[\mathcal{A} \text{ wins} \mid (X_b, Y_b) \in C \times D] = \Pr[b = 0 | (X_b, Y_b) \in C \times D]$.
So, rewriting Eq. 4.2 assuming $P_r = C \times D$, we get that $\Pr[(X_b, Y_b) \in C \times D \wedge b = 0] - \frac{1}{2} \cdot \Pr[(X_b, Y_b) \in C \times D] > \varepsilon/2$. This implies, $\frac{1}{2} \cdot (p_1 + \varepsilon') - \frac{1}{2} \cdot \frac{1}{2} \cdot (p_1 + p_1 + \varepsilon') > \varepsilon/2$, which is equivalent to $\varepsilon' > 2\varepsilon$, which is a contradiction. $\qquad \square$

Remark 4. The above reduction is in the split-state model. It may be interesting to note that the only place that we use a particular property of this model is Eq. 4.1, which can be generalized to saying that the random variable I combined with the output of tampering experiment should not reveal the message. It is also obvious that if this statement does not hold for some model then the reduction will not hold. That means that the above mentioned statement is in some sense a necessary and sufficient property of a tampering model in which the main reduction of this section is true.

5 Super Strong NMCs from Super NMCs via Inception Coding

In this section, we will show that any super non-malleable code in the split-state model can be converted into a super-strong non-malleable code in the split-state model. The main technique used here and called by us 'inception' is described in 5.2 (i.e. Definition 9). However before we start the actual definition and construction let us define some auxiliary objects in Sect. 5.1.

5.1 Check Functions

In order to detect possible tampering with a string x, we introduce the following variant of *Universal Hashing Family*.

Definition 7. *A function $C : \{0,1\}^s \times \{0,1\}^n \to \{0,1\}^t$ is called an ε-check if for any $x, y \in \{0,1\}^n$ such that $x \neq y$,*

$$\Pr_{R \leftarrow \{0,1\}^s} (C(R, x) = C(R, y)) \leq \varepsilon$$

Remark 5. Every ε-check is also $(\varepsilon \cdot 2^t - 1)$-universal hashing family. Due to unnecessarily complicated normalization of parameters in standard UHF definition it is simply more convenient for us to use the *check* notion all through the paper.

In this section we give a construction of an efficient check function that has a short output length, short seed and has preimages with affine structure. Consider the following function.

Definition 8. *Let $q, t, n > 0$ be integers. Let $\mathsf{Check}_1 : \{0,1\}^n \to \{0,1\}^{q \log n}$ be such that for all $x \in \{0,1\}^n$, $x \| \mathsf{Check}_1(x)$ is a valid Reed-Solomon code.[3] Let $\mathsf{Check}_2 : \{0,1\}^{t \log n} \times \{0,1\}^n \to \{0,1\}^t$ be a simple sampler function defined as follows. Let $r = r_1 \| r_2 \| \cdots \| r_t$ be such that each r_j is a $\log n$-bit string. Then $\mathsf{Check}_2(r, x) := x_{r_1} \ldots x_{r_t}$, where x_{r_j} is the bit of x at position r_j, when written in binary form. Then we define the function $C_0 : \{0,1\}^{t \log(n)} \times \{0,1\}^n \to \{0,1\}^{q \log n + t}$ as $C_0(r, x) := \mathsf{Check}_1(x) \| \mathsf{Check}_2(r, x)$.*

Lemma 5. *The function C_0 defined above is a $e^{-\frac{qt}{n}}$-check.*

Proof. We want to bound the probability that for any two distinct $x, y \in \{0,1\}^n$ and $R = R_1 \| \ldots \| R_t$ chosen uniformly at random from $\{0,1\}^{t \log n}$, $C_0(R, x) = C_0(R, y)$.

By Lemma 2, we have that the Hamming distance between $x \| \mathsf{Check}_1(x)$ and $y \| \mathsf{Check}_1(y)$ is at least $q + 1$. Thus, if $\mathsf{Ham}(x; y) < q$ then $\mathsf{Check}_1(x) \neq \mathsf{Check}_1(y)$. So, for $C_0(R, x) = C_0(R, y)$ we must have that $\mathsf{Ham}(x; y) \geq q$. Additionally, we have that $\mathsf{Check}_2(R, x) = \mathsf{Check}_2(R, y)$ which implies $x_{R_j} = y_{R_j}$ for all $j \in [t]$. This holds if none of $R_1, \ldots, R_t$ belong to the set of positions on which x and y are not different which occurs with probability at most

$$\left(1 - \frac{q}{n}\right)^t \leq e^{-\frac{qt}{n}}.$$

$\square$

For our application, we require a check with the output having length upper bounded by n^α for a small constant $\alpha > 0$. Now, let us describe a composition lemma for check functions that will help us to reach the expected parameters.

Lemma 6. *If $C_0 : \{0,1\}^{s_1} \times \{0,1\}^n \mapsto \{0,1\}^{t_1}$ is an ε_1-check and $C : \{0,1\}^{s_2} \times \{0,1\}^{t_1} \mapsto \{0,1\}^{t_2}$ is an ε_2-check then $C_1 : \{0,1\}^{s_1 + s_2} \times \{0,1\}^n \mapsto \{0,1\}^{t_2}$ given by*

$$C_1(r_1 \| r_2, x) := C(r_2, C_0(r_1, x))$$

is an $(\varepsilon_1 + \varepsilon_2)$-check.

Proof. Let $R_1 \| R_2 \leftarrow U_{s_1 + s_2}$, and let $E_1 = E_1(R_1, x)$ be the event that $C_0(R_1, x) = C_0(R_1, y)$ and $E_2 = E_2(R_1, R_2, x)$ be the event that $C(R_2, C_0(R_1, x)) = C(R_2, C_0(R_1, y))$. Then

$$\Pr(E_2) \leq \Pr(E_1) + \Pr(E_2 \mid \overline{E_1})$$
$$\leq \varepsilon_1 + \varepsilon_2.$$

$\square$

We now apply Lemma 6 repeatedly to the construction of Lemma 5 to obtain a check with small length of both the output and the seed.

---

[3] Correctness of this definition follows from Lemma 2.

Lemma 7. *For any constant $\delta \in (0, 1/2)$ and for a large enough integer n, there exists an efficient $2^{-n^{\delta^2/5}}$-check $\mathsf{Check^\star} : \{0,1\}^s \times \{0,1\}^n \to \{0,1\}^t$ with $s \leq n^\delta$ and $t \leq n^\delta$.*

Proof. Let $\delta' = \delta/5$. We start with the construction from Lemma 5, and we set $t = n^{3\delta'}$, and $q = n^{1-2\delta'}$. Furthermore, we assume that output length $n_1 = q \log n + t \leq n^{1-\delta'}$, and $s_1 = t \log n \leq n^{4\delta'}$, which hold for a large enough n. The error is $e^{-n^{\delta'}}$.

We then define a check function for the output of length n_1, with seed length s_2 being at most $n_1^{4\delta'} \leq n^{(1-\delta')\cdot 4\delta'}$, output length n_2 being at most $n_1^{1-\delta'} \leq n^{(1-\delta')^2}$, and error is at most $e^{-n_1^{\delta'}}$.

We continue this procedure for ℓ steps until $n_\ell \leq n^\delta$. Thus $n_{\ell-1} > n^\delta$. The number of steps ℓ is upper bounded by $\log(1-\delta')/\log\delta$. Thus, using Lemma 6, the error is upper bounded by

$$\frac{\log(1-\delta')}{\log\delta} \cdot e^{-n^{5\delta'^2}} \leq 2^{-n^{5\delta'^2}}$$

and the total seed length is

$$s_1 + \cdots + s_\ell \leq n^{4\delta'} \cdot \frac{\log(1-\delta')}{\log\delta} \leq n^\delta \, ,$$

where we again used that n is large enough. $\qquad\square$

5.2   Inception Coding

In this section, we show that any super non-malleable code in the split-state model can be converted into a super-strong non-malleable code in the split-state model. Notice that for some message m with $(X, Y) \leftarrow \mathsf{Enc}(m)$, the only possible scenario in which the output of the tampering experiment in the super-strong non-malleability definition and that in the super non-malleability definition are different is when $\mathsf{Dec}(X, Y) = \mathsf{Dec}(f(X), g(Y))$ even in the case of a non-trivial tampering, i.e., $(X, Y) \neq (f(X), g(Y))$. Our idea is to use some of the least significant bits of the message to store a seed and an output of a "Check" such that if the decoder outputs the correct message in case of a non-trivial tampering, then the "Check" can detect this and force the output to be $\bot$. This technique of installing a validity check for a codeword within the message is what we call inception coding and is defined below (Fig. 1).

Definition 9. *Let $\mathsf{Enc} : \{0,1\}^k \to \{0,1\}^n \times \{0,1\}^n$, $\mathsf{Dec} : \{0,1\}^n \times \{0,1\}^n \to \{0,1\}^k \cap \{\bot\}$ be a coding scheme. Let $C : \{0,1\}^s \times \{0,1\}^n \to \{0,1\}^t$ be some function.[4] The Inception version of $(\mathsf{Enc}, \mathsf{Dec}, C)$ is a coding scheme denoted as $\mathcal{I}\mathsf{Enc} : \{0,1\}^{k-2s-2t} \to \{0,1\}^n \times \{0,1\}^n$, $\mathcal{I}\mathsf{Dec} : \{0,1\}^n \times \{0,1\}^n \to \{0,1\}^{k-2s-2t} \cup \{\bot\}$ and is defined as follows. The encoding algorithm $\mathcal{I}\mathsf{Enc}$, for a given message $m \in \{0,1\}^{k-2s-2t}$, does the following.*

---

[4] We will use this definition with C being a check function.

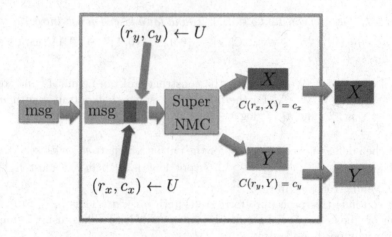

Fig. 1. Inception coding using super non-malleable code.

- *Choose uniformly at random r_x, r_y from $\{0,1\}^s$, and c_x, c_y from $\{0,1\}^t$.*
- *Sample (X, Y) as the output of the encoding algorithm* Enc *on input $(m\|r_x\|c_x\|r_y\|c_y)$ conditioned on the fact that $C(r_x, X) = c_x$ and $C(r_y, Y) = c_y$.*
- *Output (X, Y).*

The decoding algorithm $\mathcal{I}$Dec, on input $x, y \in \{0,1\}^n$, does the following.

- *Obtain* Dec$(x, y) \in \{0,1\}^k$, *and interpret the output as $(m\|r_x\|c_x\|r_y\|c_y)$, where $m \in \{0,1\}^{k-2s-2t}$, $r_x, r_y \in \{0,1\}^s$, and $c_x, c_y \in \{0,1\}^t$.*
- *If $C(r_x, x) = c_x$ and $C(r_y, y) = c_y$ then output m, else output $\perp$.*

We now state our main result.

Theorem 3. *Let $\varepsilon_1, \varepsilon_2 > 0$. $C : \{0,1\}^s \times \{0,1\}^n \to \{0,1\}^t$ be an ε_1-check. Let* Enc $: \{0,1\}^k \to \{0,1\}^n \times \{0,1\}^n$, Dec $: \{0,1\}^n \times \{0,1\}^n \to \{0,1\}^k \cap \{\perp\}$ *be a uniform ε_2-super non-malleable code in the split-state model such that for any m, r_x, c_x, r_y, c_y, there is an efficient algorithm to sample $(X, Y) \leftarrow$ Enc(m) conditioned on $C(r_x, X) = c_x$ and $C(r_y, Y) = c_y$. Then $(\mathcal{I}$Enc$, \mathcal{I}$Dec$)$ is an efficient ε'-super strong non-malleable code in the split-state model with $\varepsilon' = \frac{16\varepsilon_2}{2^{-2t}} + 2\varepsilon_1 + 3\varepsilon_2$.*

Proof. Let $f : \{0,1\}^n \mapsto \{0,1\}^n$, $g : \{0,1\}^n \mapsto \{0,1\}^n$ be arbitrary functions and $m, m' \in \{0,1\}^{k-2s-2t}$ be arbitrary messages. We will bound the statistical distance between SupStrTamp$_m^{f,g}$ and SupStrTamp$_{m'}^{f,g}$ for the encoding scheme $(\mathcal{I}$Enc$, \mathcal{I}$Dec$)$. For this purpose, we intend to use the fact that (Enc, Dec) is super non-malleable. However, the main issue with using this is that the codeword obtained by using Enc might not be a valid encoding for $\mathcal{I}$Enc. The main idea to make sure that the encoding is valid is to (artificially) do rejection sampling. We modify the tampering functions f, g to f', g' such that the tampered codeword becomes irrelevant if the code is not a valid codeword with respect to $\mathcal{I}$Enc. This is the reason that the error is blown-up by a factor 2^{2t}.

Let the space of all $x \in \{0,1\}^n$ such that $C(r,x) = c$ be $A_{r,c}$, i.e.,

$$A_{r,c} := \{x \in \{0,1\}^n \mid C(r,x) = c\} \, .$$

We choose fresh uniformly random and independent strings r_x, r_y from $\{0,1\}^s$, and c_x, c_y from $\{0,1\}^t$. Consider the following functions:

$$f'(x) := \begin{cases} f(x) \text{ if } x \in A_{r_x,c_x} \\ 0^n, \text{ otherwise.} \end{cases}$$

$$g'(y) := \begin{cases} g(y) \text{ if } y \in A_{r_y,c_y} \\ 0^n \text{ otherwise.} \end{cases}$$

Let $(X,Y) \leftarrow \mathsf{Enc}(m, r_x, c_x, r_y, c_y)$ and let $(X',Y') \leftarrow \mathsf{Enc}(m', r_x, c_x, r_y, c_y)$. We shorthand $\mathsf{SupTamp}^{f',g'}_{(m,r_x,c_x,r_y,c_y)}$ by T and $\mathsf{SupTamp}^{f',g'}_{(m',r_x,c_x,r_y,c_y)}$ by T'. The range of T and T' is $\mathcal{R} = \{0,1\}^n \times \{0,1\}^n \cup \{\bot, \mathsf{same}\}$. Also, let $\mathcal{A} = A_{r_x,c_x} \times A_{r_y,c_y}$, and let $\Pr((X,Y) \in \mathcal{A}) = p$ and $\Pr((X',Y') \in \mathcal{A}) = p'$. By Lemma 4, we have that $|p - p'| \leq \varepsilon_2$, and by the fact that $(\mathsf{Enc}, \mathsf{Dec})$ is almost uniform, we have that $p \geq 2^{-2t-1}$.

Also, if $(X,Y) \notin \mathcal{A}$, then $(f'(X), g'(Y))$ depends on at most one of X, Y, and if $(X',Y') \notin \mathcal{A}$, then $(f'(X'), g'(Y'))$ depends on at most one of X', Y'. Hence the respective tampering experiments T and T' depend on at most one of the shares and by Lemma 3, we have that in this case T and T' are statistically close, i.e.,:

$$\frac{1}{2} \cdot \sum_{z \in \mathcal{R}} |\Pr(T = z \wedge (X,Y) \notin \mathcal{A}) - \Pr(T' = z \wedge (X',Y') \notin \mathcal{A})| \leq 2\varepsilon_2 \, . \quad (5.1)$$

Also, by the super non-malleability assumption, we have that $\Delta(T; T') \leq \varepsilon_2$. Thus, using Eq. 5.1, and the triangle inequality, we have that

$$6\varepsilon_2 \geq \sum_{z \in \mathcal{R}} |\Pr(T = z \wedge (X,Y) \in \mathcal{A}) - \Pr(T' = z \wedge (X',Y') \in \mathcal{A})|$$

$$= \sum_{z \in \mathcal{R}} |\Pr(T = z \mid (X,Y) \in \mathcal{A}) \cdot p - \Pr(T' = z | (X',Y') \in \mathcal{A}) \cdot p'|$$

$$\geq p \cdot \sum_{z \in \mathcal{R}} |\Pr(T = z | (X,Y) \in \mathcal{A}) - \Pr(T' = z | (X',Y') \in \mathcal{A})| - |p - p'|$$

$$\geq (2^{-2t-1}) \cdot \sum_{z \in \mathcal{R}} |\Pr(T = z | (X,Y) \in \mathcal{A}) - \Pr(T' = z | (X',Y') \in \mathcal{A})| - 2\varepsilon_2 \, .$$

This implies that

$$\sum_{z \in \mathcal{R}} |\Pr(T = z | (X,Y) \in \mathcal{A}) - \Pr(T' = z | (X',Y') \in \mathcal{A})| \leq \frac{8\varepsilon_2}{2^{-2t-1}} \, .$$

Let $\widetilde{T}$ be the tampering experiment T conditioned on the event $(X,Y) \in \mathcal{A}$. Similarly define $\widetilde{T}'$.

We now compare the experiments $\widetilde{T}$ and $\mathsf{SupStrTamp}_m^{f,g}$. For the purpose of this comparison, we assume that the random coins needed to generate r_x, c_x, r_y, c_y, and $(X, Y) \leftarrow \mathsf{Enc}(m)$ conditioned on $(X, Y) \in \mathcal{A}$ are the same. Then, we have that if $\widetilde{T} \neq$ same, then $\mathsf{SupStrTamp}_m^{f,g}$ is equal to $\widetilde{T}$ except with probability at most ε_2. To see this, notice that if both $\widetilde{T}$ and $\mathsf{SupStrTamp}_m^{f,g}$ are not same, then they are equal. The event that $\widetilde{T} \neq$ same and $\mathsf{SupStrTamp}_m^{f,g} =$ same happens if $f(X) = X, g(Y) = Y$ but $D_{X,Y}^{f,g} = 1$. This cannot happen with probability more than ε_2, since this would mean that $T = (X, Y)$ which would immediately reveal the message thereby contradicting the non-malleability of $(\mathsf{Enc}, \mathsf{Dec})$.

Also, we claim that if $\widetilde{T} =$ same, then $\mathsf{SupStrTamp}_m^{f,g} \in \{\text{same}, \bot\}$, except with probability at most ε_1. This follows from the fact that if $\widetilde{T} =$ same, and $\mathsf{SupStrTamp}_m^{f,g} \notin \{\text{same}, \bot\}$, then this implies that at least one of $f(X) \neq X$, or $g(Y) \neq Y$ but $C(r_x, f(X)) = c_x$, and $C(r_y, g(Y)) = c_y$ which happens with probability at most ε_1.

Thus, we can bound the statistical distance between $\mathsf{SupStrTamp}_m^{f,g}$ and $\mathsf{SupStrTamp}_{m'}^{f,g}$ by

$$\frac{8\varepsilon_2}{2^{-2t-1}} + 2\varepsilon_1 + 2\varepsilon_2 + |\Pr(\mathsf{SupStrTamp}_m^{f,g} = \text{same}) - \Pr(\mathsf{SupStrTamp}_{m'}^{f,g} = \text{same})| \, .$$

Finally, using Lemma 4, we can conclude that

$$|\Pr(\mathsf{SupStrTamp}_m^{f,g} = \text{same}) - \Pr(\mathsf{SupStrTamp}_{m'}^{f,g} = \text{same})| \leq \varepsilon_2$$

by setting $A = \{x \in \{0,1\}^n : f(x) = x\}$, and $B = \{y \in \{0,1\}^n : g(y) = y\}$. □

6 Instantiating a Super Non-malleable Code

In [ADL14], Aggarwal et al. gave a construction of non-malleable codes in the split-state model. Here, we argue that the construction of [ADL14] is also super-non-malleable.

Note that for any message m with $\mathsf{Enc}(m) = (X, Y)$, and any functions f, g, the output of the tampering experiment in Definition 3 is the same as that in Definition 4 if $\mathsf{Dec}(f(X), g(Y)) = m$ or $\mathsf{Dec}(f(X), g(Y)) = \bot$. This leads to the following simple observation.

Observation 6.1. Let $\varepsilon, \varepsilon' > 0$. Let $(\mathsf{Enc} : \mathcal{M} \to \mathcal{X} \times \mathcal{X}, \mathsf{Dec} : \mathcal{X} \times \mathcal{X} \to \mathcal{M} \cup \{\bot\})$ be an ε-non-malleable code in the split-state model. Given $f, g : \mathcal{X} \mapsto \mathcal{X}$, assume there exists a partitioning $(\mathcal{S}_1, \cdots, \mathcal{S}_{s+t}, \mathcal{S}^\star)$ of $\mathcal{X} \times \mathcal{X}$ such that the following hold:

1. For all $m \in \mathcal{M}, 1 \leq i \leq s, \Pr_{(X,Y) \leftarrow \mathsf{Enc}(m)}(\mathsf{Dec}(f(X), g(Y)) \in \{m, \bot\}|(X, Y) \in \mathcal{S}_i) \geq 1 - \varepsilon'$.
2. For all $m_1, m_2 \in \mathcal{M}, s+1 \leq i \leq s+t$, let $(X_1, Y_1), (X_2, Y_2)$ be the encoding of m_1, m_2 respectively, conditioned on the fact that $(X_1, Y_1), (X_2, Y_2) \in \mathcal{S}_i$. Then $\Delta((f(X_1), g(Y_1)), (f(X_2), g(Y_2))) \leq \varepsilon'$.

3. For any $m \in \mathcal{M}$, $\Pr(\mathsf{Enc}(m) \in \mathcal{S}^\star) \leq \varepsilon'$.

Then, the scheme $(\mathsf{Enc}, \mathsf{Dec})$ is $(\varepsilon + O(\varepsilon'))$-super-non-malleable.

In the above observation, we set $D^{f,g}_{(X,Y)}$ to be 1 if $(X, Y) \in \mathcal{S}_1, \ldots, \mathcal{S}_s$, and 0, otherwise.

Before describing the encoding scheme from [ADL14], we will need the following definition of an affine-evasive function.

Definition 10. *Let* $\mathbb{F} = \mathbb{F}_p$ *be a finite field. A surjective function* $h : \mathbb{F} \mapsto \mathcal{M} \cup \{\perp\}$ *is called* (γ, δ)-*affine-evasive if or any* $a, b \in \mathbb{F}$ *such that* $a \neq 0$, *and* $(a, b) \neq (1, 0)$, *and for any* $m \in \mathcal{M}$,

1. $\Pr_{U \leftarrow \mathbb{F}}(h(aU + b) \neq \perp) \leq \gamma$
2. $\Pr_{U \leftarrow \mathbb{F}}(h(aU + b) \neq \perp \mid h(U) = m) \leq \delta$
3. *A uniformly random* X *such that* $h(X) = m$ *is efficiently samplable.*

Aggarwal [Agg15] showed the following.

Lemma 8. *There exists an efficiently computable* $(p^{-3/4}, \Theta(|\mathcal{M}| \log p \cdot p^{-1/4}))$-*affine-evasive function* $h : \mathbb{F} \mapsto \mathcal{M} \cup \{\perp\}$.

We now describe the coding scheme from [ADL14] combined with the affine-evasive function promised by Lemma 8. Let $\mathcal{M} = \{1, \ldots, K\}$ and $\mathcal{X} = \mathbb{F}^N$, where $\mathbb{F}$ is a finite field of prime order p such that $p \geq (K/\varepsilon)^{16}$, and N chosen as $C \log^6 p$, where C is some universal constant.

Then for any $m \in \mathcal{M}$, $\mathsf{Enc}(m) = \mathsf{Enc}_1 \circ \mathsf{Enc}_2(m)$, where for any $m \in \mathcal{M}$, $\mathsf{Enc}_2(m)$ is X where X is uniformly random such that $h(X) = m$, where h is affine-evasive function defined earlier, and for any $x \in \mathbb{F}$, $\mathsf{Enc}_1(x) = (L, R)$, where $L, R \in \mathbb{F}^N$ are uniform such that $\langle L, R \rangle = x$.

The decoding algorithm is as follows. For $\ell, r \in \mathbb{F}^N \times \mathbb{F}^N$, $\mathsf{Dec}(\ell, r) = \mathsf{Dec}_2 \circ \mathsf{Dec}_1(\ell, r)$, where for any $\ell, r \in \mathbb{F}^N$, $\mathsf{Dec}_1(\ell, r) = \langle \ell, r \rangle$, and for any $x \in \mathbb{F}$, $\mathsf{Dec}_2(x) = h(x)$.

The following is implicit in [ADL14].

Theorem 4. *Let* $f, g : \mathbb{F}^N \mapsto \mathbb{F}^N$ *be arbitrary functions. Let* $s = \lfloor N/20 \rfloor$, *and let* $t = \lfloor \frac{s^{1/6}}{c \log p} \rfloor$, *for some universal constant* c. *Then, there exists a set* $\mathcal{S} \subset \mathbb{F}^N \times \mathbb{F}^N$ *of size at most* p^{2N-s} *such that* $\mathbb{F}^N \times \mathbb{F}^N \setminus \mathcal{S}$ *can be partitioned into sets of the form*

1. $\mathcal{L} \times \mathcal{R}$ *such that* $(\langle L', R' \rangle, \langle f(L'), g(R') \rangle)$ *is* p^{-t}-*close to uniform for* L', R' *uniform in* $\mathcal{L}, \mathcal{R}$ *respectively.*
2. $\mathcal{L} \times \mathcal{R}$, *such that* $|\mathcal{L} \times \mathcal{R}| \geq p^{2N-7s}$, *and there exists* $A \in \mathbb{F}^{N \times N}$, $a \neq 0 \in \mathbb{F}$, $b \in \mathbb{F}^n$ *such that* $f(\ell) = A\ell$ *for all* $\ell \in \mathcal{L}$, *and* $A^T g(r) = ar + b$ *for all* $r \in \mathcal{R}$.
3. $\mathcal{L} \times \mathcal{R}$, *such that* $|\mathcal{L} \times \mathcal{R}| \geq p^{2N-7s}$, *and there exists* $y \in \mathbb{F}^N$, *such that* $g(r) = y$ *for all* $y \in \mathcal{R}$.

To argue that the construction given above is also super-non-malleable, we will need the following:

Lemma 9. *Let L and R be independent random variables over $\mathbb{F}^N$. If*

$$\mathbf{H}_\infty(L) + \mathbf{H}_\infty(R) \geq (N+1)\log p + 2\log\left(\frac{1}{\varepsilon}\right),$$

then

$$\Delta((L, \langle L, R\rangle) \; ; \; (L, U_\mathbb{F})) \leq \varepsilon \text{ and } \Delta((R, \langle L, R\rangle) \; ; \; (R, U_\mathbb{F})) \leq \varepsilon.$$

Lemma 10. *Let $X_1, Y_1 \in \mathcal{A}$, and $X_2, Y_2 \in \mathcal{B}$ be random variables such that $\Delta((X_1, X_2) \; ; \; (Y_1, Y_2)) \leq \varepsilon$. Then, for any non-empty set $\mathcal{A}_1 \subseteq \mathcal{A}$, we have*

$$\Delta(X_2 \mid X_1 \in \mathcal{A}_1 \; ; \; Y_2 \mid Y_1 \in \mathcal{A}_1) \leq \frac{2\varepsilon}{\Pr(X_1 \in \mathcal{A}_1)}.$$

Theorem 5. *The scheme* (Enc, Dec) *is almost uniform, $O(\varepsilon)$-super-non-malleable code in the split-state model.*

Proof. We first show that the scheme is a super non-malleable code in the split-state model. We will argue that each partition promised by Theorem 4 is one of $\mathcal{S}_1, \ldots, \mathcal{S}_{s+t}, \mathcal{S}^\star$ as in Observation 6.1 with $\varepsilon' = \varepsilon$. Clearly, for any $m \in \mathcal{M}$, $\Pr(\mathsf{Enc}(m) \in \mathcal{S}) \leq p^{-s+1} \leq \varepsilon$, and hence we can set $\mathcal{S}^\star = \mathcal{S}$. So, we consider the partitioning of $\mathbb{F}^n \times \mathbb{F}^n \setminus \mathcal{S}$.

1. $\mathcal{L} \times \mathcal{R}$ such that $(\langle L', R'\rangle, \langle f(L'), g(R')\rangle)$ is p^{-t}-close to uniform for L', R' uniform in $\mathcal{L}, \mathcal{R}$ respectively. In this case, for any message m, if $(L, R) \leftarrow \mathsf{Enc}(m)$, then $\mathsf{Dec}(f(L), g(R))$ conditioned on $(L, R) \in \mathcal{L} \times \mathcal{R}$ is $h(\langle f(L'), g(R')\rangle)$ conditioned on $h(\langle L', R'\rangle) = m$. By Lemma 10, we have that this is $2 \cdot p^{-t+1}$-close to uniform, and hence, by Lemma 8, we have that $h(\langle f(L'), g(R')\rangle) = \bot$ with probability at least $1 - p^{-3/4} - p^{-t+1} \geq 1 - \varepsilon$.
2. $\mathcal{L} \times \mathcal{R}$, such that $|\mathcal{L} \times \mathcal{R}| \geq p^{2N-7s}$, and there exists $A \in \mathbb{F}^{N\times N}$, $a \in \mathbb{F}, b \in \mathbb{F}^N$ such that $f(\ell) = A\ell$ for all $\ell \in \mathcal{L}$, and $A^T g(r) = ar + b$ for all $r \in \mathcal{R}$. In this case, using the same argument as in the previous item, we have that $\mathsf{Dec}(f(L), g(R))$ conditioned on $(L, R) \in \mathcal{L} \times \mathcal{R}$ is $\bot$ with probability at least $1 - p^{-1/4}\log p - p^{-t+1} \geq 1 - \varepsilon$.
3. $\mathcal{L} \times \mathcal{R}$, such that $|\mathcal{L} \times \mathcal{R}| \geq p^{2N-7s}$, and there exists $y \in \mathbb{F}^N$, such that $g(r) = y$ for all $y \in \mathcal{R}$. Let L', R' uniform in $\mathcal{L}, \mathcal{R}$, respectively. Then, using Lemma 9, we have that $\langle L', R'\rangle$ is $p^{-(N-7s-1)/2}$-close to uniform given $f(L')$, and $g(R') = y$, and so, using Lemma 10, this partition satisfies item 2 from Observation 6.1.

The result then follows from Observation 6.1.

We now show that the scheme is uniform. Let $\mathcal{X}_0, \mathcal{Y}_0 \subset \mathbb{F}^N$ such that $|\mathcal{X}_0| = p^{c_1 N}$, and $|\mathcal{Y}_0| = p^{c_2 N}$ for some $c_1, c_2 \in (1/2, 1)$, and let $\mathcal{X}_1 = \mathbb{F}^N \setminus \mathcal{X}_0$, and

$\mathcal{Y}_1 = \mathbb{F}^N \setminus \mathcal{Y}_0$. Let X_0, X_1, Y_0, Y_1 be uniform in $\mathcal{X}_0, \mathcal{X}_1, \mathcal{Y}_0, \mathcal{Y}_1$, respectively. Then by Lemma 9, there exists $c > 0$, such that for $i, j \in \{0, 1\}$,

$$\Delta(\langle X_i, Y_j \rangle \; ; \; U_{\mathbb{F}}) \le p^{-cN} \,.$$

Thus, for any $a \in \mathbb{F}_p$, the number of $x \in \mathcal{X}_i, y \in \mathcal{Y}_j$ such that $\langle x, y \rangle = a$ is

$$|\mathcal{X}_i| \cdot |\mathcal{Y}_j| \cdot (\frac{1}{p} \pm p^{-cN}) \,.$$

Thus the fraction of $(x, y) \in \mathcal{X}_0 \times \mathcal{Y}_0$ such that $\langle x, y \rangle = a$ is in the interval

$$\left(\frac{|\mathcal{X}_i| \cdot |\mathcal{Y}_j|}{p^{2N}} \cdot \frac{1 - p^{-cN+1}}{1 + p^{-cN+1}}, \; \frac{|\mathcal{X}_i| \cdot |\mathcal{Y}_j|}{p^{2N}} \cdot \frac{1 + p^{-cN+1}}{1 - p^{-cN+1}} \right) ,$$

which implies the result. $\qquad\square$

7 Final Proof of the Main Result

Theorem 5 proves that non-malleable code from [ADL14] is super non-malleable. The only additional requirement that needs to be fulfilled in order to be able to use this code to obtain super strong non-malleable codes using Theorem 3 is that there is an efficient algorithm to sample $(X, Y) \leftarrow \mathsf{Enc}(m)$ conditioned on $C(r_x, X) = c_x$ and $C(r_y, Y) = c_y$ for some given r_x, r_y, c_x, c_y, m. Note that here, $X, Y \in \mathbb{F}^N$, which is thought of as being embedded in to $\{0, 1\}^n$ for $n = N\lceil \log p \rceil$. A way to sample this will be to sample $a \leftarrow \mathsf{Enc}_2(m) \in \mathbb{F}_p$, and then try to sample X, Y such that $\langle X, Y \rangle = a$ (where X, Y are interpreted as elements of $\mathbb{F}^N$) and $C(r_x, X) = c_x$ and $C(r_y, Y) = c_y$ (where X, Y are interpreted as elements of $\{0, 1\}^n$).

Since we don't know how to sample this efficiently, we resolve this issue by introducing an alternate definition of inception coding, which we call partial inception coding, that installs only a check for X into the message.

Definition 11. *Let* $\mathsf{Enc} : \{0, 1\}^k \to \{0, 1\}^n \times \{0, 1\}^n$, $\mathsf{Dec} : \{0, 1\}^n \times \{0, 1\}^n \to \{0, 1\}^k \cap \{\bot\}$ *be a coding scheme. Let* $C : \{0, 1\}^s \times \{0, 1\}^n \to \{0, 1\}^t$ *be some function.*[5] *The* Partial Inception *version of* $(\mathsf{Enc}, \mathsf{Dec}, C)$ *is a coding scheme denoted as* $\mathcal{I}\mathsf{Enc} : \{0, 1\}^{k-s-t} \to \{0, 1\}^n \times \{0, 1\}^n$, $\mathcal{I}\mathsf{Dec} : \{0, 1\}^n \times \{0, 1\}^n \to \{0, 1\}^{k-s-t} \cup \{\bot\}$ *and is defined as follows. The encoding algorithm* $\mathcal{I}\mathsf{Enc}$, *for a given message* $m \in \{0, 1\}^{k-s-t}$, *does the following.*

- *Choose uniformly at random* r_x *from* $\{0, 1\}^s$, *and* c_x *from* $\{0, 1\}^t$.
- *Sample* (X, Y) *as the output of the encoding algorithm* Enc *on input* $(m\|r_x\|c_x)$ *conditioned on the fact that* $C(r_x, X) = c_x$.
- *Output* (X, Y).

The decoding algorithm $\mathcal{I}\mathsf{Dec}$, *on input* $x, y \in \{0, 1\}^n$, *does the following.*

---

[5] We will use this definition with C being a check function.

- *Obtain $\mathsf{Dec}(x,y) \in \{0,1\}^k$, and interpret the output as $(m\|r_x\|c_x)$, where $m \in \{0,1\}^{k-s-t}$, $r_x \in \{0,1\}^s$, and $c_x \in \{0,1\}^t$.*
- *If $C(r_x,x) = c_x$ then output m, else output $\bot$.*

Then, it is easy to sample from the desired distribution. One can efficiently sample X conditioned on $C(X,r_X) = c_X$ since for any $r \in \{0,1\}^s$ and any $c \in \{0,1\}^t$ the set of all x such that $C(r,x) = c$ is an affine subspace of $\{0,1\}^n$. This follows immediately from Lemma 2 and Definition 8. Then, Y can be sampled easily conditioned on the constraint that $\langle X,Y \rangle = a$.

However, this introduces an additional requirement on the non-malleable code that the adversary cannot decode to the same message by changing just one part of the codeword, i.e., for any function $g : \{0,1\}^n \mapsto \{0,1\}^n$, and any message m with $(X,Y) \leftarrow \mathsf{Enc}(m)$, the probability that $g(Y) \neq Y$ and $\mathsf{Dec}(X,g(Y)) = m$ is small. This condition, fortunately, is immediate from the proof of Theorem 5, where item (2) with A being the identity matrix corresponds to this case, and unless g is also the identity function, we conclude that $\mathsf{Dec}(X,g(Y)) = m$ with probability at most ε.

Remark 6. The main reason that we did not define partial inception coding to start with is because we did not want to restrict Theorem 3 in the sense that it only works if we instantiate it with a non-malleable code that has the special property that the probability that $g(Y) \neq Y$ and $\mathsf{Dec}(X,g(Y)) = m$ is small. This, we believe is just a minor technicality since we are having difficulty in sampling X,Y conditioned on $C(r_X,X) = c_X$, $C(r_Y,Y) = c_Y$ and $\langle X,Y \rangle = a$. Perhaps using a clever sampling algorithm like the one used by Chattopadhyay and Zuckerman [CZ14], such a sampling is possible. Even if this is not the case, we want Theorem 3 to be general enough so that it can be instantiated with other super non-malleable codes.

Thus, using a result analogous to Theorem 3 for the case of Partial Inception coding introduced in Definition 11 and instantiating it with $(\mathsf{Enc}, \mathsf{Dec})$ from [ADL14] gives us the following result.

Theorem 6. *There exists an efficient $2^{-k^{\Omega(1)}}$-super-strong non-malleable code in the split-state model from k-bit messages to k^7-bit codewords.*

Combining Theorem 6 with Theorem 2 gives us the main result of the paper, i.e., a construction of a persistent continuous non-malleable code in the split-state model.

Theorem 7. *There exists an efficient $(T, (T+1) \cdot 2^{-k^{\Omega(1)}})$-continuous $[1,1]$ non-malleable code in the split-state model from k-bit messages to k^7-bit codewords.*

A   Equivalence of Our Non-malleable Codes Definition (Def. 3) with that of [DPW10]

Theorem 8. *If $(\mathsf{Enc}, \mathsf{Dec})$ is an $\varepsilon-$non-malleable code then it is also an $\varepsilon-$non-malleable code according to the definition from [DPW10].*

Proof. Let us define transform $T_m : \mathcal{M} \cup \{\bot, \mathsf{same}\} \to \mathcal{M} \cup \{\bot\}$ as follows: for any $m' \in \mathcal{M}$ let $T_m(m') = m'$, $T_m(\bot) = \bot$, $T_m(\mathsf{same}) = m$. Notice that $T_m(\mathsf{Tamp}_m^{f,g}) = \mathsf{DPWTamp}_m^{f,g}$. Fix any message m_0, and take $D^{f,g} = \mathsf{Tamp}_{m_0}^{f,g}$. We know that $\mathsf{Tamp}_m^{f,g} \approx_\varepsilon \mathsf{Tamp}_{m_0}^{f,g}$ for any functions f, g and any message m. Thus

$$T_m(\mathsf{Tamp}_m^{f,g}) \approx_\varepsilon T_m(\mathsf{Tamp}_{m_0}^{f,g}),$$

$$\mathsf{DPWTamp}_m^{f,g} \approx_\varepsilon T_m(D^{f,g}).$$

$\square$

Theorem 9. *If* $(\mathsf{Enc}, \mathsf{Dec})$ *is an* $\varepsilon-$*non-malleable code according to the definition from* [DPW10], *then it is* $4\varepsilon-$*non-malleable code.*

Proof. Using the notation from Theorem 8, we know that, irrespective of the choice of $D_{x,y}^{f,g}$ distributions, the following is true:

$$T_m(\mathsf{Tamp}_m^{f,g}) = \mathsf{DPWTamp}_m^{f,g}.$$

Now let $D_{x,y}^{f,g}$ as follows:

$$\Pr(D_{x,y}^{f,g} = 0) = \min \left\{ \frac{\Pr(D^{f,g} = \mathsf{same})}{\Pr(\mathsf{DPWTamp}_{\mathsf{Dec}(x,y)}^{f,g} = \mathsf{Dec}(x,y))}, 1 \right\}$$

if $\Pr(\mathsf{DPWTamp}_{\mathsf{Dec}(x,y)}^{f,g} = \mathsf{Dec}(x,y)) \neq 0$. Otherwise let $\Pr(D_{x,y}^{f,g} = 0) = 0$. Notice that now

$$|\Pr(\mathsf{Tamp}_m^{f,g} = \mathsf{same}) - \Pr(D^{f,g} = \mathsf{same})| < \varepsilon.$$

By DPW-non-malleable codes definition we get

$$T_m(\mathsf{Tamp}_m^{f,g}) \approx_\varepsilon T_m(D^{f,g})$$

thus

$$\mathsf{Tamp}_m^{f,g} \approx_{2\varepsilon} D^{f,g},$$

and thus that for any m_0, m_1 we get

$$\mathsf{Tamp}_{m_0}^{f,g} \approx_{4\varepsilon} \mathsf{Tamp}_{m_1}^{f,g}.$$

$\square$

References

[AAnHKM+16] Aggarwal, D., Agrawal, S., Gupta, D., Maji, H.K., Pandey, O., Prabhakaran, M.: Optimal computational split state non-malleable codes. To appear in TCC 16-A (2016)

[ADKO15a] Aggarwal, D., Dodis, Y., Kazana, T., Obremski, M.: Leakage-resilient non-malleable codes. In: The 47th ACM Symposium on Theory of Computing (STOC) (2015)

[ADKO15b] Aggarwal, D., Dziembowski, S., Kazana, T., Obremski, M.: Leakage-resilient non-malleable codes. In: Dodis, Y., Nielsen, J.B. (eds.) TCC 2015. LNCS, vol. 9014, pp. 398–426. Springer, Heidelberg (2015). doi:10.1007/978-3-662-46494-6_17

[ADL14] Aggarwal, D., Dodis, Y., Lovett, S.: Non-malleable codes from additive combinatorics. In: STOC. ACM (2014)

[Agg15] Aggarwal, D.: Affine-evasive sets modulo a prime. Inf. Process. Lett. 115(2), 382–385 (2015)

[AGM+15a] Agrawal, S., Gupta, D., Maji, H.K., Pandey, O., Prabhakaran, M.: Explicit non-malleable codes resistant to permutations. In: Advances in Cryptology - CRYPTO (2015)

[AGM+15b] Agrawal, S., Gupta, D., Maji, H.K., Pandey, O., Prabhakaran, M.: A rate-optimizing compiler for non-malleable codes against bit-wise tampering and permutations. In: Dodis, Y., Nielsen, J.B. (eds.) TCC 2015. LNCS, vol. 9014, pp. 375–397. Springer, Heidelberg (2015). doi:10.1007/978-3-662-46494-6_16

[CDTV16] Coretti, S., Dodis, Y., Tackmann, B., Venturi, D.: Non-malleable encryption: simpler, shorter, stronger. In: Proceedings of 13th International Conference on Theory of Cryptography - TCC 2016-A, Tel Aviv, Israel, 10-13 January 2016, Part I, pp. 306–335 (2016)

[CG14a] Cheraghchi, M., Guruswami, V.: Capacity of non-malleable codes. In: ITCS (2014)

[CG14b] Cheraghchi, M., Guruswami, V.: Non-malleable coding against bit-wise and split-state tampering. In: TCC (2014)

[CGL15] Chattopadhyay, E., Goyal, V., Li, X.: Non-malleable extractors and codes, with their many tampered extensions. CoRR, abs/1505.00107 (2015)

[CGM+15] Chandran, N., Goyal, V., Mukherjee, P., Pandey, O., Upadhyay, J.: Block-wise non-malleable codes. IACR Cryptology ePrint Archive, 2015:129 (2015)

[CKM11] Choi, S.G., Kiayias, A., Malkin, T.: BiTR: built-in tamper resilience. In: Lee, D.H., Wang, X. (eds.) ASIACRYPT 2011. LNCS, vol. 7073, pp. 740–758. Springer, Heidelberg (2011). doi:10.1007/978-3-642-25385-0_40

[CMTV15] Coretti, S., Maurer, U., Tackmann, B., Venturi, D.: From single-bit to multi-bit public-key encryption via non-malleable codes. In: Proceedings of 12th Theory of Cryptography Conference on Theory of Cryptography - TCC 2015, Warsaw, Poland, 23-25 March 2015, Part I, pp. 532–560 (2015)

[CZ14] Chattopadhyay, E., Zuckerman, D.: Non-malleable codes in the constant split-state model. In: FOCS (2014)

[DDN00] Dolev, D., Dwork, C., Naor, M.: Nonmalleable cryptography. SIAM 30, 391–437 (2000)

[DKO13] Dziembowski, S., Kazana, T., Obremski, M.: Non-malleable codes from two-source extractors. In: Canetti, R., Garay, J.A. (eds.) CRYPTO 2013. LNCS, vol. 8043, pp. 239–257. Springer, Heidelberg (2013). doi:10.1007/978-3-642-40084-1_14

[DNO16] Döttling, N., Nielsen, J.B., Obremski, M.: Information theoretic continuously non-malleable codes in the constant split-state model. In: Presented at IMS Workshop on Information Theoretic Cryptography in NUS, Singapore (2016, unpublished Manuscript)

[DORS08] Dodis, Y., Ostrovsky, R., Reyzin, L., Smith, A.: Fuzzy extractors: how to generate strong keys from biometrics and other noisy data. SIAM J. Comput. **38**(1), 97–139 (2008)

[DPW10] Dziembowski, S., Pietrzak, K., Wichs, D.: Non-malleable codes. In: ICS, pp. 434–452. Tsinghua University Press (2010)

[DW09] Dodis, Y., Wichs, D.: Non-malleable extractors and symmetric key cryptography from weak secrets. In: Mitzenmacher, M. (ed.) Proceedings of the 41st Annual ACM Symposium on Theory of Computing, Bethesda, MD, USA, pp. 601–610. ACM (2009)

[FMNV14] Faust, S., Mukherjee, P., Nielsen, J.B., Venturi, D.: Continuous non-malleable codes. In: Lindell, Y. (ed.) TCC 2014. LNCS, vol. 8349, pp. 465–488. Springer, Heidelberg (2014). doi:10.1007/978-3-642-54242-8_20

[FMVW14] Faust, S., Mukherjee, P., Venturi, D., Wichs, D.: Efficient non-malleable codes and key-derivation for poly-size tampering circuits. In: Nguyen, P.Q., Oswald, E. (eds.) EUROCRYPT 2014. LNCS, vol. 8441, pp. 111–128. Springer, Heidelberg (2014). doi:10.1007/978-3-642-55220-5_7

[GLM+03] Gennaro, R., Lysyanskaya, A., Malkin, T., Micali, S., Rabin, T.: Algorithmic Tamper-Proof (ATP) security: theoretical foundations for security against hardware tampering. In: Naor, M. (ed.) TCC 2004. LNCS, vol. 2951, pp. 258–277. Springer, Heidelberg (2004). doi:10.1007/978-3-540-24638-1_15

[IPSW06] Ishai, Y., Prabhakaran, M., Sahai, A., Wagner, D.: Private circuits ii: keeping secrets in tamperable circuits. In: Vaudenay, S. (ed.) EUROCRYPT 2006. LNCS, vol. 4004, pp. 308–327. Springer, Heidelberg (2006). doi:10.1007/11761679_19

[ISW03] Ishai, Y., Sahai, A., Wagner, D.: Private circuits: securing hardware against probing attacks. In: Boneh, D. (ed.) CRYPTO 2003. LNCS, vol. 2729, pp. 463–481. Springer, Heidelberg (2003). doi:10.1007/978-3-540-45146-4_27

[JW15] Jafargholi, Z., Wichs, D.: Tamper detection and continuous non-malleable codes. In: Dodis, Y., Nielsen, J.B. (eds.) TCC 2015. LNCS, vol. 9014, pp. 451–480. Springer, Heidelberg (2015). doi:10.1007/978-3-662-46494-6_19

[KKS11] Kalai, Y.T., Kanukurthi, B., Sahai, A.: Cryptography with tamperable and leaky memory. In: Rogaway, P. (ed.) CRYPTO 2011. LNCS, vol. 6841, pp. 373–390. Springer, Heidelberg (2011). doi:10.1007/978-3-642-22792-9_21

[Li16] Li, X.: Improved non-malleable extractors, non-malleable codes and independent source extractors (2016)

[LL12] Liu, F.-H., Lysyanskaya, A.: Tamper and leakage resilience in the split-state model. In: Safavi-Naini, R., Canetti, R. (eds.) CRYPTO 2012. LNCS, vol. 7417, pp. 517–532. Springer, Heidelberg (2012). doi:10.1007/978-3-642-32009-5_30

[RU08] Richardson, T., Urbanke, R.: Modern Coding Theory. Cambridge University Press, New York (2008)

Four-State Non-malleable Codes with Explicit Constant Rate

Bhavana Kanukurthi[1](✉), Sai Lakshmi Bhavana Obbattu[1](✉),
and Sruthi Sekar[2](✉)

[1] Department of Computer Science and Automation, Indian Institute of Science,
Bangalore, India
bhavana@iisc.ac.in, oslbhavana@gmail.com
[2] Department of Mathematics, Indian Institute of Science, Bangalore, India
sruthi.sekar1@gmail.com

Abstract. Non-malleable codes (NMCs), introduced by Dziembowski, Pietrzak and Wichs (ITCS 2010), generalize the classical notion of error correcting codes by providing a powerful guarantee even in scenarios where error correcting codes cannot provide any guarantee: a decoded message is either the same or completely independent of the underlying message, regardless of the number of errors introduced into the codeword. Informally, NMCs are defined with respect to a family of tampering functions $\mathcal{F}$ and guarantee that any tampered codeword either decodes to the same message or to an independent message, so long as it is tampered using a function $f \in \mathcal{F}$.

Nearly all known constructions of NMCs are for the t-split-state family, where the adversary tampers each of the t "states" of a codeword, arbitrarily but independently. Cheraghchi and Guruswami (TCC 2014) obtain a Rate-1 non-malleable code for the case where $t = \mathcal{O}(n)$ with n being the codeword length and, in (ITCS 2014), show an upper bound of $1 - 1/t$ on the best achievable rate for any t-split state NMC. For $t = 10$, Chattopadhyay and Zuckerman (FOCS 2014) achieve a constant rate construction where the constant is unknown. In summary, there is no known construction of an NMC with an explicit constant rate for any $t = o(n)$, let alone one that comes close to matching Cheraghchi and Guruswami's lowerbound!

In this work, we construct an efficient non-malleable code in the t-split-state model, for $t = 4$, that achieves a constant rate of $\frac{1}{3+\zeta}$, for any constant $\zeta > 0$, and error $2^{-\Omega(\ell/log^{c+1}\ell)}$, where ℓ is the length of the message and $c > 0$ is a constant.

1 Introduction

Error correcting codes allow for the correction of errors introduced in data. However, their applicability is limited by the fact that they can only correct a bounded number of errors. When data is completely overwritten, no protection can be guaranteed. Non-malleable codes, introduced in the work of Dziembowski et al. [15], guarantee that, errors caused to the data will render it either independent of the underlying message or leave it unchanged.

© International Association for Cryptologic Research 2017
Y. Kalai and L. Reyzin (Eds.): TCC 2017, Part II, LNCS 10678, pp. 344–375, 2017.
https://doi.org/10.1007/978-3-319-70503-3_11

Non-malleable codes are parameterized by a family of *tampering* functions, $\mathcal{F}$, and they guarantee non-malleability only when $m^* = \mathsf{Dec}(f(\mathsf{Enc}(m)))$ where $f \in \mathcal{F}$ and $\mathsf{Enc}, \mathsf{Dec}$ are the encode and decode functions respectively. (In other words, there is no guarantee when $f \notin \mathcal{F}$.) Informally, given a tampering family $\mathcal{F}$, a non-malleable code ($\mathsf{Enc}, \mathsf{Dec}$) encodes a given message m into a codeword $c \leftarrow \mathsf{Enc}(m)$ s.t. if c is modified to $\tilde{c} = f(c)$ by some $f \in \mathcal{F}$, then the message $\tilde{m} = \mathsf{Dec}(\tilde{c})$ contained in the modified codeword, is either the original message m or is "unrelated" to and "independent" of m.

To understand the motivation of studying non-malleable codes, consider their application to cryptography. In any standard cryptographic security game, security is typically guaranteed even when the adversary has access to some permissible input-output behaviour on the secret key sk.[1] If the adversary is allowed to observe input-output behaviour with respect to some modified sk^*, we can no longer guarantee *any* security with respect to the original key sk. Consider a situation where sk^*, if different from sk, is guaranteed to be independent of sk. In such a case, no input-output behaviour on sk^* can help break the security with respect to sk. (After all, if obtaining information about an independent sk^* can help break the security with respect to sk, then an adversary for sk can generate this information on his own.) If sk is encoded with a non-malleable code, then non-malleability will prevent sk^* from ever taking a related value and the scheme will continue to remain secure with respect to sk.

It is no surprise that, since their introduction, non-malleable codes have found many applications such as in securing functionalities against physical – leakage and tampering– attacks [15,21], domain extension of CCA secure encryption [8] and non-malleable commitments [17]. Additionally, non-malleable codes have inspired an impressive line of theoretical research drawing connections across topics such as non-malleable extractors, additive combinatorics and so on. Researchers have been fascinated with two aspects of non-malleable codes:

(a) the richness of the tampering function family which NMCs can protect against and

(b) the *rate* ($= \frac{\text{messagelength}}{\text{codewordlength}}$) they achieve.

Our work too falls into this domain with a specific focus on the rate.

1.1 Related Work

In [15], Dziembowski et al. observe that it is impossible to build non-malleable codes which are secure with respect to the class of *all* functions. The intuition behind this is that, this class would contain the function which decodes $\mathsf{Enc}(m)$ and re-encodes it into a related value m^*. Further, [15] proves an existential result for non-malleable codes w.r.t tampering families of size less than 2^{2^n}.

---

[1] For example, this input-output behaviour may be decryption of ciphertexts in the case of Chosen Ciphertext Security of Encryption or signatures of messages in the case of Digital Signatures.

A natural but restricted class of tampering functions is the class of *bit-wise tampering functions* which modify each bit of the codeword independently. Dziembowski et al. [15] presented a construction of non-malleable codes with respect to this family. Their construction used a composition of Linear error correcting secret sharing scheme (LECSS)[2] and Algebraic Manipulation Detection codes (AMD codes)[3]. Following this, Cheraghchi and Guruswami [7] gave an explicit construction of an *optimal rate* NMC w.r.t. bit-wise tampering family. Their construction combines the properties of a LECSS scheme, a sub-optimal NMC for small messages and pseudorandom permutations.

A natural generalization of the bit-wise tampering family is the split-state tampering family, where a codeword is split into blocks (typically of equal length though not necessarily) and each block of the codeword, called a *state*, is tampered independently. A t-split-state family consists of a family of t functions acting independently on a state of length n/t, where n is the codeword length[4].

Improving on an existential result due to Dziembowski et al. [15], in [6], Cheraghchi and Guruswami show that for a t-split state family, with each state of codeword containing n/t bits, the upper bound on best achievable rate is $1 - 1/t$. Both [6,15] give a Monte-Carlo construction of non-malleable codes for the 2-split-state model which show the existence of such codes in the random oracle model. The work of [7] also makes an elegant connection between seedless t-source non-malleable extractors and non-malleable codes in the t-split-state model.

In spite of the progress on bit-wise tampering function family, the first efficient constructions of split-state non-malleable codes made strong assumptions such as the random oracle model [15] or were in the computational setting [21][5]. Dziembowski et al. [14] were the first to present an explicit construction of a non-malleable code for the split-state model. Specifically, they used the inner product extractor to construct a non-malleable code for 1-bit messages in the 2-split-state model. Improving upon this result, Aggarwal et al. [3] gave the first information theoretic construction for k-bit messages in 2-split-state model, achieving rate $\Omega(n^{-6/7})$. This construction relies on an elegant property of inner-

---

[2] LECSS ensures that the bits of codeword are t-wise independent and detects tampering if the codeword is modified by an offset Δ, when Δ is not a valid codeword of the scheme.

[3] AMD codes detect tampering attacks that add some pre-determined offset Δ to the codeword.

[4] This tampering family captures other tampering attacks such as bit-wise tampering, identity function, constant function etc. A motivation to study this model comes from practical applications like cloud storage, where a single file may be stored in t parts at t different locations and an adversary tampers each of these parts independent of the other. It is therefore both of theoretical as well as practical interest to obtain non-malleable codes for t-split state family where $t > 1$ is as small as possible.

[5] Specifically, Liu and Lysyanskaya [21] present a computational non-malleable code w.r.t. split-state tampering functions in the common reference string (CRS) model, using number theoretic assumptions and assuming existence of robust non-interactive zero-knowledge proof systems for an appropriate NP language.

product functions, which is obtained using results from additive combinatorics, including the *Quasi-polynomial Freiman-Ruzsa Theorem.*

NMC with Improved Rates: All of the above works focused on improving the richness of tampering functions which NMCs can tolerate. However, none of them, barring the codes of [7] for the bit-wise tampering family, achieve optimal rate. Chattopadhyay and Zuckerman [5] were the first to construct an efficient constant rate non-malleable code in 10-split-state model. Unfortunately, the rate they achieve is an *unknown* constant which is typically undesirable while building information-theoretic primitives. Additionally, as observed in [2], the rate is likely to be a small (i.e., poor) constant due to their use of additive combinatorics.

For the 2-split-state model, the construction by Li in [20] achieves the best known rate to date, of $\Omega(1/\log n)$. Both these works use the connection between seedless t-source non-malleable extractors and non-malleable codes in t-split-state model, due to [7]. The work of Aggarwal et al. [2] gives beautiful connections between various split-state models. Unfortunately, due to a subtle error pointed by Li [20], their proposed construction of a 2-split state, constant rate, non-malleable code no longer holds, making Li's result the best known for the 2-split state model. However, there are two *conjectured* constant-rate NMC constructions. Specifically, in [3], under an inner product conjecture, the authors get a constant-rate 2-split-state scheme. Further, while [2], as it stands, gives a linear-rate code using existing methods, it gives a constant-rate 2-split-state under an appropriate conjecture.

We know the following, about the best achievable rate, from [6]:

Lemma 1. [6, Sect. 1.1]. *For non-malleable codes in the t-split-state model, with each state of equal length, the best achievable rate is $1 - \frac{1}{t}$.*

While Cheraghchi et al. in [7], obtain a Rate-1 (optimal) NMC for $t = \mathcal{O}(n)$, there is no known construction for $t = o(n)$, which achieves the optimal rate $1 - \frac{1}{t}$, for t-split-state family. In this work, we construct a non-malleable code with rate $\frac{1}{3+\zeta}$, for any constant $\zeta > 0$ in the 4-split-state model.

Computational Setting: If we resort to computational assumptions, Aggarwal et al. [1] show that a NMC with the best possible rate as well as the least restricted of the t-split-state families can obtained. Concretely, they obtain a rate 1 computational NMC w.r.t. 2-split-state tampering function family. Unfortunately, despite significant efforts, there has been a large gap between the rates of the best known constructions in the computational setting and the information-theoretic setting.

We give an overview of the Rate-1 construction in the computational setting due to Aggarwal et al. [1] and then highlight the challenges of building such codes in the information-theoretic setting. Their construction works by choosing a key k_{ae} to a computational authenticated encryption scheme. It encodes this key with a poor-rate 2-split-state non-malleable code to get states c_1, c_2. This key is used to compute an authenticated encryption ciphertext (c_3) of the message to be encoded. This gives a three state nmc: (c_1, c_2, c_3). (They obtain a two-split-state construction by using an enhanced notion of *"augmented"* non-malleable codes. They also prove that the 2-state construction of [3] achieves augmented non-malleability.) The key behind the optimality of the rate is the observation that the length of the key for authenticated encryption (in the computational setting) can be short (and independent of the message length).

We have summarized the prior work on NMCs for the t-split-state model in Fig. 1.

Work by	No. of states	Rate
Dziembowski, Pietrzak and Wichs (ICS 2010) **Introduced NMCs**	n	• Existential result for family of size $\log(\log(|\mathcal{F}|)) < n$ • Rate < 1 (explicit const.)
Cheraghchi and Guruswami (TCC 2014)	n	$1 - o(1)$ (optimal rate)
Cheraghchi and Guruswami (ITCS 2014)	t	$1 - 1/t$ (Existential, optimal achievable rate)
Dziembowski, Kazana, Obremski (CRYPTO 2013)	2	$\Omega(n^{-1})$ (for 1-bit messages)
Aggarwal, Dodis and Lovett (STOC 2014)	2	$\Omega(n^{-6/7})$
Chattopadhyay and Zuckerman (FOCS 2014)	10	$\Omega(1)$ (explicit constant not given)
Li (STOC 2017)	2	$\Omega(1/\log n)$
Aggarwal, Agrawal, Gupta, Maji, Pandey and Prabhakaran (TCC 2016) **Computational NMC**	2	$1 - o(1)$ (optimal rate computational NMC)
OUR RESULT **(Kanukurthi, Obbattu, Sekar)**	4	**1/3 (first explicit constant rate)**

Fig. 1. Summarizing prior work on t-split-state family

1.2 Our Result

Informally, in this work, we obtain information-theoretic constant-rate non-malleable codes in the 4-split-state model. The fact that we make no computational assumptions brings up some unique challenges in both the construction as well as the proof, which we now highlight. As a starting point, consider the same construction [1] described above but replace the computational authenticated encryption scheme with an information-theoretic one: we would still obtain a secure non-malleable code. However, for an information-theoretic encryption scheme to be secure, we require the length of the key to be as much as the length of the message. This means that to obtain good rate, the split-state non-malleable code used as a building block should have good rate as it is encoding a key that is as long as the message – this is precisely the problem we are trying to solve!

To resolve this chicken-and-egg problem, we observe that an authenticated encryption scheme can be modularly decomposed into an authentication scheme and an encryption scheme: namely, encrypting a message first with a generic (one-time) encryption scheme and then authenticating it with a one-time message authentication code, gives us a construction of an (one-time) authenticated encryption scheme. The good news is that message authentication codes only require short keys (informally, as long as the security parameter) and can, therefore, be encoded using a non-malleable code without compromising on the rate. This leads to the following approach: *can we leverage the non-malleability of authentication key to non-malleably encode larger messages?*

We shall motivate our construction by discussing some incorrect constructions. Consider the following attempt: $c_1 = (\mathsf{Enc}_{k_e}(m), \mathsf{Tag}_{k_a}(\mathsf{Enc}_{k_e}(m))); c_2 = k_e;$ $(c_3, c_4) = \mathsf{NMEnc}(k_a)$ where Enc is just a one-time pad encryption, MAC = (Tag, Vrfy) is a one-time message authentication code, NMEnc is a 2-split-state non-malleable code and $\{c_i\}_{i \in [4]}$ are all stored in separate states. A fundamental problem with this proposal is that the encryption key is not encoded with a non-malleable code. By simply changing the key k_e and leaving the rest of the encoding unchanged, the adversary can relate the tampered message $\tilde{m}$ to the underlying message m. We can fix this problem by requiring the encryption key to be authenticated as well. Let $c_1 = (\mathsf{Enc}_{k_e}(m), \mathsf{Tag}_{k_a}(\mathsf{Enc}_{k_e}(m)||k_e)); \quad c_2 = k_e; \quad (c_3, c_4) = \mathsf{NMEnc}(k_a)$. While the authenticity of k_e may no longer be an issue, this introduces another problem: c_1 contains a MAC value computed on the key k_e and could reveal some information about k_e and therefore, the ciphertext c_1 may no longer be secure. The standard definition of a one-time MAC does not guarantee privacy of the underlying message. (We could consider specific MACs which do guarantee privacy as well but such information-theoretic MACs cannot have short keys, which we require, as mentioned above.) Let us try to remove this dependency by encoding the tag using the non-malleable code. Let $c_1 = (\mathsf{Enc}_{k_e}(m)); c_2 = k_e; (c_3, c_4) = \mathsf{NMEnc}(k_a, \mathsf{Tag}_{k_a}(\mathsf{Enc}_{k_e}(m)||k_e))$.

This leads to the following candidate construction to encode a message m:

1. Choose a key k_e for one-time pad encryption (Enc) and a key k_a for a one-time message authentication code (MAC).
2. Compute $c_1 = \mathsf{Enc}_{k_e}(m)$, tag $t = \mathsf{Tag}_{k_a}(c_1||k_e)$ and set $c_2 = k_e$.
3. Compute $(c_3, c_4) \leftarrow \mathsf{NMEnc}(k_a, t)$, using a 2-split-state non-malleable code with poor rate.
4. Output c_1, c_2, c_3, c_4 as the four states of the non-malleable code.

Intuitively, this might seem secure as the encryption key k_e is authenticated and its' tag is non-malleably encoded. Therefore, at best, the tampering function can make the tampered $\tilde{k}_a, \tilde{t}$ become independent of the underlying values. Assuming that the MAC verifies on the tampered key and tag, one might like to believe that it guarantees independence of $\tilde{k}_e$ and, therefore, of the underlying message $\tilde{m}$ as well. Unfortunately, this reasoning is not true for message authentication codes with short tags. Specifically, when tags are much shorter than the

message, there will necessarily be collisions in the tag space of a given key –
i.e., on a given key, there could be multiple message that map to the same tag
value.[6] As we describe in the attack below, these "collisions" can be exploited
to make the code "malleable".

Attack on the Candidate Construction: To describe an attack, we need to specify
tampering functions f_1, f_2, f_3, f_4. We use $x[0]$ to denote the least significant bit
of the binary string x in the description below.

1. Choose constants k_0, k_1 from encryption key space, ct_0, ct_1 from ciphertext space such that $ct_0[0] = k_0[0] = 0$, $ct_1[0] = k_1[0] = 1$ and a tag t^*
   and a key k_a^* such that $\mathsf{Tag}_{k_a^*}(ct_0 \| k_0) = \mathsf{Tag}_{k_a^*}(ct_0 \| k_1) = \mathsf{Tag}_{k_a^*}(ct_1 \| k_0) = \mathsf{Tag}_{k_a^*}(ct_1 \| k_1) = t^*$. Observe that these values are all independent of the mes-
   sage as well as the randomness of the encoding scheme described above. Now
   we describe the four tampering functions.
2. $f_1(c_1)$: If $c_1[0] = 0$, set $c_1^* = ct_0$ otherwise $c_1^* = ct_1$.
3. $f_2(c_2)$: If $c_2[0] = 0$, set $c_2^* = k_0$ otherwise $c_2^* = k_1$.
4. Compute $c_3^*, c_4^* = \mathsf{NMEnc}(k_a^*, t^*)$.
5. $f_3(c_3) = c_3^*$.
6. $f_4(c_4) = c_4^*$.

Carefully working through our choice of the various constants will show us
that the tampered message will retain the least significant bit of the underlying
message i.e., $\tilde{m}[0] = m[0]$, where $\tilde{m}$ is the tampered message. Furthermore, collisions in the MAC scheme have been exploited to ensure that tag of the tampered
message and key will always verify. Thus any tampering is undetected and reveals
information about the underlying message, thus violating non-malleability.

Analyzing the intuition behind the attack, we observe that the main challenge
is that, even though the key and the ciphertext are tampered independently,
jointly they may retain information about the original message. To overcome
this issue, we modify the construction to ensure that the tampered key is never
related to the original key. Ensuring this independence proves to be our major
bottleneck. We are able to overcome this bottleneck through a somewhat sur-
prising use of (strong) randomness extractors.

Using Randomness Extractors to "Amplify" Non-malleability: Informally, randomness extractors allow us to transform non-uniform randomness into uniform randomness. Here we use randomness extractors to generate the key k_e
i.e., $k_e = \mathsf{Ext}(w; s)$ where w and s are uniformly random string of appropriate
lengths. At the outset, this might seem completely pointless: after all, extractors
are typically used in settings where one does not have perfect randomness. This
is clearly not the case here: indeed, the encoding scheme is allowed to choose its'
own randomness! *How can choosing k_e as the output of an extractor be of any*

---

[6] This problem does not arise with a MAC such as $ax + b$ where (a, b) is the MAC
key and x is the underlying message. There, for a fixed key and fixed tag, there is a
unique message which satisfies the linear equation.

help? Showing how the randomness extractor helps in this scenario is the crux of our proof. We consider the following cases:

1. s, w are both unchanged: In this case, the extracted encryption key remains unchanged. While it remains unclear how to argue non-malleability in this scenario, for now, it suffices to note that the attack described above is no longer relevant and, therefore, we defer a discussion on this case to later.
2. s is changed to an independent seed $\tilde{s}$:[7] In this case, $\tilde{k}_e$ is independent of k_e, regardless of how $\tilde{w}$ depends on w. As mentioned earlier, here too the attack described above is no longer relevant.
3. s is unchanged but w is changed in a related manner: In this case, $\tilde{k}_e$ could contain information about k_e.

Case 3 seems to still retain our original bottleneck and we handle it by ensuring that, in our construction, whenever the source w is changed, the seed s also needs to be changed. This reduces it to Case 2. What remains, is to show how we can ensure this through a delicate use of randomness extractors, message authentication codes and non-malleable codes.

Overview of Our Construction: We use the following tools in our construction: (a) A non-malleable code for 2-split-state model achieving rate $\Omega(1/\log n)$ [20] where n is the block-length; (b) a one-time information theoretic message authentication code; (c) an average-case strong randomness extractor; (d) a perfectly secure encryption scheme, like One Time Pad.

Step I: We use a randomness extractor (which typically have short seeds) to extract the encryption key.
Step II: We encrypt the message using the extracted key.
Step III: To detect modification of the source (used to extract the key) and the ciphertext, we authenticate them using two different one time MACs[8].
Step IV: Finally, we encode the authentication keys and tags along with the seed (used to extract the key) using a 2-state non-malleable code. We output the 2-state codeword, the source and the ciphertext.

The non-malleable encoding in Step IV ties various key components of our construction together and is crucial in overcoming the challenge described in Case 3.

Proof Techniques: We prove non-malleability via a series of statistically-close hybrids which take us from the tampered game to a simulated game. But some non-trivial challenges arise in our proof: firstly, there are dependencies across states (e.g.: we include the source in one state and the encoding of its tag in another). So, even though the states are modified independently, the modifications will be interlinked through this dependency. Secondly, even though in our encoding, we choose the source uniformly at random, the decode process reveals

---

[7] We ensure this by encoding s using a non-malleable code.
[8] It is crucial to authenticate them separately as, a construction where we do not authenticate them separately is insecure. This is brought out in the security proof later.

information about the source. This will prevent us from using extractor security directly. The trick that helps us here is that we capture all the information learnt via the decoding using auxiliary information that is *independent* of the seed. This will allow us to use the crucial extractor security in our proof.

1.3 Organization of the Paper

We describe preliminaries and building blocks of the construction in Sects. 2 and 3, respectively. We then give the main construction in Sect. 4.2, followed by the proof in Sect. 4.3. We then give a detailed analysis of the rate and error in Sects. 4.4, 4.5, 4.6 and 4.7.

2 Preliminaries

Notation. κ denotes security parameter throughout. $s \in_R S$ denotes uniform sampling from set S. $x \leftarrow X$ denotes sampling from a probability distribution X. $x \| y$ represents concatenation of two binary strings x and y. $|x|$ denotes length of binary string x. U_l denotes the uniform distribution on $\{0, 1\}^l$. All logarithms are base 2.

Statistical Distance and Entropy. Let X_1, X_2 be two probability distributions over some set S. Their *statistical distance* is

$$\mathbf{SD}\,(X_1, X_2) \overset{\text{def}}{=} \max_{T \subseteq S}\{\Pr[X_1 \in T] - \Pr[X_2 \in T]\} = \frac{1}{2}\sum_{s \in S}\left|\Pr_{X_1}[s] - \Pr_{X_2}[s]\right|$$

(they are said to be ε-close if $\mathbf{SD}\,(X_1, X_2) \leq \varepsilon$ and denoted by $X_1 \approx_\varepsilon X_2$). The *min-entropy* of a random variable W is $\mathbf{H}_\infty(W) = -\log(\max_w \Pr[W = w])$. For a joint distribution (W, E), define the (average) conditional min-entropy of W given E [12] as

$$\widetilde{\mathbf{H}}_\infty(W \mid E) = -\log(\mathbf{E}_{e \leftarrow E}(2^{-\mathbf{H}_\infty(W|E=e)}))$$

(here the expectation is taken over e for which $\Pr[E = e]$ is nonzero). For a random variable W over $\{0, 1\}^n$, $W|E$ is said to be an (n, t) - source if $\widetilde{\mathbf{H}}_\infty(W|E) \geq t$.

Proposition 1. *Let $A_1, \ldots, A_n$ be mutually exclusive and exhaustive events. Then, for probability distributions X_1, X_2 over some set S, we have:*

$$\mathbf{SD}\,(X_1, X_2) \leq \sum_{i=1}^{n} \Pr[A_i].\mathbf{SD}\,(X_1|A_i, X_2|A_i)$$

where $X_j|A_i$ is the distribution of X_j conditioned on the event A_i.

Proof.

$$2\mathbf{SD}\,(X_1, X_2) = \sum_{s \in S} \Big| \Pr[X_1 = s] - \Pr[X_2 = s] \Big|$$

$$= \sum_{s \in S} \Big| \sum_{i=1}^{n} \big(\Pr[A_i] \Pr[X_1 = s|A_i] - \Pr[A_i] \Pr[X_2 = s|A_i] \big) \Big|$$

$$\leq \sum_{s \in S} \sum_{i=1}^{n} \Pr[A_i] \Big| \Pr[X_1 = s|A_i] - \Pr[X_2 = s|A_i] \Big|$$

$$= \sum_{i=1}^{n} \Pr[A_i] \sum_{s \in S} \Big| \Pr[X_1 = s|A_i] - \Pr[X_2 = s|A_i] \Big|$$

$$= 2 \sum_{i=1}^{n} \Pr[A_i] \mathbf{SD}\,(X_1|A_i, X_2|A_i)$$

Lemma 2. *For any random variables A, B, C if $(A, B) \approx_\epsilon (A, C)$, then $B \approx_\epsilon C$.*

Lemma 3. *For any random variables A, B if $A \approx_\epsilon B$, then for any function f, $f(A) \approx_\epsilon f(B)$.*

Lemma 4. *Let A, B be correlated random variables over $\mathcal{A}, \mathcal{B}$. For randomized functions $F : \mathcal{A} \to \mathcal{X}$, $G : \mathcal{A} \to \mathcal{X}$ (randomness used is independent of B) if $\forall\, a \in \mathcal{A}, F(a) \approx_\epsilon G(a)$, then $(B, A, F(A)) \approx_\epsilon (B, A, G(A))$*

Proof. $2\mathbf{SD}\,((B, A, F(A)), (B, A, G(A)))$

$$= \sum_{b \in \mathcal{B}, a \in \mathcal{A}, x \in \mathcal{X}} \Big| \Pr[B = b \wedge A = a \wedge F(A) = x] - \Pr[B = b \wedge A = a \wedge G(A) = x] \Big|$$

$$= \sum_{b \in \mathcal{B}, a \in \mathcal{A}, x \in \mathcal{X}} \Pr[B = b] \Big| \Pr[A = a \wedge F(A) = x|B = b] - \Pr[A = a \wedge G(A) = x|B = b] \Big|$$

$$= \sum_{b \in \mathcal{B}, a \in \mathcal{A}, x \in \mathcal{X}} \Pr[B = b] \Pr[A = a|B = b].$$

$$\Big| \Pr[F(A) = x|A = a, B = b] - \Pr[G(A) = x|A = a, B = b] \Big|$$

$$= \sum_{b \in \mathcal{B}, a \in \mathcal{A}, x \in \mathcal{X}} \Pr[B = b] \Pr[A = a|B = b].$$

$$\Big| \Pr[F(a) = x|B = b] - \Pr[G(a) = x|B = b] \Big|$$

$$= \sum_{b \in \mathcal{B}, a \in \mathcal{A}, x \in \mathcal{X}} \Pr[B = b] \Pr[A = a|B = b] \Big| \Pr[F(a) = x] - \Pr[G(a) = x] \Big|$$

$$= \sum_{b \in \mathcal{B}, a \in \mathcal{A}} \Pr[A = a \wedge B = b] \sum_{x \in \mathcal{X}} \Big| \Pr[F(a) = x] - \Pr[G(a) = x] \Big|$$

$$\leq \sum_{b \in \mathcal{B}, a \in \mathcal{A}} \Pr[A = a \wedge B = b] \cdot 2\epsilon = 2\epsilon$$

We also use the following lemma [12, Lemma 2.2b], which says that average min-entropy of a random variable does not decrease by more than the length of the correlated random variable.

Lemma 5. *If B has at most 2^λ possible values, then $\widetilde{\mathbf{H}}_\infty(A \mid B) \geq \mathbf{H}_\infty(A, B) - \lambda \geq \mathbf{H}_\infty(A) - \lambda$. And, more generally, $\widetilde{\mathbf{H}}_\infty(A \mid B, C) \geq \widetilde{\mathbf{H}}_\infty(A, B \mid C) - \lambda \geq \widetilde{\mathbf{H}}_\infty(A \mid C) - \lambda$.*

2.1 Definitions

Definition 1 [7]. *A (possibly randomized) function* $\mathsf{Enc} : \{0,1\}^l \to \{0,1\}^n$ *and a deterministic function* $\mathsf{Dec} : \{0,1\}^n \to \{0,1\}^l \cup \{\bot\}$ *is said to be a coding scheme if* $\forall\ m \in \{0,1\}^l$, $\Pr[\mathsf{Dec}(\mathsf{Enc}(m)) = m] = 1$. l *is called the message length and* n *is called the block length or the codeword length. Rate of a coding scheme is given by* $\dfrac{l}{n}$.

Definition 2 [7]. *A coding scheme* $(\mathsf{Enc}, \mathsf{Dec})$ *with message and codeword spaces as* $\{0,1\}^l, \{0,1\}^n$ *respectively, is* ϵ- *non-malleable with respect to a function family* $\mathcal{F} \subseteq \{f : \{0,1\}^n \to \{0,1\}^n\}$ *if* $\forall\ f \in \mathcal{F}$, $\exists$ *a distribution* Sim_f *over* $\{0,1\}^l \cup \{same^*, \bot\}$ *such that* $\forall\ m \in \{0,1\}^l$

$$\mathsf{Tamper}_f^m \approx_\epsilon \mathsf{Copy}_{Sim_f}^m$$

where Tamper_f^m *denotes the distribution* $\mathsf{Dec}(f(\mathsf{Enc}(m)))$ *and* $\mathsf{Copy}_{Sim_f}^m$ *is defined as*

$$\tilde{m} \leftarrow Sim_f$$

$$\mathsf{Copy}_{Sim_f}^m = \begin{cases} m\ if\ \tilde{m} = same^* \\ \tilde{m}\ otherwise \end{cases}$$

Sim_f *should be efficiently samplable given oracle access to* $f(.)$.

3 Building Blocks

We use information-theoretic message authentication codes, strong average case extractor and an existing 2-split state non-malleable codes construction by Li [20], as building blocks to our construction. We briefly discuss about these building blocks below.

3.1 One-Time Message Authentication Codes

A family of pair of functions $\{\mathsf{Tag}_{k_a} : \{0,1\}^\gamma \to \{0,1\}^\delta, \mathsf{Vrfy}_{k_a} : \{0,1\}^\gamma \times \{0,1\}^\delta \to \{0,1\}\}_{k_a \in \{0,1\}^\tau}$ is said to be a $\mu -$ secure one time MAC if

1. For $k_a \in_R \{0,1\}^\tau$, $\forall\ m \in \{0,1\}^\gamma$, $\Pr[\mathsf{Vrfy}_{k_a}(m, \mathsf{Tag}_{k_a}(m)) = 1] = 1$.
2. For any $m \neq m', t, t'$, $\Pr_{k_a}[\mathsf{Tag}_{k_a}(m) = t | \mathsf{Tag}_{k_a}(m') = t'] \leq \mu$ for $k_a \in_R \{0,1\}^\tau$.

3.2 Average-Case Extractors

Extractors [22] yield a close-to-uniform string from a random variable with high min-entropy, using a uniformly random seed i as a kind of catalyst. Strong extractors are ones in which the extracted string looks random even in the presence of the seed. (We will use only strong extractors in this paper and thus sometimes omit the adjective "strong.") If an extractor works when the guarantee on W is for conditional min-entropy rather than min-entropy, it is called an *average-case* extractor.

Definition 3 [12, Sect. 2.5]. *Let $Ext : \{0,1\}^n \times \{0,1\}^d \rightarrow \{0,1\}^l$ be a polynomial time computable function. We say that Ext is an efficient average-case (n,t,d,l,ϵ)-strong extractor if for all pairs of random variables (W,I) such that W is an n-bit string satisfying $\widetilde{\mathbf{H}}_\infty(W|I) \geq t$, we have $\mathbf{SD}\,((Ext(W;X),X,I), (U,X,I))$, where X is uniform on $\{0,1\}^d$.*

3.3   Li's Construction of 2-Split State Non-malleable Code

Lemma 6 [20, Theorem 7.12]. *For any $\beta \in \mathbb{N}$ there exists an explicit non-malleable code with efficient encoder/decoder in 2-split state model with block length 2β, rate $\Omega\left(\dfrac{1}{\log\,\beta}\right)$ and error $= 2^{-\Omega\left(\frac{\beta}{\log\,\beta}\right)}$.*

Let the message length be α for the non-malleable code in Lemma 6. By Lemma 6, we have

$$\frac{\alpha}{2\beta} = \Omega\left(\frac{1}{\log\beta}\right)$$

$$\Rightarrow \alpha = \Omega\left(\frac{\beta}{\log(\beta)}\right)$$

By Lemma 10, we have

$$\beta = \mathcal{O}(\alpha.\log(\alpha)) \tag{1}$$

4   Construction

Before we present our construction, we briefly summarize some important points that we discussed in Sect. 1. We observe that a non-malleable code is unlikely to be secure if the message m is revealed in the clear in any of the states. If it did, then the tampering function for that state could choose whether or not to tamper depending on the information it learns. It is for this reason that, in our construction, we need to encrypt the message (using a one-time pad) and then store the key as well as the ciphertext in separate states. To prevent the adversary from tampering with these in a related manner, we authenticate it using a key k_a. We encode k_a as well as the tags using a non-malleable code to ensure that any non-trivial tampering will render these independent of the underlying k_a and tags. However, as described in Sect. 1, if we store the encryption key k in the clear, then using the collisions in MAC, we can tamper the key and the ciphertext in a related way, hence leading to a related tampered message. We observe that if we are able to relate the tampered cipher-text but not the tampered encryption key $\tilde{k}$ to k, then the attack described in Sect. 1 no longer holds. Therefore, a key concern we address as we design our scheme is the following: *can we ensure the independence of any tampered encryption key $\tilde{k}$ from the underlying encryption key k?*

We show that a use of randomness extractors to generate k, combined with a careful use of message authentication codes helps us achieve this independence.

4.1 Notation

- NMEnc, NMDec be an ε_1-secure two split state non-malleable code over message and codeword spaces as $\{0,1\}^\alpha$, $\{0,1\}^{\beta_1} \times \{0,1\}^{\beta_2}$ respectively (as in Lemma 6), with the message length α and the length of the two states, β_1, β_2, respectively. NMTamper$^m_{f_1,f_2}$, NMSim$_{f_1,f_2}$ denote the tampered message distribution of m and the simulator of NMEnc, NMDec with respect to tampering functions f_1, f_2.
- Tag, Vrfy be an information theoretic ε_2 secure one time MAC (as in Lemma 9) over key, message, tag spaces as $\{0,1\}^{\tau_1}, \{0,1\}^n, \{0,1\}^{\delta_1}$ respectively.
- Tag', Vrfy' be an information theoretic ε_3 secure one time MAC (as in Lemma 9) over key, message, tag spaces as $\{0,1\}^{\tau_2}, \{0,1\}^l, \{0,1\}^{\delta_2}$ respectively.
- Ext be an $(n, t, d, l, \varepsilon_4)$ average case strong extractor.

The parameters will be chosen such that $\alpha = \tau_1 + \tau_2 + \delta_1 + \delta_2 + d$ and $n > 1 + \tau_2 + \delta_2 + l + t$. (Refer to Sect. 4.5 for details)

4.2 Construction Overview

We now define a construction for l bit messages in the four split state model. The idea is to use a randomness extractor (which typically have short seeds) to extract the key and then encode the seed using the underlying non-malleable code. Further, the source and the ciphertext are stored in separate parts of the codeword. We then authenticate the source and the ciphertext using two different one time MAC schemes and then encode the authentication keys and tags using the underlying non-malleable code. In other words, we define an encoder, which sends the ciphertext, the source (used to extract the encryption key) and the 2-state codeword encoding the two pairs of authentication keys and tags and the seed. The construction is described below:

Enc(m) :

- $w \in_R \{0,1\}^n$, $s \in_R \{0,1\}^d$
- $k_{a_1} \in_R \{0,1\}^{\tau_1}, k_{a_2} \in_R \{0,1\}^{\tau_2}$
- $k = \text{Ext}(w, s)$
- $C = m \oplus k$
- $t_1 = \text{Tag}_{k_{a_1}}(w)$, $t_2 = \text{Tag}'_{k_{a_2}}(C)$
- $(L, R) = \text{NMEnc}(k_{a_1}||k_{a_2}||t_1||t_2||s)$
- output : (L, R, w, C)

Dec(L, R, w, C) :

- $k_{a_1}||k_{a_2}||t_1||t_2||s = \text{NMDec}(L, R)$
- If $k_{a_1}||k_{a_2}||t_1||t_2||s = \bot$ output $\bot$
- else if $\text{Vrfy}_{k_{a_1}}(w, t_1) = 1$
  $\wedge$ $\text{Vrfy}'_{k_{a_2}}(C, t_2) = 1$
  output $C \oplus \text{Ext}(w, s)$
- else output $\bot$

Theorem 1. *Let* NMEnc, NMDec *be an* ε_1-*secure two split state non-malleable code,* Tag, Vrfy *be an information theoretic* ε_2 *secure one time* MAC *and* Tag', Vrfy' *be an information theoretic* ε_3 *secure one time* MAC *as given above. Let* Ext *be an* $(n, t, d, l, \varepsilon_4)$ *average case strong extractor. Let* $\alpha = \tau_1 + \tau_2 + \delta_1 + \delta_2 + d$ *and* $n > 1 + \tau_2 + \delta_2 + l + t$.

For any constant $\zeta > 0$, *messages of length* l, *any* κ *such that* $\kappa = o\left(\dfrac{l}{\log l}\right)$, *the construction in the figure above is a non-malleable code that has block length* $(3 + \zeta)l + o(l)$ *and there by achieves asymptotic rate* $\dfrac{1}{3 + \zeta}$ *and error* $2^{-\kappa}$.

Proof. We give the proof in two steps. Firstly, we prove that the proposed construction is a non-malleable coding scheme (Sect. 4.3). Secondly, we set the parameters to achieve the desired rate and error (Sect. 4.4).

4.3 Security Proof

Define the 4-split-state tampering family for the above construction as

$$\mathcal{F} = \{(h_1, h_2, f, g) : h_1 : \{0,1\}^{\beta_1} \to \{0,1\}^{\beta_1}, h_2 : \{0,1\}^{\beta_2} \to \{0,1\}^{\beta_2},$$

$$f : \{0,1\}^n \to \{0,1\}^n, g : \{0,1\}^l \to \{0,1\}^l\}$$

To show that (Enc, Dec) is non-malleable we need to show that $\forall (h_1, h_2, f, g) \in \mathcal{F}, \exists Sim_{h_1, h_2, f, g}$ such that $\forall m \in \{0,1\}^l$

$$Tamper_{h_1, h_2, f, g}^m \approx_\varepsilon Copy_{Sim_{h_1, h_2, f, g}}^m$$

Let $(h_1, h_2, f, g) \in \mathcal{F}$. We define the following simulator:

$Sim_{h_1, h_2, f, g}$:

1. $k \in_R \{0,1\}^l$
2. $C = 0 \oplus k$
3. $w \in_R \{0,1\}^n$
4. $(\tilde{w}, \tilde{C}) = (f(w), g(C))$
5. $\tilde{k_{a_1}} || \tilde{k_{a_2}} || \tilde{t_1} || \tilde{t_2} || \tilde{s} \leftarrow$ NMSim$_{h_1, h_2}$
6. If $\tilde{k_{a_1}} || \tilde{k_{a_2}} || \tilde{t_1} || \tilde{t_2} || \tilde{s} = \perp$, output $\perp$
7. else if $\tilde{k_{a_1}} || \tilde{k_{a_2}} || \tilde{t_1} || \tilde{t_2} || \tilde{s} = same^*$
      a. If $\tilde{w} = w$ and $\tilde{C} = C$ output $same^*$
      b. else output $\perp$
8. else if Vrfy$_{\tilde{k_{a_1}}}(\tilde{w}, \tilde{t_1}) = 1 \wedge$ Vrfy'$_{\tilde{k_{a_2}}}(\tilde{C}, \tilde{t_2}) = 1$ output $\tilde{C} \oplus$ Ext$(\tilde{w}; \tilde{s})$
9. else output $\perp$

We now prove the statistical closeness of the tampered random variable and the simulated random variable through a sequence of hybrids.

Proof Overview. At a high level, our goal is to remove the dependency of $\tilde{m}$ on m, through a series of hybrids. The codeword depends on m, directly or indirectly, through various random variables such as the seed s, w, the authentication keys as well as the tags. To begin with, we wish to remove the dependence of the tampered extracted key (used to decrypt the codeword) on the original extracted key. Through a series of hybrids, we achieve this by removing the dependence of the tampered extracted key on the seed s. Once we do this, we use the extractor property, to remove the dependency of C on w and s. Finally, we use perfect security of the one-time pad to remove dependency of $\tilde{C}$ on m.

Going from Tamper *experiment to* $\mathsf{Hybrid1}^m_{h_1,h_2,f,g}$: $\mathsf{Hybrid1}^m_{h_1,h_2,f,g}$ is the same as the standard tampering experiment except that we use the simulator for the underlying non-malleable code to generate the tampered random variable $\tilde{k}_{a_1}||\tilde{k}_{a_2}||\tilde{t}_1||\tilde{t}_2||\tilde{s}$.

Claim. If $(\mathsf{NMEnc}, \mathsf{NMDec})$ is an ε_1-secure non-malleable code, then $\mathsf{Tamper}^m_{h_1,h_2,f,g} \approx_{\varepsilon_1} \mathsf{Hybrid1}^m_{h_1,h_2,f,g}$

$\mathsf{Tamper}^m_{h_1,h_2,f,g}$:	$\mathsf{Hybrid1}^m_{h_1,h_2,f,g}$:
1. $w \in_R \{0,1\}^n$, $s \in_R \{0,1\}^d$	1. $w \in_R \{0,1\}^n$, $s \in_R \{0,1\}^d$
2. $k_{a_1} \in_R \{0,1\}^{\tau_1}$, $k_{a_2} \in_R \{0,1\}^{\tau_2}$	2. $k_{a_1} \in_R \{0,1\}^{\tau_1}$, $k_{a_2} \in_R \{0,1\}^{\tau_2}$
3. $k = \mathsf{Ext}(w; s)$	3. $k = \mathsf{Ext}(w; s)$
4. $C = m \oplus k$	4. $C = m \oplus k$
5. $t_1 = \mathsf{Tag}_{k_{a_1}}(w)$, $t_2 = \mathsf{Tag}'_{k_{a_2}}(C)$	5. $t_1 = \mathsf{Tag}_{k_{a_1}}(w)$, $t_2 = \mathsf{Tag}'_{k_{a_2}}(C)$
6. $(\tilde{w}, \tilde{C}) = (f(w), g(C))$	6. $(\tilde{w}, \tilde{C}) = (f(w), g(C))$
7. $\tilde{k}_{a_1}||\tilde{k}_{a_2}||\tilde{t}_1||\tilde{t}_2||\tilde{s} \leftarrow$ $\mathsf{NMTamper}^{k_{a_1}||k_{a_2}||t_1||t_2||s}_{h_1,h_2}$	7a. $\tilde{k}_{a_1}||\tilde{k}_{a_2}||\tilde{t}_1||\tilde{t}_2||\tilde{s} \leftarrow \mathsf{NMSim}_{h_1,h_2}$
	7b. If $\tilde{k}_{a_1}||\tilde{k}_{a_2}||\tilde{t}_1||\tilde{t}_2||\tilde{s} = same^*$, assign $\tilde{k}_{a_1}||\tilde{k}_{a_2}||\tilde{t}_1||\tilde{t}_2||\tilde{s} = k_{a_1}||k_{a_2}||t_1||t_2||s$
8. If $\tilde{k}_{a_1}||\tilde{k}_{a_2}||\tilde{t}_1||\tilde{t}_2||\tilde{s} = \bot$, output $\bot$	8. If $\tilde{k}_{a_1}||\tilde{k}_{a_2}||\tilde{t}_1||\tilde{t}_2||\tilde{s} = \bot$, output $\bot$
9. else if $\mathsf{Vrfy}_{\tilde{k}_{a_1}}(\tilde{w}, \tilde{t}_1) = 1 \wedge \mathsf{Vrfy}'_{\tilde{k}_{a_2}}(\tilde{C}, \tilde{t}_2) = 1$ output $\tilde{C} \oplus \mathsf{Ext}(\tilde{w}; \tilde{s})$	9. else if $\mathsf{Vrfy}_{\tilde{k}_{a_1}}(\tilde{w}, \tilde{t}_1) = 1 \wedge \mathsf{Vrfy}'_{\tilde{k}_{a_2}}(\tilde{C}, \tilde{t}_2) = 1$ output $\tilde{C} \oplus \mathsf{Ext}(\tilde{w}; \tilde{s})$
10. else output $\bot$	10. else output $\bot$

Proof. We wish to use the statistical closeness of the tampered and simulated random variables corresponding to $(\mathsf{NMEnc}, \mathsf{NMDec})$, to prove the claim.

Now, we apply Lemma 4, taking $B = (w, C)$, $A = (k_{a_1}||k_{a_2}||t_1||t_2||s)$, and the functions as $\mathsf{NMTamper}_{h_1,h_2}$, $\mathsf{Copy}_{\mathsf{NMSim}_{h_1,h_2}}$ to get:

$$\text{Since,} \quad \mathsf{NMTamper}_{h_1,h_2}^{k_{a_1}||k_{a_2}||t_1||t_2||s} \approx_{\varepsilon_1} \mathsf{Copy}_{\mathsf{NMSim}_{h_1,h_2}}^{k_{a_1}||k_{a_2}||t_1||t_2||s}$$

hence we get,

$$(w, C, k_{a_1}||k_{a_2}||t_1||t_2||s, \mathsf{NMTamper}_{h_1,h_2}^{k_{a_1}||k_{a_2}||t_1||t_2||s}) \approx_{\varepsilon_1}$$
$$(w, C, k_{a_1}||k_{a_2}||t_1||t_2||s, \mathsf{Copy}_{\mathsf{NMSim}_{h_1,h_2}}^{k_{a_1}||k_{a_2}||t_1||t_2||s})$$

$$\implies \text{By Lemma 2,} (w, C, \mathsf{NMTamper}_{h_1,h_2}^{k_{a_1}||k_{a_2}||t_1||t_2||s}) \approx_{\varepsilon_1} (w, C, \mathsf{Copy}_{\mathsf{NMSim}_{h_1,h_2}}^{k_{a_1}||k_{a_2}||t_1||t_2||s})$$

$$\implies \text{By Lemma 3,} (\tilde{w}, \tilde{C}, \mathsf{NMTamper}_{h_1,h_2}^{k_{a_1}||k_{a_2}||t_1||t_2||s}) \approx_{\varepsilon_1} (\tilde{w}, \tilde{C}, \mathsf{Copy}_{\mathsf{NMSim}_{h_1,h_2}}^{k_{a_1}||k_{a_2}||t_1||t_2||s})$$
$$\tag{2}$$

Now, we express the outputs of the hybrids as a deterministic function, Q, of the above variables, to apply Lemma 3 and hence prove the claim.
$Q(\tilde{w}, \tilde{C}, \tilde{k_{a_1}}||\tilde{k_{a_2}}||\tilde{t_1}||\tilde{t_2}||\tilde{s})$:

- If $\tilde{k_{a_1}}||\tilde{k_{a_2}}||\tilde{t_1}||\tilde{t_2}||\tilde{s} = \bot$, output $\bot$
- else if $\mathsf{Vrfy}_{\tilde{k_{a_1}}}(\tilde{w}, \tilde{t_1}) = 1 \wedge \mathsf{Vrfy}'_{\tilde{k_{a_2}}}(\tilde{C}, \tilde{t_2}) = 1$ output $\tilde{C} \oplus \mathsf{Ext}(\tilde{w}; \tilde{s})$
- else output $\bot$

Then, using Eq. 2 and Lemma 3, we get

$$Q(\tilde{w}, \tilde{C}, \mathsf{NMTamper}_{h_1,h_2}^{k_{a_1}||k_{a_2}||t_1||t_2||s}) \approx_{\varepsilon_1} Q(\tilde{w}, \tilde{C}, \mathsf{Copy}_{\mathsf{NMSim}_{h_1,h_2}}^{k_{a_1}||k_{a_2}||t_1||t_2||s})$$

$$\implies \mathsf{Tamper}_{h_1,h_2,f,g}^m \approx_{\varepsilon_1} \mathsf{Hybrid1}_{h_1,h_2,f,g}^m$$

Going from $\mathsf{Hybrid1}_{h_1,h_2,f,g}^m$ *to* $\mathsf{Hybrid2}_{h_1,h_2,f,g}^m$: As will become evident later, $\mathsf{Hybrid1}_{h_1,h_2,f,g}^m$ is what will allow us to argue that, in the restricted case where $\tilde{s} \neq s$, the extracted key $\tilde{k}$ is independent of s. We now move to $\mathsf{Hybrid2}_{h_1,h_2,f,g}^m$ which is the same as $\mathsf{Hybrid1}_{h_1,h_2,f,g}^m$ except for the case where s is unchanged. In this case, as we show in $\mathsf{Hybrid2}_{h_1,h_2,f,g}^m$, the output of the experiment can be computed without evaluating $\tilde{k}$. We prove that $\mathsf{Hybrid1}_{h_1,h_2,f,g}^m$ and $\mathsf{Hybrid2}_{h_1,h_2,f,g}^m$ are statistically close by using the unforgeability of the message authentication scheme.

Claim. If $(\mathsf{Tag}, \mathsf{Vrfy})$ and $(\mathsf{Tag}', \mathsf{Vrfy}')$ are ε_2-, ε_3-secure information theoretic one-time MAC (respectively), then $\mathsf{Hybrid1}_{h_1,h_2,f,g}^m \approx_{\varepsilon_2+\varepsilon_3} \mathsf{Hybrid2}_{h_1,h_2,f,g}^m$.

$\mathsf{Hybrid1}^m_{h_1,h_2,f,g}$:	$\mathsf{Hybrid2}^m_{h_1,h_2,f,g}$:
1. $w \in_R \{0,1\}^n$, $s \in_R \{0,1\}^d$	1. $w \in_R \{0,1\}^n$, $s \in_R \{0,1\}^d$
2. $k_{a_1} \in_R \{0,1\}^{\tau_1}, k_{a_2} \in_R \{0,1\}^{\tau_2}$	
3. $k = \mathsf{Ext}(w;s)$	3. $k = \mathsf{Ext}(w;s)$
4. $C = m \oplus k$	4. $C = m \oplus k$
5. $t_1 = \mathsf{Tag}_{k_{a_1}}(w)$, $t_2 = \mathsf{Tag}'_{k_{a_2}}(C)$	
6. $(\tilde{w}, \tilde{C}) = (f(w), g(C))$	6. $(\tilde{w}, \tilde{C}) = (f(w), g(C))$
7. $\tilde{k_{a_1}} \| \tilde{k_{a_2}} \| \tilde{t_1} \| \tilde{t_2} \| \tilde{s} \leftarrow \mathsf{NMSim}_{h_1,h_2}$	7. $\tilde{k_{a_1}} \| \tilde{k_{a_2}} \| \tilde{t_1} \| \tilde{t_2} \| \tilde{s} \leftarrow \mathsf{NMSim}_{h_1,h_2}$
8. If $\tilde{k_{a_1}} \| \tilde{k_{a_2}} \| \tilde{t_1} \| \tilde{t_2} \| \tilde{s} = same^*$, assign $\tilde{k_{a_1}} \| \tilde{k_{a_2}} \| \tilde{t_1} \| \tilde{t_2} \| \tilde{s} = k_{a_1} \| k_{a_2} \| t_1 \| t_2 \| s$	8. If $\tilde{k_{a_1}} \| \tilde{k_{a_2}} \| \tilde{t_1} \| \tilde{t_2} \| \tilde{s} = same^*$ • If $\tilde{w} = w$ and $\tilde{C} = C$ output m • else output $\perp$
9. If $\tilde{k_{a_1}} \| \tilde{k_{a_2}} \| \tilde{t_1} \| \tilde{t_2} \| \tilde{s} = \perp$, output $\perp$	9. If $\tilde{k_{a_1}} \| \tilde{k_{a_2}} \| \tilde{t_1} \| \tilde{t_2} \| \tilde{s} = \perp$, output $\perp$
10. else if $\mathsf{Vrfy}_{k_{a_1}^-}(\tilde{w}, \tilde{t_1}) = 1 \wedge \mathsf{Vrfy}'_{k_{a_2}^-}(\tilde{C}, \tilde{t_2}) = 1$ output $\tilde{C} \oplus \mathsf{Ext}(\tilde{w}; \tilde{s})$	10. else if $\mathsf{Vrfy}_{k_{a_1}^-}(\tilde{w}, \tilde{t_1}) = 1 \wedge \mathsf{Vrfy}'_{k_{a_2}^-}(\tilde{C}, \tilde{t_2}) = 1$ output $\tilde{C} \oplus \mathsf{Ext}(\tilde{w}; \tilde{s})$
11. else output $\perp$	11. else output $\perp$

Proof. If $same^*$ is not the value sampled from NMSim_{h_1,h_2}, then $\mathsf{Hybrid1}^m_{h_1,h_2,f,g}$ and $\mathsf{Hybrid2}^m_{h_1,h_2,f,g}$ can be evaluated without steps $(2, 5, 8)$ and (8) respectively. The output of the two hybrids are identical in this case. Therefore, the statistical distance is zero in this case. When $same^*$ is sampled, the key difference between $\mathsf{Hybrid1}^m_{h_1,h_2,f,g}$ and $\mathsf{Hybrid2}^m_{h_1,h_2,f,g}$ is that, corresponding to this case, we remove the two verify checks (of Step 10) in $\mathsf{Hybrid2}^m_{h_1,h_2,f,g}$ and simply replace it with the checks shown in Step 8. By Proposition 1 and above observation, we get:

$$\mathbf{SD}\left(\mathsf{Hybrid1}^m_{h_1,h_2,f,g}; \mathsf{Hybrid2}^m_{h_1,h_2,f,g}\right) \leq \Pr[\mathsf{NMSim}_{h_1,h_2} = same^*] \cdot$$
$$\mathbf{SD}\left(\mathsf{Hybrid1}^m_{h_1,h_2,f,g} | \mathsf{NMSim}h_1, h_2 = same^*; \mathsf{Hybrid2}^m_{h_1,h_2,f,g} | \mathsf{NMSim}h_1, h_2 = same^*\right)$$

So, now remains the case when NMSim_{h_1,h_2} outputs $same^*$. By using unforgeability of $(\mathsf{Tag}, \mathsf{Vrfy})$ and $(\mathsf{Tag}', \mathsf{Vrfy}')$ we show the that two hybrids are statistically close.

- Let E be the event that $same^*$ is sampled from NMSim_{h_1,h_2} and $\tilde{E}$ be its compliment.
- Let F be the event that $\tilde{w} = w \wedge \tilde{C} = C$ and $\tilde{F}$ its complement.
- E and F are independent because $\tilde{w}, \tilde{C}$ are deterministic functions of w and C respectively (which are independent of $\mathsf{NMSim}h_1, h_2$) and $\mathsf{NMSim}h_1, h_2$ does not take any input except for the a-priori fixed tampering functions h_1, h_2.

$2\mathbf{SD}\left(\mathsf{Hybrid1}^m_{h_1,h_2,f,g};\mathsf{Hybrid2}^m_{h_1,h_2,f,g}\right)$

$$= \sum_{\tilde{m}\in\{0,1\}^l\cup\{\bot\}} \left| \Pr[\mathsf{Hybrid1}^m_{h_1,h_2,f,g}=\tilde{m}] - \Pr[\mathsf{Hybrid2}^m_{h_1,h_2,f,g}=\tilde{m}] \right|$$

$$= \sum_{\tilde{m}\in\{0,1\}^l\cup\{\bot\}} \Big| \Pr[E]\big(\Pr[\mathsf{Hybrid1}^m_{h_1,h_2,f,g}=\tilde{m}|E] - \Pr[\mathsf{Hybrid2}^m_{h_1,h_2,f,g}=\tilde{m}|E]\big)$$

$$+ \Pr[\tilde{E}] \underbrace{\big(\Pr[\mathsf{Hybrid1}^m_{h_1,h_2,f,g}=\tilde{m}|\tilde{E}] - \Pr[\mathsf{Hybrid2}^m_{h_1,h_2,f,g}=\tilde{m}|\tilde{E}]\big)}_{=0 \text{ as given } \tilde{E} \text{ both the hybrids are identical.}} \Big|$$

$$= \sum_{\tilde{m}\in\{0,1\}^l\cup\{\bot\}} \Pr[E]\Big| \Pr[\mathsf{Hybrid1}^m_{h_1,h_2,f,g}=\tilde{m}|E] - \Pr[\mathsf{Hybrid2}^m_{h_1,h_2,f,g}=\tilde{m}|E]\Big|$$

$$= \Pr[E] \sum_{\tilde{m}\in\{0,1\}^l\cup\{\bot\}} \Big| \Pr[F|E].$$

$$\Big(\underbrace{\Pr[\mathsf{Hybrid1}^m_{h_1,h_2,f,g}=\tilde{m}|E,F] - \Pr[\mathsf{Hybrid2}^m_{h_1,h_2,f,g}=\tilde{m}|E,F]}_{=0 \text{ as given E and F both the hybrids output} m.\text{So for any} \tilde{m} \text{ the difference is } 0} \Big) + \Pr[\tilde{F}|E].$$

$$\Big(\Pr[\mathsf{Hybrid1}^m_{h_1,h_2,f,g}=\tilde{m}|E,\tilde{F}] - \Pr[\mathsf{Hybrid2}^m_{h_1,h_2,f,g}=\tilde{m}|E,\tilde{F}]\Big) \Big|$$

$$= \Pr[E] \sum_{\tilde{m}\in\{0,1\}^l\cup\{\bot\}} \Big| \Pr[\tilde{F}]\big(\Pr[\mathsf{Hybrid1}^m_{h_1,h_2,f,g}=\tilde{m}|E,\tilde{F}]-$$

$$\Pr[\mathsf{Hybrid2}^m_{h_1,h_2,f,g}=\tilde{m}|E,\tilde{F}]\big)\Big|$$

$$= \Pr[E]\Pr[\tilde{F}] \sum_{\tilde{m}\in\{0,1\}^l} \Big| \Pr[\mathsf{Hybrid1}^m_{h_1,h_2,f,g}=\tilde{m}|E,\tilde{F}] - \Pr[\mathsf{Hybrid2}^m_{h_1,h_2,f,g}=\tilde{m}|E,\tilde{F}]\Big|$$

$$+ \Big| \Pr[\mathsf{Hybrid1}^m_{h_1,h_2,f,g}=\bot|E,\tilde{F}] - \underbrace{\Pr[\mathsf{Hybrid2}^m_{h_1,h_2,f,g}=\bot|E,\tilde{F}]}_{=1 \text{ as given E},\tilde{F} \text{ Hybrid 2 outputs } \bot} \Big|$$

$$= \Pr[E]\Pr[\tilde{F}] \sum_{\tilde{m}\in\{0,1\}^l} \Pr[\mathsf{Hybrid1}^m_{h_1,h_2,f,g}=\tilde{m}|E,\tilde{F}] + 1$$

$$- \Pr[\mathsf{Hybrid1}^m_{h_1,h_2,f,g}=\bot|E,\tilde{F}]$$

$$= 2\Pr[E]\Pr[\tilde{F}]\big(\Pr[\mathsf{Hybrid1}^m_{h_1,h_2,f,g}\neq\bot|E,\tilde{F}]\big)$$

$$\leq 2\Pr[E]\Pr[\tilde{F}]\Pr[\mathsf{Vrfy}_{k_{a_1}^{-}}(\tilde{w},\tilde{t}_1)=1 \wedge \mathsf{Vrfy'}_{k_{a_2}^{-}}(\tilde{C},\tilde{t}_2)=1|t_1=\mathsf{Tag}_{k_{a_1}}(w),$$

$$t_2 = \mathsf{Tag'}_{k_{a_2}}(C),E,\tilde{F}]$$

$$\leq 2\Pr[E]\Pr[\tilde{F}]\Pr[\mathsf{Vrfy}_{k_{a_1}}(\tilde{w},t_1)=1 \wedge \mathsf{Vrfy'}_{k_{a_2}}(\tilde{C},t_2)=1|t_1=\mathsf{Tag}_{k_{a_1}}(w),$$

$$t_2 = \mathsf{Tag'}_{k_{a_2}}(C),\tilde{F}]$$

$$\leq 2(\varepsilon_2 + \varepsilon_3)$$

$$\therefore \ \mathsf{Hybrid1}^m_{h_1,h_2,f,g} \approx_{\varepsilon_2+\varepsilon_3} \mathsf{Hybrid2}^m_{h_1,h_2,f,g}$$

Rewriting $\mathsf{Hybrid2}^m_{h_1,h_2,f,g}$ *as* $\mathsf{Hybrid3}^m_{h_1,h_2,f,g}$: Now we simply rewrite the $\mathsf{Hybrid2}^m_{h_1,h_2,f,g}$, starting with sampling from NMSim_{h_1,h_2}.

$\mathsf{Hybrid2}^m_{h_1,h_2,f,g}$:	$\mathsf{Hybrid3}^m_{h_1,h_2,f,g}$:

1. $w \in_R \{0,1\}^n$, $s \in_R \{0,1\}^d$
 2. $k = \mathsf{Ext}(w; s)$
 3. $C = m \oplus k$
 4. $(\tilde{w}, \tilde{C}) = (f(w), g(C))$
 5. $\tilde{k_{a_1}}||\tilde{k_{a_2}}||\tilde{t_1}||\tilde{t_2}||\tilde{s} \leftarrow \mathsf{NMSim}_{h_1,h_2}$
 6. If $\tilde{k_{a_1}}||\tilde{k_{a_2}}||\tilde{t_1}||\tilde{t_2}||\tilde{s} = same^*$
     • If $\tilde{w} = w$ and $\tilde{C} = C$ output m
     • else output $\perp$
 7. If $\tilde{k_{a_1}}||\tilde{k_{a_2}}||\tilde{t_1}||\tilde{t_2}||\tilde{s} = \perp$, output $\perp$
 8. else if $\mathsf{Vrfy}_{\tilde{k_{a_1}}}(\tilde{w}, \tilde{t_1}) = 1 \wedge$
     $\mathsf{Vrfy'}_{\tilde{k_{a_2}}}(\tilde{C}, \tilde{t_2}) = 1$
     output $\tilde{C} \oplus \mathsf{Ext}(\tilde{w}; \tilde{s})$
 9. else output $\perp$
	1. $\tilde{k_{a_1}}||\tilde{k_{a_2}}||\tilde{t_1}||\tilde{t_2}||\tilde{s} \leftarrow \mathsf{NMSim}_{h_1,h_2}$
	 2. $w \in_R \{0,1\}^n$, $s \in_R \{0,1\}^d$
	 3. $k = \mathsf{Ext}(w; s)$
	 4. $C = m \oplus k$
	 5. $(\tilde{w}, \tilde{C}) = (f(w), g(C))$
	 6. If $\tilde{k_{a_1}}||\tilde{k_{a_2}}||\tilde{t_1}||\tilde{t_2}||\tilde{s} = same^*$
	     • If $\tilde{w} = w$ and $\tilde{C} = C$ output m
	     • else output $\perp$
	 7. If $\tilde{k_{a_1}}||\tilde{k_{a_2}}||\tilde{t_1}||\tilde{t_2}||\tilde{s} = \perp$, output $\perp$
	 8. else if $\mathsf{Vrfy}_{\tilde{k_{a_1}}}(\tilde{w}, \tilde{t_1}) = 1 \wedge$
	     $\mathsf{Vrfy'}_{\tilde{k_{a_2}}}(\tilde{C}, \tilde{t_2}) = 1$
	     output $\tilde{C} \oplus \mathsf{Ext}(\tilde{w}; \tilde{s})$
	 9. else output $\perp$

It is easy to see that we have rearranged the steps without changing the distributions of any of the random variable, $\mathsf{Hybrid2}^m_{h_1,h_2,f,g} \equiv \mathsf{Hybrid3}^m_{h_1,h_2,f,g}$.

Going from $\mathsf{Hybrid3}^m_{h_1,h_2,f,g}$ *to* $\mathsf{Hybrid4}^m_{h_1,h_2,f,g}$: We now wish to remove dependency of the ciphertext on the source. This removes the dependency across the two states containing w and C, which might have led to related tampering of the message. To do this we would like to use the security of our randomness extractor and replace the extracted key k by uniform. The main challenge in doing so is that, the decoded (tampered) message might itself reveal information about the key k. This is a challenge because this information is learnt after the seed s is chosen. This is the main bottleneck of our proof. The way we overcome it is by carefully arguing that the information revealed by the decoded message might be learnt from auxiliary information. Importantly, this auxiliary information is completely independent of s and therefore, we can use extractor security.

Claim. If Ext is an $(n, t, d, l, \varepsilon_4)$ average case extractor, then $\mathsf{Hybrid3}^m_{h_1,h_2,f,g} \approx_{\varepsilon_4} \mathsf{Hybrid4}^m_{h_1,h_2,f,g}$

Hybrid3$_{h_1,h_2,f,g}^{m}$:	Hybrid4$_{h_1,h_2,f,g}^{m}$:
1. $\tilde{k_{a_1}}\|\tilde{k_{a_2}}\|\tilde{t_1}\|\tilde{t_2}\|\tilde{s} \leftarrow \mathsf{NMSim}_{h_1,h_2}$	1. $\tilde{k_{a_1}}\|\tilde{k_{a_2}}\|\tilde{t_1}\|\tilde{t_2}\|\tilde{s} \leftarrow \mathsf{NMSim}_{h_1,h_2}$
2. $w \in_R \{0,1\}^n, s \in_R \{0,1\}^d$	2. $w \in_R \{0,1\}^n$
3. $k = \mathsf{Ext}(w; s)$	3. $k \in_R \{0,1\}^l$
4. $C = m \oplus k$	4. $C = m \oplus k$
5. $(\tilde{w}, \tilde{C}) = (f(w), g(C))$	5. $(\tilde{w}, \tilde{C}) = (f(w), g(C))$
6. If $\tilde{k_{a_1}}\|\tilde{k_{a_2}}\|\tilde{t_1}\|\tilde{t_2}\|\tilde{s} = same^*$	6. If $\tilde{k_{a_1}}\|\tilde{k_{a_2}}\|\tilde{t_1}\|\tilde{t_2}\|\tilde{s} = same^*$
• If $\tilde{w} = w$ and $\tilde{C} = C$ output m	• If $\tilde{w} = w$ and $\tilde{C} = C$ output m
• else output $\perp$	• else output $\perp$
7. else if $\tilde{k_{a_1}}\|\tilde{k_{a_2}}\|\tilde{t_1}\|\tilde{t_2}\|\tilde{s} = \perp$, output $\perp$	7. else if $\tilde{k_{a_1}}\|\tilde{k_{a_2}}\|\tilde{t_1}\|\tilde{t_2}\|\tilde{s} = \perp$, output $\perp$
8. else if $\mathsf{Vrfy}_{\tilde{k_{a_1}}}(\tilde{w}, \tilde{t_1}) = 1 \wedge \mathsf{Vrfy'}_{\tilde{k_{a_2}}}(\tilde{C}, \tilde{t_2}) = 1$ output $\tilde{C} \oplus \mathsf{Ext}(\tilde{w}; \tilde{s})$	8. else if $\mathsf{Vrfy}_{\tilde{k_{a_1}}}(\tilde{w}, \tilde{t_1}) = 1 \wedge \mathsf{Vrfy'}_{\tilde{k_{a_2}}}(\tilde{C}, \tilde{t_2}) = 1$ output $\tilde{C} \oplus \mathsf{Ext}(\tilde{w}; \tilde{s})$
9. else output $\perp$	9. else output $\perp$

Proof. As explained in the motivation to this claim, we wish to replace the extractor output with a uniform string. But the main challenge in this, is to capture the security, given an auxiliary information. We consider two cases and carefully analyze the auxiliary information that we use in each of them. We show that in both these cases, the auxiliary information is completely independent of s. We then use the average extractor property to argue security. We define two mutually exclusive events:

– Let $Case1$ denote the event that $\tilde{k_{a_1}}\|\tilde{k_{a_2}}\|\tilde{t_1}\|\tilde{t_2}\|\tilde{s} = same^*$.
– Let $Case2$ denote the event that $\tilde{k_{a_1}}\|\tilde{k_{a_2}}\|\tilde{t_1}\|\tilde{t_2}\|\tilde{s} \neq same^*$.

By Proposition 1, we get:
SD $\left(\mathsf{Hybrid3}_{h_1,h_2,f,g}^{m}, \mathsf{Hybrid4}_{h_1,h_2,f,g}^{m} \right)$

$$\leq Pr[Case1] \ \textbf{SD} \left(\mathsf{Hybrid3}_{h_1,h_2,f,g}^{m}|Case1, \mathsf{Hybrid4}_{h_1,h_2,f,g}^{m}|Case1 \right)$$

$$+ Pr[Case2] \ \textbf{SD} \left(\mathsf{Hybrid3}_{h_1,h_2,f,g}^{m}|Case2, \mathsf{Hybrid4}_{h_1,h_2,f,g}^{m}|Case2 \right) \quad (3)$$

We now use the security of the average case extractor to get the desired statistical closeness in each of the two cases separately. The auxiliary information in each case is different.

Case1 : $\tilde{k_{a_1}}\|\tilde{k_{a_2}}\|\tilde{t_1}\|\tilde{t_2}\|\tilde{s} = same^*$
In this case, the auxiliary information just includes a single bit, indicating whether w is modified or remains the same. So, we first define this indicator function:

$$eq(w) = \begin{cases} 0 \ if \ f(w) \neq w \\ 1 \ if \ f(w) = w \end{cases}$$

Let the auxiliary information be denoted by $E_1 \equiv (eq(W))$. E_1 is independent of S because E_1 is determined given W and W is independent of S. Now, E_1 and W are correlated and E_1 can take at most two possible values.

Hence, $\widetilde{\mathbf{H}}_\infty(W|E_1) \geq \mathbf{H}_\infty(W) - 1 = n - 1$ by Lemma 5. As $n - 1 > t$, by security of average case extractor, we get:

$$E_1, \mathsf{Ext}(W; S) \approx_{\varepsilon_4} E_1, U_l$$

As m is independent of (W, S), we get:

$$m, E_1, \mathsf{Ext}(W; S) \approx_{\varepsilon_4} m, E_1, U_l \qquad (4)$$

Now, we wish to apply Lemma 3, for which, we express the output of the hybrids in $Case1$ as a deterministic function of the variables above. Let $Q_1(m, eq(w), k)$:

- $C = m \oplus k$
- $\tilde{C} = g(C)$
- If $eq(w) = 1$ and $\tilde{C} = C$ output m
- else output $\perp$

Then, the outputs of $\mathsf{Hybrid3}_{h_1,h_2,f,g}^m|Case1$ and $\mathsf{Hybrid4}_{h_1,h_2,f,g}^m|Case1$ are expressible by Q_1 above.

Hence, $Eq.4 \implies$ By Lemma 3, $Q_1(m, E_1, \mathsf{Ext}(W; S)) \approx_{\varepsilon_4} Q_1(m, E_1, U_l)$

i.e., $\mathsf{Hybrid3}_{h_1,h_2,f,g}^m|Case1 \approx_{\varepsilon_4} \mathsf{Hybrid4}_{h_1,h_2,f,g}^m|Case1$

$$(5)$$

Case2 : $\tilde{k_{a_1}}||\tilde{k_{a_2}}||\tilde{t_1}||\tilde{t_2}||\tilde{s} \neq$ same*
This case is further divided into two mutually exclusive events of Case2.

Case2a : $\tilde{k_{a_1}}||\tilde{k_{a_2}}||\tilde{t_1}||\tilde{t_2}||\tilde{s} = \perp$
Given $\tilde{k_{a_1}}||\tilde{k_{a_2}}||\tilde{t_1}||\tilde{t_2}||\tilde{s} = \perp$ both hybrids output $\perp$ with probability 1. Therefore

$$\mathbf{SD}\left(\mathsf{Hybrid3}_{h_1,h_2,f,g}^m|case2a, \mathsf{Hybrid4}_{h_1,h_2,f,g}^m|case2a\right) = 0 \qquad (6)$$

Case2b : $\tilde{k_{a_1}}||\tilde{k_{a_2}}||\tilde{t_1}||\tilde{t_2}||\tilde{s} \neq \perp \wedge \tilde{k_{a_1}}||\tilde{k_{a_2}}||\tilde{t_1}||\tilde{t_2}||\tilde{s} \neq$ same*
When $\tilde{k_{a_1}}||\tilde{k_{a_2}}||\tilde{t_1}||\tilde{t_2}||\tilde{s} \neq (same^*, \perp)$, the auxiliary information consists of an indicator of verification of $\tilde{w}$, the simulated authentication key and tag (corresponding to the ciphertext) distributions and the modified encryption key. We first define the indicator of verification bit:

$$Verify(w) = \mathsf{Vrfy}_{\tilde{k_{a_1}}}(f(w), \tilde{t_1})$$

Now, let the auxiliary information be denoted by $E_2 \equiv (Verify(W), \tilde{K_{a_2}}, \tilde{T_2}, \mathsf{Ext}(\tilde{W}; \tilde{S}))$, where $\tilde{K_{a_1}}, \tilde{K_{a_2}}, \tilde{T_1}, \tilde{T_2}, \tilde{S}$ denote the distributions on the authentication key, tag spaces and the seed, when sampled from the simulator conditioned on the event Case2b. E_2 is clearly a deterministic function of $\tilde{K_{a_1}}, \tilde{K_{a_2}}, \tilde{W}, \tilde{T_1}, \tilde{T_2}, \tilde{S}$, all of which are independent of S (as we use the simulator). Hence, E_2 is independent of S. Now, E_2 and W are correlated. E_2 can take at most $2^{1+\tau_2+\delta_2+l}$ possible values.

Hence, $\widetilde{\mathbf{H}}_\infty(W|E_2) \geq \mathbf{H}_\infty(W) - (1 + \tau_2 + \delta_2 + l) = n - (1 + \tau_2 + \delta_2 + l)$, by Lemma 5. As $n - (1 + \tau_2 + \delta_2 + l) > t$ (due to the way we set parameters in Sect. 4.5), by security of average case extractor, we get:

$$E_2, \mathsf{Ext}(W; S) \approx_{\varepsilon_4} E_2, U_l$$

As m is independent of (W, S), we get:

$$m, E_2, \mathsf{Ext}(W; S) \approx_{\varepsilon_4} m, E_2, U_l \tag{7}$$

Now, we wish to apply Lemma 3 and again, we express the outputs of $\mathsf{Hybrid3}^m_{h_1,h_2,f,g}|Case2b$ and $\mathsf{Hybrid4}^m_{h_1,h_2,f,g}|Case2b$ as a deterministic function of the variables above. Define function Q_2 as follows.
$Q_2(m, Verify(w), \tilde{k}_{a_2}, \tilde{t}_2, \mathsf{Ext}(\tilde{w}; \tilde{s}), k)$:

 - $C = m \oplus k$
 - $\tilde{C} = g(C)$
 - If $Verify(w) = 1$ and $\mathsf{Vrfy}'_{\tilde{k}_{a_2}}(\tilde{C}, \tilde{t}_2) = 1$ output $\tilde{C} \oplus \mathsf{Ext}(\tilde{w}; \tilde{s})$
 - else output $\perp$

Then, the outputs of $\mathsf{Hybrid3}^m_{h_1,h_2,f,g}|Case2b$ and $\mathsf{Hybrid4}^m_{h_1,h_2,f,g}|Case2b$ are expressible by Q_2 above.

Hence, $Eq. 7 \implies$ By Lemma 3, $Q_2(m, E_2, \mathsf{Ext}(W; S)) \approx_{\varepsilon_4} Q_2(m, E_2, U_l)$
i.e., $\mathsf{Hybrid3}^m_{h_1,h_2,f,g}|Case2b \approx_{\varepsilon_4} \mathsf{Hybrid4}^m_{h_1,h_2,f,g}|Case2b$ (8)

Hence, by Proposition 1, Eqs. 3, 5, 6 and 8 above, we get:

$$\mathsf{Hybrid3}^m_{h_1,h_2,f,g} \approx_{\varepsilon_4} \mathsf{Hybrid4}^m_{h_1,h_2,f,g}$$

Remark on Auxiliary Information. We first observe that the auxiliary information in both the cases contains the additional information required to get the outputs of the hybrids, which are independent of the seed. In $Case1$, we just have a single bit of auxiliary information, which is independent of s. In $Case2$ however, as we add the verification bit to E_2, it is important that this verification check is independent of s. If we authenticate w and C together, under a single MAC, then the verify check would be dependent on C as well, which in turn depends on s in the third hybrid. So, it is important that we authenticate w and C using separate one time MAC. Then, we give the modified authentication key and tag corresponding to C in E_2, which are independent of s.

Rewriting $\mathsf{Hybrid4}^m_{h_1,h_2,f,g}$ *as* $\mathsf{Hybrid5}^m_{h_1,h_2,f,g}$: We again rewrite $\mathsf{Hybrid4}^m_{h_1,h_2,f,g}$ such that we first choose the encryption key k uniformly at random, to get $\mathsf{Hybrid5}^m_{h_1,h_2,f,g}$. This reordering of steps is to stress on the fact that, we have now removed the dependency of the encryption key on w and s and we sample it uniformly at random.

Hybrid4$_{h_1,h_2,f,g}^m$:	Hybrid5$_{h_1,h_2,f,g}^m$:
1. $\tilde{k_{a_1}}\|\tilde{k_{a_2}}\|\tilde{t_1}\|\tilde{t_2}\|\tilde{s} \leftarrow$ NMSim$_{h_1,h_2}$	1. $k \in_R \{0,1\}^l$
2. $w \in_R \{0,1\}^n$	2. $C = m \oplus k$
3. $k \in_R \{0,1\}^l$	3. $w \in_R \{0,1\}^n$
4. $C = m \oplus k$	4. $(\tilde{w}, \tilde{C}) = (f(w), g(C))$
5. $(\tilde{w}, \tilde{C}) = (f(w), g(C))$	5. $\tilde{k_{a_1}}\|\tilde{k_{a_2}}\|\tilde{t_1}\|\tilde{t_2}\|\tilde{s} \leftarrow$ NMSim$_{h_1,h_2}$
6. If $\tilde{k_{a_1}}\|\tilde{k_{a_2}}\|\tilde{t_1}\|\tilde{t_2}\|\tilde{s} = same^*$	6. If $\tilde{k_{a_1}}\|\tilde{k_{a_2}}\|\tilde{t_1}\|\tilde{t_2}\|\tilde{s} = same^*$
• If $\tilde{w} = w$ and $\tilde{C} = C$ output m	• If $\tilde{w} = w$ and $\tilde{C} = C$ output m
• else output $\perp$	• else output $\perp$
7. else if $\tilde{k_{a_1}}\|\tilde{k_{a_2}}\|\tilde{t_1}\|\tilde{t_2}\|\tilde{s} = \perp$, output $\perp$	7. else if $\tilde{k_{a_1}}\|\tilde{k_{a_2}}\|\tilde{t_1}\|\tilde{t_2}\|\tilde{s} = \perp$, output $\perp$
8. else if $\text{Vrfy}_{\tilde{k_{a_1}}}(\tilde{w}, \tilde{t_1}) = 1 \wedge \text{Vrfy}'_{\tilde{k_{a_2}}}(\tilde{C}, \tilde{t_2}) = 1$ output $\tilde{C} \oplus \text{Ext}(\tilde{w}; \tilde{s})$	8. else if $\text{Vrfy}_{\tilde{k_{a_1}}}(\tilde{w}, \tilde{t_1}) = 1 \wedge \text{Vrfy}'_{\tilde{k_{a_2}}}(\tilde{C}, \tilde{t_2}) = 1$ output $\tilde{C} \oplus \text{Ext}(\tilde{w}; \tilde{s})$
9. else output $\perp$	9. else output $\perp$

As we have only reordered the steps without changing any of the distributions, clearly Hybrid4$_{h_1,h_2,f,g}^m \equiv$ Hybrid5$_{h_1,h_2,f,g}^m$.

Going from Hybrid5$_{h_1,h_2,f,g}^m$ _to_ Hybrid6$_{h_1,h_2,f,g}^m$: In the final hybrid, Hybrid6$_{h_1,h_2,f,g}^m$, we use the perfect security of the one time pad to remove the dependency of C (and hence, of $\tilde{C}$) on m. This gives us the simulated view, independent of m.

Claim. Hybrid5$_{h_1,h_2,f,g}^m \equiv$ Hybrid6$_{h_1,h_2,f,g}^m$ by perfect security of One Time Pad encryption.

Proof. We begin by expressing the hybrid outputs as a deterministic function of the message and the ciphertext. Define function Q_3 as follows:
$Q_3(m, C)$:

- $\tilde{k_{a_1}}\|\tilde{k_{a_2}}\|\tilde{t_1}\|\tilde{t_2}\|\tilde{s} \leftarrow$ NMSim$_{h_1,h_2}$
- $w \in_R \{0,1\}^n$
- $(\tilde{w}, \tilde{C}) = (f(w), g(C))$
- If $\tilde{k_{a_1}}\|\tilde{k_{a_2}}\|\tilde{t_1}\|\tilde{t_2}\|\tilde{s} = same^*$
  • If $\tilde{w} = w$ and $\tilde{C} = C$ output m
  • else output $\perp$

$\text{Hybrid5}^m_{h_1,h_2,f,g}:$	$\text{Hybrid6}^m_{h_1,h_2,f,g}:$
1. $k \in_R \{0,1\}^l$	1. $k \in_R \{0,1\}^l$
2. $C = m \oplus k$	2. $C = 0 \oplus k$
3. $w \in_R \{0,1\}^n$	3. $w \in_R \{0,1\}^n$
4. $(\tilde{w}, \tilde{C}) = (f(w), g(C))$	4. $(\tilde{w}, \tilde{C}) = (f(w), g(C))$
5. $\tilde{k}_{a_1}\|\tilde{k}_{a_2}\|\tilde{t}_1\|\tilde{t}_2\|\tilde{s} \leftarrow \text{NMSim}_{h_1,h_2}$	5. $\tilde{k}_{a_1}\|\tilde{k}_{a_2}\|\tilde{t}_1\|\tilde{t}_2\|\tilde{s} \leftarrow \text{NMSim}_{h_1,h_2}$
6. If $\tilde{k}_{a_1}\|\tilde{k}_{a_2}\|\tilde{t}_1\|\tilde{t}_2\|\tilde{s} = same^*$	6. If $\tilde{k}_{a_1}\|\tilde{k}_{a_2}\|\tilde{t}_1\|\tilde{t}_2\|\tilde{s} = same^*$
• If $\tilde{w} = w$ and $\tilde{C} = C$ output m	• If $\tilde{w} = w$ and $\tilde{C} = C$ output m
• else output $\perp$	• else output $\perp$
7. else if $\tilde{k}_{a_1}\|\tilde{k}_{a_2}\|\tilde{t}_1\|\tilde{t}_2\|\tilde{s} = \perp$, output $\perp$	7. else if $\tilde{k}_{a_1}\|\tilde{k}_{a_2}\|\tilde{t}_1\|\tilde{t}_2\|\tilde{s} = \perp$, output $\perp$
8. else if $\text{Vrfy}_{\tilde{k}_{a_1}}(\tilde{w},\tilde{t}_1) = 1 \wedge \text{Vrfy}'_{\tilde{k}_{a_2}}(\tilde{C},\tilde{t}_2) = 1$ output $\tilde{C} \oplus \text{Ext}(\tilde{w};\tilde{s})$	8. else if $\text{Vrfy}_{\tilde{k}_{a_1}}(\tilde{w},\tilde{t}_1) = 1 \wedge \text{Vrfy}'_{\tilde{k}_{a_2}}(\tilde{C},\tilde{t}_2) = 1$ output $\tilde{C} \oplus \text{Ext}(\tilde{w};\tilde{s})$
9. else output $\perp$	9. else output $\perp$

- else if $\tilde{k}_{a_1}\|\tilde{k}_{a_2}\|\tilde{t}_1\|\tilde{t}_2\|\tilde{s} = \perp$, output $\perp$
- else If $\text{Vrfy}_{\tilde{k}_{a_1}}(\tilde{w},\tilde{t}_1) = 1$ and $\text{Vrfy}'_{\tilde{k}_{a_2}}(\tilde{C},\tilde{t}_2) = 1$ Output $\tilde{C} \oplus \text{Ext}(\tilde{w},\tilde{s})$
- else Output $\perp$.

Replace sequence of steps 3–9 with an output of $Q_3(m,C)$ in both the hybrids. By perfect security of OTP encryption, for any message m and a uniformly random key k

$$(m,(m \oplus k)) \equiv (m,(0 \oplus k))$$

$$Q_3(m,(m \oplus k)) \equiv Q_3(m,(0 \oplus k))$$

$$\text{Hybrid5}^m_{h_1,h_2,f,g} \equiv \text{Hybrid6}^m_{h_1,h_2,f,g}$$

Combining results of above claims in Sect. 4.3, we get

$$Tamper^m_{h_1,h_2,f,g} \approx_{\varepsilon_1} \text{Hybrid1}^m_{h_1,h_2,f,g} \approx_{\varepsilon_2+\varepsilon_3} \text{Hybrid2}^m_{h_1,h_2,f,g} \equiv \text{Hybrid3}^m_{h_1,h_2,f,g}$$

$$\text{Hybrid3}^m_{h_1,h_2,f,g} \approx_{\varepsilon_4} \text{Hybrid4}^m_{h_1,h_2,f,g} \equiv \text{Hybrid5}^m_{h_1,h_2,f,g}$$

$$\text{Hybrid5}^m_{h_1,h_2,f,g} \equiv \text{Hybrid6}^m_{h_1,h_2,f,g} \equiv Copy^m_{Sim_{h_1,h_2,f,g}}$$

$$\implies Tamper^m_{h_1,h_2,f,g} \approx_{\varepsilon_1+\varepsilon_2+\varepsilon_3+\varepsilon_4} Copy^m_{Sim_{h_1,h_2,f,g}}$$

4.4 Rate and Error Analysis

We now present the details of the rate of the code as well as the error it achieves. As we are encoding the seed of the extractor using the underlying non-malleable code, it is important that the strong extractor we use has short seed length. This is guaranteed by the following lemma.

Lemma 7 [18]. *For every constant $\nu > 0$ all integers $n \geq t$ and all $\epsilon \geq 0$, there is an explicit (efficient) (n,t,d,l,ϵ)–strong extractor with $l = (1 - \nu)t - \mathcal{O}(\log(n) + \log(\frac{1}{\epsilon}))$ and $d = \mathcal{O}(\log(n) + \log(\frac{1}{\epsilon}))$.*

Now, as we give some auxiliary information about the source, we require the security of the extractor to hold, even given this information. Hence, we use average case extractors, given in the following lemma.

Lemma 8 [12]. *For any $\mu > 0$, if* Ext *is a (worst case)$(n, t, d, l, \epsilon)-$strong extractor, then* Ext *is also an average-case $(n, t + \log(\frac{1}{\mu}), d, l, \epsilon + \mu)$ strong extractor.*

We now combine the Lemmata 7 and 8 to get an average case extractor with optimal seed length.

Corollary 1. *For any $\mu > 0$ and every constant $\nu > 0$ all integers $n \geq t$ and all $\epsilon \geq 0$, there is an explicit (efficient) $(n, t + \log(\frac{1}{\mu}), d, l, \epsilon + \mu)-$ average case strong extractor with $l = (1 - \nu)t - \mathcal{O}(\log(n) + \log(\frac{1}{\epsilon}))$ and $d = \mathcal{O}(\log(n) + \log(\frac{1}{\epsilon}))$.*

Now, we also encode the authentication keys and tags using the underlying non-malleable code. Hence, we require them to have short lengths. This is guaranteed by the following lemma.

Lemma 9 [13, Lemma 26]. *For any $n', \varepsilon_2 > 0$ there is an efficient ε_2-secure one time* MAC *with $\delta \leq (\log(n') + \log(\frac{1}{\varepsilon_2}))$, $\tau \leq 2\delta$, where τ, n', δ are key, message, tag length respectively.*

We refer the reader to [11] for a construction satisfying these parameters.

4.5 Setting Parameters

– Set all the error parameters $\epsilon, \mu, \epsilon_1 \epsilon_2, \epsilon_3 = 2^{-\lambda}$ and $\epsilon_4 = \epsilon + \mu$
– The codeword of the construction in Fig. 1 has four states: a two-split state NMC codeword(L, R), source(w), ciphertext(C). In order to estimate the rate we need to estimate the length of each of these states.
– Let l be the length of the message for construction in Fig. 1. As we are using the one-time pad encryption scheme, $|C| = l$.
– We now estimate the length of the source - n. Although the source has full entropy (i.e., uniformly random), there is some auxiliary information revealed about it. (For details, see the proof of statistical closeness of Hybrid$3_{h_1, h_2, f, g}^m$ and Hybrid$4_{h_1, h_2, f, g}^m$). Specifically, the highest entropy loss occurs in Case 2b of the proof and this is the quantity that we need to upper-bound. This auxiliary information consists of an indicator bit, the key, tag of cipher text, and an extractor output. Of these, we know that the extractor output is of length l bits and the indicator is just one bit. So we need to estimate the length of the authentication key, tag pair of the cipher text.
– τ_2, δ_2 - length of key, tag to authenticate cipher text (C) of length l.

- Applying Lemma 9 with $n' = l, \epsilon_3 = 2^{-\lambda}$ gives $\delta_2 \leq (\log(l) + \lambda)$ and $\tau_2 \leq 2\delta_2$. Therefore

$$\tau_2 + \delta_2 \leq 3(\log(l) + \lambda) \tag{9}$$

- By Lemma 5, the average entropy of the source given auxiliary information is at least $n - \underbrace{(1 + \tau_2 + \delta_2 + l)}_{length\ of\ aux\ info}$ which is at least $n - (1 + 3\log(l) + 3\lambda + l)$.

- Also we need to make sure that the average entropy we are left with is at least the entropy threshold $(t + \log(\frac{1}{\mu}))$. So we need to estimate t

  - By Corollary 1, we have $t = (l + \mathcal{O}(\log(n) + \log(\frac{1}{\epsilon})))\frac{1}{1-\nu}$

  - It is necessary and sufficient if $n - (1 + 3\log(l) + 3\lambda + l) > t + \log(\frac{1}{\mu})$

$$\Rightarrow n \geq (1 + \frac{1}{1-\nu})l + 3\log(l) + 4(\lambda) + \mathcal{O}(\log(n) + \lambda)$$

As ν can be very small constant thats close to 0, fixing $n = (2 + \zeta)l + \mathcal{O}(\log(l) + \lambda)$ for some constant ζ close to 0, would satisfy the above equation.

We now estimate the length of the codeword of the underlying NMC. We encode an authentication key, tag pair of ciphertext, authentication key, tag pair of the source, extractor seed. The length of the authentication key, tag pair of ciphertext is given in Eq. 9. We estimate the lengths of the remaining variables below.

- d - seed length of the extractor.

  - From Corollary 1. We have $d = \mathcal{O}(\log(n) + \log(\frac{1}{\epsilon}))$.

  - Substituting $n = (2 + \zeta)l + \mathcal{O}(\log(l) + \lambda)$ and $\epsilon = 2^{-\lambda}$ gives

$$d = \mathcal{O}(\log((2+\zeta)l + \mathcal{O}(\log(l)+\lambda)) + \lambda) = \mathcal{O}(\log(l+\lambda) + \lambda) = \mathcal{O}(\log(l) + \lambda) \tag{10}$$

- τ_1, δ_1 - length of key, tag to authenticate source (W) of length n.

  - Applying Lemma 9 with $n' = n, \epsilon_2 = 2^{-\lambda}$ gives $\delta_1 \leq (\log(n) + \lambda)$ and $\tau_1 \leq 2\delta_1$. Therefore

$$\tau_1 + \delta_1 \leq 3(\log(n) + \lambda) \tag{11}$$

- $\alpha = \tau_1 + \tau_2 + \delta_1 + \delta_2 + d$ - length of message that we are encoding using NMC in [20].

  - By Eqs. 9, 10, 11

$$\alpha \leq (c+1)(\log(l) + \lambda) + 3(\log(l) + \lambda) + 3(\log(n) + \lambda)$$

By the same argument as in Eq. 10

$$\alpha = \mathcal{O}(\log(l) + \lambda) \tag{12}$$

- 2β - codeword length of NMC in [20].

- By Eq. 1, we have $\beta = \mathcal{O}(\alpha \log(\alpha))$
  By Eq. 12, we have

$$\alpha \log(\alpha) = \mathcal{O}((\log(l)+\lambda).\log(\log(l)+\lambda)) = \mathcal{O}((\log(l))^2 + \lambda.\log(\lambda) + 2.\lambda.\log(l))) \tag{13}$$

Therefore,

$$\beta = \mathcal{O}((\log(l))^2 + \lambda \log(\lambda) + 2\lambda \log(l))) \tag{14}$$

- Now we have upper bound on the length of all states of the codeword in terms of l and λ.

4.6   Rate

Let R denote the rate of proposed construction.

$$R = \frac{l}{2\beta + n + l}$$

Substituting n and β (by Eq. 14)

$$= \frac{l}{\mathcal{O}((\log(l))^2 + \lambda.\log(\lambda) + 2.\lambda.\log(l)) + (2+\zeta)l + \mathcal{O}(\log(l)+\lambda) + l}$$

For some constant c

$$\geq \frac{l}{c((\log(l))^2 + \lambda\log(\lambda) + 2\lambda\log(l)) + (2+\zeta)l + \mathcal{O}(\log(l)+\lambda) + l}$$

$$= \frac{1}{\dfrac{c((\log(l))^2 + \lambda\log(\lambda) + 2\lambda\log(l)) + (2+\zeta)l + \mathcal{O}(\log(l)+\lambda) + l}{l}}$$

For large l

$$= \frac{1}{\dfrac{c(\lambda\log(\lambda) + 2\lambda\log(l)) + \mathcal{O}(\lambda)}{l} + 3 + \zeta}$$

For $\lambda = o\left(\dfrac{l}{\log l}\right)$

$$= \frac{1}{3+\zeta}$$

Construction in Fig. 1 achieves rate that is at least $\dfrac{1}{3+\zeta}$, for some ζ very close to 0.

4.7   Error

Error of the proposed construction is $\varepsilon_1 + \varepsilon_2 + \varepsilon_3 + \varepsilon_4 = 5(2^{-\lambda})$. Because $\lambda = o\left(\dfrac{l}{\log l}\right)$ the error will be at least $2^{-\frac{l}{\log l}}$. For any $\rho > 0$, fixing $\lambda = \dfrac{l}{\log^{\rho+1} l}$, the error would be at most $5.2^{-\frac{l}{\log^{\rho+1} l}}$. Setting $\kappa = \lambda - \log 5$ the error would be $2^{-\kappa} = 2^{-\Omega(l/\log^{\rho+1} l)}$.

5   Conclusion

In this work, we constructed an efficient non-malleable code in the t-split-state model, for $t = 4$, that achieves a constant rate of $\frac{1}{3+\zeta}$, for any constant $\zeta > 0$ and error $2^{-\Omega(\ell/\log^{c+1}\ell)}$, where ℓ is the length of the message and $c > 0$ is a constant. This improves the constant-rate constructions of Cheraghchi and Guruswami [7] (by bringing down the number of states from n to 4) and Chattopadhyay and Zuckerman [5] (by making the "constant" in the rate explicit and by bringing down the number of states from 10 to 4). We stress that, as is the case with all information-theoretic primitives, optimizing constant factors in achieving key parameters, such as, in this case, the rate/number of states etc., is both crucial and challenging.

While we obtain our specific parameters by using the 2 state non-malleable code construction due to [20], our techniques are general and uses the underlying NMC in a black-box. Hence, our construction can be generalized to obtain a $(t + 2)$-state NMC from any t-state NMC, leading to interesting trade-offs between the rate vs the number of states depending on the parameters of underlying NMC (Appendix A).

An interesting open problem would be to see if our techniques can be used to improve the rate of non-malleable codes with special features such as "locality" [4,9,10], security against continuous tampering [16,19], and leakage-resilience [2].

Acknowledgments. We thank Yevgeniy Dodis for insightful comments related to the generalization in Appendix A We also thank the anonymous referees for several helpful comments. Research of the first author was supported, in part, by Department of Science and Technology Inspire Faculty Award.

A   Appendix I

A.1   Building Constant Rate $(t + 2)$ - State NMC from Any t-state NMC with Inverse Polynomial Rate

Theorem 2. *Let* NMEnc, NMDec *be an* ε_1-*secure* t-*split state non-malleable code with rate* $\omega\left(\dfrac{1}{\alpha^a}\right)$, *for some constant* a *and message length* α. *The algorithms* (Tag, Vrfy), (Tag′, Vrfy′), Ext *be as a specified in Sect. 4.1.*

For any constant $\zeta > 0$, *messages of length* l, *any* κ *such that* $\kappa = o\left(\dfrac{l}{l^{a+1}}\right)$, *the* $(t + 2)$-*split state construction in figure below has block length* $(3 + \zeta)l + o(l)$, *there by achieves asymptotic rate* $\dfrac{1}{3 + \zeta}$ *and error* $2^{-\kappa}$.

Enc(m) :	Dec($L_1, L_2, \cdots, L_t, w, C$) :
$- w \in_R \{0,1\}^n, \ s \in_R \{0,1\}^d$ $- k_{a_1} \in_R \{0,1\}^{\tau_1}, k_{a_2} \in_R \{0,1\}^{\tau_2}$ $- k = \text{Ext}(w,s)$ $- C = m \oplus k$ $- t_1 = \text{Tag}_{k_{a_1}}(w), \ t_2 = \text{Tag}'_{k_{a_2}}(C)$ $- (L_1, L_2, \cdots, L_t) =$ $\quad \text{NMEnc}(k_{a_1}\|k_{a_2}\|t_1\|t_2\|s)$ $- \text{Output} :(L_1, L_2, \cdots, L_t, w, C)$	$- k_{a_1}\|k_{a_2}\|t_1\|t_2\|s =$ $\quad \text{NMDec}(L_1, L_2, \cdots, L_t)$ $- \text{If } k_{a_1}\|k_{a_2}\|t_1\|t_2\|s = \perp \text{ output } \perp$ $- \text{else if } \text{Vrfy}_{k_{a_1}}(w, t_1) = 1$ $\quad \wedge \text{Vrfy}'_{k_{a_2}}(C, t_2) = 1$ $\quad \text{output } C \oplus \text{Ext}(w, s)$ $- \text{else output } \perp$

Proof. The construction in figure above is a secure $(t+2)$- state NMC. The security proof is similar to the proof in Sect. 4.3.

Set parameters $\kappa, \epsilon, \mu, \epsilon_1 \epsilon_2, \epsilon_3, \epsilon_4, n, \alpha$ in terms of l, λ as in Sect. 4.5.

- Let β be length of t-state codeword of (NMEnc, NMDec) for messages of length α.
- $\beta = O(\alpha^{a+1})$
- The rate r of the $(t+2)-$state NMC (Enc, Dec) is

$$r = \frac{l}{\beta + n + l}$$

Substituting n and β

$$= \frac{l}{\mathcal{O}(\alpha^{a+1}) + (2+\zeta)l + \mathcal{O}(\log(l)+\lambda) + l}$$

Substituting $\alpha = \mathcal{O}(\log(l) + \lambda)$

$$= \frac{l}{\mathcal{O}((\log(l)+\lambda)^{a+1}) + (2+\zeta)l + \mathcal{O}(\log(l)+\lambda) + l}$$

For some constant c

$$\geq \frac{1}{\dfrac{c((\log(l)+\lambda)^{a+1}) + (2+\zeta)l + \mathcal{O}(\log(l)+\lambda) + l}{l}}$$

For large l

$$= \frac{1}{\dfrac{c((\log(l)+\lambda)^{a+1}) + \mathcal{O}(\lambda)}{l} + 3 + \zeta}$$

For $\lambda = o\left(\dfrac{l}{l^{a+1}}\right)$ $\qquad\qquad r = \dfrac{1}{3+\zeta}$

Error analysis is similar to analysis in Sect. 4.7.

B Appendix II

Lemma 10. If $\alpha = \Omega(\frac{\beta}{\log(\beta)})$, then $\beta = \mathcal{O}(\alpha.\log(\alpha))$

Proof. By the definition of Ω, $\exists$ a constant $c > 0$ such that for large α, β

$$0 \leq c.\frac{\beta}{\log(\beta)} \leq \alpha \tag{15}$$

$$c\beta \leq \alpha.\log(\beta)$$

$$c\beta \leq \alpha\sqrt{\beta}$$

If $c \geq 1$

$$\sqrt{\beta} \leq \alpha$$

$$\log(\beta) \leq 2.\log(\alpha)$$

Multiplying with Eq. 15, we get

$$0 \leq \frac{c}{2}.\beta \leq \alpha \log(\alpha) \tag{16}$$

If $c < 1$, let $c' = \frac{1}{c}$

$$\sqrt{\beta} \leq c'.\alpha$$

$$\log(\beta) \leq 2(\log(c') + \log(\alpha))$$

$$\log(\beta) \leq 4.\log(\alpha)$$

Multiplying with Eq. 15

$$0 \leq \frac{c}{4}.\beta \leq \alpha \log(\alpha) \tag{17}$$

In either case, for large α, β, for a constant $\frac{c}{4} > 0$

$$0 \leq \frac{c}{4}.\beta \leq \alpha \log(\alpha)$$

$$\implies \alpha \log(\alpha) = \Omega(\beta)$$

$$\implies \beta = \mathcal{O}(\alpha \log(\alpha))$$

References

1. Aggarwal, D., Agrawal, S., Gupta, D., Maji, H.K., Pandey, O., Prabhakaran, M.: Optimal computational split-state non-malleable codes. In: Kushilevitz, E., Malkin, T. (eds.) TCC 2016. LNCS, vol. 9563, pp. 393–417. Springer, Heidelberg (2016). https://doi.org/10.1007/978-3-662-49099-0_15
2. Aggarwal, D., Dodis, Y., Kazana, T., Obremski, M.: Non-malleable reductions and applications. In: Proceedings of the Forty-Seventh Annual ACM on Symposium on Theory of Computing, STOC 2015, Portland, OR, USA, 14–17 June 2015, pp. 459–468 (2015)

3. Aggarwal, D., Dodis, Y., Lovett, S.: Non-malleable codes from additive combinatorics. In: Symposium on Theory of Computing, STOC 2014, New York, NY, USA, 31 May–03 June 2014, pp. 774–783 (2014)

4. Chandran, N., Kanukurthi, B., Raghuraman, S.: Information-theoretic local nonmalleable codes and their applications. In: Kushilevitz, E., Malkin, T. (eds.) TCC 2016. LNCS, vol. 9563, pp. 367–392. Springer, Heidelberg (2016). https://doi.org/10.1007/978-3-662-49099-0_14

5. Chattopadhyay, E., Zuckerman, D.: Non-malleable codes against constant splitstate tampering. In: 55th IEEE Annual Symposium on Foundations of Computer Science, FOCS 2014, Philadelphia, PA, USA, 18–21 October 2014, pp. 306–315 (2014)

6. Cheraghchi, M., Guruswami, V.: Capacity of non-malleable codes. In: Innovations in Theoretical Computer Science, ITCS 2014, Princeton, NJ, USA, 12–14 January 2014, pp. 155–168 (2014)

7. Cheraghchi, M., Guruswami, V.: Non-malleable coding against bit-wise and splitstate tampering. In: Lindell, Y. (ed.) TCC 2014. LNCS, vol. 8349, pp. 440–464. Springer, Heidelberg (2014). https://doi.org/10.1007/978-3-642-54242-8_19

8. Coretti, S., Maurer, U., Tackmann, B., Venturi, D.: From single-bit to multi-bit public-key encryption via non-malleable codes. IACR Cryptology ePrint Archive 2014:324 (2014)

9. Dachman-Soled, D., Kulkarni, M., Shahverdi, A.: Tight upper and lower bounds for leakage-resilient, locally decodable and updatable non-malleable codes. IACR Cryptology ePrint Archive 2017:15 (2017)

10. Dachman-Soled, D., Liu, F., Shi, E., Zhou, H.: Locally decodable and updatable non-malleable codes and their applications. IACR Cryptology ePrint Archive 2014:663 (2014)

11. Dodis, Y., Kanukurthi, B., Katz, J., Reyzin, L., Smith, A.: Robust fuzzy extractors and authenticated key agreement from close secrets. IEEE Trans. Inf. Theory **58**(9), 6207–6222 (2012)

12. Dodis, Y., Ostrovsky, R., Reyzin, L., Smith, A.: Fuzzy extractors: how to generate strong keys from biometrics and other noisy data. SIAM J. Comput. **38**(1), 97–139 (2008). arXiv:cs/0602007

13. Dodis, Y., Wichs, D.: Non-malleable extractors and symmetric key cryptography from weak secrets. In: Proceedings of the Forty-First Annual ACM Symposium on Theory of Computing, Bethesda, Maryland, 31 May–2 June 2009, pp. 601–610 (2009)

14. Dziembowski, S., Kazana, T., Obremski, M.: Non-malleable codes from twosource extractors. In: Canetti, R., Garay, J.A. (eds.) CRYPTO 2013. LNCS, vol. 8043, pp. 239–257. Springer, Heidelberg (2013). https://doi.org/10.1007/978-3-642-40084-1_14

15. Dziembowski, S., Pietrzak, K., Wichs, D.: Non-malleable codes. In: Proceedings of the Innovations in Computer Science - ICS 2010, Tsinghua University, Beijing, China, 5–7 January 2010, pp. 434–452 (2010)

16. Faust, S., Mukherjee, P., Nielsen, J.B., Venturi, D.: Continuous non-malleable codes. In: Lindell, Y. (ed.) TCC 2014. LNCS, vol. 8349, pp. 465–488. Springer, Heidelberg (2014). https://doi.org/10.1007/978-3-642-54242-8_20

17. Goyal, V., Pandey, O., Richelson, S.: Textbook non-malleable commitments. In: Proceedings of the 48th Annual ACM SIGACT Symposium on Theory of Computing, STOC 2016, Cambridge, MA, USA, 18–21 June 2016, pp. 1128–1141 (2016)

18. Guruswami, V., Umans, C., Vadhan, S.P.: Unbalanced expanders and randomness extractors from Parvaresh-Vardy codes. In: IEEE Conference on Computational Complexity, pp. 96–108 (2007)
19. Jafargholi, Z., Wichs, D.: Tamper detection and continuous non-malleable codes. In: Dodis, Y., Nielsen, J.B. (eds.) TCC 2015. LNCS, vol. 9014, pp. 451–480. Springer, Heidelberg (2015). https://doi.org/10.1007/978-3-662-46494-6_19
20. Li, X.: Improved non-malleable extractors, non-malleable codes and independent source extractors. In: Symposium on Theory of Computing, STOC 2017, Montreal, Canada, 19–23 June 2017 (2017)
21. Liu, F., Lysyanskaya, A.: Tamper and leakage resilience in the split-state model. IACR Cryptology ePrint Archive 2012:297 (2012)
22. Nisan, N., Zuckerman, D.: Randomness is linear in space. J. Comput. Syst. Sci. 52(1), 43–53 (1996)

Secret Sharing

Evolving Secret Sharing: Dynamic Thresholds and Robustness

Ilan Komargodski[1]([⊠]) and Anat Paskin-Cherniavsky[2]

[1] Cornell Tech, New York, USA
komargodski@cornell.edu
[2] Department of Computer Science, Ariel University, Ariel, Israel
anatpc@ariel.ac.il

Abstract. Threshold secret sharing schemes enable a dealer to share a secret among n parties such that only subsets of parties of cardinality at least $k = k(n)$ can reconstruct the secret. Komargodski, Naor and Yogev (TCC 2016-B) proposed an efficient scheme for sharing a secret among an *unbounded* number of parties such that only subsets of k parties can recover the secret, where k is any fixed constant. This access structure is known as k-threshold. They left open the possibility of an efficient scheme for the *dynamic threshold* access structure, in which the qualified sets are of increasing size as the number of parties increases. We resolve this open problem and present a construction in which the share size of the t-th party is $O(t^4 \cdot \log t)$ bits.

Furthermore, we show how to generically translate any scheme for k-threshold into a scheme which is *robust*, where a shared secret can be recovered even if some parties hand-in incorrect shares. This answers another open problem of Komargodski et al. Our construction is based on the construction of robust (classical) secret sharing schemes of Cramer et al. (EUROCRYPT 2008) using algebraic manipulation detection codes.

1 Introduction

Secret sharing schemes, introduced by Shamir [17] and Blakley [5], are methods that enable a dealer, that holds a secret piece of information, to distribute this secret among n parties such that predefined qualified subsets can reconstruct the secret, while others learn nothing about it. The monotone collection of qualified subsets is known as an *access structure*. Secret sharing schemes are a basic primitive and have found numerous applications in cryptography and distributed computing; see the extensive survey of Beimel [2] and the book of Cramer et al. [9]. Any access structure admits a secret sharing scheme but the share size could be as large as $O(2^n)$, the maximal number of possible qualified sets [12].

This paper incorporates the manuscript of Paskin-Cherniavsky [15].

I. Komargodski—Supported in part by Elaine Shi's Packard Foundation Fellowship. Part of this work done while being a Ph.D student at the Weizmann Institute of Science, supported in part by grants from the Israel Science Foundation and by a Levzion Fellowship.

Y. Kalai and L. Reyzin (Eds.): TCC 2017, Part II, LNCS 10678, pp. 379–393, 2017.
https://doi.org/10.1007/978-3-319-70503-3_12

A significant goal in secret sharing is thus to minimize the share size, namely, the amount of information distributed to the parties.[1]

Almost all known secret sharing schemes assume that the number of parties n and the access structure are known in advance. However, in many scenarios these assumptions have a cost: First, the eventual set might turn out to be much smaller than n. Second, the access structure may change with time, forcing the dealer to re-share its secret. In a recent work, Komargodski et al. [14] initiated the study of secret sharing schemes for the case where the set of parties is *not* known in advanced and could potentially be infinite (or even more generally the access structure may change). Specifically, parties arrive one by one and whenever a party arrives there is no communication to the parties that have already received shares, i.e. the dealer distributes a share only to the new party. In the most general case, a qualified subset is revealed to the dealer only when the last party in that subset arrives. In special cases, the dealer knows the access structure to begin with, just does not have an upper bound on the number of parties. We assume that the changes to the access structure are monotone, namely, parties are only added and qualified sets remain qualified as more and more parties join. We call this an evolving access structure.

When designing a secret sharing scheme for an evolving access structure, the goal is to minimize the share size of the tth party arriving as a function of t. Komargodski et al. showed that *any* evolving access structure can be realized albeit the share size of the tth party is 2^{t-1}. Then, they consider the evolving k-threshold access structure for $k \in \mathbb{N}$, where at any point in time any k parties can reconstruct the secret but no $k-1$ parties can learn anything about the secret and showed an efficient scheme for it in which the share size of the tth party is bounded by roughly $k \cdot \log t$ bits (see Theorem 2.5 for a precise statement). Their scheme was shown to be optimal in terms of share size for $k = 2$.

One of the main open problems left open by their work was to construct an efficient secret sharing scheme for the *evolving majority* access structure in which qualified subsets are the ones which form a *majority* of the present parties at *some* point in time. More precisely, a set of k parties with indices $i_1 < \ldots < i_k$ is qualified if and only if there exists an index $j \in [k]$ such that

$$|\{i_1, \ldots, i_j\}| \geq \frac{1}{2} \cdot i_j.$$

The $1/2$ threshold above is arbitrary and could be replaced with any other constant in $(0, 1)$ or even with a sequence of growing threshold $k_1 \leq k_2 \leq \ldots$ such that the qualified sets at time t are those sets of cardinality at least k_t. We resolve this open problem and construct a secret sharing scheme for this evolving majority access structure in which the share size of the tth party is $O(t^4 \cdot \log t)$ bits. Our scheme is linear in the sense that reconstruction is done by applying a linear function on the shares [1, Sect. 4.1]. This property is desirable since it is useful in applications such as secure multiparty computation [3,8].

---

[1] Whether having exponentially large shares is necessary is a major open problem. The best lower bound known to date is (almost) linear by Csirmaz [11].

Another question left open in [14] was to construct *robust* secret sharing schemes for evolving access structures. In the setting described so far, secret sharing schemes assume the parties are honest and upon reconstruction provide their *correct* shares. However, in most cryptographic settings it is often the case that we need to handle malicious parties that manipulate their shares. For this, the strengthened notion of *robust* secret sharing was proposed by Ben-Or and Rabin [16]. This notion requires that the shared secret can be recovered even if some parties hand-in incorrect shares.

In the original construction of Ben-Or and Rabin each party authenticates the share of every other party using a MAC having unforgeability security $2^{-\lambda}$ (the reconstruction procedure checks that the majority of the tags are verified). When the number of parties is unbounded, it is unclear how to implement such a solution as the first party has to authenticate all future parties (which is an unbounded number). Several follow-up constructions of robust secret sharing schemes with smaller shares [4,6], rely on the same high-level idea of parties authenticating share of other parties (in a pairwise manner) and thus seem unsuitable for our setting.

We observe that a different line of works on robust secret sharing, ones based on algebraic manipulation detection (AMD) codes [7,10] can be adapted to the evolving setting. We thus present an efficient robust secret sharing scheme for the evolving k-threshold access structure such that as long as an adversary corrupts at most $k-1$ parties, from any set of $2k-1$ parties, one can recover the secret. The failure probability of our reconstruction procedure is $2^{-\lambda}$ and the share size is bounded by roughly $k \cdot \log t + \lambda$ bits.

2   Preliminaries

For an integer $n \in \mathbb{N}$ we denote by $[n]$ the set $\{1, \ldots, n\}$. We denote by $\log$ the base 2 logarithm and assume that $\log 0 = -\infty$. For a set $\mathcal{X}$ we denote by $x \leftarrow \mathcal{X}$ the process of sampling a value x from the uniform distribution over $\mathcal{X}$. A function $\mathsf{neg} \colon \mathbb{N} \to \mathbb{R}^+$ is *negligible* if for every constant $c > 0$ there exists an integer N_c such that $\mathsf{neg}(\lambda) < \lambda^{-c}$ for all $\lambda > N_c$.

We start by briefly recalling the standard setting of (perfect) secret sharing. Let $\mathcal{P}_n = \{1, \ldots, n\}$ be a set of n parties. A collection of subsets $\mathcal{A} \subseteq 2^{\mathcal{P}_n}$ is *monotone* if for every $B \in \mathcal{A}$, and $B \subseteq C$ it holds that $C \in \mathcal{A}$.

Definition 2.1 (Access structure). *An* access structure $\mathcal{A} \subseteq 2^{\mathcal{P}_n}$ *is a monotone collection of subsets. Subsets in* $\mathcal{A}$ *are called* qualified *and subsets not in* $\mathcal{A}$ *are called* unqualified.

A secret sharing scheme involves a dealer who has a secret, a set of n parties, and an access structure $\mathcal{A}$. A secret sharing scheme for $\mathcal{A}$ is a method by which the dealer distributes shares to the parties such that any subset in $\mathcal{A}$ can reconstruct the secret from its shares, while any subset not in $\mathcal{A}$ cannot reveal any information on the secret.

Definition 2.2. *A secret sharing scheme $\mathcal{S}$ for an access structure $\mathcal{A}$ consists of a pair of algorithms* (SHARE, RECON). SHARE *is a probabilistic procedure that gets as input a secret s (from a domain of secrets S such that $|S| \geq 2$) and a number n, and generates n shares $\Pi_1^{(s)}, \ldots, \Pi_n^{(s)}$.* RECON *is a deterministic procedure that gets as input the shares of a subset B and outputs a string. The requirements are:*

1. **Correctness:** *For every secret $s \in S$ and every qualified set $B \in \mathcal{A}$, it holds that*

$$\Pr[\mathsf{RECON}(\{\Pi_i^{(s)}\}_{i \in B}, B) = s] = 1,$$

   where the probability is over the randomness of the sharing procedure.
2. **Security:** *For every unqualified set $B \notin \mathcal{A}$ and every two different secrets $s_1, s_2 \in S$, it holds that the distributions $(\{\Pi_i^{(s_1)}\}_{i \in B})$ and $(\{\Pi_i^{(s_2)}\}_{i \in B})$ are identical.*

The *share size* of a scheme $\mathcal{S}$, denoted by $\mathsf{SS}(\mathcal{S})$, is the maximum number of bits each party holds in the worst case over all parties and all secrets. For an access structure $\mathcal{A}$ we denote by $\mathsf{SS}(\mathcal{A})$ the minimum of $\mathsf{SS}(\mathcal{S})$ over all schemes $\mathcal{S}$ for the access structure $\mathcal{A}$.

Linear schemes. An important subclass of secret sharing schemes are *linear* schemes. In such a scheme the secret is viewed as an element of a finite field, and the shares are obtained by applying a linear mapping to the secret and several independent random field elements. Equivalently, a linear scheme is defined by requiring that each qualified set reconstructs the secret by applying a linear function to its shares [1, Sect. 4.1]. We denote by $\mathsf{lin\text{-}SS}(\mathcal{A})$ the minimum value of $\mathsf{SS}(\mathcal{S})$ over all *linear* schemes $\mathcal{S}$ for the access structure $\mathcal{A}$.

2.1 Evolving Secret Sharing

We recall the notion of an evolving access structure and the corresponding notion of secret sharing defined by [14]. Roughly speaking, these definitions capture the scenario in which the access structure is *not* fully known to the sharing procedure at once but is rather revealed in an online manner. Concretely, parties arrive one by one and, in the most general case, a qualified subset is revealed only when all parties in that subset are present (in special cases the access structure is known to begin with, but there is no upper bound on the number of parties). To make sense of sharing a secret with respect to such a sequence of access structures, we require that the changes to the access structure are monotone, namely, parties are only added and qualified sets remain qualified.

Definition 2.3 (Evolving access structure). *An evolving access structures $\mathcal{A} \subseteq 2^{\mathbb{N}}$ is a (possibly infinite) monotone collection of subsets of the natural numbers such that for any $t \in \mathbb{N}$, the collection of subsets $\mathcal{A}_t \triangleq \mathcal{A} \cap [t]$ is an access structure (as in Definition 2.1).*

Below we give a generalization of the definition of a standard secret sharing scheme (see Definition 2.2) to apply for evolving access structures as in [14]. Intuitively, in this setting, at any point $t \in \mathbb{N}$ in time, there is an access structure $\mathcal{A}_t$ which defines the qualifies and unqualified subsets of parties.

Definition 2.4 (Secret sharing for evolving access structures). *Let* $\mathcal{A} = \{\mathcal{A}_t\}_{t \in \mathbb{N}}$ *be an evolving access structure. Let* S *be a domain of secrets, where* $|S| \geq 2$. *A secret sharing scheme* $\mathcal{S}$ *for* $\mathcal{A}$ *and* S *consists of a pair of algorithms* (SHARE, RECON). *The probabilistic sharing procedure* SHARE *and the deterministic reconstruction procedure* RECON *satisfy the following requirements:*

1. SHARE$(s, \{\Pi_1^{(s)}, \ldots, \Pi_{t-1}^{(s)}\})$ *gets as input a secret* $s \in S$ *and the secret shares of parties* $1, \ldots, t-1$. *It outputs a share for the* t^{th} *party. For* $t \in \mathbb{N}$ *and secret shares* $\Pi_1^{(s)}, \ldots, \Pi_{t-1}^{(s)}$ *generated for parties* $\{1, \ldots, t-1\}$, *respectively, we let*

$$\Pi_t^{(s)} \leftarrow \text{SHARE}(s, \{\Pi_1^{(s)}, \ldots, \Pi_{t-1}^{(s)}\})$$

   be the secret share of party t.

   We abuse notation and sometimes denote by $\Pi_t^{(s)}$ *the random variable that corresponds to the secret share of party* t *generated as above.*

2. *Correctness: For every secret* $s \in S$ *and every* $t \in \mathbb{N}$, *every qualified subset in* $\mathcal{A}_t$ *can reconstruct the secret. That is, for* $s \in S$, $t \in \mathbb{N}$, *and* $B \in \mathcal{A}_t$, *it holds that*

$$\Pr\left[\text{RECON}(\{\Pi_i^{(s)}\}_{i \in B}, B) = s\right] = 1,$$

   where the probability is over the randomness of the sharing procedure.

3. *Secrecy: For every* $t \in \mathbb{N}$, *every unqualified subset* $B \notin \mathcal{A}_t$, *and every two secret* $s_1, s_2 \in S$, *the distribution of the secret shares of parties in* B *generated with secret* s_1 *and the distribution of the shares of parties in* B *generated with secret* s_2 *are identical. Namely, the distributions* $(\{\Pi_i^{(s_1)}\}_{i \in B})$ *and* $(\{\Pi_i^{(s_2)}\}_{i \in B})$ *are identical.*

The *share size* of the tth party in a scheme for an evolving access structure is $\max|\Pi_t|$, namely the number of bits party t holds in the worst case over all secrets and previous assignments.[2]

In [14] it was shown how to construct a secret sharing scheme for any evolving access structure. This scheme results, for party t, with a share of size exponential in t. They further showed that in many special cases one can do much better. For example, in the evolving k-threshold access structure which contains all subsets of size k (where k is known), they gave a scheme in which the share size depends logarithmically on t.

---

[2] This means that the share size is bounded, which is almost always the case. An exception is the scheme (for rational secret sharing) of Kol and Naor [13] in which the share size does not have a fixed upper bound.

Theorem 2.5 [14]. *There is a secret sharing scheme for sharing a 1-bit secret for any evolving access structure in which for every $t \in \mathbb{N}$ the share size of the tth party is 2^{t-1}.*

For the special case of the evolving k-threshold access structure for a fixed $k \in \mathbb{N}$, there is a secret sharing scheme for sharing an ℓ-bit secret such that for every $t \in \mathbb{N}$ the share size of the tth party is $(k-1) \cdot \log t + \mathsf{poly}(k, \ell) \cdot o(\log t)$.

On choosing the access structure adaptively. One can also consider a stronger definition in which $\mathcal{A}_t$ is chosen at time t (rather than ahead of time) as long as the sequence of access structures $\mathcal{A} = \{\mathcal{A}_1, \ldots, \mathcal{A}_t\}$ is evolving. In this variant, the SHARE and RECON procedures get the access structure $\mathcal{A}_t$ as an additional parameter. An illustrative example where $\mathcal{A}_t$ is known ahead of time is the evolving k-threshold access structure mentioned above. (In this case k is fixed and is independent of t.) We will consider (in Sect. 3) a natural generalization in which there is a sequence of growing thresholds $k_1 < k_2 \ldots$ that say how many parties should be present as a function of the indices of the present parties themselves. This sequence of thresholds does not have to be known in advance.

2.2 Algebraic Manipulation Detection Codes

In our robust evolving secret sharing scheme we will use algebraic manipulation codes [10]. Originally, they were used to transform standard secret sharing schemes into robust ones.

Definition 2.6. *An (S, G, δ)-AMD code is a probabilistic encoding map $E \colon \mathcal{S} \to \mathcal{G}$ for a set $\mathcal{S}$ of size S and a group $\mathcal{G}$ of size G together with a deterministic decoding function $D \colon \mathbb{Z}_G \to [S] \cup \{\bot\}$ such that $D(E(s)) = s$ with probability 1 for every $s \in [S]$. Furthermore, for any $s \in [S]$ and $\Delta \in \mathbb{Z}_G$ it holds that*

$$\Pr_E[D(E(s) + \Delta) \notin \{s, \bot\}] \leq \delta.$$

The AMD code is called systematic *if $\mathcal{S}$ is a group, the encoding is of the form $E \colon \mathcal{S} \to \mathcal{S} \times \mathcal{G}_1 \times \mathcal{G}_2$ and $E(s)$ has the form $(s, x, f(x, s))$ for some function f and $x \in_R \mathcal{G}_1$. The decoding function of a systematic AMD code is given by $D(s', x', \sigma') = s'$ if $\sigma' = f(s', x')$ and $\bot$ otherwise.*

Theorem 2.7 [10]. *Let $\mathbb{F}$ be a field of size q and characteristic p, and let d be an integer such that $d + 2$ is not divisible by p. There exists a construction of a systematic $(q^d, q^{d+2}, (d+1)/q)$-AMD code. The encoding function maps $\mathbb{F}^d$ to $\mathbb{F}^d \times \mathbb{F} \times \mathbb{F}$.*

To achieve error parameter γ, and input domain S we will instantiate the above scheme with $\mathcal{G} = \mathbb{F}_2^t, d = 1$ where $t = \log S + \gamma + O(1)$. We refer to this construction as $\mathsf{AMD}_{S,\gamma}$.

3   A Scheme for Dynamic Threshold

In this section we present a secret sharing scheme for the evolving dynamic threshold access structure. This access structure is parametrized by a sequence of threshold values $k_1 \leq k_2 \leq \ldots$ such that at time t the qualified sets are those of cardinality at least k_t. The condition that $k_t \leq k_{t+1}$ is necessary for the monotonicity of the sequence of access structures, namely for the sequence of access structures to be a valid evolving structure.

Definition 3.1 (Dynamic threshold). *The dynamic threshold access structure is parametrized by a (possibly infinite) sequence of number $k_1 \leq k_2 \leq \ldots$. For any $t \in \mathbb{N}$, the set $\mathcal{A}_t$ of qualified sets at time t contains all those sets of cardinality at least k_t.*

Of particular interest is the following special case of dynamic threshold access structures in which the threshold at any point in time is a fixed function. Specifically, the function that we focus on is the one in which in time t the qualified sets are those of cardinality at least $\gamma \cdot t$ for fixed $\gamma \in (0,1)$.

Definition 3.2 (γ-dynamic threshold). *For a parameter $\gamma \in (0,1)$, the γ-dynamic threshold access structure is the above dynamic threshold access structures with sequence of numbers $\gamma \cdot 1, \gamma \cdot 2, \ldots$. That is, k parties $i_1 < \cdots < i_k$ is qualified iff there exists an index $j \in [k]$ such that $|\{i_1, \ldots, i_j\}| \geq \gamma \cdot i_j$.*

The main result of this section is summarized in the following theorem:

Theorem 3.3. *For any sequence of threshold values $\{k_t\}_{t \in \mathbb{N}}$ that define a dynamic threshold access structures, there exists a secret sharing scheme for sharing a 1-bit secret in which the share size of the t-th party is bounded by $O(t^4 \cdot \log t)$ bits.*

High level idea. The main idea is to represent the access structure as an infinite decision tree where the nodes in layer i are labeled by x_i. Turning such an infinite decision tree into an evolving secret sharing scheme can be done essentially generically via an evolving secret sharing scheme for undirected st-connectivity. This was done somewhat implicitly in [14] so we omit details here, but we just mention that the eventual share size is proportional to the tree size. Thus, using this naively gives us not very efficient schemes. In particular, for the dynamic threshold scheme it gives a scheme with exponential share size.

To improve this we observe that this decision tree can be "squashed" such that now each layer is labeled by a sequence of variables $x_i, \ldots, x_j$ and not just x_i. We call such a sequence a *generation*. Now, since every layer is labeled by a sequence of variables, we define each edge to be some *monotone* Boolean function of the variables in the generation. This operation potentially reduces the number of edges in the tree. If, in addition, this monotone function is simple enough (i.e. there is an efficient secret sharing scheme for it), this will eventually reduce the share size of our construction. Indeed, we can share the secret according to the new decision tree (with the squashed layers) to a virtual set of (much fewer) parties that correspond to the squashed sets and then re-sharing those shares via a secret sharing scheme among the parties inside a generation.

In the case of dynamic majority, each edge between two generation is labeled by the number of parties in the generation that arrived. This is the only information we need to remember for each generation in our structure. Now, if enough parties come so that we can reconstruct the secret, the decision tree must contain a path that leads to an accepting node (and vice versa). Luckily, this access structure (that counts how many parties arrived from a specific generation) can be implemented very efficiently using Shamir's scheme.

It remains to explain how we set the size of a generation. If we set it too low, then we do not save much in the decision tree size. If we set it too high, then we have a lot of parties in each generation and the first party in that generation will have to pay too much. The exact choice really depends on the access structure in hand, but it turns out that for the dynamic threshold case, the optimal setting of generation size is so that it increases in a specific polynomial rate, namely, the i-th generation size is square of the $(i-1)$-th generation size.

The above overview was slightly over-simplified and the actual construction requires some more care. In particular, we present the scheme directly and not as a composition of many schemes as it does not require familiarity with the st-connectivity scheme, and it allows us to prove its security directly via induction.

Proof. We begin by recalling Shamir's scheme [17] which will be heavily used in our scheme. Shamir's scheme is a scheme for sharing a 1-bit secret s among n parties for the k-out-of-n access structure (which contains all subsets of cardinality at least k). The share size in his scheme is $\log q$ bits, where $q > n$ is a prime number (or a power of a prime). We denote this scheme by $\mathsf{Shamir}(n, k, s)$. Note that in the cases where $k = 1$ or $k = n$, there are more efficient schemes: for $k = 1$, each party gets the secret and for $k = n$, each party gets a random value conditioned on their XOR being the secret. In these cases, the share size is a single bit (and it is, in particular, independent of n).

We assign to each arriving party $t \in \mathbb{N}$ a generation $\mathsf{GenOf}(t)$. The size of generation i is doubly exponential, namely, $\mathsf{GenSz}(i) = 2^{2^i}$. Thus, the t-th party is part of the $\lceil \log \log t \rceil$-th generation (at most) which includes at most t^2 parties. The first party in generation g is $\sum_{i=1}^{g} \mathsf{GenSz}(i) = \sum_{i=1}^{g} 2^{2^i}$. The state of the dealer after generation g ends consists of strings s_A, where A ranges over all tuples $(c_0, \ldots, c_g)$ such that $c_i \in [2^{2^i}]$. In other words, the dealer maintains a string s_A for each $A = (c_0, \ldots, c_g) \in [\mathsf{GenSz}(0)] \times \ldots \times [\mathsf{GenSz}(g)]$, where $\mathsf{GenSz}(i) = 2^{2^i}$. The number c_i, in some sense, represents the number of parties present from generation i.

For the ith party in the gth generation, denote by $\mathsf{IdxOf}(G, i)$ the overall index of this party since the beginning of time. Denote by s the secret to be shared and set $s_{(0)} = s$. When the $(g + 1)$-th generation begins, the dealer does the following for every $(c_0, \ldots, c_g) \in [\mathsf{GenSz}(0)] \times \ldots \times [\mathsf{GenSz}(g)]$:

1. For each party $i \in [\mathsf{GenSz}(g + 1)]$ do:
   (a) Share the secret $s_{(c_0, \ldots, c_g)}$ via a $(k_{\mathsf{IdxOf}(G+1,i)} - \sum_{i=1}^{g} c_i)$-out-of-$i$ to get shares $\Pi_1, \ldots, \Pi_i$.
   (b) For each $j \in [i]$, give share Π_j to the jth party in the generation.

2. For each $c_{g+1} \in [\mathsf{GenSz}(g+1)]$
   (a) Sample $r_{(c_0,\dots,c_{g+1})} \leftarrow \{0,1\}$ uniformly at random.
   (b) Share $r_{(c_0,\dots,c_{g+1})}$ via a c_g-ouf-of-$\mathsf{GenSz}(g+1)$ scheme among the parties of the $(g+1)^{\text{th}}$ generation.
   (c) Set $s_{(c_0,\dots,c_{g+1})} = s_{(c_0,\dots,c_g)} \oplus r_{(c_0,\dots,c_{g+1})}$.

For correctness we observe that if c_i parties arrive from generation i for every $i \in [g+1]$, then by the correctness of Shamir's scheme they can recover $r_{(c_0)}$, $r_{(c_0,c_1)}$ and all the way through $r_{(c_0,\dots,c_g)}$. Assume that the present set is qualified while the most recent party is the i-th party in generation $g+1$. Moreover, assume that from the $(g+1)^{\text{th}}$ generation there are ℓ parties present from the first i parties. Since the set is qualified, $\sum_{i=0}^{g} c_i + \ell \geq k_{\mathsf{IdxOf}(G+1,i)}$. Thus, the set of parties can further recover $s_{(c_0,\dots,c_g)}$ (again, by the correctness of Shamir's scheme). The latter is $s_{(c_0,\dots,c_g)} = s_{(c_0,\dots,c_{g-1})} \oplus r_{(c_0,\dots,c_g)}$, from which we can recover $s_{(c_0,\dots,c_{g-1})}$ (since we know $r_{(c_0,\dots,c_g)}$). Continuing in this manner, we can compute $s_{(c_0,\dots,c_{g-2})}$ and then $s_{(c_0,\dots,c_{g-3})}$ until we recover $s_{(0)}$ which is equal to the secret we shared.

For security we need to show that an unqualified set has no information regarding s, the secret that was shared. The proof is by induction on the number of generations. Assume that the scheme is secure for parties coming from g generations and we will show that it is secure for parties coming from the first $g+1$ generations. The base case follows immediately from the security of Shamir's scheme. Let the dealer share the secret among the parties in the first generation. Now, we observe that what the dealer does in the remaining sharing procedure is to share $\mathsf{GenSz}(0)$ secrets among the remaining g generations with slightly modified access structures. That is, it shares the secret $s_{(i)}$ for $i \in [\mathsf{GenSz}(0)]$ according to the sequence of dynamic thresholds $k_1 - i, k_2 - i, \dots,$. We claim that the remaining satisfies one of two cases: (1) it is unqualified in the new access structure and therefore its shares are independent of $s_{(i)}$, or (2) it is qualified so can learn $s_{(i)}$ but in this case it won't be able to recover the masking of s (by the security Shamir's scheme). The third option where it is both qualified and can learn the masking of s cannot occur since the set is unqualified to begin with.

Now, we apply the induction hypothesis and get that the shares held by the adversary according to each of these schemes are independent of the secret. Moreover, the sharing is done independently among these access structures and therefore the combination of all of these shares is independent of the secret.

The share size. The share size of a party in generation g consists of two parts corresponding to the above two Shamir sharing procedures. The first part, stemming from Item 1 above, is of size at most

$$\prod_{j=1}^{g} \mathsf{GenSz}(j) \cdot \log(\mathsf{GenSz}(g)) = \prod_{j=1}^{g} 2^{2^j} \cdot 2^g = 2^{\sum_{j=1}^{g} 2^j} \cdot 2^g \leq 2^{2^{g+1}} \cdot 2^g.$$

The second part, stemming from Item 2 above, is (again) of size at most

$$\prod_{j=1}^{g} \mathsf{GenSz}(j) \cdot \log(\mathsf{GenSz}(g)) \leq 2^{2^{g+1}} \cdot 2^g.$$

In total, the share size is bounded by $2^{2^{g+1}} \cdot 2^g \cdot 2$. The t-th party is in generation $g = \lceil \log \log t \rceil$ which means that its share size is bounded by $4t^4 \cdot \log t$.   ∎

On our generation size. The choice of parameters where generation sizes grows as $\mathsf{GenSz}(g+1) = (\mathsf{GenSz}(g))^2$ were carefully chosen to obtain optimal share complexity. The "generation-like" schemes of [14] were always growing by a linear factor and such choice in our case results with an inefficient scheme in which shares are of super-polynomial size. Specifically, our goal is to minimize the value of the product:

$$\prod_{j=1}^{g} \mathsf{GenSz}(j) \cdot \log(\mathsf{GenSz}(g)).$$

Choosing generations of linearly growing size gives that $\mathsf{GenSz}(j)$ is roughly 2^j (which is indeed small for the t-th party which is in generation roughly $\log t$) but there are now logarithmically many terms in the product which results with super-polynomial share size. A further inspection gives that our choice of the constant 2 in the exponent gives the best share size.

On sharing longer secrets. The above scheme can be generalized to support sharing of longer secrets more efficiently than sharing it bit by bit. Roughly speaking, this follows since Shamir's threshold scheme can be used to share a secret longer than 1 bit without increasing the share size. More precisely, Shamir's scheme allows to share a secret of length ℓ with shares of size $\max\{\ell, \log q\}$ (where $q > n$ is a prime number as above and n is the number of parties among which we share the secret). So, even for long secrets, for large enough party index $t \in \mathbb{N}$, we will apply Shamir's scheme on a very large set such that $\max\{\ell, \log q\} = \log q$ and therefore the analysis from above will hold. For parties with low index (where $\max\{\ell, \log q\} = \ell$) we do pay a price proportional to ℓ in the share size.

3.1   A General Framework

Our scheme is a special case of the following approach that can be used for more general evolving access structures. These access structures have the property that (1) parties can be split into generations of growing size, where the size of generation g is denoted by $\mathsf{GenSz}(g)$, (2) within each generation "not too much" information has to be remembered for the future, and (3) it is possible to efficiently "combine" all this information from different generations and decide whether a set is qualified or not.

The access structure at time $t \in \mathbb{N}$, denoted by $\mathcal{A}_t$, is a function of indicator bits representing the presence of each party in the reconstruction process. Namely, we can think of the function $\mathcal{A}_t(x_1, \ldots, x_t)$ as the indicator function of the access structure (where each x_i indicates whether the ith party is present). Denote by X_g the set of parties in generation g. Associate with each generation g, monotone functions $\Psi_0^g, \ldots, \Psi_{\ell_g}^g : \{0,1\}^{X_g} \to \{0,1\}$ that gets the indicator of the parties in the generation and output one bit (where ℓ_g is a parameter). Moreover, for each $(c_0, \ldots, c_{g-1}) \in \{0,1\}^{\ell_0} \times \ldots \times \{0,1\}^{\ell_{g-1}}$, associate a monotone function $\Phi_{c_0,\ldots,c_{g-1}} : \{0,1\}^{X_g} \to \{0,1\}$ such that the indicator of a set of parties $x_1, \ldots, x_t$ (where the generation of party t is g^*) is qualified in $\mathcal{A}_t$ iff

$$\mathcal{A}_t(x_1, \ldots, x_t) = 1 \iff \tag{3.1}$$
$$\exists c_0, \ldots, c_{g^*-1} \in [\ell_0] \times \ldots \times [\ell_{g^*-1}] : \Phi_{\Psi_{c_0}^0(X_0),\ldots,\Psi_{c_{g^*-1}}^{g^*-1}(X_{g^*-1})}(X_{g^*}).$$

Such an association always exists by setting each Ψ_i' to be the identity function that outputs the ith bit (i.e., $\ell_g = \mathsf{GenSz}(g)$) and letting $\Phi_{c_0,\ldots,c_g}$ correspond to $\mathcal{A}_t$ (for the appropriate value of t) where the output of Ψ_i for each $i \in [g-1]$ is fixed and only the last generation is not. In some cases, however, there is a more efficient mapping. For example, in the dynamic threshold considered above, we set each Ψ_i to count how many parties come from that generation, namely, $\ell_i = \mathsf{GenSz}(i)$, and the monotone function $\Phi_{\ell_0,\ldots,\ell_g}$, on input $x_1, \ldots, x_{\mathsf{GenSz}(g)}$ is naturally defined to be the one that checks for each $j \in [\mathsf{GenSz}(g)]$ whether $\sum_{i=0}^{g} \ell_i + \sum_{i=1}^{j} x_i$ is at least as large as the required threshold.

The point in making the above mapping is that now the original access structure $\mathcal{A}$ can be viewed as a composition of many access structures of the form $\Psi_{c_i}^g$ and $\Phi_{c_0,\ldots,c_g}$. If we choose the generations to be large enough but keep the ℓ_i's not too large, and moreover have efficient schemes for the above structures, we can overall have an efficient scheme. We describe this general scheme next. The state of the dealer after generation g ends consists of strings s_A, where A ranges over all tuples $(c_0, \ldots, c_g)$ such that $c_i \in \{0,1\}^{\ell_i}$. Denote by $s \in \{0,1\}$ the secret to be shared and set $s_{(0)} = s$. When the $(g+1)$-th generation begins, the dealer does the following for every $(c_0, \ldots, c_g) \in [\ell_0] \times \ldots \times [\ell_g]$:

1. Share the secret $s_{(c_0,\ldots,c_g)}$ via a $\Phi_{c_0,\ldots,c_g}$ among the parties in generation $g+1$.
2. For each $c_{g+1} \in [\ell_{g+1}]$
   (a) Sample $r_{(c_0,\ldots,c_{g+1})} \leftarrow \{0,1\}$ uniformly at random.
   (b) Share $r_{(c_0,\ldots,c_{g+1})}$ via a $\Psi_{c_{g+1}}^{g+1}$ among the parties of generation $g+1$.
   (c) Set $s_{(c_0,\ldots,c_{g+1})} = s_{(c_0,\ldots,c_g)} \oplus r_{(c_0,\ldots,c_{g+1})}$.

The correctness and security of the scheme follows by identity 3.1, similarly to how we proved correctness and security for the dynamic threshold scheme. We omit further details here.

The share size of a party in generation $g+1$ consists of two parts corresponding to the above two Φ and Ψ sharing procedures. We assume that the share size of each $\Phi_{c_0,\ldots,c_g}$ upper bounded by $\phi_{c_0,\ldots,c_g}$ and that the share size of each $\Psi_{c_g}^g$

is upper bounded by $\psi_{c_g}^g$. The first part, stemming from Item 1 above, is of size at most

$$\prod_{c_0 \in [\ell_0]} \cdots \prod_{c_g \in [\ell_g]} \phi_{c_0,\ldots,c_g}.$$

The second part, stemming from Item 2 above, is of size at most

$$\prod_{c_0[\ell_0]} \cdots \prod_{c_g \in [\ell_g]} \prod_{c_{g+1} \in [\ell_{g+1}]} \psi_{c_g}^g.$$

In total, the share size of party t that resides in generation g is bounded by the sum of the two terms above.

Instantiations. The above general blueprint captures not only the dynamic threshold scheme we presented above, but also can be used to capture the scheme for general access structures and the scheme for k-threshold for constant values of k of [14]. However, the choice of the generation size is different in each case. In the general case, the generations are of size 1 (as we cannot gain anything from squashing since the structure is completely arbitrary), and in the k-threshold case, the generations are growing in *linear* rate (linear in k) rather than polynomial in t as we have in the dynamic threshold case.

4   Robust Evolving Secret Sharing

In this section we show how to generically make any k-threshold scheme robust in the sense that even if some parties hand-in incorrect shares, the correct secret can be recovered. The formalization of this notion is done by augmenting a standard secret sharing for evolving access structures with an additional procedure called R-RECON which gets as input the shares of a set of parties A from which it can recover the secret. The adversary is allowed to corrupt any set $B \subseteq A$ such that $A \backslash B$ is still qualified. The aforementioned reconstruction procedure succeeds with all but $2^{-\lambda}$ probability, where λ is a parameter that is fixed during the sharing procedure.

Definition 4.1 (Robust evolving secret sharing). *A robust secret sharing scheme $\mathcal{R}$ is described by three procedures* (SHARE, RECON, R-RECON). *The procedures* (SHARE, RECON) *form an evolving secret sharing scheme (as in Definition 2.4) in which the procedure SHARE is augmented with an additional input 1^λ for a security parameter λ. The additional procedure R-RECON satisfies the following requirement:*

3 *Robust reconstruction: The secret s is shared using SHARE($1^\lambda, s$). An adversary $\mathcal{A}$ chooses a time t and two subsets of parties $A, B \subseteq [t]$ such that (1) $B \subseteq A$, (2) B is unqualified, and (3) $A \backslash B$ is qualified. The adversary $\mathcal{A}$ is then given the shares of the parties in B, denoted by Π_B^s, and it changes it arbitrarily to get $\Pi_B^s{}'$. Finally, the value of $s' = $ R-RECON($1^\lambda, \Pi_A^s \cup \Pi_B^s{}'$) is output.*

We say that the scheme is λ-robust if for any such adversary $\mathcal{A}$ if it holds that

$$\Pr[s' \neq s] \leq 2^{-\lambda}.$$

The next theorem shows how to obtain a robust secret sharing scheme for the evolving k-threshold access structure in which qualified sets are those of size at least k.

Theorem 4.2. *Let $k \in \mathbb{N}^+$ and $\lambda > 0$. Assume there exists a linear evolving (family of) schemes for k-threshold such that for the domain of secrets $\mathcal{S}$, it is linear over the field $\mathbb{F} = \mathbb{F}_2^t$ ($t \geq \log|\mathcal{S}|$).*

Then, there exists an evolving λ-robust secret sharing scheme for the evolving k-threshold access structure. The overhead in the share for party t is an additive factor of $O(\lambda + k \cdot \log k)$ bits relatively to the share size of the original scheme (for a sufficiently large domain $\mathcal{S}$, otherwise the overhead is multiplicative).

We prove the theorem, by adapting the robust (standard) secret sharing scheme of [10] to the evolving setting. Then, we use the linear scheme of [14] for the evolving k-threshold access structure and transform it into a robust one.[3] The high-level idea of the construction is, instead of sharing the secret itself, to share an AMD encoding of the secret (see Definition 2.6). Roughly speaking, the resulting scheme is robust since AMD codes protect information against additive attacks and our secret sharing scheme is linear.

Proof of Theorem 4.2. Our construction assumes a linear evolving scheme $\mathcal{E} = (\mathsf{SHARE}, \mathsf{RECON})$ for a k-threshold access structure and turns it into a robust evolving scheme for the same structure. We share secrets from domain $\mathcal{S}$. As an instantiation of the base scheme, we use the construction from [14] for the evolving k-threshold access structure over a sufficiently large secret space. The share size for the t-th party in their scheme is roughly $\sigma(t) = k \log t$ bits for large enough t. Fix a $\gamma' = (\lambda + k \log k)$-AMD code (E, D) for secret domain $|\mathcal{S}|$. Concretely, we use $\mathsf{AMD}_{\sigma, \gamma'}$.

Our new robust secret sharing scheme is described next:

1. The new sharing procedure $\mathsf{SHARE}'(1^\lambda, \Pi_1^s, \ldots, \Pi_{t-1}^s, s)$ gets as input a robustness parameter 1^λ, the shares of parties $1, \ldots, t-1$ and the original secret s and generates the share for the t-th party as follows. At the beginning of time (before the first party arrives), it computes an AMD encoding of s, denoted $\hat{s} = E(s)$, and shares this value using the underlying scheme by running (in the t-th time step) the procedure $\mathsf{SHARE}(\Pi_1^s, \ldots, \Pi_{t-1}^s, \hat{s})$ and giving the t-th party this value.

---

[3] Observe that the construction from [14] for the evolving k-threshold access structure are "almost" of the right form. One minor issue is that the field over which the various instances of Shamir operate grow as more parties arrive. Using extension fields, the shares can be viewed as a vector of linear combinations over a single field $\mathbb{F}_2^t$ of a suitable size, and the proof applies in a similar way. Our scheme from Theorem 3.3 has the same property.

2. The reconstruction procedure $\text{RECON}'(\Pi_B^s, B)$ on input the shares of a subset of parties B applies the original reconstruction procedure of the underlying scheme $\text{RECON}(\Pi_B^s, B)$ to obtain an AMD encoding $\hat{s}$. Then, it outputs the AMD decoding of this value $s = D(\hat{s})$.

3. The robust reconstruction procedure $\text{R-RECON}(1^\lambda, \Pi_B^s, B)$ on input the robustness parameter 1^λ and the shares of a set of parties B works as follows. Let B' denote the set of the first $\min\{2k - 1, |B|\}$ parties in B. Go over all minterms $T \subseteq B'$ (sets of size exactly k), and apply the reconstruction procedure on each of them: $\hat{s}_T = \text{RECON}'(1^\lambda, \Pi_T^s, T)$. If all $\hat{s}_T$ are $\bot$, output $\bot$. Otherwise, output the first value which is not $\bot$.

   Notice that since k is constant, the running time of this procedure is polynomial in its input size.

We proceed with the correctness, security and robustness of the above construction. As the original scheme is an evolving k-threshold scheme, and as the AMD scheme is perfectly correct the resulting scheme satisfies perfect correctness and privacy. As to robustness, first observe that $|B'| \leq 2k - 1$, and it must contain a qualified subset T' in which no party is malicious. Indeed, if $B' = B$, this follows by our guarantee on the choice of the malicious parties the adversary is allowed to make (otherwise, the adversary chose a qualified set which is illegal). If $|B'| = 2k - 1$, then the set of honest parties in this subset is of size k, and is therefore qualified.

Next, we prove that with probability at least $1 - 2^{-\lambda}$, the robust reconstruction procedure R-RECON outputs the shared secret s. By perfect correctness of the AMD scheme, $\hat{s}_{T'} = s$. It remains to show that for all other minterms T, it holds that $\hat{s}_T \in \{s, \bot\}$ with probability $1 - 2^{-\lambda}$ (the proof is similar to the one in [10], and is included here for completeness). For each T, consider any possible shift Δ_T in the shares chosen by the adversary. This shift naturally corresponds to an additive shift on the total set of shares used for reconstruction, as thus on the shared value (since the scheme basic evolving k-threshold scheme is linear).

By the security of the secret sharing scheme, the adversary's view (i.e. the shares of the parties he controls) does not depend on $\hat{s}$. Thus the distribution of shifted shares is also independent of the secret $\hat{s}$. Now, by the security of the AMD code, $\hat{s}_T \notin \{s, \bot\}$ with probability at most $2^{-\lambda + k \cdot (\log k + 1)}$. As there are at most $\binom{|B'|}{k} \leq \binom{2k-1}{k}$ possible different sets T (minterms), we can apply a union bound and get that the probability that this happens for *some* $\hat{s}_T$ is at most

$$(2k)^k \cdot 2^{-\lambda + k \cdot (\log k + 1)} = 2^{k \cdot (\log k + 1)} \cdot 2^{-\lambda + k \cdot (\log k + 1)} \leq 2^{-\lambda},$$

as required.   ∎

Acknowledgments. We thank Amos Beimel and the anonymous reviewers for their comments and suggestions.

References

1. Beimel, A.: Secure schemes for secret sharing and key distribution. Ph.D. thesis, Technion - Israel Institute of Technology (1996). http://www.cs.bgu.ac.il/beimel/ Papers/thesis.ps
2. Beimel, A.: Secret-sharing schemes: a survey. In: Chee, Y.M., Guo, Z., Ling, S., Shao, F., Tang, Y., Wang, H., Xing, C. (eds.) IWCC 2011. LNCS, vol. 6639, pp. 11–46. Springer, Heidelberg (2011). doi:10.1007/978-3-642-20901-7_2
3. Ben-Or, M., Goldwasser, S., Wigderson, A.: Completeness theorems for non-cryptographic fault-tolerant distributed computation (extended abstract). In: Proceedings of the 20th Annual ACM Symposium on Theory of Computing, STOC, pp. 1–10 (1988)
4. Bishop, A., Pastro, V., Rajaraman, R., Wichs, D.: Essentially optimal robust secret sharing with maximal corruptions. In: Fischlin, M., Coron, J.-S. (eds.) EUROCRYPT 2016. LNCS, vol. 9665, pp. 58–86. Springer, Heidelberg (2016). doi:10. 1007/978-3-662-49890-3_3
5. Blakley, G.R.: Safeguarding cryptographic keys. In: Proceedings of the AFIPS National Computer Conference, vol. 22, pp. 313–317 (1979)
6. Cevallos, A., Fehr, S., Ostrovsky, R., Rabani, Y.: Unconditionally-secure robust secret sharing with compact shares. In: Pointcheval, D., Johansson, T. (eds.) EUROCRYPT 2012. LNCS, vol. 7237, pp. 195–208. Springer, Heidelberg (2012). doi:10.1007/978-3-642-29011-4_13
7. Cramer, R., Damgård, I., Fehr, S.: On the cost of reconstructing a secret, or VSS with optimal reconstruction phase. In: Kilian, J. (ed.) CRYPTO 2001. LNCS, vol. 2139, pp. 503–523. Springer, Heidelberg (2001). doi:10.1007/3-540-44647-8_30
8. Cramer, R., Damgård, I., Maurer, U.: General secure multi-party computation from any linear secret-sharing scheme. In: Preneel, B. (ed.) EUROCRYPT 2000. LNCS, vol. 1807, pp. 316–334. Springer, Heidelberg (2000). doi:10.1007/3-540-45539-6_22
9. Cramer, R., Damgård, I., Nielsen, J.B.: Secure Multiparty Computation and Secret Sharing. Cambridge University Press, Cambridge (2015)
10. Cramer, R., Dodis, Y., Fehr, S., Padró, C., Wichs, D.: Detection of algebraic manipulation with applications to robust secret sharing and fuzzy extractors. In: Smart, N. (ed.) EUROCRYPT 2008. LNCS, vol. 4965, pp. 471–488. Springer, Heidelberg (2008). doi:10.1007/978-3-540-78967-3_27
11. Csirmaz, L.: The size of a share must be large. J. Cryptol. 10(4), 223–231 (1997)
12. Ito, M., Saito, A., Nishizeki, T.: Multiple assignment scheme for sharing secret. J. Cryptol. 6(1), 15–20 (1993)
13. Kol, G., Naor, M.: Games for exchanging information. In: Proceedings of the 40th Annual ACM Symposium on Theory of Computing, STOC, pp. 423–432 (2008)
14. Komargodski, I., Naor, M., Yogev, E.: How to share a secret, infinitely. In: Hirt, M., Smith, A. (eds.) TCC 2016. LNCS, vol. 9986, pp. 485–514. Springer, Heidelberg (2016). doi:10.1007/978-3-662-53644-5_19
15. Paskin-Cherniavsky, A.: How to infinitely share a secret more efficiently. IACR Cryptol. ePrint Arch. 2016, 1088 (2016)
16. Rabin, T., Ben-Or, M.: Verifiable secret sharing and multiparty protocols with honest majority (extended abstract). In: Proceedings of the 21st Annual ACM Symposium on Theory of Computing, pp. 73–85 (1989)
17. Shamir, A.: How to share a secret. Commun. ACM 22(11), 612–613 (1979)

Linear Secret-Sharing Schemes for Forbidden Graph Access Structures

Amos Beimel[1]($\boxtimes$), Oriol Farràs[2], Yuval Mintz[1], and Naty Peter[1]

[1] Ben Gurion University of the Negev, Be'er Sheva, Israel
amos.beimel@gmail.com, mintzyuval@gmail.com, naty@post.bgu.ac.il
[2] Universitat Rovira i Virgili, Tarragona, Catalonia, Spain
oriol.farras@urv.cat

Abstract. A secret-sharing scheme realizes the forbidden graph access structure determined by a graph $G = (V, E)$ if a pair of vertices can reconstruct the secret if and only if it is an edge in G. Secret-sharing schemes for forbidden graph access structures of bipartite graphs are equivalent to conditional disclosure of secrets protocols, a primitive that is used to construct attributed-based encryption schemes.

We study the complexity of realizing a forbidden graph access structure by linear secret-sharing schemes. A secret-sharing scheme is linear if the reconstruction of the secret from the shares is a linear mapping. In many applications of secret-sharing, it is required that the scheme will be linear. We provide efficient constructions and lower bounds on the share size of linear secret-sharing schemes for sparse and dense graphs, closing the gap between upper and lower bounds: Given a sparse graph with n vertices and at most $n^{1+\beta}$ edges, for some $0 \leq \beta < 1$, we construct a linear secret-sharing scheme realizing its forbidden graph access structure in which the total size of the shares is $\tilde{O}(n^{1+\beta/2})$. We provide an additional construction showing that every dense graph with n vertices and at least $\binom{n}{2} - n^{1+\beta}$ edges can be realized by a linear secret-sharing scheme with the same total share size.

We provide lower bounds on the share size of linear secret-sharing schemes realizing forbidden graph access structures. We prove that for most forbidden graph access structures, the total share size of every linear secret-sharing scheme realizing these access structures is $\Omega(n^{3/2})$, which shows that the construction of Gay, Kerenidis, and Wee [CRYPTO 2015] is optimal. Furthermore, we show that for every $0 \leq \beta < 1$ there exist a graph with at most $n^{1+\beta}$ edges and a graph with at least $\binom{n}{2} - n^{1+\beta}$ edges, such that the total share size of every linear secret-sharing scheme realizing these forbidden graph access structures is $\Omega(n^{1+\beta/2})$. This shows that our constructions are optimal (up to poly-logarithmic factors).

Keywords: Secret-sharing · Share size · Monotone span program · Conditional disclosure of secrets

The first and the forth authors are supported by ISF grants 544/13 and 152/17 and by the Frankel center for computer science. The second author is supported by the European Union through H2020-ICT-2014-1-644024 and H2020-DS-2015-1-700540, and by the Spanish Government through TIN2014-57364-C2-1-R.

Y. Kalai and L. Reyzin (Eds.): TCC 2017, Part II, LNCS 10678, pp. 394–423, 2017.
https://doi.org/10.1007/978-3-319-70503-3_13

1   Introduction

A secret-sharing scheme, introduced by [14,35,43], is a method in which a dealer, which holds a secret, can distribute shares to a set of parties, enabling only predefined subsets of parties to reconstruct the secret from their shares. These subsets are called authorized, and the family of authorized subsets is called the access structure of the scheme. The original motivation for defining secret-sharing was robust key management schemes for cryptographic systems. Nowadays, they are used in many secure protocols and applications, such as multiparty computation [11,21,23], threshold cryptography [27], access control [41], attribute-based encryption [34,48], and oblivious transfer [44,47].

In this paper we study secret-sharing schemes for forbidden graph access structures, first introduced by Sun and Shieh [46]. The forbidden graph access structure determined by a graph $G = (V, E)$ is the collection of all pairs of vertices in E and all subsets of vertices of size greater than two. Secret-sharing schemes for forbidden graph access structure determined by bipartite graphs are equivalent to conditional disclosure of secrets protocols. Following [7,8], we study the complexity of realizing a forbidden graph, and provide efficient constructions for sparse and dense graphs.

A secret-sharing scheme is linear if the shares are a linear function of the secret and random strings that are taken from some finite field. Equivalently, a scheme is linear if the reconstruction of the secret from the shares is a linear mapping. A linear secret-sharing can be constructed from a monotone span program, a computational model which introduced by Karchmer and Wigderson [37], and every linear secret-sharing scheme implies a monotone span program. See [4], for discussion on equivalent definitions of linear secret-sharing schemes. In many of the applications of secret-sharing mentioned above, it is required that the scheme will be linear. For example, Cramer et al. [23] construct general secure multiparty computation protocols, i.e., protocols which are secure against an arbitrary adversarial structure, from any linear secret-sharing scheme realizing the access structure in which a set is authorized if and only if it is not in the adversarial structure. Furthermore, it was shown by Attrapadung [3] and Wee [49] that linear secret-sharing schemes realizing forbidden graphs access structures are a central ingredient for constructing public-key (multi-user) attribute-based encryption. These applications motivate the study in this paper of linear secret-sharing schemes for forbidden graph access structures.

1.1   Related Work

Secret-Sharing Schemes for Arbitrary Access Structures. Secret-sharing schemes were introduced by Shamir [43] and Blakley [14] for the threshold case, and by Ito, Saito, and Nishizeki [35] for the general case. Threshold access structures, in which the authorized sets are all the sets containing at least t parties (for some threshold t), can be realized by secret-sharing schemes in which the size of each share is the size of the secret [14, 43]. There are other access structures that have secret-sharing schemes in which the size of the shares is small, i.e., polynomial (in the number of parties) share size [12, 13, 17, 37]. In particular, Benaloh and Leichter [12] proved that if an access structure can be described by a small monotone formula, then it has an efficient secret-sharing scheme. Improving on this result, Karchmer and Wigderson [37] showed that if an access structure can be described by a small monotone span program, then it has an efficient secret-sharing scheme.

The best known schemes for general access structures (e.g., [13, 17, 35, 37]) are highly inefficient, i.e., they have total share size of $2^{O(n)}$ (where n is the number of parties). The best known lower bound on the total share size of secret-sharing schemes realizing an access structure is $\Omega(n^2/\log n)$ [24, 25]; this lower bound is very far from the upper bound.

Graph Access Structures. A secret-sharing scheme realizes the graph access structure determined by a given graph if every two vertices connected by an edge can reconstruct the secret and every independent set in the graph does not get any information on the secret. The trivial secret-sharing scheme for realizing a graph access structure is sharing the secret independently for each edge; this results in a scheme whose total share size is $O(n^2)$ (times the length of the secret, which will be ignored in the introduction). This can be improved – every graph access structure can be realized by a linear secret-sharing scheme in which the total size of the shares is $O(n^2/\log n)$ [19, 29]. Graph access structures have been studied in many works, such as [7–9, 15, 16, 18, 20, 26, 45]. In particular, Beimel et al. [7] showed that a graph with n vertices that contains $\binom{n}{2} - n^{1+\beta}$ edges for some constant $0 \le \beta < 1$ can be realized by a scheme in which the total share size is $\tilde{O}(n^{5/4+3\beta/4})$.

Forbidden Graph Access Structures. Gay et al. [32] have proved that every forbidden graph access structure can be realized by a linear secret-sharing scheme in which the total size of the shares is $O(n^{3/2})$. Liu et al. [38] have recently shown that every forbidden graph access structure can be realized by a *non-linear* secret-sharing scheme in which the total size of the shares is $n^{1+o(1)}$.

Beimel et al. [8] showed that any graph with n vertices and with at least $\binom{n}{2} - n^{1+\beta}$ edges (for some constant $0 \le \beta < \frac{1}{2}$) can be realized by a linear secret-sharing scheme in which the total share size is $O(n^{7/6+2\beta/3})$. They also showed that if less than $n^{1+\beta}$ edges are removed from an arbitrary graph that can be realized by a secret-sharing scheme with total share size m, then the resulting graph can be realized by a secret-sharing scheme in which the total share size is $O(m + n^{7/6+2\beta/3})$. These results are improved in this paper.

Secret-sharing schemes for graph access structures and forbidden graph access structures have similar requirements, however, the requirements for graph access structures are stronger, since in graph access structures independent sets of vertices should not get any information on the secret. Given a secret-sharing scheme for a graph access structure, we can construct a secret-sharing scheme for the forbidden graph access structure: We can independently share the secret using the scheme for the graph access structure and the 3-out-of-n scheme of Shamir [43]. The total share size of the new scheme is slightly greater than the former. Therefore, upper bounds on the share size for graph access structures imply the same upper bounds on the share size for forbidden graph access structures.

Conditional Disclosure of Secrets. Gertner et al. [33] defined conditional disclosure of secrets (CDS). In this problem, two parties Alice and Bob want to disclose a secret to a referee if and only if their inputs (strings of N bits) satisfy some predicate (e.g., if their inputs are equal). To achieve this goal, each party computes one message based on its input, the secret, and a common random string, and sends the message to the referee. If the predicate holds, then the referee, which knows the two inputs, can reconstruct the secret from the messages it received. In [33], CDS is used to efficiently realize symmetrically-private information retrieval protocols. In [32], it is shown that CDS can be used to construct attribute-based encryption, a cryptographic primitive introduced in [34, 42].

We can represent the CDS for some predicate as the problem of realizing a secret-sharing scheme for a forbidden graph access structure of a bipartite graph and vice-versa: Every possible input for Alice is a vertex in the first part of the graph and every possible input for Bob is a vertex in the second part of the graph, and there is an edge between two vertices from different parts if and only if the two corresponding inputs satisfy the predicate. Given a CDS protocol for a predicate, we construct a secret-sharing scheme realizing the bipartite graph defined by the predicate in which the share of party z is the message sent in the CDS protocol to the referee by Alice or Bob (depending on z's part of the graph) when they hold the input z. Thus, given a predicate P, we get a bipartite graph with $n = 2^N$ vertices in each part (where N is the size of the input of the parties) such that the length of the messages required in a CDS for P is the length of the shares required by a secret-sharing realizing the forbidden graph access structure.

Gertner et al. [33] have proved that if a predicate P has a (possibly non-monotone) formula of size S, then there is a CDS protocol for P in which the length of the messages is S. A similar result holds if the predicate has a (possibly non-monotone) span program, or even a non-monotone secret-sharing scheme (this is a secret-sharing scheme realizing an access structure defined in [33] in which for every bit in the input there are two parties, one for every value of the bit). This result provides a rich class of predicates for which there are efficient CDS protocols. Thus, there is a rich class of forbidden graph access structures that can be realized by efficient secret-sharing schemes (by the equivalence between CDS and secret-sharing schemes for forbidden graph access structures).

It was shown in [32] that for every predicate there exists a linear CDS such that the size of each of the messages sent by the two parties to the referee is

$2^{N/2}$.[1] This implies that for every bipartite graph there exists a linear secret-sharing scheme realizing the forbidden graph access structure in which the size of each share is $O(n^{1/2})$ (where n is the number of the parties); in particular, the total share size of this scheme is $O(n^{3/2})$.

Liu et al. [38] have recently shown that every predicate has a non-linear CDS scheme in which the size of the messages the parties send to the referee is $2^{O(\sqrt{N \log N})}$. As a corollary, we get a non-linear secret-sharing scheme realizing the forbidden graph access structure for every bipartite graph with n vertices, in which the size of each share is $n^{O(\sqrt{\log\log n/\log n})} = n^{o(1)}$; in particular, the total share size of this scheme is $n^{1+O(\sqrt{\log\log n/\log n})} = n^{1+o(1)}$. By a transformation of [8,10], the above two results hold for every graph (not necessarily bipartite).

Applebaum et al. [2] and Ambrona et al. [1] have shown that if we have a linear CDS for some predicate P with message length c and shared random string length r, then we can construct a linear CDS for the complement predicate $\overline{P}$ in which the message length and the shared random string length is linear in c and r. Translated to secret-sharing, we conclude that if we have a linear secret-sharing scheme that uses r random field elements in the generation of the shares and realizes the forbidden graph access structure of a bipartite graph G, then we can realize its complement bipartite graph $\overline{G}$ with a linear scheme in which the size of each share is $O(r)$.

Another result shown in [2] is that for every predicate there exists a linear CDS for secrets of k bits, where k is double-exponential in N, such that the size of each of the messages sent by the two parties to the referee is $O(k \cdot N)$. This gives us an amortized size of $O(N)$ bits per each bit of the secret, much better than the size of $2^{N/2}$ for one-bit secret that was shown in [32]. When considering forbidden graph access structures, we get that for every forbidden bipartite graph access structure with n vertices there exists a linear secret-sharing scheme with secrets of length k and total share size of $O(kn\log n)$, provided that the size of the secret k is exponential in n.

1.2 Our Results

The main result we show in this paper is the construction of linear secret-sharing schemes realizing forbidden graph access structures for sparse graphs and dense graphs. We also prove tight lower bounds on the share size of linear secret-sharing schemes realizing forbidden graph access structures.

Constructions. Our main constructions of linear secret-sharing schemes are the following ones:

– Given a sparse graph with n vertices and at most $n^{1+\beta}$ edges, for some $0 \leq \beta < 1$, we construct a linear secret-sharing scheme that realizes its forbidden graph access structure, in which the total size of the shares is $\tilde{O}(n^{1+\beta/2})$. The

---

[1] A linear CDS is a CDS in which if the predicate holds, then the reconstruction function of the referee is linear.

best previously known linear secret-sharing scheme for such graphs is the trivial scheme that independently shares the secret for each edge; the total share size of this scheme is $O(n^{1+\beta})$.

- Given a dense graph with n vertices and at least $\binom{n}{2} - n^{1+\beta}$ edges, for some $0 \leq \beta < 1$, we construct a linear secret-sharing scheme that realizes its forbidden graph access structure with total share size $\tilde{O}(n^{1+\beta/2})$. The best previously known linear secret-sharing scheme for such graphs is the scheme of [8], which has total share size $O(n^{7/6+2\beta/3})$.

- As a corollary, we construct a secret-sharing scheme for forbidden graph access structures of graphs obtained by changing (adding or removing) few edges from an arbitrary graph G. If the forbidden graph access structure determined by a graph G can be realized by a secret-sharing scheme with total share size m and G' is obtained from G by changing at most $n^{1+\beta}$ edges, for some $0 \leq \beta < 1$, then we construct a secret-sharing scheme realizing the forbidden graph access structure of G' with total share size $m+\tilde{O}(n^{1+\beta/2})$. If the secret-sharing scheme realizing the forbidden graph access structure determined by G is linear, then the resulting scheme realizing the forbidden graph access structure determined by G' is also linear.

Overview of Our Constructions. We construct the secret-sharing scheme realizing forbidden graph access structures determined by sparse graphs in few stages, where in each stage we restrict the forbidden graph access structures that we can realize. We start by realizing fairly simple bipartite graphs, and in each stage we realize a wider class of graphs using the schemes constructed in previous stages.

Our basic construction, described in Lemma 1, is a linear secret-sharing scheme realizing a forbidden graph access structure for a bipartite graph $G = (A, B, E)$, where A is small and the degree of each vertex in B is at most d, for some $d < n$. To construct this scheme, we construct a linear subspace V_a for each vertex $a \in A$, and a vector $\mathbf{z_b}$ for every vertex $b \in B$, such that $\mathbf{z_b} \in V_a$ if and only if $(a, b) \in E$. The total size of the shares in the scheme we construct is $O(d|A| + |B|)$. A naive scheme for this graph, which shares the secret independently for each edge, has total share size $O(d|B|)$. Our scheme is much more efficient than the naive scheme when A is small and B is big. This is the scheme that enables us to construct efficient schemes for sparse forbidden graph access structures.

In the second stage, we construct, in Lemma 3, a secret-sharing scheme for a forbidden graph access structure for a bipartite graph $G = (A, B, E)$, where the degree of every vertex in B is at most d (and there is no restriction that A is small). The total size of the shares in this scheme is $O(n\sqrt{d}\log n)$, where $|A| = |B| = n$. The idea of this construction is to *randomly* partition the set A to $\ell = O(\sqrt{d}\ln n) = \tilde{O}(\sqrt{d})$ "small" sets $A_1, \ldots, A_\ell$. We prove that with high probability, for every $1 \leq i \leq \ell$, the degree of every vertex $b \in B$ in the bipartite graph $G_i = (A_i, B, E \cap (A_i \times B))$ is at most $O(\sqrt{d})$ (compared to its degree in

G, which can be at most d). We now realize each sparse graph G_i using the basic scheme.

In the third stage, we construct, in Theorem 2, a secret-sharing scheme for a bipartite graph $G = (A, B, E)$, where the number of edges in G is at most $n^{1+\beta}$ for some $0 \le \beta < 1$ (where $|A| = |B| = n$). That is, we realize forbidden graph access structures for bipartite graphs where the *average* degree of each vertex in B is at most n^{β}. To this purpose, we use an idea from [7] (also used in [8]). Fix some degree d, and let B_{big} be the vertices in B whose degree is at least d. Furthermore, let $B_{\text{small}} = B \backslash B_{\text{big}}$. Since the number of edges in G is at most $n^{1+\beta}$, the size of B_{big} is at most $n^{1+\beta}/d$. Using the fact that B_{big} is small (however, the degree of each vertex in B_{big} can be n), the secret-sharing scheme of [32] (alternatively, the scheme of Lemma 3) realizes the graph $G_{\text{big}} = (A, B_{\text{big}}, E \cap (A \times B_{\text{big}}))$ with "quite small" shares. Using the fact that the degree of each vertex in B_{small} is small, the secret-sharing scheme of Lemma 3 realizes $G_{\text{small}} = (A, B_{\text{small}}, E \cap (A \times B_{\text{small}}))$ with total share size $O(n\sqrt{d}\log n)$. By taking the appropriate value for d, we get a secret-sharing scheme realizing G in which (for small enough values of β) the total share size is $o(n^{1+\beta})$, but still larger than the promised total share size. To get a secret-sharing scheme realizing G with total share size $\tilde{O}(n^{1+\beta/2})$, we group the vertices in B into $O(\log n)$ sets according to their degree, where the ith set B_i contains the vertices whose degree is between $n/2^{i+1}$ and $n/2^i$. We realize each graph $G_i = (A, B_i, E \cap (A \times B_i))$ independently using the secret-sharing scheme of Lemma 3.

In the last stage, we construct, in Theorem 3, a secret-sharing scheme for any forbidden graph access structure with the promised total share size. That is, if the number of edges in G is at most $n^{1+\beta}$ for some $0 \le \beta < 1$ (where $|V| = n$), then the total share size is $\tilde{O}(n^{1+\beta/2})$. The last stage is done using a generic transformation of [8,10], which constructs a secret-sharing scheme for any graph from secret-sharing schemes for bipartite graphs.

To summarize, there are 4 stages in our construction for sparse graphs. The first two stages are the major new steps in our construction. The third stage uses ideas from [7], however, it requires designing appropriate secret-sharing schemes in the first two stages. In the last stage, we use a transformation of [8,10] as a black-box. The construction for forbidden graph access structures determine by dense graphs is similar, however, we construct a different scheme for the first stage.

The construction of a scheme realizing a forbidden graph access structure determined by a graph G' obtained by adding or removing few edges from a graph G is done using ideas from [8] as follows: First, we share the secret s using the secret-sharing scheme realizing the sparse graph containing all edges added to G (we add at most $n^{1+\beta}$ to G). In addition, we share the secret s using a 2-out-of-2 secret-sharing scheme. That is, we choose two random elements s_1 and s_2 such that $s = s_1 \oplus s_2$. We share s_1 using the scheme of the graph G and share s_2 using the secret-sharing scheme realizing the dense graph containing all possible edges except for the edges removed from G (this graph is a dense graph with at least $\binom{n}{2} - n^{1+\beta}$ edges, since we remove at most $n^{1+\beta}$ from G).

Lower Bounds. We prove that for most forbidden graph access structures, the total share size of every linear secret-sharing scheme realizing these access structures, with a one-bit secret, is $\Omega(n^{3/2})$, which shows that the construction of Gay et al. [32] is optimal. This also shows a separation between the total share size in non-linear secret-sharing schemes realizing forbidden graph access structures, which is $n^{1+o(1)}$ by [38], and the total share size required in linear secret-sharing schemes realizing forbidden graph access structures. This lower bound implies that, for most predicates $P : \{0,1\}^N \times \{0,1\}^N \to \{0,1\}$, in every linear CDS protocol for P the length of the messages is $\Omega(2^{N/2})$.

Furthermore, we show that for every $0 \leq \beta < 1$ there exist a graph with at most $n^{1+\beta}$ edges and a graph with at least $\binom{n}{2} - n^{1+\beta}$ edges, such that the total share size of every linear secret-sharing scheme realizing their forbidden graph access structures is $\Omega(n^{1+\beta/2})$. This shows that our constructions are optimal (up to poly-logarithmic factors). Our lower bounds are existential and use counting arguments. They previously appeared (in a somewhat less general form) in the master thesis of the third author of this paper [39].

2   Preliminaries

We denote the logarithmic function with base 2 and base e by log and ln, respectively. We denote vectors by bold letters, e.g., $\mathbf{v}$.

2.1   Secret-Sharing

We present the definition of secret-sharing scheme as given in [6,22]. For more information about this definition and secret-sharing in general, see [5].

Definition 1 (Secret-Sharing Schemes). *Let $P = \{p_1, \ldots, p_n\}$ be a set of parties. A collection $\Gamma \subseteq 2^P$ is* monotone *if $B \in \Gamma$ and $B \subseteq C$ imply that $C \in \Gamma$. An* access structure *is a monotone collection $\Gamma \subseteq 2^P$ of non-empty subsets of P. Sets in Γ are called* authorized, *and sets not in Γ are called* unauthorized. *The family of minimal authorized subsets is denoted by* min Γ.

A distribution scheme *$\Sigma = \langle \Pi, \mu \rangle$ with domain of secrets K is a pair, where μ is a probability distribution on some finite set R called the set of random strings and Π is a mapping from $K \times R$ to a set of n-tuples $K_1 \times K_2 \times \cdots \times K_n$, where K_j is called the* domain of shares *of p_j. A dealer distributes a secret $k \in K$ according to Σ by first sampling a random string $r \in R$ according to μ, computing a vector of shares $\Pi(k,r) = (s_1, \ldots, s_n)$, and privately communicating each share s_j to party p_j. For a set $A \subseteq P$, we denote $\Pi_A(k,r)$ as the restriction of $\Pi(k,r)$ to its A-entries (i.e., the shares of the parties in A).*

Given a distribution scheme, define the size of the secret *as $\log|K|$, the (normalized)* share size of party p_j *as $\log|K_j|/\log|K|$, the (normalized)* max share size *as $\max_{1 \leq j \leq n} \log|K_j|/\log|K|$, and the (normalized)* total share size *of the distribution scheme as $\sum_{1 \leq j \leq n} \log|K_j|/\log|K|$.*

Let K be a finite set of secrets, where $|K| \geq 2$. A distribution scheme $\langle \Pi, \mu \rangle$ with domain of secrets K is a secret-sharing scheme realizing an access structure Γ if the following two requirements hold:

CORRECTNESS. The secret k can be reconstructed by any authorized set of parties. That is, for any set $B = \{p_{i_1}, \ldots, p_{i_{|B|}}\} \in \Gamma$, there exists a reconstruction function $\mathrm{Recon}_B : K_{i_1} \times \ldots \times K_{i_{|B|}} \to K$ such that for every secret $k \in K$ and every random string $r \in R$,

$$\mathrm{Recon}_B\left(\Pi_B(k, r)\right) = k.$$

PRIVACY. Every unauthorized set cannot learn anything about the secret (in the information theoretic sense) from their shares. Formally, for any set $T \notin \Gamma$, every two secrets $a, b \in K$, and every possible vector of shares $\langle s_j \rangle_{p_j \in T}$,

$$\Pr[\,\Pi_T(a, r) = \langle s_j \rangle_{p_j \in T}\,] = \Pr[\,\Pi_T(b, r) = \langle s_j \rangle_{p_j \in T}\,].$$

when the probability is over the choice of r from R at random according to μ.

Definition 2 (Linear Secret-Sharing Scheme). Let $\Sigma = \langle \Pi, \mu \rangle$ be a secret-sharing scheme with domain of secrets K, where μ is a probability distribution on a set R and Π is a mapping from $K \times R$ to $K_1 \times K_2 \times \cdots \times K_n$. We say that Σ is a linear secret-sharing scheme over a finite field $\mathbb{F}$ if $K = \mathbb{F}$, the sets $R, K_1, \ldots, K_n$ are vector spaces over $\mathbb{F}$, Π is a $\mathbb{F}$-linear mapping, and μ is the uniform probability distribution.

2.2 Monotone Span Programs

Monotone span programs (abbreviated MSPs) are a linear-algebraic model of computation introduced by Karchmer and Wigderson [37]. As explained below in Claim 1, MSPs over finite fields are equivalent to linear secret-sharing schemes.

Definition 3 (Monotone Span Programs [37]). A monotone span program is a quadruple $\widehat{M} = \langle \mathbb{F}, M, \delta, \mathbf{v} \rangle$, where $\mathbb{F}$ is a field, M is an $a \times b$ matrix over $\mathbb{F}$, $\delta : \{1, \ldots, a\} \to P$ (where P is a set of parties) is a mapping labeling each row of M by a party,[2] and $\mathbf{v}$ is a non-zero vector in $\mathbb{F}^b$, called the target vector. The size of $\widehat{M}$ is the number of rows of M (i.e., a). For any set $A \subseteq P$, let M_A denote the sub-matrix obtained by restricting M to the rows labeled by parties in A. We say that $\widehat{M}$ accepts a set $B \subseteq P$ if the rows of M_B span the vector $\mathbf{v}$. We say that $\widehat{M}$ accepts an access structure Γ where $\widehat{M}$ accepts a set B if and only if $B \in \Gamma$.

By applying a linear transformation to the rows of M, the target vector can be changed to any non-zero vector without changing the size of the MSP. The default value for the target vector is $\mathbf{e_1} = (1, 0, \ldots, 0)$, but in this work we also use other vectors, e.g., $\mathbf{1}$ (the all one's vector).

---

[2] We label a row by a party rather than by a variable x_j as done in [37].

Claim 1 ([4,37]). *Let $\mathbb{F}$ be a finite field. There exists a linear secret-sharing scheme over $\mathbb{F}$ realizing Γ with total share size a if and only if there exists an MSP over $\mathbb{F}$ of size a accepting Γ.*

For the sake of completeness, we explain how to construct a linear secret-sharing scheme from an MSP. Given an MSP $\widehat{M} = \langle \mathbb{F}, M, \delta, \mathbf{e_1} \rangle$ accepting Γ, where M is an $a \times b$ matrix over $\mathbb{F}$, define a linear secret-sharing scheme as follows:

- **Input:** a secret $k \in \mathbb{F}$.
- Choose $b - 1$ random elements $r_2, \ldots, r_b$ independently with uniform distribution from $\mathbb{F}$ and define $\mathbf{r} = (k, r_2, \ldots, r_b)$.
- Evaluate $(s_1, \ldots, s_a) = M\mathbf{r}^T$, and distribute to each party $p \in P$ the entries corresponding to rows labeled by p.

In this linear secret-sharing scheme, every set in Γ can reconstruct the secret: Let $B \in \Gamma$ and $N = M_B$, thus, the rows of N span $\mathbf{e_1}$, and there exists some vector $\mathbf{v}$ such that $\mathbf{e_1} = \mathbf{v}N$. Notice that the shares of the parties in B are $N\mathbf{r}^T$. The parties in B can reconstruct the secret by computing $\mathbf{v}(N\mathbf{r}^T)$, since

$$\mathbf{v}(N\mathbf{r}^T) = (\mathbf{v}N)\mathbf{r}^T = \mathbf{e_1} \cdot \mathbf{r}^T = k.$$

The proof of the privacy of this scheme can be found in [5,37].

2.3 Graphs and Forbidden Graph Access Structures

Recall that a *bipartite graph* $G = (A, B, E)$ is a graph where the vertices are $A \cup B$ (A and B are called the parts of G) and $E \subseteq A \times B$. A bipartite graph is *complete* if $E = A \times B$.

Definition 4 (The Bipartite Complement). *Let $G = (A, B, E)$ be a bipartite graph. The bipartite complement of G is the bipartite graph $\overline{G} = (A, B, \overline{E})$, where every $a \in A$ and $b \in B$ satisfy $(a, b) \in \overline{E}$ if and only if $(a, b) \notin E$.*

Definition 5 (Forbidden Graph Access Structures). *Let $G = (V, E)$ be a graph. The* forbidden graph access structure *defined by G is the collection of all pairs of vertices in E and all subsets of vertices of size greater than two.*[3]

Remark 1 When we say that a secret-sharing scheme realizes a graph G, we mean that the scheme realizes the forbidden graph access structure of the graph G.

Remark 2 In applications of secret-sharing schemes for forbidden graph access structures (e.g., conditional disclosure of secrets), the only requirement is that pairs of vertices can reconstruct the secret if and only if they are connected by an edge. To fully specify the access structure of a forbidden graph, we also require that all sets of 3 or more vertices are authorized. This additional requirement

---

[3] In [46], the access structure is specified by the complement graph, i.e., by the edges that are forbidden from learning information on the secret.

only slightly increases the total share size required to realize forbidden graph access structures, since we can independently share the secret using the 3-out-of-n scheme of Shamir [43], in which the size of the share of every party is the size of the secret (when the size of the secret is at least $\log n$). To simplify the description of our schemes, in all our construction in Sects. 3 to 5 we implicitly assume that we share the secret using Shamir's 3-out-of-n secret-sharing scheme.

2.4   Conditional Disclosure of Secrets

For completeness, we present the definition of conditional disclosure of secrets, originaly defined in [33].

Definition 6 (Conditional Disclosure of Secrets). *Let* $P : \{0,1\}^N \times \{0,1\}^N \to \{0,1\}$ *be some predicate, and let* $\text{ENC}_A : \{0,1\}^N \times S \times R \to M_A$, $\text{ENC}_B : \{0,1\}^N \times S \times R \to M_B$ *be deterministic functions, where S is the domain of secrets and R is the domain of the common random strings, and* $\text{DEC} : \{0,1\}^N \times \{0,1\}^N \times M_A \times M_B \to S$ *be a deterministic function. Then,* $(\text{ENC}_A, \text{ENC}_B, \text{DEC})$ *is a conditional disclosure of secrets (CDS) protocol for the predicate P if the following two requirements hold:*

CORRECTNESS. *For every $x, y \in \{0,1\}^N$ with $P(x,y) = 1$, every secret $s \in S$, and every common random string $r \in R$,*

$$\text{DEC}(x, y, \text{ENC}_A(x, s, r), \text{ENC}_B(y, s, r)) = s.$$

PRIVACY. *For every $x, y \in \{0,1\}^N$ with $P(x,y) = 0$, every two secrets $s_1, s_2 \in S$, and every messages $m_A \in M_A, m_B \in M_B$:*

$$\Pr[\text{ENC}_A(x, s_1, r) = m_A \text{and} \text{ENC}_B(y, s_1, r) = m_B]$$
$$= \Pr[\text{ENC}_A(x, s_2, r) = m_A \text{and} \text{ENC}_B(y, s_2, r) = m_B],$$

when the probability is over the choice of r from R at random with uniform distribution.

3   The Basic Construction for Graphs of Low Degree

Our basic construction requires the following construction of linear spaces, which will be used both for sparse graphs and for dense graphs.

Claim 2. *Let $G = (A, B; E)$ be a bipartite graph with $A = \{a_1, \ldots, a_m\}$, $B = \{b_1, \ldots, b_n\}$ such that the degree of every vertex in B is at most d and let $\mathbb{F}$ be a finite field with $|\mathbb{F}| \geq m$. Then, there are m linear subspaces $V_1, \ldots, V_m \subseteq \mathbb{F}^{d+1}$ of dimension d and $n + 1$ vectors $\mathbf{z}_1, \ldots, \mathbf{z_n}, \mathbf{w} \in \mathbb{F}^{d+1}$ such that*

$$\mathbf{z_j} \in V_i \text{ if and only if } (a_i, b_j) \in E,$$

and $\mathbf{w} \notin V_i$ for every $1 \leq i \leq m$.

Proof. We identify vectors in $\mathbb{F}^{d+1}$ with polynomials of degree at most d in the indeterminate X. That is, for a vector $\mathbf{v} \in \mathbb{F}^{d+1}$ we consider a polynomial $v(X) \in \mathbb{F}[X]$ of degree d in which the coefficient of degree i is the $(i+1)$-th coordinate of $\mathbf{v}$.

For each vertex $a_i \in A$, we associate a distinct element $\alpha_i \in \mathbb{F}$. We define the subspace $V_i \subseteq \mathbb{F}^{d+1}$ of dimension d as the one associated to the space of polynomials $P(X)$ of degree at most d such that $P(\alpha_i) = 0$, i.e., the space of polynomials spanned by $\{(X - \alpha_i), (X^2 - \alpha_i \cdot X), \ldots, (X^d - \alpha_i \cdot X^{d-1})\}$. Since these d polynomials are independent, the dimension of each V_i is d. Furthermore, for a vertex $b_j \in B$, whose neighbors are $a_{i_1}, a_{i_2}, \ldots, a_{i_{d'}}$ (for some $d' \leq d$), we define

$$z_j(X) = (X - \alpha_{i_1}) \cdot (X - \alpha_{i_2}) \cdot \ldots \cdot (X - \alpha_{i_{d'}}).$$

Note that $\mathbf{z_j} \in V_i$ if and only if $z_j(\alpha_i) = 0$ if and only if $\alpha_i \in \{\alpha_{i_1}, \alpha_{i_2}, \ldots, \alpha_{i_{d'}}\}$ if and only if $(a_i, b_j) \in E$.

Finally, define $w(X) = 1$. For every $1 \leq i \leq m$, since $w(\alpha_i) = 1$ and $v(\alpha_i) = 0$ for every $\mathbf{v} \in V_i$, the vector $\mathbf{w}$ is not in V_i. $\qquad\square$

Lemma 1. *Let $G = (A, B, E)$ be a bipartite graph with $|A| = m$, $|B| = n$, such that the degree of every vertex in B is at most d. Then, there is a linear secret-sharing scheme realizing G with total share size $n + (d+1)m$.*

Proof. Denote $A = \{a_1, \ldots, a_m\}$, $B = \{b_1, \ldots, b_n\}$, and let $V_1, \ldots, V_m$ and $\mathbf{z_1}, \ldots, \mathbf{z_n}$ be the linear subspaces and vectors guaranteed by Claim 2. We construct a monotone span program accepting G, where there are $d+1$ rows labeled by a_i for every $1 \leq i \leq m$ and one row labeled by b_j for every $1 \leq j \leq n$. By Claim 1, this implies the desired linear secret-sharing scheme.

Let $\{\mathbf{v_{i,1}}, \ldots, \mathbf{v_{i,d}}\}$ be a basis of V_i, and for $1 \leq \ell \leq d$, define $\mathbf{v'_{i,\ell}} = (0, 0, \mathbf{v_{i,\ell}})$ (that is, $\mathbf{v'_{i,\ell}}$ is a vector in $\mathbb{F}^{d+3}$ whose first two coordinates are 0 followed by the vector $\mathbf{v_{i,\ell}}$). The rows labeled by a_i are $\mathbf{v'_{i,1}}, \ldots, \mathbf{v'_{i,d}}$ and $(0, 1, 0, \ldots, 0)$. The row labeled by b_j is $\mathbf{z'_j} = (1, 0, \mathbf{z_j})$. The target vector is $(1, 1, 0, \ldots, 0)$. The monotone span program accepts (a_i, b_j) if and only if $(1, 1, 0, \ldots, 0) \in$ span $\{\mathbf{z'_j}, \mathbf{v'_{i,1}}, \ldots, \mathbf{v'_{i,d}}, (0, 1, 0, \ldots, 0)\}$ if and only if $\mathbf{z_j} \in$ span $\{\mathbf{v_{i,1}}, \ldots, \mathbf{v_{i,d}}\}$ if and only if $\mathbf{z_j} \in V_i$ if and only if $(a_i, b_j) \in E$.

Furthermore, two vertices from the same part do not span $(1, 1, 0, \ldots, 0)$: For two vertices in A, this follows since the first coordinate in all vectors they label is 0. For two vertices in B, this follows since the second coordinate in the vectors they label is 0. Therefore, the monotone span program accepts G. $\qquad\square$

We next show that Lemma 1 can be used to realize every bipartite graph by a linear secret-sharing scheme with total share size $O(n^{3/2})$. This scheme has the same total share size as the linear secret-sharing scheme of [32]. This construction is presented as a warmup for our construction for bipartite graphs with bounded degree.

Lemma 2. *Let $G = (A, B, E)$ be a bipartite graph such that $|A| = |B| = n$. Then, there is a linear secret-sharing scheme realizing G with total share size $O(n^{3/2})$.*

Proof. We arbitrarily partition A into $\sqrt{n}$ sets, $A_1, \ldots, A_{\sqrt{n}}$, each set of size at most $\sqrt{n}$. By Lemma 1, the bipartite graph $(A_i, B, E \cap (A_i \times B))$ (in which every vertex in B has at most $|A_i| = \sqrt{n}$ neighbors) can be realized by a linear secret-sharing scheme with total share size $O(n + (\sqrt{n} + 1)\sqrt{n}) = O(n)$. We use this construction for each of the $\sqrt{n}$ sets $A_1, \ldots, A_{\sqrt{n}}$. Hence, the total share size of the resulting scheme is $O(n^{3/2})$.   □

It can be verified that in the secret-sharing scheme of Lemma 2, the size of the share of each vertex is $O(n^{1/2})$.

4   Secret-Sharing Schemes for Sparse Graphs

In this section we present efficient secret-sharing schemes for forbidden graph access structures of sparse graphs, that is, graphs with at most $n^{1+\beta}$ edges for some $0 \leq \beta < 1$. The main result is Theorem 3, where we show that these graphs admit secret-sharing schemes with total share size $O(n^{1+\beta/2} \log^3 n)$. Its proof is involved, and we use several intermediate results. First, we construct an efficient secret-sharing schemes for sparse bipartite graphs. In the construction for a sparse bipartite graph $G = (A, B, E)$ in Theorem 2 we partition the vertices in B into $O(\log n)$ sets according to their degree, that is, the vertices in the ith set B_i are the vertices whose degrees are between $n/2^{i+1}$ and $n/2^i$. We realize each graph $G_i = (A, B_i, E \cap (A \times B_i))$ independently using the secret-sharing scheme of Lemma 3. This methodology is the same as in [7,8]. The main new technical result in this section is Lemma 3, and it is the basis of this construction. Finally, using a transformation that appeared in [10], we use the schemes for sparse bipartite graphs to construct a scheme for general sparse graphs.

Lemma 3. *Let* $G = (A, B, E)$ *be a bipartite graph with* $|A| = n$, $|B| \leq n$ *such that the degree of each vertex in* B *is at most* d *for some* $d \leq n$. *If* $d|B| \geq n \log^2 n$, *then there is a linear secret-sharing scheme realizing* G *with total share size* $O\left(\sqrt{n|B|d} \log n\right)$.

Proof. Let $\delta = \log_n d$ (that is, $d = n^{\delta}$), $\gamma = \log_n |B|$ (i.e., $|B| = n^{\gamma}$), and

$$\alpha = \frac{1}{2} + \frac{\gamma}{2} - \frac{\delta}{2}, \tag{1}$$

and denote $\ell = 2n^{1-\alpha} \ln n$. We first prove that there are sets $A_1, \ldots, A_\ell \subset A$ of size n^α that satisfy the following properties:

(I) $\bigcup_{i=1}^{\ell} A_i = A$, and
(II) for every $1 \leq i \leq \ell$, the degree of the vertices in B in the graph $G_i = (A_i, B, E \cap (A_i \times B))$ is at most $12n^{\alpha+\delta-1}$.

For each $1 \leq i \leq \ell$, we independently choose A_i with uniform distribution among the subsets of A of size n^α. We show that, with positive probability, $A_1, \ldots, A_\ell$ satisfy properties (I) and (II).

First, we analyze the probability that (I) does not hold.

$$\Pr\left[A \neq \cup A_i\right] \leq \sum_{a \in A} \Pr\left[a \notin \cup A_i\right] = \sum_{a \in A} \prod_{i=1}^{\ell} \Pr\left[a \notin A_i\right] = \sum_{a \in A} \left(1 - \frac{n^{\alpha}}{n}\right)^{\ell}$$

$$\leq \sum_{a \in A} e^{-\ell/n^{1-\alpha}} = n\frac{1}{n^2} = \frac{1}{n}.$$

Now we show that the probability that the sets $A_1, \ldots, A_\ell$ do not satisfy Property (II) is less than $1/4$. Fix an index $1 \leq i \leq \ell$ and a vertex $b \in B$. We analyze the probability that the degree of b in G_i is larger than $12n^{\alpha+\delta-1}$. We view the choice of the random set A_i as a process of n^{α} steps, where in the jth step we uniformly choose a vertex $a_j \in A$ amongst the vertices that have not been chosen in the first $j-1$ steps. Using this view of choosing A_i, we define the following binary random variables $Z_1, \ldots, Z_{n^{\alpha}}$, where $Z_j = 1$ if (a_j, b) is an edge of G_i, and 0 otherwise. Then, we consider $Z = \sum_{j=1}^{n^{\alpha}} Z_j$, that is, Z is the degree of b in G_i.

We would like to apply a Chernoff bound to these variables, however, they are not independent. We use $Z_1, \ldots, Z_{n^{\alpha}}$ to define new random variables $Z_1', \ldots, Z_{n^{\alpha}}'$ that are independent. For every vector $\mathbf{z} = (z_t)_{t \neq j}$, let

$$p_{\mathbf{z}} = \Pr[Z_j = 1 | Z_t = z_t \text{ for all } t \neq j].$$

By convention, if $\Pr[Z_t = z_t \text{ for all } t \neq j] = 0$, then $p_{\mathbf{z}} = 0$. Note that

$$p_{\mathbf{z}} \leq \frac{n^{\delta}}{n - n^{\alpha}} \leq \frac{2}{n^{1-\delta}},$$

where $d = n^{\delta}$ is the upper bound on the degree of b given in the lemma. Observe that the last inequality follows because $n^{1/2} \leq n^{\delta/2+\gamma/2}/\log n$, and so

$$n^{\alpha} = n^{1/2+\gamma/2-\delta/2} \leq n^{(\delta/2+\gamma/2)+\gamma/2-\delta/2}/\log n \leq n/2,$$

obtaining that $n - n^{\alpha} \geq n/2$.

The random variables $Z_1', \ldots, Z_{n^{\alpha}}'$ are defined as follows: Let $z_1, \ldots, z_n$ be the values given to $Z_1, \ldots, Z_n$. If $z_j = 1$, then $Z_j' = 1$ and if $z_j = 0$, then $Z_j' = 1$ with probability $(2/n^{1-\delta} - p_{\mathbf{z}})/(1 - p_{\mathbf{z}})$ and $Z_j' = 0$ otherwise. Thus, $\Pr[Z_j' = 1 | Z_t = z_t \text{ for all } t \neq j] = 2/n^{1-\delta}$. Therefore, Z_j' is independent of $(Z_t)_{t \neq j}$, and, hence, independent of $(Z_t')_{t \neq j}$.

Let $Z' = \sum_{j=1}^{n^{\alpha}} Z_j'$. The expected value of Z' is $n^{\alpha} \cdot 2/n^{1-\delta} = 2n^{\alpha+\delta-1}$. Using a Chernoff bound [40, Theorem 4.4, (4.3)], we obtain

$$\Pr\left[Z > 12n^{\alpha+\delta-1}\right] \leq \Pr\left[Z' > 12n^{\alpha+\delta-1}\right] \leq 2^{-12n^{\alpha+\delta-1}}.$$

By (1) and since $n^{\gamma+\delta} \geq n \log^2 n$, we obtain $n^{\alpha+\delta-1} = n^{\gamma/2+\delta/2-1/2} \geq \log n$. Thus,

$$\Pr\left[Z > 12n^{\alpha+\delta-1}\right] \leq 1/n^{12} \leq 1/(4n\ell).$$

Property (II) holds if for every $b \in B$ and every $1 \le i \le \ell$, the degree of b in G_i is at most $12n^{\alpha+\delta-1}$. By the union bound, the probability that (II) does not hold is at most $1/4$. Thus, again by the union bound, the probability that random sets $A_1, \ldots, A_\ell$ satisfy properties (I) and (II) is greater than $1/2$, and, in particular, such sets exist.

Given valid sets $A_1, \ldots, A_\ell$, we construct a secret-sharing scheme for each bipartite graph $G_i = (A_i, B, E \cap (A_i \times B))$ using Lemma 1. In each one of these subgraphs, the degree of each vertex in B is at most $12n^{\alpha+\delta-1}$. Hence, the total share size of the resulting scheme will be

$$\sum_{i=1}^{\ell} \left(|B| + |A_i| \cdot (12n^{\alpha+\delta-1} + 1) \right) = O\left(\ell(n^\gamma + n^\alpha n^{\alpha+\delta-1}) \right)$$

$$= O\left(n^{1-\alpha} \ln n (n^\gamma + n^{2\alpha+\delta-1}) \right)$$

$$= O\left(\log n (n^{1+\gamma-\alpha} + n^{\alpha+\delta}) \right).$$

This value is minimized when $1 + \gamma - \alpha = \alpha + \delta$, that is, when $\alpha = \frac{1}{2} + \frac{\gamma}{2} - \frac{\delta}{2}$ (this explains our choice of α). Using this value of α, we obtain total share size of $O(n^{1/2+\gamma/2+\delta/2} \log n)$. $\qquad\square$

The following theorem is a special case of the above lemma, when $|A| = |B|$. In the proof of Theorem 2 below, we also use Lemma 3.

Theorem 1. *Let $G = (A, B, E)$ be a bipartite graph such that $|A| = |B| = n$ and the degree of every vertex in B is at most d for some $d \le n$. Then, there is a linear secret-sharing scheme realizing G in which the share size of each vertex is $O(\sqrt{d} \log n)$. The total share size of this scheme is $O(n\sqrt{d} \log n)$.*

Proof. If $d < \log^2 n$, we use the trivial secret-sharing scheme, where we share the secret independently for each edge; in this scheme the share size of each vertex is $O(d) = O(\sqrt{d} \log n)$, and the total share size is $O(n\sqrt{d} \log n)$.

Otherwise, $d \ge \log^2 n$, and let $\delta = \log_n d$, $\ell = 2n^{\delta/2} \ln n$, and $A_1, \ldots, A_\ell \subset A$ be the sets of size $n^{1-\delta/2}$ guaranteed from Lemma 3 (taking $\gamma = 1$). We can assume that each vertex in A is a member of exactly one set (by removing the vertex from every set except from one). Note that the sets still satisfy the two desired properties.

Next, as in Lemma 3, we construct a secret-sharing scheme for each bipartite graph $G_i = (A_i, B, E \cap (A_i \times B))$ (for $1 \le i \le \ell$) using the scheme of Lemma 1. The degree of each vertex in B in the graph G_i is at most $12n^{\delta/2} = O(\sqrt{d})$. Every vertex in B participates in ℓ schemes, and gets a share of size one in each of these schemes. Hence, the share size of every vertex in B is $\ell = O(\sqrt{d} \log n)$. Every vertex in A participates in one scheme, and gets a share of size $12n^{\delta/2} + 1 = O(\sqrt{d})$ in this scheme. Overall, the share size of each vertex in the resulting scheme is $O(\sqrt{d} \log n)$, and the total share size is $O(n\sqrt{d} \log n)$. $\qquad\square$

Theorem 2. *Let $G = (A, B, E)$ be a bipartite graph with $|A| = |B| = n$ and with at most $n^{1+\beta}$ edges, for some constant $0 \le \beta < 1$. Then, there is a linear secret-sharing scheme realizing G with total share size $O(n^{1+\beta/2} \log^2 n)$.*

Proof. If $n^\beta \leq \log^2 n$, we use the trivial secret-sharing scheme, where we share the secret independently for each edge; in this scheme the total share size is $O(n^{1+\beta}) = O(n^{1+\beta/2} \log n)$.

We next deal with the interesting case where $n^\beta > \log^2 n$. In this case, we partition the vertices in B according to their degree, that is, for $i = 0, \ldots, (1-\beta) \log n - 1$, define

$$B_i = \left\{ b \in B : \frac{n}{2^{i+1}} < \deg(b) \leq \frac{n}{2^i} \right\}$$

and $B_{\text{small}} = \{b \in B : \deg(b) \leq n^\beta\}$, and $G_i = (A, B_i, E \cap (A \times B_i))$.

We realize each graph G_i, for $i = 0, \ldots, (1 - \beta) \log n - 1$, using Lemma 3. Since the number of edges in G is at most $n^{1+\beta}$ and the degree of every vertex in B_i is at least $n/2^{i+1}$, the number of vertices in B_i is at most $\frac{n^{1+\beta}}{n/2^{i+1}} = 2^{i+1} n^\beta$. By adding dummy vertices to B_i with degree 0, we can assume that $|B_i| = 2^{i+1} n^\beta$. By Lemma 3, there is a secret-sharing scheme realizing the forbidden graph access structure of G_i with total share size $O(\sqrt{n \cdot 2^{i+1} n^\beta \cdot n/2^i} \cdot \log n) = O(n^{1+\beta/2} \log n)$. Note that, as required in Lemma 3, $d|B_i| = n/2^i \cdot 2^{i+1} n^\beta \geq n \log^2 n$.

Finally, we realize $(A, B_{\text{small}}, E \cap (A \times B_{\text{small}}))$ using the secret-sharing scheme of Theorem 1; the total share size of this scheme is $O(n^{1+\beta/2} \log n)$ as well. Since we use $1 + (1 - \beta) \log n$ schemes, the total share size of the resulting scheme is $O(n^{1+\beta/2} \log^2 n)$. □

Theorem 3. *Let $G = (V, E)$ be a graph with n vertices and with at most $n^{1+\beta}$ edges for some constant $0 \leq \beta < 1$. Then, there is a linear secret-sharing scheme realizing G with total share size $O(n^{1+\beta/2} \log^3 n)$.*

Proof. To simplify notation, assume that n is a power of 2. As in [10], we cover G by $\log n$ bipartite graphs, each graph having at most $n^{1+\beta}$ edges. We assume that $V = \{v_1, \ldots, v_n\}$, and for a vertex v_i we consider i as a binary $\log n$ string $i = (i_1, \ldots, i_{\log n})$. For every $1 \leq t \leq \log n$, we define the bipartite graph $H_t = (A_t, B_t, F_t)$ as the subgraph of G in which A_t is the set of vertices whose t-th bit is 0, B_t is the set of vertices whose t-th bit is 1, and $F_t = E \cap (A_t \times B_t)$, i.e., F_t is the set of edges in E between the vertices of A_t and B_t.

To share a secret s, for every $1 \leq t \leq \log n$, we share s independently using the secret-sharing scheme of Theorem 2 realizing the bipartite graph H_t with total share size $O(n^{1+\beta/2} \log^2 n)$. Since we use $\log n$ schemes, the total share size in the scheme realizing G is $O(n^{1+\beta/2} \log^3 n)$.

For an edge $(v_i, v_j) \in E$, where $i = (i_1, \ldots, i_{\log n})$ and $j = (j_1, \ldots, j_{\log n})$, there is at least one $1 \leq t \leq \log n$ such that $i_t \neq j_t$, thus, $(v_i, v_j) \in F_t$ and $\{v_i, v_j\}$ can reconstruct the secret using the shares of the scheme realizing H_t. If $(v_i, v_j) \notin E$, then $(v_i, v_j) \notin F_t$ for every $1 \leq t \leq \log n$, and, hence, $\{v_i, v_j\}$ have no information on the secret. □

5   Secret-Sharing Schemes for Dense Graphs

In this section we study forbidden graph access structures of dense graphs. The main result of this section is Theorem 6, where for every dense graph we present a linear secret-sharing scheme realizing its forbidden graph access structure. For sparse graphs, we designed a general construction starting from a basic secret-sharing scheme, described in Lemma 1. For dense graphs, we follow the same strategy, replacing the basic construction with a different scheme, given in Lemma 4.

Lemma 4. *Let $G = (A, B, E)$ be a bipartite graph with $|A| = m$, $|B| = n$, such that the degree of every vertex in B is at least $m - d$. Then, there is a linear secret-sharing scheme realizing G with total share size $2n + (d + 1)m$.*

Proof. Denote $A = \{a_1, \ldots, a_m\}$, $B = \{b_1, \ldots, b_n\}$. Let $\overline{G} = (A, B, \overline{E})$ be the bipartite complement of G, and let $V_1, \ldots, V_m \subseteq \mathbb{F}^{d+1}$ be the linear subspaces of dimension d and $\mathbf{z_1}, \ldots, \mathbf{z_n}, \mathbf{w} \in \mathbb{F}^{d+1}$ be the vectors guaranteed by Claim 2 for the graph $\overline{G}$. As proved in Claim 2, $\mathbf{z_j} \in V_i$ if and only if $(a_i, b_j) \notin E$ and $\mathbf{w} \notin V_i$ for every $1 \leq i \leq m$.

Next, we construct a monotone span program where there are $d + 1$ rows labeled by a_i for every $1 \leq i \leq m$ and two rows labeled by b_j for every $1 \leq j \leq n$. Let $\{\mathbf{v_{i,1}}, \ldots, \mathbf{v_{i,d}}\}$ be a basis of V_i. The rows labeled by a_i are $(0, 0, \mathbf{v_{i,1}}), \ldots, (0, 0, \mathbf{v_{i,d}}), (0, 1, 0, \ldots, 0)$ and the rows labeled by b_j are $(0, 0, \mathbf{z_j})$ and $(1, 0, \ldots, 0)$. We take $(1, 1, \mathbf{w})$ as the target vector.

We first prove that the span program accepts an edge $(a_i, b_j) \in E$. Since $(a_i, b_j) \in E$, it holds that $\mathbf{z_j} \notin V_i$ and so the dimension of span $\{\mathbf{z_j}, \mathbf{v_{i,1}}, \ldots, \mathbf{v_{i,d}}\}$ is 1 plus the dimension of V_i, i.e., span $\{\mathbf{z_j}, \mathbf{v_{i,1}}, \ldots, \mathbf{v_{i,d}}\} = \mathbb{F}^{d+1}$, and in particular,

$$\mathbf{w} \in \text{span} \{\mathbf{z_j}, \mathbf{v_{i,1}}, \ldots, \mathbf{v_{i,d}}\}.$$

Thus, $(1, 1, \mathbf{w})$ is in the span of the vectors labeled by a_i and b_j.

We next prove that this monotone span program does not accept any pair $(a_i, b_j) \notin E$ where $a_i \in A$ and $b_j \in B$. By Claim 2, $\mathbf{w} \notin V_i$. Since $(a_i, b_j) \notin E$, it holds that $\mathbf{z_j} \in V_i$ and so $\mathbf{w} \notin \text{span} \{\mathbf{z_j}, \mathbf{v_{i,1}}, \ldots, \mathbf{v_{i,d}}\} = V_i$. Thus, $(1, 1, \mathbf{w})$ is not in the span of the vectors labeled by a_i and b_j

Furthermore, two vertices from the same part do not span $(1, 1, \mathbf{w})$: For two vertices in A, this follows since the first coordinate in all vectors they label is 0. For two vertices in B, this follows since the second coordinate in the vectors they label is 0. Therefore, the monotone span program accepts G. $\square$

Lemma 5. *Let $G = (A, B, E)$ be a bipartite graph with $|A| = n$, $|B| \leq n$, and let $\overline{G} = (A, B, \overline{E})$ be the bipartite complement of G. If the degree of B in $\overline{G}$ is at most d, for some d satisfying $d \leq n$ and $d|B| \geq n \log^2 n$, then there is a linear secret-sharing scheme realizing G with total share size $O(\sqrt{n|B|d} \log n)$.*

Proof. We use the techniques presented in the proof of Lemma 3. We take $\delta = \log_n d$, $\gamma = \log_n |B|$, $\alpha = \frac{1}{2} + \frac{\gamma}{2} - \frac{\delta}{2}$, and $\ell = 2n^{1-\alpha} \ln n$. By the proof of Lemma 3, there exist sets $A_1, \ldots, A_\ell \subset A$ of size n^α that satisfy:

(I) $\bigcup_{i=1}^{\ell} A_i = A$, and

(II) for every $1 \leq i \leq \ell$, the degree of the vertices in B in the graph $\overline{G}_i = (A_i, B, \overline{E} \cap (A_i \times B))$ is at most $12n^{\alpha+\delta-1}$.

Then, we construct a secret-sharing scheme for each bipartite graph $G_i = (A_i, B, E \cap (A_i \times B))$ using Lemma 4. The degree of each vertex in B in the graph G_i is at least $|A_i| - 12n^{\alpha+\delta-1}$, so the total share size will be

$$O\left(\sum_{i=1}^{\ell} |B| + |A_i| \cdot 12n^{\alpha+\delta-1}\right) =$$
$$= O\left(\ln n(n^{1+\gamma-\alpha} + n^{\alpha+\delta})\right) = O(n^{1/2+\gamma/2+\delta/2}\log n).$$

$\square$

Theorem 4. *Let $G = (A, B, E)$ be a bipartite graph such that $|A| = |B| = n$ and the degree of every vertex in B is at least $n-d$ for some $d \leq n$. Then, there is a linear secret-sharing scheme realizing G in which the share size of each vertex is $O(\sqrt{d}\log n)$. The total share size of this scheme is $O(n\sqrt{d}\log n)$.*

Proof. If $d < \log^2 n$, we use the construction in [8, Lemma 3.8]; in this scheme the share size of each vertex is $O(d) = O(\sqrt{d}\log n)$, and the total share size is $O(n\sqrt{d}\log n)$.[4]

Otherwise, $d \geq \log^2 n$, and let $\delta = \log_n d$, $\ell = 2n^{\delta/2}\ln n$, and $A_1, \ldots, A_\ell \subset A$ be the sets of size $n^{1-\delta/2}$ guarantied from Lemma 5 (taking $\gamma = 1$). As in Theorem 1, we can assume that each vertex in A is a member of exactly one set, and the sets still satisfy the two desired properties.

Next, as in Lemma 5, we construct a secret-sharing scheme for each bipartite graph $G_i = (A_i, B, E \cap (A_i \times B))$ (for $1 \leq i \leq \ell$) using the scheme of Lemma 4. The degree of each vertex in B in the bipartite complement of G_i is at most $12n^{\delta/2} = O(\sqrt{d})$. Every vertex in B participates in ℓ schemes, and gets a share of size two in each of these schemes. Hence, the share size of every vertex in B is $2\ell = O(\sqrt{d}\log n)$. Every vertex in A participates in one scheme, and gets a share of size $12n^{\delta/2} + 1 = O(\sqrt{d})$ in this scheme. Overall, the share size of each vertex in the resulting scheme is $O(\sqrt{d}\log n)$, and the total share size is $O(n\sqrt{d}\log n)$.

$\square$

Theorem 5. *Let $G = (A, B, E)$ be a bipartite graph with $|A| = |B| = n$ such that its bipartite complement $\overline{G} = (A, B, \overline{E})$ has at most $n^{1+\beta}$ edges, for some constant $0 \leq \beta < 1$. Then, there is a linear secret-sharing scheme realizing G with total share size $O(n^{1+\beta/2}\log^2 n)$.*

Proof. As in the proof of Theorem 2, for $i = 0, \ldots, (1 - \beta)\log n - 1$, define $B_i = \{b \in B : \frac{n}{2^{i+1}} < \deg_{\overline{G}}(b) \leq \frac{n}{2^i}\}$ and $B_{\text{small}} = \{b \in B : \deg_{\overline{G}}(b) \leq n^\beta\}$.

For every $0 \leq i \leq (1 - \beta)\log n - 1$, we use Lemma 5 to construct a secret-sharing scheme realizing the graph $(A, B_i, E \cap (A \times B_i))$; the total share size

---

[4] In [8, Lemma 3.8], it is only stated that the total share size in the scheme is $O(nd)$, however, in their scheme the size of the share of each vertex is $O(d)$.

of this scheme is $O(\sqrt{n \cdot 2^{i+1} n^\beta \cdot n/2^i} \cdot \log n) = O(n^{1+\beta/2} \log n)$. Finally, we realize $(A, B_{\text{small}}, E \cap (A \times B_{\text{small}}))$ using the secret-sharing scheme of Theorem 4; the total share size of this scheme is $O(n^{1+\beta/2} \log n)$ as well. Since we use $1 + (1 - \beta) \log n$ schemes, the total share size of the resulting scheme is $O(n^{1+\beta/2} \log^2 n)$.   □

Theorem 6. *Let $G = (V, E)$ be a graph with n vertices and with at least $\binom{n}{2} - n^{1+\beta}$ edges, for some constant $0 \le \beta < 1$. Then, there is a secret-sharing scheme realizing G with total share size $O(n^{1+\beta/2} \log^3 n)$.*

Proof. For every $1 \le t \le \log n$, we define the bipartite graph $H_t = (A_t, B_t, F_t)$ as in Theorem 3. The bipartite complements of these bipartite graphs have at most $n^{1+\beta}$ edges. By Theorem 5, each such bipartite graph admits a secret-sharing scheme with total share size $O(n^{1+\beta/2} \log^2 n)$. The total share size of the resulting scheme is $O(n^{1+\beta/2} \log^3 n)$.   □

We use Theorems 3 and 6 to show that the total share sizes required to realize two graphs that differ in a few edges is close.

Corollary 1. *Let $G = (V, E)$ be a graph with n vertices that can be realized by a secret-sharing scheme in which the total share size is m, and let G' be a graph obtained from G by adding and removing $n^{1+\beta}$ edges, for some constant $0 \le \beta < 1$. Then, there is a secret-sharing scheme realizing G' with total share size $O(m + n^{1+\beta/2} \log^3 n)$.*

Proof. Let s be the secret, $E' \subset E$ be the set of edges removed from G, and E'' (where $E'' \cap E = \emptyset$) be the set of edges added to G. Note that $G' = (V, (E \backslash E') \cup E'')$ and $|E'|, |E''| \le n^{1+\beta}$. First, we share the secret s using the secret-sharing scheme of Theorem 3 realizing the sparse graph (V, E'') with total share size $O(n^{1+\beta/2} \log^3 n)$. Next, we independently share the secret s using a 2-out-of-2 secret-sharing scheme. I.e., let s_1, s_2 be two random elements such that $s = s_1 \oplus s_2$ (i.e., s_1 is chosen at random and $s_2 = s_1 \oplus s$). We independently share s_1 using the scheme realizing G with total share size m, and share s_2 using the secret-sharing scheme of Theorem 6 realizing the dense graph $(V, \overline{E'})$ (note that $|\overline{E'}| \ge \binom{n}{2} - n^{1+\beta}$) with total share size $O(n^{1+\beta/2} \log^3 n)$. The total share size of the resulting scheme is $O(m + n^{1+\beta/2} \log^3 n)$.

For an edge e in the graph G', if $e \in E''$, then it can reconstruct the secret using the scheme of Theorem 3 realizing (V, E''), and if $e \in E \backslash E' = E \cap \overline{E'}$, then it can reconstruct s_1 using the scheme realizing G and can reconstruct s_2 using the scheme of Theorem 6 realizing $(V, \overline{E'})$, and, hence, can reconstruct the secret s.

For an edge e not in the graph G', if $e \in E'$, then it cannot get information on the secret s from the scheme realizing (V, E'') (since $E'' \cap E' = \emptyset$, which implies that $e \notin E''$), and it cannot learn information on s_2 from the scheme realizing $(V, \overline{E'})$, and, hence, it cannot get information on the secret s from the 2-out-of-2 scheme. Otherwise, if $e \in \overline{E \cup E''}$, then it cannot get information on the secret s from the scheme realizing (V, E'') (since $e \notin E''$), and it cannot learn information on s_1 from the scheme realizing G (since $e \notin E$), and, hence, it cannot get information on the secret s from the 2-out-of-2 scheme. $\square$

6   Lower Bounds for Linear Secret-Sharing Schemes

In this section, we prove that for most forbidden graph access structures with n parties, the total share size required by any linear secret-sharing scheme realizing these access structures, with a one-bit secret, is $\Omega(n^{3/2})$. We then use this result to prove that for most forbidden graph access structures with n parties and at most $n^{1+\beta}$ edges, the total share size required by any linear secret-sharing scheme realizing these access structures, with a one-bit secret, is $\Omega(n^{1+\beta/2})$. As we show in this paper, this bound is tight up to a poly-logarithmic factor. Furthermore, we bound the share size of families of access structures whose size of minimal authorized sets is small. Since linear secret-sharing schemes are equivalent to monotone span programs (see Claim 1), we prove the lower bounds using MSP terminology.

The section is organized as follows: We start with some definitions, then in Sect. 6.1 we discuss dual access structures and the dual of MSPs. In Sect. 6.2, we prove lower bounds for MSPs in which each party labels a bounded number of rows; this implies lower bounds for the max share size in linear secret-sharing schemes. In Sect. 6.3, we prove a stronger result – the same lower bounds hold for the size of MSPs; this implies lower bounds for the total share size in linear secret-sharing schemes (this result uses the results of Section 6.2).

Definition 7. *Let $\widehat{M} = \langle \mathbb{F}, M, \delta, \mathbf{1} \rangle$ be an MSP accepting an access structure Γ. Define $\rho_i(\widehat{M})$ as the number of rows labeled by i, and define $\rho(\widehat{M})$ as the maximal number of rows labeled by a single label: $\rho(\widehat{M}) \overset{def}{=} \max_{i \in P} \rho_i(\widehat{M})$. Define $\rho_q(\Gamma)$ as the minimum $\rho(\widehat{M})$ over all MSPs accepting the access structure Γ over $\mathbb{F}_q$.*

Define $\mathrm{size}(\widehat{M})$ as the number of rows in the matrix M and $\mathrm{size}_q(\Gamma)$ as the minimum $\mathrm{size}(\widehat{M})$ over all MSPs accepting the access structure Γ over $\mathbb{F}_q$.

Notice that $\rho_q(\Gamma)$ is the minimal max share size of all linear secret-sharing schemes accepting Γ over $\mathbb{F}_q$, and $\mathrm{size}_q(\Gamma)$ is the minimal total share size of all linear secret-sharing schemes accepting Γ over $\mathbb{F}_q$.

Definition 8. *We say that an access structure Γ has rank r if the size of every minimal authorized set in Γ is at most r.*

By counting arguments it is possible to prove lower bounds on the monotone span program size for most access structures: Assume that every access structure can be accepted by an MSP of size S. The number of MSPs with n parties over $\mathbb{F}_q$ whose size is at most S is at most $n^S q^{S^2}$ (as proved in Proposition 1 below, we can consider MSPs in which the number of columns in the matrix of the MSP is at most S, thus, there are q^{S^2} possible matrices and n^S possible ways to label the rows, where n is the number of parties). Since the number of monotone access structures is at least $2^{2^n/\sqrt{n}}$ and every MSP accepts one monotone access structure, it must be that $n^S q^{S^2} \geq 2^{2^n/\sqrt{n}}$, i.e., $S \log n + S^2 \log q \geq 2^n/\sqrt{n}$, which implies that $S \log q > S\sqrt{\log q} = \Omega(2^{n/2}/n^{1/4})$ (where $S \log q$ is the non-normalized total share size of the scheme).

It is not clear how to use direct counting arguments to prove lower bounds on the size of MSPs accepting forbidden graph access structures: the number of graphs is $2^{O(n^2)}$, thus, we get that $n^S q^{S^2} \geq 2^{O(n^2)}$, which only implies the trivial lower bound $S \log q > S\sqrt{\log q} = \Omega(n)$.

6.1   Dual of Monotone Span Programs

We use the notion of *dual access structures* and *dual MSPs*, since their properties would enable us to use a counting argument that will yield tight lower bounds on the size of MSPs accepting forbidden graph access structures. Such dual's were studied in many papers, e.g., [28,30,31,36].

Definition 9 (Dual Access Structure). *Given an access structure* $\Gamma \subseteq 2^P$, *its* dual access structure $\Gamma^\perp$ *is defined as*

$$\Gamma^\perp \stackrel{def}{=} \{B \subseteq P : P\backslash B \notin \Gamma\}.$$

For example, for the *t-out-of-n* access structure $\Gamma_t = \{B \subseteq P : |B| \geq t\}$ (where $|P| = n$),

$$\Gamma_t^\perp = \{B \subseteq P : |P\backslash B| < t\} = \{B \subseteq P : |B| > n - t\}.$$

Given an MSP, we can define its *dual MSP*. For this construction, recall that given an MSP $\langle \mathbb{F}, M, \delta, \mathbf{1} \rangle$ accepting Γ, for every authorized set $A \in \Gamma$ there exists a reconstruction vector $\mathbf{r_A}$ such that $\mathbf{r_A} M = \mathbf{1}$, and $(\mathbf{r_A})^T$ is non-zero only in rows labeled by A.

Constructions 1 (Dual MSP). *Given an MSP* $\widehat{M} = \langle \mathbb{F}, M, \delta, \mathbf{1} \rangle$ *accepting* Γ *over* $\mathbb{F}$, *construct an MSP* $\widehat{M^\perp} = \langle \mathbb{F}, M^\perp, \delta, \mathbf{1} \rangle$ *in which for every minimal authorized set* $A \in \min \Gamma$ *there exists a column* $(\mathbf{r_A})^T$ *in* $M^\perp$, *where* $\mathbf{r_A}$ *is a reconstruction vector for* A *in* M. *The MSP* $\widehat{M^\perp} = \langle \mathbb{F}, M^\perp, \delta, \mathbf{1} \rangle$ *is called the* dual MSP.

The following claim can be found in [31]. For completeness, we include its proof.

Claim 3. *Let* $\widehat{M} = \langle \mathbb{F}, M, \delta, \mathbf{1} \rangle$ *be an MSP accepting an access structure* $\Gamma \subseteq 2^P$. *The dual MSP* $\widehat{M^\perp} = \langle \mathbb{F}, M^\perp, \delta, \mathbf{1} \rangle$, *as defined in Construciton 1, is an MSP accepting the dual access structure* $\Gamma^\perp$. *The sizes of* $\widehat{M} = \langle \mathbb{F}, M, \delta, \mathbf{1} \rangle$ *and* $\widehat{M^\perp} = \langle \mathbb{F}, M^\perp, \delta, \mathbf{1} \rangle$ *are the same.*

Proof. We begin by proving that for every authorized set $A \in \Gamma$, the set $B = P\backslash A$ is rejected by $\widehat{M^\perp}$. It suffices to consider only minimal authorized sets

$A \in \min \Gamma$. The reconstruction vector $\mathbf{r_A}$ of A is a column of $M^{\perp}$, and has non-zero entries only in rows labeled by A. The rows labeled by $B = P \backslash A$ cannot span $\mathbf{1}$, since in the column $(\mathbf{r_A})^T$ all entries labeled by B are zero.

Now, assume that $A \notin \Gamma$. In this case, the rows of M labeled by elements from A do not linearly span $\mathbf{1}$. By orthogonality arguments, there is a column vector $\mathbf{v}$ such that $\mathbf{1} \cdot \mathbf{v} = 1$ and $M_A \mathbf{v} = \mathbf{0}$, where M_A are the rows of M labeled by elements from A. Denote $\mathbf{w} = (M\mathbf{v})^T$. We prove that $\mathbf{w} M^{\perp} = \mathbf{1}$, i.e., $\mathbf{w}$ is a reconstruction vector of $B = P \backslash A$ in $\widehat{M^{\perp}}$. For every column $\mathbf{r_C}$ of $M^{\perp}$ the following is true:

$$\mathbf{w} \cdot (\mathbf{r_C})^T = (M\mathbf{v})^T \cdot (\mathbf{r_C})^T = \mathbf{v}^T M^T (\mathbf{r_C})^T = \mathbf{v}^T (\mathbf{r_C} M)^T = \mathbf{v}^T \cdot \mathbf{1}^T = 1.$$

This implies that $\mathbf{w} \cdot M^{\perp} = \mathbf{1}$. Furthermore, the vector $\mathbf{w}^T$ is non-zero only in rows labeled by $B = P \backslash A$ (since $M_A \mathbf{v} = 0$). Thus, the set B has a reconstruction vector for the MSP $\widehat{M^{\perp}}$, and, therefore, is accepted by $\widehat{M^{\perp}}$.

Since the MSP and its dual MSP have the same labeling, the size of the MSP and the dual MSP are the same. □

Claim 3 implies that lower bounds on the size of the dual MSPs over $\mathbb{F}$ for forbidden graph access structures yield lower bounds on the total share size of linear secret-sharing schemes over $\mathbb{F}$ for forbidden graph access structures. The following simple proposition bounds the number of columns of an MSP.

Proposition 1. *For every non-empty access structure Γ and every prime-power q, there is an MSP $\widehat{M} = \langle \mathbb{F}_q, M, \delta, \mathbf{1} \rangle$ accepting Γ such that $\mathrm{size}(\widehat{M}) = \mathrm{size}_q(\Gamma)$ and the number of columns in M is at most $\mathrm{size}(\widehat{M})$.*

Proof. Let $\widehat{M'} = \langle \mathbb{F}_q, M', \delta, \mathbf{1} \rangle$ be an MSP accepting Γ such that $\mathrm{size}(\widehat{M'}) = \mathrm{size}_q(\Gamma)$. We remove all dependent columns from the MSP $\widehat{M'}$; this does not change the sets accepted by the MSP. We obtain an MSP $\widehat{M} = \langle \mathbb{F}_q, M, \delta, \mathbf{1} \rangle$ accepting Γ such that all columns of M are linearly independent. Since column rank equals row rank, the number of columns in M is at most the number of rows in M, which is the number of rows in M'.[5] □

Given an access structure Γ of rank r and an MSP $\widehat{M} = \langle \mathbb{F}, M, \delta, \mathbf{1} \rangle$ accepting Γ, we consider its dual $\widehat{M^{\perp}} = \langle \mathbb{F}, M^{\perp}, \delta, \mathbf{1} \rangle$ which accepts $\Gamma^{\perp}$. We can assume that $M^{\perp}$ has at most S independent columns that form a basis spanning all reconstruction vectors $\{\mathbf{r_A}\}_{A \in \min \Gamma}$ (where S is the size of the MSPs $\widehat{M}$ and $\widehat{M^{\perp}}$). In particular, for every column in $M^{\perp}$ there is a set of parties A of size at most r such that the non-zero elements in the column are only in rows labeled by A.

---

[5] Notice that the rows are not necessarily linearly independent (since rows labeled by different parties can be dependent). Therefore, the number of columns can actually be smaller than the number of rows.

6.2   Counting Monotone Span Programs with Small Max Share Size

We next compute the number of access structures of rank r that have an MSP such that each party labels at most s rows and prove that there are at most $2^{O(rns^2 \log q)}$ such access structures.

Theorem 7. *Let q be a prime power and s, r, n be integers such that $s > \log n$. The number of access structures Γ with n parties, rank r, and $\rho_q(\Gamma) \leq s$ is at most $2^{2rns^2 \log q}$.*

Proof. If $\rho_q(\Gamma) \leq s$, then, as explained above, there is an MSP $\widehat{M^\perp} = \langle \mathbb{F}, M^\perp, \delta, \mathbf{1} \rangle$ accepting $\Gamma^\perp$ of the following form:

- $M^\perp$ is an $ns \times ns$ matrix (this can be achieved without changing the validity of the MSP by adding zero rows or duplicating columns).
- δ is fixed and $\delta(i) = \lceil \frac{i}{s} \rceil$, i.e., the first s rows are labeled by the first party, the next s rows are labeled by the second party, and so on.
- Every column of $M^\perp$ is a reconstruction vector of some minimal authorized set $A \in \min \Gamma$ (by Claim 3).

Every dual of a rank r access structure has an MSP of this form, and the number of these MSPs is bounded by the number of possible matrices. Every matrix has ns columns, each is a reconstruction vector of some $A \in \min \Gamma$. By the definition of reconstruction vectors, the columns can have non-zero values only in entries labeled by some $i \in A$, that is, at most rs entries can be non-zero. Therefore, the number of possible column vectors for a given minimal authorized set $A \in \min \Gamma$ is at most $|\mathbb{F}_q|^{rs} = q^{rs}$. Since we allow the entries in rows labeled by A to be zero, we can assume that the size of A is exactly r. The number of sets of size r that can label a column is $\binom{n}{r} < n^r < 2^{rs}$ (since $s > \log n$). Thus, since the number of columns is ns, the number of such matrices is at most

$$(2^{rs} q^{rs})^{ns} < 2^{2rns^2 \log q}.$$

$\square$

Theorem 7 bounds the number of MSPs over a given finite field. We use this result to give a lower bound on the share size in sharing a one-bit secret for forbidden graph access structures by a linear secret-sharing schemes over all finite fields.

Theorem 8. *For most forbidden graph access structures, the max share size for sharing a one-bit secret in a linear secret-sharing scheme is $\Omega(\sqrt{n})$.*

Proof. If we share a one-bit secret using an MSP $\widehat{M}$ over $\mathbb{F}_q$ with $\rho(\widehat{M}) = s$, then the size of the share of at least one party is $s \log q$. For the max share size to be less than $\sqrt{n}$, it must be that $q \leq 2^{\sqrt{n}}$ (otherwise, every share contains at least $\sqrt{n}$ bits), and, furthermore, $s \log q \leq \sqrt{n}$.

We next bound the number of forbidden graph access structures that can be realized by a secret-sharing scheme with max share size at most θ. Recall that in forbidden graph access structures all sets of size 3 are authorized. On one hand, by Theorem 7, the number of forbidden graph access structures Γ, each one of them has rank at most 3, with n parties and $\rho_q(\Gamma) \leq \theta/\log q$, is at most $2^{6n(\theta/\log q)^2 \log q} < 2^{6n\theta^2}$. Since we are counting linear schemes, we need to sum the number of the MSPs for every possible finite field (there are at most $2^{\sqrt{n}}$ such fields, because $q \leq 2^{\sqrt{n}}$). Consider the MSPs for which the max share size in the secret-sharing schemes defined by the MSPs is at most $\theta < \sqrt{n}$. The number of such MSPs is at most $2^{\sqrt{n}} \cdot 2^{6n\theta^2} \ll 2^{7n\theta^2}$. On the other hand, the number of graphs is $2^{\binom{n}{2}} \approx 2^{n^2/2}$. Thus, if half of the forbidden graph access structures have a linear secret-sharing scheme with max share size θ, then $2^{7n\theta^2} > \frac{1}{2} \cdot 2^{n^2/2}$, i.e., $\theta = \Omega(\sqrt{n})$. $\qquad\square$

Since CDS protocols are equivalent to secret-sharing schemes for forbidden graph access structures, we get the following corollary.

Corollary 2. *For most functions $f : \{0,1\}^N \times \{0,1\}^N \to \{0,1\}$, the communication complexity of every linear conditional disclosure of secrets protocol for f is $\Omega(2^{N/2})$.*

The same lower bound holds for graph access structures. Furthermore, if we take sparse forbidden graphs with at most $n^{1+\beta}$ edges for some constant $0 \leq \beta < 1$, then the number of such graphs is at least

$$\binom{n^2/2}{n^{1+\beta}} \geq \left(\frac{n^2/2}{n^{1+\beta}}\right)^{n^{1+\beta}} = 2^{\Omega(n^{1+\beta} \log n)}.$$

Thus, the max share size θ for such forbidden graph access structures has to satisfy $n\theta^2 > \Omega(n^{1+\beta} \log n)$, i.e., $\theta = \Omega(n^{\beta/2}\sqrt{\log n})$.

6.3 Counting Monotone Span Programs with Small Total Share Size

Theorem 7 counts the number of rank r access structures with $\rho_q(\Gamma) \leq s$. The total share size of access structures with max share size s can still be small, i.e., $n + s$. Next, we count the number of forbidden graph access structures with MSPs of size at most S.

Theorem 9. *Let q be a prime power and S, n be integers such that $S > n \log n$. The number of forbidden graph access structures Γ with n parties and $\mathrm{size}_q(\Gamma) \leq S$ is at most $2^{n^2/3+(72S^2 \log q)/n}$.*

Proof. Let $\widehat{M} = \langle \mathbb{F}, M, \delta, \mathbf{1} \rangle$ be a monotone span program accepting a forbidden graph access structure Γ of a graph $G = (V, E)$ with n parties $V = \{v_1, \ldots, v_n\}$ such that $\mathrm{size}(\widehat{M}) \leq S$. Let $B \subseteq V$ be the set of parties such that each one of the parties in B labels more than $4S/n$ rows in $\widehat{M}$. The size of B must be at most $n/4$. Let $\widehat{M}' = \langle \mathbb{F}, M', \delta', \mathbf{1} \rangle$ be the monotone span program obtained from $\widehat{M}$

by removing the rows of M labeled by parties in B. Notice that $\rho(\widehat{M'}) \leq 4S/n$. Furthermore, $\widehat{M'}$ accepts the forbidden graph access structure Γ' obtained from Γ by removing all the authorized sets containing parties from B. That is, Γ' is the forbidden graph access structure of the graph G' obtained by removing B from G (i.e., $G' = (V\backslash B, E \cap (V\backslash B) \times (V\backslash B)))$.

We say that a forbidden graph access structure Γ is efficient if $\text{size}_q(\Gamma) \leq S$. For every efficient forbidden graph access structure Γ of a graph G with n parties, arbitrarily choose an MSP $\widehat{M_G}$ accepting it whose size is exactly S,[6] choose a set B_G of size exactly $n/4$ such that each party in $V\backslash B_G$ labels at most $4S/n$ rows in $\widehat{M_G}$, and let H_G be the graph obtained by removing B_G from G. As explained above, if Γ is efficient then $\rho(\widehat{M'}) \leq 4S/n$.

Fix a set $B \subset V$ of size $n/4$ and a graph $H = (V_H, E_H)$ such that $V_H \subset \{v_1, \ldots, v_n\}$ and $|V_H| = 3n/4$. We next give an upper-bound on the number of efficient forbidden graph access structures Γ such that $B_G = B$ and $H_G = H$. The number of graphs $G = (V, E)$ such that H is obtained by removing B from G is at most $2^{\binom{n/4}{2}} \cdot 2^{\frac{n}{4} \cdot \frac{3n}{4}} \leq 2^{n^2/4}$ (where the first term corresponds to possible edges between vertices in B and the second term corresponds to possible edges between a vertex in B and a vertex in $V\backslash B$),

To conclude, the number of efficient forbidden graph access structures over $\mathbb{F}_q$ is at most

$$\binom{n}{n/4} \cdot 2^{n^2/4} \cdot 2^{6(3n/4)(4S/n)^2 \log q} \leq 2^{n^2/3 + 72(S^2/n) \log q},$$

where the first term is the number of possible choices of B, the second term is an upper bound on the number of graphs such that the graph obtained by removing B from these graph is the same, and the third term is an upper bound on the number of forbidden graph access structures Γ' whose set of parties is $V\backslash B$ and $\rho_q(\Gamma') \leq 4S/n$.   □

Corollary 3. *For most forbidden graph access structures, the total share size for sharing a one-bit secret in a linear secret-sharing scheme is $\Omega(n^{3/2})$.*

Proof. If we share a one-bit secret using an MSP $\widehat{M}$ over $\mathbb{F}_q$ with $\text{size}_q(\widehat{M}) = S$, then the total share size is $S \log q$. For the total share size to be less than $n^{3/2}$, it must be that $q \leq 2^{\sqrt{n}}$ (otherwise, each share contains more than $\sqrt{n}$ bits, and, in total, the share size is more than $n^{3/2}$), and, furthermore, $S \log q \leq n^{3/2}$.

On one hand, by Theorem 9, the number of forbidden graph access structures Γ with n parties and $\text{size}_q(\Gamma) \leq \Theta/\log q$ is at most

$$2^{n^2/3 + (72(\Theta/\log q)^2 \log q)/n} < 2^{n^2/3 + 72\Theta^2/n}.$$

Since we are counting linear schemes, we need to sum the number of the MSPs for every possible finite field (there are at most $2^{\sqrt{n}}$ such fields, because $q \leq 2^{\sqrt{n}}$).

---

[6] By adding all-zero rows we can assume that the size is exactly S.

Consider the MSPs for which the total share size in the secret-sharing schemes defined by the MSPs is at most $\Theta < n^{3/2}$. The number of such MSPs is at most

$$2^{\sqrt{n}} \cdot 2^{n^2/3 + 72\Theta^2/n}.$$

On the other hand, the number of graphs is $2^{\binom{n}{2}} \approx 2^{n^2/2}$. Thus, if half of the forbidden graph access structures have a linear secret-sharing scheme with total share size Θ, then $\sqrt{n} + n^2/3 + 72\Theta^2/n > n^2/2 - 1$, i.e., $\Theta = \Omega(n^{3/2})$. □

We cannot apply Theorem 9 directly to prove lower bounds on the total share size of linear schemes for sparse or dense forbidden graph access structures, since the term of $2^{n^2/3}$ in Theorem 9 dominates the number of sparse graphs. To prove lower bounds for sparse forbidden graph access structures, we use an idea from [7].

Corollary 4. *Let $0 \leq \beta < 1$ be a constant. There exists a forbidden graph access structure with at most $n^{1+\beta}$ edges such that the total share size for sharing a one-bit secret in a linear secret-sharing scheme is $\Omega(n^{1+\beta/2})$. Furthermore, there exists a forbidden graph access structure with at least $\binom{n}{2} - n^{1+\beta}$ edges such that the total share size for sharing a one-bit secret in a linear secret-sharing scheme is $\Omega(n^{1+\beta/2})$.*

Proof. By Corollary 3, for every n there exists a graph with n vertices such that the total share size in any linear secret-sharing scheme realizing its forbidden graph access structure is $\Omega(n^{3/2})$. We use such a graph (with fewer vertices) to construct a sparse graph $G = (V, E)$ with n vertices. We partition the vertices of G into $n^{1-\beta}$ disjoint sets of vertices $V_1, \ldots, V_{n^{1-\beta}}$, where $|V_i| = n^\beta$ for $1 \leq i \leq n^{1-\beta}$. We construct the edges as follows: For every i (where $1 \leq i \leq n^{1-\beta}$), we construct a copy of a graph from Corollary 3 with n^β vertices among the vertices of V_i. We denote this graph by G_i. There are no edges between vertices in different sets.

Since all edges in the above construction are between vertices in the same part, the number of edges is at most $\binom{n^\beta}{2} n^{1-\beta} < n^{1+\beta}$. The total share size of any linear secret-sharing scheme realizing G_i (for $1 \leq i \leq n^{1-\beta}$) is $\Omega((n^\beta)^{3/2}) = \Omega(n^{3\beta/2})$. Thus, the total share size of any linear secret-sharing scheme realizing G is $\Omega(n^{1-\beta} n^{3\beta/2}) = \Omega(n^{1+\beta/2})$.

To construct a dense graph with at least $\binom{n}{2} - n^{1+\beta}$ edges that requires large shares in every linear scheme realizing its forbidden graph access structure, we use a similar construction, however, we add all edges between different sets. Similar analysis implies that the resulting graph has at least $\binom{n}{2} - n^{1+\beta}$ edges and the total share size of any linear secret-sharing scheme realizing the graph is $\Omega(n^{1+\beta/2})$. □

Theorem 10. *Let q be a prime power and S, n, r be integers such that $S > n \log n$. The number of rank r access structures with n parties and $\text{size}_q(\Gamma) \leq S$ is at most*

$$\exp\left(O\left((1 - (3/4)^r)\binom{n}{r} + \frac{rS^2 \log q}{n}\right)\right).$$

Proof. The proof is similar to the proof of Theorem 9, i.e., given an MSP of size S, we find a set B of size at most $n/4$ containing all parties such that each one of these parties labels more than $4S/n$ rows. Let Γ' be an access structure over $3n/4$ parties such that each one of them label at most $4S/n$ rows. To complete the proof, we need to upper bound the number of rank r access structures with n parties whose restriction to $3n/4$ parties is Γ'. The number of sets of size r that intersect B is the number of sets of size r minus the number of sets of size r contained in $P \backslash B$ i.e.,

$$\binom{n}{r} - \binom{3n/4}{r} > (1 - (3/4)^r)\binom{n}{r}.$$

Thus, the number of rank r access structures with an MSP over $\mathbb{F}_q$ of size at most S is at most

$$\binom{n}{n/4} \cdot 2^{(1-(3/4)^r)\binom{n}{r}} \cdot 2^{2r(3n/4)(4S/n)^2 \log q} =$$

$$= \exp\left(O\left((1-(3/4)^r)\binom{n}{r} + \frac{rS^2 \log q}{n}\right)\right).$$

□

We conclude that for most rank r access structures with n parties, the size of the shares in every linear secret-sharing scheme realizing the access structure with a one-bit secret is $\Omega(n^{(r+1)/2})$.

References

1. Ambrona, M., Barthe, G., Schmidt, B.: Generic transformations of predicate encodings: constructions and applications. In: Katz, J., Shacham, H. (eds.) CRYPTO 2017. LNCS, vol. 10401, pp. 36–66. Springer, Cham (2017). https://doi.org/10.1007/978-3-319-63688-7_2
2. Applebaum, B., Arkis, B., Raykov, P., Vasudevan, P.N.: Conditional disclosure of secrets: amplification, closure, amortization, lower-bounds, and separations. In: Katz, J., Shacham, H. (eds.) CRYPTO 2017. LNCS, vol. 10401, pp. 727–757. Springer, Cham (2017). https://doi.org/10.1007/978-3-319-63688-7_24
3. Attrapadung, N.: Dual system encryption via doubly selective security: framework, fully secure functional encryption for regular languages, and more. In: Nguyen, P.Q., Oswald, E. (eds.) EUROCRYPT 2014. LNCS, vol. 8441, pp. 557–577. Springer, Heidelberg (2014). https://doi.org/10.1007/978-3-642-55220-5_31
4. Beimel, A.: Secure schemes for secret sharing and key distribution. Ph.D. thesis, Technion (1996). www.cs.bgu.ac.il/beimel/pub.html
5. Beimel, A.: Secret-sharing schemes: a survey. In: Chee, Y.M., Guo, Z., Ling, S., Shao, F., Tang, Y., Wang, H., Xing, C. (eds.) IWCC 2011. LNCS, vol. 6639, pp. 11–46. Springer, Heidelberg (2011). https://doi.org/10.1007/978-3-642-20901-7_2
6. Beimel, A., Chor, B.: Universally ideal secret sharing schemes. IEEE Trans. Inf. Theory 40(3), 786–794 (1994)

7. Beimel, A., Farràs, O., Mintz, Y.: Secret-sharing schemes for very dense graphs. J. Cryptology **29**(2), 336–362 (2016)
8. Beimel, A., Farràs, O., Peter, N.: Secret sharing schemes for dense forbidden graphs. In: Zikas, V., De Prisco, R. (eds.) SCN 2016. LNCS, vol. 9841, pp. 509–528. Springer, Cham (2016). https://doi.org/10.1007/978-3-319-44618-9_27
9. Beimel, A., Gál, A., Paterson, M.: Lower bounds for monotone span programs. Comput. Complex. **6**(1), 29–45 (1997)
10. Beimel, A., Ishai, Y., Kumaresan, R., Kushilevitz, E.: On the cryptographic complexity of the worst functions. In: Lindell, Y. (ed.) TCC 2014. LNCS, vol. 8349, pp. 317–342. Springer, Heidelberg (2014). https://doi.org/10.1007/978-3-642-54242-8_14
11. Ben-Or, M., Goldwasser, S., Wigderson, A.: Completeness theorems for noncryptographic fault-tolerant distributed computations. In: Proceedings of the 20th ACM Symposium on the Theory of Computing, pp. 1–10 (1988)
12. Benaloh, J., Leichter, J.: Generalized secret sharing and monotone functions. In: Goldwasser, S. (ed.) CRYPTO 1988. LNCS, vol. 403, pp. 27–35. Springer, New York (1990). https://doi.org/10.1007/0-387-34799-2_3
13. Bertilsson, M., Ingemarsson, I.: A construction of practical secret sharing schemes using linear block codes. In: Seberry, J., Zheng, Y. (eds.) AUSCRYPT 1992. LNCS, vol. 718, pp. 67–79. Springer, Heidelberg (1993). https://doi.org/10.1007/3-540-57220-1_53
14. Blakley, G.R.: Safeguarding cryptographic keys. In: Proceedings of the 1979 AFIPS National Computer Conference. AFIPS Conference proceedings, vol. 48, pp. 313–317. AFIPS Press (1979)
15. Blundo, C., De Santis, A., de Simone, R., Vaccaro, U.: Tight bounds on the information rate of secret sharing schemes. Des. Codes Crypt. **11**(2), 107–122 (1997)
16. Blundo, C., De Santis, A., Stinson, D.R., Vaccaro, U.: Graph decomposition and secret sharing schemes. J. Cryptology **8**(1), 39–64 (1995)
17. Brickell, E.F.: Some ideal secret sharing schemes. J. Comb. Math. Comb. Comput. **6**, 105–113 (1989)
18. Brickell, E.F., Davenport, D.M.: On the classification of ideal secret sharing schemes. J. Cryptology **4**(73), 123–134 (1991)
19. Bublitz, S.: Decomposition of graphs and monotone formula size of homogeneous functions. Acta Inf. **23**(6), 689–696 (1986)
20. Capocelli, R.M., De Santis, A., Gargano, L., Vaccaro, U.: On the size of shares for secret sharing schemes. J. Cryptology **6**(3), 157–168 (1993)
21. Chaum, D., Crépeau, C., Damgård, I.: Multiparty unconditionally secure protocols. In: Proceedings of the 20th ACM Symposium on the Theory of Computing, pp. 11–19 (1988)
22. Chor, B., Kushilevitz, E.: Secret sharing over infinite domains. J. Cryptology **6**(2), 87–96 (1993)
23. Cramer, R., Damgård, I., Maurer, U.: General secure multi-party computation from any linear secret-sharing scheme. In: Preneel, B. (ed.) EUROCRYPT 2000. LNCS, vol. 1807, pp. 316–334. Springer, Heidelberg (2000). https://doi.org/10.1007/3-540-45539-6_22
24. Csirmaz, L.: The dealer's random bits in perfect secret sharing schemes. Studia Sci. Math. Hungar. **32**(3–4), 429–437 (1996)
25. Csirmaz, L.: The size of a share must be large. J. Cryptology **10**(4), 223–231 (1997)
26. Csirmaz, L.: Secret sharing schemes on graphs. Technical Report 2005/059, Cryptology ePrint Archive (2005). eprint.iacr.org/

27. Desmedt, Y., Frankel, Y.: Shared generation of authenticators and signatures. In: Feigenbaum, J. (ed.) CRYPTO 1991. LNCS, vol. 576, pp. 457–469. Springer, Heidelberg (1992). https://doi.org/10.1007/3-540-46766-1_37
28. Dijk, M.V., Jackson, W., Martin, K.M.: A note on duality in linear secret sharing schemes. Bull. Inst. Comb. Appl. **19**, 98–101 (1997)
29. Erdös, P., Pyber, L.: Covering a graph by complete bipartite graphs. Discrete Math. **170**(1–3), 249–251 (1997)
30. Fehr, S.: Efficient construction of the dual span program (1999). Manuscript
31. Gál, A.: Combinatorial methods in boolean function complexity. Ph.D. thesis, University of Chicago (1995). www.eccc.uni-trier.de/eccc-local/ECCC-Theses/gal.html
32. Gay, R., Kerenidis, I., Wee, H.: Communication complexity of conditional disclosure of secrets and attribute-based encryption. In: Gennaro, R., Robshaw, M. (eds.) CRYPTO 2015. LNCS, vol. 9216, pp. 485–502. Springer, Heidelberg (2015). https://doi.org/10.1007/978-3-662-48000-7_24
33. Gertner, Y., Ishai, Y., Kushilevitz, E., Malkin, T.: Protecting data privacy in private information retrieval schemes. J. Comput. Syst. Sci. **60**(3), 592–629 (2000)
34. Goyal, V., Pandey, O., Sahai, A., Waters, B.: Attribute-based encryption for fine-grained access control of encrypted data. In: Proceedings of the 13th ACM Conference on Computer and Communications Security, pp. 89–98 (2006)
35. Ito, M., Saito, A., Nishizeki, T.: Secret sharing schemes realizing general access structure. In: Proceedings of the IEEE Global Telecommunication Conference, Globecom, vol. 87, pp. 99–102 (1987). Journal version: multiple assignment scheme for sharing secret. J. Cryptology **6**(1), 15–20 (1993)
36. Jackson, W., Martin, K.M.: Geometric secret sharing schemes and their duals. Des. Codes Crypt. **4**, 83–95 (1994)
37. Karchmer, M., Wigderson, A.: On span programs. In: Proceedings of the 8th IEEE Structure in Complexity Theory, pp. 102–111 (1993)
38. Liu, T., Vaikuntanathan, V., Wee, H.: Conditional disclosure of secrets via non-linear reconstruction. In: Katz, J., Shacham, H. (eds.) CRYPTO 2017. LNCS, vol. 10401, pp. 758–790. Springer, Cham (2017). https://doi.org/10.1007/978-3-319-63688-7_25
39. Mintz, Y.: Information ratios of graph secret-sharing schemes. Master's thesis, Department of Computer Science, Ben Gurion University (2012)
40. Mitzenmacher, M., Upfal, E.: Probability and Computing. Cambridge University Press, Cambridge (2005)
41. Naor, M., Wool, A.: Access control and signatures via quorum secret sharing. In: 3rd ACM Conference on Computer and Communications Security, pp. 157–167 (1996)
42. Sahai, A., Waters, B.: Fuzzy identity-based encryption. In: Cramer, R. (ed.) EUROCRYPT 2005. LNCS, vol. 3494, pp. 457–473. Springer, Heidelberg (2005). https://doi.org/10.1007/11426639_27
43. Shamir, A.: How to share a secret. Commun. ACM **22**, 612–613 (1979)
44. Shankar, B., Srinathan, K., Rangan, C.P.: Alternative protocols for generalized oblivious transfer. In: Rao, S., Chatterjee, M., Jayanti, P., Murthy, C.S.R., Saha, S.K. (eds.) ICDCN 2008. LNCS, vol. 4904, pp. 304–309. Springer, Heidelberg (2007). https://doi.org/10.1007/978-3-540-77444-0_31
45. Stinson, D.R.: Decomposition construction for secret sharing schemes. IEEE Trans. Inf. Theory **40**(1), 118–125 (1994)
46. Sun, H., Shieh, S.: Secret sharing in graph-based prohibited structures. In: Proceedings IEEE INFOCOM 1997, pp. 718–724 (1997)

47. Tassa, T.: Generalized oblivious transfer by secret sharing. Des. Codes Crypt. **58**(1), 11–21 (2011)

48. Waters, B.: Ciphertext-policy attribute-based encryption: an expressive, efficient, and provably secure realization. In: Catalano, D., Fazio, N., Gennaro, R., Nicolosi, A. (eds.) PKC 2011. LNCS, vol. 6571, pp. 53–70. Springer, Heidelberg (2011). https://doi.org/10.1007/978-3-642-19379-8_4

49. Wee, H.: Dual system encryption via predicate encodings. In: Lindell, Y. (ed.) TCC 2014. LNCS, vol. 8349, pp. 616–637. Springer, Heidelberg (2014). https://doi.org/10.1007/978-3-642-54242-8_26

Near-Optimal Secret Sharing and Error Correcting Codes in AC^0

Kuan Cheng[1]([✉]), Yuval Ishai[2,3], and Xin Li[1]

[1] Department of Computer Science, Johns Hopkins University, Baltimore, USA
kcheng17@jhu.edu, lixints@cs.jhu.edu
[2] Department of Computer Science, Technion, Haifa, Israel
yuvali@cs.technion.ac.il
[3] UCLA, Los Angeles, USA

Abstract. We study the question of minimizing the computational complexity of (robust) secret sharing schemes and error correcting codes. In standard instances of these objects, both encoding and decoding involve linear algebra, and thus cannot be implemented in the class AC^0. The feasibility of non-trivial secret sharing schemes in AC^0 was recently shown by Bogdanov et al. (Crypto 2016) and that of (locally) decoding errors in AC^0 by Goldwasser et al. (STOC 2007).

In this paper, we show that by allowing some slight relaxation such as a small error probability, we can construct much better secret sharing schemes and error correcting codes in the class AC^0. In some cases, our parameters are close to optimal and would be impossible to achieve without the relaxation. Our results significantly improve previous constructions in various parameters.

Our constructions combine several ingredients in pseudorandomness and combinatorics in an innovative way. Specifically, we develop a general technique to simultaneously amplify security threshold and reduce alphabet size, using a two-level concatenation of protocols together with a random permutation. We demonstrate the broader usefulness of this technique by applying it in the context of a variant of secure broadcast.

1 Introduction

The motivation for this paper comes from two different sources. The first is the general theme of improving performance at the price of allowing some small probability of error or failure. This is evident throughout computer science. For example, randomized algorithms tend to be much more efficient than their deterministic counterparts. In cryptography and coding theory, randomization with small failure probability can often be used to amplify security or improve efficiency. This is arguably a good tradeoff in practice.

The second source of motivation is the goal of minimizing the computational complexity of cryptographic primitives and related combinatorial objects. For example, a line of work on the parallel complexity of cryptography [2, 3, 16, 18, 29]

A full version of this paper appears in [13].

© International Association for Cryptologic Research 2017
Y. Kalai and L. Reyzin (Eds.): TCC 2017, Part II, LNCS 10678, pp. 424–458, 2017.
https://doi.org/10.1007/978-3-319-70503-3_14

successfully constructed one way functions and other cryptographic primitives in the complexity class NC^0 based on different kinds of assumptions, including very standard cryptographic assumptions. Works along this line have found several unexpected applications, most recently in the context of general-purpose obfuscation [24]. The study of low-complexity cryptography is also motivated by the goal of obtaining stronger *negative results*. For instance, low-complexity pseudo-random functions imply stronger hardness results for learning [30] and stronger natural proof barriers [27], and low-complexity decryption [8] implies a barrier for function secret sharing [10].

In this paper, we address the question of minimizing the complexity of secret sharing schemes and error correcting codes by introducing additional randomization and allowing for a small failure probability. We focus on the complexity class AC^0, which is the lowest class for which a secret can be reconstructed or a message be decoded with negligible error probability. We show that the randomization approach can be used towards obtaining much better parameters than previous constructions. In some cases, our parameters are close to optimal and would be impossible to achieve without randomization.

We now give a more detailed account of our results, starting with some relevant background.

1.1 (Robust) Secret Sharing in AC^0

A secret sharing scheme allows a dealer to randomly split a secret between n parties so that qualified subsets of parties can reconstruct the secret from their shares while unqualified subsets learn nothing about the secret. We consider here a variant of threshold secret sharing (also known as a "ramp scheme"), where any k parties can learn nothing about the secret, whereas all n parties together can recover the secret from their shares. We also consider a robust variant where the secret should be correctly reconstructed even if at most d shares are corrupted by an adversary, possibly in an adaptive fashion. We formalize this below.

Definition 1 (secret sharing). *An (n, k) secret sharing scheme with message alphabet Σ_0, message length m, and share alphabet Σ is a pair of functions (Share, Rec), where Share : $\Sigma_0^m \to \Sigma^n$ is probabilistic and Rec : $\Sigma^n \to \Sigma_0^m$ is deterministic, which satisfy the following properties.*

- *Privacy: For a privacy threshold k, the adversary can choose a sequence $W = (w_1, \ldots, w_k) \in [n]^k$ of share indices to observe, either adaptively (where each w_i depends on previously observed shares Share$(x)_{w_1}, \ldots,$ Share$(x)_{w_{i-1}}$) or non-adaptively (where W is picked in one shot). We say that the scheme is ϵ-private if for every such strategy, there is a share distribution $\mathcal{D}$ over Σ^k such that for every secret message $x \in \Sigma_0^m$, Share$(x)_W$ is ϵ-close (in statistical distance) to $\mathcal{D}$. We refer to ϵ as the privacy error and say that the scheme has perfect privacy if $\epsilon = 0$.*
- *Reconstruction: We say that the scheme has reconstruction error η if for every $x \in \Sigma_0^m$,*

$$\Pr[\mathsf{Rec}(\mathsf{Share}(x)) = x] \geq 1 - \eta.$$

We say the scheme has perfect reconstruction *if $\eta = 0$.*

We are also interested in robust secret sharing, *where an adversary is allowed to modify at most d shares.*

– *Robustness: For any secret $x \in \Sigma_0^m$, let $Y = \mathsf{Share}(x)$. Consider an arbitrary adversary who (adaptively or non-adaptively) observes d shares and can then arbitrarily change these d shares, transforming Y to Y'. The scheme is d-robust if for every such adversary,*

$$\Pr[\mathsf{Rec}(Y') = x] \geq 1 - \eta.$$

If the share alphabet and the message alphabet are both Σ, then we simply say the alphabet of the scheme is Σ. By saying that a secret sharing scheme is in AC^0, we mean that both the sharing function and the reconstruction function can be computed by (uniform) AC^0 circuits.

A recent work of Bogdanov et al. [7] considers the complexity of sharing and reconstructing secrets. The question is motivated by the observation that almost all known secret sharing schemes, including the well known Shamir's scheme [31], require the computation of linear functions over finite fields, and thus cannot be implemented in the class AC^0 (i.e., constant depth circuits). Thus a natural question is whether there exist secret sharing schemes in AC^0 with good parameters. In the case of threshold secret sharing, Bogdanov et al. [7] showed a relation between the approximate degree[1] of a function and the privacy threshold of a secret sharing scheme. Using this and known approximate degree lower bounds, they obtained several secret sharing schemes with sharing and reconstruction functions computable in AC^0. However, to achieve a large privacy threshold (e.g., $k = \Omega(n)$) their construction needs to use a large alphabet (e.g., size $2^{\mathsf{poly}(n)}$). In the case of binary alphabet, they can only achieve privacy threshold $\Omega(\sqrt{n})$ with perfect reconstruction and privacy threshold $\Omega((n/\log n)^{2/3})$ with constant reconstruction error $\eta < 1/2$. This limit is inherent without improving the best known approximate degree of an AC^0 function [11]. Furthermore, their schemes only share one bit, and a naive approach of sharing more bits by repeating the scheme multiple times will lead to a bad information rate. This leaves open the question of improving these parameters. Ideally, we would like to share many bits (e.g., $\Omega(n)$), obtain a large privacy threshold (e.g., $\Omega(n)$), and achieve perfect reconstruction and small alphabet size at the same time.

In order to improve the AC^0 secret sharing schemes from [7], we relax their perfect privacy requirement and settle for the notion of ϵ-privacy from Definition 1. (This relaxation was recently considered in [9], see discussion below.) Note that this relaxation is necessary to improve the privacy threshold of AC^0 secret sharing schemes, unless one can obtain better approximate degree lower bounds of an explicit AC^0 function (as [7] showed that an explicit AC^0 secret

---

[1] The approximate degree of a Boolean function is the lowest degree of a real polynomial that can approximate the function within, say, an additive difference of $1/3$ on every input.

sharing scheme with privacy threshold k and perfect privacy also implies an explicit function in AC^0 with approximate degree at least k). Like most schemes in [7], we only require that the secret can be reconstructed by all n parties. On the other hand, we always require perfect reconstruction. We show that under this slight relaxation, we can obtain much better secret sharing schemes in AC^0. For an adaptive adversary, we can achieve both a constant information rate and a large privacy threshold ($k = \Omega(n)$) over a binary alphabet. In addition, our privacy error is exponentially small. Specifically, we have the following theorem.

Theorem 1 (adaptive adversary). *For every $n \in \mathbb{N}$ and constant $\gamma \in (0, 1/4)$, there exists an explicit $(n, \Omega(n))$ secret sharing scheme in AC^0 with alphabet $\{0, 1\}$, secret length $m = \Omega(n)$, adaptive privacy error $2^{-\Omega(n^{\frac{1}{4}-\gamma})}$ and perfect reconstruction.*

Note that again, by using randomization and allowing for a small privacy error, we can significantly improve both the privacy threshold and the information rate, while also making the scheme much more efficient by using a smaller alphabet.

Remark 1. We note that a recent paper by Bun and Thaler [11] gave improved lower bounds for the approximate degree of AC^0 functions. Specifically, for any constant $\alpha > 0$ they showed an explicit AC^0 function with approximate degree at least $n^{1-\alpha}$, and by the relation established in [7] this also gives a secret sharing scheme in AC^0 with privacy threshold $n^{1-\alpha}$. However, our results are stronger in the sense that we can achieve threshold $\Omega(n)$, and furthermore we can achieve perfect reconstruction while the secret sharing scheme in [11] only has constant reconstruction error.

Remark 2. Our construction of AC^0 secret sharing schemes is actually a general transformation and can take any such scheme in [7] or [11] as the starting point. The error $2^{-\Omega(n^{\frac{1}{4}-\gamma})}$ in Theorem 1 comes from our use of the one-in-a-box function [28], which has approximate degree $n^{1/3}$. We can also use the new AC^0 function of [11] with approximate degree $n^{1-\alpha}$, which will give us an error of $2^{-\Omega(n^{\frac{1}{2}-\gamma})}$ but the reconstruction error will become a constant. We note that the privacy error of our construction is also close to optimal, without further improvement on the lower bounds of approximate degree of AC^0 functions. This is because a privacy error of 2^{-s} will imply an AC^0 function of approximate degree $\Omega(s/\log n)$. Thus if one can achieve a sufficiently small privacy error (e.g., $2^{-\Omega(n)}$), then this will give an improved approximate degree lower bound for an AC^0 function. See Appendix A of the full version for a more detailed explanation.

A very recent paper by Bogdanov and Williamson [9] considered a similar relaxation as ours. Specifically, they showed how to construct two distributions over n bits that are (k, ϵ)-wise indistinguishable, but can be distinguished with advantage $1 - \eta$ by some AC^0 function. Here (k, ϵ)-wise indistinguishable means that if looking at any subset of k bits, the two distributions have statistical distance at most ϵ. Translating into the secret sharing model, this roughly implies an AC^0 secret sharing scheme with binary alphabet, privacy threshold k, privacy error ϵ and reconstruction error η. Bogdanov and Williamson [9] obtained several results in this case. Specifically, they showed a pair of such distributions for any $k \leq n/2$ with $\epsilon = 2^{-\Omega(n/k)}$, that can be distinguished with $\eta = \Omega(1)$ by the OR function; or for any k with $\epsilon = 2^{-\Omega((n/k)^{1-1/d})}$, that can be distinguished with $\eta = 0$ by a depth-d AND-OR tree.

We note the following important differences between our results and the corresponding results by Bogdanov and Williamson [9]: first, the results in [9], in the language of secret sharing, only consider a 1-bit secret, while our results can share $\Omega(n)$ bits with the same share size. Thus our information rate is much larger than theirs. Second, we can achieve a privacy threshold of $k = \Omega(n)$ while simultaneously achieving an exponentially small privacy error of $\epsilon = 2^{-n^{\Omega(1)}}$ and perfect reconstruction ($\eta = 0$). In contrast, the results in [9], when going into the range of $k = \Omega(n)$, only have constant privacy error. In short, our results are better than the results in [9], in the sense that we can simultaneously achieve asymptotically optimal information rate and privacy threshold, exponentially small privacy error and perfect reconstruction. As a direct corollary, we have the following result, which is incomparable to the results in [9].

Corollary 1. *There exists a constant $\alpha > 0$ such that for every n and $k \leq \alpha n$, there exists a pair of $(k, 2^{-n^{\Omega(1)}})$-wise indistinguishable distributions X, Y over $\{0,1\}^n$ and an AC^0 function D such that $\Pr[D(X)] - \Pr[D(Y)] = 1$.*

Next, we extend our AC^0 secret sharing schemes to the robust case, where the adversary can tamper with several parties' shares. Our goal is to simultaneously achieve a large privacy threshold, a large tolerance to errors, a large information rate and a small alphabet size. We can achieve a constant information rate with privacy threshold and error tolerance both $\Omega(n)$, with constant size alphabet, exponentially small privacy error and polynomially small reconstruction error. However, here we can only handle a non-adaptive adversary. Specifically, we have the following theorem.

Theorem 2 (non-adaptive adversary). *For every $n \in \mathbb{N}$, every $\eta = \frac{1}{\mathrm{poly}(n)}$, there exists an explicit $(n, \Omega(n))$ robust secret sharing scheme in AC^0 with share alphabet $\{0,1\}^{O(1)}$, message alphabet $\{0,1\}$, message length $m = \Omega(n)$, non-adaptive privacy error $2^{-n^{\Omega(1)}}$, non-adaptive robustness $\Omega(n)$ and reconstruction error η.*

1.2   Error Correcting Codes for Additive Channels in AC^0

Robust secret sharing schemes are natural generalizations of error correcting codes. Thus our robust secret sharing schemes in AC^0 also give error correcting codes with randomized AC^0 encoding and deterministic AC^0 decoding. The model of our error correcting codes is the same as that considered by Guruswami and

Smith [20]: stochastic error correcting codes for additive channels. Here, the code has a randomized encoding function and a deterministic decoding function, while the channel can add an arbitrary error vector $e \in \{0,1\}^n$ of Hamming weight at most ρn to the transmitted codeword of length n. As in [20], the error may depend on the message but crucially does not depend on the randomness used by the encoder. Formally, we have the following definition.

Definition 2. *For any* $n, m \in \mathbb{N}$, *any* $\rho, \epsilon > 0$, *an* (n, m, ρ) *stochastic binary error correcting code* (Enc, Dec) *with randomized encoding function* Enc : $\{0,1\}^m \to \{0,1\}^n$, *deterministic decoding function* Dec : $\{0,1\}^n \to \{0,1\}^m$ *and decoding error* ϵ, *is such that for every* $x \in \{0,1\}^m$, *every* $e = (e_1, \ldots, e_m) \in \{0,1\}^m$ *with hamming weight at most* ρn,

$$\Pr[\mathsf{Dec}(\mathsf{Enc}(x) + e) = x] \geq 1 - \epsilon.$$

An (n, m, ρ) *stochastic error correcting code* (Enc, Dec) *can be computed by* AC⁰ *circuits if both* Enc *and* Dec *can be computed by* AC⁰ *circuits.*

Previously, Guruswami and Smith [20] constructed such codes that approach the Shannon capacity $1 - H(\rho)$. Their encoder and decoder run in polynomial time and have exponentially small decoding error. Here, we aim at constructing such codes with AC⁰ encoder and decoder. In a different setting, Goldwasser et al. [19] gave a construction of *locally decodable* codes that can tolerate a constant fraction of errors and have AC⁰ decoding. Their code has deterministic encoding but randomized decoding. By repeating the local decoder for each bit for $O(\log n)$ times and taking majority, one can decode each bit in AC⁰ with error probability $1/\mathsf{poly}(n)$ and thus by a union bound the original message can also be decoded with error probability $1/\mathsf{poly}(n)$. However we note that the encoding function of [19] is not in AC⁰, and moreover their message rate is only polynomially small. In contrast, our code has constant message rate and can tolerate a constant fraction of errors (albeit in a weaker model) when the decoding error is $1/\mathsf{poly}(n)$ or even $2^{-\mathsf{poly}\log(n)}$. The rate and tolerance are asymptotically optimal. We can achieve even smaller error $(2^{-\Omega(r/\log n)})$ with message rate $1/r$. Furthermore both our encoding and decoding are in AC⁰. Specifically, we have the following theorems.

Theorem 3 (error-correcting codes). *For any* $n \in \mathbb{N}$ *and* $\epsilon = 2^{-\mathsf{poly}\log(n)}$, *there exists an* $(n, \Omega(n), \Omega(1))$ *stochastic binary error correcting code with decoding error* ϵ, *which can be computed by* AC⁰ *circuits.*

Theorem 4 (error-correcting codes with smaller decoding error). *For any* $n, r \in \mathbb{N}$, *there exists an* $(n, m = \Omega(n/r), \Omega(1))$ *stochastic binary error correcting code with decoding error* $2^{-\Omega(r/\log n)}$, *which can be computed by* AC⁰ *circuits.*

Note that Theorem 4 is interesting mainly in the case where r is at least $\mathsf{poly}\log n$.

Remark 3. We note that, without randomization, it is well known that deterministic AC^0 circuits cannot compute asymptotically good codes [25]. Thus the randomization in our AC^0 encoding is necessary here. For deterministic AC^0 decoding, only very weak lower bounds are known. In particular, Lee and Viola [23] showed that any depth-c AC^0 circuit with parity gates cannot decode beyond error $(1/2 - 1/O(\log n)^{c+2})d$, where d is the distance of the code. While the repetition code can be decoded in AC^0 with a near-optimal fraction of errors by using approximate majority, obtaining a similar positive result for codes with a significantly better rate is open.

1.3   Secure Broadcasting with an External Adversary

We apply our ideas and technical approach to the following flavor of secure broadcasting in the presence of an adversary. The problem can be viewed as a generalization of a one-time pad encryption. In a one-time pad encryption, two parties share a secret key which can be used to transmit messages with information-theoretic security. Suppose that each party wants to transmit an m-bit string to the other party. If an external adversary can see the entire communication, then it is well known that to keep both messages secret, the parties must share a secret key of length at least $2m$. This can be generalized to the case of n parties, where we assume that they have access to a public broadcast channel, and each party wants to securely communicate an m-bit string to all other parties. This problem can be useful, for example, when n collaborating parties want to compute a function of their secret inputs without revealing the inputs to an external adversary. Again, if the adversary can see the entire communication, then the parties need to share a secret key of length at least nm.

Now, what if we relax the problem by restricting the adversary's power? Suppose that instead of seeing the entire communication, the adversary can only see some fraction of the communicated messages. Can we get more efficient solutions? We formally define this model below, requiring not only the secrecy of the inputs but also correctness of the outputs in the presence of adaptive tampering with a bounded fraction of messages.

Definition 3. *Let $n, m \in \mathbb{N}$ and $\alpha, \epsilon > 0$. An $(n, m, \alpha, \epsilon, \eta)$-secure broadcasting protocol is an n-party protocol with the following properties. Initially, each party i has a local input $x_i \in \{0,1\}^m$ and the parties share a secret key. The parties can then communicate over a public broadcast channel. At the end of the communication, each party computes a local output. We require the protocol to satisfy the following security properties.*

- *(Privacy) For any adaptive adversarial observation W which observes at most $1 - \alpha$ fraction of the messages, there is a distribution $\mathcal{D}$, such that for any inputs $x = (x_1, \ldots, x_n) \in (\{0,1\}^m)^n$ leading to a sequence of messages Y, the distribution Y_W of observed messages is ϵ-close to $\mathcal{D}$.*
- *(Robustness) For any adaptive adversary that corrupts at most $1 - \alpha$ fraction of the messages, and any n-tuple of inputs $x = (x_1, \ldots, x_n) \in (\{0,1\}^m)^n$, all*

n parties can reconstruct x correctly with probability at least $1 - \eta$ after the communication.

The naive solution of applying one-time pad still requires a shared secret key of length at least nm, since otherwise even if the adversary only sees part of the communication, he may learn some information about the inputs. However, by using randomization and allowing for a small error, we can achieve much better performance. Specifically, we have the following theorem.

Theorem 5 (secure broadcasting). *For any $n, m, r \in \mathbb{N}$ with $r \leq m$, there exists an explicit $(n, m, \alpha = \Omega(1), n2^{-\Omega(r)}, n2^{-\Omega(r)} + nm2^{-\Omega(m/r)})$ secure broadcasting protocol with communication complexity $O(nm)$ and shared secret key of length $O(r \log(nr))$.*

1.4   Overview of the Techniques

Secret sharing. Here we give an overview of the techniques used in our constructions of AC^0 secret sharing schemes and error correcting codes. Our constructions combine several ingredients in pseudorandomness and combinatorics in an innovative way, so before describing our constructions, we will first describe the important ingredients used.

The secret sharing scheme in [7]. As mentioned before, Bogdanov et al. [7] were the first to consider secret sharing schemes in AC^0. Our constructions will use one of their schemes as the starting point. Specifically, since we aim at perfect reconstruction, we will use the secret sharing scheme in [28] based on the so called "one-in-a-box function" or Minsky-Papert CNF function. This scheme can share one bit among n parties, with binary alphabet, privacy threshold $\Omega(n^{1/3})$ and perfect reconstruction.

Random permutation. Another important ingredient, as mentioned before, is random permutation. Applying a random permutation, in many cases, reduces worst case errors to random errors, and the latter is much more convenient to handle. This property has been exploited in several previous work, such as the error correcting codes by Guruswami and Smith [20]. We note that a random permutation from $[n]$ to $[n]$ can be computed in AC^0 [22,26,33].

K-wise independent generators. The third ingredient of our construction is the notion of k-wise independent pseudorandom generators. This is a function that stretches some r uniform random bits to n bits such that any subset of k bits is uniform. Such generators are well studied, while for our constructions we need such generators which can be computed by AC^0 circuits. This requirement is met by using k-wise independent generators based on unique neighbor expander graphs, such as those constructed by Guruswami et al. [21] which use seed length $r = k\text{poly}\log(n)$.

Secret sharing schemes based on error correcting codes. Using asymptotically good linear error correcting codes, one can construct secret sharing schemes that simultaneously achieve constant information rate and privacy threshold $\Omega(n)$ (e.g., [12]). However, certainly in general these schemes are not in AC^0 since they need to compute linear functions such as parity. For our constructions, we will use these schemes with a small block length (e.g., $O(\log n)$ or $\mathsf{poly}\log(n)$) such that parity with such input length can be computed by constant depth circuits. For robust secret sharing, we will also be using robust secret sharing schemes based on codes, with constant information rate, privacy threshold and tolerance $\Omega(n)$ (e.g., [15]), with a small block length.

The constructions. We can now give an informal description of our constructions. As mentioned before, our construction is a general transformation and can take any scheme in [7] or [11] as the starting point. A specific scheme of interest is the one in [7] based on the one-in-a-box function, which has perfect reconstruction. Our goal then is to keep the property of perfect reconstruction, while increasing the information rate and privacy threshold. One naive way to share more bits is to repeat the scheme several times, one for each bit. Of course, this does not help much in boosting the information rate. Our approach, on the other hand, is to use this naive repeated scheme to share a short random seed R. Suppose this gives us n parties with privacy threshold k_0. We then use R and the k-wise independent generator G mentioned above to generate an n-bit string Y, and use Y to share a secret X by computing $Y \oplus X$.

Note that now the length of the secret X can be as large as n and thus the information rate is increased to $1/2$. To reconstruct the secret, we can use the first n parties to reconstruct R, then compute Y and finally X. Note that the whole computation can be done in AC^0 since the k-wise independent generator G is computable in AC^0. The privacy threshold, on the other hand, is the minimum of k_0 and k. This is because if an adversary learns nothing about R, then Y is k-wise independent and thus by looking at any k shares in $Y \oplus X$, the adversary learns nothing about X. This is the first step of our construction.

In the next step, we would like to boost the privacy threshold to $\Omega(n)$ while decreasing the information rate by at most a constant factor. Our approach for this purpose can be viewed as concatenating a larger outer protocol with a smaller inner protocol, which boosts the privacy threshold while keeping the information rate and the complexity of the whole protocol. More specifically, we first divide the parties obtained from the first step into small blocks, and then for each small block we use a good secret sharing scheme based on error correcting codes. Suppose the adversary gets to see a constant fraction of the shares, then on average for each small bock the adversary also gets to see only a constant fraction of the shares. Thus, by Markov's inequality and adjusting the parameters, the adversary only gets to learn the information from a constant fraction of the blocks. However, this is still not enough for us, since the outer protocol only has threshold $n^{\Omega(1)}$.

We solve this problem by using a threshold amplification technique. This is one of our main innovations, and a key step towards achieving both constant information rate and privacy threshold $\Omega(n)$ without sacrificing the error. On a high level, we turn the inner protocol itself into another concatenated protocol (i.e., a larger outer protocol combined with a smaller inner protocol), and then apply a random permutation. Specifically, we choose the size of the block mentioned above to be something like $O(\log^2 n)$, apply a secret sharing scheme based on asymptotically good error correcting codes and obtain $O(\log^2 n)$ shares. We then divide these shares further into $O(\log n)$ smaller blocks each of size $O(\log n)$ (alternatively, this can be viewed as a secret sharing scheme using alphabet $\{0,1\}^{O(\log n)}$), and now we apply a random permutation of these smaller blocks. If we are to use a slightly larger alphabet, we can now store each block together with its index before the permutation as one share. Note that we need the index information when we try to reconstruct the secret, and the reconstruction can be done in AC^0.

Now, suppose again that the adversary gets to see some small constant fraction of the final shares, then since we applied a random permutation, we can argue that each smaller block gets learned by the adversary only with some constant probability. Thus, in the larger block of size $O(\log^2 n)$, by a Chernoeff type bound, except with probability $1/\mathsf{poly}(n)$, we have that only some constant fraction of the shares are learned by the adversary. Note that here by using two levels of blocks, we have reduced the probability that the adversary learns some constant fraction of the shares from a constant to $1/\mathsf{poly}(n)$, which is much better for the outer protocol as we shall see soon. By adjusting the parameters we can ensure that the number of shares that the adversary may learn is below the privacy threshold of the larger block and thus the adversary actually learns nothing. Now, going back to the outer protocol, we know that the expected number of large blocks the adversary can learn is only $n/\mathsf{poly}(n)$; and again by a Chernoff type bound, except with probability $2^{-n^{\Omega(1)}}$, the outer protocol guarantees that the adversary learns nothing. This gives us a secret sharing scheme with privacy threshold $\Omega(n)$ while the information rate is still constant since we only increased the number of shares by a constant factor. With the $O(\log n)$ size alphabet, we can actually achieve privacy threshold $(1-\alpha)n'$ for any constant $0 < \alpha < 1$, where n' is the total number of final parties.

To reduce to the binary alphabet, we can apply another secret sharing scheme based on error correcting codes to each share of length $O(\log n)$. In this case then we won't be able to achieve privacy threshold $(1-\alpha)n'$, but we can achieve $\beta n'$ for some constant $\beta > 0$. This is because if the adversary gets to see a small constant fraction of the shares, then by Markov's inequality only for some constant fraction of the smaller blocks the adversary can learn some useful information. Thus the previous argument still holds.

As described above, our general construction uses two levels of concatenated protocols, which corresponds to two levels of blocks. The first level has larger blocks of size $O(\log^2 n)$, where each larger block consists of $O(\log n)$ smaller blocks of size $O(\log n)$. We use this two-level structure to reduce the probability that an adversary can learn some constant fraction of shares, and this enables us to amplify the privacy threshold to $\Omega(n)$. We choose the smaller block to have size $O(\log n)$ so that both a share from the larger block with length $O(\log n)$ and its index information can be stored in a smaller block. This ensures that the information rate is still a constant even if we add the index information. Finally, the blocks in the second level are actually the blocks that go into the random permutation. This general strategy is one of our main contributions and we hope that it can find other applications.

The above construction gives an AC^0 secret sharing scheme with good parameters. However, it is not a priori clear that it works for an adaptive adversary. In standard secret sharing schemes, a non-adaptive adversary and an adaptive adversary are almost equivalent since usually we have privacy error 0. More specifically, a secret sharing scheme for a non-adaptive adversary with privacy error ϵ and privacy threshold k is also a secret sharing scheme for an adaptive adversary with privacy error $n^k \epsilon$ and privacy threshold k. However in our AC^0 secret sharing scheme the error ϵ is not small enough to kill the n^k factor. Instead, we use the property of the random permutation to argue that our final distribution is essentially symmetric; and thus informally no matter how the adversary picks the shares to observe adaptively, he will not gain any advantage. This will show that our AC^0 secret sharing scheme also works for an adaptive adversary.

To extend to robust secret sharing, we need to use robust secret sharing schemes instead of normal schemes for the first and second level of blocks. Here we use the nearly optimal robust secret sharing schemes based on various codes by Cheraghchi [15]. Unfortunately since we need to use it on a small block length of $O(\log n)$, the reconstruction error becomes $1/\mathsf{poly}(n)$. Another tricky issue here is that an adversary may modify some of the indices. Note that we need the correct index information in order to know which block is which before the random permutation. Suppose the adversary does not modify any of the indices, but only modify the shares, then the previous argument can go through exactly when we change the secret sharing schemes based on error correcting codes into robust secret sharing schemes. However, if the adversary modifies some indices, then we could run into situations where more than one block have the same index and thus we cannot tell which one is correct (and it's possible they are all wrong). To overcome this difficulty, we store every index multiple times among the blocks in the second level. Specifically, after we apply the random permutation, for every original index we randomly choose $O(\log n)$ blocks in the second level to store it. As the adversary can only corrupt a small constant fraction of the blocks in the second level, for each such block, we can correctly recover its original index with probability $1 - 1/\mathsf{poly}(n)$ by taking the majority of the backups of its index. Thus by a union bound with probability $1 - 1/\mathsf{poly}(n)$ all original indices can be correctly recovered. In addition, we use the same randomness for each block to pick the $O(\log n)$ blocks, except we add a different shift to the selected blocks. This way, we can ensure that for each block the $O(\log n)$ blocks are randomly selected and thus the union bound still holds. Furthermore the randomness used here is also stored in every block in the second level, so that we can take the majority to reconstruct it correctly. In the above description, we sometimes need to take majority for n inputs, which is not computable in AC^0. However, we note that by adjusting parameters we can ensure that at least say $2/3$ fraction of the inputs are the same, and in this case it suffices to take *approximate majority*, which can be computed in AC^0 [32].

For our error correcting codes, the construction is a simplified version of the robust secret sharing construction. Specifically, we first divide the message itself into blocks of the first level, and then encode every block using an asymptotically good code and divide the obtained codeword into blocks of the second level. Then we apply a random permutation to the blocks of the second level as before, and we encode every second level block by another asymptotically good code. In short, we replace the above mentioned robust secret sharing schemes by asymptotically good error correcting codes. We use the same strategy as in robust secret sharing to identify corrupted indices. Using a size of $O(\log^2 n)$ for blocks in the first level will result in decoding error $1/\mathsf{poly}(n)$, while using larger block size (e.g., $\mathsf{poly}\log(n)$) will result in decoding error $2^{-\mathsf{poly}\log(n)}$. This gives Theorem 3. To achieve even smaller error, we can first repeat each bit of the message r times for some parameter r. This serves as an outer error correcting code, which can tolerate up to $r/3$ errors, and can be decoded in in AC^0 by taking approximate majority. The two-level block structure and the argument we described before can now be used to show a smaller decoding error of $2^{-\Omega(r/\log^2 n)}$. This gives Theorem 4.

Secure broadcasting. Rather than use the naive approach of one-time pad, here a more clever solution is to use secret sharing (assuming that each party also has access to local private random bits). By first applying a secret sharing scheme to the input and then broadcasting the shares, a party can ensure that if the adversary only gets to see part of the messages (below the secrecy threshold), then the adversary learns nothing. In this case the parties do not even need shared secret key. However, one problem with this solution is that the adversary cannot be allowed to see more than $1/n$ fraction of the messages, since otherwise he can just choose the messages broadcasted from one particular party, and then the adversary learns the input of that party. This is the place where randomization comes into play. If in addition, we allow the parties to share a small number of secret random bits, then the parties can use this secret key to *randomly permute* the order in which the they broadcast their messages (after applying the secret sharing scheme). Since the adversary does not know the secret key, we can argue that with high probability only a small fraction of each party's secret shares are observed. Therefore, by the properties of secret sharing we can say that the adversary learns almost nothing about each party's input. The crucial features of this solution are that first, the adversary can see some fixed fraction of messages, which is independent of the number of parties n (and thus can be much larger than $1/n$). Second, the number of shared secret random bits is much smaller than the naive approach of one-time pad. Indeed, as we show in Theorem 23, to achieve security parameter roughly r it is enough for the parties to share $O(r(\log n + \log r))$ random bits. Finally, by using an appropriate secret sharing scheme, the communication complexity of our protocol for each party is $O(m)$, which is optimal up to a constant factor. Note that here, by applying random permutation and allowing for a small probability of error, we simultaneously improve the security threshold (from $1/n$ to $\Omega(1)$) and the length of the shared secret key (from nm to $O(r(\log n + \log r))$).

Discussions and open problems. In this paper we continue the line of work on applying randomization and allowing a small failure probability for minimizing the computational complexity of cryptographic primitives and related combinatorial objects while maximizing the level of achievable security. In the context of secret sharing in AC^0, we show how to get much better parameters by allowing an (exponentially) small privacy error. We note that achieving exponentially small error here is non-trivial. In fact, if we allow for a larger error then (for a non-adaptive adversary) there is a simple protocol for AC^0 secret sharing: one can first take a random seed R of length $\Omega(n)$, and then apply a deterministic AC^0 extractor for bit-fixing sources to obtain an output Y of length $\Omega(n)$. The secret X can then be shared by computing the parity of Y and X. This way, one can still share $\Omega(n)$ bits of secret, and if the adversary only learns some small fraction of the seed, then the output Y is close to uniform by the property of the extractor, and thus X remains secret. However, by the lower bound of [14], the error of such AC^0 extractors (or even for the stronger seeded AC^0 extractors) is at least $2^{-\operatorname{poly}\log(n)}$. Therefore, one has to use additional techniques to achieve exponentially small error. We also extended our techniques to robust AC^0 secret sharing schemes, stochastic error correcting codes for additive channels, and secure broadcasting. Several intriguing open problems remain.

First, in our robust AC^0 secret sharing schemes, we only achieve reconstruction error $1/\operatorname{poly}(n)$. This is because we need to use existing robust secret sharing schemes on a block of size $O(\log n)$. Is it possible to avoid this and make the error exponentially small? Also, again in this case we can only handle non-adaptive adversaries, and it would be interesting to obtain a robust AC^0 secret sharing scheme that can handle adaptive adversaries. These questions are open also for AC^0 stochastic error correcting codes.

Second, as we mentioned in Remark 2 (see also [9]), a sufficiently small privacy error in an AC^0 secret sharing scheme would imply an improved approximate degree lower bound for AC^0 functions. Is it possible to improve our AC^0 secret sharing scheme, and use this approach to obtain better approximate degree lower bound for AC^0 functions? This seems like an interesting direction.

In addition, the privacy threshold amplification technique we developed, by using two levels of concatenated protocols together with a random permutation, is quite general and we feel that it should have applications elsewhere. We note that the approach of combining an "outer scheme" with an "inner scheme" to obtain the best features of both has been applied in many previous contexts. For instance, it was used to construct better codes [1,20] or better secure multiparty computation protocols [17]. However, in almost all of these previous applications, one starts with an outer scheme with a very good threshold (e.g., the Reed-Solomon code which has a large distance) and the goal is to use the inner scheme to inherit this good threshold while improving some other parameters (such as alphabet size). Thus, one only needs one level of concatenation. In our case, instead, we start with an outer scheme with a very weak threshold (e.g., the one-in-a-box function which only has privacy threshold $n^{1/3}$). By using two levels of concatenated protocols together with a random permutation, we can actually amplify this threshold to $\Omega(n)$ while simultaneously reducing the alphabet size. This is an important difference to previous constructions and one of our main contributions. We hope that these techniques can find other applications in similar situations.

Finally, since secret sharing schemes are building blocks of many other important cryptographic applications, it is an interesting question to see if the low-complexity secret sharing schemes we developed here can be used to reduce the computational complexity of other cryptographic primitives.

Paper organization. We introduce some notation and useful results in Sect. 2. In Sect. 3 we give our privacy threshold amplification techniques. In Sect. 4, we show how to increase the information rate using k-wise independent generators. Combining all the above techniques, our final construction of AC^0 secret sharing schemes is given in Sect. 5. Instantiations appear in Sect. 6. Finally, we give our constructions of robust AC^0 secret sharing schemes, AC^0 error correcting codes, and secure broadcast protocols in Sect. 7. Some proofs and additional details have been deferred to the full version [13].

2 Preliminaries

Let $|\cdot|$ denote the size of the input set or the absolute value of an input real number, based on contexts.

For any set I of integers, for any $r \in \mathbb{Z}$, we denote $r + I$ or $I + r$ to be $\{i' : i' = i + r, i \in I\}$.

We use Σ to denote the alphabet. Readers can simply regard Σ as $\{0,1\}^l$ for some $l \in \mathbb{N}$. For $\sigma \in \Sigma$, let $\sigma^n = (\sigma, \sigma, \ldots, \sigma) \in \Sigma^n$. For any sequence $s = (s_1, s_2, \ldots, s_n) \in \Sigma^n$ and sequence of indices $W = (w_1, \ldots, w_t) \in [n]^t$ with $t \leq n$, let s_W be the subsequence $(s_{w_1}, s_{w_2}, \ldots, s_{w_t})$.

For any two sequences $a \in \Sigma^n, b \in \Sigma'^{n'}$ where $a = (a_1, a_2, \ldots, a_n), b = (b_1, b_2, \ldots, b_{n'})$, let $a \circ b = (a_1, \ldots, a_n, b_1, \ldots, b_{n'}) \in \Sigma^n \times \Sigma'^{n'}$.

Let $\mathsf{supp}(\cdot)$ denote the support of the input random variable. Let $I(\cdot)$ be the indicator function.

Definition 4 (Statistical Distance). *The statistical distance between two random variables X and Y over Σ^n for some alphabet Σ, is $\mathsf{SD}(X,Y)$ which is defined as follows,*

$$\mathsf{SD}(X,Y) = 1/2 \sum_{a \in \Sigma^n} |\Pr[X = a] - \Pr[Y = a]|.$$

Here we also say that X is $\mathsf{SD}(X,Y)$-close to Y.

Lemma 1 (Folklore Properties of Statistical Distance [4]).

1. (Triangle Inequality) For any random variables X, Y, Z over Σ^n, we have

$$\mathsf{SD}(X,Y) \leq \mathsf{SD}(X,Z) + \mathsf{SD}(Y,Z).$$

2. $\forall n, m \in \mathbb{N}$, any deterministic function $f : \{0,1\}^n \to \{0,1\}^m$ and any random variables X, Y over Σ^n,

$$\mathsf{SD}(f(X), f(Y)) \leq \mathsf{SD}(X, Y).$$

We will use the following well known perfect XOR secret sharing scheme.

Theorem 6 (Folklore XOR secret sharing). *For any finite field $\mathbb{F}$, define* $\mathsf{Share}_+ : \mathbb{F} \to \mathbb{F}^n$ *and* $\mathsf{Rec}_+ : \mathbb{F}^n \to \mathbb{F}$, *such that for any secret $x \in \mathbb{F}$, $\mathsf{Share}_+(x) = y$ such that y is uniformly chosen in $\mathbb{F}^n$ conditioned on $\sum_{i \in [n]} y_i = x$ and Rec_+ is taking the sum of its input.*

($\mathsf{Share}_+, \mathsf{Rec}_+$) is an $(n, n-1)$ secret sharing scheme with share alphabet and message alphabet both being $\mathbb{F}$, message length 1, perfect privacy and reconstruction.

Definition 5 (Permutation). *For any $n \in \mathbb{N}$, a permutation over $[n]$ is defined to be a bijective function $\pi : [n] \to [n]$.*

Definition 6 (k-wise independence). *For any set S, let $X_1, \ldots, X_n$ be random variables over S. They are k-wise independent (and uniform) if any k of them are independent (and uniformly distributed).*

For any $r, n, k \in \mathbb{N}$, a function $g : \{0,1\}^r \to \Sigma^n$ is a k-wise (uniform) independent generator, if for $g(U) = (Y_1, \ldots, Y_n)$, $Y_1, \ldots, Y_n$ are k-wise independent (and uniform). Here U is the uniform distribution over $\{0,1\}^r$.

Definition 7 [21]. *A bipartite graph with N left vertices, M right vertices and left degree D is a (K, A) expander if for every set of left vertices $S \subseteq [N]$ of size K, we have $|\Gamma(S)| > AK$. It is a $(\leq K_{max}, A)$ expander if it is a (K, A) expander for all $K \leq K_{max}$.*

Here $\forall x \in [N]$, $\Gamma(x)$ outputs the set of all neighbours of x. It is also a set function which is defined accordingly. Also $\forall x \in [N], d \in [D]$, the function $\Gamma : [N] \times [D] \to [M]$ is such that $\Gamma(x, d)$ is the dth neighbour of x.

Theorem 7 [21]. *For all constants $\alpha > 0$, for every $N \in \mathbb{N}$, $K_{max} \leq N$, and $\epsilon > 0$, there exists an explicit $(\leq K_{max}, (1-\epsilon)D)$ expander with N left vertices, M right vertices, left degree $D = O((\log N)(\log K_{max})/\epsilon)^{1+1/\alpha}$ and $M \leq D^2 K_{max}^{1+\alpha}$. Here D is a power of 2.*

For any circuit C, the size of C is denoted as $\mathsf{size}(C)$. The depth of C is denoted as $\mathsf{depth}(C)$. Usually when we talk about computations computable by AC^0 circuits, we mean uniform AC^0 circuits, if not stated specifically.

Lemma 2 (Folklore properties of AC^0 circuits [4,19]**).** *For every $n \in \mathbb{N}$,*

1. *([4] Folklore) every Boolean function $f : \{0,1\}^{l = \Theta(\log n)} \to \{0,1\}$ can be computed by an AC^0 circuit of size $\mathsf{poly}(n)$ and depth 2.*
2. *[19] for every $c \in \mathbb{N}$, every integer $l = \Theta(\log^c n)$, if the function $f_l : \{0,1\}^l \to \{0,1\}$ can be computed by a circuit with depth $O(\log l)$ and size $\mathsf{poly}(l)$, then it can be computed by a circuit with depth $c+1$ and size $\mathsf{poly}(n)$.*

Remark 4. We briefly describe the proof implied in [19] for the second property of our Lemma 2. As there exists an NC^1 complete problem which is downward self-reducible, the function f_l can be reduced to (AC^0 reduction) a function with input length $O(\log n)$. By Lemma 2 part 1, and noting that the reduction here is an AC^0 reduction, f_l can be computed by an AC^0 circuit.

3   Random Permutation

3.1   Increasing the Privacy Threshold

The main technique we use here is random permutation.

Lemma 3 [22,26,33]. *For any constant $c \geq 1$, there exists an explicit AC^0 circuit $C : \{0,1\}^r \to [n]^n$ with size $poly(n)$, depth $O(1)$ and $r = O(n^{c+1} \log n)$ such that with probability $1 - 2^{-n^c}$, $C(U_r)$ gives a uniform random permutation of $[n]$; When this fails the outputs are not distinct.*

In the following we give a black box AC^0 transformation of secret sharing schemes increasing the privacy threshold.

Construction 1. *For any $n, k, m \in \mathbb{N}$ with $k \leq n$, any alphabet Σ, Σ_0, let* (Share, Rec) *be an (n, k) secret sharing scheme with share alphabet Σ, message alphabet Σ_0, message length m.*

Let (Share$_+$, Rec$_+$) *be a $(t, t-1)$ secret sharing scheme with alphabet Σ by Theorem 6.*

For any constant $a \geq 1, \alpha > 0$, large enough $b \geq 1$, we can construct the following $(n' = tn\bar{n}, k' = (1-\alpha)n')$ secret sharing scheme (Share$'$, Rec$'$) *with share alphabet $\Sigma \times [n']$, message alphabet Σ_0, message length $m' = m\bar{n}$, where $t = O(\log n), \bar{n} = bn^{a-1}$.*

Function Share$' : \Sigma_0^{m'} \to (\Sigma \times [n'])^{n'}$ *is as follows.*

1. *On input secret $x \in \Sigma_0^{m\bar{n}}$, parse x to be $(x_1, x_2, \ldots, x_{\bar{n}}) \in (\Sigma_0^m)^{\bar{n}}$.*
2. *Compute $y = (y_1, \ldots, y_{\bar{n}}) = (\mathsf{Share}(x_1), \ldots, \mathsf{Share}(x_{\bar{n}}))$ and parse it to be $\hat{y} = (\hat{y}_1, \ldots, \hat{y}_{n\bar{n}}) \in \Sigma^{n\bar{n}}$. Note that* Share *is from Σ_0^m to Σ^n.*
3. *Compute $(\mathsf{Share}_+(\hat{y}_1), \ldots, \mathsf{Share}_+(\hat{y}_{n\bar{n}})) \in (\Sigma^t)^{n\bar{n}}$ and split every entry to be t elements in Σ to get $y' = (y'_1, \ldots, y'_{n'}) \in \Sigma^{n'}$. Note that* Share$_+$ *is from Σ to Σ^t.*
4. *Generate π by Lemma 3 which is uniformly random over permutations of $[n']$. If it fails, which can be detected by checking element distinctness, set π to be such that $\forall i \in [n'], \pi(i) = i$.*
5. *Let*

$$\mathsf{Share}'(x) = (y'_{\pi^{-1}(1)} \circ \pi^{-1}(1), \ldots, y'_{\pi^{-1}(n')} \circ \pi^{-1}(n')) \in (\Sigma \times [n'])^{n'}.$$

Function Rec$' : (\Sigma \times [n'])^{n'} \to \Sigma_0^{m'}$ *is as follows.*

1. *Parse the input to be* $(y'_{\pi^{-1}(1)} \circ \pi^{-1}(1), \ldots, y'_{\pi^{-1}(n')} \circ \pi^{-1}(n'))$.
2. *Compute* $y' = (y'_1, \ldots, y'_{n'})$ *according to the permutation.*
3. *Apply* Rec$_+$ *on* y' *for every successive* t *entries to get* $\hat{y}$.
4. *Parse* $\hat{y}$ *to be* y.
5. *Compute* x *by applying* Rec *on every entry of* $\hat{y}$.
6. *Output* x.

Lemma 4. *If* Share *and* Rec *can be computed by* AC^0 *circuits, then* Share$'$ *and* Rec$'$ *can also be computed by* AC^0 *circuits.*

Proof. As Share can be computed by an AC^0 circuit, y can be computed by an AC^0 circuit (uniform). By Lemma 2 part 1, we know that (Share$_+$, Rec$_+$) both can be computed by AC^0 circuits. By Lemma 3, $(\pi^{-1}(1), \pi^{-1}(2), \ldots, \pi^{-1}(n'))$ can be computed by an AC^0 circuit. Also

$$\forall i \in [n'], y'_{\pi^{-1}(i)} = \bigvee_{j \in [n']} (y'_j \wedge (j = \pi^{-1}(i))). \tag{1}$$

Thus Share$'$ can be computed by an AC^0 circuit.

For Rec$'$, $\forall i \in [n'], y'_i = \bigvee_{j \in [n']} (y'_{\pi^{-1}(j)} \wedge (\pi^{-1}(j) = i))$. As Rec$_+$ can be computed by an AC^0 circuit, y can be computed by an AC^0 circuit. As Rec can be computed by an AC^0 circuit, Rec$'$ can be computed by an AC^0 circuit. $\square$

Lemma 5. *If the reconstruction error of* (Share, Rec) *is* η, *then the reconstruction error of* (Share$'$, Rec$'$) *is* $\eta' = \bar{n}\eta$.

Proof. According to the construction, as (Share$_+$, Rec$_+$) has perfect reconstruction by Lemma 6, the y computed in Rec$'$ is exactly (Share$(x_1), \ldots$, Share$(x_{\bar{n}})$). As $\forall i \in [\bar{n}], \Pr[\mathsf{Rec}(\mathsf{Share}(x_i)) = x_i] \geq 1 - \eta$,

$$\Pr[\mathsf{Rec}'(\mathsf{Share}'(x)) = x] = \Pr[\bigwedge_{i \in [\bar{n}]} (\mathsf{Rec}(\mathsf{Share}(x_i)) = x_i)] \geq 1 - \bar{n}\eta, \tag{2}$$

by the union bound. $\square$

In order to show privacy, we need the following Chernoff Bound.

Definition 8 (Negative Correlation [5,6]). *Binary random variables* $X_1, X_2, \ldots, X_n$ *are negative correlated, if* $\forall I \subseteq [n]$,

$$\Pr[\bigwedge_{i \in I} (X_i = 1)] \leq \prod_{i \in I} \Pr[X_i = 1] \ \text{and} \ \Pr[\bigwedge_{i \in I} (X_i = 0)] \leq \prod_{i \in I} \Pr[X_i = 0].$$

Theorem 8 (Negative Correlation Chernoff Bound [5,6]). *Let* $X_1, \ldots, X_n$ *be negatively correlated random variables with* $X = \sum_{i=1}^n X_i$, $\mu = \mathbb{E}[X]$.

– *For any* $\delta \in (0, 1)$,

$$\Pr[X \leq (1 - \delta)\mu] \leq e^{-\delta^2 \mu/2} \ \text{and} \ \Pr[X \geq (1 + \delta)\mu] \leq e^{-\delta^2 \mu/3}.$$

– *For any* $d \geq 6\mu, \Pr[X \geq d] \leq 2^{-d}$.

Lemma 6. *Let $\pi : [n] \to [n]$ be a random permutation. For any set $S, W \subseteq [n]$, let $u = \frac{|W|}{n}|S|$. Then the following holds.*

– for any constant $\delta \in (0, 1)$,

$$\Pr[|\pi(S) \cap W| \le (1 - \delta)\mu] \le e^{-\delta^2 \mu / 2},$$

$$\Pr[|\pi(S) \cap W| \ge (1 + \delta)\mu] \le e^{-\delta^2 \mu / 3}.$$

– for any $d \ge 6\mu$, $\Pr[|\pi(S) \cap W| \ge d] \le 2^{-d}$.

Proof. For every $s \in S$, let X_s be the indicator such that $X_s = 1$ is the event that $\pi(s)$ is in W. Let $X = \sum_{s \in S} X_s$. So $|\pi(S) \cap W| = X$. Note that $\Pr[X_s = 1] = |W|/n$. So $\mu = \mathbb{E}(X) = \frac{|W|}{n}|S|$.

For any $I \subseteq S$,

$$\Pr[\bigwedge_{i \in I}(X_i = 1)] = \frac{|W|}{n} \cdot \frac{|W| - 1}{n - 1} \cdots \frac{|W| - |I|}{n - |I|}, \tag{3}$$

(if $|W| < |I|$, it is 0). This is because the random permutation can be viewed as throwing elements $1, \ldots, n$ into n boxes uniformly one by one, where every box can have at most one element. We know that for $j = 1, \ldots, |I|$, $\frac{|W| - j}{n - j} \le \frac{|W|}{n}$ as $|W| \le n$. So $\Pr[\bigwedge_{i \in I}(X_i = 1)] \le \prod_{i \in I} \Pr[X_i = 1]$. In the same way, for any $I \subseteq [n]$,

$$\Pr[\bigwedge_{i \in I}(X_i = 0)] = \frac{n - |W|}{n} \cdot \frac{n - |W| - 1}{n - 1} \cdots \frac{n - |W| - |I|}{n - |I|}, \tag{4}$$

(if $n - |W| < |I|$, it is 0). Thus $\forall I \subseteq [n], \Pr[\bigwedge_{i \in I}(X_i = 0)] \le \prod_{i \in I} \Pr[X_i = 0]$. By Theorem 8, the conclusion follows.

We can get the following more general result by using Lemma 6.

Lemma 7. *Let $\pi : [n] \to [n]$ be a random permutation. For any $W \subseteq [n]$ with $|W| = \gamma n$, any constant $\delta \in (0, 1)$, any $t, l \in \mathbb{N}^+$ such that $tl \le \frac{0.9\delta}{1 + 0.9\delta}\gamma n$, any $S = \{S_1, \ldots, S_l\}$ such that $\forall i \in [l], S_i \subseteq [n]$ are disjoint sets and $|S_i| = t$, let X_i be the indicator such that $X_i = 1$ is the event $|\pi(S_i) \cap W| \ge (1 + \delta)\gamma t$. Let $X = \sum_{i \in [l]} X_i$. Then for any $d \ge 0$,*

$$\Pr[X \ge d] \le e^{-2d + (e^2 - 1)e^{-\Omega(\gamma t)}l}.$$

Proof. For any $s > 0$, $\Pr[X \ge d] = \Pr[e^{sX} \ge e^{sd}] \le \frac{\mathbb{E}[e^{sX}]}{e^{sd}}$ by Markov's inequality. For every $i \in [l]$, $\forall x_1, \ldots, x_{i-1} \in \{0, 1\}$, consider $p = \Pr[X_i = 1 | \forall j < i, X_j = x_j]$. Let $\bar{S}_i = \bigcup_{j=1}^{i} S_j$ for $i \in [l]$. Note that the event $\forall j < i, X_j = x_j$ is the union of exclusive events $\pi(\bar{S}_{i-1}) = V, \forall j < i, X_j = x_j$ for $V \subseteq [n]$ with $|V| = (j - 1)t$ and $\pi(\bar{S}_{i-1}) = V$ does not contradict $\forall j < i, X_j = x_j$. Conditioned on any one of those events, saying $\pi(\bar{S}_{i-1}) = V, \forall j < i, X_j = x_j$, π is a random bijective mapping from $[n] - \bar{S}_i$ to $[n] - V$. Note that $\frac{|W \cap ([n]-V)|}{n-(i-1)t} \leq \frac{\gamma n}{n - \frac{0.9\delta}{1+0.9\delta}\gamma n} \leq \frac{\gamma n}{n - \frac{0.9\delta}{1+0.9\delta}n} \leq (1 + 0.9\delta)\gamma n$, since $(i-1)t \leq lt \leq \frac{0.9\delta}{1+0.9\delta}\gamma n$. So $\mathbb{E}[\pi(S_i) \cap W | \pi(\bar{S}_{i-1}) = V, \forall j < i, X_j = x_j] \leq (1 + 0.9\delta)\gamma t$. By Lemma 6, $\Pr[X_i = 1 | \pi(\bar{S}_{i-1}) = V, \forall j < i, X_j = x_j] = \Pr[|\pi(S_i) \cap W| \geq (1+\delta)\gamma t | \pi(\bar{S}_{i-1}) = V, \forall j < i, X_j = x_j] \leq e^{-\Omega(\gamma t)}$. Thus $p \leq e^{-\Omega(\gamma t)}$. Next note that

$$\mathbb{E}[e^{s\sum_{k=i}^{l} X_k} | \forall j < i, X_j = x_j]$$

$$= p e^s \mathbb{E}[e^{s\sum_{k=i+1}^{l} X_k} | \forall j < i, X_j = x_j, X_i = 1]$$

$$+ (1-p)\mathbb{E}[e^{s\sum_{k=i+1}^{l} X_k} | \forall j < i, X_j = x_j, X_i = 0]$$

$$\leq (p e^s + 1 - p) \max(\mathbb{E}[e^{s\sum_{k=i+1}^{l} X_k} | \forall j < i, X_j = x_j, X_i = 1],$$

$$\mathbb{E}[e^{s\sum_{k=i+1}^{l} X_k} | \forall j < i, X_j = x_j, X_i = 0]) \qquad (5)$$

$$\leq e^{p(e^s - 1)} \max(\mathbb{E}[e^{s\sum_{k=i+1}^{l} X_k} | \forall j < i, X_j = x_j, X_i = 1],$$

$$\mathbb{E}[e^{s\sum_{k=i+1}^{l} X_k} | \forall j < i, X_j = x_j, X_i = 0])$$

$$\leq e^{e^{-\Omega(\gamma t)}(e^s - 1)} \max(\mathbb{E}[e^{s\sum_{k=i+1}^{l} X_k} | \forall j < i, X_j = x_j, X_i = 1],$$

$$\mathbb{E}[e^{s\sum_{k=i+1}^{l} X_k} | \forall j < i, X_j = x_j, X_i = 0]).$$

As this holds for every $i \in [l]$ and every $x_1, \ldots, x_{i-1} \in \{0,1\}$, we can iteratively apply the inequality and get the result that there exists $x'_1, \ldots, x'_l \in \{0,1\}$ such that

$$\mathbb{E}[e^{sX}] \leq e^{e^{-\Omega(\gamma t)}(e^s - 1)} \mathbb{E}[e^{s\sum_{k=2}^{l} X_k} | X_1 = x'_1]$$

$$\leq e^{2e^{-\Omega(\gamma t)}(e^s - 1)} \mathbb{E}[e^{s\sum_{k=3}^{l} X_k} | X_1 = x'_1, X_2 = x'_2]$$

$$\leq \cdots \leq e^{(l-1)e^{-\Omega(\gamma t)}(e^s - 1)} \mathbb{E}[e^{sX_l} | X_1 = x'_1, X_2 = x'_2, \ldots, X_{l-1} = x'_{l-1}]$$

$$\leq e^{e^{-\Omega(\gamma t)}(e^s - 1)l}.$$

$$(6)$$

Let's take $s = 2$. So $\Pr[X \geq d] \leq \frac{\mathbb{E}[e^{sX}]}{e^{sd}} \leq e^{-2d + (e^2 - 1)e^{-\Omega(\gamma t)}l}$.

Let's first show the non-adaptive privacy of this scheme.

Lemma 8. *If the non-adaptive privacy error of* (Share, Rec) *is* ϵ*, then the non-adaptive privacy error of* (Share', Rec') *is* $\bar{n}(\epsilon + 2^{-\Omega(k)})$.

Proof. We show that there exists a distribution $\mathcal{D}$ such that for any string $x \in \Sigma_0^{m'}$, for any sequence of distinct indices $W = (w_1, w_2, \ldots, w_{k'}) \in [n']^{k'}$ (chosen before observation),

$$\mathsf{SD}(\mathsf{Share}'(x)_W, \mathcal{D}) \leq \bar{n}(\epsilon + 2^{-\Omega(k)}).$$

For every $i \in [n\bar{n}]$, the block $\mathsf{Share}_+(\hat{y}_i)$ has length t. Let the indices of shares in $\mathsf{Share}_+(\hat{y}_i)$ be $S_i = \{(i-1)t + 1, \ldots, it\}$.

For every $i \in [\bar{n}]$, let E_i be the event that for at most k of $j \in \{(i-1)n + 1, \ldots, in\}$, $\pi(S_j) \subseteq W$. Let $E = \bigcap_{i \in [\bar{n}]} E_i$. We choose b to be such that $tn \leq \frac{0.9\alpha}{1+0.9\alpha}|W|$. So by Lemma 7, $\Pr[E_i] \geq 1 - e^{-\Omega(k)+(e^2-1)e^{-\Omega((1-\alpha)t)}n}$. We choose a large enough $t = O(\log n)$ such that $\Pr[E_i] \geq 1 - e^{-\Omega(k)}$. So $\Pr[E] \geq 1 - \bar{n}e^{-\Omega(k)}$ by the union bound.

Let's define the distribution $\mathcal{D}$ to be $\mathsf{Share}'(\sigma)_W$ for some $\sigma \in \Sigma_0^{m'}$. We claim that $\mathsf{Share}'(x)_W | E$ and $\mathcal{D}|E$ have statistical distance at most $\bar{n}\epsilon$. The reason is as follows.

Let's fix a permutation π for which E happens. We claim that $\mathsf{Share}'(x)_W$ is a deterministic function of at most k entries of each y_i for $i \in [\bar{n}]$ and some extra uniform random bits. This is because, as E happens, for those $i \in [n\bar{n}]$ with $\pi(S_i) \not\subseteq W$, the shares in $\pi(S_i) \cap W$ are independent of the secret by the privacy of $(\mathsf{Share}_+, \mathsf{Rec}_+)$. Note that they are also independent of other shares since the construction uses independent randomness for $\mathsf{Share}_+(\hat{y}_i), i \in [n\bar{n}]$. For those $i \in [n\bar{n}]$ with $\pi(S_i) \subseteq W$, the total number of them is at most k. So the claim holds. Hence by the privacy of $(\mathsf{Share}, \mathsf{Rec})$ with noting that $y_i, i \in [\bar{n}]$ are generated using independent randomness,

$$\mathsf{SD}(\mathsf{Share}'(x)_W, \mathcal{D}) \leq \bar{n}\epsilon. \tag{7}$$

So with probability at least $1 - \bar{n}e^{-\Omega(k)}$ over the fixing of π, $\mathsf{Share}'(x)_W$ and $\mathcal{D}$ have statistical distance at most $\bar{n}\epsilon$, which means that

$$\mathsf{SD}(\mathsf{Share}'(x)_W, \mathcal{D}) \leq \bar{n}(\epsilon + 2^{-\Omega(k)}). \tag{8}$$

Next we show the adaptive privacy.

Lemma 9. *For any alphabet Σ, any $n, k \in \mathbb{N}$ with $k \leq n$, for any distribution $X = (X_1, \ldots, X_n)$ over Σ^n, let $Y = ((X_{\pi^{-1}(1)} \circ \pi^{-1}(1)), \ldots, (X_{\pi^{-1}(n)} \circ \pi^{-1}(n)))$ where π is a random permutation over $[n] \to [n]$. For any adaptive observation W with $|W| = k$, Y_W is the same distribution as $Y_{[k]}$.*

Proof. Let $W = (w_1, \ldots, w_k)$.

We use induction.

For the base step, for any $x \in \Sigma$, any $i \in [n]$,

$$\Pr[Y_{w_1} = (x, i)] = \Pr[X_i = x]/n, \tag{9}$$

while

$$\Pr[Y_1 = (x, i)] = \Pr[X_i = x]/n. \tag{10}$$

So Y_{w_1} and Y_1 are the same distributions.

For the inductive step, assume that $Y_{W_{[i]}}$ and $Y_{[i]}$ are the same distributions. We know that for any $u \in (\Sigma \times [n])^i$,

$$\Pr[Y_{W_{[i]}} = u] = \Pr[Y_{[i]} = u]. \tag{11}$$

Fix a $u \in (\Sigma \times [n])^i$. For any $v = (v_1, v_2) \in (\Sigma \times [n])$, where $v_1 \in \Sigma, v_2 \in [n]$, $\Pr[Y_{w_{i+1}} = v | Y_{W_{[i]}} = u] = 0$ if v_2 has already been observed in the previous i

observations; otherwise $\Pr[Y_{W_{i+1}} = v | Y_{W_{[i]}} = u] = \frac{\Pr[X_{v_2}=v_1]}{n-i}$. Also $\Pr[Y_{i+1} = v | Y_{[i]} = u] = 0$ if v_2 has already been observed in the previous i observations; otherwise $\Pr[Y_{i+1} = v | Y_{[i]} = u] = \frac{\Pr[X_{v_2}=v_1]}{n-i}$.

Thus $Y_{W_{[i+1]}}$ and $Y_{[i+1]}$ are the same distributions. This finishes the proof.

Lemma 10. *If* (Share, Rec) *has non-adaptive privacy error* ϵ, *then* (Share', Rec') *has adaptive privacy error* $\bar{n}(\epsilon + 2^{-\Omega(k)})$.

Proof. First we assume that the adaptive observer always observes k' shares. For every observer M which does not observe k' shares, there exists another observer M' which can observe the same shares as M and then observe some more shares. That is to say that if the number of observed shares is less than k', M' will choose more unobserved shares (sequentially in a fixed order) to observe until k' shares are observed. Since we can use a deterministic function to throw away the extra observes of M' to get what M should observe, by Lemma 1 part 2, if the privacy holds for M' then the privacy holds for M. As a result, we always consider observers which observe k' shares.

By Lemma 9, for any $s \in \Sigma_0^{m'}$, any adaptive observation W, Share'$(s)_W$ is the same distribution as Share'$(s)_{W'}$ where $W = \{w_1, w_2, \ldots, w_{k'}\}$, $W' = [k']$. As W' is actually a non-adaptive observation, by Lemma 8, for distinct $s, s' \in \{0, 1\}^{m'}$, $\mathsf{SD}(\mathsf{Share}'(s)_{W'}, \mathsf{Share}'(s')_{W'}) \leq \bar{n}(\epsilon + 2^{-\Omega(k)})$. So

$$\mathsf{SD}(\mathsf{Share}'(s)_W, \mathsf{Share}'(s')_W) = \mathsf{SD}(\mathsf{Share}'(s)_{W'}, \mathsf{Share}'(s')_{W'}) \leq \bar{n}(\epsilon + 2^{-\Omega(k)}). \tag{12}$$

The theorem below now follows from Construction 1, Lemmas 4, 5 and 10.

Theorem 9. *For any* $n, m \in \mathbb{N}, m \leq n$, *any* $\epsilon, \eta \in [0, 1]$ *and any constant* $a \geq 1, \alpha \in (0, 1]$, *if there exists an explicit* (n, k) *secret sharing scheme in* AC^0 *with share alphabet* Σ, *message alphabet* Σ_0, *message length* m, *non-adaptive privacy error* ϵ *and reconstruction error* η, *then there exists an explicit* $(n' = O(n^a \log n), (1 - \alpha)n')$ *secret sharing scheme in* AC^0 *with share alphabet* $\Sigma \times [n']$, *message alphabet* Σ_0, *message length* $\Omega(mn^{a-1})$, *adaptive privacy error* $O(n^{a-1}(\epsilon + 2^{-\Omega(k)}))$ *and reconstruction error* $O(n^{a-1}\eta)$.

3.2 Binary Alphabet

In this subsection, we construct AC^0 secret sharing schemes with binary alphabet based on some existing schemes with binary alphabets, enlarging the privacy threshold.

We use some coding techniques and secret sharing for small blocks.

Lemma 11 ([12] Sect. 4). *For any* $n \in \mathbb{N}$, *any constant* $\delta_0, \delta_1 \in (0, 1)$, *let* $C \subseteq \mathbb{F}_2^n$ *be an asymptotically good* $(n, k = \delta_0 n, d = \delta_1 n)$ *linear code.*

1. There exists an (n, d) *secret sharing scheme* (Share, Rec) *with alphabet* $\{0, 1\}$, *message length* k, *perfect privacy and reconstruction. Here* $\forall x \in \{0, 1\}^k$,

Share$(x) = f(x) + c$ with c drawn uniform randomly from $C^{\perp}$ (the dual code of C) and f is the encoding function from $\{0,1\}^k$ to C. For $y \in \{0,1\}^n$, Rec(y) is to find x such that there exists a $c \in C^{\perp}$ with $f(x) + c = y$.

2. For any $p = \mathsf{poly}(n)$, there exists an explicit (n,d) secret sharing scheme (Share, Rec) with alphabet $\{0,1\}^p$, message length k, perfect privacy and reconstruction.

3. If the codeword length is logarithmic (say $n = O(\log N)$ for some $N \in \mathbb{N}$), then both schemes can be constructed explicitly in AC^0 (in N).

Proof. The first assertion is proved in [12].

The second assertion follows by applying the construction of the first assertion in parallel p times.

The third assertion holds because, when the codeword length is $O(\log N)$, both encoding and decoding functions have input length $O(\log N)$. For encoding, we can use any classic methods for generating asymptotically good binary codes. For decoding, we can try all possible messages to uniquely find the correct one. By Lemma 2, both functions can be computed by AC^0 circuits.

Now we give the secret sharing scheme in AC^0 with a constant privacy rate while having binary alphabet.

Construction 2. *For any $n, k, m \in \mathbb{N}$ with $k, m \leq n$, let (Share, Rec) be an (n,k) secret sharing scheme with alphabet $\{0,1\}$, message length m.*

Let (Share$_C$, Rec$_C$) be an (n_C, k_C) secret sharing scheme with alphabet $\{0,1\}^p$, $p = O(\log n)$, message length m_C by Lemma 11, where $m_C = \delta_0 n_C$, $k_C = \delta_1 n_C$, $n_C = O(\log n)$ for some constants δ_0, δ_1.

Let (Share$_0$, Rec$_0$) be an (n_0, k_0) secret sharing scheme with alphabet $\{0,1\}$, message length m_0 by Lemma 11, where $m_0 = \delta_0 n_0 = p + O(\log n)$, $k_0 = \delta_1 n_0$.

For any constant $a \geq 1$, we can construct the following $(n' = O(n^a), k' = \Omega(n'))$ secret sharing scheme (Share$'$, Rec$'$) with alphabet $\{0,1\}$, message length $m' = m\bar{n}$, where $\bar{n} = \Theta(n^{a-1})$ is large enough.

Function Share$' : \{0,1\}^{m'} \to \{0,1\}^{n'}$ is as follows.

1. *On input $x \in \{0,1\}^{m\bar{n}}$, parse it to be $(x_1, x_2, \ldots, x_{\bar{n}}) \in (\{0,1\}^m)^{\bar{n}}$.*

2. *Compute $y = (y_1, \ldots, y_{\bar{n}}) = (\mathsf{Share}(x_1), \ldots, \mathsf{Share}(x_{\bar{n}})) \in (\{0,1\}^n)^{\bar{n}}$. Split each entry to be blocks each has length pm_C to get $\hat{y} = (\hat{y}_1, \ldots, \hat{y}_{\tilde{n}}) \in (\{0,1\}^{pm_C})^{\tilde{n}}$, where $\tilde{n} = \bar{n}\lceil \frac{n}{pm_C} \rceil$.*

3. *Let $y^* = (\mathsf{Share}_C(\hat{y}_1), \ldots, \mathsf{Share}_C(\hat{y}_{\tilde{n}}))$. Parse it to be $y^* = (y_1^*, \ldots, y_{n^*}^*) \in (\{0,1\}^p)^{n^*}$, $n^* = \tilde{n}n_C$.*

4. *Generate π by Lemma 3 which is uniform random over permutations of $[n^*]$. If it failed, which can be detected by checking element distinctness, set π to be such that $\forall i \in [n^*], \pi(i) = i$.*

5. *Compute*

$$z(x) = (\mathsf{Share}_0(y^*_{\pi^{-1}(1)} \circ \pi^{-1}(1)), \ldots, \mathsf{Share}_0(y^*_{\pi^{-1}(n^*)} \circ \pi^{-1}(n^*)))$$
$$\in (\{0,1\}^{n_0})^{n^*}.$$

6. *Parse $z(x)$ to be bits and output.*

   Function $\mathsf{Rec}' : \{0,1\}^{n'=n_0 n^*} \to \{0,1\}^{m'}$ is as follows.

1. *Parse the input bits to be $z \in (\{0,1\}^{n_0})^{n^*}$ and compute*

$$(y^*_{\pi^{-1}(1)} \circ \pi^{-1}(1), \ldots, y^*_{\pi^{-1}(n^*)} \circ \pi^{-1}(n^*)) = (\mathsf{Rec}_0(z_1), \ldots, \mathsf{Rec}_0(z_{n^*})).$$

2. *Compute $y^* = (y^*_1, \ldots, y^*_{n^*})$.*
3. *Compute $\hat{y}$ by applying Rec_C on y^* for every successive n_C entries.*
4. *Parse $\hat{y}$ to be y.*
5. *Compute x by applying Rec on every entry of y.*

We have the following two lemmas, whose proofs are deferred to the full version.

Lemma 12. *If Share and Rec can be computed by AC^0 circuits, then Share' and Rec' can be computed by AC^0 circuits.*

Lemma 13. *If the reconstruction error of $(\mathsf{Share}, \mathsf{Rec})$ is η, then the reconstruction error of $(\mathsf{Share}', \mathsf{Rec}')$ is $\eta' = \bar{n}\eta$.*

Lemma 14. *If the non-adaptive privacy error of $(\mathsf{Share}, \mathsf{Rec})$ is ϵ, then the nonadaptive privacy error of $(\mathsf{Share}', \mathsf{Rec}')$ is $\bar{n}(\epsilon + 2^{-\Omega(k/\log^2 n)})$.*

Proof. Let $k' = 0.9\delta_1^2 n'$. We show that there exists a distribution $\mathcal{D}$ such that for any string $x \in \{0,1\}^m$, for any $W \subseteq [n']$ with $|W| \le k'$,

$$\mathsf{SD}(\mathsf{Share}'(x)_W, \mathcal{D}) \le \bar{n}(\epsilon + 2^{-\Omega(k/\log^2 n)}). \tag{13}$$

Let $\mathcal{D}$ be $\mathsf{Share}'(\sigma)_W$ for some $\sigma \in \{0,1\}^{m'}$.

Consider an arbitrary observation $W \subseteq [n']$, with $|W| \le k'$. Note that for at least $1 - 0.9\delta_1$ fraction of all blocks $z_i \in \{0,1\}^{n_0}, i = 1, \ldots, n^*$, at most δ_1 fraction of the bits in the block can be observed. Otherwise the number of observed bits is more than $0.9\delta_1 \times \delta_1 n'$. Let W^* be the index set of those blocks which have more than δ_1 fraction of bits being observed.

For every $i \in [n^*]\backslash W^*$, z_i is independent of $y^*_{\pi^{-1}(i)} \circ \pi^{-1}(i)$ by the privacy of $(\mathsf{Share}_0, \mathsf{Rec}_0)$. Note that z_i is also independent of $z_{i'}, i' \in [n^*], i' \ne i$ since it is independent of $y^*_{\pi^{-1}(i)} \circ \pi^{-1}(i)$ (its randomness is only from the randomness of the Share_0 function) and every Share_0 function uses independent randomness. So we only have to show that

$$\mathsf{SD}(z_{W^*}(x), z_{W^*}(\sigma)) \le \bar{n}(\epsilon + 2^{-\Omega(k/\log^2 n)}). \tag{14}$$

For every $i \in [\tilde{n}]$, let $S_i = \{(i-1)n_C + 1, \ldots, in_C\}$. Let X_i be the indicator that $|\pi(S_i) \cap W^*| > k_C, i \in [\tilde{n}]$. Note that $\mathbb{E}[|\pi(S_i) \cap W^*|] \le 0.9\delta_1 n_C = 0.9k_C$.

For every $i \in [\bar{n}]$, let E_i be the event that $\sum_{j=(i-1)\lceil \frac{n}{pm_C}\rceil+1}^{i\lceil \frac{n}{pm_C}\rceil} X_j \le \frac{k}{pm_C}$. Let $E = \bigcap_{i\in[\bar{n}]} E_i$. We take $\bar{n}$ to be large enough such that $n_C\lceil \frac{n}{pm_C}\rceil \le \frac{0.9\times0.1}{1+0.9\times0.1}|W^*|$. For every $i \in [\bar{n}]$, by Lemma 7,

$$1 - \Pr[E_i] \le e^{-2k/(pm_C)+(e^2-1)e^{-\Omega(0.9\delta_1^2 n_C)}\lceil \frac{n}{pm_C}\rceil}. \tag{15}$$

We take $n_C = O(\log n)$ to be large enough such that the probability is at most

$$e^{-\Omega(k/(pm_C))} \leq e^{-\Omega(k/\log^2 n)}. \tag{16}$$

Next we do a similar argument as that in the proof of Lemma 8. We know that $\Pr[E] \geq 1 - \bar{n}e^{-\Omega(k/\log^2 n)}$. We claim that $z_{W^*}(x)|E$ and $z_{W^*}(\sigma)|E$ have statistical distance at most $\bar{n}\epsilon$. The reason follows.

Let's fix a permutation π for which E happens. We claim that $z_{W^*}(x)$ is a deterministic function of at most k bits of each y_i for $i \in [\bar{n}]$ and some extra uniform random bits. This is because, as E happens, for those $i \in [\bar{n}]$ with $|\pi(S_i) \cap W^*| \leq k_C$, the shares in $\pi(S_i) \cap W^*$ are independent of the secret by the privacy of $(\text{Share}_C, \text{Rec}_C)$. Note that they are also independent of other shares since the construction uses independent randomness for $\text{Share}_C(\hat{y}_i), i \in [\bar{n}]$. For those $i \in [\bar{n}]$ with $|\pi(S_i) \cap W^*| > k_C$, the total number of them is at most $\frac{k}{pm_C}$. By the construction, $\text{Share}'(x)_{W^*}$ is computed from at most $\frac{k}{pm_C} \times pm_C = k$ bits of each y_i for $i \in [\bar{n}]$ and some extra uniform random bits. Hence by the privacy of $(\text{Share}, \text{Rec})$ and noting that $y_i, \in [\bar{n}]$ are generated using independent randomness,

$$\text{SD}(z_{W^*}(x), z_{W^*}(\sigma)) \leq \bar{n}\epsilon. \tag{17}$$

Thus with probability at least $1 - \bar{n}e^{-\Omega(k/\log^2 n)}$ over the fixing of π, $z_{W^*}(x)$ and $z_{W^*}(\sigma)$ have statistical distance at most $\bar{n}\epsilon$, which means that

$$\text{SD}(z_{W^*}(x), z_{W^*}(\sigma)) \leq \bar{n}(\epsilon + e^{-\Omega(k/\log^2 n)}). \tag{18}$$

Lemma 15. *For any alphabet Σ, any $n \in \mathbb{N}$, Let $X = (X_1, \ldots, X_n)$ be an arbitrary distribution over Σ^n. For any $n_0, k_0 \in \mathbb{N}$ with $k_0 \leq n_0$, let $(\text{Share}_0, \text{Rec}_0)$ be an arbitrary (n_0, k_0)-secret sharing scheme with binary alphabet, message length $m_0 = \log|\Sigma| + O(\log n)$, perfect privacy. Let*

$$Y = (\text{Share}_0(X_{\pi^{-1}(1)} \circ \pi^{-1}(1)), \ldots, \text{Share}_0(X_{\pi^{-1}(n)} \circ \pi^{-1}(n)))$$

where π is a random permutation over $[n] \rightarrow [n]$. For any $t \leq n \cdot k_0$, let W be an any adaptive observation which observes t shares. Then there exists a deterministic function $f : \{0,1\}^{\text{poly}(n)} \rightarrow \{0,1\}^t$ such that Y_W has the same distribution as $f(Y_{W'} \circ S)$, where S is uniform over $\{0,1\}^{\text{poly}(n)}$ and $W' = [t'n_0], t' = \lceil \frac{t}{k_0} \rceil$.

Proof. For every $i \in [n]$, Let $B_i = \{(i-1)n_0 + 1, \ldots, in_0\}$. Assume the adaptive adversary is M.

Let f be defined as in Algorithm 1.

Let $W = (w_1, \ldots, w_t) \in [n \cdot n_0]^t$, $Z = f(Y_{W'} \circ S)$. Let $R \in \{0,1\}^{nn_0}$ be the random variable corresponds to r.

We use induction to show that Y_W has the same distribution as Z.

For the base case, the first bits of both random variables have the same distributions by the perfect privacy of $(\text{Share}_0, \text{Rec}_0)$.

For the inductive step, assume that, projected on the first d bits, the two distributions are the same. Fix the first d observed bits for both Y_W and Z to

---

Algorithm 1. $f(\cdot)$

Input: $y \in \{0,1\}^{t'n_0}$, $s \in \{0,1\}^{\text{poly}(n)}$
Let $c = 1$;
$\forall i \in [n], l_i \in [n] \cup \{\text{null}\}$ is assigned to be null;
Compute the secrets for the t' blocks y, which are

$$(x_1, \ldots, x_{t'}) \in (\{0,1\}^{m_0})^{t'};$$

Compute $(\text{Share}_0(\sigma), \ldots, \text{Share}_0(\sigma)) \in (\{0,1\}^{n_0})^n$ and parse it to be
$r \in \{0,1\}^{n_0 n}$, for an arbitrary $\sigma \in \Sigma$. Here for each Share_0 function, we take
some unused bits from s as the random bits used in that function.
Next f does the following computation by calling M;
while M *wants to observe the ith bit which is not observed previously* **do**
    Find $j \in [n]$ such that $i \in B_j$;
    if *the number of observed bits in the jth block is less than k_0* **then**
    | Let M observe r_i;
    else
        Let I_j be the indices of the observed bits in the jth block. (The indices
        here are the relative indices in the jth block)
        if $l_j = \text{null}$ **then**
        | $l_j = c$;
        | $c = c+1$;
        | Draw a string v^j from $\text{Share}_0(x_c)|_{\text{Share}_0(x_c)_{I_j} = r_{(j-1)n_0 + I_j}}$ by using
        | some unused bits of s;
        end
        Let M observe $v^j_{i-(j-1)n_0}$;
    end
end

---

be $\bar{y} \in \{0,1\}^d$. Assume that the $(d+1)$th observation is to observe the w_dth bit where w_d is in B_j for some j.

If the number of observed bits in the jth block is less than k_0 then $Y_{\{w_1,\ldots,w_{d+1}\} \cap B_j}$ has the same distribution as $R_{\{w_1,\ldots,w_{d+1}\} \cap B_j}$, following the privacy of $(\text{Share}_0, \text{Rec}_0)$. Note that the blocks $Y_{\{w_1,\ldots,w_{d+1}\} \cap B_i}$, $i \in [n]$ are independent. The blocks $R_{\{w_1,\ldots,w_{d+1}\} \cap B_i}$, $i \in [n]$ are also independent. As f will output $R_{w_{d+1}}$, the conclusion holds for $d+1$.

Else, if the number of observed bits in the jth block is at least k_0, it is sufficient to show that $Y_{w_{d+1}}|_{Y_{\{w_1,\ldots,w_d\}} = \bar{y}}$ has the same distribution as that of $Z_{d+1}|_{Z_{\{1,\ldots,d\}} = \bar{y}}$. Note that there are c blocks such that W observes more than k_0 bits for each of them. Let $q_1, \ldots, q_c$ denote those blocks. Let $I = ((q_1 - 1)n_0 + I_{q_1}, \ldots, (q_c - 1)n_0 + I_{q_c})$, which is the set of indices of all observed bits. Note that $I \subseteq \{w_1, \ldots, w_d\}$.

By the privacy of the secret sharing scheme, for those blocks which have at most k_0 bits being observed, they are independent of the secret and hence independent of other blocks. So $Y_{w_{d+1}}|_{Y_{\{w_1,\ldots,w_d\}} = \bar{y}}$ is in fact $Y_{w_{d+1}}|_{Y_I = y^*}$ where y^* are the corresponding bits from $\bar{y}$ with a proper rearrangement according to

I. From the definition of f we know that for $i \in [c]$, the observed bits in the q_ith block is exactly the same distribution as $(Y_{B_{l_{q_i}}})_{I_{q_i}} = \mathsf{Share}_0(x_{l_{q_i}})_{I_{q_i}}$. So for $Z_{d+1}|_{Z_{\{1,\ldots,d\}}=\bar{y}}$, it is the same distribution as

$$T = (Y_{B_{l_j}})_{w_d-(j-1)n_0} |\wedge_{i=1}^c ((Y_{B_{l_{q_i}}})_{I_{q_i}} = y^*_{(q_i-1)n_0+I_{q_i}})$$
$$= \mathsf{Share}_0(x_{l_j})_{w_d-(j-1)n_0} |\wedge_{i=1}^c (\mathsf{Share}_0(x_{l_{q_i}})_{I_{q_i}} = y^*_{(q_i-1)n_0+I_{q_i}}). \tag{19}$$

By Lemma 9, $(Y_{B_{q_1}}, \ldots, Y_{B_{q_c}})$ has the same distribution as $(Y_{B_{l_{q_1}}}, \ldots, Y_{B_{l_{q_c}}})$ as they both are the same distribution as $(\mathsf{Share}_0(x_1), \ldots, \mathsf{Share}_0(x_c))$. Thus $Y_{w_{d+1}}|_{Y_I=y^*}$ has the same distribution as T, as $Y_{w_{d+1}}|_{Y_I=y^*}$ is the distribution of some bits in $(Y_{B_{q_1}}, \ldots, Y_{B_{q_c}})$ and T is the distribution of the corresponding bits (same indices) in $(Y_{B_{l_{q_1}}}, \ldots, Y_{B_{l_{q_c}}})$. So we know that $Y_{w_{d+1}}|_{Y_{\{w_1,\ldots,w_d\}}=\bar{y}}$ has the same distribution as $Z_{d+1}|_{Z_{\{1,\ldots,d\}}=\bar{y}}$ and this shows our conclusion.

Lemma 16. *If the non-adaptive privacy error of* (Share, Rec) *is ϵ, then the adaptive privacy error of* (Share′, Rec′) *is $\bar{n}(\epsilon + 2^{-\Omega(k/\log^2 n)})$.*

Proof. Let W be an adaptive observation. Let $W' = [\lceil |W|/k_0 \rceil n_0]$. Let $|W| = \Omega(n')$ be small enough such that $|W'| \le 0.9\delta_1^2 n'$. By Lemma 15, there exists a deterministic function f such that for any $x, x' \in \{0,1\}^{m'}$,

$$\mathsf{SD}(\mathsf{Share}'(x)_W, \mathsf{Share}(x')_W) = \mathsf{SD}(f(\mathsf{Share}'(x)_{W'} \circ S), f(\mathsf{Share}'(x')_{W'} \circ S)), \tag{20}$$

where S is the uniform distribution as defined in Lemma 15 which is independent of $\mathsf{Share}'(x)_{W'}$ or $\mathsf{Share}'(x')_{W'}$. By Lemma 1, we know that

$$\mathsf{SD}(f(\mathsf{Share}'(x)_{W'} \circ S), f(\mathsf{Share}'(x')_{W'} \circ S)) \le \mathsf{SD}(\mathsf{Share}'(x)_{W'}, \mathsf{Share}'(x')_{W'}). \tag{21}$$

By Lemma 14 we know that

$$\mathsf{SD}(\mathsf{Share}'(x)_{W'}, \mathsf{Share}'(x')_{W'}) \le \bar{n}(\epsilon + 2^{-\Omega(k/\log^2 n)}). \tag{22}$$

Hence

$$\mathsf{SD}(\mathsf{Share}'(x)_W, \mathsf{Share}'(x')_W) \le \bar{n}(\epsilon + 2^{-\Omega(k/\log^2 n)}). \tag{23}$$

Theorem 10. *For any $n, m \in \mathbb{N}, m \le n$, any $\epsilon, \eta \in [0,1]$ and any constant $a \ge 1$, if there exists an explicit (n, k) secret sharing scheme in AC^0 with alphabet $\{0,1\}$, message length m, non-adaptive privacy error ϵ and reconstruction error η, then there exists an explicit $(n' = O(n^a), k' = \Omega(n'))$ secret sharing scheme in AC^0 with alphabet $\{0,1\}$, message length $\Omega(mn^{a-1})$, adaptive privacy error $O(n^{a-1}(\epsilon + 2^{-\Omega(k/\log^2 n)}))$ and reconstruction error $O(n^{a-1}\eta)$.*

Proof. It follows from Construction 2, Lemmas 12, 13 and 16.

4   k-Wise Independent Generator in AC^0

In this section we focus on increasing the secret length to be linear of the number of shares while keeping the construction in AC^0. The privacy rate is not as good as the previous section. The main technique is to use the following well known k-wise independent generator which is constructed from expander graphs.

Theorem 11 [29]. *For any $N, D, M \in \mathbb{N}$, any $\epsilon > 0$, if there exists a $(\leq K_{\max}, (\frac{1}{2} + \epsilon)D)$ expander with left set of vertices $[N]$, right set of vertices $[M]$, left degree D, then the function $g : \{0,1\}^M \to \{0,1\}^N$, defined by $g(x)_i = \bigoplus_{j \in [D]} x_{\Gamma(i,j)}, i = 1, 2, \dots, N$, is a $K_{\max}$-wise uniform independent generator.*

Next we directly give the main results for this section. Detailed proofs are deferred to the full version.

Theorem 12. *For any $M \in \mathbb{N}$, $N = \mathsf{poly}(M)$, any alphabets Σ_0, Σ, any constant $\gamma \in (0,1]$, there exists an explicit K-wise independent generator $g : \Sigma_0^M \to \Sigma^N$ in AC^0, where $K = (\frac{M \log |\Sigma_0|}{\log |\Sigma|})^{1-\gamma}$.*

Now we give the construction of secret sharing schemes in AC^0 with large message rate (saying $1 - 1/\mathsf{poly}(n)$).

Construction 3. *For any $n, k, m \in \mathbb{N}$ with $k \leq n$, any alphabets Σ_0, Σ, let $(\mathsf{Share}, \mathsf{Rec})$ be an (n, k) secret sharing scheme with share alphabet Σ, message alphabet Σ_0, message length m.*

For any constant $a > 1, \gamma \in (0,1]$, we construct the following $(n' = n + m', k' = \min(k, l))$ secret sharing scheme $(\mathsf{Share}', \mathsf{Rec}')$ with alphabet Σ, message length $m' = \Omega(n^a)$, where $l = \Theta(\frac{m \log |\Sigma_0|}{\log |\Sigma|})^{1-\gamma}$.

The function $\mathsf{Share}' : \Sigma^{m'} \to \Sigma^{n'}$ is as follows.

1. *Let $g_\Gamma : \Sigma_0^m \to \Sigma^{m'}$ be the l-wise independent generator by Theorem 12.*
2. *For secret $x \in \Sigma^{m'}$, we draw r uniform randomly from Σ_0^m let*

$$\mathsf{Share}'(x) = (\mathsf{Share}(r), g_\Gamma(r) \oplus x).$$

The function $\mathsf{Rec}' : \Sigma^{n'} \to \Sigma^{m'}$ is as follows.

1. *The input is $y = (y_1, y_2)$ where $y_1 \in \Sigma^n, y_2 \in \Sigma^{m'}$.*
2. *Let*

$$\mathsf{Rec}'(y) = g_\Gamma(\mathsf{Rec}(y_1)) \oplus y_2.$$

Theorem 13. *For any $n, m \in \mathbb{N}, m \leq n$, any $\epsilon, \eta \in [0,1]$, any constant $\gamma \in (0,1]$, any $m' = \mathsf{poly}(n)$ and any alphabets Σ_0, Σ, if there exists an explicit (n, k) secret sharing scheme in AC^0 with share alphabet Σ, message alphabet Σ_0, message length m, non-adaptive privacy error ϵ and reconstruction error η, then there exists an explicit $(n + m', \min(k, (\frac{m \log |\Sigma_0|}{\log |\Sigma|})^{1-\gamma}))$ secret sharing scheme in AC^0 with alphabet Σ, message length m', non-adaptive privacy error ϵ and reconstruction error η.*

5 Final Construction

In this section we give our final AC^0 construction of secret sharing schemes which has constant message rate and constant privacy rate.

Our construction will use both random permutation and k-wise independent generator proposed in the previous sections.

Construction 4. *For any $n, k, m \in \mathbb{N}$ with $k, m \leq n$, let (Share, Rec) be an (n, k) secret sharing scheme with alphabet $\{0, 1\}$, message length m.*

Let $(\text{Share}_C, \text{Rec}_C)$ be an (n_C, k_C) secret sharing scheme from Lemma 11 with alphabet $\{0, 1\}^{p=O(\log n)}$, message length m_C, where $m_C = \delta_0 n_C$, $k_C = \delta_1 n_C$, $n_C = O(\log n)$ for some constants δ_0, δ_1.

Let $(\text{Share}_C^*, \text{Rec}_C^*)$ be an (n_C^*, k_C^*) secret sharing scheme from Lemma 11 with alphabet $\{0, 1\}$, message length large enough m_C^*, where $m_C^* = \delta_0 n_C^* = p + O(\log n)$, $n_C^* = \delta_1 n_C^*$.

For any constant $a > 1, \gamma > 0$, we can construct the following $(n' = O(n^a), k' = \Omega(n'))$ secret sharing scheme $(\text{Share}', \text{Rec}')$ with alphabet $\{0, 1\}$, message length $m' = \Omega(n')$.

The function $\text{Share}' : \{0, 1\}^{m'} \rightarrow \{0, 1\}^{n'}$ is as follows.

1. *Let $\bar{n} = \Theta(n^{a-1})$ where the constant factor is large enough.*
2. *Let $g_\Gamma : \{0, 1\}^{m\bar{n}} \rightarrow \{0, 1\}^{m'}$ be the l-wise independent generator by Theorem 12, where $l = \Omega(mn^{a-1})^{1-\gamma}$.*
3. *For secret $x \in \{0, 1\}^{m'}$, we draw a string $r = (r_1, \ldots, r_{\bar{n}})$ uniform randomly from $(\{0, 1\}^m)^{\bar{n}}$.*
4. *Let $y = (y_s, y_g)$, where*

$$y_s = (y_{s,1}, \ldots, y_{s,\bar{n}}) = (\text{Share}(r_1), \ldots, \text{Share}(r_{\bar{n}})) \in (\{0, 1\}^n)^{\bar{n}}, \quad (24)$$

$$y_g = (y_{g,1}, \ldots, y_{g,m'}) = g_\Gamma(r) \oplus x \in \{0, 1\}^{m'}. \quad (25)$$

5. *Compute $\hat{y}_s \in ((\{0, 1\}^p)^{m_C})^{n_s}$ from y_s by parsing $y_{s,i}$ to be blocks over $(\{0, 1\}^p)^{m_C}$ for every $i \in [\bar{n}]$, where $n_s = \lceil \frac{n}{pm_C} \rceil \bar{n}$.*
6. *Compute $\hat{y}_g \in ((\{0, 1\}^p)^{m_C})^{n_g}$ from y_g by parsing y_g to be blocks over $(\{0, 1\}^p)^{m_C}$, where $n_g = \lceil \frac{m'}{pm_C} \rceil$.*
7. *Let*

$$y' = (\text{Share}_C(\hat{y}_{s,1}), \ldots, \text{Share}_C(\hat{y}_{s,n_s}), \text{Share}_C(\hat{y}_{g,1}), \ldots, \text{Share}_C(\hat{y}_{g,n_g})).$$

Parse y' as $(y_1', \ldots, y_{n^*}') \in (\{0, 1\}^p)^{n^*}$, where $n^* = (n_s + n_g)n_C$.

8. *Generate a random permutation $\pi : [n^*] \rightarrow [n^*]$ and compute*

$$z(x) = (\text{Share}_C^*(y_{\pi^{-1}(1)}' \circ \pi^{-1}(1)), \ldots, \text{Share}_C^*(y_{\pi^{-1}(n^*)}' \circ \pi^{-1}(n^*)))$$

$$\in (\{0, 1\}^{n_C^*})^{n^*}.$$

9. *Parse $z(x)$ to be bits and output.*

The function $\text{Rec}' : \{0, 1\}^{n'} \rightarrow \{0, 1\}^{m'}$ is as follows.

1. *Parse the input bits to be* $z = (z_1, \ldots, z_{n^*}) \in (\{0,1\}^{n_C^*})^{n^*}$.
2. *For every* $i \in [n^*]$, *let* $(y'_{\pi^{-1}(i)} \circ \pi^{-1}(i)) = \mathsf{Rec}_C^*(z_i)$ *to get* y'.
3. *Parse* $y' = (y'_s, y'_g)$, *where* $y'_s = (y'_{s,1}, \ldots, y'_{s,n_s}) \in (\{0,1\}^{p n_C})^{n_s}$ *and* $y'_g = (y'_{g,1}, \ldots, y'_{g,n_g}) \in (\{0,1\}^{p n_C})^{n_g}$.
4. *Let*

$$\hat{y}_s = (\mathsf{Rec}_C(y'_{s,1}), \ldots, \mathsf{Rec}_C(y'_{s,n_s})), \hat{y}_g = (\mathsf{Rec}_C(y'_{g,1}), \ldots, \mathsf{Rec}_C(y'_{g,n_g})).$$

5. *Parse* $\hat{y}_s$ *to get* y_s.
6. *Parse* $\hat{y}_g$ *to get* y_g
7. *Let* $r = (\mathsf{Rec}(y_{s,1}), \ldots, \mathsf{Rec}(y_{s,\bar{n}}))$.
8. *Output*

$$\mathsf{Rec}'(z) = g_\Gamma(r) \oplus y_g.$$

We have the following lemmas, whose proofs are similar to previous ones and deferred to the full version.

Lemma 17. *If* $(\mathsf{Share}, \mathsf{Rec})$ *can be computed by* AC^0 *circuits, then* $(\mathsf{Share}', \mathsf{Rec}')$ *can be computed by* AC^0 *circuits.*

Lemma 18. *If the reconstruction error of* $(\mathsf{Share}, \mathsf{Rec})$ *is* η, *then the reconstruction error of* $(\mathsf{Share}', \mathsf{Rec}')$ *is* $\eta' = \bar{n}\eta$.

Lemma 19. *If the non-adaptive privacy error of* $(\mathsf{Share}, \mathsf{Rec})$ *is* ϵ, *then the non-adaptive privacy error of* $(\mathsf{Share}', \mathsf{Rec}')$ *is* $\bar{n}(\epsilon + e^{-\Omega(k/\log^2 n)}) + e^{-\Omega(l/\log^2 n)}$.

Lemma 20. *If the non-adaptive privacy error of* $(\mathsf{Share}, \mathsf{Rec})$ *is* ϵ, *then the adaptive privacy error of* $(\mathsf{Share}', \mathsf{Rec}')$ *is* $\bar{n}(\epsilon + e^{-\Omega(k/\log^2 n)}) + e^{-\Omega(l/\log^2 n)}$.

Theorem 14. *For any* $\epsilon, \eta \in [0,1]$, *any* $n, m \in \mathbb{N}, m \leq n$ *and any constant* $a > 1, \gamma > 0$, *if there exists an explicit* (n, k) *secret sharing scheme in* AC^0 *with alphabet* $\{0,1\}$, *message length* m, *non-adaptive privacy error* ϵ *and reconstruction error* η, *then there exists an explicit* $(n' = O(n^a), \Omega(n'))$ *secret sharing scheme in* AC^0 *with alphabet* $\{0,1\}$, *message length* $\Omega(n')$, *adaptive privacy error* $O(n^{a-1}(\epsilon + 2^{-\Omega(k/\log^2 n)}) + 2^{-\Omega((mn^{a-1})^{1-\gamma}/\log^2 n)})$ *and reconstruction error* $O(n^{a-1}\eta)$.

Proof. It follows from Construction 4, Lemmas 17, 18, 20.

6   Instantiation

The Minsky-Papert function [28] gives a secret sharing scheme in AC^0 with perfect privacy.

Theorem 15 [7,28]. *For any* $n \in \mathbb{N}$, *there exists an explicit* $(n, n^{\frac{1}{3}})$ *secret sharing scheme in* AC^0 *with alphabet* $\{0,1\}$, *message length* 1, *perfect privacy and reconstruction.*

Combining our techniques with Theorem 15, we have the following results. The detailed proofs are deferred to the full version.

Theorem 16. *For any $n \in \mathbb{N}$, any constant $\alpha \in (0,1], \beta \in [0,1)$, there exists an explicit $(n, (1-\alpha)n)$ secret sharing scheme in AC^0 with share alphabet $\{0,1\}^{O(\log n)}$, message alphabet $\{0,1\}$, message length $m = n^\beta$, adaptive privacy error $2^{-\Omega((\frac{n}{m \log n})^{1/3})}$ and perfect reconstruction.*

Theorem 17. *For any $n \in \mathbb{N}$, for any constant $\gamma \in (0,1/4)$, there exists an explicit $(n, \Omega(n))$ secret sharing scheme in AC^0 with alphabet $\{0,1\}$, message length $m = \Omega(n)$, adaptive privacy error $2^{-\Omega(n^{\frac{1}{4}-\gamma})}$ and perfect reconstruction.*

7 Extensions and Other Applications

The detailed constructions and proofs in this section appear in the full version.

7.1 Robust Secret Sharing

Our secret sharing schemes can be made robust by using robust secret sharing schemes and authentication techniques in small blocks.

We first recall the following robust secret sharing scheme.

Theorem 18 [15]. *For any $n \in \mathbb{N}$, any constant $\rho < 1/2$, there is an $(n, \Omega(n))$ robust secret sharing scheme, with alphabet $\{0,1\}^{O(1)}$, message length $\Omega(n)$, perfect privacy, robustness parameter $d = \rho n$ and reconstruction error $2^{-\Omega(n)}$.*

We use concatenations of the schemes from Theorem 18 to get the following robust secret sharing scheme in AC^0 with poly-logarithmic number of shares.

Lemma 21. *For any $n \in \mathbb{N}$, any constant $a \in \mathbb{N}$, any $\epsilon = 1/\text{poly}(n)$, there exists an $(n_0 = O(\log^a n), k_0 = \Omega(n_0))$ robust secret sharing scheme in AC^0 (in n), with share alphabet $\{0,1\}^{O(1)}$, message alphabet $\{0,1\}$, message length $\Omega(n_0)$, perfect privacy, robustness parameter $\Omega(n_0)$, reconstruction error ϵ.*

Next, we give our construction of robust secret sharing scheme with "asymptotically good" parameters.

Theorem 19. *For any $n \in \mathbb{N}$, any $\eta = \frac{1}{\text{poly}(n)}$, there exists an explicit $(n, \Omega(n))$ robust secret sharing scheme in AC^0 with share alphabet $\{0,1\}^{O(1)}$, message alphabet $\{0,1\}$, message length $m = \Omega(n)$, non-adaptive privacy error $2^{-n^{\Omega(1)}}$, non-adaptive robustness $\Omega(n)$ and reconstruction error η.*

7.2   Stochastic Error Correcting Code

Using our general strategy, we can also construct stochastic error correcting codes in AC^0 which can resist additive errors [20].

One important component of our construction is the following "tiny" codes. It is constructed by classic code concatenation techniques.

Lemma 22. *For any $n \in \mathbb{N}$, any constant $a \in \mathbb{N}$, there exists an asymptotically good binary $(n = O(\log^a n), m, d)$ code C such that the encoding and decoding can both be computed by AC^0 circuits of size $\mathsf{poly}(n)$.*

Here we give the construction of stochastic error correcting codes in AC^0 which are "asymptotically good".

Construction 5. *For any $n \in \mathbb{N}$, we construct the following $(n, m = \Omega(n), \rho = \Omega(1))$ stochastic error correcting code.*

Let δ_0, δ_1 be some proper constants in $(0, 1)$.

Let $(\mathsf{Enc}_0, \mathsf{Dec}_0)$ be an asymptotically good (n_0, m_0, d_0) error correcting code with alphabet $\{0, 1\}^p$, $n_0 = O(\log n)$, $m_0 = \delta_0 n_0$, $d_0 = \delta_1 n_0$. In fact we can realize this code by applying an asymptotically good binary code, having the same rate, in parallel p times.

Let $(\mathsf{Enc}_1, \mathsf{Dec}_1)$ be an asymptotically good (n_1, m_1, d_1) error correcting code from Lemma 22 with alphabet $\{0, 1\}$, $n_1 = p + O(\log n)$, $m_1 = \delta_0 n_1 = O(p)$, $d_1 = \delta_1 n_0$.

Encoding function $\mathsf{Enc} : \{0, 1\}^{m = \Omega(n)} \to \{0, 1\}^n$ is a random function which is as follows.

1. *On input $x \in \{0, 1\}^m$, split x into blocks of length pm_0 such that $x = (\bar{x}_1, \ldots, \bar{x}_{m/(pm_0)}) \in (\{0, 1\}^{pm_0})^{m/(pm_0)}$.*
2. *Let $y = (y_1, \ldots, y_{n'}) = (\mathsf{Enc}_0(\bar{x}_1), \ldots, \mathsf{Enc}_0(\bar{x}_{m/(pm_0)})) \in (\{0, 1\}^p)^{n'}$, $n' = m/(\delta_0 p)$*
3. *Generate a random permutation $\pi : [n'] \to [n']$.*
4. *Randomly pick $l = O(\log n)$ different indices $r_1, \ldots, r_l \in [n']$ and let $r = (r_1, \ldots, r_l)$.*
5. *For every $i \in [n']$, let $\tilde{y}_i = (y_{\pi^{-1}(i)}, \pi^{-1}(i), \pi^{-1}(i \gg r_1), \ldots, \pi^{-1}(i \gg r_l), r)$.*
6. *Output $z = (\mathsf{Enc}_1(\tilde{y}_1), \ldots, \mathsf{Enc}_1(\tilde{y}_{n'})) \in (\{0, 1\}^{n_1})^{n'}$.*

Decoding function $\mathsf{Dec} : \{0, 1\}^{n = n_1 n'} \to \{0, 1\}^m$ is as follows.

1. *On the input z, apply Dec_1 on every block of length n_0 to get $\tilde{y}$.*
2. *Take the majority of the r in every $\tilde{y}_i, i \in [n']$ to get r.*
3. *$\forall i \in [n']$, we do the following. Check that for every $j \in [l]$, the corresponding backup of $\pi^{-1}(i)$ in the $(i \ll r_j)$th block is equal to the one stored in the ith block. Take the approximate majority of these l tests, if the output is true then mark $\tilde{y}_i$ as good, otherwise mark it as bad.*
4. *Compute the entries of y from shares that are marked as good. Other entries are set as blank.*
5. *Apply Dec_0 on every block of y of length pn_0 to get x.*

Theorem 20. *For any $n \in \mathbb{N}$ and any $\epsilon = 1/\mathrm{poly}(n)$, there exists an explicit $(n, m = \Omega(n), \rho = \Omega(1))$ stochastic binary error correcting code with decoding error ϵ, which can be computed by AC^0 circuits.*

Note that if we set both levels of codes in our construction to be from Lemma 22 with length $\mathrm{poly}\log n$ and l to be also $\mathrm{poly}\log n$, we can get quasi-polynomially small decoding error following the same proof. The result is stated as the follows.

Theorem 21. *For any $n \in \mathbb{N}$, any $\epsilon = 2^{-\mathrm{poly}\log n}$, there exists an explicit $(n, m = \Omega(n), \rho = \Omega(1))$ stochastic binary error correcting code with decoding error ϵ, which can be computed by AC^0 circuits.*

We can use duplicating techniques to make the decoding error to be even smaller, however with a smaller message rate.

Theorem 22. *For any $n, r \in \mathbb{N}$, there exists an $(n, m = \Omega(n/r), \rho = \Omega(1))$ stochastic binary error correcting code with decoding error $2^{-\Omega(r/\log n)}$, which can be computed by AC^0 circuits.*

7.3 Secure Broadcasting

We give a protocol that allows n parties to securely communication their secret inputs to each other using only a small amount of common secret randomness and communication over a public broadcast channel. The protocol should be secure against an external adversary who can (adaptively) observe and tamper with a constant fraction of the messages. This notion is formalized in Definition 3.

Protocol 1. *For any $n, m \in \mathbb{N}$, for any $i \in [n]$, let $x_i \in \{0, 1\}^m$ be the input of party i. Let the security parameter be $r \in \mathbb{N}$ with $r \leq m$.*

Let $(\mathsf{RShare}_0, \mathsf{RRec}_0)$ be an $(n_0, k_0 = \delta_0 n_0)$ robust secret sharing scheme with share alphabet $\{0, 1\}^{p=O(1)}$, secret length $m_0 = m = \delta n_0$ and robustness parameter $d_0 = \delta_1 n_0$, as given by Theorem 18 for some constant $\delta, \delta_0, \delta_1$ with $\delta_0 \geq \delta_1$.

Let $(\mathsf{RShare}_1, \mathsf{RRec}_1)$ be an $(n_1, k_1 = \delta_0 n_1)$ robust secret sharing scheme with share alphabet $\{0, 1\}^{p=O(1)}$, secret length $m_1 = p n_0/r = \delta n_1$ and robustness parameter $d_1 = \delta_1 n_1$, by Theorem 18.

Assume that all parties have a common secret key $s \in \{0, 1\}^{O(r \log(nr))}$.

The i-th party does the following.

1. *Generate a $2^{-\Omega(r)}$-almost r-wise independent random permutation π over $[nr]$ using s.*
2. *Compute the secret shares $y_i = \mathsf{RShare}_0(x_i) \in (\{0, 1\}^p)^{n_0}$. Split y_i into r blocks each of length $p n_0/r$ such that $y_i = (y_{i,1}, \dots, y_{i,r})$.*
3. *View the communication procedure as having $[nr]$ time slots. For $j \in [r]$, on the $\pi((i-1)r + j)$'s time slot, send message $z_{i,j} = \mathsf{RShare}_1(y_{i,j})$.*

4. For every $i \in [n], j \in [r]$, compute $y_{i,j} = \mathsf{RRec}_1(z_{i,j})$, where $z_{i,j}$ is the message received in the $\pi((i-1)r + j)$'s time slot.
5. For every $i \in [n]$ get $y_i = (y_{i,1}, \ldots, y_{i,r})$.
6. For every $i \in [n]$, $x_i = \mathsf{RRec}_0(y_i)$.

Theorem 23. For any $n, m, r \in \mathbb{N}$ with $r \leq m$, there exists an explicit $(n, m, \alpha = \Omega(1), n2^{-\Omega(r)}, n2^{-\Omega(r)} + nm2^{-\Omega(m/r)})$ secure broadcasting protocol with communication complexity $O(nm)$ and secret key length $O(r \log(nr))$.

Acknowledgements. This collaboration started at the DIMACS Workshop on Cryptography and its Interactions. The first and third authors were supported by NSF Grant CCF-1617713. The second author was supported by a DARPA/ARL SAFE-WARE award, NSF Frontier Award 1413955, NSF grants 1619348, 1228984, 1136174, and 1065276, NSF-BSF grant 2015782, ERC grant 742754, ISF grant 1709/14, BSF grant 2012378, a Xerox Faculty Research Award, a Google Faculty Research Award, an equipment grant from Intel, and an Okawa Foundation Research Grant. This material is based upon work supported by the Defense Advanced Research Projects Agency through the ARL under Contract W911NF-15-C-0205. The views expressed are those of the authors and do not reflect the official policy or position of the Department of Defense, the National Science Foundation, or the U.S. Government.

References

1. Alon, N., Bruck, J., Naor, J., Naor, M., Roth, R.M.: Construction of asymptotically good low-rate error-correcting codes through pseudo-random graphs. IEEE Trans. Inf. Theory **38**(2), 509–516 (1992)
2. Applebaum, B., Ishai, Y., Kushilevitz, E.: Cryptography in NC^0. SIAM J. Comput. **36**(4), 845–888 (2006)
3. Applebaum, B., Ishai, Y., Kushilevitz, E.: On pseudorandom generators with linear stretch in NC^0. Comput. Complex. **17**(1), 38–69 (2008)
4. Arora, S., Barak, B.: Computational Complexity: A Modern Approach. Cambridge University Press, Cambridge (2009)
5. Auger, A., Doerr, B.: Theory of Randomized Search Heuristics: Foundations and Recent Developments, vol. 1. World Scientific, Singapore (2011)
6. Bishop, A., Pastro, V., Rajaraman, R., Wichs, D.: Essentially optimal robust secret sharing with maximal corruptions. In: Fischlin, M., Coron, J.-S. (eds.) EURO-CRYPT 2016. LNCS, vol. 9665, pp. 58–86. Springer, Heidelberg (2016). https://doi.org/10.1007/978-3-662-49890-3_3
7. Bogdanov, A., Ishai, Y., Viola, E., Williamson, C.: Bounded indistinguishability and the complexity of recovering secrets. In: Robshaw, M., Katz, J. (eds.) CRYPTO 2016. LNCS, vol. 9816, pp. 593–618. Springer, Heidelberg (2016). https://doi.org/10.1007/978-3-662-53015-3_21
8. Bogdanov, A., Lee, C.H.: Homomorphic evaluation requires depth. In: Kushilevitz, E., Malkin, T. (eds.) TCC 2016. LNCS, vol. 9562, pp. 365–371. Springer, Heidelberg (2016). https://doi.org/10.1007/978-3-662-49096-9_15
9. Bogdanov, A., Williamson, C.: Approximate bounded indistinguishability. In: ICALP (2017)

10. Boyle, E., Gilboa, N., Ishai, Y.: Function secret sharing. In: Oswald, E., Fischlin, M. (eds.) EUROCRYPT 2015. LNCS, vol. 9057, pp. 337–367. Springer, Heidelberg (2015). https://doi.org/10.1007/978-3-662-46803-6_12

11. Bun, M., Thaler, J.: A nearly optimal lower bound on the approximate degree of AC^0. In: FOCS (2017)

12. Chen, H., Cramer, R., Goldwasser, S., de Haan, R., Vaikuntanathan, V.: Secure computation from random error correcting codes. In: Naor, M. (ed.) EUROCRYPT 2007. LNCS, vol. 4515, pp. 291–310. Springer, Heidelberg (2007). https://doi.org/10.1007/978-3-540-72540-4_17

13. Cheng, K., Ishai, Y., Li, X.: Near-optimal secret sharing and error correcting codes in AC^0. Cryptology ePrint Archive, Report 2017/927 (2017). http://eprint.iacr.org/2017/927

14. Cheng, K., Li, X.: Randomness extraction in AC^0 and with small locality. arXiv preprint arXiv:1602.01530 (2016)

15. Cheraghchi, M.: Nearly optimal robust secret sharing. In: 2016 IEEE International Symposium on Information Theory (ISIT), pp. 2509–2513. IEEE (2016)

16. Cryan, M., Miltersen, P.B.: On pseudorandom generators in NC^0. In: Sgall, J., Pultr, A., Kolman, P. (eds.) MFCS 2001. LNCS, vol. 2136, pp. 272–284. Springer, Heidelberg (2001). https://doi.org/10.1007/3-540-44683-4_24

17. Damgård, I., Ishai, Y., Krøigaard, M., Nielsen, J.B., Smith, A.: Scalable multiparty computation with nearly optimal work and resilience. In: Wagner, D. (ed.) CRYPTO 2008. LNCS, vol. 5157, pp. 241–261. Springer, Heidelberg (2008). https://doi.org/10.1007/978-3-540-85174-5_14

18. Goldreich, O.: Candidate one-way functions based on expander graphs. In: Goldreich, O. (ed.) Studies in Complexity and Cryptography. Miscellanea on the Interplay between Randomness and Computation. LNCS, vol. 6650, pp. 76–87. Springer, Heidelberg (2011). https://doi.org/10.1007/978-3-642-22670-0_10

19. Goldwasser, S., Gutfreund, D., Healy, A., Kaufman, T., Rothblum, G.N.: Verifying and decoding in constant depth. In: STOC, pp. 440–449. ACM (2007)

20. Guruswami, V., Smith, A.: Optimal rate code constructions for computationally simple channels. J. ACM (JACM) **63**(4), 35 (2016)

21. Guruswami, V., Umans, C., Vadhan, S.: Unbalanced expanders and randomness extractors from Parvaresh-Vardy codes. J. ACM **56**(4), 20 (2009)

22. Hagerup, T.: Fast parallel generation of random permutations. In: Albert, J.L., Monien, B., Artalejo, M.R. (eds.) ICALP 1991. LNCS, vol. 510, pp. 405–416. Springer, Heidelberg (1991). https://doi.org/10.1007/3-540-54233-7_151

23. Lee, C.H., Viola, E.: Some limitations of the sum of small-bias distributions. In: ECCC, vol. 22, p. 5. Citeseer (2015)

24. Lin, H.: Indistinguishability obfuscation from constant-degree graded encoding schemes. In: Fischlin, M., Coron, J.-S. (eds.) EUROCRYPT 2016. LNCS, vol. 9665, pp. 28–57. Springer, Heidelberg (2016). https://doi.org/10.1007/978-3-662-49890-3_2

25. Lovett, S., Viola, E.: Bounded-depth circuits cannot sample good codes. In: CCC, pp. 243–251. IEEE (2011)

26. Matias, Y., Vishkin, U.: Converting high probability into nearly-constant time with applications to parallel hashing. In: STOC, pp. 307–316. ACM (1991)

27. Miles, E., Viola, E.: Substitution-permutation networks, pseudorandom functions, and natural proofs. J. ACM **62**(6), 46:1–46:29 (2015)

28. Minsky, M., Papert, S.: Perceptrons. MIT Press, Cambridge (1988)

29. Mossel, E., Shpilka, A., Trevisan, L.: On ε-biased generators in NC^0. Random Struct. Algorithms **29**(1), 56–81 (2006)

30. Naor, M., Reingold, O.: Synthesizers and their application to the parallel construction of pseudo-random functions. J. Comput. Syst. Sci. **58**(2), 336–375 (1999)
31. Shamir, A.: How to share a secret. Commun. ACM **22**(11), 612–613 (1979)
32. Viola, E.: On approximate majority and probabilistic time. Comput. Complex. **18**(3), 337 (2009)
33. Viola, E.: The complexity of distributions. SIAM J. Comput. **41**, 191–218 (2012)

OT Combiners

Resource-Efficient OT Combiners
with Active Security

Ignacio Cascudo[1]([✉]), Ivan Damgård[2], Oriol Farràs[3], and Samuel Ranellucci[4,5]

[1] Aalborg University, Aalborg, Denmark
ignacio@math.aau.dk
[2] Aarhus University, Aarhus, Denmark
ivan@cs.au.dk
[3] Universitat Rovira i Virgili, Tarragona, Spain
oriol.farras@urv.cat
[4] University of Maryland, College Park, USA
samuel@umd.edu
[5] George Mason University, Fairfax, USA

Abstract. An OT-combiner takes n candidate implementations of the oblivious transfer (OT) functionality, some of which may be faulty, and produces a secure instance of oblivious transfer as long as a large enough number of the candidates are secure. We see an OT-combiner as a 2-party protocol that can make several black-box calls to each of the n OT candidates, and we want to protect against an adversary that can corrupt one of the parties and a certain number of the OT candidates, obtaining their inputs and (in the active case) full control of their outputs.

In this work we consider perfectly (unconditionally, zero-error) secure OT-combiners and we focus on *minimizing the number of calls* to the candidate OTs.

First, we construct a single-use (one call per OT candidate) OT-combiner which is perfectly secure against active adversaries corrupting one party and a constant fraction of the OT candidates. This extends a previous result by Ishai et al. (ISIT 2014) that proves the same fact for passive adversaries.

Second, we consider a more general asymmetric corruption model where an adversary can corrupt different sets of OT candidates depending on whether it is Alice or Bob who is corrupted. We give sufficient and nec-

I. Cascudo—Acknowledges support from the Danish Council for Independent Research, grant no. DFF-4002-00367.
I. Damgård—This project has received funding from the European Research Council (ERC) under the European Unions's Horizon 2020 research and innovation programme under grant agreement No 669255 (MPCPRO).
O. Farràs—Supported by the European Union through H2020-ICT-2014-1-644024 and H2020-DS-2015-1-700540, and by the Spanish Government through TIN2014-57364-C2-1-R.
S. Ranellucci—Supported by NSF grants #1564088 and #1563722. Any opinions, findings, and conclusions or recommendations expressed in this material are those of the authors and do not necessarily reflect the views of the National Science Foundation.

Y. Kalai and L. Reyzin (Eds.): TCC 2017, Part II, LNCS 10678, pp. 461–486, 2017.
https://doi.org/10.1007/978-3-319-70503-3_15

essary conditions for the existence of an OT combiner with a given number of calls to the candidate OTs in terms of the existence of secret sharing schemes with certain access structures and share-lengths. This allows in some cases to determine the optimal number of calls to the OT candidates which are needed to construct an OT combiner secure against a given adversary.

1   Introduction

1-out-of-2 bit oblivious transfer [EGL82] (OT) is a well-known cryptographic primitive between two parties, a sender Alice and a receiver Bob, in which the sender has as input two one-bit messages and the receiver chooses to learn one of them; in addition, two other guarantees hold, namely the sender does know which of her two messages was chosen by the receiver and the receiver obtains no information about the message that he did not choose to learn.

OT is a fundamental primitive for secure multiparty computation. In fact it is known that secure multiparty computation protocols can be entirely based on OT [Kil88, IPS08]. However, unconditionally secure two-party computation is not possible in the plain model, even if we only assume that one of the parties may be passively corrupted. Hence, OT is likewise impossible to be attained unless we assume the existence of some additional resource or some restriction on the capabilities of the parties. Examples of such situations include: physical assumptions such as the existence of a noisy channel between the sender and the receiver [CK88, IKO+11], hardware tokens [GIS+10], or the premise that one of the parties has bounded memory [CCM98]; and computational assumptions, where we assume that the parties are computationally bounded and we base the security of the OT protocol on the hardness of some problem, for example hardness of factoring [Rab81], the DDH assumption [BM89, AIR01], hardness of decoding [DvdGMN08], the quadratic residuosity assumption, and worst-case lattice assumptions [PVW08].

However, a particular assumption may at some point become compromised (e.g. computational assumptions may be broken, a hardware token may be corrupted, or a party may be in possession of a better-than-expect reception equipment in the case of a protocol based on noisy channels) and this would consequently jeopardize the security of an OT protocol based on such assumption. This motivates the notion of an OT combiner, a protocol between Alice and Bob that makes black-box calls to n candidate implementations of OT, and produces an instance of OT which is secure as long as a certain number of the candidates were secure to start with. In this way, we do not need to rely on a particular OT candidate being secure.

OT combiners can also be seen as a *server-aided* oblivious transfer protocol, where the resource that Alice and Bob have at their disposal is the existence of n servers, each of which is supposed to implement the OT functionality. Alice and Bob can call each of the servers several times, where for each execution a server receives two bits from Alice and one bit from Bob, and outputs the resulting bit to Bob. Therefore, in particular, there is no need of direct communication between servers; in fact, the servers do not even need to be aware of each other. We adopt this view of OT combiners in what follows.

OT combiners were introduced in [HKN+05] and further studied in several articles such as [HIKN08, PW08, IMSW14]. In this work we are interested in minimizing the number of calls to each of the servers, and we take as starting point [IMSW14], where the authors focus on *single-use* OT combiners, in which each OT server is used only once. In their work, they consider an adversary that may corrupt Alice and up to t_A servers or Bob and up to t_B servers, thereby obtaining all information seen during the protocol by the corrupted servers and party. We will call this adversary a (t_A, t_B)-adversary. It is shown that for large enough n, there exists a single-use OT combiner which is perfectly secure against a *passive* (t_A, t_B)-adversary where $t_A = t_B = \Omega(n)$. More precisely this holds for $t_A = t_B = 0.11n$. Furthermore, they show that the existence of single-use OT combiners implies the existence of a certain secret sharing scheme whose privacy and reconstruction thresholds are related to t_A and t_B and where the shares are of constant size. By applying certain bounds on secret sharing over small alphabets [CCX13], they conclude among other facts that unconditionally secure single-use OT-combiners cannot exist when $t_A + t_B = n - O(1)$ (it is easy to show that perfectly secure OT combiners, single-use or not, cannot exist if $t_A + t_B \geq n$).

In this work, we first show a construction of single-use OT-combiners which are perfectly secure against an *active* adversary corrupting the same sets as in [IMSW14], namely:

Theorem 1. *For any large enough n, there exists an n-server single-use OT-combiner which is perfectly secure against an active $(0.11n, 0.11n)$-adversary.*

In fact, this theorem is a special case of a more general result, that represents a tight link between secret sharing schemes and OT combiners.

In order to explain this result, we first need to consider a slightly more general adversary that can corrupt either Alice and a set $A \in \mathcal{A}$ of servers, or Bob and a set $B \in \mathcal{B}$ of servers. Here $\mathcal{A}$ and $\mathcal{B}$ are two adversary structures[1] on the set of servers $\{1, \ldots, n\}$. We say that a pair $(\mathcal{A}, \mathcal{B})$ of adversary structures is $\mathcal{R}_2$ if for all $A \in \mathcal{A}$ and $B \in \mathcal{B}$ we have $A \cup B \neq \{1, \ldots, n\}$. Our result is then as follows.

Theorem 2. *Let $\mathcal{A}, \mathcal{B}$ be adversary structures on the set of servers $\{1, \ldots, n\}$. Suppose that the following conditions are true:*

- *$(\mathcal{A}, \mathcal{B})$ is an $\mathcal{R}_2$ pair of structures.*
- *There exists a secret sharing scheme S for the set of participants $\{1, \ldots, n\}$ with the following properties:*
  1. *It is a linear secret sharing scheme.*
  2. *The domain of secrets is $\{0, 1\}$ and for $i = 1, \ldots, n$ the domain of the i-th share is $\{0, 1\}^{\ell_i}$, for some $\ell_i > 0$.*
  3. *Every set $A \in \mathcal{A}$ is unqualified in S and for every set $B \in \mathcal{B}$, its complement $\overline{B}$ is qualified in S.*

---

[1] An adversary (or anti-monotone) structure $\mathcal{A}$ is a family of subsets of $\{1, \ldots, n\}$ such that if $A \in \mathcal{A}$ and $A' \subseteq A$, then $A' \in \mathcal{A}$.

Then there exists a OT-combiner which is perfectly secure against any active $(\mathcal{A}, \mathcal{B})$-adversary and uses the i-th server exactly ℓ_i times.

Therefore we can see that a single-use OT combiner exists in the cases where an *ideal* (i.e. every share is one bit long) linear secret sharing scheme $\mathcal{S}$ exists with a fitting access structure. Theorem 1 is obtained by plugging into Theorem 2 secret sharing schemes constructed from families of binary linear codes such that both them and their duals are on the Gilbert-Varshamov bound [CCG+07] (see Sect. 5.3 for more details).

An interesting fact about Theorem 2 is that it is close to give a tight characterization of unconditionally secure OT combiners in terms of secret sharing schemes, since one can extend the arguments in [IMSW13] to prove the following result.

Theorem 3. *Let $\mathcal{A}$, $\mathcal{B}$ be adversary structures on the set of servers $\{1, \ldots, n\}$. If there exists a perfectly secure OT-combiner which is secure against any active $(\mathcal{A}, \mathcal{B})$-adversary and uses server S_i exactly ℓ_i times, then:*

- *$(\mathcal{A}, \mathcal{B})$ is an $\mathcal{R}_2$ pair of structures.*
- *There exists a secret sharing scheme $\mathcal{S}$ for the set of participants $\{1, \ldots, n\}$ with the following properties:*
  1. *The domain of secrets is $\{0, 1\}$ and for $i = 1, \ldots, n$ the domain of the i-th share is $\{0, 1\}^{\ell_i}$, for some $\ell_i > 0$.*
  2. *Every set $A \in \mathcal{A}$ is unqualified in $\mathcal{S}$ and for every set $B \in \mathcal{B}$, its complement $\overline{B}$ is qualified in $\mathcal{S}$.*

If we compare both Theorems 2 and 3 we see there is just one gap regarding sufficient and necessary conditions, namely that our construction from Theorem 2 requires a linear secret sharing scheme, while we do not know if this is strictly necessary. Nevertheless, Theorems 2 and 3 can be used to determine the exact minimal number of calls that are sufficient and necessary for a perfectly secure OT combiner in some cases. For example, we can determine that if there are 3 servers and the adversary can be corrupt one party and one server, then the optimal number of OT calls is 5 (Sect. 8).

1.1 Details and Techniques

Our construction of an OT combiner showing Theorem 2 relies on the combination of two secret sharing schemes. The first one is the secret sharing scheme $\mathcal{S}$ assumed by the theorem, which is used by Bob in order to secret share his input among the servers. The other secret sharing scheme is a multi-secret sharing scheme Σ with some unusual properties, whose construction may be of independent interest. This will be used by Alice in order to secret share her inputs among the servers.

Such secret sharing scheme takes a 2-bit secret (m_0, m_1) and, in the simplified "single-use" case of our theorem where all $\ell_i = 1$ (which is enough to show Theorem 1), splits it into $2n$ shares, indexed by pairs (i, j), where $i = 1, \ldots, n$, and $j = 0, 1$. The secret sharing scheme is such that a set of participants of the form $\{(1, v_1), (2, v_2), \ldots, (n, v_n)\}$ (where $v_i \in \{0,1\}$) can reconstruct the message m_0 if and only if the bit-string $(v_1, \ldots, v_n)$ belongs to some given vector space V, while it can reconstruct m_1 if and only if $(v_1, \ldots, v_n)$ belongs to some affine space $t + V$ for some given vector t. Further, these sets are the only minimally qualified sets for each of the messages.

If they were the only requirements, the existence of such a secret sharing scheme would be guaranteed by known general results in secret sharing (where each coordinate m_0 and m_1 would then be independently shared with a secret sharing scheme with potentially exponentially long shares). But what makes the problem interesting is that we have an additional requirement: *every share is one bit long*. This rules out the solution above and therefore the question of how the requirements on the access structures of m_0 and m_1 can be realized simultaneously is not trivial. Moreover, given that m_0 and m_1 cannot be shared independently, it is also necessary to exact some conditions preventing certain sets of shares from leaking correlations between m_0 and m_1 even if they give no information about either individual message. We show that we can achieve all these properties by a relatively simple construction.

With all these elements in hand, it is now easy to explain how our OT combiner works. Alice will use a secret sharing scheme as specified above where V is the set of all possible sharings of 0 in the scheme $\mathcal{S}$ used by Bob, and t is a sharing of 1 in $\mathcal{S}$. In this situation $t + V$ is the set of all sharings of 1 in $\mathcal{S}$ by linearity of $\mathcal{S}$. She then sends the $(i, 0)$ and $(i, 1)$-th shares to the i-th server. If Bob has used $b_1, \ldots, b_n$ as input for the servers, he will receive the shares of (m_0, m_1) with indices $(1, b_1), \ldots, (n, b_n)$. By the properties of the scheme Σ given that set of shares he can now reconstruct m_0 if $(b_1, \ldots, b_n)$ was a sharing of 0 with $\mathcal{S}$, and m_1 if $(b_1, \ldots, b_n)$ was a sharing of 1 with $\mathcal{S}$. Of course this only shows the correctness of the protocol when Alice and Bob are honest. We need to take into account that Bob can corrupt a set $B \in \mathcal{B}$ of servers, obtaining both of Alice's shares corresponding to those servers. Furthermore, in the active case, he can also submit values that do not correspond to a valid sharing of a bit with $\mathcal{S}$. However, we show that even using both strategies simultaneously will not give him information about more than one of Alice's messages.

1.2 Other Related Work

[HKN+05] introduced the notion of OT combiners. Several different flavours are introduced; the notion we are considering in this paper corresponds to the one they call third-party black-box combiners. They consider threshold security with $t_A = t_B = t$, and show that passively unconditionally secure OT combiners cannot exist for $n = 2$, $t = 1$. On the other hand, they give a concrete construction of a secure OT combiner for $n = 3$, $t = 1$ making 2 calls to each OT-candidate (giving a total number of calls of 6, which as mentioned above can be brought down to 5 by our construction).

In [HIKN08], OT-combiners are constructed from secure multiparty computation protocols. Again, the threshold case with $t_A = t_B = t$ is considered. They show how to construct OT combiners which are statistically secure against a (t, t)-adversary with $t = \Omega(n)$ which make $O(1)$ calls to each server. Furthermore they achieve constant production rate, meaning that their construction allows to produce $\Theta(n)$ instances of OT (in this work, we are only concerned about producing one instance). Furthermore, they show a variant of their protocol that is computationally secure against active adversaries. Subsequently [IPS08] shows, as one of the applications of their compiler, that the latter construction can be turned into a statistically secure OT-combiner, still achieving constant production rate and being secure against an active (t, t)-adversary with $t = \Omega(n)$.

In [PW08] an oblivious linear function evaluation (OLFE) combiner is constructed where each server executes a single instance of OLFE and the construction achieves perfect security whenever $t_A + t_B < n$. OLFE is a functionality where Alice has as input two values a, b in a finite field $\mathbb{F}_q$ of q elements, Bob has as input $x \in \mathbb{F}_q$ and receives $ax + b$ as output. Even though OLFE is a generalization of OT (OT is equivalent to OLFE over $\mathbb{F}_2$), the construction in [PW08] requires $q > n$, since it uses Shamir secret sharing in order to share the parties' inputs among the servers.

Finally, it is interesting to point out that [BI01] and [VV15] consider, in different contexts, secret sharing schemes with access structures that are somewhat related to the ones we need. Given a language $L \subseteq \{0, 1\}^n$, their secret sharing schemes for $2n$ participants have as minimally qualified subsets all those of the form $\{(1, v_1), (2, v_2), \ldots, (n, v_n)\}$ where $(v_1, v_2, \ldots, v_n) \in L$. However, both works also include the sets of the form $\{(i, 0), (i, 1)\}$ as minimally qualified.

1.3 Extensions and Open Questions

We briefly consider some possible extensions of our result that we do not fully address in this paper. First, [IMSW14] also presents a single-use OT combiner that achieves statistical security against a passive adversary corrupting one of Alice and Bob and up to $n/2 - \omega(\log \kappa)$ servers, where κ is the security parameter. We sketch in Sect. 5.3 how we think our construction from Theorem 1 can be modified in order to achieve a similar result as [IMSW14] against a static active adversary.

Moreover, in this paper we have focused in minimizing the number of OT calls when we want to produce a single secure instance of OT. It is an interesting open question to understand whether our constructions can be extended to achieve constant production rate for perfect actively secure combiners. This raises the question whether our multi-secret sharing scheme can be modified so that it handles secrets of size $O(n)$.

Finally, we only consider adversaries that corrupt one of the parties Alice and Bob together with a subset of servers. Our model does not consider corruption of only servers. It is easy to see that if an OT combiner is secure against a passive $(\mathcal{A}, \mathcal{B})$-adversary, then it is also secure against passive corruption of a server set C

which lies in both $\mathcal{A}$ and $\mathcal{B}$. This is because such "external" adversary corrupting only C cannot obtain more information about Alice's (resp. Bob's) input than an adversary corrupting C and Bob (resp. Alice). However, when considering and active adversary we also need to guarantee the correctness of the combiner, i.e., that the external adversary is not able to make Bob output a value that is inconsistent with Alice's inputs. We can in fact identify situations where the $\mathcal{R}_2$ condition is not enough to achieve security against such adversaries. We discuss this in Sect. 9. It is an open question to determine in which conditions security is possible against corruption of servers only.

1.4 Overview

Section 2 contains preliminaries on secret sharing and adversary structures, although we also introduce the notion of $\mathcal{R}_2$ pair. Section 3 describes our model. Section 4 gives a construction of a multi-secret sharing scheme with certain properties regarding its access structure; this will be the secret sharing scheme used by Alice in our construction. In Sect. 5 we show Theorem 2 in the case where $\mathcal{S}$ can be taken to be an ideal secret sharing scheme (i.e. every share is a bit long). This is enough to show Theorem 1. In Sect. 6 we show Theorem 2 in the general case. In Sect. 7 we show Theorem 3. In Sect. 8 we apply our results to determine the minimal number of calls which are required for a 3-server OT combiner to be secure against an active (1,1)-adversary. Finally Sect. 9 contains our considerations on the case where an adversary corrupts only servers.

2 Preliminaries

2.1 Adversary Structures and $\mathcal{R}_2$ Pairs of Structures

We denote by $\mathcal{P}_n$ the set $\{1, 2, \ldots, n\}$. Furthermore, $2^{\mathcal{P}_n}$ is the family of all subsets of $\mathcal{P}_n$.

Definition 1. An adversary (or antimonotone) structure $\mathcal{A} \subseteq 2^{\mathcal{P}_n}$ is a family of subsets of $\mathcal{P}_n$ such that $\emptyset \in \mathcal{A}$ and for every $A \in \mathcal{A}$ and $B \subseteq A$ we have $B \in \mathcal{A}$.

Definition 2. We say that a pair $(\mathcal{A}, \mathcal{B})$ of adversary structures is $\mathcal{R}_2$ if for all $A \in \mathcal{A}$, $B \in \mathcal{B}$, we have $A \cup B \neq \mathcal{P}_n$.

$\mathcal{R}_2$ is a generalization of the well known notion of a $\mathcal{Q}_2$ adversary structure (an adversary structure $\mathcal{A}$ is $\mathcal{Q}_2$ if for all $A, B \in \mathcal{A}$, we have $A \cup B \neq \mathcal{P}_n$). More precisely, the pair of adversary structures $(\mathcal{A}, \mathcal{A})$ is $\mathcal{R}_2$ if and only if $\mathcal{A}$ is $\mathcal{Q}_2$. However, there exist adversary structures $\mathcal{A}, \mathcal{B}$ such that neither $\mathcal{A}$ nor $\mathcal{B}$ are $\mathcal{Q}_2$, while the pair $(\mathcal{A}, \mathcal{B})$ is $\mathcal{R}_2$. For example: $n = 4$, and $\mathcal{A}$ and $\mathcal{B}$ are the adversary structures with maximal sets $\{1, 2\}, \{3, 4\}$ in the case of $\mathcal{A}$, and $\{1, 3\}, \{2, 4\}$ in the case of $\mathcal{B}$.

2.2 Secret Sharing

Our protocols rely heavily on secret sharing, a well-known cryptographic primitive introduced by Shamir [Sha79] and, independently, Blakley [Bla79]. We recall some terminology and results which will be needed later.

A secret sharing scheme for the set of participants $\mathcal{P}_n$ is given by a probabilistic algorithm $\mathtt{Share}_\mathcal{S}$ that takes as input a secret s and outputs values $a_1, a_2, \ldots, a_n$ known as shares. The vector $(a'_1, a'_2, \ldots, a'_n)$ is called a sharing of s if on input s $\mathtt{Share}_\mathcal{S}$ outputs the values a'_i as shares with non-zero probability.

We say that a set $A \subseteq \mathcal{P}_n$ is unqualified if for any secret s and any sharing $(a_1, a_2, \ldots, a_n)$ for it, the vector $(a_i)_{i \in A}$ gives no information about the secret, i.e., the probability that the values $(a_i)_{i \in A}$ are outputted (as shares for A) by $\mathtt{Share}_\mathcal{S}$ on input s is the same as the probability of the same event when the input is s'. Note that the family $\mathcal{A} \subseteq 2^{\mathcal{P}_n}$ of all unqualified sets of $\mathcal{S}$ is an adversary structure. We say that a set $A \subseteq \mathcal{P}_n$ is qualified if for any secret s and any sharing $(a_1, a_2, \ldots, a_n)$ for it, the vector $(a_i)_{i \in A}$ uniquely determines the secret, i.e. there is a unique secret for which $\mathtt{Share}_\mathcal{S}$ can output those values as shares for A. The family of all qualified sets is called the access structure of $\mathcal{S}$. We say that a secret sharing scheme is perfect if every set $A \subseteq \mathcal{P}_n$ is either qualified or unqualified (there are no sets of shares which give partial information about the secret).

We also define $\mathtt{Reconstruct}_\mathcal{S}$, an algorithm that takes as input a set of pairs $\{(i, a_i) : i \in A\}$ where $A \subseteq \mathcal{P}_n$ and outputs s if A is a qualified set for $\mathcal{S}$ and the values $(a_i)_{i \in A}$ are part of a valid sharing of the secret s, and $\perp$ otherwise.

Let $\mathbb{F}$ be a finite field. A linear secret sharing scheme $\mathcal{S}$ (over $\mathbb{F}$), LSSS for short, is a secret sharing scheme where the space of secrets is a vector space $\mathbb{F}^{\ell_0}$, the space of the i-th shares is $\mathbb{F}^{\ell_i}$ for $i = 1, \ldots, n$, and there exists an integer e and a map $M : \mathbb{F}^{\ell_0 + e} \to \mathbb{F}^{\ell_1} \times \cdots \times \mathbb{F}^{\ell_n}$ such that $\mathtt{Share}_\mathcal{S}$ consists in choosing a uniformly random vector $\mathbf{u} \in \mathbb{F}^e$ and outputting $M(s, \mathbf{u})$ as shares. We denote by $[s, \mathbf{u}]_\mathcal{S} \in \mathbb{F}^\ell$ this sharing, where $\ell = \sum_{i=1}^n \ell_i$. Given a set $A \subseteq \mathcal{P}_n$ we use $[s, \mathbf{u}]_\mathcal{S}^{(A)}$ to denote the vector consisting only of the shares corresponding to A. When we do not need to make the randomness explicit, then we write $[s]_\mathcal{S}$ and $[s]_\mathcal{S}^{(A)}$. Moreover, we say that ℓ is the complexity of $\mathcal{S}$. We note that $\mathtt{Share}_\mathcal{S}$ runs in polynomial time in ℓ. The set of possible sharings in a LSSS is a vector space and for all $\lambda_1, \lambda_2 \in \mathbb{F}$ we have $\lambda_1 [s_1, \mathbf{u_1}]_\mathcal{S} + \lambda_2 [s_2, \mathbf{u_2}]_\mathcal{S} = [\lambda_1 s_1 + \lambda_2 s_2, \lambda_1 \mathbf{u_1} + \lambda_2 \mathbf{u_2}]_\mathcal{S}$, i.e. a linear combination of sharings is a sharing for the same linear combination applied to the secrets. An immediate implication is that $\mathtt{Reconstruct}_\mathcal{S}$, on input a qualified set A and a set of shares for it, acts by applying a linear function to these shares.

We need a few facts about when sets are qualified and unqualified in a linear secret sharing scheme. First, consider the case $\ell_0 = 1$, where the secret is just an element in $\mathbb{F}$. In that case a LSSS is perfect, and we have:

Lemma 1. *Let $\mathcal{S}$ be a LSSS with secrets in $\mathbb{F}$. A set $A \subseteq \mathcal{P}_n$ is unqualified if and only if there exists a vector $\mathbf{u}$, such that $[1, \mathbf{u}]_\mathcal{S}^{(A)} = \mathbf{0}$, i.e., if we share the secret*

1 *using randomness* $\mathbf{u}$, *the shares corresponding to* A *are all zero. Otherwise, it is qualified.*

This can be easily derived by taking into account that, if the condition above is satisfied, then $[s, \mathbf{t}]_S$ and $[s', \mathbf{t}']_S = [s, \mathbf{t}]_S + (s' - s)[1, \mathbf{u}]_S$ are sharings of s and s' such that all the shares in A coincide.

Now suppose that in addition $\mathbb{F} = \mathbb{F}_2$, so we are dealing with binary LSSS; and that every share is one bit long, i.e., $\ell_i = 1$. Since given a qualified set A, the reconstruction algorithm in a LSSS consists of applying a linear function on the corresponding shares, under the conditions above the secret needs to equal the sum of the shares of a fixed subset $A' \subseteq A$. Therefore we can characterize the minimally qualified sets (those qualified sets such that none of their subsets are qualified) as follows.

Lemma 2. *Let* S *be a LSSS with secrets in* $\mathbb{F}_2$ *and shares in* $\mathbb{F}_2$. *A set* A *is minimally qualified if and only if for any secret* $s \in \mathbb{F}_2$ *and any sharing* $(a_1, a_2, \ldots, a_n) = [s]_S$, *we have that* $s = \sum_{i \in A} a_i$.

In this work it will also be essential to understand LSSSs where $\ell_0 = 2$ and $\mathbb{F}$ is the binary field $\mathbb{F}_2$. In general, if $\ell_0 > 1$, the situation is more complicated than in the case $\ell_0 = 1$ since there may be sets $A \subseteq \mathcal{P}_n$ which can obtain partial information about the secret. The generalization of Lemma 1 is as follows. Let $T_A \subseteq \mathbb{F}^{\ell_0}$ be the set of secrets s such that there exists $\mathbf{u}$ with $[s, \mathbf{u}]_S^{(A)} = \mathbf{0}$. Then for any secret m, when given $[m]_S^{(A)}$, any element in $m + T_A$ has the same probability of being the secret and any element not in $m + T_A$ can be ruled out. Furthermore, T_A is always a vector space. In the case $\ell_0 = 2$, $\mathbb{F} = \mathbb{F}_2$, this means that a set A can be either qualified, unqualified or learn one bit of information about the secret $m = (m_0, m_1)$, and this partial information can be of three types, corresponding to the three different subspaces of $\mathbb{F}_2^2$ of dimension 1: either it learns one coordinate m_0 and has no information about the other m_1, or viceversa, or it learns $m_0 + m_1$ and nothing else. A LSSS Σ with secrets (m_0, m_1) in $\mathbb{F}_2^2$ induces a perfect LSSS Σ_0 for the secret m_0 (by considering m_1 as randomness) and similarly, perfect LSSSs Σ_1 and Σ_2 for m_1 and $m_0 + m_1$ respectively. Therefore we can talk about qualified sets and unqualified sets for m_0 (resp. m_1, $m_0 + m_1$) and we will use Lemmas 1 and 2 for these individual secrets later on. We are therefore seeing Σ as a multi-secret sharing scheme (in a multi-secret sharing scheme [JMO93] several secret values are distributed among a set of users, and each secret may have different qualified subsets). Moreover, we can clearly define a reconstruction algorithm for the individual secrets m_0 and m_1, which we call $\mathtt{Reconstruct}_\Sigma^0$ and $\mathtt{Reconstruct}_\Sigma^1$ respectively.

As for the existence of LSSS, it is well known [ISN87] that every adversary structure is the adversary structure of a LSSS.

Theorem 4. *For every finite field* $\mathbb{F}$ *and integer* $\ell_0 \geq 1$ *and for every adversary structure* $\mathcal{A}$ *there exists a perfect LSSS* S *with secrets in* $\mathbb{F}^{\ell_0}$ *and adversary structure* $\mathcal{A}$.

In general the complexity of the LSSS $\mathcal{S}$ constructed with the methods used in [ISN87] is exponential in n. We say that a LSSS is ideal if $\ell_0 = 1$ and $\ell_i = 1$ for all i. The complexity of an ideal LSSS is n, which is the smallest possible. Given a finite field $\mathbb{F}$ most adversary structures $\mathcal{A}$ do not admit ideal LSSSs over $\mathbb{F}$.

3   OT-Combiners

We describe our model in more detail. Alice has a pair of inputs $m_0, m_1 \in \{0, 1\}$ and Bob has an input a selection bit $b \in \{0, 1\}$. They execute a protocol π whose goal is to implement the functionality $\mathcal{F}_{OT}$ securely (in the presence of an adversary which we specify below) on those inputs. The protocol π consists only of local computations by each of the parties and oracle calls to servers $S_1, \ldots, S_n$ (in particular, we do not need a direct communication channel between Alice and Bob). If the server S_i is not corrupted, then it executes a copy of the functionality $\mathcal{F}_{OT}$ and may be called several times. Each time a server is called, it receives a new pair of inputs $x_0, x_1 \in \{0, 1\}$ from Alice and c from Bob, and executes the functionality $\mathcal{F}_{OT}$ on these inputs, therefore outputting the message x_c towards Bob (Fig. 1).

Functionality $\mathcal{F}_{OT}$

1. On input (**transfer**, b) from Bob, send (**ready**) to Alice.
2. On input (**send**, m_0, m_1) from Alice, if (**transfer**, b) has been received previously from Bob, send (**sent**, m_b) to Bob.

Fig. 1. Functionality $\mathcal{F}_{OT}$

We consider a static adversary Adv characterized by a pair of adversary structures $(\mathcal{A}, \mathcal{B})$ each contained in $2^{\{S_1, \ldots, S_n\}}$, which we call an $(\mathcal{A}, \mathcal{B})$-adversary. Such adversary can corrupt, before the protocol starts, either Alice and a set of servers $A \in \mathcal{A}$ or Bob and a set of servers $B \in \mathcal{B}$. If the adversary is passive, then it obtains all information seen bys the corrupted party and servers during the protocol, but cannot make them deviate from the protocol. If the adversary is active, it can in addition make the corrupted party and servers deviate arbitrarily from the protocol.

In these conditions, we say that the protocol π is an n-server OT-combiner secure against Adv if it securely implements the functionality $\mathcal{F}_{OT}$ in the presence of this adversary. In this paper we will prove security using the Universal Composability framework [Can01], see [CDN15] for more information.

Let $1 \le t_A, t_B \le n$. If there exist $\mathcal{A}$ and $\mathcal{B}$ such that $\mathcal{A}$ contains all subsets of size t_A of $\{1, \ldots, n\}$ and $\mathcal{B}$ contains all subsets of size t_B of $\{1, \ldots, n\}$ and if π is an n-server OT-combiner secure against any $(\mathcal{A}, \mathcal{B})$-adversary, then we say that π is an n-server OT-combiner secure against a (t_A, t_B)-adversary.

4 A Multi-secret Sharing Scheme

As we mentioned in Sect. 1.1, our OT combiners rely on the combination of two linear secret sharing schemes S and Σ. S is given by the statement of Theorem 2 and is used by Bob. The secret sharing scheme Σ, used by Alice, is a multi-secret sharing scheme satisfying a number of properties that we need in order to achieve security of our combiner.

In this section, we abstract the properties that we will need for Σ, and we give a construction achieving these properties. How this will play a role in our OT-combiners will become apparent in the next sections.

Proposition 1. *Let ℓ be an integer, $V \subsetneq \mathbb{F}_2^\ell$ be a vector subspace, $\mathbf{t} \in \mathbb{F}_2^\ell$ be a vector such that $\mathbf{t} \notin V$ and let W be the affine space $W = \mathbf{t} + V$. Finally for $I \subseteq \{1, \ldots, \ell\}$ let $\mathbf{e}_I \in \mathbb{F}_2^\ell$ denote the vector with 1's in the I-coordinates and 0's in the rest.*

Then the linear secret sharing scheme Σ for 2ℓ participants (indexed by pairs (i, j)) with secrets in $\{0, 1\}^2$ and shares in $\{0, 1\}$, given in Fig. 2, is such that the following properties hold:

1. *The minimally qualified sets for reconstructing the first coordinate m_0 of the secret are exactly the sets of the form*
$$\{(i, a_i) : i = 1, \ldots, n, (a_1, \ldots, a_n) \in V\}.$$

2. *The minimally qualified sets for reconstructing the second coordinate m_1 of the secret are exactly the sets of the form*
$$\{(i, a_i) : i = 1, \ldots, n, (a_1, \ldots, a_n) \in W\}.$$

3. *The minimally qualified sets for reconstructing the sum $m_0 + m_1$ are those of the form*
$$\{(i, c) : i \in H, c = 0, 1\},$$
where H is such that $\mathbf{e}_H \in W$ and $\mathbf{e}_{H'} \notin W$ for $H' \subsetneq H$.

Before starting with the proof, we need some definitions. Let U be the vector space spanned by the set $V \cup \{\mathbf{t}\}$. Note $U = V + W$. We define
$$Z_0 = U^\perp = \{\mathbf{h} \in \mathbb{F}_2^\ell : \mathbf{h} \in V^\perp, <\mathbf{t}, \mathbf{h}> = 0\}$$
and
$$Z_1 = \{\mathbf{h} \in \mathbb{F}_2^\ell : \mathbf{h} \in V^\perp, <\mathbf{t}, \mathbf{h}> = 1\}.$$

Note since $\mathbf{b} \notin V$, then Z_1 is non-empty and $Z_1 = Z_0 + \mathbf{g}$ for some $\mathbf{g}$ such that $<\mathbf{t}, \mathbf{g}> = 1$.

We also need the following lemma, which is a basic fact of linear algebra.

Lemma 3. *For every $\mathbf{u} \notin U$, the random variable $<\mathbf{u}, \mathbf{h}>$, where $\mathbf{h}$ is chosen uniformly at random in Z_0 (resp. Z_1), is uniformly distributed in $\mathbb{F}_2$.*

The multi-secret sharing scheme Σ

Let $V^\perp$ be the orthogonal space to V, i.e.,

$$V^\perp = \{\mathbf{h} \in \mathbb{F}_2^\ell : \langle \mathbf{v}, \mathbf{h} \rangle = 0 \text{ for all } \mathbf{v} \in V\}.$$

To share $(m_0, m_1) \in \mathbb{F}_2^2$:

- Sample uniformly at random $r_1, \ldots, r_{\ell-1} \in \mathbb{F}_2$ and let $r_\ell = m_0 - \sum_{i=1}^{\ell-1} r_i$.
- Sample $\mathbf{h} = (h_1, h_2, \ldots, h_\ell)$ uniformly at random in the space

$$\{\mathbf{h} \in \mathbb{F}_2^\ell : \mathbf{h} \in V^\perp, < \mathbf{t}, \mathbf{h} >= m_0 + m_1\}.$$

- Send $a_{(i,j)} = r_i + jh_i \in \mathbb{F}_2$ to participant (i,j)

Fig. 2. The multi-secret sharing scheme Σ

Now we can proceed with the proof of Proposition 1

Proof of Proposition 1. Clearly Σ is linear, since a fixed linear combination of the sharings is a sharing for the same linear combination applied to the secrets. Nevertheless we can also make the linearity of the construction more explicit by showing how the shares are constructed as a linear function of the secret (m_0, m_1) and a uniform random vector in some space $\mathbb{F}_2^e$, as follows. Note that $V^\perp$ is a vector subspace. The set Z_0 is also a vector subspace which will have a basis $\{\mathbf{z}^{(1)}, \mathbf{z}^{(2)}, \ldots, \mathbf{z}^{(s)}\}$.

A uniformly random element in $\{\mathbf{h} \in \mathbb{F}_2^\ell : \mathbf{h} \in V^\perp, <\mathbf{t}, \mathbf{h}> = m_0 + m_1\}$ can be then sampled by sampling independent uniform random elements $d_1, \ldots, d_s \in \mathbb{F}_2$ and outputting $d_1\mathbf{z}^{(1)} + \cdots + d_s\mathbf{z}^{(s)} + (m_0 + m_1)\mathbf{g}$. The elements h_i in our construction are simply the coordinates $d_1 z_i^{(1)} + \cdots + d_s z_i^{(s)} + (m_0 + m_1)g_i$. Therefore, the shares can be written as a linear combination of uniformly random elements $r_1, \ldots, r_{\ell-1}, d_1, \ldots, d_s \in \mathbb{F}_2$ and the values m_0, m_1.

Now we need to argue about the access structure of the secret sharing schemes for the different pieces of information m_0, m_1 and $m_0 + m_1$.

By Lemma 2, in the conditions of these scheme (linear, binary, every share is a bit) a set is minimally qualified for m_0 (resp. m_1, $m_0 + m_1$) if and only if the corresponding shares always sum up to m_0 (resp. m_1, $m_0 + m_1$) and there is no stricty smaller subset satisfying the same.

Fix $A \subseteq \{1, 2, \ldots, \ell\} \times \{0, 1\}$ a set of indices. We define two sets $I_1, I_2 \subseteq \{1, 2, \ldots, \ell\}$ as follows:

$$I_1 = \{i : \text{exactly one of } (i,0) \text{ and } (i,1) \text{ is in } A\}$$

and

$$I_2 = \{i : (i,1) \in A\}.$$

Then

$$\sum_{(i,j) \in A} a_{(i,j)} = \sum_{i \in I_1} r_i + \sum_{i \in I_2} h_i = \sum_{i \in I_1} r_i + <\mathbf{e}_{I_2}, \mathbf{h}>$$

where $\mathbf{e}_{I_2}$ is the vector with 1's in the positions of I_2 and 0's in the rest.

Note that if $I_1 \neq \emptyset, \{1, \ldots, \ell\}$, then $\sum_{i \in I_1} r_i$ is uniformly distributed in $\mathbb{F}_2$ over the choice of the r_i's. Furthermore, $\sum_{i \in I_1} r_i$ is clearly independent from $<\mathbf{e}_{I_2}, \mathbf{h}>$. Hence the sum $\sum_{(i,j) \in A} a_{(i,j)}$ is uniformly distributed in $\mathbb{F}_2$.

Likewise if $\mathbf{e}_{I_2} \notin U = V \cup W$ then $<\mathbf{e}_{I_2}, \mathbf{h}>$ is uniformly distributed in $\mathbb{F}_2$ by Lemma 3 (regardless of whether $m_0 + m_1 = 0$ or $m_0 + m_1 = 1$). Therefore, the only cases where A can be minimally qualified for either m_0, m_1, $m_0 + m_1$ are the following:

- $I_1 = \{1, \ldots, \ell\}$, $\mathbf{e}_{I_2} \in V$. This case corresponds to

$$A = \{(1, b_1), (2, b_2), \ldots, (n, b_n)\}$$

  where $(b_1, b_2, \ldots, b_n) = \mathbf{e}_{I_2} \in V$. Moreover $\sum_{(i,j) \in A} a_{(i,j)} = m_0 + <\mathbf{h}, \mathbf{e}_{I_2}> = m_0$, so this set is minimally qualified for m_0, since clearly there cannot be smaller subsets satisfying the same property.
- $I_1 = \{1, \ldots, \ell\}$, $\mathbf{e}_{I_2} \in W$. This case corresponds to

$$A = \{(1, b_1), (2, b_2), \ldots, (n, b_n)\}$$

  where $(b_1, b_2, \ldots, b_n) = \mathbf{e}_{I_2} \in W$. Moreover $\sum_{(i,j) \in A} a_{(i,j)} = m_0 + <\mathbf{h}, \mathbf{e}_{I_2}> = m_1$, so this set is minimally qualified for m_1, since clearly there cannot be smaller subsets satisfying the same property.
- $I_1 = \emptyset$, $\mathbf{e}_{I_2} \in V$: in this case,

$$A = \{(i, 0) : i \in I_2\} \cup \{(i, 1) : i \in I_2\}.$$

  However $\sum_{(i,j) \in A} a_{(i,j)} = <\mathbf{h}, \mathbf{e}_{I_2}> = 0$, so this set is not minimally qualified for any of the secrets.
- $I_1 = \emptyset$, $\mathbf{e}_{I_2} \in W$: in this case, again

$$A = \{(i, 0) : i \in I_2\} \cup \{(i, 1) : i \in I_2\}.$$

Now $\sum_{(i,j) \in A} a_{(i,j)} = <\mathbf{h}, \mathbf{e}_{I_2}> = m_0 + m_1$, so this set is minimally qualified for $m_0 + m_1$ unless there is a smaller subset $I_2' \subseteq I_2$ such that $\mathbf{e}_{I_2'} \in W$. □

5   Construction of OT-Combiners When $\mathcal{S}$ is Ideal

In this section we will show Theorem 2, under the additional assumption that the secret sharing scheme $\mathcal{S}$ is also ideal. That is, we show:

Theorem 2 case $\mathcal{S}$ ideal. *Let $\mathcal{A}$, $\mathcal{B} \subseteq 2^{\mathcal{P}_n}$ be adversary structures such that $(\mathcal{A}, \mathcal{B})$ is a $\mathcal{R}_2$ pair. Suppose there exists a linear secret sharing scheme $\mathcal{S}$ for n participants where the secret is in $\{0, 1\}$ and every share is in $\{0, 1\}$, and such that every set $A \in \mathcal{A}$ is unqualified in $\mathcal{S}$ and the complement $\overline{B}$ of every set $B \in \mathcal{B}$ is qualified in $\mathcal{S}$.*

Then there exists a single-use n-server OT combiner which is perfectly secure against any active $(\mathcal{A}, \mathcal{B})$-adversary.

This result is enough to show Theorem 1, which is proven at the end of this section.

5.1   The Protocol

Our protocol π_{OT} described in Fig. 3 works as follows: Bob computes a secret sharing of his input b with the ideal linear secret sharing scheme S promised above, therefore creating n shares b_i, each of which is a bit since the scheme is ideal. On the other hand, Alice will secret share her input (m_0, m_1) with a secret sharing scheme Σ that is defined as follows: Σ is the secret sharing scheme given by Proposition 1 where $\ell = n$, V is the set of all possible sharings $[0, \mathbf{u}]_S$ of 0 with S (which is a vector space because S is linear) and $\mathbf{t}$ will be one sharing of 1 with S (for example $\mathbf{t} = [1, \mathbf{0}]_S$). By linearity, W is the set of all possible sharings of 1.

Now Alice an Bob call each OT server once, the inputs to the i-th server being $a_{(i,0)}$ and $a_{(i,1)}$, in this order, on Alice's side, and b_i on Bob's side. Assuming that there is no active corruption, Bob will receive $a_{(i,b_i)}$ from the servers. By definition of Σ he has enough information to reconstruct m_b by running the corresponding reconstruction algorithm (if the reconstruction fails, because Alice's shares were malformed, Bob outputs 0 by default).

Oblivious transfer protocol π_{OT}

Let (m_0, m_1) be Alice's input and b be Bob's input.

1. Local computation:
   Alice creates a sharing $[(m_0, m_1)]_\Sigma = (a_{(i,j)})_{(i,j)\in\mathcal{P}_{n,2}}$ of her input.
   Bob creates a sharing $[b]_S = (b_1, \ldots, b_n)$ of his input. Note that each $b_i \in \{0,1\}$ because S is ideal.
2. Use of the OT servers:
   For $i \in \{1, \ldots, n\}$, Alice and Bob use server S_i to execute an OT with inputs $(a_{i,0}, a_{i,1})$ for Alice and b_i for Bob. Let y_i denote the output of Bob.
3. Local computation: If $b = 0$, Bob constructs m'_0 by applying

$$\texttt{Reconstruct}^0_\Sigma(\{((i, b_i), y_i) : i \in \mathcal{P}_n\}).$$

   Similarly, if $b = 1$, Bob constructs m'_1 by applying

$$\texttt{Reconstruct}^1_\Sigma(\{(i, b_i), y_i) : i \in \mathcal{P}_n\}).$$

   In any of the cases, if the reconstruction fails, output 0. Otherwise output the reconstructed m'_b.

Fig. 3. Protocol π_{OT} for ideal LSSSs.

Proposition 2. *If Alice and Bob follow the protocol semi-honestly, then π_{OT} (Fig. 3) implements OT with perfect correctness.*

Proof. If Alice and Bob follow the protocol (semi-)honestly, at the end of the protocol Bob will have received all values $m_b^{(i,b_i)}, i = 1, \ldots, n$, for some sharing $[b]_\mathcal{S} = (b_1, \ldots, b_n)$. By Proposition 1, $\{(1, b_1), \ldots, (n, b_n)\}$ is qualified for reconstructing m_b (because $(b_1, \ldots, b_n) \in V$ if $b = 0$ and $(b_1, \ldots, b_n) \in W$ if $b = 1$). $\square$

5.2   Security

In order to guarantee the privacy of Alice's input, the first thing that we need to observe is that Bob does not learn m_b from $a_{(i, b_i)}$ if $(b_1, \ldots, b_n)$ is not a valid sharing of b with $\mathcal{S}$, since in that case $\{(1, b_1), \ldots, (n, b_n)\}$ is not qualified for m_b by Proposition 1. However, this only guarantees privacy against a very weak semi-honest adversary corrupting Bob and no servers. Note that, first of all, the adversary can corrupt some set $B \in \mathcal{B}$ of servers, thereby obtaining both $a_{(i,0)}$ and $a_{(i,1)}$ for all $i \in B$. Moreover, if the adversary is malicious, it can also make Bob submit values b_i such that $(b_1, \ldots, b_n)$ is not a valid sharing $[b]_\mathcal{S}$. Finally, remember that in Sect. 2.2 we argued that given an ideal LSSS with secrets in $\mathbb{F}_2$, like it is the case with Σ, it may in principle happen that some sets of shares allow to reconstruct $m_0 + m_1$ even if they do not get any information about the individual m_0 and m_1. Therefore we also need to ensure that these cases will not happen in our problem.

We show how the properties we have guaranteed in Proposition 1 take care of all these and prevent the potentially malicious Bob from learning other information than he should.

Proposition 3. *Suppose $(\mathcal{A}, \mathcal{B})$ is an $\mathcal{R}_2$ pair of adversary structures and $\mathcal{S}$ and Σ are defined as above. Let (m_0, m_1) be shared with Σ. Fix $B \in \mathcal{B}$ and $(b'_1, \ldots, b'_n) \in \mathbb{F}_2^n$, and define the set of indices*

$$\mathcal{H} = \{(i, b'_i) : i \in \overline{B}\} \cup \{(i, j) : i \in B, j \in \{0, 1\}\}.$$

Then:

- *If the set $\{b'_i : i \in \overline{B}\}$ is not part of any sharing $[c]_\mathcal{S}$ for any $c \in \{0, 1\}$ then the values $a_{(i,j)}, (i, j) \in I'$ give no information about the pair (m_0, m_1).*
- *If the set $\{b'_i : i \in \overline{B}\}$ is a part of a sharing $[c]_\mathcal{S}$ of some $c \in \{0, 1\}$ then the values $a_{(i,j)}, (i, j) \in I'$ give full information about m_c but no information about m_{1-c}.*

Proof. By the considerations in Sect. 2.2, we know that in principle a set of shares could either be unqualified (give no information about (m_0, m_1)), qualified (give full information) or give partial information, which in turn can be of three types: either it gives information about one of the coordinates m_d and no information about m_{1-d} or it could give information about $m_0 + m_1$ and nothing else. On the other hand, Proposition 1 describes the minimally qualified sets for m_0, m_1 and $m_0 + m_1$.

We show first that the set $\mathcal{H}$ is not qualified for $m_0 + m_1$ in any case. If that were the case, then there would exist a set $I \subseteq \mathcal{P}_n$ such that $\mathcal{H}$ would contain all indices of the form $(i, 0)$, $(i, 1)$ with $i \in I$ and such that $\mathbf{e}_I \in \mathbb{F}_2^n$ is a sharing of 1 with $\mathcal{S}$. $\mathcal{H}$ contains both $(i,0)$ and $(i,1)$ exactly for those $i \in B$. But assume there existed an $I \subseteq B$ such that $\mathbf{e}_I \in \mathbb{F}_2^n$ were a sharing of 1. Now we get a contradiction as follows: from the assumptions, $\overline{B}$ is qualified in $\mathcal{S}$. Therefore by linearity of $\mathcal{S}$ there cannot be a sharing of 1, $[1]_{\mathcal{S}}$, such that $[1]_{\mathcal{S}}^{\overline{B}} = \mathbf{0}$. But on the other hand $\mathbf{e}_I \in \mathbb{F}_2^n$ is a sharing of 1 which satisfies that $[1]_{\mathcal{S}}^{\overline{I}}$ is zero, and since $\overline{B} \subseteq \overline{I}$ both statements are contradictory.

Now note that the minimally qualified sets for m_0 (resp. m_1) are those of the form $\{(1,b_1),\ldots,(n,b_n)\} \subseteq \mathcal{P}_{n,2}$ where $(b_1,\ldots,b_n)$ is a sharing of 0 (resp. 1) with $\mathcal{S}$. This implies that if $\mathcal{H}$ is qualified for m_0 (resp. m_1) then necessarily $\{b_i' : i \in \overline{B}\}$ needs to be part of a sharing $[0]_{\mathcal{S}}$ (respectively $[1]_{\mathcal{S}}$). $\qquad\square$

These elements are enough to formally show the security of our construction.

Theorem 5. *The protocol π_{OT} UC-implements the functionality $\mathcal{F}_{OT}$ in the presence of an $(\mathcal{A},\mathcal{B})$-adversary.*

Proof. **Alice honest, Bob malicious:**

We will suppose without loss of generality that corrupted servers act as a dummy adversary. Let B denote the set of corrupted servers.

First, Sim awaits $(\textbf{ready},i)$ for $i \in B$ and that the environment has sent b_i' for each $i \in \overline{B}$. Then it executes $\texttt{Reconstruct}_{\mathcal{S}}(\{(i,b_i') : i \in \overline{B}\})$. If the reconstruction fails then Sim chooses random messages $\tilde{m}_0$, $\tilde{m}_1$. If the reconstruction succeeds, let b be its output; then Sim sends the command $(\textbf{transfer}, b)$ to $\mathcal{F}_{OT}$, receives message $(\textbf{sent}, m_b)$ and sets $\tilde{m}_b := m_b$; it selects a random message $\tilde{m}_{1-b} \in \mathcal{M}$.

In any case, Sim generates a sharing $(a_{(i,j)})_{(i,j)\in\mathcal{P}_{n,2}} = [(\tilde{m}_0,\tilde{m}_1)]_{\Sigma}$.

Finally, in parallel Sim sends the following to the environment: for each $i \in \overline{B}$, it sends $a_{(i,b_i')}$, and for each $i \in B$, it sends the entire vectors $a_{(i,0)}$, $a_{(i,1)}$.

We need to prove now that the distribution of these values is indistinguishable from the ones obtained in the interaction with the actual protocol. We should first note that since the set $\overline{B}$ is qualified for $\mathcal{S}$, the values $\{b_i' : i \in \overline{B}\}$ cannot be part of both a sharing $[0]_{\mathcal{S}}$ and a sharing $[1]_{\mathcal{S}}$. Using Proposition 3, this implies that the distribution of the set of shares $(\tilde{m}_0)_{(i,j)}$, $(\tilde{m}_1)_{(i,j)}$, for $i \in B$ and $j \in \{0,1\}$ and $(\tilde{m}_0)_{(i,b_i')})$, $(\tilde{m}_1)_{(i,b_i')})$ for $i \in \overline{B}$ obtained in the simulation is the same as the corresponding distribution in the actual protocol.

Alice malicious, Bob honest:

We will suppose without loss of generality that corrupted servers act as a dummy adversary. Let $A \in \mathcal{A}$ be the set of corrupted servers. The simulator works as follows:

Upon receiving $(\textbf{ready})$ from the ideal functionality $\mathcal{F}_{OT}$, Sim generates uniformly random sharings of $b = 0$ and $b' = 1$ in $\mathcal{S}$ subject to the only condition that if $i \in A$, then $b_i = b_i'$. Note that this is possible since A is unqualified for $\mathcal{S}$. Then, in parallel Sim sends b_i to the environment for each $i \in A$. Sim now awaits that for each $i \in \overline{A}$, the environment sends $a_{(i,0)}$ and $a_{(i,1)}$ and that for each $i \in A$ the environment sends $a_{(i,b_i)}$.

For $k = 0, 1$, if m_k is not already set to 0 then Sim computes

$$m_k = \text{Reconstruct}_\Sigma^k(\{((i, b_i), a_{(i, b_i)}) : i \in \mathcal{P}_n\})$$

If the reconstruction of m_k fails, Sim sets $m_k = 0$. Finally, it sends (send, m_0, m_1) to $\mathcal{F}_{OT}$.

By construction, the shares b_i corresponding to the set A of corrupt servers that the environment receives are indistinguishable from the A-shares in a uniformly random sharing of b, regardless of whether $b = 0$ or $b = 1$. Hence these b_i do not allow the receiver to distinguish the real and ideal world. Now, since after that step there is no further interaction, it suffices to show that the messages sent to Bob are indistinguishable from the ones sent in the real world.

This is the case since the shares have been chosen with the distribution Bob would use and since the simulator reconstructs the messages m_0 and m_1 in exactly the same way as Bob would reconstruct m_b in the real protocol, if b is his input. Therefore the real and ideal world are indistinguishable. □

We note that the simulators in the proof above run in polynomial time.

5.3 Threshold Adversaries

We now consider threshold (t_A, t_B)-adversaries, which corrupt Alice and up to t_A servers or Bob and up to t_B servers. Our main result is Theorem 1, which we recall next.

Theorem 1. *For any large enough n, there exists an n-server single-use OT-combiner which is perfectly secure against an active $(0.11n, 0.11n)$-adversary.*

This and other statements we claim below will be a consequence of the following lemma.

Lemma 4. *If there exists a linear error-correcting code C over the binary field with length n, minimum distance d satisfying $d \geq t_B + 2$, and such that the minimum distance $d^\perp$ of its dual $C^\perp$ satisfies $d^\perp \geq t_A + 2$, then there exists a single-use OT-combiner for n servers which is perfectly secure against an active (t_A, t_B)-adversary.*

Proof. We know from [Mas93] (see also [CCG+07, Theorem 1]) that given a linear code C (over a field $\mathbb{F}_q$) with length $n + 1$, one can construct a linear secret sharing scheme for n participants with secret and shares in the same field $\mathbb{F}_q$ as follows. Namely, given a secret $s \in \mathbb{F}_q$, choose a codeword from C whose first coordinate is s, and define the remaining coordinates as the n shares. Then, if the code has minimum distance d and its dual code $C^\perp$ has minimum distance $d^\perp$, then any set of $d^\perp - 2$ participants in this LSSS is unqualified and any set of $n - d + 2$ participants is qualified. Hence the conditions of the lemma guarantee the existence of a ideal binary LSSS $\mathcal{S}$ for n participants where every set of t_A participants is unqualified and every set of $n - t_B$ participants is qualified. Plugging this $\mathcal{S}$ into Theorem 2 (in the ideal case we have already proved in this section) shows the result. □

Theorem 1 is then derived from the following result

Theorem 6. *For large enough n, there exists a linear binary code with length $n+1$ and $d, d^{\perp} \geq 0.11n$.*

The proof of this result essentially follows the steps from [CCG+07], and is based on the well-known Gilbert-Varshamov theorem from coding theory.

Theorem 7 (Gilbert-Varshamov). *For every $0 \leq \delta < 1/2$ and any $0 < \epsilon < 1 - h_2(\delta)$ (where $h(\cdot)$ denotes the binary entropy function), if a linear code is chosen uniformly at random among all linear codes over $\mathbb{F}_2$ of length $n+1$ and dimension $k = \lceil (1 - h_2(\delta) - \epsilon)(n+1) \rceil$, then with probability $1 - 2^{-\Omega(n)}$ the code has minimum distance at least $\delta(n+1)$.*

Proof of Theorem 6. Choosing $\delta = 0.11$ (which guarantees $h_2(\delta) < 1/2$), and $\epsilon = 1/2 - h_2(\delta)$, Theorem 7 states that for large n, a uniformly random binary linear code of dimension $(n+1)/2$ has minimum distance $\delta(n+1)$ with very large probability. Now the dual of a code of dimension $(n+1)/2$ also has dimension $(n+1)/2$. So one can use Gilbert-Varshamov bound (applied to both a code and its dual, whose distribution is clearly also uniformly random among all codes of dimension $(n+1)/2$) and a union bound argument and the observations above about the relationship between codes and secret sharing schemes to conclude the result.   □

Proof of Theorem 1. This is now straightforward from Lemma 4 and Theorem 6.
                                                                                            □

We can also give non-asymptotic statements, at the cost of a small loss in the constant 0.11.

Theorem 8. *For $n \geq 21$, there exists an n-server single-use OT-combiner which is perfectly secure against an active $(\lfloor 0.1n \rfloor, \lfloor 0.1n \rfloor)$-adversary.*

Proof [CCG+07, Corollary 2]. (see also Definition 5 in the same paper) guarantees that for $n \geq 21$, there exists a binary linear code with both $d, d^{\perp} \geq \lfloor 0.1n \rfloor$. Again applying Lemma 4 we obtain the result.   □

Theorem 1 is an existence result, and explicit constructions of codes attaining the Gilbert-Varshamov bound over the binary field are not known. We can only guarantee that choosing a random code of length $n+1$ and dimension $(n+1)/2$ will with high probability yield a linear secret sharing scheme with the desired guarantees. Explicit constructions of perfectly secure OT-combiners against an active $(\Omega(n), \Omega(n))$-adversary can be obtained from algebraic geometric codes, but the underlying constant is worse than 0.11. For small values of n one can also obtain explicit constructions of ideal binary LSSS with relatively good privacy and reconstruction thresholds. One possibility is to use self-dual codes (i.e. codes that are their own duals), since in that case the minimum distance of the code and its dual is the same. Tables of self-dual codes with the largest known minimum distance for their lengths are available at [Gab]. These tables show for instance the existence of a binary self-dual code of length 8 and minimum distance 4, which yields a single-use 7-server OT-combiner with perfect security against an active $(2, 2)$-adversary.

Finally, while in this paper we focus on perfect security, we briefly sketch a modification of our protocol towards the goal of achieving statistical security against a stronger threshold adversary that corrupts $n/2 - \omega(\log \kappa)$ servers, for a security parameter κ, following the ideas of [IMSW14] who obtained a similar result for passive adversaries. In this case, we need to assume the existence of a direct communication channel between Alice and Bob and we assume that the static adversary corrupts a set of servers and one of the parties prior to the beginning of the protocol. The idea is to use our construction from Theorem 1 but, rather than fixing a LSSS S prior to the start of the protocol as we do in Theorem 1, in the statistical version we would let Alice and Bob choose a random linear code and hence its associated LSSS as the first step of the protocol, after corruption of the servers (and one of the parties) has taken place. They do this by means of a secure coin tossing protocol. According to the arguments in Theorem 2, the adversary can only break the security of the protocol if it was able to corrupt either Alice and a set of servers A which is qualified in the corresponding LSSS scheme S or Bob and a set of servers B such that the complement $\overline{B}$ is not qualified in S. However, the adversary does not know the LSSS at the time of the corruption, so he must basically guess which set to corrupt. The results about LSSS constructed from codes in [Mas93, CCG+07] imply that the adversary succeeds if he corrupts a set of servers such that there exists a codeword in either C or $C^\perp$ with a 1 in the first coordinate and the rest of its support is contained in the set of indices corresponding to the corrupted set. However, one can show by a simple counting argument that the probability that this bad event happens is negligible in κ.

6 Construction of OT-Combiners in the General Case

In this section we present the general version of the protocol π_{OT} from the previous Sect. 5, when the adversary structure $\mathcal{A}$ is not necessarily the adversary structure of an ideal LSSS over $\mathbb{F}_2$. Note that many interesting access structures, for example most threshold structures, do not admit an ideal LSSS over $\mathbb{F}_2$.

Theorem 2. Let $\mathcal{A}, \mathcal{B} \subseteq 2^{\mathcal{P}_n}$ be adversary structures such that $(\mathcal{A}, \mathcal{B})$ is a $\mathcal{R}_2$ pair. Suppose there exists a linear secret sharing scheme S for n participants where the secret is in $\{0, 1\}$ and the i-th share is in $\{0, 1\}^{\ell_i}$, and such that every set $A \in \mathcal{A}$ is unqualified in S and the complement $\overline{B}$ of every set $B \in \mathcal{B}$ is qualified in S.

Then there exists an OT combiner which calls the i-th server ℓ_i times and is perfectly secure against any active $(\mathcal{A}, \mathcal{B})$-adversary.

Let S be a possibly non-ideal perfect secret sharing scheme with adversary structure $\mathcal{A}$. For $i = 1, \ldots, n$ the i-th share of S belongs to some vector space $U_i = \{0, 1\}^{\ell_i}$ for some integer $\ell_i \geq 1$. Let $\ell = \sum_{i=1}^{n} \ell_i$ be the complexity of S.

Oblivious transfer protocol π_{OT} (non-ideal S case)

We use the index $i \in \{1, \ldots, n\}$ for the servers, $k_i \in \{1, \ldots, \ell_i\}$ to index the bits of the i-th share of S and $j \in \{0, 1\}$ to index the bits in Alice's input to each instance of OT.

1. Local computation:
   Bob creates a sharing $[b]_S = (b_i)_{i \in \{1,\ldots,n\}}$, where each $b_i \in \{0,1\}^{\ell_i}$ is parsed as $(b_{i,1}, b_{i,2}, \ldots, b_{i,\ell_i})$ with $b_{i,k} \in \{0,1\}$.
   Alice creates a sharing

   $$[(m_0, m_1)]_\Sigma = (a_{(i,k,j)})_{i \in \{1,\ldots,n\}, k \in \{1,\ldots,\ell_i\}, j \in \{0,1\}}.$$

2. Use of the OT servers:
   For $i \in \{1, \ldots, n\}$ and for each $k \in \{1, \ldots, \ell_i\}$, Alice and Bob use server S_i to execute an OT with inputs $(a_{i,k,0}, a_{i,k,1})$ for Alice and $b_{i,k}$ for Bob. Let $y_{i,k}$ denote the output of Bob in instance (i, k).

3. Local computation:
   If $b = 0$, Bob constructs m'_0 by applying

   $$\mathtt{Reconstruct}^0_\Sigma(\{((i,k,b_{i,k}), y_{i,k}) : i \in \mathcal{P}_n, k \in \{1, \ldots, \ell_i\}\}).$$

   Similarly, if $b = 1$, Bob constructs m'_1 by applying

   $$\mathtt{Reconstruct}^1_\Sigma(\{((i,k,b_{i,k}), y_{i,k}) : i \in \mathcal{P}_n, k \in \{1, \ldots, \ell_i\}\}).$$

   In any of the cases, if the reconstruction fails, output $\mathbf{0}$. Otherwise output the reconstructed m'_b.

Fig. 4. Protocol π_{OT} for general LSSSs.

The idea of the generalization is simple. The i-th server is split in ℓ_i subservers, each of which will receive one different bit of the i-th share of Bob's input. These subservers will now work as the servers did in the protocol from Sect. 5 (we remark however that the adversaries corrupt full servers and not individual subservers). For that we need to modify the secret sharing scheme Σ used by Alice accordingly. More precisely, let $V, W \subseteq U_1 \times \cdots \times U_n$ be the sets of all possible sharings of 0 and 1 respectively. We can think of the elements of V and W as ℓ-bit strings, and we index their coordinates by pairs (i, k) where the (i, k)-th coordinate of a sharing is the k-th bit of the i-th share. Now we can define Σ as in Proposition 1 for these V and W (and setting $\mathbf{t}$ to be some sharing $[1]_S$). Everything works therefore the same as in Sect. 5.1 except that Σ will now have 2ℓ shares. The set of shares will be indexed by $\mathcal{P}_{\ell,2} := \{(i, k, j) : i = 1, \ldots, n, \ k = 1, \ldots, \ell_i, \ j = 0, 1\}$. The general protocol is given in Fig. 4. The security proofs work essentially as in the case presented in Sect. 5.

7 Necessary Conditions for the Existence of OT Combiners

In this section we show Theorem 3.

Theorem 3. *Let $\mathcal{A}$, $\mathcal{B}$ be adversary structures on the set of servers $\{S_1, \ldots, S_n\}$. If there exists a perfectly secure OT-combiner which is secure against any passive $(\mathcal{A}, \mathcal{B})$-adversary and uses server S_i exactly ℓ_i times, then $(\mathcal{A}, \mathcal{B})$ is an $\mathcal{R}_2$ pair of structures and there exists a secret sharing scheme for n participants with secret in $\{0,1\}$, the i-th share in $\{0,1\}^{\ell_i}$, for $i = 1, \ldots, n$ and such that every set $A \in \mathcal{A}$ is unqualified in S and the complement $\overline{B}$ of any set every set $B \in \mathcal{B}$ is qualified in S.*

First we show that if $(\mathcal{A}, \mathcal{B})$ were not $\mathcal{R}_2$ then the existence of an unconditionally secure OT combiner would imply the existence of a 2-party unconditionally secure OT protocol. Indeed if $(\mathcal{A}, \mathcal{B})$ is not $\mathcal{R}_2$, then there exists $A \in \mathcal{A}$ and $B \in \mathcal{B}$ such that $A \cup B$ is the set of all servers. Then the entire protocol can be emulated by two parties: Alice', who plays the joint role of Alice and all the servers in A and Bob' who plays for Bob and all servers in B. This is then a two-party protocol in the plain model which is unconditionally secure against a semi-honest adversary who can corrupt either of the parties Alice' and Bob'. This is known to be impossible.

Next, we prove the existence of a secret sharing scheme with the properties mentioned in the theorem. In fact, we simply reproduce the arguments from [IMSW13] in our setting. Assume we have an OT combiner which is perfectly secure against an $(\mathcal{A}, \mathcal{B})$-adversary and where the i-th server is used ℓ_i times. Then Bob's inputs to the OT servers must have been computed from his global input to the OT combiner by some probabilistic algorithm `AlgBob`. We now consider a secret sharing scheme S whose sharing algorithm is `AlgBob` (understanding that the i-th share is the bit-string containing all ℓ_i inputs bits to the i-th OT server produced by `AlgBob`). Since the OT combiner is secure against and adversary corrupting Alice and a set $A \in \mathcal{A}$, this means that every $A \in \mathcal{A}$ must be unqualified in S. Next we show that for every $B \in \mathcal{B}$, its complement $\overline{B}$ must be a reconstructing set for S. Consider a party Alice' who plays the role of Alice and the servers in $\overline{B}$ in the OT-combiner and a party Bob', who plays the role of Bob and the servers in B. Assume that the inputs of Alice and Bob are independent. We then have a protocol between Alice' and Bob' in the plain model, which correctly implements the OT functionality and in which, by security of the OT combiner and since $B \in \mathcal{B}$, Bob' obtains no information about the input (m_0, m_1) of Alice' after the protocol has been executed. In these conditions, it follows from standard arguments about the impossibility of two party computation in the plain model (see e.g. [CDN15]) that Alice' not only obtains information about the input of Bob', but in fact she recovers it with probability 1. Given that all the information that Alice' has learned during the execution of the protocol is the input bits to the servers in $\overline{B}$, we conclude that $\overline{B}$ is a reconstructing set for S.

8   2-Out-of-3 OT-Combiners

As an application of Theorems 2 and 3 we determine the minimal number of calls for a perfectly secure OT combiner where we have 3 servers, and 2 of them are secure. In other words, we want perfect security against an $(1,1)$-adversary, i.e. $\mathcal{A} = \mathcal{B} = \{\{1\},\{2\},\{3\}\}$. By Theorem 2, we are then interested in finding a linear secret sharing scheme over $\mathbb{F}_2$ for 3 participants such that it has 1-privacy (every single participant is unqualified) and it has 2-reconstruction (every set of two participants is qualified). Note that we want to find a threshold secret sharing scheme, but Shamir's scheme cannot be used directly over $\mathbb{F}_2$ (we would tolerate at most 2 participants). One could instead use Shamir's scheme over the extension field $\mathbb{F}_4$, and in this case we have shares which are each in $\{0,1\}^2$. This yields an OT-combiner where each server is called twice, which matches the number of calls in a construction in [HKN+05]. However, we show that one can do better with the following LSSS $\mathcal{S}$.

Secret sharing scheme $\mathcal{S}$

To share $s \in \{0,1\}$.

- Sample r and r' uniformly at random in $\{0,1\}$.
- Send:
    1. r to Participant 1.
    2. $(s-r, r')$ to Participant 2.
    3. $(s-r, s-r')$ to Participant 3.

Fig. 5. A 2-out-of-3 threshold linear secret sharing scheme $\mathcal{S}$

Lemma 5. $\mathcal{S}$ has 2-reconstruction and 1-privacy.

Corollary 1. There exists an OT combiner for 3 OT servers which is perfectly secure against an $(1,1)$-adversary and makes 1 call to one of the OT servers and 2 calls to each of the other 2 servers.

Now we apply Theorem 3 in combination with the results from [CCX13] to show that this is optimal in the total number of server calls. Theorem 3 states that given an OT-combiner in the conditions above, there needs to exist a secret sharing scheme (linear or not) for 3 participants with 1-privacy, 2-reconstruction and share lengths matching the number of calls to the OT-servers. On the other hand we have

Theorem 9 [CCX13]. Suppose there exists a secret sharing scheme for n participants, where the i-th share takes values in an alphabet A_i, and such that it has

t-privacy and r-reconstruction. Let $\bar{q} = \frac{1}{n} \sum_{i=1}^{n} |A_i|$ be the average cardinality of the share-alphabets. Then

$$r - t \geq \frac{n - t + 1}{\bar{q}}.$$

Therefore, a secret sharing in the conditions above must satisfy that the average cardinality of the share-alphabets is $\bar{q} \geq 3$. Now note that in our case the shares are in $\{0, 1\}^{\ell_i}$, which are alphabets of cardinality 2^{ℓ_i}, and we can rule out degenerate cases where $\ell_i = 0$ (since in that case, clearly it cannot happen simultaneously that $\{i, j\}$ is qualified and $\{j\}$ is unqualified). Under all these conditions, one can easily check that $\sum_{i=1}^{3} \ell_i < 5$ and $\bar{q} = \frac{1}{3} \sum_{i=1}^{3} 2^{\ell_i} \geq 3$ cannot be achieved simultaneously. Therefore,

Corollary 2. *The minimal number of calls for a OT combiner for 3 OT servers which is perfectly secure against an $(1, 1)$-adversary is 5.*

9 Security Against Corruptions of Only Servers

Our model does not consider corruption of only servers, and our security proofs therefore do not directly guarantee any security in case the adversaries corrupt only a set of servers. Nevertheless, we can argue that some security properties are satisfied even in case of server-only corruption.

Let Adv be an adversary that corrupts a set C of servers only. Alice and Bob are both honest and have inputs $(m_0, m_1), b$ respectively. Let us first consider the case where Adv is semi-honest and corrupts only a set $S \in \mathcal{B}$ of servers. If a protocol π is secure in our model, it is easy to see that it will compute the correct result $(\perp, m_b)$ (meaning Bob receives m_b and Alice receives nothing) also in this case and that Adv will learn nothing more than at most b, m_b. This follows, since if Adv had also corrupted Bob semi-honestly, he would have learned at least as much and we can use security of π to conclude that in that case the correct result is computed and Adv learns nothing more than b, m_b. In particular, the view of Adv can be simulated perfectly based on b, m_b. A similar conclusion holds if we switch the roles of Alice and Bob, i.e. if Adv is semi-honest and corrupts only a set $S \in \mathcal{A}$ of servers, his view can be simulated perfectly based only on m_0, m_1.

Now, consider the case where $S \in \mathcal{A}$ and $S \in \mathcal{B}$. We can then conclude that the view of Adv can be simulated perfectly based on m_0, m_1 and also based on b, m_b. But this must mean that the distribution of this view does not depend on any of these values: assume for contradiction that there existed m_0, m_1 such that the distribution of the view of S given $(0, m_0)$ is different from the one given $(1, m_1)$. Now compare the two cases where we run the protocol on inputs $(m_0, m_1, 0)$ respectively $(m_0, m_1, 1)$. Then the simulation based on m_0, m_1 would output the same distribution in both cases, so it cannot be consistent with both the distribution resulting from $(m_0, m_1, 0)$ and from $(m_0, m_1, 1)$. So we have

Proposition 4. *If protocol π is perfectly secure in our model, it is also secure against semi-honest corruption of a set of servers that is in both $\mathcal{A}$ and $\mathcal{B}$, except that the simulation may not in general be efficient.*

Let us now consider malicious corruption: Alice and Bob are honest and Adv is malicious and corrupts only a set $C \in \mathcal{B}$ of servers. Note that from Alice's point of view, the situation is indistinguishable from a case where Adv also corrupts Bob but lets him play honestly. Security of π now implies that Adv learns nothing more than b and $m_{b'}$ for some well defined input b' that is determined by the behaviour of the malicious servers. Note that we are not guaranteed that b' is equal to the honest input b, even though Bob plays honestly. Similarly, for $C \in \mathcal{A}$, Adv will learn nothing about b.

We observe that if S is in both $\mathcal{A}$ and $\mathcal{B}$, then both the honest Alice and honest Bob are guaranteed privacy: By running π, I will give away only the function evaluated in my own input and some input from the other party. But Alice and Bob are not guaranteed to agree on the result, so we do not get security in the standard single adversary sense against malicious corruption of C.

We can in fact argue that this cannot in general be achieved in our model, even if C is in both $\mathcal{A}$ and $\mathcal{B}$: Consider a case with 3 servers $1, 2, 3$ and let $\mathcal{A} = \{\{1\}, \{2\}\}$ and $\mathcal{B} = \{\{2\}, \{3\}\}$. This is clearly $\mathcal{R}_2$, so our model applies. Now, it is easy to see that a secure protocol π in our sense will in this case also be semi-honestly secure against single-adversary corruption of $\{Alice, 1\}$, as well as $\{Bob, 3\}$. So if π was also single adversary maliciously secure against corruption of $\{2\}$, then we would have a situation where the whole player set is covered by 2 sets that are semi-honestly corruptible and 1 set that is maliciously corruptible, while π remains secure. And where furthermore the malicious server 2 has no inputs or outputs. We are precisely in the case where the proof of Theorem 1 in [FHM99] rules out the possibility of having a secure protocol.

Acknowledgments. We thank the anonymous reviewers for their suggestions, which have helped us to improve this work.

References

[AIR01] Aiello, B., Ishai, Y., Reingold, O.: Priced oblivious transfer: how to sell digital goods. In: Pfitzmann, B. (ed.) EUROCRYPT 2001. LNCS, vol. 2045, pp. 119–135. Springer, Heidelberg (2001). https://doi.org/10.1007/3-540-44987-6_8

[BI01] Beimel, A., Ishai, Y.: On the power of nonlinear secret-sharing. In: Proceedings of the 16th Annual IEEE Conference on Computational Complexity, Chicago, Illinois, USA, 18–21 June 2001, pp. 188–202 (2001)

[Bla79] Blakley, G.R.: Safeguarding cryptographic keys. In: Proceedings of the 1979 AFIPS National Computer Conference, vol. 48, pp. 313–317, June 1979

[BM89] Bellare, M., Micali, S.: Non-interactive oblivious transfer and applications. In: Brassard, G. (ed.) CRYPTO 1989. LNCS, vol. 435, pp. 547–557. Springer, New York (1990). https://doi.org/10.1007/0-387-34805-0_48

[Can01] Canetti, R.: Universally composable security: a new paradigm for cryptographic protocols. In: 42nd IEEE Symposium on Foundations of Computer Science, Proceedings. pp. 136–145. IEEE (2001)

[CCG+07] Chen, H., Cramer, R., Goldwasser, S., de Haan, R., Vaikuntanathan, V.: Secure computation from random error correcting codes. In: Naor, M. (ed.) EUROCRYPT 2007. LNCS, vol. 4515, pp. 291–310. Springer, Heidelberg (2007). https://doi.org/10.1007/978-3-540-72540-4_17

[CCM98] Cachin, C., Crépeau, C., Marcil, J.: Oblivious transfer with a memory-bounded receiver. In: 39th Annual Symposium on Foundations of Computer Science, FOCS 1998, 8–11 November 1998, Palo Alto, California, USA, pp. 493–502 (1998)

[CCX13] Cascudo, I., Cramer, R., Xing, C.: Bounds on the threshold gap in secret sharing and its applications. IEEE Trans. Inf. Theory **59**(9), 5600–5612 (2013)

[CDN15] Cramer, R., Damgård, I., Nielsen, J.B.: Secure multiparty computation and secret sharing. Cambridge University Press, Cambridge (2015)

[CK88] Crépeau, C., Kilian, J.: Achieving oblivious transfer using weakened security assumptions (extended abstract). In: 29th Annual Symposium on Foundations of Computer Science, White Plains, New York, USA, 24–26 October 1988, pp. 42–52 (1988)

[DvdGMN08] Dowsley, R., van de Graaf, J., Müller-Quade, J., Nascimento, A.C.A.: Oblivious transfer based on the McEliece assumptions. In: Safavi-Naini, R. (ed.) ICITS 2008. LNCS, vol. 5155, pp. 107–117. Springer, Heidelberg (2008). https://doi.org/10.1007/978-3-540-85093-9_11

[EGL82] Even, S., Goldreich, O., Lempel, A.: A randomized protocol for signing contracts. In: Chaum, D., Rivest, R.L., Sherman, A.T. (eds.) Advances in Cryptology, pp. 205–210. Springer, Boston (1982). https://doi.org/10.1007/978-1-4757-0602-4_19

[FHM99] Fitzi, M., Hirt, M., Maurer, U.: General adversaries in unconditional multi-party computation. In: Lam, K.-Y., Okamoto, E., Xing, C. (eds.) ASIACRYPT 1999. LNCS, vol. 1716, pp. 232–246. Springer, Heidelberg (1999). https://doi.org/10.1007/978-3-540-48000-6_19

[Gab] Gaborit, P.: Tables of self-dual codes. http://www.unilim.fr/pages_perso/philippe.gaborit/SD/

[GIS+10] Goyal, V., Ishai, Y., Sahai, A., Venkatesan, R., Wadia, A.: Founding cryptography on tamper-proof hardware tokens. In: Micciancio, D. (ed.) TCC 2010. LNCS, vol. 5978, pp. 308–326. Springer, Heidelberg (2010). https://doi.org/10.1007/978-3-642-11799-2_19

[HIKN08] Harnik, D., Ishai, Y., Kushilevitz, E., Nielsen, J.B.: OT-combiners via secure computation. In: Canetti, R. (ed.) TCC 2008. LNCS, vol. 4948, pp. 393–411. Springer, Heidelberg (2008). https://doi.org/10.1007/978-3-540-78524-8_22

[HKN+05] Harnik, D., Kilian, J., Naor, M., Reingold, O., Rosen, A.: On robust combiners for oblivious transfer and other primitives. In: Cramer, R. (ed.) EUROCRYPT 2005. LNCS, vol. 3494, pp. 96–113. Springer, Heidelberg (2005). https://doi.org/10.1007/11426639_6

[IKO+11] Ishai, Y., Kushilevitz, E., Ostrovsky, R., Prabhakaran, M., Sahai, A., Wullschleger, J.: Constant-rate oblivious transfer from noisy channels. In: Rogaway, P. (ed.) CRYPTO 2011. LNCS, vol. 6841, pp. 667–684. Springer, Heidelberg (2011). https://doi.org/10.1007/978-3-642-22792-9_38

[IMSW13] Ishai, Y., Maji, H.K., Sahai, A., Wullschleger, J.: Single-use oblivious transfer combiners (2013). Full version of [IMSW14] https://www.cs.purdue.edu/homes/hmaji/papers/IshaiMaSaWu13.pdf

[IMSW14] Ishai, Y., Maji, H.K., Sahai, A., Wullschleger, J.: Single-use OT combiners with near-optimal resilience. In: 2014 IEEE International Symposium on Information Theory, Honolulu, HI, USA, 29 June – 4 July 2014, pp. 1544–1548 (2014)

[IPS08] Ishai, Y., Prabhakaran, M., Sahai, A.: Founding cryptography on oblivious transfer – efficiently. In: Wagner, D. (ed.) CRYPTO 2008. LNCS, vol. 5157, pp. 572–591. Springer, Heidelberg (2008). https://doi.org/10.1007/978-3-540-85174-5_32

[ISN87] Ito, M., Saito, A., Nishizeki, T.: Secret sharing schemes realizing general access structures. In: Proceedings of IEEE GlobeCom 1987 Tokyo, pp. 99–102 (1987)

[JMO93] Jackson, W.-A., Martin, K.M., O'Keefe, C.M.: Multisecret threshold schemes. In: Stinson, D.R. (ed.) CRYPTO 1993. LNCS, vol. 773, pp. 126–135. Springer, Heidelberg (1994). https://doi.org/10.1007/3-540-48329-2_11

[Kil88] Kilian, J.: Founding cryptography on oblivious transfer. In: Proceedings of the 20th Annual ACM Symposium on Theory of Computing, 2–4 May 1988, Chicago, Illinois, USA, pp. 20–31 (1988)

[Mas93] Massey, J.L.: Minimal codewords and secret sharing. In: Proceedings of the 6th Joint Swedish-Russian International Workshop on Information Theory, pp. 276–279 (1993)

[PVW08] Peikert, C., Vaikuntanathan, V., Waters, B.: A framework for efficient and composable oblivious transfer. In: Wagner, D. (ed.) CRYPTO 2008. LNCS, vol. 5157, pp. 554–571. Springer, Heidelberg (2008). https://doi.org/10.1007/978-3-540-85174-5_31

[PW08] Przydatek, B., Wullschleger, J.: Error-Tolerant Combiners for Oblivious Primitives. In: Aceto, L., Damgård, I., Goldberg, L.A., Halldórsson, M.M., Ingólfsdóttir, A., Walukiewicz, I. (eds.) ICALP 2008. LNCS. Springer, Heidelberg (2008). https://doi.org/10.1007/978-3-540-70583-3_38

[Rab81] Rabin, M.: How to exchange secrets with oblivious transfer. Technical report, Aiken Computation Lab, Harvard University (1981)

[Sha79] Shamir, A.: How to share a secret. Commun. ACM **22**, 612–613 (1979)

[VV15] Vaikuntanathan, V., Vasudevan, P.N.: Secret sharing and statistical zero knowledge. In: Iwata, T., Cheon, J.H. (eds.) ASIACRYPT 2015. LNCS, vol. 9452, pp. 656–680. Springer, Heidelberg (2015). https://doi.org/10.1007/978-3-662-48797-6_27

Signatures

An Equivalence Between Attribute-Based Signatures and Homomorphic Signatures, and New Constructions for Both

Rotem Tsabary[(✉)]

Weizmann Institute of Science, Rehovot, Israel
rotem.ts0@gmail.com

Abstract. In Attribute-Based Signatures (ABS; first defined by Maji, Prabhakaran and Rosulek, CT-RSA 2011) an authority can generate multiple signing keys, where each key is associated with an attribute x. Messages are signed with respect to a constraint f, such that a key for x can sign messages respective to f only if $f(x) = 0$. The security requirements are unforgeability and key privacy (signatures should not expose the specific signing key used). In (single-hop) Homomorphic Signatures (HS; first defined by Boneh and Freeman, PKC 2011), given a signature for a data-set x, one can evaluate a signature for the pair $(f(x), f)$, for functions f. In *context-hiding* HS, evaluated signatures do not reveal information about the original (pre-evaluated) signatures.

In this work we start by showing that these two notions are in fact equivalent. The first implication of this equivalence is a new lattice-based ABS scheme for polynomial-depth circuits, based on the HS construction of Gorbunov, Vaikuntanathan and Wichs (GVW; STOC 2015).

We then construct a new ABS candidate from a worst case lattice assumption (SIS), with different parameters. Using our equivalence again, now in the opposite direction, our new ABS implies a new lattice-based HS scheme with different parameter trade-off, compared to the aforementioned GVW.

1 Introduction

In a standard digital signature scheme an authority generates a public verification key vk and a secret signing key sk. Given sk, it is possible to sign any message, and signatures can be verified publicly with vk. Recent works study more powerful notions of digital signatures, where the authority can generate multiple signing keys, each with limited signing permissions. An example use case is when an organization wants to allow its employees to sign on behalf of its name, while controlling which messages each employee can sign. A signature should not reveal any information about the signing permissions of the signer, other than whether he is allowed to sign the message corresponding to the same

---

R. Tsabary—Supported by the Israel Science Foundation (Grant No. 468/14) and Binational Science Foundation (Grant No. 712307).

Y. Kalai and L. Reyzin (Eds.): TCC 2017, Part II, LNCS 10678, pp. 489–518, 2017.
https://doi.org/10.1007/978-3-319-70503-3_16

signature. In stronger notions, the signature should not reveal any information about the *identity* of the signer. Main notions of this form are attribute-based signatures (ABS) [MPR11], policy-based signatures (PBS) [BF14], constrained signatures (CS) [BZ14] and functional signatures (FS) [BGI14]. In this work we use a slightly modified definition of *constrained signatures*, with two flavors that capture ABS and PBS for languages in $\mathbf{P}$.

In a homomorphic signatures (HS) scheme, given a signature for a data-set x, one can evaluate a signature for the pair $(f(x), f)$, for any f in the supported function space of the scheme. Context-hiding HS has the security guarantee that an evaluated signature does not reveal information about the original (pre-evaluated) signature. In particular, it does not reveal x. Context-hiding homomorphic signatures are useful, for example, when one wants to prove that he has a signature for a data-set which satisfies some condition, without revealing the data-set itself. We show in this work that CS is equivalent to context-hiding 1-hop HS.

1.1   Overview

Two flavors of CS will be alternately used throughout this work. In *key-policy constrained signatures*, each signing key sk_f is associated with a circuit $f : \{0, 1\}^* \to \{0, 1\}$, which we refer to as the *constraint*, and a key sk_f can sign an *attribute* $x \in \{0, 1\}^*$ only if $f(x) = 0$. In *message-policy constrained signatures*, each key is associated with an attribute $x \in \{0, 1\}^*$, and a key sk_x can sign a constraint $f : \{0, 1\}^* \to \{0, 1\}$ only if $f(x) = 0$. Message-policy CS is equivalent to attribute-based signatures, and key-policy CS is equivalent policy-based signatures for languages in $\mathbf{P}^1$. When presented as two flavors of a single primitive, we can take advantage of the similarities and alternately use the definition that best fits the context. Note that the flavors are interchangeable up to switching the constraint space and attribute space.

Security. We consider two aspects of security – unforgeability and key privacy. Unforgeability requires that an adversary cannot sign a message which it does not have a permission to sign, even after seeing other signatures. We also define a relaxed notion where the adversary has only a single key, and a selective notion where the adversary has to announce the message for which it is going to forge a signature before seeing any public data. Key privacy bounds the information revealed by a signature regarding the key that was used to produce it. In the strongest notion, *key-hiding* privacy, the signature completely hides the key. In particular, it is impossible to determine whether two signatures were derived from the same key. In *constraint-hiding* privacy (or *attribute-hiding* privacy, in the message-policy flavor) we only aim to hide the constraint (or to hide the

---

[1] The original definition of ABS [MPR11] (PBS [BF14]) considers an additional message space $\mathcal{M}$, where messages $m \in \mathcal{M}$ are signed respective to an attribute (a policy). The two definitions are equivalent since m can always be encoded into the signed attribute (policy).

attribute, in the message-policy flavor), possibly leaving the identity of the signing key public. We note that without any privacy requirements, CS are trivial to achieve using standard signatures.

Delegation. A CS scheme can be extended to support key delegation. In this setting, a party with a singing key sk_f can derive a signing key $\mathsf{sk}_{(f,g)}$ that is authorized to sign a message x only when $f(x) = 0$ *and* $g(x) = 0$. Note that the permissions of $\mathsf{sk}_{(f,g)}$ are never stronger than the permissions of sk_f, since otherwise the scheme is forgeable.

Motivation. CS is weaker than PBS for **NP** but strong enough for some of the motivations that lead to the study of PBS, such as constructing group signatures and attribute-based signatures. See the applications discussion in [BF14] for details. We exploit this gap and construct CS with a different approach than previous results that were using variations of NIZK. Indeed, as noted in [BF14], PBS for general languages in **NP** implies simulation-extractable NIZK proofs. We also see in this work a contribution to the understanding of homomorphic signatures – prior to this work there was only a single known construction of (leveled) fully HS [GVW15].

1.2 Results

Unforgeability Amplification. In our first construction we assume a (key-policy) CS scheme with *single-key-selective unforgeability*. This notion is captured by a security game where the adversary is only allowed to query for a single key sk_f, and it has to announce f before seeing any public data. It wins if it manages to forge a signature for an attribute x that is not authorized by f, i.e. where $f(x) = 1$. We use a standard signatures scheme to construct a (key-policy) CS scheme with full unforgeability. The downside of this general amplification is the loss in key privacy – while the new CS scheme is constraint-hiding (i.e. it hides the functionality of the signing key, as long as the underlying CS scheme does as well), signatures reveal other key-specific information and therefore it is not key-hiding (i.e. one can learn from a signature the identity of the signing key). The amplification maintains the delegation properties of the underlying CS scheme.

Equivalence of CS and Homomorphic Signatures. We first construct a (message-policy) CS scheme which is *single-key-selective unforgeable* and *key-hiding*, from context-hiding 1-hop homomorphic signatures. [GVW15] construct a context-hiding HS scheme which is secure under the Short Integer Solution (SIS) hardness assumption. When used as the underlying HS scheme to our construction, this results in a SIS-based (message-policy) CS scheme with bounded attribute space, and constraint space of boolean circuits with bounded depth. In the other direction, we construct a selectively-unforgeable context-hiding 1-hop HS scheme from a single-key-selective unforgeable key-hiding (message-policy) CS scheme. As shown in [GVW15], it is possible to amplify the unforgeability of such HS scheme to the adaptive notion.

CS from Lattice Trapdoors. We construct a (key-policy) CS scheme from lattice trapdoors, which is *message-selective unforgeable* and *key-hiding*. The key privacy is statistical, and the unforgeability relies on the Short Integers Solution (SIS) hardness assumption. The construction supports attribute space of fixed size and constraint space of boolean circuits with bounded depth. When translated to the message-policy flavor, the attribute space is unbounded and the policy space is bounded in depth and size.

A New Homomorphic Signatures Construction. An immediate conclusion of the above two results is a new lattice-based (leveled) fully homomorphic signatures scheme, where fresh signatures are of fixed size (independent of the signed dataset size), and evaluated signatures grow with the size of the policy description. It means that for any policy with a short description succinctness is maintained.

Two New CS Constructions. Combining the first two results gives a new CS construction – first construct the HS-based (message-policy) CS scheme which is single-key-selective unforgeable, and then amplify it to full unforgeability, while compromising on key privacy. We summarize the different properties of this CS construction and the lattice-based CS construction in the table below. Note that the HS-based scheme is presented in the message-policy flavor, and the lattice-based scheme is presented in the key-policy flavor. Implementing each of them in the opposite flavor will result in a constraint space of bounded depth *and size*, and an *unbounded* attribute space.

	HS-based message-policy CS	Lattice-based key-policy CS
Assumption	SIS	SIS
Attribute space	Fixed	Fixed
Constraint space	Bounded depth	Bounded depth
Unforgeability	Full	Message-selective
Privacy	Constraint-hiding	Key-hiding
Supports delegation	No	Yes

1.3 Technical Overview

Definition of CS. A (key-policy) CS scheme consists of 4 algorithms (Setup, Keygen, Sign, Ver). Setup is an initialization algorithm that generates a verification key vk and a master signing key msk. Keygen produces constrained signing keys – it takes as input the master signing key msk and a constraint f, and outputs a constrained key sk_f. The signing algorithm Sign takes as input an attribute x and a constrained singing key sk_f, and outputs a signature σ_x, which is valid if and only if $f(x) = 0$. The verification algorithm Ver takes an attribute x and a signature σ_x, and either accepts or rejects.

Unforgeability Amplification. We now give a brief description of the amplification. Assume a (key-policy) constrained signatures scheme CS′ which is single-key-selective unforgeable, constraint-hiding and possibly supports delegation. Let S be an existentially unforgeable standard signatures scheme. The construction is as follows. In Setup, the authority initializes S and sets $(\text{vk}, \text{msk}) = (\text{S.vk}, \text{S.sk})$. Every time a key is generated, the authority initializes a fresh instance of CS′ and generates a constrained key for the desired f under this instance: $(\text{CS}′.\text{vk}′, \text{CS}′.\text{sk}_f′)$. It also generates a fresh instance of $\text{S} : (\text{S.vk}″, \text{S.sk}″)$. The authority then signs $(\text{CS}′.\text{vk}′, \text{S.vk}″)$ under the standard scheme S using $\text{msk} = \text{S.sk}$ and gets $\text{S}.\sigma_{(\text{vk}′,\text{vk}″)}$. The constrained key is therefore $\text{sk}_f = (\text{CS}′.\text{vk}, \text{CS}′.\text{sk}_f, \text{S.vk}″, \text{S.sk}″, \text{S}.\sigma_{(\text{vk}′,\text{vk}″)})$. To sign an attribute x with a key of this form, one signs x with $(\text{CS}′.\text{vk}, \text{CS}′.\text{sk}_f)$, signs x with $(\text{S.vk}″, \text{S.sk}″)$ and outputs these signatures along with $\text{S}.\sigma_{(\text{vk}′,\text{vk}″)}$. Verification is done by verifying the signatures for x under $\text{CS}′.\text{vk}′$ and $\text{S.vk}″$, and verifying $\text{S}.\sigma_{(\text{vk}′,\text{vk}″)}$ under S.vk. Since for each instance of CS′ the authority only generates a single key, the unforgeability for each such instance is maintained. The existential unforgeability of S guarantees that it is not possible to forge a signature for an instance of CS′ that was not initialized by the authority. Note that CS′.vk is a part of the signature, and since this value is different for each key, it reveals the identity of the key. For that reason the construction is not key-hiding but solely constraint-hiding.

CS from Homomorphic Signatures. The construction of (message-policy) CS from context-hiding HS works as follows. The CS authority initializes the HS scheme. In order to produce a CS key for an attribute x, it signs x under the HS scheme and outputs $\text{sk}_x = \text{HS}.\sigma_x$. A signature for a policy f is derived from sk_x by homomorphically evaluating f on $\text{HS}.\sigma_x$. This results in an HS signature for the pair $(f, f(x))$. In order to verify one checks the validity of the HS signature, and that $f(x) = 0$. The context-hiding property of HS ensures that $\sigma_{(f,f(x))}$ reveals nothing about σ_x, and thus the construction is key-hiding.

Homomorphic Signatures from CS. The construction of context-hiding 1-hop HS from (message-policy) CS works as follows. The HS authority initializes the CS scheme. In order to sign a data-set x, generate a CS key for the attribute x and outputs $\sigma_x = \text{CS.sk}_x$. To homomorphically evaluate a function f on a signature σ_x, first compute $y = f(x)$, then define the function f_y that on input $x′$ outputs 0 if and only if $f(x′) = y$. Sign the constraint f_y under the CS scheme (using CS.sk_x) and output this CS signature: $\text{HS}.\sigma_{(f,y)} = \text{CS}.\sigma_{f_y}$. In order to verify one checks the validity of the CS signature. The key-hiding property of CS ensures that $\text{CS}.\sigma_{f_y}$ reveals nothing about CS.sk_x, and thus the construction is context-hiding.

CS from Lattice Trapdoors. We use techniques that were developed in [GVW13, BGG+14] for the purpose of attribute-based encryption (ABE). Let ℓ be the attribute length, i.e. $x \in \{0,1\}^\ell$. The constraint space is all the circuits $f : \{0,1\}^\ell \rightarrow \{0,1\}$ of bounded depth. The verification key vk consists of a uniformly sampled matrix $\vec{\mathbf{A}} = [\mathbf{A}_1 \| \ldots \| \mathbf{A}_{\ell_x}]$ and a close-to-uniform matrix $\mathbf{A}$, and the master signing key msk is a trapdoor for $\mathbf{A}$, i.e. $\mathbf{A}_{\tau_0}^{-1}$. A valid signature for an attribute x is a non-zero short-entries vector $\mathbf{v}_x$ such that $[\mathbf{A}\|\vec{\mathbf{A}} - x \otimes \mathbf{G}] \cdot \mathbf{v}_x = \mathbf{0}$, where $\mathbf{G}$ is a special fixed gadget matrix. The constrained signing key sk_f respective to a circuit f is a trapdoor $[\mathbf{A}\|\mathbf{A}_f]_\tau^{-1}$, where $\mathbf{A}_f$ is computed from $\vec{\mathbf{A}}$ and f. Given $\mathsf{msk} = \mathbf{A}_{\tau_0}^{-1}$ it is possible to generate a trapdoor $[\mathbf{A}\|\mathbf{M}]_\tau^{-1}$ for any matrix $\mathbf{M}$, so the authority can generate such keys efficiently. For any pair (x, f), a trapdoor $[\mathbf{A}\|\vec{\mathbf{A}} - x \otimes \mathbf{G}]_{\tau'}^{-1}$ can be derived from the trapdoor $[\mathbf{A}\|\mathbf{A}_f - f(x)\mathbf{G}]_\tau^{-1}$. This implies that when $f(x) = 0$, it can be derived from the signing key $\mathsf{sk}_f = [\mathbf{A}\|\mathbf{A}_f]_\tau^{-1}$. The trapdoor $[\mathbf{A}\|\vec{\mathbf{A}} - x \otimes \mathbf{G}]_{\tau'}^{-1}$ allows to sample a short vector $\mathbf{v}_x$ which is a valid signature for x. Since the signature is sampled from the same distribution regardless of the signing key, the scheme is statistically key-hiding. The proof of message-selective unforgeability is similar to the selective security proof in [BGG+14]. Recall that the adversary has to announce x for which it is going to forge a signature at the beginning of the game. The matrix $\vec{\mathbf{A}}$ is then generated from $\mathbf{A}$ based on x in such way that it is possible to generate a key for any function f for which $f(x) = 1$ without $\mathbf{A}_{\tau_0}^{-1}$. It is then shown that forging a signature for x implies breaking SIS respective to the matrix $\mathbf{A}$.

1.4   Related Work

Policy-based signatures were introduced in [BF14], where it was also shown that PBS for **NP** can be constructed from NIZK. [CNW16] construct lattice-based PBS in the random oracle model. [MPR11] introduced attribute-based signatures, and suggested a general framework for constructing ABS from NIZK. In [SAH16] ABS for circuits is constructed from bilinear maps. [BK16] construct ABS for threshold functions and $(\vee, \wedge)$- functions from lattice assumptions. Our construction in Sect. 6 is the first ABS candidate for circuits that does not use NIZK or non-standard assumptions.

[Fuc14, CRV14] define *constrained verifiable random functions* (CVRF), which are constraint PRFs where given a constraint key one can compute, in addition to the function value, a non-interactive proof for the computed function value, where the proof is key-hiding. ABS can be constructed from CVRF trivially, however the pseudo-randomness property of known CVRF constructions implies *single-key* unforgeability of the derived ABS. [Fuc14, CRV14] show existence of CVRFs for poly-sized circuits, where the constructions assume mulitilinar-maps and the multilinear DDH assumption respectively.

Homomorphic signatures were constructed in [BF11, CFW14] for polynomials, and later in [GVW15] for boolean circuits. [LTWC16] define *multi-key* homomorphic signatures and show how to derive ABS from it. [FMNP16] define multi-key homomorphic MACS and signatures, and extend the [GVW15] HS construction to support multi-key evaluation.

Other notions of digital signatures with fine-grained control over signing permissions are *functional signatures* (FE) [BGI14] and *delegatable functional signatures* [BMS16]. In FE, a key respective to a function f can sign a message y

if and only if the signer provides a preimage x such that $f(x) = y$. When the function space consists of efficiently invertible functions, finding such x is trivial whenever it exists, and FE can be derived from (key-policy) CS: a FE key for f will be a CS key for the function that computes $f \circ f^{-1}$ and returns 0 if and only if the output is equal to the input.

2 Preliminaries

2.1 Digital Signatures

Definition 1 ((Standard) Signature Scheme). *A signature scheme is a tuple of PPT algorithms* (Setup, Sign, Ver) *with the following syntax.*

- Setup(1^λ) $\rightarrow$ (vk, sk) *takes as input the security parameter λ and outputs a verification key* vk *and a signing key* sk.
- Sign(sk, m) $\rightarrow$ σ_m *takes as input a signing key* sk *and a message m, and outputs a signature σ_m for m.*
- Ver$_{vk}$(m, σ_m) *takes as input a message m and a signature σ_m, and either accepts or rejects.*

Correctness. The scheme is correct for a message space $\mathcal{M}$, if for all $m \in \mathcal{M}$ it holds that Ver$_{vk}$(m, Sign(sk, m)) = *accept, where* (sk, vk) $\leftarrow$ Setup(1^λ).

Existential Unforgeability. The scheme is existentially unforgeable for a message space $\mathcal{M}$ if every PPTM adversary $\mathcal{A}$ has no more than negligible advantage in the following game:

1. *The challenger computes* (sk, vk) $\leftarrow$ Setup(1^λ) *and sends* vk *to $\mathcal{A}$.*
2. *$\mathcal{A}$ makes queries: it sends $m \in \mathcal{M}$ and gets in response $\sigma_m \leftarrow$ Sign(m, sk).*
3. *$\mathcal{A}$ wins if it manages to output (m^*, σ_{m^*}) such that* Ver$_{vk}$(m^*, σ_{m^*}) = *accept, where $m^* \neq m$ for any signature queried by $\mathcal{A}$ for a message $m \in \mathcal{M}$.*

2.2 Short Integer Solution (SIS)

Below is the definition and hardness assumption of SIS, as phrased in [Pei16].

Definition 2 (Short Integer Solution (SIS$_{n,q,B,m}$)). *Given a uniformly random matrix $\mathbf{A} \in \mathbb{Z}_q^{n \times m}$, find a nonzero integer vector $\mathbf{r} \in \mathbb{Z}^m$ of norm $\|\mathbf{r}\|_\infty \leq B$ such that $\mathbf{Ar} = \mathbf{0}$.*

Theorem 1 [Ajt96, Mic04, MR07, MP13]. *For any $m = \text{poly}(n)$, $B > 0$, and sufficiently large $q \geq B \cdot \text{poly}(n)$, solving SIS$_{n,q,B,m}$ with non-negligible probability is at least as hard as solving the decisional approximate shortest vector problem GapSVP$_\gamma$ and the approximate shortest independent vectors problem SIVP$_\gamma$ on arbitrary n-dimensional lattices (i.e., in the worst case) with overwhelming probability, for some $\gamma = B \cdot \text{poly}(n)$.*

2.3 Lattice Trapdoors

Let $n, q \in \mathbb{Z}$, $\mathbf{g} = (1, 2, 4, \ldots, 2^{\lceil \log q \rceil - 1}) \in \mathbb{Z}_q^{\lceil \log q \rceil}$ and $m = n \lceil \log q \rceil$. The *gadget matrix* $\mathbf{G}$ is defined as the diagonal concatenation of $\mathbf{g}$ n times. Formally, $\mathbf{G} = \mathbf{g} \otimes \mathbf{I}_n \in \mathbb{Z}_q^{n \times m}$. For any $t \in \mathbb{Z}$, the function $\mathbf{G}^{-1} : \mathbb{Z}_q^{n \times t} \to \{0, 1\}^{m \times t}$ expands each entry $a \in \mathbb{Z}_q$ of the input matrix into a column of size $\lceil \log q \rceil$ consisting of the bits representation of a. For any matrix $\mathbf{A} \in \mathbb{Z}_q^{n \times t}$, it holds that $\mathbf{G} \cdot \mathbf{G}^{-1}(\mathbf{A}) = \mathbf{A}$.

The (centered) discrete Gaussian distribution over $\mathbb{Z}^m$ with parameter τ, denoted $D_{\mathbb{Z}^m, \tau}$, is the distribution over $\mathbb{Z}^m$ where for all $\mathbf{x}$, $\Pr[\mathbf{x}] \propto e^{-\pi \|\mathbf{x}\|^2 / \tau^2}$. Let $n, m, q \in \mathbb{N}$ and consider a matrix $\mathbf{A} \in \mathbb{Z}_q^{n \times m}$. For all $\mathbf{v} \in \mathbb{Z}_q^n$ we let $\mathbf{A}_\tau^{-1}(\mathbf{v})$ denote the random variable whose distribution is the Discrete Gaussian $D_{\mathbb{Z}^m, \tau}$ conditioned on $\mathbf{A} \cdot \mathbf{A}_\tau^{-1}(\mathbf{v}) = \mathbf{v}$.

A τ-trapdoor for $\mathbf{A}$ is a procedure that can sample from a distribution within 2^{-n} statistical distance of $\mathbf{A}_\tau^{-1}(\mathbf{v})$ in time $\text{poly}(n, m, \log q)$, for any $\mathbf{v} \in \mathbb{Z}_q^n$. We slightly overload notation and denote a τ-trapdoor for $\mathbf{A}$ by $\mathbf{A}_\tau^{-1}$. The following properties had been established in a long sequence of works.

Corollary 1 (Trapdoor Generation [Ajt96, MP12]). *There exists an efficiently computable value* $m_0 = O(n \log q)$ *and an efficient procedure* $\text{TrapGen}(1^n, q, m)$ *such that for all* $m \geq m_0$ *outputs* $(\mathbf{A}, \mathbf{A}_{\tau_0}^{-1})$, *where* $\mathbf{A} \in \mathbb{Z}_q^{n \times m}$ *is* 2^{-n}*-uniform and* $\tau_0 = O(\sqrt{n \log q \log n})$.

We use the most general form of trapdoor extension as formalized in [MP12].

Theorem 2 (Trapdoor Extension [ABB10, MP12]). *Given* $\bar{\mathbf{A}} \in \mathbb{Z}_q^{n \times m}$ *with a trapdoor* $\bar{\mathbf{A}}_\tau^{-1}$, *and letting* $\bar{\mathbf{B}} \in \mathbb{Z}_q^{n \times m'}$ *be s.t.* $\bar{\mathbf{A}} = \bar{\mathbf{B}} \mathbf{S}$ (mod q) *where* $\mathbf{S} \in \mathbb{Z}^{m' \times m}$ *with largest singular value* $s_1(\mathbf{S})$, *then* $(\bar{\mathbf{A}}_\tau^{-1}, \mathbf{S})$ *can be used to sample from* $\bar{\mathbf{B}}_{\tau'}^{-1}$ *for any* $\tau' \geq \tau \cdot s_1(\mathbf{S})$.

A few additional important corollaries are derived from this theorem. We recall that $s_1(\mathbf{S}) \leq \sqrt{m'm} \|\mathbf{S}\|_\infty$ and that a trapdoor $\mathbf{G}_{O(1)}^{-1}$ is trivial. The first is a trapdoor extension that follows by taking $\mathbf{S} = [\mathbf{I}_{m'} \| \mathbf{0}_m]^T$.

Corollary 2. *Given* $\mathbf{A} \in \mathbb{Z}_q^{n \times m'}$, *with a trapdoor* $\mathbf{A}_\tau^{-1}$, *it is efficient to generate a trapdoor* $[\mathbf{A} \| \mathbf{B}]_{\tau'}^{-1}$ *for all* $\mathbf{B} \in \mathbb{Z}_q^{n \times m}$, *for any* $m \in \mathbb{N}$ *and any* $\tau' \geq \tau$.

Next is a trapdoor extension that had been used extensively in prior work. It follows from Theorem 2 with $\mathbf{S} = [-\mathbf{R}^T \| \mathbf{I}_m]^T$.

Corollary 3. *Given* $\mathbf{A} \in \mathbb{Z}_q^{n \times m'}$, *and* $\mathbf{R} \in \mathbb{Z}^{m' \times m}$ *with* $m = n \lceil \log q \rceil$, *it is efficient to compute* $[\mathbf{A} \| \mathbf{A}\mathbf{R} + \mathbf{G}]_\tau^{-1}$ *for* $\tau = O(\sqrt{mm'} \|\mathbf{R}\|_\infty)$.

Note that by taking $\mathbf{A}$ uniform and $\mathbf{R}$ to be a high entropy small matrix, e.g. uniform in $\{-1, 0, 1\}$, and relying on the leftover hash lemma, Corollary 1 is in fact a special case of this one.

It is also possible to permute trapdoors in the following manner.

Corollary 4. *Given* $[\mathbf{A}_1 \| \ldots \| \mathbf{A}_t]_\tau^{-1}$ *and a permutation* $\rho : \mathbb{Z}_t \to \mathbb{Z}_t$, *it is efficient to compute* $[\mathbf{A}_{\rho(1)} \| \ldots \| \mathbf{A}_{\rho(t)}]_\tau^{-1}$.

2.4   Lattice Evaluation

The following is an abstraction of the evaluation procedure in recent LWE based FHE and ABE schemes, that developed in a long sequence of works [ABB10, MP12, GSW13, AP14, BGG+14, GVW15]. We use a similar formalism to [BV15, BCTW16] but slightly rename the functions.

Theorem 3. *There exist efficient deterministic algorithms* EvalF *and* EvalFX *such that for all* $n, q, \ell \in \mathbb{N}$, *and for any sequence of matrices* $\vec{\mathbf{A}} = (\mathbf{A}_1, \ldots, \mathbf{A}_\ell) \in (\mathbb{Z}_q^{n \times n \lceil \log q \rceil})^\ell$, *for any depth* d *boolean circuit* $f : \{0,1\}^\ell \to \{0,1\}$ *and for every* $\mathbf{x} = (x_1, \ldots, x_\ell) \in \{0,1\}^\ell$, *the outputs* $\mathbf{H}_f = \mathsf{EvalF}(f, \vec{\mathbf{A}})$ *and* $\mathbf{H}_{f,x} = \mathsf{EvalFX}(f, x, \vec{\mathbf{A}})$ *are both in* $\mathbb{Z}^{(\ell n \lceil \log q \rceil) \times n \lceil \log q \rceil}$ *and it holds that* $\|\mathbf{H}_f\|_\infty, \|\mathbf{H}_{f,x}\|_\infty \leq (2n \lceil \log q \rceil)^d$ *and* $(\vec{\mathbf{A}} - \mathbf{x} \otimes \mathbf{G}) \cdot \mathbf{H}_{f,\mathbf{x}} = \vec{\mathbf{A}} \cdot \mathbf{H}_f - f(\mathbf{x})\mathbf{G}$ (mod q).

3   Definition of Constrained Signatures (CS)

We now define constrained signatures, along with a number of security notions that will be used throughout this work. The definitions are presented in the key-policy flavor. See Appendix A for definitions in the message-policy flavor. Lastly we define key delegation in the context of constrained signatures.

Definition 3 ((Key-Policy) Constrained Signatures). *Let* $\mathcal{X}$ *be an attribute space and* $\mathcal{F}$ *be a function space of the form* $f \in \mathcal{F} \implies f : \mathcal{X}' \to \{0,1\}$ *where* $\mathcal{X}' \subseteq \mathcal{X}$. *A constrained signatures scheme for* $(\mathcal{X}, \mathcal{F})$ *is a tuple of algorithms:*

- Setup(1^λ) → (msk, vk) *takes as input the security parameter* λ *and possibly a description of* $(\mathcal{X}, \mathcal{F})$, *and outputs a master signing key* msk *and a public verification key* vk.
- Keygen(f, msk) → sk$_f$ *takes as input a function* $f \in \mathcal{F}$ *and the master signing key* msk, *and outputs a signing key* sk$_f$.
- Sign(x, sk$_f$) → σ_x *takes as input an attribute* $x \in \mathcal{X}$ *and a signing key* sk$_f$, *and outputs a signature* σ_x.
- Ver$_{\mathsf{vk}}$(x, σ_x) → {*accept*, *reject*} *takes as input an attribute* $x \in \mathcal{X}$ *and a signature* σ_x, *and either accepts or rejects.*

Correctness. The scheme is correct if for all $x \in \mathcal{X}$ *and* $f \in \mathcal{F}$ *for which* $f(x) = 0$, *it holds that with all but negligible probability* Ver$_{\mathsf{vk}}$(x, σ_x) = *accept, where* (msk, vk) ← Setup(1^λ) *and* σ_x = Sign(x, Keygen(f, msk)).

Privacy. Privacy bounds the information revealed by a signature about the signing key that was used to produce it. We define two notions of privacy. In constraint-hiding privacy, a signature should not reveal the signing key's functionality f, *however it might be possible to retrieve other information such as whether two signatures were produced using the same key. In key-hiding privacy, a signature should not reveal any information at all about the signing key.*

Definition 4 (Privacy of (Key-Policy) Constrained Signatures). *The scheme is* constraint-hiding *if any* PPT *adversary* $\mathcal{A}$ *has no more than negligible advantage in the following game.*

1. *The challenger computes and outputs* $(\mathsf{msk}, \mathsf{vk}) \leftarrow \mathsf{Setup}(1^\lambda)$.
2. $\mathcal{A}$ *sends* (f_0, f_1, x) *such that* $f_0(x) = f_1(x) = 0$.
3. *The challenger computes* $\mathsf{sk}_{f_0} = \mathsf{Keygen}(f_0, \mathsf{msk})$ *and* $\mathsf{sk}_{f_1} = \mathsf{Keygen}(f_1, \mathsf{msk})$. *It then samples* $b \xleftarrow{\$} \{0, 1\}$ *and computes* $\sigma_{x,b} \leftarrow \mathsf{Sign}(x, \mathsf{sk}_{f_b})$. *It sends* $\sigma_{x,b}$ *to* $\mathcal{A}$.
4. $\mathcal{A}$ *outputs* $b' \in \{0, 1\}$ *and wins if and only if* $b' = b$.

The scheme is key-hiding *if any* PPT *adversary* $\mathcal{A}$ *has no more than negligible advantage in the above game, where in step 3 the challenger sends* $(\mathsf{sk}_{f_0}, \mathsf{sk}_{f_1}, \sigma_{x,b})$ *to* $\mathcal{A}$.

Unforgeability. We consider *full unforgeability* vs. *message-selective unforgeability*. These notions are caputred by a security game between a challenger and an adversary. In the full unforgeability game, the adversary can adaptively make queries of three types: (1) query for constrained keys, (2) query for signatures under a specified constraint, and (3) query for signatures that are generated with an existing key from a type (2) query. In order to win the adversary has to forge a signature for an attribute x^* that is not authorized by any of the queried keys, and does not appear in any of the type (2) and (3) signature queries. In the message-selective game, the adversary has to announce x^* before seeing the verification key. The construction in Sect. 6 is message-selective unforgeable.

Definition 5 (Unforgeability of (Key-Policy) Constrained Signatures). *The scheme is* fully unforgeable *if every PPTM adversary* $\mathcal{A}$ *has no more than negligible advantage in the following game:*

1. *The challenger computes* $(\mathsf{msk}, \mathsf{vk}) \leftarrow \mathsf{Setup}(1^\lambda)$ *and sends* vk *to* $\mathcal{A}$.
2. $\mathcal{A}$ *makes queries of three types:*
   - Key Queries. $\mathcal{A}$ *sends* $f \in \mathcal{F}$ *and gets back* $\mathsf{sk}_f \leftarrow \mathsf{Keygen}(f, \mathsf{msk})$.
   - Signature Queries. $\mathcal{A}$ *sends* $(f, x) \in \mathcal{F} \times \mathcal{X}$ *such that* $f(x) = 0$. *The challenger computes* $\mathsf{sk}_f \leftarrow \mathsf{Keygen}(f, \mathsf{msk})$ *and sends back* $\sigma_x \leftarrow \mathsf{Sign}(x, \mathsf{sk}_f)$.
   - Repeated Signature Queries. $\mathcal{A}$ *sends* $i \in \mathbb{N}$ *and* $x \in \mathcal{X}$. *If there were less than* i *signature queries at this point of the game, the challenger returns* $\perp$. *Otherwise, let* f *denote the constraint that was sent at the* i*th signature query and let* sk_f *denote the key that was generated by the challenger when answering this query. If* $f(x) \neq 0$, *the challenger returns* $\perp$. *Otherwise it returns* $\sigma_x \leftarrow \mathsf{Sign}(x, \mathsf{sk}_f)$.
3. $\mathcal{A}$ *wins if it manages to output* (x^*, σ_{x^*}) *such that* $\mathsf{Ver}_{\mathsf{vk}}(x^*, \sigma_{x^*}) = accept$ *and the following restrictions hold:*
   - *For any key queried by* $\mathcal{A}$ *respective to* $f \in \mathcal{F}$, *it holds that* $f(x^*) = 1$.
   - *For any signature* σ_x *queried by* $\mathcal{A}$, *it holds that* $x \neq x^*$.

The scheme is message-selective unforgeable *if any PPT* $\mathcal{A}$ *that announces* x^* *before seeing* vk *has no more than negligible advantage in the game.*

We also define a relaxed notion, *single-key-selective unforgeability*, which is useful as a building block towards full unforgeability, as shown in Sect. 4. In this security game, the adversary is restricted to a single key query and no signatures queries. It also has to announce the queried constraint at the beginning of the game.

Definition 6 (Single-Key-Selective Unforgeability of (Key-Policy) Constrained Signatures). *The scheme is* single-key-selective *unforgeable if every PPTM adversary $\mathcal{A}$ has no more than negligible advantage in the following game:*

1. *$\mathcal{A}$ sends $f^* \in \mathcal{F}$ to the challenger.*
2. *The challenger computes $(\mathsf{msk}, \mathsf{vk}) \leftarrow \mathsf{Setup}(1^\lambda)$ and $\mathsf{sk}_{f^*} \leftarrow \mathsf{Keygen}(f^*, \mathsf{msk})$, and sends $(\mathsf{vk}, \mathsf{sk}_{f^*})$ to $\mathcal{A}$.*
3. *$\mathcal{A}$ wins if it manages to output $(x^*, \sigma_{(x^*)})$ such that $\mathsf{Ver}_{\mathsf{vk}}(x^*, \sigma_{x^*}) = accept$ and $f^*(x^*) = 1$.*

3.1 Key Delegation

Given a key sk_f for a constraint $f \in \mathcal{F}$, it might be useful to generate a key with limited capabilities, i.e. a key $\mathsf{sk}_{(f,g)}$ for a constraint that requires $f(x) = 0$ and $g(x) = 0$ for some function $g \in \mathcal{F}$. In this setting, any attribute $x \in \mathcal{X}$ that can be signed by $\mathsf{sk}_{(f,g)}$ can also be signed by sk_f, but the other direction is not guaranteed since it might be the case that $f(x) = 0$ but $g(x) = 1$. Key delegation can therefore be though of as restricting the signing permissions of a given key.

We now give a formal definition of the key delegation algorithm, along with definitions for correctness, privacy and unforgeability. Note that it captures multiple levels of delegation. The unforgeability game is analogouse to the non-delegatable unforgeability game, where the adversary can in addition query for delegated keys.

Definition 7 (Delegation of (Key-Policy) Constrained Signatures). *A constrained signatures scheme $\mathsf{CS} = (\mathsf{Setup}, \mathsf{Keygen}, \mathsf{Sign}, \mathsf{Ver})$ with attribute space $\mathcal{X}$, function space $\mathcal{F}$ and key space $\mathcal{K}$ supports delegation if there exists a PPT algorithm DelKey with the syntax*

- $\mathsf{DelKey}(\mathsf{sk}_{(f_1,\ldots,f_t)}, f_{t+1}) \rightarrow \mathsf{sk}_{(f_1,\ldots,f_{t+1})}$: *takes as input a constrained key $\mathsf{sk}_{(f_1,\ldots,f_t)} \in \mathcal{K}$ and a function $f_{t+1} \in \mathcal{F}$, and outputs a delegated constrained key $\mathsf{sk}_{(f_1,\ldots,f_{t+1})} \in \mathcal{K}$.*

such that it satisfies correctness, privacy and unforgeability as defined below. For any $t \geq 1$ and $F = (f_1, \ldots, f_t) \in \mathcal{F}^t$, write $F(x) = 0$ to denote that $f \in F \Rightarrow f(x) = 0$. Moreover, denote $\mathsf{sk}_F = \mathsf{sk}_{(f_1,\ldots,f_t)}$, where $\forall i \in [2\ldots t] : \mathsf{sk}_{(f_1,\ldots,f_i)} = \mathsf{DelKey}(\mathsf{sk}_{(f_1,\ldots,f_{i-1})}, f_i)$ and $\mathsf{sk}_{f_1} = \mathsf{Keygen}(f_1, \mathsf{msk})$ for some $(\mathsf{msk}, \mathsf{vk}) \leftarrow \mathsf{Setup}(1^\lambda)$ which is clear from the context.

Correctness. Consider $(\mathsf{msk}, \mathsf{vk}) \leftarrow \mathsf{Setup}(1^\lambda)$. The scheme is correct for a function family $\mathcal{F}$ and attribute space $\mathcal{X}$, if for all $t \in \mathbb{N}$, $(x, F) \in \mathcal{X} \times \mathcal{F}^t$ for which

$F(x) = 0$, *it holds with all but negligible probability that* $\mathsf{Ver}_{\mathsf{vk}}(x, \mathsf{Sign}(x, \mathsf{sk}_F)) = accept$.

Privacy. *The scheme is* constraint-hiding *if any* PPT *adversary* $\mathcal{A}$ *has no more than negligible advantage in the following game.*

1. *The challenger computes and outputs* $(\mathsf{msk}, \mathsf{vk}) \leftarrow \mathsf{Setup}(1^\lambda)$.
2. $\mathcal{A}$ *sends* (t, F_0, F_1, x), *where* $\forall b \in \{0, 1\} : F_b = (f_1^b, \ldots, f_t^b)$ *and* $F_b(x) = 0$.
3. *The challenger computes* sk_{F_0} *and* sk_{F_1}. *It then samples* $b \xleftarrow{\$} \{0, 1\}$ *and computes* $\sigma_{x,b} \leftarrow \mathsf{Sign}(x, \mathsf{sk}_{F_b})$. *It sends* $\sigma_{x,b}$ *to* $\mathcal{A}$.
4. $\mathcal{A}$ *outputs* $b' \in \{0, 1\}$ *and wins if and only if* $b' = b$.

The scheme is key-hiding *if any* PPT *adversary* $\mathcal{A}$ *has no more than negligible advantage in the above game, where in step 3 the challenger sends* $(\mathsf{sk}_{F_0}, \mathsf{sk}_{F_1}, \sigma_{x,b})$ *to* $\mathcal{A}$.

Full Unforgeability. *The scheme is* fully unforgeable *if every PPTM adversary* $\mathcal{A}$ *has no more than negligible advantage in the following game:*

1. *The challenger computes* $(\mathsf{msk}, \mathsf{vk}) \leftarrow \mathsf{Setup}(1^\lambda)$ *and sends* vk *to* $\mathcal{A}$.
2. $\mathcal{A}$ *makes queries of three types:*
   - Key Queries. $\mathcal{A}$ *sends* $t \in \mathbb{N}$, $F \in \mathcal{F}^t$ *and gets back* sk_F.
   - Signature Queries. $\mathcal{A}$ *sends* $t \in \mathbb{N}$, $(F, x) \in \mathcal{F}^t \times \mathcal{X}$ *such that* $F(x) = 0$. *The challenger computes* sk_F *as described above and returns* $\sigma_x \leftarrow \mathsf{Sign}(x, \mathsf{sk}_F)$.
   - Repeated Signature Queries. $\mathcal{A}$ *sends* $i \in \mathbb{N}$ *and* $x \in \mathcal{X}$. *If there were less than* i *signature queries at this point of the game, the challenger returns* $\bot$. *Otherwise, let* F *denote the set of constraints that was sent at the* ith *signature query and let* sk_F *denote the key that was generated by the challenger when answering this query. If* $\exists f \in F$ *s.t.* $f(x) \neq 0$, *the challenger returns* $\bot$. *Otherwise it returns* $\sigma_x \leftarrow \mathsf{Sign}(x, \mathsf{sk}_f)$.
3. $\mathcal{A}$ *wins if it manages to output* (x^*, σ_{x^*}) *such that* $\mathsf{Ver}_{\mathsf{vk}}(x^*, \sigma_{x^*}) = accept$ *and the following restrictions hold:*
   - *For any key queried by* $\mathcal{A}$ *respective to* $t \in \mathbb{N}$, $F \in \mathcal{F}^t$, *it holds that* $\exists f \in F$ *such that* $f(x^*) = 1$.
   - *For any signature* σ_x *queried by* $\mathcal{A}$, *it holds that* $x \neq x^*$.

Message-Selective Unforgeability. *The scheme maintains* message-selective unforgeability *if any PPT* $\mathcal{A}$ *that announces* x^* *before seeing* vk *has no more than negligible advantage in the game.*

Single-Key-Selective Unforgeability. *The scheme is* single-key-selective unforgeable *if every PPTM adversary* $\mathcal{A}$ *has no more than negligible advantage in the following game:*

1. $\mathcal{A}$ *sends* $t \in \mathbb{N}, F \in \mathcal{F}^t$ *to the challenger.*
2. *The challenger computes* $(\mathsf{msk}, \mathsf{vk}) \leftarrow \mathsf{Setup}(1^\lambda)$ *and* sk_F, *and sends* $(\mathsf{vk}, \mathsf{sk}_F)$ *to* $\mathcal{A}$.
3. $\mathcal{A}$ *wins if it manages to output* (x^*, σ_{x^*}) *such that* $\mathsf{Ver}_{\mathsf{vk}}(x^*, \sigma_{x^*}) = accept$ *and* $\exists f \in F$ *such that* $f(x^*) = 1$.

4 From Single-Key-Selective Unforgeability to Full Unforgeability

We show how any standard digital signatures scheme can be used to amplify the security guarantee of a (key-policy) CS scheme from *single-key-selective* to *full* unforgeability. This comes with a partial loss in key privacy – while the underlying scheme might be either key-hiding or solely constraint-hiding, the amplified scheme reveals key-specific information as part of the signature, and thus it is only constraint-hiding.

Let $\mathsf{CS} = (\mathsf{Setup}', \mathsf{Keygen}', \mathsf{Sign}', \mathsf{Ver}')$ be a single-key selectively unforgeable constraint-hiding constrained signature scheme with attribute space $\mathcal{X}'$, constraint space $\mathcal{F}'$ and verification-key space $\mathcal{VK}'$. Let $\mathsf{S} = (\mathsf{S.Setup}, \mathsf{S.Sign}, \mathsf{S.Ver})$ be a standard signature scheme with verification-key space $\mathcal{VK}$ and message space $\mathcal{X}$ such that $\mathcal{VK}' \times \mathcal{VK} \subseteq \mathcal{X}$. The construction is as follows.

- $\mathsf{Setup}(1^\lambda)$. Compute $(\mathsf{S.vk}, \mathsf{S.sk}) \leftarrow \mathsf{S.Setup}(1^\lambda)$. Output $\mathsf{vk} = \mathsf{S.vk}$ and $\mathsf{msk} = \mathsf{S.sk}$.
- $\mathsf{Keygen}(f, \mathsf{msk})$. Generate $(\mathsf{vk}', \mathsf{msk}') \leftarrow \mathsf{Setup}'(1^\lambda)$. Compute $k'_f \leftarrow \mathsf{Keygen}'(\mathsf{msk}', f)$. Generate $(\mathsf{vk}'', \mathsf{sk}'') \leftarrow \mathsf{S.Setup}(1^\lambda)$. Sign $(\mathsf{vk}', \mathsf{vk}'')$ using msk: $\sigma_{(\mathsf{vk}', \mathsf{vk}'')} \leftarrow \mathsf{S.Sign}(\mathsf{S.sk}, (\mathsf{vk}', \mathsf{vk}''))$. Output $k_f = (\mathsf{vk}', k'_f, \mathsf{vk}'', \mathsf{sk}'', \sigma_{(\mathsf{vk}', \mathsf{vk}'')})$.
- $\mathsf{Sign}(x, k_f)$. Compute $\sigma'_x = \mathsf{Sign}'(x, k'_f)$ and $\sigma''_x = \mathsf{S.Sign}(\mathsf{sk}'', x)$. Output $\sigma_x = (\mathsf{vk}', \sigma'_x, \mathsf{vk}'', \sigma''_x, \sigma_{(\mathsf{vk}', \mathsf{vk}'')})$.
- $\mathsf{Ver}_{\mathsf{vk}}(x, \sigma_x)$.
  Accept only if $\mathsf{S.Ver}(\sigma_{(\mathsf{vk}', \mathsf{vk}'')}, (\mathsf{vk}', \mathsf{vk}'')) = accept$, $\mathsf{Ver}'_{\mathsf{vk}'}(x, \sigma'_x) = accept$ and $\mathsf{S.Ver}_{\mathsf{vk}''}(x, \sigma''_x) = accept$.

Lemma 1 (Correctness). *The scheme is correct for* $(\mathcal{F}', \mathcal{X}')$.

Proof. Fix $x \in \mathcal{X}'$ and $f \in \mathcal{F}'$ such that $f(x) = 0$, and consider $(\mathsf{msk}, \mathsf{vk}) \leftarrow \mathsf{Setup}(1^\lambda)$ and $\sigma_x = \mathsf{Sign}(x, \mathsf{Keygen}(f, \mathsf{msk}))$. Denote $\sigma_x = (\mathsf{vk}', \sigma'_x, \mathsf{vk}'', \sigma''_x, \sigma_{(\mathsf{vk}', \mathsf{vk}'')})$, then by Sign and Keygen it holds that $\sigma'_x = \mathsf{Sign}'(x, k'_f) = \mathsf{Sign}'(x, \mathsf{Keygen}'(\mathsf{msk}', f))$, and since $f(x) = 0$ it holds that $\mathsf{Ver}'_{\mathsf{vk}'}(\sigma'_x, x) = accept$ by the correctness of CS'. Moreover, $\mathsf{S.Ver}_{\mathsf{vk}''}(x, \sigma''_x) = \mathsf{S.Ver}_{\mathsf{vk}''}(x, \mathsf{S.Sign}(\mathsf{sk}'', x) = accept$ and $\mathsf{S.Ver}(\sigma_{(\mathsf{vk}', \mathsf{vk}'')}, (\mathsf{vk}', \mathsf{vk}'')) = \mathsf{S.Ver}(\mathsf{S.Sign}(\mathsf{S.sk}, (\mathsf{vk}', \mathsf{vk}'')), (\mathsf{vk}', \mathsf{vk}'')) = accept$ by the correctness of S. Therefore, $\mathsf{Ver}_{\mathsf{vk}}(x, m, \sigma_x)$ accepts.

Lemma 2 (Privacy). *The scheme is constraint-hiding for* $(\mathcal{F}', \mathcal{X}')$.

Proof. Assume towards contradiction an adversary $\mathcal{A}$ that wins the constraint-hiding privacy game with some significant probability, and use it to break the constraint-hiding privacy of CS as follows:

1. Receive $(\mathsf{vk}', \mathsf{msk}') \leftarrow \mathsf{Setup}'(1^\lambda)$ from the CS challenger.
2. Compute $(\mathsf{S.vk}, \mathsf{S.sk}) \leftarrow \mathsf{S.Setup}(1^\lambda)$ and send $(\mathsf{msk} = \mathsf{S.sk}, \mathsf{vk} = \mathsf{S.vk})$ to $\mathcal{A}$.
3. $\mathcal{A}$ returns (f_0, f_1, x) such that $f_0(x) = f_1(x) = 0$. Forward (f_0, f_1, x) to the CS challenger.

4. The CS challenger samples $b \xleftarrow{\$} \{0,1\}$ and returns $\sigma'_{x,b}$. Now generate $(\mathsf{vk}'', \mathsf{sk}'') \leftarrow \mathsf{S.Setup}(1^\lambda)$, sign $(\mathsf{vk}', \mathsf{vk}'')$ with the standard signature scheme: $\sigma_{(\mathsf{vk}', \mathsf{vk}'')} \leftarrow \mathsf{S.Sign}(\mathsf{S.sk}, (\mathsf{vk}', \mathsf{vk}''))$, sign x with the standard signature scheme: $\sigma''_x \leftarrow \mathsf{S.Sign}(\mathsf{sk}'', x)$ and send to $\mathcal{A}$ the signature $\sigma_{x,b} = (\mathsf{vk}', \sigma'_{x,b}, \mathsf{vk}'', \sigma''_x, \sigma_{(\mathsf{vk}', \mathsf{vk}'')})$.
5. Get b' from $\mathcal{A}$ and forward it to the CS challenger. Clearly, any advantage of $\mathcal{A}$ induces an advantage of the reduction.

Lemma 3 (Unforgeability). *The scheme is fully unforgeable for $(\mathcal{F}', \mathcal{X}')$.*

Proof. Assume towards contradiction an adversary $\mathcal{A}$ that wins the security game. We show that it can be used to break either S or CS. Let $\mathcal{Q}_{key}, \mathcal{Q}_{sig}, \mathcal{Q}_{rep}$ be the sets of key queries, signature queries and repeated signature queries made by $\mathcal{A}$ during the security game. Recall that $\mathcal{Q}_{key} \in \mathcal{F}'$, $\mathcal{Q}_{sig} \in \mathcal{F}' \times \mathcal{X}'$ and $\mathcal{Q}_{rep} \in \mathbb{N} \times \mathcal{X}'$. In particular, each query $q_i \in \mathcal{Q}_{key} \bigcup \mathcal{Q}_{sig}$ contains an element $f_i \in \mathcal{F}$. Moreover, every response of the challenger (whether it is a key or a signature) contains a pair $(\mathsf{vk}'_i, \mathsf{vk}''_i)$ that is generated during $\mathsf{Keygen}(f_i, \mathsf{msk})$. $\mathcal{A}$ wins the game, it therefore outputs a successful forgery (x^*, σ_{x^*}), where $\sigma_{x^*} = (\mathsf{vk}'_*, \sigma'_{x^*}, \mathsf{vk}''_*, \sigma''_{x^*}, \sigma_{(\mathsf{vk}'_*, \mathsf{vk}''_*)})$. Since $\mathsf{Ver}_{\mathsf{vk}}(x^*, \sigma_{(x^*, m^*)}) = accept$, it holds that $\mathsf{S.Ver}(\sigma_{\mathsf{vk}'_*}, \mathsf{vk}'_*)$ accepts, $\mathsf{Ver}'_{\mathsf{vk}'_*}(x^*, \sigma'_{x^*})$ accepts and $\mathsf{S.Ver}_{\mathsf{vk}''}(x^*, \sigma''_{x^*})$ accepts. Consider three cases:

- If $\exists q_i \in \mathcal{Q}_{key}$ such that $(\mathsf{vk}'_i, \mathsf{vk}''_i) = (\mathsf{vk}'_*, \mathsf{vk}''_*)$, then (x^*, σ'_{x^*}) is a valid forgery to the CS instance that was initialized during $\mathsf{Keygen}(f_i, \mathsf{msk})$. Note that since $q_i \in \mathcal{Q}_{key}$, $f_i(x^*) = 1$. We show a reduction from the selective-single-key security game of CS to this game:
  1. Initialize $(\mathsf{S.vk}, \mathsf{S.sk}) \leftarrow \mathsf{S.Setup}(1^\lambda)$ as in the real scheme and send $\mathsf{S.vk}$ to $\mathcal{A}$.
  2. Queries phase:
     - Answer all queries except of the ith as in the real unforgeability game.
     - Upon receiving form $\mathcal{A}$ the query $q_i \in \mathcal{Q}_{key}$, send f_i to the ith CS challenger and get back $(\mathsf{vk}'_i, k'_{f_i})$. Generate $(\mathsf{vk}''_i, \mathsf{sk}''_i) \leftarrow \mathsf{S.Setup}(1^\lambda)$, sign $(\mathsf{vk}'_i, \mathsf{vk}''_i)$ with the standard scheme: $\sigma_{(\mathsf{vk}'_i, \mathsf{vk}''_i)} \leftarrow \mathsf{S.Sign}(\mathsf{S.sk}, (\mathsf{vk}'_i, \mathsf{vk}''_i))$. Send to $\mathcal{A}$ the key $k_{f_i} = (\mathsf{vk}'_i, k'_{f_i}, \mathsf{vk}''_i, \mathsf{sk}''_i, \sigma_{(\mathsf{vk}'_i, \mathsf{vk}''_i)})$.
  3. When $\mathcal{A}$ sends the forgery (x^*, σ_{x^*}), send (x^*, σ'_{x^*}) to the ith CS challenger to win the selective-single-key game.
- If $\exists q_i \in \mathcal{Q}_{sig}$ such that $(\mathsf{vk}'_i, \mathsf{vk}''_i) = (\mathsf{vk}'_*, \mathsf{vk}''_*)$, then (x^*, σ''_{x^*}) is a valid forgery to the S instance that was initialized during $\mathsf{Keygen}(f_i, \mathsf{msk})$. Note that $\forall q_i \in \mathcal{Q}_{sig}$, where $q_i = (f_i, x_i)$, it holds that $x_i \neq x^*$. We show a reduction from the security game of $\mathcal{S}$ to this game:
  1. Initialize $(\mathsf{S.vk}, \mathsf{S.sk}) \leftarrow \mathsf{S.Setup}(1^\lambda)$ as in the real scheme and send $\mathsf{S.vk}$ to $\mathcal{A}$.
  2. Queries phase:
     - Answer all queries up to q_i as in the real unforgeability game.

- Upon receiving form $\mathcal{A}$ the query $q_i \in \mathcal{Q}_{sig}$, instantiate a game against the ith S challenger and get vk_i''. Query a signature for x_i and get back σ_{x_i}''. Generate $(\mathsf{vk}_i', \mathsf{msk}_i') \leftarrow \mathsf{Setup}'(1^\lambda)$ and $k_{f_i}' \leftarrow \mathsf{Keygen}'(\mathsf{msk}_i', f_i)$, sign $\sigma_{x_i}' \leftarrow \mathsf{Sign}'(x_i, k_{f_i}')$. Sign $(\mathsf{vk}_i', \mathsf{vk}_i'')$ with the standard signature scheme: $\sigma_{(\mathsf{vk}_i', \mathsf{vk}_i'')} \leftarrow \mathsf{S.Sign}(\mathsf{S.sk}, (\mathsf{vk}_i', \mathsf{vk}_i''))$. Send $\mathcal{A}$ the signature $\sigma_{x_i} = (\mathsf{vk}_i', \sigma_{x_i}', \mathsf{vk}_i'', \sigma_{x_i}'', \sigma_{(\mathsf{vk}_i', \mathsf{vk}_i'')})$.
- Answer all queries as in the real game, except of repeated signature queries that reference q_i. For these, do as described above with the same $\mathsf{vk}_i', \mathsf{vk}_i'', \sigma_{(\mathsf{vk}_i', \mathsf{vk}_i'')}, k_{f_i}'$.
  3. When $\mathcal{A}$ sends the forgery (x^*, σ_{x^*}), send (x^*, σ_{x^*}'') to the ith S challenger to win the game.
- Otherwise $\forall q_i \in \mathcal{Q}_{key} \bigcup \mathcal{Q}_{sig}$ $(\mathsf{vk}_i', \mathsf{vk}_i'') \neq (\mathsf{vk}_*', \mathsf{vk}_*'')$, and thus $(\sigma_{(\mathsf{vk}_*', \mathsf{vk}_*'')}, (\mathsf{vk}_*', \mathsf{vk}_*''))$ is a valid forgery to S. We show a reduction from the security game of S to this game:
  1. Receive S.vk from the S challenger and send it to $\mathcal{A}$.
  2. Answer queries from $\mathcal{A}$ as in the real game, except the way $\sigma_{(\mathsf{vk}_i', \mathsf{vk}_i'')}$ is computed: instead of signing $(\mathsf{vk}_i', \mathsf{vk}_i'')$ with $\mathsf{msk} = \mathsf{S.sk}$ (which we don't have), query the S challenger and get $\sigma_{(\mathsf{vk}_i', \mathsf{vk}_i'')}$.
  3. When $\mathcal{A}$ sends the forgery (x^*, σ_{x^*}), send $(\sigma_{(\mathsf{vk}_*', \mathsf{vk}_*'')}, (\mathsf{vk}_*', \mathsf{vk}_*''))$ to the S challenger to win the game.

4.1 Key Delegation

If the underlying scheme CS supports delegation, i.e. there exists an algorithm $\mathsf{DelKey}'(k_{(f_1,\ldots,f_t)}', f_{t+1}) \rightarrow k_{(f_1,\ldots,f_t,f_{t+1})}'$ and CS is correct, constraint-hiding and single-key-selectively unforgeable as per Definition 7, then also the amplified construction is. The amplified delegation algorithm delegates the key of CS. It also initializes a new instance of S with each delegation, which is used either to sign x, when the key is used in Sign, or to sign the verification keys of every two neighboring delegation levels, when the key is delegated.

- $\mathsf{DelKey}(\mathsf{sk}_{(f_1,\ldots,f_t)}, f_{t+1})$ takes a key $\mathsf{sk}_{(f_1,\ldots,f_t)} = (\mathsf{vk}', k_{(f_1,\ldots,f_t)}', \{\mathsf{vk}_i''\}_{i\in[t]}, \mathsf{sk}_t''; \sigma_{(\mathsf{vk}', \mathsf{vk}_1'')}, \{\sigma_{(\mathsf{vk}_i'', \mathsf{vk}_{i+1}'')}\}_{i\in[t-1]})$ and a constraint $f_{t+1} \in \mathcal{F}'$. It computes $k_{(f_1,\ldots,f_t,f_{t+1})}' \leftarrow \mathsf{DelKey}'(k_{(f_1,\ldots,f_t)}', f_{t+1})$. It then generates $(\mathsf{sk}_{t+1}'', \mathsf{vk}_{t+1}'') \leftarrow \mathsf{S.Setup}(1^\lambda)$, signs $\sigma_{(\mathsf{vk}_t'', \mathsf{vk}_{t+1}'')} \leftarrow \mathsf{S.Sign}(\mathsf{sk}_t'', (\mathsf{vk}_t'', \mathsf{vk}_{t+1}''))$ and outputs $\mathsf{sk}_{(f_1,\ldots,f_t,f_{t+1})} = (\mathsf{vk}', k_{(f_1,\ldots,f_{t+1})}', \{\mathsf{vk}_i''\}_{i\in[t+1]}, \mathsf{sk}_{t+1}'', \sigma_{(\mathsf{vk}', \mathsf{vk}_1'')}, \{\sigma_{(\mathsf{vk}_i'', \mathsf{vk}_{i+1}'')}\}_{i\in[t]})$.
- $\mathsf{Sign}(x, \mathsf{sk}_{(f_1,\ldots,f_t)})$ takes a key $\mathsf{sk}_{(f_1,\ldots,f_t)} = (\mathsf{vk}', k_{(f_1,\ldots,f_t)}', \{\mathsf{vk}_i''\}_{i\in[t]}, \mathsf{sk}_t'', \sigma_{(\mathsf{vk}', \mathsf{vk}_1'')}, \{\sigma_{(\mathsf{vk}_i'', \mathsf{vk}_{i+1}'')}\}_{i\in[t-1]})$ and an attribute $x \in \mathcal{X}'$. It computes $\sigma_x' \leftarrow \mathsf{Sign}'(x, k_{(f_1,\ldots,f_t)}')$ and $\sigma_x'' \leftarrow \mathsf{S.Sign}(\mathsf{sk}_t'', x)$. It outputs $\sigma_x = (\mathsf{vk}', \sigma_x', \{\mathsf{vk}_i''\}_{i\in[t]}, \sigma_x'', \sigma_{(\mathsf{vk}', \mathsf{vk}_1'')}, \{\sigma_{(\mathsf{vk}_i'', \mathsf{vk}_{i+1}'')}\}_{i\in[t-1]})$.
- $\mathsf{Ver}_{\mathsf{vk}}(x, \sigma_x)$ accepts only when all of the following conditions hold: $\mathsf{Ver}_{\mathsf{vk}'}'(x, \sigma_x')$ accepts; $\mathsf{S.Ver}_{\mathsf{S.vk}}(\sigma_{(\mathsf{vk}', \mathsf{vk}_1'')}, (\mathsf{vk}', \mathsf{vk}_1''))$ accepts; $\forall i \in [t-1]$, $\mathsf{S.Ver}_{\mathsf{vk}_i''}(\sigma_{(\mathsf{vk}_i'', \mathsf{vk}_{i+1}'')}, (\mathsf{vk}_i'', \mathsf{vk}_{i+1}''))$ accepts; $\mathsf{S.Ver}_{\mathsf{vk}_t''}(\sigma_x'', x)$ accepts.

See Appendix B for correctness, privacy and unforgeability proofs.

5 Equivalence of CS and Homomorphic Signatures

5.1 Recap on Homomorphic Signatures

Our starting point is a (single-data selectively secure) homomorphic signature scheme, which is also context hiding. We use a simplified version of the definition in [GVW15] that suffices for our needs.

Definition 8 (Single-Data Homomorphic Signature). *A single-data homomorphic signature scheme is a 4-tuple of PPT algorithms* (HS.Setup, HS.Sign, HS.Eval, HS.Ver) *with the following syntax.*

- HS.Setup$(1^\lambda) \to$ (vk, sk) *takes as input the security parameter λ and possibly a description of the data-set space $\mathcal{X}$ and the functions space $\mathcal{G}$. It outputs a verification key* vk *and a signing key* sk.
- HS.Sign(sk, x) $\to \sigma_x$ *takes as input a signing key* sk *and a data-set $x \in \mathcal{X}$, and outputs a signature σ_x.*
- HS.Eval$(g, \dot{x}, \sigma_x) \to \sigma_{(g,g(x))}$ *takes as input a data-set $x \in \mathcal{X}$ and a function $g \in \mathcal{G}$ such that $g(x)$ is defined, and a signature σ_x. It outputs a signature for the pair $(g, g(x))$: $\sigma_{(g,g(x))}$.*
- HS.Ver$_{vk}(g, y, \sigma_{(g,y)})$ *takes as input a function $g \in \mathcal{G}$, a value y and a signature $\sigma_{(g,y)}$, and either accepts or rejects.*

Correctness. The scheme is correct for a function family $\mathcal{G}$ and data-set space $\mathcal{X}$ if for all $x \in \mathcal{X}$ and $g \in \mathcal{G}$ such that $g(x)$ is defined, it holds that HS.Ver$_{vk}(g, g(x), \sigma_{(g,g(x))}) = accept$, *where* $\sigma_{(g,g(x))} = $ HS.Eval(g, x, σ_x), $\sigma_x = $ HS.Sign(sk, x) *and* (vk, sk) $\gets$ HS.Setup(1^λ).

Single-Data Selective Unforgeability. Fix $\mathcal{X}, \mathcal{G}$ and consider the following game between an adversary $\mathcal{A}$ and a challenger:

- *$\mathcal{A}$ sends $x \in \mathcal{X}$ to the challenger.*
- *The challenger computes* (sk, vk) $\gets$ HS.Setup(1^λ) *and* $\sigma_x \gets$ HS.Sign$_{vk}$(sk, x). *It sends to $\mathcal{A}$ the values* (vk, σ_x).
- *$\mathcal{A}$ outputs $(g, y, \sigma_{(g,y)})$. It wins if $g \in \mathcal{G}$,* HS.Ver$_{vk}(g, y, \sigma_{(g,y)}) = accept$ *and $y \neq g(x)$.*

The scheme is secure for $\mathcal{X}, \mathcal{G}$ if any PPT $\mathcal{A}$ has no more than negligible advantage in this game.

Context Hiding. The scheme is context hiding for $\mathcal{X}, \mathcal{G}$ if any PPT *adversary $\mathcal{A}$ has no more than negligible advantage in the following game.*

1. *The challenger computes and outputs* (sk, vk) $\gets$ HS.Setup(1^λ).
2. *$\mathcal{A}$ sends $(g, x_0, x_1) \in \mathcal{G} \times \mathcal{X} \times \mathcal{X}$ such that $g(x_0) = g(x_1)$. Denote this value by y.*
3. *The challenger computes $\sigma_{x_0} \gets$* HS.Sign(sk, x_0) *and $\sigma_{x_1} \gets$* HS.Sign(sk, x_1). *It then samples $b \xleftarrow{\$} \{0, 1\}$ and computes $\sigma_{(g,y)} \gets$* HS.Eval(g, x_b, σ_{x_b}). *It sends $(\sigma_{x_0}, \sigma_{x_1}, \sigma_{(g,y)})$ to $\mathcal{A}$.*

4. $\mathcal{A}$ outputs $b' \in \{0,1\}$ and wins if and only if $b' = b$.

Note that the correctness requirement also captures the validity of a non-evaluated signature: a signature σ_x for a data-set $x \in \mathcal{X}$ can be verified bit-by-bit using the functions $\{g_i\}_{i \in [\|x\|]}$, where $g_i(x)$ outputs the ith bit of x. The context hiding property requires that an evaluated signature will not reveal anything about the original (pre-evaluated) signature, other than the evaluation result along with a signature for it.

5.2 Constrained Signatures from Homomorphic Signatures

In this section we construct a (message-policy) CS scheme from context-hiding homomorphic signatures. We assume that the underlying HS scheme is context-hiding and single data-set unforgeable, and show that the resulting CS scheme is single-key-selective unforgeable and key-hiding. Combined with the security amplification from Sect. 4 (which downgrades the key privacy), this results in a scheme that is fully unforgeable and attribute-hiding.

Let HS $=$ (Setup, Sign, Eval, Ver) be a homomorphic signature scheme with data-space $\mathcal{X}$ and functions space $\mathcal{F}$. We construct CS $=$ (Setup, Keygen, Sign, Ver) for $(\mathcal{X}, \mathcal{F})$.

- CS.Setup(1^λ). Initialize the HS scheme (HS.sk, HS.vk) $\leftarrow$ HS.Setup(1^λ) and output vk $=$ HS.vk and msk $=$ HS.sk.
- CS.Keygen(x, msk). Sign x using HS: HS.$\sigma_x \leftarrow$ HS.Sign(HS.sk, x). Output sk$_x =$ HS.σ_x.
- CS.Sign(f, sk$_x$). Use σ_x to homomorphically compute a context-hiding signature for $y = f(x)$. That is, compute and output $\sigma_f =$ HS.$\sigma_{(f, f(x))} \leftarrow$ HS.Eval(f, x, σ_x).
- CS.Ver$_{vk}$(f, σ_f). Accept if and only if HS.Ver$_{vk}$($f, 0, \sigma_f$) accepts.

Lemma 4 (Correctness). *The scheme is correct for* $(\mathcal{F}, \mathcal{X})$.

Proof. Fix $(x, f) \in \mathcal{X} \times \mathcal{F}$ such that $f(x) = 0$. Consider (msk, vk) $\leftarrow$ CS.Setup(1^λ), sk$_x \leftarrow$ CS.Keygen(x, msk) and $\sigma_f =$ CS.Sign(f, sk$_x$). Then it holds that $\sigma_f \leftarrow$ HS.Eval($f, x,$ HS.Sign(HS.sk, x)). We need to show that Ver$_{vk}$(f, σ_f) $=$ *accept*, i.e. that HS.Ver$_{vk}$($f, 0,$ HS.$\sigma_{(f, f(x))}$) accepts. Indeed, $f(x) = 0$ by assumption, thus the result follows by the correctness of HS.

Lemma 5 (Privacy). *The scheme is key-hiding for* $(\mathcal{F}, \mathcal{X})$.

Proof. Assume towards contradiction an adversary $\mathcal{A}_c$ that wins the privacy game with noticeable advantage and use it to break the context hiding property of the underlying HS scheme as follows:

1. Receive (HS.sk, HS.vk) $\leftarrow$ HS.Setup(1^λ) from the HS challenger and forward it to $\mathcal{A}_c$ as (msk, vk).
2. Receive from $\mathcal{A}_c$ a tuple (x_0, x_1, f) such that $f(x_0) = f(x_1) = 0$. Forward (x_0, x_1, f) to the HS challenger.

3. Receive from the HS challenger the challenge $(\mathsf{HS}.\sigma_{x_0}, \mathsf{HS}.\sigma_{x_1}, \mathsf{HS}.\sigma_{(f,0)})$ and forward it to $\mathcal{A}_c$ as $(\mathsf{sk}_{x_0}, \mathsf{sk}_{x_1}, \sigma_f)$.
4. Get b' from $\mathcal{A}_c$ and forward it to the HS challenger. Clearly, any advantage of $\mathcal{A}_c$ induces an advantage of the reduction.

Lemma 6 (Unforgeability). *The scheme is single-key-selectively unforgeable for* $(\mathcal{F}, \mathcal{X})$.

Proof. Consider the CS single-key selective security game against an adversary $\mathcal{A}_c$. Let $x \in \mathcal{X}$ be the attribute sent by $\mathcal{A}_c$, and assume towards contradiction that it wins the game. Then $\mathcal{A}_c$ outputs (f, σ_f) such that $\mathsf{CS}.\mathsf{Ver}_{\mathsf{vk}}(f, \sigma_f) = accept$ and $f(x) \neq 0$. Such adversary can be used to break the unforgeability of HS:

1. Upon receiving x from $\mathcal{A}_c$, send it to the HS challenger.
2. The HS challenger sends back $\mathsf{HS}.\mathsf{vk}$ and $\mathsf{HS}.\sigma_x = \mathsf{HS}.\mathsf{Sign}(\mathsf{HS}.\mathsf{sk}, x)$, which is exactly $(\mathsf{vk}, \mathsf{sk}_x)$ that we have to send to $\mathcal{A}_c$.
3. $\mathcal{A}_c$ sends back (f, σ_f) such that $\mathsf{Ver}_{\mathsf{vk}}(f, \sigma_f) = accept$ and $f(x) \neq 0$. Denoting $\sigma_f = \mathsf{HS}.\sigma_{(f, f(x))}$, it means that $\mathsf{HS}.\mathsf{Ver}_{\mathsf{vk}}(f, 0, \mathsf{HS}.\sigma_{(f, f(x))}) = accept$ while $f(x) \neq 0$, therefore $\mathsf{HS}.\sigma_{(f_m, f_m(x))}$ is a successful forgery against HS.

5.3 Homomorphic Signatures from Constrained Signatures

We show how to construct a context-hiding 1-hop homomorphic signatures scheme from (message-policy) CS. We assume that the underlying CS scheme is single-key-selective unforgeable and key-hiding, and show that the resulting HS scheme is context-hiding and selectively unforgeable. As shown in [GVW15], it is possible to construct an adaptively unforgeable HS scheme from a selectively unforgeable HS scheme.

Let $\mathsf{CS} = (\mathsf{Setup}, \mathsf{Keygen}, \mathsf{Sign}, \mathsf{Ver})$ be a constrained signatures scheme with attribute space $\mathcal{X}$ and constraint space $\mathcal{F}$. We construct $\mathsf{HS} = (\mathsf{Setup}, \mathsf{Sign}, \mathsf{Eval}, \mathsf{Ver})$ for data-set space $\mathcal{X}$ and functions space $\mathcal{G} : \mathcal{X} \to \mathcal{Y}$, where the requirement is that for any $(g, y) \in \mathcal{G} \times \mathcal{Y}$, it holds that $f_{(g,y)} \in \mathcal{F}$, where $f_{(g,y)} : \mathcal{X} \to \{0, 1\}$ is a function that on input x returns 0 if and only if $g(x) = y$.

- $\mathsf{HS}.\mathsf{Setup}(1^\lambda)$. Initialize the CS scheme: compute $(\mathsf{CS}.\mathsf{msk}, \mathsf{CS}.\mathsf{vk}) \leftarrow \mathsf{CS}.\mathsf{Setup}(1^\lambda)$. Output $\mathsf{vk} = \mathsf{CS}.\mathsf{vk}$ and $\mathsf{sk} = \mathsf{CS}.\mathsf{msk}$.
- $\mathsf{HS}.\mathsf{Sign}(x, \mathsf{sk})$. Compute and output $\sigma_x = \mathsf{CS}.\mathsf{sk}_x \leftarrow \mathsf{CS}.\mathsf{Keygen}(x, \mathsf{CS}.\mathsf{msk})$.
- $\mathsf{HS}.\mathsf{Eval}(g, \sigma_x)$. Let $y = g(x)$. Define the circuit $f_{(g,y)} : \mathcal{X} \to \{0, 1\}$ that on input x returns 0 if and only if $g(x) = y$. Use $\mathsf{CS}.\mathsf{sk}_x$ to sign the policy $f_{(g,y)}$. That is, compute and output $\sigma_{(g,y)} = \mathsf{CS}.\sigma_{f_{(g,y)}} \leftarrow \mathsf{CS}.\mathsf{Sign}(f_{(g,y)}, \mathsf{CS}.\mathsf{sk}_x)$.
- $\mathsf{HS}.\mathsf{Ver}_{\mathsf{vk}}(g, y, \sigma_{(g,y)})$. Accept if and only if $\mathsf{CS}.\mathsf{Ver}_{\mathsf{vk}}(f_{(g,y)}, \mathsf{CS}.\sigma_{f_{(g,y)}})$ accepts.

Lemma 7 (Correctness). *The scheme is correct for* $(\mathcal{G}, \mathcal{X})$.

Proof. Fix $(x, g) \in \mathcal{X} \times \mathcal{G}$. Consider $(\mathsf{sk}, \mathsf{vk}) \leftarrow \mathsf{HS.Setup}(1^\lambda)$, $\sigma_x \leftarrow \mathsf{HS.Sign}(x, \mathsf{sk})$ and $\sigma_{(g,y)} = \mathsf{HS.Eval}(g, \sigma_x)$, where $y = g(x)$. Then it holds that $\sigma_{(g,y)} = \mathsf{CS}.\sigma_{f_{(g,y)}} = \mathsf{CS.Sign}(f_{(g,y)}, \mathsf{CS.sk}_x)$, where $\mathsf{CS.sk}_x \leftarrow \mathsf{CS.Keygen}(x, \mathsf{CS.msk})$. We need to show that $\mathsf{HS.Ver}_{\mathsf{vk}}(g, y, \sigma_{(g,y)}) = accept$, i.e. that $\mathsf{CS.Ver}_{\mathsf{vk}}(f_{(g,y)}, \mathsf{CS}.\sigma_{f_{(g,y)}})$ accepts. Indeed, $g(x) = y$ and therefore $f_{(g,y)}(x) = 0$, and thus $\mathsf{CS.Ver}_{\mathsf{vk}}(f_{(g,y)}, \mathsf{CS}.\sigma_{f_{(g,y)}})$ accepts by the correctness of CS.

Lemma 8 (Privacy). *The scheme is context-hiding for* $(\mathcal{G}, \mathcal{X})$.

Proof. Assume towards contradiction an adversary $\mathcal{A}_h$ that wins the context-hiding game with noticeable advantage, and use it to break the key-privacy the underlying MPCS scheme as follows:

1. Receive $(\mathsf{CS.msk}, \mathsf{CS.vk}) \leftarrow \mathsf{CS.Setup}(1^\lambda)$ from the CS challenger and forward it to $\mathcal{A}_h$ as $(\mathsf{sk}, \mathsf{vk})$.
2. Receive from $\mathcal{A}_h$ a tuple (g, x_0, x_1) such that $g(x_0) = g(x_1)$ and denote this value by y. Forward $(x_0, x_1, f_{(g,y)})$ to the CS challenger.
3. Receive from the CS challenger the challenge $(\mathsf{CS.sk}_{x_0}, \mathsf{CS.sk}_{x_1}, \mathsf{CS}.\sigma_{f_{(g,y)}})$ and forward it to $\mathcal{A}_h$ as $(\sigma_{x_0}, \sigma_{x_1}, \sigma_{(g,y)})$.
4. Get b' from $\mathcal{A}_h$ and forward it to the CS^y challenger. Clearly, any advantage of $\mathcal{A}_h$ induces an advantage of the reduction.

Lemma 9 (Unforgeability). *The scheme is single-data selectively unforgeable for* $(\mathcal{G}, \mathcal{X})$.

Proof. Consider the HS single-data selective unforgeability game against an adversary $\mathcal{A}_h$. Let $x \in \mathcal{G}$ be the data-set sent by $\mathcal{A}_h$, and assume towards contradiction that it wins the game. Then $\mathcal{A}_h$ outputs $(g, y, \sigma_{(g,y)})$ such that $\mathsf{HS.Ver}_{\mathsf{vk}}(g, y, \sigma_{(g,y)}) = accept$ and $g(x) \neq y$. Such adversary can be used to break the unforgeability of MPCS:

1. Upon receiving x from $\mathcal{A}_h$, send it to the CS challenger.
2. The CS challenger sends back $\mathsf{CS.sk}_x = \mathsf{CS.Keygen}(\mathsf{CS.msk}, x)$ and $\mathsf{CS.vk}$, which is exactly (σ_x, vk) that we have to send to $\mathcal{A}_h$.
3. $\mathcal{A}_h$ sends back $(g, y, \sigma_{(g,y)})$ such that $\mathsf{HS.Ver}_{\mathsf{vk}}(g, y, \sigma_{(g,y)}) = accept$ and $g(x) \neq y$. Denoting $\sigma_{(g,y)} = \mathsf{CS}.\sigma_{f_{(g,y)}}$, it means that $\mathsf{CS.Ver}_{\mathsf{vk}}(f_{(g,y)}, \mathsf{CS}.\sigma_{f_{(g,y)}}) = accept$, however $g(x) \neq y$ and therefore $f_{(g,y)}(x) \neq 0$, thus $\mathsf{CS}.\sigma_{f_{(g,y)}}$ is a successful forgery against CS.

6 CS Construction from Lattice Trapdoors

In this section we construct a (key-policy) CS scheme from lattices trapdoors, using techniques that were developed in [GVW13, BGG+14]. The resulting scheme supports a fixed attribute space, and the constraint space consists of boolean circuits with a bound on depth. We prove message-selective unforgeability based on the SIS hardness assumption, and statistical key-hiding. Lastly we show how to extend the scheme to support key delegation.

The initialization parameters are (ℓ, d), where the attribute space is $\mathcal{X} = \{0,1\}^\ell$ and the constraint space is all d-depth bounded circuits $\mathcal{F}_d = \{f : \{0,1\}^\ell \to \{0,1\}\}$.

6.1   The Scheme

Initialize the parameters $n, m, m', q, B, \tau_0, \tau_k, \tau_s$ respective to λ, d, ℓ as described below.

- $\mathsf{Setup}(1^\lambda) \to (\mathsf{msk}, \mathsf{vk})$: Generate a matrix $\mathbf{A} \in \mathbb{Z}_q^{n \times m'}$ with its trapdoor $\mathbf{A}_{\tau_0}^{-1}$ (see Corollary 1). Sample uniformly a matrix $\vec{\mathbf{A}} \xleftarrow{\$} \mathbb{Z}_q^{n \times (m \times \ell)}$. Output $\mathsf{vk} = (\mathbf{A}, \vec{\mathbf{A}})$ and $\mathsf{msk} = \mathbf{A}_{\tau_0}^{-1}$.
- $\mathsf{Keygen}_{\mathsf{vk}}(f, \mathsf{msk}) \to \mathsf{sk}_f$: Compute $\mathbf{H}_f = \mathsf{EvalF}(f, \vec{\mathbf{A}})$ (see Theorem 3) and $\mathbf{A}_f = \vec{\mathbf{A}} \cdot \mathbf{H}_f$, then use $\mathbf{A}_{\tau_0}^{-1}$ to compute $\mathsf{sk}_f = [\mathbf{A} \| \mathbf{A}_f]_{\tau_k}^{-1}$ (see Corollary 2).
- $\mathsf{Sign}_{\mathsf{pp}}(x, \mathsf{sk}_f) \to \sigma_x$: If $f(x) \neq 0$ return $\perp$. Otherwise, compute $\mathbf{H}_{f,x} = \mathsf{EvalFX}(f, x, \vec{\mathbf{A}})$ (see Theorem 3). Note that by this theorem, $[\vec{\mathbf{A}} - x \otimes \mathbf{G}] \cdot \mathbf{H}_{f,x} = \mathbf{A}_f - f(x)\mathbf{G} = \mathbf{A}_f$. Now apply trapdoor extension (see Theorem 2) with

$$\bar{\mathbf{A}} = [\mathbf{A} \| \mathbf{A}_f], \quad \bar{\mathbf{B}} = [\mathbf{A} \| \vec{\mathbf{A}} - x \otimes \mathbf{G}], \quad \mathbf{S} = \begin{bmatrix} \mathbf{I}_{m'} & \mathbf{0} \\ \mathbf{0} & \mathbf{H}_{f,x} \end{bmatrix}$$

(using $\mathsf{sk}_f = [\mathbf{A} \| \mathbf{A}_f]_{\tau_k}^{-1} = \bar{\mathbf{A}}_{\tau_k}^{-1}$), and achieve $\bar{\mathbf{B}}_{\tau_s}^{-1} = [\mathbf{A} \| \vec{\mathbf{A}} - x \otimes \mathbf{G}]_{\tau_s}^{-1}$. Sample $\sigma_x \xleftarrow{\$} [\mathbf{A} \| \vec{\mathbf{A}} - x \otimes \mathbf{G}]_{\tau_s}^{-1}(\mathbf{0})$ and output σ_x.
  Note that by Theorem 3, $\mathbf{H}_{f,x} \in \mathbb{Z}^{\ell m \times m}$ and $\|\mathbf{H}_{f,x}\|_\infty \leq (2m)^d$, and thus the largest singular value $s_1(\mathbf{S}) = \max\{1, s_1(\mathbf{H}_{f,x})\} \leq \sqrt{\ell} 2^d m^{d+1}$. Hence $\tau_k \cdot s_1(\mathbf{S}) \leq \tau_s = \tau_k \cdot \sqrt{\ell} 2^d m^{d+1}$, as required by the conditions of Theorem 2.
- $\mathsf{Ver}_{\mathsf{pp}}(x, \sigma_x) \to \{accept, reject\}$: Output $accept$ if and only if the following conditions hold: $\sigma_x \neq \perp$, $\sigma_x \neq \mathbf{0}$, $[\mathbf{A} \| \vec{\mathbf{A}} - x \otimes \mathbf{G}] \cdot \sigma_x = \mathbf{0}$ and $\|\sigma_x\|_\infty \leq B$.

Choice of Parameters. The SIS parameters n, q, B' are chosen according to constraints from the correctness and security analyses that follow. We require that $n \geq \lambda$, $q \leq 2^n$ and recall that $\ell = \text{poly}(\lambda) \leq 2^n$. We set $m = n\lceil \log q \rceil$, $m' = \max\{m_0, (n+1)\lceil \log q \rceil + 2\lambda\}$, where m_0 is as required by $\mathsf{TrapGen}$ (see Corollary 1), $\tau_0 = O(\sqrt{n\lceil \log q \rceil} \log n)$ as required by $\mathsf{TrapGen}$ (see Corollary 1), $\tau_k = \max\{\sqrt{m'} \ell 2^d m^{1.5+d}, \tau_0\}$, $\tau_s = \tau_k \cdot \sqrt{\ell} 2^d m^{d+1}$, $B = \tau_s \sqrt{m' + \ell \cdot m}$, and we require that $(\ell m + 1)B \leq B'$, i.e. that $(\ell m + 1)\sqrt{m'} \ell^{1.5} 2^{2d} m^{2d+2.5} \sqrt{m' + \ell \cdot m} \leq B'$, while keeping $\mathsf{SIS}_{n,q,B',m'}$ hard as per Theorem 1. These constraints can be met by setting $n = d^{\frac{1}{\epsilon}} + \ell$, $B' = 2^{n^\epsilon}$ and then choosing q accordingly based on Theorem 1. Note that it guarantees that indeed $q \leq 2^n$ and $(\ell m + 1)\sqrt{m'} \ell^{1.5} 2^{2d} m^{2d+2.5} \sqrt{m' + \ell \cdot m} \leq B'$.

Correctness and Security. We prove correctness and security for the attribute space $\mathcal{X} = \{0,1\}^\ell$ and function family $\mathcal{F}_d = \{f : \{0,1\}^\ell \to \{0,1\}\}$ of circuits with depth at most d.

Lemma 10 (Correctness). *The scheme is correct for $(\mathcal{X}, \mathcal{F})$.*

Proof. Fix $x \in \mathcal{X}$ and $f \in \mathcal{F}$ for which $f(x) = 0$, and consider $(\mathsf{msk}, \mathsf{vk}) \leftarrow$ $\mathsf{Setup}(1^\lambda)$ and $\sigma_x = \mathsf{Sign}_{\mathsf{vk}}(x, \mathsf{Keygen}_{\mathsf{vk}}(f, \mathsf{msk}))$. Then since $f(x) = 0$, $\sigma_x \in$ $[\mathbf{A} \| \vec{\mathbf{A}} - x \otimes \mathbf{G}]_{\tau_s}^{-1}(\mathbf{0})$ and therefore $[\mathbf{A} \| \vec{\mathbf{A}} - x \otimes \mathbf{G}] \cdot \sigma_x = 0$. By the properties of lattice trapdoors, samples from $[\mathbf{A} \| \vec{\mathbf{A}} - x \otimes \mathbf{G}]_{\tau_s}^{-1}(\mathbf{0})$ are within 2^{-n} statistical distance from a discrete Gaussian distribution over $\mathbb{Z}_q^{m'+\ell \cdot m}$ with parameter τ_s. Therefore, with all but $2^{-(m'+\ell \cdot m)} = \mathsf{negl}(\lambda)$ probability, $\|\sigma_{(x,m)}\|_\infty \leq$ $\tau_s \sqrt{m' + \ell \cdot m} = B$ and hence $\mathsf{Ver}_{\mathsf{vk}}(x, \sigma_x) = accept$.

Lemma 11 (Privacy). *The scheme is statistically key-hiding for $(\mathcal{X}, \mathcal{F})$.*

Proof. Consider the key-hiding privacy game from Definition 4. Change the way that $\sigma_{x,b}$ is generated in the challenge: use $\mathsf{msk} = \mathbf{A}_{\tau_0}^{-1}$ to compute $[\mathbf{A} \| \vec{\mathbf{A}} - x \otimes \mathbf{G}]_{\tau_s}^{-1}$ (note that $\tau_s \geq \tau_0$ and see Corollary 2), then sample and output $\sigma_{x,b} \overset{\$}{\leftarrow} [\mathbf{A} \| \vec{\mathbf{A}} - x \otimes \mathbf{G}]_{\tau_s}^{-1}(\mathbf{0})$. The distribution from which $\sigma_{x,b}$ is sampled remains the same, therefore this change is statistically indistinguishable. In this setting, the challenge is independent of b and thus any adversary has no advantage in the game.

Lemma 12 (Unforgeability). *The scheme is message-selective unforgeable for $(\mathcal{X}, \mathcal{F})$.*

Proof. The proof proceeds with a sequence of hybrids and follows similar lines to [BGG+14].

Hybrid $\mathcal{H}_0$. The message-selective unforgeability game from Definition 5.

Hybrid $\mathcal{H}_1$. Upon receiving x^*, the challenger generates vk as follows: it generates $\mathbf{A}$ along with $\mathbf{A}_{\tau_0}^{-1}$ as before, then it samples a matrix $\vec{\mathbf{R}}_A \overset{\$}{\leftarrow} \{0,1\}^{m' \times \ell \times m}$ and computes $\vec{\mathbf{A}} = \mathbf{A}\vec{\mathbf{R}}_A + x^* \otimes \mathbf{G}$. Indistinguishability follows from the extended leftover hash lemma, since $m' \geq (n+1)\lceil \log q \rceil + 2\lambda$ and $\mathbf{A}$ is statistically-close to uniform by Corollary 1.

Hybrid $\mathcal{H}_2$. Change the way that the challenger answers key queries. Let f be a query, then $f(x^*) = 1$ and thus $f(x^*) = 1$, thus by Theorem 3

$$[\mathbf{A} \| \mathbf{A}_f - \mathbf{G}] = [\mathbf{A} \| \mathbf{A}_f - f(x^*)\mathbf{G}] = [\mathbf{A} \| [\vec{\mathbf{A}} - x^* \otimes \mathbf{G}] \cdot \mathbf{H}_{f,x^*}] = [\mathbf{A} \| \mathbf{A} \cdot \vec{\mathbf{R}}_A \cdot \mathbf{H}_{f,x^*}].$$

Hence $[\mathbf{A} \| \mathbf{A}_f] = [\mathbf{A} \| \mathbf{A} \cdot \vec{\mathbf{R}}_A \cdot \mathbf{H}_{f,x^*} + \mathbf{G}]$, and by Corollary 3 it is possible to compute $\mathsf{sk}_f = [\mathbf{A} \| \mathbf{A}_f]_{\tau_k}^{-1} = [\mathbf{A} \| \mathbf{A} \cdot \vec{\mathbf{R}}_A \cdot \mathbf{H}_{f,x^*} + \mathbf{G}]_{\tau_k}^{-1}$ given $\mathbf{A}, \vec{\mathbf{R}}_A$ and $\mathbf{H}_{f,x^*}$, since $\|\mathbf{H}_{f,x}\|_\infty \leq (2m)^d$ and thus

$$\sqrt{m'm} \left\| \vec{\mathbf{R}}_A \cdot \mathbf{H}_{f,x} \right\|_\infty \leq \sqrt{m'\ell} m^{1.5} \cdot \left\| \vec{\mathbf{R}}_A \right\|_\infty \cdot \|\mathbf{H}_{f,x}\|_\infty \leq \sqrt{m'\ell} 2^d m^{1.5+d} \leq \tau_k.$$

The distribution of sk_f remains the same, thus the hybrids are statistically indistinguishable.

Hybrid $\mathcal{H}_3$. Change the way that the challenger answers signature queries. Let (f, x) be a query, then $x \neq x^*$ and $f(x) = 0$. Consider the function

$f_x : \{0,1\}^\ell \to \{0,1\}$ that returns 0 if the input is x, and 1 otherwise. Then since $x \neq x^*$, $f_x(x^*) = 1$, hence we can generate a sk_{f_x} respective to the function f_x as described in the previous hybrid. In this hybrid we compute a signature for x using this sk_{f_x}, i.e. output $\mathsf{Sign}_{\mathsf{vk}}(x, \mathsf{sk}_{f_x})$. Since $f_x(x) = 0$ and the scheme is statistically constraint-hiding, this change is statistically indistinguishable.

Hybrid $\mathcal{H}_4$. Change the way that the challenger answers repeated signature queries. Let $(i,x) \in \mathbb{N} \times \mathcal{X}$ be a query. Compute and output $\mathsf{Sign}_{\mathsf{vk}}(x, \mathsf{sk}_{f_x})$, where sk_{f_x} is as described above. Since the scheme is statistically key-hiding, this change is statistically indistinguishable.

Hybrid $\mathcal{H}_5$. At this point the challenger does not use $\mathbf{A}_{\tau_0}^{-1}$ anymore. We switch to sampling $\mathbf{A}$ uniformly without $\mathbf{A}_{\tau_0}^{-1}$, which is statistically indistinguishable by Corollary 1.

Finally we show that if $\mathcal{A}$ wins the game in this hybrid then it breaks $\mathsf{SIS}_{n,q,B'}$: Let $\mathbf{A}$ be a $\mathsf{SIS}_{n,q,B',m'}$ challenge. Initialize a game against $\mathcal{A}$ as in this hybrid using the matrix $\mathbf{A}$. Assume that $\mathcal{A}$ produces a valid forgery σ_{x^*} for x^*. Then $\sigma_{x^*} \neq \mathbf{0}$, $\|\sigma_{x^*}\|_\infty \leq B$ and

$$0 = [\mathbf{A}\|\vec{\mathbf{A}} - x^* \otimes \mathbf{G}] \cdot \sigma_{x^*} = [\mathbf{A}\|\mathbf{A}\vec{\mathbf{R}}_A] \cdot \sigma_{x^*} = \mathbf{A} \cdot [\mathbf{I}\|\vec{\mathbf{R}}_A] \cdot \sigma_{x^*}.$$

Since

$$\left\| [\mathbf{I}\|\vec{\mathbf{R}}_A] \cdot \sigma_{x^*} \right\|_\infty \leq (\ell m + 1) \|\sigma_{x^*}\|_\infty = (\ell m + 1) B \leq B',$$

$[\mathbf{I}\|\vec{\mathbf{R}}_A] \cdot \sigma_{x^*}$ is a valid solution to $\mathsf{SIS}_{n,q,B',m'}^\ell$.

6.2   Adding Key Delegation

It is possible to extend the construction to support key delegation as per Definition 7. We define an alternative Sign^{del} algorithm along with a new DelKey algorithm. Note that by definition each key maintains its delegation history: an ordered list of constraints which define the permissions of the key. Upon computing $\mathsf{DelKey}_{\mathsf{vk}}(\mathsf{sk}_{(f_1,\ldots,f_t)}, f_{t+1}) \to \mathsf{sk}_{(f_1,\ldots,f_{t+1})}$, the delegated key $\mathsf{sk}_{(f_1,\ldots,f_{t+1})}$ contains the constraints list of $\mathsf{sk}_{(f_1,\ldots,f_t)}$ and the new constraint f_{t+1}. The scheme should be parameterized with an upper bound t' to the delegation depth (i.e. the list length). The other parameters are initialized as before, with the only differences $\tau_s = \tau_k \cdot \sqrt{\ell t'} 2^d m^{d+1}$ and $n = d^{\frac{1}{\epsilon}} + \ell t'$. Hence the scheme can be initializes with any $t' = \mathsf{poly}(\lambda)$.

- $\mathsf{DelKey}_{\mathsf{vk}}(\mathsf{sk}_{(f_1,\ldots,f_t)}, f_{t+1}) \to \mathsf{sk}_{(f_1,\ldots,f_{t+1})}$: Recall that when $t = 1$, $\mathsf{sk}_f = [\mathbf{A}\|\mathbf{A}_f]_{\tau_k}^{-1}$. Assume that for any $t \geq 1$, $\mathsf{sk}_{f_1,\ldots,f_t} = [\mathbf{A}\|\mathbf{A}_{f_1}\|\ldots\|\mathbf{A}_{f_t}]_{\tau_k}^{-1}$, and compute the new key as follows: Compute $\mathbf{H}_{f_{t+1}} = \mathsf{EvalF}(f_{t+1}, \vec{\mathbf{A}})$ (see Theorem 3) and $\mathbf{A}_{f_{t+1}} = \vec{\mathbf{A}} \cdot \mathbf{H}_{f_{t+1}}$, then use $[\mathbf{A}\|\mathbf{A}_{f_1}\|\ldots\|\mathbf{A}_{f_t}]_{\tau_k}^{-1}$ to compute and output $sk_{f_1,\ldots,f_{t+1}} = [\mathbf{A}\|\mathbf{A}_{f_1}\|\ldots\|\mathbf{A}_{f_{t+1}}]_{\tau_k}^{-1}$ (see Corollary 2).

– $\mathsf{Sign}_{\mathsf{pp}}(x, sk_{f_1,...,f_t}) \to \sigma_x$: If $\exists i \in [t]$ s.t. $f_i(x) \neq 0$, return $\bot$. Otherwise, for $i \in [t]$ compute $\mathbf{H}_{f_i,x} = \mathsf{EvalFX}(f_i, x, \vec{\mathbf{A}})$ (see Theorem 3). Note that by this theorem, $[\vec{\mathbf{A}} - x \otimes \mathbf{G}] \cdot \mathbf{H}_{f_i,x} = \mathbf{A}_{f_i} - f_i(x)\mathbf{G} = \mathbf{A}_{f_i} - f_i(x)\mathbf{G} = \mathbf{A}_{f_i}$. Now apply the Trapdoor Extension Theorem (2) with

$$\bar{\mathbf{A}} = [\mathbf{A}\|\mathbf{A}_{f_1}\| \ldots \|\mathbf{A}_{f_t}], \quad \bar{\mathbf{B}} = [\mathbf{A}\|\vec{\mathbf{A}} - x \otimes \mathbf{G}], \quad \mathbf{S} = \begin{bmatrix} \mathbf{I}_{m'} & 0 & \cdots 0 \\ 0 & \mathbf{H}_{f_1,x} & \cdots \mathbf{H}_{f_t,x} \end{bmatrix}$$

(using $sk_f = \bar{\mathbf{A}}_{\tau_k}^{-1}$), and achieve $\bar{\mathbf{B}}_{\tau_s}^{-1} = [\mathbf{A}\|\vec{\mathbf{A}} - x \otimes \mathbf{G}]_{\tau_s}^{-1}$. Finally sample and output $\sigma_x \xleftarrow{\$} [\mathbf{A}\|\vec{\mathbf{A}} - x \otimes \mathbf{G}]_{\tau_s}^{-1}(0)$.

Note that by Theorem 3, $\forall i \in [t] : \mathbf{H}_{f_i,x} \in \mathbb{Z}^{\ell m \times m}$ and $\|\mathbf{H}_{f_i,x}\|_\infty \leq (2m)^d$, and thus the largest singular value $s_1(\mathbf{S}) \leq \sqrt{\ell t} 2^d m^{d+1}$. Hence $\tau_k \cdot s_1(\mathbf{S}) \leq \tau_k \cdot \sqrt{\ell t'} 2^d m^{d+1} = \tau_s$, as required by the conditions of Theorem 2.

Correctness and Security. Correctness and statistical key-hiding can be proved the same way as in the non-delegatable scheme, since for each x the valid signatures distribution remains the same: $[\mathbf{A}\|\vec{\mathbf{A}} - x \otimes \mathbf{G}]_{\tau_s}^{-1}(0)$. We now prove message-selective unforgeability as per Definition 7.

Lemma 13. *The scheme is message-selective unforgeable for $(\mathcal{X}, \mathcal{F})$.*

Proof. We first define the procedure $\mathsf{PermuteKey}(sk_{f_1,...,f_t}, \rho) \to sk_{f_{\rho(1)},...,f_{\rho(t)}}$ that takes as input a signing key $sk_{f_1,...,f_t}$ and a permutation $\rho : \mathbb{Z}_t \to \mathbb{Z}_t$, and outputs a key of the permuted constraints $sk_{f_{\rho(1)},...,f_{\rho(t)}}$. $\mathsf{PermuteKey}$ works as follows: Recall that $sk_{f_1,...,f_t} = [\mathbf{A}\|\mathbf{A}_{f_1}\| \ldots \|\mathbf{A}_{f_t}]_{\tau_k}^{-1}$, thus by Corollary 4, it is efficient to compute $sk_{f_{\rho(1)},...,f_{\rho(t)}} = [\mathbf{A}\|\mathbf{A}_{f_{\rho(1)}}\| \ldots \|\mathbf{A}_{f_{\rho(t)}}]_{\tau_k}^{-1}$.

The security proof goes by reduction to the security of the non-delegatable scheme. Assume an adversary $\mathcal{A}_{del}$ that wins the delegation security game, and use it to win the security game without delegation against a challenger $\mathsf{Challenger}$ as follows:

1. Receive x^* from $\mathcal{A}_{del}$ and forward it to $\mathsf{Challenger}$.
2. Receive vk from $\mathsf{Challenger}$ and forward it to $\mathcal{A}_{del}$.
3. Answer $\mathcal{A}_{del}$'s queries as follows:
   – If the query is a key query, i.e. it is of the form $t \in \mathbb{N}$, $F \in \mathcal{F}^t$ such that $\exists f \in F$ for which $f(x^*) = 1$, request sk_{f_i} from $\mathsf{Challenger}$. Then compute $sk_{(f,F/f)}$ using DelKey $|F| - 1$ times and sk_f. Finally compute sk_F using $\mathsf{PermuteKey}$ and $sk_{(f,F/f)}$, and send it to $\mathcal{A}_{del}$.
   – If the query is a signature query, i.e. it is of the form $t \in \mathbb{N}$, $(F, x) \in \mathcal{F}^t \times \mathcal{X}$ such that $x \neq x^*$ and $\forall f \in F : f(x) = 0$, request σ_x from $\mathsf{Challenger}$ using an arbitrary $f \in F$, i.e. send (x, f) and get back σ_x. Forward the signature to $\mathcal{A}_{del}$. Recall that in the unforgeability game, those queries should be answered by computing $\sigma_x \leftarrow \mathsf{Sign}(x, sk_F)$. Since the construction is key-hiding, this is indistinguishable to $\mathcal{A}_{del}$.
   – If the query is a repeated signature query, i.e. it is of the form $i \in \mathbb{N}$, $x \in \mathcal{X}$ such that $x \neq x^*$ and the ith signature query (F_i, x_i) satisfies

$\forall f \in F_i : f(x) = 0$, answer it as described above as if it were a signature query of the form (F_i, x). Recall that in the unforgeability game, those queries should be answered by computing $\sigma_x \leftarrow \text{Sign}(x, \text{sk}_{F_i})$, where sk_{F_i} is a key that was generated when the ith signature query was answered. Since the construction is key-hiding, this is indistinguishable to $\mathcal{A}_{del}$.

4. Get a forgery σ_{x^*} from $\mathcal{A}_{del}$ and forward it to Challenger.

If $\mathcal{A}_{del}$ wins the game then also the reduction does, with contradiction to the security of the non-delegatable scheme.

A   Definitions of Message-Policy CS

Definition 9 ((Message-Policy) Constrained Signatures). *Let $\mathcal{X}$ be an attribute space and $\mathcal{F}$ be a function space of the form $f \in \mathcal{F} \implies f : \mathcal{X}' \to \{0, 1\}$ where $\mathcal{X}' \subseteq \mathcal{X}$. A constrained signatures scheme for $(\mathcal{X}, \mathcal{F})$ is a tuple of algorithms:*

- $\text{Setup}(1^\lambda) \to (\text{msk}, \text{vk})$ *takes as input the security parameter λ and possibly a description of $(\mathcal{X}, \mathcal{F})$, and outputs a master signing key msk and a public verification key vk.*
- $\text{Keygen}(x, \text{msk}) \to \text{sk}_x$ *takes as input an attribute $x \in \mathcal{X}$ and the master signing key msk, and outputs a signing key sk_x.*
- $\text{Sign}(f, \text{sk}_f) \to \sigma_f$ *takes as input a policy $f \in \mathcal{F}$ and a signing key sk_x, and outputs a signature σ_f.*
- $\text{Ver}_{\text{vk}}(f, \sigma_f) \to \{accept, reject\}$ *takes as input a policy $f \in \mathcal{F}$ and a signature σ_f, and either accepts or rejects.*

Correctness. The scheme is correct if for all $x \in \mathcal{X}$ and $f \in \mathcal{F}$ for which $f(x) = 0$, it holds that with all but negligible probability $\text{Ver}_{\text{vk}}(f, \sigma_f) = accept$, where $(\text{msk}, \text{vk}) \leftarrow \text{Setup}(1^\lambda)$ and $\sigma_f = \text{Sign}(f, \text{Keygen}(x, \text{msk}))$.

Definition 10 (Privacy of (Message-Policy) Constrained Signatures). *The scheme is attribute-hiding if any PPT adversary $\mathcal{A}$ has no more than negligible advantage in the following game.*

1. *The challenger computes and outputs $(\text{msk}, \text{vk}) \leftarrow \text{Setup}(1^\lambda)$.*
2. *$\mathcal{A}$ sends (x_0, x_1, f) such that $f(x_0) = f(x_1) = 0$.*
3. *The challenger computes $\text{sk}_{x_0} = \text{Keygen}(x_0, \text{msk})$ and $\text{sk}_{x_1} = \text{Keygen}(x_1, \text{msk})$. It then samples $b \xleftarrow{\$} \{0, 1\}$ and computes $\sigma_{f,b} \leftarrow \text{Sign}(f, \text{sk}_{x_b})$. It sends $\sigma_{f,b}$ to $\mathcal{A}$.*
4. *$\mathcal{A}$ outputs $b' \in \{0, 1\}$ and wins if and only if $b' = b$.*

The scheme is key-hiding if any PPT adversary $\mathcal{A}$ has no more than negligible advantage in the above game, where in step 2 the challenger sends $(\text{sk}_{x_0}, \text{sk}_{x_1}, \sigma_{f,b})$ to $\mathcal{A}$.

Definition 11 (Unforgeability of (Message-Policy) Constrained Signatures). *The scheme is* fully unforgeable *if every PPTM adversary $\mathcal{A}$ has no more than negligible advantage in the following game:*

1. *The challenger computes* $(\mathsf{msk}, \mathsf{vk}) \leftarrow \mathsf{Setup}(1^\lambda)$ *and sends* vk *to* $\mathcal{A}$.
2. $\mathcal{A}$ *makes queries of three types:*
   - Key Queries. $\mathcal{A}$ *sends* $x \in \mathcal{X}$ *and gets back* $\mathsf{sk}_x \leftarrow \mathsf{Keygen}(x, \mathsf{msk})$.
   - Signature Queries. $\mathcal{A}$ *sends* $(f, x) \in \mathcal{F} \times \mathcal{X}$ *such that* $f(x) = 0$. *The challenger computes* $\mathsf{sk}_x \leftarrow \mathsf{Keygen}(x, \mathsf{msk})$ *and sends back* $\sigma_f \leftarrow \mathsf{Sign}(f, \mathsf{sk}_x)$.
   - Repeated Signature Queries. $\mathcal{A}$ *sends* $i \in \mathbb{N}$ *and* $f \in \mathcal{F} \times \mathcal{M}$. *If there were less than i signature queries at this point of the game, the challenger returns* $\perp$. *Otherwise, let x denote the attribute that was sent at the ith signature query and let sk_x denote the key that was generated by the challenger when answering this query. If $f(x) \neq 0$, the challenger returns* $\perp$. *Otherwise it returns* $\sigma_f \leftarrow \mathsf{Sign}(f, \mathsf{sk}_x)$.
3. $\mathcal{A}$ *wins if it manages to output* (f^*, σ_{f^*}) *such that* $\mathsf{Ver}_{\mathsf{vk}}(f^*, \sigma_{f^*}) = accept$ *and the following restrictions hold:*
   - *For any key queried by $\mathcal{A}$ respective to $x \in \mathcal{X}$, it holds that* $f^*(x) = 1$.
   - *For any signature σ_f queried by $\mathcal{A}$, it holds that* $f \neq f^*$.

The scheme maintains message-selective *unforgeability if any PPT $\mathcal{A}$ that announces f^* before seeing vk has no more than negligible advantage in the game.*

Definition 12 (Single-Key-Selective Unforgeability of (Message-Policy) Constrained Signatures). *The scheme is* single-key selectively unforgeable *if every PPTM adversary $\mathcal{A}$ has no more than negligible advantage in the following game:*

1. $\mathcal{A}$ *sends* $x^* \in \mathcal{F}$ *to the challenger.*
2. *The challenger computes* $(\mathsf{msk}, \mathsf{vk}) \leftarrow \mathsf{Setup}(1^\lambda)$ *and* $\mathsf{sk}_{x^*} \leftarrow \mathsf{Keygen}(x^*, \mathsf{msk})$, *and sends* $(\mathsf{vk}, \mathsf{sk}_{x^*})$ *to* $\mathcal{A}$.
3. $\mathcal{A}$ *wins if it manages to output* (f^*, σ_{f^*}) *such that* $\mathsf{Ver}_{\mathsf{vk}}(f^*, \sigma_{f^*}) = accept$ *and* $f^*(x^*) = 1$.

B Proofs for Sect. 4.1

For any $t \geq 1$ and $F = (f_1, \ldots, f_t) \in \mathcal{F}^t$, write $F(x) = 0$ to denote that $f \in F \Rightarrow f(x) = 0$. Moreover, denote $\mathsf{sk}_F = \mathsf{sk}_{(f_1, \ldots, f_t)}$, where $\forall i \in [2 \ldots t]$: $\mathsf{sk}_{(f_1, \ldots, f_i)} = \mathsf{DelKey}(\mathsf{sk}_{(f_1, \ldots, f_{i-1})}, f_i)$ and $\mathsf{sk}_{f_1} = \mathsf{Keygen}(f_1, \mathsf{msk})$ for some $(\mathsf{msk}, \mathsf{vk}) \leftarrow \mathsf{Setup}(1^\lambda)$ which is clear from the context.

Lemma 14 (Correctness). *The scheme from Sect. 4.1 is correct for* $(\mathcal{F}', \mathcal{X}')$.

Proof. Fix $x \in \mathcal{X}'$, $t \in \mathbb{N}$ and $F \in \mathcal{F}'^t$ such that $F(x) = 0$, and consider $(\mathsf{msk}, \mathsf{vk}) \leftarrow \mathsf{Setup}(1^\lambda)$. Consider sk_F as described above and $\sigma_x = \mathsf{Sign}(x, \mathsf{sk}_F)$.

Denote

$$\sigma_x = (\mathsf{vk}', \sigma_x', \{\mathsf{vk}_i''\}_{i \in [t]}, \sigma_x'', \sigma_{(\mathsf{vk}', \mathsf{vk}_1'')}, \{\sigma_{(\mathsf{vk}_i'', \mathsf{vk}_{i+1}'')}\}_{i \in [t-1]}),$$

then by Sign, Keygen and DelKey it holds that $\sigma_x' = \mathsf{Sign}'(x, \mathsf{sk}_F')$, and since $F(x) = 0$ it holds that $\mathsf{Ver}_{\mathsf{vk}'}'(\sigma_x', x) = accept$ by the correctness of CS'. Moreover,

$$\mathsf{S.Ver}_{\mathsf{vk}_t''}(x, \sigma_x'') = \mathsf{S.Ver}_{\mathsf{vk}_t''}(x, \mathsf{S.Sign}(\mathsf{sk}_t'', x)) = accept,$$

$$\mathsf{S.Ver}_{\mathsf{S.vk}}(\sigma_{(\mathsf{vk}', \mathsf{vk}_1'')}, (\mathsf{vk}', \mathsf{vk}_1'')) = \mathsf{S.Ver}_{\mathsf{S.vk}}(\mathsf{S.Sign}(\mathsf{S.sk}, (\mathsf{vk}', \mathsf{vk}_1'')), (\mathsf{vk}', \mathsf{vk}_1'')) = accept,$$

and for all $i = 1 \ldots t - 1$,

$$\mathsf{S.Ver}_{\mathsf{vk}_i''}(\sigma_{(\mathsf{vk}_i'', \mathsf{vk}_{i+1}'')}, (\mathsf{vk}_i'', \mathsf{vk}_{i+1}'')) = \mathsf{S.Ver}_{\mathsf{vk}_i''}(\mathsf{S.Sign}(\mathsf{sk}_i'', (\mathsf{vk}_i'', \mathsf{vk}_{i+1}'')), (\mathsf{vk}_i'', \mathsf{vk}_{i+1}'')) = accept.$$

by the correctness of S. Therefore, $\mathsf{Ver}_{\mathsf{vk}}(x, \sigma_x)$ accepts.

Lemma 15 (Privacy). *The scheme from Sect. 4.1 is constraint-hiding for* $(\mathcal{F}', \mathcal{X}')$.

Proof. Assume towards contradiction an adversary $\mathcal{A}$ that wins the constraint-hiding privacy game with some significant probability, and use it to break the constraint-hiding privacy of CS as follows:

1. Receive $(\mathsf{vk}', \mathsf{msk}') \leftarrow \mathsf{Setup}'(1^\lambda)$ from the CS challenger.
2. Compute $(\mathsf{S.vk}, \mathsf{S.sk}) \leftarrow \mathsf{S.Setup}(1^\lambda)$ and send $(\mathsf{msk} = \mathsf{S.sk}, \mathsf{vk} = \mathsf{S.vk})$ to $\mathcal{A}$.
3. $\mathcal{A}$ returns (t, F_0, F_1, x), where $\forall b \in \{0,1\} : F_b = (f_1^b, \ldots, f_t^b)$ and $F_b(x) = 0$. Forward (t, F_0, F_1, x) to the CS challenger.
4. The CS challenger samples $b \xleftarrow{\$} \{0,1\}$ and returns $\sigma_{x,b}'$.
   Now for $i \in [t]$ generate $(\mathsf{vk}_1'', \mathsf{sk}_t'') \leftarrow \mathsf{S.Setup}(1^\lambda)$, sign $(\mathsf{vk}', \mathsf{vk}_1'')$ with the standard signature scheme: $\sigma_{(\mathsf{vk}', \mathsf{vk}_1'')} \leftarrow \mathsf{S.Sign}(\mathsf{S.sk}, (\mathsf{vk}', \mathsf{vk}_1''))$ and for each $i \in [t - 1]$ sign $\sigma_{(\mathsf{vk}_i'', \mathsf{vk}_{i+1}'')} \leftarrow \mathsf{S.Sign}(\mathsf{sk}_i'', (\mathsf{vk}_i'', \mathsf{vk}_{i+1}''))$. Finally sign $\sigma_x'' \leftarrow \mathsf{S.Sign}(\mathsf{sk}_t'', x)$ and send to $\mathcal{A}$ the signature $\sigma_{x,b} = (\mathsf{vk}', \sigma_{x,b}', \{\mathsf{vk}_i''\}_{i \in [t]}, \sigma_x'', \sigma_{(\mathsf{vk}', \mathsf{vk}_1'')}, \{\sigma_{(\mathsf{vk}_i'', \mathsf{vk}_{i+1}'')}\}_{i \in [t-1]})$.
5. Get b' from $\mathcal{A}$ and forward it to the CS challenger. Clearly, any advantage of $\mathcal{A}$ induces an advantage of the reduction.

Lemma 16 (Unforgeability). *The scheme from Sect. 4.1 is fully unforgeable for* $(\mathcal{F}', \mathcal{X}')$.

Proof. Assume towards contradiction an adversary $\mathcal{A}$ that wins the security game. We show that it can be used to break either S or CS. Let $\mathcal{Q}_{key}, \mathcal{Q}_{sig}, \mathcal{Q}_{rep}$ be the sets of key queries, signature queries and repeated signature queries made by $\mathcal{A}$ during the security game. Recall that each query $q_i \in \mathcal{Q}_{key}$ is of the form $(t_i, (f_1^i, \ldots, f_{t_i}^i))$ and each query $q_i \in \mathcal{Q}_{sig}$ is of the form $(t_i, (f_1^i, \ldots, f_{t_i}^i, x_i))$, where $t_i \in \mathbb{Z}, f_j^i \in \mathcal{F}', x_i \in \mathcal{X}'$. In particular, each query $q_i \in \mathcal{Q}_{key} \bigcup \mathcal{Q}_{sig}$ contains a set $(f_1^i, \ldots, f_{t_i}^i) \in \mathcal{F}'^{t_i}$. Moreover, every response of the challenger (whether it is a key or a signature) contains a tuple $(\mathsf{vk}'^i, \{\mathsf{vk}_j''^i\}_{j \in [t_i]})$ that is generated during Keygen and DelKey. $\mathcal{A}$ wins the game, it therefore outputs a successful forgery (x^*, σ_{x^*}), where $\sigma_{x^*} = (\mathsf{vk}'^*, \sigma_{x^*}', \{\mathsf{vk}_j''^*\}_{j=1\ldots t}, \sigma_{x^*}'', \sigma_{(\mathsf{vk}'^*, \mathsf{vk}_1''^*)}, \{\sigma_{(\mathsf{vk}_j''^*, \mathsf{vk}_{j+1}''^*)}\}_{j=1\ldots t-1})$. Consider three cases:

- If $\exists q_i \in \mathcal{Q}_{key}$ such that $(\mathsf{vk}'^i, \{\mathsf{vk}_j''^i\}_{j \in [t_i]}) = (\mathsf{vk}'^*, \{\mathsf{vk}_j''^*\}_{j \in [t_i]})$, then (x^*, σ_{x^*}') is a valid forgery to the delegatable CS instance that was initialized during $\mathsf{Keygen}(f_i, \mathsf{msk})$. Note that since $q_i \in \mathcal{Q}_{key}$, $\exists j \in [1 \dots t_i]$ such that $f_j^i(x^*) = 1$, therefore $(t_i, f_1^i, \dots, f_{t_i}^i)$ is a valid delegated-key query to the underlying CS challenger. We show a reduction from the selective-single-key security game of CS to this game:
  1. Initialize $(\mathsf{S.vk}, \mathsf{S.sk}) \leftarrow \mathsf{S.Setup}(1^\lambda)$ as in the real scheme and send $\mathsf{S.vk}$ to $\mathcal{A}$.
  2. Queries phase:
     - Answer all queries except of the ith as in the real unforgeability game.
     - Upon receiving form $\mathcal{A}$ the query $q_i \in \mathcal{Q}_{key}$, send $(t_i, f_1^i, \dots, f_{t_i}^i)$ to the ith CS challenger and get back $(\mathsf{vk}_i', k_{(f_1^i, \dots, f_{t_i}^i)}')$. For $j \in [t_i]$, generate $(\mathsf{vk}_j''^i, \mathsf{sk}_j''^i) \leftarrow \mathsf{S.Setup}(1^\lambda)$. Compute $\sigma_{(\mathsf{vk}_i', \mathsf{vk}_1''^i)} \leftarrow \mathsf{S.Sign}(\mathsf{S.sk}, (\mathsf{vk}_i', \mathsf{vk}_1''^i))$ and for each $j \in [1 \dots t_i - 1]$ compute $\sigma_{(\mathsf{vk}_j''^i, \mathsf{vk}_{j+1}''^i)} \leftarrow \mathsf{S.Sign}(\mathsf{sk}_j''^i, (\mathsf{vk}_j''^i, \mathsf{vk}_{j+1}''^i))$. Send to $\mathcal{A}$ the key $\mathsf{sk}_{(f_1^i, \dots, f_{t_i}^i)} = (\mathsf{vk}_i', k_{(f_1^i, \dots, f_{t_i}^i)}', \{\mathsf{vk}_j''^i\}_{j \in [t_i]}, \mathsf{sk}_{t_i}''^i, \sigma_{(\mathsf{vk}_i', \mathsf{vk}_1''^i)}, \{\sigma_{(\mathsf{vk}_j''^i, \mathsf{vk}_{j+1}''^i)}\}_{j \in [t_i - 1]})$.
  3. When $\mathcal{A}$ sends the forgery (x^*, σ_{x^*}), send (x^*, σ_{x^*}') to the ith CS challenger to win the selective-single-key game.
- If $\exists q_i \in \mathcal{Q}_{sig}$ such that $(\mathsf{vk}'^i, \{\mathsf{vk}_j''^i\}_{j \in [t_i]}) = (\mathsf{vk}'^*, \{\mathsf{vk}_j''^*\}_{j \in [t_i]})$, then (x^*, σ_{x^*}'') is a valid forgery to the S instance that was initialized during $\mathsf{DelKey}(k_{(f_1^i, \dots, f_{t_i-1}^i)}', f_{t_i}^i)$. Note that $\forall q_i \in \mathcal{Q}_{sig}$, it holds that $x_i \neq x^*$. We show a reduction from the security game of $\mathcal{S}$ to this game:
  1. Initialize $(\mathsf{S.vk}, \mathsf{S.sk}) \leftarrow \mathsf{S.Setup}(1^\lambda)$ as in the real scheme and send $\mathsf{S.vk}$ to $\mathcal{A}$.
  2. Queries phase:
     - Answer all queries up to q_i as in the real unforgeability game.
     - Upon receiving form $\mathcal{A}$ the query $q_i \in \mathcal{Q}_{sig}$, compute $k_{(f_1^i, \dots, f_{t_i-1}^i)}'$ as in the real game, then instantiate a game against the S challenger and get $\mathsf{vk}_{t_i}''^i$. Query a signature for (x_i, m_i) and get back $\sigma_{(x_i, m_i)}''$. Sign $\sigma_{(\mathsf{vk}_{t_i-1}''^i, \mathsf{vk}_{t_i}''^i)} \leftarrow \mathsf{S.Sign}(\mathsf{sk}_{t_i-1}''^i, (\mathsf{vk}_{t_i-1}''^i, \mathsf{vk}_{t_i}''^i))$. Compute $k_{(f_1^i, \dots, f_{t_i}^i)}' \leftarrow \mathsf{DelKey}'(k_{(f_1^i, \dots, f_{t_i-1}^i)}', f_{t_i}^i)$ and $\sigma_{(x_i, m_i)}' \leftarrow \mathsf{Sign}'(x_i, m_i, k_{(f_1^i, \dots, f_{t_i}^i)}')$. Send to $\mathcal{A}$: $\sigma_{x_i} = (\mathsf{vk}_i', \sigma_{x_i}', \{\mathsf{vk}_j''^i\}_{j \in [t_i]}, \sigma_{(x_i, m_i)}'', \sigma_{(\mathsf{vk}_i', \mathsf{vk}_1''^i)}, \{\sigma_{(\mathsf{vk}_j''^i, \mathsf{vk}_{j+1}''^i)}\}_{j \in [t_i - 1]})$.
     - Answer all queries as in the real game, except of repeated signature queries that reference q_i. For these, do as described above with the values $\mathsf{vk}_i', \{\mathsf{vk}_j''^i\}_{j \in [t_i]}, \sigma_{(\mathsf{vk}_i', \mathsf{vk}_1''^i)}, \{\sigma_{(\mathsf{vk}_j''^i, \mathsf{vk}_{j+1}''^i)}\}_{j \in [t_i - 1]}, k_{(f_1^i, \dots, f_{t_i}^i)}'$ that were generated when q_i was answered.
  3. When $\mathcal{A}$ sends the forgery (x^*, σ_{x^*}), send (x^*, σ_{x^*}'') to the ith S challenger to win the game.
- If $\forall d \in [1 \dots t_i]$ and $\forall q_i \in \mathcal{Q}_d^* = \{q_i \in \mathcal{Q}_{key} \bigcup \mathcal{Q}_{sig} : (\mathsf{vk}_i', \{\mathsf{vk}_j''^i\}_{j=1 \dots d-1}) = (\mathsf{vk}_*', \{\mathsf{vk}_j''^*\}_{j=1 \dots d-1})\}$ it holds that $\mathsf{vk}_d''^* \neq \mathsf{vk}_d''^i$, then $(\sigma_{(\mathsf{vk}_{d-1}''^*, \mathsf{vk}_d''^*)},$

$((\mathsf{vk}''^*_{d-1}, \mathsf{vk}''^*_d))$ is a valid forgery to the S instance with the verification key $\mathsf{vk}''^*_{d-1} = \mathsf{vk}''^i_{d-1}$. The reduction follows similar lines to the reduction from the previous case.

- Otherwise $\forall q_i \in \mathcal{Q}_{key} \bigcup \mathcal{Q}_{sig}$ $(\mathsf{vk}'_i, \mathsf{vk}''^i_1) \neq (\mathsf{vk}'_*, \mathsf{vk}''^*_1)$, and thus $(\sigma_{(\mathsf{vk}'_*, \mathsf{vk}''^*_1)}, (\mathsf{vk}'_*, \mathsf{vk}''^*_1))$ is a valid forgery to S. We show a reduction from the security game of S to this game:

  1. Receive S.vk from the S challenger and send it to $\mathcal{A}$.
  2. Answer queries from $\mathcal{A}$ as in the real game, except the way $\sigma_{(\mathsf{vk}'_*, \mathsf{vk}''^*_1)}$ is computed: instead of signing $(\mathsf{vk}'_*, \mathsf{vk}''^*_1)$ with $\mathsf{msk} = \mathsf{S.sk}$, query the S challenger and get $\sigma_{(\mathsf{vk}'_*, \mathsf{vk}''^*_1)}$.
  3. When $\mathcal{A}$ sends the forgery (x^*, σ_{x^*}), send $(\sigma_{(\mathsf{vk}'_*, \mathsf{vk}''^*_1)}, (\mathsf{vk}'_*, \mathsf{vk}''^*_1))$ to the S challenger to win the game.

References

[ABB10] Agrawal, S., Boneh, D., Boyen, X.: Lattice basis delegation in fixed dimension and shorter-ciphertext hierarchical IBE. In: Rabin, T. (ed.) CRYPTO 2010. LNCS, vol. 6223, pp. 98–115. Springer, Heidelberg (2010). doi:10.1007/978-3-642-14623-7_6

[Ajt96] Ajtai, M.: Generating hard instances of lattice problems (extended abstract). In: Miller, G.L. (ed.) Proceedings of the Twenty-Eighth Annual ACM Symposium on the Theory of Computing, Philadelphia, Pennsylvania, USA, 22–24 May 1996, pp. 99–108. ACM (1996)

[AP14] Alperin-Sheriff, J., Peikert, C.: Faster bootstrapping with polynomial error. In: Garay, J.A., Gennaro, R. (eds.) CRYPTO 2014. LNCS, vol. 8616, pp. 297–314. Springer, Heidelberg (2014). doi:10.1007/978-3-662-44371-2_17

[BCTW16] Brakerski, Z., Cash, D., Tsabary, R., Wee, H.: Targeted homomorphic attribute-based encryption. In: Hirt, M., Smith, A. (eds.) TCC 2016. LNCS, vol. 9986, pp. 330–360. Springer, Heidelberg (2016). doi:10.1007/978-3-662-53644-5_13

[BF11] Boneh, D., Freeman, D.M.: Linearly homomorphic signatures over binary fields and new tools for lattice-based signatures. In: Catalano, D., Fazio, N., Gennaro, R., Nicolosi, A. (eds.) PKC 2011. LNCS, vol. 6571, pp. 1–16. Springer, Heidelberg (2011). doi:10.1007/978-3-642-19379-8_1

[BF14] Bellare, M., Fuchsbauer, G.: Policy-based signatures. In: Krawczyk, H. (ed.) PKC 2014. LNCS, vol. 8383, pp. 520–537. Springer, Heidelberg (2014). doi:10.1007/978-3-642-54631-0_30

[BGG+14] Boneh, D., Gentry, C., Gorbunov, S., Halevi, S., Nikolaenko, V., Segev, G., Vaikuntanathan, V., Vinayagamurthy, D.: Fully key-homomorphic encryption, arithmetic circuit ABE and compact garbled circuits. In: Nguyen, P.Q., Oswald, E. (eds.) EUROCRYPT 2014. LNCS, vol. 8441, pp. 533–556. Springer, Heidelberg (2014). doi:10.1007/978-3-642-55220-5_30

[BGI14] Boyle, E., Goldwasser, S., Ivan, I.: Functional signatures and pseudorandom functions. In: Krawczyk, H. (ed.) PKC 2014. LNCS, vol. 8383, pp. 501–519. Springer, Heidelberg (2014). doi:10.1007/978-3-642-54631-0_29

[BK16] El Bansarkhani, R., El Kaafarani, A.: Post-quantum attribute-based signatures from lattice assumptions. Cryptology ePrint Archive, Report 2016/823 (2016). http://eprint.iacr.org/2016/823

[BMS16] Backes, M., Meiser, S., Schröder, D.: Delegatable functional signatures. In: Cheng, C.-M., Chung, K.-M., Persiano, G., Yang, B.-Y. (eds.) PKC 2016. LNCS, vol. 9614, pp. 357–386. Springer, Heidelberg (2016). doi:10.1007/978-3-662-49384-7_14

[BV15] Brakerski, Z., Vaikuntanathan, V.: Constrained key-homomorphic PRFs from standard lattice assumptions - or: how to secretly embed a circuit in your PRF. In: Dodis, Y., Nielsen, J.B. (eds.) TCC 2015. LNCS, vol. 9015, pp. 1–30. Springer, Heidelberg (2015). doi:10.1007/978-3-662-46497-7_1

[BZ14] Boneh, D., Zhandry, M.: Multiparty key exchange, efficient traitor tracing, and more from indistinguishability obfuscation. In: Garay, J.A., Gennaro, R. (eds.) CRYPTO 2014. LNCS, vol. 8616, pp. 480–499. Springer, Heidelberg (2014). doi:10.1007/978-3-662-44371-2_27

[CFW14] Catalano, D., Fiore, D., Warinschi, B.: Homomorphic signatures with efficient verification for polynomial functions. In: Garay, J.A., Gennaro, R. (eds.) CRYPTO 2014. LNCS, vol. 8616, pp. 371–389. Springer, Heidelberg (2014). doi:10.1007/978-3-662-44371-2_21

[CHKP12] Cash, D., Hofheinz, D., Kiltz, E., Peikert, C.: Bonsai trees, or how to delegate a lattice basis. J. Cryptol. **25**(4), 601–639 (2012)

[CNW16] Cheng, S., Nguyen, K., Wang, H.: Policy-based signature scheme from lattices. Des. Codes Cryptogr. **81**, 43–74 (2016)

[CRV14] Chandran, N., Raghuraman, S., Vinayagamurthy, D.: Constrained pseudorandom functions: verifiable and delegatable (2014). http://eprint.iacr.org/2014/522

[FMNP16] Fiore, D., Mitrokotsa, A., Nizzardo, L., Pagnin, E.: Multi-key homomorphic authenticators. In: Cheon, J.H., Takagi, T. (eds.) ASIACRYPT 2016. LNCS, vol. 10032, pp. 499–530. Springer, Heidelberg (2016). doi:10.1007/978-3-662-53890-6_17

[Fuc14] Fuchsbauer, G.: Constrained verifiable random functions. In: Abdalla, M., De Prisco, R. (eds.) SCN 2014. LNCS, vol. 8642, pp. 95–114. Springer, Cham (2014). doi:10.1007/978-3-319-10879-7_7

[GPV08] Gentry, C., Peikert, C., Vaikuntanathan, V.: Trapdoors for hard lattices and new cryptographic constructions. In: Dwork, C. (ed.) Proceedings of the 40th Annual ACM Symposium on Theory of Computing, Victoria, British Columbia, Canada, 17–20 May 2008, pp. 197–206. ACM (2008)

[GSW13] Gentry, C., Sahai, A., Waters, B.: Homomorphic encryption from learning with errors: conceptually-simpler, asymptotically-faster, attribute-based. In: Canetti, R., Garay, J.A. (eds.) CRYPTO 2013. LNCS, vol. 8042, pp. 75–92. Springer, Heidelberg (2013). doi:10.1007/978-3-642-40041-4_5

[GVW13] Gorbunov, S., Vaikuntanathan, V., Wee, H.: Attribute-based encryption for circuits. In: Boneh, D., Roughgarden, T., Feigenbaum, J. (eds.) Symposium on Theory of Computing Conference, STOC 2013, Palo Alto, CA, USA, 1–4 June 2013, pp. 545–554. ACM (2013)

[GVW15] Gorbunov, S., Vaikuntanathan, V., Wichs, D.: Leveled fully homomorphic signatures from standard lattices. In: Servedio, R.A., Rubinfeld, R. (eds.) Proceedings of the Forty-Seventh Annual ACM on Symposium on Theory of Computing, STOC 2015, Portland, OR, USA, 14–17 June 2015, pp. 469–477. ACM (2015)

[LTWC16] Lai, R.W.F., Tai, R.K.H., Wong, H.W.H., Chow, S.S.M.: A zoo of homomorphic signatures: multi-key and key-homomorphism (2016). http://eprint.iacr.org/2016/834

[Mic04] Micciancio, D.: Almost perfect lattices, the covering radius problem, and applications to ajtais connection factor. SIAM J. Comput. **34**(1), 118–169 (2004)

[MP12] Micciancio, D., Peikert, C.: Trapdoors for lattices: simpler, tighter, faster, smaller. In: Pointcheval, D., Johansson, T. (eds.) EUROCRYPT 2012. LNCS, vol. 7237, pp. 700–718. Springer, Heidelberg (2012). doi:10.1007/978-3-642-29011-4_41

[MP13] Micciancio, D., Peikert, C.: Hardness of SIS and LWE with small parameters. In: Canetti, R., Garay, J.A. (eds.) CRYPTO 2013. LNCS, vol. 8042, pp. 21–39. Springer, Heidelberg (2013). doi:10.1007/978-3-642-40041-4_2

[MPR11] Maji, H.K., Prabhakaran, M., Rosulek, M.: Attribute-based signatures. In: Kiayias, A. (ed.) CT-RSA 2011. LNCS, vol. 6558, pp. 376–392. Springer, Heidelberg (2011). doi:10.1007/978-3-642-19074-2_24

[MR07] Micciancio, D., Regev, O.: Worst-case to average-case reductions based on gaussian measures. SIAM J. Comput. **37**(1), 267–302 (2007)

[Pei16] Peikert, C.: A decade of lattice cryptography. Found. Trends Theor. Comput. Sci. **10**, 283–424 (2016)

[SAH16] Sakai, Y., Attrapadung, N., Hanaoka, G.: Attribute-based signatures for circuits from bilinear map. In: Cheng, C.-M., Chung, K.-M., Persiano, G., Yang, B.-Y. (eds.) PKC 2016. LNCS, vol. 9614, pp. 283–300. Springer, Heidelberg (2016). doi:10.1007/978-3-662-49384-7_11

On the One-Per-Message Unforgeability
of (EC)DSA and Its Variants

Manuel Fersch[1]([✉]), Eike Kiltz[1], and Bertram Poettering[1,2]

[1] Horst Görtz Institute for IT Security, Ruhr University Bochum, Bochum, Germany
{manuel.fersch,eike.kiltz}@rub.de
[2] Information Security Group, Royal Holloway, University of London, London, UK
bertram.poettering@rhul.ac.uk

Abstract. The American signature standards DSA and ECDSA, as
well as their Russian and Chinese counterparts GOST 34.10 and SM2,
are of utmost importance in the current security landscape. The mentioned schemes are all rooted in the Elgamal signature scheme (1984)
and use a hash function and a cyclic group as building blocks. Unfortunately, authoritative security guarantees for the schemes are still due:
All existing positive results on their security use aggressive idealization
approaches, like the generic group model, leading to debatable overall
results.

In this work we conduct security analyses for a set of classic signature
schemes, including the ones mentioned above, providing positive results
in the following sense: If the hash function (which is instantiated with
SHA1 or SHA2 in a typical DSA/ECDSA setup) is modeled as a random
oracle, and the signer issues at most one signature per message, then the
schemes are unforgeable if and only if they are key-only unforgeable,
where the latter security notion captures that the adversary has access
to the verification key but not to sample signatures. Put differently, for
the named signature schemes, in the one-signature-per-message setting
the signature oracle is redundant.

Keywords: Elgamal signatures · DSA · ECDSA · GOST · SM2

1 Introduction

DIGITAL SIGNATURES. Digital signature schemes are a ubiquitous cryptographic
primitive. They are extensively used for message and entity authentication and
find widespread application in real-world protocols. The signature schemes most
often used in practice are likely the RSA-based PKCS#1v1.5, and the DLP-
based DSA and ECDSA [20]. For instance, current versions of TLS exclusively
employ signatures of these types to authenticate servers. Standardized schemes

The full version of this work can be found on the *IACR Cryptology ePrint
Archive* [12].

Y. Kalai and L. Reyzin (Eds.): TCC 2017, Part II, LNCS 10678, pp. 519–534, 2017.
https://doi.org/10.1007/978-3-319-70503-3_17

that share a great similarity with (EC)DSA are the Russian GOST 34.10 [9] and the Chinese SM2 [19]. In the following we describe those schemes in more detail.

DSA AND ECDSA. The signature schemes DSA and ECDSA build on ideas of ElGamal [10] and are defined over a cyclic group $\mathbb{G} = \langle g \rangle$ of prime order q. They utilize two independent hash functions, H and f, that map messages and group elements, respectively, into the exponent space $\mathbb{Z}_q$. Function f is called the *conversion function*. While for DSA the group $\mathbb{G}$ is a prime-order subgroup of the multiplicative group of some prime field $GF(p)$ with the canonical representation of group elements as integers in $\{1, \ldots, p-1\}$, and f is defined as $A \mapsto (A \bmod p)$ $\bmod q$, for ECDSA the group is a subgroup of an elliptic curve over some field $GF(p^n)$, and f is defined as $A \mapsto A.x \bmod q$ where $A.x$ is an encoding of the x-coordinate of elliptic curve point A as an integer.

The signature schemes GOST and SM2 use similar settings. After having fixed the cyclic group $\mathbb{G}$, the hash function H, and the conversion function f, if x is a signing key and $X = g^x$ the corresponding verification key, an (EC)DSA signature on a message m is a pair (s, t) such that $s = (H(m) + xt)/r$ and $t = f(g^r)$, where r is freshly picked in each signing operation. In GOST and SM2, different equations that values s, t, r, x have to fulfill are used. (For details see Fig. 2.)

PRIOR ANALYSES OF ELGAMAL-TYPE SIGNATURE SCHEMES. The first positive results on (unmodified) ECDSA are due to Brown. In [4–6] he proves security of ECDSA in the *generic group model* [27]. Unfortunately, some crucial formal aspects of his idealization remain unclear, for instance that his modeling approach for the group *implicitly* also idealizes the conversion function f. This has unexpected impact: he *de facto* proves that ECDSA signatures are strongly unforgeable, while in practice this is obviously not the case. See the discussions in [11,28] for more details. Further, as Brown reports, his arguments are applicable to ECDSA only, but not to the (closely-related) DSA.

Independently of the findings discussed above, in [4,6,7] Brown identifies both sufficient and necessary conditions on H, f for the security of ECDSA. However, the sufficient ones are significantly stronger than the discrete logarithm problem.

In an informal discussion, in [6, II.4.4], Brown mentions that for ECDSA, in the random oracle model, unforgeability against adversaries that have access to the verification key but not to a signing oracle implies unforgeability against adversaries that can request signatures, but at most one per message. No formal argument is given for this claim. We work out the details in the current article. As our treatment shows, a formal proof requires careful consideration and additional techniques.

In [11] the current authors propose GenDSA, a signature framework that subsumes both DSA and ECDSA in unmodified form, and prove the unforgeability of corresponding signatures using a novel approach of idealization: They decompose the conversion function into three independent functions, where the outer two mimic algebraic properties of the conversion function's domain and range, and the inner function is modeled as a bijective random oracle.[1] In the full version they extend their results to also cover GOST and SM2. To the best of our knowledge, this is the only existing security proof for GOST signatures. For SM2, the only other security evaluation is in the generic group model [31].

In comparison to [5,11] the current work takes a conservative approach: We idealize neither the group nor the conversion function but rather model a hash function as a random oracle. As this hash function is typically instantiated with a dedicated construction like SHA1 or SHA2, we believe our assumptions are weaker and thus preferable to those used in [5,11,31]. We caution, however, that also our results are weaker for not giving a reduction to the DLP, but to a different (non-interactive) assumption.

FURTHER RELATED WORK. The works discussed next do not establish security results for standardized schemes like DSA/GOST/SM2: Some works instead target modified versions of these schemes, others give implementation advice.

Brickell et al. [3] define a framework for signature schemes called *Trusted El Gamal Type Signature Scheme* and prove its unforgeability in the random oracle model. Among the instantiations of their framework are the schemes DSA-I (reportedly due to Brickell, 1996) in which the conversion function f is replaced by a random oracle, and DSA-II (due to [26]) that deviates from DSA for applying the hash function H to both the message and the ephemeral value $f(g^r)$. The framework of [3] cannot be instantiated such that unmodified (EC)DSA, GOST, or SM2 is covered.

Similarly, Malone-Lee and Smart [22] propose the variants ECDSA-II and ECDSA-III of ECDSA. In order to make certain attacks impossible (like duplicate signatures [28] where one signature is valid for two messages), and for obtaining tighter security reductions, the authors diverge from the original ECDSA scheme.

Other work on the security of DSA and ECDSA, identifying necessary conditions for the security of the schemes or analyzing their robustness against flaws in implementations and parameter selection, was conducted by Vaudenay [29,30], Howgrave-Graham and Smart [18], Nguyen and Shparlinski [24], Leadbitter et al. [21], García et al. [13], and Genkin et al. [14].

Our Contribution

Our contribution is threefold. First, we describe the abstract signature scheme GenElgamal that, among others, subsumes DSA, ECDSA, and GOST in unmodified, and SM2 in an equivalent form. Second, we show that in the random oracle model (for H), forging signatures in the presence of a signing oracle that can be queried at most once on each message (one-per-message unforgeability, uf-cma1) is as hard, but with a non-tight security reduction, as without such an oracle (key-only unforgeability, uf-koa). This means for the named schemes that the

---

[1] A bijective random oracle is an idealized public bijection that is accessible, in both directions, via oracles; cryptographic constructions that build on such objects include the Even–Mansour blockcipher and the SHA3 hash function.

(restricted) signing oracle is actually redundant. Third, we generalize the notion of *intractable semi-logarithm* from [6] and show that it is equivalent, for some schemes, to key-only unforgeability. In the following we describe these three parts in more detail.

GENERIC ELGAMAL SIGNATURES. The GenElgamal signature scheme is defined in the DLP setting relative to a hash function H, a conversion function f, a so-called *defining equation E*, and a set $\mathbb{D}$ that enforces some restrictions on the signature values. See Sect. 3 for the details. Different choices of these parameters lead to different signature schemes, including DSA, ECDSA, GOST, and SM2.

PROVING THE SECURITY OF GENELGAMAL. Consider GenElgamal and assume H is a random oracle. In Sect. 4 we prove that, in this setting, key-only unforgeability implies one-per-message unforgeability. (The latter notion is not only of theoretical interest; as we elaborate in Sect. 2 it is sufficient in many practical scenarios.) This observation can be traced back to Brown [6, II.4.4] for the case of ECDSA, but previously it has not been proved formally. Surprisingly, our security reduction requires a Coron-like partitioning argument [8]. We note that our reduction is not tight but loses a factor of about Q_s (the number of queries to the signing oracle).

INTRACTABLE SEMI-LOGARITHM. The notion of intractable semi-logarithm was introduced by Brown [6, II.2.2] to analyze the security of ECDSA. The idea is effectively to remove hash function H from the assumption that ECDSA is unforgeable. In brief, a semi-logarithm challenge consists of computing, given g and $X = g^x$, a pair (s,t) such that $t = f((gX^t)^{1/s})$. We formalize and generalize the semi-logarithm assumption in Sect. 5 and show that, in the random oracle model, its hardness is equivalent to the key-only unforgeability of the signature schemes considered in this article (except for SM2).

2 Preliminaries

NOTATION. For a set $\mathbb{A}$ we write $\mathbb{A}^n$ for the n-fold Cartesian product. We denote random sampling from a finite set $\mathbb{A}$ according to the uniform distribution with $a \xleftarrow{\$} \mathbb{A}$. We use symbol $\xleftarrow{\$}$ also for assignments from randomized algorithms, while we denote assignments from deterministic algorithms and calculations with $\leftarrow$. All algorithms are randomized unless explicitly noted. When using symbols like $\perp$ we mean special symbols that do not appear as elements of sets (e.g., key spaces). Any computation involving $\perp$ results in $\perp$, in particular for every function f we have $f(\perp) = \perp$.

If q is a prime number, we write $\mathbb{Z}_q$ for the field $\mathbb{Z}/q\mathbb{Z}$ and assume the canonic representation of its elements as a natural number in the interval $[0, q-1]$. That is, an element $a \in \mathbb{Z}_q$ is invertible iff $a \neq 0$. We denote prime-order groups with $(\mathbb{G}, g, q)$ where $\mathbb{G}$ is (the description of) a cyclic group, its order $q = |\mathbb{G}|$ is a prime number, and g is a generator such that $\mathbb{G} = \langle g \rangle$. We write 1 for the neutral element of $\mathbb{G}$ and $\mathbb{G}^* = \mathbb{G}\backslash\{1\}$ for the set of its generators.

Our security definitions are game based and expressed via program code. As data structures, besides sets our code may use associative arrays (look-up tables). We use notation $A[\cdot] \leftarrow \varnothing$ to initialize all cells of an array A to empty. A game G consists of an INIT procedure, one or more procedures to respond to adversary oracle queries, and a FIN procedure. G is executed with an adversary $\mathcal{A}$ as follows: INIT is always run first and its outputs are the inputs to $\mathcal{A}$. Next, the oracle queries of $\mathcal{A}$ are answered by the corresponding procedures of G. Finally, $\mathcal{A}$ calls FIN and terminates. Whenever the Stop command is invoked in a game, the execution of game and adversary is halted and the command's argument is considered the output of the game. We write 'Abort' as a shortcut for 'Stop with 0'. By $G^{\mathcal{A}} \Rightarrow$ out we denote the event that game G executed with $\mathcal{A}$ invokes the Stop command with argument out.

SIGNATURE SCHEMES. A *signature scheme* consists of algorithms KGen, Sign, Verify such that: algorithm KGen generates a signing key sk and a verification key pk; on input a signing key sk and a message m algorithm Sign generates a signature σ or the failure indicator $\perp$; on input a verification key pk, a message m, and a candidate signature σ, deterministic algorithm Verify outputs 0 or 1 to indicate rejection and acceptance, respectively. A signature scheme is correct if for all key pairs (sk, pk) created by KGen and all messages m, an invocation of Sign(sk, m) results in a signature with overwhelming probability, and if it does so then Verify accepts it.

We specify three security notions for signature schemes: uf-cma, uf-cma1, and uf-koa. The standard goal is *unforgeability under chosen-message attack* (uf-cma), meaning that no adversary can produce a valid signature on a fresh message, even if it sees signatures on messages of its choosing. A slightly weaker notion is *one-per-message unforgeability* (uf-cma1) [2,15,25] that adds the restriction that the adversary can see at most one signature per message. The weakest notion considered in this paper is *key-only unforgeability* (uf-koa) where the adversary sees no sample signature but only the verification key. The corresponding security games are in Fig. 1. Note that the uf-cma1 game aborts if the adversary queries the signing oracle a second time on any message, and that in the uf-koa game there is no signing oracle.

Definition 1 (Unforgeability). *For a signature scheme, a forger $\mathcal{F}$ is said to (τ, Q_s, ε)-break uf-cma (uf-cma1, uf-koa) security if it runs in at most time τ, poses at most Q_s queries to the SIGN oracle, and achieves a forging advantage of $\varepsilon = \Pr[G^{\mathcal{F}} \Rightarrow 1]$, where G is the corresponding game in Fig. 1. (In the uf-koa case we require $Q_s = 0$.)*

If the signature scheme is specified in relation to some idealized primitive that is accessed via oracles, we also annotate the maximum number of corresponding queries; for instance, in the random oracle model for a hash function H we use the expression $(\tau, Q_s, Q_H, \varepsilon)$. We always assume that forgers that output a forgery attempt (m^*, σ^*) pose a priori all (public) queries that the verification in FIN will require.

Note that, while the uf-cma1 notion is technically weaker than uf-cma security, for many practical applications the former is natural and sufficient. For instance, in Signed-Diffie-Hellman key agreement users exchange messages of

Procedure INIT	**Procedure** FIN(m^*, σ^*)
00 $\mathcal{L} \leftarrow \emptyset$	07 If $m^* \in \mathcal{L}$: Abort
01 $(sk, pk) \xleftarrow{\$} \mathsf{KGen}$	08 If $\mathsf{Verify}(pk, m^*, \sigma^*) = 0$: Abort
02 Return pk	09 Stop with 1
Procedure SIGN(m) (uf-cma)	**Procedure** SIGN(m) (uf-cma1)
$\vdots$	10 If $m \in \mathcal{L}$: Abort
03 $\sigma \xleftarrow{\$} \mathsf{Sign}(sk, m)$	11 $\sigma \xleftarrow{\$} \mathsf{Sign}(sk, m)$
04 If $\sigma = \bot$: Return $\bot$	12 If $\sigma = \bot$: Return $\bot$
05 $\mathcal{L} \leftarrow \mathcal{L} \cup \{m\}$	13 $\mathcal{L} \leftarrow \mathcal{L} \cup \{m\}$
06 Return σ	14 Return σ

Fig. 1. The vertical space above Line 03 is exclusively for aligning the SIGN oracles of variant uf-cma and of variant uf-cma1 (that adds Line 10). In variant uf-koa the SIGN oracle does not exist.

the form $g^x \parallel \mathsf{Sign}(sk, g^x)$, where exponent x is fresh for each execution and thus no value g^x is ever signed twice. For cases where uf-cma security is not sufficient, [2] propose efficient generic transformations that turn uf-cma1 secure signature schemes into ones secure in the uf-cma sense. Concretely, one possibility is to derandomize the signing algorithm by obtaining the randomness from a secretly keyed function applied to the message.

3   The Generic Elgamal Framework

We recall the abstract signature framework GenElgamal from [23, Sect. 11] that is defined relative to a group $\mathbb{G}$, a hash function H, a conversion function f, and an equation $E(s, h, t, r, x)$ called the *defining equation* of GenElgamal. To the latter is also associated a set $\mathbb{D}$. In GenElgamal, the hash function H is used to hash messages to elements of field $\mathbb{Z}_q$, and the conversion function f is used to transform group elements to elements of $\mathbb{Z}_q$. Intuitively, a signature consists of a solution s of E for values $h = H(m)$, $t = f(g^r)$ where r is the signing randomness, and signing key x. As we will see, to ensure functionality and security, certain such solutions need to be excluded. This is implemented by filtering them out by requiring containedness of corresponding triples (s, h, t) in set $\mathbb{D}$. As it turns out, some standards are overly restrictive on the set of possible signatures (i.e., set $\mathbb{D}$ is specified smaller than it could be; an example is SGenSM2 where $s = 0$ is not allowed). Nevertheless, in this document we stick to the sets specified by the standard documents unless further noted.

Different choices of the defining equation E (and set $\mathbb{D}$) lead to different signature schemes. See Fig. 2 for an overview of classic ones. All these schemes are rooted in the Elgamal signature scheme [10].

Definition 2 (Defining Equation). *Let $\mathbb{D} \subseteq \mathbb{Z}_q^3$ be a set. An equation*

$$E = E(s, h, t, r, x) \text{ over } \mathbb{D} \times (\mathbb{Z}_q^*)^2$$

is said to be defining (a signature scheme) if E has the form

$$E(s, h, t, r, x) = C_0(s, h, t) + r\, C_r(s, h, t) + x\, C_x(s, h, t),$$

where C_0, C_x are functions $\mathbb{D} \to \mathbb{Z}_q$, and C_r is a function $\mathbb{D} \to \mathbb{Z}_q^*$. With other words, E is defining if it is affine linear in x and r, and E can always be solved for r.

Figure 2 lists possible defining equations together with common names for the corresponding signature schemes. Concretely, we consider all variants of Elgamal signatures mentioned in the Handbook of Applied Cryptography [23], and in addition SM2.[2] Of course there are also other possible choices for E; for example, [17] lists a total of 18 configurations.

Scheme			E	$\mathbb{D}$
GenDSA	(V1)	[20]	$h + tx = rs$	$\mathbb{Z}_q^* \times \mathbb{Z}_q \times \mathbb{Z}_q^*$
GenGOST	(V3)	[9]	$hr + tx = s$	$\mathbb{Z}_q^* \times \mathbb{Z}_q^* \times \mathbb{Z}_q^*$
SGenSM2		[19]	$h + r + t = sx$	$\mathbb{D}_{\mathrm{SM}}(t)$
GenAMV	(V2)	[1]	$h = rt + sx$	$\mathbb{Z}_q \times \mathbb{Z}_q \times \mathbb{Z}_q^*$
GenHarn	(V6)	[16]	$hsx + r = st$	$\mathbb{Z}_q^* \times \mathbb{Z}_q \times \mathbb{Z}_q^*$
no name	(V4)	[23]	$hx + rt = s$	$\mathbb{Z}_q \times \mathbb{Z}_q \times \mathbb{Z}_q^*$
no name	(V5)	[23]	$hr + t = sx$	$\mathbb{Z}_q \times \mathbb{Z}_q^* \times \mathbb{Z}_q^*$

Fig. 2. Defining equations of a selection of established signature schemes. The variant number (Vi) refers to [23, Table 11.5]. $\mathbb{D}_{\mathrm{SM}}(t)$ is defined as $\{(s, h, t) \in \mathbb{Z}_q^* \times \mathbb{Z}_q^2 : t + h \neq 0, s - t - h \neq 0\}$.

Definition 3 (Signing and Verification Function). *Let E be a defining equation. Then we define the signing function $\mathsf{S}^E(h, t, r, x) = \mathsf{S}_x^E(h, t, r)$ as follows: if there exists a unique s such that $E(s, h, t, r, x)$ is satisfied, S^E returns s; otherwise, the function returns $\perp$.*

Further, we define the verification function $\mathsf{V}^E(g, s, h, t, x) = \mathsf{V}_{g,x}^E(s, h, t)$ with respect to a prime-order group $(\mathbb{G}, g, q)$ as follows: if r is the (unique) solution of $E(s, h, t, r, x)$ then V^E returns g^r.

Note that the affine linear form of E makes it possible to efficiently evaluate V^E given just s, h, t, g^x, i.e., without knowing x explicitly.

Definition 4 (GenElgamal Framework). *Let $(\mathbb{G}, g, q)$ be a prime-order group, $\mathbb{D} \subseteq \mathbb{Z}_q^3$ a set, and $H: \{0, 1\}^* \to \mathbb{Z}_q$ a hash function. Let further $f: \mathbb{G}^* \to \mathbb{Z}_q$ be a function and E a defining equation as in Definition 2. Then GenElgamal (relative to $E, \mathbb{G}, H, f, \mathbb{D}$) is defined by the algorithms of Fig. 3.*

---

[2] More precisely, we consider SGenSM2 which is an equivalent variant of SM2. Concretely, $(\hat{s}, \hat{t})$ is a valid SM2 signature on a message m for the verification key $\hat{X}$ if and only if $(s, t) = (\hat{s} + \hat{t}, \hat{t} - H(m))$ is a valid SGenSM2 signature on m for the verification key $X = g\hat{X}$. As all these transformations are public and reversible, the functionality and security of SM2 and SGenSM2 are the same.

Proc KGen	**Proc** Sign(sk, m)	**Proc** Verify$(pk, m, (s, t))$
00 $x \xleftarrow{\$} \mathbb{Z}_q^*; X \leftarrow g^x$	03 $r \xleftarrow{\$} \mathbb{Z}_q; R \leftarrow g^r$	11 $h \leftarrow H(m)$
01 $sk := x; pk := X$	04 If $R = 1$: Return $\bot$	12 If $(s, h, t) \notin \mathbb{D}$:
02 Return (sk, pk)	05 $t \leftarrow f(R)$	13 Return 0
	06 $h \leftarrow H(m)$	14 $\hat{R} \leftarrow \mathsf{V}_{g,x}^E(s, h, t)$
	07 $s \leftarrow \mathsf{S}_x^E(h, t, r)$	15 If $\hat{R} = 1$: Return 0
	08 If $(s, h, t) \notin \mathbb{D}$:	16 $\hat{t} \leftarrow f(\hat{R})$
	09 Return $\bot$	17 If $t \neq \hat{t}$: Return 0
	10 Return (s, t)	18 Return 1

Fig. 3. The GenElgamal signature scheme with defining equation E. Functions S^E and V^E are as in Definition 3. If S^E returns $\bot$ in Line 07 then Sign returns $\bot$ in Line 09.

We define a notion of *simulatability* that will be used in the GenElgamal security proof (in Sect. 4). It captures the fact that, in the random oracle model, it is possible to simulate (almost) correctly distributed GenElgamal signatures without knowledge of the signing key.

Definition 5 (δ-**Simulatability**). *Let* $(E, \mathbb{G}, H, f, \mathbb{D})$ *be an instantiation of* GenElgamal *as in Definition 4. We say the scheme is* δ-simulatable *if there exists a function* $\mathsf{Sim}^E : \mathbb{Z}_q^3 \to \mathbb{Z}_q^2 \cup \{\bot\}$ *that is computable in about the same time as* S^E *such that for all* $x \in \mathbb{Z}_q^*$ *the statistical distance between the outputs of the two protocols depicted in Fig. 4 is at most* δ.

Protocol $\mathsf{P}_{\mathsf{real}}(x)$	**Protocol** $\mathsf{P}_{\mathsf{sim}}(g^x)$
00 $r \xleftarrow{\$} \mathbb{Z}_q$	08 $a, b \xleftarrow{\$} \mathbb{Z}_q$
01 $R \leftarrow g^r$	09 $R \leftarrow X^a g^b$
02 If $R = 1$: Return $\bot$	10 If $R = 1$: Return $\bot$
03 $t \leftarrow f(R)$	11 $t \leftarrow f(R)$
04 $h \xleftarrow{\$} \mathbb{Z}_q$	12 $(s, h) \leftarrow \mathsf{Sim}^E(a, b, t)$
05 $s \leftarrow \mathsf{S}_x^E(h, t, r)$	$\vdots$
06 If $(s, h, t) \notin \mathbb{D}$: Return $\bot$	13 If $(s, h, t) \notin \mathbb{D}$: Return $\bot$
07 Return (s, h, t)	14 Return (s, h, t)

Fig. 4. Simulatability of an instantiation of GenElgamal. If Sim^E outputs $\bot$ in Line 12 then $\mathsf{P}_{\mathsf{sim}}$ outputs $\bot$ in Line 13. The vertical space between Lines 12 and 13 is exclusively for aligning the two protocols.

Lemma 1. *All of the instantiations of* GenElgamal *described in Fig. 2 are* δ-simulatable with $\delta \leq 2/q$.

Proof. Consider any of the instantiations. Let $x \in \mathbb{Z}_q^*$ be arbitrary. In $\mathsf{P}_{\mathsf{sim}}$ the random value r is implicitly computed in the exponent as $ax + b$ and by choice of a and b uniformly distributed on $\mathbb{Z}_q$, so the t-values in both protocols are distributed identically.

Next, we want to show that for fixed r, t, x the value a is almost always a function in h and vice versa. To this end we show that for each instantiation there exist sets $\mathbb{A}, \mathbb{H} \subseteq \mathbb{Z}_q$ (depending on $r, t = f(g^r), x$) with $|\mathbb{H}| \geq q - 2$ and a bijection $\pi_{x,r} \colon \mathbb{H} \to \mathbb{A}$. The bijection and its inverse function can be computed directly from the respective defining equation, see Fig. 5. Note that $\pi_{x,r}^{-1}$ actually is a function of a, b, t, but for fixed x, r the value of b is uniquely determined by the choice of a as $b = r - ax$ and the value of t is uniquely determined as $t = f(g^r)$. Now when sampling $a \xleftarrow{\$} \mathbb{Z}_q$ and computing h as $\pi_{x,r}^{-1}(a, r - ax, f(g^r))$ in $\mathsf{P}_{\mathrm{sim}}(x)$ (setting $\pi_{x,r}^{-1}(a, r - ax, f(g^r)) = \bot$ for $a \notin \mathbb{A}$, which happens with probability at most $2/q$ since $|\mathbb{Z}_q \backslash \mathbb{A}| \leq 2$) instead of directly sampling h uniformly random from $\mathbb{Z}_q$ in $\mathsf{P}_{\mathrm{real}}(x)$, the statistical distance between the h-values is at most $2/q$.

Scheme	$\mathbb{H}$	$\mathbb{A}$	$\pi_{x,r}$	$\pi_{x,r}^{-1}$	$\xi_{x,r}$	δ
GenDSA	$\mathbb{Z}_q \backslash \{-xt\}$	$\mathbb{Z}_q^*$	$rt/(h+xt)$	bt/a	t/a	$1/q$
GenGOST	$\mathbb{Z}_q^*$	$\mathbb{Z}_q^*$	$-1/h$	$-1/a$	$-b/a$	$1/q$
SGenSM2	$\mathbb{Z}_q \backslash \{-t-r\}$	$\mathbb{Z}_q^*$	$(h+r+t)/x$	$-(b+t)$	a	$1/q$
GenAMV	$\mathbb{Z}_q \backslash \{rt\}$	$\mathbb{Z}_q^*$	$(h-rt)/tx$	bt	$-at$	$1/q$
GenHarn	$\mathbb{Z}_q^* \backslash \{t/x\}$	$\mathbb{Z}_q^* \backslash \{r/x\}$	$hr/(hx-t)$	$-at/b$	b/t	$2/q$
(V4)	$\mathbb{Z}_q^*$	$\mathbb{Z}_q^*$	$-h/t$	$-at$	bt	$1/q$
(V5)	$\mathbb{Z}_q^* \backslash \{-t/r\}$	$\mathbb{Z}_q^* \backslash \{r/x\}$	$(hr+t)/hx$	$-t/b$	$-at/b$	$2/q$

Fig. 5. Sets $\mathbb{H}$ and $\mathbb{A}$ and functions $\pi_{x,r}(h)$, $\pi_{x,r}^{-1}(a, b, t)$, and $\xi_{x,r}(a, b, t)$ for the schemes from Fig. 2. We write $t = f(g^r)$. The last column shows the δ-values for the simulatability of the instantiation (see Definition 5).

Now once x, a, b, t, h are fixed, since the defining equation has to hold, s can be computed deterministically by a function $\xi_{x,r}$, also displayed in Fig. 5. Note that both $\pi_{x,r}^{-1}$ and $\xi_{x,r}$ can be computed without explicit knowledge of x, r for all of the instantiations. So if we set

$$\mathsf{Sim}^E(a, b, t) = (\xi_{x,r}(a, b, t), \pi_{x,r}^{-1}(a, b, t)),$$

the statistical distance between the outputs of the two protocols from Fig. 4 is at most $2/q$. $\square$

4   Security of GenElgamal in the ROM

We examine the security of GenElgamal, showing that if the hash function H is modeled as a random oracle, key-only unforgeability implies one-per-message unforgeability. This was already suggested in [6, II.4.4] for the case of GenDSA, but no formal treatment was given. We here provide a formal statement and a proof for the general case. Interestingly, our argument involves Coron-type partitioning [8].

Theorem 1. *Let $E, \mathbb{G}, H, f, \mathbb{D}$ be a δ-simulatable instantiation of GenElgamal. Then if H is modeled as a random oracle, for every forger $\mathcal{F}$ that $(\tau, Q_s, Q_H, \varepsilon)$-breaks the one-per-message unforgeability of this instantiation there also exists a forger $\mathcal{F}'$ that $(\tau', 0, Q_H, \varepsilon')$-breaks the key-only unforgeability of this instantiation, where*

$$\varepsilon' \geq \varepsilon/(e^2(Q_s + 1)) - Q_s\delta \qquad and \qquad \tau' = \tau + \mathcal{O}(Q_H).$$

Proof. Let $\mathcal{F}$ be a forger that $(\tau, Q_s, Q_H, \varepsilon)$-breaks the one-per-message unforgeability of the scheme under consideration. Let **Game G_0** be the standard uf-cma1 game with the algorithms of Fig. 3 plugged in and an additional random oracle RO for H that is implemented by lazy sampling (see Fig. 6). We assume without loss of generality that $\mathcal{F}$ queries RO on m before calling SIGN or FIN involving the same message. We have

$$\Pr[G_0^{\mathcal{F}} \Rightarrow 1] = \varepsilon.$$

The idea of the reduction is that we respond to each hash query $\mathrm{RO}(m)$ by selecting the hash value in a specific though uniform way (such that we can simulate signatures on m), except for the value of m^*, which we want to forward to the random oracle RO^* of the uf-koa security game in a reduction later. But m^* is not yet known at the time of simulating the hash queries, so in **Game G_1** (see Fig. 6) we apply the partitioning technique from [8] and toss a biased coin that takes value 0 with probability $Q_s/(Q_s + 1)$ and value 1 with probability

Procedure INIT	**Procedure** RO(m)	
00 $\mathcal{L} \leftarrow \emptyset$	14 If $H[m] \neq \emptyset$:	
01 $H[\cdot] \leftarrow \emptyset; c[\cdot] \leftarrow \emptyset$	15 $\quad$ Return $H[m]$	
02 $x \xleftarrow{\$} \mathbb{Z}_q^*; X \leftarrow g^x$	16 $c[m] \xleftarrow{\$} \mathrm{Ber}(\gamma)$	(G_1)
03 Return X	17 $h \xleftarrow{\$} \mathbb{Z}_q$	
	18 $H[m] \leftarrow h$	
Procedure SIGN(m)	19 Return h	
04 If $m \in \mathcal{L}$: Abort		
05 If $c[m] \neq 0$: Abort $\quad (G_1)$	**Procedure** FIN$(m^*, (s^*, t^*))$	
06 $r \xleftarrow{\$} \mathbb{Z}_q; R \leftarrow g^r$	20 If $m^* \in \mathcal{L}$: Abort	
07 If $R = 1$: Return $\perp$	21 If $c[m^*] \neq 1$: Abort $\quad (G_1)$	
08 $t \leftarrow f(R)$	22 $h^* \leftarrow H[m^*]$	
09 $h \leftarrow H[m]$	23 If $(s^*, h^*, t^*) \notin \mathbb{D}$: Abort	
10 $s \leftarrow \mathsf{S}_x^E(h, t, r)$	24 $R^* \leftarrow \mathsf{V}_{g,x}^E(s^*, h^*, t^*)$	
11 If $(s, h, t) \notin \mathbb{D}$: Return $\perp$	25 If $R^* = 1$: Abort	
12 $\mathcal{L} \leftarrow \mathcal{L} \cup \{m\}$	26 If $f(R^*) \neq t^*$: Abort	
13 Return (s, t)	27 Stop with 1	

Fig. 6. Games G_0 and G_1. Ber is the Bernoulli distribution with bias $\gamma = 1/(Q_s + 1)$, i.e., in Line 16 $c[m]$ takes the value 1 with probability $1/(Q_s + 1)$. Note that Line 20 is redundant in G_1.

$\gamma = 1/(Q_s + 1)$ for every queried message, and we hope that it takes the value 0 for all messages used in signature queries and the value 1 for m^*.

We now analyze the probability that one of the coins takes an unwanted value, i.e., the probability of an abort in Lines 05 and 21. To do this, we consider the complementary probability. Since for all messages m, $c[m]$ is distributed according to the Bernoulli distribution $\text{Ber}(\gamma)$ with $\gamma = 1/(Q_s + 1)$ and independently of all other coins, the probability that no abort happens in these lines is

$$(1 - \gamma)^{Q_s} \gamma \geq (1 - 1/Q_s)^{Q_s}(1/(Q_s + 1)) \geq 1/e^2(Q_s + 1),$$

where the last inequality is a standard result in calculus and holds for $Q_s \geq 2$. The case $Q_s = 1$ is trivial. It follows that

$$\Pr[G_0^{\mathcal{F}} \Rightarrow 1] \leq e^2(Q_s + 1)\Pr[G_1^{\mathcal{F}} \Rightarrow 1].$$

In **Game G_2** (see Fig. 7) we introduce two changes: (a) when processing a random oracle query on a message m, a signature for m is precomputed and stored, and (b) the way of signing messages is changed so that signatures are generated without knowing the signing key. Note that change (a) is possible only because the SIGN oracle may be queried on each message at most once. Change (b) exploits the assumed simulatability (see Definition 5) of GenElgamal.

Procedure INIT	**Procedure** RO(m)
00 $\mathcal{L} \leftarrow \emptyset$	09 If $H[m] \neq \emptyset$: Return $H[m]$
01 $H[\cdot] \leftarrow \emptyset; c[\cdot] \leftarrow \emptyset$	10 $c[m] \stackrel{\$}{\leftarrow} \text{Ber}(\gamma)$
02 $\sigma[\cdot] \leftarrow \emptyset$	11 $h \stackrel{\$}{\leftarrow} \mathbb{Z}_q$
03 $x \stackrel{\$}{\leftarrow} \mathbb{Z}_q^*; X \leftarrow g^x$	12 If $c[m] = 0$:
04 Return X	13 $\quad a, b \stackrel{\$}{\leftarrow} \mathbb{Z}_q$
	14 $\quad R \leftarrow X^a g^b$
Procedure SIGN(m)	15 $\quad$ If $R = 1$:
05 If $m \in \mathcal{L}$: Abort	16 $\qquad \sigma[m] \leftarrow \perp$; Goto Line 22
06 If $c[m] \neq 0$: Abort	17 $\quad t \leftarrow f(R)$
07 $\mathcal{L} \leftarrow \mathcal{L} \cup \{m\}$	18 $\quad (s, h) \leftarrow \text{Sim}^E(a, b, t)$
08 Return $\sigma[m]$	19 $\quad$ If $(s, h, t) \notin \mathbb{D}$:
	20 $\qquad \sigma[m] \leftarrow \perp$; Goto Line 22
Procedure FIN$(m^*, (s^*, t^*))$	21 $\quad \sigma[m] \leftarrow (s, t)$
$\quad$ as in G_1 (Fig. 6)	22 $H[m] \leftarrow h$
	23 Return h

Fig. 7. Game G_2

We argue that the adversary can distinguish G_1 and G_2 with probability at most $Q_s \delta$. To see this, note that change (a) is a pure rewriting step and does not influence the output of the game. Concerning change (b), consider first the case that the adversary queries SIGN or RO on a message m with $c[m] = 1$. For the random oracle, the response h is picked uniformly at random in Line 11, and the signing oracle aborts, so the distribution is exactly as in G_1.

Consider next the case that the adversary queries one of the oracles on a message m with $c[m] = 0$. Observe then that Lines 06 to 11 in G_1 correspond exactly to the protocol $\mathsf{P_{real}}$ from Fig. 4, and Lines 13 to 20 in G_2 correspond exactly to the protocol $\mathsf{P_{sim}}$. Thus, switching the way of computing signatures introduces, for each call to the signing oracle, a statistical distance between the two games that is bounded by δ. We obtain

$$\left| \Pr[G_1^{\mathcal{F}} \Rightarrow 1] - \Pr[G_2^{\mathcal{F}} \Rightarrow 1] \right| \leq Q_s \delta.$$

Now construct a uf-koa forger $\mathcal{F}'$ against GenElgamal in the random oracle model as in Fig. 8.

Procedure INIT	**Procedure** SIGN(m)
replace Line 03 with	as in G_2 (Fig. 7)
03 $X \xleftarrow{\$} \text{INIT}^*$	
Procedure RO(m)	**Procedure** FIN$(m^*, (s^*, t^*))$
replace Line 11 with	replace Lines 22–27 in Fig. 6 with
11 $h \leftarrow \text{RO}^*(m)$	22 Invoke FIN$^*(m^*, (s^*, t^*))$

Fig. 8. Construction of uf-koa forger $\mathcal{F}'$ from $\mathcal{F}$ by changing Game G_2 as specified. INIT*, RO*, and FIN* are the procedures from the uf-koa security game run by $\mathcal{F}'$. Procedure SIGN is as in Game G_2.

The coin tosses in Line 10 of Fig. 7 ensure that $\mathcal{F}'$ only has to provide signatures on messages for which it programmed the random oracle itself; it thus simulates the signing procedure of G_2 perfectly. Further, the coin tosses guarantee that the forgery is consistent with RO*, so $\mathcal{F}'$ wins its game exactly if $\mathcal{F}$ produces a valid forgery. This means that

$$\Pr[G_2^{\mathcal{F}} \Rightarrow 1] = \varepsilon',$$

and the statement follows.   □

5   The Semi-Logarithm Problem

We formalize and generalize the notion of intractable *semi-logarithm problem* (SLP), a notion introduced by Brown for the analysis of signature schemes.

His motivation for studying the SLP is "to isolate the role of the hash function and the group in analyzing the security of ECDSA" [6, p. 25]. Effectively, the SLP is a number-theoretic hardness assumption related to the search problem of finding a valid GenElgamal signature for a (unknown) message m with hash value $H(m) = 1$.

As we show, the key-only unforgeability of an instantiation of GenElgamal is characterized by the intractability of the corresponding variant of the semi-logarithm problem (in the random oracle model), potentially establishing a simplified target for cryptanalysis. Note that a suitable SLP variant does not exist for all GenElgamal instantiations: for SM2 there is apparently no corresponding SLP definition.

Definition 6. *Let $(\mathbb{G}, g, q)$ be a prime-order group and let $f: \mathbb{G}^* \to \mathbb{Z}_q$ and $\rho_0, \rho_1: \mathbb{Z}_q^2 \to \mathbb{Z}_q$ be functions. We say that an algorithm $\mathcal{I}$ (τ, ε)-breaks the semi-logarithm problem (SLP) in $\mathbb{G}$ with respect to f, ρ_0, ρ_1 if it runs in time at most τ and achieves probability*

$$\varepsilon = \Pr[X \xleftarrow{\$} \mathbb{G}; (u, v) \xleftarrow{\$} \mathcal{I}(g, X) : v = f(g^{\rho_0(u,v)} X^{\rho_1(u,v)})].$$

Definition 7. *Let $E = E(s, h, t, r, x)$ be a defining equation with corresponding set $\mathbb{D}$ (see Definition 2). We say that E is h-decomposable (with respect to $\mathbb{D}$) if there exist functions*

$$\eta_0, \eta_1: \mathbb{Z}_q \to \mathbb{Z}_q \qquad and \qquad \rho_0, \rho_1: \mathbb{Z}_q^2 \to \mathbb{Z}_q$$

such that $\eta_0(h), \eta_1(h) \neq 0$ if $h \neq 0$ and

$$r = \eta_0(h)\rho_0(s, t) + x\,\eta_1(h)\rho_1(s, t)$$

for all $(s, h, t) \in \mathbb{D}$ and $r, x \in \mathbb{Z}_q^*$ satisfying $E(s, h, t, r, x)$.

All defining equations from Fig. 2, except for SGenSM2, are h-decomposable. The corresponding components $\eta_0, \rho_0, \eta_1, \rho_1$ are listed in Fig. 9.

Scheme	$\eta_0(h)$	$\rho_0(s,t)$	$\eta_1(h)$	$\rho_1(s,t)$
GenDSA (V1)	h	$1/s$	1	t/s
GenGOST (V3)	$1/h$	s	$-1/h$	t
GenAMV (V2)	h	$1/t$	-1	s/t
GenHarn (V6)	1	st	$-h$	s
no name (V4)	1	s/t	$-h$	$1/t$
no name (V5)	$-1/h$	t	$1/h$	s

Fig. 9. Components $\eta_0, \rho_0, \eta_1, \rho_1$ of the h-decomposable defining equations from Fig. 2.

Theorem 2. *Let $(\mathbb{G}, g, q)$ be a prime-order group, let E be a defining equation with corresponding set $\mathbb{D}$, and let $f: \mathbb{G}^* \to \mathbb{Z}_q$ and $H: \{0,1\}^* \to \mathbb{Z}_q$ be functions. If E is h-decomposable with functions ρ_0, ρ_1, and H is modeled as a random oracle, then the semi-logarithm problem in $\mathbb{G}$ with respect to f, ρ_0, ρ_1 is non-tightly equivalent to the key-only unforgeability of GenElgamal when instantiated with $E, \mathbb{G}, H, f, \mathbb{D}$.*

More precisely, for any adversary $\mathcal{I}$ that (τ, ε)-breaks SLP, there exists a forger $\mathcal{F}$ that (τ', ε)-breaks the key-only unforgeability of GenElgamal, where $\tau \approx \tau'$.

Conversely, for any forger $\mathcal{F}$ that (τ, Q_H, ε)-breaks the key-only unforgeability of GenElgamal, *there exists an adversary $\mathcal{I}$ that $(\tau', \varepsilon/Q_H - 1/q)$-breaks SLP, where $\tau' \approx \tau$ and Q_H is the number of random oracle queries posed by $\mathcal{F}$.*

Proof. Given an adversary $\mathcal{I}$ that (τ, ε)-breaks SLP, we construct a forger $\mathcal{F}$ that (τ', ε)-breaks key-only unforgeability of GenElgamal, for any hash function H. (For the particular case of ECDSA, this result is due to Brown [6].) On input, $\mathcal{F}$ obtains g, X (from pk). It picks any message m (independently of X) such that $H(m) \neq 0$, computes $h \leftarrow H(m)$, $g' \leftarrow g^{\eta_0(h)}$, and $X' \leftarrow X^{\eta_1(h)}$, and lets $\mathcal{I}$ compute a semi-logarithm as per $(u, v) \overset{\$}{\leftarrow} \mathcal{I}(g', X')$. Then (u, v) is a valid signature on m (with respect to g, X). Indeed, since E is h-decomposable, by definition of $\mathsf{V}^E_{g,x}$ (see Definition 3) it holds that in Verify (see Line 14 in Fig. 3) we have

$$\hat{R} = \mathsf{V}^E_{g,x}(u, h, v) = g^{\eta_0(h)\rho_0(u,v)} X^{\eta_1(h)\rho_1(u,v)} = (g')^{\rho_0(u,v)}(X')^{\rho_1(u,v)},$$

and thus $f(\hat{R}) = v$.

Let now $\mathcal{F}$ be a forger that (τ, Q_H, ε)-breaks the key-only unforgeability of GenElgamal. We construct an adversary $\mathcal{I}$ against SLP from it. On input of (g, X), it draws $a \overset{\$}{\leftarrow} \mathbb{Z}_q$, aborts if $a = 0$, sets $g' \leftarrow g^{1/\eta_0(a)}$ and $X' \leftarrow X^{1/\eta_1(a)}$, and starts $\mathcal{F}$ on input $pk = (g', X')$. If m^* denotes the message on which $\mathcal{F}$ forges a signature, we assume w.l.o.g. that $\mathcal{F}$ queries $H(m^*)$ before outputting the latter. $\mathcal{I}$ initially guesses the index $j \in \{1, \ldots, Q_H\}$ of the corresponding query to H. It then responds to the jth random oracle query by programming it via $H(m_j) \leftarrow a$, and answers all other queries with uniform values. Once $\mathcal{F}$ outputs its forgery $(m^*, (s, t))$, adversary $\mathcal{I}$ forwards (s, t) to its own challenger. Since E is h-decomposable and $g = (g')^{\eta_0(H(m^*))}$ and $X = (X')^{\eta_1(H(m^*))}$, it holds that

$$g^{\rho_0(s,t)} X^{\rho_1(s,t)} = ((g')^{\eta_0(H(m^*))})^{\rho_0(s,t)}((X')^{\eta_1(H(m^*))})^{\rho_1(s,t)}$$
$$= \mathsf{V}^E_{g',x'}(s, H(m^*), t),$$

where $x' = \log_{g'} X'$. That is, $\mathcal{I}$ wins in the SLP game if it didn't abort when sampling a, its guess for index j was correct, and $\mathcal{F}$ forges successfully. $\qquad \square$

Acknowledgments. The first author was supported by DFG SPP 1736 Big Data. The second author was supported in part by ERC Project ERCC (FP7/615074) and by DFG SPP 1736 Big Data. The third author was supported in part by ERC Project ERCC (FP7/615074).

References

1. Agnew, G., Mullin, R., Vanstone, S.: Improved digital signature scheme based on discrete exponentiation. Electron. Lett. **26**(14), 1024–1025 (1990)
2. Bellare, M., Poettering, B., Stebila, D.: From identification to signatures, tightly: a framework and generic transforms. In: Cheon, J.H., Takagi, T. (eds.) ASIACRYPT 2016. LNCS, vol. 10032, pp. 435–464. Springer, Heidelberg (2016). doi:10.1007/978-3-662-53890-6_15

3. Brickell, E., Pointcheval, D., Vaudenay, S., Yung, M.: Design validations for discrete logarithm based signature schemes. In: Imai, H., Zheng, Y. (eds.) PKC 2000. LNCS, vol. 1751, pp. 276–292. Springer, Heidelberg (2000). doi:10.1007/978-3-540-46588-1_19
4. Brown, D.R.L.: Generic groups, collision resistance, and ECDSA. Cryptology ePrint Archive, Report 2002/026 (2002). http://eprint.iacr.org/2002/026
5. Brown, D.R.L.: Generic groups, collision resistance, and ECDSA. Des. Codes Crypt. **35**(1), 119–152 (2005)
6. Brown, D.R.L.: On the provable security of ECDSA. In: Blake, I.F., Seroussi, G., Smart, N.P. (eds.) Advances in Elliptic Curve Cryptography, pp. 21–40. Cambridge University Press, Cambridge (2005). doi:10.1017/CBO9780511546570.004
7. Brown, D.R.L.: One-up problem for (EC)DSA. Cryptology ePrint Archive, Report 2008/286 (2008). http://eprint.iacr.org/2008/286
8. Coron, J.-S.: On the exact security of full domain hash. In: Bellare, M. (ed.) CRYPTO 2000. LNCS, vol. 1880, pp. 229–235. Springer, Heidelberg (2000). doi:10.1007/3-540-44598-6_14
9. Dolmatov, V., Degtyarev, A.: GOST R 34.10-2012: Digital Signature Algorithm. RFC 7091 (Informational), December 2013. http://www.ietf.org/rfc/rfc7091.txt
10. ElGamal, T.: A public key cryptosystem and a signature scheme based on discrete logarithms. In: Blakley, G.R., Chaum, D. (eds.) CRYPTO 1984. LNCS, vol. 196, pp. 10–18. Springer, Heidelberg (1985). doi:10.1007/3-540-39568-7_2
11. Fersch, M., Kiltz, E., Poettering, B.: On the provable security of (EC)DSA signatures. In: Weippl, E.R., Katzenbeisser, S., Kruegel, C., Myers, A.C., Halevi, S. (eds.) ACM CCS 16, Vienna, Austria, 24–28 October 2016, pp. 1651–1662. ACM Press (2016)
12. Fersch, M., Kiltz, E., Poettering, B.: On the one-per-message unforgeability of (EC)DSA and its variants. Cryptology ePrint Archive, Report 2017/890 (2017). http://eprint.iacr.org/2017/890
13. García, C.P., Brumley, B.B., Yarom, Y.: Make sure DSA signing exponentiations really are constant-time. In: Weippl, E.R., Katzenbeisser, S., Kruegel, C., Myers, A.C., Halevi, S. (eds.) ACM CCS 2016, Vienna, Austria, 24–28 October 2016, pp. 1639–1650. ACM Press (2016)
14. Genkin, D., Pachmanov, L., Pipman, I., Tromer, E., Yarom, Y.: ECDSA key extraction from mobile devices via nonintrusive physical side channels. In: Weippl, E.R., Katzenbeisser, S., Kruegel, C., Myers, A.C., Halevi, S. (eds.) ACM CCS 2016, Vienna, Austria, 24–28 October 2016, pp. 1626–1638. ACM Press (2016)
15. Gentry, C., Peikert, C., Vaikuntanathan, V,: Trapdoors for hard lattices and new cryptographic constructions. In: Ladner, R.E., Dwork, C. (eds.) 40th ACM STOC, Victoria, British Columbia, Canada, 17–20 May 2008, pp. 197–206. ACM Press (2008)
16. Harn, L.: New digital signature scheme based on discrete logarithm. Electron. Lett. **30**(5), 396–398 (1994)
17. Harn, L., Xu, Y.: Design of generalised ElGamal type digital signature schemes based on discrete logarithm. Electron. Lett. **30**(24), 2025–2026 (1994)
18. Howgrave-Graham, N., Smart, N.P.: Lattice attacks on digital signature schemes. Des. Codes Crypt. **23**(3), 283–290 (2001)
19. ISO/IEC 11889:2015: Information technology—Trusted Platform Module library (2013). https://www.iso.org/
20. Kerry, C.F., Gallagher, P.D.: FIPS PUB 186-4 Federal Information Processing Standards publication: Digital Signature Standard (DSS) (2013). doi:10.6028/NIST.FIPS.186-4

21. Leadbitter, P.J., Page, D., Smart, N.P.: Attacking DSA under a repeated bits assumption. In: Joye, M., Quisquater, J.-J. (eds.) CHES 2004. LNCS, vol. 3156, pp. 428–440. Springer, Heidelberg (2004). doi:10.1007/978-3-540-28632-5_31
22. Malone-Lee, J., Smart, N.P.: Modifications of ECDSA. In: Nyberg, K., Heys, H. (eds.) SAC 2002. LNCS, vol. 2595, pp. 1–12. Springer, Heidelberg (2003). doi:10. 1007/3-540-36492-7_1
23. Menezes, A.J., van Oorschot, P.C., Vanstone, S.A.: Handbook of Applied Cryptography. The CRC Press Series on Discrete Mathematics and Its Applications. CRC Press, Boca Raton (1997). 2000 N.W. Corporate Blvd., FL 33431–9868, USA
24. Nguyen, P.Q., Shparlinski, I.: The insecurity of the elliptic curve digital signature algorithm with partially known nonces. Des. Codes Crypt. **30**(2), 201–217 (2003)
25. Poettering, B., Stebila, D.: Double-authentication-preventing signatures. In: Kutyłowski, M., Vaidya, J. (eds.) ESORICS 2014. LNCS, vol. 8712, pp. 436–453. Springer, Cham (2014). doi:10.1007/978-3-319-11203-9_25
26. Pointcheval, D., Vaudenay, S.: On provable security for digital signature algorithms. Technical report LIENS-96-17, LIENS (1996)
27. Shoup, V.: Lower bounds for discrete logarithms and related problems. In: Fumy, W. (ed.) EUROCRYPT 1997. LNCS, vol. 1233, pp. 256–266. Springer, Heidelberg (1997). doi:10.1007/3-540-69053-0_18
28. Stern, J., Pointcheval, D., Malone-Lee, J., Smart, N.P.: Flaws in applying proof methodologies to signature schemes. In: Yung, M. (ed.) CRYPTO 2002. LNCS, vol. 2442, pp. 93–110. Springer, Heidelberg (2002). doi:10.1007/3-540-45708-9_7
29. Vaudenay, S.: Hidden collisions on DSS. In: Koblitz, N. (ed.) CRYPTO 1996. LNCS, vol. 1109, pp. 83–88. Springer, Heidelberg (1996). doi:10.1007/ 3-540-68697-5_7
30. Vaudenay, S.: The security of DSA and ECDSA. In: Desmedt, Y.G. (ed.) PKC 2003. LNCS, vol. 2567, pp. 309–323. Springer, Heidelberg (2003). doi:10.1007/ 3-540-36288-6_23
31. Zhang, Z., Yang, K., Zhang, J., Chen, C.: Security of the SM2 signature scheme against generalized key substitution attacks. In: Chen, L., Matsuo, S. (eds.) SSR 2015. LNCS, vol. 9497, pp. 140–153. Springer, Cham (2015). doi:10.1007/ 978-3-319-27152-1_7

Verifiable Random Functions

A Generic Approach to Constructing and Proving Verifiable Random Functions

Rishab Goyal[1(✉)], Susan Hohenberger[2], Venkata Koppula[1], and Brent Waters[1]

[1] University of Texas at Austin, Austin, USA
{rgoyal,kvenkata,bwaters}@cs.utexas.edu
[2] Johns Hopkins University, Baltimore, USA
susan@cs.jhu.edu

Abstract. Verifiable Random Functions (VRFs) as introduced by Micali, Rabin and Vadhan are a special form of Pseudo Random Functions (PRFs) wherein a secret key holder can also prove validity of the function evaluation relative to a statistically binding commitment.

Prior works have approached the problem of constructing VRFs by proposing a candidate under a specific number theoretic setting — mostly in bilinear groups — and then grappling with the challenges of proving security in the VRF environments. These constructions achieved different results and tradeoffs in practical efficiency, tightness of reductions and cryptographic assumptions.

In this work we take a different approach. Instead of tackling the VRF problem as a whole, we demonstrate a simple and generic way of building Verifiable Random Functions from more basic and narrow cryptographic primitives. Then we can turn to exploring solutions to these primitives with a more focused mindset. In particular, we show that VRFs can be constructed generically from the ingredients of: (1) a 1-bounded constrained pseudo random function for a functionality that is "admissible hash friendly", (2) a non-interactive statistically binding commitment scheme (without trusted setup) and (3) non-interactive witness indistinguishable proofs or NIWIs. The first primitive can be replaced with a more basic puncturable PRF constraint if one is willing to settle for selective security or assume sub-exponential hardness of assumptions.

In the second half of our work, we support our generic approach by giving new constructions of the underlying primitives. We first provide new constructions of perfectly binding commitments from the Learning with Errors (LWE) and Learning Parity with Noise (LPN) assumptions. Second, we give two new constructions of 1-bounded constrained PRFs for admissible hash friendly constructions. Our first construction is from the n-powerDDH assumption. The next is from the ϕ hiding assumption.

1 Introduction

Verifiable Random Functions (VRFs) as introduced by Micali et al. [30] are a special form of Pseudo Random Functions (PRFs) [20] wherein a secret key holder can also prove validity of the function evaluation relative to a statistically

© International Association for Cryptologic Research 2017
Y. Kalai and L. Reyzin (Eds.): TCC 2017, Part II, LNCS 10678, pp. 537–566, 2017.
https://doi.org/10.1007/978-3-319-70503-3_18

binding commitment. The caveat being that the pseudorandomness of the function on other points should not be sacrificed even after providing polynomially many proofs. The VRF definition forbids *interactivity* or any *setup assumption*, thereby disallowing trivial extensions of PRFs making the problem more challenging and interesting.

Prior works [13, 14, 22, 24, 25, 29] have approached the problem of constructing VRFs by proposing a candidate under a specific number theoretic setting — mostly in bilinear groups — and then grappling with the challenges of proving security in the VRF environments. These constructions achieved different results and tradeoffs in practical efficiency, tightness of reductions and cryptographic assumptions.

In this work we take a different approach. Instead of tackling the VRF problem as a whole, we demonstrate a simple and generic way of building Verifiable Random Functions from more basic and narrow cryptographic primitives. Then we can turn to exploring solutions to these primitives with a more focused mindset.

In particular, we show that VRFs can be constructed generically from the ingredients of: (1) a 1-bounded constrained pseudo random function [8, 10, 27] for a functionality that is "admissible hash friendly", (2) a non-interactive statistically binding commitment scheme (without trusted setup) and (3) non-interactive witness indistinguishable proofs or NIWIs [16]. The first primitive can be replaced with a more basic puncturable PRF [36] constraint if one is willing to settle for selective security or assume sub-exponential hardness of assumptions.

The first benefit of our approach is that by generically breaking down the problem we expose and separate the core features of VRFs. Namely, we can see that in spirit any reduction must both develop a way of constraining itself from knowing the output of the entire PRF space while at the same time be able to develop non-interactive proofs without a common setup. Second, with the VRF problem dissected into constituent parts, we can explore and develop number theoretic solutions to each piece. Ideally, this breakdown will help us develop a wider array of solutions and in particular break away from the dependence on bilinear maps. We now look at each primitive in turn.

Beginning with constrained PRFs, our goal is to build them for constraints that we call admissible hash [7] compatible. In particular, we need a constrained key that can be associated with a string $z \in \{0, 1, \perp\}^n$ where the constrained key can be evaluated on any input $x \in \{0, 1\}^n$ where $x \neq z$. For our purposes such a scheme only needs to be secure in the model where an attacker is allowed a single key query. The recent work of Brakerski and Vaikuntanthan [11] construct 1-bounded constrained PRFs under the learning with errors (LWE) [35] assumption that can handle any constraint in $\mathbf{NC}^1$ which encompasses the admissible hash compatible functionality.

We complement this by providing a new construction of constrained PRFs that is admissible hash friendly in the setting of non-bilinear groups. Our construction is proven secure under the n-powerDDH problem. Informally, one is given $g, g^a, g^{a^2}, \ldots, g^{a^{n-1}}$, it is hard to distinguish g^{a^n} from a random group element. We note that this problem in composite order groups reduces to the subgroup decision problem [12]. In addition, as mentioned above if we assume sub-exponential hardness of our assumptions or relax to selective security we can instead rely on puncturable PRFs which are realizable from any one way function.

We next turn to constructing non-interactive perfectly binding commitments. The main challenge here is any solution must not utilize a trusted setup since a trusted setup is disallowed in the VRF setting. Naor [32] showed how any certifiably injective one way function gives rise to such a commitment scheme. Injective functions can in turn be based on (certifiable) groups where discrete log is hard.

We develop new constructions for non-interactive perfectly binding commitments from noisy cryptographic assumptions. We show and prove a construction under the Learning with Errors and Learning Parity with Noise (LPN) assumptions. Our LPN solution uses a low-noise variant ($\beta \approx \frac{1}{\sqrt{n}}$) of the LPN assumption that has been used in previous public key encryption schemes [1]. We also develop an approach for proving security under LPN with constant noise. Our solution requires the existence of an explicit error correcting code with certain properties. We leave finding such a code as an interesting open problem.

Finally, we arrive at NIWIs. There are three basic approaches to building NIWIs. First, in the bilinear setting, it is known [21] how to construct NIWIs from the decision linear assumption. Second, Barak, Ong and Vadhan (BOV) [4] showed that two-message public-coin witness indistinguishable proofs (a.k.a. ZAPs [15]) imply NIWIs under certain complexity theoretic assumptions that allow for derandomization. Finally, indistinguishability obfuscation [18] gives rise to NIWI constructions [6].

Taking a step back we can see that our approach already leads to constructions of VRFs with new properties. For example, if we build ZAPs from trapdoor permutations and apply the BOV theorem we can achieve multiple constructions of adaptively secure VRFs *without* complexity leveraging that do not use bilinear groups. In addition, given the wide array of choices for building our commitments and constrained PRFs, our work reveals developing new techniques for building and proving NIWIs as the primary bottleneck for progress towards VRFs.

1.1 Technical Overview

We now give a high level overview of our technical approach. A formal treatment is given in the main body. We break our overview into three pieces. First we describe our generic construction of Verifiable Random Functions. Next, we define admissible hash compatible constrained PRFs and go over our non-bilinear group solution. Finally, we overview our LWE and LPN solutions to non-interactive perfectly binding commitments.

Constructing VRFs Generically. We first briefly review the definition of a Verifiable Random Function. In the VRF framework, a party runs the Setup algorithm to generate a pair of secret key SK and public verification key VK. Using the secret key SK, it could efficiently evaluate the function $F_{SK}(\cdot)$ on any input x as well as a proof Π of the statement $y = F_{SK}(x)$. The verification key could be considered as a statistically binding commitment to the underlying pseudorandom function. A third party verification algorithm Verify is used to verify a proof Π which takes the verification key VK, function evaluation y, and message x as additional inputs. First, the soundness condition dictates that for each (VK, x) pair there should be at most one output y such that $\mathsf{Verify}(VK, x, y, \pi) = 1$. Importantly, VRFs do not make use of any setup assumption and soundness should hold even in the case of a *maliciously generated* VK. Second, it should also hold that the output of function $F_{SK}(\cdot)$ is indistinguishable from a random string even after observing polynomially many evaluations and proofs at adversarially chosen points. The latter is formalized as pseudorandomness property of the VRF.

We now give a simple construction from the aforementioned primitives. The VRF setup proceeds as follows. First, a constrained PRF key K is sampled and kept as part of the secret key. Next, a sequence of three independent commitments c_1, c_2, c_3 is computed such that each commitment c_i opens to the key K.[1] The triple of commitments (c_1, c_2, c_3) is stored as the public verification key and the corresponding randomness used during commitment is included in the secret key. For evaluating the VRF on any input x, we first apply an admissible hash function on x and then evaluate the constrained PRF on the output of admissible hash. In short, the VRF output on some input x is $\mathsf{PRF}_K(h(x))$. For proving correctness of evaluation, we use non-interactive witness indistinguishable proofs (NIWIs). In particular, to prove that the output of VRF on some input x is y, we create a NIWI proof for the statement that *at least two out of three* commitments (c_1, c_2, c_3) (in the verification key) open to keys K_1, K_2 such that $y = \mathsf{PRF}_{K_1}(h(x)) = \mathsf{PRF}_{K_2}(h(x))$ (the idea of a majority-based decoding (i.e., two out of three trick) was also used in [2]). We would like to emphasize that keys K_1 and K_2 need not be identical as the only constraint that must hold is that the PRF evaluation of input $h(x)$ must be equal to y irrespective of the key (out of K_1, K_2) used. The proof verification can be done in a straightforward manner as it simply involves running the NIWI verifier.

Now we briefly sketch the idea behind pseudorandomness proof in the adaptive setting. To prove security we use a "partitioning" argument where roughly $1/Q$ fraction of inputs can be used as challenge and remaining $1 - 1/Q$ fraction will be used for answering evaluation queries, where Q is the number of queries made by an attacker. First step in the reduction is to concretely define the challenge and non-challenge partitions using admissible hash function. Next, we leverage the facts that all the evaluation queries will lie outside the challenge

---

[1] Looking ahead, it will be crucial for proving the unique provability property that the commitment scheme used is perfectly binding.

partition[2] and for generating the evaluation proofs we only need openings of two key commitments out of three. At a high level, our goal is to switch all three commitments c_1, c_2, c_3 such that they commit to the constrained key K' instead of key K, where K' could be used to evaluate the VRF on all points outside the challenge partition. To this end, the reduction proceeds as follows.

First, the challenger makes two crucial modifications — (1) it generates a constrained PRF key K' along with the master key K, (2) it computes c_3 as a commitment to key K' instead of key K. Such a hybrid jump is indistinguishable by the hiding property of the commitment scheme as for generating all the evaluation proofs it does not need the opening for c_3. Next, we switch the NIWI witness used to generate the proof. In particular, the challenger now uses openings of c_2, c_3 as the NIWI witnesses. This only results in a negligible dip in the adversary's advantage because for all inputs outside the challenge partition, the PRF evaluation using the master key K and constrained key K' is identical, thus the openings of any two commitments out of c_1, c_2, c_3 could be used as the NIWI witness. Applying similar modifications as above in succession, all three commitments c_1, c_2, c_3 could be switched to commitments of the constrained key K'. If all three commitments open to the constrained key K', then the challenger could directly reduce an attack on the VRF pseudorandomness to an attack on the constrained pseudorandomness of the PRF.

It is also interesting to note that if we use a puncturable PRF instead of an admissible hash compatible constrained PRF, then the same construction could be proven to be selectively secure with only polynomial security loss to the underlying assumptions. The major difference in the proof being the partitioning step, where instead of using the admissible hash function to perform partitioning and aborting in case of bad partitions, the reduction already knows the challenge input at the start, thus it only needs to puncture the PRF key on the challenge input in order to use the same sequence of hybrids. This is discussed in detail in Sect. 3.

Admissible Hash Compatible Constrained PRFs. A constrained PRF family consists of a setup algorithm that outputs the master PRF key, a constrain algorithm that takes as input the master PRF key and a constraint, and outputs a constrained PRF key. The constrained PRF key can be used to evaluate the PRF at all points satisfied by the constraint. As mentioned in the previous paragraph, for constructing adaptively secure VRFs, we require constrained PRFs for a special class of "admissible hash compatible" constraints. Each constraint is specified by a string $u \in \{0, 1, \perp\}^n$. Given a constrained key for u, it can be used to evaluate the PRF at all points x such that there exists an index $i \leq n$ where $u_i \neq \perp$ and $x_i \neq u_i$. For this work, we require a weaker notion of security which we call 'single-key no-query' security. Here, the adversary first sends a constrained key query u. After receiving the constrained key, it sends a challenge point x such

---

[2] The challenger needs to perform an abort step in case of bad partitioning, however for the above informal exposition we avoid discussing it. More details are provided in Sect. 3.

that it does not satisfy the constraint (that is, for all $i \leq n$, either $u_i = \perp$, or $x_i = u_i$). It then receives either the PRF evaluation at x or a uniformly random string, and it must distinguish between the two scenarios.

Powers-DDH Construction. This construction, at a high level, is similar to the Naor-Reingold PRF construction. The PRF key consists of $2n$ integers $\{c_{i,b}\}_{i \leq n, b \in \{0,1\}}$ and a group element g. To evaluate at a point x, we first choose n out of the $2n$ integers, depending on the bits of x. Let t denote the product of these n integers. The PRF evaluation is g^t. A constrained key for constraint $u \in \{0, 1, \perp\}^n$ consists of n powers of a random integer a in the exponent of g: $(g, g^a, \ldots, g^{a^{n-1}})$ and $2n$ integers $\{v_{i,b}\}$. Each $v_{i,b}$ is set to be either $c_{i,b}$ or $c_{i,b}/a$, depending on u_i. Using the $v_{i,b}$ and an appropriate g^{a^k} term, one can compute the PRF evaluation at any point x such that it satisfies the constraint (that is, if there exists an $i \leq n$ such that $u_i \neq \perp$ and $x_i \neq u_i$). However, if x does not satisfy the constraint, then one needs to compute g^{a^n} to compute the PRF evaluation at x. Using the n-powerDDH assumption, we can argue that if an adversary can distinguish between the PRF evaluation and a truly random string, then one can use this adversary to distinguish between g^{a^n} and a random group element.

Phi-Hiding Construction. In this scheme, the PRF key consists of an RSA modulus N, its factorization (p, q), $2n$ integers $c_{i,b}$, a base integer h and a strong extractor seed $\mathfrak{s}$. The PRF evaluation on an n bit strings is performed as follows: first choose n out of the $2n$ integers depending on the input, compute their product, then compute this product in the exponent of h and finally apply a strong extractor on the product with seed $\mathfrak{s}$. A constrained key for constraint $u \in \{0, 1, \perp\}^n$ consists of $2n$ integers $\{v_{i,b}\}$, integers e and h^e, and seed $\mathfrak{s}$. Each $v_{i,b}$ is set to be either $(c_{i,b} - 1) \cdot e^{-1}$ or $c_{i,b} \cdot e^{-1}$, depending on u_i. Integers $v_{i,b}$ are set such that the PRF evaluation at any point x satisfying the constraint is of the form $\mathsf{Ext}(h^{e\alpha}, \mathfrak{s})$, where α could be computed only using $v_{i,b}$'s and e. However, for all unsatisfying points x, the output is of the form $\mathsf{Ext}(h^{1+e\alpha}, \mathfrak{s})$. Using the phi-hiding assumption, we can argue that an adversary can not distinguish between the cases where e is co-prime with respect to $\phi(N)$, and when e divides $\phi(N)$. Note that in the latter case, there are e distinct e^{th} roots of h^e. Thus, for any challenge point, the term $h^{1+e\alpha}$ will have large min-entropy, and by strong extractor guarantee we could conclude that it looks uniformly random to the adversary.

We could also show that the above construction is a secure constrained unpredictable function under the RSA assumption. Note that constrained unpredictability is a weaker notion of security than constrained pseudorandomness in which the adversary must guess the PRF evaluation on the challenge point.

New Constructions of Non-Interactive Perfectly Binding Commitments. Finally, the third component required for our VRF construction is a non-interactive perfectly binding commitment scheme (without trusted setup). In this work, we give new constructions for this primitive based on the Learning with Errors (LWE) and Learning Parity with Noise (LPN) assumptions. (We emphasize that such commitments have applications beyond VRFs. For example, they are a key ingredient in building verifiable functional encryption [2].) Our LPN construction can be proven secure under the LPN with low noise assumption. Finally, we also give an approach for proving security under LPN with constant noise. This approach relies on the existence of special error correcting codes with 'robust' generator matrix. Currently, we do not have any explicit constructions for this combinatorial object. For simplicity, we only consider single bit commitment schemes.

LWE Construction. In this scheme, we will be working in $\mathbb{Z}_q$ for a suitably large prime q. The commitment to a bit b consists of a randomly chosen vector $\mathbf{w}$ and $\mathbf{w}^T\mathbf{s} + \mathsf{noise} + b(q/2)$, where $\mathbf{s}$ is a randomly chosen secret vector. However, to ensure perfect binding, we need to have some additional components. The scheme also chooses a random matrix $\mathbf{B}$ from a distribution $\mathcal{D}_1$ and outputs $\mathbf{B}, \mathbf{B}^T\mathbf{s} + \mathsf{noise}$. This distribution has the special property that all matrices from this distribution have 'medium norm' rowspace. This property ensures that there does not exist two distinct vectors $\mathbf{s}_1$ and $\mathbf{s}_2$ such that $\mathbf{B}^T\mathbf{s}_1 + \mathsf{noise}_1 = \mathbf{B}^T\mathbf{s}_2 + \mathsf{noise}_2$. Finally, to argue computational hiding, we require that a random matrix from this distribution looks uniformly random. If this condition is satisfied, then we can use the LWE assumption to argue that $\mathbf{w}^T\mathbf{s} + \mathsf{noise}$ and $\mathbf{B}^T\mathbf{s} + \mathsf{noise}'$ look uniformly random, thereby hiding the committed bit. Sampling a matrix from the distribution $\mathcal{D}_1$ works as follows: first choose a uniformly random matrix $\mathbf{A}$, then choose a matrix $\mathbf{C}$ with low norm entries, matrix $\mathbf{D}$ with 'medium' entries and output $[\mathbf{A} \mid \mathbf{AC} + \mathbf{D} + \mathsf{noise}]$. For any non zero vector $\mathbf{s}$, if $\mathbf{A}^T\mathbf{s}$ has low norm, then $\mathbf{C}^T\mathbf{A}^T\mathbf{s}$ also has low norm, but $\mathbf{D}^T\mathbf{s}$ has medium norm entries, and therefore $[\mathbf{A} \mid \mathbf{AC} + \mathbf{D} + \mathsf{noise}]^T\mathbf{s}$ has medium norm entries.

Low Noise LPN construction. This scheme is similar to the LWE construction. Here also, the commitment to a bit b consists of $\mathbf{w}$ and $\mathbf{w}^T\mathbf{s} + b$, where $\mathbf{w}$ and $\mathbf{s}$ are uniformly random vectors in $\mathbb{Z}_2^n$. To ensure that there can be only one vector $\mathbf{s}$, we also choose a matrix $\mathbf{B}$ from a special distribution $\mathcal{D}_2$ and output $\mathbf{B}, \mathbf{B}^T\mathbf{s} + \mathsf{noise}$. In this case, the distribution $\mathcal{D}_2$ is such that all matrices from this distribution have high hamming weight rowspace. To sample from the distribution $\mathcal{D}_2$, one chooses a uniformly random matrix $\mathbf{A}$, a matrix $\mathbf{C}$ with low hamming weight rows and outputs $[\mathbf{A} \mid \mathbf{AC} + \mathbf{G}]$, where $\mathbf{G}$ is the generator matrix of an error correcting code. Here the role of $\mathbf{G}$ is similar to the role of $\mathbf{D}$ in the previous solution: to map any non-zero vector to a high hamming weight vector. An important point here is that we need the rows of $\mathbf{C}$ to have low ($O(\sqrt{n})$) hamming weight. This is because we want to argue that if $\mathbf{A}^T\mathbf{s}$ has low hamming weight, then so does $\mathbf{C}^T\mathbf{A}^T\mathbf{s}$. Finally, to argue that $\mathcal{D}_2$ looks like the uniform distribution, we need the LPN assumption with low noise[3] (since $\mathbf{C}$ has low ($O(\sqrt{n})$) hamming weight rows).

---

[3] We will be using the (low noise) Knapsack LPN assumption. The Knapsack LPN assumption states that for a uniformly random matrix $\mathbf{A}$ and a matrix $\mathbf{E}$ such that each entry is 1 with probability p and $\mathbf{A}$ has fewer rows than columns, then $(\mathbf{A}, \mathbf{AE})$ look like uniformly random matrices.

This construction bears some similarities to the CCA secure encryption scheme of Kiltz et al. [28].

Standard LPN construction. Finally, we describe an approach for constructing a commitment scheme that can be proven secure under the standard LPN assumption (with constant noise). For this approach, we require a deterministic procedure that can output ℓ matrices $\mathbf{G}_1, \ldots, \mathbf{G}_\ell$ with the following property: for any matrix $\mathbf{A}$, there exists an index i such that the rowspace of $\mathbf{A} + \mathbf{G}_i$ has high hamming weight. Given such a procedure, our commitment scheme works as follows. The commitment algorithm, on input message b, chooses a uniformly random matrix $\mathbf{A}$ and generates ℓ sub-commitments. The ith sub-commitment chooses uniformly random vectors $\mathbf{s}_i, \mathbf{w}_i$ and outputs $(\mathbf{A} + \mathbf{G}_i)^T \mathbf{s}_i + \mathsf{noise}$, $\mathbf{w}_i$ and $\mathbf{w}_i^T \mathbf{s}_i + b$. For perfect binding, we will use the guarantee that there exists an i such that the rowspace of $\mathbf{A} + \mathbf{G}_i$ has high hamming weight. This implies that if $(\mathbf{A} + \mathbf{G}_i)^T \mathbf{s}_1 + \mathsf{noise} = (\mathbf{A} + \mathbf{G}_i)^T \mathbf{s}_2 + \mathsf{noise}$, then $\mathbf{s}_1 = \mathbf{s}_2$. For computational hiding, we need a hybrid argument to switch each sub-commitment to uniformly random.

1.2 Concurrent Work

Independently and concurrently, Bitansky [5] gave a very similar construction of VRFs from NIWIs, perfectly binding commitments and puncturable PRFs/constrained PRFs for admissible hash friendly constraints.

The notable differences in the two works are with respect to the new realizations of commitments and constrained PRFs. Both works give a constrained PRF under the n-powerDDH assumption for admissible hash friendly constraints. Bitansky was able to further prove this construction secure under the DDH assumption. Interestingly, the result was achieved by considering constrained PRFs for a more general notion of partitioning than admissible hash. We also construct admissible hash friendly constrained PRFs based on the phi-hiding assumption as well as constrained unpredictable functions based on the more standard RSA assumption. Finally, we also provide new constructions for perfectly binding commitments based on the LWE and LPN assumption.

Subsequently, Badrinarayanan et al. [3] gave an alternate construction of VRFs from puncturable PRFs/constrained PRFs for admissible hash friendly constraints and Verifiable Functional Encryption [2], which in turn can be constructed from NIWIs, injective one-way functions and secret key functional encryption schemes secure against single ciphertext and unbounded key queries.

2   Preliminaries

2.1   Verifiable Random Functions

Verifiable random functions (VRFs) were introduced by Micali, Rabin and Vadhan [30]. VRFs are keyed functions with input domain $\{\mathcal{X}_\lambda\}_\lambda$, output range $\{\mathcal{Y}_\lambda\}_\lambda$ and consist of three polynomial time algorithms Setup, Evaluate and Verify described as follows:

- Setup(1^λ) is a randomized algorithm that on input the security parameter, outputs (SK, VK). SK is called secret key, and VK verification key.
- Evaluate(SK, x) is a (possibly randomized) algorithm, and on input the secret key SK and $x \in \mathcal{X}_\lambda$, it outputs an evaluation $y \in \mathcal{Y}_\lambda$ and a proof $\pi \in \{0, 1\}^*$.
- Verify(VK, x, y, π) is a (possibly randomized) algorithm which uses verification key VK and proof π to verify that y is the correct evaluation on input x. It outputs 1 (accepts) if verification succeeds, and 0 (rejects) otherwise.

Definition 1 *(Adaptively-secure VRF). A pair of polynomial time algorithms* (Setup, Evaluate, Verify) *is an adaptively-secure verifiable random function if it satisfies the following conditions:*

- *(Correctness) For all* (SK, VK) $\leftarrow$ Setup(1^λ), *and all* $x \in \mathcal{X}_\lambda$, *if* $(y, \pi) \leftarrow$ Evaluate(SK, x), *then* $\Pr[\text{Verify}(\text{VK}, x, y, \pi) = 1] = 1$.
- *(Unique Provability) For every* (VK, $x, y_1, \pi_1, y_2, \pi_2$) *such that* $y_1 \neq y_2$, *the following holds for at least one* $i \in \{1, 2\}$:

$$\Pr[\text{Verify}(\text{VK}, x, y_i, \pi_i) = 1] \leq 2^{-\Omega(\lambda)}.$$

- *(Pseudorandomness) For any PPT adversary* $\mathcal{A} = (\mathcal{A}_0, \mathcal{A}_1)$ *there exists a negligible function* negl($\cdot$), *such that for all* $\lambda \in \mathbb{N}$, $\text{Adv}_{\mathcal{A}}^{\text{adp-VRF}}(\lambda) \leq negl(\lambda)$, *where advantage of* $\mathcal{A}$ *is defined as*

$$\text{Adv}_{\mathcal{A}}^{\text{adp-VRF}}(\lambda) = \Pr \left[\mathcal{A}_1^{\mathcal{O}_{x^*}}(\text{st}, y_b) = b : \begin{array}{l} (\text{SK}, \text{VK}) \leftarrow \text{Setup}(1^\lambda); \\ (x^*, \text{st}) = \mathcal{A}_0^{\text{Evaluate}(\text{SK}, \cdot)}(\text{VK}) \\ (y_1, \pi) \leftarrow \text{Evaluate}(\text{SK}, x^*); \\ y_0 \leftarrow \mathcal{Y}_\lambda; \quad b \leftarrow \{0, 1\} \end{array} \right] - \frac{1}{2},$$

where x^* *should not have been queried by* $\mathcal{A}_0$, *and oracle* $\mathcal{O}_{x^*}$ *on input* x^* *outputs* $\bot$, *otherwise behaves same as* Evaluate(SK, $\cdot$).

A weaker notion of security for VRFs is selective pseudorandomness where the adversary must commit to its challenge x^* at the start of the game, that is before the challenger sends VK to $\mathcal{A}$. Then during evaluation phase, $\mathcal{A}$ is allowed to query on polynomially many messages $x \neq x^*$, and $\mathcal{A}$ wins if its guess $b' = b$. The advantage of $\mathcal{A}$ is defined to be $\text{Adv}_{\mathcal{A}}^{\text{sel-VRF}}(\lambda) = |\Pr[\mathcal{A} \text{ wins}] - 1/2|$.

Definition 2 *(Selectively-secure VRF). A pair of polynomial time algorithms* (Setup, Evaluate, Verify) *is called a selectively-secure verifiable random function if it satisfies correctness and unique provability properties (as in Definition 1), and for all PPT adversaries* $\mathcal{A}$, $\text{Adv}_{\mathcal{A}}^{\text{sel-VRF}}(\lambda)$ *is negligible in the security parameter* λ.

2.2 Non-interactive Witness Indistinguishable Proofs

Witness indistinguishable (WI) proofs were introduced by Feige and Shamir [16] as a natural weakening of zero-knowledge (ZK) proofs. At a high level, the witness indistinguishability property says that a proof must not reveal the witness used to prove the underlying statement even if it reveals all possible witnesses corresponding to the statement. Unlike ZK proofs, WI proofs without interaction in the standard model are known to be possible. Barak et al. [4] provided constructions for one-message (completely non-interactive, with no shared random string or setup assumptions) witness indistinguishable proofs (NIWIs) based on ZAPs (i.e., two-message public-coin witness indistinguishable proofs) and Nisan-Wigderson type pseudorandom generators [34]. Groth et al. [21] gave the first NIWI construction from a standard cryptographic assumption, namely the decision linear assumption. Recently, Bitansky and Paneth [6] constructed NIWI proofs assuming iO and one-way permutations.

Definition 3 *(NIWI). A pair of PPT algorithms* $(\mathcal{P}, \mathcal{V})$ *is a NIWI for a language* $\mathcal{L} \in \mathbf{NP}$ *with witness relation* $\mathcal{R}$ *if it satisfies the following conditions:*

– *(Perfect Completeness) For all* (x, w) *such that* $\mathcal{R}(x, w) = 1$,

$$\Pr[\mathcal{V}(x, \pi) = 1 : \pi \leftarrow \mathcal{P}(x, w)] = 1.$$

– *(Statistical Soundness) For every* $x \notin \mathcal{L}$ *and* $\pi \in \{0, 1\}^*$,

$$\Pr[\mathcal{V}(x, \pi) = 1] \leq 2^{-\Omega(|x|)}.$$

– *(Witness Indistinguishability) For any sequence* $\mathcal{I} = \{(x, w_1, w_2) : \mathcal{R}(x, w_1) = 1 \wedge \mathcal{R}(x, w_2) = 1\}$

$$\{\pi_1 : \pi_1 \leftarrow \mathcal{P}(x, w_1)\}_{(x, w_1, w_2) \in \mathcal{I}} \approx_c \{\pi_2 : \pi_2 \leftarrow \mathcal{P}(x, w_2)\}_{(x, w_1, w_2) \in \mathcal{I}}$$

2.3 Perfectly Binding Commitments (with No Setup Assumptions)

A commitment scheme with message space $\{\mathcal{M}_\lambda\}_\lambda$, randomness space $\{\mathcal{R}_\lambda\}_\lambda$ and commitment space $\{\mathcal{C}_\lambda\}_\lambda$ consists of two polynomial time algorithms — Commit and Verify with the following syntax.

– Commit($1^\lambda, m \in \mathcal{M}_\lambda; r \in \mathcal{R}_\lambda$): The commit algorithm is a randomized algorithm that takes as input the security parameter λ, message m to be committed and random coins r. It outputs a commitment c.
– Verify($m \in \mathcal{M}_\lambda, c \in \mathcal{C}_\lambda, o \in \mathcal{R}_\lambda$): The verification algorithm takes as input the message m, commitment c and an opening o. It outputs either 0 or 1.

For simplicity, we assume that the opening for a commitment is simply the randomness used during the commitment phase. As a result, we do not have a separate 'reveal' algorithm. Below we formally define perfectly binding computationally hiding (PB-CH) commitment schemes with no setup assumptions (i.e., without trusted setup and CRS).

Definition 4 *(PB-CH Commitments). A pair of polynomial time algorithms* (Commit, Verify) *is a perfectly binding computationally hiding (PB-CH) commitment scheme if it satisfies the following conditions:*

- *(Perfect Correctness)* For all security parameters $\lambda \in \mathbb{N}$, message $m \in \mathcal{M}_\lambda$ and randomness $r \in \mathcal{R}_\lambda$, if $c = \mathsf{Commit}(1^\lambda, m; r)$, then $\mathsf{Verify}(m, c, r) = 1$.
- *(Perfect Binding)* For every (c, m_1, r_1, m_2, r_2) such that $m_1 \neq m_2$, the following holds for at least one $i \in \{1, 2\}$:

$$\Pr[\mathsf{Verify}(m_i, c, r_i) = 1] = 0.$$

- *(Computationally Hiding)* For all security parameters $\lambda \in \mathbb{N}$, messages $m_1, m_2 \in \mathcal{M}_\lambda$,

$$\left\{ c_1 : \begin{matrix} c_1 \leftarrow \mathsf{Commit}(1^\lambda, m_1; r_1); \\ r_1 \leftarrow \mathcal{R}_\lambda \end{matrix} \right\} \approx_c \left\{ c_2 : \begin{matrix} c_2 \leftarrow \mathsf{Commit}(1^\lambda, m_2; r_2); \\ r_2 \leftarrow \mathcal{R}_\lambda \end{matrix} \right\}$$

Perfectly binding commitments (without trusted setup) can be constructed from *certifiably injective* one-way functions. In this work, we show how to construct them under the Learning Parity with Low Noise assumption [1] and Learning with Errors assumption [35]. We would like to point out that the 'no trusted setup' requirement for commitments is essential for our VRF construction. We already know how to construct perfectly binding commitments *with trusted setup* from the LPN assumption [26], however it is not sufficient for our VRF construction as VRFs disallow trusted setup.

2.4   Admissible Hash Functions

A commonly used technique for achieving adaptive security is the *partitioning strategy* where the input space is partitioned into a 'query partition' and a 'challenge partition'. This partitioning is achieved using *admissible hash functions* introduced by Boneh and Boyen [7]. Here we state a simplified definition from [23].

Definition 5. *Let* k, ℓ *and* θ *be efficiently computable univariate polynomials. Let* $h\colon \{0,1\}^{k(\lambda)} \to \{0,1\}^{\ell(\lambda)}$ *be an efficiently computable function and* $\mathsf{AdmSample}$ *a PPT algorithm that takes as input* 1^λ *and an integer* Q, *and outputs* $u \in \{0, 1, \perp\}^{\ell(\lambda)}$. *For any* $u \in \{0, 1, \perp\}^{\ell(\lambda)}$, *define* $P_u : \{0,1\}^{k(\lambda)} \to \{0,1\}$ *as follows:*

$$P_u(x) = \begin{cases} 1 & \text{if for } j \leq \ell(\lambda), \quad u_j = h(x)_j \vee u_j = \perp \\ 0 & \text{otherwise.} \end{cases}$$

We say that $(h, \mathsf{AdmSample})$ *is* θ-*admissible if the following condition holds:*

For any efficiently computable polynomial Q, *for all* $x_1, \ldots, x_{Q(\lambda)}, x^* \in \{0,1\}^{k(\lambda)}$, *where* $x^* \notin \{x_i\}_1^{Q(\lambda)}$,

$$\Pr[(\forall i \leq Q(\lambda), P_u(x_i) = 0) \wedge P_u(x^*) = 1] \geq \frac{1}{\theta(Q(\lambda))}$$

where the probability is taken over $u \leftarrow \mathsf{AdmSample}(1^\lambda, Q(\lambda))$.

Theorem 1 (Admissible Hash Function Family [7], simplified proof in [17]). *For any efficiently computable polynomial k, there exist efficiently computable polynomials ℓ, θ such that there exist θ-admissible function families mapping k bits to ℓ bits.*

Note that the above theorem is information theoretic, and is not based on any cryptographic assumption.

2.5 Constrained Pseudorandom and Unpredictable Functions

Constrained pseudorandom functions, introduced by [8,10,27], are an extension of pseudorandom functions [20] where a party having the master PRF key can compute keys corresponding to any constraint from a constraint class. A constrained key for constraint C can be used to evaluate the PRF on inputs x that satisfy the constraint $C(x) = 0$.[4] However, the constrained key should not reveal PRF evaluations at points not satisfied by the constraint. Constrained PRFs for general circuit constraints can be constructed using multilinear maps [8], indistinguishability obfuscation [9] and the learning with errors assumption [11]. Note that the construction from LWE only allows a single constrained key query, which is a weaker security definition than the standard fully 'collusion-resistant' notion.

In this work, we will be using a special constraint family which we call 'admissible hash compatible', and the security definition will also be weaker than the standard (fully collusion-resistant) security for constrained PRFs. This enables us to construct this primitive from weaker and standard cryptographic assumptions such as the n-powerDDH assumption.

Definition 6. *Let $\mathcal{Z}_n = \{0, 1, \perp\}^n$. An admissible hash compatible function family $\mathcal{P}_n = \{P_z : \{0,1\}^n \to \{0,1\} \mid z \in \mathcal{Z}_n\}$ is defined exactly as the predicate $P_u(\cdot)$ in Definition 5.*

Looking ahead the above admissible hash compatible function family will correspond to the family of constraints for which we assume constrained PRFs. Next, we formally define the syntax, correctness and security properties of constrained PRFs.

Syntax. Let $n(\cdot)$ be a polynomial. A constrained pseudorandom function CPRF with domain $\{\mathcal{X}_\lambda = \{0,1\}^{n(\lambda)}\}_\lambda$, range $\mathcal{Y} = \{\mathcal{Y}_\lambda\}_\lambda$, key space $\mathcal{K} = \{\mathcal{K}_\lambda\}_\lambda$ and constrained key space $\mathcal{K}^c = \{\mathcal{K}^c_\lambda\}_\lambda$ for a family of admissible hash compatible constraints $\{\mathcal{C}_\lambda = \mathcal{P}_{n(\lambda)}\}_\lambda$ consists of three algorithms Setup, Constrain, Evaluate defined as follows. For simplicity of notation, we will refer to z as the constraint instead of P_z.

---

[4] We would like to point out that our notation departs from what has been used in the literature. Traditionally, it is considered that the constrained key allows PRF evaluation on points that satisfy $C(x) = 1$. However, we switch the constraint to $C(x) = 0$ for convenience.

- Setup(1^λ): The setup algorithm takes as input the security parameter λ and outputs a PRF key $K \in \mathcal{K}_\lambda$.
- Constrain($K, z \in \{0, 1, \perp\}^{n(\lambda)}$): The constrain algorithm takes as input a master PRF key $K \in \mathcal{K}_\lambda$, a constraint $z \in \{0, 1, \perp\}^{n(\lambda)}$ and outputs a constrained key $K_z \in \mathcal{K}_\lambda^c$.
- Evaluate($K \in \mathcal{K}_\lambda \cup \mathcal{K}_\lambda^c, x \in \{0, 1\}^{n(\lambda)}$): The evaluation algorithm takes as input a PRF key K (master or constrained), and outputs $y \in \mathcal{Y}$.

We would like to point out that in the above description there is a common evaluation algorithm that accepts both the PRF master key as well as the constrained key. Such an abstraction helps us in simplifying our VRF construction later in Sect. 3. Note that this is not a restriction on the constrained PRFs as it can achieved without loss of generality from any constrained PRF. Below we define the *single-key no-query* constrained pseudorandomness security notion for constrained PRFs.

Definition 7. *A pair of polynomial time algorithms* (Setup, Constrain, Evaluate) *is a* single-key no-query *secure constrained pseudorandom function for admissible hash compatible constraint family if it satisfies the following conditions:*

- *(Correctness) For every security parameter $\lambda \in \mathbb{N}$, master PRF key $K \leftarrow$* Setup(1^λ), *constraint $z \in \{0, 1, \perp\}^{n(\lambda)}$, constrained key $K_z \leftarrow$* Constrain(K, z) *and input $x \in \{0, 1\}^{n(\lambda)}$ such that $P_z(x) = 0$,* Evaluate(K, x) $=$ Evaluate(K_z, x).
- *(Single-key No-query Constrained Pseudorandomness) For any PPT adversary $\mathcal{A} = (\mathcal{A}_0, \mathcal{A}_1, \mathcal{A}_2)$ there exists a negligible function $\text{negl}(\cdot)$, such that for all $\lambda \in \mathbb{N}$,* $\text{Adv}_\mathcal{A}^{\text{CPRF}}(\lambda) \le \text{negl}(\lambda)$, *where advantage of $\mathcal{A}$ is defined as*

$$\text{Adv}_\mathcal{A}^{\text{CPRF}}(\lambda) = \left| \Pr \left[\mathcal{A}_2(\widetilde{\text{st}}, y_b) = b : \begin{array}{c} K \leftarrow \text{Setup}(1^\lambda); \quad (z, \text{st}) = \mathcal{A}_0(1^\lambda) \\ K_z \leftarrow \text{Constrain}(K, z) \\ (x, \widetilde{\text{st}}) \leftarrow \mathcal{A}_1(\text{st}, K_z); \quad b \leftarrow \{0, 1\} \\ y_1 = \text{Evaluate}(K, x); \quad y_0 \leftarrow \mathcal{Y}_\lambda \end{array} \right] - \frac{1}{2} \right|.$$

Also, the challenge point x chosen by $\mathcal{A}$ must satisfy the constraint $P_z(x) = 1$, i.e. it should not be possible to evaluate the PRF on x using constrained key K_z.

Note that the above security notion is weaker than the standard fully collusion-resistant security notion, since the adversary gets one constrained key, and then it must distinguish between a random string and the PRF evaluation at a point not satisfying the constraint. This is weaker than the standard security definition in two ways. First, there is only one constrained key query, and second, there are no evaluation queries. However, as we will see in Sect. 3, this suffices for our construction. Looking ahead, the high level idea is that we will partition the VRF input space using an admissible hash function, and to answer each evaluation query we only need a constrained key since a constrained key lets us evaluate at all points in the query partition.

Remark 1. Additionally, we want that there exists a polynomial $s(\cdot)$ such that $\forall \lambda \in \mathbb{N}$, $K \in \mathcal{K}_\lambda \cup \mathcal{K}_\lambda^c$, $|K| \le s(\lambda)$, i.e. size of each PRF key is polynomially bounded.

We could also define constrained PRFs for an even weaker constraint family which is the puncturing constraint function family.

Definition 8. *A puncturing constraint function family* $\mathcal{P}_n = \{P_z : \{0,1\}^n \to \{0,1\} \mid z \in \{0,1\}^n\}$ *is defined exactly as the predicate* $P_u(\cdot)$ *in Definition 5.*

Definition 9. *A set of polynomial time algorithms* (Setup, Puncture, Evaluate) *is a secure puncturable pseudorandom function if it is a* single-key no-query *secure constrained pseudorandom function (Definition 7) for puncturing constraint function family.*

We also define the notion of constrained unpredictable functions which are syntactically the same as constrained PRFs with the difference only being that they only need to satisfy a weaker security requirement. Below we formally define constrained unpredictable functions.

Definition 10. *A pair of polynomial time algorithms* (Setup, Constrain, Evaluate) *is a* single-key no-query *secure constrained unpredictable function for admissible hash compatible constraint family if it satisfies the correctness condition (as in Definition 7) and it also satisfies the following:*

– *(Single-key No-query Constrained Unpredictability) For any PPT adversary* $\mathcal{A} = (\mathcal{A}_0, \mathcal{A}_1)$ *there exists a negligible function* $\mathsf{negl}(\cdot)$, *such that for all* $\lambda \in \mathbb{N}$, $\mathsf{Adv}_{\mathcal{A}}^{\mathsf{CUF}}(\lambda) \le \mathsf{negl}(\lambda)$, *where advantage of* $\mathcal{A}$ *is defined as*

$$\mathsf{Adv}_{\mathcal{A}}^{\mathsf{CUF}}(\lambda) = \Pr\left[y = \mathsf{Evaluate}(K, x) : \begin{array}{c} K \leftarrow \mathsf{Setup}(1^\lambda); \quad (z, \mathsf{st}) = \mathcal{A}_0(1^\lambda) \\ K_z \leftarrow \mathsf{Constrain}(K, z); \\ (x, y) = \mathcal{A}_1(\mathsf{st}, K_z) \end{array} \right].$$

Also, the challenge point x *chosen by* $\mathcal{A}$ *must satisfy the constraint* $P_z(x) = 1$, *i.e. it should not be possible to evaluate the PRF on* x *using constrained key* K_z.

2.6   Strong Extractors

Extractors are combinatorial objects used to 'extract' uniformly random bits from a source that has high randomness, but is not uniformly random. In this work, we will be using seeded extractors. In a seeded extractor, the extraction algorithm takes as input a sample point x from the high randomness source $\mathcal{X}$, together with a short seed s, and outputs a string that looks uniformly random. Here, we will be using strong extractors, where the extracted string looks uniformly random even when the seed is given.

Definition 11. *A* (k, ϵ) *strong extractor* $\mathsf{Ext} : \mathbb{D} \times \mathbb{S} \to \mathbb{Y}$ *is a deterministic algorithm with domain* $\mathbb{D}$, *range* $\mathbb{Y}$ *and seed space* $\mathbb{S}$ *such that for every source* $\mathcal{X}$ *on* $\mathbb{D}$ *with min-entropy at least* k, *the following two distributions have statistical distance at most* ϵ:

$$\mathcal{D}_1 = \{(\mathfrak{s}, \mathsf{Ext}(x, \mathfrak{s})) : \mathfrak{s} \leftarrow \mathbb{S}, x \leftarrow \mathcal{X}\}, \mathcal{D}_2 = \{(\mathfrak{s}, y) : \mathfrak{s} \leftarrow \mathbb{S}, y \leftarrow \mathbb{Y}\}$$

Using the Leftover Hash Lemma, we can construct strong extractors from pairwise-independent hash functions. More formally, let $\mathcal{H} = \{h : \{0,1\}^n \to \{0,1\}^m\}$ be a family of pairwise independent hash functions, and let $m = k - 2\log(1/\epsilon)$. Then $\mathsf{Ext}(x, h) = h(x)$ is a strong extractor with h being the seed. Such hash functions can be represented using $O(n)$ bits.

2.7 Lattice Preliminaries

Given positive integers n, m, q and a matrix $\mathbf{A} \in \mathbb{Z}_q^{n \times m}$, we let $\Lambda_q^{\perp}(\mathbf{A})$ denote the lattice $\{\mathbf{x} \in \mathbb{Z}^m : \mathbf{A} \cdot \mathbf{x} = \mathbf{0} \mod q\}$. For $\mathbf{u} \in \mathbb{Z}_q^n$, we let $\Lambda_q^{\mathbf{u}}(\mathbf{A})$ denote the coset $\{\mathbf{x} \in \mathbb{Z}^m : \mathbf{A} \cdot \mathbf{x} = \mathbf{u} \mod q\}$.

Discrete Gaussians. Let σ be any positive real number. The Gaussian distribution $\mathcal{D}_\sigma$ with parameter σ is defined by the probability distribution function $\rho_\sigma(\mathbf{x}) = \exp(-\pi \cdot ||\mathbf{x}||^2/\sigma^2)$. For any set $\mathrm{L} \subset \mathcal{R}^m$, define $\rho_\sigma(\mathrm{L}) = \sum_{\mathbf{x} \in \mathrm{L}} \rho_\sigma(\mathbf{x})$. The discrete Gaussian distribution $\mathcal{D}_{\mathrm{L},\sigma}$ over L with parameter σ is defined by the probability distribution function $\rho_{\mathrm{L},\sigma}(\mathbf{x}) = \rho_\sigma(\mathbf{x})/\rho_\sigma(\mathrm{L})$ for all $\mathbf{x} \in \mathrm{L}$.

The following lemma (Lemma 4.4 of [19,31]) shows that if the parameter σ of a discrete Gaussian distribution is small, then any vector drawn from this distribution will be short (with high probability).

Lemma 1. *Let* m, n, q *be positive integers with* $m > n$, $q \geq 2$. *Let* $\mathbf{A} \in \mathbb{Z}_q^{n \times m}$ *be a matrix of dimensions* $n \times m$, *and* $L = \Lambda_q^{\perp}(\mathbf{A})$. *Then*

$$\Pr[||\mathbf{x}|| > \sqrt{m} \cdot \sigma : \mathbf{x} \leftarrow \mathcal{D}_{L,\sigma}] \leq negl(n).$$

3   Constructing Verifiable Random Functions

In this section, we give a generic construction of VRFs from admissible hash functions, perfectly binding commitments, NIWIs and constrained pseudorandom functions for admissible hash compatible constraints. We also prove that it satisfies correctness, unique provability and pseudorandomness properties (as described in Definition 1). Later in Sect. 3.3, we give a slightly modified construction for VRF that is selectively-secure assuming only puncturable pseudorandom functions.

Let $(h, \mathsf{AdmSample})$ be an admissible hash function that hashes $n(\lambda)$ bits to $\ell(\lambda)$ bits, $(\mathcal{P}, \mathcal{V})$ be a NIWI proof system for language $\mathcal{L}$ (where the language will be defined later), $(\mathsf{CS.Commit}, \mathsf{CS.Verify})$ be a perfectly binding commitment scheme with $\{\mathcal{M}_\lambda\}_\lambda, \{\mathcal{R}_\lambda\}_\lambda$ and $\{\mathcal{C}_\lambda\}_\lambda$ as the message, randomness and commitment space, and CPRF = (CPRF.Setup, CPRF.Constrain, CPRF.Eval) be a constrained pseudorandom function with $\{\mathcal{X}_\lambda\}_\lambda$, $\{\mathcal{Y}_\lambda\}_\lambda$, $\{\mathcal{K}_\lambda\}_\lambda$ and $\{\mathcal{K}_\lambda^c\}_\lambda$ as its domain, range, key and constrained key spaces. For simplicity assume that $\mathcal{K}_\lambda \cup \mathcal{K}_\lambda^c \subseteq \mathcal{M}_\lambda$, or in other words, all the PRF master keys and constrained keys lie in the message space of the commitment scheme. Also, let $\mathcal{X}_\lambda = \{0,1\}^{\ell(\lambda)}$.

First, we define the language $\mathcal{L}$. It contains instances of the form $(c_1, c_2, c_3, x, y) \in \mathcal{C}_\lambda^3 \times \{0,1\}^{n(\lambda)} \times \mathcal{Y}_\lambda$ with the following witness relation:

$$\exists\, i, j \in \{1, 2, 3\},\ K, K' \in \mathcal{K}_\lambda \cup \mathcal{K}_\lambda^c,\ r, r' \in \mathcal{R}_\lambda \text{ such that}$$
$$i \neq j \wedge \mathsf{CS.Verify}(K, c_i, r) = 1 \wedge \mathsf{CS.Verify}(K', c_j, r') = 1 \wedge$$
$$\mathsf{CPRF.Eval}(K, h(x)) = \mathsf{CPRF.Eval}(K', h(x)) = y.$$

Clearly the above language is in **NP** as it can be verified in polynomial time. Next we describe our construction for VRFs with message space $\{0,1\}^{n(\lambda)}$ and range space $\{\mathcal{Y}_\lambda\}_\lambda$.

3.1   Construction

- Setup(1^λ) → (SK, VK). It generates a PRF key for constrained pseudorandom function as $K \leftarrow \mathsf{CPRF.Setup}(1^\lambda)$. It also generates three independent commitments to the key K as $c_i \leftarrow \mathsf{CS.Commit}(1^\lambda, K; r_i)$ for $i \leq 3$ where r_i is sampled as $r_i \leftarrow \mathcal{R}_\lambda$, and sets the secret-verification key pair as $\mathrm{SK} = \left(K, \{(c_i, r_i)\}_{i \leq 3}\right)$, $\mathrm{VK} = (c_1, c_2, c_3)$.
- Evaluate(SK, x) → (y, π). Let $\mathrm{SK} = \left(K, \{(c_i, r_i)\}_{i \leq 3}\right)$. It runs the PRF evaluation algorithm on x as $y = \mathsf{CPRF.Eval}(K, h(x))$. It also computes a NIWI proof π for the statement $(c_1, c_2, c_3, x, y) \in \mathcal{L}$ using NIWI prover algorithm $\mathcal{P}$ with $(i = 1, j = 2, K, K, r_1, r_2)$ as the witness, and outputs y and π as the evaluation and corresponding proof.
- Verify(VK, x, y, π) → $\{0, 1\}$. Let $\mathrm{VK} = (c_1, c_2, c_3)$. It runs NIWI verifier to check proof π as $\mathcal{V}((c_1, c_2, c_3, x, y), \pi)$ and accepts the proof (outputs 1) iff $\mathcal{V}$ outputs 1.

3.2   Correctness, Unique Provability and Pseudorandomness

Theorem 2. *If $(h, \mathsf{AdmSample})$ is an admissible hash function, (CS.Commit, CS.Verify) is a secure perfectly binding commitment scheme, $(\mathcal{P}, \mathcal{V})$ is a secure NIWI proof system for language $\mathcal{L}$, and CPRF is a secure single-key constrained pseudorandom function according to Definitions 5, 4, 3, and 7 (respectively), then the above construction forms an adaptively-secure VRF satisfying correctness, unique provability and pseudorandomness properties as described in Definition 1.*

Correctness. For every well-formed secret and verification key pair (SK, VK) ← Setup(1^λ), we know that both c_1 and c_2 are commitments to PRF key K with r_1 and r_2 as the corresponding openings, where $\mathrm{SK} = \left(K, \{(c_i, r_i)\}_{i \leq 3}\right)$. Therefore, by perfect correctness of the constrained PRF and NIWI proof system, we can conclude that the above construction satisfies the VRF correctness condition.

Unique Provability. We will prove this by contradiction. Assume that the above construction does not satisfy unique provability property. This implies that there exists $(\text{VK}, x, y_1, \pi_1, y_2, \pi_2)$ such that $y_1 \neq y_2$ and $\Pr[\text{Verify}(\text{VK}, x, y_i, \pi_i) = 1] > 2^{-\Omega(\lambda)}$ for both $i \in \{1, 2\}$. To prove that this is not possible, we show that at least one of these proof verifications must involve verifying a NIWI proof for an invalid instance. Formal arguments proceed as follows:

- Let $\text{VK} = (c_1, c_2, c_3)$. Since the commitment scheme is *perfectly binding*, we know that for each $i \in \{1, 2, 3\}$ there exists *at most* one key K_i such that there exists an r_i which is a valid opening for c_i, i.e. $\text{CS.Verify}(K_i, c_i, r_i) = 1$.
- Suppose c_i is a commitment to key K_i for $i \leq 3$, and $\text{CPRF.Eval}(K_1, x) = \text{CPRF.Eval}(K_2, x) = y_1$. Now since $y_1 \neq y_2$, thus even when $\text{CPRF.Eval}(K_3, x) = y_2$ holds, we know that $(c_1, c_2, c_3, x, y_2) \notin \mathcal{L}$ as no two keys out of K_1, K_2, K_3 evaluate to y_2 on input x. Therefore, at least one proof out of π_1 and π_2 is a proof for an incorrect statement.
- However, by statistical soundness of NIWI proof system, we know that for all instances not in $\mathcal{L}$, probability that any proof gets verified is at most $2^{-\Omega(\lambda)}$. Therefore, if the above construction does not satisfy unique provability, then the NIWI proof system is not statistically sound which contradicts our assumption. Hence, unique provability follows from perfect binding property of the commitment scheme and statistical soundness of NIWI proof system.

Pseudorandomness. The pseudorandomness proof follows from a sequence of hybrid games. The high level proof idea is as follows. We start by partitioning the input space into query and challenge partition using the admissible hash function. After partitioning we observe that to answer evaluation queries we only need a constrained PRF key which can evaluate on inputs in the query partition, however to give a proof we still need the master PRF key. Next we note that to compute the NIWI proofs we only need openings for any two commitments out of the three. Thus, we could switch one of the strings c_i to commit to the constrained key instead. This follows from the hiding property of the commitment scheme. Now we observe that we only need to compute NIWI proofs for the inputs in the query partition, thus we could use a master key - constrained key pair instead of using the master key - master key pair as the NIWI witness. This follows from witness indistinguishability property of NIWI proof system and the fact that the constrained and master key compute the same output on query partition. Using the same trick two more times, we could move to a hybrid game in which all three strings c_i's are commitments of the constrained key. Finally, in this hybrid we could directly reduce the pseudorandomness security of VRF to constrained pseudorandomness security of the single-key secure constrained PRF. Due to space constraints, the formal proof has been provided in the full version.

Remark 2. We would like to note that if we use a constrained unpredictable function instead of a constrained PRF in the above construction, then it results in an adaptively-secure VUF (verifiable unpredictable function).

3.3 Selectively-Secure VRFs

In this section, we give a modified construction which assumes puncturable PRFs instead of constrained PRFs for admissible hash compatible constraints. The trade-off is that we could only prove selective security of this construction. However, if we make sub-exponential security assumptions, then it could be proven to be adaptively-secure as well.

Let $(\mathcal{P}, \mathcal{V})$ be a NIWI proof system for language $\widetilde{\mathcal{L}}$ (where the language will be defined later), $(\mathsf{CS.Commit}, \mathsf{CS.Verify})$ be a perfectly binding commitment scheme with $\{\mathcal{M}_\lambda\}_\lambda, \{\mathcal{R}_\lambda\}_\lambda$ and $\{\mathcal{C}_\lambda\}_\lambda$ as the message, randomness and commitment space, and $\mathsf{PPRF} = (\mathsf{PPRF.Setup}, \mathsf{PPRF.Puncture}, \mathsf{PPRF.Eval})$ be a constrained pseudorandom function with $\{\mathcal{X}_\lambda\}_\lambda, \{\mathcal{Y}_\lambda\}_\lambda, \{\mathcal{K}_\lambda\}_\lambda$ and $\{\mathcal{K}_\lambda^p\}_\lambda$ as its domain, range, key and constrained key spaces. For simplicity assume that $\mathcal{K}_\lambda \cup \mathcal{K}_\lambda^p \subseteq \mathcal{M}_\lambda$, or in other words, all the PRF master keys and constrained keys lie in the message space of the commitment scheme.

First, we define the language $\widetilde{\mathcal{L}}$. It contains instances of the form $(c_1, c_2, c_3, x, y) \in \mathcal{C}_\lambda^3 \times \mathcal{X}_\lambda \times \mathcal{Y}_\lambda$ with the following witness relation:

$$\exists\, i, j \in \{1, 2, 3\},\ K, K' \in \mathcal{K}_\lambda \cup \mathcal{K}_\lambda^p,\ r, r' \in \mathcal{R}_\lambda \text{ such that}$$
$$i \neq j \wedge \mathsf{CS.Verify}(K, c_i, r) = 1 \wedge \mathsf{CS.Verify}(K', c_j, r') = 1 \wedge$$
$$\mathsf{PPRF.Eval}(K, x) = \mathsf{PPRF.Eval}(K', x) = y.$$

Clearly the above language is in **NP** as it can be verified in polynomial time. Next we describe our construction for selectively-secure VRFs with message space $\{\mathcal{X}_\lambda\}_\lambda$ and range space $\{\mathcal{Y}_\lambda\}_\lambda$.

- $\mathsf{Setup}(1^\lambda) \to (\mathrm{SK}, \mathrm{VK})$. It generates a PRF key for punctured pseudorandom function as $K \leftarrow \mathsf{PPRF.Setup}(1^\lambda)$. It also generates three independent commitments to the key K as $c_i \leftarrow \mathsf{CS.Commit}(1^\lambda, K; r_i)$ for $i \leq 3$ where r_i is sampled as $r_i \leftarrow \mathcal{R}_\lambda$, and sets the secret-verification key pair as $\mathrm{SK} = \left(K, \{(c_i, r_i)\}_{i \leq 3}\right), \mathrm{VK} = (c_1, c_2, c_3)$.

- $\mathsf{Evaluate}(\mathrm{SK}, x) \to (y, \pi)$. Let $\mathrm{SK} = \left(K, \{(c_i, r_i)\}_{i \leq 3}\right)$. It runs the PRF evaluation algorithm on x as $y = \mathsf{PPRF.Eval}(K, x)$. It also computes a NIWI proof π for the statement $(c_1, c_2, c_3, x, y) \in \widetilde{\mathcal{L}}$ using NIWI prover algorithm $\mathcal{P}$ with $(i = 1, j = 2, K, K, r_1, r_2)$ as the witness, and outputs y and π as the evaluation and corresponding proof.

- $\mathsf{Verify}(\mathrm{VK}, x, y, \pi) \to \{0, 1\}$. Let $\mathrm{VK} = (c_1, c_2, c_3)$. It runs NIWI verifier to check proof π as $\mathcal{V}((c_1, c_2, c_3, x, y), \pi)$ and accepts the proof (outputs 1) iff $\mathcal{V}$ outputs 1.

Theorem 3. *If* $(\mathsf{CS.Commit}, \mathsf{CS.Verify})$ *is a secure perfectly binding commitment scheme,* $(\mathcal{P}, \mathcal{V})$ *is a secure NIWI proof system for language* $\widetilde{\mathcal{L}}$, *and* PPRF *is a secure puncturable pseudorandom function according to Definitions 4, 3, and 9 (respectively), then the above construction forms a selectively-secure VRF satisfying correctness, unique provability and pseudorandomness properties as described in Definition 2.*

Proof Sketch. Correctness and unique provability of the above scheme could be proven similar to as in Sect. 3.2. The proof of pseudorandomness is also similar to that provided before with the following differences — (1) since we are only targeting selective security, the reduction algorithm receives the challenge input from the adversary at the start of the game, thus it does not need to perform any partitioning or abort, (2) in the final hybrid game, the reduction algorithm uses the adversary to attack the punctured pseudorandomness property. The main idea in the reduction to punctured pseudorandomness is that since at the start of the game adversary sends the challenge input to the reduction algorithm, the reduction algorithm could get a punctured key from the PRF challenger and use it inside the commitments as well as to answer each evaluation query.

4   Perfectly Binding Commitment Schemes

In this section, we give new constructions of perfectly binding non-interactive commitments from the Learning with Errors assumption and the Learning Parity with Noise assumption. These constructions are in the standard model without trusted setup. As mentioned in the introduction, there are already simple solutions [26] known from LWE/LPN when there is a trusted setup.

We will first present a construction based on the LWE assumption. Next, we will adapt this solution to work with the LPN assumption. However, this adaptation only works with low noise (that is, the Bernoulli parameter is $1/\sqrt{n}$). We also propose a different approach for constructing perfectly binding non-interactive commitments from the standard constant noise LPN problem. This approach reduces to finding error correcting codes with 'robust' generator matrices. Currently, we do not have any explicit[5] constructions for such error correcting codes, and finding such a family of generator matrices is an interesting open problem.

4.1   Construction from Learning with Errors

In this commitment scheme, our message space is $\{0, 1\}$ for simplicity. To commit to a bit x, one first chooses two vectors $\mathbf{s}$, $\mathbf{w}$ and outputs $\mathbf{w}$ and $\mathbf{w}^T \mathbf{s} + x$. Clearly, this is not binding since there could be different $\mathbf{s}$ vectors that open to different messages. Therefore, we need to ensure that the vector $\mathbf{s}$ is fixed. To address this, we choose a matrix $\mathbf{B}$ with certain structure and output $\mathbf{B}$ and $\mathbf{B}^T \mathbf{s}$+noise. The special structure of the matrix ensures that there cannot be two different vectors $\mathbf{s}_1, \mathbf{s}_2$ and noise vectors $\mathsf{noise}_1, \mathsf{noise}_2$ such that $\mathbf{B}^T \mathbf{s}_1 + \mathsf{noise}_1 = \mathbf{B}^T \mathbf{s}_2 + \mathsf{noise}_2$. Computational hiding of the committed bit follows from the fact that even though $\mathbf{B}$ has special structure, it 'looks' like a random matrix, and therefore we can use the LWE assumption to argue that $\mathbf{B}^T \mathbf{s} + \mathsf{noise}$ looks random, and therefore the message x is hidden.

We will now describe the algorithms formally. Let $\lfloor \cdot \rfloor$ denote the floor operation, i.e. $\lfloor x \rfloor = \max\{y \in \mathbb{Z} : y \leq x\}$.

---

[5] We note that most randomly chosen linear codes satisfy this property.

- Commit($1^n, x \in \{0,1\}$): The commitment algorithm first sets the LWE modulus $p = 2^{n^\epsilon}$ for some $\epsilon < 1/2$ and error distribution $\chi = \mathcal{D}_\sigma$ where $\sigma = n^c$ for some constant c. Next, it chooses a matrix $\mathbf{A} \leftarrow \mathbb{Z}_p^{n \times n}$, low norm matrices $\mathbf{C} \leftarrow \chi^{n \times n}$, $\mathbf{E} \leftarrow \chi^{n \times n}$ and constructs $\mathbf{D} = \lfloor p/(4n^{c+1}) \rfloor \cdot \mathbf{I}$ (here $\mathbf{I}$ is the $n \times n$ identity matrix). Let $\mathbf{B} = [\mathbf{A} \mid \mathbf{AC} + \mathbf{D} + \mathbf{E}]$.

  It then chooses vectors $\mathbf{s} \leftarrow \chi^n$, $\mathbf{w} \leftarrow \mathbb{Z}_p^n$, $\mathbf{e} \leftarrow \chi^{2n}$ and $f \leftarrow \chi$, and computes $\mathbf{y} = \mathbf{B}^T\mathbf{s} + \mathbf{e}$ and $z = \mathbf{w}^T\mathbf{s} + x(p/2) + f$. If either $\|\mathbf{C}\| > n^{c+2}$ or $\|\mathbf{E}\| > n^{c+2}$ or $\|\mathbf{e}\| > 2n^{c+1}$ or $\|\mathbf{s}\| > n^{c+1}$ or $f > \lfloor p/100 \rfloor$, the commitment algorithm outputs x as the commitment. Else, the commitment consists of $(p, c, \mathbf{B}, \mathbf{w}, \mathbf{y}, z)$.

- Verify(com, x, $(\mathbf{C}, \mathbf{E}, \mathbf{e}, \mathbf{s}, f)$): Let com $= (p, c, \mathbf{B}, \mathbf{w}, \mathbf{y}, z)$. The verification algorithm first checks if $\|\mathbf{C}\| \leq n^{c+2}$, $\|\mathbf{E}\| \leq n^{c+2}$, $\|\mathbf{e}\| \leq 2n^{c+1}$, $\|\mathbf{s}\| \leq n^{c+1}$ and $f \leq \lfloor p/100 \rfloor$. Next, it checks that $\mathbf{B} = [\mathbf{A} \mid \mathbf{AC} + \mathbf{D} + \mathbf{E}]$, $\mathbf{B}^T\mathbf{s} + \mathbf{e} = \mathbf{y}$ and $\mathbf{w}^T\mathbf{s} + x(p/2) + f = z$, where $\mathbf{D} = \lfloor p/(4n^{c+1}) \rfloor \cdot \mathbf{I}$. If all these checks pass, it outputs 1.

Theorem 4. *If $(n, m, 2^{n^\epsilon}, \mathcal{D}_{n^c})$-LWE-ss assumption holds, then the above construction is a perfectly binding computationally hiding commitment scheme as per Definition 4.*

Perfect Correctness. Suppose there exist two different openings for the same commitment. Let $\mathbf{s}_1, \mathbf{e}_1, f_1, \mathbf{C}_1, f_1$ and $\mathbf{s}_2, \mathbf{e}_2, f_2, \mathbf{C}_2, f_2$ be the two openings. We will first show that $\mathbf{s}_1 = \mathbf{s}_2$ and $\mathbf{e}_1 = \mathbf{e}_2$. Next, we will argue that if $\mathbf{s}_1 = \mathbf{s}_2$, then the commitment cannot be opened to two different bits.

Suppose $\mathbf{s}_1 \neq \mathbf{s}_2$. Since $\mathbf{B}^T\mathbf{s}_1 + \mathbf{e}_1 = \mathbf{B}^T\mathbf{s}_2 + \mathbf{e}_2$, it follows that $\mathbf{B}^T(\mathbf{s}_1 - \mathbf{s}_2) = \mathbf{e}_2 - \mathbf{e}_1$. Let $\mathbf{e}_1^1$ and $\mathbf{e}_2^1$ denote the first n components of $\mathbf{e}_1$ and $\mathbf{e}_2$ respectively. Then $\mathbf{A}^T(\mathbf{s}_1 - \mathbf{s}_2) = \mathbf{e}_1^1 - \mathbf{e}_2^1$. Note that $\|\mathbf{e}_2 - \mathbf{e}_1\| \leq 4n^{c+1}$, and therefore, $\|\mathbf{A}^T(\mathbf{s}_1 - \mathbf{s}_2)\| \leq 4n^{c+1}$.

Since $\mathbf{C}_1$ and $\mathbf{C}_2$ are matrices with low norm entries, it follows that $\|\mathbf{C}_1\| \leq n^{c+2}$ and $\|\mathbf{C}_2\| \leq n^{c+2}$. This implies $\|\mathbf{C}_1^T\mathbf{A}^T(\mathbf{s}_1 - \mathbf{s}_2)\| \leq 4n^{2c+3}$. Similarly, since $\|\mathbf{E}_1\| \leq n^{c+2}$, $\|\mathbf{E}_1^T(\mathbf{s}_1 - \mathbf{s}_2)\| \leq 2n^{2c+3}$. However, since the matrix $\mathbf{D}$ has 'medium-sized' entries, if $\mathbf{s}_1 \neq \mathbf{s}_2$, it follows that $\|\mathbf{D}^T(\mathbf{s}_1 - \mathbf{s}_2)\|_\infty \geq \lfloor p/(4n^{c+1}) \rfloor$. Additionally, since $\mathbf{D}$ has medium-sized entries, we could also say that each entry of vector $\mathbf{D}^T(\mathbf{s}_1 - \mathbf{s}_2)$ is at most $p/2$. This is because $\|\mathbf{D}^T(\mathbf{s}_1 - \mathbf{s}_2)\|_\infty \leq \|\mathbf{D}^T\|_\infty \cdot \|\mathbf{s}_1 - \mathbf{s}_2\|_\infty \leq \lfloor p/(4n^{c+1}) \rfloor \cdot 2n^{c+1} \leq p/2$. Therefore, the vector $\mathbf{D}^T(\mathbf{s}_1 - \mathbf{s}_2)$ is sufficiently long, i.e. $\|\mathbf{D}^T(\mathbf{s}_1 - \mathbf{s}_2)\|_\infty \in [\lfloor p/(4n^{c+1}) \rfloor, p/2]$.

Next, let us consider the norm of vector $\mathbf{B}^T(\mathbf{s}_1 - \mathbf{s}_2)$. Recall that $\mathbf{B} = [\mathbf{A} \mid \mathbf{AC} + \mathbf{D} + \mathbf{E}]$. Consider the matrix $\mathbf{X} = [\mathbf{A} \mid \mathbf{AC} + \mathbf{E}]$, i.e. it is same as $\mathbf{B}$ except it does not contain matrix $\mathbf{D}$. Using triangle inequality, we can write that $\|\mathbf{X}^T(\mathbf{s}_1 - \mathbf{s}_2)\| \leq \|\mathbf{A}^T(\mathbf{s}_1 - \mathbf{s}_2)\| + \|\mathbf{C}_1^T\mathbf{A}^T(\mathbf{s}_1 - \mathbf{s}_2)\| + \|\mathbf{E}_1^T(\mathbf{s}_1 - \mathbf{s}_2)\| \leq 8n^{2c+3}$. Therefore, we could also say that each entry of vector $\mathbf{X}^T(\mathbf{s}_1 - \mathbf{s}_2)$ is at most $8n^{2c+3}$, i.e. $\|\mathbf{X}^T(\mathbf{s}_1 - \mathbf{s}_2)\|_\infty \leq 8n^{2c+3}$.

We know that $\mathbf{B}^T(\mathbf{s}_1 - \mathbf{s}_2) = \mathbf{X}^T(\mathbf{s}_1 - \mathbf{s}_2) + [\mathbf{0} \mid \mathbf{D}]^T(\mathbf{s}_1 - \mathbf{s}_2)$. Therefore, given the above bounds, we could conclude that $\lfloor p/(4n^{c+1}) \rfloor - 8n^{2c+3} \leq$

$\left\| \mathbf{B}^T(\mathbf{s}_1 - \mathbf{s}_2) \right\|_\infty \leq p/2 + 8n^{2c+3}$. Since, $p = 2^{n^\varepsilon}$, we know that for suffi-
ciently large values of n, $\lfloor p/(8n^{c+1}) \rfloor \leq \left\| \mathbf{B}^T(\mathbf{s}_1 - \mathbf{s}_2) \right\|_\infty < p$. However, this
is a contradiction since $\mathbf{B}^T(\mathbf{s}_1 - \mathbf{s}_2) = \mathbf{e}_2 - \mathbf{e}_1$ and $\|\mathbf{e}_2 - \mathbf{e}_1\| \leq 4n^{c+1}$, thus
$\left\| \mathbf{B}^T(\mathbf{s}_1 - \mathbf{s}_2) \right\|_\infty < 4n^{c+1}$.

Now, if $\mathbf{s}_1 = \mathbf{s}_2$ and f_1, f_2 are both at most $\lfloor p/100 \rfloor$, then $\mathbf{w}^T \mathbf{s}_1 + f_1$ cannot
be equal to $\mathbf{w}^T \mathbf{s}_2 + f_2 + p/2$. This implies that any commitment cannot be opened
to two different bits.

Computational Hiding. Due to space constraints, we defer the formal proof
to the full version of our paper.

4.2   Construction from Learning Parity with Low Noise

We will now construct a perfectly binding non-interactive commitment scheme
that can be proven secure under the low noise LPN assumption. At a high level,
this solution is similar to our LWE solution. The message space is $\{0, 1\}$, and to
commit to a bit x, we choose a vector $\mathbf{w}$, secret vector $\mathbf{s}$ and output $\mathbf{w}, \mathbf{w}^T \mathbf{s} + x$ as
part of the commitment. However, this is not enough, as there could exist $\mathbf{s}_1, \mathbf{s}_2$
such that $\mathbf{w}^T \mathbf{s}_1 + 1 = \mathbf{w}^T \mathbf{s}_2$. To prevent this, the commitment also consists of a
matrix $\mathbf{B}$ chosen from a special distribution, and $\mathbf{B}^T \mathbf{s} + \text{noise}'$ fixes the vector
$\mathbf{s}$. Drawing parallels with the LWE solution, we use an error correcting code's
generator matrix $\mathbf{G}$ instead of the matrix $\mathbf{D}$ used in the LWE solution. Both
these matrices have a similar role: to map non-zero vectors to vectors with high
hamming weight/high norm.

An important point to note here is that the Bernoulli parameter needs to
be $O(1/\sqrt{n})$. This is necessary for proving perfect binding. Recall, in the LWE
perfect binding proof, we argue that since $\mathbf{A}^T \mathbf{s}$ has low norm, $\mathbf{C}^T \mathbf{A}^T \mathbf{s}$ also
has low norm. For the analogous argument to work here, the error distribution
must be $O(1/\sqrt{n})$. In that case, we can argue that if the error distribution has
hamming weight fraction at most $1/100\sqrt{n}$ and each row of $\mathbf{C}$ has hamming
weight fraction at most $1/100\sqrt{n}$, then $\mathbf{C}^T \mathbf{A}^T \mathbf{s}$ has hamming weight fraction
at most $1/10000$. If the noise rate was constant, then we cannot get an upper
bound on the hamming weight fraction of $\mathbf{C}^T \mathbf{A}^T \mathbf{s}$.

We will now describe the formal construction. Let $\beta = 1/(100\sqrt{n})$ and $\chi =
\text{Ber}_\beta$ the noise distribution. Let $\{\mathbf{G}_n \in \mathbb{Z}_2^{n \times 10n}\}_{n \in \mathbb{N}}$ be a family of generator
matrices for error correcting codes where the distance of the code generated by
$\mathbf{G}_n$ is at least $4n$.

- Commit($1^n, x \in \{0, 1\}$): Let $m = 10n$. Choose random matrices $\mathbf{A} \leftarrow \mathbb{Z}_2^{n \times m}$,
  $\mathbf{w} \leftarrow \mathbb{Z}_2^n$ and $\mathbf{C} \leftarrow \chi^{m \times m}$. Let $\mathbf{B} = [\mathbf{A} \mid \mathbf{AC} + \mathbf{G}]$. Choose secret vector
  $\mathbf{s} \leftarrow \mathbb{Z}_2^n$, error vector $\mathbf{e} \leftarrow \chi^{2m}$ and set $\mathbf{y} = \mathbf{B}^T \mathbf{s} + \mathbf{e}$. If either Ham-Wt($\mathbf{e}$) $>$
  $m/(25\sqrt{n})$ or there exists some row $\mathbf{c}_i$ of matrix $\mathbf{C}$ such that Ham-Wt($\mathbf{c}_i$) $>$
  $m/(50\sqrt{n})$, output the message x in clear as the commitment. Else, let $z =
  \mathbf{w}^T \mathbf{s} + x$. The commitment string com is set to be $(\mathbf{B}, \mathbf{w}, \mathbf{y}, z)$.

- Verify(com, x, $(\mathbf{s}, \mathbf{e}, \mathbf{C})$): Let com $= (\mathbf{B}, \mathbf{w}, \mathbf{y}, z)$. The verification algorithm first checks that Ham-Wt($\mathbf{e}$) $\leq m/(25\sqrt{n})$ and all rows $\mathbf{c}_i$ of $\mathbf{C}$ satisfy Ham-Wt($\mathbf{c}_i$) $\leq m/(50\sqrt{n})$. Next, it checks if $\mathbf{B} = [\mathbf{A} \mid \mathbf{AC} + \mathbf{G}]$, $\mathbf{y} = \mathbf{B}^T\mathbf{s} + \mathbf{e}$ and $z = \mathbf{w}^T\mathbf{s} + x$. If all checks pass, it outputs 1, else it outputs 0.

Theorem 5. *Assuming the Extended Learning Parity with Noise problem* LPN$_{n,m,p}$ *and Knapsack Learning Parity with Noise problem* KLPN$_{n,m,\beta}$ *(for $\beta = 1/(100\sqrt{n})$) is hard, the above construction is a perfectly binding computationally hiding commitment scheme as per Definition 4.*

Perfect Correctness. First, we will argue perfect correctness. Suppose there exists a commitment com $= (\mathbf{B}, \mathbf{w}, \mathbf{y}, z)$ that can be opened to two different messages. Then there exist two different reveals $(\mathbf{s}_1, \mathbf{e}_1, \mathbf{C}_1)$ and $(\mathbf{s}_2, \mathbf{e}_2, \mathbf{C}_2)$ such that $\mathbf{B}^T\mathbf{s}_1 + \mathbf{e}_1 = \mathbf{y} = \mathbf{B}^T\mathbf{s}_2 + \mathbf{e}_2$, $\mathbf{w}^T\mathbf{s}_1 + 0 = z = \mathbf{w}^T\mathbf{s}_2 + 1$ and $[\mathbf{A}|\mathbf{AC}_1 + \mathbf{G}] = \mathbf{B} = [\mathbf{A}|\mathbf{AC}_2 + \mathbf{G}]$. We will first show that $\mathbf{s}_1 = \mathbf{s}_2$, and then show that this implies perfect binding.

For proving that $\mathbf{s}_1 = \mathbf{s}_2$ and $\mathbf{e}_1 = \mathbf{e}_2$, notice that $\mathbf{B}^T(\mathbf{s}_1 + \mathbf{s}_2) = \mathbf{e}_1 + \mathbf{e}_2$, which implies that Ham-Wt($[\mathbf{A}|\mathbf{AC}_1 + \mathbf{G}]^T(\mathbf{s}_1 + \mathbf{s}_2)$) $\leq 2m/(25\sqrt{n})$ (recall, the hamming weight of $\mathbf{e}_1 + \mathbf{e}_2$ is at most $2m/(25\sqrt{n})$).

This implies, in particular, Ham-Wt($\mathbf{A}^T(\mathbf{s}_1 + \mathbf{s}_2)$) $\leq 2m/(25\sqrt{n})$. Since each row of $\mathbf{C}_1$ and $\mathbf{C}_2$ has hamming weight at most $m/(50\sqrt{n})$, Ham-Wt($(\mathbf{AC}_1)^T(\mathbf{s}_1 + \mathbf{s}_2)$) $\leq m^2/(625n) < n$. As a result, Ham-Wt($[\mathbf{A}|\mathbf{AC}_1]^T(\mathbf{s}_1 + \mathbf{s}_2)$) $< 2n$. But if $\mathbf{s}_1 \neq \mathbf{s}_2$, then Ham-Wt($\mathbf{G}^T(\mathbf{s}_1 + \mathbf{s}_2)$) $\geq 4n$ which implies, using triangle inequality, that Ham-Wt($\mathbf{B}^T(\mathbf{s}_1 + \mathbf{s}_2)$) $\geq 2n$. This brings us to a contradiction since Ham-Wt($\mathbf{e}_1 + \mathbf{e}_2$) $\leq 2m/(25\sqrt{n}) < n$.

Next, given that $\mathbf{s}_1 = \mathbf{s}_2$, it follows that $\mathbf{w}^T\mathbf{s}_1 + 1 \neq \mathbf{w}^T\mathbf{s}_2$. This concludes our proof.

Computational Hiding. Due to space constraints, we defer the proof to the full version of our paper.

4.3   Construction from Learning Parity with Constant Noise

For this construction, we will require a polynomial time algorithm GenECC that generates 'robust' error correcting code generator matrices. More formally, GenECC(1^n) takes as input a parameter n and outputs ℓ matrices $\mathbf{G}_1, \ldots, \mathbf{G}_\ell$ of dimension $n \times m$ such that the following property holds: for every matrix $\mathbf{A} \in \mathbb{Z}_2^{n \times m}$, there exists an $i \in [\ell]$ such that every non-zero vector in the rowspace of $\mathbf{A} + \mathbf{G}_i$ has hamming weight at least $m/3$. Let $\beta = 1/100$ denote the error rate.

- Commit(1^n, $x \in \{0, 1\}$): The commitment algorithm first computes $(\mathbf{G}_1, \ldots, \mathbf{G}_\ell) \leftarrow$ GenECC(1^n), where $\mathbf{G}_i \in \mathbb{Z}_2^{n \times m}$. Next, it chooses $\mathbf{A} \leftarrow \mathbb{Z}_2^{n \times m}$ and sets $\mathbf{D}_i = [\mathbf{A} + \mathbf{G}_i]$. It chooses secret vectors $\mathbf{s}_i \leftarrow \mathbb{Z}_2^n$ and error vectors $\mathbf{e}_i \leftarrow \chi^m$ for $i \leq \ell$. If any of the error vectors have hamming weight greater than $2m\beta$, then the algorithm outputs x in the clear. Else, it chooses $\mathbf{w} \leftarrow \mathbb{Z}_2^n$, sets $\mathbf{y}_i \leftarrow \mathbf{D}_i^T \mathbf{s}_i + \mathbf{e}_i$ for $i \in [\ell]$, $z_i = \mathbf{w}^T \mathbf{s}_i + x$ and outputs $\mathsf{com} = (\mathbf{A}, \{\mathbf{y}_i, z_i\})$ as the commitment.

- $\mathsf{Verify}(\mathsf{com}, x, (\{\mathbf{s}_i, \mathbf{e}_i\}))$: Let $\mathsf{com} = (\mathbf{A}, \{\mathbf{y}_i, z_i\})$. The verification algorithm first checks that $\mathbf{y}_i = [\mathbf{A} + \mathbf{G}_i]^T \mathbf{s}_i + \mathbf{e}_i$ for all $i \in [\ell]$ and $z_i = \mathbf{w}^T \mathbf{s}_i + x$. Next, it checks that each error vector has hamming weight less than $2m\beta$. If all these checks pass, it outputs 1, else it outputs 0.

Perfect Correctness. This will crucially rely the robustness property of GenECC algorithm. Suppose there exist two sets of vectors $\{\mathbf{s}_i^1\}, \{\mathbf{s}_i^2\}$ and error vectors $\{\mathbf{e}_i^1\}$ and $\{\mathbf{e}_i^2\}$ such that $\mathbf{D}_i^T \mathbf{s}_i^1 + \mathbf{e}_i^1 = \mathbf{D}_i^T \mathbf{s}_i^2 + \mathbf{e}_i^2$. Then, for all $i \leq \ell$, $\mathbf{D}_i^T(\mathbf{s}_i^1 + \mathbf{s}_i^2)$ has hamming weight at most $4m\beta$. This implies that for all $i \leq \ell$, there exists at least one non-zero vector in the rowspace of $\mathbf{D}_i$ that has hamming weight at most $4m\beta$. But by the robustness property, for every $\mathbf{A} \in \mathbb{Z}_2^{n \times m}$, there exists at least one index $i \in [\ell]$ such that the row space of $\mathbf{A} + \mathbf{G}_i$ has hamming weight at least $m/3$. This brings us to a contradiction.

Computational Hiding Proof Sketch. The proof is fairly simple, and follows from the LPN assumption. First we introduce ℓ hybrid experiments, where in the ith experiment, $(\mathbf{y}_j, \mathbf{z}_j)$ are random for all $j \leq i$. The remaining $(\mathbf{y}_j, \mathbf{z}_j)$ components are same as in the actual construction. The only difference between the $(i-1)^{th}$ and i^{th} hybrid is the distribution of $(\mathbf{y}_i, \mathbf{z}_i)$.

Hybrid Hybrid_i. In this experiment, the challenger chooses a matrix $\mathbf{A} \leftarrow \mathbb{Z}_2^{n \times m}$, vector $\mathbf{w} \leftarrow \mathbb{Z}_2^n$ and sets $\mathbf{D}_i = \mathbf{A} + \mathbf{G}_i$. Next, it chooses $\mathbf{s}_j \leftarrow \mathbb{Z}_2^n$ and $\mathbf{e}_j \leftarrow \mathsf{Ber}_\beta^m$ for all $j \leq \ell$. For $j \leq i$, it chooses $y_j \leftarrow \mathbb{Z}_2^m$ and $z_j \leftarrow \mathbb{Z}_2$. For $j > i$, it chooses the commitment bit $b \leftarrow \{0,1\}$, sets $\mathbf{y}_j = \mathbf{D}_j^T \mathbf{s}_j + \mathbf{e}_j$ and $z_j = \mathbf{w}^T \mathbf{s}_j + b$. It sends $(\mathbf{A}, \mathbf{w}, \{\mathbf{y}_i, z_i\}_i)$ to the adversary. The adversary outputs a bit b' and wins if $b = b'$.

Suppose there exists an adversary $\mathcal{A}$ that can distinguish between these two hybrids. Then we can construct a reduction algorithm $\mathcal{B}$ that can break the extended LPN assumption. $\mathcal{B}$ receives $(\mathbf{X}, \mathbf{w}, \mathbf{y}, z)$ from the LPN challenger, where $\mathbf{y} = \mathbf{X}^T \mathbf{s} + \mathbf{e}$ or is random, and $z = \mathbf{w}^T \mathbf{s}$. It sets $\mathbf{A} = \mathbf{X} - \mathbf{G}_i$. The remaining components can be generated using $\mathbf{A}$ (note that there is a different $\mathbf{s}_i$ for each i, so the reduction algorithm does not need the LPN secret $\mathbf{s}$ to generate the remaining components). Depending on whether $\mathbf{y}$ is random or not, $\mathcal{B}$ either simulates Hybrid i or Hybrid $i - 1$.

5   Constrained PRFs for Admissible Hash Compatible Constraints

In this section, we will provide two separate constructions of constrained PRFs for admissible hash compatible constraints. We prove security of the first construction under the n-$\mathsf{powerDDH}$ assumption and the second construction is proven to be secure under the $\mathsf{Phi}\text{-}\mathsf{Hiding}$ assumption.

5.1   Constrained PRFs from n-powerDDH Assumption

At a high level, our base PRF looks like the Naor-Reingold PRF [33]. The PRF key consists of $2n$ integers and a random group generator g. The PRF evaluation on an n bit strings is performed as follows: first choose n out of the $2n$ integers depending on the input, compute their product and then output this product in the exponent of g.

- Setup(1^λ): The setup algorithm takes as input the security parameter λ. It first generates a group of prime order as $(p, \mathbb{G}, g) \leftarrow \mathcal{G}(1^\lambda)$, where p is a prime, $\mathbb{G}$ is a group of order p and g is a random generator. Next, it chooses $2n$ integers $c_{i,b} \leftarrow \mathbb{Z}_p^*$ for $i \leq n$, $b \in \{0,1\}$. It sets the master PRF key as $K = ((p, \mathbb{G}, g), \{c_{i,b}\}_{i \leq n, b \in \{0,1\}})$.
- Constrain($K, u \in \{0, 1, \perp\}^n$): The constrain algorithm takes as input the master PRF key $K = ((p, \mathbb{G}, g), \{c_{i,b}\}_{i,b})$ and constraint $u \in \{0, 1, \perp\}^n$. It first chooses an integer $a \in \mathbb{Z}_p^*$ and computes, for all $i \leq n$, $b \in \{0,1\}$,

$$v_{i,b} = \begin{cases} c_{i,b}/a & \text{if } u_i = b \lor u_i = \perp \\ c_{i,b} & \text{otherwise.} \end{cases}$$

  It sets the constrained key as $K_u = ((p, \mathbb{G}, g), u, \{g, g^a, g^{a^2}, \ldots, g^{a^{n-1}}\}, \{v_{i,b}\}_{i,b})$.
- Evaluate($K, x \in \{0,1\}^n$): The evaluation algorithm takes as input a PRF key K (which could be either the master PRF key or constrained PRF key) and an input string $x \in \{0,1\}^n$.

  If K is a master PRF key, then it can be parsed as $K = ((p, \mathbb{G}, g), \{c_{i,b}\}_{i,b})$. The evaluation algorithm computes $t = \prod_{i \leq n} c_{i,x_i}$ and outputs g^t.

  If K is a constrained key, then it consists of the group description $(p, \mathbb{G}, g)$, constraint $u \in \{0, 1, \perp\}^n$, group elements $(g_0, g_1, \ldots, g_{n-1})$ and $2n$ integers $\{v_{i,b}\}_{i,b}$. The evaluation algorithm first checks if $P_u(x) = 0$. If not, it outputs $\perp$. Else, it computes the product $v = \prod_{i \leq n} v_{i,x_i}$. Next, it counts the number of positions s such that $u_i = x_i \lor u_i = \perp$. It outputs the evaluation as g_s^v (note that since $P_u(x) = 0$, $0 \leq s < n$, and therefore the output is well defined).

Theorem 6. *If n-powerDDH assumption holds over $\mathcal{G}$, then the above construction is a secure single-key no-query secure constrained pseudorandom function for admissible hash compatible constraint family as per Definition 7.*

Correctness. We need to show that for any PRF key K, any constraint $u \in \{0, 1, \perp\}^n$, any key K_u constrained at u and any input $x \in \{0,1\}^n$ such that $P_u(x) = 0$, evaluation at x using the master PRF key K matches the evaluation at x using the constrained key K_u.

More formally, let $K \leftarrow$ Setup(1^n), and let $K = ((p, \mathbb{G}, g), \{c_{i,b}\})$. Let $u \in \{0, 1, \perp\}^n$ be any constraint, and let $K_u = ((p, \mathbb{G}, g), u, \{g, g^a, \ldots, g^{a^{n-1}}\}, \{v_{i,b}\})$ be the constrained key. On input $x \in \{0,1\}^n$, the PRF evaluation using the master PRF key computes $t = \prod c_{i,x_i}$ and outputs $h = g^t$.

Let $S = \{i \; : \; u_i = x_i \lor u_i = \perp\}$, and let $s = |S|$. Since $P_u(x) = 0$, it follows that $s < n$ (since there is at least one index where $u_i \neq \perp \land x_i \neq u_i$). For all $i \in S$, v_{i,x_i} is set to be $c_{i,x_i}/a$, and for all $i \notin S$, $v_{i,x_i} = c_{i,x_i}$. As a result, $v = \prod_i v_{i,x_i} = (\prod_i c_{i,x_i})/a^s$. Therefore, $(g^{a^s})^v = g^t = h$, which is equal to the master key evaluation.

Security. We will now show that the construction described above is secure as per Definition 7. Recall, in the single-key no-query security game, the adversary is allowed to query for a single constrained key, after which the adversary must output a challenge point not in the constrained set and then distinguish between the PRF evaluation at the challenge point and a truly random string. We will show that such an adversary can be used to break the n-powerDDH assumption. The reduction algorithm receives as challenge $(g, g^a, g^{a^2}, \ldots, g^{a^{n-1}})$ and T, where $T = g^{a^n}$ or a uniformly random group element. The reduction algorithm then receives a constrained key query u from the adversary. The reduction algorithm chooses $2n$ random integers and sends them along with $(g, g^a, \ldots, g^{a^{n-1}})$. Now, the adversary sends a point x such that $P_u(x) = 1$. The reduction algorithm will use T to respond to the adversary. The crucial point here is that the reduction does not need to know a to construct this response.

Lemma 2. *Assuming the n-powerDDH assumption, for any $\mathcal{A}$, $\mathsf{Adv}_{\mathcal{A}}^{\mathrm{CPRF}}(n) \leq negl(n)$.*

Proof. Suppose there exists an adversary $\mathcal{A}$ such that $\mathsf{Adv}_{\mathcal{A}}^{\mathrm{CPRF}}(n) = \epsilon$. We will use $\mathcal{A}$ to construct a reduction algorithm $\mathcal{B}$ that breaks the n-powerDDH assumption. The reduction algorithm receives the group description $(p, \mathbb{G}, g)$, n group elements $(g_0, g_1, \ldots, g_{n-1})$ and the challenge term T from the challenger. It then chooses $2n$ random integers $v_{i,b} \leftarrow \mathbb{Z}_p^*$ for all $i \leq n, b \in \{0, 1\}$. It receives constrained key query u from $\mathcal{A}$, and sends $((p, \mathbb{G}, g), u, \{g_0, \ldots, g_{n-1}\}, \{v_{i,b}\}_{i,b})$ to $\mathcal{A}$. Next, it receives the challenge input $x \in \{0, 1\}^n$ from $\mathcal{A}$ such that $P_u(x) = 1$. The reduction algorithm computes $v = \prod_i v_{i,x_i}$ and sends T^v to the adversary. If $\mathcal{A}$ guesses that the challenge string is random, then $\mathcal{B}$ guesses that T is random, else it guesses that $T = g^{a^n}$, where $g_i = g^{a^i}$.

We now need to argue that $\mathcal{B}$ perfectly simulates the single-key no-query constrained PRF game. First, let us consider the case when $g_i = g^{a^i}$ and $T = g^{a^n}$. The constrained key is distributed as in the actual security game. The reduction algorithm implicitly sets $c_{i,b} = v_{i,b}a$ for all i, b such that $u_i = b \lor u_i = \perp$. On challenge input x such that $P_u(x) = 1$, let $v = \prod_i v_{i,x_i}$. Note that $t = \prod_i c_{i,x_i} = a^n v$. As a result, its outputs $T^v = g^t$ is the correct PRF evaluation at x.

Now, suppose T is a uniformly random group element. Then, once again, the constrained key's distribution is identical to the real security game distribution, and the response to PRF challenge is a uniformly random group element. This implies that $\mathcal{B}$ can break the n-powerDDH assumption with advantage ϵ.

5.2   Constrained PRFs from Phi-Hiding Assumption

The PRF key consists of a RSA modulus, its factorization, $2n$ integers, a random group generator h and a strong extractor seed. The PRF evaluation on an n bit strings is performed as follows: first choose n out of the $2n$ integers depending on the input, compute their product, then compute this product in the exponent of h and finally apply a strong extractor on the product.

- Setup(1^λ): The setup algorithm takes as input the security parameter λ. It first sets input length $n = \lambda$, parameter $\ell_{\mathrm{RSA}} = 20(n+1)$, generates RSA modulus $N = pq$, where p, q are primes of $\ell_{\mathrm{RSA}}/2$ bits each. Next, it chooses $2n$ integers $c_{i,b} \leftarrow \mathbb{Z}_{\phi(N)}$ for $i \le n$, $b \in \{0,1\}$ and $h \leftarrow \mathbb{Z}_N^*$. Finally, it sets $\ell_s = O(n)$ and chooses an extractor seed $\mathfrak{s} \leftarrow \{0,1\}^{\ell_s}$. It sets the master PRF key as $K = ((N, p, q), \{c_{i,b}\}_{i \le n, b \in \{0,1\}}, h, \mathfrak{s})$.
- Constrain($K, u \in \{0, 1, \perp\}^n$): The constrain algorithm takes as input the master PRF key $K = ((N, p, q), \{c_{i,b}\}_{i,b}, h, \mathfrak{s})$ and constraint $u \in \{0, 1, \perp\}^n$. It first chooses an integer $e \in \mathbb{Z}_{\phi(N)}^*$ and computes, for all $i \le n$, $b \in \{0, 1\}$,

$$v_{i,b} = \begin{cases} (c_{i,b} - 1) \cdot e^{-1} \mod \phi(N) & \text{if } u_i = b \vee u_i = \perp \\ c_{i,b} \cdot e^{-1} \mod \phi(N) & \text{otherwise.} \end{cases}$$

It sets the constrained key as $K_u = (N, u, e, \{v_{i,b}\}_{i,b}, h^e, \mathfrak{s})$.
- Evaluate($K, x \in \{0,1\}^n$): The evaluation algorithm takes as input a PRF key K (which could be either the master PRF key or constrained PRF key) and an input string $x \in \{0,1\}^n$.

  If K is a master PRF key, then $K = ((N, p, q), \{c_{i,b}\}_{i \le n, b \in \{0,1\}}, h, \mathfrak{s})$. The evaluation algorithm computes $t = \prod_{i \le n} c_{i,x_i}$ and outputs $\mathsf{Ext}(h^t, \mathfrak{s})$.

  If K is a constrained key, then $K = (N, u, e, \{v_{i,b}\}_{i \le n, b \in \{0,1\}}, g, \mathfrak{s})$. Recall g is set to be h^e. The evaluation algorithm first checks if $P_u(x) = 0$. If not, it outputs $\perp$. Since $P_u(x) = 0$, there exists an index i such that $u_i \ne \perp$ and $u_i \ne x_i$. Let i^* be the first such index. For all $i \ne i^*$, compute $w_{i,b} = v_{i,b} \cdot e + 1$ if $u_i = b \vee u_i = \perp$, else $w_{i,b} = v_{i,b} \cdot e$. Finally, set $w_{i^*, x_{i^*}} = v_{i^*, x_{i^*}}$ and compute $t' = \prod w_{i,x_i}$. Output $\mathsf{Ext}(g^{t'}, \mathfrak{s})$.

Theorem 7. *If Phi-Hiding assumption holds and* Ext *is a* $(\ell_{\mathrm{RSA}}/5, 1/2^{2n})$ *strong extractor as per Definition 11, then the above construction is a secure single-key no-query secure constrained pseudorandom function for admissible hash compatible constraint family as per Definition 7.*

Correctness. We need to show that for any PRF key K, any constraint $u \in \{0, 1, \perp\}^n$, any key K_u constrained at u and any input $x \in \{0,1\}^n$ such that $P_u(x) = 0$, evaluation at x using the master PRF key K matches the evaluation at x using the constrained key K_u.

More formally, let $K \leftarrow \mathsf{Setup}(1^n)$, and let $K = ((N, p, q), \{c_{i,b}\}, h, \mathfrak{s})$. Let $u \in \{0, 1, \perp\}^n$ be any constraint, and let $K_u = (N, u, e, \{v_{i,b}\}, h^e, \mathfrak{s})$ be the constrained key. On input $x \in \{0,1\}^n$, the PRF evaluation using the master PRF key computes $t = \prod c_{i,x_i}$ and outputs $\mathsf{Ext}(h^t, \mathfrak{s})$.

Since $P_u(x) = 0$, there is at least one index i^* where $u_{i^*} \ne \perp \wedge x_{i^*} \ne u_{i^*}$. As a result, $v_{i^*, x_{i^*}} = c_{i^*, x_{i^*}} \cdot e^{-1}$. For all $i \ne i^*$, we can compute $c_{i,b}$ given $v_{i,b}$ and e. Therefore, if we define $w_{i,b}$ as in the evaluation algorithm and compute

$t' = \prod_i w_{i,x_i}$, then $(h^e)^{t'} = h^{\prod c_{i,x_i}}$. Since both the constrained key evaluation and PRF key evaluation use the same extractor seed, the evaluation using the constrained key is correct.

Security. If $P_u(x) = 1$, then there exists no i such that $v_{i,x_i} = c_{i,x_i} \cdot e^{-1}$. As a result, suppose there exists an adversary $\mathcal{A}$ that can win the single-key no-query constrained PRF security game. Then we can use $\mathcal{A}$ to break the Phi-hiding assumption. We will prove security via a sequence of hybrid experiments. First, we will switch the exponent e in the constrained key from being a random element (co-prime w.r.t. $\phi(N)$) to a factor of $\phi(N)$. This step will rely on the Phi-hiding assumption. Next, we will show that any adversary has negligible advantage if e divides $\phi(N)$. Intuitively, this step will follow because the quantity $\gamma = h^e$ in the constrained key does not reveal h — there could be e different e^{th} roots of γ. As a result, running the extractor on $h^{\prod c_{i,x_i}}$ outputs a uniformly random bit. Due to space constraints, we defer the formal proof to the full version of our paper.

5.3   Constrained Unpredictable Functions from RSA Assumption

The PRF key consists of a RSA modulus, its factorization, $2n$ integers and a random group generator h. The PRF evaluation on an n bit strings is performed as follows: first choose n out of the $2n$ integers depending on the input, compute their product and then output this product in the exponent of h.

- Setup(1^λ): The setup algorithm takes as input the security parameter λ. It first generates RSA modulus $N = pq$, where p, q are primes of $\ell_{\mathrm{RSA}}/2$ bits each. Next, it chooses $2n$ integers $c_{i,b} \leftarrow \mathbb{Z}_{\phi(N)}$ for $i \le n$, $b \in \{0,1\}$ and $h \leftarrow \mathbb{Z}_N^*$. It sets the master PRF key as $K = ((N, p, q), \{c_{i,b}\}_{i \le n, b \in \{0,1\}}, h)$.
- Constrain($K, u \in \{0, 1, \perp\}^n$): The constrain algorithm takes as input the master PRF key $K = ((N, p, q), \{c_{i,b}\}_{i,b}, h)$ and constraint $u \in \{0, 1, \perp\}^n$. It first chooses an integer $e \in \mathbb{Z}_{\phi(N)}^*$ and computes, for all $i \le n$, $b \in \{0,1\}$,

$$v_{i,b} = \begin{cases} (c_{i,b} - 1) \cdot e^{-1} \mod \phi(N) & \text{if } u_i = b \vee u_i = \perp \\ c_{i,b} \cdot e^{-1} \mod \phi(N) & \text{otherwise.} \end{cases}$$

It sets the constrained key as $K_u = (N, u, e, \{v_{i,b}\}_{i,b}, h^e)$.
- Evaluate($K, x \in \{0, 1\}^n$): The evaluation algorithm takes as input a PRF key K (which could be either the master PRF key or constrained PRF key) and an input string $x \in \{0, 1\}^n$.

    If K is a master PRF key, then $K = ((N, p, q), \{c_{i,b}\}_{i \le n, b \in \{0,1\}}, h)$. The evaluation algorithm computes $t = \prod_{i \le n} c_{i,x_i}$ and outputs h^t.

    If K is a constrained key, then $K = (N, u, e, \{v_{i,b}\}_{i \le n, b \in \{0,1\}}, g)$. Recall g is set to be h^e. The evaluation algorithm first checks if $P_u(x) = 0$. If not, it outputs $\perp$. Since $P_u(x) = 0$, there exists an index i such that $u_i \ne \perp$ and $u_i \ne x_i$. Let i^* be the first such index. For all $i \ne i^*$, compute $w_{i,b} = v_{i,b} \cdot e + 1$ if $u_i = b \vee u_i = \perp$, else $w_{i,b} = v_{i,b} \cdot e$. Finally, set $w_{i^*,x_{i^*}} = v_{i^*,x_{i^*}}$ and compute $t' = \prod w_{i,x_i}$. Output $g^{t'}$.

Correctness. The proof of correctness is identical to that provided for correctness of constrained PRF in Sect. 5.2.

Security. If $P_u(x) = 1$, then there exists no i such that $v_{i,x_i} = c_{i,x_i} \cdot e^{-1}$. As a result, suppose there exists an adversary $\mathcal{A}$ that can win the single-key no-query constrained unpredictable function security game. Then we can use $\mathcal{A}$ to break the RSA assumption. We will prove security via a sequence of hybrid experiments. The idea is to set h^e to be the RSA challenge. At a high level, if the adversary can win the unpredictability game (i.e., correctly output $h^{\prod c_{i,x_i}}$ at point x such that $P_u(x) = 0$), then it must have computed the eth root of h^e. The detailed proof can be found in the full version of our paper.

Acknowledgements. We give a large thanks to David Zuckerman for helpful discussions regarding the error correcting code described in Sect. 4.3. The second author is supported by the National Science Foundation (NSF) CNS-1228443 and CNS-1414023, the Office of Naval Research under contract N00014-14-1-0333, and a Microsoft Faculty Fellowship. The fourth author is supported by NSF CNS-1228599 and CNS-1414082, DARPA SafeWare, Microsoft Faculty Fellowship, and Packard Foundation Fellowship.

References

1. Alekhnovich, M.: More on average case vs approximation complexity. In: Proceedings of the 44th Annual IEEE Symposium on Foundations of Computer Science (2003)
2. Badrinarayanan, S., Goyal, V., Jain, A., Sahai, A.: Verifiable functional encryption. In: Cheon, J.H., Takagi, T. (eds.) ASIACRYPT 2016. LNCS, vol. 10032, pp. 557–587. Springer, Heidelberg (2016). doi:10.1007/978-3-662-53890-6_19
3. Badrinarayanan, S., Goyal, V., Jain, A., Sahai, A.: A note on VRFs from verifiable functional encryption. Cryptology ePrint Archive, Report 2017/051 (2017). http://eprint.iacr.org/2017/051
4. Barak, B., Ong, S.J., Vadhan, S.: Derandomization in cryptography. SIAM J. Comput. **37**, 380–400 (2007)
5. Bitansky, N.: Verifiable random functions from non-interactive witness-indistinguishable proofs. Cryptology ePrint Archive, Report 2017/018 (2017). http://eprint.iacr.org/2017/018
6. Bitansky, N., Paneth, O.: ZAPs and non-interactive witness indistinguishability from indistinguishability obfuscation. In: Dodis, Y., Nielsen, J.B. (eds.) TCC 2015. LNCS, vol. 9015, pp. 401–427. Springer, Heidelberg (2015). doi:10.1007/978-3-662-46497-7_16
7. Boneh, D., Boyen, X.: Secure identity based encryption without random oracles. In: Franklin, M. (ed.) CRYPTO 2004. LNCS, vol. 3152, pp. 443–459. Springer, Heidelberg (2004). doi:10.1007/978-3-540-28628-8_27
8. Boneh, D., Waters, B.: Constrained pseudorandom functions and their applications. In: Sako, K., Sarkar, P. (eds.) ASIACRYPT 2013. LNCS, vol. 8270, pp. 280–300. Springer, Heidelberg (2013). doi:10.1007/978-3-642-42045-0_15
9. Boneh, D., Zhandry, M.: Multiparty key exchange, efficient traitor tracing, and more from indistinguishability obfuscation. In: Garay, J.A., Gennaro, R. (eds.) CRYPTO 2014. LNCS, vol. 8616, pp. 480–499. Springer, Heidelberg (2014). doi:10.1007/978-3-662-44371-2_27

10. Boyle, E., Goldwasser, S., Ivan, I.: Functional signatures and pseudorandom functions. In: Krawczyk, H. (ed.) PKC 2014. LNCS, vol. 8383, pp. 501–519. Springer, Heidelberg (2014). doi:10.1007/978-3-642-54631-0_29

11. Brakerski, Z., Vaikuntanathan, V.: Constrained key-homomorphic PRFs from standard lattice assumptions - or: how to secretly embed a circuit in your PRF. In: Dodis, Y., Nielsen, J.B. (eds.) TCC 2015. LNCS, vol. 9015, pp. 1–30. Springer, Heidelberg (2015). doi:10.1007/978-3-662-46497-7_1

12. Chase, M., Meiklejohn, S.: Déjà Q: using dual systems to revisit q-type assumptions. In: Nguyen, P.Q., Oswald, E. (eds.) EUROCRYPT 2014. LNCS, vol. 8441, pp. 622–639. Springer, Heidelberg (2014). doi:10.1007/978-3-642-55220-5_34

13. Dodis, Y.: Efficient construction of (distributed) verifiable random functions. In: Desmedt, Y.G. (ed.) PKC 2003. LNCS, vol. 2567, pp. 1–17. Springer, Heidelberg (2003). doi:10.1007/3-540-36288-6_1

14. Dodis, Y., Yampolskiy, A.: A verifiable random function with short proofs and keys. In: Vaudenay, S. (ed.) PKC 2005. LNCS, vol. 3386, pp. 416–431. Springer, Heidelberg (2005). doi:10.1007/978-3-540-30580-4_28

15. Dwork, C., Naor, M.: Zaps and their applications. In: FOCS, pp. 283–293 (2000)

16. Feige, U., Shamir, A.: Witness indistinguishable and witness hiding protocols. In: STOC, pp. 416–426 (1990)

17. Freire, E.S.V., Hofheinz, D., Paterson, K.G., Striecks, C.: Programmable hash functions in the multilinear setting. In: Canetti, R., Garay, J.A. (eds.) CRYPTO 2013. LNCS, vol. 8042, pp. 513–530. Springer, Heidelberg (2013). doi:10.1007/978-3-642-40041-4_28

18. Garg, S., Gentry, C., Halevi, S., Raykova, M., Sahai, A., Waters, B.: Candidate indistinguishability obfuscation and functional encryption for all circuits. In: FOCS (2013)

19. Gentry, C., Peikert, C., Vaikuntanathan, V.: Trapdoors for hard lattices and new cryptographic constructions. In: STOC, pp. 197–206 (2008)

20. Goldreich, O., Goldwasser, S., Micali, S.: How to construct random functions (extended abstract). In: FOCS, pp. 464–479 (1984)

21. Groth, J., Ostrovsky, R., Sahai, A.: New techniques for noninteractive zero-knowledge. J. ACM 59(3), 11 (2012)

22. Hofheinz, D., Jager, T.: Verifiable random functions from standard assumptions. In: Kushilevitz, E., Malkin, T. (eds.) TCC 2016. LNCS, vol. 9562, pp. 336–362. Springer, Heidelberg (2016). doi:10.1007/978-3-662-49096-9_14

23. Hohenberger, S., Sahai, A., Waters, B.: Replacing a random oracle: full domain hash from indistinguishability obfuscation. In: Nguyen, P.Q., Oswald, E. (eds.) EUROCRYPT 2014. LNCS, vol. 8441, pp. 201–220. Springer, Heidelberg (2014). doi:10.1007/978-3-642-55220-5_12

24. Hohenberger, S., Waters, B.: Constructing verifiable random functions with large input spaces. In: Gilbert, H. (ed.) EUROCRYPT 2010. LNCS, vol. 6110, pp. 656–672. Springer, Heidelberg (2010). doi:10.1007/978-3-642-13190-5_33

25. Jager, T.: Verifiable random functions from weaker assumptions. In: Dodis, Y., Nielsen, J.B. (eds.) TCC 2015. LNCS, vol. 9015, pp. 121–143. Springer, Heidelberg (2015). doi:10.1007/978-3-662-46497-7_5

26. Jain, A., Krenn, S., Pietrzak, K., Tentes, A.: Commitments and efficient zero-knowledge proofs from learning parity with noise. In: Wang, X., Sako, K. (eds.) ASIACRYPT 2012. LNCS, vol. 7658, pp. 663–680. Springer, Heidelberg (2012). doi:10.1007/978-3-642-34961-4_40

27. Kiayias, A., Papadopoulos, S., Triandopoulos, N., Zacharias, T.: Delegatable pseudorandom functions and applications. In: ACM Conference on Computer and Communications Security, pp. 669–684 (2013)
28. Kiltz, E., Masny, D., Pietrzak, K.: Simple chosen-ciphertext security from low-noise LPN. IACR Cryptology ePrint Archive 2015, 401 (2015). http://eprint.iacr.org/2015/401
29. Lysyanskaya, A.: Unique signatures and verifiable random functions from the DH-DDH separation. In: Yung, M. (ed.) CRYPTO 2002. LNCS, vol. 2442, pp. 597–612. Springer, Heidelberg (2002). doi:10.1007/3-540-45708-9_38
30. Micali, S., Rabin, M., Vadhan, S.: Verifiable random functions. In: Proceedings 40th IEEE Symposium on Foundations of Computer Science (FOCS), pp. 120–130. IEEE (1999)
31. Micciancio, D., Regev, O.: Worst-case to average-case reductions based on Gaussian measures. SIAM J. Comput. 37(1), 267–302 (2007)
32. Naor, M.: Bit commitment using pseudorandomness. J. Cryptol. 4(2), 151–158 (1991)
33. Naor, M., Reingold, O.: Number-theoretic constructions of efficient pseudo-random functions. J. ACM 51(2), 231–262 (2004)
34. Nisan, N., Wigderson, A.: Hardness vs randomness. J. Comput. Syst. Sci. 49(2), 149–167 (1994). http://dx.doi.org/10.1016/S0022-0000(05)80043-1
35. Regev, O.: On lattices, learning with errors, random linear codes, and cryptography. In: Proceedings of the 37th Annual ACM Symposium on Theory of Computing, Baltimore, MD, USA, 22–24 May 2005, pp. 84–93 (2005)
36. Sahai, A., Waters, B.: How to use indistinguishability obfuscation: deniable encryption, and more. In: STOC, pp. 475–484 (2014)

Verifiable Random Functions from Non-interactive Witness-Indistinguishable Proofs

Nir Bitansky[✉]

Tel Aviv University, Tel Aviv, Israel
nirbitan@tau.ac.il

Abstract. *Verifiable random functions* (VRFs) are pseudorandom functions where the owner of the seed, in addition to computing the function's value y at any point x, can also generate a non-interactive proof π that y is correct, without compromising pseudorandomness at other points. Being a natural primitive with a wide range of applications, considerable efforts have been directed towards the construction of such VRFs. While these efforts have resulted in a variety of algebraic constructions (from bilinear maps or the RSA problem), the relation between VRFs and other general primitives is still not well understood.

We present new constructions of VRFs from general primitives, the main one being *non-interactive witness-indistinguishable proofs* (NIWIs). This includes:

- A selectively-secure VRF assuming NIWIs and non-interactive commitments. As usual, the VRF can be made adaptively-secure assuming subexponential hardness of the underlying primitives.
- An adaptively-secure VRF assuming (polynomially-hard) NIWIs, noninteractive commitments, and *(single-key) constrained pseudorandom functions* for a restricted class of constraints.

The above primitives can be instantiated under various standard assumptions, which yields corresponding VRF instantiations, under different assumptions than were known so far. One notable example is a non-uniform construction of VRFs from subexponentially-hard trapdoor permutations, or more generally, from *verifiable pseudorandom generators* (the construction can be made uniform under a standard derandomization assumption). This partially answers an open question by Dwork and Naor (FOCS '00).

The construction and its analysis are quite simple. Both draw from ideas commonly used in the context of *indistinguishability obfuscation*.

1 Introduction

Verifiable random functions (VRFs), introduced by Micali et al. [39], are pseudorandom functions (PRFs) [27] where it is possible to verify that a given output y corresponds to a correct evaluation of the function on any given input x. Such a VRF is associated with a secret key SK and a corresponding public

© International Association for Cryptologic Research 2017
Y. Kalai and L. Reyzin (Eds.): TCC 2017, Part II, LNCS 10678, pp. 567–594, 2017.
https://doi.org/10.1007/978-3-319-70503-3_19

verification key VK. The secret key allows anyone to compute the function $y = \mathsf{VRF.Eval}_{SK}(x)$ at any point x, and also to compute a proof $\pi_{x,y}$ that y was computed correctly. Here, by "computed correctly", we mean that any verification key VK^*, even a maliciously chosen one, is a commitment to the entire function—it uniquely determines the value y of the function at any point x, and accepting proofs only exist for this value y. The pseudorandomness requirement generalizes that of plain PRFs—the value y of the function at any point x should be pseudorandom, even after evaluating the function and obtaining proofs of correctness for an arbitrary polynomial number of points $\{x_i \neq x\}$. The standard definition is *adaptive*, allowing the point x to be chosen at any point, and we can also consider a *selective* definition, where the adversary chooses the challenge x, before getting the verification key VK, and before any evaluation query.

Constructions. VRFs are a natural primitive with a variety of applications (listed for instance in [1]), and considerable effort has been invested in the pursuit of constructions, aiming to diversify and simplify the underlying assumptions [1,11,12,19,21,22,26,33,35,36,38,39]. Despite the progress made, almost all known constructions are of an algebraic nature, and are based directly either on the (strong) RSA assumption, or on different assumptions related to bilinear (or multilinear) maps. Attempts to construct VRFs from more general assumptions have been limited to constructions from *VRF-suitable identity-based encryption* [1], or from indistinguishability obfuscation (IO) and injective one-way functions [45]. In both cases, concrete instantiations are, again, only known based on bilinear or multilinear maps.[1] Alternatively, *weak VRFs*, which are the verifiable analog of *weak PRFs* [42], can be constructed from (doubly enhanced) trapdoor permutations [16].

In terms of barriers, VRFs imply [29] non-interactive zero-knowledge proofs (NIZKs) [10], and accordingly constructing VRFs from symmetric-key primitives like one-way functions, or collision-resistant hashing, seems out of reach for existing techniques. In contrast, NIZKs can be constructed from (doubly enhanced) trapdoor permutations (TDPs) [6,24,28], and we may hope that so can VRFs. As possible evidence that this is a false hope, Fiore and Schröder show that there is no *black-box* reduction from VRFs to (doubly enhanced) TDPs [25].

1.1   This Work

We present new constructions of VRFs from general assumptions, the main one being *non-interactive witness-indistinguishable proofs* (NIWIs), which were introduced by Barak et al. [4].

Our most basic result is a selectively-secure construction based on NIWIs, non-interactive commitments, and *puncturable PRFs* [13,15,37,45] (these are in

---

[1] The construction based on IO is also limited to either selective security, or reliance on subexponential hardness.

turn implied by one-way functions and thus also by non-interactive commitments). As usual, adaptive security of the construction can be shown assuming all primitives are subexponentially-secure.

Theorem 1 (informal). *Assuming the existence of NIWIs and non-interactive commitments, there exist selectively-secure VRFs. Further assuming subexponential hardness of these primitives, there exist adaptively-secure VRFs.*

Aiming to avoid subexponential assumptions, our more general construction replaces puncturable PRFs with more general types of *single-key constrained PRF* (CPRFs) [13,15,37] and achieves adaptive security from polynomial assumptions.

Theorem 2 (informal). *Assuming the existence of NIWIs, non-interactive commitments, and single-key CPRFs (for some restricted class of constraints), there exist adaptively-secure VRFs.*

Given the reliance on generic primitives, the above theorems already allow (and may further allow in the future) to base VRFs on different assumptions. We now review the (generic and specific) assumptions under which the above primitives are known, and derive corresponding corollaries. (For now, we focus on the implications of the theorems. We recall the definitions of NIWIs and CPRFs later, in the technical overview.)

NIWIs. Dwork and Naor [23] gave a non-uniform construction of NIWIs from NIZKs (which can be constructed from doubly enhanced TDPs). Barak et al. [4] showed that the construction can be made uniform assuming also the existence of a problem solvable in deterministic time $2^{O(n)}$ with non-deterministic circuit complexity $2^{\Omega(n)}$. The latter is a worst-case assumption previously used to derandomize **AM** [40], and can be seen as an extension of the assumption that **EXP** $\not\subseteq$ **NP/poly** (see further discussion in [4]). Groth et al. [32] then constructed NIWIs based on standard assumptions on bilinear maps such as the Decision Linear (DLIN) assumption, the Symmetric External Diffie Hellman (SXDH) assumption, or the Subgroup Decision Assumption. In [8], NIWIs are constructed from IO and one-way permutations.

Non-interactive Commitments. Such commitments are known from any family of injective one-way functions [9]. Naor [41] gave a non-uniform construction from plain one-way functions, which can be made uniform under the same derandomization assumption mentioned above [4].

CPRFs. Theorem 2 relies on single-key CPRFs for certain specific classes of constraints (see the technical outline below). It can be instantiated either by the CPRFs of Brakerski and Vaikuntanathan [17], based on LWE and 1D-SIS, or

from those of Boneh and Zhandry, based on IO [14]. We also give new instantiations under the DDH assumption.[2]

We can now combine the above in different ways to get instantiations of
(adaptively-secure) VRFs from different assumptions, several of which were previously unknown. For example:

- A non-uniform construction from subexponential hardness of (doubly
  enhanced) TDPs. This should be contrasted with the black-box barrier of
  Fiore and Schröder mentioned above. The barrier does not apply to this construction both due to non-uniformity, and also non-black-box use of some of
  the underlying primitives, such as the commitments or puncturable PRFs.
- By instantiating these TDPs with a variant of the Rabin construction [28], we
  get a non-uniform construction from subexponential hardness of Factoring.
  This should be compared with the construction from subexponential hardness
  of strong RSA [39]. (We can avoid subexponential hardness relying on DDH
  or LWE and 1D-SIS. We can further make the construction uniform under
  the above mentioned derandomization assumption.)
- Constructions from simple assumptions on bilinear groups, such as DLIN or
  SXDH. Indeed, the past decade has seen gradual progress toward this goal,
  starting from [38], through [1,11,12,21,22,35,36], and culminating in [33],
  with a construction from the n-Linear assumption. While the result obtained
  here *does not* improve on [33], it provides a quite different solution.
- A construction from polynomially hard IO and one-way permutations. In
  comparison, the existing construction mentioned above [45] required subexponential hardness for adaptive security.

An Equivalence Between Nonuniform VRFs, VPRGs, and NIZKs.
Dwork and Naor [23] defined a verifiable version of pseudo-random generators
(VPRGs) and showed their equivalence to NIZKs. Such VPRGs (or NIZKs) are
implied (even by selectively-secure) VRFs. Dwork and Naor raised the question of whether the converse holds: *do VPRGs imply VRFs? (Analogously to
the fact that PRGs imply PRFs.)* Our result shows that for non-uniform constructions this is indeed the case—VPRGs imply selectively-secure VRFs (or
adaptively-secure if they are subexponentially-hard). For uniform constructions,
we only establish this equivalence conditioned on the mentioned derandomization assumption.

1.2   Techniques

We now explain the main ideas behind our constructions.

A Naïve Idea: NIWIs instead of NIZKs. Our starting point is the simple
construction of VRFs in the common random string model [39]—to construct a
VRF, let the verification key VK be a commitment $c = Com(F)$ to a function F

---

[2] We also give a simpler construction under the stronger d-power DDH assumption.

drawn at random from a PRF family [27], and store F along with the commitment randomness as the private evaluation key SK. The value of the function at any point x is simply $y = F(x)$, and the proofs of correctness $\pi_{x,y}$ are simply NIZKs that y is consistent with the commitment c.

This solution works as expected, but requires a common random string. Aiming to get a construction in the plain model, a natural direction is to replace NIZKs with NIWIs, which exist in the plain model and still offer some level of privacy. Concretely, NIWIs guarantee absolute soundness (convincing proofs for false statements simply do not exist), and witness indistinguishability—a proof for a statement with multiple witnesses leaks no information about which witness was used in the proof; namely, proofs that use different witnesses are computationally indistinguishable. It is not hard see, however, that this relaxed privacy guarantee does not allow using NIWIs *as is* in the above solution. Indeed, since F is uniquely determined by the commitment c, a NIWI proof may very well leak it in full, without ever compromising witness indistinguishability.

Indeed, leveraging witness indistinguishability would require a different function commitment mechanism that would not *completely* determine the underlying description of the function F. This may appear to conflict with the uniqueness requirement of VRFs, which in the naïve construction was guaranteed exactly due to the fact that the commitment fixes the function's description. However, we observe that there is still some wiggle room here—uniqueness of VRFs only requires that the *functionality* $\{F(x)\}_x$ is fixed (rather than the description F of the function). Our solution will take advantage of this fact.

Function Commitments: Indistinguishability instead of Simulation. At high level, our first step is to consider, and instantiate, a function commitment mechanism so that on one hand, any verification key VK^* completely determines the underlying function, but on the other hand, does not leak which specific (circuit) description is used in the commitment. The second step will be to show that such function commitments can be combined with appropriate PRFs to obtain VRFs.

This approach bears similarity to a common approach in obfuscation-based applications. There, typically, a given application easily follows from the simulation-based notion of *virtual black-box obfuscation*. The challenge is to recover the application using the weaker indistinguishability-based notion of IO, which hides which circuit was obfuscated (among different circuit descriptions for the same function). In our context, the NIZK-based VRF solution corresponds to simulation-based function commitments where the verification key, function values, and proofs can all be efficiently simulated given black-box access to the underlying function, in which case, any PRF would be enough to get VRFs. Our challenge will be to obtain VRFs from an indistinguishability-based notion of function commitments. Indeed, our second step will rely on techniques from the IO regime, such as *puncturing* [45]. Details follow.

Step 1: Indistinguishability-Based Function Commitments. The function commitment notion we consider requires that verification keys VK, VK' corresponding to two circuits F, F' would be indistinguishable given evaluations y_i, with proofs of consistency π_{x_i, y_i}, for an arbitrary polynomial number of points x_i, provided that the circuits agree on these points, namely $\mathsf{F}(x_i) = \mathsf{F}'(x_i)$. This is on top of the usual binding requirement saying that any verification key VK^* uniquely determines the underlying function (but not its circuit description).

This notion is dual and equivalent to a notion of *functional (bit-string) commitments* considered in [2, Appendix G] where the commitment is to an input x, and evaluations correspond to $f_i(x)$ for different functions f_i. In [2], such functional commitments are constructed from *single-ciphertext verifiable functional encryption* (SCT-VFE), which in turn is constructed from commitments, NIWIs, and plain, non-verifiable, SCT-FE (known from one-way functions [30,44]). This, in particular, gives an instantiation for the required function commitments.

Here we give a simple construction of the required function commitments directly from NIWIs and commitments (avoiding FE altogether). Concretely, a verification key VK for a circuit F consists of three commitments (c_1, c_2, c_3) to the circuit F. The secret key SK consists of F and the randomness for the commitments. To prove correctness of $y = \mathsf{F}(x)$, we give a NIWI that y is consistent with two out of the three commitments; namely, there exist $1 \leq i < j \leq 3$ so that c_i, c_j are commitments to circuits $\mathsf{F}_i, \mathsf{F}_j$, and $y = \mathsf{F}_i(x) = \mathsf{F}_j(x)$.

The binding of commitments and soundness of NIWIs, guarantee that any verification key corresponds to at most a single function, which at any point returns the majority value of the functions underlying the commitments (for malicious verification keys, a majority may not exist, in which case no value will be accepted). At the same time, the required indistinguishability can be shown by a simple hybrid argument. Throughout this argument, NIWI proofs use as the witness the randomness and underlying plaintext for any two of the three commitments, allowing to invoke the hiding of the third commitment. For example, at first, proofs will use the randomness for c_1 and c_2, allowing to change the third commitment c_3 from the circuit F to the circuit F'. Then, assuming F' and F agree on all evaluation queries x_i, we can rely on witness-indistinguishability, and now use instead the randomness for two different commitments, say c_1 and c_3 to compute NIWI proofs. Now, we can change c_2 to F', and so on.

Step 2: From Function Commitments to VRFs. Our construction of VRFs then proceeds by combining function commitments such as those above with carefully chosen PRFs. Indeed, while we might not be able to use any PRF (as in the simulation-based function commitments from NIZKs), the indistinguishability guarantee that we have suggests a natural solution. Specifically, if we could replace the committed PRF circuit F, with a circuit F' that agrees with F on all of the adversary's evaluation queries x_i, and yet does not leak information on the function's value $\mathsf{F}(x)$ at the challenge point x, then we could satisfy the pseudorandomness requirement of VRFs. *Can we generate such a circuit F'?* We first observe that in the case of a selective adversary (that announces the challenge

x before even getting the verification key), we certainly can—via puncturable PRFs [13,15,37]. Recall that in such PRFs, we can puncture the PRF circuit F at any point x, so that the new punctured circuit $F'_{\{x\}}$ retains the functionality of F at any point other than x, whereas the value $F(x)$ at the punctured point x remains pseudorandom.

Concretely, our security reduction will use any selective adversary against the VRF to break the pseudorandomness at the punctured point x. The reduction will generate a commitment (namely, verification key) for the punctured $F'_{\{x\}}$, and use this punctured circuit to compute the answers (y_i, π_{x_i, y_i}), for all the queries $x_i \neq x$. By the function-commitment indistinguishability, the adversary could not distinguish between this and the real VRF experiment where the unpunctured F would be used, as the two completely agree on all evaluations points x_i. Accordingly, any successful adversary in the VRF game can be used by the reduction to distinguish $F(x)$ from a truly random output.

Adaptive Security via Constrained PRFs. As mentioned, selective security implies adaptive security if we assume subexponential hardness—the reduction basically guesses the challenge, incurring a $2^{|x|}$ security loss. To obtain adaptive security from polynomial assumptions, we follow a common path in adaptive-security proofs, relying on the idea of *partitioning*. Roughly speaking, the idea is that instead of guessing the challenge (which is successful with exponentially-small probability), the reduction guesses a partition $(S, X\backslash S)$ of the query space X, aiming that with noticeable (rather than exponentially-small) probability, all evaluation queries x_i will fall outside S, but the challenge x will fall inside S.

In our case, given such a partition scheme, we aim to follow the same approach as above (for the selective case), only that now instead of creating a circuit $F'_{\{x\}}$ that is punctured at a single point, we would like to create a circuit F'_S that is punctured at the entire set S; namely, it retains the functionality of F on any point in $X\backslash S$, but the value $F(x)$ is pseudorandom for any $x \in S$. This more general notion is indeed known as constrained PRFs (CPRF). Here we only need *single-key* CPRFs in the sense that security holds in the presence of a single constrained PRF. Also, we do not need constraining for arbitrary sets S, but just for the sets S in the support of the partition scheme we use. We give three examples of such partition schemes, one that aligns with the common notion of *admissible hash functions* [11], a second one that generalizes admissible hashing to large alphabets, and a third one based on universal hashing [18]. As stated in the previous subsection, we demonstrate corresponding CPRFs based on different (polynomial) assumptions. Overall, the construction is exactly the same as before only that we instantiate the PRF with a CPRF for constrained sets in the support of one of the above partition schemes.[3]

---

[3] In the body, we further allow the partition scheme to involve some *encoding* of the input space X into a more structured input space $\widehat{X}$, and then consider applying the CPRF and partitioning for encoded inputs in the new space $\widehat{X}$. See Definition 4 and Sect. 3 for more details.

Fulfilling the above approach involves certain technical subtleties, most of which are common to typical partitioning proofs. One notorious issue concerns the fact that, while overall noticeable, the probability of successful partition may vary with how the adversary chooses its queries. In particular, it may potentially be the case that conditioned on a successful partition, the adversary's advantage in the VRF game becomes negligible (see more elaborate discussion in [46]). There are several approaches for dealing with this in the literature (the most common one is perhaps the artificial abort technique in [46]). We follow an approach suggested by Jager [36] of requiring that the partition schemes in use are *balanced* in the sense that the probability of partition does not change by much over different choices of queries. See further details in Sects. 2.4 and 3.3.

1.3 Concurrent and Subsequent Work

In concurrent and independent work, Goyal et al. [31] present a similar approach for constructing VRFs. The general construction and underlying primitives are essentially the same as ours. There are some differences regarding the instantiations provided for the underlying primitives and the presentation. We summarize the symmetric difference below.

– **Underlying Primitives.** In terms of CPRF instantiations, apart from the instantiations common to both works, they give an instantiation based on the Phi-Hiding assumption, and we give an instantiations based on the DDH assumption. They also give new instantiations for commitment schemes based on LWE and LPN, which we do not.
– **Presentation and Abstractions.** For modularity, we chose to use the abstraction of function commitments. Effectively, the same function commitment construction is present in both works. Also, to get adaptive security, they rely on the standard notion of *admissible hash functions*, whereas we chose to consider a somewhat more general notion of *partition schemes*, with the aim of giving more flexibility when designing corresponding CPRFs; indeed, this allows us to get our DDH-based instantiation.
– **Analysis.** To prove adaptive security, they use the technique of *artificial aborts* [46], whereas we instead use a slightly stronger notion of partition schemes (or admissible hash functions) that are also balanced [36]. (The balance property does not require any additional assumptions and is essentially obtained for free in the considered constructions).

In a subsequent note [3], Badrinarayanan et al. suggest an alternative construction of VRFs from *single-ciphertext verifiable functional-encryption* (SCT-VFE). Their construction can be interpreted as following our two-step construction where the first step—function commitments—is realized using SCT-VFE (the second step, of using puncturable or constrained PRFs, is identical). As mentioned, SCT-VFE was constructed in [2] from commitments, NIWIs, and plain (non-verifiable) SCT-FE. We give a simple construction of the required function commitments directly from NIWIs and commitments.

Organization. In Sect. 2, we define the primitives used in this work. In Sect. 3, we present the main construction and its analysis. In Sect. 4, we discuss possible instantiations, induced by different partition schemes and CPRFs. Some of the basic definitions and proofs are Omitted and can be found in the full version.

2   Preliminaries

In this section, we give the basic definitions used throughout the paper. For lack of space, some of the standard definitions can be found in the full version.

2.1   Verifiable Random Functions

We define verifiable random functions (VRFs).

Definition 1 (VRF [39]). *Let n, m, k be polynomially bounded functions. A verifiable random function VRF = (VRF.Gen, VRF.Eval, VRF.P, VRF.V) consists of the following polynomial-time algorithms:*

- *a probabilistic key sampler VRF.Gen(1^λ) that given a security parameter 1^λ outputs a secret key SK and public verification key $VK \in \{0,1\}^{k(\lambda)}$,*
- *an evaluator VRF.Eval$_{SK}(x)$ that given the secret key and $x \in \{0,1\}^{n(\lambda)}$ outputs $y \in \{0,1\}^{m(\lambda)}$,*
- *a prover VRF.P$_{SK}(x)$ that given x and the secret key produces a proof π that y is consistent with the verification key VK,*
- *and verifier VRF.V$_{VK}(\pi, x, y)$ that verifies the proof.*

We make the following requirements:

1. *Completeness: For every security parameter $\lambda \in \mathbb{N}$ and input $x \in \{0,1\}^{n(\lambda)}$,*

$$\Pr\left[\text{VRF.V}_{VK}(\pi, x, y) = 1 \; \middle| \; \begin{array}{l} (SK, VK) \leftarrow \text{VRF.Gen}(1^\lambda) \\ y = \text{VRF.Eval}_{SK}(x) \\ \pi \leftarrow \text{VRF.P}_{SK}(x) \end{array} \right] = 1.$$

2. *Uniqueness: For every security parameter $\lambda \in \mathbb{N}$, input $x \in \{0,1\}^{n(\lambda)}$, and arbitrary verification key $VK^* \in \{0,1\}^{k(\lambda)}$, there exists at most a single $y \in \{0,1\}^{m(\lambda)}$ for which there exists an accepting proof π. That is,*

$$\text{if} \quad \text{VRF.V}_{VK^*}(\pi_0, x, y_0) = \text{VRF.V}_{VK^*}(\pi_1, x, y_1) = 1 \quad \text{then} \quad y_0 = y_1.$$

3. *Adaptive Indistinguishability: For any adversary $\mathcal{A}(1^\lambda)$, consider the following game $\mathcal{G}_{\mathcal{A}}^{\text{vrf}}$:*
   (a) *The VRF challenger samples $(SK, VK) \leftarrow \text{VRF.Gen}(1^\lambda)$, and sends VK to $\mathcal{A}$.*
   (b) *$\mathcal{A}$ submits to a challenger evaluation queries $x_1, \ldots, x_Q$, and gets back from the challenger $(y_1, \pi_1), \ldots, (y_Q, \pi_Q)$, where $y_i = \text{VRF.Eval}_{SK}(x_i)$, $\pi_i \leftarrow \text{VRF.P}(x_i, SK)$.*

(c) *At any point, including between evaluation queries, $\mathcal{A}$ may submit a challenge input $x_* \in \{0,1\}^{n(\lambda)}$. The challenger then sets $y_*^0 = \mathsf{VRF.Eval}_{SK}(x_*), y_*^1 \leftarrow \{0,1\}^{m(\lambda)}$, samples $b \leftarrow \{0,1\}$, and sends y_*^b to $\mathcal{A}$. (The adversary $\mathcal{A}$ may then make additional evaluation queries.)*

(d) *At the end, $\mathcal{A}$ outputs a guess b'. The result of the game $\mathcal{G}_{\mathcal{A}}^{vrf}(\lambda)$ is 1 if $b' = b$, and 0 otherwise.*

*We say that $\mathcal{A}$ is **admissible** if in the above game it is always the case that $x_* \notin \{x_i \mid i \in [Q]\}$. We require that any polynomial-size admissible adversary wins the game with negligible advantage:*

$$\mathsf{Adv}_{\mathcal{A}}^{vrf} := \left| \Pr\left[\mathcal{G}_{\mathcal{A}}^{vrf}(\lambda) = 1\right] - \frac{1}{2} \right| \leq \mathrm{negl}(\lambda).$$

We say that the VRF satisfies <u>Selective Indistinguishability</u> (rather than adaptive) if $\mathcal{A}$ submits the challenge query x_* at the beginning of the game, before getting VK and making any evaluation query.

2.2   Sets with Efficient Representation

We consider collections of sets with efficient representation.

Definition 2 (Efficient Representation of Sets). $\mathcal{S} = \{\mathcal{S}_\lambda\}_{\lambda \in \mathbb{N}}$ *is a collection of sets with efficient representation if there is a polynomial poly such that any set $S \in \mathcal{S}_\lambda$ can be represented by a circuit C_S of size $\mathrm{poly}(\lambda)$ such that $C_S(s) = 1$ if $s \in S$ and $C_S(s) = 0$ otherwise. We further require that given C_S, it is possible to efficiently sample some $s \in S$.*

It will be convenient to identify any set S with its circuit representation C_S. In particular, when an algorithm gets as input a set S that is super-polynomially large, we mean that it gets as input its efficient representation C_S.

2.3   Constrained Pseudo-Random Functions

We next define constrained pseudo-random functions (CPRFs).

Definition 3 (Constrained PRFs [13,15,37]). *Let n, m, k be polynomially-bounded functions. Let $\mathcal{S} = \left\{\mathcal{S}_\lambda \subseteq 2^{\{0,1\}^{n(\lambda)}}\right\}_{\lambda \in \mathbb{N}}$ be a collection of sets with efficient representation. A constrained PRF $\mathsf{CPRF} = (\mathsf{CPRF.Gen}, \mathsf{CPRF.Eval}, \mathsf{CPRF.Cons})$ for $\mathcal{S}$ consists of the following polynomial-time algorithms:*

- *a probabilistic key sampler $\mathsf{CPRF.Gen}(1^\lambda)$ that given a security parameter 1^λ outputs a key $K \in \{0,1\}^{k(\lambda)}$,*
- *an evaluator $\mathsf{CPRF.Eval}_K(x)$ that given as input the key K and $x \in \{0,1\}^{n(\lambda)}$ outputs $y \in \{0,1\}^{m(\lambda)}$,*
- *and a constraining algorithm that given as input the key K and a set $S \in \mathcal{S}_\lambda$, outputs a constrained key $K_S \in \{0,1\}^{k(\lambda)}$.*

We make the following requirements:

1. *Functionality: For every security-parameter $\lambda \in \mathbb{N}$, set $S \in \mathcal{S}_\lambda$, and input $x \in \{0,1\}^{n(\lambda)} \backslash S$,*

$$\Pr\left[\mathsf{CPRF.Eval}_{K_S}(x) = \mathsf{CPRF.Eval}_K(x) \; \middle| \; \begin{array}{l} K \leftarrow \mathsf{CPRF.Gen}(1^\lambda) \\ K_S \leftarrow \mathsf{CPRF.Cons}(K, S) \end{array}\right] = 1.$$

2. *(Single-Key) Indistinguishability: For any adversary $\mathcal{B}(1^\lambda)$, consider the following game $\mathcal{G}_\mathcal{B}^{\mathsf{cprf}}$:*

   (a) *$\mathcal{B}$ submits a constraint S to a CPRF challenger.*

   (b) *The CPRF challenger samples $K \leftarrow \mathsf{CPRF.Gen}(1^\lambda)$, computes a constrained key $K_S \leftarrow \mathsf{CPRF.Cons}(K, S)$, and sends K_S to $\mathcal{B}$.*

   (c) *$\mathcal{B}$, given K_S, chooses a challenge input $x_* \in \{0,1\}^{n(\lambda)}$, and sends it to the challenger.*

   (d) *The challenger sets $\begin{array}{l} y_*^0 = \mathsf{CPRF.Eval}_K(x_*), \\ y_*^1 \leftarrow \{0,1\}^{m(\lambda)} \end{array}$, samples $b \leftarrow \{0,1\}$, and sends y_*^b to $\mathcal{B}$.*

   (e) *$\mathcal{B}$, given y_*^b, outputs a guess b'. The result of the game $\mathcal{G}_\mathcal{B}^{\mathsf{cprf}}(\lambda)$ is 1 if $b' = b$, and 0 otherwise.*

   *We say that $\mathcal{B}$ is **admissible** if in the above game it is always the case that $S \in \mathcal{S}_\lambda$ and $x_* \in S$. We require that any polynomial-size admissible adversary wins the game with negligible advantage:*

$$\mathsf{Adv}_\mathcal{B}^{\mathsf{cprf}} := \left| \Pr\left[\mathcal{G}_\mathcal{B}^{\mathsf{cprf}}(\lambda) = 1\right] - \frac{1}{2} \right| \leq \mathsf{negl}(\lambda).$$

Remark 1 (Key Size). In the above definition, constrained keys and unconstrained keys have the same description size k. Furthermore, we have a single evaluation algorithm for both constrained and unconstrained keys. Both of these assumptions are without loss of generality and are just meant to simplify presentation in our construction.

Remark 2 (Computational Functionality). We can also consider a relaxed computational functionality requirement [17], which essentially says that inputs outside the constrained set S, on which functionality isn't preserved, may exist, but are hard to find. Formally,

1. *Computational Functionality: For any polynomial-size adversary $\mathcal{A}$, any $\lambda \in \mathbb{N}$, and any $S \in \mathcal{S}_\lambda$:*

$$\Pr\left[\begin{array}{c} x \notin S \\ \mathsf{CPRF.Eval}_{K_S}(x) \neq \mathsf{CPRF.Eval}_K(x) \end{array} \; \middle| \; \begin{array}{l} K \leftarrow \mathsf{CPRF.Gen}(1^\lambda) \\ K_S \leftarrow \mathsf{CPRF.Cons}(K, S) \\ x \leftarrow \mathcal{A}^{\mathsf{CPRF.Eval}_K(\cdot)}(K_S) \end{array}\right] \leq \mathsf{negl}(\lambda).$$

2.4 Partition Schemes

We define *partition schemes*, which generalize the concept of *admissible hash functions* [11] often used in the literature to prove adaptive security.

Such a scheme for a domain $\{0,1\}^n$ provides a way to efficiently encode any element $x \in \{0,1\}^n$ to an element $\widehat{x} = \mathsf{PAR.Enc}(x)$ in a new domain $\{0,1\}^{\widehat{n}}$. The new domain is associated with a partition sampler $\mathsf{PAR.Gen}$ that samples a partition $(S, \overline{S})$, where $\overline{S} = \{0,1\}^{\widehat{n}} \backslash S$. The main guarantee is that for any set of Q elements $X \subseteq \{0,1\}^n$ and any $x_* \notin X$, with high probability $\widehat{x}_* \in S$ and $\widehat{X} \subseteq \overline{S}$; namely, x_* and X are split by the partition. We shall further require that the scheme is balanced, roughly meaning that the probability that the above occurs does not change much between different choices of (X, x_*). This property was suggested in [36] for admissible hash functions as an alternative to the artificial abort technique in partition-based proofs [46], inspired by [5].

Definition 4 (Partition Schemes). *Let $n, \widehat{n}$ be polynomially bounded functions, $\tau < 1$ an inverse-polynomial function, and $\mathcal{S} = \left\{ \mathcal{S}_\lambda \subseteq 2^{\{0,1\}^{\widehat{n}(\lambda)}} \right\}_{\lambda \in \mathbb{N}}$ a collection of sets with efficient representation. A partition scheme $\mathsf{PAR} = (\mathsf{PAR.Enc}, \mathsf{PAR.Gen})$ parameterized by $(n, \widehat{n}, \tau, \mathcal{S})$ consists of the following polynomial-time algorithms*

- *a deterministic encoder $\mathsf{PAR.Enc}(x)$ that maps any $x \in \{0,1\}^{n(\lambda)}$ to $\widehat{x} \in \{0,1\}^{\widehat{n}(\lambda)}$*
- *a probabilistic sampler $\mathsf{PAR.Gen}(1^\lambda, Q, \delta)$ that given security parameter 1^λ, integer Q, and balance parameter δ, outputs a set $S \in \mathcal{S}_\lambda$, interpreted as a partition $(S, \overline{S})$ of $\{0,1\}^{\widehat{n}(\lambda)}$.[4]*

Fix $\lambda, Q \in \mathbb{N}, \delta < 1$. Let $\mathcal{X}$ be a distribution on pairs (X, x_*) such that $X := (x_1, \ldots, x_Q) \in \{0,1\}^{n(\lambda) \times Q}$ and $x_* \in \{0,1\}^{n(\lambda)} \backslash X$. We define the probability that (X, x_*) are split by the sampled partition:

$$P_\mathcal{X}(\lambda, Q, \delta) := \Pr\left[\widehat{x}_* \in S, \widehat{X} \subseteq \overline{S} \;\middle|\; \begin{array}{c} (X, x_*) \leftarrow \mathcal{X}, \\ \widehat{x}_* = \mathsf{PAR.Enc}(x_*), \\ \widehat{X} = \{\mathsf{PAR.Enc}(x_i) \mid x_i \in X\}, \\ S \leftarrow \mathsf{PAR.Gen}(1^\lambda, Q, \delta) \end{array} \right].$$

For every $\lambda, Q \in \mathbb{N}, \delta < 1$, and any two distributions $\mathcal{X}, \mathcal{X}'$ as above, we require:

1. Probable Partitioning:

$$P_\mathcal{X}(\lambda, Q, \delta) \geq \tau(\lambda, Q, \delta^{-1}) = \left(\frac{\delta}{Q \cdot \lambda} \right)^{O(1)},$$

---

[4] We note that the set S has efficient representation in terms of λ, and does not grow with Q, δ^{-1}. Indeed, throughout this paper, Q, δ^{-1}, will be arbitrary polynomials in λ that depend on the adversary. In our partition schemes, the representation of sets will only scale with $\min\{\log(Q/\delta), n(\lambda)\}$.

2. _Balance:_

$$1 - \delta \leq \frac{P_{\mathcal{X}}(\lambda, Q, \delta)}{P_{\mathcal{X}'}(\lambda, Q, \delta)} \leq 1 + \delta.$$

Remark 3 (Admissible Hash Functions). Admissible hash functions [11] are a special case of partition schemes where the partitions considered are of a specific kind—namely S is always the set of all strings that contain a certain substring (we call these _substring matching_ in Sect. 4). For our construction, we may use other partition schemes as well (we give such an example in Sect. 4).

We also note that the balance requirement is inspired by the definition in [36] for balanced admissible hash functions. There, the requirements of probable partition and balanced are unified to one requirement. We find that the above formulation captures the balance requirement in a somewhat more intuitive way.

3   The Construction

In this section, we present our VRF construction. For this purpose we first define and construct verifiable function commitments. We then use this primitive in conjunction with constrained PRFs to obtain our VRFs.

3.1   A Verifiable Function Commitment

We define verifiable function commitment schemes (VFCs). At high-level such a scheme has a similar syntax to that of a VRF, it allows to commit to a function and then verify its uniquely determined values. Security of such commitments says that commitments to two circuits C_0, C_1 remain indistinguishable, as long as the attacker only sees evaluations (with proofs) on inputs x such that $C_0(x) = C_1(x)$.

Definition 5 (Verifiable Function Commitment). _Let n, m, k be polynomially bounded functions. A verifiable function commitment_ VFC $=$ (VFC.Gen, VFC.P, VFC.V) _consists of the following polynomial-time algorithms:_

- _a probabilistic key sampler_ VFC.Gen$(1^\lambda, C)$ _that given a security parameter 1^λ and a circuit C: $\{0,1\}^{n(\lambda)} \to \{0,1\}^{m(\lambda)}$ outputs a secret key SK and public verification key $VK \in \{0,1\}^{k(\lambda)}$,_
- _a prover_ VFC.P$_{SK}(x)$ _that given x and the secret key produces a proof π that $y = C(x)$ is consistent with the verification key VK,_
- _and verifier_ VFC.V$_{VK}(\pi, x, y)$ _that verifies the proof._

We make the following requirements (the first two analogous to those of a VRF):

1. _Completeness: For every security parameter $\lambda \in \mathbb{N}$, input $x \in \{0,1\}^{n(\lambda)}$, and circuit C,_

$$\Pr\left[\text{VFC.V}_{VK}(\pi, x, y) = 1 \;\middle|\; \begin{array}{l} (SK, VK) \leftarrow \text{VFC.Gen}(1^\lambda, C) \\ y = C(x) \\ \pi \leftarrow \text{VFC.P}_{SK}(x) \end{array} \right] = 1.$$

2. *Uniqueness:* For every security parameter $\lambda \in \mathbb{N}$, input $x \in \{0,1\}^{n(\lambda)}$, and arbitrary verification key $VK^* \in \{0,1\}^{k(\lambda)}$, there exists at most a single $y \in \{0,1\}^{m(\lambda)}$ for which there exists an accepting proof π. That is,

if $\mathsf{VFC.V}_{VK^*}(\pi_0, x, y_0) = \mathsf{VFC.V}_{VK^*}(\pi_1, x, y_1) = 1$ then $y_0 = y_1$.

3. *Indistinguishability:* For any adversary $\mathcal{A}(1^\lambda)$, consider the following game $\mathcal{G}_{\mathcal{A}}^{\mathsf{vfc}}$:

(a) $\mathcal{A}$ submits to the challenger two circuits C_0, C_1.

(b) The challenger samples $b \leftarrow \{0,1\}$, $(SK, VK) \leftarrow \mathsf{VFC.Gen}(1^\lambda, C_b)$, and sends VK to $\mathcal{A}$.

(c) $\mathcal{A}$ submits to a challenger evaluation queries $x_1, \ldots, x_Q$, and gets back from the challenger $\pi_1, \ldots, \pi_Q$, where $\pi_i \leftarrow \mathsf{VFC.P}(x_i, SK)$.

(d) At the end, $\mathcal{A}$ outputs a guess b'. The result of the game $\mathcal{G}_{\mathcal{A}}^{\mathsf{vfc}}(\lambda)$ is 1 if $b' = b$, and 0 otherwise.

We say that $\mathcal{A}$ is **admissible** if in the above game the circuits C_0, C_1 map $\{0,1\}^{n(\lambda)}$ to $\{0,1\}^{m(\lambda)}$ are of the same size and $C_0(x_i) = C_1(x_i)$ for all $i \in [Q]$. We require that any polynomial-size admissible adversary wins the game with negligible advantage:

$$\mathsf{Adv}_{\mathcal{A}}^{\mathsf{vfc}} := \left| \Pr\left[\mathcal{G}_{\mathcal{A}}^{\mathsf{vfc}}(\lambda) = 1\right] - \frac{1}{2} \right| \leq \mathsf{negl}(\lambda).$$

We now show how to construct such a VFC.

Ingredients:

- A non-interactive commitment Com.
- A non-interactive witness-indistinguishable proof system NIWI.

The Construction:

- The key sampler $\mathsf{VRF.Gen}(1^\lambda, C)$:
  - Compute three commitments $\{c_i := \mathsf{Com}(C; r_i)\}_{i \in [3]}$, using randomness $r_i \leftarrow \{0,1\}^\lambda$.
  - Output the secret key $SK = (C, r_2, r_3)$ and public key $VK = (c_1, c_2, c_3)$.
- The prover $\mathsf{VRF.P}_{SK}(x)$:
  - Construct the statement $\Psi = \Psi(c_1, c_2, c_3, x, y)$ asserting that y is consistent with the function value given by the majority of the commitments:

$$1 \leq i < j \leq 3,$$
$$\exists((i, r_i, C_i), (j, r_j, C_j)) : c_i = \mathsf{Com}(C_i; r_i), c_j = \mathsf{Com}(C_j; r_j),$$
$$y = C_i(x) = C_j(x).$$

  - Output a NIWI proof $\pi \leftarrow \mathsf{NIWI.P}(\Psi, (2, r_2, C), (3, r_3, C), 1^\lambda)$ for the statement Ψ, using the commitment randomness r_2, r_3 and the circuit C as the witness.

- The verifier $\mathsf{VRF.V}_{VK}(\pi, x, y)$:
  - Construct Ψ as above.
  - Run the NIWI verifier $\mathsf{NIWI.V}(\pi, \Psi)$ and output the same answer.

Completeness and Uniqueness. The completeness of the scheme follows readily from the completeness of the NIWI system. The uniqueness follows from the perfect binding of the commitment as well as the soundness of the NIWI. Indeed, given the verification key $VK = (\mathsf{c}_1, \mathsf{c}_2, \mathsf{c}_3)$, binding implies that for each commitment c_i, there exists at most a single circuit C_i such that c_i is a valid commitment to C_i. Thus, also for any input x, each c_i is consistent with at most a single value $y_i = C_i(x)$. By the soundness of the NIWI, any accepted y must be consistent with the majority of value y_1, y_2, y_3.

Indistinguishability. We prove the security of the scheme.

Proposition 1. *For any polynomial-size admissible adversary $\mathcal{A}$, it holds that* $\mathsf{Adv}^{\mathsf{vfc}}_{\mathcal{A}}(\lambda) \leq \mathsf{negl}(\lambda)$.

The proof proceeds by a standard hybrid argument and is given in the full version.

3.2   The VRF

We now present the VRF construction based on verifiable function commitments and constrained pseudorandom functions. We first list the required ingredients.

Ingredients:

- A partition scheme PAR parameterized by $(n, \widehat{n}, \tau, \mathcal{S})$ for a collection of sets $\mathcal{S} = \{\mathcal{S}_\lambda\}_{\lambda \in \mathbb{N}}$ with efficient representation.
- A constrained pseudo-random function CPRF for the collection $\mathcal{S}$, mapping $\widehat{n}$ bits to m bits. (For simplicity, we assume perfect functionality. We later observe that the construction works also given computational functionality.)
- A verifiable function commitment VFC for circuits mapping $\widehat{n}$ bits to m bits.

The Construction:

- The key sampler $\mathsf{VRF.Gen}(1^\lambda)$:
  - Sample a CPRF key $K \leftarrow \mathsf{CPRF.Gen}(1^\lambda)$, and consider the circuit $C_K(\cdot) = \mathsf{CPRF.Eval}_K(\cdot)$.
  - Sample VFC keys $(\overline{SK}, \overline{VK}) \leftarrow \mathsf{VFC.Gen}(1^\lambda, C_K)$.
  - Output the secret key $SK = (K, \overline{SK})$ and public key $VK = \overline{VK}$.
- The evaluator $\mathsf{VRF.Eval}_{SK}(x)$:
  - Compute $\widehat{x} = \mathsf{PAR.Enc}(x)$.
  - Output $y := \mathsf{CPRF.Eval}_K(\widehat{x})$.
- The prover $\mathsf{VRF.P}_{SK}(x)$:
  - Output a VFC proof $\pi \leftarrow \mathsf{VFC.P}_{\overline{SK}}(\widehat{x})$ for the consistency of $y = C_K(\widehat{x})$ with $\overline{VK}$.
- The verifier $\mathsf{VRF.V}_{VK}(\pi, x, y)$:
  - Run the VFC verifier $\mathsf{VFC.V}_{\overline{VK}}(\pi, \widehat{x}, y)$ and output the same answer.

Completeness and Uniqueness. Completeness and uniqueness follow readily from those of the VFC.

3.3   Security Analysis

We now prove the security of the VRF constructed above. Concretely, given an admissible adversary $\mathcal{A}$ against the VRF, we construct an admissible adversary $\mathcal{B}$ against the underlying constrained PRF. Throughout, we assume that $\mathcal{A}$ makes (w.l.o.g exactly) $Q = Q(\lambda)$ evaluation queries in the VRF game, for some polynomially bounded $Q(\lambda)$, and denote its advantage $\mathsf{Adv}_{\mathcal{A}}^{\mathsf{vrf}}(\lambda)$ by $\delta = \delta(\lambda)$.

The CPRF adversary. Adversary $\mathcal{B}(1^\lambda)$ operates as follows:

1. Initializes a variable $\mathsf{result} = \mathsf{succ}$.
2. Invokes $\mathsf{PAR.Gen}(1^\lambda, Q, \delta)$ to sample a partition set $S \in \mathcal{S}_\lambda$.
3. Submits S to the CPRF challenger as the constraint, and obtains a constrained key K_S.
4. It now emulates $\mathcal{A}$ in $\mathcal{G}_{\mathcal{A}}^{\mathsf{vrf}}$ as follows:
   (a) Computes the constrained evaluation circuit $C_{K_S}(\cdot) = \mathsf{CPRF.Eval}_{K_S}(\cdot)$, samples corresponding VFC keys $(\overline{SK}, \overline{VK}) \leftarrow \mathsf{VFC.Gen}(1^\lambda, C_{K_S})$, and sends $VK = \overline{VK}$ to $\mathcal{A}$.
   (b) When $\mathcal{A}$ makes an evaluation query $x_i \in \{0,1\}^n$, for $i \in [Q]$,
       i. $\mathcal{B}$ computes the encoding $\widehat{x}_i$ of x_i.
       ii. If $\widehat{x}_i \in S$, sets $\mathsf{result} = \mathtt{fail}$, and jumps to the last step 4d.
       iii. Otherwise, computes $y_i = C_{K_S}(\widehat{x}_i)$, and a VFC proof $\pi_i \leftarrow \mathsf{VFC.P}_{SK}(\widehat{x}_i)$ that y_i is consistent with $\overline{VK}$. Sends (y_i, π_i) to $\mathcal{A}$.
   (c) When $\mathcal{A}$ makes the challenge query $x_* \in \{0,1\}^n$,
       i. As before, $\mathcal{B}$ computes the encoding $\widehat{x}_*$ of x_*.
       ii. If $\widehat{x}_* \notin S$, sets $\mathsf{result} = \mathtt{fail}$, and jumps to the last step 4d.
       iii. Otherwise, submits $\widehat{x}_*$ to the CPRF challenger as the challenge query, obtains y_*^b, and sends it to $\mathcal{A}$ as the VRF challenge.
   (d) At the end of the game, if $\mathsf{result} = \mathtt{fail}$, $\mathcal{B}$ acts as follows:
       i. If a challenge query $\widehat{x}_*$ has not yet been submitted to the CPRF challenger (due to a pre-challenge failure in step 4(b)ii or 4(c)ii), samples some $z \in S$ and submits it as the challenge. Disregards the challenger's answer.
       ii. Outputs a random guess $b' \leftarrow \{0,1\}$.
       If $\mathsf{result} = \mathsf{succ}$, $\mathcal{B}$ obtains a guess b' from $\mathcal{A}$, and outputs b'.

Note that $\mathcal{B}$ is admissible by construction (it always respects the constraint S). We now show that the advantage of $\mathcal{B}$ in the CPRF game is as large as the advantage δ of $\mathcal{A}$ in the VRF game, up to some loss τ that depends on the partition scheme (the guaranteed partition probability).

Proposition 2. $\mathsf{Adv}_{\mathcal{B}}^{\mathsf{cprf}}(\lambda) \geq \tau(\lambda, Q, \delta^{-1}) \cdot \frac{\delta}{2} - \mathsf{negl}(\lambda) \geq \left(\frac{\delta}{\lambda \cdot Q}\right)^{O(1)} - \mathsf{negl}(\lambda)$.

Proof. To prove the claim we examine a sequence of hybrid CPRF games $\{\mathcal{G}_{\alpha}^{\mathsf{cprf}}\}$, each with a corresponding adversary $\mathcal{B}_{\alpha}$ and challenger $\mathcal{CH}_{\alpha}$, which slightly augment the adversary and challenger of the previous hybrid. In all games, as in the original CPRF game, the result of the game is 1 if and only if the adversary $\mathcal{B}_{\alpha}$ guesses correctly the challenge bit, i.e. $b' = b$.

Hybrid $\mathcal{G}_0^{\mathsf{cprf}}$: This corresponds to the game $\mathcal{G}_{\mathcal{B}}^{\mathsf{cprf}}$ described above. Namely $\mathcal{B}_0$ is the above described $\mathcal{B}$ and $\mathcal{CH}_0$ is the usual CPRF challenger.

Hybrid $\mathcal{G}_1^{\mathsf{cprf}}$: In this game, the CPRF challenger $\mathcal{CH}_1$ also provides $\mathcal{B}_1$ with the unconstrained key K, and $\mathcal{B}_1$ generates the VFC keys $(\overline{SK}, \overline{VK}) \leftarrow$ VFC.Gen$(1^\lambda, C_K)$ corresponding to the circuit $C_K(\cdot) = \mathsf{CPRF.Eval}_K(\cdot)$ instead of the constrained circuit C_{K_S}.

We argue that by the indistinguishability of the VFC scheme

$$\left| \Pr\left[\mathcal{G}_1^{\mathsf{cprf}}(\lambda) = 1 \right] - \Pr\left[\mathcal{G}_0^{\mathsf{cprf}}(\lambda) = 1 \right] \right| \leq \mathsf{negl}(\lambda).$$

Indeed, any noticeable difference between the games, leads to an efficient distinguisher $\mathcal{D}$ that can break the VFC scheme. The distinguisher $\mathcal{D}$ will submit to the VFC challenger the circuits $C_0 = C_{K_S}, C_1 = C_K$, and then will emulate $\mathcal{B}$ only that instead of generating $(\overline{SK}, \overline{VK})$ and the proofs π_i by itself, it will use the verification key $\overline{VK}$ and proofs π_i given by the VFC challenger. First, note that this always induces an admissible VFC adversary. Indeed, $\mathcal{B}$ only answers the queries x_i of $\mathcal{A}$ as long as they are such that $\widehat{x}_i \notin S$, meaning that $C_{K_S}(\widehat{x}_i) = C_K(\widehat{x}_i)$. It is left to note that when the challenge bit is b, the emulated $\mathcal{B}$ acts exactly as $\mathcal{B}_b$ in $\mathcal{G}_b^{\mathsf{cprf}}$.

Hybrid $\mathcal{G}_2^{\mathsf{cprf}}$: In this game, the adversary $\mathcal{B}_2$ and challenger $\mathcal{CH}_2$ act differently given evaluation queries x_i, or the challenge query x_*, from the emulated $\mathcal{A}$. $\mathcal{B}_2$ does not check right away whether $\widehat{x}_i$, or $\widehat{x}_*$ are in S. Instead, first all evaluation queries are answered according to the unconstrained circuit C_K, and the challenge is also answered according to this circuit, or a random string, depending on the challenge bit b. Namely, this part exactly emulates the real VRF game $\mathcal{G}_{\mathcal{A}}^{\mathsf{vrf}}$.

Having finished emulating $\mathcal{A}$ as above, and recording its output guess b', $\mathcal{B}_2$ now checks that for all evaluation queries x_i made $\widehat{x}_i \notin S$ and for the challenge query $\widehat{x}_* \in S$. If this is the case, it outputs the recorded b' (previously output by $\mathcal{A}$) as the guess. Otherwise, it outputs a random guess $b' \leftarrow \{0, 1\}$.

We argue that

$$\Pr\left[\mathcal{G}_1^{\mathsf{cprf}}(\lambda) = 1 \right] = \Pr\left[\mathcal{G}_2^{\mathsf{cprf}}(\lambda) = 1 \right].$$

Indeed, consider in either game the event **bad** that either $\widehat{x}_i \in S$ for some evaluation query by $\mathcal{A}$ or $\widehat{x}_* \notin S$ for the challenge query by $\mathcal{A}$. Then, until the first query that induces **bad**, the view of $\mathcal{A}$ in the two experiments is distributed exactly the same. This also implies that **bad** occurs in both experiments with exactly the same probability. Furthermore, if **bad** does occur, then from that point on, $\mathcal{A}$'s emulation is disregarded and the two experiments again have exactly the same output distribution, a random b'. The required equality follows.

The Advantage in $\mathcal{G}_2^{\mathsf{cprf}}$. To conclude the proof, we show that

$$\left| \Pr\left[\mathcal{G}_2^{\mathsf{cprf}}(\lambda) = 1 \right] - \frac{1}{2} \right| \geq \tau(\lambda, Q, \delta^{-1}) \cdot \frac{\delta}{2}.$$

Let us denote by win the event that in $\mathcal{G}_2^{\mathsf{cprf}}$ the adversary $\mathcal{A}$ emulated in the first part correctly guesses the challenge bit b. We continue to denote by bad the event that either $\widehat{x}_i \in S$ for some evaluation query by $\mathcal{A}$ or $\widehat{x}_* \notin S$ for the challenge query by $\mathcal{A}$.

Then, we have that

$$\Pr\left[\mathcal{G}_2^{\mathsf{cprf}}(\lambda) = 1\right]$$

$$= \Pr\left[\mathsf{bad}\right] \cdot \Pr\left[\mathcal{G}_2^{\mathsf{cprf}}(\lambda) = 1 \;\middle|\; \mathsf{bad}\right] + \Pr\left[\mathcal{G}_2^{\mathsf{cprf}}(\lambda) = 1 \wedge \overline{\mathsf{bad}}\right]$$

$$= \left(1 - \Pr\left[\overline{\mathsf{bad}}\right]\right) \cdot \frac{1}{2} + \Pr\left[\mathsf{win}\right] \cdot \Pr\left[\mathcal{G}_2^{\mathsf{cprf}}(\lambda) = 1 \wedge \overline{\mathsf{bad}} \;\middle|\; \mathsf{win}\right]$$

$$\quad + \Pr\left[\overline{\mathsf{win}}\right] \cdot \Pr\left[\mathcal{G}_2^{\mathsf{cprf}}(\lambda) = 1 \wedge \overline{\mathsf{bad}} \;\middle|\; \overline{\mathsf{win}}\right]$$

$$= \left(1 - \Pr\left[\overline{\mathsf{bad}}\right]\right) \cdot \frac{1}{2} + \Pr\left[\mathsf{win}\right] \cdot \Pr\left[\overline{\mathsf{bad}} \;\middle|\; \mathsf{win}\right] \cdot \Pr\left[\mathcal{G}_2^{\mathsf{cprf}}(\lambda) = 1 \;\middle|\; \mathsf{win} \wedge \overline{\mathsf{bad}}\right]$$

$$\quad + \Pr\left[\overline{\mathsf{win}}\right] \cdot 0 = \left(1 - \Pr\left[\overline{\mathsf{bad}}\right]\right) \cdot \frac{1}{2} + \Pr\left[\mathsf{win}\right] \cdot \Pr\left[\overline{\mathsf{bad}} \;\middle|\; \mathsf{win}\right] \cdot 1$$

$$= \frac{1}{2} + \Pr\left[\overline{\mathsf{bad}} \;\middle|\; \mathsf{win}\right]\left(\Pr\left[\mathsf{win}\right] - \frac{1}{2} \cdot \frac{\Pr\left[\overline{\mathsf{bad}}\right]}{\Pr\left[\overline{\mathsf{bad}} \;\middle|\; \mathsf{win}\right]}\right).$$

We next note that by the probable partition and balance properties of the underlying partition schemes:

$$\Pr\left[\overline{\mathsf{bad}} \;\middle|\; \mathsf{win}\right] \geq \tau(Q, \lambda, \delta^{-1}),$$

$$\frac{\Pr\left[\overline{\mathsf{bad}}\right]}{\Pr\left[\overline{\mathsf{bad}} \;\middle|\; \mathsf{win}\right]} \in [1 - \delta, 1 + \delta].$$

Indeed, $\overline{\mathsf{bad}}$ is exactly the event of successful partition where $(X = \{x_1, \ldots, x_q\}, x_*)$ are sampled according to $\mathcal{A}$'s queries in the VRF game. $\overline{\mathsf{bad}}|\mathsf{win}$ is the event of successful partition when (X, x_*) are sampled from a different distribution—the one induced by $\mathcal{A}$ in the VRF game, but conditioned on $\mathcal{A}$ winning.

In addition, since the view of the emulated $\mathcal{A}$ in $\mathcal{G}_2^{\mathsf{cprf}}$ is identical to its view in $\mathcal{G}_{\mathcal{A}}^{\mathsf{vrf}}$, it holds that

$$\Pr\left[\mathsf{win}\right] = \Pr\left[\mathcal{G}_{\mathcal{A}}^{\mathsf{vrf}}(\lambda) = 1\right].$$

It now follows that

$$\left|\Pr\left[\mathcal{G}_2^{\mathsf{cprf}}(\lambda) = 1\right] - \frac{1}{2}\right|$$

$$= \Pr\left[\overline{\mathsf{bad}} \;\middle|\; \mathsf{win}\right] \cdot \left|\Pr\left[\mathcal{G}_{\mathcal{A}}^{\mathsf{vrf}}(\lambda) = 1\right] - \frac{1}{2} \cdot \frac{\Pr\left[\overline{\mathsf{bad}}\right]}{\Pr\left[\overline{\mathsf{bad}} \;\middle|\; \mathsf{win}\right]}\right|$$

$$\geq \tau(\lambda, Q, \delta^{-1}) \cdot \left(\left|\Pr\left[\mathcal{G}_{\mathcal{A}}^{\mathsf{vrf}}(\lambda) = 1\right] - \frac{1}{2}\right| - \frac{1}{2} \cdot \left|\frac{\Pr\left[\overline{\mathsf{bad}}\right]}{\Pr\left[\overline{\mathsf{bad}} \;\middle|\; \mathsf{win}\right]} - 1\right|\right)$$

$$\geq \tau(\lambda, Q, \delta^{-1}) \cdot \left(\delta - \frac{\delta}{2}\right) = \tau(\lambda, Q, \delta^{-1}) \cdot \frac{\delta}{2}.$$

Extending the Proof for CPRFs with Computational Functionality.
We observe that the proof extends when relying on CPRFs with computational
(and not perfect) functionality (Remark 2). First, note that the place where we
rely on the functionality of the CPRF is in the transition between $\mathcal{G}_0^{\mathsf{cprf}}$ to $\mathcal{G}_1^{\mathsf{cprf}}$.
There, to argue that both C_K and C_{K_S} agree on any $\mathcal{A}$-query x_i (thus making
the VCF attacker admissible), we rely on the fact that for $x_i \notin S$, the two circuits
agree. For CPRFs with perfect functionality, this agreement is guaranteed.

To extend the analysis to the case of computational functionality, we will
argue that in the above transition, the VCF distinguisher $\mathcal{D}$ considered still
does not *violate functionality*—namely, it does not output any evaluation query
$x_i \notin S$ such that $\mathsf{CPRF.Eval}_{K_S}(x_i) \neq \mathsf{CPRF.Eval}_K(x_i)$—except with negligible
probability. Concretely, if it outputs with non-negligible probability $x_i \notin S$ that
violates functionality, we can construct from it an adversary that breaks the
computational functionality of the CPRF.

First, we argue that if the VCF attacker $\mathcal{D}$ violates functionality with non-
negligible probability when the VCF challenge bit b is chosen at random, then it
also does so when we restrict $b = 0$; that is, when VFC keys always correspond to
$C_0 = C_{K_S}$. Indeed, until the point that $\mathcal{D}$ outputs x_i that violates functionality,
the case that $b = 0$ and $b = 1$ are indistinguishable by the VFC guarantee;
furthermore, the event that x_i violates functionality is efficiently testable.

We now observe that in the restricted VFC experiment where $b = 0$, can
be perfectly emulated given only the constrained key K_S and oracle access to
$\mathsf{CPRF.Eval}_K$ (needed to compute the answer to the challenge query). Thus, we
can use $\mathcal{D}$ to break the computational functionality of the CPRF.

4   Instantiations

In this section, we discuss possible instantiations for the underlying partition
scheme and constrained PRF. We consider both adaptive security and selective
security. For adaptive security, we consider instantiations based on various polynomial assumptions (such as LWE and 1D-SIS, DDH, or IO), or instantiations
based on sub-exponential one-way functions. For selective security, we can rely
on polynomial one-way functions. (The assumptions mentioned above are those
required for appropriate CPRFs. For the CPRFs themselves, we still need NIWIs
and non-interactive commitments).

4.1   Adaptive Security from Polynomial Assumptions

To obtain adaptive security from polynomial assumptions, we describe three partition schemes for three different collections of partition sets $\mathcal{S}$. We then exhibit
the existence of CPRFs for these collections based on different assumptions.

Partition Schemes. We give three examples of partition schemes. The first is a
code-based scheme that aligns with the common notion of (balanced) admissible
hash functions from the literature. The second is a variant of the first to large

alphabets (which will be useful later on for simplifying the assumptions behind CPRFs). The third is a simple scheme based on universal hashing [18], which is omitted here and can be found in the full version.

Substring Matching over Binary Alphabet. We first describe an existing partition scheme considered first in [38] for the collection substring matching sets, which aligns with the notion of admissible hash functions. The scheme was also shown to be balanced in [36]. Given that our definition is slightly different than that in [36], and for the sake of completeness, we describe the scheme and its analysis.

- The partition scheme's encoding function $\mathsf{PAR.Enc}(x)$ is any binary error correcting code with constant distance $c < 1$.[5] Each element $x \in \{0,1\}^n$ is encoded by an element $\widehat{x} \in \{0,1\}^{\widehat{n}}$.
- The collection of sets $\mathcal{S}_\lambda$ that partitions $\{0,1\}^{\widehat{n}(\lambda)}$ consists of sets S_s parameterized by a string $s \in \{0,1,\star\}^{\widehat{n}(\lambda)}$ containing wildcard symbols $\star$. For an element $z \in \{0,1\}^{\widehat{n}(\lambda)}$, we say that $z \in S_s$ if every non-wildcard bit of s agrees with z; namely, if $s_i \neq \star$, then $s_i = z_i$. We call such a set S_s a *substring matching set*.
- The partition sampler $\mathsf{PAR.Gen}(1^\lambda, Q, \delta)$ works as follows:
  - Let $d := \log(2Q/\delta)/\log(\frac{1}{1-c})$.
  - Sample a random set of d indices $D \leftarrow \binom{[\widehat{n}]}{d}$.
  - For $i \in D$ sample $s_i \leftarrow \{0,1\}$ at random. For $i \notin D$ set $s_i = \star$.
  - Output S_s.

We will now prove probable partition and balance.

For $(X = (x_1, \ldots, x_Q), x_*)$, and consistently with Definition 4, define:

$$P_{X,x_*}(\lambda, Q, \delta) := \Pr\left[\widehat{x}_* \in S, \widehat{X} \subseteq \overline{S} \;\middle|\; \begin{array}{l} \widehat{x}_* = \mathsf{PAR.Enc}(x_*), \\ \widehat{X} = \{\widehat{x}_i \mid x_i \in X\}, \\ S \leftarrow \mathsf{PAR.Gen}(1^\lambda, Q, \delta) \end{array}\right].$$

Further define

$$\overline{P} = \max_{(X,x_*):x^* \notin X} P_{X,x_*}(\lambda, Q, \delta), \qquad \underline{P} = \min_{(X,x_*):x^* \notin X} P_{X,x_*}(\lambda, Q, \delta).$$

First, note that for any fixed $(X = \{x_1, \ldots, x_Q\}, x_*)$ and any $x_i \in X$, it holds that

$$\Pr_D[\widehat{x}_i|D = \widehat{x}_*|D] = \prod_{i \in [d]} \left(1 - \frac{cn + i - 1}{n}\right) \leq (1-c)^d.$$

Also, for any fixed D,

$$\Pr_{s|D \leftarrow \{0,1\}^d}[s|D = \widehat{x}_*|D] = 2^{-d}.$$

---

[5] Recall that in a code with (relative) distance c, each two codewords agree on at most a c-fraction of symbols.

Combining the first fact, a union bound over all $x_i \in X$, and the second fact, we have

$$\underline{P} \geq 2^{-d}(1 - Q(1 - c)^d) = 2^{-d}(1 - \delta/2) \geq (\delta/Q)^{O(1)}.$$

Thus, probable partitioning holds with $\tau(\lambda, Q, \delta^{-1}) = (\delta/Q)^{O(1)}$.

Furthermore, we know that

$$\overline{P} \leq \max_{x_*, D} \Pr_{s|D} [s|D = \widehat{x}_* | D] = 2^{-d}.$$

This in turn implies that

$$1 - \delta \leq 1 - \delta/2 \leq \underline{P}/\overline{P} \leq \overline{P}/\underline{P} \leq \frac{1}{1 - \delta/2} \leq 1 + \delta.$$

Since for every two distributions $\mathcal{X}, \mathcal{X}'$ on pairs (X, x_*) it holds that

$$\underline{P}/\overline{P} \leq \frac{P_{\mathcal{X}}(\lambda, Q, \delta)}{P_{\mathcal{X}'}(\lambda, Q, \delta)} \leq \overline{P}/\underline{P},$$

the balance property follows.

Substring Matching over Polynomial Alphabet. We describe a variant of the above that will have a polynomial alphabet and will require supporting d-symbol substrings only for a *constant* d, which will be useful in the construction of corresponding CPRFs. We shall restrict attention to a relatively simple setting of parameters, which will be enough for our purpose. (Conceivably, setting the parameters more carefully may lead to more efficient constructions.)

- Let $\Sigma \supseteq \{0, 1\}$ be an alphabet of size $\sigma = O(n^2)$. The partition scheme's encoding function PAR.Enc(x) is an efficient error correcting code mapping Σ^n to $\Sigma^m \cong \{0, 1\}^{\widehat{n}}$ with distance $1 - \frac{1}{n}$. Each element $x \in \{0, 1\}^n$ is encoded by an element $\widehat{x} \in \{0, 1\}^{\widehat{n}}$. For example, we can take the Reed-Solomon code consisting of degree n polynomials over a field $\mathbb{F}_{2^k}$ of size $O(n^2)$ (so $\widehat{n} = m \times k$).
- The collection of sets $\mathcal{S}_\lambda$ that partitions $\Sigma^m \cong \{0, 1\}^{\widehat{n}}$ consists of sets S_s parameterized by a string $(s \in \Sigma \cup \{\star\})^m$ containing wildcard symbols $\star$. For an element $z \in \Sigma^m$, we say that $z \in S_s$ if every non-wildcard symbol of s agrees with z; namely, if $s_i \neq \star$, then $s_i = z_i$. Again, we call such a set S_s a *substring matching set*.
- The partition sampler PAR.Gen$(1^\lambda, Q, \delta)$ works as follows:
  - Let $d := \log(2Q/\delta)/\log(n)$. (In our setting, both Q/δ and n are polynomial in λ and $d = O(1)$.)
  - Sample a random set of d indices $D \leftarrow \binom{[m]}{d}$.
  - For $i \in D$ sample $s_i \leftarrow \Sigma$ at random. For $i \notin D$ set $s_i = \star$.
  - Output S_s.

The proof of probable partition and balance naturally generalizes that of the previous partition scheme.

Constrained PRFs. We now discuss possible CPRF instantiations for the above collections.

Existing Constructions. We start by noting that CPRFs for all set collections with efficient representation, with computational functionality, are known based on the standard lattice assumptions—LWE and 1D-SIS [17]. We also note that such CPRFs with perfect correctness are known from indistinguishability obfuscation (IO) [14]. In particular, we can rely on the above CPRFs with either one of the partition schemes presented above.

A Construction for Substring Matching Sets over Binary Alphabet. We now give a construction that can be used together with the first partition scheme for substring matching sets over binary alphabet. The construction is based on the d-power DDH assumption (for logarithmic d), which in turn can be reduced to the subgroup hiding assumption in composite DDH groups [20,34]. Later on, we will show how to reduce the assumption to plain DDH, by generalizing this construction.

Assumption 41 (d-Power DDH). *There exists a polynomial-time sampler* $\mathcal{G}(1^\lambda)$ *that outputs a group* $\mathbb{G}$ *and* $g \in \mathbb{G}$, *such that for any polynomial-size adversary* $\mathcal{A}$, *and any* $d(\lambda) = O(\log \lambda)$,

$$\mathsf{Adv}_{\mathcal{A}}^{\mathsf{dpdh}}(\lambda) := \left| \Pr \left[\mathcal{A}(\mathbb{G}, g, g^\alpha, \dots, g^{\alpha^{d-1}}, g^{\gamma_b}) = b \;\middle|\; \begin{matrix} (\mathbb{G}, g) \leftarrow \mathcal{G}(1^\lambda) \\ \alpha, \beta \leftarrow \mathbb{Z}_{|\mathbb{G}|}^* \\ \gamma_0 = \alpha^d, \gamma_1 \leftarrow \beta \\ b \leftarrow \{0,1\} \end{matrix} \right] - \frac{1}{2} \right| \leq \mathsf{negl}(\lambda).$$

We next describe the construction, which is inspired by the Naor-Reingold PRF [43] and a construction of adaptive puncturable PRFs from [34] from indistinguishability obfuscation and d-Power DDH. The security notion considered in that work is stronger than the one considered in this work (Definition 3), where the constraining set is chosen ahead of time and not adaptively. In particular, it will not require indistinguishability obfuscation and will handle the collection of constraints $\mathcal{S}$ considered in this section.

For domain $\{0,1\}^{\widehat{n}}$, the function is defined as follows:

- Each (unconstrained) key K consists of $\widehat{n}$ pairs $\left(k_{i,b} \leftarrow \mathbb{Z}_{|\mathbb{G}|}^* \right)_{i \in [\widehat{n}], b \in \{0,1\}}$, as well as $(\mathbb{G}, g)$.
- The value of the function is given by $\mathsf{CPRF.Eval}_K(x) = g^{\prod_{i \in [\widehat{n}]} k_{i,x_i}}$.
- The constraining algorithm $\mathsf{CPRF.Cons}(K, s)$, given a key K and a string $s \in \{0, 1, \star\}^{\widehat{n}}$, with d non-wildcards at positions $D \subseteq [\widehat{n}]$, works as follows:
  • Samples $\alpha \leftarrow \mathbb{Z}_{\mathbb{G}}^*$.
  • Outputs a constrained key K_{S_s} consisting of $(s, \mathbb{G}, g, g^\alpha, \dots, g^{\alpha^{d-1}})$ and a new set $\left(k'_{i,b} \right)_{i,b}$, where

$$k'_{i,b} = \begin{cases} \alpha^{-1} \cdot k_{i,b} & i \in D, b = s_i \\ k_{i,b} & \text{otherwise} \end{cases}.$$

- To evaluate the function on $x \in \{0,1\}^{\widehat{n}} \backslash S_s$ using the constrained key K_{S_s}:
  - Let d' be the number of indices $i \in D$ such that $x_i = s_i$ (note that $d' < d$ since $x \notin S_s$).
  - Output $\left(g^{\alpha^{d'}} \right)^{\prod_{i \in [\widehat{n}]} k'_{i,x_i}}$.

Functionality. By definition,

$$\mathsf{CPRF.Eval}_{K_{S_s}}(x) = \left(g^{\alpha^{d'}} \right)^{\prod_{i \in [\widehat{n}]} k'_{i,x_i}} = \left(g^{\alpha^{d'}} \right)^{\alpha^{-d'} \prod_{i \in [\widehat{n}]} k_{i,x_i}}$$

$$= g^{\prod_{i \in [\widehat{n}]} k_{i,x_i}} = \mathsf{CPRF.Eval}_K(x).$$

Indistinguishability. We now prove the indistinguishability property of the constructed CPRF. Given an (admissible) adversary $\mathcal{B}$ that breaks the indistinguishability of the CPRF, we construct and adversary $\mathcal{A}$ that breaks the d-Power DDH assumption with the same advantage.

The breaker $\mathcal{A}$. Given $(\mathbb{G}, g, g^\alpha, \ldots, g^{\alpha^{d-1}}, g^{\gamma_b})$, the adversary $\mathcal{A}$ emulates $\mathcal{B}$ as follows:

1. When $\mathcal{B}$ submits $s \in \{0, 1, \star\}^{\widehat{n}}$ to the CPRF challenger, where s has d non-wildcard entries on an index set $D \subseteq [\widehat{n}]$, $\mathcal{A}$ samples $\left(k'_{i,b} \leftarrow \mathbb{Z}^*_{|G|} \right)_{i,b}$. It then sends $K_{S_s} := \left(s, \mathbb{G}, g, g^\alpha, \ldots, g^{\alpha^{d-1}}, \left(k'_{i,b} \right)_{i,b} \right)$ to $\mathcal{B}$.
2. Then $\mathcal{B}$ gives $x \in S_s$ as the challenge query, $\mathcal{A}$ returns $g^{\gamma_b \prod_{i \in \widehat{n}} k'_{i,x_i}}$.
3. When $\mathcal{B}$ outputs a guess b', $\mathcal{A}$ outputs the same guess.

We observe that the view of the emulated $\mathcal{B}$ is identical to its view in the CPRF game, where the induced unconstrained key is given by

$$k_{i,b} = \begin{cases} \alpha \cdot k'_{i,b} & i \in D, b = s_i \\ k_{i,b} & \text{otherwise} \end{cases}.$$

When $\gamma_b = \alpha^d$, this corresponds to the case that the CPRF value is returned, and when $\gamma_b \leftarrow \mathbb{Z}^*_{|G|}$ is random, this corresponds to the case that a random element $g^\beta, \beta \leftarrow \mathbb{Z}^*_{|G|}$ is returned.[6]

It follows that

$$\mathsf{Adv}^{\mathsf{dpdh}}_{\mathcal{A}}(\lambda) = \mathsf{Adv}^{\mathsf{cfprf}}_{\mathcal{B}}(\lambda).$$

A Construction for Substring Matching Sets over Polynomial Alphabet. We now give a construction that can be used together with the second

---

[6] The above distribution is not necessarily random over strings. In any natural instantiation of the group, e.g. as a prime order group for a large prime, or a composite group of smooth order, g^β is also random in the group $\mathbb{G}$. In any case, and as usual, if one insists, on outputting a random string, we can further apply a randomness extractor (see for example, [43]).

partition scheme for substring matching sets over polynomial alphabet. The construction is based on the Generalized Decision Diffie Hellman Assumption (GDDH), which follows from DDH [43].

Assumption 42 (GDDH). *There exists a polynomial-time sampler $\mathcal{G}(1^\lambda)$ that outputs a group $\mathbb{G}$ and $g \in \mathbb{G}$, such that for any polynomial-size adversary $\mathcal{A}$, and any $d = O(1)$,*[7]

$$\mathsf{Adv}_{\mathcal{A}}^{\mathsf{gddh}}(\lambda) := \left| \Pr\left[\mathcal{A}\left(\mathbb{G}, \left(g^{\Pi_{i \in S}\, \alpha_i} \mid S \subsetneq [d]\right), g^{\gamma_b}\right) = b \; \middle| \begin{array}{l} (\mathbb{G}, g) \leftarrow \mathcal{G}(1^\lambda) \\ \alpha_1, \ldots, \alpha_d, \beta \leftarrow \mathbb{Z}_{|\mathbb{G}|}^* \\ \gamma_0 = \Pi_{i \in [d]}\, \alpha_i, \gamma_1 = \beta \\ b \leftarrow \{0,1\} \end{array} \right] - \frac{1}{2} \right| \le \mathsf{negl}(\lambda).$$

We next describe the construction, which is a carefully augmented variant of the previous construction. At first, it might be tempting to use the previous CPRF construction (with binary substring matching partition) as before, only that instead of using the same pad α, we would use independent pads $\alpha_1, \ldots, \alpha_d$ for each of the d padded coordinates. The problem with this approach is that the constrained key will need to include all the elements $\left(g^{\Pi_{i \in S}\, \alpha_i} \mid S \subsetneq [d]\right)$. Here, as long as we use the first partition scheme, over binary alphabet, $d \approx \log Q/\delta$. Thus, the size of the above set is roughly Q/δ, which is too large. (It is a polynomial in λ, but a polynomial that depends on the adversary's number of queries and advantage, which are not apriori bounded. Before, this was not an issue as we only considered the set of all powers of the same element α.)

To circumvent the above we use the second partition scheme presented over a polynomial alphabet that has a constant d. This requires a natural augmentation of the construction, which we present now.

For domain $\{0,1\}^{\widehat{n}} \cong \Sigma^m$, where Σ is of size $\sigma = O(n^2)$, the function is defined as follows:

- Each (unconstrained) key K consists of an $m \times \sigma$ matrix $\left(k_{i,j} \leftarrow \mathbb{Z}_{|\mathbb{G}|}^*\right)_{i \in [m], j \in \Sigma}$, as well as $\mathbb{G}, g$.
- The value of the function on $x \in \Sigma^m$ is given by $\mathsf{CPRF.Eval}_K(x) = g^{\Pi_{i \in [m]}\, k_{i, x_i}}$.
- The constraining algorithm $\mathsf{CPRF.Cons}(K, s)$, given a key K and a string $s \in (\Sigma \cup \{\star\})^m$, with d non-wildcards at positions $\{i_1, \ldots, i_d\} = D \subseteq [m]$, works as follows:
  - Samples $\alpha_{i_1}, \ldots, \alpha_{i_d} \leftarrow \mathbb{Z}_{\mathbb{G}}^*$.
  - Outputs a constrained key K_{S_s} consisting of $s, \mathbb{G}, \left(g^{\Pi_{\ell \in S}\, \alpha_{i_\ell}} \mid S \subsetneq [d]\right)$, and a new set $\left(k'_{i,j}\right)_{i,j}$, where

$$k'_{i,j} = \begin{cases} \alpha_i^{-1} \cdot k_{i,j} & i \in D, j = s_i \\ k_{i,j} & \text{otherwise} \end{cases}.$$

---

[7] This is a weaker variant of the usual GDDH assumption where d may be polynomial (and the elements are given by an oracle). This weaker variant will be sufficient for us.

- To evaluate the function on $x \in \Sigma^m \setminus S_s$ using the constrained key K_{S_s}:
  - Let $D' \subseteq D$ be the subset of indices such that $x_i = s_i$ (note that $D' \neq D$ since $x \notin S_s$).
  - Output $\left(g^{\prod_{\ell \in D'} \alpha_{i_\ell}}\right)^{\prod_{i \in [m]} k'_{i,x_i}}$.

First, we note that as long as $d \leq c \log n$ for some fixed constant c, all the algorithms, including the constraining algorithm run in fixed polynomial time as required. When combining this scheme with the substring matching partition scheme over large alphabets, it is always the case that $d = O(1) \ll \log n$. Proving functionality and security of the CPRF is similar to the previous CPRF (from d-power DDH), and can be found in the full version.

Remark 4 (Resulting VRFs from Bilinear Maps). Using the above construction, we get VRFs from simple assumptions on bilinear maps—DLIN and SXDH. Indeed, both SXDH and DLIN imply DDH in plain (non-bilinear) groups,[8] as required for the above CPRFs, as well as commitments and NIWIs.

Remark 5 (Verifiable Unpredictable Function from Factoring). We note that a computational (rather than decisional) version of GDH holds assuming it is hard to factor Blum integers [7]. In this version, the value $g^{\prod_{\ell \in D} \alpha_{i_\ell}}$ is only unpredictable and not necessarily pseudorandom. It is not hard to see that the same construction as above, would give in this case a corresponding notion of unpredictable CPRFs. Plugging this in our general construction would readily give a Verifiable Unpredictable Function [39], instead of a VRF.

4.2   Selective Security

We now discuss how to obtain selective security based on plain puncturable PRFs, instead of the more general CPRFs considered above. As usual, this also gives an adaptively-secure constructions assuming subexponential hardness.

Puncturable PRFs are a special case of constrained PRFs where the collection of sets $\mathcal{S}$ includes singletons $S_x = \{x\}$; namely, every constrained key $K_{\{x\}}$ allows computing the PRF everywhere, but at the point x. As shown in [13,15,37], the GGM [27] PRF yield puncturable PRFs. In particular, (subexponential) puncturable PRFs can be constructed from (subexponential) one-way functions.

Recall that in the case of selective security (see Definition 3), the VRF adversary announces the challenge query x_* ahead of time, before obtaining the verification key, or performing any evaluation query. In this case, we can avoid using partition schemes, and replace use puncturable PRFs as our CPRFs. Alternatively, we can think of a trivial partition scheme for the collection of singletons where the encoding is the identity, and the partition sampler also gets the challenges x_* as input, and outputs it as the partition, corresponding to the case that successful partition occurs with probability $\tau = 1$. The same analysis as in Sect. 3.3 now applies.

---

[8] For SXDH, DDH holds in the based groups. For DLIN, DDH holds in the target group. We thank Brent Waters for pointing out this last fact.

By taking all the underlying primitives to be subexponentially hard (say $2^{\lambda^{\varepsilon}}$-hard), the scheme is adaptively secure (when setting the underlying security parameter to $n^{1/\varepsilon}$). This follows by a standard reduction (see for example [1]).

Acknowledgements. Member of the Check Point Institute of Information Security. Supported by the Alon Young Faculty Fellowship. Part of this research was done while at MIT. Supported by NSF Grants CNS-1350619 and CNS-1414119 and DARPA and ARO under Contract No. W911NF-15-C-0236. Any opinions, findings and conclusions or recommendations expressed in this material are those of the author(s) and do not necessarily reflect the views of the DARPA and ARO. Part of this research was done while visiting Tel Aviv University and supported by the Leona M. & Harry B. Helmsley Charitable Trust and Check Point Institute for Information Security.

References

1. Abdalla, M., Catalano, D., Fiore, D.: Verifiable random functions: relations to identity-based key encapsulation and new constructions. J. Cryptol. **27**(3), 544–593 (2014)
2. Badrinarayanan, S., Goyal, V., Jain, A., Sahai, A.: Verifiable functional encryption. In: Cheon, J.H., Takagi, T. (eds.) ASIACRYPT 2016. LNCS, vol. 10032, pp. 557–587. Springer, Heidelberg (2016). doi:10.1007/978-3-662-53890-6_19
3. Badrinarayanan, S., Goyal, V., Jain, A., Sahai, A.: A note on VRFs from verifiable functional encryption. Cryptology ePrint Archive 2017/051 (2017)
4. Barak, B., Ong, S.J., Vadhan, S.P.: Derandomization in cryptography. SIAM J. Comput. **37**(2), 380–400 (2007)
5. Bellare, M., Ristenpart, T.: Simulation without the artificial abort: simplified proof and improved concrete security for waters' IBE scheme. In: Joux, A. (ed.) EUROCRYPT 2009. LNCS, vol. 5479, pp. 407–424. Springer, Heidelberg (2009). doi:10.1007/978-3-642-01001-9_24
6. Bellare, M., Yung, M.: Certifying permutations: noninteractive zero-knowledge based on any trapdoor permutation. J. Cryptol. **9**(3), 149–166 (1996)
7. Biham, E., Boneh, D., Reingold, O.: Breaking generalized Diffie-Hellmann modulo a composite is no easier than factoring. Inf. Process. Lett. **70**(2), 83–87 (1999)
8. Bitansky, N., Paneth, O.: ZAPs and non-interactive witness indistinguishability from indistinguishability obfuscation. In: Dodis, Y., Nielsen, J.B. (eds.) TCC 2015. LNCS, vol. 9015, pp. 401–427. Springer, Heidelberg (2015). doi:10.1007/978-3-662-46497-7_16
9. Blum, M.: Coin flipping by telephone. In: IEEE Workshop on Communications Security Advances in Cryptology: A Report on CRYPTO 1981, Santa Barbara, California, USA, pp. 11–15, 24–26 August 1981
10. Blum, M., De Santis, A., Micali, S., Persiano, G.: Noninteractive zero-knowledge. SIAM J. Comput. **20**(6), 1084–1118 (1991)
11. Boneh, D., Boyen, X.: Secure identity based encryption without random oracles. In: Franklin, M. (ed.) CRYPTO 2004. LNCS, vol. 3152, pp. 443–459. Springer, Heidelberg (2004). doi:10.1007/978-3-540-28628-8_27
12. Boneh, D., Montgomery, H.W., Raghunathan, A.: Algebraic pseudorandom functions with improved efficiency from the augmented cascade. In: Proceedings of the 17th ACM Conference on Computer and Communications Security, CCS 2010, Chicago, Illinois, USA, pp. 131–140, 4–8 October 2010

13. Boneh, D., Waters, B.: Constrained pseudorandom functions and their applications. In: Sako, K., Sarkar, P. (eds.) ASIACRYPT 2013. LNCS, vol. 8270, pp. 280–300. Springer, Heidelberg (2013). doi:10.1007/978-3-642-42045-0_15
14. Boneh, D., Zhandry, M.: Multiparty key exchange, efficient traitor tracing, and more from indistinguishability obfuscation. In: Garay, J.A., Gennaro, R. (eds.) CRYPTO 2014. LNCS, vol. 8616, pp. 480–499. Springer, Heidelberg (2014). doi:10.1007/978-3-662-44371-2_27
15. Boyle, E., Goldwasser, S., Ivan, I.: Functional signatures and pseudorandom functions. In: Krawczyk, H. (ed.) PKC 2014. LNCS, vol. 8383, pp. 501–519. Springer, Heidelberg (2014). doi:10.1007/978-3-642-54631-0_29
16. Brakerski, Z., Goldwasser, S., Rothblum, G.N., Vaikuntanathan, V.: Weak verifiable random functions. In: Reingold, O. (ed.) TCC 2009. LNCS, vol. 5444, pp. 558–576. Springer, Heidelberg (2009). doi:10.1007/978-3-642-00457-5_33
17. Brakerski, Z., Vaikuntanathan, V.: Constrained key-homomorphic PRFs from standard lattice assumptions. In: Dodis, Y., Nielsen, J.B. (eds.) TCC 2015. LNCS, vol. 9015, pp. 1–30. Springer, Heidelberg (2015). doi:10.1007/978-3-662-46497-7_1
18. Carter, L., Wegman, M.N.: Universal classes of hash functions. J. Comput. Syst. Sci. **18**(2), 143–154 (1979)
19. Chandran, N., Raghuraman, S., Vinayagamurthy, D.: Constrained pseudorandom functions: verifiable and delegatable. Cryptology ePrint Archive, 2014/522 (2014)
20. Chase, M., Meiklejohn, S.: Déjà Q: using dual systems to revisit q-type assumptions. In: Nguyen, P.Q., Oswald, E. (eds.) EUROCRYPT 2014. LNCS, vol. 8441, pp. 622–639. Springer, Heidelberg (2014). doi:10.1007/978-3-642-55220-5_34
21. Dodis, Y.: Efficient construction of (distributed) verifiable random functions. In: Desmedt, Y.G. (ed.) PKC 2003. LNCS, vol. 2567, pp. 1–17. Springer, Heidelberg (2003). doi:10.1007/3-540-36288-6_1
22. Dodis, Y., Yampolskiy, A.: A verifiable random function with short proofs and keys. In: Vaudenay, S. (ed.) PKC 2005. LNCS, vol. 3386, pp. 416–431. Springer, Heidelberg (2005). doi:10.1007/978-3-540-30580-4_28
23. Dwork, C., Naor, M.: ZAPs and their applications. SIAM J. Comput. **36**(6), 1513–1543 (2007)
24. Feige, U., Lapidot, D., Shamir, A.: Multiple noninteractive zero knowledge proofs under general assumptions. SIAM J. Comput. **29**(1), 1–28 (1999)
25. Fiore, D., Schröder, D.: Uniqueness is a different story: impossibility of verifiable random functions from trapdoor permutations. In: Cramer, R. (ed.) TCC 2012. LNCS, vol. 7194, pp. 636–653. Springer, Heidelberg (2012). doi:10.1007/978-3-642-28914-9_36
26. Fuchsbauer, G.: Constrained verifiable random functions. In: Abdalla, M., Prisco, R. (eds.) SCN 2014. LNCS, vol. 8642, pp. 95–114. Springer, Cham (2014). doi:10.1007/978-3-319-10879-7_7
27. Goldreich, O., Goldwasser, S., Micali, S.: How to construct random functions. J. ACM **33**(4), 792–807 (1986)
28. Goldreich, O., Rothblum, R.D.: Enhancements of trapdoor permutations. J. Cryptol. **26**(3), 484–512 (2013)
29. Goldwasser, S., Ostrovsky, R.: *Invariant* signatures and non-interactive zero-knowledge proofs are equivalent. In: Brickell, E.F. (ed.) CRYPTO 1992. LNCS, vol. 740, pp. 228–245. Springer, Heidelberg (1993). doi:10.1007/3-540-48071-4_16
30. Gorbunov, S., Vaikuntanathan, V., Wee, H.: Functional encryption with bounded collusions via multi-party computation. In: Safavi-Naini, R., Canetti, R. (eds.) CRYPTO 2012. LNCS, vol. 7417, pp. 162–179. Springer, Heidelberg (2012). doi:10.1007/978-3-642-32009-5_11

31. Goyal, R., Hohenberger, S., Koppula, V., Waters, B.: A generic approach to constructing and proving verifiable random functions. Cryptology ePrint Archive 2017/21 (2017)

32. Groth, J., Ostrovsky, R., Sahai, A.: New techniques for noninteractive zero-knowledge. J. ACM **59**(3), 11 (2012)

33. Hofheinz, D., Jager, T.: Verifiable random functions from standard assumptions. In: Kushilevitz, E., Malkin, T. (eds.) TCC 2016. LNCS, vol. 9562, pp. 336–362. Springer, Heidelberg (2016). doi:10.1007/978-3-662-49096-9_14

34. Hohenberger, S., Koppula, V., Waters, B.: Adaptively secure puncturable pseudorandom functions in the standard model. In: Iwata, T., Cheon, J.H. (eds.) ASIACRYPT 2015. LNCS, vol. 9452, pp. 79–102. Springer, Heidelberg (2015). doi:10.1007/978-3-662-48797-6_4

35. Hohenberger, S., Waters, B.: Constructing verifiable random functions with large input spaces. In: Gilbert, H. (ed.) EUROCRYPT 2010. LNCS, vol. 6110, pp. 656–672. Springer, Heidelberg (2010). doi:10.1007/978-3-642-13190-5_33

36. Jager, T.: Verifiable random functions from weaker assumptions. In: Dodis, Y., Nielsen, J.B. (eds.) TCC 2015. LNCS, vol. 9015, pp. 121–143. Springer, Heidelberg (2015). doi:10.1007/978-3-662-46497-7_5

37. Kiayias, A., Papadopoulos, S., Triandopoulos, N., Zacharias, T.: Delegatable pseudorandom functions and applications. In: Sadeghi, A.-R., Gligor, V.D., Yung, M. (eds.) 20th Conference on Computer and Communications Security, ACM CCS 2013, pp. 669–684. ACM Press, Berlin (2013)

38. Lysyanskaya, A.: Unique signatures and verifiable random functions from the DH-DDH separation. In: Yung, M. (ed.) CRYPTO 2002. LNCS, vol. 2442, pp. 597–612. Springer, Heidelberg (2002). doi:10.1007/3-540-45708-9_38

39. Micali, S., Rabin, M.O., Vadhan, S.P.: Verifiable random functions. In: 40th Annual Symposium on Foundations of Computer Science, FOCS 1999, New York, NY, USA, pp. 120–130, 17–18 October 1999

40. Miltersen, P.B., Vinodchandran, N.V.: Derandomizing Arthur-Merlin games using hitting sets. In: 40th Annual Symposium on Foundations of Computer Science, FOCS 1999, New York, NY, USA, pp. 71–80, 17–18 October 1999

41. Naor, M.: Bit commitment using pseudorandomness. J. Cryptol. **4**(2), 151–158 (1991)

42. Naor, M., Reingold, O.: Synthesizers and their application to the parallel construction of pseudo-random functions. J. Comput. Syst. Sci. **58**(2), 336–375 (1999)

43. Naor, M., Reingold, O.: Number-theoretic constructions of efficient pseudo-random functions. J. ACM **51**(2), 231–262 (2004)

44. Sahai, A., Seyalioglu, H.: Worry-free encryption: functional encryption with public keys. In: Proceedings of the 17th ACM Conference on Computer and Communications Security, CCS 2010, Chicago, Illinois, USA, pp. 463–472, 4–8 October 2010

45. Sahai, A., Waters, B.: How to use indistinguishability obfuscation: deniable encryption, and more. In: Shmoys, D.B. (ed.) 46th Annual ACM Symposium on Theory of Computing, pp. 475–484. ACM Press, New York (2014)

46. Waters, B.: Efficient identity-based encryption without random oracles. In: Cramer, R. (ed.) EUROCRYPT 2005. LNCS, vol. 3494, pp. 114–127. Springer, Heidelberg (2005). doi:10.1007/11426639_7

Fully Homomorphic Encryption

Batched Multi-hop Multi-key FHE from Ring-LWE with Compact Ciphertext Extension

Long Chen[1,2], Zhenfeng Zhang[1,2(✉)], and Xueqing Wang[1,3]

[1] University of Chinese Academy of Sciences, Beijing, China
[2] Trusted Computing and Information Assurance Laboratory, Institute of Software, Chinese Academy of Sciences, Beijing, China
{chenlong,zfzhang}@tca.iscas.ac.cn
[3] State Key Laboratory of Information Security, Institute of Information Engineering, Chinese Academy of Sciences, Beijing, China
wangxueqing@iie.ac.cn

Abstract. Traditional fully homomorphic encryption (FHE) schemes support computation on data encrypted under a single key. In STOC 2012, López-Alt et al. introduced the notion of multi-key FHE (MKFHE), which allows homomorphic computation on ciphertexts encrypted under different keys. In this work, we focus on MKFHE constructions from standard assumptions and propose a new construction of ring-LWE-based multi-hop MKFHE scheme. Our work is based on Brakerski-Gentry-Vaikuntanathan (BGV) FHE scheme where, in contrast, all the previous works on multi-key FHE with standard assumptions were based on Gentry-Sahai-Waters (GSW) FHE scheme. Therefore, our construction can encrypt a ring element rather than a single bit and naturally inherits the advantages in aspects of the ciphertext/plaintext ratio and the complexity of homomorphic operations. Moveover, our MKFHE scheme supports the Chinese Remainder Theorem (CRT)-based ciphertexts packing technique, achieves $poly(k, L, \log n)$ computation overhead for k users, circuits with depth at most L and an n dimensional lattice, and gives the first batched MKFHE scheme based on standard assumptions to our knowledge. Furthermore, the ciphertext extension algorithms of previous schemes need to perform complex computation on each ciphertext, while our extension algorithm just needs to generate evaluation keys for the extended scheme. So the complexity of ciphertext extension is only dependent on the number of associated parities but not on the number of ciphertexts. Besides, our scheme also admits a threshold decryption protocol from which a generalized two-round MPC protocol can be similarly obtained as prior works.

1 Introduction

Fully homomorphic encryption (FHE) is a very attractive cryptography primitive that allows computation on encrypted data and has numerous theoretical and practical applications [Gen09, BV11b, DPSZ12, GSW13]. In STOC 2012, López-Alt et al. introduced a notion of multi-key FHE (MKFHE) [LATV12], which

© International Association for Cryptologic Research 2017
Y. Kalai and L. Reyzin (Eds.): TCC 2017, Part II, LNCS 10678, pp. 597–627, 2017.
https://doi.org/10.1007/978-3-319-70503-3_20

is a variant of FHE allowing computation on data encrypted under different and independent keys. One of the most appealing applications of MKFHE is to construct on-the-fly multiparty computation (MPC) protocols.

López-Alt et al. [LATV12] proposed the first MKFHE construction based on the NTRU cryptosystem [HPS98], which was optimized later in [DHS16]. However, the security of this construction is based on a new and somewhat non-standard assumption on polynomial rings. Clear and McGoldrick [CM15] proposed an LWE-based MKFHE construction for an unlimited number of keys using the Gentry-Sahai-Waters (GSW) FHE scheme [GSW13, ASP14]. In EUROCRYPT 2016, Mukherjee and Wichs [MW16] presented a construction of MKFHE based on LWE that simplifies the scheme of Clear and McGoldrick [CM15] and admits a simple 1-round threshold decryption protocol. Based on this threshold MKFHE, they successfully constructed a general two-round MPC protocol upon it in the common random string model.

The schemes in [CM15, MW16] need to determine all the involved parties before the homomorphic computation and do not allow any new party to join in, which called *single-hop* MKFHE in [PS16]. Recently, Peikert and Shiehian [PS16] proposed a notion of *multi-hop* MKFHE, in which the result ciphertexts of homomorphic evaluations can be used in further homomorphic computations involving additional parties (secret keys). In multi-hop MKFHE, any party can dynamically join the homomorphic computation at any time. A similar notion named *fully dynamic* MKFHE was proposed by Brakerski and Perlman in [BP16]. A slight difference is that in fully dynamic MKFHE the bound of the number of users does not need to be input during the setup procedure.

The method to construct multi-hop MKFHE in [PS16] is maintaining commitment randomness relative to a fixed public parameter, along with an encryption of that randomness. Their homomorphic evaluation algorithm requires only a few standard GSW-style matrix operations. This comes at the cost of relatively larger ciphertexts, which grow at least quadratically in the maximum number of keys. In [BP16], Brakerski and Perlman provided a fully dynamic MKFHE scheme with an approach of extending the refresh keys to the ones under a joint secret key at first and then bootstrapping the ciphertexts by the extended refresh keys. Specifically, their multi-key ciphertexts grow only linearly in the number of different involving secret keys. In addition, they described an "on-the-fly" bootstrapping algorithm that requires only a linear amount of "local" memory. However, as [PS16] analyzed, [BP16] is comparatively inefficient since their bootstrapping is generally very costly and some efficient bootstrapping techniques such as [ASP13, HS15, DM15] seem not to be applicable here.[1] From above, one can obverse that MKFHE is still far from practical, even comparing with existing results of single key FHE.

---

[1] Most of practical bootstrapping techniques [ASP13, HS15, DM15] are based on ring-LWE schemes and few can be applied to the LWE-based GSW scheme like that used in [BP16].

1.1 Motivations

Encrypting a ring element. There are two most widely studied single-key FHE schemes based on standard assumptions, the BGV type scheme [BV11a, BGV12, GHS12b, HS15] and the GSW type scheme [GSW13, BV14, ASP14]. Both of them have an LWE version and a ring-LWE version. As the analysis in [GSW13], the most efficient one among them is the ring-LWE based BGV scheme in aspects of the ciphertext/plaintext ratio and the complexity of homomorphic operations. Actually, the plaintext of ring-LWE BGV scheme is a ring element, while both the LWE version and ring-LWE version of GSW scheme can only encrypt one bit for each ciphertext according to [GSW13]. The major reason is that the GSW noise depends also on the plaintext size after a homomorphic multiplication. Consequently, MKFHE from the GSW scheme [CM15, MW16, BP16, PS16] can only encrypt a single bit even based on the ring-LWE assumption. Therefore, if we can encrypt a ring element in MKFHE schemes, the efficiency will be improved considerably.

SIMD operations. Currently, the most efficient FHE schemes are those that allow SIMD (Single Instruction Multiple Data) style operations, by packing some plaintexts into the same number of independent "slots" as the plaintext space. Gentry et al. [GHS12b] showed that if the circuit $\mathcal{C}$ has size $t = poly(\lambda)$, depth L, and average width $w = O(\lambda)$, and we set the packing parameter as $l = \Theta(\lambda)$, then we get an $O(L \cdot \log \lambda)$-depth implementation of $\mathcal{C}$ using $O(t/\lambda \cdot poly \log(\lambda))$ l-fold gates. If implementing each l-fold gates takes $\tilde{O}(L^b \lambda^c)$ time, then the total time to evaluate $\mathcal{C}$ is no more than $\tilde{O}(t \cdot L^b \cdot \lambda^{c-1})$. Smart and Vercauteren described a ciphertext-packing technique based on polynomial-CRT [SV14], and Gentry et al. [GHS12b] used the technique to achieve a nearly optimal homomorphic evaluation (up to poly-logarithmic factors). Besides, two other ciphertexts packing techniques have been proposed [BGH13, HAO15] so far, both of which are based on kinds of matrix operations rather than the algebra structure of the rings. However, it is not clear how ciphertext packing techniques can be applied to standard assumption based MKFHE schemes [CM15, MW16, BP16, PS16] so far.

Generally, since existing MKFHE schemes [CM15, MW16, BP16, PS16] from standard assumptions are all based on GSW scheme, one interesting theoretical problem is that *whether we can construct MKFHE from other existing standard assumption based single key FHE schemes?*

Compact ciphertext extension. In the MKFHE schemes [CM15, MW16, BP16, PS16], each party's messages are encrypted by different public keys at first, and the original ciphertexts correspond to different secret keys. When several parties decide to jointly evaluate a circuit, a *ciphertext extension* algorithm is used to transform the original ciphertexts to larger dimensional ciphertexts under a same new secret key which is a concatenation of all the involved parities' secret keys. Generally, the outputs of ciphertext extension can be viewed as the ciphertexts in a single-key FHE scheme with a larger dimensional secret key. After that, the circuit is finally evaluated under the new larger dimensional single-key FHE scheme. Particularly, in [CM15, MW16], a GSW ciphertext is extended to a k times dimensional ciphertext matrix, by adding sub-blocks which are derived from the encryption of randomness. The ciphertext extension in [PS16] is similar to that in [CM15, MW16], while the additional sub-blocks are derived from commitment randomness relative to a fixed public parameter, along with an encryption of that randomness. In [BP16], the ciphertext extension of a GSW ciphertext is completed by bootstrapping the ciphertext with an extended refreshed key which needs to be generated in advance. All of their ciphertext extension algorithms need to perform complex computations for each ciphertext, which will be a heavy burden if the number of ciphertexts is large. We observe that such a ciphertext extension procedure is not needed in [LATV12]. For a standard assumption based MKFHE scheme, a natural question is whether one can directly compute homomorphic operations for the ciphertexts under different keys and reduce the dependence of the computation cost of ciphertext extension (if necessary) on the number of ciphertexts.

1.2 Our Contributions

Note that all previous MKFHE [CM15, MW16, BP16, PS16] are all constructed from the GSW scheme. In this paper, we construct a new ring-LWE based multi-hop MKFHE scheme from the BGV scheme, so our work naturally inherits the advantages of the second generation FHE [Lin]. For example, our scheme can encrypt a ring element and support the CRT-based ciphertexts packed technique. So it is much more efficient than prior works in aspects of the ciphertext/plaintext ratio, the complexity of homomorphic operations and other computation overhead. The detailed comparisons are provided in Tables 1, 2 and 3 in Subsect. 4.7. Similar to [PS16], a priori bound on the number of users is required at the setup phase. Our scheme also admit a threshold decryption protocol as [MW16], so a 2-round MPC can be similarly obtained from our construction.

A simple ciphertext extension is also used in our construction to transform BGV ciphertexts under different secret keys to larger dimensional ciphertexts under the concatenation of all involving secret keys, which is realized by just padding the ciphertext vectors with zeros. However, due to the structure of the BGV cryptosystem, the generation of new evaluation keys is needed. As the result, the complexity of the extension procedure is dependent only on the number of involved secret keys *but not on the number of ciphertexts*. The evaluation keys are generated in the key-generation phase, and can be pre-computed before encryption and even be publicly stored for the next time evaluation if the involved parties are unchanged. This is beneficial for a possible scenario where multiple ciphertexts are encrypted with the same key.

Generally, both the LWE version and the ring-LWE version of our construction can be provided. In the text, we choose to present the ring-LWE version. It is easy for readers to get the analogous LWE version without much effort. Moreover, our technique of constructing MKFHE can be extended to other (ring-)LWE based second generation FHE schemes such as [BV11a, Bra12], and all optimization techniques about these FHE schemes [GHS12a, GHS12c, GHPS13, ASP13, HS14, HS15, CP16] also can apply here.

From a technical point of view, we show the evaluation key of BGV scheme can be generated from a GSW encryption of a secret key the first time. We believe this technique can help us to better understand the internal connection between these two famous FHE schemes.

1.3   Technique Overview

In the ring-LWE based BGV scheme, given level-l ciphertexts $\mathbf{c}_l = (\langle \mathbf{a}, \mathbf{z}_l \rangle + 2e + \mu, \mathbf{a}) \in R_q^2$ under the secret key $\mathbf{s}_l = (1, -\mathbf{z}_l) \in R_q^2$ and $\mathbf{c}_l' = (\langle \mathbf{a}', \mathbf{z}_l' \rangle + 2e' + \mu', \mathbf{a}') \in R_q^2$ under the secret key $\mathbf{s}_l' = (1, -\mathbf{z}_l') \in R_q^2$, one can trivially extend them to ciphertexts $\bar{\mathbf{c}}_l = (\mathbf{c}_l, \mathbf{0}) \in R_q^4$ and $\bar{\mathbf{c}}_l' = (\mathbf{0}, \mathbf{c}_l') \in R_q^4$ under the same secret key $\bar{\mathbf{s}}_l = (\mathbf{s}_l, \mathbf{s}_l') \in R_q^4$ which is a concatenation of the two parties' secret keys. For extended ciphertexts, the homomorphic addition is just the vector addition. But for homomorphic multiplication, one need to compute the tensor product of the two ciphertexts, then use the evaluation key to relinearization the ciphertext. Since the corresponding secret key of $\bar{\mathbf{c}}_l \otimes \bar{\mathbf{c}}_l' \in R_q^{16}$ is $\hat{\mathbf{s}}_l = \bar{\mathbf{s}}_l \otimes \bar{\mathbf{s}}_l \in R_q^{16}$, the required evaluation key is

$$evk_l = \left\{ \left(\langle \mathbf{a}_{i,j}, \mathbf{z}_{l-1}^* \rangle + 2e_{i,j} + 2^j \hat{\mathbf{s}}_l[i], \mathbf{a}_{i,j} \right)_{i=1,\dots,16,\ j=0,\dots,\lfloor \log q \rfloor} \right\} \tag{1}$$

for next level secret key $\bar{\mathbf{s}}_{l-1} = (1, -\mathbf{z}_{l-1}^*) \in R_q^4$ and some $\mathbf{a}_{i,j} \in R_q^3$. So the main obstacle is to generate the evaluation key evk_l.

Generating BGV's evk from GSW scheme. Intuitively, evk_l can be viewed as a kind of "encryption" of each element of $\hat{\mathbf{s}}_l \in R_q^{16}$. Our first observation is that evk_l of the BGV scheme can be generated from a GSW encryption of $\hat{\mathbf{s}}_l$. In fact, the variant of GSW encryption for the plaintext $\hat{\mathbf{s}}_l[i]$ is

$$\mathsf{GSW.Enc}_{\bar{\mathbf{s}}_{l-1}}(\hat{\mathbf{s}}_l[i]) = r \left(\mathbf{A}\mathbf{z}_{l-1}^* + 2\mathbf{e}, \mathbf{A} \right) + 2\mathbf{E} + \hat{\mathbf{s}}_l[i] \cdot \mathbf{G} \in R_q^{(\lfloor \log q \rfloor + 1)4 \times 4}.$$

Here

$$\mathbf{G} = \left(1, \dots, 2^{\lfloor \log q \rfloor} \right)^T \otimes \mathbf{I}_4 \in \mathbb{Z}_q^{(\lfloor \log q \rfloor + 1)4 \times 4}$$

is the gadget matrix, $\mathbf{A} \in R_q^{4(\lfloor \log q \rfloor + 1) \times 3}$ is a random matrix, $r \in R_q$ and $\mathbf{E} \in R^{4(\lfloor \log q \rfloor + 1) \times 4}$. Note that the plaintext is encrypted in low bits, which is different from the original GSW scheme in [GSW13, ASP14]. Then the j-th row has the form $(\langle \mathbf{a}_j, \mathbf{z}_{l-1}^* \rangle + 2e_j + 2^j \hat{\mathbf{s}}_l[j], \mathbf{a}_j) \in R_q^4$ for some random vector $\mathbf{a}_j \in R_q^3$. This gives the evaluation key evk_l we need.

The next task is to generate $\mathsf{GSW.Enc}_{\bar{\mathbf{s}}_{l-1}}(\hat{\mathbf{s}}_l[i])$. Our basic idea is to take advantage of the ciphertext extension method in [CM15, MW16]. Specifically, each element of $\hat{\mathbf{s}}_l$ is a product of two elements of $\bar{\mathbf{s}}_l$, where $\bar{\mathbf{s}}_l$ is the concatenation of each party's secret key. So if one party's public key includes $\mathsf{GSW.Enc}_{\mathbf{s}_{l-1}}(\mathbf{s}_l[i]), i = 1, 2$, it can be extended to a larger dimensional ciphertext $\mathsf{GSW.Enc}_{\bar{\mathbf{s}}_{l-1}}(\mathbf{s}_l[i])$ under the secret key $\bar{\mathbf{s}}_{l-1} = (\mathbf{s}_{l-1}, \mathbf{s}_{l-1}') \in R_q^4$, and also

GSW.Enc$_{\mathbf{s}'_{l-1}}$($\mathbf{s}'_l[i]$) can be extended to GSW.Enc$_{\bar{\mathbf{s}}_{l-1}}$($\mathbf{s}'_l[i]$). If we can homomorphically multiply GSW.Enc$_{\bar{\mathbf{s}}_{l-1}}$($\mathbf{s}_l[i]$) and GSW.Enc$_{\bar{\mathbf{s}}_{l-1}}$($\mathbf{s}'_l[i']$), $i, i' = 1, 2$, we get all the element of GSW.Enc$_{\bar{\mathbf{s}}_{l-1}}$($\hat{\mathbf{s}}_l[i]$), $i = 1, \ldots, 16$. Then we can derive $\lfloor \log q \rfloor + 1$ BGV ciphertexts

$$(\langle \mathbf{a}_j, \mathbf{z}^*_{l-1} \rangle + 2e_j + 2^j \hat{\mathbf{s}}_l[j], \mathbf{a}_j) \in R^4_q, j = 0, \ldots, \lfloor \log q \rfloor$$

under the secret key $\bar{\mathbf{s}}_{l-1} = (\mathbf{s}_{l-1}, \mathbf{s}'_{l-1}) = (1, -\mathbf{z}^*_{l-1})$ from each GSW encryption GSW.Enc$_{\bar{\mathbf{s}}_{l-1}}$($\hat{\mathbf{s}}_l[i]$), and therefore get the supposed evaluation key.

GSW Scheme with ring element plaintext. However, the plaintext of the traditional GSW scheme is in $\{0, 1\}$ while we encrypt $\hat{\mathbf{s}}_l[i] \in R_q$. When the plaintext is an element in R_q, the homomorphic multiplication can not work normally as explained before since the noise will be out of control. To deal with this problem, we propose a variant of GSW scheme with ring element plaintext. Specifically, we observe that when we compute GSW.Enc(a) $\odot$ GSW.Enc(b) for some $a, b \in R_q$, the noise in the result ciphertext only depends on b *but not on* a. So we can compute

$$\sum_{i=0}^{\lfloor \log q \rfloor} \text{GSW.Enc}\,(\text{Powersof2}(a)[i]) \odot \text{GSW.Enc}\,(\text{BitDecomp}(b)[i]).$$

Such a homomorphic multiplication in our GSW scheme with ring element plaintext can *only be performed once*, but it is enough for us to successfully compute GSW.Enc$_{\bar{\mathbf{s}}_{l-1}}$($\hat{\mathbf{s}}_l[i]$).

1.4   Organization

In Sect. 2, some background knowledge is provided. We introduce a special GSW scheme with ring element plaintext which is used to generate evaluation keys and existing techniques about the BGV scheme in Sect. 3. In Sect. 4, we give a formal description of our ring-LWE based MKFHE construction. Finally, in Sect. 5, we present a threshold decryption mechanism and a two round MPC protocol from our scheme. The conclusion is provided in Sect. 6.

2   Preliminaries

In this paper, we use bold lower case letters to denote vectors and bold upper case letters to denote matrices. All vectors are represented as columns. For a matrix $\mathbf{A}$, we use $\mathbf{A}[i, :]$ to denote the i-th row vector, and $\mathbf{A}[i, j]$ to denote the entry in the i-th row and j-th column. For a vector $\mathbf{a}$, $\mathbf{a}[i]$ denotes the i-th entry.

For a positive integer m, let $\Phi_m(X)$ be the m-th cyclotomic polynomial which has degree $n = \phi(m)$ where $\phi(\cdot)$ is the Euler's function. We will use the ring $R = \mathbb{Z}[X]/\Phi_m(X)$ and its localization R_N, for some modulus N. When dealing with R_N, we assume that the coefficients are in $[-N/2, N/2)$ (except for R_2 whose coefficients are in $\{0, 1\}$). Given a polynomial $a \in R$, we denote by $\|a\|_\infty = \max_{0 \leq j \leq n-1} |a_j|$ the standard l_∞-norm and $\|a\|_1 = \sum_{j=0}^{n-1} |a_j|$ the standard l_1-norm.

2.1 Hardness Assumption

The ring-LWE problem introduced by [LPR13a] can be seen as a ring version of the LWE problem [Reg09]. Now we recall its definition. Let K be the m-th cyclotomic number field having dimension $n = \phi(m)$ and $R = \mathcal{O}_K$ be its ring of integers which embeds as a lattice. $R^\vee \subset K$ is the dual fractional ideal of R. The noise estimation can be taken with respect to the canonical embedding norm $\|a\|_\infty^{can} = \|\sigma(a)\|_\infty$, where σ is the canonical embedding defined in [LPR13a]. To map from norms in the canonical embedding to norms on the coefficients of the polynomial, we have

$$\|a\|_\infty \le c_m \|a\|_\infty^{can}, \tag{2}$$

where c_m is the ring expansion factor, see [DPSZ12] for more details.

Definition 1 (Ring-LWE [LPR13a, LPR13b]). *For an $s \in R_q^\vee$ and a distribution χ over the field tensor product $K_\mathbb{R} = K \otimes_\mathbb{Q} \mathbb{R}$, a sample from the ring-LWE distribution $A_{s,\chi}$ over $R_q \times K_\mathbb{R}/qR^\vee$ is generated by choosing $a \leftarrow R_q$ uniformly at random, choosing $e \leftarrow \chi$, and outputting $(a, b = a \cdot s + e)$.*

The decisional version of the ring-LWE problem, denoted R-DLWE$_{q,\chi}$, is to distinguish with non-negligible advantage between independent samples from $A_{s,\chi}$, where s is uniformly chosen from $R_q^\vee$ once and for all, and the same number of uniformly random and independent samples from $R_q \times K_\mathbb{R}/qR^\vee$.

On the hardness, the theorem below captures reductions from GapSVP (GapSIVP) on ideal lattices to ring-LWE for certain parameters. We state the result in terms of canonical norm B-bounded distributions over the ring. Hereafter, "canonical norm" sometimes will be omit.

Definition 2 (B-bounded distribution over the ring). *A distribution ensemble $\{\chi_n\}_{n \in \mathbb{N}}$, supported over $K_\mathbb{R}$, is called (canonical norm) B-bounded if*

$$\Pr_{e \leftarrow \chi_n} [\|e\|_\infty^{can} > B] = negl(n).$$

Theorem 1 [LPR13a, LPR13b]. *Let R be the m-th cyclotomic ring, having dimension $n = \phi(m)$. Let $q = q(n)$, $q = 1 \bmod m$ be a poly(n)-bounded integer, and $B = \omega(\sqrt{n \log n})$. There is a poly$(n)$-time quantum reduction from $n^{\omega(1)}q/B$-approximate SIVP (or SVP) on ideal lattices in R to solve R-DLWE$_{q,\chi}$ where χ is a distribution bounded by B with overwhelming probability.*

It has been shown for ring-LWE that one can equivalently assume that s is alternatively sampled from the noise distribution χ [LPR13a].

2.2 Smudging Lemma

We rely on the following lemma, which says that adding large noise "smudges out" any small values.

Lemma 1 [AJL+12]. *Let $B_1 = B_1(\lambda)$, and $B_2 = B_2(\lambda)$ be positive integers and let $e_1 \in [-B_1, B_1]$ be a fixed integer. Let the integer $e_2 \in [-B_2, B_2]$ be chosen uniformly at random. Then the distribution of e_2 is statistically indistinguishable from that of $e_2 + e_1$ as long as $B_1/B_2 = negl(\lambda)$.*

Similarly, when $R = \mathbb{Z}[X]/\Phi_m(X)$, let $e_1 \in R_q$ be a fixed ring element where $\|e_1\|_\infty \leq B_1$, and e_2 be another ring element whose coefficients are chosen uniformly at random from $[-B_2, B_2]$. Then the distribution of e_2 is statistically indistinguishable from that of $e_2 + e_1$ as long as $B_1/B_2 = negl(\lambda)$.

2.3 Bit Decomposition Technique

The bit decomposition technique is first introduced in [BV11a] and widely used in FHE schemes. Let $\beta = \lfloor \log q \rfloor + 1$. We describe the subroutines as follows.

- BitDecomp($\mathbf{V} \in \mathbb{Z}_q^{n \times d}$): Decompose each coefficient of $\mathbf{V}$ in bit representation. Namely, write $\mathbf{V} = \sum_{j=0}^{\lfloor \log q \rfloor} 2^j \cdot \mathbf{U}_j$, with all $\mathbf{U}_j \in \{0,1\}^{n \times d}$, and output $[\mathbf{U}_0, \mathbf{U}_1, \ldots, \mathbf{U}_{\lfloor \log q \rfloor}] \in \{0,1\}^{n \times d\beta}$.
- Powersof2($\mathbf{V} \in \mathbb{Z}_q^{n \times d}$): Let $\mathbf{W}_j = 2^j \mathbf{V} \mod q \in \mathbb{Z}_q^{n \times d}$, $j = 0, \ldots, \lfloor \log q \rfloor$ and output $[\mathbf{W}_0, \mathbf{W}_1, \ldots, \mathbf{W}_{\lfloor \log q \rfloor}] \in \mathbb{Z}_q^{n \times d\beta}$.

Obviously, BitDecomp($\mathbf{U}$)·Powerof2($\mathbf{V}$)^T = $\mathbf{U} \cdot \mathbf{V}^T$, where $\mathbf{U}, \mathbf{V} \in \mathbb{Z}_q^{n \times d}$. Consequently, let $\mathbf{g} = (1, 2, \ldots, 2^{\lfloor \log q \rfloor})^T \in \mathbb{Z}_q^\beta$, $\mathbf{I}_d$ be the d dimensional identity matrix and $\mathbf{G} = \mathbf{g} \otimes \mathbf{I}_d \in \mathbb{Z}_q^{d\beta \times d}$. For any matrix $\mathbf{C} \in \mathbb{Z}_q^{n \times d}$, $\bar{\mathbf{C}} = $ BitDecomp($\mathbf{C}$) $\in \mathbb{Z}_q^{n \times d\beta}$ and $\bar{\mathbf{C}} \cdot \mathbf{G} = \mathbf{C}$. Moreover, when a is an element in the ring $R_q = R/qR$ where $R = \mathbb{Z}[x]/\Phi_m[X]$, a can be represented as a vector in $\mathbb{Z}_q^n$ and we can apply BitDecomp and Powersof2 algorithms to a as well.

2.4 Cryptographic Definitions

Definition 3. *A leveled multi-hop, multi-key FHE scheme is a tuple of efficient randomized algorithms (Setup, Gen, Enc, Dec, Eval) described as follows:*

- *Setup($1^\lambda, 1^K, 1^L$): Given the security parameter λ, a bound K on the number of keys, and a bound L on the circuit depth, output a public parameter pp.*
- *Gen(pp): Given the public parameter pp, output public key pk_i and secret key sk_i ($i = 1, \ldots, K$) for each party.*
- *Enc(pp, pk_i, μ): Given the public key pk_i of party i and a message μ, output a ciphertext ct_i. Without loss of generality, ct_i contains the index of corresponding secret key and the level tag.*
- *Dec(pp, $(sk_{i_1}, sk_{i_2}, \ldots, sk_{i_k}), ct_S$): Given a ciphertext ct_S corresponding to a set of parties $S = \{i_1, \ldots, i_k\} \subseteq [K]$ and their secret keys $sk_{i_1}, sk_{i_2}, \ldots, sk_{i_k}$, output the message μ.*
- *Eval(pp, $\mathcal{C}, (ct_{S_1}, pk_{S_1}), \ldots, (ct_{S_t}, pk_{S_t})$): Given (a description of) a boolean circuit $\mathcal{C}$ along with t tuples (ct_{S_i}, pk_{S_i}), each comprising of a ciphertext ct_{S_i} corresponding to a set of secret keys indexed by $S_i = \{i_1, \ldots, i_{k_i}\} \subseteq [K]$ and a set of public keys $pk_{S_i} = \{pk_j, \forall j \in S_i\}$, output a ciphertext ct corresponding to the set of secret keys indexed by $S = \bigcup_{i=1}^t S_i \subseteq [K]$.*

Notice that the input ciphertexts of Eval can be fresh or the intermediate results of any homomorphic operations, which is allowed by the multi-hop property.

Definition 4 (Correctness). *A leveled multi-hop, multi-key FHE scheme is correct if for any circuit C of depth at most L having t input wires and any tuples $\{(ct_{S_i}, pk_{S_i})\}_{i \in [t]}$, letting $\mu_i = Dec(sk_{S_i}, ct_{S_i})$, where $sk_{S_i} = \{sk_j, \forall j \in S_i\}$, $i = 1, \ldots t$, it holds that*

$$\Pr\left[Dec(sk_S, Eval(C, (ct_{S_1}, pk_{S_1}), \ldots, (ct_{S_t}, pk_{S_t}))) \neq C(\mu_1, \ldots, \mu_t)\right] = negl(\lambda),$$

where $S = \bigcup_{i=1}^{t} S_i$, $pp \leftarrow Setup(1^\lambda, 1^K, 1^L)$, $(pk_j, sk_j) \leftarrow Gen(pp)$ for $j \in [S]$.

Definition 5 (Compactness). *A leveled multi-hop, multi-key FHE scheme is compact if there exists a polynomial $poly(\cdot, \cdot, \cdot)$ such that in Definition 3, $|ct| \leq poly(\lambda, K, L)$. In other words, the length of ct is independent of the size of C, but can depend polynomially on λ, K, and L.*

3 GSW Scheme with Ring Element Plaintext

In this section, we describe a variant of ring-LWE based GSW scheme with ring element plaintext, which can also be converted to a MKFHE scheme using the key extension technique in [CM15, MW16]. As explained in the introduction, this scheme will be used for the evaluation key generation in the Eval algorithm of the MKFHE scheme. The analogous LWE based scheme can be similarly constructed without effort, so we omit the description.

3.1 Basic Scheme

Here we present basic algorithms of our ring-GSW scheme. The differences between our scheme and the original ring-LWE based GSW scheme in [GSW13] include the following. First, the plaintext here is a R_q ring element instead of one bit, so our scheme do not support the general homomorphic multiplication gate. But we show that in a special case that the second plaintext has a small l_1 norm, one homomorphic multiplication is allowed. Second, the plaintext in our scheme is encrypted in low bits for the convenience of transformation to the evaluation key of the BGV scheme. Third, the decryption algorithm of our scheme is not presented, since it will not be used in our construction.

Our scheme is parameterized by an integer m (that defines the cyclotomic polynomial Φ_m and $\phi(m) = n$), a modulus $q(= poly(n))$, a small constant integer p, a (canonical norm) B-bounded discrete distribution χ in $R = \mathbb{Z}[X]/\Phi_m$ for $B \ll q$ and an integer $N = O(n \log q)$. Let $\beta = \lfloor \log q \rfloor + 1$. We use ring $R_q = R/qR$.

RGSW.Keygen(1^n): Sample $z \in R$ with a distribution χ, then we define the secret key as a vector $\mathbf{s} = (1, -z)^T \in R_q^2$. Pick a random vector $\mathbf{a} \in R_q^{2\beta}$ uniformly at random and vectors $\mathbf{e} \in R^{2\beta}$ with a distribution $\chi^{2\beta}$. Output the public key as

$$\mathbf{P} = [\mathbf{a}z + p\mathbf{e}, \mathbf{a}] = [\mathbf{b}, \mathbf{a}] \in R_q^{2\beta \times 2}.$$

*RGSW.EncRand(μ,**P**):* This procedure is to generate the encryption of randomness that is used in the real encryption. When input $\mu \in R_q$, pick β ring elements $r_i \leftarrow \chi$ for $i = 1, \ldots, \beta$ and two vectors $\mathbf{e}_1', \mathbf{e}_2' \leftarrow \chi^\beta$, and output

$$\mathsf{RGSW.EncRand_s}(\mu) = \mathbf{F} = [\mathbf{f}_1, \mathbf{f}_2] \in R_q^{\beta \times 2},$$

where for $i = 1 \ldots \beta$,

$$\mathbf{f}_1[i] = \mathbf{b}[i]r_i + p\mathbf{e}_1'[i] + \mathsf{Powersof2}(\mu)[i] \in R_q$$

and

$$\mathbf{f}_2[i] = \mathbf{a}[i]r_i + p\mathbf{e}_2'[i] \in R_q.$$

Notice that $\mathbf{Fs} = p\tilde{\mathbf{e}} + \mathsf{Powersof2}(\mu)^T \in R_q^\beta$ for some small $\tilde{\mathbf{e}} \in R^\beta$. In fact, $\tilde{\mathbf{e}}[i] = \mathbf{e}[i]r_i + \mathbf{e}_1'[i] - \mathbf{e}_2'[i]z$ for $i = 1, \ldots, \beta$.

*RGSW.Enc(μ,**P**):* On inputs $\mu \in R_q$ and the public key $\mathbf{P}$, pick a random ring element $r \xleftarrow{\$} \chi$ and an error matrix $\mathbf{E} = [\mathbf{e}_1, \mathbf{e}_2] \leftarrow \chi^{2\beta \times 2}$, and output

$$\begin{aligned}
\mathsf{RGSW.Enc}(\mu)_s = \mathbf{C} &= r\mathbf{P} + p\mathbf{E} + \mu\mathbf{G} \\
&= [r\mathbf{b}, r\mathbf{a}] + p\mathbf{E} + \mu\mathbf{G} \\
&= [raz + p(re + \mathbf{e}_1), ra + p\mathbf{e}_2] + \mu\mathbf{G} \in R_q^{2\beta \times 2},
\end{aligned}$$

where $\mathbf{G} = (\mathbf{I}, 2\mathbf{I}, \ldots, 2^{\beta-1}\mathbf{I})^T \in R_q^{2\beta \times 2}$, and

$$\mathsf{RGSW.EncRand}(r, \mathbf{P}) = \mathbf{F} \in R_q^{\beta \times 2}.$$

Notice that $\mathbf{C} \cdot \mathbf{s} = p\tilde{\mathbf{e}} + \mu\mathbf{Gs} \in R_q^{2\beta}$ for some small $\tilde{\mathbf{e}}$. The corresponding decryption algorithm is not provided.

RGSW.HomAdd($\mathbf{C}_1, \mathbf{C}_2$): Addition of two ciphertext matrices is just standard addition in R_q.

RGSW.HomMult($\mathbf{C}_1, \mathbf{C}_2$): On input two ciphertexts $\mathbf{C}_1, \mathbf{C}_2 \in R_q^{2\beta \times 2}$, first computes the bit decomposition $\overline{\mathbf{C}}_1 = [\mathbf{D}_0, \ldots, \mathbf{D}_{\beta-1}]^T \in R_q^{2\beta \times 2\beta}$ of $\mathbf{C}_1$ such that $\mathbf{C}_1 = \sum_{i=0}^{\beta-1} 2^i \mathbf{D}_i$, and then present the multiplication as

$$\mathbf{C}_1 \odot \mathbf{C}_2 := \overline{\mathbf{C}}_1 \cdot \mathbf{C}_2.$$

The homomorphic multiplication can be accelerated using FFT/NTT as [DM15]. Notice that RGSW.HomMult operation can not always output a legal ciphertext with small noise. But in a special case that $\mathbf{C}_2$ encrypts a plaintext with a small l_1 norm, the noise in the output will be small. A rigorous analysis will be provided in Subsect. 3.3.

RGSW.CTExt $(\mathbf{C}_i, \mathbf{F}_i, \{\mathbf{P}_j, j = 1, \ldots, k\})$: given a ciphertext $\mathbf{C}_i \in R_q^{2\beta \times 2}$, an encryption of randomness $\mathbf{F}_i$ and public keys of all parties, output an extended ciphertext as

$$\bar{\mathbf{C}} = \begin{bmatrix} \mathbf{C}_i & \cdots & \mathbf{X}_1 & \cdots & 0 \\ 0 & \ddots & \vdots & & 0 \\ \vdots & & \mathbf{C}_i & & \vdots \\ & & \vdots & \ddots & \\ 0 & \cdots & \mathbf{X}_k & \cdots & \mathbf{C}_i \end{bmatrix} \in R_q^{2k\beta \times 2k} \tag{3}$$

where each sub block $\mathbf{X}_j \in R_q^{2\beta \times 2}$ is constructed from $\mathbf{F}_i$ and $\{\mathbf{P}_j\}_{j=1,\ldots,k}$ as $\mathbf{X}_j[u, :] = \mathsf{BitDecomp}(\tilde{\mathbf{b}}_j[u])\mathbf{F}_i \in R_q^2$ for $u = 1, \ldots, 2\beta$.

3.2 Security

The view of the attacker is the following distribution $(\mathbf{P}, \mathbf{F}, \mathbf{C})$ generated via, $(sk, pk = \mathbf{P}) \leftarrow \mathsf{RGSW.Keygen}(params)$, $\mathbf{F} \leftarrow \mathsf{RGSW.EncRand}(r, \mathbf{P})$ and $\mathbf{C} \leftarrow \mathsf{RGSW.Enc}(\mu, \mathbf{P})$. We prove semantic security of our GSW scheme with ring element plaintext by relying on the semantic security of the underlying ring-LWE scheme [LPR13a,LPR13b]. The proof consists of the following hybrids:

- First, we change the public key $\mathbf{P}$ to a random matrix $R_q^{2\beta \times 2}$ according the ring LWE assumption.
- Second, we change the encryption of randomness $\mathbf{F}$ to β ring LWE encryption of 0.
- Third, we change the encryption $\mathbf{C}$ to 2β ring LWE encryption of 0.

Finally, this distribution is completely independent of the plaintext μ which concludes the proof of security.

3.3 Noise Growth

The noise growth by the evaluation of the homomorphic operation can be analysed by the following lemma.

Lemma 2. *Let* $\beta = \lfloor \log q \rfloor + 1$ *and* $k \geq 1$. *Let* $\mathbf{s} \in R_q^{2k}$ *be a secret key. Let* $\mathbf{C}_1, \mathbf{C}_2 \in R_q^{2k\beta \times 2k}$ *be ciphertexts that encrypt* $\mu_1, \mu_2 \in R_q$ *with noise vectors* $\mathbf{e}_1, \mathbf{e}_2 \in R^{2k\beta}$, *respectively. Let* $\mathbf{C}_{add} := \mathbf{C}_1 \oplus \mathbf{C}_2$ *and* $\mathbf{C}_{mult} := \mathbf{C}_1 \odot \mathbf{C}_2$. *Then, we have*

$$\mathbf{C}_{add}\mathbf{s} = p\mathbf{e}_{add} + (\mu_1 + \mu_2)\mathbf{Gs},$$

$$\mathbf{C}_{mult}\mathbf{s} = p\mathbf{e}_{mult} + (\mu_1 \mu_2)\mathbf{Gs},$$

where $\mathbf{e}_{add} := \mathbf{e}_1 + \mathbf{e}_2$ *and* $\mathbf{e}_{mult} := \overline{\mathbf{C}}_1 \mathbf{e}_2 + \mu_2 \mathbf{e}_1$. *In particular,* $\|\mathbf{e}_{mult}\|_\infty^{can} \leq \tilde{O}(\phi(m)k)\|\mathbf{e}_2\|_\infty^{can} + \|\mu_2\|_1\|\mathbf{e}_1\|_\infty^{can}$.

Proof. The statements for $\mathbf{C}_{add}$ can be immediately proved. For $\mathbf{C}_{mult}$, we have

$$
\begin{aligned}
\mathbf{C}_{mult}\mathbf{s} &= \overline{\mathbf{C}}_1 \cdot \mathbf{C}_2\mathbf{s} \\
&= \overline{\mathbf{C}}_1 \cdot (p\mathbf{e}_2 + \mu_2\mathbf{G}\mathbf{s}) \\
&= p\overline{\mathbf{C}}_1 \cdot \mathbf{e}_2 + \mu_2\mathbf{C}_1\mathbf{s} \\
&= p(\overline{\mathbf{C}}_1 \cdot \mathbf{e}_2 + \mu_2\mathbf{e}_1) + (\mu_1\mu_2)\mathbf{G}\mathbf{s}.
\end{aligned}
$$

Remind that $\overline{\mathbf{C}}_1 = \sum_{i=1}^{\beta} 2^i \mathbf{D}_i$, where each $\mathbf{D}_i \in R_q^{2k\beta \times 2k}$ has entries with coefficients in $\{0,1\}$. So the canonical norm of them are bounded by $\phi(m)$. Then we have

$$
\|\mathbf{e}_{mult}\|_\infty^{can} \leq \tilde{O}(\phi(m)k)\|\mathbf{e}_2\|_\infty^{can} + \|\mu_2\|_1\|\mathbf{e}_1\|_\infty^{can}.
$$

$\square$

From the above lemma, we can see that the noise term in $\mathbf{C}_{mult}$ is only concerned with the l_1 norm of μ_2. From this observation, we get the following important corollary.

Corollary 1. *Let* $\beta = \lfloor \log q \rfloor + 1$, $k \geq 1$ *and* $\phi(m) = n$. *Let* $\mathbf{C}_1, \mathbf{C}_2 \in R_q^{2k\beta \times 2k}$ *be ciphertexts that encrypt* $\mu_1, \mu_2 \in R_q$ *with B bounded distribution noise vectors* $\mathbf{e}_1, \mathbf{e}_2 \in R^{2\beta} \simeq \mathbb{Z}^{2\beta\phi(m)}$, *respectively.* $\mathbf{C}_{mult}$ *and* $\mathbf{e}_{mult}$ *is defined as before. If* $\|\mu_2\|_\infty \leq 1$, *we have* $\| \mathbf{e}_{mult} \|_\infty \leq \tilde{O}(n) \cdot B$.

Proof. From Lemma 2, we have

$$
\|\mathbf{e}_{mult}\|_\infty^{can} \leq \tilde{O}(k\phi(m))\|\mathbf{e}_2\|_\infty^{can} + \|\mu_2\|_1\|\mathbf{e}_1\|_\infty^{can}.
$$

Since $\|\mu_2\|_\infty \leq 1$, $\|\mu_2\|_1 \leq n$. So by (2) we have

$$
\| \mathbf{e}_{mult} \|_\infty \leq c_m \| \mathbf{e}_{mult} \|_\infty^{can} \leq \tilde{O}(kn) \cdot B.
$$

$\square$

3.4 Correctness of Ciphertext Extension

In this subsection, we will explain the method of [CM15, MW16] to extend GSW ciphertexts corresponding to one single secret key to larger dimensional GSW ciphertexts corresponding to a concatenation of multiple keys.

Specifically, let $\mathbf{C}_i \in R_q^{2\beta \times 2}$ be a GSW ciphertext encrypting the message μ under secret key $\mathbf{s}_i = (1, -z_i)^T \in R_q^2$, i.e.,

$$
\begin{aligned}
\mathbf{C}_i &= r_i[az_i + pe_i, a] + \mathbf{E} + \mu\mathbf{G} \\
&= r_i[az_i + pe_i, a] + \mathbf{E} + \mu\mathbf{G} \in R_q^{2\beta \times 2}.
\end{aligned}
\tag{4}
$$

Given a sequence of public vectors from different parties

$$
\mathbf{b}_j = az_j + pe_j \in R_q^{2\beta}, j = 1, \ldots, i-1, i+1, \ldots, k
$$

and the i-th party's encryptions of the randomness

$$\mathsf{RGSW.EncRand}(r_i, pk_i) = \mathbf{F}_i \in R_q^{\beta \times 2},$$

we show that the $\mathbf{C}_i$ can be extended to a larger GSW ciphertext $\bar{\mathbf{C}} \in R_q^{2k\beta \times 2k}$ encrypting the same message μ under the secret key $\bar{\mathbf{s}} = (\mathbf{s}_1 | \ldots | \mathbf{s}_k) \in R_q^{2k}$ for $\mathbf{s}_j = (1, -z_j)^T \in R_q^2$, $j \in [k]$, such that

$$\bar{\mathbf{C}} \cdot \bar{\mathbf{s}} = p\mathbf{e} + \mu \bar{\mathbf{G}} \bar{\mathbf{s}},$$

where $\tilde{\mathbf{e}} \in R^{2k\beta}$ is a small noise vector. Here the matrix $\bar{\mathbf{G}}$ can be written as

$$\bar{\mathbf{G}} = \left[\mathbf{I}_{2k}, 2\mathbf{I}_{2k}, \ldots, 2^{\lfloor \log q \rfloor} \mathbf{I}_{2k} \right]^T \in R_q^{2k\beta \times 2k}.$$

Let the extended ciphertext

$$\bar{\mathbf{C}} = \begin{bmatrix} \mathbf{C}_i & \cdots & \mathbf{X}_1 & \cdots & 0 \\ 0 & \ddots & \vdots & & 0 \\ \vdots & & \mathbf{C}_i & & \vdots \\ & & \vdots & \ddots & \\ 0 & \cdots & \mathbf{X}_k & \cdots & \mathbf{C}_i \end{bmatrix} \in R_q^{2k\beta \times 2k} \tag{5}$$

to be a matrix whose sub blocks in $R_q^{2\beta \times 2}$ are all zero except the ones in the diagonal line and the ith column. Since $\mathbf{C}_i \mathbf{s}_i = p\mathbf{e}_i + \mu \mathbf{G} \mathbf{s}_i$, we also need to make sure that

$$\mathbf{X}_j \mathbf{s}_i + \mathbf{C}_i \mathbf{s}_j = p\tilde{\mathbf{e}} + \mu \mathbf{G} \mathbf{s}_j, \tag{6}$$

where $\tilde{\mathbf{e}} \in R^{2\beta}$ is a small noise vector.

Therefore, for $\mathbf{s}_i = (1, -z_i)^T$ and $\mathbf{s}_j = (1, -z_j)^T$, we can define

$$\tilde{\mathbf{b}}_j = \mathbf{b}_j - \mathbf{b}_i \in R_q^{2\beta}.$$

Let the uth row of $\mathbf{X}_j$ be

$$\mathbf{X}_j[u, :] = \mathsf{BitDecomp}(\tilde{\mathbf{b}}_j[u])\mathbf{F}_i \in R_q^2 \tag{7}$$

for $u = 1, \ldots, 2\beta$. Hence

$$\begin{aligned} \mathbf{X}_j[u, :]\mathbf{s}_i &= \left(\mathsf{BitDecomp}(\tilde{\mathbf{b}}_j[v])\mathbf{F}_i \right) \mathbf{s}_i \\ &= \mathsf{BitDecomp}(\tilde{\mathbf{b}}_j[v]) \cdot \left(p\mathbf{e} + \mathsf{Powersof2}(r_i)^T \right) \\ &= p\mathbf{e}' + \tilde{\mathbf{b}}_j[v] \cdot r_i, \end{aligned}$$

and

$$\mathbf{X}_j \mathbf{s}_i = p\mathbf{e}' + r_i \tilde{\mathbf{b}}_j \tag{8}$$

where e' is bounded by βB (canonical norm). According to the Eq. (4), we have

$$\mathbf{C}_i \mathbf{s}_j = r_i(\mathbf{a} z_i + p\mathbf{e}) - r_i \mathbf{a} z_j + \mathbf{E} \mathbf{s}_j + \mu \mathbf{G} \mathbf{s}_j$$
$$= r_i(\mathbf{b}_i - \mathbf{b}_j) + \mathbf{E} \mathbf{s}_j + \mu \mathbf{G} \mathbf{s}_j \quad .$$

Therefore, as the Eq. (6) holds for $\tilde{\mathbf{e}} = \mathbf{e}' + \mathbf{E} \mathbf{s}_j$ which is bounded by βB^2 (canonical norm).

Formally, the ciphertext extension algorithm can be described as follow.

- RGSW.CTExt $(\mathbf{C}_i, \mathbf{F}_i, \{\mathbf{P}_j, j = 1, \dots, k\})$, given a ciphertext $\mathbf{C}_i \in R_q^{2\beta \times 2}$, an encryption of randomness $\mathbf{F}_i$ and public keys of all parties, output an extended ciphertext as (5) where each sub block $\mathbf{X}_j \in R_q^{2\beta \times 2}$ is constructed from $\mathbf{F}_i$ and $\{\mathbf{P}_j\}_{j=1,\dots,k}$ as (7).

4   New Construction of Ring-LWE MKFHE

In this section, we present the details of our method to extend the BGV scheme to a MKFHE scheme. As explained in Definition 3, MKFHE consists of five algorithms, i.e., MKFHE.Setup, MKFHE.Gen, MKFHE.Enc, MKFHE.Dec and MKFHE.Eval. For convenience, in the following we use RGSW.Enc$_{\mathbf{s}}(\mu)$ (presented in Sect. 3) to denote a GSW ciphertext (which may be not fresh) that can be decrypted to μ with the secret key $\mathbf{s}$. Also we directly adopt the same subroutines such as modulus switching ModulusSwitch and key switching SwitchKey as the single key BGV scheme. For details of the original BGV scheme, see Appendix A.

4.1   Basic Schemes

MKFHE.Setup$(1^\lambda, 1^K, 1^L)$: Given the security parameter λ, a bound K on the number of keys, and a bound L on the circuit depth, generate the noise distribution $\chi = \chi(\lambda, K, L)$ which is a B-bounded distribution over R, L decreasing modules $q_L \gg q_{L-1} \gg \dots \gg q_0$ for each level and a small integer p coprime with all q_l's. Let $\beta_l = \lfloor \log q_l \rfloor + 1$, and choose $L + 1$ random public vectors $\mathbf{a}_l \in R_{q_l}^{2\beta_l}$ for $l = L, \dots, 0$. All the following algorithms implicitly take the public parameter $pp = (R, \chi, B, \{q_l, \mathbf{a}_l\}_{l \in \{L,\dots,0\}}, p)$ as input.

MKFHE.Gen$(j \in [K])$: Generate keys for the j-th party. For l from L down to 0, do the following:

1. Choose $z_{l,j} \leftarrow \chi$, and set $\mathbf{s}_{l,j} := (1, -z_{l,j})^T \in R_{q_l}^2$. The secret key for the j-th party is $sk_j = \{\mathbf{s}_{l,j}\}_{l \in \{L,\dots,0\}}$.
2. Generate $2\beta_l$ ring-LWE instances

$$pt_{l,j} := [\mathbf{b}_{l,j} = \mathbf{a}_l z_{l,j} + p\mathbf{e}_{l,j}, \mathbf{a}_l] \in R_{q_l}^{2\beta_l \times 2},$$

where $\mathbf{e}_{l,j} \leftarrow \chi^{2\beta_l}$. The public key pk_j for the j-th party consists of all the $pt_{l,j}$, $l = L, \dots, 0$.

3. For $i = 1, \ldots, 2\beta_l$, compute RGSW.Enc $(\text{Powersof2}(s_{l,j})[i], pt_{l-1,j})$ and get

$$\Phi_{i,l,j} = \text{RGSW.Enc}_{s_{l-1,j}} \left(\text{Powersof2}(\mathbf{s}_{l,j})[i] \right)$$
$$= r_{i,l,j} \left[\mathbf{b}_{l-1,j}, \mathbf{a}_{l-1} \right] + p\mathbf{E}_{i,l,j} + \text{Powersof2}(\mathbf{s}_{l,j})[i]\mathbf{G}$$

together with

$$\mathbf{F}_{i,l,j} = \text{RGSW.EncRand}(r_{i,l,j}, pt_{l-1,j}) \in R_{q_l}^{\beta_l \times 2}.$$

Also compute

$$\Psi_{i,l,j} = \text{RGSW.Enc}_{s_{l-1,j}} \left(\text{BitDecomp}(\mathbf{s}_{l,j})[i] \right)$$
$$= r'_{i,l,j} \left[\mathbf{b}_{l-1,j}, \mathbf{a}_{l-1} \right] + p\mathbf{E}'_{i,l,j} + \text{BitDecomp}(\mathbf{s}_{l,j})[i]\mathbf{G}$$

together with

$$\mathbf{F}'_{i,l,j} = \text{RGSW.EncRand}(r'_{i,l,j}, pt_{l-1,j}) \in R_{q_l}^{\beta_l \times 2}.$$

The evaluation key generation material is

$$em_j = \left\{ (\Phi_{i,l,j}, \mathbf{F}_{i,l,j}), (\Psi_{i,l,j}, \mathbf{F}'_{i,l,j}) \right\}_{i \in [2\beta_l], l \in [L]}.$$

Later, the em_j will be used to generate evaluation keys for the homomorphic evaluation algorithm.

MKFHE.Enc(pk_j, μ): Given the public key pk_j of the j-th party and a message $\mu \in R_p$, choose a random ring element $r \in R_2$. Similar to the BGV scheme, the level-L ciphertext $\mathbf{c} = (c^0, c^1) \in R_{q_L}^2$ encrypts a plaintext element $\mu \in R_p$ with respect to $\mathbf{s}_L = (1, -z_L)$, where

$$c^0 = r\mathbf{b}_{L,j}[1] + pe + \mu \in R_{q_L} \text{ and } c^1 = r\mathbf{a}_L[1] + pe' \in R_{q_L}.$$

Let S be an ordered set containing all indexes of the parities that the ciphertext corresponding to. Without loss of generality, we assume that the indexes in S are always arranged from small to large and S has no duplicate elements. Here we set $S = \{j\}$. Usually, the ciphertext ct contains $\mathbf{c}$, the set S and a tag l to label the number of the level. Finally, output a tuple $ct = (\mathbf{c}, \{j\}, L)$.

MKFHE.Dec$(sk_S, ct = (\mathbf{c}, S, l))$: Suppose $S = \{j_1, \ldots, j_k\}$ and sk_S consists of all the parties' secret keys whose indexes are contained in S, i.e., $sk_S = \{sk_{j_1}, \ldots, sk_{j_k}\}$. Let

$$\bar{\mathbf{s}}_l = (\mathbf{s}_{l,j_1} | \mathbf{s}_{l,j_2} | \cdots | \mathbf{s}_{l,j_k}) \in R_{q_l}^{2k},$$

where $\mathbf{s}_{l,j}$ is the key of the j-th party to decrypt level-l ciphertexts. Once given a level-l ciphertext $\mathbf{c} \in R_{q_l}^{2k}$, compute

$$\mu = \langle \mathbf{c}, \bar{\mathbf{s}}_l \rangle \mod q_l \mod p.$$

$MKFHE.Eval((pk_{i_1}, \ldots, pk_{i_k}), em_S, \mathcal{C}, (ct_1, \ldots, ct_t))$: Assume that the sequence of ciphertexts are at the same level-l (If needed, use SwitchKey and ModulusSwitch to make it so). For $j \in [t]$, parse ct_j as $(\mathbf{c}_j, S_j, l)$, let $|S_j| = k_j$, $S = \bigcup_{j=1}^{t} S_j = \{i_1, \ldots, i_k\}$, $pk_S = (pk_{i_1}, \ldots, pk_{i_k})$, and thus $\mathbf{c}_j \in R_{q_l}^{2k_j}$. Then the outline of the evaluation of the Boolean circuit $\mathcal{C}$ is as follows.

1. For $j \in [t]$, compute $MKFHE.CTExt(\mathbf{c}_j, S) = \bar{\mathbf{c}}_j$ to get extended $2k$ dimensional ciphertexts which encrypts the same message under the key $\bar{\mathbf{s}}_l$. Here $\bar{\mathbf{s}}_l := (\mathbf{s}_{l,i_1}, \ldots, \mathbf{s}_{l,i_k})$ is indexed by S.
2. Compute $MKFHE.EVKGen(em_S) = evk_S$ to generate the evaluation key for the extended scheme.
3. Call the two basic homomorphic operations for the extended ciphertexts $MKFHE.EvalAdd(evk_S, \bar{\mathbf{c}}_i, \bar{\mathbf{c}}_j)$ and $MKFHE.EvalMult(evk_S, \bar{\mathbf{c}}_i, \bar{\mathbf{c}}_j)$ to evaluate each gate of the circuit $\mathcal{C}$.

Note that, we have given a detailed description of the first four algorithms MKFHE.Setup, MKFHE.Gen, MKFHE.Enc and MKFHE.Dec. For MKFHE.Eval, we just provided an outline of the algorithm. In the following subsections, we will detail the ciphertext extension algorithm MKFHE.CTExt and the evaluation key generation algorithm MKFHE.EVKGen. Also, we will explain how to call the algorithm MKFHE.EvalAdd and MKFHE.EvalMult to evaluate addition and multiplication for larger dimensional ciphertexts.

4.2   The Ciphertext Extension

In this subsection, we detail the ciphertext extension algorithm MKFHE.CTExt which converts a BGV ciphertext to a larger dimensional ciphertext under a new larger dimensional secret key. In fact, the new secret key is a concatenation of secret keys from a larger set of parties.

$MKFHE.CTExt(ct, S')$: On input a ciphertext $ct = (\mathbf{c}, S, l)$ and a set of parties's indexes S' for $S \subseteq S'$, where S has k members $\{i_1, i_2, \ldots, i_k\}$ and S' has k' members $\{j_1, j_2, \ldots, j_{k'}\}$ for $k' > k$. $\mathbf{c} \in R_{q_l}^{2k}$ corresponds to the decryption key $\mathbf{s}_l \in R_{q_l}^{2k}$, so $\langle \mathbf{c}, \mathbf{s}_l \rangle \bmod q_l = pe + \mu$. Sequentially divide $\mathbf{c}$ into k sub-vectors which can be indexed by $S = \{i_1, i_2, \ldots, i_k\}$, i.e.,

$$\mathbf{c} = (\mathbf{c}_{i_1} | \mathbf{c}_{i_2} | \cdots | \mathbf{c}_{i_k}) \in R_{q_l}^{2k}$$

where each $\mathbf{c}_{i_1} \in R_{q_l}^2$. The extended ciphertext $\bar{\mathbf{c}} \in R_{q_l}^{2k'}$ consists of k' sequential sub-vectors of 2 dimensional, which can be indexed by $S' = \{j_1, j_2, \ldots, j_{k'}\}$, i.e.,

$$\bar{\mathbf{c}} = \left(\mathbf{c}'_{j_1} | \mathbf{c}'_{j_2} | \cdots | \mathbf{c}'_{j_{k'}} \right) \in R_{q_l}^{2k'}.$$

If an index j in S' is also included in S, we set $\mathbf{c}'_j = \mathbf{c}_j$, otherwise $\mathbf{c}'_j = 0$.

Obviously, $\bar{\mathbf{c}}$ corresponds to the secret key

$$\bar{\mathbf{s}}_l = (\mathbf{s}_{j_1,l} | \mathbf{s}_{j_2,l} | \cdots | \mathbf{s}_{j_{k'},l}) \in R_{q_l}^{2k'},$$

where $s_{j,l}$ is the key of the j-th party to decrypt the level-l ciphertexts. And the decryption is performed by the inner product and modulus, i.e.,

$$\langle \bar{\mathbf{c}}, \bar{\mathbf{s}}_l \rangle = \sum_{t=1}^{k'} \langle \mathbf{c}'_{j_t}, \mathbf{s}_{j_t,l} \rangle = \sum_{\iota=1}^{k} \langle \mathbf{c}_{i_\iota}, \mathbf{s}_{i_\iota,l} \rangle = \langle \mathbf{c}, \mathbf{s}_l \rangle = pe + \mu, \qquad (9)$$

and $\mu = \langle \bar{\mathbf{c}}, \bar{\mathbf{s}}_l \rangle \mod q_l \mod p$. The second equality in (9) holds because other $\mathbf{c}'_j$'s are all 0.

4.3 Homomorphic Operations

In this subsection, we explain how to perform the algorithms MKFHE.EvalAdd and MKFHE.EvalMult on extended ciphertexts when a proper evaluation key is provided. The evaluation key we needed is

$$\tau_{\bar{\mathbf{s}}'_l \to \bar{\mathbf{s}}_{l-1}} = \{\mathcal{K}_{t,\varsigma}\}_{t=1,\dots,\beta_l; \varsigma=1,\dots,4k^2} \qquad (10)$$

for $\bar{\mathbf{s}}'_l = \bar{\mathbf{s}}_l \otimes \bar{\mathbf{s}}_l$ and $\mathcal{K}_{t,\varsigma} \in R_{q_l}^{2k}$ such that $\langle \mathcal{K}_{t,\varsigma}, \bar{\mathbf{s}}_{l-1} \rangle = pe_{t,\varsigma} + 2^{t-1}\bar{\mathbf{s}}'_l[\varsigma] \in R_{q_l}$ and the canonical norm of $e_{t,\varsigma}$ is small.

MKFHE.EvalAdd$(evk_S, \bar{\mathbf{c}}_1, \bar{\mathbf{c}}_2)$: Take two (extended) ciphertexts $\bar{\mathbf{c}}_1, \bar{\mathbf{c}}_2 \in R_{q_l}^{2k}$ at the same level-l under the same $\bar{\mathbf{s}}_l$ as inputs (If needed, use SwitchKey and ModulusSwitch to make it so). First, compute $\bar{\mathbf{c}}'_3 \leftarrow \bar{\mathbf{c}}_1 + \bar{\mathbf{c}}_2 \mod q_l$ under the secret key $\bar{\mathbf{s}}_l \in R_{q_l}^{2k}$. Second, use SwitchKey$(\bar{\mathbf{c}}'_3, \tau_{\bar{\mathbf{s}}'_l \to \bar{\mathbf{s}}_{l-1}}, q_l)$ to generate ciphertext $\bar{\mathbf{c}}''_3$ under the secret key $\bar{\mathbf{s}}_{l-1}$ ($\bar{\mathbf{s}}'_l$'s coefficients include all of $\bar{\mathbf{s}}_l$'s since $\bar{\mathbf{s}}'_l = \bar{\mathbf{s}}_l \otimes \bar{\mathbf{s}}_l$ and $\bar{\mathbf{s}}_l$'s first coefficient is 1). Third, compute $\bar{\mathbf{c}}_3 = \text{ModulusSwitch}(\bar{\mathbf{c}}''_3, l)$.

MKFHE.EvalMult$(evk_S, \bar{\mathbf{c}}_1, \bar{\mathbf{c}}_2)$: Take two (extended) ciphertexts $\bar{\mathbf{c}}_1, \bar{\mathbf{c}}_2 \in R_{q_l}^{2k}$ at the same level-l under the same $\bar{\mathbf{s}}_l$. (If needed, use SwitchKey and ModulusSwitch to make it so). First, compute $\bar{\mathbf{c}}'_3 \leftarrow \bar{\mathbf{c}}_1 \otimes \bar{\mathbf{c}}_2 \mod q_l$ under the secret key $\bar{\mathbf{s}}_l \in R_{q_l}^{2k}$. Second, use SwitchKey$(\bar{\mathbf{c}}'_3, \tau_{\bar{\mathbf{s}}'_l \to \bar{\mathbf{s}}_{l-1}}, q_l)$ to generate a ciphertext $\bar{\mathbf{c}}''_3$ under the secret key $\bar{\mathbf{s}}'_l = \bar{\mathbf{s}}_l \otimes \bar{\mathbf{s}}_l$. Third, compute $\bar{\mathbf{c}}_3 = \text{ModulusSwitch}(\bar{\mathbf{c}}''_3, l)$.

4.4 Evaluation Key Generation

In this subsection, we detail the evaluation key generation algorithm EVKGen, which inputs the public keys of involved parties and outputs the extended BGV evaluation key as (10). Remind that all parties share L common random public matrices $\mathbf{a}_l \in R_{q_l}^{2\beta_l}$ for $l = L, \dots, 0$ and $\beta_l = \lfloor \log q_l \rfloor + 1$. The evaluation key generation material em_j for the jth party consists of all the $\Phi_{i,l,j}$, $\Psi_{i,l,j}$, $\mathbf{F}_{i,l,j}$ and $\mathbf{F}'_{i,l,j}$ for $l = L, \dots, 0$ and $i = 1, \dots, 2\beta_l$.

MKFHE.EVKGen(em_S, pk_S). Notice that S contains k elements, and em_S consists of a collection of evaluation key generation materials $\{em_{j_1}, \dots, em_{j_k}\}$ and the public keys $\{pk_{j_1}, \dots, pk_{j_k}\}$ belonging to parties in S. To generate a level-l evaluation key as (10), compute as follows.

1. For each $j^* \in S$, use the GSW extend algorithm to get larger dimensional ciphertexts under a key $\bar{\mathbf{s}}_{l-1}$

$$\bar{\Phi}_{i,l,j^*} = \mathsf{RGSW.CTExt}\left(\Phi_{i,l,j^*}, pk_S, \mathbf{F}_{i,l,j^*}\right)$$
$$= \mathsf{RGSW.Enc}_{\bar{\mathbf{s}}_{l-1}}\left(\mathsf{Powersof2}(\mathbf{s}_{l,j^*})[i]\right)$$

and

$$\bar{\Psi}_{i,l,j^*} = \mathsf{RGSW.CTExt}\left(\Psi_{i,l,j^*}, pk_S, \mathbf{F}'_{i,l,j^*}\right)$$
$$= \mathsf{RGSW.Enc}_{\bar{\mathbf{s}}_{l-1}}\left(\mathsf{BitDecomp}(\mathbf{s}_{l,j^*})[i]\right)$$

where $\bar{\mathbf{s}}_{l-1} = (\mathbf{s}_{l-1,j_1}|\mathbf{s}_{l-1,j_2}|\cdots|\mathbf{s}_{l-1,j_k}) \in R_{q_l}^{2k}$.

2. Set $\bar{\mathbf{s}}_l = (\mathbf{s}_{l,j_1}|\mathbf{s}_{l,j_2}|\cdots|\mathbf{s}_{l,j_k}) \in R_{q_l}^{2k}$ and $\bar{\mathbf{s}}'_l = \bar{\mathbf{s}}_l \otimes \bar{\mathbf{s}}_l \in R_{q_l}^{4k^2}$. If we can compute $\mathsf{RGSW.Enc}_{\bar{\mathbf{s}}_{l-1}}\left(\bar{\mathbf{s}}_l[\zeta] \cdot \bar{\mathbf{s}}_l[\zeta']\right)$ from $\{\bar{\Phi}_{i,l,j}, \bar{\Psi}_{i,l,j}\}$ and $\{\bar{\Phi}_{i',l,j'}, \bar{\Psi}_{i',l,j'}\}$, where $\bar{\mathbf{s}}_l[\zeta]$ and $\bar{\mathbf{s}}_l[\zeta']$ are any two elements of $\bar{\mathbf{s}}_l$, we have the GSW encryptions of all the elements of $\bar{\mathbf{s}}'_l$ under the key $\bar{\mathbf{s}}_{l-1}$. The details of how to accomplish this task will be explained later.

3. Given the $\mathsf{RGSW.Enc}_{\bar{\mathbf{s}}_{l-1}}\left(\bar{\mathbf{s}}'_l[\zeta]\right)$, compute

$$\tau_{\bar{\mathbf{s}}'_l \to \bar{\mathbf{s}}_{l-1}} = \{\mathcal{K}_{t,\varsigma}\}_{t=1,\ldots,\beta_l;\varsigma=1,\ldots,4k^2} \tag{11}$$

for $\mathcal{K}_\varsigma \in R_{q_l}^{2k}$ such that $\langle \mathcal{K}_{t,\varsigma}, \bar{\mathbf{s}}_{l-1} \rangle = pe_{t,\varsigma} + 2^{t-1}\bar{\mathbf{s}}'_l[\zeta] \in R_{q_l}$. Also, the details will be provided later.

Details of Step 2. Since we need to compute the GSW encryptions of $\bar{\mathbf{s}}[\zeta] \cdot \bar{\mathbf{s}}[\zeta']$, the intuition may be the homomorphic multiplication of the GSW encryptions of $\bar{\mathbf{s}}[\zeta]$ and $\bar{\mathbf{s}}[\zeta'] \in R_q$. But the noise will be out of control in this way according to Lemma 2, because the absolute value of the message $\bar{\mathbf{s}}[\zeta']$ can be larger than $q_l/2$. Alternatively, we know that $\langle \mathsf{Powersof2}(\bar{\mathbf{s}}_l[\zeta]), \mathsf{BitDecomp}(\bar{\mathbf{s}}_l[\zeta']) \rangle = \bar{\mathbf{s}}_l[\zeta] \cdot \bar{\mathbf{s}}_l[\zeta']$. So we homomorphically compute the inner product of the GSW encryptions of $\mathsf{Powersof2}(\bar{\mathbf{s}}_l[\zeta]) = \mathsf{Powersof2}(\mathbf{s}_{l,j}[t])$ and $\mathsf{BitDecomp}(\bar{\mathbf{s}}_l[\zeta']) = \mathsf{BitDecomp}(\mathbf{s}_{l,j'}[t'])$, since $\zeta = 2(j-1) + t$ and $\zeta' = 2(j'-1) + t'$, $1 \le j \le k$, $t = 1$ or 2. Namely we compute

$$\mathsf{RGSW.Enc}_{\bar{\mathbf{s}}_{l-1}}(\bar{\mathbf{s}}_l[\zeta] \cdot \bar{\mathbf{s}}_l[\zeta'])$$

$$= \sum_{\iota=1}^{\beta_l}\left(\mathsf{RGSW.Enc}_{\bar{\mathbf{s}}_{l-1}}\left(\mathsf{Powersof2}(\bar{\mathbf{s}}_l[\zeta])[\iota]\right) \odot \mathsf{RGSW.Enc}_{\bar{\mathbf{s}}_{l-1}}\left(\mathsf{BitDecomp}(\bar{\mathbf{s}}_l[\zeta'])[\iota]\right)\right)$$

$$= \sum_{\iota=1}^{\beta_l}\left(\mathsf{RGSW.Enc}_{\bar{\mathbf{s}}_{l-1}}\left(\mathsf{Powersof2}(\mathbf{s}_{l,j}[t])[\iota]\right) \odot \mathsf{RGSW.Enc}_{\bar{\mathbf{s}}_{l-1}}\left(\mathsf{BitDecomp}(\mathbf{s}_{l,j'}[t'])[\iota]\right)\right)$$

$$= \sum_{\iota=1}^{\beta_l} \bar{\Phi}_{\beta_l(t-1)+\iota,l,j} \odot \bar{\Psi}_{\beta_l(t'-1)+\iota,l,j'}. \tag{12}$$

The l_∞ norm of $\mathsf{BitDecomp}(\mathbf{s}_{l,j'}[t'])[\iota]$ is less than 1. According to Corollary 1, the canonical norm of the noise in the result ciphertext of homomorphic multiplication is bounded by $\tilde{O}(n)B^*$ if the noise in the input ciphertexts is bounded by B^*. So the noise in the final output ciphertext $\mathsf{RGSW.Enc}_{\bar{\mathbf{s}}_{l-1}}(\bar{\mathbf{s}}_l[\zeta] \cdot \bar{\mathbf{s}}_l[\zeta'])$ of (12) is bounded by $\tilde{O}(n\beta_l^2)B^2$ for $\beta_l = \lfloor \log q_l \rfloor + 1$ if the noise in em_j is bounded by B.

Details of Step 3. After above procedure, we have the GSW ciphertext

$$\mathsf{RGSW.Enc}_{\bar{\mathbf{s}}_{l-1}}(\bar{\mathbf{s}}_l'[\zeta]) = \mathbf{C}_\zeta \in R_{q_l}^{2k\beta_l \times 2k}$$

so that

$$\mathbf{C}_\zeta \bar{\mathbf{s}}_{l-1} = p\mathbf{e} + \bar{\mathbf{s}}_l'[\zeta]\mathbf{G}\bar{\mathbf{s}}_{l-1}.$$

Since

$$\mathbf{G} = \left[\mathbf{I}_{2k}, 2\mathbf{I}_{2k}, \ldots, 2^{\lfloor \log q \rfloor}\mathbf{I}_{2k}\right]^T \in R_{q_l}^{2k\beta_l \times 2k},$$

let the $2t \cdot k + 1$th row of $\mathbf{C}_\zeta$ be $\mathbf{c}_{t,\zeta} \in R_{q_l}^{2k}$, so we have

$$\langle \mathbf{c}_{t,\zeta}, \bar{\mathbf{s}}_{l-1} \rangle = pe_{t,\zeta} + 2^{t-1}\bar{\mathbf{s}}_l'[\zeta] \in R_{q_l}$$

for some small $e_{t,\zeta}$. This is the evaluation key as (10).

4.5   Packing Ciphertexts

We show that if the underlying single key BGV ciphertexts is batched, we can get a batched multi-key FHE scheme. The extended ciphertext $\bar{\mathbf{c}} = (\mathbf{c}_1 | \ldots | \mathbf{c}_k) \in R_{q_l}^{2k}$ has $O(n)$ plaintext slots if the plaintext $\mu \in R_p$ has $O(n)$ slots by the Chinese Remainder Theorem. The $O(n)$-fold addition gate and the $O(n)$-fold multiplication gate can be evaluated directly by MKFHE.EvalAdd and MKFHE.EvalMult since the plaintext space is R_p. In the following we provide the homomorphic permutation operation. Given the extended ciphertext $\bar{\mathbf{c}} \in R_{q_l}^{2k}$, we first apply the automorphisms ρ_i as (15) to each ring element of **c**. Since

$$\langle \bar{\mathbf{c}}, \bar{\mathbf{s}}_l \rangle = pe + \mu + k[X]\Phi_m[X],$$

we have the equality

$$\langle \bar{\mathbf{c}}[X^i], \bar{\mathbf{s}}[X^i]_l \rangle = pe[X^i] + \mu[X^i] + k[X^i]\Phi_m[X^i].$$

In view of $\Phi(X)$ divides $\Phi(X^i)$ for $i \in \mathbb{Z}_m^*$, $\bar{\mathbf{c}}[X^i] \in R_{q_l}^{2k}$ is an encryption of $\mu[X^i]$ under the key $\bar{\mathbf{s}}[X^i]$. So the homomorphic permutation is completed by KeySwitching and get an level-$(l-1)$ ciphertext which encrypts $\mu[X^i]$ under the key $\bar{\mathbf{s}}_{l-1}$.

In this case, the evaluation key generation material for the jth party should also include the RGSW.Enc $(s_{l,j}[X^i], pt_{l-1,j})$ for $i \in \mathbb{Z}_m^*$. By applying the GSW ciphertext extension and extracting certain rows, we can successfully compute the evaluation key

$$\tau_{\bar{\mathbf{s}}_l'[X^i] \to \bar{\mathbf{s}}_{l-1}} = \{\mathcal{K}_{t,\zeta}\}_{t=1,\ldots,\beta_l; \zeta=1,\ldots,4k^2}$$

for $\mathcal{K}_\zeta \in R_{q_l}^{2k}$ such that $\langle \mathcal{K}_{t,\zeta}, \bar{\mathbf{s}}_{l-1} \rangle = pe_\zeta + 2^{t-1}\bar{\mathbf{s}}_l'[\zeta][X^i] \in R_{q_l}$.

4.6 Analysis

An analysis of the evaluation key generation procedure is as follows.

Lemma 3. *Assume the noise in each $\Phi_{i,l,j}$ and $\Psi_{i,l,j}$ is bounded by B, and k is the number of the parities involved in the evaluation. The noise of each evaluation key in (11) is bounded by $\tilde{O}(nk)B^2$.*

Proof. For $\beta_l = \lfloor \log q_l \rfloor + 1$, if the noise in each $\Phi_{i,l,j}$ and $\Psi_{i,l,j}$ is bounded by B, the noise in each $\bar{\Phi}_{i,l,j}$ and $\bar{\Psi}_{i,l,j}$ is bounded by $\beta_l B^2$ (canonical norm). According to Corollary 1, the noise in $\bar{\Phi}_{\beta_l(t-1)+\iota,l,j} \odot \bar{\Psi}_{\beta_l(t'-1)+\iota,l,j'}$ is bounded by $O(nk\beta_l)B^2$. So the noise in ciphertext $\mathsf{RGSW.Enc}_{\bar{\mathbf{s}}_{l-1}}(\bar{\mathbf{s}}_l[\zeta] \cdot \bar{\mathbf{s}}_l[\zeta'])$ in (12) is bounded by $O(nk\beta_l^2 B^2)$. The final evaluation key in (10) is just derived from the $\mathsf{RGSW.Enc}_{\bar{\mathbf{s}}_{l-1}}(\bar{\mathbf{s}}_l[\zeta] \cdot \bar{\mathbf{s}}_l[\zeta'])$, so the bound of noise is also $O(nk\beta_l^2)B^2 = \tilde{O}(nk)B^2$. $\qquad\square$

An analysis of the homomorphic operation procedure is as follows.

Definition 6. *We say an (extended) BGV ciphertext $\bar{\mathbf{c}} \in R_{q_l}^{2k}$ $(k \geq 1)$ encrypts $\mu \in R_p$ under a key $\bar{\mathbf{s}}_l \in R_{q_l}^{2k}$ if $\langle \bar{\mathbf{c}}, \bar{\mathbf{s}}_l \rangle \bmod q_l = pe + \mu$.*

Lemma 4. *If the (extended) ciphertexts $\bar{\mathbf{c}}_1, \bar{\mathbf{c}}_2 \in R_{q_l}^{2k}$ $(k \geq 1)$ encrypt $\mu_1, \mu_2 \in R_p$, respectively, under a key $\bar{\mathbf{s}}_l \in R_{q_l}^{2k}$, the extended ciphertext $\bar{\mathbf{c}}_1 + \bar{\mathbf{c}}_2 \in R_{q_l}^{2k}$ encrypts $\mu_1 + \mu_2 \in R_p$ under the decryption key $\bar{\mathbf{s}}_l \in R_{q_l}^{2k}$.*

Lemma 5. *If the (extended) ciphertexts $\bar{\mathbf{c}}_1, \bar{\mathbf{c}}_2 \in R_{q_l}^{2k}$ $(k \geq 1)$ encrypt $\mu_1, \mu_2 \in R_p$, respectively, under the decryption key $\bar{\mathbf{s}}_l \in R_{q_l}^{2k}$, the extended ciphertext $\bar{\mathbf{c}}_1 \otimes \bar{\mathbf{c}}_2 \in R_{q_l}^{4k^2}$ encrypts the $\mu_1 \cdot \mu_2 \in R_p$ under the key $\bar{\mathbf{s}}_l' = \bar{\mathbf{s}}_l \otimes \bar{\mathbf{s}}_l \in R_{q_l}^{4k^2}$. Moreover, given the evaluation key as (10) where the canonical norm of $e_{t,\zeta}$ is bounded by B, we can use $\mathsf{SwitchKey}(\tau_{\bar{\mathbf{s}}_l' \to \bar{\mathbf{s}}_{l-1}}, \bar{\mathbf{c}}_1 \otimes \bar{\mathbf{c}}_2)$ to get $\bar{\mathbf{c}}^* \in R_{q_l}^{2k}$ which encrypts $\mu_1 \cdot \mu_2 \in \mathbb{Z}_p$ under the key $\bar{\mathbf{s}}_{l-1} \in R_{q_l}^{2k}$ with the noise bounded by $O(k^2\beta_l) \cdot B$. Here*

$$\bar{\mathbf{s}}_{l-1} = (\mathbf{s}_{l-1,j_1} | \mathbf{s}_{l-1,j_2} | \cdots | \mathbf{s}_{l-1,j_k}) \in R_{q_l}^{2k}, \tag{13}$$

where $\mathbf{s}_{l-1,j}$ is the key of the jth party to decrypt level-$(l-1)$ ciphertexts and the first entry of $\mathbf{s}_{l-1,j}$ is 1.

Assuming the noise in the public key pt_j and the evaluation key generation material em_j is bounded by B, the noise in the evaluation key is bounded by $\tilde{O}(kn) \cdot B$ according to Lemma 3. If the level-l ciphertexts have a noise bounded by B_l, the ciphertexts after homomorphic operations and before modulus switching have a noise bounded by $B_l^2 + \tilde{O}(k^3 n) \cdot B$ by Lemma 5. Finally, we apply the Scale function. The noise is now at most

$$B_{l-1} = \frac{q_{l-1}}{q_l} \left(B_l^2 + \tilde{O}(k^3 n) \cdot B^2 \right) + \eta_{\mathsf{Scale},l}$$

where $\eta_{\mathsf{Scale},l}$ is an additive term. Let B_l be bounded by B_{max} for all l. Also we let $B_{max} \geq 2\left(\tilde{O}\left(K^3 n\right) \cdot B^2 + \eta_{\mathsf{Scale},l}\right)$ for all l and the upper bound of the parties' number K, and $q_l/q_{l-1} \geq 2 \cdot B_{max}$ for all l. Then we have

$$B_{l-1} = \frac{q_{l-1}}{q_l}\left(B_l^2 + \tilde{O}(k^3 n) \cdot B^2\right) + \eta_{\mathsf{Scale},l}$$

$$\leq \frac{q_{l-1}}{q_l}B_{max}^2 + \tilde{O}(k^3 n) \cdot B^2 + \eta_{\mathsf{Scale},l}$$

$$\leq \frac{1}{2 \cdot B_{max}}B_{max}^2 + \frac{1}{2}B_{max}$$

$$\leq B_{max}.$$

Therefore, it is enough to set B_{max} as $poly(n, K)$ and the largest modulus q_L as $poly(n, K)^L$. For approximation factors of the presumed hardness, our scheme is $poly(n, K)^L$ due to the above analysis. So our scheme can similarly bootstrap as [BGV12].

4.7   Parameters and Comparisons

The comparisons of main properties of various schemes are provided in Tables 1, 2 and 3. To ensure security, we can set the dimension of the underlying (ring-) LWE problem as $n = O(\lambda \log q_L) = \tilde{O}(\lambda L)$ for our scheme and $n = O(\lambda)$ for previous schemes, where λ is the security parameter.

Comparison with [LATV12]. The first advantage over [LATV12] is that the security of our scheme is based on the LWE assumption or the ring-LWE assumption which is currently supported by a worst-case hardness theorem, but not on a somewhat non-standard assumption on polynomial rings such as the decisional small polynomial ratio (DSPR) assumption. The second advantage is that our construction admits a threshold decryption protocol, therefore can obtain a 2-round MPC, while only a "on-the-fly" MPC can be obtained from [LATV12]. Moreover, when [LATV12] is modified to avoid the recent subexponential attacks on the NTRU problem, our scheme still holds some advantages in efficiency. In fact, the attacks [ABD16, MSZ16, CJL16] have complexity $2^{\tilde{O}(\sqrt{n}/\log q)}$, where n is the degree of the ring, and q is the largest modulus in the modulus chain. To get security against attacks running in time 2^λ, we need $\log q > K \cdot L$ to support noise growth and $n > (\lambda K L)^2$ to thwart the attacks. This gives public key of size $\lambda^2 K^4 L^5$ and ciphertext of size $\lambda^2 K^3 L^3$ for [LATV12], while our ring-LWE based scheme has public key of size $\lambda^2 L^6$ and ciphertext of size $\lambda k L^2$.

Comparison with [PS16] *and* [BP16]. For approximation factors of the presumed hardness, our scheme is $poly(K, n)^L$ due to the above analysis, while [PS16] is $poly(K, n, L)^{K+L}$ and [BP16] is $poly(K, n)$. Comparing to [BP16], our scheme needs to take larger dimensions to compensate for larger approximation factors when L is large. But thanks to the ring element plaintext space and the

SIMD operations, our construction has much better amortized per-bit timing. Moreover, when considering the threshold decryption protocol, because of the Smudging Lemma, [PS16] and [BP16] also need exponential large modulus/error rate in λ and K as well as our scheme. In this case, [PS16] and [BP16] do not own an advantage in hardness assumptions when constructing a 2-round MPC protocol.

Table 1. Main properties comparisons. k denotes the actual number of parties involved in the evaluation, with a designed bound of K in [PS16]. L denotes the circuit depth that the scheme is designed to homomorphically evaluate.

Scheme	Assumption	Public key	Ciphertext/plaintext	Key hops	Batch
[CM15]	LWE	$\tilde{O}(\lambda^2 L^2)$	$\tilde{O}(k^2 \lambda^2 L^2)$	Single	No
[CM15]	ring-LWE	$\tilde{O}(\lambda L^2)$	$\tilde{O}(k^2 \lambda L^2)$	Single	No
[BP16]	LWE	$\tilde{O}(\lambda^3)$	$\tilde{O}(k\lambda)$	Multiple	No
[PS16] scheme #1	LWE	$\tilde{O}(\lambda(K+L)^2)$	$\tilde{O}(k\lambda^3(K+L)^4)$	Multiple	No
[PS16] scheme #2	LWE/KDM	$\tilde{O}(\lambda^4(K+L)^4)$	$\tilde{O}(k^2\lambda^2(K+L)^2)$	Multiple	No
Our scheme	LWE	$\tilde{O}(\lambda^3 L^7)$	$\tilde{O}(k\lambda L)$	Multiple	No
Our scheme	ring-LWE	$\tilde{O}(\lambda^2 L^6)$	$\tilde{O}(kL)$	Multiple	Yes

Table 2. Complexity of party extension. The meanings of the symbols are as same as Table 1. $t(\geq k)$ denotes the number of involved ciphertexts in an evaluation. The ciphertexts extension in [BP16] denotes the evluation of the circuit $\mathcal{C}(x,y) = \mathsf{NAND}\,(\mathsf{Dec}_x(c_1), \mathsf{Dec}_y(c_2))$, and the evaluation key generation is to generate the extended refresh key. The matrix multiplication is performed by the algorithm in [WV12], which has complexity of $O(n^{2.37})$ for n dimensional square matrices. It is hard to give an exact complexity for multiplication of rectangular matrices with the algorithm in [WV12], so we just provide the upper bound of the complexity by the naive algorithm.

Scheme	Assumption	Approximate factor	Ciphertexts extension	Evaluation key generation
[CM15]	LWE	$poly(K, \lambda)^L$	$t \cdot \tilde{O}(k\lambda^{4.37}L^{4.37})$	***
[CM15]	ring-LWE	$poly(K, \lambda)^L$	$t \cdot \tilde{O}(k\lambda L)$	***
[BP16]	LWE	$poly(K, \lambda)$	$\tilde{O}(k^2\lambda^4)$	$\tilde{O}(k\lambda^{4.37})$
[PS16] scheme #1	LWE	$poly(K, \lambda, L)^{K+L}$	$< t \cdot \tilde{O}(k^2\lambda^4(K+L)^4)$	***
[PS16] scheme #2	LWE/KDM	$poly(K, \lambda, L)^{K+L}$	$< t \cdot \tilde{O}(k^2\lambda^5(K+L)^4)$	***
Our scheme	LWE	$poly(K, \lambda, L)^L$	$\tilde{O}(1)$	$\tilde{O}(k^{4.37}\lambda^{4.37}L^{7.37})$
Our scheme	ring-LWE	$poly(K, \lambda, L)^L$	$\tilde{O}(1)$	$\tilde{O}(k^3\lambda^3 L^6)$

5   Threshold Decryption and Two Round MPC

We now show how to implement a threshold decryption for the MKFHE construction presented in the previous section, hence a 2-round MPC protocol can be constructed according to the result of [MW16].

Table 3. Complexity of evaluation. The meanings of the symbols are as same as Tables 1 and 2. Also we just provide the complexity of the naive algorithm as the upper bound of rectangular matrix multiplication complexity.

Scheme	Assumption	Per gate complexity	Overhead
[CM15]	LWE	$\tilde{O}(k^{2.37}\lambda^{2.37}L^{2.37})$	$\tilde{O}(k^{2.37}\lambda^{2.37}L^{3.37})$
[CM15]	ring-LWE	$\tilde{O}(k^3\lambda L^2)$	$\tilde{O}(k^3\lambda L^2)$
[BP16]	LWE	$\tilde{O}(k^2\lambda^4)$	$\tilde{O}(k^2\lambda^4)$
[PS16] scheme #1	LWE	$< \tilde{O}(k^2\lambda^5(K+L)^7)$	$< \tilde{O}(k^2\lambda^5(K+L)^7)$
[PS16] scheme #2	LWE/KDM	$\tilde{O}(k^{2.37}\lambda^{2.37}(K+L)^{2.37})$	$\tilde{O}(k^{2.37}\lambda^{2.37}(K+L)^{2.37})$
Our scheme	LWE	$\tilde{O}(k^3\lambda^3L^5)$	$\tilde{O}(k^3\lambda^3L^5)$
Our scheme	ring-LWE	$\tilde{O}(k^2\lambda L^3)$	$\tilde{O}(k^2L^2)$

5.1 Definitions

Definition 7 [MW16]. *A Threshold multi-key FHE scheme (TMKFHE) is a MKFHE scheme with two additional algorithms MFHE.PartDec, MFHE.FinDec described as follows:*

- $\rho_i \leftarrow$ *MFHE.PartDec$(ct, (pk_1, \ldots, pk_K), i, sk_i)$: On input an expanded ciphertext under a sequence of K keys and the i-th secret key, output a partial decryption ρ_i.*
- $\mu \leftarrow$ *MFHE.FinDec$(\rho_1, \ldots, \rho_K)$: On input K partial decryption, output the plaintext μ.*

Along with the properties of multi-key FHE we require the scheme to satisfy the following properties.

Correctness. The following holds with probability 1:

$$\text{MKFHE.FinDec}(\rho_1, \ldots, \rho_N) = \mathcal{C}(\mu_1, \ldots, \mu_h)$$

where $\{\rho_i \leftarrow \text{MKFHE.PartDec}(ct, (pk_1, \ldots, pk_K), i, sk_i)\}_{i \in [K]}$ are the partial decryptions and ct is the final output ciphertext by the evaluation algorithm for the circuit $\mathcal{C}$.

Simulatability. There exists a PPT simulator $\mathcal{S}^{thr}$ which, on input index $i \in [K]$, all but the i-th keys $\{sk_j\}_{j \in [K]/\{i\}}$, the evaluated ciphertext ct and the output message $\mu := \mathcal{C}(\mu_1, \ldots, \mu_h)$, produces a simulated partial decryption $\rho_i' \leftarrow \mathcal{S}^{thr}(\mu, ct, i, \{sk_j\}_{j \in [K]/\{i\}})$ such that

$$\rho_i \approx \rho_i'$$

where $\rho_i \leftarrow \text{MFHE.PartDec}(ct, (pk_1, \ldots, pk_N), i, sk_i)$. Note that the randomness is only over the random coins of the simulator and the MFHE.PartDec procedure, and all other values are assumed to be fixed (and known).

Theorem 2 [MW16]. *Given any threshold multi-key fully homomorphic scheme defined as above, one can construct a two-round MPC protocol for any circuit which achieves honest-but-curious security in the CRS model. Additionally assuming the existence of NIZKs, then one can construct a two-round MPC protocol for any circuit which achieves fully malicious security in the UC framework in the CRS model.*

5.2 Construction

We now show how to implement a threshold decryption for the MKFHE construction presented in the previous section. Since Smudging Lemma 1 is involved to ensure the simulatability, we should choose the modulus q_L as large as $2^{O(K,\lambda,L)}$, which implies the approximate factor for the underlying problem to be exponentially large. Note that the same problem exists in [MW16] as well.

MKFHE.PartDec$(\bar{c}, (pk_1, \ldots, pk_k), i, sk_i)$: On input an expanded ciphertext $\bar{c} \in R_q^{2k}$ under a sequence of keys $(pk_1, \ldots, pk_k)$ and the ith secret key at level-l $\mathbf{s}_{l,i} \in R_q^2$, do the following:

- Parse $\bar{c}$ as a concatenation of k sub-vectors $\mathbf{c}_i \in R_q^2$ such that $\bar{c} = (\mathbf{c}_1 | \ldots | \mathbf{c}_k)$.
- Then compute $\gamma_i = \langle \mathbf{s}_i, \mathbf{c}_i \rangle \in R_q$ and output $\rho_i = \gamma_i + e_i^{sm} \in R_q$, where each coefficient of the random "smudging noise" e_i^{sm} is uniformly sampled from $[-B_{smdg}^{dec}, B_{smdg}^{dec}]$ for $B_{smdg}^{dec} = 2^\lambda B_{max}$ and $B_{max} = \tilde{O}(\lambda K)$.

MFHE:FinDec$(p_1, \ldots, p_k)$: Given $\rho_1, \ldots, \rho_k$, compute the sum $\rho := \sum_{i=1}^k \rho_i$. Output $\mu := \rho \mod p$.

5.3 Correctness and Simulation Security

Theorem 3. *The above threshold decryption procedures for MKFHE satisfy the correctness and the (statistical) simulation security.*

Correctness. The entire scheme is the same as MKFHE except the decryption. If $\mathcal{C}$ is an evaluated ciphertext encrypting a bit μ and the secret keys are $\bar{\mathbf{s}}_l = (s_{l,1}, \ldots, s_{l,k})$, by the correctness analysis of the non-threshold MKFHE, we have

$$\langle \bar{\mathbf{s}}_l, \bar{c} \rangle = \sum_{i \in [k]} \langle \mathbf{s}_{l,i}, \mathbf{c}_i \rangle = \mu + pe,$$

where $\|e\|_\infty \leq K \cdot B_0$. Therefore, if the partial decryptions ρ_i are computed as above, we have

$$\sum_{i \in [k]} \rho_i = \sum_{i \in [k]} \gamma_i + p \sum_{i \in [k]} e_i^{sm}$$

$$= \sum_{i \in [k]} \langle \mathbf{s}_{l,i}, \mathbf{c}_i \rangle + pe^{sm} \tag{14}$$

$$= \mu + pe + pe^{sm},$$

where $e^{sm} = \sum_{i \in [k]} e_i^{sm}$ has norm $\|e^{sm}\|_\infty \leq K \cdot B_{smdg}^{dec} \leq K \cdot 2^{O(\lambda)} B_{max}$ and e has norm $\|e\|_\infty \leq B_{max}$. If we set $q_0 = 4K \cdot 2^\lambda B_{max}$, then $\|e_0 + e_{sm}\| < q/4$ and the correctness holds immediately.

Simulatability. The simulator $\mathcal{S}^{thr} \left(\mu, \hat{\mathbf{c}}, i, \{s_{l,j}\}_{j \in [k]/\{i\}} \right)$ takes as inputs the secrets keys $\{s_{l,j}\}_{j \in [k]/\{i\}}$, the evaluated ciphertext $\hat{\mathbf{c}} \in R_q^{2k}$ and the output value $\mu = \mathcal{C}(\mu_1, \ldots, \mu_k)$ encrypted in $\hat{\mathbf{c}}$. It outputs the simulated partial decryption as

$$\rho_i' = \mu + p e_i^{sm} - p \sum_{i \neq j} \gamma_i$$

for $e^{sm} \in [-B_{smdg}^{dec}, B_{smdg}^{dec}]$ where $\gamma_i = \langle \mathbf{s}_{l,i}, \mathbf{c}_i \rangle$. To see the indistinguishability, note that if $\rho_i = \gamma_i + e_i^{sm}$ is the real partial decryption then according to (14)

$$\rho_i = \mu + pe + pe_i^{sm} - p \sum_{i \neq j} \gamma_i.$$

The difference between the real value ρ_i and the simulated value ρ_i' is the noise e of norm $\|e\|_\infty \leq B_{max}$. By Lemma 1, the distributions of e_i^{sm} and $e_i^{sm} + e$ are statistically close since each coefficient of e_i^{sm} is uniformly sampled from $[-B_{smdg}^{dec}, B_{smdg}^{dec}]$ where $B_{smdg}^{dec} = 2^\lambda B_{max}$, so that $B_{smdg}^{dec}/\|e\|_\infty \geq 2^\lambda$. Therefore, the simulated partial decryption and the real one are statistically indistinguishable.

6   Conclusion

In this paper, we show the multi-hop multi-key FHE can be achieved from the BGV scheme. Therefore, the scheme inherits the advantages of the BGV scheme, for example, it can encrypt a ring element as the plaintext and support the CRT-based packed ciphertexts technique. Moreover, the complexity of the ciphertext extension procedure in out scheme is dependent only on the number of involved secret keys but not on the number of ciphertexts.

Acknowledgement. We would like to thank Jiang Zhang and Qiang Tang for thoughtful discussions. Also we would like to thank the anonymous reviewers for their valuable comments. The work is supported by the National Key Research and Development Program of China (Nos. 2017YFB0802005, 2017YFB0802504) the National Natural Science Foundation of China (No. U1536205) and the National Basic Research Program of China (No. 2013CB338003).

A   The BGV Cryptosystem

In this section, we revisit the BGV scheme from [BGV12]. As explained in the introduction, our MKFHE is based on the BGV FHE scheme.

A.1   Modulus Switching

In the BGV LFHE scheme, since the noise term grows with homomorphic operations of the cryptosystem, switching modulus from q_{i+1} to q_i is used to decrease the noise term roughly by the ratio q_{i+1}/q_i.

– ModulusSwitch($\mathbf{c}, i$): The operation takes a ciphertext $\mathbf{c} = (c_0, c_1)$ defined modulo q_i as input, and produces a ciphertext $\mathbf{c}' = (c_0', c_1')$ defined modulus q_{i-1}, such that $[c_0 - z \cdot c_1]_{q_i} \equiv [c_0' - z \cdot c_1']_{q_{i-1}} \pmod{p}$. Then change the level tag from i to $i - 1$.

The Modulus Switching procedure makes use of the function $\mathsf{Scale}(x, q, q')$ that takes an element $x \in R_q$ as input and returns an element $y \in R_{q'}$ such that in coefficient representation it holds that $y \equiv x \pmod{p}$, and y is the closest element to $(q'/q) \cdot x$ that satisfies this mod-p condition for $p \ll q$. The details are available in [BGV12, GHS12c]. Once we have a level-0 ciphertext ct, we can no longer use modulus switching technique to reduce the noise. Then the bootstrapping technique is needed to regain a fresh cipher.

Lemma 6 [BGV12, GHS12c]. *Let $q_i > q_{i-1} > p$ be positive integers satisfying $q_i = q_{i-1} = 1 (\bmod\ p)$. Let c, s be two ring elements over $R = \mathbb{Z}[X]/\Phi_m(X)$ such that*

$$\|c \cdot s\|_{q_i}^{can} < q_i/2 - \frac{q_i}{q_{i-1}} pn \cdot \phi(m) \|s\|^{can},$$

and let $c' = \mathsf{Scale}(c, q_i, q_{i-1}, p)$. Denoting $e = cs \bmod \Phi_m(X)$ and $e' = c's \bmod \Phi_m(X)$ (arithmetic in $\mathbb{Z}[X] = \Phi_m(X)$), it holds that $e \bmod q_{i-1} \bmod p \equiv e' \bmod q_i \bmod p$ in coefficient representation, and

$$\|e'\|_{q_{i-1}}^{can} < \frac{q_{i-1}}{q_i} \cdot \|e\|_{q_i}^{can} + pn \cdot \phi(m) \cdot \|s\|^{can}.$$

A.2   Key Switching

After some homomorphic evaluation operations, we have on our hands not a "normal" ciphertext which is valid relative to a "normal" secret key, but an "extended ciphertext" which is valid with respect to an "extended secret key". Let $\beta = \lfloor \log q \rfloor + 1$. The key switching approach consists of two procedures, i.e.,

– SwitchKeyGen($\mathbf{s}_1 \in R_q^k, \mathbf{s}_2 = (1, -z_2)^T \in R_q^2$): Compute $\bar{\mathbf{s}} = \mathsf{Powersof2}(\mathbf{s}_1) \in R_q^{k\beta}$, sample $k \cdot \beta$ ring-LWE instances $(a_i, a_i z_2 + pe_i), i = 1, \cdots, k\beta$, and output

$$\tau_{\mathbf{s}_1 \to \mathbf{s}_2} := \{\mathcal{K}_i = (a_i z_2 + pe_i + \bar{\mathbf{s}}[i], a_i) \in R_q^2\}_{i=1,\cdots,k\beta}.$$

– SwitchKey($\tau_{\mathbf{s}_1 \to \mathbf{s}_2}, \mathbf{c} \in R_q^k$): Since $\bar{\mathbf{c}} = \mathsf{BitDecomp}(\mathbf{c})$, output

$$\mathbf{c}' = \sum_i \bar{\mathbf{c}}[i] \mathcal{K}_i$$

as the new ciphertext under the secret key $\mathbf{s}_2$. The correctness requires that $\langle \mathcal{K}_i, \mathbf{s}_2 \rangle = pe + \mathsf{Powersof2}(\mathbf{s}_1)[i]$ for a small norm e.

A.3   BGV LFHE Scheme

Following we list the basic algorithms of BGV schemes. See [BGV12, GHS12c] for details. Specifically, the BGV scheme is parameterized by a sequence of decreasing module $q_L \gg q_{L-1} \gg \cdots \gg q_0$, and an "level-$l$ ciphertext" in the scheme is $\mathbf{c} = (c^0, c^1) \in R_{q_l}^2$. Let $\beta_l = \lfloor \log q_l \rfloor + 1$ for $l = L, \ldots, 0$. After each homomorphic operation, modulus q_l at level-l is switched to q_{l-1} at level-$l-1$. Also, the corresponding secret key is switched.

$BGV.KeyGen(1^\lambda, 1^L)$: Given the security parameter λ and L, choose the noise distribution $\chi = \chi(\lambda, L)$ which is a B-bounded distribution over R, L decreasing module $q_L \gg q_{L-1} \gg \cdots \gg q_0$ for each level, and a small integer p coprime with all q_l's. For l from L down to 0, do the following:

1. Choose a vector $z_l \leftarrow \chi$, and set $\mathbf{s}_l := (1, -z_l)^T \in R_{q_l}^2$.
2. Generate ring-LWE instances $pt_l := (b_l = a_l \cdot z_l + pe_l \bmod q_l, a_l) \in R_{q_l}^2$ for $a_l \in R_{q_l}$, set pt_l 'as the level-l public key relative to the secret key $\mathbf{s}_l$.
3. Set $\mathbf{s}_l' = \mathbf{s}_l \otimes \mathbf{s}_l \in R_{q_l}^4$, run $\tau_{\mathbf{s}_l' \to \mathbf{s}_{l-1}} \leftarrow SwitchKeyGen(\mathbf{s}_l', \mathbf{s}_{l-1})$ (omit this step when $l = 0$).

The public key is $pk = \{pt_l\}_{l \in \{L, \ldots, 0\}}$, the evaluation key is $evk = \{\tau_{\mathbf{s}_l' \to \mathbf{s}_{l-1}}\}_{l \in [L]}$ and the secret key is $sk = \{\mathbf{s}_l\}_{l \in \{L, \ldots, 0\}}$.

$BGV.Enc(pk, \mu)$: To encrypt an element $\mu \in R_p$, choose two random elements $r, e \leftarrow \chi$ and output level-L ciphertext $\mathbf{c} = (c^0, c^1) \in R_{q_L}^2$ where

$$c^0 = rb_L + pe + \mu \in R_{q_L} \text{ and } c^1 = ra_L \in R_{q_L}.$$

$BGV.Dec(sk, \mathbf{c}, l)$: Given a level-$l$ ciphertext $\mathbf{c} = (c^0, c^1) \in R_{q_l}^2$, compute

$$\mu = \langle \mathbf{c}_1, \mathbf{s}_l \rangle \bmod q_l \bmod p.$$

$BGV.HomAdd(evk, \mathbf{c}_1, \mathbf{c}_2)$: Take two ciphertexts $\mathbf{c}_1$ and $\mathbf{c}_2$ at the same level-l under the same $\mathbf{s}_l$ as inputs (If needed, use SwitchKey and ModulusSwitch to make it so). First, compute $\mathbf{c}_1 + \mathbf{c}_2 \bmod q_l$ and pad zeros to get $\mathbf{c}_3' \in R_{q_l}^4$ under the key $\mathbf{s}_l' := \mathbf{s}_l \otimes \mathbf{s}_l$. Second, use $SwitchKey(\tau_{\mathbf{s}_l' \to \mathbf{s}_{l-1}}, \mathbf{c}_3')$ to generate a ciphertext $\bar{\mathbf{c}}_3$ under the secret key $\mathbf{s}_{l-1}$ ($\mathbf{s}_l'$'s coefficients include all of $\mathbf{s}_l$s since $\mathbf{s}_l' = \mathbf{s}_l \otimes \mathbf{s}_l$ and $\mathbf{s}_l$'s first coefficient is 1). Third, compute $\mathbf{c}_3 = ModulusSwitch(\bar{\mathbf{c}}_3, l)$.

$BGV.HomMult(evk, \mathbf{c}_1, \mathbf{c}_2)$: Take two ciphertexts $\mathbf{c}_1$ and $\mathbf{c}_2$ at same level-l under the same $\mathbf{s}_l$ as inputs (If needed, use SwitchKey and ModulusSwitch to make it so). First, compute $\tilde{\mathbf{c}}_3 = \mathbf{c}_1 \otimes \mathbf{c}_2$ under the secret key $\mathbf{s}_l' = \mathbf{s}_l \otimes \mathbf{s}_l$. Second, use $SwitchKey(\tilde{\mathbf{c}}_3, \tau_{\mathbf{s}_l' \to \mathbf{s}_{l-1}}, q_l)$ to generate a ciphertext $\mathbf{c}_3'$ under the secret key $\mathbf{s}_{l-1}$. Third, compute $\mathbf{c}_3 = ModulusSwitch(\mathbf{c}_3', l)$.

A.4   Packing Ciphertexts

Let p be a prime integer, coprime to m, and R_p be the localisation of R at p. The polynomial $\Phi_m(X)$ factors modulo p into $k^{(R)}$ irreducible factors, i.e., $\Phi_m(X) \equiv \prod_{i=1}^{k^{(R)}} F_i(X) \pmod{p}$. Each $F_i(X)$ has degree $d^{(R)} = \phi(m)/k^{(R)}$, where $d^{(R)}$ is the multiplicative order of p in $\mathbb{Z}_m^*$. In the packed ciphertext scheme, each of these $k^{(R)}$ factors corresponds to a "plaintext slot", i.e.

$$R_p \cong \mathbb{Z}_p[X]/F_1(X) \times \cdots \times \mathbb{Z}_p[X]/F_{k^{(R)}}(X) \cong (\mathbb{F}_{p^{d^{(R)}}})^{k^{(R)}}.$$

More precisely, we have $k^{(R)} = |\mathbb{Z}_m^* / \langle p \rangle|$ isomorphisms

$$\psi_i : \mathbb{Z}_p[X]/F_i(X) \to \mathbb{F}_{p^{d^{(R)}}}, i = 1, \ldots, k^{(R)},$$

that allow to represent $k^{(R)}$ plaintext elements of $\mathbb{F}_{p^d}$ as a single element in R_p. By the Chinese Remainder Theorem, addition and multiplication correspond to the SIMD operations on the slots, which allows us to process $k^{(R)}$ input values at once.

Beyond addition and multiplications, we can also manipulate elements in R_p using a set of automorphisms on R_p of the form $a(X) \mapsto a(X^j)$, or in more detail

$$\rho_j : R_p \to R_p, \, a(X) + (p, \Phi_m(X)) \mapsto a(X^j) + (p, \Phi_m(X)) \, (j \in \mathbb{Z}_m^*). \quad (15)$$

Actually, the Galois group $\mathcal{G}al(\mathbb{Q}[X]/\Phi_m(X))$ consists of all the transformations $X \mapsto X^i$ for $i \in \mathbb{Z}_m^*$, hence there are exactly $\phi(m)$ of them. Specifically, $\mathcal{G}al(Q[X]/\Phi_m(X))$ contains a subgroup $\mathcal{G} = \{(X \mapsto X^{p^i}) : j = 0, 1, \ldots, d-1\}$ corresponding to the Frobenius automorphisms modulo p. This subgroup does not permute the slots at all, but the quotient group $H = \mathcal{G}al/\mathcal{G}$ does. Clearly, $\mathcal{G}$ has order d and H has order $\phi(m)/d = k$. We can homomorphically evaluate these automorphisms by applying them to the batched BGV ciphertext elements and then preforming a "key switching". As discussed in [GHS12b], the combinations of automorphisms in H can induce any permutations on the plaintext slots.

Theorem 4 [GHS12b]. *Let l, t, ω and W be parameters. Then any t-gate fan-in-2 arithmetic circuit C with average width ω and maximum width W, can be evaluated using a network of $O\left(\lceil t/l \rceil \cdot \lceil l/w \rceil \cdot \log W \cdot poly \log(l)\right)$ l-fold gates of types l-Add, l-Mult, and l-Permute. The depth of this network of l-fold gates is at most $O(\log W)$ times that of the original circuit C, and the description of the network can be computed in time $\tilde{O}(t)$ given the description of C.*

Using this theorem, Gentry et al. showed, as the batched BGV scheme with bootstrapping [BGV12], the total overhead is polylogarithmic in the security parameter.

References

[ABD16] Albrecht, M., Bai, S., Ducas, L.: A subfield lattice attack on overstretched NTRU assumptions. In: Robshaw, M., Katz, J. (eds.) CRYPTO 2016. LNCS, vol. 9814, pp. 153–178. Springer, Heidelberg (2016). doi:10.1007/978-3-662-53018-4_6

[AJL+12] Asharov, G., Jain, A., López-Alt, A., Tromer, E., Vaikuntanathan, V., Wichs, D.: Multiparty computation with low communication, computation and interaction via threshold FHE. In: Pointcheval, D., Johansson, T. (eds.) EUROCRYPT 2012. LNCS, vol. 7237, pp. 483–501. Springer, Heidelberg (2012). doi:10.1007/978-3-642-29011-4_29

[ASP13] Alperin-Sheriff, J., Peikert, C.: Practical bootstrapping in quasilinear time. In: Canetti, R., Garay, J.A. (eds.) CRYPTO 2013. LNCS, vol. 8042, pp. 1–20. Springer, Heidelberg (2013). doi:10.1007/978-3-642-40041-4_1

[ASP14] Alperin-Sheriff, J., Peikert, C.: Faster bootstrapping with polynomial error. In: Garay, J.A., Gennaro, R. (eds.) CRYPTO 2014. LNCS, vol. 8616, pp. 297–314. Springer, Heidelberg (2014). doi:10.1007/978-3-662-44371-2_17

[BGH13] Brakerski, Z., Gentry, C., Halevi, S.: Packed ciphertexts in LWE-based homomorphic encryption. In: Kurosawa, K., Hanaoka, G. (eds.) PKC 2013. LNCS, vol. 7778, pp. 1–13. Springer, Heidelberg (2013). doi:10.1007/978-3-642-36362-7_1

[BGV12] Brakerski, Z., Gentry, C., Vaikuntanathan, V.: (Leveled) fully homomorphic encryption without bootstrapping. In: Proceedings of the 3rd Innovations in Theoretical Computer Science Conference, pp. 309–325. ACM (2012)

[BP16] Brakerski, Z., Perlman, R.: Lattice-based fully dynamic multi-key FHE with short ciphertexts. In: Robshaw, M., Katz, J. (eds.) CRYPTO 2016. LNCS, vol. 9814, pp. 190–213. Springer, Heidelberg (2016). doi:10.1007/978-3-662-53018-4_8

[Bra12] Brakerski, Z.: Fully homomorphic encryption without modulus switching from classical GapSVP. In: Safavi-Naini, R., Canetti, R. (eds.) CRYPTO 2012. LNCS, vol. 7417, pp. 868–886. Springer, Heidelberg (2012). doi:10.1007/978-3-642-32009-5_50

[BV11a] Brakerski, Z., Vaikuntanathan, V.: Efficient fully homomorphic encryption from (standard) LWE. In: 52 Annual IEEE Symposium on Foundations of Computer Science, vol. 2011, no. 2, pp. 97–106 (2011)

[BV11b] Brakerski, Z., Vaikuntanathan, V.: Fully homomorphic encryption from ring-LWE and security for key dependent messages. In: Rogaway, P. (ed.) CRYPTO 2011. LNCS, vol. 6841, pp. 505–524. Springer, Heidelberg (2011). doi:10.1007/978-3-642-22792-9_29

[BV14] Brakerski, Z., Vaikuntanathan, V.: Lattice-based FHE as secure as PKE. In: Proceedings of the 5th Conference on Innovations in Theoretical Computer Science, pp. 1–12. ACM (2014)

[CJL16] Cheon, J.H., Jeong, J., Lee, C.: An algorithm for NTRU problems, cryptanalysis of the GGH multilinear map without a low-level encoding of zero. LMS J. Comput. Math. 19(A), 255–266 (2016)

[CM15] Clear, M., McGoldrick, C.: Multi-identity and multi-key leveled FHE from learning with errors. In: Gennaro, R., Robshaw, M. (eds.) CRYPTO 2015. LNCS, vol. 9216, pp. 630–656. Springer, Heidelberg (2015). doi:10.1007/978-3-662-48000-7_31

[CP16]   Crockett, E., Peikert, C.: Λολ: functional lattice cryptography. In: Proceedings of the 2016 ACM SIGSAC Conference on Computer and Communications Security, pp. 993–1005 (2016)

[DHS16]   Doröz, Y., Hu, Y., Sunar, B.: Homomorphic AES evaluation using the modified LTV scheme. Des. Codes Crypt. **80**(2), 333–358 (2016)

[DM15]   Ducas, L., Micciancio, D.: FHEW: bootstrapping homomorphic encryption in less than a second. In: Oswald, E., Fischlin, M. (eds.) EUROCRYPT 2015. LNCS, vol. 9056, pp. 617–640. Springer, Heidelberg (2015). doi:10.1007/978-3-662-46800-5_24

[DPSZ12] Damgård, I., Pastro, V., Smart, N., Zakarias, S.: Multiparty computation from somewhat homomorphic encryption. In: Safavi-Naini, R., Canetti, R. (eds.) CRYPTO 2012. LNCS, vol. 7417, pp. 643–662. Springer, Heidelberg (2012). doi:10.1007/978-3-642-32009-5_38

[Gen09]   Gentry, C.: Fully homomorphic encryption using ideal lattices. In: STOC, vol. 9, pp. 169–178 (2009)

[GHPS13] Gentry, C., Halevi, S., Peikert, C., Smart, N.P.: Field switching in BGV-style homomorphic encryption. J. Comput. Secur. **21**(5), 663–684 (2013)

[GHS12a] Gentry, C., Halevi, S., Smart, N.P.: Better bootstrapping in fully homomorphic encryption. In: Fischlin, M., Buchmann, J., Manulis, M. (eds.) PKC 2012. LNCS, vol. 7293, pp. 1–16. Springer, Heidelberg (2012). doi:10.1007/978-3-642-30057-8_1

[GHS12b] Gentry, C., Halevi, S., Smart, N.P.: Fully homomorphic encryption with polylog overhead. In: Pointcheval, D., Johansson, T. (eds.) EUROCRYPT 2012. LNCS, vol. 7237, pp. 465–482. Springer, Heidelberg (2012). doi:10.1007/978-3-642-29011-4_28

[GHS12c] Gentry, C., Halevi, S., Smart, N.P.: Homomorphic evaluation of the AES circuit. In: Safavi-Naini, R., Canetti, R. (eds.) CRYPTO 2012. LNCS, vol. 7417, pp. 850–867. Springer, Heidelberg (2012). doi:10.1007/978-3-642-32009-5_49

[GSW13]   Gentry, C., Sahai, A., Waters, B.: Homomorphic encryption from learning with errors: conceptually-simpler, asymptotically-faster, attribute-based. In: Canetti, R., Garay, J.A. (eds.) CRYPTO 2013. LNCS, vol. 8042, pp. 75–92. Springer, Heidelberg (2013). doi:10.1007/978-3-642-40041-4_5

[HAO15]   Hiromasa, R., Abe, M., Okamoto, T.: Packing messages and optimizing bootstrapping in GSW-FHE. In: Katz, J. (ed.) PKC 2015. LNCS, vol. 9020, pp. 699–715. Springer, Heidelberg (2015). doi:10.1007/978-3-662-46447-2_31

[HPS98]   Hoffstein, J., Pipher, J., Silverman, J.H.: NTRU: a ring-based public key cryptosystem. In: Buhler, J.P. (ed.) ANTS 1998. LNCS, vol. 1423, pp. 267–288. Springer, Heidelberg (1998). doi:10.1007/BFb0054868

[HS14]   Halevi, S., Shoup, V.: Algorithms in HElib. In: Garay, J.A., Gennaro, R. (eds.) CRYPTO 2014. LNCS, vol. 8616, pp. 554–571. Springer, Heidelberg (2014). doi:10.1007/978-3-662-44371-2_31

[HS15]   Halevi, S., Shoup, V.: Bootstrapping for HElib. In: Oswald, E., Fischlin, M. (eds.) EUROCRYPT 2015. LNCS, vol. 9056, pp. 641–670. Springer, Heidelberg (2015). doi:10.1007/978-3-662-46800-5_25

[LATV12] López-Alt, A., Tromer, E., Vaikuntanathan, V.: On-the-fly multiparty computation on the cloud via multikey fully homomorphic encryption. In: Proceedings of the Forty-Fourth Annual ACM Symposium on Theory of Computing, pp. 1219–1234. ACM (2012)

[Lin]   Lindell, Y.: Tutorials on the foundations of cryptography
[LPR13a]   Lyubashevsky, V., Peikert, C., Regev, O.: On ideal lattices and learning
           with errors over rings. J. ACM (JACM) **60**(6), 43 (2013)
[LPR13b]   Lyubashevsky, V., Peikert, C., Regev, O.: A toolkit for ring-LWE cryp-
           tography. In: Johansson, T., Nguyen, P.Q. (eds.) EUROCRYPT 2013.
           LNCS, vol. 7881, pp. 35–54. Springer, Heidelberg (2013). doi:10.1007/
           978-3-642-38348-9_3
[MSZ16]   Miles, E., Sahai, A., Zhandry, M.: Annihilation attacks for multilinear maps:
           cryptanalysis of indistinguishability obfuscation over GGH13. In: Robshaw,
           M., Katz, J. (eds.) CRYPTO 2016. LNCS, vol. 9815, pp. 629–658. Springer,
           Heidelberg (2016). doi:10.1007/978-3-662-53008-5_22
[MW16]   Mukherjee, P., Wichs, D.: Two round multiparty computation via multi-
           key FHE. In: Fischlin, M., Coron, J.-S. (eds.) EUROCRYPT 2016.
           LNCS, vol. 9666, pp. 735–763. Springer, Heidelberg (2016). doi:10.1007/
           978-3-662-49896-5_26
[PS16]   Peikert, C., Shiehian, S.: Multi-key FHE from LWE, revisited. In: Hirt,
           M., Smith, A. (eds.) TCC 2016. LNCS, vol. 9986, pp. 217–238. Springer,
           Heidelberg (2016). doi:10.1007/978-3-662-53644-5_9
[Reg09]   Regev, O.: On lattices, learning with errors, random linear codes, and cryp-
           tography. J. ACM (JACM) **56**(6), 34 (2009)
[SV14]   Smart, N.P., Vercauteren, F.: Fully homomorphic SIMD operations. Des.
           Codes Crypt. **71**(1), 57–81 (2014)
[WV12]   Williams, V.V.: Multiplying matrices faster than Coppersmith-Winograd.
           In: Proceedings of the Annual ACM Symposium on Theory of Computing,
           vol. 129, no. 8, 887–898 (2012)

Database Privacy

Strengthening the Security of Encrypted Databases: Non-transitive JOINs

Ilya Mironov[1], Gil Segev[2(⊠)], and Ido Shahaf[2(⊠)]

[1] Jerusalem, Israel
[2] School of Computer Science and Engineering,
Hebrew University of Jerusalem, 91904 Jerusalem, Israel
{segev,ido.shahaf}@cs.huji.ac.il

Abstract. Database management systems that operate over encrypted data are gaining significant commercial interest. CryptDB is one such notable system supporting a variety SQL queries over encrypted data (Popa et al., SOSP '11). It is a practical system obtained by utilizing a number of encryption schemes, together with a new cryptographic primitive for supporting SQL's join operator.

This new primitive, an *adjustable join scheme*, is an encoding scheme that enables to generate tokens corresponding to any two database columns for computing their join given only their encodings. Popa et al. presented a framework for modeling the security of adjustable join schemes, but it is not completely clear what types of potential adversarial behavior it captures. Most notably, CryptDB's join operator is *transitive*, and this may reveal a significant amount of sensitive information.

In this work we put forward a strong and intuitive notion of security for adjustable join schemes, and argue that it indeed captures the security of such schemes: We introduce, in addition, natural simulation-based and indistinguishability-based notions (capturing the "minimal leakage" of such schemes), and prove that our notion is positioned between their adaptive and non-adaptive variants.

Then, we construct an adjustable join scheme that satisfies our notion of security based on the linear assumption (or on the seemingly stronger matrix-DDH assumption for improved efficiency) in bilinear groups. Instantiating CryptDB with our scheme strengthens its security by providing a *non-transitive join operator*, while increasing the size of CryptDB's encodings from one group element to four group elements based on the linear assumption (or two group elements based on the matrix-DDH assumption), and increasing the running time of the adjustment operation from that of computing one group exponentiation to that of computing four bilinear maps based on the linear assumption (or two bilinear maps based on the matrix-DDH assumption). Most importantly, however, the most critical and frequent operation underlying our scheme is comparison of single group elements as in CryptDB's join scheme.

I. Mironov and G. Segev—Work initiated at Microsoft Research Silicon Valley.

Y. Kalai and L. Reyzin (Eds.): TCC 2017, Part II, LNCS 10678, pp. 631–661, 2017.
https://doi.org/10.1007/978-3-319-70503-3_21

1   Introduction

Database management systems operating over encrypted data are gaining significant commercial interest. CryptDB, designed by Popa et al. [37–40], is one such notable system that supports a variety of SQL queries over encrypted databases. It is a practical system offering a throughput loss of only 26% as compared to MySQL. We refer the reader to CryptDB's project page for the growing list of companies and organizations that have already either adopted CryptDB or designed similar systems directly inspired by CryptDB.[1]

CryptDB operates in a setting that consists of two main parties, a proxy and a server, with the goal of enabling the server to execute SQL queries on encrypted data almost as if it were executing the same queries on the data itself. The only difference is that the operators corresponding to the SQL queries, such as selections, projections, joins, aggregates, and orderings, are performed using possibly modified operators (see, for example, [18,19,23–25,28] and the references therein, as well as our discussion in Sect. 1.3, for additional approaches and systems for executing SQL queries on encrypted data).

Specifically, for our purposes it is sufficient to consider a proxy that holds a secret key sk, and a server that holds a database encrypted using sk. Such a database consists of a number of tables, where each table consists of several data records that are vertically-partitioned into columns. Whenever the proxy would like the server to execute an SQL query, it uses its secret key sk for generating a token allowing the server to execute the given query over the encrypted database. This is realized in CryptDB by utilizing a number of existing encryption schemes, together with a new cryptographic primitive for supporting SQL's join operator (see Fig. 1 for a simplified description of SQL's join operator[2]).

Adjustable join schemes. Supporting SQL's join operator within CryptDB is essentially equivalent to identifying the matching pairs of values for two encrypted columns, and this has motivated Popa et al. to introduce the notion of an *adjustable join scheme*. This is a symmetric-key encoding scheme supporting the following two operations: (1) Given the secret key sk it is possible to generate an encoding $\mathsf{Enc}_{\mathsf{sk}}(m, \mathsf{col})$ of any message m relative to any column label col, and (2) given the secret key sk it is possible to generate a token $\mathsf{TokenGen}_{\mathsf{sk}}(\mathsf{col}, \mathsf{col}')$ enabling to compute the join of any two given columns labeled by col and col′ (we refer the reader to Sect. 3 for the formal definition of such schemes). Popa and Zeldovich initiated the study of adjustable join schemes, and presented the first construction of such a scheme, which they have incorporated into the design of CryptDB.

The security of CryptDB's adjustable join. In terms of functionality, a server that is given an encrypted database and a token for computing the join

---

[1] CryptDB's project page is available at css.csail.mit.edu/cryptdb.

[2] The example described in Fig. 1 considers the *inner* join operator, and we note that all of our contributions in this work equally apply to various other join operators, such as right join, left join, full join, and self join.

of two columns, should be able to identify all pairs of encodings from these two columns that correspond to identical messages. At the same time, in terms of security, we would like the server not to learn any additional information. Generally speaking, this intuitive requirement can be viewed as a specific instantiation of the security requirement underlying private-key two-input functional encryption (e.g., [5,7,21]): Encryption of messages $m_1, \ldots, m_k$ and functional keys corresponding to functions $f_1, \ldots, f_n$ should not reveal any information other than the values $\{f_\ell(m_i, m_j)\}_{i,j \in [k], \ell \in [n]}$.

Popa and Zeldovich [40] formalized a specific notion of security for adjustable join schemes, aiming to capture the above intuitive requirement, and proved that CryptDB's adjustable join scheme indeed satisfies their notion. However, unlike the recently-introduced security notions for private-key functional encryption, it is not completely clear what types of potential adversarial behavior it actually captures.

Most notably, due to efficiency considerations, Popa et al. have chosen to consider a notion of security that does not capture transitivity: For any three columns col_i, col_j and col_k, tokens for computing the joins between col_i and col_k and between col_k and col_j should ideally not allow computing the join between col_i and col_j. Moreover, it is not only that their notion does not capture transitivity, but in fact CryptDB's adjustable join scheme is indeed transitive by design due to efficiency considerations: Given tokens for computing the joins between col_i and col_k and between col_k and col_j, it is easy to compute the join between columns col_i and col_j.

Using our example from Fig. 1, this means that given a token for computing the join between the "Students" and "Terrorists" tables (via their "Name" column), and a token for computing the join between the "Terrorists" and "Firearm Holders" tables (again via their "Name" column), the CryptDB server learns that the "Students" and "Firearm Holders" tables have matching records *which were not included in the results of these two join operations* (those matching records belong to David – who is not a terrorist). This may leak significantly more information than one would expect when executing SQL queries over encrypted databases (specifically, in our example, this leaks the fact that among the non-terrorist students there is a student that has two firearms in his or her possession).

In light of the growing commercial interest in CryptDB and in various other similar systems, this state of affairs suggests that a more in-depth security treatment of adjustable join schemes is required, and raises the concrete goal of strengthening the security of CryptDB's adjustable join scheme. Offering a new trade-off between the security of CryptDB and its efficiency is of significant importance especially given the various recent attacks on CryptDB and other similar systems (see, for example, [22,31,35,41]).

1.1 Our Contributions

In this work we first put forward a fine-grained definitional framework for adjustable join schemes. Then, we design a new adjustable join scheme for

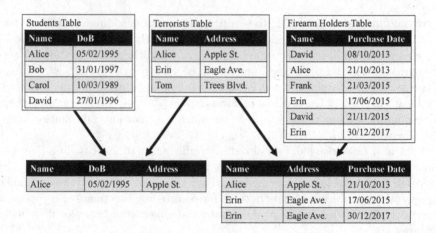

Fig. 1. SQL's join operator takes as input two tables, and one or more column labels, and outputs all records that have matching values with respect to the given column labels. There are different types of join operators, depending on the subset of the data records one would like to select from the two given tables. The above example shows the result of joining the "Students" and "Terrorists" tables via their "Name" column, and joining the "Terrorists" and "Firearm Holders" tables via their "Name" column.

CryptDB that satisfies our strong notions of security, thus offering a new trade-off between the security of CryptDB and its efficiency. In addition, we discusses various extensions of our scheme (e.g., supporting multi-column joins), which can be used for fine-tuning its efficiency, while providing different levels of security, ranging from the security guarantees of CryptDB's join scheme to the stronger security guarantees of our new scheme.

Although our strengthening of CryptDB's security does not directly mitigate the recent attacks on CryptDB (e.g., [35,41]), our new trade-off constitutes a first step towards demonstrating that the security of CryptDB (and, potentially, of other similar systems) can be gradually improved in various aspects. Given the promising applications of such systems and the growing commercial interest in such systems, obtaining a better understanding of such potential trade-offs is an important goal.

We emphasize that an adjustable join scheme is a general and system-independent cryptographic primitive. Although our work is motivated by CryptDB, adjustable join schemes can be used by any database system that would like to support join queries over encrypted data, and not only by CryptDB (see, for example, [18,19,25,28] and the references therein). Moreover, while our specific construction is designed to be compatible with that of CryptDB, our framework for modeling and defining the security of adjustable join schemes is completely system-independent and is rather likely to find additional applications in various other database systems.

Strengthening the definitional framework. We put forward strong and realistic notions of security for adjustable join schemes, identify the relations among them, and their relations to the notion of security suggested by Popa and Zeldovich [40].

Specifically, we first extend the notion of security considered by Popa and Zeldovich (which we denote by 2Partition) that does not capture transitivity due to efficiency considerations, into a new notion (which we denote by 3Partition) that does capture transitivity. At a first glance, our new notion may still seem rather arbitrary, and it is not immediately clear what types of potential adversarial behaviour it actually captures.

Then, we show that our new notion indeed captures the security of adjustable join schemes: We formalize new simulation-based and indistinguishability-based notions of security, capturing the "minimal leakage" of adjustable join schemes, and prove that 3Partition is positioned between their adaptive variants and non-adaptive variants (i.e., we prove that their adaptive variants imply 3Partition, and that 3Partition implies their non-adaptive variants). We refer the reader to Fig. 2 for an illustration of our notions of security and the relations among them, and to Sect. 1.2 for an overview of our new definitional framework.

Constructing a non-transitive adjustable join scheme. We construct an adjustable join scheme that satisfies our strong notions of security based on the linear assumption [4]. Instantiating CryptDB with our scheme strengthens its security by providing a *non-transitive join operator*, at the expense of increasing the size of CryptDB's encodings from one group element to four group elements, and increasing the running time of the adjustment operation from that of computing one group exponentiation to that of computing four bilinear maps. Most importantly, however, our join operation (which is typically much more frequent than the adjust operation) relies on one comparison of single group elements as in CryptDB.

Moreover, by relying on the seemingly stronger matrix-DDH assumption due to Escala et al. [16], we obtain a significant improvement to the efficiency of our scheme while still satisfying our strong notion of security. Specifically, basing our scheme on the matrix-DDH assumption results in increasing the size of CryptDB's encodings from one group element to only *two* group elements, and increasing the running time of the adjustment operation from that of computing one group exponentiation to that of computing only *two* bilinear maps (see Sect. 1.4).

1.2 Overview of Our Contributions

In this section we provide a high-level overview of our contributions. First, we briefly describe the notion of an adjustable join scheme. Then, we discuss the notion of security considered by Popa and Zeldovich [40] for such schemes, and CryptDB's transitive join scheme. Finally, we turn to describe our strengthened definitional framework, and the main technical ideas underlying our new scheme.

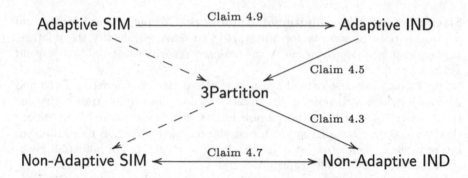

Fig. 2. An illustration of our notions of security for adjustable join schemes. Solid arrows represent our claims, and dashed arrows follow by transitivity.

Adjustable join schemes. As discussed above, an adjustable join scheme [40] is a symmetric-key encoding scheme that enables to generate an encoding $c \leftarrow \mathsf{Enc}_{\mathsf{sk}}(m, \mathsf{col})$ of any message m relative to any column label col, and to generate a pair of tokens $(\tau, \tau') \leftarrow \mathsf{TokenGen}_{\mathsf{sk}}(\mathsf{col}, \mathsf{col}')$ enabling to compute the join of any two given columns labeled by col and col'. The join is computed publicly via an adjustment algorithm Adj with the following guarantee: For any two column labels col and col' with corresponding tokens $(\tau, \tau') \leftarrow \mathsf{TokenGen}_{\mathsf{sk}}(\mathsf{col}, \mathsf{col}')$, and for any two messages m and m', it holds that

$$m = m' \iff \mathsf{Adj}\left(\tau, \mathsf{Enc}_{\mathsf{sk}}\left(m, \mathsf{col}\right)\right) = \mathsf{Adj}\left(\tau', \mathsf{Enc}_{\mathsf{sk}}\left(m', \mathsf{col}'\right)\right).$$

That is, the scheme adjusts each encoding using its corresponding part of the token, and compares the resulting encodings. It should be noted that we consider schemes that may adjust both columns, whereas CryptDB's scheme adjusts only one of the columns. As far as we can tell, adjusting both columns is fully compatible with the design of CryptDB, and allows for more flexibility when designing adjustable join schemes. We refer the reader to Sect. 3.1 for a more detailed description of adjustable join schemes.

The security of CryptDB's join scheme. The adjustable join scheme proposed by Popa and Zeldovich [40], as well as the scheme that we proposed in this work, are based on a deterministic encoding algorithm. Clearly, whenever a deterministic encoding algorithm is used, an unavoidable leakage is the equality pattern within each column. When considering, in addition, the functionality of a join scheme, an additional unavoidable leakage is the equality pattern between each pair of columns for which a join token was provided (and this leakage is inherent due to the functionality of the scheme even if the encoding is randomized). However, CryptDB's join scheme leaks significantly more information than the minimal leakage, and our goal is to avoid any unnecessary leakage (as will be formally captured by our notions of security).

Specifically, the notion of security introduced by Popa and Zeldovich, that we denote by 2Partition, considers an experiment in which an adversary may adaptively define two disjoint sets of columns, which we refer to as a "left" set L and a "right" set R. The adversary is given the ability to compute joins inside L and joins inside R, but it should not be able to compute the join between any column in L and any column in R.

However, this intuitive requirement does not capture transitivity: Assume that there is a certain column col* that does not belong to either L or R, then the ability to compute the join between col* and columns in L, and to compute the join between col* and columns in R, may imply the ability to compute the join between columns in L and columns in R. Moreover, it is not only that 2Partition does not capture transitivity, but in fact the adjustable join scheme of Popa and Zeldovich (that satisfies 2Partition) is indeed transitive due to efficiency considerations (recall our example based on Fig. 1). We refer the reader to Sect. 3.2 for a more detailed discussion of the 2Partition notion and of the adjustable join scheme of Popa and Zeldovich.

Our definitional framework. As our first step, we introduce a new notion of security, denoted 3Partition, which strictly extends 2Partition. Our notion considers a partitioning of the columns into *three* disjoint sets in a manner that enables it to properly model non-transitive joins. Specifically, we consider adversaries that may adaptively define three disjoint sets of columns, which we refer to as a "left" set L, a "right" set R, and a "middle" set M. The adversary is given the ability to compute joins inside L, inside M, and inside R, as well as joins between L and M and between R and M, but it should not be able to compute the join between any column in L and any column in R.

Intuitively, partitioning the columns into three disjoint sets is inherent when attacking an adjustable join scheme. Consider, for example, a natural security notion asking that an adversary should not be able to distinguish encodings of two databases even when given tokens for computing joins (clearly, this only makes sense as long as the actual results of the join operations do not trivially distinguish the two databases). Then, we claim that the difference between the two databases can be gradually divided into small "changes", each of them implicitly defines a partition into three disjoint sets: There is the set of columns that contain this change, the set of columns that are joined with those columns (and are thus limited to not reveal the difference), and the set of all other columns (which are not subject to any restrictions).

At this point one may ask whether partitioning the columns into three disjoint sets is sufficient for capturing the security of adjustable join schemes, or whether we should also consider partitioning the columns into more than three sets. We show that partitioning the columns into three disjoint sets is sufficient, and that 3Partition indeed captures the security of adjustable join schemes: We formalize new simulation-based and indistinguishability-based notions of security, capturing the "minimal leakage" of adjustable join schemes, and prove that 3Partition in positioned between their adaptive variants and non-adaptive variants (recall Fig. 2 for an illustration of our notions of security and the relations among them). We refer the reader to Sect. 4 for a detailed description and analysis of our definitional framework.

Our adjustable join scheme. Our scheme is inspired by that of Popa [37–40]. Their scheme uses a group $\mathbb{G}$ of prime order p that is generated by an element $g \in \mathbb{G}$, and a pseudorandom function for identifying messages and column labels as pseudorandom $\mathbb{Z}_p$ elements. The encoding of a message m for a column col is the group element $g^{a_{\mathsf{col}} \cdot x_m} \in \mathbb{G}$, where a_{col} and x_m are the pseudorandom $\mathbb{Z}_p$ elements corresponding to col and m, respectively. A token for computing the join between columns col_i and col_j is the element $\tau_{i,j} = a_{\mathsf{col}_i} \cdot a_{\mathsf{col}_j}^{-1} \in \mathbb{Z}_p$, and thus it is clear that such tokens enable transitive joins: Given the tokens $\tau_{i,k} = a_{\mathsf{col}_i} \cdot a_{\mathsf{col}_k}^{-1} \in \mathbb{Z}_p$ and $\tau_{k,j} = a_{\mathsf{col}_k} \cdot a_{\mathsf{col}_j}^{-1} \in \mathbb{Z}_p$, one can efficiently compute the token $\tau_{i,j} = \tau_{i,k} \cdot \tau_{k,j}^{-1}$.

The main idea underlying our scheme is to introduce additional structure into both the encodings and the tokens, and to rely on a bilinear map $\hat{e} : \mathbb{G} \times \mathbb{G} \to \mathbb{G}_T$ for computing the adjusted encodings. First, instead of applying a pseudorandom function for identifying messages and column labels as pseudorandom $\mathbb{Z}_p$ elements, we apply a pseudorandom function for identifying messages as pseudorandom $\mathbb{Z}_p^4$ vectors, and column labels as pseudorandom invertible $\mathbb{Z}_p^{4 \times 4}$ matrices. In what follows, for a matrix $A = [a_{ij}] \in \mathbb{Z}_p^{a \times b}$ we define $g^A = [g^{a_{ij}}]_{ij} \in \mathbb{G}^{a \times b}$, and for matrices $H = [h_{ij}] \in \mathbb{G}^{a \times b}$ and $H' = [h'_{ij}] \in \mathbb{G}^{b \times c}$ we define $\hat{e}(H, H') = [\prod_{k=1}^{b} \hat{e}(h_{ik}, h'_{kj})]_{ij} \in \mathbb{G}_T^{a \times c}$ (thus, for matrices A and B of appropriate dimensions it holds that $\hat{e}(g^A, g^B) = \hat{e}(g, g)^{AB}$).

Equipped with this notation, the encoding of a message m for a column label col is defined as $c = g^{A_{\mathsf{col}} x_m} \in \mathbb{G}^4$, where $x_m \in \mathbb{Z}_p^4$ and $A_{\mathsf{col}} \in \mathsf{Rk}_4(\mathbb{Z}_p^{4 \times 4})$ are the pseudorandom vector and matrix associated with m and col, respectively. Our token-generation algorithm takes as input two column labels, col_i and col_j, uniformly samples a vector $v \leftarrow \mathbb{Z}_p^4$, and outputs the adjustment tokens $g^{v^{\mathsf{T}} A_{\mathsf{col}_i}^{-1}} \in \mathbb{G}^4$ and $g^{v^{\mathsf{T}} A_{\mathsf{col}_j}^{-1}} \in \mathbb{G}^4$. Adjusting an encoding $c \in \mathbb{G}^4$ using a token $\tau \in \mathbb{G}^4$ is computed as $\hat{e}(\tau^{\mathsf{T}}, c) \in \mathbb{G}_T$, and we prove that correctness holds with an overwhelming probability: For any two column labels col_i and col_j, and for any two messages m_i and m_j, it holds that $m_i = m_j$ if and only if $\hat{e}(g^{v^{\mathsf{T}} A_{\mathsf{col}_i}^{-1}}, g^{A_{\mathsf{col}_i} x_{m_i}}) = \hat{e}(g^{v^{\mathsf{T}} A_{\mathsf{col}_j}^{-1}}, g^{A_{\mathsf{col}_j} x_{m_j}})$ with all but a negligible probability. We refer the reader to Sect. 5.1 for the formal description of our scheme.

One may wonder why we use matrices and vectors instead of scalars (as in [40], as well as in [19,25]). Otherwise, the scheme is trivially broken, because of the presence of a bilinear map unless rather non-standard assumptions are made (such as the new assumption introduced by Furukawa and Isshiki [19] for the purpose of their analysis). In particular, for distinct messages m, m', m'' and columns $\mathsf{col}_i, \mathsf{col}_j$, an adversary can distinguish between $(g^{a_{\mathsf{col}_i} x_m}, g^{a_{\mathsf{col}_i} x_{m'}}, g^{a_{\mathsf{col}_j} x_m}, g^{a_{\mathsf{col}_j} x_{m'}})$ and $(g^{a_{\mathsf{col}_i} x_m}, g^{a_{\mathsf{col}_i} x_{m'}}, g^{a_{\mathsf{col}_j} x_m}, g^{a_{\mathsf{col}_j} x_{m''}})$ by comparing the bilinear image of the first and fourth elements to the bilinear image of the second and third elements.

Our proof of security. For proving the security of our scheme, we first observe that the linear assumption [4] implies that the two distributions $(g^A, g^{Ax}, g^B, g^{By})$ and $(g^A, g^{Ax}, g^B, g^{Bx})$ are computationally indistinguishable, where

$A, B \leftarrow \mathbb{Z}_p^{4 \times 4}$ and $x, y \leftarrow \mathbb{Z}_p^4$. Intuitively, this enables us to view A and B as $\mathbb{Z}_p^{4 \times 4}$ matrices corresponding to two different column labels, and x and y as $\mathbb{Z}_p^4$ vectors corresponding to two different messages. Without being explicitly given a token for computing the join between the columns A and B, an adversary should not be able to distinguish between an encoding g^{Bx} of x to the column B and an encoding g^{By} of y to the column B, even when given an encoding g^{Ax} of x to the column A in both cases.

Our proof of security realizes this intuition, showing that given $(g^A, g^{Ax}, g^B, g^{By})$ or $(g^A, g^{Ax}, g^B, g^{Bx})$ as input we can essentially generate an entire encoding of an adversarially-chosen database, as well as generate all join tokens of the adversary's choice, as long as no token is requested for the join of A and B. Most importantly, although we do not explicitly know either A or B, for any column C we can generate tokens for computing the join between A and C, and the join between C and B. The main challenge, however, is that in our 3Partition notion, the adversary is not limited to only one such pair A and B, and more generally, we do not know in advance the entire structure of the database or the pairs of columns for which the adversary will request join tokens.

Recall that our 3Partition notion considers adversaries that may adaptively define three disjoint sets of columns, which we refer to as a "left" set L, a "right" set R, and a "middle" set M. The adversary is given the ability to compute joins inside L, inside M, and inside R, as well as joins between L and M and between R and M, but it is not given the ability to compute the join between any column in L and any column in R. We rely on this structure for reusing the matrix A for all columns in L and for reusing the matrix B for all columns in R, where in both cases this is done via an appropriate re-randomization. The fact that the adversary is not allowed to request join tokens between L and R guarantees that we are able to generate all required join tokens. We refer the reader to Sect. 5.2 for our proof of security.

1.3 Additional Related Work

Supporting join queries over encrypted data. Additional approaches for supporting join queries over encrypted data include those of Furukawa and Isshiki [19], Hang et al. [25], and Kamara and Moataz [28] which we now discuss.

Furukawa and Isshiki [19] consider a notion of security for join schemes which is seemingly weaker compared to our 3Partition notion, and captures non-transitivity to a certain extent (it is essentially equivalent to a non-adaptive variant of our 3Partition notion). However, as we pointed out in Sect. 1.1, without also including more standard indistinguishability-based and simulation-based notions (as we do in our work), it is far from being clear that such a notion indeed captures the security of join schemes. Furukawa and Isshiki also propose a specific scheme that can be viewed as based on a simplified variant of our scheme where scalars are used instead of matrices and vectors. As discussed in Sect. 1.2, such a scheme is trivially insecure with respect to our notions of security unless rather non-standard assumptions are made (specifically, Furukawa and Isshiki introduced a new and non-standard assumption for the purpose of their analysis).

Hang et al. [25] frame their approach in terms of deterministic proxy re-encryption. However, they propose a weak notion of security which does not seem to capture non-transitivity, and their proposed scheme does not satisfy any of our notions of security (or even the notion of security considered by Popa and Zeldovich [40]) under any assumption. As far as we can tell, our scheme is fully compatible with their approach and design goals.

Kamara and Moataz [28] recently proposed the first solution for supporting SQL queries on encrypted databases that does not make use of deterministic encodings of the data. Their approach avoids the usage of property-preserving encryption techniques (that are known to be susceptible to various attacks [22, 31,35]) and of general-purpose primitives such as fully-homomorphic encryption or oblivious RAM (that are currently somewhat unlikely to lead to practical schemes). Their scheme provides strong security guarantees, and in particular a non-transitive join operator. However, their scheme is based on essentially computing all possible joins in advance, and then the problem can be solved via symmetric searchable encryption techniques. Thus, their approach both requires a significant amount of storage (may be quadratic in the size of the database – and thus potentially impractical), and does not seem to support dynamic updates to either the structure or the content of the database.

Proxy re-encryption schemes. Proxy re-encryption schemes (e.g., [2,3,27]) have various applications to distributed storage systems. However, the known constructions and notions of security for proxy re-encryption typically focus on randomized schemes, and therefore (in general) even after invoking the re-encryption algorithm it is not directly clear how to compare two encrypted messages without providing a decryption key – which results in a transitive scheme. Deterministic variants of proxy re-encryption may support such comparisons, as suggested by Hang et al. [25] and discussed above.

Private set intersection. Adjustable join schemes are somewhat related to the classic problem of designing private set-intersection protocols both in terms of techniques and in terms of security notions. However, in the setting of adjustable join schemes all elements are encoded using a shared secret key sk, whereas in the setting of private set-intersection protocols the parties are not assumed to share any secrets. Moreover, the approach underlying the existing practical protocols does not seem to rely on establishing shared secrets as part of the protocol (see, for example, [17,26,36] and the references therein).

Searchable encryption. Adjustable join schemes may also seem somewhat related to symmetric searchable encryption [1,6,8–15,20,29,30,32,33,42,43]. However, in the setting of symmetric searchable encryption a search token is associated with a specific message and enables to identify encryptions of that message, whereas in an adjustable join schemes a join token enables to reveal the equality pattern between two sets of encryptions. As a result, both our notions of security and our techniques are significantly different from those of symmetric searchable encryption. Nevertheless, it would be intriguing to explore any potential applications of our techniques to symmetric searchable encryption.

1.4   Extensions and Open Problems

Multi-column joins. Following the work of Popa et al. [37–39] we have considered joins according to two columns (and thus two tables). Our adjustable join scheme can in fact be extended to support multi-column joins by modifying its token-generation algorithm (and without modifying its encoding or adjustment algorithms). This enables to join multiple tables more efficiently (compared to successively applying two-column joins), and leads to reducing the space overhead by using a smaller number of adjusted encodings.

Specifically, our token-generation algorithm can be modified as follows. On input $\mathsf{params} = (\mathbb{G}, \mathbb{G}_T, g, p, \hat{e})$, $\mathsf{sk} = (K_1, K_2)$ and an arbitrary number $k = k(\lambda)$ column labels $\mathsf{col}_1, \ldots, \mathsf{col}_k \in \mathcal{L}_\lambda$, the modified token-generation algorithm uniformly samples $v \leftarrow \mathbb{Z}_p^4 \setminus \{(0,0,0,0)\}$, computes $A_{\mathsf{col}_i} = \mathsf{PRF}_{K_2}(\mathsf{col}_i) \in \mathsf{Rk}_4(\mathbb{Z}_p^{4 \times 4})$ for every $i \in [k]$, and outputs the tuple $\left(g^{v^\top A_{\mathsf{col}_1}^{-1}}, \ldots, g^{v^\top A_{\mathsf{col}_k}^{-1}} \right) \in \left(\mathbb{G}^4 \right)^k$ of adjustment tokens. Moreover, we can generate such a multi-join adjustment tokens even when not all k columns are known in advance, as long as we securely store the value v (or, possibly, regenerate it using a pseudorandom function), then compute the value $g^{v^\top A_{\mathsf{col}_i}^{-1}}$ only when col_i is determined.

This allows to reduce space usage (and time as well), by storing adjusted encodings for cliques of joined columns, instead of storing adjusted encodings for each pair of them. Moreover, this allows tuning a trade-off between privacy and efficiency in space and time, by using multiple-column join encodings for the less sensitive data. At the extreme end, one can store only one column of adjusted encodings for each column, by using multiple-column encodings for disjoint sets of columns, and obtain security guarantees that are similar to the 2Partition-security of [40]. Overall, our support for multi-column joins enables to fine-tune the efficiency of our scheme, while providing different levels of security, ranging from the security guarantees of CryptDB's join scheme to the stronger security guarantees of our new scheme.

Improved efficiency via the matrix-DDH assumption. The security of our adjustable join scheme is based on the assumption the two distributions $(\mathsf{params}, g^A, g^{Ax}, g^B, g^{By})$ and $(\mathsf{params}, g^A, g^{Ax}, g^B, g^{Bx})$ are computationally indistinguishable, where $\mathsf{params} = (\mathbb{G}, \mathbb{G}_T, g, p, \hat{e}) \leftarrow \mathcal{G}(1^\lambda)$, $A, B \leftarrow \mathsf{Rk}_4(\mathbb{Z}_p^{4 \times 4})$ and $x, y \leftarrow \mathbb{Z}_p^4$. This assumption is the reason that we increase the size of CryptDB's encodings from one group element to four group elements, and increase the running time of the adjustment operation from that of computing one group exponentiation to that of computing four bilinear maps.

Claim 2.5 (which we prove in the full version of this paper [34]) states that this assumption is implied by the linear assumption [4]. The seemingly stronger $\mathcal{U}_{4,2}$-MDDH assumption due to Escala et al. [16], states that our underlying assumption holds already for 2×2 matrices instead of 4×4 matrices. In turn, based on the $\mathcal{U}_{4,2}$-MDDH assumption we obtain a more efficient scheme, increasing the size of CryptDB's encodings from one group element to two group elements, and increasing the running time of the adjustment operation from that of computing one group exponentiation to that of computing two bilinear maps. This more efficient scheme is directly obtained from our scheme by simply modifying the dimensions of all 4×4 matrices and 4×1 vectors to dimensions 2×2 and 2×1, respectively (and without any additional modification to either the construction or the proof of security).

Adaptive security. Our adjustable join scheme satisfies our strong 3Partition notion, which considers adversaries that may determine databases of any polynomial size (i.e., databases containing any polynomial number columns and records). When considering databases with a logarithmic number of columns (but still allowing any polynomial number of records!), it is possible to prove that our scheme satisfies our even stronger, adaptive, indistinguishability-based notion.

This is done by "guessing" the partitioning of the columns into three disjoint sets, as implicitly defined by the adversary's token-generation queries within our adaptive indistinguishability experiment – thus leading to only a polynomial security loss as the number of such partitions is polynomial assuming that the number of columns is logarithmic (a rather standard argument shows that the notion of security obtained from 3Partition by not asking the adversary to explicitly partition the columns into three sets, is equivalent to our adaptive indistinguishability-based notion). Similarly, by relying on the standard sub-exponential variant of the linear assumption, we can prove adaptive indistinguishability-based security for databases with any a-priori bounded polynomial number of columns (without requiring any a-priori bound on the polynomial number of records). We leave the task of formalizing these intuitions to future work. An intriguing open problem is to achieve such a level of security without relying on sub-exponential assumptions or without an a-priori bound on the number of columns.

Deterministic vs. randomized encodings. Our encoding algorithm is deterministic similarly and in compatibility with that of CryptDB. An intriguing open problem is to explore the possibility and the potential advantages of join schemes that are based on a randomized encoding algorithm. Given the inherent leakage of the join operation itself, it is not immediately clear that using a randomized encoding algorithm may offer any clear advantage except for avoiding the inherent leakage of deterministic encoding (i.e., the equality pattern within each column).

1.5   Paper Organization

The remainder of this paper is organized as follows. In Sect. 2 we introduce the basic tools and computational assumptions underlying our contributions. In Sect. 3 we present the notion of an adjustable join scheme, and discuss the weakness of the notion of security for such schemes that was put forward by

Popa and Zeldovich [40]. In Sect. 4 we introduce our new and refined framework for capturing the security of adjustable join schemes. In Sect. 5 we present our new adjustable join scheme and prove its security.

2   Preliminaries

In this section we present the notation and basic definitions that are used in this work. For a distribution X we denote by $x \leftarrow X$ the process of sampling a value x from the distribution X. Similarly, for a set $\mathcal{X}$ we denote by $x \leftarrow \mathcal{X}$ the process of sampling a value x from the uniform distribution over $\mathcal{X}$. For an integer $n \in \mathbb{N}$ we denote by $[n]$ the set $\{1, \dots, n\}$, and for two random variables X and Y we denote by $\Delta(X, Y)$ their statistical distance. The following two facts follow directly from notion of statistical distance:

Fact 2.1. *Let X and Y be two random variables over Ω. Then, for any (possibly randomized) function $f : \Omega \to \Omega'$ it holds that $\Delta(f(X), f(Y)) \leq \Delta(X, Y)$.*

Fact 2.2. *Let X and Y be a random variables over Ω such that $\Pr[Y = \omega] = \Pr[X = \omega \mid A^c]$ for some event A and for all $\omega \in \Omega$. Then, it holds that $\Delta(X, Y) \leq \Pr[A]$.*

Throughout the paper, we denote by $\lambda \in \mathbb{N}$ the security parameter. A function $\nu : \mathbb{N} \to \mathbb{R}^+$ is *negligible* if for every constant $c > 0$ there exists an integer N_c such that $\nu(\lambda) < \lambda^{-c}$ for all $\lambda > N_c$. Two sequences of random variables $X = \{X_\lambda\}_{\lambda \in \mathbb{N}}$ and $Y = \{Y_\lambda\}_{\lambda \in \mathbb{N}}$ are *statistically indistinguishable* (denoted $X \approx_s Y$) if $\Delta(X_\lambda, Y_\lambda)$ is negligible in λ. Two sequences of random variables $X = \{X_\lambda\}_{\lambda \in \mathbb{N}}$ and $Y = \{Y_\lambda\}_{\lambda \in \mathbb{N}}$ are *computationally indistinguishable* (denoted $X \approx_c Y$) if for any probabilistic polynomial-time algorithm $\mathcal{A}$ it holds that $\left| \Pr_{x \leftarrow X_\lambda}[\mathcal{A}(1^\lambda, x) = 1] - \Pr_{y \leftarrow Y_\lambda}[\mathcal{A}(1^\lambda, y) = 1] \right|$ is negligible in λ. The following fact follows directly from notion of computational indistinguishability:

Fact 2.3. *Let $X = \{X_\lambda\}_{\lambda \in \mathbb{N}}$ and $Y = \{Y_\lambda\}_{\lambda \in \mathbb{N}}$ be computationally indistinguishable. Then, for any probabilistic polynomial-time algorithm $\mathcal{A}$ it holds that $\mathcal{A}(X)$ and $\mathcal{A}(Y)$ are computationally indistinguishable.*

2.1   Pseudorandom Functions

Let $\{\mathcal{K}_\lambda, \mathcal{X}_\lambda, \mathcal{Y}_\lambda\}_{\lambda \in \mathbb{N}}$ be a sequence of sets and let $\mathsf{PRF} = (\mathsf{PRF.Gen}, \mathsf{PRF.Eval})$ be a function family with the following syntax:

- $\mathsf{PRF.Gen}$ is a probabilistic polynomial-time algorithm that takes as input the unary representation of the security parameter λ, and outputs a key $K \in \mathcal{K}_\lambda$.
- $\mathsf{PRF.Eval}$ is a deterministic polynomial-time algorithm that takes as input a key $K \in \mathcal{K}_\lambda$ and a value $x \in \mathcal{X}_\lambda$, and outputs a value $y \in \mathcal{Y}_\lambda$.

The sets $\mathcal{K}_\lambda$, $\mathcal{X}_\lambda$, and $\mathcal{Y}_\lambda$ are referred to as the *key space*, *domain*, and *range* of the function family, respectively. For ease of notation we may denote by $\mathsf{PRF.Eval}_K(\cdot)$ or $\mathsf{PRF}_K(\cdot)$ the function $\mathsf{PRF.Eval}(K, \cdot)$ for $K \in \mathcal{K}_\lambda$. The following is the standard definition of a pseudorandom function family.

Definition 2.4. *A function family* $\mathsf{PRF} = (\mathsf{PRF.Gen}, \mathsf{PRF.Eval})$ *is pseudorandom if for every probabilistic algorithm* $\mathcal{A}$ *there exists a negligible function* $\nu(\cdot)$ *such that*

$$\mathsf{Adv}_{\mathsf{PRF}, \mathcal{A}}(\lambda) \overset{\text{def}}{=} \left| \Pr_{K \leftarrow \mathsf{PRF.Gen}(1^\lambda)} \left[\mathcal{A}^{\mathsf{PRF.Eval}_K(\cdot)}(1^\lambda) = 1 \right] - \Pr_{f \leftarrow F_\lambda} \left[\mathcal{A}^{f(\cdot)}(1^\lambda) = 1 \right] \right|$$
$$\leq \nu(\lambda),$$

for all sufficiently large $\lambda \in \mathbb{N}$, *where* F_λ *is the set of all functions that map* $\mathcal{X}_\lambda$ *into* $\mathcal{Y}_\lambda$.

2.2 Computational Assumptions

Let $\mathcal{G}$ be a probabilistic polynomial-time algorithm that takes as input the security parameter 1^λ, and outputs a tuple $(\mathbb{G}, \mathbb{G}_T, g, p, \hat{e})$, where p is a λ-bit prime number, $\mathbb{G}$ and $\mathbb{G}_T$ are groups of order p, g is a generator of $\mathbb{G}$, and $\hat{e} : \mathbb{G} \times \mathbb{G} \to \mathbb{G}_T$ is a non-degenerate efficiently-computable bilinear map.

For a matrix $A = [a_{ij}] \in \mathbb{Z}_p^{a \times b}$ we define $g^A = [g^{a_{ij}}]_{ij} \in \mathbb{G}^{a \times b}$, and for matrices $H = [h_{ij}] \in \mathbb{G}^{a \times b}$ and $H' = [h'_{ij}] \in \mathbb{G}^{b \times c}$ we define $\hat{e}(H, H') = [\prod_{k=1}^b \hat{e}(h_{ik}, h'_{kj})]_{ij} \in \mathbb{G}_T^{a \times c}$ (thus, for matrices A and B of appropriate dimensions it holds that $\hat{e}(g^A, g^B) = \hat{e}(g, g)^{AB}$). We denote by $\mathsf{Rk}_r(\mathbb{Z}_p^{a \times b})$ the set of all $a \times b$ matrices over $\mathbb{Z}_p$ of rank r.

The linear assumption [4] states that for $\mathsf{params} \leftarrow \mathcal{G}(1^\lambda)$, $g_1, g_2, g_3 \leftarrow \mathbb{G}$ and $r_1, r_2, r_3 \leftarrow \mathbb{Z}_p$, the two distributions $(\mathsf{params}, g_1, g_2, g_3, g_1^{r_1}, g_2^{r_2}, g_3^{r_3})$ and $(\mathsf{params}, g_1, g_2, g_3, g_1^{r_1}, g_2^{r_2}, g_3^{r_1 + r_2})$ are computationally indistinguishable. The security of our scheme relies on the following assumption – which we prove to follow from the linear assumption:

Claim 2.5. *The linear assumption implies that the two distributions* $(\mathsf{params}, g^A, g^{Ax}, g^B, g^{By})$ *and* $(\mathsf{params}, g^A, g^{Ax}, g^B, g^{Bx})$ *are computationally indistinguishable, where* $\mathsf{params} = (\mathbb{G}, \mathbb{G}_T, g, p, \hat{e}) \leftarrow \mathcal{G}(1^\lambda)$, $A, B \leftarrow \mathsf{Rk}_4(\mathbb{Z}_p^{4 \times 4})$ *and* $x, y \leftarrow \mathbb{Z}_p^4$.

As discussed in Sect. 1.4, a variant of the above claim for 2×2 matrices is implied by the matrix-DDH assumption due to Escala et al. [16]. Specifically, their $\mathcal{U}_{4,2}$-MDDH assumption states that the two distributions $(\mathsf{params}, g^C, g^{Cv})$ and $(\mathsf{params}, g^C, g^u)$ are computationally indistinguishable, where $\mathsf{params} = (\mathbb{G}, \mathbb{G}_T, g, p, \hat{e}) \leftarrow \mathcal{G}(1^\lambda)$, $C \leftarrow \mathbb{Z}_p^{4 \times 2}$, $v \leftarrow \mathbb{Z}_p^2$ and $u \leftarrow \mathbb{Z}_p^4$.

Claim 2.6. *The* $\mathcal{U}_{4,2}$-MDDH *assumption implies that the two distributions* $(\mathsf{params}, g^A, g^{Ax}, g^B, g^{By})$ *and* $(\mathsf{params}, g^A, g^{Ax}, g^B, g^{Bx})$ *are computationally indistinguishable, where* $\mathsf{params} = (\mathbb{G}, \mathbb{G}_T, g, p, \hat{e}) \leftarrow \mathcal{G}(1^\lambda)$, $A, B \leftarrow \mathsf{Rk}_2(\mathbb{Z}_p^{2 \times 2})$ *and* $x, y \leftarrow \mathbb{Z}_p^2$.

The proof of Claim 2.6 is rather straightforward. Given $(\mathsf{params}, g^C, g^u)$, where either $u \leftarrow \mathbb{Z}_p^4$ or $u = Cv$ where $v \leftarrow \mathbb{Z}_p^2$, we view C and u as consisting of two equal-sized matrices and vectors, respectively,

$$C = \begin{bmatrix} A \\ B \end{bmatrix}, \quad u = \begin{bmatrix} w \\ z \end{bmatrix},$$

and rearrange the tuple as $(\mathsf{params}, g^A, g^w, g^B, g^z)$. Since the probability that A or B are not invertible is negligible, by Fact 2.2 we may assume that they are invertible. Now, for $x, y \leftarrow \mathbb{Z}_p^2$, it holds that Ax and By are independent, uniformly distributed, and independent of A and B. So, if $u \leftarrow \mathbb{Z}_p^4$, then w and z are distributed as Ax and By. On the other hand, if $u = Cv$ where $v \leftarrow \mathbb{Z}_p^2$, then $w = Av$ and $z = Bv$. So, distinguishing between the two ensembles in Claim 2.6 would result in contradicting the $\mathcal{U}_{4,2}$-MDDH assumption.

3 Adjustable Join Schemes and Their Security

In this section we first present the notion of an adjustable join scheme [37–40]. Then, we present the notion of security introduced by Popa and Zeldovich [40] for such schemes, that we denote by 2Partition, and observe that it does not guarantee non-transitive joins.

3.1 Adjustable Join Schemes

An adjustable join scheme for a message space $\mathcal{M} = \{\mathcal{M}_\lambda\}_{\lambda \in \mathbb{N}}$, an encoding space $\mathcal{C} = \{\mathcal{C}_\lambda\}_{\lambda \in \mathbb{N}}$ and a column label space $\mathcal{L} = \{\mathcal{L}_\lambda\}_{\lambda \in \mathbb{N}}$, is a 4-tuple $\Pi = (\mathsf{KeyGen}, \mathsf{Enc}, \mathsf{TokenGen}, \mathsf{Adj})$ of polynomial-time algorithms with the following properties:

- The key-generation algorithm, KeyGen, is a probabilistic algorithm that takes as input a unary representation 1^λ of the security parameter $\lambda \in \mathbb{N}$, and outputs a secret key sk and public parameters params.
- The encoding algorithm, Enc, is a deterministic algorithm that takes as input a secret key sk, a message $m \in \mathcal{M}_\lambda$ and a column label $\mathsf{col} \in \mathcal{L}_\lambda$, and outputs an encoding $c \in \mathcal{C}_\lambda$.
- The token-generation algorithm, $\mathsf{TokenGen}$, is a probabilistic algorithm that takes as input a secret key sk and two column labels $\mathsf{col}_i, \mathsf{col}_j \in \mathcal{L}_\lambda$, and outputs a pair (τ_i, τ_j) of adjustment tokens.
- The adjustment algorithm, Adj, is a deterministic algorithm that takes as input the public parameters params, an encoding $c \in \mathcal{C}_\lambda$ and an adjustment token τ, and outputs an encoding $c' \in \mathcal{C}_\lambda$.

Correctness. In terms of correctness, we require that for all sufficiently large $\lambda \in \mathbb{N}$, and for any two column labels $\mathsf{col}_i, \mathsf{col}_j \in \mathcal{L}_\lambda$ and two messages $m_i, m_j \in \mathcal{M}_\lambda$, it holds that

$$m_i = m_j \iff \mathsf{Adj}\left(\mathsf{params}, \tau_i, \mathsf{Enc}_{\mathsf{sk}}\left(m_i, \mathsf{col}_i\right)\right) = \mathsf{Adj}\left(\mathsf{params}, \tau_j, \mathsf{Enc}_{\mathsf{sk}}\left(m_j, \mathsf{col}_j\right)\right)$$

with an overwhelming probability over the choice of $(\mathsf{sk}, \mathsf{params}) \leftarrow \mathsf{KeyGen}(1^\lambda)$ and $(\tau_i, \tau_j) \leftarrow \mathsf{TokenGen}_{\mathsf{sk}}(\mathsf{col}_i, \mathsf{col}_j)$.

A comparison with the notion of Popa and Zeldovich [40]. The above notion of an adjustable join scheme is essentially identical to the one originally formalized by Popa and Zeldovich [40] except for the following minor difference: When computing the join of columns i and j, we allow the scheme to apply the adjustment algorithm to the encodings of column i and to the encodings of column j, whereas Popa and Zeldovich allow the scheme to apply the adjustment algorithm only to the encodings of column j. As far as we can tell, applying the adjustment algorithm to the encodings of both columns is fully compatible with the design of CryptDB.

3.2 The 2Partition Security Notion and its Weakness

The notion of security introduced by Popa and Zeldovich [40], that we denote by 2Partition, considers an experiment in which an adversary may adaptively define two disjoint sets of columns, which we refer to as a "left" set L and a "right" set R. The adversary is given the ability to compute joins inside L and joins inside R, but it should not be able to compute the join between any column in L and any column in R. Specifically, at any point in time the adversary can insert any column to either L or R, and to obtain encodings of messages of her choice relative to any of these columns. In addition, the adversary may obtain tokens for computing the join of all columns col_i and col_j such that $\mathsf{col}_i, \mathsf{col}_j \in L$ or $\mathsf{col}_i, \mathsf{col}_j \in R$.

The 2Partition notion of security asks that such an adversary should not be able to compute the join of any two columns $\mathsf{col}_i \in L$ and $\mathsf{col}_j \in R$. This is modeled in the experiment by enabling the adversary to output a pair of messages, m_0 and m_1, and providing the adversary either with the encodings of m_0 for all columns in R or with the encodings of m_1 for all columns in R. The adversary should not be able to distinguish these two cases with a non-negligible advantage (of course, as long as the adversary did not explicitly ask for an encoding of m_0 or m_1 relative to some column label in R).

A comparison with the notion of Popa and Zeldovich [40]. The above informal description is in fact a simplification of the notion considered by Popa and Zeldovich [40], but a straightforward hybrid argument shows that the two are in fact equivalent (whenever the message space is not too small). Specifically, whereas in the above description the adversary obtains *either* encodings of m_0 for all columns in R *or* encodings of m_1 for all columns in R, Popa and Zeldovich provide the adversary with encodings of *both* m_0 and m_1 for all columns in R but in a shuffled order. We refer the reader to [40, Sect. 3.1] for a more formal description of their notion.

2Partition does not capture transitivity. Intuitively, the 2Partition notion guarantees that for any two disjoint sets of columns, L and R, the ability to compute joins inside L and joins inside R, does not imply the ability to compute the join between any column in L and any column in R. However, this does not capture transitivity: Assume that there is a certain column col^* that does not belong to either L or R, then the ability to compute the join between col^* and columns in L, and to compute the join between col^* and columns in R, may imply the ability to compute the join between columns in L and columns in R.

Moreover, it is not only that 2Partition does not capture transitivity, but in fact the adjustable join scheme of Popa and Zeldovich [40] is completely transitive (due to efficiency considerations) although it satisfies 2Partition: For any three columns col_i, col_j and col_k, given tokens for computing the joins between col_i and col_k and between col_k and col_j, it is easy to efficiently construct a token for computing the join between col_i and col_j.

Specifically, as pointed out in Sect. 1.2, their scheme uses a group $\mathbb{G}$ of prime order p that is generated by an element $g \in \mathbb{G}$, and a pseudorandom function PRF mapping column labels and messages into $\mathbb{Z}_p^*$ with keys sk_col and sk_msg, respectively (Popa et al. use a pseudorandom permutation, but in fact any pseudorandom function suffices as any specific collision occurs with only a negligible probability whenever the range of the function is of size super-polynomial in the security parameter). The encoding of a message m for a column col_i is the group element $g^{\mathsf{PRF}_{\mathsf{sk}_\mathsf{col}}(\mathsf{col}_i) \cdot \mathsf{PRF}_{\mathsf{sk}_\mathsf{msg}}(m)} \in \mathbb{G}$, and a token for computing the join between columns col_i and col_j is the element $\tau_{i,j} = \mathsf{PRF}_{\mathsf{sk}_\mathsf{col}}(\mathsf{col}_i) \cdot \mathsf{PRF}_{\mathsf{sk}_\mathsf{col}}(\mathsf{col}_j)^{-1} \in \mathbb{Z}_p$. Thus, it is clear that given the tokens $\tau_{i,k} = \mathsf{PRF}_{\mathsf{sk}_\mathsf{col}}(\mathsf{col}_i) \cdot \mathsf{PRF}_{\mathsf{sk}_\mathsf{col}}(\mathsf{col}_k)^{-1} \in \mathbb{Z}_p$ and $\tau_{k,j} = \mathsf{PRF}_{\mathsf{sk}_\mathsf{col}}(\mathsf{col}_k) \cdot \mathsf{PRF}_{\mathsf{sk}_\mathsf{col}}(\mathsf{col}_j)^{-1} \in \mathbb{Z}_p$, one can efficiently compute the token $\tau_{i,j} = \tau_{i,k} \cdot \tau_{k,j}$.

4   Strengthening the Definitional Framework

In this section we introduce our new and refined framework for capturing the security of adjustable join schemes. First, in Sect. 4.1, we introduce a new notion of security, denoted 3Partition, which strictly strengthens 2Partition. Our notion considers a partitioning of the columns into *three* disjoint sets (instead of two disjoint sets as in the 2Partition notion) in a manner that enables it to properly model non-transitive joins.

As discussed in Sect. 1.2, partitioning the columns into three disjoint sets is intuitively inherent for capturing the security of adjustable join schemes. In Sects. 4.2 and 4.3 we show that partitioning the columns into three sets is indeed sufficient and captures the security of adjustable join schemes in a natural manner: We formalize natural simulation-based and indistinguishability-based security notion, capturing the "minimal leakage" of join schemes without any explicit partitioning of the columns, and prove that 3Partition in positioned between their adaptive variants and their non-adaptive variant. Finally, in Sect. 4.4 we include some additional remarks regarding the standard aspects of column privacy and leakage of frequency characteristics that arise in our notions of security.

4.1   The 3Partition Security Notion

Our 3Partition notion of security considers an adversary that may adaptively define three disjoint sets of columns, which we refer to as a "left" set L, a "right" set R, and a "middle" set M. The adversary is given the ability to compute joins inside L, inside M, and inside R, as well as joins between L and M and between R and M, but it should not be able to compute the join between any column in L and any column in R. Specifically, at any point in time the adversary can insert any column to either L, R or M, and to obtain encodings of messages of her choice relative to any of these columns. In addition, the adversary may obtain tokens for computing the join of all columns col_i and col_j such that $col_i, col_j \in L \cup M$ or $col_i, col_j \in R \cup M$.

The 3Partition notion of security asks that such an adversary should not be able to compute the join of any two columns $col_i \in L$ and $col_j \in R$. This is modeled by enabling the adversary to output a pair of messages, m_0 and m_1, and providing the adversary either with the encodings of m_0 for all columns in R or with the encodings of m_1 for all columns in R. The adversary should not be able to distinguish these two cases with a non-negligible advantage (of course, as long as the adversary did not explicitly ask for an encoding of m_0 or m_1 relative to some column label in $R \cup M$).

Definition 4.1. *A join scheme* $\Pi = (\mathsf{KeyGen}, \mathsf{Enc}, \mathsf{TokenGen}, \mathsf{Adj})$ *is 3Partition-secure if for any probabilistic polynomial-time adversary* $\mathcal{A}$ *there exists a negligible function* $\nu(\cdot)$ *such that*

$$\mathsf{Adv}^{\mathsf{3Par}}_{\Pi,\mathcal{A}}(\lambda) \stackrel{\mathrm{def}}{=} \left| \Pr\left[\mathsf{Exp}^{\mathsf{3Par}}_{\Pi,\mathcal{A}}(\lambda, 0) = 1\right] - \Pr\left[\mathsf{Exp}^{\mathsf{3Par}}_{\Pi,\mathcal{A}}(\lambda, 1) = 1\right] \right| \le \nu(\lambda)$$

for all sufficiently large $\lambda \in \mathbb{N}$, *where for each* $b \in \{0, 1\}$ *the experiment* $\mathsf{Exp}^{\mathsf{3Par}}_{\Pi,\mathcal{A}}(\lambda, b)$ *is defined as follows:*

1. *Setup phase: Sample* $(\mathsf{sk}, \mathsf{params}) \leftarrow \mathsf{KeyGen}(1^\lambda)$, *and initialize* $L = R = M = \emptyset$. *The public parameters* params *are given as input to the adversary* $\mathcal{A}$.
2. *Pre-challenge query phase:* $\mathcal{A}$ *may adaptively issue* AddColumn, Enc *and* TokenGen *queries, which are defined as follows.*
   - AddColumn(col, S): *Adds the column label* col *to the set* S, *where* $S \in \{\text{"}L\text{"}, \text{"}R\text{"}, \text{"}M\text{"}\}$. $\mathcal{A}$ *is not allowed to add a column label into more than one set (i.e., the sets* L, R *and* M *must always be pairwise disjoint).*
   - Enc(m, col): *Computes and returns to* $\mathcal{A}$ *an encoding* $c \leftarrow \mathsf{Enc}_{\mathsf{sk}}(m, col)$, *where* $col \in L \cup R \cup M$.
   - TokenGen(col_i, col_j): *Computes and returns to* $\mathcal{A}$ *a pair of tokens* (τ_i, τ_j) $\leftarrow \mathsf{TokenGen}_{\mathsf{sk}}(col_i, col_j)$, *where* $col_i, col_j \in L \cup M$ *or* $col_i, col_j \in R \cup M$.
3. *Challenge phase:* $\mathcal{A}$ *chooses messages* m_0 *and* m_1 *subject to the constraint that* $\mathcal{A}$ *did not previously issue a query of the form* Enc(m, col) *where* $m \in \{m_0, m_1\}$ *and* $col \in R \cup M$. *As a response,* $\mathcal{A}$ *obtains an encoding* $c \leftarrow \mathsf{Enc}_{\mathsf{sk}}(m_b, col)$ *for every* $col \in R$.
4. *Post-challenge query phase: As in the pre-challenge query phase, with the restriction that* $\mathcal{A}$ *is not allowed to issue a query of the form* Enc(m, col) *where* $m \in \{m_0, m_1\}$ *and* $col \in R \cup M$. *In addition, for each* AddColumn$(col, \text{"}R\text{"})$ *query,* $\mathcal{A}$ *is also provided with* $c \leftarrow \mathsf{Enc}_{\mathsf{sk}}(m_b, col)$.

5. *Output phase: $\mathcal{A}$ outputs a value $\sigma \in \{0,1\}$ which is defined as the value of the experiment.*

Our 3Partition notion clearly strengthens the 2Partition notion of Popa and Zeldovich [40] by considering a partitioning of the column labels into three sets instead of two sets. Moreover, as shown in Sect. 3.2, the adjustable join scheme of Popa and Zeldovich is not a 3Partition-secure scheme, although they proved it to be a 2Partition-secure scheme, and thus our 3Partition notion strictly strengthens the 2Partition notion.

4.2   Indistinguishability-Based Security Notions

We first introduce some basic notation that will be helpful in formalizing our indistinguishability-based security notions. A *database* DB of dimensions $\dim = \dim(\mathsf{DB}) = (t, (n_i)_{i=1}^t)$ consists of a list of distinct column labels, denoted $\mathsf{Cols} = \mathsf{Cols}(\mathsf{DB}) = (\mathsf{col}_1, \ldots, \mathsf{col}_t)$, and of a list of distinct messages $L_i = (m_1^i, \ldots, m_{n_i}^i)$ for each column label $\mathsf{col}_i \in \mathsf{Cols}$. The size of a database is defined as $\mathsf{size}(\mathsf{DB}) = \sum_{i=1}^t n_i$ (i.e., the total number of messages in DB). We let

$$V = V(\dim) = \{(i,k) | i \in [t], k \in [n_i]\}$$

and view the messages of the database as a map $\mathsf{m} = \mathsf{m}(\mathsf{DB}) : V \to \mathcal{M}_\lambda$ by setting $\mathsf{m}(i,k) = m_k^i$. A map m is "valid" (i.e., can be a part of a description of a database) if and only if $\mathsf{m}(i,k) \neq \mathsf{m}(i,\ell)$ for all $i \in [t]$ and $k \neq \ell \in [n_i]$.

Given an adjustable join scheme $\Pi = (\mathsf{KeyGen}, \mathsf{Enc}, \mathsf{TokenGen}, \mathsf{Adj})$ we extend its encoding algorithm from encoding single messages to encoding a complete database by defining $\mathsf{Enc}_{\mathsf{sk}}(\mathsf{DB}) = \{(i, k, \mathsf{Enc}_{\mathsf{sk}}(\mathsf{m}(i,k), \mathsf{col}_i))\}_{i \in [t], k \in [n_i]}$. Similarly, given a list of pairs of indices $I = ((i_1, j_1), \ldots, (i_s, j_s)) \in ([t] \times [t])^*$, we extend its token-generation algorithm by defining

$$\mathsf{TokenGen}_{\mathsf{sk}}(\mathsf{DB}, I) = \{(i, j, \mathsf{TokenGen}_{\mathsf{sk}}(\mathsf{col}_i, \mathsf{col}_j))\}_{(i,j) \in I}.$$

In addition, for such a list I and a database DB we define

$$\mathsf{Join}_{\mathsf{DB}}(i,j) = \{(k, \ell) \in [n_i] \times [n_j] : \mathsf{m}(i,k) = \mathsf{m}(j,\ell)\},$$

and we define the leakage of (DB, I) to be

$$\mathcal{L}(\mathsf{DB}, I) = \left(\dim(\mathsf{DB}), \mathsf{Cols}(\mathsf{DB}), I, \{(i, j, \mathsf{Join}_{\mathsf{DB}}(i,j))\}_{(i,j) \in I}\right).$$

Non-adaptive IND security. Our non-adaptive indistinguishability-based notion is perhaps the most simplistic and natural notion: It considers an adversary that obtains the public parameters of the scheme, and then chooses two databases, DB_0 and DB_1, and a list I of pairs of indices such that $\mathcal{L}(\mathsf{DB}_0, I) = \mathcal{L}(\mathsf{DB}_1, I)$ (i.e., the functionality of the scheme does not trivially distinguish DB_0 and DB_1). We ask that such an adversary has only a negligible advantage in distinguishing between $(\mathsf{Enc}_{\mathsf{sk}}(\mathsf{DB}_0), \mathsf{TokenGen}_{\mathsf{sk}}(\mathsf{DB}_0, I))$ and $(\mathsf{Enc}_{\mathsf{sk}}(\mathsf{DB}_1),$

$\mathsf{TokenGen_{sk}(DB_1}, I))$. That is, the adversary should essentially not be able to distinguish between an encoding of $\mathsf{DB_0}$ and an encoding of $\mathsf{DB_1}$, where in both cases she is given tokens for computing the joins of all column label pairs corresponding to the pair of indices in I.

Definition 4.2 (Non-adaptive IND security). *A join scheme* $\Pi =$ $(\mathsf{KeyGen, Enc, TokenGen, Adj})$ *is* non-adaptively IND-secure *if for any probabilistic polynomial-time adversary* $\mathcal{A}$ *there exists a negligible function* $\nu(\cdot)$ *such that*

$$\mathsf{Adv}_{\Pi,\mathcal{A}}^{\mathsf{naIND}}(\lambda) \stackrel{\text{def}}{=} \left| \Pr\left[\mathsf{Exp}_{\Pi,\mathcal{A}}^{\mathsf{naIND}}(\lambda, 0) = 1 \right] - \Pr\left[\mathsf{Exp}_{\Pi,\mathcal{A}}^{\mathsf{naIND}}(\lambda, 1) = 1 \right] \right| \leq \nu(\lambda)$$

for all sufficiently large $\lambda \in \mathbb{N}$, *where for each* $b \in \{0, 1\}$ *the experiment* $\mathsf{Exp}_{\Pi,\mathcal{A}}^{\mathsf{naIND}}(\lambda, b)$ *is defined as follows:*

1. *Setup phase: Sample* $(\mathsf{sk, params}) \leftarrow \mathsf{KeyGen}(1^\lambda)$. *The public parameters* params *are given as input to the adversary* $\mathcal{A}$.
2. *Challenge phase:* $\mathcal{A}$ *chooses two databases,* $\mathsf{DB_0}$ *and* $\mathsf{DB_1}$, *and a list* I *of column label pairs such that* $\mathcal{L}(\mathsf{DB_0}, I) = \mathcal{L}(\mathsf{DB_1}, I)$. *As a response,* $\mathcal{A}$ *obtains* $\mathsf{Enc_{sk}(DB_b)}$ *and* $\mathsf{TokenGen_{sk}(DB_b}, I)$.
3. *Output phase:* $\mathcal{A}$ *outputs a value* $\sigma \in \{0, 1\}$ *which is defined as the value of the experiment.*

The following claim, which is proved in the full version of this paper [34], states that non-adaptive IND security is implied by 3Partition security.

Claim 4.3. *Any* 3Partition-*secure join scheme that supports a message space of super-polynomial size (in the security parameter* $\lambda \in \mathbb{N}$) *is a non-adaptively* IND-*secure join scheme.*

Adaptive IND security. We consider an adaptive flavor of Definition 4.2 by considering adversaries that can adaptively issue encoding queries and token-generation queries. Each encoding query consists of a pair of messages, m_0 and m_1, and a column label col, and the adversary obtains an encoding $\mathsf{Enc_{sk}}(m_b, \mathsf{col})$ (where $b \in \{0, 1\}$ is fixed throughout the experiment). The adversary's encoding queries define two databases, $\mathsf{DB_0}$ and $\mathsf{DB_1}$, of the same dimension that have the same column label set. Each token-generation query consists of a pair of column labels, and the adversary obtains a token for computing the join of these columns. The adversary's token-generation queries define a set I of all column label pairs for which the adversary has obtained tokens. Such an adversary is called "valid" if at the end of the experiment it holds that $\mathcal{L}(\mathsf{DB_0}, I) = \mathcal{L}(\mathsf{DB_1}, I)$.

Definition 4.4 (Adaptive IND security). *A join scheme* $\Pi = (\mathsf{KeyGen, Enc,}$ $\mathsf{TokenGen, Adj})$ *is* IND-secure *if for any probabilistic polynomial-time valid adversary* $\mathcal{A}$ *there exists a negligible function* $\nu(\cdot)$ *such that*

$$\mathsf{Adv}_{\Pi,\mathcal{A}}^{\mathsf{IND}}(\lambda) \stackrel{\text{def}}{=} \left| \Pr\left[\mathsf{Exp}_{\Pi,\mathcal{A}}^{\mathsf{IND}}(\lambda, 0) = 1 \right] - \Pr\left[\mathsf{Exp}_{\Pi,\mathcal{A}}^{\mathsf{IND}}(\lambda, 1) = 1 \right] \right| \leq \nu(\lambda)$$

for all sufficiently large $\lambda \in \mathbb{N}$, *where for each* $b \in \{0, 1\}$ *the experiment* $\mathsf{Exp}_{\Pi,\mathcal{A}}^{\mathsf{IND}}(\lambda, b)$ *is defined as follows:*

1. *Setup phase: Sample* (sk, params) ← KeyGen(1^λ). *The public parameters* params *are given as input to the adversary* $\mathcal{A}$.
2. *Query phase:* $\mathcal{A}$ *may adaptively issue* Enc *and* TokenGen *queries, which are defined as follows.*
    - Enc(m_0, m_1, col): *Computes an encoding* $c \leftarrow$ Enc$_{sk}(m_b$, col), *and returns* c *to* $\mathcal{A}$.
    - TokenGen(col$_i$, col$_j$): *Computes a token* $(\tau_i, \tau_j) \leftarrow$ TokenGen$_{sk}$(col$_i$, col$_j$), *and returns* (τ_i, τ_j) *to* $\mathcal{A}$.
3. *Output phase:* $\mathcal{A}$ *outputs a value* $\sigma \in \{0,1\}$ *which is defined as the value of the experiment.*

The following claim states that adaptive IND security implies 3Partition security.

Claim 4.5. *Any adaptively* IND-*secure join scheme is a* 3Partition-*secure join scheme.*

The proof of Claim 4.5 is straightforward, as the IND-security experiment is essentially less restrictive than the 3Partition-security experiment. Specifically, given an adversary to the 3Partition-security experiment we can construct an adversary to the IND-security experiment (having the exact same advantage) as follows:

- All queries of the form AddColumn(col, S) are ignored. However, the adversary keeps track of the set R.
- Any query of the form Enc(m, col) is converted into a query Enc(m, m, col).
- Any query of the form TokenGen(col$_i$, col$_j$) is forwarded as without any modification.
- The challenge (m_0, m_1) is converted into queries of the form Enc(m_0, m_1, col) for each col $\in R$.
- Any query of the form AddColumn(col, "R") in the post-challenge query phase is converted into a query Enc(m_0, m_1, col).

4.3 Simulation-Based Security Notions

As with our indistinguishability-based notions, we first formalize a non-adaptive simulation-based notion, which we then generalize to an adaptive one.

Non-adaptive SIM security. Our non-adaptive simulation-based notion considers an adversary $\mathcal{A}$ and a simulator $\mathcal{S}$. In the real-world experiment, the adversary $\mathcal{A}$ interacts with the scheme in the following non-adaptive manner: It obtains the public parameters of the scheme, chooses a databases DB and a list I of column label pairs, and then obtains an encoding of DB and tokens for all column label pairs in I. In the ideal-world experiment, the simulator has to produce a view that is indistinguishable from the real world when given only the "minimal" leakage $\mathcal{L}(\text{DB}, I)$, and without being given the database DB (recall that the leakage function $\mathcal{L}$ was defined in Sect. 4.2).

Formally, for an adjustable join scheme Π and an adversary $\mathcal{A}$, we consider the experiment Real$_{\Pi, \mathcal{A}}^{\text{naSIM}}(\lambda)$ which is defined as follows:

1. Setup phase: Sample $(\mathsf{sk}, \mathsf{params}) \leftarrow \mathsf{KeyGen}(1^\lambda)$. The public parameters params are given as input to the adversary $\mathcal{A}$.
2. Challenge phase: $\mathcal{A}$ chooses a databases DB and a list I of column label pairs. As a response, $\mathcal{A}$ obtains $\mathsf{Enc}_{\mathsf{sk}}(\mathsf{DB})$ and $\mathsf{TokenGen}_{\mathsf{sk}}(\mathsf{DB}, I)$.
3. Output phase: $\mathcal{A}$ outputs a value $\sigma \in \{0, 1\}$ which is defined as the value of the experiment.

In addition, given an adversary $\mathcal{A}$ and a simulator $\mathcal{S}$, we consider the experiment $\mathsf{Ideal}^{\mathsf{naSIM}}_{\mathcal{A},\mathcal{S}}(\lambda)$ which is defined as follows:

1. Setup phase: The simulator $\mathcal{S}$ produces the public parameters params, which are given as input to the adversary $\mathcal{A}$.
2. Challenge phase: $\mathcal{A}$ chooses a databases DB and a list I of column label pairs. The simulator is given $\mathcal{L}(\mathsf{DB}, I)$ and produces a database encoding and a list of tokens, which are given to $\mathcal{A}$.
3. Output phase: $\mathcal{A}$ outputs a value $\sigma \in \{0, 1\}$ which is defined as the value of the experiment.

Definition 4.6 (Non-adaptive SIM security). *A join scheme $\Pi = (\mathsf{KeyGen},$ $\mathsf{Enc}, \mathsf{TokenGen}, \mathsf{Adj})$ is non-adaptively SIM-secure if for any probabilistic polynomial-time adversary $\mathcal{A}$ there exist a probabilistic polynomial-time simulator $\mathcal{S}$ and a negligible function $\nu(\cdot)$ such that*

$$\mathsf{Adv}^{\mathsf{naSIM}}_{\Pi,\mathcal{A},\mathcal{S}}(\lambda) \overset{\mathsf{def}}{=} \left| \Pr\left[\mathsf{Real}^{\mathsf{naSIM}}_{\Pi,\mathcal{A}}(\lambda) = 1\right] - \Pr\left[\mathsf{Ideal}^{\mathsf{naSIM}}_{\mathcal{A},\mathcal{S}}(\lambda) = 1\right] \right| \leq \nu(\lambda)$$

for all sufficiently large $\lambda \in \mathbb{N}$.

The following claim, which is proved in the full version of this paper [34], states that non-adaptive SIM security is equivalent to non-adaptive IND security.

Claim 4.7. *Any join scheme Π that supports a message space of super-polynomial size (in the security parameter $\lambda \in \mathbb{N}$) is non-adaptively SIM secure if and only if it is non-adaptive IND secure.*

Adaptive SIM security. We consider an adaptive flavor of Definition 4.6 by naturally generalizing the above real-world and ideal-world experiments. Specifically, for an adjustable join scheme Π and an adversary $\mathcal{A}$, we consider the experiment $\mathsf{Real}^{\mathsf{SIM}}_{\Pi,\mathcal{A}}(\lambda)$ which is defined as follows:

1. Setup phase: Sample $(\mathsf{sk}, \mathsf{params}) \leftarrow \mathsf{KeyGen}(1^\lambda)$. The public parameters params are given as input to the adversary $\mathcal{A}$.
2. Query phase: $\mathcal{A}$ may adaptively issue Enc and TokenGen queries, which are defined as follows.
   - $\mathsf{Enc}(m, \mathsf{col})$: Computes an encoding $c \leftarrow \mathsf{Enc}_{\mathsf{sk}}(m, \mathsf{col})$, and returns c to $\mathcal{A}$.
   - $\mathsf{TokenGen}(\mathsf{col}_i, \mathsf{col}_j)$: Computes a token $(\tau_i, \tau_j) \leftarrow \mathsf{TokenGen}_{\mathsf{sk}}(\mathsf{col}_i, \mathsf{col}_j)$, and returns (τ_i, τ_j) to $\mathcal{A}$.

3. Output phase: $\mathcal{A}$ outputs a value $\sigma \in \{0,1\}$ which is defined as the value of the experiment.

In addition, given an adversary $\mathcal{A}$ and a simulator $\mathcal{S}$, we consider the experiment $\mathsf{Ideal}^{\mathsf{SIM}}_{\mathcal{A},\mathcal{S}}(\lambda)$ which is defined as follows:

1. Setup phase: The simulator $\mathcal{S}$ produces the public parameters params, which are given as input to the adversary $\mathcal{A}$. An empty database DB and an empty list I of column label pairs are initialized.
2. Query phase: $\mathcal{A}$ may adaptively issue Enc and TokenGen queries, which are defined as follows.
   - Enc(m, col): The pair (m, col) is inserted into the database DB, and $\mathcal{S}$ obtains $\mathcal{L}(\mathsf{DB}, I)$. Then, $\mathcal{S}$ provides $\mathcal{A}$ with an encoding c.
   - TokenGen($\mathsf{col}_i, \mathsf{col}_j$): The pair $(\mathsf{col}_i, \mathsf{col}_j)$ is inserted into the list I, and $\mathcal{S}$ obtains $\mathcal{L}(\mathsf{DB}, I)$. Then, $\mathcal{S}$ provides $\mathcal{A}$ with a pair (τ_i, τ_j).
3.. Output phase: $\mathcal{A}$ outputs a value $\sigma \in \{0,1\}$ which is defined as the value of the experiment.

Definition 4.8 (Adaptive SIM security). *A join scheme* $\Pi = (\mathsf{KeyGen}, \mathsf{Enc}, \mathsf{TokenGen}, \mathsf{Adj})$ *is* SIM*-secure if for any probabilistic polynomial-time adversary* $\mathcal{A}$ *there exist a probabilistic polynomial-time simulator* $\mathcal{S}$ *and a negligible function* $\nu(\cdot)$ *such that*

$$\mathsf{Adv}^{\mathsf{SIM}}_{\Pi,\mathcal{A},\mathcal{S}}(\lambda) \stackrel{\mathsf{def}}{=} \left| \Pr\left[\mathsf{Real}^{\mathsf{SIM}}_{\Pi,\mathcal{A}}(\lambda) = 1\right] - \Pr\left[\mathsf{Ideal}^{\mathsf{SIM}}_{\mathcal{A},\mathcal{S}}(\lambda) = 1\right] \right| \leq \nu(\lambda)$$

for all sufficiently large $\lambda \in \mathbb{N}$.

The following claim states that adaptive SIM security implies adaptive IND security.

Claim 4.9. *Any* SIM*-secure join scheme is an* IND*-secure join scheme.*

The proof idea of Claim 4.9 is similar to the non-adaptive case: The adversary cannot distinguish between DB_0 and the simulation, and between the simulation and DB_1, hence cannot distinguish between DB_0 and DB_1. In more details, given an adversary $\mathcal{B}$ to the IND-security experiment, we construct an adversary $\mathcal{A}$ to the SIM-security experiment, which samples $c \leftarrow \{0,1\}$, and converts each query of the form Enc(m_0, m_1, col) into a query Enc(m_c, col). Finally, when $\mathcal{B}$ halts and outputs $\sigma \in \{0,1\}$ then $\mathcal{A}$ halts and outputs $\sigma \oplus c$. A similar argument to the one in the proof of Claim 4.7 shows that

$$\mathsf{Adv}^{\mathsf{IND}}_{\Pi,\mathcal{B}}(\lambda) = 2 \cdot \mathsf{Adv}^{\mathsf{SIM}}_{\Pi,\mathcal{A},\mathcal{S}}(\lambda),$$

where $\mathcal{S}$ is the simulator for which $\mathsf{Adv}^{\mathsf{SIM}}_{\Pi,\mathcal{A},\mathcal{S}}(\lambda)$ is negligible. Therefore, the SIM-security of Π implies its IND-security.

4.4 Additional Remarks

Column privacy. Our notions of security include the column labels Cols(DB) of the encrypted databases as explicit leakage (either as part of the experiment or via leakage functions). In fact, our scheme in Sect. 5 does not leak the column labels. All of our security notions can be naturally refined to model column privacy in addition to message privacy. Although the task of guaranteeing column privacy is well motivated, in this paper we focus on message privacy in order to simplify our notions of security.

Implicit (and unavoidable) leakage. Our notions of security assume that the given encrypted databases are "valid" in the sense that no message appears more than once in each column. An alternative approach (e.g., [13,15]) is to avoid this assumption, and explicitly include a leakage function that specifies the frequency characteristics of each column. For deterministic encodings of messages (where such leakage is unavoidable), these two approaches are equivalent. Therefore, we do not explicitly include such a leakage function, but rather incorporate this unavoidable leakage directly into our security notions.

5 Our Adjustable Join Scheme

In this section we present an adjustable join scheme that satisfies our 3Partition security notion. In Sect. 5.1 we describe our scheme and prove its correctness, and in Sect. 5.2 we prove its security.

5.1 The Scheme

Let $\mathsf{PRF} = (\mathsf{PRF.Gen}, \mathsf{PRF.Eval})$ be a pseudorandom function family, and let $\mathcal{G}$ be a probabilistic polynomial-time algorithm that takes as input the security parameter 1^λ, and outputs a triplet $(\mathbb{G}, \mathbb{G}_T, g, p, \hat{e})$, where p is a λ-bit prime number, $\mathbb{G}$ and $\mathbb{G}_T$ are groups of order p, g is a generator of $\mathbb{G}$, and $\hat{e} : \mathbb{G} \times \mathbb{G} \to \mathbb{G}_T$ is a non-degenerate efficiently-computable bilinear map. The scheme $\Pi = (\mathsf{KeyGen}, \mathsf{Enc}, \mathsf{TokenGen}, \mathsf{Adj})$ is defined as follows.

- **Key generation.** On input 1^λ the key-generation algorithm KeyGen samples $(\mathbb{G}, \mathbb{G}_T, g, p, \hat{e}) \leftarrow \mathcal{G}(1^\lambda)$, $K_1 \leftarrow \mathsf{PRF.Gen}(1^\lambda)$, and $K_2 \leftarrow \mathsf{PRF.Gen}(1^\lambda)$. For each $i \in \{1, 2\}$ we let $\mathsf{PRF}_{K_i}(\cdot) = \mathsf{PRF.Eval}(K_i, \cdot)$, and we assume that $\mathsf{PRF}_{K_1} : \mathcal{M}_\lambda \to \mathbb{Z}_p^4$ and $\mathsf{PRF}_{K_2} : \mathcal{L}_\lambda \to \mathsf{Rk}_4(\mathbb{Z}_p^{4\times 4})$, where $\mathcal{M} = \{\mathcal{M}_\lambda\}_{\lambda \in \mathbb{N}}$ and $\mathcal{L} = \{\mathcal{L}_\lambda\}_{\lambda \in \mathbb{N}}$ are the message space and the column label space, respectively. The algorithm outputs $\mathsf{params} = (\mathbb{G}, \mathbb{G}_T, g, p, \hat{e})$ and $\mathsf{sk} = (K_1, K_2)$.

  For the above description, recall that $\mathsf{Rk}_4(\mathbb{Z}_p^{4\times 4})$ denotes the set of all invertible 4×4 matrices over $\mathbb{Z}_p$. Note that a pseudorandom function $\mathsf{PRF}_{K_2} : \mathcal{M}_\lambda \to \mathsf{Rk}_4(\mathbb{Z}_p^{4\times 4})$ can be constructed, for example, by taking any pseudorandom function $\mathsf{PRF}_{K_2} : \mathcal{M}_\lambda \to \mathbb{Z}_p^{4\times 4}$ and substituting each non-invertible output with the identity matrix.

- **Encoding.** On input params $= (\mathbb{G}, \mathbb{G}_T, g, p, \hat{e})$, sk $= (K_1, K_2)$, a column label col $\in \mathcal{L}_\lambda$ and a message $m \in \mathcal{M}_\lambda$, the encoding algorithm Enc computes $A_{\mathsf{col}} = \mathsf{PRF}_{K_2}(\mathsf{col}) \in \mathsf{Rk}_4(\mathbb{Z}_p^{4\times4})$ and $x_m = \mathsf{PRF}_{K_1}(m) \in \mathbb{Z}_p^4$, and then outputs $c = g^{A_{\mathsf{col}} x_m} \in \mathbb{G}^4$.
- **Token generation.** On input params $= (\mathbb{G}, \mathbb{G}_T, g, p, \hat{e})$, sk $= (K_1, K_2)$ and two column labels col, col$' \in \mathcal{L}_\lambda$, the token-generation algorithm TokenGen uniformly samples $v \leftarrow \mathbb{Z}_p^4 \setminus \{(0,0,0,0)\}$, computes $A_{\mathsf{col}} = \mathsf{PRF}_{K_2}(\mathsf{col}) \in \mathsf{Rk}_4(\mathbb{Z}_p^{4\times4})$ and $A_{\mathsf{col}'} = \mathsf{PRF}_{K_2}(\mathsf{col}') \in \mathsf{Rk}_4(\mathbb{Z}_p^{4\times4})$, and then outputs the pair of adjustment tokens $\left(g^{v^\mathsf{T} A_{\mathsf{col}}^{-1}}, g^{v^\mathsf{T} A_{\mathsf{col}'}^{-1}}\right) \in \mathbb{G}^4 \times \mathbb{G}^4$.
- **Adjustment.** On input params $= (\mathbb{G}, \mathbb{G}_T, g, p, \hat{e})$, an adjustment token $\tau \in \mathbb{G}^4$, and an encoding $c \in \mathbb{G}^4$, the adjustment algorithm Adj outputs $\hat{e}(\tau^\mathsf{T}, c) \in \mathbb{G}_T$.

Correctness. For any two column labels col, col$' \in \mathcal{L}_\lambda$ and for any two messages $m, m' \in \mathcal{M}_\lambda$ it holds that

$$\mathsf{Adj}\left(\tau, \mathsf{Enc}_{\mathsf{sk}}(m, \mathsf{col})\right) = \hat{e}\left(g^{v^\mathsf{T} A_{\mathsf{col}}^{-1}}, g^{A_{\mathsf{col}} x_m}\right)$$
$$= \hat{e}(g, g)^{v^\mathsf{T} A_{\mathsf{col}}^{-1} A_{\mathsf{col}} x_m} = \hat{e}(g, g)^{v^\mathsf{T} x_m}$$
$$\mathsf{Adj}\left(\tau', \mathsf{Enc}_{\mathsf{sk}}(m', \mathsf{col}')\right) = \hat{e}\left(g^{v^\mathsf{T} A_{\mathsf{col}'}^{-1}}, g^{A_{\mathsf{col}'} x_{m'}}\right)$$
$$= \hat{e}(g, g)^{v^\mathsf{T} A_{\mathsf{col}'}^{-1} A_{\mathsf{col}'} x_{m'}} = \hat{e}(g, g)^{v^\mathsf{T} x_{m'}},$$

where (sk, params) $\leftarrow$ KeyGen(1^λ) and $(\tau, \tau') \leftarrow$ Adj(sk, col, col$'$). Therefore, it holds that
$$\mathsf{Adj}\left(\tau, \mathsf{Enc}_{\mathsf{sk}}(m, \mathsf{col})\right) = \mathsf{Adj}\left(\tau', \mathsf{Enc}_{\mathsf{sk}}(m', \mathsf{col}')\right)$$
if and only if $v^\mathsf{T} x_m = v^\mathsf{T} x_{m'}$. Note that if $m = m'$ then the equality always holds. In addition, if $m \neq m'$ then with an overwhelming probability $x_m \neq x_{m'}$ (since PRF is a pseudorandom function), and since v is uniform then the probability that $v^\mathsf{T} x_m = v^\mathsf{T} x_{m'}$ is at most $1/p$. We conclude that if $m \neq m'$ then $v^\mathsf{T} x_m \neq v^\mathsf{T} x_{m'}$ with an overwhelming probability.

5.2 Proof of Security

We prove the following theorem:

Theorem 5.1. *Assuming that* PRF *is a pseudorandom function family and that the linear assumption holds relative to* $\mathcal{G}$*, then* Π *is a* 3Partition*-secure adjustable join scheme.*

For proving Theorem 5.1, we introduce a scheme $\hat{\Pi}$ which is obtained from Π by replacing its TokenGen and Adj algorithms with the followings algorithms:

- **Token generation.** On input params $= (\mathbb{G}, \mathbb{G}_T, g, p, \hat{e})$, sk $= (K_1, K_2)$ and two column labels col, col$' \in \mathcal{L}_\lambda$, the modified token-generation algorithm TokenGen uniformly samples $V \leftarrow \mathsf{Rk}_4(\mathbb{Z}_p^{4\times4})$, computes $A_{\mathsf{col}} =$

$\mathsf{PRF}_{K_2}(\mathsf{col}) \in \mathsf{Rk}_4(\mathbb{Z}_p^{4\times 4})$ and $A_{\mathsf{col}'} = \mathsf{PRF}_{K_2}(\mathsf{col}') \in \mathsf{Rk}_4(\mathbb{Z}_p^{4\times 4})$, and then outputs $\left(g^{VA_{\mathsf{col}}^{-1}}, g^{VA_{\mathsf{col}'}^{-1}}\right) \in \mathbb{G}^{4\times 4} \times \mathbb{G}^{4\times 4}$.

- **Adjustment.** On input params $= (\mathbb{G}, \mathbb{G}_T, g, p, \hat{e})$, an adjustment token $\mathcal{T} \in \mathbb{G}^{4\times 4}$, and an encoding $c \in \mathbb{G}^4$, the modified adjustment algorithm Adj outputs $\hat{e}(\mathcal{T}, c) \in \mathbb{G}_T^4$.

Note that Π can be obtained from $\hat{\Pi}$ by viewing any $v \in \mathbb{Z}_p^4 \setminus \{(0,0,0,0)\}$ that is produced by Π's token-generation algorithm as the first row of the matrix $V \in \mathsf{Rk}_4(\mathbb{Z}_p^{4\times 4})$ that is produced by $\hat{\Pi}$ token-generation algorithm. That is, Π's token-generation algorithm can be obtained from $\hat{\Pi}$'s token-generation algorithm by outputting only the first rows of its tokens. Thus, there is no information that Π reveals and $\hat{\Pi}$ does not, and therefore it suffices to prove the security of $\hat{\Pi}$.

For each $b \in \{0,1\}$ and an adversary $\mathcal{A}$, let $\mathsf{Exp}^{\mathsf{3Par}}_{\mathsf{Rand},\mathcal{A}}(\lambda, b)$ denote the experiment obtained from $\mathsf{Exp}^{\mathsf{3Par}}_{\hat{\Pi},\mathcal{A}}(\lambda, b)$ by replacing the pseudorandom functions $\mathsf{PRF}_{K_1} : \mathcal{M}_\lambda \to \mathbb{Z}_p^4$ and $\mathsf{PRF}_{K_2} : \mathcal{L}_\lambda \to \mathsf{Rk}_4(\mathbb{Z}_p^{4\times 4})$ with truly random functions $f_1 : \mathcal{M}_\lambda \to \mathbb{Z}_p^4$ and $f_2 : \mathcal{L}_\lambda \to \mathsf{Rk}_4(\mathbb{Z}_p^{4\times 4})$. By the pseudorandomness property of the pseudorandom function family PRF, it holds that for any $b \in \{0,1\}$ and any probabilistic polynomial-time adversary $\mathcal{A}$, the advantage of $\mathcal{A}$ in distinguishing between the experiments $\mathsf{Exp}^{\mathsf{3Par}}_{\hat{\Pi},\mathcal{A}}(\lambda, b)$ and $\mathsf{Exp}^{\mathsf{3Par}}_{\mathsf{Rand},\mathcal{A}}(\lambda, b)$ is negligible. Therefore, in order to prove the 3Partition-security of $\hat{\Pi}$ it suffices to show that the advantage of any adversary $\mathcal{A}$ in distinguishing between the experiments $\mathsf{Exp}^{\mathsf{3Par}}_{\mathsf{Rand},\mathcal{A}}(\lambda, 0)$ and $\mathsf{Exp}^{\mathsf{3Par}}_{\mathsf{Rand},\mathcal{A}}(\lambda, 1)$ is negligible.

By Claim 2.5 and Fact 2.3, it follows that under the linear assumption it holds that

$$\left(\mathsf{params}, g^A, g^{Ax}, g^{Ay}, g^B, g^{Bx}\right) \approx_c \left(\mathsf{params}, g^A, g^{Ax}, g^{Ay}, g^B, g^{Bz}\right)$$
$$\approx_c \left(\mathsf{params}, g^A, g^{Ax}, g^{Ay}, g^B, g^{By}\right),$$

where $\mathsf{params} \leftarrow \mathcal{G}(1^\lambda)$, $A, B \leftarrow \mathsf{Rk}_4(\mathbb{Z}_p^{4\times 4})$ and $x, y, z \leftarrow \mathbb{Z}_p^4$. We denote by X and Y the computationally indistinguishable ensembles $X = (\mathsf{params}, g^A, g^{Ax}, g^{Ay}, g^B, g^{Bx})$ and $Y = (\mathsf{params}, g^A, g^{Ax}, g^{Ay}, g^B, g^{By})$. Assume for now that during the pre-challenge query phase, the adversary $\mathcal{A}$ does not issue a query of the form $\mathsf{Enc}(m_0, \mathsf{col})$ or $\mathsf{Enc}(m_1, \mathsf{col})$, from any column label col, where m_0 and m_1 are the challenge messages. We claim that there exists a polynomial-time challenger Chal, such that it holds that $\mathsf{Chal}^{\mathcal{A}}(X) \equiv \mathsf{Exp}^{\mathsf{3Par}}_{\mathsf{Rand},\mathcal{A}}(\lambda, 0)$ and $\mathsf{Chal}^{\mathcal{A}}(Y) \equiv \mathsf{Exp}^{\mathsf{3Par}}_{\mathsf{Rand},\mathcal{A}}(\lambda, 0)$ as distributions (and this implies that the advantage of $\mathcal{A}$ in distinguishing between the experiments $\mathsf{Exp}^{\mathsf{3Par}}_{\mathsf{Rand},\mathcal{A}}(\lambda, 0)$ and $\mathsf{Exp}^{\mathsf{3Par}}_{\mathsf{Rand},\mathcal{A}}(\lambda, 1)$ is negligible subject to the above assumption on $\mathcal{A}$). Given $(\mathsf{params}, g^A, g^{Ax}, g^{Ay}, g^B, g^{Bz})$ as input and $\mathcal{A}$ as oracle, the challenger Chal works as follows:

Setup phase. Chal provides $\mathcal{A}$ with params.

Pre-challenge query phase. We specify how Chal handles $\mathcal{A}$'s queries:

- AddColumn(col, S): Chal adds the column label col to the set S, where $S \in \{"L", "R", "M"\}$. In addition, Chal samples $R_{col} \leftarrow \mathsf{Rk}_4(\mathbb{Z}_p^{4 \times 4})$, and denotes

$$A_{col} = \begin{cases} R_{col} A & col \in L \\ R_{col} B & col \in R \\ R_{col} & col \in M \end{cases}.$$

Note that since Chal does not explicitly know A and B, he does not explicitly know A_{col} in case that $col \in L \cup R$.

- Enc(m, col): Chal samples $x_m \leftarrow \mathbb{Z}_p^4$, unless it was already sampled before. Then, Chal returns $c = g^{A_{col} x_m}$ to $\mathcal{A}$. We need to show that Chal can efficiently compute c, and we show this by cases:
  1. $col \in M$: Chal explicitly knows $A_{col} = R_{col}$ and x_m, so he can efficiently compute $g^{A_{col} x_m}$.
  2. $col \in L$: Since Chal knows g^A, R_{col} and x_m, he can efficiently compute $g^{A_{col} x_m} = {}^{R_{col}} \left(g^A\right)^{x_m}$.
  3. $col \in R$: Similar to the previous case, but with g^B.

- TokenGen(col_i, col_j): Chal returns to $\mathcal{A}$ the pair of tokens $\left(g^{V A_{col_i}^{-1}}, g^{V A_{col_j}^{-1}}\right)$ where $V \leftarrow \mathsf{Rk}_4(\mathbb{Z}_p^{4 \times 4})$ is freshly sampled. We show that Chal is able to efficiently compute τ by cases:
  1. $col_i, col_j \in M$: Since Chal explicitly knows $A_{col_i} = R_{col_i}$ and $A_{col_j} = R_{col_j}$, he can simply sample $V \leftarrow \mathsf{Rk}_4(\mathbb{Z}_p^{4 \times 4})$, and compute $g^{V A_{col_i}^{-1}}$ and $g^{V A_{col_j}^{-1}}$.
  2. $col_i, col_j \in L$: Denote $U = V A_{col_i}^{-1}$ and $W = V A_{col_j}^{-1}$. Chal needs to be able to compute g^U and g^W. Fixing A_{col_i} and A_{col_j}, both U and W are uniform in $\mathsf{Rk}_4(\mathbb{Z}_p^{4 \times 4})$, but dependent of each other by the relation $U A_{col_i} = W A_{col_j}$. In our case, $A_{col_i} = R_{col_i} A$ and $A_{col_j} = R_{col_j} A$, so the relation turns into $U R_{col_i} = W R_{col_j}$, and Chal can sample $U \leftarrow \mathsf{Rk}_4(\mathbb{Z}_p^{4 \times 4})$ and take $W = U R_{col_i} R_{col_j}^{-1}$. Since Chal explicitly knows U and W, he can compute g^U and g^W efficiently.
  3. $col_i, col_j \in R$: Similar to the previous case.
  4. $col_i \in L$ and $col_j \in M$: In this case, $A_{col_i} = R_{col_i} A$ and $A_{col_j} = R_{col_j}$, so the relation $U A_{col_i} = W A_{col_j}$ turns into $U R_{col_i} A = W R_{col_j}$. So Chal can sample $U \leftarrow \mathsf{Rk}_4(\mathbb{Z}_p^{4 \times 4})$ and take $W = U R_{col_i} A R_{col_j}^{-1}$. Since Chal explicitly knows U, he can compute g^U. Since he knows U, R_{col_i}, R_{col_j} and g^A, he can efficiently compute $g^W = {}^{U R_{col_i}} \left(g^A\right)^{R_{col_j}^{-1}}$.
  5. $col_i \in R$ and $col_j \in M$: Similar to the previous case.
  6. $col_i \in L$ and $col_j \in R$: This case is not allowed by the definition of 3Partition-security.

Challenge phase. $\mathcal{A}$ chooses messages m_0 and m_1. As a response, Chal returns to $\mathcal{A}$ an encoding $c = g^{A_{col} z}$ for every $col \in R$. Since $c = {}^{R_{col}} \left(g^{Bz}\right)$, and Chal knows R_{col} and g^{Bz}, it can efficiently compute c.

Post-challenge query phase. The only differences from the pre-challenge query phase are the followings:

- AddColumn(col, S): In case that S="R", Chal provides $\mathcal{A}$ with $c = g^{A_{col}z}$, which we already saw that Chal can efficiently compute.
- Enc(m, col): In case that $m = m_0$ or $m = m_1$, by the definition of 3Partition-security it must be that col $\in L$, and Chal return to $\mathcal{A}$ the encoding $g^{A_{col}x}$ or $g^{A_{col}y}$, respectively. Since $g^{A_{col}x} = {}^{R_{col}}(g^{Ax})$ and $g^{A_{col}y} = {}^{R_{col}}(g^{Ay})$, Chal can efficiently compute them.

Output phase. Chal outputs the value $\sigma \in \{0, 1\}$ that $\mathcal{A}$ outputs.

This completes the description of Chal. Denote $x_{m_0} = x$ and $x_{m_1} = y$. It does not cause ambiguity in the notation because we assume that $\mathcal{A}$ does not query m_0 or m_1 in the pre-challenge query phase, so Chal never samples x_{m_0} and x_{m_1} by himself. Every $x_m \in \mathbb{Z}_p^4$ and $A_{col} \in \mathsf{Rk}_4(\mathbb{Z}_p^{4\times4})$ are uniformly random. So Chal returns to $\mathcal{A}$ encodings and tokens with respect to truly random functions. In the case that Chal is given as input $X = (\mathsf{params}, g^A, g^{Ax}, g^{Ay}, g^B, g^{Bx})$, it answers the challenge with encodings of m_0, so we obtain the experiment $\mathsf{Exp}_{\mathsf{Rand},\mathcal{A}}^{\mathsf{3Par}}(\lambda, 0)$. Similarly, in the case Chal is given $Y = (\mathsf{params}, g^A, g^{Ax}, g^{Ay}, g^B, g^{By})$, we obtain the experiment $\mathsf{Exp}_{\mathsf{Rand},\mathcal{A}}^{\mathsf{3Par}}(\lambda, 1)$. This completes the proof of security for adversaries that fulfill the aforementioned assumption.

When dealing with adversaries that may query m_0 and m_1 in the pre-challenge phase, the problem is that Chal does not know when he queried on m_0 and m_1. If he knew that, then he could respond in the same way he does in the post-challenge query phase. So to solve this, Chal guesses when it is queried with m_0 or m_1. More precisely, let $q(\lambda)$ be a bound on the number of queries that $\mathcal{A}$ performs. Chal samples $t_0, t_1 \leftarrow \{0, \ldots, q(\lambda)\}$. During the pre-challenge phase, if Chal is queried for an encoding of a message m that is the t_0-th or t_1-th distinct message so far, then he acts as if it was queried on m_0 or m_1 respectively, that is, he returns to $\mathcal{A}$ the encoding $g^{A_{col}x}$ or $g^{A_{col}y}$, respectively. Then, in the challenge phase, if it turns out that the guess was wrong, or if Chal was queried on less than $\max\{t_0, t_1\}$ distinct messages, then Chal aborts and outputs 0. Since until the challenge phase, the view of $\mathcal{A}$ is independent of the sampling of t_0 and t_1, it holds that the guess of Chal succeeds with probability of exactly $1/(q(\lambda)+1)^2$, and that the success probability is independent of the behavior of $\mathcal{A}$, so it holds that,

$$\left| \Pr\left[\mathsf{Exp}_{\mathsf{Rand},\mathcal{A}}^{\mathsf{3Par}}(\lambda, 0) = 1\right] - \Pr\left[\mathsf{Exp}_{\mathsf{Rand},\mathcal{A}}^{\mathsf{3Par}}(\lambda, 1) = 1\right] \right| \tag{1}$$

$$= (q(\lambda)+1)^2 \cdot \left| \Pr\left[\mathsf{Chal}^{\mathcal{A}}(X) = 1\right] - \Pr\left[\mathsf{Chal}^{\mathcal{A}}(Y) = 1\right] \right|. \tag{2}$$

For any probabilistic polynomial-time adversary $\mathcal{A}$, the bound $q(\lambda)$ on its number of queries is polynomial in the security parameter λ. The linear assumption implies that the expression in Eq. (2) is negligible, and therefore also the expression in Eq. (1) is negligible, and this concludes the proof.

Acknowledgments. We thank Zvika Brakerski for fruitful discussions and the TCC reviewers for their valuable comments.

Gil Segev and Ido Shahaf are supported by the European Union's 7th Framework Program (FP7) via a Marie Curie Career Integration Grant (Grant No. 618094), by the European Union's Horizon 2020 Framework Program (H2020) via an ERC Grant (Grant No. 714253), by the Israel Science Foundation (Grant No. 483/13), by the Israeli Centers of Research Excellence (I-CORE) Program (Center No. 4/11), by the US-Israel Binational Science Foundation (Grant No. 2014632), and by a Google Faculty Research Award.

References

1. Asharov, G., Naor, M., Segev, G., Shahaf, I..: Searchable symmetric encryption: Optimal locality in linear space via two-dimensional balanced allocations. In: Proceedings of the 48th Annual ACM Symposium on Theory of Computing, pp. 1101–1114 (2016)
2. Ateniese, G., Fu, K., Green, M., Hohenberger, S.: Improved proxy re-encryption schemes with applications to secure distributed storage. ACM Trans. Inf. Syst. Secur. **9**(1), 1–30 (2006)
3. Blaze, M., Bleumer, G., Strauss, M.: Divertible protocols and atomic proxy cryptography. In: Nyberg, K. (ed.) EUROCRYPT 1998. LNCS, vol. 1403, pp. 127–144. Springer, Heidelberg (1998). https://doi.org/10.1007/BFb0054122
4. Boneh, D., Boyen, X., Shacham, H.: Short group signatures. In: Franklin, M. (ed.) CRYPTO 2004. LNCS, vol. 3152, pp. 41–55. Springer, Heidelberg (2004). https://doi.org/10.1007/978-3-540-28628-8_3
5. Boneh, D., Lewi, K., Raykova, M., Sahai, A., Zhandry, M., Zimmerman, J.: Semantically secure order-revealing encryption: multi-input functional encryption without obfuscation. In: Oswald, E., Fischlin, M. (eds.) EUROCRYPT 2015. LNCS, vol. 9057, pp. 563–594. Springer, Heidelberg (2015). https://doi.org/10.1007/978-3-662-46803-6_19
6. Bösch, C., Hartel, P.H., Jonker, W., Peter, A.: A survey of provably secure searchable encryption. ACM Comput. Surv. **47**(2), 1–18 (2014)
7. Brakerski, Z., Komargodski, I., Segev, G.: Multi-input functional encryption in the private-key setting: stronger security from weaker assumptions. In: Fischlin, M., Coron, J.-S. (eds.) EUROCRYPT 2016. LNCS, vol. 9666, pp. 852–880. Springer, Heidelberg (2016). https://doi.org/10.1007/978-3-662-49896-5_30
8. Cash, D., Grubbs, P., Perry, J., Ristenpart, T.: Leakage-abuse attacks against searchable encryption. In: Proceedings of the 22nd ACM Conference on Computer and Communications Security, pp. 668–679 (2015)
9. Cash, D., Jaeger, J., Jarecki, S., Jutla, C.S., Krawczyk, H., Rosu, M., Steiner, M.: Dynamic searchable encryption in very-large databases: data structures and implementation. In: Proceedings of the 21st Annual Network and Distributed System Security Symposium (2014)
10. Cash, D., Jarecki, S., Jutla, C., Krawczyk, H., Roşu, M.-C., Steiner, M.: Highly-scalable searchable symmetric encryption with support for Boolean queries. In: Canetti, R., Garay, J.A. (eds.) CRYPTO 2013. LNCS, vol. 8042, pp. 353–373. Springer, Heidelberg (2013). https://doi.org/10.1007/978-3-642-40041-4_20
11. Cash, D., Tessaro, S.: The locality of searchable symmetric encryption. In: Nguyen, P.Q., Oswald, E. (eds.) EUROCRYPT 2014. LNCS, vol. 8441, pp. 351–368. Springer, Heidelberg (2014). https://doi.org/10.1007/978-3-642-55220-5_20

12. Chang, Y.-C., Mitzenmacher, M.: Privacy preserving keyword searches on remote encrypted data. In: Proceedings of the 3rd International Conference on Applied Cryptography and Network Security, pp. 442–455 (2005)
13. Chase, M., Kamara, S.: Structured encryption and controlled disclosure. In: Abe, M. (ed.) ASIACRYPT 2010. LNCS, vol. 6477, pp. 577–594. Springer, Heidelberg (2010). https://doi.org/10.1007/978-3-642-17373-8_33
14. Curtmola, R., Garay, J.A., Kamara, S., Ostrovsky, R.: Searchable symmetric encryption: improved definitions and efficient constructions. In: Proceedings of the 13th ACM Conference on Computer and Communications Security, pp. 79–88 (2006)
15. Curtmola, R., Garay, J.A., Kamara, S., Ostrovsky, R.: Searchable symmetric encryption: improved definitions and efficient constructions. J. Comput. Secur. **19**(5), 895–934 (2011)
16. Escala, A., Herold, G., Kiltz, E., Ràfols, C., Villar, J.L.: An algebraic framework for Diffie-Hellman assumptions. J. Cryptol. **30**(1), 242–288 (2017)
17. Freedman, M.J., Hazay, C., Nissim, K., Pinkas, B.: Efficient set intersection with simulation-based security. J. Cryptol. **29**(1), 115–155 (2016)
18. Fuller, B., Varia, M., Yerukhimovich, A., Shen, E., Hamlin, A., Gadepally, V., Shay, R., Mitchell, J.D., Cunningham, R.K.: SoK: cryptographically protected database search. In: Proceedings of the 38th IEEE Symposium on Security and Privacy, pp. 172–191 (2017)
19. Furukawa, J., Isshiki, T.: Controlled joining on encrypted relational database. In: Abdalla, M., Lange, T. (eds.) Pairing 2012. LNCS, vol. 7708, pp. 46–64. Springer, Heidelberg (2013). https://doi.org/10.1007/978-3-642-36334-4_4
20. Goh, E.: Secure indexes. Cryptology ePrint Archive, Report 2003/216 (2003)
21. Goldwasser, S., Gordon, S.D., Goyal, V., Jain, A., Katz, J., Liu, F.-H., Sahai, A., Shi, E., Zhou, H.-S.: Multi-input functional encryption. In: Nguyen, P.Q., Oswald, E. (eds.) EUROCRYPT 2014. LNCS, vol. 8441, pp. 578–602. Springer, Heidelberg (2014). https://doi.org/10.1007/978-3-642-55220-5_32
22. Grubbs, P., Sekniqi, K., Bindschaedler, V., Naveed, M., Ristenpart, T.: Leakage-abuse attacks against order-revealing encryption. In: 2017 IEEE Symposium on Security and Privacy, pp. 655–672 (2017)
23. Hacigümüs, H., Iyer, B.R., Li, C., Mehrotra, S.: Executing SQL over encrypted data in the database-service-provider model. In: Proceedings of the ACM SIGMOD International Conference on Management of Data, pp. 216–227 (2002)
24. Hacigümüş, H., Iyer, B., Mehrotra, S.: Efficient execution of aggregation queries over encrypted relational databases. In: Lee, Y.J., Li, J., Whang, K.-Y., Lee, D. (eds.) DASFAA 2004. LNCS, vol. 2973, pp. 125–136. Springer, Heidelberg (2004). https://doi.org/10.1007/978-3-540-24571-1_10
25. Hang, I., Kerschbaum, F., Damiani, E.: ENKI: access control for encrypted query processing. In: Proceedings of the 2015 ACM SIGMOD International Conference on Management of Data, pp. 183–196 (2015)
26. Huang, Y., Evans, D., Katz, J.: Private set intersection: are garbled circuits better than custom protocols? In: 19th Annual Network and Distributed System Security Symposium, NDSS 2012 (2012)
27. Ivan, A., Dodis, Y.: Proxy cryptography revisited. In: Proceedings of the 10th Annual Network and Distributed System Security Symposium (2003)
28. Kamara, S., Moataz, T.: SQL on structurally-encrypted databases. Cryptology ePrint Archive, Report 2016/453 (2016)

29. Kamara, S., Papamanthou, C.: Parallel and dynamic searchable symmetric encryption. In: Proceedings of the 16th International Conference on Financial Cryptography and Data Security, pp. 258–274 (2013)
30. Kamara, S., Papamanthou, C., Roeder, T.: Dynamic searchable symmetric encryption. In: Proceedings of the 19th ACM Conference on Computer and Communications Security, pp. 965–976 (2012)
31. Kellaris, G., Kollios, G., Nissim, K., O'Neill, A.: Generic attacks on secure outsourced databases. In: Proceedings of the 2016 ACM SIGSAC Conference on Computer and Communications Security, pp. 1329–1340 (2016)
32. Kurosawa, K., Ohtaki, Y.: UC-secure searchable symmetric encryption. In: Keromytis, A.D. (ed.) FC 2012. LNCS, vol. 7397, pp. 285–298. Springer, Heidelberg (2012). https://doi.org/10.1007/978-3-642-32946-3_21
33. Kurosawa, K., Ohtaki, Y.: How to update documents *verifiably* in searchable symmetric encryption. In: Abdalla, M., Nita-Rotaru, C., Dahab, R. (eds.) CANS 2013. LNCS, vol. 8257, pp. 309–328. Springer, Cham (2013). https://doi.org/10.1007/978-3-319-02937-5_17
34. Mironov, I., Segev, G., Shahaf, I.: Strengthening the security of encrypted databases: non-transitive JOINs. Cryptology ePrint Archive, Report 2017/883 (2017)
35. Naveed, M., Kamara, S., Wright, C.V.: Inference attacks on property-preserving encrypted databases. In: Proceedings of the 22nd ACM SIGSAC Conference on Computer and Communications Security, pp. 644–655 (2015)
36. Pinkas, B., Schneider, T., Segev, G., Zohner, M.: Phasing: private set intersection using permutation-based hashing. In: Proceedings of the 24th USENIX Security Symposium, pp. 515–530 (2015)
37. Popa, R.A.: Building practical systems that compute on encrypted data. Ph.D. thesis, Massachusetts Institute of Technology (2014). http://www.eecs.berkeley.edu/~raluca/Thesis.pdf
38. Popa, R.A., Redfield, C.M.S., Zeldovich, N., Balakrishnan, H.: CryptDB: protecting confidentiality with encrypted query processing. In: Proceedings of the 23rd ACM Symposium on Operating Systems Principles, pp. 85–100 (2011)
39. Popa, R.A., Redfield, C.M.S., Zeldovich, N., Balakrishnan, H.: CryptDB: processing queries on an encrypted database. Commun. ACM **55**(9), 103–111 (2012)
40. Popa, R.A., Zeldovich, N.: Cryptographic treatment of CryptDB's adjustable join. Technical report MIT-CSAIL-TR-2012-006 (2012). http://people.csail.mit.edu/nickolai/papers/popa-join-tr.pdf
41. Popa, R.A., Zeldovich, N., Balakrishnan, H.: Guidelines for using the CryptDB system securely. Cryptology ePrint Archive, Report 2015/979 (2015)
42. Song, D.X., Wagner, D., Perrig, A.: Practical techniques for searches on encrypted data. In: Proceedings of the 21st Annual IEEE Symposium on Security and Privacy, pp. 44–55 (2000)
43. van Liesdonk, P., Sedghi, S., Doumen, J., Hartel, P.H., Jonker, W.: Computationally efficient searchable symmetric encryption. In: Proceedings of 7th VLDB Workshop on Secure Data Management, pp. 87–100 (2010)

Can We Access a Database Both Locally and Privately?

Elette Boyle[1]([✉]), Yuval Ishai[2,3], Rafael Pass[4], and Mary Wootters[5]

[1] IDC Herzliya, Herzliya, Israel
elette.boyle@idc.ac.il
[2] Technion, Haifa, Israel
yuvali@cs.technion.ac.il
[3] UCLA, Los Angeles, USA
[4] Cornell University, Ithaca, USA
rafael@cs.cornell.edu
[5] Stanford University, Stanford, USA
marykw@stanford.edu

Abstract. We consider the following strong variant of private information retrieval (PIR). There is a large database x that we want to make publicly available. To this end, we post an encoding X of x together with a short public key pk in a publicly accessible repository. The goal is to allow any client who comes along to retrieve a chosen bit x_i by reading a small number of bits from X, whose positions may be randomly chosen based on i and pk, such that even an adversary who can fully observe the access to X does not learn information about i.

Towards solving this problem, we study a weaker secret key variant where the data is encoded and accessed by the same party. This primitive, that we call an *oblivious locally decodable code* (OLDC), is independently motivated by applications such as searchable symmetric encryption. We reduce the public-key variant of PIR to OLDC using an ideal form of obfuscation that can be instantiated heuristically with existing indistinguishability obfuscation candidates, or alternatively implemented with small and stateless tamper-proof hardware.

Finally, a central contribution of our work is the first proposal of an OLDC candidate. Our candidate is based on a secretly permuted Reed-Muller code. We analyze the security of this candidate against several natural attacks and leave its further study to future work.

1 Introduction

A private information retrieval (PIR) protocol allows a client to retrieve an item from a remote database while hiding which item is retrieved even from the servers storing the database. PIR has been studied both in a multi-server setting, where security should only hold against non-colluding servers [9,10], and in a single-server setting [27]. In both settings, the main focus of the large body of work on PIR has been on minimizing the *communication complexity*.

© International Association for Cryptologic Research 2017
Y. Kalai and L. Reyzin (Eds.): TCC 2017, Part II, LNCS 10678, pp. 662–693, 2017.
https://doi.org/10.1007/978-3-319-70503-3_22

Improving the *computational complexity* of PIR turned out to be much more challenging. If no preprocessing of the database is allowed, the computational complexity of the servers must be at least linear in the database size [4]. While preprocessing was shown to be helpful in the multi-server setting [4], the existence of sublinear-time single-server PIR protocols has been a longstanding open question, with no negative results or (even heuristic) candidate solutions.

In this work we consider the following strong variant of sublinear-time PIR that we call *public-key PIR* (pk-PIR). Suppose we want to allow efficient and privacy-preserving access to a large database $x \in \{0,1\}^n$. To this end, we encode x into a (possibly bigger) database $X = (X_1, \ldots, X_N)$ and post X together with a short public key pk in a publicly accessible repository. We want to allow any client who comes along to retrieve a chosen bit x_i by reading a small number of bits from X (sublinear in n), where the positions of these bits may be randomly chosen based on i and pk. (Note that X can be over any alphabet, but the total number of *bits* read by the decoder should be $o(n)$.) More concretely, there is a randomized decoder that given i and pk picks a small set $I \subset [N]$ of positions to be read, and using X_I, pk, and its secret randomness recovers x_i.

We would like to achieve the following strong security guarantee: even an adversary who knows pk and can fully observe the access to X, including both the positions I and the contents X_I of symbols being read, does not learn information about i. Since we are interested in efficient solutions that transfer less than n bits of information, one should settle for computational (rather than information-theoretic) security against computationally bounded observers [10].

Our notion of pk-PIR can be viewed as a variant of single-server PIR with preprocessing [4] (see Sect. 1.1 for a detailed discussion). It can also be viewed as a variant of oblivious RAM (ORAM) [19] which is weaker in that it only supports "read" operations, but is qualitatively stronger in that the same encrypted database can be repeatedly used without being updated. Unlike the standard notion of ORAM, pk-PIR can support a virtually unlimited number of accesses by an arbitrary number of stateless clients who do not trust each other. An efficient realization of pk-PIR can be extremely useful for enabling privacy-preserving public access to a large static database.

Main tool: OLDC. We reduce pk-PIR to the design of a new primitive that we call an *oblivious locally decodable code* (OLDC). Intuitively, OLDC can be thought of as a simpler secret-key variant of pk-PIR. An OLDC encoder randomly maps the database x into an encoded database X by using a short secret key sk. The decoder may use sk to determine the set I of symbols of X it reads and also for recovering x_i from X_I, where the same key sk can be used for polynomially many invocations of the decoder. As in pk-PIR (and standard LDC), we require the decoder to have sublinear locality, namely to read $o(n)$ bits of X. There are two significant differences in the notion of security. First, the observer does not have access to the secret key sk used for decoding. Second, it does not even have access to the contents of the symbols X_I. All the observer can see is the positions I of the symbols being read.

On the non-triviality of OLDC. The relaxed security goal makes OLDC conceivably easier to realize than pk-PIR. However, whether such OLDC exists is still far from obvious. In fact, one might be tempted to try to prove that OLDC is just too strong to exist. In Appendix A we argue that ruling out the existence of OLDC is unlikely, as it would require proving strong data structure lower bounds that seem beyond the reach of current techniques.

On the other hand, there is also no hope to prove the existence of OLDC unconditionally; in fact, we prove that any OLDC implies a one-way function. Another source of non-triviality comes from the following general property of OLDC. With overwhelming probability over the choice of sk, the encoder and (probabilistic) decoder defined by sk should satisfy the following requirement: the probability that a given codeword symbol is read by the decoder is essentially independent of the query index i. Using known results, this means that any OLDC can be easily converted into a closely related "smooth code"[1] [24], or even into a standard LDC that allows for local decoding in the presence of a constant fraction of *errors* [26]. Since there is only a handful of known smooth code and LDC constructions, this severely limits the pool of potential OLDC candidates.

On the usefulness of OLDC. Unlike standard notions of PIR (but similarly to ORAM), OLDC does not apply to the case of publicly accessible data, in the sense that a client who has the key to access the encoded data can learn the queries i of others who access the same encoded data. However, OLDC can still be useful in many application scenarios. For instance, by applying an OLDC on top of a data structure (e.g., one supporting near-neighbor searches), one can implement general forms of searchable symmetric encryption [13,36], avoiding the access pattern leakage of current practical approaches without the need to update the encoded data as in an ORAM-based approach.

From OLDC to pk-PIR. Before describing our candidate OLDC construction, we explain the transformation from OLDC to pk-PIR. Conceptually, the transformation is similar to an obfuscation-based construction of public-key encryption from secret-key encryption. The idea is to have the pk-PIR encoder produce an encrypted and authenticated version of the symbols of the OLDC encoding X, and emulate the OLDC decoder by obfuscating the code for generating I from i and pk together with the code for recovering x_i from X_I. An additional authentication mechanism is needed to ensure that the decoder is indeed fed with X_I for the same I it generated.

Unlike the simpler case of encryption [34], here we cannot instantiate the construction using indistinguishability obfuscation (iO). Instead, we need to rely on an ideal "virtual black-box" obfuscation primitive [3]. This primitive can be heuristically instantiated using existing iO candidates (e.g., the ones from [14,15]) or provably instantiated by relying on ideal multi-linear maps [2].

---

[1] A smooth code supports a local decoding procedure in which each codeword symbol is read with roughly the same probability.

Alternatively, the decoder can be implemented directly by using small and stateless tamper-proof hardware or a secure co-processor. The latter setting does not seem to trivialize the problem, and can potentially provide an implementable variant of our construction that is not curbed by the inefficiency of current software-based obfuscation methods.

An OLDC candidate. A central contribution of our work is the first proposal of an OLDC candidate, which we describe below. The encoding is just a secretly permuted version of a standard locally decodable code obtained from Reed-Muller codes (cf. [24]): the secret key defines a (pseudo-)random permutation, and the encoder applies a Reed-Muller encoding to x and then permutes the result according to the permutation defined by the secret key. The parameters are chosen such that decoding is done by probing $O(\lambda \cdot n^\epsilon)$ (permuted) points along a degree-λ curve, where λ is a security parameter and $\epsilon > 0$ can be an arbitrarily small constant that determines the (polynomial) storage overhead. Decoding is done via interpolation, where it is crucial that the interpolation points be kept secret to defeat a simple linearization attack we describe.

Assuming the security of this OLDC candidate, we get pk-PIR based on ideal obfuscation and one-way functions, where the client reads $\mathsf{poly}(\lambda) \cdot n^\epsilon$ bits for an arbitrarily small constant $\epsilon > 0$. As noted above, ideal obfuscation can be heuristically replaced by existing iO candidates, leading to an explicit candidate construction of pk-PIR. Alternatively, it can be implemented by small and stateless tamper-proof hardware.

Roughly speaking, the security of our OLDC candidate reduces to an intractability assumption defined by a "randomized puzzle" obtained by first sampling polynomially many random low-degree curves (where each curve has a different color), and then randomly shuffling the pieces of the puzzle, i.e., the colored points of the space. The assumption is that it is hard to distinguish the shuffled pieces of the puzzle from pieces of a similar puzzle where the low-degree curves are replaced by high-degree curves, or even by totally random functions. Note that unlike standard physical puzzles, or computational puzzles that are motivated by problems such as DNA sequencing, the local independence property of random low-degree curves ensures that there is no local information to help determine whether two pieces are likely to fit next to each other.

Being unable to reduce the security of our OLDC candidate to any well studied assumption, we establish its plausible security by showing that it defeats several relevant types of attacks. This may be an inevitable state of affairs, as it is often the case in cryptography that ambitious new goals call for new assumptions. On the other hand, we show that several weaker variants of the construction can be broken by linearization attacks. This includes variants in which the global permutation is replaced by one that randomly permutes only one of the coordinates in the space.

Finally, it is useful to note that other ad-hoc pseudorandomness assumptions related to specific classes of efficiently decodable codes have successfully withstood the test of time. This includes the conjectured pseudorandomness of noisy Reed-Solomon codes [31] (despite early attacks on a specialized variant [6,7]) and assumptions related to unbroken instances of the McEliece cryptosystem [28] (despite some broken variants [35]). In contrast, several attempts to base single-server PIR or public-key encryption on noisy Reed-Muller or Reed-Solomon codes have been irreparably broken [5,11,12,25]. Our OLDC candidate does not fit in the latter category, since neither the OLDC primitive nor our concrete intractability assumption seem to imply single-server PIR or even public-key encryption.

Future directions. The problem considered in this work is a rare remaining example for a major "feasibility" goal in cryptography that is not clearly impossible to achieve, and yet is not readily solved by using an ideal form of obfuscation and standard cryptographic assumptions. The main question we leave open is that of further evaluating the security of our OLDC candidate, either by showing it insecure or by reducing its security (or the security of another candidate) to a well studied assumption. There is of course a third possibility that the candidate will survive the test of time and become "well studied" without a security reduction to an earlier assumption. A second natural open question is to obtain a construction of pk-PIR from OLDC via iO. Some evidence against this is given by the fact that single-server PIR cannot be based on iO and one-way functions using standard proof techniques [1]. Finally, it would be very interesting to come up with a direct candidate construction of pk-PIR that does not rely on any form of general-purpose obfuscation.

1.1   Related Work

Sublinear-time PIR. The question of PIR with sublinear server computation was first studied in [4]. The main model considered in [4] is that of PIR with polynomial-time preprocessing. This model allows each server to apply a one-time, polynomial-time preprocessing to the database in order to enable faster processing of queries.

Our notion of pk-PIR can be seen as a variant of the single-server model from [4] (Definition 2) with the following differences. Our model is more restrictive in that it does not allow the client to send a query which is answered by the server. This has the advantage of not requiring the data to be stored on a single computer—the encoded database can be dispersed over the network, or written "up in the sky" or on the pages of a book, and can be accessed by clients directly. By default, we also restrict the decoder to be non-adaptive (given the public key), whereas the general version of the model from [4] can use multiple rounds of interaction. On the other hand, our model is more liberal in that it allows the encoding of the database to be randomized. This randomization is essential for our solutions, even in the secret-key case of OLDC.

The results of [4] on PIR with preprocessing include a weak lower bound on the tradeoff between storage and server computation, positive results in the multi-server model, and a barrier to proving strong negative results for single-server solutions with adaptive queries (see Appendix A). They also obtain positive results for sublinear-time PIR in alternative models, including the case of amortizing the computational work required for processing multiple queries simultaneously and protocols with single-use preprocessing. The question of reducing the amortized computational cost of multi-query PIR was subsequently studied in [21,22].

Other notions of keyed LDC. A very different notion of LDC with (private or public) keys was considered in [20,33]. The goal of these works is to make use of the keys towards improving the efficiency of LDCs, rather than hide the access pattern.

1.2   Independent Work

The problem we consider has been independently studied by Canetti et al. [8]. The two works consider the same problem of sublinear-time PIR with preprocessing and propose similar candidate solutions based on secretly permuted Reed-Muller codes. The notion of OLDC (resp., pk-PIR) from the present work corresponds to the notion of designated-client (resp., public-client) doubly-efficient PIR from [8]. (In this work we make the additional restriction of non-adaptive queries.) We provide an overview of the main differences between the two works below.

The main contributions of [8] beyond those of this work include: (1) A different variant of the designated-client (OLDC) candidate in which the curve evaluation points used by the decoder are fixed (or made public) but some of the points on the curve are replaced by random noise. A combination of random noise with secret evaluation points is also proposed as a potentially more conservative candidate. (2) A search-to-decision reduction for a restricted case of the above fixed-evaluation-point variant, where the location of the noise elements is the same for all queries. (3) An efficient variant of the designated client scheme, that is secure in the *bounded-query* case assuming one way functions.

The main contributions of this work beyond those of [8] include: (1) A general transformation from (designated-client) OLDC to (public-client) pk-PIR by applying VBB obfuscation to the query generation algorithm and an authenticated version of the decoding algorithm. This yields an explicit candidate construction of pk-PIR. (2) Two types of barriers: A "data structures barrier," suggesting that even a very strong form of pk-PIR, with deterministic encoder and non-adaptive queries, would be difficult to unconditionally rule out; and an "LDC barrier," showing that OLDC implies traditional LDC, effectively imposing a limitation on the space of possible candidates. (3) Ruling out (under standard assumptions) a natural "learning" approach for generically breaking constructions based on secret linear codes, by using the power of span programs. (4) A proof that any OLDC implies a one-way function.

2   Preliminaries

Notation. The security parameter is denoted by λ. A function $\nu : \mathbb{N} \to \mathbb{N}$ is said to be *negligible* if for every positive polynomial $p(\cdot)$ and all sufficiently large λ it holds that $\nu(\lambda) < 1/p(\lambda)$. We use $[n]$ to denote the set $\{1, \ldots, n\}$. We use $d \leftarrow \mathcal{D}$ to denote the process of sampling d from the distribution $\mathcal{D}$ or, if $\mathcal{D}$ is a set, a uniform choice from it. We denote by S_N the symmetric group on N elements.

2.1 Standard Cryptographic Tools

We refer the reader to, e.g. [17] for treatment of standard cryptographic primitives, including pseudorandom function (PRF) families (Gen, Eval), pseudorandom permutations PRP, semantically secure symmetric-key encryption schemes (Gen, Enc, Dec), and message authentication codes (Gen, Tag, Verify).

2.2 Virtual Black-Box Obfuscation

Intuitively, a program obfuscator serves to "scramble" a program, hiding implementation details, while preserving its input/output functionality. The notion of *Virtual Black-Box (VBB)* obfuscation was first formally studied by [3]. We consider a notion with auxiliary input.

Definition 1 (VBB Obfuscator [3]). *Let $\mathcal{C} = \{\mathcal{C}_n\}_{n \in \mathbb{N}}$ be a family of polynomial-size circuits, where $\mathcal{C}_n$ is a set of boolean circuits operating on inputs of length n. And let $\mathcal{O}$ be a PPT algorithm, which takes as input an input length $n \in \mathbb{N}$, a circuit $C \in \mathcal{C}_n$, a security parameter 1^λ, and outputs a boolean circuit $\mathcal{O}(C)$ (not necessarily in $\mathcal{C}$). $\mathcal{O}$ is a virtual black-box (VBB) obfuscator for the circuit family $\mathcal{C}$ if there exists a negligible function ν such that:*

1. *(Preserving Functionality): For every $n \in \mathbb{N}$, and every $C \in \mathcal{C}_n$, and every $x \in \{0,1\}^n$, with all but $\nu(\lambda)$ probability over the coins of $\mathcal{O}$, we have $(\mathcal{O}(C, 1^n, 1^\lambda))(x) = C(x)$.*
2. *(Polynomial Slowdown): There exists a polynomial $p(\cdot)$ such that for every $n, \lambda \in \mathbb{N}$ and $C \in \mathcal{C}$, the circuit $\mathcal{O}(C, 1^n, 1^\lambda)$ is of size at most $p(|C|, n, \lambda)$.*
3. *(Virtual Black-Box): For every (non-uniform) polynomial-size adversary $\mathcal{A}$, there exists a (non-uniform) polynomial-size simulator $\mathcal{S}$ such that, for every $n \in \mathbb{N}$ every $C \in \mathcal{C}_n$ and every auxiliary input z,*

$$\left| \Pr[\tilde{C} \leftarrow \mathcal{O}(C, 1^\lambda, 1^n); b \leftarrow \mathcal{A}(\tilde{C}, z) : b = 1] \right.$$
$$\left. - \Pr[b \leftarrow \mathcal{S}^C(1^{|C|}, 1^n, 1^\lambda, z) : b = 1] \right| \leq \nu(\lambda).$$

3 Oblivious LDC and Public-Key PIR

In this section, we formally introduce the notions of oblivious locally decodable codes and public-key private information retrieval. For simplicity, we consider a database x consisting of n bits.

3.1 Oblivious LDC

A standard locally decodable code (LDC) is an error-correcting code that simultaneously offers resilience to errors and a local decoding procedure, which can recover any message bit x_i with good success probability by probing few, randomly selected, bits of the encoding. Intuitively, an oblivious LDC (OLDC) is an LDC with the additional property that the sets of symbols being read computationally do not reveal the respective queried indices i. Unlike the standard goal of LDCs, we do not explicitly require any error correction capability, but such a capability is in some sense implied by our security requirement (see Remark 2 below).

Note that Oblivious LDC is a "secret-key" notion of public-key PIR, where to generate valid queries one must hold the secret key sk that was used within the encoding procedure. As in other secret key primitives, we need to ensure that the same sk can be used to hide any polynomial number of queries.

Definition 2 (Oblivious LDC). *An Oblivious LDC is a tuple of PPT algorithms* $(\mathsf{G}, \mathsf{E}, \mathsf{Q}, \mathsf{D})$ *with the following syntax:*

$\mathsf{G}(1^\lambda)$ *is a probabilistic key generation algorithm, which takes as input a security parameter* 1^λ *and outputs a secret sampling key* sk.

$\mathsf{E}(1^\lambda, \mathsf{sk}, x)$ *is a probabilistic encoder, which takes as input a security parameter* 1^λ, *secret key* sk, *and database* $x = (x_1, \ldots, x_n)$ *with* $x_i \in \{0, 1\}$, *and outputs* $X = (X_1, \ldots, X_N)$ *with* $X_i \in \{0, 1\}^L$.

$\mathsf{Q}(1^\lambda, 1^n, i, \mathsf{sk}; r)$ *is a probabilistic query sampler which takes as input: a security parameter* 1^λ, *database size* 1^n, *index* $i \in [n]$, *secret key* sk, *and randomness* r *used within the query generation, and outputs a list of* q *indices* $I \in [N]^q$.

$\mathsf{D}(1^\lambda, 1^n, i, X_I, \mathsf{sk}, r)$ *is a deterministic decoder. It takes as input: a security parameter* 1^λ, *database size* 1^n, *an index* $i \in [n]$, *a vector of* q *queried database symbols* $X_I \in (\{0, 1\}^L)^q$, *secret key* sk, *and secret randomness* r *used within the corresponding execution of* Q. *The output of* D *is a decoded database symbol (presumably* x_i).

The algorithms $(\mathsf{G}, \mathsf{E}, \mathsf{Q}, \mathsf{D})$ *should satisfy the following correctness, non-triviality and security guarantees:*

Correctness: *Honest execution of* $\mathsf{G}, \mathsf{E}, \mathsf{Q}, \mathsf{D}$, *successfully returns the requested data items. That is, for every* $x = (x_1, \ldots, x_n)$ *and every* $i \in [n]$,

$$\Pr\left[\mathsf{sk} \leftarrow \mathsf{G}(1^\lambda); X \leftarrow \mathsf{E}(1^\lambda, \mathsf{sk}, x); I \leftarrow \mathsf{Q}(1^\lambda, 1^n, i, \mathsf{sk}; r); \right.$$
$$\left. x_i' = \mathsf{D}(1^\lambda, 1^n, i, X_I, \mathsf{sk}, r) : x_i' = x_i\right] = 1.$$

Non-triviality: *There exists* $\epsilon > 0$ *such that for every* λ, *and all sufficiently large* n, *the number of queried bits satisfies* $Lq < n^{1-\epsilon}$.

Security: *No efficient adversary can distinguish the memory accesses dictated by* Q *on input query index* i_0 *and* i_1, *for a randomly sampled* sk. *Namely,* *for every non-uniform PPT adversary $\mathcal{A}$, there exists a negligible function ν such that the distinguishing advantage of $\mathcal{A}$ in the following game is bounded by $\nu(\lambda)$:*

1. $\mathsf{sk} \leftarrow \mathsf{G}(1^\lambda)$: *The challenger samples a secret key* sk.
2. $(i_0, i_1, \mathsf{aux}) \leftarrow \mathcal{A}^{\mathsf{Q}_{\mathsf{sk}}(\cdot)}(1^\lambda)$: $\mathcal{A}$ *selects a challenge index pair* $i_0 \neq i_1 \in [n]$, *and auxiliary information* aux, *given oracle access to the randomized functionality* $\mathsf{Q}_{\mathsf{sk}}(\cdot)$, *which on input* $i \in [n]$ *outputs a list of indices* $I \in [N]^q$ *sampled as* $I \leftarrow \mathsf{Q}(1^\lambda, 1^n, i, \mathsf{sk})$.
3. $b \leftarrow \{0,1\}$; $I^* \leftarrow \mathsf{Q}(1^\lambda, 1^n, i_b, \mathsf{sk})$: *The challenger selects a random bit and generates a sample query for the chosen index* i_b.
4. $b' \leftarrow \mathcal{A}^{\mathsf{Q}_{\mathsf{sk}}(\cdot)}(\mathsf{aux}, I^*)$: $\mathcal{A}$ *outputs a guess for* b, *given the challenge* I^*, *and continued oracle access to* $\mathsf{Q}_{\mathsf{sk}}(\cdot)$ *as defined above.*
5. $\mathcal{A}$*'s advantage in the challenge game is defined as* $\Pr[b' = b] - 1/2$, *over the randomness of the challenger (and* $\mathcal{A}$*).*

Remark 1. The above security definition is specified for a *single* challenge query. However, since security holds also given access to the query ("encrypt") oracle, then by a straightforward hybrid argument, this definition directly implies computational indistinguishability for any polynomial number of queries, analogous to semantic security of symmetric-key encryption.

Remark 2 (Relation to LDC). Analogous to PIR, OLDCs are a close relative to standard LDCs, whose focus is on local recoverability of data given symbol errors or erasures. Indeed, the OLDC security requirement implies that with overwhelming probability over the choice of sk, the encoder and (probabilistic) decoder defined by sk must read any given codeword symbol with probability essentially independent of the queried index i. This property holds directly for information theoretic PIR; for OLDC, the security guarantees are only computational, but such a probability disparity would constitute an efficient distinguisher (and thus cannot exist). Thus, in a similar fashion to the PIR-implies-LDC construction, a simple modification to the OLDC (by dropping "low-weight" symbols and duplicating "high-weight" ones) then yields a related *smooth code* (i.e., with a local decoding procedure where each codeword symbol is read with roughly *equal* probability); see "Smooth encodings and PIR" in [24]. This in turn directly yields an LDC correctable against erasures, or against errors in a low but nontrivial error regime, and can further be transformed into a standard LDC that allows for local decoding in the presence of a constant fraction of errors [26]. This means that future OLDC candidates inherently must come out of LDC techniques.

We prove that within the nontrivial regime of parameters, OLDC necessarily implies the existence of *one-way functions*. Interestingly, several straightforward approaches toward this assertion are not valid. In particular, one cannot make a direct use of an OLDC to devise a symmetric-key encryption scheme, since correctness of OLDC decoding is only guaranteed given the randomness used to generate the query indices, and indistinguishability of OLDC query index sets is only guaranteed when the corresponding codeword symbols themselves are unknown. The proof considers two distributions: One with a list of query sets I_{r_i} for random query indices r_i together with the *real* indices r_i, and the second with a similar list of query sets I_{r_i} together with *uncorrelated* random indices r_i'. Note that we must necessarily make use of the fact that the OLDC decoder can make many queries, as bounded-query OLDC exists unconditionally (e.g., using a k-wise independent functions).

Proposition 1 (OLDC Implies OWF). *Suppose OLDC exists. Then one-way functions must exist.*

Proof. Let $(\mathsf{G}, \mathsf{E}, \mathsf{Q}, \mathsf{D})$ be an OLDC with parameters as above. We demonstrate two distributions which are (by OLDC security) computationally indistinguishable, but are (by OLDC correctness) statistically far [16]. Consider the following pair of distributions, for a parameter $\ell \in \mathbb{N}$:

$$D_1(1^\lambda, \ell) := \left\{ ((I_{r_1}, r_1), \ldots, (I_{r_\ell}, r_\ell)) : \begin{array}{c} \mathsf{sk} \leftarrow \mathsf{G}(1^\lambda); \\ r_1, \ldots, r_\ell \leftarrow [n]^\ell; \\ \forall i \in [\ell], I_{r_i} \leftarrow \mathsf{Q}(1^\lambda, 1^n, r_i, \mathsf{sk}) \end{array} \right\}$$

$$D_2(1^\lambda, \ell) := \left\{ ((I_{r_1}, r_1'), \ldots, (I_{r_\ell}, r_\ell')) : \begin{array}{c} \mathsf{sk} \leftarrow \mathsf{G}(1^\lambda); \\ r_1, \ldots, r_\ell \leftarrow [n]^\ell; \\ r_1', \ldots, r_\ell' \leftarrow [n]^\ell; \\ \forall i \in [\ell], I_{r_i} \leftarrow \mathsf{Q}(1^\lambda, 1^n, r_i, \mathsf{sk}) \end{array} \right\}.$$

OLDC security directly dictates that $D_1(1^\lambda, \ell), D_2(1^\lambda, \ell)$ are computationally indistinguishable for any polynomial $\ell = \ell(\lambda)$. We now argue that for appropriate choice of ℓ they must be statistically far.

To do so, we first consider an intermediate step, roughly corresponding to the above distributions *together with the secret key* sk. Given sk, the OLDC decoding correctness will require the distributions to be statistically far (by the impossibility of information theoretic PIR). This does not yet suffice for our final goal, as given sk the distributions are no longer computationally close. However, with some amplification this will enable us to prove that the distributions remain statistically far even when sk is removed.

For any sk in the support of $\mathsf{G}(1^{\mathsf{sk}})$, consider a related pair of distributions $D_1^{\mathsf{sk}}, D_2^{\mathsf{sk}}$ sampled as

$$D_1^{\mathsf{sk}} := \left\{ (\mathsf{sk}, (I_r, r)) : \begin{array}{c} r \leftarrow [n]; \\ I_r \leftarrow \mathsf{Q}(1^\lambda, 1^n, r, \mathsf{sk}) \end{array} \right\}.$$

$$D_2^{\mathsf{sk}} := \left\{ (\mathsf{sk}, (I_r, r')) : \begin{array}{c} r, r' \leftarrow [n]; \\ I_r \leftarrow \mathsf{Q}(1^\lambda, 1^n, r, \mathsf{sk}) \end{array} \right\}.$$

For any ensemble of keys $\{\mathsf{sk}_\lambda\}_\lambda$ in the support of G, the statistical distance between $D_1^{\mathsf{sk}_\lambda}$ and $D_2^{\mathsf{sk}_\lambda}$ must be non-negligible, as the contrary would imply the existence of information theoretically secure 1-server PIR with server-to-client communication sublinear in n:

- To query index $i \in [n]$, the client samples $(\mathsf{sk}, (I_r, r)) \leftarrow D_1^{\mathsf{sk}_\lambda}$ (where the execution of Q takes randomness rand) and sends the tuple $(\mathsf{sk}, (I_r, r - i))$ to the server.
- On input $(\mathsf{sk}, (I, r'))$, the server responds by OLDC-encoding the r'-shifted database (i.e., x' where $x'_j = x_{j+r' \pmod n} \; \forall j \in [n]$) as $X \leftarrow \mathsf{E}(1^\lambda, \mathsf{sk}, x')$, and sending the codeword symbols X_I.
- To decode, the client executes $x_i = \mathsf{D}(1^\lambda, 1^n, i, X_I, \mathsf{sk}, \mathsf{rand})$.

Correctness and communication complexity follow from OLDC decoding and non-triviality. Note that the desired x_i will be be mapped to position r via the $(r - i)$ shift. Statistical privacy of the PIR holds by the statistical indistinguishability of D'_1 and D'_2 (by implying an index-i query $(\mathsf{sk}, (I_r, r + i))$ is statistically close to $(\mathsf{sk}, (I_r, r' + i))$, which is the query distribution for a random index).

As the final step, we show that if we consider several such (I_r, r) query pairs, then non-negligible statistical distance must be maintained even when we remove sk from the distribution (at which point we can no longer use OLDC correctness arguments directly). Intuitively, this must hold, otherwise omitting sk would yield a secret-key encryption scheme with *information theoretic* security.

More formally, since the sampling of (I_r, r) and (I_r, r') are independent conditioned on a given value of sk, we may directly amplify the (non-negligible) statistical distance of $D_1^{\mathsf{sk}_\lambda}$ and $D_2^{\mathsf{sk}_\lambda}$ to be $1 - \nu(\lambda)$ for negligible function ν by including a sufficiently large polynomial number $\ell_1(\lambda)$ of sample pairs (I_{r_i}, r_i) or (I_{r_i}, r'_i), respectively (as in $D_1(1^\lambda)$ and $D_2(1^\lambda)$ above), together with sk. In particular, for any choice of $\{\mathsf{sk}_\lambda\}_\lambda$, one can reliably transmit a bit (with possibly inefficient decoding) $b \in \{0, 1\}$ by sending a sample

$$(\mathsf{sk}_\lambda, (I_{r_1}, r_1), \ldots, (I_{r_{\ell_1(\lambda)}}, r_{\ell_1(\lambda)})) \text{ if } b = 0, \text{ or}$$

$$(\mathsf{sk}_\lambda, (I_{r_1}, r'_1), \ldots, (I_{r_{\ell_1(\lambda)}}, r'_{\ell_1(\lambda)})) \text{ if } b = 1,$$

(where this notation is shorthand for the distributions described above). This is preserved for the larger value $\ell^*(\lambda) = 2|\mathsf{sk}_\lambda|\ell_1(\lambda)$, enabling reliable transmission of $2|\mathsf{sk}_\lambda|$ bits of information. Further, it is maintined over a random choice of $\mathsf{sk}_\lambda \leftarrow \mathsf{G}(1^\lambda)$.

Now, suppose that for this choice of ℓ^* the original pair of distributions $D_1(1^\lambda, \ell^*(\lambda)), D_2(1^\lambda, \ell^*(\lambda))$ are statistically close. These distributions correspond directly to the $\ell^*(\lambda)$-sample distributions above (which enable transmission of $2|\mathsf{sk}_\lambda|$ bits) but with sk omitted. That is, we have just demonstrated an *information theoretically* secure symmetric-key encryption scheme for messages of length greater than twice the key size $|\mathsf{sk}_\lambda|$, a contradiction to Shannon's impossibility. Thus, assuming OLDC it must be that $D_1(1^\lambda, \ell^*(\lambda)), D_2(1^\lambda, \ell^*(\lambda))$ are computationally indistinguishable but statistically far.

3.2   Public-Key PIR

Definition 3 (pk-PIR). *A Public-Key PIR (with preprocessing) is a tuple of PPT algorithms* (Gen, Encode, Query, Decode) *acting on a size-n database with the following syntax:*

$\mathsf{Gen}(1^\lambda)$: *On input the security parameter,* Gen *outputs a secret encoding key* sk *and a public sampling key* pk.

$\mathsf{Encode}(1^\lambda, \mathsf{sk}, x)$: *On input a secret encoding key and database* $x \in \{0,1\}^n$, Encode *outputs a compiled database* $X \in (\{0,1\}^L)^N$.

$\mathsf{Query}(\mathsf{pk}, i)$: *On input the public key and index* $i \in [n]$, *the algorithm* Query *outputs a sample-specific decoding key* sk_i *and a list of indices* $I \in [N]^q$ *for some* q.

$\mathsf{Decode}(\mathsf{sk}_i, X_I)$: *On input a query-specific decoding key* sk_i *(as generated by* Query*) and values* $X_I \in (\{0,1\}^L)^q$, *the algorithm outputs a decoded value* $x' \in \{0,1\}$.

The algorithms $(\mathsf{Gen}, \mathsf{Encode}, \mathsf{Query}, \mathsf{Decode})$ *should satisfy the following correctness and security guarantees:*

Correctness: *Honest execution of* $\mathsf{Gen}, \mathsf{Encode}, \mathsf{Query},$ *and* Decode *successfully recovers requested data items. That is, for every* $i \in [n]$,

$$\Pr\Big[(\mathsf{sk}, \mathsf{pk}) \leftarrow \mathsf{Gen}(1^\lambda); X \leftarrow \mathsf{Encode}(1^\lambda, \mathsf{sk}, x);$$

$$(\mathsf{sk}_i, I) \leftarrow \mathsf{Query}(\mathsf{pk}, i); x'_i = \mathsf{Decode}(\mathsf{sk}_i, X_I) : x'_i = x_i\Big] = 1.$$

Non-triviality: *There exists* $\epsilon > 0$ *such that for every* λ, *and all sufficiently large* n, *the number of queried bits satisfies* $Lq < n^{1-\epsilon}$.

Security: *No efficient adversary, given access to a public key and encoded database, can distinguish the memory accesses dictated by* Query *on input query index* i_0 *and* i_1. *Namely, for every non-uniform PPT adversary* $\mathcal{A}$, *there exists a negligible function* ν *such that the distinguishing advantage of* $\mathcal{A}$ *in the following game is bounded by* $\nu(\lambda)$:

1. $(x, \mathsf{aux}) \leftarrow \mathcal{A}(1^\lambda)$: $\mathcal{A}$ *selects a database* $x \in \{0,1\}^n$ *and auxiliary information* aux.
2. $(\mathsf{sk}, \mathsf{pk}) \leftarrow \mathsf{Gen}(1^\lambda); X \leftarrow \mathsf{Encode}(1^\lambda, \mathsf{sk}, x)$: *The challenger samples a key pair and encodes the database* x.
3. $(i_0, i_1, \mathsf{aux}') \leftarrow \mathcal{A}(\mathsf{pk}, X, \mathsf{aux})$: $\mathcal{A}$ *selects a challenge index pair* $i_0 \neq i_1 \in [n]$.
4. $b \leftarrow \{0,1\}; (\mathsf{sk}_i, I^*) \leftarrow \mathsf{Query}(\mathsf{pk}, i_b)$: *The challenger selects a random bit and generates a sample query (and key* sk_i*) for the chosen index* i_b.
5. $b' \leftarrow \mathcal{A}(\mathsf{aux}', I^*)$: $\mathcal{A}$ *outputs a guess for* b, *given the challenge index list* I^*.
6. $\mathcal{A}$'s *advantage in the challenge game is defined as* $\Pr[b' = b] - 1/2$, *over the randomness of the challenger (and* $\mathcal{A}$*).*

Remark 3. As with OLDCs, the pk-PIR security definition is specified for a single challenge query, but extends via a straightforward hybrid argument for any polynomial number of queries (this time analogous to semantic security of *public*-key encryption).

4   Oblivious LDC Candidate

We propose an approach for constructing Oblivious LDCs via Reed-Muller codes. At a high level, we use the standard LDC based on Reed-Muller codes (with a constant number of variables m and query complexity $\tilde{O}(n^{1/m})$), except that we randomly permute the codeword symbols. A more explicit description follows.

Let $\mathbb{F}$ be a finite field and let $d, m \in \mathbb{N}$ with $d\lambda + 1 < |\mathbb{F}|$. We consider an (m, d)-Reed-Muller code over $\mathbb{F}$, namely the code defined by m-variate polynomials of degree $\leq d$ over $\mathbb{F}$. The codeword corresponding to a polynomial p consists of the values of p on all points in $\mathbb{F}^m$. We use a secret (pseudo-random) permutation over $\mathbb{F}^m$ to order the codeword symbols (e.g., [30]). To decode the value of the polynomial p at a target point $\alpha \in \mathbb{F}^m$, the decoder picks a random degree-λ parameterized curve beginning at α, and recovers $p(\alpha)$ by reading the values of p on a random sequence of $d\lambda + 1$ distinct parameter values along the curve (excluding the initial parameter value).

We formally describe the construction below, viewing the number of variables m and degree bound d as parameters that determine the database size n.

Construction 1 ((m, d) RM-Based Oblivious LDC Candidate). *Let* $n = \binom{m+d}{d}$. *Fix a canonical set of n points in $\mathbb{F}^m$ in general position, denoted by α_i for $i \in [n]$. Let $N = |\mathbb{F}|^m$, and fix a correspondence between $\boldsymbol{a} \in \mathbb{F}^m$ and $j_{\boldsymbol{a}} \in [N]$. Consider the following tuple of PPT algorithms.*

$G(1^\lambda)$: *Sample a key describing a pseudorandom permutation $\pi \in S_N$, via $\pi \leftarrow$ $\mathsf{PRP}(1^\lambda)$. Output $\mathsf{sk} = \pi$.*

$E(1^\lambda, \mathsf{sk}, x)$:

1. *For message $x = (x_1, \ldots, x_n) \in \mathbb{F}^n$, define the corresponding m-variable d-degree polynomial $P_x \in \mathbb{F}[Z_1, \ldots, Z_m]$ as the low-degree interpolation of evaluations $P_x(\boldsymbol{\alpha}_i) = x_i$. Denote the resulting codeword by $X' \in \mathbb{F}^N$ indexed by points $\boldsymbol{a} \in \mathbb{F}^m$ (recall $N = |\mathbb{F}|^m$), given componentwise as the evaluations of P_x at every point in $\mathbb{F}^m$: i.e., $\forall \boldsymbol{a} \in \mathbb{F}^m$, take $X'[\boldsymbol{a}] := P_x(\boldsymbol{a})$.*

2. *Permute the indices of X' via π. That is, let $X = (X'_{\pi(1)}, \ldots, X'_{\pi(N)})$.*

3. *Output X.*

$Q(1^\lambda, 1^n, i, \mathsf{sk}; r)$:

1. *Parse $\mathsf{sk} = \pi \in S_N$.*

2. *Sample a random degree-λ parametric curve $C = \{(p_1(t), \ldots, p_m(t)) : t \in \mathbb{F}\} \subset \mathbb{F}^m$ that intersects the ith distinguished point $\alpha_i \in \mathbb{F}^m$, for queried index $i \in [n]$. Concretely, C is defined by letting p_h be a random univariate polynomial of degree $\leq \lambda$ such that $p_h(0) = (\alpha_i)_h$.*

3. *Select a random sequence $(t_0, \ldots, t_{d\lambda}) \in \mathbb{F}^{d\lambda+1}$ of $d\lambda + 1$ distinct nozero parameter values, using the randomness r. For each $\ell = 0, \ldots, d\lambda$, let $\boldsymbol{b}_\ell = (p_1(t_\ell), \ldots, p_m(t_\ell)) \in \mathbb{F}^m$ be the corresponding point on C, and let $j_{\boldsymbol{b}_\ell} \in [N]$ be the associated index.*

4. *Output $I = (\pi(j_{\boldsymbol{b}_0}), \ldots, \pi(j_{\boldsymbol{b}_{d\lambda}})) \in [N]^{d\lambda}$ (i.e., the list of π-permuted indices) as the list of query indices.*

$\mathsf{D}(1^\lambda, 1^n, i, X_I, \mathsf{sk}, r)$:

1. *Parse* $X_I = (X_0, \ldots, X_{d\lambda})$, $\mathsf{sk} = \pi$ *the pseudorandom permutation, and* $r = (t_0, \ldots, t_{d\lambda})$.
2. *The choice of parameter evaluation points* $t_1, \ldots, t_{d\lambda}$ *determines a corresponding list of Lagrange polynomial interpolation coefficients* $c_0, \ldots, c_{d\lambda} \in \mathbb{F}$.
3. *Output the linear combination* $x'_i = \sum_{\ell=0}^{d\lambda} c_\ell X_\ell \in \mathbb{F}$.

Choice of parameters. Viewing the number of variables $m \geq 2$ as constant, the code dimension is $\Theta(d^m)$. We can therefore encode $x \in \{0,1\}^n$ by letting $d = O(n^{1/m})$ and $|\mathbb{F}| = O(d\lambda)$. The code length is now $|\mathbb{F}|^m = O(\lambda^m \cdot n)$ and the number of queries used for local decoding is $d\lambda + 1 = O(\lambda \cdot n^{1/m})$.

Consider the Oblivious LDC security game for the candidate construction above. The challenger samples a random secret permutation π of the points in $\mathbb{F}^m$ (corresponding to $[N]$). The adversary is given oracle access to the query-generation algorithm Q_{sk}. In this case, the index set $I \leftarrow \mathsf{Q}_{\mathsf{sk}}(i)$ corresponds to a collection of π-permuted points in the space $\mathbb{F}^m$ which (before the permutation) were an oversampling of a low-degree curve in $\mathbb{F}^m$.

Security of the candidate would say that, given access to polynomial many samples of this type for desired query indices i, an efficient adversary still cannot discern a fresh query index sample for some i_0 from i_1. In particular, it must be the case that he cannot learn the secret permutation given access to these samples.

We treat the security of the proposed scheme with respect to the following conjecture. Roughly, it states that a permuted "puzzle" of colored low-degree curves in m-dimensional space $\mathbb{F}^m$ is computationally indistinguishable from the same number of colored points selected at random from $\mathbb{F}^m$.

Conjecture 1 (Permuted Low-Degree Polynomials). Let $m \in \mathbb{N}$ be a dimension parameter and $d = d_m(n)$ the minimal integer for which $n \geq \binom{m+d}{d}$. For every efficient non-uniform $\mathcal{A} = (\mathcal{A}_1, \mathcal{A}_2)$ there exists a negligible ν such that

$$\Pr \left[\begin{array}{l} (1^n, 1^{|\mathbb{F}|}, \mathsf{aux}) \leftarrow \mathcal{A}_1(1^\lambda); \\ \pi \leftarrow S_{(\mathbb{F}^m)}; b \leftarrow \{0,1\}; \quad : \quad b' = b \\ b' \leftarrow \mathcal{A}_2^{\mathsf{Samp}_b(\pi, \cdot)}(1^n, \mathsf{aux}) \end{array} \right] \leq 1/2 + \nu(\lambda),$$

where $\mathbb{F}$ is a finite field satisfying $|\mathbb{F}| > d\lambda + 1$, and for any $\pi \in S_{(\mathbb{F}^m)}$ and $v \in \mathbb{F}^m$, the probabilistic algorithm $\mathsf{Samp}_b(\pi, v)$ does the following:

- If $b = 0$:
  1. Select m random degree-λ polynomials $p_1, \ldots, p_m \leftarrow \mathbb{F}[Z]$ where $\forall i \in [m]$, $p_i(0) = v_i$. This determines a curve in $\mathbb{F}^m$, given by the points $\{(p_1(t), \ldots, p_m(t)) : t \in \mathbb{F}\}$.
  2. Sample $d\lambda + 1$ distinct random points on this curve, defined by *nonzero* parameters $t_0, \ldots, t_{d\lambda} \leftarrow \mathbb{F}$.

3. Output these points (in order), but with *each point permuted* by $\pi : \mathbb{F}^m \to \mathbb{F}^m$. That is,

$$\left(\pi\big(p_1(t_i), \ldots, p_m(t_i)\big) \right)_{i=0}^{d\lambda} \in (\mathbb{F}^m)^{d\lambda+1}.$$

- If $b = 1$: Output $d\lambda + 1$ random points in $\mathbb{F}^m$: $(w_0, \ldots, w_{d\lambda}) \leftarrow (\mathbb{F}^m)^{d\lambda+1}$.

Proposition 2. *Suppose that Conjecture 1 holds for dimension $m \geq 2$. Then Construction 1 is a secure Oblivious LDC with communication complexity $\lambda^m \cdot \tilde{O}(n^{1/m})$.*

Proof. The complexity is derived in "Choice of parameters" above. For the security of the OLDC it suffices to prove a version of Conjecture 1 with the following changes. In the first step $\mathcal{A}_1$ picks a pair of points (v_0, v_1). After the second step, $\mathcal{A}_2$ is given a single instance of $\mathsf{Samp}_0(\pi, v_b)$. Finally, the third step is modified so that Samp_0 is used instead of Samp_b. Conjecture 1 implies that for both choices of b, the view of $\mathcal{A}_2$ is indistinguishable from a random and independent set of points. Hence, the advantage of $\mathcal{A}_2$ in guessing b is negligible.

We remark that we choose to present the simplest proposed candidate in this style whose security is plausible. One may consider several natural more complex extensions, such as including additional "distractor" indices in the query list I whose values will be ignored within the decoding. Such inclusion will correspond to introduction of error symbols within the permuted codeword.

4.1   Generalized and Toy Versions of Conjecture

We explore both a generalization and a specific instance of the Permuted Low-Degree Polynomials conjecture above.

Generalization: Permuted Puzzles. As discussed in the Introduction, our main conjecture is a particular instance of a broader class of distinguishing tasks of "permuted puzzles." We think of a puzzle as describing: (1) a distribution of structured functions from $\mathbb{F}^m$ to some range R (e.g., the class of pixel maps defining images of dogs), and (2) a corresponding distribution of unstructured functions (e.g., the class of all pixel maps with the same general color balance). The corresponding Permuted Puzzle Conjecture considers a random secret permutation π of the "puzzle pieces" (i.e., the input space $\mathbb{F}^m$), and states that one cannot efficiently distinguish between an arbitrary polynomial collection of permuted samples from Structured from permuted samples from Unstructured, where each sample is permuted with the *same* π.

Definition 4 (Puzzle). *We refer to an m-dimensional puzzle over $\mathbb{F}$ with range R as defined by a pair of efficiently samplable distributions* (Structured, Unstructured), *each over the class of functions* $\{f : \mathbb{F}^m \to R\}$.

Conjecture 2 (Permuted Puzzle Conjecture). The *Permuted Puzzle Conjecture* with respect to the m-dimensional puzzle (Structured, Unstructured) states that for every efficient non-uniform $\mathcal{A}$, there exists a negligible ν such that

$$\Big| \Pr[\pi \leftarrow \mathsf{PRP}(1^\lambda); b' \leftarrow \mathcal{A}^{\mathcal{O}_\pi(\mathsf{struct})}(1^\lambda) : b' = 1]$$

$$- \Pr[\pi \leftarrow \mathsf{PRP}(1^\lambda); b' \leftarrow \mathcal{A}^{\mathcal{O}_\pi(\mathsf{unstruct})}(1^\lambda) : b' = 1] \Big| \leq \nu(\lambda),$$

where $\mathcal{O}_\pi$ is an oracle that takes as input $b \in \{\mathsf{struct}, \mathsf{unstruct}\}$ and performs the following:

- If $b = \mathsf{struct}$: Sample $f \leftarrow$ Structured, output $f \circ \pi$.
- If $b = \mathsf{unstruct}$: Sample $f \leftarrow$ Unstructured, output $f \circ \pi$.

For example, the Permuted Low-Degree Polynomials Conjecture 1 is a particular case of the permuted puzzle conjecture, where Structured consists of functions $f : \mathbb{F}^m \to \{0,1\}$ which evaluate to 1 precisely on $(d\lambda+1)$ points on a degree-λ parametric curve, and Unstructured consists of *all* functions $\mathbb{F}^m \to \{0,1\}$ which have $(d\lambda + 1)$ nonzero outputs (but in an arbitrary placement).

Specific Instance: Toy Conjecture. To encourage investigation of the core Permuted Low-Degree Polynomials conjecture, we put forth a simple toy variant, which constitutes an easier version of the simplest parameter setting. In particular, it considers the case of dimension $m = 2$, and takes the first-coordinate polynomial to be the *identity* function: that is, including the value of the curve parameter explicitly. This variant brings the problem closer to typical settings of coding theory, and may thus be a useful starting point toward addressing coding-based cryptanalytic attacks. We pursue this strategy in the discussion of cryptanalysis in Sect. 4.2 below.

Conjecture 3 (Toy Conjecture). Let $|\mathbb{F}| \approx \lambda^2$. Let $p_1, \ldots, p_m$ be random degree-λ polynomials over $\mathbb{F}$, for $m = \lambda^{100}$. Let $q_1, \ldots, q_m$ be random functions from $\mathbb{F}$ to $\mathbb{F}$.

Then the following two distributions are computationally indistinguishable, over the choice of random permutation $\pi \leftarrow S_{\mathbb{F} \times \mathbb{F}}$ over $\mathbb{F} \times \mathbb{F}$. Here, elements of each set S_i or T_i appear in canonical sorted order (not ordered by $x \in \mathbb{F}$).

1. Permuted low-degree polynomials: $(S_1, \ldots, S_m)$, for $S_i = \{\pi(x, p_i(x)) : x \in \mathbb{F}\}$.
2. Permuted random functions: $(T_1, \ldots, T_m)$, for $T_i = \{\pi(x, q_i(x)) : x \in \mathbb{F}\}$.

4.2   Discussion on Cryptanalysis

We briefly address a selection of relevant cryptanalytic techniques with respect to the candidate construction, as well as attacks on simplified versions of the construction. We focus on the Toy Conjecture 3 (i.e., $m = 2$ dimensions, where the first-coordinate polynomial is the identity function), as an attack on the primary conjecture is necessarily also an attack on this easier version.

Permuting Individual Coordinates. To develop intuition, we first consider weaker (i.e., easier to break) variants of the Toy Conjecture, and show that these are *not* secure. In these variants, instead of choosing the permutation π from the entire space $S_{\mathbb{F} \times \mathbb{F}}$, we sample from a restricted class that permutes one or both coordinates of $\mathbb{F} \times \mathbb{F}$ independently. In particular:

1. Permute only second coordinate: $\pi \leftarrow id \times S_{\mathbb{F}}$. In this case, the permuted low-degree curves are given as sets of points $\{(t, \pi_2(p(t)))\} \subseteq \mathbb{F} \times \mathbb{F}$.

   This weakened version is not secure. The exposure of the parameter values t themselves in the clear reveals a linear constraint on the corresponding second coordinate symbols, corresponding to Lagrange interpolation where the coefficients are known. As discussed and generalized in the second category of Linearization attacks below, this enables an adversary with sufficiently many samples to learn the preimages of π.

2. Permute only first coordinate: $\pi \leftarrow S_{\mathbb{F}} \times id$. In this case, the permuted low-degree curves are given as sets of points $\{(\pi_1(t), p(t))\} \subseteq \mathbb{F} \times \mathbb{F}$.

   This weakened version is also not secure. One can view this as the problem of distinguishing "noisy" Reed-Solomon codewords from uniformly random vectors in $\mathbb{F}^{|\mathbb{F}|}$, where the "noise" is a permutation of the codeword symbols. Since the resulting "noisy" codewords are still codewords in a linear code, they are contained in some low-dimensional subspace. Thus, the adversary may simply check the dimension of the span of sufficiently many samples to determine whether the structured or unstructured case holds.

Standard Decoding Attacks. Coding-theoretic attacks are a natural attempt to refute the Toy Conjecture 3; as above, the attacker's task is similar to the task of distinguishing "noisy" Reed-Solomon codewords from uniformly random vectors. As noted above, when the "noise" is a permutation acting on either coordinate independently, the linearity of the underlying code provides an attack. Similarly, if the "noise" did not include a permutation, and only included standard coding-theoretic noise (that is, if S_i were of the form $\{(x, p_i(x) + e_i(x)) : x \in \mathbb{F}\}$ for a sparse $e_i(x)$), then standard decoding algorithms (for example Reed-Solomon list-decoding, or the multi-dimensional extension of Coppersmith and Sudan [11]) might apply. However, because the noise takes the form of a permutation, it is not at all clear how to apply such techniques in this setting.

Similarly, an attacker might hope to adapt attacks on instantiations of the McEliece cryptosystem [28] with Reed-Solomon codes in the place of Goppa codes, since these attacks are aimed at distinguishing a permutation applied to a Reed-Solomon generator matrix from uniformly random; such attacks might apply directly in the setting where the S_i are of the form $\{(\pi(x), p_i(x) + e_i(x)) : x \in \mathbb{F}\}$. However, there are two reasons that these sorts of attacks are not directly applicable to the general Toy Conjecture 3. First, the permuation acts on the entire space $\mathbb{F} \times \mathbb{F}$, rather than just on the first coordinate. Second, these attacks require knowledge of the public key—the scrambled generator matrix—and in the Oblivious LDC setting the attacker is not privy to this information.

Linearization Attacks. Generalizing the discussion above on permuting individual coordinates, linearization-style attacks can be used to break any version of the above candidate construction satisfying the following simplified properties:

1. Encoding is linear & public:
   In this case, each encoded database entry X_j corresponds to a known linear combination of the original database entries x_j, i.e. to a known n-dimensional coefficient vector $c^{(j)} \in \mathbb{F}^n$ for which $X_j = \sum_{i=1}^n c_i^{(j)} x_i$. In this case we can assume without loss of generality that the decoder is also linear. Indeed, for a random database x, a set of linear combinations of x_j can be used to infer a given target x_i with better than $1/2$ success probability if and only if it spans x_i. Given a query set $I \in [N]^q$, we can simply determine whether a given basis vector e_i lies in the span of the vectors $c^{(j)}$ corresponding to the queried locations. By correctness and linearity of the decoder, this must be the case for the true queried index i. But, since the number of queries $q < n/2$, this cannot be the case for most indices $i' \neq i$.

   In particular, this means that if Encode is a linear procedure, then it must utilize *secret randomness*. In our candidate construction, this is achieved by use of the secret permutation π. Namely, Encode corresponds to implementing a fixed public linear Reed-Muller encoding procedure composed with a random permutation matrix.

2. Decoding is linear & public, encoding is linear:
   In this case, even if the encoding is randomized and secret, but the *decoding* is linear and public, we can launch a simple linearization attack. As above, linear encoding means each encoded symbol X_j corresponds to some n-dimensional coefficient vector $c^{(j)} \in \mathbb{F}^n$ (for which $X_j = \sum_{i=1}^n c_i^{(j)} x_i$). Define nN linearization variables, corresponding to the unknown values of $\{c_i^{(j)}\}_{i \in [n], j \in [N]}$. Plugging in the known linear decoding function, each received query sample $I \in [N]^q$ on input $i \in [n]$ (whose data value x_i is known) yields a fresh linear constraint on these variables.

   In particular, this means that a simplified version of our candidate construction in which the $d\lambda + 1$ parameter values $t_0, \ldots, t_{d\lambda} \in \mathbb{F}$ are *fixed* (and public) would be broken, as well as the simplified variant discussed in "Permuting Individual Coordinates" above where the parameter values are random but public. We avoid this issue in our proposed candidate by sampling a random set of such values for each query, and passing this information along to the decoder (but *not* revealing it directly). In effect, each distinct subset of parameter values induces a distinct linear function for the decoding, corresponding to the different value of Lagrange interpolation coefficients.

Generic Learning Approach. Assuming the existence of pseudorandom functions in NC^1 [18,32] (a mild assumption that follows from most standard cryptographic assumptions), we can rule out the following hypothetical generic attack that applies to constructions based on permuted linear LDCs. The generic attack views every symbol of X as a hidden vector which specifies some linear combination of x. By repeatedly invoking the decoder on index i, one can get polynomially many samples of sets of hidden vectors which span a given target vector t. If this information could be used to learn the hidden vectors, or even just distinguish between samples that span t and ones that do not, this would give rise to a distinguishing attack.

However, the existence of pseudorandom functions in NC^1, together with the fact that span programs [23] can efficiently simulate NC^1 functions, imply that an attack as above cannot work in general. For simplicity we restrict the attention to the case where t is the unit vector e_1 and the field size is fixed.

Proposition 3. *Suppose there is a pseudorandom function in NC^1. Then, for any finite field $\mathbb{F}$, there are PPT algorithms (Gen, Query) such that $\mathsf{Gen}(1^\lambda)$, on a security parameter λ, outputs a secret key sk and a matrix $M \in \mathbb{F}^{N \times n}$, and $\mathsf{Query}(\mathsf{sk}, b)$ outputs a row index set $I_b \subseteq [N]$, and the following conditions hold.*

- *For the pair (M, I_1) obtained by running $\mathsf{Gen}(1^\lambda)$ and then $\mathsf{Query}(\mathsf{sk}, 1)$, the set of I_1-rows of M spans the unit vector $e_1 \in \mathbb{F}^n$ except with $\mathsf{neg}(\lambda)$ failure probability.*
- *For the pair (M, I_0) obtained by running $\mathsf{Gen}(1^\lambda)$ and then $\mathsf{Query}(\mathsf{sk}, 0)$, the set of I_0-rows of M does not span e_1 except with $\mathsf{neg}(\lambda)$ failure probability.*
- *For any polynomial $p(\lambda)$, the distribution ensembles $\{(I_0^1, \ldots, I_0^{p(\lambda)})\}_\lambda$ and $\{(I_1^1, \ldots, I_1^{p(\lambda)})\}_\lambda$ are computationally indistinguishable, where $(I_b^1, \ldots, I_b^{p(\lambda)})_\lambda$ is obtained by letting $(\mathsf{sk}, M) \leftarrow \mathsf{Gen}(1^\lambda)$ and then $I_b^j \leftarrow \mathsf{Query}(\mathsf{sk}, b)$ for $j = 1, \ldots, p(\lambda)$.*

Proof. Let $\mathsf{Gen}(1^\lambda)$ generate a boolean formula F of size N computing a PRF described by a secret evaluation key sk on an input $x \in \{0, 1\}^\lambda$. (The existence of polynomial-time Gen follows from the existence of a PRF in NC^1.) Using the known simulation of formulas by span programs [23], one can efficiently construct 2λ matrices $M_{i,0}, M_{i,1}$ over $\mathbb{F}$, $1 \le i \le \lambda$, each with $n \le N$ columns and a *total* of N rows, such that $F(x) = 1$ if and only if the unit vector $e_1 \in \mathbb{F}^n$ is spanned by the rows of the λ matrices M_{i,x_i}. The matrix M output by Gen is the matrix whose rows contain all rows of $M_{i,b}$ in order.

The algorithm $\mathsf{Query}(\mathsf{sk}, b)$ samples a random x such that $F(x) = b$, and outputs the index set I_b of the rows of M_{i,x_i} as rows of M. Since $F = F_{\mathsf{sk}}$ is a PRF, $F(x) = b$ holds for roughly a half of the inputs, and so such an x can be sampled with negligible failure probability by trying λ random candidates. Finally, since F is indistinguishable from a random function, polynomially many samples of inputs x for which $F(x) = 0$ are indistinguishable from polynomially many samples of inputs x for which $F(x) = 1$. Since the row indices in I_b are determined by the input, this implies the required indistinguishability condition.

Overall, while there are certainly some simplified variants of the Toy Conjecture 3 that are not secure, it seems that the stated version is not immediately susceptible to natural attack strategies. We hope that this Toy Conjecture will be the subject of further study (either with the goal of refuting or confirming it), as this will lead to a better understanding of our core Permuted Low-Degree Polynomials Conjecture.

5   Oblivious LDC to Public-Key PIR

We demonstrate a general transformation from any Oblivious LDC to a construction of Public-Key PIR, assuming virtual black-box program obfuscation. Recall the core differences between the two primitives are: (1) querying an OLDC (and decoding the retrieved values) requires the secret encoding key, and (2) OLDC security holds only if the codeword remains private. The transformation uses obfuscation to safely enable public querying and decoding (without revealing sk directly). The codeword will be published in encrypted form, and the obfuscated program will additionally contain the decryption key. Finally, to protect against malicious decoding queries, all queries generated by the obfuscated program will be authenticated by a MAC, which will be verified before answering.

Theorem 2. *Suppose Oblivious LDCs exist. Then, assuming one-way functions, there exists a secure Public-Key PIR in the virtual black-box obfuscation hybrid model.*

Proof. We present a general transformation from any oblivious LDC (G, E, Q, D) to a public-key PIR scheme $(\mathsf{Gen}, \mathsf{Encode}, \mathsf{Query}, \mathsf{Decode})$ in Construction 3, assuming the following tools (each of which, aside from VBB obfuscation itself, are implied by one-way functions):

- Let $\mathcal{O}$ be a VBB circuit obfuscator secure with auxiliary input.
- Let $(\mathsf{Gen_{SKE}}, \mathsf{Enc}, \mathsf{Dec})$ be a semantically secure symmetric encryption scheme.
- Let $(\mathsf{Gen_{MAC}}, \mathsf{Tag}, \mathsf{Verify})$ be a secure deterministic MAC.[2]
- Let $(\mathsf{Gen_{PRF}}, \mathsf{Eval_{PRF}})$ be a pseudorandom function family.

Construction 3 (pk-PIR from Oblivious LDC)

$\mathsf{Gen}(1^\lambda, x)$:
1. *Sample* $P \leftarrow \mathsf{Samp}(1^\lambda)$, *defined as follows:*
   - *Sample an oblivious LDC key* $\mathsf{sk_{LDC}} \leftarrow G(1^\lambda)$.
   - *Sample a SKE key* $\mathsf{sk_{SKE}} \leftarrow \mathsf{Gen_{SKE}}(1^\lambda)$.
   - *Sample a MAC key* $\mathsf{sk_{MAC}} \leftarrow \mathsf{Gen_{MAC}}(1^\lambda)$.
   - *Sample a PRF key* $k \leftarrow \mathsf{Gen_{PRF}}(1^\lambda)$.
   - *Let* P *be as in Fig. 1, with* $\mathsf{sk_{LDC}}, \mathsf{sk_{SKE}}, \mathsf{sk_{MAC}}, k$ *hardcoded.*
2. *Obfuscate the program as* $\tilde{P} \leftarrow \mathcal{O}(P, 1^\lambda, 1^n)$.
3. *Output* $\mathsf{sk} := (\mathsf{sk_{LDC}}, \mathsf{sk_{SKE}}, \mathsf{sk_{MAC}}, k)$ *and* $\mathsf{pk} := \tilde{P}$.

$\mathsf{Encode}(1^\lambda, \mathsf{sk}, x)$:
1. *Encode* x *using the oblivious LDC: i.e.,* $X'' \leftarrow E(1^\lambda, \mathsf{sk_{LDC}}, x)$.
2. *Encrypt each item in the encoded database (using* $\mathsf{sk_{SKE}}$ *from above):*
   For $j = 1, \ldots, N$, *let* $X'_j \leftarrow \mathsf{Enc_{sk_{SKE}}}(X''_j)$.
3. *MAC each item in the encrypted database (using* $\mathsf{sk_{MAC}}$ *from above):*
   For $j = 1, \ldots, N$, *compute* $\mathsf{tag}_j = \mathsf{Tag}(\mathsf{sk_{MAC}}, (j, X'_j))$, *and define* $X_j = (X'_j, \mathsf{tag}_j)$.
4. *Output the database* $X = (X_1, \ldots, X_N)$.

---

[2] Note that a pseudorandom function can also be used directly for this purpose; however, we use separate notation for clarity to emphasize the two uses.

Query(pk, i): *Sample randomness* $r \leftarrow \{0,1\}^{\lambda}$. *Evaluate* $(I, c, \mathsf{tag}_Q) = \tilde{P}(\text{"query"}, i, r)$. *Output* $\mathsf{sk}_i = (c, \mathsf{tag}_Q)$ *and query index set* I.

Decode(sk_i, X_I): *Parse* $\mathsf{sk}_i = (c, \mathsf{tag}_Q)$. *Output* $v = \tilde{P}(\text{"decode"}, (i, I, c, \mathsf{tag}_Q, X_I))$.

Public Key Program P

Hardcoded: Oblivious LDC key $\mathsf{sk}_{\mathsf{LDC}}$, SKE key $\mathsf{sk}_{\mathsf{SKE}}$, MAC key $\mathsf{sk}_{\mathsf{MAC}}$, PRF key k.

- Input ("query", i, r):
    1. Let $(r_1, r_2) = \mathsf{Eval}_{\mathsf{PRF}}(0, i, r)$. This will serve as the randomness.
    2. Let $I = \mathsf{Q}(1^{\lambda}, 1^n, i, \mathsf{sk}_{\mathsf{LDC}}; r_1)$. Sample the LDC query set, using randomness r_1.
    3. Let $c = \mathsf{Enc}_{\mathsf{sk}_{\mathsf{SKE}}}(r_1; r_2)$. Encrypt the randomness r_1 (using randomness r_2).
    4. Let $\mathsf{tag}_Q = \mathsf{MAC}_{\mathsf{sk}_{\mathsf{MAC}}}(i, I, c)$.
    5. Output (I, c, tag_Q).
- Input ("decode", $(i, I, c, \mathsf{tag}_Q, (\mathsf{dataCT}_j, \mathsf{tag}_j)_{j \in I})$):
    1. Test $1 \overset{?}{=} \mathsf{Verify}(\mathsf{sk}_{\mathsf{MAC}}, (i, I, c), \mathsf{tag}_Q)$. That is, verify the query MAC tag.
    2. For each $j \in I$:
        (a) Test $1 \overset{?}{=} \mathsf{Verify}(\mathsf{sk}_{\mathsf{MAC}}, (j, \mathsf{dataCT}_j), \mathsf{tag}_j)$. That is, verify the submitted MAC on message (j, dataCT) consisting of the index and submitted encrypted data value.
        (b) Decrypt $\mathsf{data}_j = \mathsf{Dec}_{\mathsf{sk}_{\mathsf{SKE}}}(\mathsf{dataCT}_j)$.
    3. Decrypt $r_1 = \mathsf{Dec}_{\mathsf{sk}_{\mathsf{SKE}}}(c)$.
    4. If any MACs did not properly verify, output $\perp$.
       Otherwise, output $D(1^{\lambda}, 1^n, i, (\mathsf{data}_j)_{j \in I}, \mathsf{sk}_{\mathsf{LDC}}, r_1)$.

Fig. 1. Query/Decode program whose obfuscation will constitute the pk-PIR public key.

Suppose, for contradiction, that Construction 3 is not a secure pk-PIR: that is, that there exists a non-negligible function α and non-uniform polynomial-time $\mathcal{A} = (\mathcal{A}_1, \mathcal{A}_2, \mathcal{A}_3)$ who wins in the pk-PIR security challenge game with advantage α. We will demonstrate a contradiction via a sequence of related games.

Game 0. Real pk-PIR security game.

By definition of the pk-PIR security game, we have that $\mathcal{A}$ satisfies

$$\Pr\Big[(x, \mathsf{aux}) \leftarrow \mathcal{A}_1(1^{\lambda}); (\mathsf{sk}, \mathsf{pk}) \leftarrow \mathsf{Gen}(1^{\lambda}); X \leftarrow \mathsf{Encode}(1^{\lambda}, \mathsf{sk}, x);$$
$$(i_0, i_1, \mathsf{aux}') \leftarrow \mathcal{A}_2(\mathsf{pk}, X, \mathsf{aux}); b \leftarrow \{0,1\}; (\mathsf{sk}_{i_b}, I) \leftarrow \mathsf{Query}(\mathsf{pk}, i_b);$$
$$b' \leftarrow \mathcal{A}_3(\mathsf{aux}', I) : b' = b\Big] \geq \alpha. \quad (1)$$

Game 1. VBB security. In this step, we show that the adversary $\mathcal{A}$ must still be able to successfully distinguish in the pk-PIR security game given only *black-box* access to the program P in the place of seeing the actual obfuscated code $\mathsf{pk} = \tilde{P}$.

Formally, consider Expression (1) above. By the pigeonhole principle applied over index pairs $(i_0, i_1) \in [n^2]$, there must exist a fixed choice of $(i_0^*, i_1^*) \in [n]^2$ for which

$$\Pr\Big[(x, \mathsf{aux}) \leftarrow \mathcal{A}_1(1^\lambda); (\mathsf{sk}, \mathsf{pk}) \leftarrow \mathsf{Gen}(1^\lambda); X \leftarrow \mathsf{Encode}(1^\lambda, \mathsf{sk}, x);$$
$$(i_0, i_1, \mathsf{aux}') \leftarrow \mathcal{A}_2(\mathsf{pk}, X, \mathsf{aux}); b \leftarrow \{0, 1\}; (\mathsf{sk}_{i_b}, I) \leftarrow \mathsf{Query}(\mathsf{pk}, i_b);$$
$$b' \leftarrow \mathcal{A}_3(\mathsf{aux}', I) : (b' = b) \wedge \big[(i_0, i_1) = (i_0^*, i_1^*)\big]\Big] \geq \alpha/n^2.$$

For this choice of $(i_0^*, i_1^*) \in [n]^2$, define a new adversary $\mathcal{A}_{(i_0^*, i_1^*)} = (\mathcal{A}_1, \mathcal{A}_2, \mathcal{A}_3')$ where $\mathcal{A}_3'(\mathsf{aux}', I)$ outputs $\mathcal{A}_3(\mathsf{aux}', I)$ if $(i_0, i_1) = (i_0^*, i_1^*)$ and $\perp$ otherwise. Then

$$\Pr\Big[(x, \mathsf{aux}) \leftarrow \mathcal{A}_1(1^\lambda); (\mathsf{sk}, \mathsf{pk}) \leftarrow \mathsf{Gen}(1^\lambda); X \leftarrow \mathsf{Encode}(1^\lambda, \mathsf{sk}, x);$$
$$(i_0, i_1, \mathsf{aux}') \leftarrow \mathcal{A}_2(\mathsf{pk}, X, \mathsf{aux}); b \leftarrow \{0, 1\}; (\mathsf{sk}_{i_b}, I) \leftarrow \mathsf{Query}(\mathsf{pk}, i_b);$$
$$b' \leftarrow \mathcal{A}_3'(\mathsf{aux}', I) : b' = b\Big] \geq \alpha/n^2.$$

Plugging in the particular procedure for Gen (consisting of sampling $(P, \mathsf{sk}) \leftarrow \mathsf{Samp}(1^\lambda)$ and then obfuscating $\tilde{P} \leftarrow \mathcal{O}(P, 1^\lambda, 1^n)$, and taking $\mathsf{pk} := \tilde{P}$), of Query (which samples randomness $r \leftarrow \{0, 1\}^\lambda$ and evaluates the obfuscated program at input $(\mathsf{sk}_i, I) = \tilde{P}(\text{"query"}, i, r))$, and making use of the correctness of the obfuscator (so that $\tilde{P}(\text{"query"}, i, r) = P(\text{"query"}, i, r)$), this implies

$$\Pr\Big[(x, \mathsf{aux}) \leftarrow \mathcal{A}_1(1^\lambda); (P, \mathsf{sk}) \leftarrow \mathsf{Samp}(1^\lambda); \tilde{P} \leftarrow \mathcal{O}(P, 1^\lambda, 1^n);$$
$$X \leftarrow \mathsf{Encode}(1^\lambda, \mathsf{sk}, x); (i_0, i_1, \mathsf{aux}') \leftarrow \mathcal{A}_2(\tilde{P}, X, \mathsf{aux}); b \leftarrow \{0, 1\}; r \leftarrow \{0, 1\}^\lambda;$$
$$(\mathsf{sk}_{i_b}, I) = P(\text{"query"}, i_b, r); b' \leftarrow \mathcal{A}_3'(\mathsf{aux}', I) : b' = b\Big] \geq \alpha/n^2.$$

For $i \in [n]$, define the distribution $(P, (\mathsf{aux}, X, I)) \leftarrow \mathsf{InstSamp}_i(1^\lambda)$ by:

1. $(x, \mathsf{aux}) \leftarrow \mathcal{A}_1(1^\lambda)$.
2. $(P, \mathsf{sk}) \leftarrow \mathsf{Samp}(1^\lambda)$ (where Samp samples keys and takes $\mathsf{sk} = (\mathsf{sk}_{\mathsf{LDC}}, \mathsf{sk}_{\mathsf{SKE}}, \mathsf{sk}_{\mathsf{MAC}}, k)$ as specified in Gen in Construction 3).
3. $X \leftarrow \mathsf{Encode}(1^\lambda, \mathsf{sk}, x)$ (where Encode is specified in Construction 3).
4. $r \leftarrow \{0, 1\}^\lambda; (\mathsf{sk}_i, I) = P(\text{"query"}, i, r)$.
5. Output $(P, (\mathsf{aux}, X, I))$.

Then (for the same $(i_0^*, i_1^*) \in [n]^2$ as above) we have

$$\Pr\Big[b \leftarrow \{0, 1\}; (P, (\mathsf{aux}, X, I)) \leftarrow \mathsf{InstSamp}_{i_b^*}(1^\lambda); \tilde{P} \leftarrow \mathcal{O}(P, 1^\lambda, 1^n);$$
$$(i_0, i_1, \mathsf{aux}') \leftarrow \mathcal{A}_2(\tilde{P}, X, \mathsf{aux}); b' \leftarrow \mathcal{A}_3'(\mathsf{aux}', I) : b' = b\Big] \geq \alpha/n^2$$

Note that while the challenge I is sampled using either i_0^* or i_1^* instead of i_0 or i_1 as selected by $\mathcal{A}$, this does not affect the probabilities since $\mathcal{A}_3'$ will anyway output $\perp$ in the case that $(i_0, i_1) \neq (i_0^*, i_1^*)$.

For the same $(i_0^*, i_1^*) \in [n]^2$ as above, define the algorithm $\mathcal{B}_{(i_0^*, i_1^*)}$ that, on input an obfuscated program $\tilde{P}$, and a triple (aux, X, I), executes as follows:
1. Run $(i_0, i_1, \mathsf{aux}') \leftarrow \mathcal{A}_2(\tilde{P}, X, \mathsf{aux})$.
2. Output $b' \leftarrow \mathcal{A}_3'(\mathsf{aux}', I)$.

Then, plugging in $\mathcal{B}_{(i_0^*, i_1^*)}$ notation to the expression above we have

$$\Pr\Big[b \leftarrow \{0,1\}; (P, (\mathsf{aux}, X, I)) \leftarrow \mathsf{InstSamp}_{i_b^*}(1^\lambda);$$
$$\tilde{P} \leftarrow \mathcal{O}(P, 1^\lambda, 1^n); b' \leftarrow \mathcal{B}_{(i_0^*, i_1^*)}(\tilde{P}, (\mathsf{aux}, X, I)) : b' = b\Big] \geq \alpha/n^2.$$

Now, by the VBB security of the obfuscator $\mathcal{O}$, then for the algorithm $\mathcal{B}_{(i_0^*, i_1^*)}$ there exists a corresponding simulator $\mathcal{S}_{(i_0^*, i_1^*)}$ such that for every auxiliary input $z = (\mathsf{aux}, X, I)$,

$$\Big| \Pr[\tilde{P} \leftarrow \mathcal{O}(P, 1^\lambda, 1^n); b' \leftarrow \mathcal{B}_{(i_0^*, i_1^*)}^{\mathsf{aux}}(\tilde{P}, (\mathsf{aux}, X, I)) : b' = 1]$$
$$- \Pr[b' \leftarrow (\mathcal{S}_{(i_0^*, i_1^*)})^{P(\cdot)}(1^{|P|}, 1^n, 1^\lambda, (\mathsf{aux}, X, I)) : b' = 1]\Big| \leq \nu(\lambda).$$

Therefore it must be the case that

$$\Pr\Big[b \leftarrow \{0,1\}; (P, (\mathsf{aux}, X, I)) \leftarrow \mathsf{InstSamp}_{i_b^*}(1^\lambda);$$
$$b' \leftarrow (\mathcal{S}_{(i_0^*, i_1^*)})^{P(\cdot)}(1^{|P|}, 1^n, 1^\lambda, (\mathsf{aux}, X, I)) : b' = b\Big] \geq \alpha/n^2 - 2\nu(\lambda). \quad (2)$$

That is, the simulator $(\mathcal{S}_{(i_0^*, i_1^*)})$ wins an analogous pk-PIR challenge (on a fixed choice of challenge indices (i_0^*, i_1^*)), given only black-box oracle access to the program P instead of its obfuscated code.

Game 2. MAC security. In this game, we consider the same experiment as in Eq. (2), but where the simulator $\mathcal{S}_{(i_0^*, i_1^*)}$ instead interacts with a modified (stateful) oracle, P_{MAC} defined below. P_{MAC} acts precisely as P but self destructs if it ever receives as input a valid MAC tag that was not generated by the program itself (or appearing in the given encoded database X).

(Stateful) program P_{MAC}:
    Hardcoded: Program P, and encoded database $X = ((\mathsf{dataCT}_1^{\mathsf{real}}, \mathsf{tag}_1^{\mathsf{real}}), \ldots, (\mathsf{dataCT}_N^{\mathsf{real}}, \mathsf{tag}_N^{\mathsf{real}}))$.

- Initialize $\mathsf{ValidTagList} \leftarrow \emptyset$.
- For each input ("query", i, r):

1. Let $(I, c, \mathsf{tag}_Q) = P(\text{"query"}, i, r)$.
2. Add new message-tag pair to the list: ValidTagList $\leftarrow$ ValidTagList $\cup$ $\{((i, I, c), \mathsf{tag}_Q)\}$.
3. Output (I, c, tag_Q).

- For each input ("decode", $(i, I, c, \mathsf{tag}_Q, (\mathsf{dataCT}_j, \mathsf{tag}_j)_{j \in I}))$:

  1. If either of the following holds, set ForgedTag $\leftarrow$ 1. Otherwise, ForgedTag $\leftarrow$ 0.
     - For some $j \in I$, Verify($\mathsf{sk}_{\mathsf{MAC}}, (j, \mathsf{dataCT}_j), \mathsf{tag}_j) = 1$ and $\mathsf{dataCT}_j \neq \mathsf{dataCT}_j^{\mathsf{real}}$.
     - Verify($\mathsf{sk}_{\mathsf{MAC}}, (i, I, c), \mathsf{tag}_Q) = 1$ and $((i, I, c), \mathsf{tag}_Q) \notin$ ValidTagList.
  2. If ForgedTag $= 1$: then selfdestruct.
  3. Else, output $P(\text{"decode"}, (i, I, c, \mathsf{tag}_Q, (\mathsf{dataCT}_j, \mathsf{tag}_j)_{j \in I}))$.

Claim. For (i_0^*, i_1^*), InstSamp defined in Game 1, and P_{MAC} as above, there exists a negligible function ν_2 for which

$$\Pr\Big[b \leftarrow \{0, 1\}; (P, (\mathsf{aux}, X, I)) \leftarrow \mathsf{InstSamp}_{i_b^*}(1^\lambda);$$

$$b' \leftarrow (\mathcal{S}_{(i_0^*, i_1^*)})^{P_{\mathsf{MAC}}(\cdot)}(1^{|P|}, 1^n, 1^\lambda, (\mathsf{aux}, X, I)) : b' = b \Big] \geq \alpha/n^2 - \nu_2(\lambda). \quad (3)$$

Proof. Follows directly by the security of the MAC. Namely, if the expression in Eq. (3) differs from that in Eq. (2) by more than a negligible amount, this would imply that the non-uniform polynomial algorithm $\mathcal{S}_{(i_0^*, i_1^*)}$ succeeds with non-negligible probability in generating a fresh message-tag pair, given black-box access to the program P. But, such an algorithm can be directly used to win with non-negligible probability in the MAC security game, since the outputs of the program P can be simulated given only query access to the algorithms Tag and Verify for a challenge key.

Game 3. Correctness of SKE and Oblivious LDC. In this step, instead of actually running the oblivious LDC decoder D on a "decode" request to the program, we will respond in one of two ways: (1) if the request is invalid or includes message-tag pair that was not generated earlier by the program or X (i.e., the case where P_{MAC} would self-destruct) then output $\perp$; (2) otherwise, the decode request corresponds directly to a previously asked "query" request for some index $i \in [n]$, in which case we will directly output the database value x_i.

(Stateful) program P_{correct}:
   Hardcoded: Program P, plaintext database $x = x_1, \ldots, x_n$, encoded database $X = ((\mathsf{dataCT}_1^{\mathsf{real}}, \mathsf{tag}_1^{\mathsf{real}}), \ldots, (\mathsf{dataCT}_N^{\mathsf{real}}, \mathsf{tag}_N^{\mathsf{real}}))$.

- Initialize QueryList $\leftarrow \emptyset$.
- For each input ("query", i, r):

  1. Let $(I, c, \mathsf{tag}_Q) = P(\text{"query"}, i, r)$.
  2. Add new query pair to the list: QueryList $\leftarrow$ QueryList $\cup \{((i, I, c), \mathsf{tag}_Q)\}$.
  3. Output (I, c, tag_Q).

- For each input ("decode", $(i, I, c, \mathsf{tag}_Q, (\mathsf{dataCT}_j, \mathsf{tag}_j)_{j \in I}))$:
  1. If either of the following holds, set ForgedTag $\leftarrow$ 1. Otherwise, ForgedTag $\leftarrow$ 0.
     - For some $j \in I$, Verify($\mathsf{sk}_{\mathsf{MAC}}, (j, \mathsf{dataCT}_j), \mathsf{tag}_j) = 1$ and $\mathsf{dataCT}_j \neq \mathsf{dataCT}_j^{\mathsf{real}}$.
     - Verify($\mathsf{sk}_{\mathsf{MAC}}, (i, I, c), \mathsf{tag}_Q) = 1$ and $((i, I, c), \mathsf{tag}_Q) \notin \mathsf{QueryList}$.
  2. If ForgedTag = 1: then selfdestruct.
  3. If $((i, I, c), \mathsf{tag}_Q) \in \mathsf{QueryList}$, output x_i.
  4. Else output $\perp$.

Claim. For (i_0^*, i_1^*), InstSamp defined in Game 1, and P_{correct} as above, there exists a negligible function ν_3 for which

$$\Pr\left[b \leftarrow \{0,1\}; (P, (\mathsf{aux}, X, I)) \leftarrow \mathsf{InstSamp}_{i_b^*}(1^\lambda);\right.$$
$$\left. b' \leftarrow (\mathcal{S}_{(i_0^*, i_1^*)})^{P_{\mathsf{correct}}(\cdot)}(1^{|P|}, 1^n, 1^\lambda, (\mathsf{aux}, X, I)) : b' = b\right] \geq \alpha/n^2 - \nu_3(\lambda). \quad (4)$$

Proof. Note that P_{MAC} and P_{correct} identically treat "query" inputs (including an identical update of respective lists ValidTagList and QueryList). Suppose an input is received of the form ("decode", $(i, I, c, \mathsf{tag}_Q, (\mathsf{dataCT}_j, \mathsf{tag}_j)_{j \in I}))$, for which ForgedTag = 0 (otherwise, if ForgedTag = 1, both P_{MAC} and P_{correct} self destruct). In particular, this means two things:

- The triple (I, c, tag_Q) was generated as the output of the program on some input ("query", i, r). By the definition of the "query" portion of the programs, this means there exists (r_1, r_2) for which $I = \mathsf{Q}(1^\lambda, 1^n, i, \mathsf{sk}_{\mathsf{LDC}}; r_1)$ and $c = \mathsf{Enc}_{\mathsf{sk}_{\mathsf{SKE}}}(r_1; r_2)$.
- The input values $(\mathsf{dataCT}_j)_{j \in I}$ are the *true* values of the encoded database at the indices specified by I (i.e., X_I). Now, recall that X was generated (within $\mathsf{InstSamp}_{i_b^*}$, defined in Game 1, where Samp, Encode are defined as in Fig. 1) by: sampling an oblivious LDC key as $\mathsf{sk}_{\mathsf{LDC}} \leftarrow \mathsf{G}(1^\lambda)$; encoding x via the oblivious LDC as $X'' \leftarrow \mathsf{E}(1^\lambda, \mathsf{sk}_{\mathsf{LDC}}, x)$; encrypting each coordinate of the encoded database as $\mathsf{dataCT}_j \leftarrow \mathsf{Enc}_{\mathsf{sk}_{\mathsf{SKE}}}(X''_j) \; \forall j \in [N]$; MACing each encrypted coordinate as $\mathsf{tag}_j \leftarrow \mathsf{Tag}(\mathsf{sk}_{\mathsf{MAC}}, (j, \mathsf{dataCT}_j)) \; \forall j \in [N]$; and taking final output values $X_j = (\mathsf{dataCT}_j, \mathsf{tag}_j) \; \forall j \in [N]$.

Now, consider the steps of the "decode" portion of P_{MAC} that are replaced within P_{correct}:

1. For each $j \in I$: Decrypt $\mathsf{data}_j = \mathsf{Dec}_{\mathsf{sk}_{\mathsf{SKE}}}(\mathsf{dataCT}_j)$.
   By correctness of the SKE, we have that $\mathsf{data}_j = X''_j$ (as defined above) for each j.
2. Decrypt $r_1 = \mathsf{Dec}_{\mathsf{sk}_{\mathsf{SKE}}}(c)$.
   By correctness of the SKE, we have that $\mathsf{Dec}_{\mathsf{sk}_{\mathsf{SKE}}}(c) = r_1$, for the randomness value r_1 used in Q to generate I.
3. Output $D(1^\lambda, 1^n, i, (\mathsf{data}_j)_{j \in I}, \mathsf{sk}_{\mathsf{LDC}}, r_1)$.
   In our notation, this is $D(1^\lambda, 1^n, i, X''_I, \mathsf{sk}_{\mathsf{LDC}}, r_1)$, where $I = \mathsf{Q}(1^\lambda, 1^n, i, \mathsf{sk}_{\mathsf{LDC}}; r_1)$.
   By correctness of decoding for the Oblivious LDC, this value is thus the queried ith data value, x_i.

Therefore, the programs P_{MAC} and P_{correct} are in fact *identical*. The claim follows.

Game 4. PRF security. We now replace the pseudorandom values (r_1, r_2) with *truly* random values.

(Stateful) program P_{PRF}:
Hardcoded: $\mathsf{sk}_{\mathsf{LDC}}, \mathsf{sk}_{\mathsf{SKE}}, \mathsf{sk}_{\mathsf{MAC}}$, Plaintext database $x = x_1, \ldots, x_n$, encoded database $X = ((\mathsf{dataCT}_1^{\mathsf{real}}, \mathsf{tag}_1^{\mathsf{real}}), \ldots, (\mathsf{dataCT}_N^{\mathsf{real}}, \mathsf{tag}_N^{\mathsf{real}}))$.

- Initialize QueryList $\leftarrow \emptyset$.
- Initialize OutputList $\leftarrow \emptyset$.
- Input ("query", i, r):
    1. If there exists a pair $(("query", i, r), (I, c, \mathsf{tag}_Q)) \in$ OutputList, then output (i, c, tag_Q).
    2. Else, let $(r_1, r_2) \leftarrow \{0,1\}^\lambda \times \{0,1\}^\lambda$. (This was previously *pseudo-randomness*).
    3. Let $I = \mathsf{Q}(1^\lambda, 1^n, i, \mathsf{sk}_{\mathsf{LDC}}; r_1)$.
    4. Let $c = \mathsf{Enc}_{\mathsf{sk}_{\mathsf{SKE}}}(r_1; r_2)$.
    5. Let $\mathsf{tag}_Q = \mathsf{MAC}_{\mathsf{sk}_{\mathsf{MAC}}}(i, I, c)$.
    6. Add new query pair to the list: QueryList $\leftarrow$ QueryList $\cup \{((i, I, c), \mathsf{tag}_Q)\}$.
    7. Add new output value to the list:
       OutputList $\leftarrow$ OutputList $\cup \{(("query", i, r), (I, c, \mathsf{tag}_Q))\}$.
    8. Output (I, c, tag_Q).
- Input ("decode", $(i, I, c, \mathsf{tag}_Q, (\mathsf{dataCT}_j, \mathsf{tag}_j)_{j \in I}))$:
  Compute and output $P_{\mathsf{correct}}(("decode", (i, I, c, \mathsf{tag}_Q, (\mathsf{dataCT}_j, \mathsf{tag}_j)_{j \in I}))$, as in Game 3.

Claim. For (i_0^*, i_1^*), InstSamp defined in Game 1, and P_{PRF} as above, there exists a negligible function ν_4 for which

$$\Pr\left[b \leftarrow \{0,1\}; (P, (\mathsf{aux}, X, I)) \leftarrow \mathsf{InstSamp}_{i_b^*}(1^\lambda); \right.$$
$$\left. b' \leftarrow (\mathcal{S}_{(i_0^*, i_1^*)})^{P_{\mathsf{PRF}}(\cdot)}(1^{|P|}, 1^n, 1^\lambda, (\mathsf{aux}, X, I)) : b' = b\right] \geq \alpha/n^2 - \nu_4(\lambda). \quad (5)$$

Proof. Follows directly by the security of the PRF. Note that Step 1 ensures consistency if the same input ("query", i, r) is received more than once.

Game 5. SKE security. We consider a new program P_{SKE} that replaces each $c \leftarrow \mathsf{Enc}(r_1)$ in P_{PRF} with an encryption of 0, i.e. $c \leftarrow \mathsf{Enc}(0)$. (Note that each encryption in P_{PRF} indeed uses true, freshly sampled randomness r_2.) In addition, we modify the InstSamp procedure so that instead of including encryptions of the encoded database as X, we now simply generate N fresh encryptions of 0 (and MAC the resulting ciphertexts).

Formally, define the new distribution $(P, (\mathsf{aux}, X, I)) \leftarrow \mathsf{InstSamp}_i^{\mathsf{Enc}(0)}(1^\lambda)$, for $i \in [n]$, by:

1. $(x, \mathsf{aux}) \leftarrow \mathcal{A}_1(1^\lambda)$.
2. $(P, \mathsf{sk}) \leftarrow \mathsf{Samp}(1^\lambda)$ (where Samp is defined in Gen in Construction 3).
3. For $j = 1, \ldots, N$:
   (a) Sample CT of 0: $\mathsf{dataCT}_j \leftarrow \mathsf{Enc}_{\mathsf{sk}_{\mathsf{SKE}}}(0)$.
   (b) MAC each item: $\mathsf{tag}_j \leftarrow \mathsf{Tag}(\mathsf{sk}_{\mathsf{MAC}}, (j, \mathsf{dataCT}_j))$.
   (c) Let $X_j = (\mathsf{dataCT}_j, \mathsf{tag}_j)$.
4. $r \leftarrow \{0,1\}^\lambda$; $(\mathsf{sk}_i, I) = P(\text{``query''}, i, r)$.
5. Output $(P, (\mathsf{aux}, X, I))$.

(Stateful) program P_{SKE}:
Hardcoded: $\mathsf{sk}_{\mathsf{LDC}}, \mathsf{sk}_{\mathsf{SKE}}, \mathsf{sk}_{\mathsf{MAC}}$, Plaintext database $x = x_1, \ldots, x_n$, encoded database $X = ((\mathsf{dataCT}_1^{\mathsf{real}}, \mathsf{tag}_1^{\mathsf{real}}), \ldots, (\mathsf{dataCT}_N^{\mathsf{real}}, \mathsf{tag}_N^{\mathsf{real}}))$.

- Initialize $\mathsf{QueryList} \leftarrow \emptyset$.
- Initialize $\mathsf{OutputList} \leftarrow \emptyset$.
- Input $(\text{``query''}, i, r)$:
   1. If there exists a pair $((\text{``query''}, i, r), (I, c, \mathsf{tag}_Q)) \in \mathsf{OutputList}$, then output (I, c, tag_Q).
   2. Let $I \leftarrow Q(1^\lambda, 1^n, i, \mathsf{sk}_{\mathsf{LDC}})$.
   3. Let $c \leftarrow \mathsf{Enc}_{\mathsf{sk}_{\mathsf{SKE}}}(0)$. (Previously encrypted the randomness used in Q.)
   4. Let $\mathsf{tag}_Q = \mathsf{MAC}_{\mathsf{sk}_{\mathsf{MAC}}}(i, I, c)$.
   5. Add new query pair to the list: $\mathsf{QueryList} \leftarrow \mathsf{QueryList} \cup \{(i, I, c)\}$.
   6. Add new output value to the list:
      $\mathsf{OutputList} \leftarrow \mathsf{OutputList} \cup \{((\text{``query''}, i, r), (I, c, \mathsf{tag}_Q))\}$
   7. Output (I, c, tag_Q).
- Input $(\text{``decode''}, (i, I, c, \mathsf{tag}_Q, (\mathsf{dataCT}_j, \mathsf{tag}_j)_{j \in I}))$:
   Compute and output $P_{\mathsf{correct}}((\text{``decode''}, (i, I, c, \mathsf{tag}_Q, (\mathsf{dataCT}_j, \mathsf{tag}_j)_{j \in I}))$, as in Game 3.

Claim. For (i_0^*, i_1^*) as in Game 1, and $\mathsf{InstSamp}_i^{\mathsf{Enc}(0)}$, P_{SKE} as above, there exists a negligible function ν_5 for which

$$\Pr\left[b \leftarrow \{0,1\}; (P, (\mathsf{aux}, X, I)) \leftarrow \mathsf{InstSamp}_{i_b^*}^{\mathsf{Enc}(0)}(1^\lambda);\right.$$
$$\left. b' \leftarrow (\mathcal{S}_{(i_0^*, i_1^*)})^{P_{\mathsf{SKE}}(\cdot)}(1^{|P|}, 1^n, 1^\lambda, (\mathsf{aux}, X, I)) : b' = b\right] \geq \alpha/n^2 - \nu_5(\lambda). \quad (6)$$

Proof. Follows by the semantic security of the SKE and a standard hybrid argument.

Game 6. Oblivious LDC security. In our final step, we argue that Eq. (6) *cannot* hold for non-negligible α. The reason is because interaction with the program P_{SKE} can be completely simulated given only access to the challenge oracle for the Oblivious LDC security game. Therefore, the combined (non-uniform polynomial-time) adversary which runs the simulator $\mathcal{S}_{(i_0^*, i_1^*)}$ and simulates the answers of its oracle $P_{\mathsf{SKE}}(\cdot)$ serves as an Oblivious LDC adversary, who successfully distinguishes between the challenge I sampled via $\mathsf{InstSamp}_{i_0^*}^{\mathsf{Enc}(0)}$ from that sampled via $\mathsf{InstSamp}_{i_1^*}^{\mathsf{Enc}(0)}$.

Claim. For (i_0^*, i_1^*) as in Game 1, and $\mathsf{InstSamp}_i^{\mathsf{Enc}(0)}, P_{\mathsf{SKE}}$ as in Game 5, there exists a negligible function ν_6 for which

$$\Pr\left[b \leftarrow \{0,1\}; (P, (\mathsf{aux}, X, I)) \leftarrow \mathsf{InstSamp}_{i_b^*}^{(\mathsf{Enc}(0))}(1^\lambda); \right.$$
$$\left. b' \leftarrow (\mathcal{S}_{(i_0^*, i_1^*)})^{P_{\mathsf{SKE}}(\cdot)}(1^{|P|}, 1^n, 1^\lambda, (\mathsf{aux}, X, I)) : b' = b \right] \leq \nu_6(\lambda). \quad (7)$$

Proof. Suppose, to the contrary, the probability expression in Eq. (7) is equal to some non-negligible function $\beta(\lambda)$.

Consider following the Oblivious LDC adversary $\mathcal{B}_{\mathsf{LDC}}$:

1. An Oblivious LDC challenge key is sampled as $\mathsf{sk} \leftarrow \mathsf{G}(1^\lambda)$. $\mathcal{B}_{\mathsf{LDC}}$ receives oracle access to $\mathsf{Q}_{\mathsf{sk}}(\cdot)$ (which on input $i \in [n]$ outputs $I \leftarrow \mathsf{Q}(1^\lambda, 1^n, i, \mathsf{sk})$).
2. $\mathcal{B}_{\mathsf{LDC}}$ simulates the remaining (non-LDC) items in $\mathsf{InstSamp}^{\mathsf{Enc}(0)}$:
   (a) Simulate $\mathcal{A}_1$ to obtain $(x, \mathsf{aux}) \leftarrow \mathcal{A}_1(1^\lambda)$.
   (b) Sample $\mathsf{sk}_{\mathsf{SKE}} \leftarrow \mathsf{Gen}_{\mathsf{SKE}}(1^\lambda); \mathsf{sk}_{\mathsf{MAC}} \leftarrow \mathsf{Gen}_{\mathsf{MAC}}(1^\lambda);$ and $k \leftarrow \mathsf{Gen}_{\mathsf{PRF}}(1^\lambda)$.
   (c) For $j = 1, \ldots, N$:
       i. Sample CT of 0: $\mathsf{dataCT}_j \leftarrow \mathsf{Enc}_{\mathsf{sk}_{\mathsf{SKE}}}(0)$.
       ii. MAC each item: $\mathsf{tag}_j \leftarrow \mathsf{Tag}(\mathsf{sk}_{\mathsf{MAC}}, (j, \mathsf{dataCT}_j))$.
       iii. Let $X_j = (\mathsf{dataCT}_j, \mathsf{tag}_j)$.
3. $\mathcal{B}_{\mathsf{LDC}}$ selects the Oblivious LDC challenge index pair $(i_0^*, i_1^*) \in [n]^2$, and receives a challenge index sequence I generated as $I \leftarrow \mathsf{Q}(1^\lambda, 1^n, i_b^*, \mathsf{sk})$ for randomly selected $b \leftarrow \{0,1\}$.
4. $\mathcal{B}_{\mathsf{LDC}}$ simulates $b' \leftarrow (\mathcal{S}_{(i_0^* i_1^*)})^{P_{\mathsf{SKE}}(\cdot)}(1^{|P|}, 1^n, 1^\lambda, (\mathsf{aux}, X, I))$, for the values of (aux, X, I) as generated in Step 2.
   For each query made by $\mathcal{S}_{(i_0^* i_1^*)}$ to the oracle $P_{\mathsf{SKE}}(\cdot)$, $\mathcal{B}_{\mathsf{LDC}}$ simulates the response:
   – In Step 2 of the computation for an input of the form ("query", i, r), $\mathcal{B}_{\mathsf{LDC}}$ makes a query to its oracle $\mathsf{Q}_{\mathsf{sk}}(\cdot)$ on the input index i.
   – In all other steps, $\mathcal{B}_{\mathsf{LDC}}$ simulates precisely.
5. $\mathcal{B}_{\mathsf{LDC}}$ outputs the guess bit b'.

By construction, the advantage of $\mathcal{B}_{\mathsf{LDC}}$ in the Oblivious LDC security challenge for $(\mathsf{G}, \mathsf{E}, \mathsf{Q}, \mathsf{D})$ is precisely β. Therefore, it must be the case that β is negligible.

Combining Games 1–6, we have that the original advantage α of the adversary $\mathcal{A}$ in the Public-Key PIR security challenge game must be negligible. That is, (Gen, Encode, Query, Decode) of Construction 3 is a secure Public-Key PIR. This concludes the proof of Theorem 2.

Combining Proposition 2 and Theorem 2, we obtain the following main theorem.

Theorem 4. *Suppose the Permuted Low-Degree Polynomials Conjecture holds (Conjecture 1), and one-way functions exist. Then given ideal obfuscation (alternatively, a poly(λ)-size, stateless hardware token), there is a pk-PIR scheme with communication and computation complexity poly$(\lambda) \cdot n^\epsilon$, for every $\epsilon > 0$.*

6 Conclusion and Open Problems

In this work we put forward two new cryptographic primitives: pk-PIR, a public-key variant of single-server PIR with preprocessing, and OLDC, its secret-key variant. We propose a candidate implementation for OLDC and reduce pk-PIR to OLDC via ideal obfuscation. Our work leaves open many interesting directions for further research. For example:

- Further study the Permuted Low-Degree Polynomials Conjecture and more general instances of the Permuted Puzzles problem.
- Can a construction of OLDC be based on standard cryptographic assumptions? Alternatively, can it be based on standard assumptions together with ideal obfuscation?
- Are there OLDC candidates that provide a better tradeoff between storage overhead and decoding complexity?
- Does a general transformation from OLDC to pk-PIR follow from indistinguishability obfuscation?
- Is there a direct candidate construction of pk-PIR that does not rely on any form of general-purpose obfuscation?

Acknowledgments. We thank David Cash, Ronald Cramer, Venkat Guruswami, Tancrède Lepoint, Daniel Wichs, and Chaoping Xing for helpful discussions.

This work was done in part while the first three authors were visiting the Simons Institute for the Theory of Computing, supported by the Simons Foundation and by the DIMACS/Simons Collaboration in Cryptography through NSF grant #CNS-1523467. EB was supported in part by ISF grant 1861/16, AFOSR Award FA9550-17-1-0069, and ERC Grant no. 307952. YI was supported in part by NSF-BSF grant 2015782, BSF grant 2012366, ISF grant 1709/14, ERC grants 259426 and 742754, DARPA/ARL SAFEWARE award, NSF Frontier Award 1413955, NSF grants 1619348, 1228984, 1136174, and 1065276, a Xerox Faculty Research Award, a Google Faculty Research Award, an equipment grant from Intel, and an Okawa Foundation Research Grant. This material is based upon work supported by the DARPA through the ARL under Contract W911NF-15-C-0205. RP was supported in part by NSF Award CNS-1561209, NSF Award CNS-1217821, AFOSR Award FA9550-15-1-0262, a Microsoft Faculty Fellowship, and a Google Faculty Research Award. MW is supported in part by NSF grant CCF-1657049. The views expressed are those of the authors and do not reflect the official policy or position of the DoD, the NSF, or the U.S. Government.

A   Barriers to Proving Impossibility of OLDC

In this section we argue that ruling out the existence of OLDC is unlikely, as it would imply data structure lower bounds that seem beyond the reach of current techniques.

When considering a relaxed notion of OLDC that allows for *adaptive decoding* (i.e., decoding proceeds in rounds, where the location of each symbol read by the decoder may depend on the contents of the previous ones) there is a known barrier which was already pointed out in [4,29]: proving strong lower bounds in the adaptive setting requires strong branching program lower bounds. However, no such connection is known in the non-adaptive case.

We argue that ruling out the existence of OLDC is very unlikely, as it would require proving strong data structure lower bounds. To be concrete, consider the following question:

> Is it possible to preprocess any circuit $C : \{0,1\}^k \to \{0,1\}$ of size k^{100} into a data structure D of size $\text{poly}(k)$ such that for any input q, $C(q)$ can be evaluated by non-adaptively probing k^{10} bits of D?

While this type of "dream data structure" seems extremely unlikely to exist, ruling it out seems beyond the reach of current techniques.[3] Given such a hypothetical data structure, we can take existing single-server PIR protocols (e.g., the one from [27]) and just let D be the data structure corresponding to the circuit C_x that computes the answer given the client's PIR query. For instance, for the concrete dream data structure formulated above, we can take an instance of the protocol from [27] where the queries are of size k, the database is of size $n = k^{98}$, and the circuit C_x is of size k^{100}. This would result in an OLDC that makes $k^{10} \ll n$ probes to the encoded database. In fact, this OLDC is stronger than our default notion in that has a *deterministic encoder* and does not make use of any secret key.

References

1. Asharov, G., Segev, G.: Limits on the power of indistinguishability obfuscation and functional encryption. In: IEEE 56th Annual Symposium on Foundations of Computer Science, FOCS 2015, Berkeley, CA, USA, 17–20 October 2015, pp. 191–209 (2015)
2. Barak, B., Garg, S., Kalai, Y.T., Paneth, O., Sahai, A.: Protecting obfuscation against algebraic attacks. In: Nguyen, P.Q., Oswald, E. (eds.) EUROCRYPT 2014. LNCS, vol. 8441, pp. 221–238. Springer, Heidelberg (2014). doi:10.1007/978-3-642-55220-5_13
3. Barak, B., Goldreich, O., Impagliazzo, R., Rudich, S., Sahai, A., Vadhan, S.P., Yang, K.: On the (im)possibility of obfuscating programs. J. ACM 59(2), 6 (2012)
4. Beimel, A., Ishai, Y., Malkin, T.: Reducing the servers computation in private information retrieval: PIR with preprocessing. In: Bellare, M. (ed.) CRYPTO 2000. LNCS, vol. 1880, pp. 55–73. Springer, Heidelberg (2000). doi:10.1007/3-540-44598-6_4
5. Bleichenbacher, D., Kiayias, A., Yung, M.: Decoding of interleaved reed solomon codes over noisy data. In: Baeten, J.C.M., Lenstra, J.K., Parrow, J., Woeginger, G.J. (eds.) ICALP 2003. LNCS, vol. 2719, pp. 97–108. Springer, Heidelberg (2003). doi:10.1007/3-540-45061-0_9
6. Bleichenbacher, D., Nguyen, P.Q.: Noisy polynomial interpolation and noisy Chinese remaindering. In: Preneel, B. (ed.) EUROCRYPT 2000. LNCS, vol. 1807, pp. 53–69. Springer, Heidelberg (2000). doi:10.1007/3-540-45539-6_4

---

[3] We ran this problem by several relevant experts, who were unaware of any negative results or implications to other well studied problems in complexity theory.

7. Boneh, D.: Finding smooth integers in short intervals using CRT decoding. J. Comput. Syst. Sci. **64**(4), 768–784 (2002)
8. Canetti, R., Holmgren, J., Richelson, S.: Towards doubly efficient private information retrieval. In: TCC 2017. IACR Cryptology ePrint Archive 2017: 568 (2017)
9. Chor, B., Gilboa, N.: Computationally private information retrieval (extended abstract). In: Proceedings of the Twenty-Ninth Annual ACM Symposium on the Theory of Computing, El Paso, Texas, USA, 4–6 May 1997, pp. 304–313 (1997)
10. Chor, B., Kushilevitz, E., Goldreich, O., Sudan, M.: Private information retrieval. J. ACM **45**(6), 965–981 (1998). Earlier version in Proceedings of FOCS 2005
11. Coppersmith, D., Sudan, M.: Reconstructing curves in three (and higher) dimensional space from noisy data. In: Proceedings of the 35th Annual ACM Symposium on Theory of Computing, 9–11 June 2003, San Diego, CA, USA, pp. 136–142 (2003)
12. Coron, J.-S.: Cryptanalysis of a public-key encryption scheme based on the polynomial reconstruction problem. In: Bao, F., Deng, R., Zhou, J. (eds.) PKC 2004. LNCS, vol. 2947, pp. 14–27. Springer, Heidelberg (2004). doi:10.1007/978-3-540-24632-9_2
13. Curtmola, R., Garay, J.A., Kamara, S., Ostrovsky, R.: Searchable symmetric encryption: Improved definitions and efficient constructions. J. Comput. Secur. **19**(5), 895–934 (2011)
14. Garg, S., Gentry, C., Halevi, S., Raykova, M., Sahai, A., Waters, B.: Candidate indistinguishability obfuscation and functional encryption for all circuits. In: FOCS (2013)
15. Garg, S., Miles, E., Mukherjee, P., Sahai, A., Srinivasan, A., Zhandry, M.: Secure obfuscation in a weak multilinear map model. In: Hirt, M., Smith, A. (eds.) TCC 2016. LNCS, vol. 9986, pp. 241–268. Springer, Heidelberg (2016). doi:10.1007/978-3-662-53644-5_10
16. Goldreich, O.: A note on computational indistinguishability. Inf. Process. Lett. **34**(6), 277–281 (1990)
17. Goldreich, O.: Foundations of Cryptography - Basic Tools. Cambridge University Press, Cambridge (2001)
18. Goldreich, O., Goldwasser, S., Micali, S.: How to construct random functions. J. ACM **33**(4), 792–807 (1986)
19. Goldreich, O., Ostrovsky, R.: Software protection and simulation on oblivious rams. J. ACM **43**(3), 431–473 (1996)
20. Hemenway, B., Ostrovsky, R.: Public-key locally-decodable codes. In: Wagner, D. (ed.) CRYPTO 2008. LNCS, vol. 5157, pp. 126–143. Springer, Heidelberg (2008). doi:10.1007/978-3-540-85174-5_8
21. Ishai, Y., Kushilevitz, E., Ostrovsky, R., Sahai, A.: Batch codes and their applications. In: Proceedings of the 36th Annual ACM Symposium on Theory of Computing, Chicago, IL, USA, 13–16 June 2004, pp. 262–271 (2004)
22. Ishai, Y., Kushilevitz, E., Ostrovsky, R., Sahai, A.: Cryptography from anonymity. In: Proceedings of 47th Annual IEEE Symposium on Foundations of Computer Science (FOCS 2006), 21–24 October 2006, Berkeley, California, USA, pp. 239–248 (2006)
23. Karchmer, M., Wigderson, A.: On span programs. In: Proceedings of the Eight Annual Structure in Complexity Theory Conference, San Diego, CA, USA, 18–21 May 1993, pp. 102–111 (1993)
24. Katz, J., Trevisan, L.: On the efficiency of local decoding procedures for error-correcting codes. In: Proceedings of the Thirty-Second Annual ACM Symposium on Theory of Computing, 21–23 May 2000, Portland, OR, USA, pp. 80–86 (2000)

25. Kiayias, A., Yung, M.: Cryptanalyzing the polynomial-reconstruction based public-key system under optimal parameter choice. In: Lee, P.J. (ed.) ASIACRYPT 2004. LNCS, vol. 3329, pp. 401–416. Springer, Heidelberg (2004). doi:10.1007/978-3-540-30539-2_28

26. Kopparty, S., Meir, O., Ron-Zewi, N., Saraf, S.: High-rate locally-correctable and locally-testable codes with sub-polynomial query complexity. In: Proceedings of the 48th Annual ACM SIGACT Symposium on Theory of Computing, STOC 2016, Cambridge, MA, USA, 18–21 June 2016, pp. 202–215 (2016)

27. Kushilevitz, E., Ostrovsky, R.: Replication is not needed: single database, computationally-private information retrieval. In: FOCS, pp. 364–373 (1997)

28. McEliece, R.J.: A public-key cryptosystem based on algebraic coding theory. Deep Space Netw. Prog. Rep. **44**, 114–116 (1978)

29. Miltersen, P.B., Nisan, N., Safra, S., Wigderson, A.: On data structures and asymmetric communication complexity. J. Comput. Syst. Sci. **57**(1), 37–49 (1998)

30. Morris, B., Rogaway, P., Stegers, T.: How to encipher messages on a small domain. In: Halevi, S. (ed.) CRYPTO 2009. LNCS, vol. 5677, pp. 286–302. Springer, Heidelberg (2009). doi:10.1007/978-3-642-03356-8_17

31. Naor, M., Pinkas, B.: Oblivious polynomial evaluation. SIAM J. Comput. **35**(5), 1254–1281 (2006)

32. Naor, M., Reingold, O.: Number-theoretic constructions of efficient pseudo-random functions. J. ACM **51**(2), 231–262 (2004)

33. Ostrovsky, R., Pandey, O., Sahai, A.: Private locally decodable codes. In: Arge, L., Cachin, C., Jurdziński, T., Tarlecki, A. (eds.) ICALP 2007. LNCS, vol. 4596, pp. 387–398. Springer, Heidelberg (2007). doi:10.1007/978-3-540-73420-8_35

34. Sahai, A., Waters, B.: How to use indistinguishability obfuscation: deniable encryption, and more. In: Symposium on Theory of Computing, STOC 2014, New York, NY, USA, 31 May–03 June 2014, pp. 475–484 (2014)

35. Sidelnikov, V.M., Shestakov, S.O.: On insecurity of cryptosystems based on generalized Reed-Solomon codes. Discret. Math. Appl. **2**, 439–444 (2009)

36. Song, D.X., Wagner, D., Perrig, A.: Practical techniques for searches on encrypted data. In: 2000 IEEE Symposium on Security and Privacy, Berkeley, California, USA, 14–17 May 2000, pp. 44–55 (2000)

Towards Doubly Efficient Private Information Retrieval

Ran Canetti[1,2], Justin Holmgren[3(✉)], and Silas Richelson[4(✉)]

[1] Boston University, Boston, USA
[2] Tel-Aviv University, Tel Aviv, Israel
[3] Massachusetts Institute of Technology, Cambridge, USA
holmgren@mit.edu
[4] University of California Riverside, Riverside, USA
silas.richelson@gmail.com

Abstract. Private Information Retrieval (PIR) allows a client to obtain data from a public database without disclosing the locations accessed. Traditionally, the stress is on preserving sublinear work for the client, while the server's work is taken to inevitably be at least linear in the database size. Beimel, Ishai and Malkin (JoC 2004) show PIR schemes where, following a linear-work preprocessing stage, the server's work per query is sublinear in the database size. However, that work only addresses the case of multiple non-colluding servers; the existence of single-server PIR with sublinear server work remained unaddressed.

We consider single-server PIR schemes where, following a preprocessing stage in which the server obtains an encoded version of the database and the client obtains a short key, the per-query work of both server and client is polylogarithmic in the database size. Concentrating on the case where the client's key is secret, we show:

- A scheme, based on one-way functions, that works for a bounded number of queries, and where the server storage is linear in the number of queries plus the database size.
- A family of schemes for an unbounded number of queries, whose security follows from a corresponding family of new hardness assumption that are related to the hardness of solving a system of noisy linear equations.

We also show the insufficiency of a natural approach for obtaining doubly efficient PIR in the setting where the preprocessing is public.

1 Introduction

Enabling clients to query remote databases while preserving privacy of the queries is a basic challenge in cryptography. With the proliferation of huge data-

Work supported by the NSF MACS project.

R. Canetti—Member of CPIIS. Supported in addition by ISF Grant 1523/14.

J. Holmgren—Supported in addition by DARPA IBM-W911NF-15C0236 and SIMONS Investigator Award.

S. Richelson—Work done while at MIT and Boston University.

Y. Kalai and L. Reyzin (Eds.): TCC 2017, Part II, LNCS 10678, pp. 694–726, 2017.
https://doi.org/10.1007/978-3-319-70503-3_23

bases stored and managed by powerful third parties, this challenge becomes ever more relevant.

One of the more basic formulations of this multi-faceted problem is the concept of *Private Information Retrieval (PIR)* [CKGS98]. Here the client is interested in learning the contents of specific addresses in the database, while preventing the server controlling the database (or, simply, the database) from learning these addresses. The goal here is to minimize communication and work for the client.

There are two general types of PIR schemes: Multi-server schemes whose security relies on the assumption that servers do not collude, but are otherwise information theoretic (see e.g. [CKGS98, BI01]), and single-server schemes which are based on computational assumptions, often of a structured nature (e.g., [KO97, CMS99]). Still, in both cases, the per-query work of the server is traditionally taken to be at least linear in the database size—else the server can "obviously" somewhat localize the requested address. Indeed, this linear server overhead is a main bottleneck for deployment (see e.g. [CSP+]).

Is this bottleneck really inevitable? A first indication that this might not be the case is the body of work on oblivious RAM [GO96, Ajt10, DMN11, SCSL11]: Here a client can indeed access a database in a privacy preserving manner, with polylogarithmic overhead for both client and database (following an initial poly-time preprocessing stage). However, oblivious RAM schemes inherently require the client to (a) keep secret state and (b) be able to update the database. This is so even if the client only wants to read from the database. Furthermore, if the database is not trusted for correctness then the client needs to be able to continually update its local state. Consequently, a database cannot serve multiple clients without having the clients continually coordinate with each other.

An indication that these restrictions might not be necessary either is the work of Beimel et al. [BIM04]. They present PIR schemes where, following an initial polynomial-time preprocessing stage, the client and servers each are stateless and incur a per-query overhead that is sublinear in the database size. However, that work considers only the multi-server setting, and furthermore the number of servers is tied to the "level of sublinearity" of the scheme. This leaves open the following question:

> Can we construct a single-server PIR scheme where the client has no updatable state and where the per-query work of both the client and the server is sublinear in the database size, potentially with a more expensive preprocessing stage?

Paraphrasing [GR17], we call this primitive doubly efficient PIR (DEPIR).

1.1 Our Contributions

We provide some positive answers to this question, along with some impossibility results and cryptanalysis of our candidate schemes. Our DEPIR schemes start with an initial preprocessing stage which takes the database as input and hands a preprocessed version of the database to the server and (short) key to the client. We distinguish between the *public preprocessing* case, where the random choices made during preprocessing are public, the *public client* case, where the preprocessing may use secret randomness but the client's long-term key is public, and the *designated client* case where the client's key remains hidden from the server. In all cases the client maintains no state across queries other than the long-term key, and the database is read-only.

We have no positive results for the first two cases. In fact, we demonstrate that a natural and general approach towards a public preprocessing solution is doomed to fail. We leave progress on this fascinating question to future research. We then concentrate on the designated client case. Here we show:

1. A designated-client scheme for a bounded number of queries, whose security can be based on any one way function. Given a bound B on the number of client queries, the size of the preprocessed database is $\tilde{O}(B + \mathsf{poly}(N))$, where N is the database size. The client keeps a short secret key of size λ, the security parameter. The per-query client and server overheads are $\lambda \cdot \mathsf{polylog}(N, B)$ and $\mathsf{polylog}(N, B)$, respectively. (We compare the performance of this scheme to that of the trivial stateful scheme where in preprocessing the client hands the server B independently permuted copies of the database, and then uses a different copy for each query. Here the online work is only $\log N$, but the size of the preprocessed database is BN. This means that the amortized space overhead in this scheme is N, whereas in our scheme it is $\mathsf{polylog}(N)$.) We then demonstrate the tightness of the analysis in two ways:
   (a) We demonstrate an efficient attack on this scheme which is applicable as soon as the number of queries exceeds the designated bound B.
   (b) We demonstrate the failure of a natural approach to extending the scheme while preserving its proof structure[1]. Along the way, we also show a tight quantitative extension of the impossibility result from [CKGS98] regarding the communication complexity in standard single-server PIR, and a tight bound on the size of the key in an information-theoretic designated-client PIR with preprocessing.
2. A candidate extension of the scheme from (1) to the case of unbounded queries. The extended scheme provides a natural tradeoff between complexity and potential security, where in the best case the complexity parameters are comparable to those of the bounded scheme with $B = 1$. We are unable to prove security of this scheme based on known assumptions. Instead, we introduce a new computational problem, which we call the hidden permutation with noise (HPN) problem, and reduce the security of our scheme to the assumption that HPN is hard. HPN is a noisy learning problem and is thus superficially similar to other "standard" cryptographic assumptions (e.g. LWE, LPN), but we do not know of any reduction to these assumptions.
3. We take first steps towards analyzing the hardness of HPN. Security of the candidate scheme from (2) can be rephrased as the hardness of the adaptive,

---

[1] Specifically, using pseudo-random functions and pseudo-random permutations to compress a long key for a statistically secure scheme.

decision version of HPN. We then prove that the adaptive decision version is no harder than the static (selective), search version. This allows future investigation of the hardness of HPN to focus on the latter version, which is structurally simpler and more basic.

4. We also consider a number of other methods for extending the scheme from (1) to the case of unbounded queries. However, while these other methods may well provide additional security on top of the HPN-based scheme described above, we are unable to make significant headways either towards cryptanalysis of these methods, or towards reducing security to a simpler problem.

In the rest of the introduction we describe our contributions in more detail.

Defining PIR security with preprocessing. We formulate the security of PIR schemes with preprocessing in a range of settings, including the ones mentioned above and some variants. A PIR scheme with preprocessing consists of five algorithms (Keygen, Process, Query, Resp, Dec), as follows. Keygen takes the security parameter λ and samples a key K. Process takes K and a database $DB \in \Sigma^N$ for some alphabet Σ and samples a preprocessed database $\widetilde{DB}$ to be handed to the server. Query takes K and an address $i \in \{1, \ldots, N\}$, and samples a query q and local state s. Resp computes the server's response d given q and RAM access to $\widetilde{DB}$, and Dec outputs the decoded value given K, s, and d. Giving Resp oracle (random-)access to $\widetilde{DB}$ enables it to be sublinear in N. It is stressed that the client is stateless, apart from the long-term key K and the short-term state s between sending a query and obtaining its response.

The correctness requirement is obvious. Double efficiency means that Query, Resp, and Dec each run in time $o(N) \cdot \text{poly}(\lambda)$ (ideally, they should be polylogarithmic in N), and additionally Process runs in time $\text{poly}(N, \lambda)$. For security, we consider three main cases (plus several variants).

In the designated client case, security is defined by requiring that for any polytime stateful adversary $\mathcal{A}$ there exists a polytime stateful simulator $\mathcal{S}$ such that $\mathcal{A}$ can distinguish between the following two games only with negligible probability: In the real game, $\mathcal{A}$ chooses a database DB, obtains a preprocessed database $\widetilde{DB} \leftarrow \text{Process}(K, DB)$ where $K \leftarrow \text{Keygen}(\lambda)$, and then repeatedly and adaptively generates an index $i \in [N]$ and obtains $\text{Query}(K, i)$. In the ideal game, $\mathcal{A}$ chooses a database DB, obtains a simulated preprocessed database $\mathcal{S}(DB)$, and then repeatedly and adaptively generates an index $i \in [N]$ and obtains $\mathcal{S}()$. (If $\mathcal{S}$ gets only N rather than DB then we say that the scheme guarantees also database privacy.)

In the public client case, the above real game is modified so that $\mathcal{A}$ obtains $K \leftarrow \text{Keygen}(\lambda)$ before generating DB; in the ideal game K is generated by $\mathcal{S}$. In the public preprocessing case we assume, in addition, that Keygen simply outputs its random input, and Process is deterministic. (Other variants are considered within.)

We remark that our definitional style is inspired by UC security. Indeed, our game-based definitions can be re-formulated as realizing the appropriate "ideal PIR functionalities".

Candidate constructions and analysis. For simplicity, we restrict attention to DEPIR schemes where the client's query consists of a list of addresses in the encoded database $\tilde{D}$, and the server answers with the contents of $\tilde{D}$ in these addresses. (Since we are shooting for polylogarithmic communication complexity, not much generality is lost by this simplification.)

When viewed this way, the encoding of a database bears resemblance to locally decodable codes: The ith symbol of D should be decodable by accessing only few locations of the encoded version $\tilde{D}$. Here however we have the added requirement that the locations queried should be simulatable without knowing the original addresses i. On the other hand, we do not have any error-correction requirements.

A natural approach, which we follow, is thus to start from an existing locally decodable code and try to modify it to obtain privacy. Specifically, we start from the following variant of Reed-Muller codes: In order to encode a database $D \in \{0,1\}^N$ choose a field $\mathbb{F}$ of size $\mathsf{polylog}(N)$ and a subset $H \subset \mathbb{F}$ of size $\log N$. The database is viewed as a function $D : H^m \to \{0,1\}$, where $m = \log N / \log \log N$ so that $|H^m| = N$. With this setup in place, $\tilde{D}$ is the truth table of the *low degree extension* of D. That is, $\tilde{D} = \{\hat{D}(x) : x \in \mathbb{F}^m\}$, where $\hat{D} : \mathbb{F}^m \to \mathbb{F}$ is the unique m-variate polynomial of degree at most $(|H| - 1)$ in each variable, such that $\hat{D}(i) = D(i)$ for all $i \in H^m$. The total degree of $\hat{D}$ is $d = O(\log^2 N)$. To query the database at $i \in H^m$ (*i.e.*, to decode $D(i)$ from $\tilde{D}$), the client chooses a line $\varphi : \mathbb{F} \to \mathbb{F}^m$ such that $\varphi(0) = i$, and sets $q = (\varphi(1), \ldots, \varphi(k))$ where $k = d + 1$. Upon receiving the server's response $(\mathbf{x}_1, \ldots, \mathbf{x}_k)$, client recovers $D(i) = \varphi(0)$ by interpolation (note that $(\mathbf{x}_1, \ldots, \mathbf{x}_k)$ all lie on a curve of degree at most d).

The above scheme is clearly insecure as the server can easily interpolate $i = \varphi(0)$ from the client's query $(\varphi(1), \ldots, \varphi(k))$. In this work we study three natural and orthogonal alterations to this basic scheme which attempt to prevent the server from interpolating, while still allowing the client to do so. As a preliminary step to all alterations, we let φ be a random degree-d' polynomial, where $d' = \mathsf{polylog}(N)$, rather than a random line. (Still, we let $D(i) = \varphi(0)$.) This means that, in order to allow the client to interpolate $\tilde{D}(\varphi(0))$, we should set $k \geq dd' + 1$. As we'll see, setting d' to be super-constant will be important for the security of our schemes in various ways. The three alterations are:

1. The client uses *secret* evaluation points $(\alpha_1, \ldots, \alpha_k)$ rather than $(1, \ldots, k)$. The evaluation points can be chosen randomly once and remain fixed throughout, or alternatively chosen anew for each query.
2. The client introduces noise by adding some random points in $\mathbb{F}^m$ to the query, at random locations. (There are a number of different variants here, depending on the noise structure.)
3. At preprocessing, the client first encrypts all elements of the database using symmetric encryption. Next it encodes the database to obtain $\tilde{D}$. Finally, it secretly and pseudorandomly permutes the elements of $\tilde{D}$ before handing it to the server. The client keeps the encryption key, as well as the key of the pseudorandom permutation.
   That is, let $\pi \in \mathsf{Perm}(\mathbb{F}^m)$ be a pseudorandom permutation. (Since the

domain is polynomial in size, use e.g. [MRS09].) The precomputed database $\tilde{D}$ is now the truth table of the function $\hat{D} \circ \pi^{-1} : \mathbb{F}^m \to \mathbb{F}$. To query address i, client draws φ and computes $(\mathbf{x}_1, \ldots, \mathbf{x}_k)$ as before, but sends the query $(\mathbf{x}'_1, \ldots, \mathbf{x}'_k)$ where $\mathbf{x}'_i = \pi(\mathbf{x}_i)$. The client uses the responses $(a_1, \ldots, a_k)$ to interpolate the encrypted $D(i)$, and then decrypts to obtain the actual value.

The various combinations of these three ideas suggest several possible DEPIR schemes. Note that a scheme based on either of the first two ideas (or both) but not the third would be public preprocessing. The third idea results in a designated client scheme. We briefly review how our main results are mapped to these three ideas.

No Public-Client DEPIR via Linear Codes: In Sect. 3, we prove that any combination of the first two ideas alone is insecure. More generally, we show that any scheme where the preprocessed database $\tilde{D}$ is obtained just by encoding D via some explicit linear code cannot be secure. This holds regardless of which query and response mechanism is used.

Bounded Security, Unbounded Insecurity via (3): In Sect. 4, we show that alteration (3) by itself suffices to obtain our bounded-query result stated above. In fact, we show that security holds even if, instead of starting from Reed-Muller codes, we start from any locally decodable code in a rather general class of codes.

On the other hand, we demonstrate an explicit attack on the scheme, for the case of Reed-Muller codes, if the client asks even slightly more queries than the bound allows.

Candidate Schemes via other combinations: We observe that the previous attack is thwarted by using either (1) and (3) together, or using (2) and (3) together. In fact, we were unable to break either one of these two candidates, with any non-trivial level of noise in (2). We thus suggest them as target for further cryptanalysis. In fact it is reasonable to also propose the scheme that combines all three ideas.

We note however that, while it is tempting to assume that adding alterations (e.g., adding noise or moving from fixed evaluation points to hidden or random evaluation points) increases security, or at least does not harm security, we cannot always back this intuition by actual reductions. For instance we do not currently see a way to argue that, a scheme that uses all three alterations is always no less secure than a scheme that uses only alterations (2) and (3).

Security reduction: We concentrate on the following "minimal" variant of a scheme that combines ideas (2) and (3): We choose a random set T of l indices in $[k + l]$. We then run alteration (3) with $k + l$ evaluation points, obtain a query $q_1, \ldots, q_{k+l}$, and then for each $j \in T$ we replace q_j with a random point in the domain. In Sect. 5, we reduce the security of this scheme to the computational hardness of a *search* problem that is roughly sketched as follows. As already mentioned, we call this the *hidden permutation with noise (HPN)* problem:

In the HPN problem, a random permutation $\pi \in \mathsf{Perm}(\mathbb{F}^m)$ is chosen, where

$|\mathbb{F}| = \text{polylog}(N)$ and $|\mathbb{F}^m| = \text{poly}(N)$. The problem is to compute π given samples chosen as follows: First a random set T of l indices out of $[k + l]$ is chosen. Next, draw $\text{poly}(N)$ samples from the following distribution $H_{\pi,T}$: Choose $z \leftarrow \mathbb{F}$, a degree-d polynomial $\varphi : \mathbb{F} \to \mathbb{F}^m$ with $\varphi(z) = 0$. Now, for $i \in T$ choose y_i randomly from $\mathbb{F}^m$. For $i \notin T$, let $y_i = \varphi(i)$. The sample is $(\pi(z), \pi(y_1), \ldots, \pi(y_{k+l}))$. The parameters are set so that $k \approx d^2$; however l can be significantly larger, so a sample may not uniquely determine φ even if π is known.

Note that a sample from $H_{\pi,T}$ directly corresponds to a query in the scheme. In other words, security of the scheme corresponds directly to a decisional variant of HPN with adaptively chosen free coefficients for φ. In contrast, the HPN problem as formulated above is a search problem with non-adaptive input.

One may of course consider also another variant of this scheme, where the client chooses a new set T for each query. While this variant indeed appears to be harder to cryptanalyze, we are not able to argue that it is no less secure than the above, fixed-T variant. Furthermore, we were unable to extend the decision-to-search reduction to this variant.

Finally, we note that only the first alteration above (namely, using random evaluation points) is specific to Reed-Muller codes. The other two are generic and apply to any locally decodable code, opening other potential routes to DEPIR schemes. In fact our bounded-query scheme in Sect. 4 is stated (and proved secure) generically in terms of *any* locally decodable code whose decoding queries are t-wise uniform for sufficiently large t.

Related Work. There are several existing hardness assumptions about polynomials in the literature, which do not appear to be related to ours. In particular, we point out the "noisy polynomial interpolation" problem, introduced by Naor and Pinkas [NP06] and (somewhat) cryptanalyzed by Bleichenbacher and Nguyen [BN00]. Two main differences between this assumption and our HPN assumption are that (i) we completely hide the algebraic structure of the underlying field by permuting the polynomial's domain, and (ii) we work with multivariate polynomials rather than univariate polynomials, which can sometimes make reconstruction problems much more difficult [GKS10].

Coppersmith and Sudan [CS03] show how to remove noise from codes based on multi-variate polynomials. However, their techniques do not appear to extend to our case of codes concatenated with a hidden permutation.

1.2   Independent Work

The problem we consider has been independently studied by Boyle et al. [BIPW17]. The two works consider the same problem of sublinear-time PIR with preprocessing and propose similar candidate solutions based on secretly permuted Reed-Muller codes.

The notions of designated-client (resp., public-client) doubly-efficient PIR from the present work correspond to the notions of OLDC (resp., pk-PIR) from [BIPW17] (with the exception that they make the additional restriction of non-adaptive queries). We provide an overview of the main differences between the two works below.

The main contributions of [BIPW17] beyond those of this work include:

1. A general transformation from (designated-client) OLDC to (public-client) pk-PIR by applying VBB obfuscation to the query generation algorithm and an authenticated version of the decoding algorithm. This yields an explicit candidate construction of pk-PIR.
2. Two types of barriers: A "data structures barrier," suggesting that even a very strong form of pk-PIR, with deterministic encoder and non-adaptive queries, would be difficult to unconditionally rule out; and an "LDC barrier," showing that OLDC implies traditional LDC, effectively imposing a limitation on the space of possible candidates.
3. Ruling out (under standard assumptions) a natural "learning" approach for generically breaking constructions based on secret linear codes, by using the power of span programs.
4. A proof that any OLDC (or, DEPIR scheme) implies a one-way function.

The main contributions of this work beyond those of [BIPW17] include:

1. A different variant of the designated-client (OLDC) candidate in which the curve evaluation points used by the decoder are fixed (or made public) but some of the points on the curve are replaced by random noise. A combination of random noise with secret evaluation points is also proposed as a potentially more conservative candidate.
2. A search-to-decision reduction for a restricted case of the above fixed-evaluation-point variant, where the location of the noise elements is the same for all queries.
3. An efficient variant of the designated client scheme, that is secure in the *bounded-query* case assuming one way functions.

2 Defining Doubly Efficient PIR

We define doubly-efficient PIR (DEPIR) schemes within a number of settings. While we only construct DEPIR schemes in few of these settings, we hope that the definitions will be useful as a basis for future work. In all settings, we consider information retrieval schemes with preprocessing that consist of the following five algorithms:

Keygen takes the security parameter 1^λ and samples a key k.
Process takes k and a database $DB \in \Sigma^N$ and outputs a preprocessed database $\widetilde{DB}$.
Query takes k and index $i \in \{1, \ldots, N\}$ and outputs a query q and local state st.

Resp takes q and $\widetilde{DB}$ and returns the server answer a.

Dec takes k, st, a and returns a data element in Σ.

The correctness and efficiency requirements are obvious:

Definition 1 (Correct and Doubly Efficient Information Retrieval).
An information retrieval scheme with preprocessing Π = (Keygen, Process, Query, Resp, Dec), *is correct if the correctness error of* Π *is negligible in* λ, *where* Π *has correctness error* ϵ *if for all* $DB \in \Sigma^N$ *and* $i \in [N]$ *we have:*

$$\Pr\left[\mathsf{Dec}(\mathsf{st}, a) \neq DB_i\right] \leq \epsilon$$

in the probability space defined by sampling

$$K \leftarrow \mathsf{Keygen}(1^\lambda), \widetilde{DB} \leftarrow \mathsf{Process}(K, DB), (q, \mathsf{st}) \leftarrow \mathsf{Query}(K, i), \ a \leftarrow \mathsf{Resp}^{\widetilde{DB}}(q)$$

If $\epsilon = 0$, *then* Π *is* perfectly correct.

Π *is* doubly efficient *if all algorithms are polynomial in* λ, $|\widetilde{DB}| = \mathrm{poly}(\lambda, N)$, *and* Query, Resp, Dec *are sublinear in* N, *where* Resp *is given RAM access to* $\widetilde{DB}$. *(Ideally, these algorithms are polylogarithmic in* N.*)*

We consider several levels of security. In all levels, the database and the indices to be read by the client are assumed to be chosen adversarially ("by the environment"). Also, in all levels we only consider honest-but-curious database servers, i.e. we trust the database server to run Resp (and sometimes also Process) as specified. We then consider three main levels with some variants:

Designated client: Here the key k is known only to the client. We consider two variants: One where the server does not even learn the database itself, and the other where the server may learn the database but does not learn the queried locations. We also consider the case of security for only a bounded number of queries.

Public client: Here k is assumed to be public (and honestly generated); however, the randomness used to generate k is assumed to remain hidden. Since Query is stateless, this means that many clients may query the database concurrently. The server learns the database but not the queried locations. Here (and in the next variant) we consider two cases, depending on whether the database is chosen before k is known, or adaptively, depending on k. We also consider the case where Keygen generates an additional secret key that is used only by Process.

Public preprocessing: This is the same as public client, except that the randomness used by Keygen is public (or, equivalently, Keygen simply outputs is random input.)

Our formal notions of security are inspired by UC security, and can be formulated via realizing appropriate variants of an "ideal PIR functionality". However, for self-containment we present them directly via the following games. (To simplify presentation the notation below considers adversaries and simulators that are stateful throughout the interaction.)

Definition 2 (Designated-Client and bounded-query DEPIR). *A DEPIR scheme* $\Pi = (\mathsf{Keygen}, \mathsf{Process}, \mathsf{Query}, \mathsf{Resp}, \mathsf{Dec})$ *is* Designated Client *if for any PPT* $\mathcal{A}$ *there exists a polytime simulator* $\mathcal{S}$ *such that* $\mathrm{REAL}_{\mathcal{A},\Pi} \approx \mathrm{IDEAL}_{\mathcal{A},\mathcal{S}}$, *where:*

$\mathrm{REAL}_{\mathcal{A},\Pi}$ *is the output of* $\mathcal{A}$ *in the following interaction:*

1. $\mathcal{A} \rightarrow \mathsf{DB} \in \Sigma^N$ *and obtains* $\widetilde{\mathsf{DB}} \leftarrow \mathsf{Process}(K, \mathsf{DB})$, *where* $K \leftarrow \mathsf{Keygen}(\lambda, N)$.
2. *Repeat until* $\mathcal{A}$ *generates final output:*
   (a) $\mathcal{A}$ *generates an index* $i \in [N]$ *and obtains* $q \leftarrow \mathsf{Query}(K, i)$.

$\mathrm{IDEAL}_{\mathcal{A},\mathcal{S}}$ *is defined as the output of* $\mathcal{A}$ *in the following interaction:*

1. $\mathcal{A}$ *outputs a database* $\mathsf{DB} \in \Sigma^N$ *and obtains* $\widetilde{\mathsf{DB}} \leftarrow \mathcal{S}(\lambda, \mathsf{DB})$;
2. *Repeat until* $\mathcal{A}$ *generates final output:*
   (a) $\mathcal{A}$ *generates an index* $i \in [N]$ *and obtains* $q \leftarrow \mathcal{S}()$.

If in the above interaction $\mathcal{S}$ *obtains only* N *rather than the entire* DB *then we say that the scheme has also* **database privacy**.

If Keygen *obtains an additional input* B, *and the privacy requirement is modified so that* $\mathcal{A}$ *can generate at most* B *queries, then we say that the scheme is* B-bounded DEPIR. *In this case we define the* **amortized storage overhead** *of the scheme to be* $|\widetilde{\mathsf{DB}}|/B$.

Definition 3 (Public-Client and Public-Preprocessing DEPIR). *A DEPIR scheme* $\Pi = (\mathsf{Keygen}, \mathsf{Process}, \mathsf{Query}, \mathsf{Resp}, \mathsf{Dec})$ *is* Public-Client *if for any polytime* $\mathcal{A}$ *there exists a polytime simulator* $\mathcal{S}$ *such that* $\mathrm{REAL}_{\mathcal{A},\Pi} \approx \mathrm{IDEAL}_{\mathcal{A},\mathcal{S}}$, *where:*

$\mathrm{REAL}_{\mathcal{A},\Pi}$ *is the output of* $\mathcal{A}$ *in the following interaction:*

1. $\mathcal{A}(K) \rightarrow \mathsf{DB} \in \Sigma^N$, *where* $K \leftarrow \mathsf{Keygen}(\lambda, N)$; $\mathcal{A}$ *obtains* $\widetilde{\mathsf{DB}} \leftarrow \mathsf{Process}(K, \mathsf{DB})$.
2. *Repeat until* $\mathcal{A}$ *generates final output:*
   (a) $\mathcal{A}$ *generates an index* $i \in [N]$ *and obtains* $q \leftarrow \mathsf{Query}(K, i)$.

$\mathrm{IDEAL}_{\mathcal{A},\mathcal{S}}$ *is defined as the output of* $\mathcal{A}$ *in the following interaction:*

1. $\mathcal{A}(K) \rightarrow \mathsf{DB} \in \Sigma^N$, *where* $K \leftarrow \mathcal{S}(\lambda, N)$; $\mathcal{A}$ *obtains* $\widetilde{\mathsf{DB}} \leftarrow \mathcal{S}(\mathsf{DB})$.
2. *Repeat until* $\mathcal{A}$ *generates final output:*
   (a) $\mathcal{A}$ *generates an index* $i \in [N]$ *and obtains* $q \leftarrow \mathcal{S}()$.

If in the above interaction Keygen *outputs its random input, and* $\mathsf{Process}$ *uses no additional randomness other than* K *then we say that the scheme is* **public preprocessing**.

If in the above interaction $\mathcal{A}$ *obtains* K *only after generating* DB *then we say that the scheme has* **non-adaptive database generation**.

If in the above interaction $\mathcal{S}$ *obtains* $K = \mathsf{Keygen}(\lambda, N)$ *rather than generating it, then we say that the scheme has* **global key generation**. *If in the above interaction* Keygen *generates an additional key that is used by* $\mathsf{Process}$ *and otherwise remains unknown, then we say that the scheme is* **public client with secret preprocessing key**.

3   Failure of a Natural Approach for Public-Preprocessing DEPIR

We present an approach for constructing public-preprocessing DEPIR, and demonstrate its failure. Whether public-preprocessing doubly efficient PIR schemes exist is left as a fascinating open question.

As sketched in the introduction, a natural approach to constructing public-preprocessing DEPIR is to view the database $\mathsf{DB} \in \{0,1\}^N$ as a function $\mathsf{DB} : H^m \to \{0,1\}$, where $H \subset \mathbb{F}$ with $|H| = \log N$, $\mathbb{F}$ is a finite field of order $\mathsf{polylog}(N)$, and $m = \frac{\log N}{\log \log N}$. The encoding of DB is done by extending it to an m-variate polynomial $\widehat{\mathsf{DB}} : \mathbb{F}^m \to \mathbb{F}$ of degree $|H| - 1$, where $\widehat{\mathsf{DB}}(x) = \mathsf{DB}(x)$ for all $x \in H^m$.

One may hope to construct query distributions $\{\mathcal{Q}_i\}_{i \in H^m}$ such that

1. (**Interpolability**) When sampling $Q \leftarrow \mathcal{Q}_i$, it holds that $\widehat{\mathsf{DB}}|_Q$ determines $\mathsf{DB}(i)$. That is, *any* m-variate polynomial g of degree $|H| - 1$ which agrees with $\widehat{\mathsf{DB}}$ on Q also agrees with $\widehat{\mathsf{DB}}$ (and therefore DB) on i.
2. (**Privacy**) $\mathcal{Q}_i$ computationally hides i. That is, for any $i \neq i'$, $\mathcal{Q}_i$ and $\mathcal{Q}_{i'}$ are computationally indistinguishable.

Such a construction would immediately give a (public-client) PIR scheme. The server just stores the truth table of $\widehat{\mathsf{DB}}$, and the client makes queries to i by sampling $Q \leftarrow \mathcal{Q}_i$, asking the server for $\widehat{\mathsf{DB}}_Q$, and interpolating the returned values to obtain $\mathsf{DB}(i)$.

For example, one may suggest to construct $\mathcal{Q}_i$ by sampling a uniformly random curve $\gamma : \mathbb{F} \to \mathbb{F}^m$ of degree $t = \log^2 k$ such that $\gamma(0) = i$. That is, $\mathcal{Q}_i$ is defined as $\{\gamma(x_i)\}_{i=0}^d$, where $\{x_i\}_{i=0}^d$ are uniformly random distinct points in $\mathbb{F} \setminus \{0\}$, and $d = t \cdot m \cdot (|H| - 1)$ is the degree of $\widehat{\mathsf{DB}} \circ \gamma$; A natural justification here is that interpolating $\{\gamma(x_i)\}$ to find $\gamma(0)$ seems to require knowledge of the evaluation points $\{x_i\}$. One can also include in the query some number of random points in $\mathbb{F}^m$ to make interpolation look even harder.

This template can be further generalized by replacing $\widehat{\mathsf{DB}}$ with any locally decodable code (LDC) encoding of DB, and appropriately adapting the notion of interpolability.

However, we show that even this general template fails, as long as the LDC in use is *linear*—which rules out the vast majority of the LDCs studied in the literature. We are inspired by a recent work of Kalai and Raz [KR17], which shows (among other things) the insecurity of the Reed-Muller instantiation of this template.

Definition 4. *Let* $\mathcal{C} : \Sigma^N \to \Sigma^M$ *be a code, and let* Q *be a subset of* $[M]$. *We say that* Q *determines* $i \in [N]$ *if for every* $m, m' \in \Sigma^N$ *for which* $\mathcal{C}(m)|_Q = \mathcal{C}(m)|_Q$, *it holds that* $m_i = m'_i$.

Proposition 1. *Let* $\mathcal{C} : \mathbb{F}^N \to \mathbb{F}^M$ *be a linear code. Then there is a* $\mathsf{poly}(M)$-*time algorithm which takes as input a set of queries* $Q \subseteq [M]$, *and outputs all* *indices* $i \in [N]$ *which are determined by* Q. *Furthermore, there are at most* $|Q|$ *such indices.*

Proof. Let $G \in \mathbb{F}^{M \times N}$ be the generator matrix for $\mathcal{C}$. Then Q determines i iff the ith standard basis vector $\mathbf{e}_i \in \mathbb{F}^N$ is spanned by the rows of G which are indexed by Q. This criterion is efficiently checkable by Gaussian elimination.

To see the "furthermore" part of the proposition, let A denote the set of $i \in [N]$ which are determined by Q. If $|A|$ were larger than $|Q|$, then $(Gm)_Q$ would be a compressed encoding of m_A, which is impossible since m_A was arbitrary. □

4   Bounded-Query Designated-Client DEPIR

We consider the case of bounded-query, designated-client DEPIR. We first present a trivial scheme with minimal online work but with large space overhead for the server which also requires a stateful client. Next we present our main bounded-query scheme, which is based on any family of locally decodable codes. When instantiated with the Reed-Muller family of codes (with a generalized decoding procedure), we obtain the following parameters, for a database of size N and query bound B:

- The prover and verifier both do $\mathsf{polylog}(N)$ online work
- The processed database size and secret key size are both $|\widetilde{\mathsf{DB}}| = \tilde{O}(B + \mathsf{poly}(N))$.

We emphasize this holds with a *stateless client*. Our construction improves significantly on the trivial scheme, which only supports a single query and cannot be simply scaled up by repetition without having the client maintain updatable long-term state.

Database Encryption. In both schemes the first step in the preprocessing of the database is to encrypt each entry, using some semantically secure symmetric encryption, with a key that's part of the clients secret key. Notice that this step makes the encrypted database computationally independent from the plaintext database. For simplicity of presentation, we omit the encryption step from the description of both schemes, and instead assume that the adversary does not see the plaintext database. Instead, it sees only the preprocessed database and the queries. (It is also possible to obtain statistical independence between the plaintext databases and the preprocessed one by using perfectly secure encryption such as one time pad, at the cost of a longer client secret key.)

Organization. The trivial, stateful scheme is presented in Sect. 4.1). The main scheme is presented and analyzed in Sect. 4.2. Optimality of the analysis is demonstrated in Sects. 4.3 and 4.4. Section 4.3 presents an efficient attack that kicks in as soon as the number of queries exceeds $|\mathbb{F}^m|$. The attack is specific for the Reed-Muller instantiation of the scheme. Section 4.4 provides a more general bound on the key size and communication complexity of any statistically-secure designated client DEPIR.

4.1   A Trivial Scheme

We note that it is trivial to construct a one-round designated-client PIR scheme with perfect correctness and perfect 1-query security, with server storage $\tilde{O}(N)$ and server work $O(1)$:

- Keygen$(1^\lambda, N)$ samples a uniformly random permutation $\pi : [N] \to [N]$, and outputs $K = \pi$.
- Process(K, DB) outputs $\widetilde{\mathsf{DB}}$, where

$$\widetilde{\mathsf{DB}} : [N] \to \{0, 1\}$$

$$\widetilde{\mathsf{DB}}(i) = \mathsf{DB}(\pi(i)).$$

- Query(K, i) outputs (q, st), where $q = \pi(i)$ and st is the empty string.
- Resp$(\widetilde{\mathsf{DB}}, q)$ outputs $\widetilde{\mathsf{DB}}(q)$.
- Dec(st, a) outputs a.

Extensions and Shortcomings. If the client is allowed to keep long-term state (i.e. remember how many queries it has made), then one can obtain a B-query scheme by concatenating B single-query schemes, resulting in server (and client) storage which is $\tilde{\Theta}(BN)$. With a *stateless* client however, it is not even clear how to support 2 queries. Furthermore, the storage cost of $\tilde{\Theta}(BN)$ leaves much to be desired.

4.2   A Scheme Based on LDCs and Random Permutations

We show a scheme with a stateless client, parameterized by a query bound B, which achieves B-bounded security and server storage of $B \cdot \mathsf{poly}(\lambda)$ (for sufficiently large B). By using pseudo-randomness, the *client* storage in our schemes can be reduced to $\mathsf{poly}(\lambda)$, where λ is a security parameter for computational hardness. We present our scheme generally based on a weak type of locally decodable code, which we now define.[2] However, we encourage readers to keep in mind the Reed-Muller based scheme mentioned in the intro. Several remarks throughout this section are designed to help in this endeavor.

Definition 5 (Locally Decodable Codes). *A locally decodable code is a tuple* (Enc, Query, Dec) *where:*

- Enc : $\Sigma^N \to \Sigma^M$ *is a deterministic "encoding" procedure which maps a message m to a codeword c. N is called the message length, and M is called the block length.*
- Query *is a p.p.t. algorithm which on input $i \in [N]$ outputs k indices $j_1, \ldots, j_k \in [M]$ along with some decoding state* st.

---

[2] Our definition differs from the standard definition of locally decodable codes in that it does not require any robustness against codeword errors, and we assume that the decoding queries are non-adaptive.

– Dec *is a p.p.t. algorithm which on input* st *and* $c_{j_1}, \ldots, c_{j_k}$ *outputs* m_i.

The locally decodable code is said to be t-smooth *if when sampling* $(\text{st}, (j_1, \ldots, j_k)) \leftarrow \text{Query}(i)$, $(j_{s_1}, \ldots, j_{s_t})$ *is uniformly distributed on* $[M]^t$ *for every distinct* $s_1, \ldots, s_t$.

The secret key is q i.i.d. uniform permutations $\pi_1, \ldots, \pi_q : [M] \to [M]$, so a lower key size can be achieved at the cost of computational security by using (small-domain) pseudo-random permutations [MRS09]. A processed database $\widetilde{\text{DB}}$ is the tuple $(\text{Enc}(\text{DB}) \circ \pi_1, \ldots, \text{Enc}(\text{DB}) \circ \pi_q)$, where composition of $\text{Enc}(\text{DB}) \in \Sigma^M$ with π_i denotes rearrangement of the elements of $\text{Enc}(\text{DB})$, as if $\text{Enc}(\text{DB})$ were a function mapping $[M]$ to Σ and $\circ$ denoted function composition.

More formally, we define a scheme template as follows.

Keygen$(1^\lambda, N, B)$: Pick a t-smooth locally decodable code $\mathcal{LDC}$ with message length N and a k-query decoding procedure, with parameters chosen so that $B k^{t-1} \left(\frac{B}{M}\right)^{\frac{t}{2}-1} \leq 2^{-\lambda-1}$. See further discussion below on the choice of parameters.

Sample i.i.d. uniform permutations $\pi_1, \ldots, \pi_k : [M] \to [M]$. Output $(\pi_1, \ldots, \pi_k)$ as the secret key. (If $\mathcal{LDC}$ has additional parameters then they should be output as well.)

Process(sk, DB): If necessary, encode each entry of DB as an element of Σ, so DB lies in Σ^N. Output $\widetilde{\text{DB}} = (\widetilde{\text{DB}}^{(1)}, \ldots, \widetilde{\text{DB}}^{(k)})$, where $\widetilde{\text{DB}}^{(i)}$ is defined by permuting the coordinates of $\mathcal{LDC}.\text{Enc}(\text{DB})$ by π_i. That is, $\widetilde{\text{DB}}^{(i)}_{\pi_i(j)} = \mathcal{LDC}.\text{Enc}(\text{DB})_j$.

Query(sk, i): Output $((\pi_1(j_1), \ldots, \pi_k(j_k)), \text{st})$, where $((j_1, \ldots, j_k), \text{st})$ is sampled according to $\mathcal{LDC}.\text{Query}(i)$.

Resp$^{\widetilde{\text{DB}}}((\tilde{j}_1, \ldots, \tilde{j}_k))$: Output $(\widetilde{\text{DB}}^{(1)}_{\tilde{j}_1}, \ldots, \widetilde{\text{DB}}^{(k)}_{\tilde{j}_k})$.

Dec$(\text{st}, (\mathbf{y}_1, \ldots, \mathbf{y}_k))$: Output $\mathcal{LDC}.\text{Dec}(\text{st}, (\mathbf{y}_1, \ldots, \mathbf{y}_k))$.

The perfect correctness of this scheme follows from the correctness of the underlying LDC.

The Reed-Muller Based Scheme. The following polynomial-based code is a natural choice for instantiating our scheme. It is t-smooth because of the t-wise independence of degree t polynomials. Choose a finite field $\mathbb{F}$, integer m and a subset $H \subset \mathbb{F}$ such that $|H|^m = N$ and $|\mathbb{F}|^m = M$. For correctness, we require that $|\mathbb{F}| \geq m \cdot t \cdot (|H| - 1) + 1$.

Enc: Identify $\text{DB} \in \{0,1\}^N$ with a map $H^m \to \{0,1\}$ and let $\widetilde{\text{DB}} : \mathbb{F}^m \to \mathbb{F}$ be the low degree extension. Output $\widetilde{\text{DB}} \in \mathbb{F}^{\mathbb{F}^m}$.

Query: Identify $i \in [N]$ with $\mathbf{z} \in H^m$ and choose a random degree-t curve $\varphi : \mathbb{F} \to \mathbb{F}^m$ such that $\varphi(0) = \mathbf{z}$. For k at least $m \cdot t \cdot (|H| - 1)$, output the query $(\mathbf{x}_1, \ldots, \mathbf{x}_k) \in \mathbb{F}^{mk}$ where $\mathbf{x}_i = \varphi(i)$.

Dec: Given responses $(a_1, \ldots, a_k) \in \mathbb{F}^k$, let $\widetilde{\varphi} : \mathbb{F} \to \mathbb{F}$ be the unique univariate polynomial of degree at most $k - 1$ such that $\widetilde{\varphi}(i) = a_i$. Output $\widetilde{\varphi}(0)$.

Let us see how the LDC constraints are satisfiable by a concrete code, and with what parameters.

Example Parameters: Low Work. For (relative) simplicity, assume that $N^4 \leq B \leq \frac{2^\lambda}{\lambda^3}$. Then one can set $|H| = \lambda$, $m = \frac{\log N}{\log \lambda}$ ($\leq \frac{\lambda}{4}$), and $|\mathbb{F}| = (2\lambda^6 B)^{1/m}$. With this choice of parameters $M = 2\lambda^6 B$, and there is a t-smooth, k-query decoding procedure (via curves) with $t = 2(\lambda + \log(2Bk) + 1)$ and $k = \lambda^3$ (as required for correctness of decoding, $|\mathbb{F}| \geq B^{1/m} \geq \lambda^4 \geq k$, and $k = \lambda^3 \geq (\lambda - 1)4(\lambda + 1)\frac{\lambda}{4} \geq (|H| - 1) \cdot m \cdot t$).

$$2Bk^{t-1} \left(\frac{B}{M} \right)^{t/2-1} = 2Bk \left(\frac{Bk^2}{M} \right)^{t/2-1} = 2Bk2^{-t/2+1} = 2^{-\lambda}$$

Thus we obtain an amortized storage overhead (defined in Sect. 2), server overhead, and client overheads which are all $\mathrm{poly}(\lambda)$ (respectively λ^6, λ^3, and λ^3).

Example Parameters: Low Server Storage. Let $\epsilon > 0$ be any constant. Let $|H| = \max(\lambda, N^\epsilon)$ and $m = \frac{\log N}{\log |H|}$ ($\leq \frac{1}{\epsilon}$). Suppose for simplicity that $\lambda \leq N^\epsilon \leq 2^\lambda$ and $B \leq 2^\lambda$. Let t and k be such that $t \geq 2(\lambda + \log(2Bk) + 1)$ and $k \geq m \cdot t \cdot (|H| - 1)$, which can be achieved by setting $k = O(\lambda \cdot N^\epsilon)$ and $t = O(\lambda)$. Let $|\mathbb{F}| = \max\left(k, (2k^2 B)^{1/m}\right)$. With this choice of parameters $M = \max(N \cdot \lambda^{1/\epsilon}, 2k^2 B)$, which in particular is $N \cdot \mathrm{poly}(\lambda)$ whenever $B = o\left(\frac{N^{1-2\epsilon}}{\lambda^2}\right)$. This yields

$$2Bk^{t-1} \left(\frac{B}{M} \right)^{t/2-1} = 2Bk \left(\frac{Bk^2}{M} \right)^{t/2-1} \leq 2^{-\lambda}$$

We leave further optimization of parameters (or instantiation with different locally decodable codes) to future work.

Proving Security

Theorem 1. *For any database size, any bound B on the number of queries, and any value λ for the security parameter, the above SSPIR scheme is a B-bounded designated client DEPIR scheme with statistical $2^{-\lambda}$-security. Furthermore, the scheme provides database privacy.*

Proof. We show that every query (for the first B queries) is statistically close to a distribution that is simulatable given the adversary's view thus far. First, by the principle of deferred decision, we can think of the random permutations $\pi_1, \ldots, \pi_k$ as being lazily defined, input-by-input as needed. Thus the adversary's view of the ℓth query $(\pi_1(j_1), \ldots, \pi_k(j_k))$ only reveals, for every $i \in [k]$, the subset of prior queries which also had $\pi_i(j_i)$ as their i^{th} coordinate. Let $S_1, \ldots, S_k \subseteq [\ell - 1]$ denote these subsets.

Next, we observe that $S_1, \ldots, S_k$ inherit t-wise independence from the underlying t-smooth LDC. Furthermore, we have for each i that $S_i = \emptyset$ with probability at least $1 - \frac{B}{M}$. Our main lemma, which at this point directly implies security of our scheme, says that all such distributions are within a total variational distance ball of diameter $\epsilon = 2k^{t-1} \left(\frac{B}{M}\right)^{t/2-1}$. The advantage of an unbounded adversary is then $B\epsilon$.

Lemma 1. Let $\bar{X} = (X_1, \ldots, X_k)$ and $\bar{Y} = (Y_1, \ldots, Y_k)$ be t-wise independent random variables with the same marginals (i.e. for each i, X_i and Y_i are identically distributed), such that for each $i \in [k]$, there is a value $\star$ such that $\Pr[X_i = \star] \geq 1 - \epsilon$. Then $d_{\mathrm{TV}}(\bar{X}, \bar{Y}) \leq (k\epsilon)^{t/2} + k^{t-1}\epsilon^{t/2-1} \leq 2k^{t-1}\epsilon^{t/2-1}$.

Proof. We first show that $\bar{X}$ and $\bar{Y}$ each have only $t/2$ non-$\star$ values, except with probability at most $(k\epsilon)^{t/2}$.

Claim 1. $\Pr\left[|\{i : X_i \neq \star\}| \geq t/2\right] \leq (k\epsilon)^{t/2}$, and the same holds with Y_i in place of X_i.

Proof. For any $I \subset [k]$ with $|I| < t$, the probability that $X_i \neq \star$ for all $i \in I$ is at most $\epsilon^{|I|}$ by t-wise independence. The number of i for which $X_i \neq \star$ is at least $t/2$ iff for some $I \subset [k]$ with $|I| \geq t/2$, it holds that for every $i \in I$, $X_i \neq \star$. So by a union bound,

$$\Pr\left[|\{i : X_i \neq \star\}| \geq t/2\right] \leq \binom{k}{t/2} \cdot \epsilon^{t/2} \leq (k\epsilon)^{t/2}.$$

$\square$

With this claim in hand, define G as the set of $z_1, \ldots, z_k$ for which $|\{i : z_i \neq \star\}| < t/2$. The above claim then says that $\Pr[\bar{X} \notin G]$ and $\Pr[\bar{Y} \notin G]$ are each at most $(k\epsilon)^{t/2}$. We then have

$$d_{\mathrm{TV}}(\bar{X}, \bar{Y}) = \frac{1}{2} \sum_{\bar{z} = z_1, \ldots, z_k} \left| \Pr[\bar{X} = \bar{z}] - \Pr[\bar{Y} = \bar{z}] \right|$$

$$\leq \frac{1}{2} \left(\Pr[\bar{X} \notin G] + \Pr[\bar{Y} \notin G] + \sum_{\bar{z} \in G} \left| \Pr[\bar{X} = \bar{z}] - \Pr[\bar{Y} = \bar{z}] \right| \right)$$

$$\leq (k\epsilon)^{t/2} + \frac{1}{2} \sum_{\bar{z} \in G} \left| \Pr[\bar{X} = \bar{z}] - \Pr[\bar{Y} = \bar{z}] \right|. \tag{1}$$

We now bound the second term of Eq. (1). We begin by rewriting, for any $\bar{z} \in G$, the event $\bar{X} = \bar{z}$ as the conjunction of two not necessarily independent events. Let I denote the set of coordinates where $\bar{z}$ is not $\star$, i.e. $I \overset{\text{def}}{=} \{i : z_i \neq \star\}$. Then $\bar{X} = \bar{z}$ iff both

1. $\bar{X}$ and $\bar{z}$ agree on their restrictions to I, i.e. $\bar{X}_I = \bar{z}_I$.
2. $X_i = \star$ for every $i \notin I$. As short-hand, we write this event as $\bar{X}_{\sim I} = \star$.

We can therefore profitably rewrite $\Pr[\bar{X} = \bar{z}] = \Pr[\bar{X}_I = \bar{z}_I] \cdot \Pr[\bar{X}_{\sim I} = \star | \bar{X}_I = \bar{z}_I]$ and similarly $\Pr[\bar{Y} = \bar{z}] = \Pr[\bar{Y}_I = \bar{z}_I] \cdot \Pr[\bar{Y}_{\sim I} = \star | \bar{Y}_I = \bar{z}_I]$. By t-wise independence, the probability that $\bar{X}_I = \bar{z}_I$ is exactly the same as the probability that $\bar{Y}_i = \bar{z}_I$ (since $|I| < t/2$). Hence the difference of these probabilities has a common factor $\bar{X}_I = \bar{z}_I = \bar{Y}_I = \bar{z}_I$, which can be factored out to yield

$$\Pr[\bar{X}_I = \bar{z}_I] \cdot \left| \Pr[\bar{X}_{\sim I} = \star | \bar{X}_I = \bar{z}_I] - \Pr[\bar{Y}_{\sim I} = \star | \bar{Y}_I = \bar{z}_I] \right| \qquad (2)$$

Claim 2. For all $I \subset [k]$ such that $|I| < t/2$, and all $\bar{z}_I$, it holds that

$$\left| \Pr[X_{\sim I} = \star | X_I = \bar{z}_I] - \Pr[Y_{\sim I} = \star | Y_I = \bar{z}_I] \right| \leq 2(k - |I|)^{t-1} \epsilon^{t/2-1}$$
$$\leq 2k^{t-1} \epsilon^{t/2-1}.$$

Proof. All we really need about the conditional distributions $X_{\sim I} | X_I = \bar{z}_I$ and $Y_{\sim I} | Y_I = \bar{z}_I$ are that they are $t/2$-wise independent. This $t/2$-wise independence follows from the fact that $\bar{X}$ and $\bar{Y}$ are t-wise independent, and the events $X_I = \bar{z}_I$ and $Y_I = \bar{z}_I$ depend on fewer than $t/2$ coordinates of $\bar{X}$ and $\bar{Y}$, respectively. We also only need, for each $i \notin I$, the single bit of whether or not $X_i = \star$.

So it suffices for us to prove the following slightly more abstract lemma. This lemma can be viewed as a special case of a natural generalization of Braverman's celebrated result that poly-logarithmic independence fools AC^0 [Bra09]. Instead of AC^0 our predicate is a single conjunction (with fan-in $n = k - |I|$), but the lemma does not follow directly from [Bra09] because any individual X_i' might not be uniformly distributed on $\{0,1\}$.

Lemma 2. *If* $(X_1', \ldots, X_n')$ *are* t'-*wise independent* $\{0,1\}$-*valued random variables such that* $\mathbb{E}[X_i'] = \Pr[X_i' = 1] \geq 1 - \epsilon$ *for all* i, *then*

$$\left| \mathbb{E}\left[\prod_{i=1}^{n} X_i' \right] - \prod_{i=1}^{n} \mathbb{E}[X_i'] \right| \leq 2n(n^2 \epsilon)^{t'-1}$$

Proof. For any subset $S \subseteq [n]$, write X_S' to denote the product $\prod_{i \in S} X_i'$. Let ϵ_i denote $1 - \mathbb{E}[X_i']$ With this notation, we want to bound $\left| \mathbb{E}[X_{[n]}'] - \prod_{i=1}^{n}(1 - \epsilon_i) \right|$. By the principle of inclusion-exclusion, we have

$$\mathbb{E}[X_{[n]}'] = 1 + \sum_{\emptyset \neq S \subseteq [n]} (-1)^{|S|} \mathbb{E}[1 - X_S']$$

$$= 1 + \sum_{0 < |S| \leq t'} (-1)^{|S|} \mathbb{E}[1 - X_S'] + \sum_{t' < |S| \leq n} (-1)^{|S|} \mathbb{E}[1 - X_S']$$

$$= 1 + \sum_{0 < |S| \leq t'} \prod_{i \in S} (-\epsilon_i) + \sum_{t' < |S| \leq n} (-1)^{|S|} \mathbb{E}[1 - X_S'], \qquad (3)$$

where the last equality is by t'-wise independence. Comparing Eq. (3) to the binomial expansion

$$\prod_{i=1}^{n}(1-\epsilon_i) = 1 + \sum_{0<|S|\leq n}\prod_{i\in S}(-\epsilon_i), \tag{4}$$

we just need to bound the last term of Eq. (3) (If C denotes a bound which holds for any $X_1', \ldots, X_n'$, then it must also apply to $\sum_{0<|S|\leq n}\prod_{i\in S}(-\epsilon_i)$. As a result we have $|\mathbb{E}[X_{[n]}'] - \prod_{i=1}^{n}(1-\epsilon_i)| \leq 2C$). We bound

$$\left|\sum_{t'<|S|\leq n}(-1)^{|S|}\mathbb{E}[1-X_S']\right| = \left|\mathbb{E}\left[\sum_{t'<|S|\leq n}(-1)^{|S|}(1-X_S')\right]\right|$$

$$\leq \mathbb{E}\left[\left|\sum_{t'<|S|\leq n}(-1)^{|S|}(1-X_S')\right|\right]$$

$$= \mathbb{E}\left[\left|\sum_{\substack{S\subseteq\{i:X_i'=0\}\\|S|>t}}(-1)^{|S|}\right|\right] \tag{5}$$

We bound Eq. (5) via the basic fact that for any B-bounded random variable Z, we have $\mathbb{E}[Z] \leq B \cdot \Pr[Z > 0]$. We apply this fact with

$$Z = \left|\sum_{\substack{S\subseteq\{i:X_i'=0\}\\|S|>t}}(-1)^{|S|}\right|.$$

Z is 0 if $\left|\{i : X_i' = 0\}\right| \leq t'$, which happens with probability at least $1 - (n\epsilon)^{t'-1}$ by Claim 1, so $\Pr[Z > 0] \leq (n\epsilon)^{t'-1}$. When this is not the case, we bound Z via the elementary combinatorial identity $\sum_{S\subseteq[n]}(-1)^{|S|} = \sum_{i=0}^{n}(-1)^i\binom{n}{i} = 0$ (this follows from the binomial expansion of $(1-1)^n$), obtaining

$$Z = \left|\sum_{\substack{S\subseteq\{i:X_i'=0\}\\|S|\leq t'}}(-1)^{|S|}\right| \leq \binom{n}{t'} \leq n^{t'}.$$

This implies $\mathbb{E}[Z] \leq (n\epsilon)^{t'-1}n^{t'} \leq n(n^2\epsilon)^{t'-1}$. Substituting into Eq. (5) concludes the proof of Lemma 2. $\qquad\square$

Claim 2 follows by applying Lemma 2 with $n = k - |I|$ and $t' = t/2$. $\qquad\square$

Substituting Eq. (2) into Eq. (1) and applying the following claim concludes the proof of Lemma 1. $\qquad\square$

Theorem 1 follows from the discussion preceding the statement of Lemma 1, and from the fact that we chose an LDC for which $2Bk^{t-1}\left(\frac{B}{M}\right)^{t/2-1} = 2^{-\lambda}$ $\qquad\square$

4.3   A Linear Attack if Too Many Queries Are Asked

In this section we describe a technique for analyzing the query data which arises when the number of queries exceeds B. Our technique gives an attack which, in some situations, breaks the (unbounded-query) security of the (bounded-query secure) scheme from Sect. 4.2. Our attack utilizes extra properties of the underlying LDC which are not without loss of generality, but are nevertheless natural and satisfied by the Reed-Muller based LDC, as well as other choices based on polynomials. Roughly speaking, our attack exploits extra linear structure in the $\mathcal{LDC}$.Query and $\mathcal{LDC}$.Dec procedures. Readers familiar with polynomial-based codes will recognize the properties we use as abstractions of properties commonly used in those settings.

Intuition and Overview

Extra Properties of $\mathcal{LDC}$. Recall $\mathcal{LDC} = (\mathcal{LDC}.\mathsf{Enc}, \mathcal{LDC}.\mathsf{Query}, \mathcal{LDC}.\mathsf{Dec})$. The encode and query procedures are randomized maps

$$\mathcal{LDC}.\mathsf{Enc} : \{0,1\}^N \to \Sigma^{[M]}; \text{ and } \mathcal{LDC}.\mathsf{Query} : [N] \to [M]^k;$$

we assume $\mathcal{LDC}$.Dec is a public operation and so $\mathcal{LDC}$.Query outputs no decoding state st. We assume that $[M]$ is a vector space over some finite field $\mathbb{F}$, and that $[N] \subset [M]$ (not necessarily a subspace). Note in our Reed-Muller example, we had $[N] = H^m \subset \mathbb{F}^m = [M]$. Moreover, we assume there exists some subspace $\mathsf{V} \subset [M]^k$ such that for each $i \in [N]$, $\mathcal{LDC}$.Query(i) outputs a random element from an affine coset of V, denoted $\mathsf{V}_i \subset [M]^k$. In the Reed-Muller case, V is the set of $(\mathbf{x}_1, \ldots, \mathbf{x}_k)$ for which there exists a curve $\varphi : \mathbb{F} \to \mathbb{F}^m$ of degree at most t satisfying $\varphi(0) = 0$ and such that $\mathbf{x}_s = \varphi(s)$ for $s = 1, \ldots, k$. The affine shift V_i for $i \in H^m$ is the set of $\mathbf{x}$ which lie on a low degree curve satisfying $\varphi(0) = i$ instead of $\varphi(0) = 0$. We furthermore assume that for any distinct $s_1, \ldots, s_{t+1} \in [k] \cup \{\mathsf{index}\}$, there exists a linear map $\psi_s : [M]^{t+1} \to [M]$ such that $\psi_s(\mathsf{V}_i|_s) = i$ for all $i \in [N]$, where $\mathsf{V}_i|_s$ denotes the projection of V_i onto the coordinates s (if $s = \mathsf{index}$ then $\mathsf{V}_i|_s = i$). For Reed-Muller, these linear maps are interpolation. Note this last property implies that $\mathcal{LDC}$.Query $: [N] \to [M]^k$ is an error-correcting code with good distance since queries to distinct $i, i' \in [N]$ can agree in at most t places. This last property also means that $\dim(\mathsf{V}) \le t \cdot \dim([M])$. Our scheme requires $\mathcal{LDC}$ to be $t-$smooth so $\dim(\mathsf{V}) \ge t \cdot \dim([M])$, thus $\dim(\mathsf{V}) = t \cdot \dim([M])$. Finally, we require that $\mathcal{LDC}$ is locally *correctable* rather than just decodeable. This means that $\mathcal{LDC}$.Query supports queries to any codeword symbol, rather than only message symbols *i.e.*, $\mathcal{LDC}$.Query supports any $i \in [M]$ rather than just $i \in [N]$. This means that the $|M|$ different affine planes $\{\mathsf{V}_i\}_{i \in [M]}$, together form a subspace $\hat{\mathsf{V}} \subset [M]^k$ of dimension $(t+1) \cdot \dim([M])$. Note that the following distributions are identical:

1. draw $i \leftarrow [M]$, $(j_1, \ldots, j_k) \leftarrow \mathsf{V}_i$, output $(i, j_1, \ldots, j_k)$;
2. draw $(j_1, \ldots, j_k) \leftarrow \hat{\mathsf{V}}$ and output $(i, j_1, \ldots, j_k)$ where $(j_1, \ldots, j_k) \in \mathsf{V}_i$.

This will be useful moving forward.

Our Attack. Concretely, we describe an attack which, given $B = M^{1+o(1)}$ queries $\{(j_{\alpha,1}, \ldots, j_{\alpha,k})\}_{\alpha=1}^{B}$ from either: (1) all from V_i for a fixed $i \in [M]$; or (2) from V_{i_α} for random $i_\alpha \leftarrow [M]$, distinguishes between (1) and (2). We emphasize that this is an attack on the $\mathcal{LDC}$ but not exactly an attack on the DEPIR scheme, because the distinguisher in the DEPIR security game only gets to see queries from V_i for $i \in [N]$ and not $i \in [M] - [N]$. This assumption is mainly to simplify the analysis; we show in Sect. 5.4 how to analyze the attack (in a different context) without making this assumption (but using more queries).

Notation. Since we are assuming that the query spaces, V_i, are affine planes, membership in the V_i is decided by the linear equation: $\mathbf{v} \in V_i$ iff $\psi_s(\mathbf{v}) = i$ for any $s \subset [k]$. From now on, however, we will not be explicit about the s or the linear maps ψ_s, we will just talk about the linear equation "$\mathbf{v} \in V_i$". (For the specific case of Reed-Muller codes, the coefficients of the linear equation are the Lagrange coefficients that correspond to the points where φ is evaluated.)

Intuition. The high-level idea of the attack is the following. First, initialize variables $\{\mathbf{v}_{s,j_s'}\}_{(s,j_s)\in[k]\times[M]}$ which take values in $[M]$. The intention is that $\mathbf{v}_{s,j_s'} = j_s$ if $\pi_s(j_s) = j_s'$. For each query $(j_{\alpha,1}', \ldots, j_{\alpha,k}')$, add the constraint $\mathbf{v}_{j_\alpha'} \in V_i$ to a list L of linear constraints on the $\{\mathbf{v}_{s,j_s}\}$ where $\mathbf{v}_{j_\alpha'}$ is shorthand for $(\mathbf{v}_{1,j_{\alpha,1}'}, \ldots \mathbf{v}_{k,j_{\alpha,k}'})$. After enough constraints have been added to L, we will be in one of two cases depending on whether the queries $(j_{\alpha,1}', \ldots, j_{\alpha,k}')$ are all to the same index or are to random indices. In the first case, there will exist non-constant assignments to the $\mathbf{v}_{s,j_s'}$ which satisfy all constraints in L; in the second case all satisfying assignments are constant. This distinction allows the two cases to be efficiently distinguished.

The QueryDist *Algorithm.* Set $B = k\lambda M^{1+o(1)}$.
Input: $\{(j_{\alpha,1}', \ldots, j_{\alpha,k}')\}_\alpha$

1. Initialize variables $\{\mathbf{v}_{s,j_s'}\}_{(s,j_s')\in[k]\times[M]}$ taking values in $[M]$, and a list L of linear constraints on the $\mathbf{v}_{s,j_s'}$ to $\emptyset$. Also fix $i \in [N]$ arbitrarily.
2. For $\alpha \in \{1, \ldots, B\}$, add $\mathbf{v}_{j_\alpha'} \in V_i$ to L, where $\mathbf{v}_{j_\alpha'}$ is short for $(\mathbf{v}_{1,j_{\alpha,1}'}, \ldots, \mathbf{v}_{k,j_{\alpha,k}'})$.
3. Checks whether there is a non-constant assignment to the $\{\mathbf{v}_{s,j_s'}\}$ which satisfies the constraints in L. If so, output <u>fixed</u>, if not output <u>random</u>. An assignment is constant if for all (s, j_s', j_s''), $\mathbf{v}_{s,j_s'} = \mathbf{v}_{s,j_s''}$.

Note that QueryDist runs in time poly(λ, B, M). Step 3 involves checking whether the space of satisfying assignments is contained in the space of constant assignments; this is possible to do efficiently using Gaussian elimination. All other steps are clearly polytime.

Lemma 3. *Assume $k > 2t$, $|\mathbb{F}|^{-t} = 2^{-\Omega(\lambda)}$, and all of the assumptions mentioned in the previous paragraph. If* QueryDist *is given inputs $\{(j_{\alpha,1}, \ldots, j_{\alpha,k})\}$ which are all queries for the same index, it outputs* <u>fixed</u> *with probability 1. If given $\{(j_{\alpha,1}, \ldots, j_{\alpha,k})\}$ which are queries to random indices, it outputs* <u>random</u> *with probability $1 - 2^{-\Omega(\lambda)}$ over the queries.*

Proof. If the $\{(j_{\alpha,1}, \ldots, j_{\alpha,k})\}$ are all queries to i, then the assignment $\mathbf{v}_{s,j'_s} = \pi_s^{-1}(j'_s)$ is non-constant and satisfies every constraint in L since $(\pi_1^{-1}(j'_{\alpha,1}), \ldots, \pi_k^{-1}(j'_{\alpha,k})) \in \mathsf{V}_i$ for all α. If they are all queries to some other $i' \neq i$, then L can be satisfied by setting $\mathbf{v}_{s,j'_s} = (\pi'_s)^{-1}(j'_s)$ where $\pi'_s = \pi_s \circ \tau_s$ and the τ_s are any permutations such that $(\tau_1, \ldots, \tau_k)(\mathsf{V}_i) = \mathsf{V}_{i'}$. Therefore, QueryDist outputs <u>fixed</u> with probability 1. We complete the proof by showing that if the $\{(j'_{\alpha,1}, \ldots, j'_{\alpha,k})\}$ are queries for random indices then with overwhelming probability, any assignment to the $\mathbf{v}_{s,j'_s}$ which satisfies all constraints in L must be constant.

Fix any assignment to the $\mathbf{v}_{s,j'_s}$ satisfying L and for $s = 1, \ldots, k$ let $\sigma_s : [M] \to [M]$ be the map which sends j'_s to the vector assigned to $\mathbf{v}_{s,j'_s}$. We will show that each σ_s is constant. Since the assignment satisfies L, for every $(j'_{\alpha,1}, \ldots, j'_{\alpha,k})$, for all α, $(\sigma_1(j'_{\alpha,1}), \ldots, \sigma_k(j'_{\alpha,k})) \in \mathsf{V}_i$. Recall that drawing $(j'_{\alpha,1}, \ldots, j'_{\alpha,k})$ consists of drawing $i_\alpha \leftarrow [N] = [M]$ and $(j_{\alpha,1}, \ldots, j_{\alpha,k}) \leftarrow \mathsf{V}_{i_\alpha}$. Therefore, every $(j_{\alpha,1}, \ldots, j_{\alpha,k}) \leftarrow \mathsf{V}_{i_\alpha}$ drawn to produce the input to QueryDist satisfies $\boldsymbol{\sigma} \circ \boldsymbol{\pi}(\boldsymbol{j}_\alpha) \in \mathsf{V}_i$, where $\boldsymbol{\sigma} \circ \boldsymbol{\pi}(\boldsymbol{j})$ is shorthand for $(\sigma_1 \circ \pi_1(j_{\alpha,1}), \ldots, \sigma_k \circ \pi_k(j_{\alpha,k}))$.

Say an assignment to $\{\mathbf{v}_{s,j'_s}\}$ is BAD if $\Pr_{(j_1,\ldots,j_k) \leftarrow \hat{\mathsf{v}}}[\boldsymbol{\sigma} \circ \boldsymbol{\pi}(\boldsymbol{j}) \in \mathsf{V}_i] < (1 - 1/|\mathbb{F}|)$. Note,

$$\Pr_{\{j_\alpha\}}[\exists \text{ BAD satisfying assignment}] < M^{kM} \cdot \left(1 - \frac{1}{|\mathbb{F}|}\right)^B = 2^{-\Omega(\lambda)},$$

when $B = k\lambda M^{1+o(1)}$, so we can assume that the assignment underlying σ is not BAD.

Now, fix $(j_1, \ldots, j_t) \in [M]^t$ such that $\Pr_{\boldsymbol{j} \leftarrow \hat{\mathsf{V}}}[\boldsymbol{\sigma}(\boldsymbol{j}) \in \mathsf{V}_i | (j_1, \ldots, j_t)] \geq (1 - 1/|\mathbb{F}|)$. Note drawing $\boldsymbol{j} \leftarrow \hat{V}$ conditioned on fixed $(j_1, \ldots, j_t)$ requires drawing just one more coordinate, say j_{t+1}, randomly from $[M]$ (using the extra property as well as interpolation). Now, having fixed $(j_1, \ldots, j_t)$, for $s \in [k]$, let $\bar{j}_s = \sigma_s \circ \pi_s(j_s)$. Let $j_{t+1}^* \in [M]$ be the unique value such that $(\bar{j}_1, \ldots, \bar{j}_t, j_{t+1}^*)$ is consistent with V_i. It follows that

$$\Pr_{j_{t+1} \leftarrow [M]}[\bar{j}_{t+1} = j_{t+1}^*] \geq 1 - \frac{1}{|\mathbb{F}|}$$

and so $\sigma_{t+1} \circ \pi_{t+1}$ (hence σ_{t+1}) takes a constant value on a $(1 - 1/|\mathbb{F}|)$−fraction of its inputs. The same is true for all of the σ_s. For each s, let $j'_s \in [M]$ be the most likely value of σ_s. We show that either $\sigma_s(j_s) = j'_s$ with probability 1 for all s, in which case the assignment is constant; or else with high probability, $\boldsymbol{\sigma} \circ \boldsymbol{\pi}(\boldsymbol{j}_\alpha) \notin \mathsf{V}_i$ for some α, so the assignment does not satisfy L.

By the t−smoothness of $\mathcal{LDC}$, Claim 1 implies

$$\Pr_{\boldsymbol{j} \leftarrow \hat{\mathsf{v}}}[^\#\{s \in [k] : \bar{j}_s \neq j'_s\} > t] \leq (k/|\mathbb{F}|)^t = 2^{-\Omega(\lambda)}.$$

It follows that with high probability, for any α, α',

$$\Delta(\boldsymbol{\sigma} \circ \boldsymbol{\pi}(\boldsymbol{j}_\alpha), \boldsymbol{\sigma} \circ \boldsymbol{\pi}(\boldsymbol{j}_{\alpha'})) \leq \Delta(\boldsymbol{\sigma} \circ \boldsymbol{\pi}(\boldsymbol{j}_\alpha), \bar{\boldsymbol{j}})) + \Delta(\bar{\boldsymbol{j}}, \boldsymbol{\sigma} \circ \boldsymbol{\pi}(\boldsymbol{j}_{\alpha'})) \leq 2t,$$

where Δ is Hamming distance. Therefore, $\sigma \circ \pi(j_\alpha)$ and $\sigma \circ \pi(j_{\alpha'})$ share at least $k - 2t > t$ of their coordinates. The interpolation assumption implies $\sigma \circ \pi(j_\alpha) = \sigma \circ \pi(j_{\alpha'})$ for all α, α'. Therefore, σ is constant and the result follows. $\square$

4.4 Limits on Statistical DEPIR

We show that in any B-bounded information-theoretically secure (designated client) PIR, either:

– The server's responses are almost as long as the database, or
– The length of the secret key is almost B.

The bound holds even for schemes with only imperfect correctness and security. This in particular implies that the bound holds even for schemes, like the one above, which provides information-theoretic security except for the use of pseudorandom permutations for permuting the database.

Answer Size in Public Client PIR. First, we show that a *public-client* PIR cannot achieve both information theoretic security and non-trivial succinctness. The intuition is that (by statistical security) a single query is indistinguishable from a query to any other index, so the server's answer contains almost all the information about the database. Let $|a|$ denote the size of a server's response – i.e. the length of an output of Resp.

Theorem 2. *In any statistically δ-secure public-client DEPIR with correctness error ϵ:*

$$|a| \geq (1 - H(\epsilon + \delta))N - O(\log N).$$

In fact, this lower bound holds even if the PIR is only non-adaptively δ-secure.

Proof. Suppose the PIR is non-adaptively δ-secure. Then

Claim. There is an algorithm Reconstruct such that for any database DB,

$$\mathbb{E}\left[\Delta(\mathsf{DB}', \mathsf{DB})\right] \geq (1 - \epsilon - \delta)N$$

in the probability space defined by sampling

$$\begin{aligned}
(\mathsf{pk}, \mathsf{sk}) &\leftarrow \mathsf{Keygen}(1^\lambda, N) \\
\widetilde{\mathsf{DB}} &\leftarrow \mathsf{Process}(\mathsf{sk}, \mathsf{DB}) \\
(q, \mathsf{st}) &\leftarrow \mathsf{Query}(\mathsf{pk}, 0) \\
a &\leftarrow \mathsf{Resp}(q, \widetilde{\mathsf{DB}}) \\
\mathsf{DB}' &\leftarrow \mathsf{Reconstruct}(\mathsf{pk}, q, a).
\end{aligned}$$

Proof. Reconstruct is an algorithm which does the following: Given (pk, q, a), it samples $\mathsf{st}_1, \ldots, \mathsf{st}_N$, where each st_i is independently sampled from the distribution of the state st obtained by sampling $(q', \mathsf{st}) \leftarrow \mathsf{Query}(\mathsf{pk}, i)$ conditioned on $q' = q$. Finally Reconstruct outputs DB' such that for each i, $\mathsf{DB}'_i = \mathsf{Dec}(\mathsf{st}_i, a)$.

By linearity of expectation, it suffices to show that for a uniformly random i, $\Pr\left[\mathsf{DB}_i = \mathsf{Dec}(\mathsf{st}_i, a)\right] \geq 1 - \epsilon - \delta$.

By the non-adaptive δ-security, if we instead sample $(q, \mathsf{st}) \leftarrow \mathsf{Query}(\mathsf{pk}, i)$, this change modifies the distribution of $(\widetilde{\mathsf{DB}}, \mathsf{pk}, q)$ by statistical distance at most δ. Since a is a function of (pk, q), and st_i is a function of (pk, q, a), the distribution of $(\widetilde{\mathsf{DB}}, a, \mathsf{st}_i)$ and therefore the probability that $\mathsf{DB}_i = \mathsf{Dec}(\mathsf{st}_i, a)$ also changes by at most δ. However, the modified experiment induces a distribution of $(\widetilde{\mathsf{DB}}, \mathsf{pk}, q, \mathsf{st}_i)$ which is exactly as if one had sampled $(q, \mathsf{st}_i) \leftarrow \mathsf{Query}(\mathsf{pk}, i)$. Thus in the modified experiment, $\Pr\left[\mathsf{DB}_i = \mathsf{Dec}(\mathsf{st}_i, a)\right] \geq 1 - \epsilon$, which means that in the original experiment $\Pr\left[\mathsf{DB}_i = \mathsf{Dec}(\mathsf{st}_i, a)\right] \geq 1 - \epsilon - \delta$. □

Claim. A random variable $X \in \{0,1\}^N$ with expected Hamming weight is at most ϵN (with $\epsilon \leq \frac{1}{2}$) has entropy at most $H(\epsilon)N + O(\log N)$.

Proof. We can partition the set of N-bit strings based on their Hamming weight. It is clear that the maximal entropy of X is achieved only when the distribution of X is uniform within each class. In other words, an entropy-maximizing distribution takes the form $\sum_{i=0}^N w_i U_i$, where U_i is the uniform distribution on strings with Hamming weight i and $\{w_i\}$ are non-negative weights summing to 1. The entropy of this distribution is $-\sum_i w_i \log w_i + \sum_i w_i H(U_i)$, which is at most $\sum_i w_i H(U_i) + \log(N+1)$. So we want to maximize $\sum_i w_i H(U_i) = \sum_i w_i \log \binom{N}{i}$ subject to the constraint that $\sum_i w_i \cdot i \leq \epsilon N$.

We have the bound

$$\sum_i w_i \log \binom{N}{i} = O(\log N) + \sum_i w_i H\left(\frac{i}{N}\right) N \quad \text{by Stirling's formula}$$

$$\leq O(\log N) + H\left(\sum_i \frac{w_i \cdot i}{N}\right) N \quad \text{by Jensen's inequality}$$

$$\leq O(\log N) + H(\epsilon) N \quad \text{because } \sum_i \frac{w_i \cdot i}{N} \leq \epsilon \leq \frac{1}{2}$$

□

To prove the theorem, we use the following basic fact. If X and Y are random variables, then

$$0 \leq H(X) - H(X|Y) \leq H(Y).$$

We apply this where $X = \mathsf{DB}$ is uniformly random (i.e. has entropy N), and $Y = a$. Conditioning on the value of a can reduce the entropy of DB by at most $|a|$. The fact that Reconstruct produces DB' which agrees in expectation with DB on at least $(1 - \epsilon - \delta)N$ locations implies that $H(\mathsf{DB}|a) \leq H(\epsilon + \delta)N + O(\log N)$. Thus

$$|a| \geq N - (H(\epsilon + \delta)N + O(\log N)) = (1 - H(\epsilon + \delta))N - O(\log N),$$

which concludes the proof of Theorem 2. □

Key Size for Designated Client PIR. The idea behind our lower bound on key size for a designated client scheme is that releasing the key turns the scheme into a public client scheme, which by Theorem 2 must be insecure. Since the key is a piece of information which causes a dramatic change in the entropy of a random variable, it must be long.

Theorem 3. *In any B-bounded-query statistically δ_{dc}-secure, $(1 - \epsilon)$-correct designated-client DEPIR, the key size $|\mathsf{sk}_{dc}|$ satisfies:*

$$|\mathsf{sk}_{dc}| \geq \left(1 - 2\delta_{dc} - H\left(\frac{1 - \delta_{pc}}{2}\right)\right) \cdot B - O(\log B)$$

where δ_{pc} is the smallest δ such that $H(\epsilon + \delta) \geq 1 - \frac{|a| + O(\log N)}{N}$. In particular, if $|a| = o(N)$, $\epsilon = o(1)$, and $\delta_{dc} = o(1)$, then $|\mathsf{sk}_{dc}| = \Omega(B)$.

Proof. Given any designated client PIR scheme with correctness error ϵ, answer size $|a|$, and B-query δ_{dc}-security, we can turn it into a public-client scheme with the same correctness probability and answer size $|a|$ by just releasing the secret key. By Theorem 2, this scheme can only be non-adaptively δ-secure if

$$H(\epsilon + \delta) \geq 1 - \frac{|a| + O(\log N)}{N}$$

Let δ_{pc} denote the minimum such δ. Note that if $\epsilon = o(1)$ and $|a| = o(N)$, then $\delta_{pc} = \frac{1}{2} - o(1)$. By definition of δ_{pc}, there exists a database DB and indices i_0 and i_1 such that the distributions $(\mathsf{pk}, \widetilde{\mathsf{DB}}, q_0)$ and $(\mathsf{pk}, \widetilde{\mathsf{DB}}, q_1)$ are δ_{pc}-far (i.e. distinguishable with probability $\frac{1 + \delta_{pc}}{2}$) in the probability space defined by sampling

$$(\mathsf{pk}_{pc}, \mathsf{sk}_{pc}) \leftarrow \mathsf{Keygen}(1^\lambda, N)$$
$$\widetilde{\mathsf{DB}} \leftarrow \mathsf{Process}(\mathsf{sk}_{pc}, \mathsf{DB})$$
$$q_0 \leftarrow \mathsf{Query}(\mathsf{pk}, i_0)$$
$$q_1 \leftarrow \mathsf{Query}(\mathsf{pk}, i_1).$$

In particular, suppose a uniformly random string $M \in \{0,1\}^B$ is chosen, and an adversary $\mathcal{A}$ is given $(\mathsf{pk}_{pc}, \widetilde{\mathsf{DB}}, q_1, \ldots, q_B)$, where $q_j \leftarrow \mathsf{Query}(\mathsf{pk}, i_{m_j})$. Then it is possible for $\mathcal{A}$ to output M' such that in expectation, $\Delta(m, m') \geq \frac{1 + \delta_{pc}}{2} \cdot B$. In other words,

$$H(M|(\mathsf{pk}_{pc}, \widetilde{\mathsf{DB}}, q_1, \ldots, q_B)) \leq H\left(\frac{1 - \delta_{pc}}{2}\right) B + O(\log B).$$

On the other hand, we can use the following lemma, proved implicitly by Bellare et al. [BTV12] and explicitly restated by Dodis [Dod12] to lower bound the entropy of M given only $\widetilde{\mathsf{DB}}, q_1, \ldots, q_B$.

Lemma 4 [BTV12]. *For any (possibly correlated) distributions M, C over some spaces $\mathcal{M}$ and $\mathcal{C}$, let*

$$\epsilon = \mathbf{SD}((M, C); M \times C)$$

where $M \times C$ is the product distribution of the independent marginal distributions M and C. Then,

$$2\epsilon^2 \leq \boldsymbol{I}(M;C) \leq 2\epsilon \cdot \log(|\mathcal{M}|/\epsilon)$$

This lemma, together with the B-bounded δ_{dc}-security of our designated client PIR, implies that

$$
\begin{aligned}
H(M|\widetilde{\mathsf{DB}}, q_1, \ldots, q_B) &\geq B - 2\delta_{dc}(B - \log \delta_{dc}) \\
&= (1 - 2\delta_{dc})B + 2\delta_{dc}\log \delta_{dc} \\
&\geq (1 - 2\delta_{dc})B - 2.
\end{aligned}
$$

$|\mathsf{pk_{pc}}| = |\mathsf{sk_{dc}}|$ must be large as the difference between these two entropies, which proves the theorem. $\qquad\square$

5   A Candidate Designated Client Scheme and HPN

In this section we propose a candidate designated-client DEPIR scheme for unbounded number of queries. We prove the security of the scheme based on the hardness of a new computational problem, called the hidden permutation with noise problem (HPN).

Our candidate scheme is similar to the bounded secure scheme of Sect. 4, except that the client adds noise to each of its queries by overwriting some of the coordinates with random values. This modification thwarts the linear attack of last section; however, due to the impossibility of statistically secure designated client DEPIR (see Sect. 4.4), the security of a scheme that follows these lines can only be computational *even if the client uses perfectly random permutations*. Thus, an additional hardness assumption is necessary.

We formulate a number of variants of HPN. The strongest variant is essentially a restatement of the privacy requirement from the scheme, as per Definition 1. It says that no PPT $\mathcal{A}$ can distinguish the queries generated by the scheme from sequences of random values in $\mathbb{F}^m$, even if $\mathcal{A}$ has full adaptive control over which addresses are queried. We then give reductions from the adaptive to static versions of HPN and from the decision version to a search version where hidden random permutations are recovered in full. This implies that our scehme is secure as long as the static, search problem remains hard.

The candidate scheme is presented in Sect. 5.1, the HPN assumption is defined in Sect. 5.2, and the reductions are proved in Sects. 5.3 and 5.4.

5.1   Candidate Scheme

Notation. Let $\mathcal{P}$ be a family of pseudorandom permutations with seed length λ. We use the same algebraic notation as in the Introduction. So let $(m, t, r, k, H, \mathbb{F})$ be such that $m < t < r < k < |\mathbb{F}|$ and $H \subset \mathbb{F}$ such that $|H|^m = N$ and $m(t-1)(|H|-1) < r$. Also, $|\mathbb{F}|^m = \mathsf{poly}(n)$ while $|\mathbb{F}|^t = n^{\omega(1)}$.

Keygen$(1^\lambda, N)$: Draw permutations $\tau \leftarrow \mathcal{P}(\mathbb{F}^{m+1})$ and $\pi \leftarrow \mathcal{P}(\mathbb{F}^m)$ and a subset $T \subset [k]$ of size $|T| = r$. Output $k = (\mathsf{seed}_\pi, \mathsf{seed}_\tau, T)$.

Process(k, DB): Interpret $\mathsf{DB} \in \{0,1\}^N$ as $\mathsf{DB} : H^m \to \{0,1\}$ using the identification of $[N]$ with (a subset of) H^m (DB is zero on any points in H^m not in the image of this identification) and let $\widehat{\mathsf{DB}} : \mathbb{F}^m \to \mathbb{F}$ be the low degree extension, so $\deg(\widehat{\mathsf{DB}}) \le m(|H| - 1)$. Output

$$\widetilde{\mathsf{DB}} = \left\{ \left(\mathbf{x}, \tau\left(\mathbf{x}, \widehat{\mathsf{DB}}(\pi^{-1}(\mathbf{x}))\right) \right) \right\}_{\mathbf{x} \in \mathbb{F}^m}.$$

Query(k, i): Let $\mathbf{z} \in H^m$ be the element corresponding to $i \in [N]$. Choose $\mathbf{x} = (\mathbf{x}_1, \ldots, \mathbf{x}_k) \leftarrow \mathsf{V}_\mathbf{z}$. Output $\mathbf{y} = (\mathbf{y}_1, \ldots, \mathbf{y}_k)$ where $\mathbf{y}_i = \pi(\mathbf{x}_i)$ if $i \in T$, and $\mathbf{y}_i \leftarrow \mathbb{F}^m$ is random otherwise. Set $\mathsf{st} = (\mathsf{seed}_\tau, T)$.

Resp$^{\widetilde{\mathsf{DB}}}(q)$: Upon receiving $q = (\mathbf{y}_1, \ldots, \mathbf{y}_k)$, for each $i = 1, \ldots, k$, find the row of $\widetilde{\mathsf{DB}}$ with first coordinate $\mathbf{y}_i$: $(\mathbf{y}_i, \mathbf{y}'_i)$. Output $a = (\mathbf{y}'_1, \ldots, \mathbf{y}'_k)$.

Dec(st, a): Parse $a = (\mathbf{y}'_1, \ldots, \mathbf{y}'_k)$ and $\mathsf{st} = (\mathsf{seed}_\tau, T)$. For $i \in T$, set $(\mathbf{x}_i, \alpha_i) = \tau_i^{-1}(\mathbf{y}'_i)$. Let $\psi : \mathbb{F} \to \mathbb{F}$ be the unique univariate polynomial of degree at most $m(t-1)(|H|-1)$ such that $\psi(i) = \alpha_i$ for all $i \in T$. Output $\perp$ if no such polynomial exists; otherwise output $\psi(0)$.

5.2   Variants of HPN

All variants of the HPN problem are defined in terms of the HPN distribution, which is essentially a noisy version of the distributions $\mathcal{D}(\{\pi_i\}, \mathbf{z})$ from the previous section. Recall this distribution: $\mathbf{x} \leftarrow \mathsf{V}_\mathbf{z}$ is drawn and $\mathbf{y}$ is output where $\mathbf{y}_i = \pi_i(\mathbf{x}_i)$. In this section we simplify notations and use the same permutation π for all coordinates $i \in [k]$. We add noise to the samples in the following way: at the beginning of the experiment a random subset $T \subset [k]$ of size $r > t$ is chosen and $\mathbf{y}_i = \pi(\mathbf{x}_i)$ only if $i \in T$; otherwise $\mathbf{y}_i$ is drawn randomly from $\mathbb{F}^m$. Intuitively, HPN says that no PPT adversary can either distinguish such samples from random (decision form) or recover the hidden permutation π (search version).

Definition 6 (HPN Distribution). *Let $(m, t, r, k, \mathbb{F})$ be such that $m < t < r < k < |\mathbb{F}|$, $|\mathbb{F}|^m = \mathsf{poly}(n)$ and $|\mathbb{F}|^t = n^{\omega(1)}$. For $\pi \in \mathsf{Perm}(\mathbb{F}^m)$, $\mathbf{z} \in \mathbb{F}^m$ and $T \subset [k]$, let $\mathcal{D}(\pi, \mathbf{z}, T)$ be the distribution which: draws $\mathbf{x} \leftarrow \mathsf{V}_\mathbf{z}$ and outputs $\mathbf{y} \in \mathbb{F}^{mk}$ where $\mathbf{y}_i = \pi(\mathbf{x}_i)$ if $i \in T$ and $\mathbf{y}_i \leftarrow \mathbb{F}^m$ otherwise.*

The static versions of the HPN assumption are formulated against a PPT adversary who gets polynomially many samples $(\mathbf{z}_\alpha, \mathbf{y}_\alpha)$ where $\mathbf{y}_\alpha \leftarrow \mathcal{D}(\pi, \mathbf{z}_\alpha, T)$ for random fixed $\pi \in \mathsf{Perm}(\mathbb{F}^m)$ and $T \subset [k]$ and random $\mathbf{z}_\alpha \leftarrow \mathbb{F}^m$. In the adaptive versions of the assumption allow the adversary to choose the $\mathbf{z}_\alpha \in \mathbb{F}^m$ adaptively as the experiment progresses. The static versions of HPN imply the adaptive versions as $|\mathbb{F}|^m = \text{poly}(n)$, and so a static adversary who receives enough random samples, will be able to provide samples to an adaptive adversary. This idea is utilized in the proof of Claim 5.2 below. In the definitions below we write $\{\mathbf{y}_\alpha\} \leftarrow \mathcal{D}(\pi, \{\mathbf{z}_\alpha\}, T)$ for the samples; it is to be understood that the indices $\{\mathbf{z}_\alpha\}$ are chosen randomly from $\mathbb{F}^m$ and made public to the adversary.

Definition 7 (The HPN Assumption). *Let $(m, t, r, k, \mathbb{F})$ be as above.*

Search Version: *For all PPT algorithms $\mathcal{A}$ and non-negligible $\delta > 0$,*

$$\Pr_{\pi, T, \{\mathbf{y}_\alpha\}}\Big[\mathcal{A}(\{\mathbf{y}_\alpha\}) = \pi\Big] < \delta.$$

The probability above is over $\pi \leftarrow \text{Perm}(\mathbb{F}^m)$, random subset $T \subset [k]$ such that $|T| = r$, and $\{\mathbf{z}_\alpha\} \leftarrow \mathbb{F}^m$, $\{\mathbf{y}_\alpha\} \leftarrow \mathcal{D}(\pi, \{\mathbf{z}_\alpha\}, T)$.

Decision Version: *For all PPT $\mathcal{A}$ and non-negligible $\delta > 0$,*

$$\Pr_{\pi, T}\Big[\Big|\Pr_{\{\mathbf{y}_\alpha\} \leftarrow \mathcal{D}(\pi, \{\mathbf{z}_\alpha\}, T)}[\mathcal{A}(\{\mathbf{y}_\alpha\}) = 1] - \Pr_{\{\mathbf{y}_\alpha\} \leftarrow \mathbb{F}^{km}}[\mathcal{A}(\{\mathbf{y}_\alpha\}) = 1]\Big| > \delta\Big] < \delta,$$

where the outer probability is over $\pi \leftarrow \text{Perm}(\mathbb{F}^m)$ and random $T \subset [k]$ such that $|T| = r$.

Claim. The candidate scheme is secure assuming decisional HPN.

Proof. The ideal world simulator for the candidate scheme simply sends a random $\mathbf{y}_\alpha \in \mathbb{F}^{km}$ anytime the adversary $\mathcal{A}$ requests a query for some index $\mathbf{z}_\alpha$. Note that decisional HPN says that the simulated transcript is indistinguishable from valid queries to a random sequence of address vectors $\mathbf{z}_\alpha \in \mathbb{F}^m$. This doesn't quite prove security since the DEPIR chooses arbitrary addresses in H^m in an adaptive fashion. However, note that since $|\mathbb{F}|^m = \text{poly}(n)$, arbitrary adaptive address choice does not grant extra power to the adversary. Indeed, if $\mathcal{A}$ requests a query to a particular address $\mathbf{z} \in H^m$, a distinguisher who gets queries corresponding to random $\mathbf{z}_\alpha \in \mathbb{F}^m$ simply asks for $|\mathbb{F}|^m \cdot n$ such queries and forwards to $\mathcal{A}$ the first one for which $\mathbf{z}_\alpha = \mathbf{z}$. With high probability, some such α will exist. □

5.3   Search to Decision Reduction

Theorem 4. *If there exists a PPT $\mathcal{A}$ which breaks the decisional HPN−assumption, then there exists PPT $\mathcal{B}$ which breaks search HPN.*

Proof. Let $\mathcal{A}$ be any PPT algorithm and $\delta > 0$ non-negligible such that

$$\Pr_{\pi, T}\Big[\Big|\Pr_{\{\mathbf{y}_\alpha\} \leftarrow \mathcal{D}(\pi, \{\mathbf{z}_\alpha\}, T)}[\mathcal{A}(\{\mathbf{y}_\alpha\}) = 1] - \Pr_{\{\mathbf{y}_\alpha\} \leftarrow \mathbb{F}^{km}}[\mathcal{A}(\{\mathbf{y}_\alpha\}) = 1]\Big| > \delta\Big] \geq \delta.$$

We construct $\mathcal{B}$ which recovers π given samples from $\mathcal{D}(\pi, \{\mathbf{z}_\alpha\}, T)$ and oracle access to $\mathcal{A}$. Our algorithm $\mathcal{B}$ will proceed in two steps. First, it will use $\mathcal{A}$ to recover a large (size at least $t + 1$) subset $T' \subset T$. We call this the "cleaning step" since $\mathcal{B}$ removes all noise from the queries: given $\mathbf{y} \leftarrow \mathcal{D}(\pi, \mathbf{z}, T)$, $(\mathbf{y})_{T'}$ consists entirely of correct permuted evaluations of a curve. Then, $\mathcal{B}$ passes the cleaned samples to the RecoverPerm algorithm, described and analyzed in Sect. 5.4. RecoverPerm outputs π given polynomially many noiseless samples, and is an extension of the distinguishing attack on the bounded scheme from Sect. 4.3. We now describe the CLEAN algorithm.

The Distribution $\mathcal{D}_S$. For $S \subset [k]$, let $\mathcal{D}_S$ be the distribution which draws $\{\mathbf{y}_\alpha\} \leftarrow \mathcal{D}(\pi, \{\mathbf{z}_\alpha\}, T)$, and outputs $\{\mathbf{y}'_\alpha\}$ where

$$\mathbf{y}'_{\alpha,i} = \begin{cases} \mathbf{y}_{\alpha,i}, & i \in S \\ \mathbf{y}'' \leftarrow \mathbb{F}^m, & i \notin S \end{cases}$$

Remark. We make the following observations about $\mathcal{D}_S$.

1. Since $\mathcal{B}$ is given samples from $\mathcal{D}(\pi, \{\mathbf{z}_\alpha\}, T)$, it can efficiently obtain samples from $\mathcal{D}_S$ for any $S \subset [k]$. Since $\mathcal{B}$ additionally gets oracle access to $\mathcal{A}$, it can approximate

$$p_S := \Pr_{\{\mathbf{y}_\alpha\} \leftarrow \mathcal{D}_S}[\mathcal{A}(\{\mathbf{y}_\alpha\}) = 1]$$

   to within arbitrary inverse polynomial accuracy in polynomial time with probability $1 - 2^{-n}$.
2. For all $S \subset [k]$, $\mathcal{D}_S$ is identically distributed to $\mathcal{D}_{S \cap T}$. In particular, if $i \notin T$ then $\mathcal{D}_S \equiv \mathcal{D}_{S \cup \{i\}}$.
3. If $S = [k]$ then $\mathcal{D}_S = \mathcal{D}(\pi, \{\mathbf{z}_\alpha\}, T)$; if $|S| \le t$ then $\mathcal{D}_S$ is the uniform distribution on $\mathbb{F}^{mk \cdot \mathrm{poly}}$ by t–wise independence of degree t curves.

Intuition. The main idea of CLEAN is the following. It samples $\{\mathbf{y}_\alpha\} \leftarrow \mathcal{D}(\pi, \{\mathbf{z}_\alpha\}, T)$, chooses $i \in [k]$ and replaces every $\mathbf{y}_{\alpha,i}$ with a random element of $\mathbb{F}^m$. If $i \notin T$, then the distribution of $\{\mathbf{y}_\alpha\}$ has not changed, if $i \in T$, then each $\mathbf{y}_\alpha$ has one fewer correct coordinate. If CLEAN was lucky in the choice of i, $\mathcal{A}$ will change its decision probability, and CLEAN decides that $i \in T$. A hybrid argument shows that if CLEAN will efficiently be able to find enough "lucky" $i \in T$, to output $T' \subset T$ of size at least $t + 1$.

The CLEAN Algorithm. For a parameter $\delta > 0$, set $M = nk^2/\delta^2$ and let c be a universal constant.

1. Use M samples from $\mathcal{D}_{[k]}$ and $\mathcal{D}_\emptyset$ to compute $\hat{p}_{[k]}$ and $\hat{p}_\emptyset$, approximations of $p_{[k]}$ and $p_\emptyset$.
2. **Initialize $T' = \emptyset$; While $|T'| \le t$:**
   - **Initialize $S = T'$, $\hat{p}_S = \hat{p}_\emptyset$; While $S \neq [k]$:**
     * Pick $i \notin S$. Use M samples from $\mathcal{D}_{S \cup \{i\}}$ to compute $\hat{p}_{S \cup \{i\}}$, an approximation of $p_{S \cup \{i\}}$.
     * If $|\hat{p}_{S \cup \{i\}} - \hat{p}_S| > \delta/2k$, $T' = T' \cup \{i\}$.
     * Redefine $S = S \cup \{i\}$, $\hat{p}_S = \hat{p}_{S \cup \{i\}}$.

3. **Output** T'.
4. **Time Out Condition:** If the total runtime ever reaches 2^{cn}, abort and output T'.

Lemma 5. *Let $(m, t, r, k, |\mathbb{F}|)$ be as above. Suppose PPT $\mathcal{A}$, non-negligible $\delta > 0$ and $\pi \in \mathsf{Perm}(\mathbb{F}^m)$, $T \subset [k]$ of size $|T| = r$ are such that*

$$\left| \Pr\nolimits_{\{\mathbf{y}_\alpha\} \leftarrow \mathcal{D}(\pi, \{\mathbf{z}_\alpha\}, T)} \left[\mathcal{A}(\{\mathbf{y}_\alpha\}) = 1 \right] - \Pr\nolimits_{\{\mathbf{y}_\alpha\} \leftarrow \mathbb{F}^{km}} \left[\mathcal{A}(\{\mathbf{y}_\alpha\}) = 1 \right] \right| > \delta.$$

Then

$$\Pr\nolimits_{\{\mathbf{y}_\alpha\} \leftarrow \mathcal{D}(\pi, \{\mathbf{z}_\alpha\}, T)} \left[\mathsf{CLEAN}^{\mathcal{A}}(\{\mathbf{y}_\alpha\}) = T' \text{ st } T' \subset T \text{ and } |T'| = t{+}1 \right] \geq 1 - 2^{-\Omega(n)}.$$

Moreover, the expected running time of CLEAN *is* $\mathcal{O}(nk^3 t / \delta^2)$.

Proof. We show that if all approximations $\hat{p}$ computed by CLEAN are within $\delta/4k$ of the true expectations p (in this case we say that the approximations are *good*) then CLEAN runs in $\mathcal{O}(Mkt)$ time and outputs $T' \subset T$ of size at least $t{+}1$. This completes the proof since by the Chernoff-Hoeffding inequality, all of CLEAN's approximations are good with probability $1 - 2^{-\Omega(n)}$; the maximum runtime is 2^{cn} because of the time-out condition, so events which occur with probability $2^{-\Omega(n)}$ may be safely ignored. Note that when CLEAN's approximations are good, the output T' is a subset of T. Indeed, the only way i gets added to T' is if $|\hat{p}_{S \cup \{i\}} - \hat{p}_S| > \delta/2k$; if $i \notin T$ and approximations are good:

$$|\hat{p}_{S \cup \{i\}} {-} \hat{p}_S| \leq |\hat{p}_{S \cup \{i\}} {-} p_{S \cup \{i\}}| + |p_{S \cup \{i\}} {-} p_S| + |\hat{p}_S {-} p_S| \leq \frac{\delta}{2k} + |p_{S \cup \{i\}} {-} p_S| = \frac{\delta}{2k},$$

by Observation 2. We show that if approximations are good then each time through the outer while loop at least one i is added to T'. This completes the proof since the time to run the inner while loop is $\mathcal{O}(Mk)$. The key point is that throughout the course of the inner loop S goes from $|S| \leq t$ (so that $p_S = p_\emptyset$ by Observation 3) to $S = [k]$. Since $\mathcal{A}$ distinguishes $\mathcal{D}(\{\pi_i\}, \{\mathbf{z}_\alpha\}, T)$ from uniform with probability at least $\delta > 0$, $|p_{[k]} - p_\emptyset| \geq \delta$. By a hybrid argument, there must exist some (S, i) encountered during the course of the inner loop so that $|p_{S \cup \{i\}} - p_S| \geq \delta/k$. Since approximations are good, $|\hat{p}_{S \cup \{i\}} - \hat{p}_S| \geq \delta/2k$ and so i is added to T'. $\qquad\square$

5.4   Recovering the Permutations

In this section we describe a protocol which is given samples from $\mathcal{D}(\pi, \{\mathbf{z}_\alpha\})$ and recovers the permutation π used to produce the samples. This attack extends to the case of many permutations $\{\pi_i\}$ instead of just one, and so constitutes a strong break of the unbounded variant of the scheme from Sect. 4. We use the same notation as in that section. This algorithm requires more samples than the one in the previous section ($\mathsf{poly}(|\mathbb{F}|^m)$ versus $|\mathbb{F}|^{m(1+o(1))}$).

The RecoverPerm *Algorithm.* Let $(m, t, k, |\mathbb{F}|)$ be such that $m < t < k < |\mathbb{F}|$ and $|\mathbb{F}|^m = \text{poly}(\lambda)$. Set $B = m\lambda|\mathbb{F}|^{3m+3}$. Let $\{\mathbf{z}_\alpha\}$ be any sequence of addresses such that every $\mathbf{z} \in H^m$ appears at least B times in $\{\mathbf{z}_\alpha\}$.
Input: $\{\mathbf{y}_\alpha\}$ drawn from $\mathcal{D}(\pi, \{\mathbf{z}_\alpha\})$.

1. Initialize variables $\{\mathbf{v_y}\}_{\mathbf{y} \in \times \mathbb{F}^m}$ taking values in $\mathbb{F}^m$, and a list L of linear constraints to $\emptyset$.
2. For all α, add the constraint $\mathbf{v_{y_\alpha}} \in \mathsf{V_{z_\alpha}}$ to L, where $\mathbf{v_{y_\alpha}}$ is shorthand for the vector $(\mathbf{v}_{y_{\alpha,1}}, .., \mathbf{v}_{y_{\alpha,k}})$.
3. If the constraints in L are inconsistent (*i.e.* no assignment to the $\mathbf{v_y}$ satisfies all constraints), abort and output $\bot$. Otherwise, choose an arbitrary assignment satisfying all constraints in L and let $\sigma : \mathbb{F}^m \to \mathbb{F}^m$ be the map which sends $\mathbf{y}$ to the vector assigned to $\mathbf{v_y}$. If σ is not a permutation, abort and output $\bot$. Otherwise, output $\pi' \in \mathsf{Perm}(\mathbb{F}^m)$ where $\pi' = \sigma^{-1}$.

Note that RecoverPerm runs in time $\text{poly}(B, |\mathbb{F}|^m, \lambda)$ since Step 3 involves solving a system of linear equations and checking whether a functions with poly-sized domain is a permutation; all other steps are efficient. The next Lemma states RecoverPerm recovers the correct π used to generate the samples with high probability.

Lemma 6. *Set $B = m\lambda|\mathbb{F}|^{3m+3}$ and let $\{\mathbf{z}_\alpha\}$ be any sequence of addresses such that each $\mathbf{z} \in H^m$ appears at least B times in $\{\mathbf{z}_\alpha\}$. Let $\pi \in \mathsf{Perm}(\mathbb{F}^m)$ be the permutation used to generate the input samples, and let $\pi' \in \mathsf{Perm}(\mathbb{F}^m)$ the output. Then with overwhelming probability: $\pi' = \pi$.*

Proof. The first failure event in Step 3, that the linear constraints in L are inconsistent, never occurs as by definition $\mathbf{v_y} = \pi^{-1}(\mathbf{y})$ satisfies every constraint. Fix any assignment to the $\mathbf{v_y}$ satisfying the constraints in L, let $\sigma : \mathbb{F}^m \to \mathbb{F}^m$ be the map which sends $\mathbf{y}$ to the vector assigned to $\mathbf{v_y}$. Since the assignment satisfies L, for every $\mathbf{y}_\alpha$, we have $\sigma(\mathbf{y}_\alpha) \in \mathsf{V_{z_\alpha}}$, where $\sigma(\mathbf{y}_\alpha)$ is shorthand for $(\sigma(\mathbf{y}_{\alpha,1}), \ldots, \sigma(\mathbf{y}_{\alpha,k}))$. Recall that drawing $\mathbf{y}_\alpha \leftarrow \mathcal{D}(\pi, \mathbf{z}_\alpha)$ consists of drawing $\mathbf{x}_\alpha \leftarrow \mathsf{V_{z_\alpha}}$ and then setting $\mathbf{y}_\alpha = \pi(\mathbf{x}_\alpha)$. Therefore, for every $\mathbf{x}_\alpha \leftarrow \mathsf{V_{z_\alpha}}$ drawn to produce the input of RecoverPerm: $\sigma \circ \pi(\mathbf{x}_\alpha) \in \mathsf{V_{z_\alpha}}$.

We say that an assignment to the $\mathbf{v_y}$ is BAD if $\Pr_{\mathbf{x} \leftarrow \mathsf{V_z}}[\sigma \circ \pi(\mathbf{x}) \in \mathsf{V_z}] < 1 - |\mathbb{F}|^{-(2m+2)}$, for some $\mathbf{z} \in H^m$. Note,

$$\Pr[\exists \text{ BAD satisfying asst}] < |\mathbb{F}|^{m|\mathbb{F}|^m} \cdot \left(1 - \frac{1}{|\mathbb{F}|^{2m+2}}\right)^B = 2^{-\Omega(\lambda)},$$

when $B = m\lambda|\mathbb{F}|^{3m+3}$. Therefore, it suffices to assume that the assignment is not BAD. Lemma 7 below shows that in this case, $\sigma \circ \pi = \mathbb{1}$. The result follows. $\qquad\square$

Lemma 7. *Suppose $f_1, \ldots, f_k : \mathbb{F}^m \to \mathbb{F}^m$ are such that $\Pr_{\mathbf{x} \leftarrow \mathsf{V_z}}[\mathbf{f}(\mathbf{x}) \in \mathsf{V_z}] \geq 1 - |\mathbb{F}|^{-(2m+2)}$ for all $\mathbf{z} \in H^m$. Then there exists a curve $\varphi : \mathbb{F} \to \mathbb{F}^m$ of degree at most t satisfying $\varphi(0) = \mathbf{0}$ such that $f_i(\mathbf{x}_i) = \mathbf{x}_i + \varphi(i)$ for all $i = 1, \ldots, k$. In particular, if all f_i are equal then each f_i is the identity function.*

Proof. The second statement follows from the first since if $\varphi(i)$ takes the same value for $i = 1, \ldots, k$ then φ must be constant, hence identically zero.

The proof of the first statement consists of three steps, described momentarily. First however we define the following random variables. Let f be functions that satisfy the lemma hypotheses. For any $\mathbf{c} \in V_0$, define $f_{\mathbf{c}}(\mathbf{x}) := f(\mathbf{x} + \mathbf{c}) - f(\mathbf{c})$. Choose $\mathbf{c} \in V_0$ so that $f_{\mathbf{c}}(\mathbf{0}) = \mathbf{0}$ and $\Pr_{\mathbf{x} \leftarrow V_{\mathbf{z}}}\left[f_{\mathbf{c}}(\mathbf{x}) \in V_{\mathbf{z}} \mid \mathbf{x}_4 = \cdots = \mathbf{x}_{t+1} = \mathbf{0}\right] \geq 1 - 1/(2|\mathbb{F}|^{2m})$ for all $\mathbf{z} \in H^m$ (random $\mathbf{c} \leftarrow V_0$ satisfies these properties with probability at least $1 - |\mathbb{F}|^{-1}$).

In the first step we show that $f_{\mathbf{c}_1,1}$ is linear, so $f_{\mathbf{c}_1,1}(\mathbf{x}_1) = \mathbf{A}_1\mathbf{x}_1$ for a matrix $\mathbf{A}_1 \in \mathbb{F}^{m \times m}$; similarly, we have $f_{\mathbf{c}_2,2}(\mathbf{x}_2) = \mathbf{A}_2\mathbf{x}_2$.

In the second step we show that $\mathbf{A}_1$ and $\mathbf{A}_2$ are equal (so drop the subscripts). In particular, it follows that f_1 and f_2 are affine with the same linear component: $f_i(\mathbf{x}_i) = f_{\mathbf{c}_i,i}(\mathbf{x}_i - \mathbf{c}_i) + f_i(\mathbf{c}_i) = \mathbf{A}\mathbf{x}_i - \left(f_{\mathbf{c}_i,i}(\mathbf{c}_i) - f_i(\mathbf{c}_i)\right)$ for $i = 1, 2$. This argument extends to all $i \in [k]$: there exists $\mathbf{A} \in \mathbb{F}^{m \times m}$ and $\mathbf{b}_1, \ldots, \mathbf{b}_k \in \mathbb{F}^m$ such that $f(\mathbf{x}) = (\mathbf{A}\mathbf{x}_1 + \mathbf{b}_1, \ldots, \mathbf{A}\mathbf{x}_k + \mathbf{b}_k)$.

Finally, we complete the proof by showing that $\mathbf{A} = \mathbb{1}$ and $\mathbf{b} \in V_0$.

To see that $f_{\mathbf{c}_1,1}$ is linear, let us first set some notation. Write $(\mathbf{x}_1, \mathbf{x}_2, \mathbf{x}_3) \in V_0'$ if there exists $\mathbf{x}' \in V_0$ such that $(\mathbf{x}_1', \mathbf{x}_2', \mathbf{x}_3') = (\mathbf{x}_1, \mathbf{x}_2, \mathbf{x}_3)$ and $\mathbf{x}_4' = \cdots = \mathbf{x}_{t+1}' = \mathbf{0}$. Clearly $(\mathbf{x}_1, \mathbf{x}_2, \mathbf{x}_3), (\mathbf{x}_1', \mathbf{x}_2, \mathbf{x}_3) \in V_0'$ implies $\mathbf{x}_1' = \mathbf{x}_1$ because of agreement considerations. Note that $V_0' \subset \mathbb{F}^{3m}$ is a $(2m)$-dimensional subspace so is closed under addition. By our choice of $\mathbf{c} \in V_0$, $\left(f_{\mathbf{c}_1,1}(\mathbf{x}_1), f_{\mathbf{c}_2,2}(\mathbf{x}_2), f_{\mathbf{c}_3,3}(\mathbf{x}_3)\right) \in V_0'$ whenever $(\mathbf{x}_1, \mathbf{x}_2, \mathbf{x}_3) \in V_0'$. Now, choose arbitrary $\mathbf{x}_1, \mathbf{x}_1' \in \mathbb{F}^m$, we will show $f_{\mathbf{c}_1,1}(\mathbf{x}_1 + \mathbf{x}_1') = \overline{\mathbf{x}}_1 + \overline{\mathbf{x}}_1'$, where $\overline{\mathbf{x}}_1 = f_{\mathbf{c}_1,1}(\mathbf{x}_1)$, $\overline{\mathbf{x}}_1' = f_{\mathbf{c}_1,1}(\mathbf{x}_1')$. Let $\mathbf{x}_2, \mathbf{x}_3 \in \mathbb{F}^m$ be so that $(\mathbf{x}_1, \mathbf{x}_2, \mathbf{0}), (\mathbf{x}_1', \mathbf{0}, \mathbf{x}_3) \in V_0'$ (such $\mathbf{x}_2, \mathbf{x}_3$ exist by interpolation). Let $\overline{\mathbf{x}}_i = f_{\mathbf{c}_i,i}(\mathbf{x}_i)$ for $i = 2, 3$. We have $(\overline{\mathbf{x}}_1, \overline{\mathbf{x}}_2, \mathbf{0}), (\overline{\mathbf{x}}_1', \mathbf{0}, \overline{\mathbf{x}}_3) \in V_0'$ (using $f_{\mathbf{c}}(\mathbf{0}) = \mathbf{0}$), and so $(\overline{\mathbf{x}}_1 + \overline{\mathbf{x}}_1', \overline{\mathbf{x}}_2, \overline{\mathbf{x}}_3) \in V_0'$. On the other hand, if we first add then apply f we get $\left(f_{\mathbf{c}_1,1}(\mathbf{x}_1 + \mathbf{x}_1'), \overline{\mathbf{x}}_2, \overline{\mathbf{x}}_3\right) \in V_0'$; $f_{\mathbf{c}_1,1}(\mathbf{x}_1 + \mathbf{x}_1') = \overline{\mathbf{x}}_1 + \overline{\mathbf{x}}_1'$ follows.

Let $\mathbf{A}_1 \in \mathbb{F}^{m \times m}$ be the matrix form of $f_{\mathbf{c}_1,1}$. As mentioned before, the above argument also shows that $f_{\mathbf{c}_2,2}$ is linear with matrix $\mathbf{A}_2 \in \mathbb{F}^{m \times m}$. We show here that $\mathbf{A}_1 = \mathbf{A}_2$. To see this, consider the linear map $\Phi : \mathbb{F}^m \to \mathbb{F}^m$ which sends $\mathbf{x}_1$ to $\mathbf{x}_2$ such that $(\mathbf{x}_1, \mathbf{x}_2, \mathbf{0}) \in V_0'$. Note that Φ is actually just multiplication by some non-zero scalar $\beta \in \mathbb{F}$ (this can be seen by writing Φ explicitly in terms of Lagrange interpolation coefficients). For any $\mathbf{x}_1 \in \mathbb{F}^m$, $(\mathbf{x}_1, \beta \cdot \mathbf{x}_1, \mathbf{0}) \in V_0'$; the properties of $f_{\mathbf{c}}$ imply that $(\mathbf{A}_1\mathbf{x}_1, \beta \cdot \mathbf{A}_2\mathbf{x}_1, \mathbf{0}) \in V_0'$; this means $\beta\mathbf{A}_2\mathbf{x}_1 = \beta\mathbf{A}_1\mathbf{x}_1$; $\mathbf{A}_1 = \mathbf{A}_2$ follows.

We have shown so far that f_1 and f_2 are affine with the same linear component. This argument extends to any f_i, f_j for $i, j \in [k]$ so, as mentioned above, there exists a single matrix $\mathbf{A} \in \mathbb{F}^{m \times m}$ and vectors $\mathbf{b}_1, \ldots, \mathbf{b}_k \in \mathbb{F}^m$ such that $f_i(\mathbf{x}_i) = \mathbf{A}\mathbf{x}_i + \mathbf{b}_i$ for all $i \in [k]$. We show that $\mathbf{A} = \mathbb{1}$ and $\mathbf{b} \in V_0$, which completes the proof. For any $\mathbf{z} \in H^m$, the affine map $f : \mathbb{F}^{mk} \to \mathbb{F}^{mk}$ maps the affine plane $V_{\mathbf{z}} \subset \mathbb{F}^{mk}$ to an affine plane in $\mathbb{F}^{mk}$. It follows that either $f(V_{\mathbf{z}}) \subset V_{\mathbf{z}}$, or $\Pr_{\mathbf{x} \leftarrow V_{\mathbf{z}}}\left[f(\mathbf{x}) \in V_{\mathbf{z}}\right] \leq |\mathbb{F}|^{-1}$ since affine planes intersect in at most $1/|\mathbb{F}|$ fraction of their points unless there is containment. We are given that $\Pr_{\mathbf{x} \leftarrow V_{\mathbf{z}}}\left[f(\mathbf{x}) \in V_{\mathbf{z}}\right] \geq 1 - |\mathbb{F}|^{-(2m+2)}$, so it must be that $f(V_{\mathbf{z}}) \subset V_{\mathbf{z}}$ for all $\mathbf{z} \in H^m$. In particular, $\mathbf{b} = f(\mathbf{0}) \in V_0$. Finally, note that

$\mathbf{x} \mapsto (\mathbf{Ax}_1, \ldots, \mathbf{Ax}_k) + \mathbf{b}$ maps V_z to $V_{\mathbf{Az}}$. Therefore, we must have $\mathbf{Az} = \mathbf{z}$ for all $\mathbf{z} \in H^m$. As H^m spans $\mathbb{F}^m$, this forces $\mathbf{A} = \mathbb{1}$ as desired. $\square$

Acknowledgments. We thank Mariana Raykova for motivational discussions in the early stages of this project, and Madhu Sudan and Yael Kalai for breaking some of our schemes.

References

[Ajt10] Ajtai, M.: Oblivious rams without cryptographic assumptions. In: STOC, pp. 181–190. ACM (2010)

[BI01] Beimel, A., Ishai, Y.: Information-theoretic private information retrieval: a unified construction. In: Orejas, F., Spirakis, P.G., van Leeuwen, J. (eds.) ICALP 2001. LNCS, vol. 2076, pp. 912–926. Springer, Heidelberg (2001). https://doi.org/10.1007/3-540-48224-5_74

[BIM04] Beimel, A., Ishai, Y., Malkin, T.: Reducing the servers' computation in private information retrieval: PIR with preprocessing. J. Cryptol. **17**(2), 125–151 (2004)

[BIPW17] Boyle, E., Ishai, Y., Pass, R., Wootters, M.: Can we access a database both locally and privately? Cryptology ePrint Archive, Report 2017/567 (2017). http://eprint.iacr.org/2017/567

[BN00] Bleichenbacher, D., Nguyen, P.Q.: Noisy polynomial interpolation and noisy chinese remaindering. In: Preneel, B. (ed.) EUROCRYPT 2000. LNCS, vol. 1807, pp. 53–69. Springer, Heidelberg (2000). https://doi.org/10.1007/3-540-45539-6_4

[Bra09] Braverman, M.: Poly-logarithmic independence fools AC^0 circuits. In: IEEE Conference on Computational Complexity, pp. 3–8. IEEE Computer Society (2009)

[BTV12] Bellare, M., Tessaro, S., Vardy, A.: Semantic security for the wiretap channel. In: Safavi-Naini, R., Canetti, R. (eds.) CRYPTO 2012. LNCS, vol. 7417, pp. 294–311. Springer, Heidelberg (2012). https://doi.org/10.1007/978-3-642-32009-5_18

[CKGS98] Chor, B., Kushilevitz, E., Goldreich, O., Sudan, M.: Private information retrieval. J. ACM **45**(6), 965–981 (1998)

[CMS99] Cachin, C., Micali, S., Stadler, M.: Computationally private information retrieval with polylogarithmic communication. In: Stern, J. (ed.) EUROCRYPT 1999. LNCS, vol. 1592, pp. 402–414. Springer, Heidelberg (1999). https://doi.org/10.1007/3-540-48910-X_28

[CS03] Coppersmith, D., Sudan, M.: Reconstructing curves in three (and higher) dimensional space from noisy data. In: Proceedings of the 35th Annual ACM Symposium on Theory of Computing, 9–11 June 2003, San Diego, CA, USA, pp. 136–142 (2003)

[CSP+] Cheng, R., Scott, W., Parno, B., Zhang, I., Krishnamurthy, A., Anderson, T.: Talek: a private publish-subscribe protocol (2016)

[DMN11] Damgård, I., Meldgaard, S., Nielsen, J.B.: Perfectly secure oblivious RAM without random oracles. In: Ishai, Y. (ed.) TCC 2011. LNCS, vol. 6597, pp. 144–163. Springer, Heidelberg (2011). https://doi.org/10.1007/978-3-642-19571-6_10

[Dod12] Dodis, Y.: Shannon impossibility, revisited. In: Smith, A. (ed.) ICITS 2012. LNCS, vol. 7412, pp. 100–110. Springer, Heidelberg (2012). https://doi.org/10.1007/978-3-642-32284-6_6

[GKS10] Gopalan, P., Khot, S., Saket, R.: Hardness of reconstructing multivariate polynomials over finite fields. SIAM J. Comput. **39**(6), 2598–2621 (2010)

[GO96] Goldreich, O., Ostrovsky, R.: Software protection and simulation on oblivious rams. J. ACM **43**(3), 431–473 (1996)

[GR17] Goldreich, O., Rothblum, G.N.: Simple doubly-efficient interactive proof systems for locally-characterizable sets. In: Electronic Colloquium on Computational Complexity (ECCC), vol. 24, p. 18 (2017)

[KO97] Kushilevitz, E., Ostrovsky, R.: Replication is NOT needed: SINGLE database, computationally-private information retrieval. In: FOCS, pp. 364–373. IEEE Computer Society (1997)

[KR17] Kalai, Y., Raz, R.: Personal communication (2017)

[MRS09] Morris, B., Rogaway, P., Stegers, T.: How to encipher messages on a small domain. In: Halevi, S. (ed.) CRYPTO 2009. LNCS, vol. 5677, pp. 286–302. Springer, Heidelberg (2009). https://doi.org/10.1007/978-3-642-03356-8_17

[NP06] Naor, M., Pinkas, B.: Oblivious polynomial evaluation. SIAM J. Comput. **35**(5), 1254–1281 (2006)

[SCSL11] Shi, E., Chan, T.-H.H., Stefanov, E., Li, M.: Oblivious RAM with $O((\log N)^3)$ worst-case cost. In: Lee, D.H., Wang, X. (eds.) ASIACRYPT 2011. LNCS, vol. 7073, pp. 197–214. Springer, Heidelberg (2011). https://doi.org/10.1007/978-3-642-25385-0_11

Assumptions

On Iterative Collision Search for LPN and Subset Sum

Srinivas Devadas, Ling Ren$^{(\boxtimes)}$, and Hanshen Xiao$^{(\boxtimes)}$

Massachusetts Institute of Technology, Cambridge, MA, USA
{devadas,renling,hsxiao}@mit.edu

Abstract. Iterative collision search procedures play a key role in developing combinatorial algorithms for the subset sum and learning parity with noise (LPN) problems. In both scenarios, the single-list pair-wise iterative collision search finds the most solutions and offers the best efficiency. However, due to its complex probabilistic structure, no rigorous analysis for it appears to be available to the best of our knowledge. As a result, theoretical works often resort to overly constrained and sub-optimal iterative collision search variants in exchange for analytic simplicity. In this paper, we present rigorous analysis for the single-list pair-wise iterative collision search method and its applications in subset sum and LPN. In the LPN literature, the method is known as the LF2 heuristic. Besides LF2, we also present rigorous analysis of other LPN solving heuristics and show that they work well when combined with LF2. Putting it together, we significantly narrow the gap between theoretical and heuristic algorithms for LPN.

1 Introduction

The Learning Parity with Noise (LPN) problem is a fundamental problem in coding theory, cryptography and machine learning. In cryptography, LPN attracts most interest from lightweight constructions, i.e., those that run efficiently on constrained devices such as RFID tags and wireless sensors. Many lightweight constructions [7,9,11,13] build on the hardness of the LPN due to the simplicity of the operations it entails. Studying the best algorithms for solving LPN is vital to determine suitable parameters for these constructions and subsequent improvements.

For a uniformly selected secret $\mathbf{s} \in \mathbb{Z}_2^n$, the LPN problem is to find $\mathbf{s}$ given input samples $\mathbf{As} + \mathbf{e}$, where $\mathbf{A}$ is uniformly random and each component of $\mathbf{e}$ is a Bernoulli noise. For ease of exposition, we follow prior work and think of LPN algorithms as consisting of two phases: a reduction phase and a solving phase. The classical algorithm for LPN is the BKW algorithm [4]. At its core is an iterative collision search procedure for the reduction phase. To start, partition the samples into $2^{\frac{n}{k+1}}$ groups such that the first $\frac{n}{k+1}$ bits are identical. Here, k is a parameter of the algorithm and is set to $\Theta(\log n)$. Then, select one sample in each group and add it to the other ones in the group to cancel out the first $\frac{n}{k+1}$ bits. Each subsequent iterative step follows the same procedure to cancel out

© International Association for Cryptologic Research 2017
Y. Kalai and L. Reyzin (Eds.): TCC 2017, Part II, LNCS 10678, pp. 729–746, 2017.
https://doi.org/10.1007/978-3-319-70503-3_24

the next $\frac{n}{k+1}$ bits. After a few iterations, the samples only depend on a single bit in the secret. These samples are the outputs of the reduction phase and we call them *reduced* samples. At this point, the algorithm enters the solving phase to guess this secret bit and tests it on the reduced samples. The algorithm then moves on to guess the next secret bit, repeating the reduction phase and the solving phase therein.

The BKW algorithm needs a sub-exponential number of input samples. Lyubashevsky [18] and Kirchner [14] modified the BKW algorithm to work with a polynomial number of samples. Outside the "limited-sample" direction, however, theoretical advances for LPN algorithms have been stagnant for more than a decade. On the other hand, heuristic and practical methods for LPN continue to develop at a fast pace. Levieil and Fouque [15] proposed two important heuristic methods. The first one, LF1, improves the solving phase by guessing multiple secret bits at a time. It is augmented with the Fast Walsh-Hadamard transform to further reduce runtime. The second method, LF2, is a more efficient iterative collision search procedure in the reduction phase. The goal is to generate more reduced samples for the solving phase. After partitioning input samples into groups sharing a chunk of bits, instead of adding one sample to the others in the group as in BKW, LF2 computes the sums of every pair in the group. Recent works [5,6,8,15,25] have applied covering codes, partial secret guessing and linear programming to improve the solving phase.

The LF1 and LF2 heuristics are two most important heuristic techniques in the LPN literature, and have been adopted by every subsequent work we know of [5,6,8,25]. The efficiency gain, however, presents a challenge for analysis since the reduced samples now depend on each other in a complex manner. (LF1 was initially presented as a rigorous algorithm [15], but Zhang et al. [25] pointed out that the original proof incorrectly assumed independence between reduced samples. Hence, LF1 should be treated as a heuristic prior to our work.) A main contribution of this paper is to provide rigorous analysis for the LF1 and LF2 methods and establish them as rigorous LPN algorithms. In particular, we compute the number of solutions (both expectation and distribution) produced by LF2 in the reduction phase. We also show that the correlation between LF2 reduced samples has little impact on the success rate of the LPN solving phase for both majority voting and LF1 Walsh-Hadamard transform. Our results significantly narrow the gap between theoretical and heuristic solutions to the LPN problem.

LPN has a close connection to the subset sum problem. As Wagner suggests [24], any improvement to the subset sum problem will also result in an improvement to LPN. In this paper, we consider the random fixed-weighted XOR variant of subset sum. Given a list L of elements sampled uniformly randomly from $\mathbb{Z}_2^n$, find 2^k elements from L such that they XOR to 0. One way is to apply Wagner's algorithm. However, Wagner's algorithm was not tailored for fixed weighted subset sum. Instead, it was presented for the generalized birthday problem [24]. In the generalized birthday problem, there are 2^k separate lists and the goal is to find one element from each list such that they XOR to 0. In order to apply Wagner's algorithm, one has to partition the single list L into 2^k smaller lists. Wagner's algorithm then places the 2^k lists as the leaves of a depth-k binary tree. In step i, every pair of sibling lists are merged into a new list at their parent node such that the i-th chunk of $\frac{n}{k+1}$ bits are canceled out. To elaborate, the merge operation searches for two elements, one from each input list, such that their i-th chunk of $\frac{n}{k+1}$ bits XOR to 0. After k steps, the elements in the last list at the root of the tree are solutions to the problem.

Clearly, the partition into 2^k separate lists is an artifact in order to invoke Wagner's algorithm. It not only increases the time complexity but also imposes an unnecessary constraint that eliminates many valid candidate solutions. It is much more natural to perform the same merge operation within the original single list L: at step i, search for pairs of distinct elements in L that cancel out the i-th chunk of $\frac{n}{k+1}$ bits, and add their XOR results to the new list for the next step. This single-list pair-wise iterative collision search very much resembles the LF2 method (there are also important differences which we describe in Sect. 3.2). Also resembling LF2, it creates difficulties for the analysis. In Wagner's algorithm, in every merge operation, the two input elements (from different lists) are independent of each other. In contrast, the single-list iterative collision search introduces dependence across steps, making it hard to reason about the expected list size after each step or the number of solutions produced in the end. With a rigorous analysis, we establish the single-list pair-wise iterative collision search as an improved algorithm over Wagner for random fixed weighted subset sum.

The rest of the paper is organized as follows. We start with the fixed weighted subset sum problem since the LPN problem additionally has to deal with the solving phase. Section 2 presents our analysis for the single-list iterative collision search algorithm for the fixed weighted subset sum problem. Section 3 presents our analysis for the LF1 and LF2 methods for LPN. We conclude in Sect. 4.

2   Random Fixed Weighted Subset Sum

2.1   Background

Definition 1 (subset sum). *Given a list* $L = \{a_1, a_2, ..., a_N\}$ *of* N *numbers from an algebraic structure and an operation* $\oplus$, *find* $\mathbf{x} \in \{0,1\}^N$ *such that* $\langle \mathbf{x}, S \rangle = x_1 a_1 \oplus x_2 a_2 \oplus ... \oplus x_N a_N = t$ *where* t *is a pre-defined target.*

The subset sum problem is one of Karp's 21 NP-complete problems [12]. The classical subset sum problem considers integers and integer addition. In the last three decades, there have also been a few important variants of the subset sum problem that attracted interest in cryptography [10,17,19].

In this paper, we focus on the random fixed weighted variant of the problem. The term fixed weighted means the solution vector $\mathbf{x}$ must have a Hamming weight of 2^k.[1] For concreteness, we start with the XOR case, i.e., $a_1, a_2, \cdots, a_N$

---

[1] Without the fixed weighted restriction, the problem can be solved with Gauss elimination easily.

are n-bit binary string drawn independently and uniformly randomly from $\mathbb{Z}_2^n$, and the operator $\oplus$ is bit-wise XOR. Later , we will extend our analysis to other groups and group operators, e.g., $\mathbb{Z}_q^n$ for some prime q and addition on $\mathbb{Z}_q^n$. We also focus on the special case where the target is $t = 0$.

Wagner's Generalized Birthday Problem and Algorithm. Wagner introduced the generalized birthday problem and an algorithm for it [24]. The generalized birthday problem bears some similarities to the random fixed-weighted subset sum problem, but is also different in a fundamental way. Instead of finding 2^k elements from a single list, the problem takes 2^k lists and finds one element from each list.

Definition 2 (generalized birthday problem). *Given* 2^k *lists* $L_1, L_2,$ $\cdots, L_{2^k}$ *each containing* N *elements in* $\mathbb{Z}_2^n$, *find one element from each list* $a_1 \in L_1, a_2 \in L_2, \cdots, a_{2^k} \in L_{2^k}$ *such that* $a_1 \oplus a_2 \oplus \cdots \oplus a_{2^k} = 0$.

Wagner's algorithm performs iterative collision search in a tree fashion in k steps. [2] Write the 2^k input lists as $L_1^{(0)}, L_2^{(0)}, ..., L_{2^k}^{(0)}$ and place them at the leaves of a binary tree of depth k. In the j-th step $(1 \leq j < k)$, for each pair of lists $L_{2i}^{(j-1)}$ and $L_{2i+1}^{(j-1)}$, find two elements $l \in L_{2i}^{(j-1)}$ and $l' \in L_{2i+1}^{(j-1)}$ such that the j-th chunk of $\frac{n}{k+1}$ bits cancel out (i.e., XOR to 0), and then add $l \oplus l'$ to a new list $L_i^{(j)}$. In the last step $j = k$, there are only two lists remaining, and the algorithm looks for two elements, one from each list, such that they cancel out the last $\frac{2n}{k+1}$ bits and XOR to 0^n. Figure 1 gives an illustration of this algorithm. There have been several improvements and analysis to Wagner's algorithm [2,14,16,20], and they all follow the tree-based collision search framework.

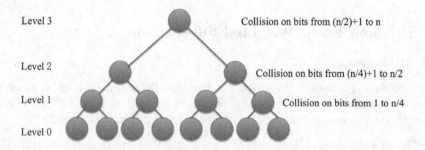

Fig. 1. An illustration of Wagner's algorithm.

To ensure at least one solution is found in expectation, the size of each input list should be at least $N \geq 2^{\frac{n}{k+1}}$. Crucially for the analysis, in each step, a pair

---

[2] Different from our notation, Wagner denoted the number of lists as k and the number of steps as $\log_2 k$ [24].

Input: A single list L, also written as $L^{(0)}$, of size N.
1. Initially, add the index alongside each element in $L^{(0)}$, i.e., each element in $L^{(0)}$ now has the form $(a_i, \{i\})$.
2. **for** $j = 1 : k - 1$ **do**

  For each pair of elements (a, α) and (a', α') in $L^{(j-1)}$, if $a \oplus a'$ cancel out the+ j-th chunk of $\frac{n}{k+1}$ bits and $\alpha \cap \alpha' = \varnothing$, then add $(a \oplus a', \alpha \cup \alpha')$ to the new list $L^{(j)}$.

end
3. At the last step, repeat the similar operation to find a pair of elements (a, α) and (a', α') such that $a \oplus a'$ cancel out the last $\frac{2n}{k+1}$ bits and $\alpha \cap \alpha' = \varnothing$. Output $L^{(k)}$.

Algorithm 1. The single-list pair-wise iterative collision search algorithm.

of elements l and l' are independent because they are sums of elements that come from disjoint lists. Thus, the expected list size at each step can be easily calculated as $N^2 \cdot 2^{-\frac{n}{k+1}} \geq N$, and in the last step, $N^2 \cdot 2^{-\frac{2n}{k+1}} \geq 1$ solutions are produced in expectation.

2.2 Single List Iterative Collision Search

The single-list pair-wise collision search algorithm is known as the LF2 method in the LPN literature [15], which was in turn inspired by Wagner's algorithm [24]. Algorithm 1 gives the pseudocode. Recently, it was also independently proposed, though seemingly by accident, in a memory hard proof-of-work scheme called Equihash [3]. The Equihash paper [3] used the above Algorithm 1 to solve the random fixed-weighted subset sum, but confusingly, claimed to be using Wagner's algorithm and solving the generalized birthday problem throughout the paper.

Complexities. Following previous works, we measure time complexity in the number of $\oplus$ operations and measure time complexity in the number list entries, essentially ignoring the number of bits $\oplus$ operates on and the number of bits in each entry. For Algorithm 1, the time complexity is roughly $O(kN)$ and the space complexity is roughly $O(N)$. As a comparison, for Wagner's algorithm, the time complexity is roughly $O(2^k N)$ and the space complexity is roughly $O(kN)$.

As we have mentioned, analyzing the single-list pair-wise collision search algorithm is much harder than analyzing Wagner's algorithm because, after the first step, elements in the list become correlated. They are no longer sums of non-overlapping elements. Rather, they are now sums that contain common addends. If the input list size at a certain step is N, the expected output list size is no longer simply $N^2 \cdot 2^{-\frac{n}{k+1}}$. Indeed, it seems difficult to derive the final expected number of solutions by calculating the expected list size at each step. In the next subsection, we approach the problem from a different angle. We will calculate the total number of distinct candidate solutions and the probability that each one is an actual solution that Algorithm 1 produces.

2.3   Expected Number of Solutions

Theorem 1. *Let* $p = 2^{-\frac{n}{k+1}}$. *The expected number of solutions produced by Algorithm 1 is*

$$\mathrm{E}\left[|L^{(k)}|\right] = 2\binom{N}{2^k}(2^k)!(p/2)^{2^k}.$$

Proof. Consider an index vector $\alpha = (i_1, i_2, ..., i_{2^k})$, and the candidate solution it defines, $\mathbf{a}_\alpha = \{a_{i_1}, a_{i_2}, \cdots, a_{i_{2^k}}\}$. Let $Y_\alpha = 1$ if $\mathbf{a}_\alpha$ is a solution produced by Algorithm 1 and $Y_\alpha = 0$ otherwise. Before we proceed, we remark that a solution to the fixed-weighted subset sum problem is not necessarily a solution that will be found by Algorithm 1. (The other direction is true). The reason is that Algorithm 1 can only find solutions that meet stringent conditions, i.e., those that cancel out a chunk of bits after each step. For example, if $\alpha = (1, 2, 3, 4)$ and $Y_\alpha = 1$, it is not only required that $a_1 \oplus a_2 \oplus a_3 \oplus a_4 = 0$, but also that $a_1 \oplus a_2$ and $a_3 \oplus a_4$ both cancel out the first chunk of bits. The iterative collision search framework in general only finds solutions with a specific structure rather than all solutions.

It is also important to note that some index vectors represent the same solution and should be counted only once. For example, if $\alpha = (1, 2, 3, 4)$ and $Y_\alpha = 1$, then for $\alpha' = (1, 2, 4, 3), (2, 1, 3, 4), (2, 1, 4, 3), (3, 4, 1, 2), (3, 4, 2, 1), (4, 3, 1, 2)$, or $(4, 3, 2, 1)$, we have $Y_{\alpha'} = 1$. However, these eight vectors all represent the same single solution that will be produced by Algorithm 1. Define I to be a maximal set of index vectors that correspond to distinct candidate solutions. To calculate $|I|$, we think of the indices in a vector as the leaves in a binary tree of depth k. (This binary tree is just a tool for analyzing Algorithm 1 and should not be confused with Wagner's tree-based iterative collision search in Fig. 1.) In the jth step, swapping the two siblings would yield the same candidate solution. Thus, for each subset of 2^k elements, there are $\frac{(2^k)!}{\prod_{j=1}^{k} 2^{2^{k-j}}} = \frac{(2^k)!}{2^{2^k-1}}$ distinct candidate solutions out of the $(2^k)!$ total possible index vectors. Therefore, $|I| = \binom{N}{2^k}\frac{(2^k)!}{2^{2^k-1}}$ is the number of distinct candidate solutions that Algorithm 1 can possibly produce. The expected number of solutions produced by Algorithm 1 can then be calculated as $\mathrm{E}\left[|L^{(k)}|\right] = \mathrm{E}\left[\sum_{\alpha \in I} Y_\alpha\right]$.

After the jth step, the list $L^{(j)}$ contains (XOR) sums of 2^j addends. We again think of the 2^j addends as leaves of a binary tree of depth j. To appear in $L^{(j)}$, the two addends need to cancel out a chunk of $\frac{n}{k+1}$ bits at each node in the tree. At each node, the probability is[3] $p = 2^{-\frac{n}{k+1}}$ and there are $2^j - 1$ nodes in a tree

---

[3] $p = 2^{-\frac{n}{k+1}}$ is used throughout the paper.

of depth j. So the probability that a sum of certain 2^j addends appear in $L^{(j)}$ is p^{2^j-1}. The expected number of elements in $L^{(j)}$ is hence

$$E\left[|L^{(j)}|\right] = |I| \cdot p^{2^j-1} = \binom{N}{2^j}\frac{(2^j)!}{2^{2^j-1}} \cdot p^{2^j-1} = \binom{N}{2^j}(2^j)!(p/2)^{2^j-1}. \quad (1)$$

The last step needs to cancel out $\frac{2n}{k+1}$ bits which happens with probability p^2. Thus, we have $\Pr(Y_\alpha = 1) = p^{2^k}$, and

$$E\left[|L^{(k)}|\right] = |I| \cdot p^{2^k} = \binom{N}{2^k}\frac{(2^k)!}{2^{2^k-1}} \cdot p^{2^k} = 2\binom{N}{2^k}(2^k)!(p/2)^{2^k}$$

Extension to $\mathbb{Z}_q^n$. Although we presented our analysis in the $\mathbb{Z}_2^n$ and XOR case for simplicity, our analysis can be easily modified to work with a larger modulus q, i.e., when the operator $\oplus$ is modular addition over $\mathbb{Z}_q^n$. The only change in the analysis above and in Sect. 2.5 is to replace $p = 2^{-\frac{n}{k+1}}$ with $p = q^{-\frac{n}{k+1}}$.

2.4 Experimental Verification

In this subsection, we provide experimental results that corroborate the expected number of solutions we derive in Theorem 1. Another purpose of this section is to correct a mistake in the Equihash scheme [3]. Specifically, Equihash adopts Algorithm 1 with a list size $N = 2^{\frac{n}{k+1}+1}$. It then claimed the expected number of solutions is $\binom{N}{2} \cdot 2^{-\frac{2n}{k+1}} \approx 2$ citing Wagner's analysis. As we mentioned, Wagner's analysis requires independence and does not hold in the single-list case.

Table 1 lists the expected number of solutions found through experiments as well as the values given by Theorem 1 under different choices of n and k. Our theorem accurately predicts the number of solutions. (Our theorem is precise. The difference is due to errors in the experiments.) Equihash claims 2 solutions in expectation under all parameter settings, which as we see can be orders of magnitude off. We note that the latter four (n,k) pairs are among the recommended parameter settings from the Equihash paper [3]. For readers who are interested, this incorrect estimation will make the difficulty of the proof-of-work scheme proportionally harder than intended. For example, if a protocol designer adopts Equihash with $(n,k) = (192,11)$, the expected time to find a valid proof-of-work will be $10^7 \times$ longer than intended!

Table 1. The expected number of solutions found through experiments and Theorem 1.

n	16	32	48	56	96	128	160	192
k	1	3	5	6	5	7	9	11
Experiments	2.00	1.90	0.76	0.03	2.00	1.8	0.8	0.0
Theorem 1	1.9961	1.8931	0.7437	0.0328	1.9924	1.8797	0.7362	2.1×10^{-7}

2.5 Distribution of Solutions

Knowing the expected number of solutions is in most cases sufficient to parameterize an algorithm. For example, to attack knapsack-based cryptosystems, one may parameterize Algorithm 1 to produce a small constant number of solutions in expectation, e.g., 1. But for a rigorous analysis, we would like to rule out a possible bad corner case. With the expectation being 1, it is possible that Algorithm 1 generates 2^{30} solutions with a 2^{-30} probability, while producing no solution most of the time. In this subsection, we study the distribution of the number of solutions produced by Algorithm 1. Aside from ruling out that bad corner case, a more precise distribution will be useful in our analysis for LPN and possibly other applications.

We will show that the distribution of solutions is close to a Poisson distribution. We will apply the Chen-Stein method of the second moment analysis as the main tool to bound the difference.

Lemma 1 (Chen-Stein [1]). Let Π be a random variable that follows a Poisson distribution with mean $\lambda = \mathrm{E}\left[|L^{(k)}|\right]$. Let J_α be the neighborhood of dependence for Y_α (which means any $Y_\beta \notin J_\alpha$ is independent of Y_α) and $J_\alpha^* = J_\alpha \setminus \{\alpha\}$ where $\setminus$ is set subtraction. Then,

$$\sum_{j=0}^{\infty} \left| P\left(|L^{(k)}| = j\right) - P(\Pi = j) \right|$$

$$\leq \frac{4(1 - e^{-\lambda})}{\lambda} \left(\sum_{\alpha \in I} \sum_{\beta \in J_\alpha} \mathrm{E}\left[Y_\alpha\right] \mathrm{E}\left[Y_\beta\right] + \sum_{\alpha \in I} \sum_{\beta \in J_\alpha^*} \mathrm{E}\left[Y_\alpha Y_\beta\right] \right).$$

Define Δ to be the right hand side of the above inequality.

The rest of this subsection bounds the two double sums in Δ separately. The first sum is

$$\sum_{\alpha \in I} \sum_{\beta \in J_\alpha} \mathrm{E}\left[Y_\alpha\right] \mathrm{E}\left[Y_\beta\right] = \mathrm{E}\left[|L^{(k)}|\right] \sum_{\beta \in J_\alpha} E(Y_\beta)$$

$$= \mathrm{E}\left[|L^{(k)}|\right] p^{2^k} \frac{(2^k)!}{2^{2^k - 1}} \sum_{i=0}^{2^k - 1} \binom{2^k}{i} \binom{N - 2^k}{i} \approx \mathrm{E}\left[|L^{(k)}|\right] \cdot p.$$

In most applications (e.g., attack hash functions), finding a few solutions is sufficient, so $\mathrm{E}\left[|L^{(k)}|\right]$ will be much less than $\frac{1}{p}$, and this first sum can be ignored.

The dominant part and also the difficulty of this analysis is the sum of the correlation terms $E(Y_\alpha Y_\beta)$. To start, we have

$$\mathrm{E}\left[Y_\alpha Y_\beta\right] = \mathrm{E}\left[\mathrm{E}\left[Y_\alpha Y_\beta | Y_\beta\right]\right] = \Pr(Y_\alpha = 1, Y_\beta = 1)$$
$$= \Pr(Y_\alpha = 1) \Pr(Y_\beta = 1 | Y_\alpha = 1).$$

The last term above depends on the overlap pattern between two index vectors (and their corresponding candidate solutions). For convenience, we denote a candidate solution by an index vector, e.g., $\alpha = (1,2,3,4)$ refers to the candidate solution $\{a_1, a_2, a_3, a_4\}$. We again treat their elements as leaves of a binary tree. For each node in the tree for β, we color it black if its XOR output is independent of α. At the leaf level, any element in β that does not appear in α is independent of α and is colored black. For each level above, a node is colored black if at least one of its two children is black. This is because XORing with an independent and uniformly random addend yields an independent and uniformly random output.

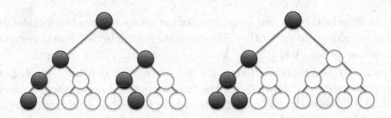

Fig. 2. Fewest black nodes occur when black nodes at the leaf level are clustered in the smallest subtree possible.

As black nodes in β's tree are independent of α, we have $P(Y_\beta = 1|Y_\alpha = 1) \leq p^{1+B}$ where B is the number of black nodes in the tree excluding the leaf level. This is because the candidate solution β needs to cancel out a chunk of bits at each node, and what happens with β at the black nodes are independent of α. The extra p is because the last step (the tree root) cancels out $\frac{2n}{k+1}$ bits which happens with p^2. p^{1+B} reaches its largest value when there are fewest black nodes in the tree. For a certain number of black nodes at the leaves (height 0), the number of black nodes in the entire tree is the fewest if all the black nodes at height 0 are contained in the smallest subtree possible. Figure 2 gives an illustration of this configuration with the minimal number of black nodes. In this case, an upper bound on the number of black nodes in the tree can be derived as follows:

$$\begin{cases} \gamma_0 = |\beta \setminus \alpha| \\ \gamma_j = \lceil \gamma_{j-1}/2 \rceil & j > 0 \\ \gamma(m) = \sum_{j=1}^{k} \gamma_j \text{ where } m = \gamma_0 \end{cases} \tag{2}$$

Then, $\gamma(|\beta \setminus \alpha|)$ is an upper bound on B, and we have

$$\mathrm{E}\left[Y_\alpha Y_\beta\right] \leq \Pr(Y_\alpha = 1) \Pr(Y_\beta = 1|Y_\alpha = 1) \leq p^{2^k + 1 + \gamma(|\beta \setminus \alpha|)} \tag{3}$$

Next, to bound $\sum_{\alpha \in I} \sum_{\beta \in J_\alpha^*} \mathrm{E}\left[Y_\alpha Y_\beta\right]$, we partition J_α^*, into disjoint parts $U_1, U_2, \cdots, U_{2^k}$ according to the number of elements that differ from α. In other words, if $\beta \in U_i$, then $|\beta \setminus \alpha| = i$. For example, for a candidate solution $\alpha = (1,2,3,4)$ (implying $k = 2$), U_1 contains $(1,2,3,5)$, $(1,6,2,3)$, etc. By a simple counting argument,

$$|U_i| = \binom{2^k}{2^k - i} \binom{N - 2^k}{i} \frac{(2^k)!}{2^{2^k - 1}} \tag{4}$$

For $\beta \in U_m$, we have derived an upper bound that $\mathrm{E}\,[Y_\alpha Y_\beta] \leq p^{2^k+1+\gamma(m)}$ in Inequality (3). In Lemma 2, we would like to bound the number of candidate solutions in U_m that can reach this upper bound. To do so, we introduce some additional notations. For an integer $0 < m < 2^k$, write m as a sum of a powers of 2 in ascending order l_i, i.e., $m = \sum_{i=1}^{\zeta} 2^{l_i}$ where $0 \leq l_1 < l_2 < \cdots l_\zeta < k$.

Lemma 2. *Let $\hat{U}_m \subset U_m$ be the set of candidate solutions that achieve the maximum correlation $p^{2^k+1+\gamma(m)}$. $|\hat{U}_m| \leq \binom{N-2^k}{m} \cdot \frac{m!}{2^{m-\zeta}} \cdot \frac{2^k}{2^{l_1}}$.*

Proof. As mentioned, the maximum correlation appears when black nodes at the leaf label are closest to each other. We calculate how many such max-correlation configurations exist. First, the 2^{l_ζ} leaves of a certain subtree of depth l_ζ should be taken up by black nodes. There are $\frac{2^k}{2^{l_\zeta}}$ subtrees of depth l_ζ in total. After choosing one subtree of depth l_ζ, all the remaining black nodes should appear in the sibling subtree of depth l_ζ. Similarly, within that sibling subtree of depth l_ζ, a certain subtree of depth $l_{\zeta-1}$ should be taken by black nodes, giving $2^{l_\zeta-l_{\zeta-1}}$ possible ways. We then repeat the above argument on the next subtree of depth $l_{\zeta-2}$ until we place all the m black nodes. Therefore, the total number of the candidate solutions in U_m that achieve the maximum correlation is at most

$$|\hat{U}_m| \leq \binom{N-2^k}{m} \cdot \frac{m!}{\prod_{i=1}^{\zeta} 2^{2^{l_i}-1}} \cdot \frac{2^k}{2^{l_\zeta}} \cdot \frac{2^{l_\zeta}}{2^{l_{\zeta-1}}} \cdot \cdots \cdot \frac{2^{l_2}}{2^{l_1}} = \binom{N-2^k}{m} \cdot \frac{m!}{2^{m-\zeta}} \cdot \frac{2^k}{2^{l_1}}$$

We can now finally bound the correlation sum in Lemma 1. While $\forall \beta \in \hat{U}_m$ achieves the maximum correlation by definition, $\forall \beta \notin \hat{U}_m$ will have a correlation that is at most p times the maximum, because its corresponding binary tree has at least one more black node. Therefore,

$$\sum_{\alpha \in I} \sum_{\beta \in J_\alpha^*} \mathrm{E}\,[Y_\alpha Y_\beta] \leq |I| \cdot \mathrm{Pr}(Y_\alpha = 1) \sum_{\beta \in J_\alpha^*} \mathrm{Pr}(Y_\beta = 1 | Y_\alpha = 1)$$

$$\leq \mathrm{E}\,\left[|L^{(k)}|\right] \cdot \sum_{i=0}^{2^k-1} \left[|\hat{U}_i| + p\left(|U_i| - |\hat{U}_i|\right)\right] p^{2^k+1+\gamma(i)}$$

where $\mathrm{E}\,\left[|L^{(k)}|\right]$ is given in Theorem 1, $|\hat{U}_i|$ is given in Lemma 2, $|U_i|$ is given in Eq. (4), $p = 2^{-\frac{n}{k+1}}$, and $\gamma(i)$ is defined in Eq. (2).

Example numerical calculation. Suppose $k = 2$. For brevity, we temporarily write $\mathrm{Pr}(Y_\beta = 1 | Y_\alpha = 1)$ as $P_{\beta\alpha}$ for short. We have

- $|U_0| = \frac{4!}{2^3} = 3$, and $\forall \beta \in U_0$, $P_{\beta\alpha} \leq p$;
- $|U_1| = 3 \cdot \binom{N-4}{1} \cdot \binom{4}{1}$, $|\hat{U}_1| = 4(N-4)$;
- $|U_2| = 3 \cdot \binom{N-4}{2} \cdot \binom{4}{2}$, $|\hat{U}_2| = 2\binom{N-4}{2}$; and $\forall \beta \in \hat{U}_1 \cup U_2$, $P_{\beta\alpha} \leq p^3$.
- $|U_3| = |\hat{U}_3| = 3 \cdot \binom{N-4}{3} \cdot \binom{4}{3}$, and $\forall \beta \in U_3$, $P_{\beta\alpha} \leq p^4$.

Denote the right hand side in Lemma 1 as Δ. Plugging in a few example values, we have

- For $n = 30$ and $N = 2 \times 2^{\frac{n}{k+1}}$, $\sum_{\beta \in J_\alpha^*} P_{\beta\alpha} < 0.021$ and $\Delta < 0.037$;
- For $n = 100$ and $N = 2 \cdot 2^{\frac{n}{k+1}}$, $\sum_{\beta \in J_\alpha^*} P_{\beta\alpha} < 2.033 \cdot 10^{-9}$ and $\Delta < 3.511 \cdot 10^{-9}$;
- For a larger list size $N = 10 \cdot 2^{\frac{n}{k+1}}$ with $n = 100$, $\sum_{\beta \in J_\alpha^*} P_{\beta\alpha} < 1.942 \cdot 10^{-7}$ and $\Delta < 3.790 \cdot 10^{-9}$;

For a few more examples,

- For $k = 3$, $n = 100$, and $N = 4 \times 2^{\frac{n}{k+1}}$, $\Delta < 2.1 \times 10^{-3}$;
- For $k = 3$, $n = 120$, and $N = 5 \times 2^{\frac{n}{k+1}}$, $\Delta < 3.1 \times 10^{-4}$;
- For $k = 3$, $n = 120$, and $N = 10 \times 2^{\frac{n}{k+1}}$, $\Delta < 3.8 \times 10^{-2}$;
- For $k = 4$, $n = 200$, and $N = 4 \times 2^{\frac{n}{k+1}}$, $\Delta < 3.8 \times 10^{-5}$;
- For $k = 4$, $n = 250$, and $N = 5 \times 2^{\frac{n}{k+1}}$, $\Delta < 1.1 \times 10^{-6}$.

The above calculations show that the distribution of the number of solutions produced by Algorithm 1 can be closely approximated by a Poisson distribution. The total variation distance Δ between the two is small.

3   Learning Parity with Noise

3.1   Background

The Learning Parity with Noise (LPN) problem is a famous open problem that is widely conjectured to be hard. It forms the foundation of several primitives in lightweight cryptography and post-quantum cryptography. It is also a special case of the Learning With Error (LWE) problem, which has a reduction from the Shortest Independent Vector Problem (SIVP) [23] and has enabled numerous works in lattice-based cryptography [21,22].

Definition 3 (LPN). *Find the secret bit vector* $\mathbf{s} \in \mathbb{Z}_2^n$, *given samples in the form* $\{(\mathbf{a}_i, b_i)\}$ *where each* $\mathbf{a}_i \in \mathbb{Z}_2^n$ *is a random n-bit string, and each* $e_i \in \{0,1\}$ *is a Bernoulli noise with parameter* $0 < \tau < 0.5$ *and* $b_i = \langle \mathbf{a}_i, \mathbf{s} \rangle \oplus e_i$

Starting from the seminal work by Blum, Kalai and Wasserman [4], LPN solving algorithms and heuristics largely follow the "reduce-and-solve" framework below.

- **The reduction phase.** Find a subset of samples $\{b_i = \langle \mathbf{a}_i, \mathbf{s} \rangle \oplus e_i\}$ such that $\sum \mathbf{a}_i$ is one of the n bases of $\mathbb{Z}_2^n$. The most popular choice is the standard orthogonal bases, in which case the reduction phase becomes a subset sum problem. For brevity and without loss of the generality, we focus on the first bit of $\mathbf{s}$, denoted by s_1. The reduction phase looks for samples such that $\sum \mathbf{a}_i = (1, 0, \cdots, 0)$. Adding up the samples yield $\hat{b} = s_1 \oplus \hat{e}$ where $\hat{b} = \sum b_i$ and $\hat{e} = \sum e_i$. We call these output samples of the reduction phase *reduced samples*.
- **The solving phase.** With abundant reduced samples $\{\hat{b}\}$, solve s_1.

LPN solving algorithms/heuristics differ in the detailed strategies for the reduction phase and the solving phase. In all existing proposals we know of, the reduction phase always uses some type of iterative collision search procedure. The reduction phase of BKW in each step adds one sample to a set of other samples to cancel out a chunk of bits in $\sum \mathbf{a}_i$, and in the end obtains one reduced sample. BKW then repeats the collision search procedure on fresh samples to obtain more independent reduced samples.

For the reduction phase, the two most popular techniques are simple majority voting and Fast Walsh-Hadamard Transform. BKW uses simple majority voting: given abundant reduced samples $\{\hat{b}\}$, if there are more 0's than 1's, guess $s_1 = 1$; otherwise, guess $s_1 = 0$. Levieil and Fouque [15] proposed recovering multiple secret bits at a time in the solving phase and using the Fast Walsh-Hadamard Transform, which we explain in Sect. 3.4.

3.2   LPN Reduction Phase Using Iterative Collision Search

The BKW algorithm only obtains one reduced sample from each run of the reduction phase in order to ensure independence among reduced samples to apply the Chernoff bound in the solving phase. As a result, BKW is extravagant in consuming input samples and does not mind "missing" many candidate reduced samples. Similar to the subset sum case, the single-list pair-wise iterative collision search, known as the LF2 method in the LPN literature, will produce far more reduced samples given the same amount of initial samples. The LF2 method has been an important technique, and has been adopted by every subsequent LPN solving work that we know of. But prior to our work, LF2 remains a heuristic with no rigorous analysis available. In particular, it remains open after a decade how many reduced samples LF2 produces, to what degree these reduced samples are correlated, and to what extent the correlation affects the solving phase. We now answer these questions with rigorous analysis.

Although the reduction phase of LPN is almost exactly the same as a subset sum problem if we think of the vectors $\{\mathbf{a}_i\}$ as the bit-strings in the list L of subset sum, several remarks should be made regarding the collision schedule, i.e., how many bits to cancel at each step.

1. There is no agreed upon collision schedule in the literature. The original LF2 method [15] was inspired by Wagner's algorithm [24], which cancels out $\frac{2n}{k+1}$ bits in the last step and $\frac{n}{k+1}$ bits in every other step. Many subsequent works define LF2 to cancel out $\frac{n}{k}$ bits in every step including the last one. Our analysis will assume the original collision search schedule by Wagner, but can be extended to other schedules. With Wagner's schedule, our analysis for the number of solutions (both expectation and distribution) in Sect. 2 would apply if we only output fixed weighted reduced samples. But we note that it is OK for the LPN reduction phase to output reduced samples with weights lower than 2^k. So the total number of reduced samples will be greater than what our analysis in Sect. 2 indicates. We omit the analysis of this effect because more reduced samples improve the success rate of the solving phase.

2. The number of input samples to the reduction phase (i.e., the original list size $N = |L^{(0)}|$) greatly influences the expected number of reduced samples output by the reduction phase. If we set $N = 2 \times 2^{\frac{n}{k+1}}$ as in Sect. 2.4, then the list size at each step roughly remains the same (or slightly decreases) and the expected number of output samples is less than 2. However, in LPN, we would like the reduction phase to produce more samples for the solving phase. An easy way to achieve this is to increase the initial list size N to be slightly larger than $2 \times 2^{\frac{n}{k+1}}$. In this case, the list size will grow after every step before the last step.

3. Another way to obtain more reduced samples is to adjust the collision search schedule to cancel out slightly fewer than $\frac{2n}{k+1}$ bits in the last step, and slightly more than $\frac{n}{k+1}$ bits in every other step. The optimal collision schedule is outside the scope of this paper.

4. Bogos et al. [5] used an oversimplified combinatorial method to estimate the expected number of reduced samples, which led to the conclusion that $N = 3 \times 2^{\frac{n}{k+1}}$ would keep the list size constant across steps. Our analysis shows this is not true. Plugging into Eq. (1), we can see that $N = 3 \times 2^{\frac{n}{k+1}}$ will cause the list size to grow exponentially after each step.

5. Another flaw in previous work is the LF(4) proposal by Zhang et al. [25]. It generalizes the LF2 method by with the intention to check all 4-tuple combinations instead of 2-tuple combinations. However, the scheme presented in [25] approximates the 4-tuple collision search using a 2-tuple collision search. This is essentially LF2 with the number of steps k doubled, and hence will not produce the claimed number of reduced samples. On the other hand, if a scheme really enumerates all 4-tuple combinations by brute force, the time complexity will become much more formidable than what's reported in [25], and it remains unclear whether the increased number of reduced samples can make up for it.

3.3 LPN Solving Phase with Majority Voting

This subsection and the next one analyze how the correlation between reduced samples affects the solving phase. Several previous works [5,8,25] have experimentally shown that the correlation does not seem to cause problems in the solving phase. Our analysis will provide theoretical support for these experimental results. We show the correlation between reduced samples produced by the iterative collision search is weak and does not affect the success rate too much. This subsection focuses on the majority voting method, while the next subsection studies the fast Walsh-Hadamard transform method.

Recall that the majority voting method tallies the reduced samples $\{\hat{b}\}$, and guesses $s_1 = 1$ if there are more 1's than 0's, and guesses 0 otherwise. Since $\hat{b} = s_1 \oplus \hat{e}$, each $\hat{e} = 1$ contributes an incorrect vote. Define $Z_\alpha = Y_\alpha \hat{e}_\alpha$ where Y_α is defined in Sect. 2 and $\hat{e}_\alpha = \oplus_{i \in \alpha} e_i$. Let $W = \sum_{\alpha \in I} Z_\alpha$. W represents the number of incorrect votes among the reduced samples. If W does not exceed one half of the reduced samples, then the majority voting will guess s_1 correctly.

If $\{Z_\alpha\}$ were independent, a Chernoff bound would suffice like in BKW [4]. The main difficulty we face is to bound $\Pr(W \geq w)$ when $\{Z_\alpha\}$ are not independent. We will show that if we calculate this bound pretending that $\{Z_\alpha\}$ are independent, the error will be very small.

Let W' be the sum of $|I|$ independent Bernoulli random variables (cf. the definition of W). Each addend Z' follows the same distribution as Z_α, i.e., $\Pr(Z' = 1) = \Pr(Z_\alpha = 1) = \Pr(Y_\alpha = 1)\Pr(\hat{e}_\alpha = 1)$. We once again invoke the Chen-Stein method [1] to bound the total variation distance between W and W',

$$\Delta' = \sum_{l=0}^{\infty} |\Pr(W = l) - \Pr(W' = l)|.$$

We introduce an intermediate random variable Π that follows a Poisson distribution with mean $\lambda' = \mathrm{E}[W]$. Using the triangle inequality, we have $\Delta' \leq \Delta'_1 + \Delta'_2$ where Δ'_1 and Δ'_2 are the total variation distances between W and Π, and between Π and W', respectively. Δ'_1 can be bounded in the same way as in Sect. 2.5. Recall that $W = \sum_{\alpha \in I} Z_\alpha$, $|L^{(k)}| = \sum_{\alpha \in I} Y_\alpha$ and $Z_\alpha = Y_\alpha \hat{e}_\alpha \leq Y_\alpha$. So Δ'_1 is no larger than Δ. (Δ is defined in Lemma 1.)

W' follows a binomial distribution, which is frequently approximated by a Poisson distribution. Concretely, we can bound their total variation distance using the Chen-Stein method. Note that for each addend Z' of W', the neighborhood of dependence of Z' is empty, so only the first double sum in the Chen-Stein method (cf. Lemma 1) remains.

$$\Delta'_2 = \sum_{l=0}^{\infty} |\Pr(W' = l) - \Pr(\Pi = l)| \leq \frac{4(1 - e^{\lambda'})}{\lambda'} \cdot |I| \cdot (\Pr(Z' = 1))^2$$

Observe that $\lambda' = \mathrm{E}[W'] = |I| \cdot \Pr(Z' = 1)$, $\Pr(Z' = 1) = \Pr(Y_\alpha = 1) \cdot \Pr(\hat{e}_\alpha = 1)$, $\Pr(Y_\alpha = 1) = p^{2^k}$, and $\Pr(\hat{e}_\alpha = 1) = \Pr(\oplus_{i \in \alpha} e_i = 1) = \frac{1 - (1 - 2\tau)^{2^k}}{2}$ [4]. Thus,

$$\Delta'_2 \leq 4(1 - e^{\lambda'}) \cdot \Pr(Z' = 1) \leq 4(1 - e^{\lambda'}) \cdot p^{2^k} \cdot \frac{1 - (1 - 2\tau)^{2^k}}{2} < 2p^{2^k}.$$

Clearly, Δ'_2 is very small compared to Δ'_1, so $\Delta' \approx \Delta'_1 \leq \Delta$.

W' is a sum of independent Bernoulli random variables, so the Chernoff bound can be applied to $\Pr(W' \geq w)$. $\Pr(W \geq w)$ can then be bounded by $\leq \Pr(W' \geq w) + \Delta'$. This means the correlation between votes (i.e., reduced samples) resulting from the reduction phase lowers the success rate by at most Δ compared to independent votes. Section 2.5 has shown that Δ is very small, ranging from 0.02 to 10^{-9}. This explains why previous works observed that majority voting using correlated reduced samples works well in reality.

3.4   LPN Solving Phase with Fast Walsh-Hadamard Transform

Levieil and Fouque [15] proposed applying the Fast Wash-Hadamard Transform (FWHT) and recovering a block of secret bits at a time. They call this method LF1. We describe the LF1 method below.

Since LF1 tries to recover a block of y secret bits at a time, it needs to modify the reduction phase to generate reduced samples that depend on y bits of the secret. This is a straightforward modification that simply involves canceling out fewer bits ($n-y$ instead of $n-1$). Denote these reduced samples as $\hat{b}_l = \langle \hat{a}_l, s \rangle \oplus \hat{e}_l$ where $\hat{a}_l, s \in Z_2^y$, i.e., we focus on the y secret bits we are trying to guess.

In the solving phase, for $x \in \{0,1\}^y$ define $f(x) = \sum_l \delta(a_l, x)(-1)^{b_l}$ where $\delta(a_l, x) = 1$ if $a_l = x$ and 0 otherwise. LF1 applies FWHT to compute for each $v \in \{0,1\}^y$,

$$\hat{f}(v) = \sum_x (-1)^{\langle x,v \rangle} f(x) = \sum_l (-1)^{\langle \hat{a}_l, s \oplus v \rangle \oplus \hat{e}_l}$$

Observe that $\hat{f}(s) = \sum_l (-1)^{\hat{e}_l}$. Since $\Pr(\hat{e}_l = 0) > \Pr(\hat{e}_l = 1)$, $f(s)$ should be noticeably larger than 0. On the other hand, for $s' \neq s$, $e'_l = \langle \hat{a}_l, s' \oplus s \rangle$ is uniformly random, and $f(s')$ should be close to 0. LF1 then picks the largest $\hat{f}(v)$ and guesses $s = v$. Thus, if there exists $s' \neq s$ such that $\hat{f}(s') \geq \hat{f}(s)$, then the LF1 method fails. For each s', the probability that $\hat{f}(s') \geq \hat{f}(s)$ is

$$\epsilon = \Pr\left(\hat{f}(s') \geq \hat{f}(s)\right) = \Pr\left(\sum_l e'_l \leq \sum_l \hat{e}_l\right) \tag{5}$$

When analyzing the success rate of LF1, there are two places that prior works argue heuristically [5,6,8,15,25]. One is that they assume reduced samples are independent. The other one is that after noting LF1's success requires $\forall s' \in \{0,1\}^y, \hat{f}(s') < \hat{f}(s)$, they assume independence between the events $\hat{f}(s') < \hat{f}(s)$ for different s' and approximate LF1's success rate as $(1-\epsilon)^{2^y-1}$.

We now present a rigorous analysis for LF1's success rate. We first bound ϵ. The difficulty again lies in analyzing $\sum_l \hat{e}_l$ for correlated $\{\hat{e}_l\}$. We use similar techniques as before. Write $S = \sum_l \hat{e}_l = \sum_{\alpha \in I} Y_\alpha \hat{e}_\alpha$ and $T = \sum_l e'_l = \sum_{\alpha \in I} Y_\alpha \cdot \langle \hat{a}_\alpha, s' \oplus s \rangle$. Define S' to be the sum of I independent Bernoulli random variables each with mean $\Pr(Y_\alpha \hat{e}_\alpha = 1) = \frac{1}{2} \cdot p^{2^k} \cdot (1 - (1 - 2\tau)^{2^k})$. Define T' to be the sum of I independent Bernoulli random variables each with mean $\Pr(e'_l = 1) = \frac{1}{2}$. We again have $\sum_{l=0}^\infty |\Pr(S = l) - \Pr(S' = l)| \leq \Delta'_3 \leq \Delta$ and $\sum_{l=0}^\infty |\Pr(T = l) - \Pr(T' = l)| \leq \Delta'_3 \leq \Delta$. Therefore,

$$\epsilon = \Pr(T \leq S) \leq \Pr(T' \leq S') + 2\Delta'_3 \leq \Pr(T' \leq S') + 2\Delta. \tag{6}$$

This means a heuristic estimation of ϵ by pretending that T and S are sums of independent random variables (T' and S') is only off by at most 2Δ, which is very small under suitable parameters as shown in Sect. 2.5. $\Pr(T' \leq S')$ can be bounded rigorously using the Hoedffing bound. We continue the analysis in the next subsection.

The second inaccuracy above can be easily fixed by a union bound. Thus, the probability that LF1 recovers y secret bits fully correctly is

$$\Pr(\text{LF1 succeeds}) < 1 - 2^y \epsilon.$$

3.5 Complexity Analysis

In this section, we analyze the time and space complexities of the LF1 + LF2 algorithm and compare it to the BKW algorithm [4] (the best previously known non-heuristic algorithm).

The LF1 solving phase with FWHT recovers multiple bits at a time. A common practice in the literature [5,25] is to recover $y = \Theta(k)$ bits at time. This way, the process of recovering the remaining $n - y$ bits (still y bits at time) combined cost roughly the same amount of time as the first y bits. This is because the runtime of the reduction phase has a $2^{\frac{n-y}{k+1}}$ term. When recovering the second batch of y bits, that term becomes $2^{\frac{n-2y}{k+1}}$, which is a constant factor smaller compared to the first batch.

Next, we determine how many reduced samples we should feed to LF1. Let this quantity be N_L. Recall that the failure probability of LF1 is $2^y \epsilon$ from Sect. 3.4). Using the Hoeffding inequality to bound $\Pr(T' \leq S')$ in Eq. (6), we can upper bound the failure probability of LF1 using N_L reduced samples by $2^y \epsilon \leq 2^y (e^{-N_L \delta^2/8} + 2\Delta)$. Here, $\delta = (1 - 2\tau)^{2^k}$ where τ is the error rate of initial input samples, and $1/2 - \delta$ is an upper bound on the error rate of the reduced samples [4]. For the LF algorithm to work, we need Δ to be small. Then, if we want the above probability to be at most θ, we need $N_L \approx 8\delta^{-2} \ln(2^y/\theta)$ reduced samples.

The number of initial samples to feed into the LF2 reduction phase is thus $(N_L)^{1/2^k} 2^{\frac{n}{k+1}+1}$. In practice, it is common to set k such that $N_L < 2^{\frac{n}{k+1}}$. The time complexity of the LF2 reduction phase is $T_{\mathrm{LF2}} = O(\sum_{i=1}^{k-1} N_L^{2^{i-k}} 2^{\frac{n}{k+1}} + N_L) = O(\sqrt{N_L} 2^{\frac{n}{k+1}})$ The time complexity of the LF1 solving phase is $T_{\mathrm{LF1}} = O(y2^y \log N_L + yN_L) = O(yN_L)$ due to [6]. Combining the two, the total time complexity is $T_{\mathrm{LF}} = T_{\mathrm{LF1}} + T_{\mathrm{LF2}} = O(\sqrt{N_L} 2^{\frac{n}{k+1}})$. The maximum space usage occurs at the $(k-1)^{th}$ collision search, which is $S_{\mathrm{LF}} = O(\sqrt{N_L} 2^{\frac{n}{k+1}})$.

Next, we analyze the time and space complexities of the BKW algorithm. In the reduction phase, BKW repeats its iterative collision search procedure many times, each time with fresh initial samples, until it obtains sufficiently many independent reduced samples. The solving phase is simply a majority vote, so the time and space complexities are dominated by the reduction phase. Again, we first need to calculate how many reduced samples are needed. Call this quantity N_B. The probability that a majority of reduced samples are erroneous is $\Pr(\sum_{l=1}^{N_B} \hat{e}_l \geq \frac{N_B}{2}) \leq e^{-\frac{N_B \delta^2}{2}}$. For a fair comparison, we want BKW to recover the first y secret bits with a success probability of $1 - \theta$. This requires $N_B \approx 2\delta^{-2} \ln(y/\theta)$. The time complexity is $T_{\mathrm{BKW}} = O(yN_B k^2 2^{\frac{n}{k+1}})$ and the space complexity is $S_{\mathrm{BKW}} = O(k2^{\frac{n}{k+1}})$.

Finally, we have

$$\frac{T_{\mathrm{BKW}}}{T_{\mathrm{LF}}} = \Theta\left(\frac{k^2 \sqrt{y} \ln y}{\delta}\right) = O(k^{2.5}(\ln k)\delta^{-1}),$$

and

$$\frac{S_{\mathrm{BKW}}}{S_{\mathrm{LF}}} = O\left(\frac{k}{\sqrt{N_L}}\right) = O(k^{0.5}\delta).$$

In conclusion, the LF1 algorithm improves runtime by a factor of (slightly more than) δ^{-1} by consuming a factor of (slightly less than) δ^{-1} more space.

4 Conclusion

Iterative collision search is a crucial technique in solving subset sum and LPN. The single-list pair-wise variant has so far been the most efficient variant for random fixed weighted subset sum and LPN, but has not been rigorously analyzed prior to our work. In this paper, we presented rigorous analysis for the single-list pair-wise iterative collision search procedure and its applications in random fixed weighted subset sum and LPN. In the LPN context, we show that while the reduced samples produced by this method are correlated, the correlation is weak and barely decreases the success rate of LPN solving. Our analysis of the single-list pair-wise iterative collision search is also applicable to LWE. It remains interesting future work to study how it interacts with other techniques in the LWE literature.

References

1. Arratia, R., Goldstein, L., Gordon, L.: Two moments suffice for poisson approximations: the chen-stein method. Ann. Probab. **17**(1), 9–25 (1989)
2. Bernstein, DJ.: Better price-performance ratios for generalized birthday attacks. In: Workshop Record of SHARCS, vol. 7, p. 160 (2007)
3. Biryukov, A., Khovratovich, D.: Equihash: asymmetric proof-of-work based on the generalized birthday problem. In: NDSS (2016)
4. Blum, A., Kalai, A., Wasserman, H.: Noise-tolerant learning, the parity problem, and the statistical query model. J. ACM **50**(4), 506–519 (2003)
5. Bogos, S., Tramer, F., Vaudenay, S.: On solving LPN using BKW and variants. Crypt. Commun. **8**(3), 331–369 (2016)
6. Bogos, S., Vaudenay, S.: Optimization of LPN solving algorithms. In: Cheon, J.H., Takagi, T. (eds.) ASIACRYPT 2016. LNCS, vol. 10031, pp. 703–728. Springer, Heidelberg (2016). doi:10.1007/978-3-662-53887-6_26
7. Gilbert, H., Robshaw, M.J.B., Seurin, Y.: HB#: increasing the security and efficiency of HB+. In: Smart, N. (ed.) EUROCRYPT 2008. LNCS, vol. 4965, pp. 361–378. Springer, Heidelberg (2008). doi:10.1007/978-3-540-78967-3_21
8. Guo, Q., Johansson, T., Löndahl, C.: Solving LPN using covering codes. In: Sarkar, P., Iwata, T. (eds.) ASIACRYPT 2014. LNCS, vol. 8873, pp. 1–20. Springer, Heidelberg (2014). doi:10.1007/978-3-662-45611-8_1
9. Hopper, N.J., Blum, M.: Secure human identification protocols. In: Boyd, C. (ed.) ASIACRYPT 2001. LNCS, vol. 2248, pp. 52–66. Springer, Heidelberg (2001). doi:10.1007/3-540-45682-1_4
10. Howgrave-Graham, N., Joux, A.: New generic algorithms for hard knapsacks. In: Gilbert, H. (ed.) EUROCRYPT 2010. LNCS, vol. 6110, pp. 235–256. Springer, Heidelberg (2010). doi:10.1007/978-3-642-13190-5_12
11. Juels, A., Weis, S.A.: Authenticating pervasive devices with human protocols. In: Shoup, V. (ed.) CRYPTO 2005. LNCS, vol. 3621, pp. 293–308. Springer, Heidelberg (2005). doi:10.1007/11535218_18

12. Karp, R.M.: Reducibility among combinatorial problems. In: Miller, R.E., Thatcher, J.W., Bohlinger, J.D. (eds.) Complexity of Computer Computations. IRSS, pp. 85–103. Springer, Boston (1972). doi:10.1007/978-1-4684-2001-2_9

13. Kiltz, E., Pietrzak, K., Cash, D., Jain, A., Venturi, D.: Efficient authentication from hard learning problems. In: Paterson, K.G. (ed.) EUROCRYPT 2011. LNCS, vol. 6632, pp. 7–26. Springer, Heidelberg (2011). doi:10.1007/978-3-642-20465-4_3

14. Kirchner, P.: Improved generalized birthday attack. Cryptology ePrint Archive, Report 2011/377 (2011)

15. Levieil, É., Fouque, P.-A.: An improved LPN algorithm. In: De Prisco, R., Yung, M. (eds.) SCN 2006. LNCS, vol. 4116, pp. 348–359. Springer, Heidelberg (2006). doi:10.1007/11832072_24

16. Lindo, A., Sagitov, S.: Asymptotic results for the number of wagner's solutions to a generalised birthday problem. Stat. Probab. Lett. **107**, 356–361 (2015)

17. Lyubashevsky, V.: On random high density subset sums. In: Electronic Colloquium on Computational Complexity (ECCC), vol. 12. Citeseer (2005)

18. Lyubashevsky, V.: The parity problem in the presence of noise, decoding random linear codes, and the subset sum problem. In: Chekuri, C., Jansen, K., Rolim, J.D.P., Trevisan, L. (eds.) APPROX/RANDOM -2005. LNCS, vol. 3624, pp. 378–389. Springer, Heidelberg (2005). doi:10.1007/11538462_32

19. Lyubashevsky, V., Micciancio, D.: Generalized compact knapsacks are collision resistant. In: Bugliesi, M., Preneel, B., Sassone, V., Wegener, I. (eds.) ICALP 2006. LNCS, vol. 4052, pp. 144–155. Springer, Heidelberg (2006). doi:10.1007/11787006_13

20. Minder, L., Sinclair, A.: The extended k-tree algorithm. In: Proceedings of the Twentieth Annual ACM-SIAM Symposium on Discrete Algorithms, pp. 586–595. SIAM (2009)

21. Peikert, C.: A decade of lattice cryptography. Found. Trends Theor. Comput. Sci. **10**(4), 283–424 (2016)

22. Pietrzak, K.: Cryptography from learning parity with noise. In: Bieliková, M., Friedrich, G., Gottlob, G., Katzenbeisser, S., Turán, G. (eds.) SOFSEM 2012. LNCS, vol. 7147, pp. 99–114. Springer, Heidelberg (2012). doi:10.1007/978-3-642-27660-6_9

23. Regev, O.: On lattices, learning with errors, random linear codes, and cryptography. J. ACM (JACM) **56**(6), 34 (2009)

24. Wagner, D.: A generalized birthday problem. In: Yung, M. (ed.) CRYPTO 2002. LNCS, vol. 2442, pp. 288–304. Springer, Heidelberg (2002). doi:10.1007/3-540-45708-9_19

25. Zhang, B., Jiao, L., Wang, M.: Faster algorithms for solving LPN. In: Fischlin, M., Coron, J.-S. (eds.) EUROCRYPT 2016. LNCS, vol. 9665, pp. 168–195. Springer, Heidelberg (2016). doi:10.1007/978-3-662-49890-3_7

Can PPAD Hardness be Based on Standard Cryptographic Assumptions?

Alon Rosen[1], Gil Segev[2], and Ido Shahaf[2(✉)]

[1] Efi Arazi School of Computer Science, IDC, Herzliya, Israel
alon.rosen@idc.ac.il
[2] School of Computer Science and Engineering,
Hebrew University of Jerusalem, 91904 Jerusalem, Israel
{segev,ido.shahaf}@cs.huji.ac.il

Abstract. We consider the question of whether PPAD hardness can be based on standard cryptographic assumptions, such as the existence of one-way functions or public-key encryption. This question is particularly well-motivated in light of new devastating attacks on obfuscation candidates and their underlying building blocks, which are currently the only known source for PPAD hardness.

Central in the study of obfuscation-based PPAD hardness is the SINK-OF-VERIFIABLE-LINE (SVL) problem, an intermediate step in constructing instances of the PPAD-complete problem SOURCE-OR-SINK. Within the framework of black-box reductions we prove the following results:

- Average-case PPAD hardness (and even SVL hardness) does not imply any form of cryptographic hardness (not even one-way functions). Moreover, even when assuming the existence of one-way functions, average-case PPAD hardness (and, again, even SVL hardness) does not imply any public-key primitive. Thus, strong cryptographic assumptions (such as obfuscation-related ones) are not essential for average-case PPAD hardness.
- Average-case SVL hardness cannot be based either on standard cryptographic assumptions or on average-case PPAD hardness. In particular, average-case SVL hardness is not essential for average-case PPAD hardness.
- Any attempt for basing the average-case hardness of the PPAD-complete problem SOURCE-OR-SINK on standard cryptographic assumptions must result in instances with a nearly-exponential number of solutions. This stands in striking contrast to the obfuscation-based approach, which results in instances having a unique solution.

Taken together, our results imply that it may still be possible to base PPAD hardness on standard cryptographic assumptions, but any such black-box attempt must significantly deviate from the obfuscation-based approach: It cannot go through the SVL problem, and it must result in SOURCE-OR-SINK instances with a nearly-exponential number of solutions.

© International Association for Cryptologic Research 2017
Y. Kalai and L. Reyzin (Eds.): TCC 2017, Part II, LNCS 10678, pp. 747–776, 2017.
https://doi.org/10.1007/978-3-319-70503-3_25

1   Introduction

In recent years there has been increased interest in the computational complexity of finding a Nash equilibrium. Towards this end, Papadimitriou defined the complexity class PPAD, which consists of all TFNP problems that are polynomial-time reducible to the SOURCE-OR-SINK problem [31].[1] Papadimitriou showed that the problem of finding a Nash equilibrium is reducible to SOURCE-OR-SINK, and thus belongs to PPAD. He also conjectured that there exists a reduction in the opposite direction, and this was proved by Daskalakis, Goldberg and Papadimitriou [18], and by Chen, Deng and Teng [11]. Thus, to support the belief that finding a Nash equilibrium may indeed be computationally hard, it became sufficient to place a conjectured computationally-hard problem within the class PPAD.

Currently, no PPAD-complete problem is known to admit a sub-exponential-time algorithm. At the same time, however, we do not know how to generate instances that defeat known heuristics for these problems (see [24] for oracle-based worst-case hard instances of computing Brouwer fixed points and [36] for finding a Nash equilibrium). This leaves us in an intriguing state of affairs, in which we know of no efficient algorithms with provable worst-case guarantees, but we are yet to systematically rule out the possibility that known heuristic algorithms perform well on the average.

"Post-obfuscation" PPAD hardness. A natural approach for arguing hardness on the average would be to reduce from problems that originate from cryptography. Working in the realm of cryptography has at least two advantages. First of all, it enables us to rely on well-studied problems that are widely conjectured to be average-case hard. Secondly, and no less importantly, cryptography supplies us with frameworks for reasoning about average-case hardness. On the positive direction, such frameworks are highly suited for designing and analyzing reductions between average-case problems. On the negative direction, in some cases it is possible to argue that such "natural" reductions do not exist [27,34].

Up until recently not much progress has been made in relating between cryptography and PPAD hardness. This has changed as a result of developments in the study of obfuscation [4,19], a strong cryptographic notion with connections to the hardness of SOURCE-OR-SINK. As shown by Bitansky, Paneth and Rosen [8] the task of breaking sub-exponentially secure *indistinguishability obfuscation* can be reduced to solving SOURCE-OR-SINK. Beyond giving the first extrinsic evidence of PPAD hardness, the result of Bitansky et al. also provided the first method to sample potentially hard-on-average SOURCE-OR-SINK instances. Their result was subsequently strengthened by Garg, Pandey and Srinivasan, who based it on indistinguishability obfuscation with standard (i.e., polynomial) hardness [20].

"Pre-obfuscation" PPAD hardness? Indistinguishability obfuscation has revealed to be an exceptionally powerful primitive, with numerous far reaching

---

[1] The name END-OF-LINE is more commonly used in the literature, however SOURCE-OR-SINK is more accurately descriptive [7].

applications. However, its existence is far from being a well-established crypto-graphic assumption, certainly not nearly as well-established as the existence of one-way functions or public-key encryption. Recently, our confidence in existing indistinguishability obfuscation candidates has somewhat been shaken, following a sequence of devastating attacks on both candidate obfuscators and on their underlying building blocks (see, for example, [10, 12–15, 17, 25, 29, 30]). It thus became natural to ask:

Can average-case PPAD hardness be based on
standard cryptographic assumptions?

By standard cryptographic assumptions we are in general referring to "pre-obfuscation" type of primitives, such as the existence of one-way functions or public-key cryptography. As mentioned above, such assumptions are currently by far more well-established than indistinguishability obfuscation, and basing average-case PPAD hardness on them would make a much stronger case.

For all we know PPAD hardness may be based on the existence of one-way functions. However, if it turned out that average-case PPAD hardness implies public-key encryption, then this would indicate that basing average-case PPAD hardness on one-way functions may be extremely challenging since we currently do not know how to base public-key encryption on one-way functions (and in fact cannot do so using black-box techniques [27]). Similarly, if it turned out that average-case PPAD hardness implies indistinguishability obfuscation, this would indicate that basing average-case PPAD average on any standard cryptographic assumption would require developing radically new techniques. More generally, the stronger the implication of PPAD hardness is, the more difficult it may be to base PPAD hardness on standard assumptions. This leads us to the following second question:

Does average-case PPAD hardness imply
any form of cryptographic hardness?

As discussed above, a negative answer to the above question would actually be an encouraging sign. It would suggest, in particular, that program obfuscation is not essential for PPAD hardness, and that there may be hope to base PPAD hardness on standard cryptographic assumptions.

1.1   Our Contributions

Motivated by the above questions, we investigate the interplay between average-case PPAD hardness and standard cryptographic assumptions. We consider this interplay from the perspective of black-box reductions, the fundamental app-roach for capturing natural relations both among cryptographic primitives (e.g., [27, 28, 34]) and among complexity classes (e.g., [7, 16]).

Average-case PPAD hardness does not imply cryptographic hardness.
Our first result shows that average-case PPAD hardness does not imply any form

of cryptographic hardness in a black-box manner (not even a one-way function). In addition, our second result shows that, even when assuming the existence of one-way functions, average-case PPAD hardness does not imply any public-key primitive (not even key agreement).[2] In fact, we prove the following more general theorems by considering the SINK-OF-VERIFIABLE-LINE (SVL) problem, introduced by Abbot et al. [1] and further studied by Bitansky et al. [8] and Garg et al. [20]:

Theorem 1.1. *There is no black-box construction of a one-way function from a hard-on-average distribution of SVL instances.*

Theorem 1.2. *There is no black-box construction of a key-agreement protocol from a one-way function and a hard-on-average distribution of SVL instances.*

Abbot et al. [1] and Bitansky et al. [8] showed that any hard-on-average distribution of SVL instances can be used in a black-box manner for constructing a hard-on-average distribution of instances to a PPAD-complete problem (specifically, instances of the SOURCE-OR-SINK problem). Thus, Theorem 1.1 implies, in particular, that there is no black-box construction of a one-way function from a hard-on-average distribution of instances to a PPAD-complete problem. Similarly, Theorem 1.2 implies, in particular, that there is no black-box construction of a key-agreement protocol from a one-way function and a hard-on-average distribution of instances to a PPAD-complete problem.

As discussed in the previous section, the fact that average-case PPAD hardness does not naturally imply any form of cryptographic hardness is an encouraging sign in the pursuit of basing average-case PPAD hardness on standard cryptographic assumptions. For example, if average-case PPAD hardness would have implied program obfuscation, this would have indicated that extremely strong cryptographic assumptions are likely to be essential for average-case PPAD hardness. Similarly, if average-case PPAD hardness would have implied public-key cryptography, this would have indicated that well-structured cryptographic assumptions are essential for average-case PPAD hardness. The fact that average-case PPAD hardness does not naturally imply any form of cryptographic hardness hints that it may be possible to base average-case PPAD hardness even on the minimal (and unstructured) assumption that one-way functions exist.

PPAD hardness vs. SVL hardness. The SVL problem played a central role in the recent breakthrough of Bitansky et al. [8] and Garg et al. [20] in constructing a hard-on-average distribution of instances to a PPAD-complete problem based on indistinguishability obfuscation. Specifically, they constructed a hard-on-average distribution of SVL instances, and then reduced it to a hard-on-average distribution of SOURCE-OR-SINK instances [1,8].

We show, however, that the SVL problem is in fact far from representing PPAD hardness: Whereas Abbot et al. [1] and Bitansky et al. [8] showed that

---

[2] Recall that although indistinguishability obfuscation does not unconditionally imply the existence of one-way functions [5], it does imply public-key cryptography when assuming the existence of one-way functions [35].

the SVL problem can be efficiently reduced to the SOURCE-OR-SINK problem (even in the worst case), we show that there is no such reduction in the opposite direction (not even an average-case one). We prove the following theorem:

Theorem 1.3. *There is no black-box construction of a hard-on-average distribution of SVL instances from a hard-on-average distribution of SOURCE-OR-SINK instances. Moreover, this holds even if the underlying SOURCE-OR-SINK instances always have a unique solution.*

On basing average-case PPAD hardness on standard assumptions. Theorem 1.1 encouragingly shows that it may still be possible to base average-case PPAD hardness on standard cryptographic assumptions, but Theorem 1.3 shows that the obfuscation-based approach (which goes through the SVL problem) may not be the most effective one. Now, we show that in fact any attempt for basing average-case PPAD hardness on standard cryptographic assumptions (e.g., on one-way functions, public-key encryption, and even on injective trapdoor functions) in a black-box manner must significantly deviate from the obfuscation-based approach. Specifically, the SOURCE-OR-SINK instances resulting from that approach have exactly one solution[3], and we show that when relying on injective trapdoor functions in a black-box manner it is essential to have a nearly-exponential number of solutions. We prove the following theorem:

Theorem 1.4. *There is no black-box construction of a hard-on-average distribution of SOURCE-OR-SINK instances over $\{0,1\}^n$ with $2^{n^{o(1)}}$ solutions from injective trapdoor functions.*

In particular, since Abbot et al. [1] and Bitansky et al. [8] showed that hard-on-average SVL instances lead to hard-on-average SOURCE-OR-SINK instances *having a unique solution*, Theorem 1.4 implies the following corollary which, when combined with Theorem 1.1, shows that average-case SVL hardness is essentially incomparable to standard cryptographic assumptions.

Corollary 1.5. *There is no black-box construction of hard-on-average distribution of SVL instances from injective trapdoor functions.*

More generally, although Theorem 1.4 and Corollary 1.5 focus on injective trapdoor functions, our impossibility result holds for a richer and larger class of building blocks. Specifically, it holds for any primitive that exists relative to a random injective trapdoor function oracle. Thus, Theorem 1.4 and Corollary 1.5 hold, for example, also for collision-resistant hash functions (which are not implied by one-way functions or injective trapdoor functions in a black-box manner [23,37]).

Taken together, our results imply that it may be possible to base average-case PPAD hardness on standard cryptographic assumptions, but any black-box attempt must significantly deviate from the obfuscation-based approach:

---

[3] Unless, of course, one allows for artificial manipulations of the instances to generate multiple (strongly related) solutions.

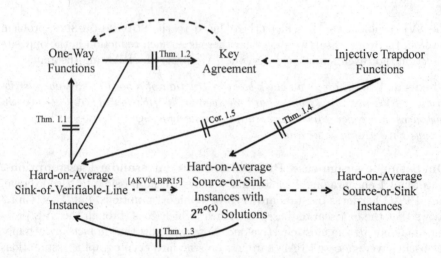

Fig. 1. An illustration of our results. Dashed arrows correspond to known implications, and solid arrows correspond to our separations.

It cannot go through the SVL problem, and it must result in SOURCE-OR-SINK instances with a nearly-exponential number of solutions. See Fig. 1 for an illustration of our results.

A wider perspective: From Rudich's impossibility to structured building blocks and bounded-TFNP hardness. Our results apply to a wide class of search problems, and not only to the specific SOURCE-OR-SINK and SVL problems. We consider the notion of TFNP instances with a guaranteed (non-trivial) upper bound on their number of existing solutions, to which we refer as *bounded-*TFNP instances. This captures, in particular, SOURCE-OR-SINK instances and (valid) SVL instances, and provides a more general and useful perspective for studying cryptographic limitations in constructing hard instances of search problems.

Equipped with such a wide perspective, our approach and proof techniques build upon, and significantly extend, Rudich's classic proof for ruling out black-box constructions of one-way permutations based on one-way functions [34]. We extend Rudich's approach from its somewhat restricted context of one-way functions (as building blocks) and one-way permutations (as target objects) to provide a richer framework that considers: (1) *significantly more structured* building blocks, and (2) *significantly less restricted* target objects. Specifically, we bound the limitations of hard-on-average SOURCE-OR-SINK and SVL instances as building blocks (instead of one-way functions), and we rule out bounded-TFNP instances as target objects (instead of one-way permutations).

1.2 Open Problems

Several interesting open problems arise directly from our results, and here we point out some of them.

- The strong structural barrier put forward in Theorem 1.4 stands in stark contrast to the approach of Bitansky et al. [8] and Garg et al. [20]. Thus, an intriguing open problem is either to extend our impossibility result to rule out constructions with any number of solutions, or to circumvent our impossibility result by designing instances with an nearly-exponential number of solutions based on standard cryptographic assumptions.
- More generally, the question of circumventing black-box impossibility results by utilizing non-black-box techniques is always fascinating. In our specific context, already the obfuscation-based constructions of Bitansky et al. [8] and Garg et al. [20] involve non-black-box techniques (e.g., they apply an indistinguishability obfuscator to a circuit that uses a pseudorandom function). However, as recently shown by Asharov and Segev [2,3], as long as the indistinguishability obfuscator itself is used in a black-box manner, such techniques can in fact be captured by refining the existing frameworks for black-box separations (specifically, the framework of Asharov and Segev captures the obfuscation-based constructions of Bitansky et al. [8] and Garg et al. [20]). Thus, an exciting open problem is to circumvent our results by utilizing non-black-box techniques while relying on standard cryptographic assumptions.
- Our impossibility results in Theorem 1.4 and Corollary 1.5 apply to any building block that exists relative to a random injective trapdoor function oracle (e.g., a collision-resistent hash function). It is not clear, however, whether similar impossibility results may apply to one-way *permutations*. Thus, an intriguing open problem is either to extend our impossibility results to rule out constructions based on one-way permutations, or to circumvent our impossibility results by designing hard-on-average instances based on one-way permutations. We note that by relying on one-way permutations it is rather trivial to construct some arbitrary hard-on-average TFNP distribution (even one with unique solutions), but it is not known how to construct less arbitrary forms of hardness, such as average-case PPAD or SVL hardness.
- The recent work of Hubáček, Naor, and Yogev [26] proposes two elegant approaches for constructing hard-on-average TFNP instances. Their first approach is based on any hard-on-average NP relation (the existence of which is implied, for example, by any one-way function) in a black-box manner, and results in TFNP instances with a possibly exponential number of solutions. Their second approach is based on any injective one-way function and a non-interactive witness-indistinguishable proof system for NP (which can be constructed based on trapdoor permutations), and results in TFNP instances having at most two solutions. An interesting question is whether their approaches imply not only average-case TFNP hardness for the particular problems defined by their underlying one-way function and proof system, but also more specific forms of TFNP hardness, such as average-case PPAD or SVL hardness.

1.3   Overview of Our Approach

In this section we provide a high-level overview of the main ideas underlying our results. Each of our results is of the form "the existence of P does not imply the existence of Q in a black-box manner", where each of P and Q is either a cryptographic primitive (e.g., a one-way function) or a hard-on-average search problem (e.g., the source-or-sink problem). Intuitively, such a statement is proved by constructing a distribution over oracles relative to which there exists an implementation of P, but any implementation of Q can be "efficiently broken". Our formal proofs properly formalize this intuition via the standard framework of black-box reductions (e.g., [21, 27, 28, 32]).

Average-case SVL hardness does not imply OWFs. Theorem 1.1 is proved by presenting a distribution of oracles relative to which there exists a hard-on-average distribution of SVL instances, but there are no one-way functions. An SVL instance is of the form $\{(\mathsf{S}_n, \mathsf{V}_n, L(n))\}_{n \in \mathbb{N}}$, where for every $n \in \mathbb{N}$ it holds that $\mathsf{S}_n : \{0,1\}^n \to \{0,1\}^n$, $\mathsf{V}_n : \{0,1\}^n \times [2^n] \to \{0,1\}$, and $L(n) \in [2^n]$. Such an instance is *valid* if for every $n \in \mathbb{N}$, $x \in \{0,1\}^n$, and $i \in [2^n]$, it holds that $\mathsf{V}_n(x, i) = 1$ if and only if $x = \mathsf{S}_n^i(0^n)$. Intuitively, the circuit S_n can be viewed as implementing the successor function of a directed graph over $\{0,1\}^n$ that consists of a single line starting at 0^n, and the circuit V_n enables to efficiently test whether a given node x is of distance i from 0^n on the line. The goal is to find the node of distance $L(n)$ from 0^n (see Sect. 2.1 for the formal definition of the SVL problem).

We consider an oracle that is a valid SVL instance $\mathcal{O}_{\mathsf{SVL}}$ corresponding to a graph with a single line $0^n \to x_1 \to \cdots \to x_{L(n)}$ of length $L(n) = 2^{n/2}$. The line is chosen uniformly among all lines in $\{0,1\}^n$ of length $L(n)$ starting at 0^n (and all nodes outside the line have self loops and are essentially irrelevant). First, we show that the oracle $\mathcal{O}_{\mathsf{SVL}}$ is indeed a hard-on-average SVL instance. This is based on the following, rather intuitive, observation: Since the line $0^n \to x_1 \to \cdots \to x_{L(n)}$ is *sparse* and *uniformly sampled*, then any algorithm performing $q = q(n)$ oracle queries should not be able to query $\mathcal{O}_{\mathsf{SVL}}$ with any element on the line beyond the first q elements $0^n, x_1, \ldots, x_{q-1}$. In particular, for our choice of parameters, any algorithm performing at most, say, $2^{n/4}$ queries, has only an exponentially-small probability of reaching $x_{L(n)}$ (where the probability is taken over the choice of the oracle $\mathcal{O}_{\mathsf{SVL}}$).

Then, we show that any oracle-aided function $F^{\mathcal{O}_{\mathsf{SVL}}}(\cdot)$ can be inverted (with high probability over the choice of the oracle $\mathcal{O}_{\mathsf{SVL}}$) by an algorithm whose query complexity is polynomially-related to that of the function $F^{\mathcal{O}_{\mathsf{SVL}}}(\cdot)$. The proof is based on the following approach. Consider a value $y = F^{\mathcal{O}_{\mathsf{SVL}}}(x)$ that we would like to invert. If F performs at most $q = q(n)$ oracle queries, the above-mentioned observation implies that the computation $F^{\mathcal{O}_{\mathsf{SVL}}}(x)$ should not query $\mathcal{O}_{\mathsf{SVL}}$ with any elements on the line $0^n \to x_1 \to \cdots \to x_{L(n)}$ except for the first q elements $x_0, x_1, \ldots, x_{q-1}$. This observation gives rise to the following inverter $\mathcal{A}$: First perform q queries to $\mathcal{O}_{\mathsf{SVL}}$ for discovering $x_1, \ldots, x_q$, and then invert $y = F^{\mathcal{O}_{\mathsf{SVL}}}(x)$ relative to the oracle $\widetilde{\mathcal{O}_{\mathsf{SVL}}}$ defined via the following successor function $\widetilde{\mathsf{S}}$:

$$\widetilde{\mathsf{S}}(\alpha) = \begin{cases} x_{i+1} \text{ if } \alpha = x_i \text{ for some } i \in \{0, \ldots, q-1\} \\ \alpha \quad \text{otherwise} \end{cases}.$$

The formal proof is in fact more subtle, and requires a significant amount of caution when inverting $y = F^{\mathcal{O}_{\mathsf{SVL}}}(x)$ relative to the oracle $\widetilde{\mathcal{O}_{\mathsf{SVL}}}$. Specifically, the inverter $\mathcal{A}$ should find an input $\widetilde{x}$ such that the computations $F^{\widetilde{\mathcal{O}_{\mathsf{SVL}}}}(\widetilde{x})$ and $F^{\mathcal{O}_{\mathsf{SVL}}}(\widetilde{x})$ do not query the oracles $\widetilde{\mathcal{O}_{\mathsf{SVL}}}$ and $\mathcal{O}_{\mathsf{SVL}}$, respectively, with any of $x_q, \ldots, x_{L(n)}$. In this case, we show that indeed $F^{\mathcal{O}_{\mathsf{SVL}}}(\widetilde{x}) = y$ and the inverter is successful. We refer the reader to Sect. 3 for more details and for the formal proof.

Average-case SVL hardness and OWFs do not imply key agreement. Theorem 1.2 is proved by showing that in any black-box construction of a key-agreement protocol based on a one-way function and a hard-on-average distribution of SVL instances, we can eliminate the protocol's need for using the SVL instances. This leads to a black-box construction of key-agreement protocol based on a one-way function, which we can then rule out by invoking the classic result of Impagliazzo and Rudich [27] and its refinement by Barak and Mahmoody-Ghidary [6].

Specifically, consider a key-agreement protocol $(\mathcal{A}^{f,\mathcal{O}_{\mathsf{SVL}}}, \mathcal{B}^{f,\mathcal{O}_{\mathsf{SVL}}})$ in which the parties have oracle access to a random function f and to the oracle $\mathcal{O}_{\mathsf{SVL}}$ used for proving Theorem 1.1. Then, if $\mathcal{A}$ and $\mathcal{B}$ perform at most $q = q(n)$ oracle queries, the observation underlying the proof of Theorem 1.1 implies that, during an execution $(\mathcal{A}^{f,\mathcal{O}_{\mathsf{SVL}}}, \mathcal{B}^{f,\mathcal{O}_{\mathsf{SVL}}})$ of the protocol, the parties should not query $\mathcal{O}_{\mathsf{SVL}}$ with any elements on the line $0^n \to x_1 \to \cdots \to x_{L(n)}$ except for the first q elements $x_0, x_1, \ldots, x_{q-1}$. This observation gives rise to a key-agreement protocol $(\widetilde{\mathcal{A}}^f, \widetilde{\mathcal{B}}^f)$ that does not require access to the oracle $\mathcal{O}_{\mathsf{SVL}}$: First, $\widetilde{\mathcal{A}}$ samples a sequence $x_1, \ldots, x_q$ of q values, and sends these values to $\widetilde{\mathcal{B}}$. Then, $\widetilde{\mathcal{A}}$ and $\widetilde{\mathcal{B}}$ run the protocol $(\mathcal{A}^{f,\mathcal{O}_{\mathsf{SVL}}}, \mathcal{B}^{f,\mathcal{O}_{\mathsf{SVL}}})$ by using the values $x_1, \ldots, x_q$ instead of accessing $\mathcal{O}_{\mathsf{SVL}}$. That is, $\widetilde{\mathcal{A}}$ and $\widetilde{\mathcal{B}}$ run the underlying protocol relative to the given oracle f and to the oracle $\widetilde{\mathcal{O}_{\mathsf{SVL}}}$ defined via the following successor function $\widetilde{\mathsf{S}}$ (which each party can compute on its own):

$$\widetilde{\mathsf{S}}(\alpha) = \begin{cases} x_{i+1} \text{ if } \alpha = x_i \text{ for some } i \in \{0, \ldots, q-1\} \\ \alpha \quad \text{otherwise} \end{cases}.$$

The formal proof is again rather subtle, and we refer the reader to the full version of this paper [33] for the formal proof.

Average-case PPAD hardness does not imply unique-TFNP hardness. Theorem 1.3 is proved by presenting a distribution of oracles relative to which there exists a hard-on-average distribution of instances of a PPAD-complete problem (specifically, we consider the source-or-sink problem), but there are no hard TFNP instances having unique solutions.

A TFNP instance with a unique solution, denoted a unique-TFNP instance, is of the form $\{C_n\}_{n \in \mathbb{N}}$, where for every $n \in \mathbb{N}$ it holds that $C_n : \{0,1\}^n \to \{0,1\}$ and there is a unique $x^* \in \{0,1\}^n$ such that $C(x) = 1$. Note that any *valid* SVL instance yields a TFNP instance that has a unique solution. Therefore, relative to our distribution over oracles any valid SVL instance can be efficiently solved.

A source-or-sink instance is of the form $\{(S_n, P_n)\}_{n \in \mathbb{N}}$, where for every $n \in \mathbb{N}$ it holds that $S_n : \{0,1\}^n \to \{0,1\}^n$ and $P_n : \{0,1\}^n \to \{0,1\}^n$. Intuitively, the circuits S_n and P_n can be viewed as implementing the successor and predecessor functions of a directed graph over $\{0,1\}^n$, where the in-degree and out-degree of every node is at most one, and the in-degree of 0^n is 0 (i.e., it is a source). The goal is to find any node, other than 0^n, with either no incoming edge and no outgoing edge. We again refer the reader to Sect. 2.1 for the formal definitions.

We consider an oracle that is a source-or-sink instance $\mathcal{O}_{\mathsf{PPAD}}$ which is based on the same sparse structure used to define the oracle $\mathcal{O}_{\mathsf{SVL}}$: It corresponds to a graph with a single line $0^n \to x_1 \to \cdots \to x_{L(n)}$ of length $L(n) = 2^{n/2}$. The line is chosen uniformly among all lines in $\{0,1\}^n$ of length $L(n)$ starting at 0^n (and all nodes outside the line have self loops). The fact that the oracle $\mathcal{O}_{\mathsf{PPAD}}$ is a hard-on-average source-or-sink instance follows quite easily from the above-mentioned observation on its sparse and uniform structure: Any algorithm performing $q = q(n)$ oracle queries should not be able to query $\mathcal{O}_{\mathsf{PPAD}}$ with any element on the line beyond the first q elements $x_0, x_1, \ldots, x_{q-1}$. In particular, for our choice of parameters, any such algorithm should have only an exponentially-small probability of reaching $x_{L(n)}$.

Solving any oracle-aided unique-TFNP instance relative to $\mathcal{O}_{\mathsf{PPAD}}$, however, turns out to be a completely different challenge. One might be tempted to follow a same approach based on the oracle's sparse and uniform structure. Specifically, let C_n be a unique-TFNP instance, and consider the unique value $x^* \in \{0,1\}^n$ for which $C_n^{\mathcal{O}_{\mathsf{PPAD}}}(x^*) = 1$. Then, if C_n issues at most $q = q(n)$ oracle queries, the computation $C_n^{\mathcal{O}_{\mathsf{PPAD}}}(x^*)$ should essentially not be able to query $\mathcal{O}_{\mathsf{PPAD}}$ with any elements on the line $0^n \to x_1 \to \cdots \to x_{L(n)}$ except for the first q elements $0^n, x_1, \ldots, x_{q-1}$. Therefore, one can define a "fake" oracle $\widetilde{\mathcal{O}_{\mathsf{PPAD}}}$ whose successor and predecessor functions agree with $\mathcal{O}_{\mathsf{PPAD}}$ on $0^n, x_1, \ldots, x_q$ (and are defined as the identity functions for all other inputs), and then find the unique $\widetilde{x}$ such that $C_n^{\widetilde{\mathcal{O}_{\mathsf{PPAD}}}}(\widetilde{x}) = 1$. This approach, however, completely fails since the solution x^* itself may depend on $\mathcal{O}_{\mathsf{PPAD}}$ in an arbitrary manner, providing the computation $C_n^{\mathcal{O}_{\mathsf{PPAD}}}(x^*)$ with sufficient information for querying $\mathcal{O}_{\mathsf{PPAD}}$ with an input x_i that is located further along the line (i.e., $q \le i \le L(n)$).

As discussed in Sect. 1.1, our proof is obtained by significantly extending Rudich's classic proof for ruling out black-box constructions of one-way permutations based on one-way functions [34]. Here, we show that his approach provides a rich framework that allows to bound not only the limitations of one-way functions as a building block, but even the limitations of *significantly more structured* primitives as building blocks. Specifically, our proof of Theorem 1.3 generalizes Rudich's technique for bounding the limitations of hard-on-average source-or-sink instances. We refer the reader to Sect. 4 for more details and for the formal proof.

Injective trapdoor functions do not imply bounded-TFNP hardness. Theorem 1.4 and Corollary 1.5 are proved by presenting a distribution of oracles relative to which there exists a collection of injective trapdoor functions, but there are no hard TFNP instances having a bounded number of solutions (specifically, our result will apply to a sub-exponential number of solutions).

A TFNP instance with bounded number $k(\cdot)$ of solutions, denoted a k-bounded TFNP instance, is of the form $\{C_n\}_{n \in \mathbb{N}}$, where for every $n \in \mathbb{N}$ it holds that $C : \{0,1\}^n \to \{0,1\}$, and there is at least one and at most $k(n)$ distinct inputs $x \in \{0,1\}^n$ such that $C(x) = 1$ (any one of these x's is a solution). In particular, as discussed above, any *valid* SVL instance yields a 1-bounded TFNP instance (i.e., a unique-TFNP instance), and therefore our result rules out black-box constructions of a hard-on-average distribution of SVL instances from injective trapdoor functions. Similarly, any source-or-sink instance which consists of at most $(k + 1)/2$ disjoint lines yields a k-bounded TFNP instance, and therefore our result rules out black-box constructions of a hard-on-average distribution of source-or-sink instances with a bounded number of disjoint lines from injective trapdoor functions.

For emphasizing the main ideas underlying our proof, in Sect. 5 we first prove our result for constructions that are based on one-way functions, and then in Sect. 6 we generalize the proof to constructions that are based on injective trapdoor functions. Each of these two parts requires introducing new ideas and techniques, and such a level of modularity is useful in pointing them out.

When considering constructions that are based on one-way functions, our proof is obtained via an additional generalization of Rudich's proof technique [34]. As discussed above, we first observe that Rudich's approach can be generalized from ruling out constructions of one-way permutations based on one-way functions to ruling out constructions of any hard-on-average distribution of unique-TFNP instances based on one-way functions. Then, by extending and refining Rudich's proof technique once again, we show that we can rule out not only constructions of unique-TFNP instances, but even constructions of bounded-TFNP instances. This require a substantial generalization of Rudich's attacker, and we refer reader to Sect. 5 for more details and for the formal proof.

Then, when considering constructions that are based on injective trapdoor functions, we show that our proof from Sect. 5 can be generalized from constructions of bounded-TFNP instances based on one-way functions to constructions of bounded-TFNP instances based on injective trapdoor functions. Combined with our the proof of Theorem 1.3, this extends Rudich's approach from its somewhat restricted context of one-way functions (as building blocks) and one-way permutations (as target objects) to provide a richer framework that considers: (1) *significantly more structured* building blocks, and (2) *significantly less restricted* target objects. We refer reader to Sect. 6 for more details and for the formal proof.

1.4   Paper Organization

The remainder of this paper is organized as follows. In Sect. 2 we introduce our notation as well as the search problems and the cryptographic primitives that we consider in this paper. In Sect. 3 we show that average-case SVL hardness does not imply one-way functions in a black-box manner (proving Theorem 1.1). In Sect. 4 we show that average-case PPAD hardness does not imply unique-TFNP hardness in a black-box manner (proving Theorem 1.3). In Sect. 5 we show that one-way functions do not imply bounded-TFNP hardness in a black-box manner, and in Sect. 6 we generalize this result, showing that even injective trapdoor functions do not imply bounded-TFNP hardness in a black-box manner (proving Theorem 1.4 and Corollary 1.5). In the full version of this paper [33] we extend our approach from Sect. 3 and show that average-case SVL hardness does not imply key agreement even when assuming the existence of one-way functions.

2   Preliminaries

In this section we present the notation and basic definitions that are used in this work. For a distribution X we denote by $x \leftarrow X$ the process of sampling a value x from the distribution X. Similarly, for a set $\mathcal{X}$ we denote by $x \leftarrow \mathcal{X}$ the process of sampling a value x from the uniform distribution over $\mathcal{X}$. For an integer $n \in \mathbb{N}$ we denote by $[n]$ the set $\{1, \ldots, n\}$. A q-query algorithm is an oracle-aided algorithm A such that for any oracle $\mathcal{O}$ and input $x \in \{0,1\}^*$, the computation $A^{\mathcal{O}}(x)$ consists of at most $q(|x|)$ oracle calls to $\mathcal{O}$.

2.1   Complexity Classes and Total Search Problems

An efficiently-verifiable search problem is described via a pair (I, R), where $I \subseteq \{0,1\}^*$ is an efficiently-recognizable set of instances, and R is an efficiently-computable binary relation. Such a search problem is *total* if for every instance $z \in I$ there exists a witness w of length polynomial in the length z such that $R(z, w) = 1$.

The class TFNP consists of all efficiently-verifiable search problem that are total, and its sub-class PPAD consists of all such problems that are polynomial-time reducible to the source-or-sink problem [31], defined as follows.

Definition 2.1 (The source-or-sink problem). *A source-or-sink instance consists of a pair of circuits* $S, P : \{0,1\}^n \to \{0,1\}^n$ *such that* $P(0^n) = 0^n \neq S(0^n)$. *The goal is to find an element* $w \in \{0,1\}^n$ *such that* $P(S(w)) \neq w$ *or* $S(P(w)) \neq w \neq 0^n$.

Intuitively, the circuits S and P can be viewed as implementing the successor and predecessor functions of a directed graph over $\{0,1\}^n$, where for each pair of nodes x and y there exists an edge from x to y if and only if $S(x) = y$ and $P(y) = x$ (note that the in-degree and out-degree of every node in this graph is at most one, and the in-degree of 0^n is 0). The goal is to find any node, other than 0^n, with either no incoming edge or no outgoing edge. Such a node must always exist by a parity argument.

The sink-of-verifiable-line (SVL) problem is a search problem introduced by Abbot et al. [1] and further studied by Bitansky et al. [8] and Garg et al. [20]. It is defined as follows:

Definition 2.2 (The sink-of-verifiable-line (SVL) problem). *An SVL instance consists of a triplet* (S, V, T), *where* $T \in [2^n]$, *and* $S : \{0,1\}^n \to \{0,1\}^n$ *and* $V : \{0,1\}^n \times [2^n] \to \{0,1\}$ *are two circuits with the guarantee that for every* $x \in \{0,1\}^n$ *and* $i \in [2^n]$ *it holds that* $V(x,i) = 1$ *if and only if* $x = S^i(0^n)$. *The goal is to find an element* $w \in \{0,1\}^n$ *such that* $V(w,T) = 1$.

Intuitively, the circuit S can be viewed as implementing the successor function of a directed graph over $\{0,1\}^n$ that consists of a single line starting at 0^n. The circuit V enables to efficiently test whether a given node x is of distance i from 0^n on the line, and the goal is to find the node of distance T from 0^n. Note that not any triplet (S, V, T) is a *valid* SVL instance (moreover, there may not be an efficient algorithm for verifying whether a triplet (S, V, T) is a valid instance).

Oracle-aided instances with private randomness. We consider source-or-sink and SVL instances that are described by oracle-aided circuits, and we would like to allow these circuits to share an oracle-dependent state that may be generated via private randomness (this clearly strengthens the class of problems that we consider, and in particular, capture those constructed by [8,20] using indistinguishability obfuscation). For this purpose, we equip the instances with an oracle-aided randomized index-generation algorithm, denoted Gen, that produces a public index σ which is then provided to all circuits of the instance (and to any algorithm that attempts to solve the instance).

Specifically, we consider source-or-sink instances of the form $\{((\mathsf{Gen}_n, \mathsf{S}_n, \mathsf{P}_n)\}_{n \in \mathbb{N}}$, where for every $n \in \mathbb{N}$ and for every index σ produced by Gen_n it holds that $\mathsf{S}_n(\sigma, \cdot) : \{0,1\}^n \to \{0,1\}^n$ and $\mathsf{P}_n(\sigma, \cdot) : \{0,1\}^n \to \{0,1\}^n$. Similarly, we consider SVL instances of the form $\{(\mathsf{Gen}_n, \mathsf{S}_n, \mathsf{V}_n, T(n))\}_{n \in \mathbb{N}}$, where for every $n \in \mathbb{N}$ and for every index σ produced by Gen_n it holds that $\mathsf{S}_n(\sigma, \cdot) : \{0,1\}^n \to \{0,1\}^n$, $\mathsf{V}_n(\sigma, \cdot, \cdot) : \{0,1\}^n \times [2^n] \to \{0,1\}$, and $T(n) \in [2^n]$. We say that an SVL instance is *valid* if for every $n \in \mathbb{N}$, σ produced by Gen_n, $x \in \{0,1\}^n$, and $i \in [2^n]$, it holds that $\mathsf{V}_n(\sigma, x, i) = 1$ if and only if $x = \mathsf{S}_n^i(\sigma, 0^n)$.

Bounded TFNP instances. As discussed in Sect. 1.1, we prove our results using the notion of *bounded*-TFNP instances, naturally generalizing source-or-sink instances (and valid SVL instances) by considering TFNP instances with a guaranteed upper bound on the number of solutions.

Definition 2.3. *A k-bounded TFNP instance is of the form* $\{\mathsf{Gen}_n, C_n\}_{n \in \mathbb{N}}$, *where for every* $n \in \mathbb{N}$ *and for every index* σ *produced by* Gen_n *it holds that* $C_n(\sigma, \cdot) : \{0,1\}^n \to \{0,1\}$, *and there is at least one and at most $k(n)$ distinct inputs* $x \in \{0,1\}^n$ *such that* $C_n(\sigma, x) = 1$ *(any one of these x's is a solution).*

Note that any *valid* SVL instance yields a 1-bounded TFNP instance (to which we refer as a *unique*-TFNP instance), and any source-or-sink instance which consists of at most $(k + 1)/2$ disjoint lines yields a k-bounded TFNP instance.

Average-case PPAD hardness and bound-TFNP hardness. The following two definitions formalize the standard notion of average-case hardness in the specific context of source-or-sink instances and k-bounded TFNP instances. These notions then serve as the basis of our definitions of black-box constructions.

Definition 2.4. *Let $t = t(n)$ and $\epsilon = \epsilon(n)$ be functions of the security parameter $n \in \mathbb{N}$. A source-or-sink instance $\{(\mathsf{Gen}_n, \mathsf{S}_n, \mathsf{P}_n)\}_{n \in \mathbb{N}}$ is (t, ϵ)-hard if for any algorithm $\mathcal{A}$ that runs in time $t(n)$ it holds that*

$$\Pr\left[\mathcal{A}\left(1^n, \sigma\right) = w \text{ s.t. } \mathsf{P}_n(\sigma, \mathsf{S}_n(\sigma, w)) \neq w \text{ or } \mathsf{S}_n(\sigma, \mathsf{P}_n(\sigma, w)) \neq w \neq 0^n\right] \leq \epsilon(n)$$

for infinitely many values of $n \in \mathbb{N}$, where the probability is taken over the choice of $\sigma \leftarrow \mathsf{Gen}_n()$ and over the internal randomness of $\mathcal{A}$.

Definition 2.5. *Let $k = k(n)$, $t = t(n)$ and $\epsilon = \epsilon(n)$ be functions of the security parameter $n \in \mathbb{N}$. A k-bounded TFNP instance $\{\mathsf{Gen}_n, C_n\}_{n \in \mathbb{N}}$ is (t, ϵ)-hard if for any algorithm $\mathcal{A}$ that runs in time $t(n)$ it holds that*

$$\Pr\left[\mathcal{A}\left(1^n, \sigma\right) = x \text{ s.t. } C_n(\sigma, x) = 1\right] \leq \epsilon(n)$$

for infinitely many values of $n \in \mathbb{N}$, where the probability is taken over the choice of $\sigma \leftarrow \mathsf{Gen}_n()$ and over the internal randomness of $\mathcal{A}$.

2.2 One-Way Functions and Injective Trapdoor Functions

We rely on the standard (parameterized) notions of a one-way function and injective trapdoor functions [22].

Definition 2.6. *An efficiently-computable function $f : \{0,1\}^* \to \{0,1\}^*$ is $(t(\cdot), \epsilon(\cdot))$-one-way if for any probabilistic algorithm A that runs in time $t(n)$ it holds that*

$$\Pr\left[A\left(f(x)\right) \in f^{-1}\left(f(x)\right)\right] \leq \epsilon(n)$$

for all sufficiently large $n \in \mathbb{N}$, where the probability is taken over the choice of $x \leftarrow \{0,1\}^n$ and over the internal randomness of A.

A collection of injective trapdoor functions is a triplet $(\mathsf{KG}, \mathsf{F}, \mathsf{F}^{-1})$ of polynomial-time algorithms. The key-generation algorithm KG is a probabilistic algorithm that on input the security parameter 1^n outputs a pair $(\mathsf{pk}, \mathsf{td})$, where pk is a public key and td is a corresponding trapdoor. For any $n \in \mathbb{N}$ and for any pair $(\mathsf{pk}, \mathsf{td})$ that is produced by $\mathsf{KG}(1^n)$, the evaluation algorithm F computes an injective function $\mathsf{F}(\mathsf{pk}, \cdot) : \{0,1\}^n \to \{0,1\}^{\ell(n)}$, and the inversion algorithm $F^{-1}(\mathsf{td}, \cdot) : \{0,1\}^{\ell(n)} \to \{0,1\}^n \cup \{\bot\}$ computes its inverse whenever an inverse exists (i.e., it outputs $\bot$ on all values y that are not in the image of the function $\mathsf{F}(\mathsf{pk}, \cdot)$). The security requirement of injective trapdoor functions is formalized as follows:

Definition 2.7. *A collection of injective trapdoor functions $(\mathsf{KG}, \mathsf{F}, \mathsf{F}^{-1})$ is $(t(\cdot), \epsilon(\cdot))$-secure if for any probabilistic algorithm A that runs in time $t(n)$ it holds that*

$$\Pr\left[A\left(\mathsf{pk}, \mathsf{F}(\mathsf{pk}, x)\right) = x\right] \leq \epsilon(n)$$

for all sufficiently large $n \in \mathbb{N}$, where the probability is taken over the choice of $(\mathsf{pk}, \mathsf{td}) \leftarrow \mathsf{KG}(1^n)$, $x \leftarrow \{0,1\}^n$, and over the internal randomness of A.

3   Average-Case SVL Hardness Does Not Imply One-Way Functions

In this section we prove that there is no fully black-box construction of a one-way function from a hard-on-average distribution of SVL instances[4] (proving Theorem 1.1). Our result is obtained by presenting a distribution of oracles relative to which the following two properties hold:

1. There exists a hard-on-average distribution of SVL instances.
2. There are no one-way functions.

Recall that an SVL instance is of the form $\{(\mathsf{Gen}_n, \mathsf{S}_n, \mathsf{V}_n, L(n))\}_{n\in\mathbb{N}}$, where for every $n \in \mathbb{N}$ and for every index σ produced by Gen_n it holds that $\mathsf{S}_n(\sigma, \cdot) : \{0,1\}^n \to \{0,1\}^n$, $\mathsf{V}_n(\sigma, \cdot, \cdot) : \{0,1\}^n \times [2^n] \to \{0,1\}$, and $L(n) \in [2^n]$. We say that an SVL instance is *valid* if for every $n \in \mathbb{N}$, σ produced by Gen_n, $x \in \{0,1\}^n$, and $i \in [2^n]$, it holds that $\mathsf{V}_n(\sigma, x, i) = 1$ if and only if $x = \mathsf{S}_n^i(\sigma, 0^n)$. The following definition tailors the standard notion of a fully black-box construction (based, for example, on [21,28,32]) to the specific primitives under consideration.

Definition 3.1. *A fully black-box construction of a one-way function from a hard-on-average distribution of SVL instances consists of an oracle-aided polynomial-time algorithm F, an oracle-aided algorithm M that runs in time $T_M(\cdot)$, and functions $\epsilon_{M,1}(\cdot)$ and $\epsilon_{M,2}(\cdot)$, such that the following conditions hold:*

- **Correctness**: *There exists a polynomial $\ell(\cdot)$ such that for any valid SVL instance $\mathcal{O}_{\mathsf{SVL}}$ and for any $x \in \{0,1\}^*$ it holds that $F^{\mathcal{O}_{\mathsf{SVL}}}(x) \in \{0,1\}^{\ell(|x|)}$.*
- **Black-box proof of security**: *For any valid SVL instance $\mathcal{O}_{\mathsf{SVL}} = \{(\mathsf{Gen}_n, \mathsf{S}_n, \mathsf{V}_n, L(n))\}_{n\in\mathbb{N}}$, for any oracle-aided algorithm $\mathcal{A}$ that runs in time $T_\mathcal{A} = T_\mathcal{A}(n)$, and for any function $\epsilon_\mathcal{A}(\cdot)$, if*

$$\Pr\left[\mathcal{A}^{\mathcal{O}_{\mathsf{SVL}}}\left(F^{\mathcal{O}_{\mathsf{SVL}}}(x)\right) \in \left(F^{\mathcal{O}_{\mathsf{SVL}}}\right)^{-1}\left(F^{\mathcal{O}_{\mathsf{SVL}}}(x)\right)\right] \geq \epsilon_\mathcal{A}(n)$$

for infinitely many values of $n \in \mathbb{N}$, where the probability is taken over the choice of $x \leftarrow \{0,1\}^n$ and over the internal randomness of $\mathcal{A}$, then

$$\Pr\left[M^{\mathcal{A},\mathcal{O}_{\mathsf{SVL}}}(1^n, \sigma) \text{ solves } (\mathsf{S}_n(\sigma, \cdot), \mathsf{V}_n(\sigma, \cdot), L(n))\right]$$
$$\geq \epsilon_{M,1}(T_\mathcal{A}(n)/\epsilon_\mathcal{A}(n)) \cdot \epsilon_{M,2}(n)$$

for infinitely many values of $n \in \mathbb{N}$, where the probability is taken over the choice of $\sigma \leftarrow \mathsf{Gen}_n()$ and over the internal randomness of M.

Following Asharov and Segev [2,3], we split the security loss in the above definition to an adversary-dependent security loss and an adversary-independent

---

[4] Recall that any hard-on-average distribution of SVL instances can be used in a black-box manner to construct a hard-on-average distribution of instances of a PPAD-complete problem [1,8]. Thus, our result implies (in particular) that average-case PPAD hardness does not imply one-way functions in a black-box manner.

security loss, as this allows us to capture constructions where one of these losses is super-polynomial whereas the other is polynomial (e.g., [8,9]). In addition, we note that the correctness requirement in the above definition may seem somewhat trivial since the fact that the output length of $F^{\mathcal{O}_{SVL}}(\cdot)$ is polynomial follows directly from the requirement that F runs in polynomial time. However, for avoiding rather trivial technical complications in the proofs of this section, for simplicity (and without loss of generality) we nevertheless ask explicitly that the output length is some fixed polynomial $\ell(n)$ for any input length n (clearly, $\ell(n)$ may depend on the running time of F, and shorter outputs can always be padded). Equipped with the above definition we prove the following theorem in the full version of this paper [33]:

Theorem 3.2. *Let $(F, M, T_M, \epsilon_{M,1}, \epsilon_{M,2})$ be a fully black-box construction of a one-way function from a hard-on-average SVL instance. Then, at least one of the following properties holds:*

1. *$T_M(n) \geq 2^{\zeta n}$ for some constant $\zeta > 0$ (i.e., the reduction runs in exponential time).*
2. *$\epsilon_{M,1}(n^c) \cdot \epsilon_{M,2}(n) \leq 2^{-n/10}$ for some constant $c > 1$ (i.e., the security loss is exponential).*

In particular, Theorem 3.2 rules out standard "polynomial-time polynomial-loss" reductions. More generally, the theorem implies that if the running time $T_M(\cdot)$ of the reduction is sub-exponential and the adversary-dependent security loss $\epsilon_{M,1}(\cdot)$ is polynomial (as expected), then the adversary-independent security loss $\epsilon_{M,2}(\cdot)$ must be exponential (thus even ruling out constructions based on SVL instances with *sub-exponential* average-case hardness).

In what follows we first describe the oracle, denoted $\mathcal{O}_{SVL}$, on which we rely for proving Theorem 3.2. Then, we describe the structure of the proof, showing that relative to the oracle $\mathcal{O}_{SVL}$ there exists a hard-on-average distribution of SVL instances, but there are no one-way functions. For the remainder of this section we remind the reader that a *q-query algorithm* is an oracle-aided algorithm A such that for any oracle $\mathcal{O}$ and input $x \in \{0,1\}^*$, the computation $A^{\mathcal{O}}(x)$ consists of at most $q(|x|)$ oracle calls to $\mathcal{O}$.

The oracle $\mathcal{O}_{SVL}$. The oracle $\mathcal{O}_{SVL}$ is a valid SVL instance $\{(S_n, V_n, L(n))\}_{n \in \mathbb{N}}$ that is sampled via the following process for every $n \in \mathbb{N}$:

- Let $L(n) = 2^{n/2}$, $x_0 = 0^n$, and uniformly sample distinct elements $x_1, \ldots, x_{L(n)} \leftarrow \{0,1\}^n \setminus \{0^n\}$.
- The successor function $S_n : \{0,1\}^n \rightarrow \{0,1\}^n$ is defined as

$$S_n(x) = \begin{cases} x_{i+1} & \text{if } x = x_i \text{ for some } i \in \{0, \ldots, L(n) - 1\} \\ x & \text{otherwise} \end{cases}.$$

- The verification function $V_n : \{0,1\}^n \times [2^n] \rightarrow \{0,1\}$ is defined in a manner that is consistent with S_n (i.e., V_n is defined such that the instance is valid).

Part I: $\mathcal{O}_{\mathsf{SVL}}$ is a hard-on-average SVL instance. We show that the oracle $\mathcal{O}_{\mathsf{SVL}}$ itself is a hard-on-average SVL instance, which implies in particular that relative to the oracle $\mathcal{O}_{\mathsf{SVL}}$ there exists a hard-on-average distribution of SVL instances. We prove the following claim stating that, in fact, the oracle $\mathcal{O}_{\mathsf{SVL}}$ is an *exponentially* hard-on-average SVL instance (even without an index-generation algorithm):

Claim 3.3. *For every $q(n)$-query algorithm M, where $q(n) \leq L(n) - 1$, it holds that*

$$\Pr\left[M^{\mathcal{O}_{\mathsf{SVL}}}(1^n) \ solves \ (\mathsf{S}_n, \mathsf{V}_n, L(n))\right] \leq \frac{(q(n)+1) \cdot L(n)}{2^n - q(n) - 1}$$

for all sufficiently large $n \in \mathbb{N}$, where the probability is taken over the choice of the oracle $\mathcal{O}_{\mathsf{SVL}} = \{(\mathsf{S}_n, \mathsf{V}_n, L(n))\}_{n \in \mathbb{N}}$ as described above.

The proof of the above claim is based on the following, rather intuitive, observation: Since the line $0^n \to x_1 \to \cdots \to x_{L(n)}$ is *sparse* and *uniformly sampled*, then any algorithm performing $q = q(n)$ oracle queries should not be able to query $\mathcal{O}_{\mathsf{SVL}}$ with any element on the line beyond the first q elements $0^n, x_1, \ldots, x_{q-1}$. In particular, for our choice of parameters, any such algorithm should have only an exponentially-small probability of reaching $x_{L(n)}$.

Part II: Inverting oracle-aided functions relative to $\mathcal{O}_{\mathsf{SVL}}$. We show that any oracle-aided function $F^{\mathcal{O}_{\mathsf{SVL}}}(\cdot)$ computable in time $t(n)$ can be inverted with high probability by an inverter that issues roughly $t(n)^4$ oracle queries. We prove the following claim:

Claim 3.4. *For every deterministic oracle-aided function F that is computable in time $t(n)$ there exists a $q(n)$-query algorithm $\mathcal{A}$, where $q(n) = O(t(n)^4)$, such that*

$$\Pr\left[\mathcal{A}^{\mathcal{O}_{\mathsf{SVL}}}\left(F^{\mathcal{O}_{\mathsf{SVL}}}(x)\right) \in \left(F^{\mathcal{O}_{\mathsf{SVL}}}\right)^{-1}\left(F^{\mathcal{O}_{\mathsf{SVL}}}(x)\right)\right] \geq \frac{1}{2}$$

for all sufficiently large $n \in \mathbb{N}$ and for every $x \in \{0,1\}^n$, where the probability is taken over the choice of the oracle $\mathcal{O}_{\mathsf{SVL}} = \{(\mathsf{S}_n, \mathsf{V}_n, L(n))\}_{n \in \mathbb{N}}$ as described above. Moreover, the algorithm $\mathcal{A}$ can be implemented in time polynomial in $q(n)$ given access to a PSPACE-complete oracle.

The proof of the above claim is based on the following approach. Consider the value $y = F^{\mathcal{O}_{\mathsf{SVL}}}(x)$ that is given as input to the inverter $\mathcal{A}$. Since F is computable in time $t = t(n)$, it can issue at most t oracle queries and therefore the observation used for proving Claim 3.3 implies that the computation $F^{\mathcal{O}_{\mathsf{SVL}}}(x)$ should not query $\mathcal{O}_{\mathsf{SVL}}$ with any elements on the line $0^n \to x_1 \to \cdots \to x_{L(n)}$ except for the first t elements $x_0, x_1, \ldots, x_{t-1}$. In this case, any S_n-query α in the computation $F^{\mathcal{O}_{\mathsf{SVL}}}(x)$ can be answered as follows: If $\alpha = x_i$ for some $i \in \{0, \ldots, t-1\}$ then the answer is x_{i+1}, and otherwise the answer is α. Similarly, any V_n-query (α, j) in the computation $F^{\mathcal{O}_{\mathsf{SVL}}}(x)$ can be answered as follows: If $(\alpha, j) = (x_i, i)$ for some $i \in \{0, \ldots, t-1\}$ then the answer is 1, and otherwise the answer is 0.

This observation gives rise to the following inverter $\mathcal{A}$: First perform t queries to S_n for discovering $x_1, \ldots, x_t$, and then invert $y = F^{\mathcal{O}_{\mathsf{SVL}}}(x)$ relative to the oracle $\widetilde{\mathcal{O}_{\mathsf{SVL}}}$ defined via the following successor function $\widetilde{\mathsf{S}}_n$:

$$\widetilde{\mathsf{S}}_n(\alpha) = \begin{cases} x_{i+1} \text{ if } \alpha = x_i \text{ for some } i \in \{0, \ldots, t-1\} \\ \alpha \quad \text{otherwise} \end{cases} .$$

The formal proof is in fact more subtle, and requires a significant amount of caution when inverting $y = F^{\mathcal{O}_{\mathsf{SVL}}}(x)$ relative to the oracle $\widetilde{\mathcal{O}_{\mathsf{SVL}}}$. Specifically, the inverter $\mathcal{A}$ should find an input $\widetilde{x}$ such that the computations $F^{\widetilde{\mathcal{O}_{\mathsf{SVL}}}}(\widetilde{x})$ and $F^{\mathcal{O}_{\mathsf{SVL}}}(\widetilde{x})$ do not query the oracles $\widetilde{\mathcal{O}_{\mathsf{SVL}}}$ and $\mathcal{O}_{\mathsf{SVL}}$, respectively, with any of $x_t, \ldots, x_{L(n)}$. In this case, we show that indeed $F^{\mathcal{O}_{\mathsf{SVL}}}(\widetilde{x}) = y$ and the inverter is successful.

4   Average-Case PPAD Hardness Does Not Imply Unique-TFNP Hardness

In this section we prove that there is no fully black-box construction of a hard-on-average distribution of TFNP instances having a unique solution from a hard-on-average distribution of instances of a PPAD-complete problem (proving, in particular, Theorem 1.3). Our result is obtained by presenting a distribution of oracles relative to which the following two properties hold:

1. There exists a hard-on-average distribution of instances of a PPAD-complete problem (specifically, we consider the source-or-sink problem).
2. There are no hard-on-average distributions over TFNP instances having a unique solution.

Recall that a TFNP instance with a unique solution, denoted a unique-TFNP instance (see Definitions 2.3 and 2.5), is of the form $\{\mathsf{Gen}_n, C_n\}_{n \in \mathbb{N}}$, where for every $n \in \mathbb{N}$ and for every index σ produced by Gen_n it holds that $C_n(\sigma, \cdot) : \{0,1\}^n \to \{0,1\}$ and there is a unique $x^* \in \{0,1\}^n$ such that $C_n(\sigma, x) = 1$. In particular, for any *valid* SVL instance $(\mathsf{Gen}, \mathsf{S}, \mathsf{V}, T)$ it holds that $(\mathsf{Gen}, \mathsf{V}(\cdot, \cdot, T))$ is a TFNP instance that has a unique solution since for every σ produced by Gen there is exactly one value x^* for which $\mathsf{V}(\sigma, x^*, T) = 1$. Therefore, our result shows, in particular, that there is no fully black-box construction of a hard-on-average distribution of SVL instances from a hard-on-average distribution of instances of a PPAD-complete problem[5].

Recall that a source-or-sink instance is of the form $\{(\mathsf{Gen}_n, \mathsf{S}_n, \mathsf{P}_n)\}_{n \in \mathbb{N}}$, where for every $n \in \mathbb{N}$ and for every index σ produced by Gen_n it holds that $\mathsf{S}_n(\sigma, \cdot) : \{0,1\}^n \to \{0,1\}^n$ and $\mathsf{P}_n(\sigma, \cdot) : \{0,1\}^n \to \{0,1\}^n$. The following definition tailors the standard notion of a fully black-box construction to the specific primitives under consideration.

---

[5] Recall that constructions in the opposite direction do exist: Any hard-on-average distribution of SVL instances can be used in a black-box manner to construct a hard-on-average distribution of instances of a PPAD-complete problem [1,8].

Definition 4.1. *A fully black-box construction of a hard-on-average distribution of unique-TFNP instances from a hard-on-average distribution of source-or-sink instances consists of a sequence of polynomial-size oracle-aided circuits* $C = \{\text{Gen}_n, C_n\}_{n \in \mathbb{N}}$, *an oracle-aided algorithm M that runs in time $T_M(\cdot)$, and functions $\epsilon_{M,1}(\cdot)$ and $\epsilon_{M,2}(\cdot)$, such that the following conditions hold:*

- **Correctness**: *For any source-or-sink instance $\mathcal{O}_{\text{PPAD}}$, for any $n \in \mathbb{N}$, and for any index σ produced by $\text{Gen}_n^{\mathcal{O}_{\text{PPAD}}}$, there exists a unique $x^* \in \{0,1\}^n$ such that $C_n^{\mathcal{O}_{\text{PPAD}}}(\sigma, x^*) = 1$.*
- **Black-box proof of security**: *For any source-or-sink instance $\mathcal{O}_{\text{PPAD}} = \{(\text{Gen}'_n, \mathsf{S}_n, \mathsf{P}_n)\}_{n \in \mathbb{N}}$, for any oracle-aided algorithm $\mathcal{A}$ that runs in time $T_{\mathcal{A}} = T_{\mathcal{A}}(n)$, and for any function $\epsilon_{\mathcal{A}}(\cdot)$, if*

$$\Pr\left[\mathcal{A}^{\mathcal{O}_{\text{PPAD}}}(1^n, \sigma) = x^* \text{ s.t. } C_n^{\mathcal{O}_{\text{PPAD}}}(\sigma, x^*) = 1\right] \geq \epsilon_{\mathcal{A}}(n)$$

for infinitely many values of $n \in \mathbb{N}$, where the probability is taken over the choice of $\sigma \leftarrow \text{Gen}_n()$ and over the internal randomness of $\mathcal{A}$, then

$$\Pr\left[M^{\mathcal{A}, \mathcal{O}_{\text{PPAD}}}(1^n, \sigma') \text{ solves } (\mathsf{S}_n(\sigma', \cdot), \mathsf{P}_n(\sigma', \cdot))\right]$$
$$\geq \epsilon_{M,1}\left(T_{\mathcal{A}}(n)/\epsilon_{\mathcal{A}}(n)\right) \cdot \epsilon_{M,2}(n)$$

for infinitely many values of $n \in \mathbb{N}$, where the probability is taken over the choice of $\sigma' \leftarrow \text{Gen}'_n()$ and over the internal randomness of M.

We note that, as in Definition 3.1, we split the security loss in the above definition to an adversary-dependent security loss and an adversary-independent security loss, as this allows us to capture constructions where one of these losses is super-polynomial whereas the other is polynomial. Equipped with the above definition we prove the following theorem in the full version of this paper [33]:

Theorem 4.2. *Let $(C, M, T_M, \epsilon_{M,1}, \epsilon_{M,2})$ be a fully black-box construction of a hard-on-average distribution of unique-TFNP instances from a hard-on-average distribution of source-or-sink instances. Then, at least one of the following properties holds:*

1. $T_M(n) \geq 2^{\zeta n}$ *for some constant $\zeta > 0$ (i.e., the reduction runs in exponential time).*
2. $\epsilon_{M,1}(n^c) \cdot \epsilon_{M,2}(n) \leq 2^{-n/10}$ *for some constant $c > 1$ (i.e., the security loss is exponential).*

In particular, Theorem 4.2 rules out standard "polynomial-time polynomial-loss" reductions. More generally, the theorem implies that if the running time $T_M(\cdot)$ of the reduction is sub-exponential and the adversary-dependent security loss $\epsilon_{M,1}(\cdot)$ is polynomial (as expected), then the adversary-independent security loss $\epsilon_{M,2}(\cdot)$ must be exponential (thus even ruling out constructions based on SVL instances with *sub-exponential* average-case hardness).

In what follows we first describe the oracle, denoted $\mathcal{O}_{\text{PPAD}}$, on which we rely for proving Theorem 4.2. Then, we describe the structure of the proof, showing that relative to the oracle $\mathcal{O}_{\text{PPAD}}$ there exists a hard-on-average distribution of source-or-sink instances, but there are no hard-on-average unique-TFNP instances. For the remainder of this section we remind the reader that a q-*query algorithm* is an oracle-aided algorithm A such that for any oracle $\mathcal{O}$ and input $x \in \{0,1\}^*$, the computation $A^{\mathcal{O}}(x)$ consists of at most $q(|x|)$ oracle calls to $\mathcal{O}$.

The oracle $\mathcal{O}_{\mathsf{PPAD}}$. The oracle $\mathcal{O}_{\mathsf{PPAD}}$ is a source-or-sink instance $\{(\mathsf{S}_n, \mathsf{P}_n)\}_{n \in \mathbb{N}}$ that is based on the same sparse structure used to define the oracle $\mathcal{O}_{\mathsf{SVL}}$ in Sect. 3. The oracle $\mathcal{O}_{\mathsf{PPAD}}$ is sampled via the following process for every $n \in \mathbb{N}$:

- Let $L(n) = 2^{n/2}$, $x_0 = 0^n$, and uniformly sample distinct elements $x_1, \ldots, x_{L(n)} \leftarrow \{0,1\}^n \setminus \{0^n\}$.
- The successor function $\mathsf{S}_n : \{0,1\}^n \to \{0,1\}^n$ is defined as

$$\mathsf{S}_n(x) = \begin{cases} x_{i+1} & \text{if } x = x_i \text{ for some } i \in \{0, \ldots, L(n) - 1\} \\ x & \text{otherwise} \end{cases}.$$

- The predecessor function $\mathsf{P}_n : \{0,1\}^n \to \{0,1\}^n$ is defined in a manner that is consistent with the successor function S_n:

$$\mathsf{P}_n(x) = \begin{cases} x_{i-1} & \text{if } x = x_i \text{ for some } i \in \{1, \ldots, L(n)\} \\ x & \text{otherwise} \end{cases}.$$

Note that the oracle $\mathcal{O}_{\mathsf{PPAD}}$ corresponds to a source-or-sink instance that consists of the single line $0^n \to x_1 \to \cdots \to x_{L(n)}$, and therefore the only solution to this instance is the element $x_{L(n)}$.

Part I: $\mathcal{O}_{\mathsf{PPAD}}$ is a hard-on-average source-or-sink instance. We show that the oracle $\mathcal{O}_{\mathsf{PPAD}}$ itself is a hard-on-average source-or-sink instance, which implies in particular that relative to the oracle $\mathcal{O}_{\mathsf{PPAD}}$ there exists a hard-on-average distribution of instances to the source-or-sink problem. We prove the following claim stating that, in fact, the oracle $\mathcal{O}_{\mathsf{PPAD}}$ is an *exponentially* hard-on-average source-or-sink instance (even without an index-generation algorithm):

Claim 4.3. *For every $q(n)$-query algorithm M, where $q(n) \leq L(n) - 1$, it holds that*

$$\Pr\left[M^{\mathcal{O}_{\mathsf{PPAD}}}(1^n) \text{ solves } (\mathsf{S}_n, \mathsf{P}_n)\right] \leq \frac{(q(n) + 1) \cdot L(n)}{2^n - q(n) - 1}$$

for all sufficiently large $n \in \mathbb{N}$, where the probability is taken over the choice of the oracle $\mathcal{O}_{\mathsf{PPAD}} = \{(\mathsf{S}_n, \mathsf{P}_n)\}_{n \in \mathbb{N}}$ as described above.

The proof of the claim, which is provided in the full version of this paper [33], is based on an observation similar to the one used for proving Claim 3.3: Since the line $0^n \to x_1 \to \cdots \to x_{L(n)}$ is *sparse* and *uniformly sampled*, then any algorithm performing $q = q(n)$ oracle queries should not be able to query $\mathcal{O}_{\mathsf{PPAD}}$ with any element on the line beyond the first q elements $x_0, x_1, \ldots, x_{q-1}$. In particular, for our choice of parameters, any such algorithm should have only an exponentially-small probability of reaching $x_{L(n)}$.

Part II: Solving oracle-aided unique-TFNP instances relative to $\mathcal{O}_{\mathsf{PPAD}}$. We show that any oracle-aided unique-TFNP instance $\{\mathsf{Gen}_n, C_n\}_{n \in \mathbb{N}}$, where Gen_n and C_n are circuits that contain at most $q(n)$ oracle gates, can always be solved by an algorithm that issues roughly $q(n)^2$ oracle queries. We prove the following claim:

Claim 4.4. *Let $C = \{\mathsf{Gen}_n, C_n\}_{n \in \mathbb{N}}$ be an oracle-aided unique-TFNP instance, where Gen_n and C_n are circuits that contain at most $q(n)$ oracle gates each for every $n \in \mathbb{N}$. If C satisfies the correctness requirement stated in Definition 4.1, then there exists an $O(q(n)^2)$-query algorithm $\mathcal{A}$ such that*

$$\Pr\left[\mathcal{A}^{\mathcal{O}_{\mathsf{PPAD}}}(1^n, \sigma) = x^* \text{ s.t. } C_n^{\mathcal{O}_{\mathsf{PPAD}}}(\sigma, x^*) = 1\right] = 1$$

for every $n \in \mathbb{N}$, where the probability is taken over the choice of the oracle $\mathcal{O}_{\mathsf{PPAD}} = \{(\mathsf{S}_n, \mathsf{P}_n)\}_{n \in \mathbb{N}}$ as described above and over the choice of $\sigma \leftarrow \mathsf{Gen}_n^{\mathcal{O}_{\mathsf{PPAD}}}()$. Moreover, the algorithm $\mathcal{A}$ can be implemented in time $q(n)^2 \cdot \mathrm{poly}(n)$ given access to a PSPACE-complete oracle.

For proving Claim 4.4, one might be tempted to follow the same approach used for proving Claim 3.4, based on the sparse and uniform structure of the oracle. However, as discussed in Sect. 1.3, this approach seems to completely fail.

Our proof of Claim 4.4, which is provided in the full version of this paper [33], is obtained by building upon Rudich's classic proof for ruling out black-box constructions of one-way permutations based on one-way functions [34]. We show, by extending and refining Rudich's proof technique, that his approach provides a rich framework that allows to bound not only the limitations of one-way functions as a building block, but even the limitations of *significantly more structured* primitives as building blocks. Specifically, our proof of Claim 4.4 extends Rudich's technique for bounding the limitations of hard-on-average source-or-sink instances.

5 One-Way Functions Do Not Imply Bounded-TFNP Hardness

In this section we prove that there is no fully black-box construction of a hard-on-average distribution of TFNP instances having a bounded number of solutions from a one-way function. Our result is obtained by presenting a distribution of oracles relative to which the following two properties hold:

1. There exists a one-way function.
2. There are no hard-on-average distributions of TFNP instances having a bounded number of solutions. Specifically, our result will apply to any sub-exponential number of solutions.

Recall that a TFNP instance with bounded number $k(\cdot)$ of solutions, denoted a k-bounded TFNP instance (see Definitions 2.3 and 2.5), is of the form $\{\mathsf{Gen}_n, C_n\}_{n \in \mathbb{N}}$, where for every $n \in \mathbb{N}$ and for every index σ produced by Gen_n it holds that $C_n(\sigma, \cdot) : \{0, 1\}^n \to \{0, 1\}$, and there is at least one and at most

$k(n)$ distinct inputs $x \in \{0,1\}^n$ such that $C_n(\sigma, x) = 1$ (any one of these x's is a solution). In particular, as discussed in Sect. 4, any *valid* SVL instance yields a 1-bounded TFNP instance (i.e., a unique-TFNP instance as defined in Sect. 4), and therefore our result rules out fully black-box constructions of a hard-on-average distribution of SVL instances from a one-way function. Similarly, any source-or-sink instance which consists of at most $(k + 1)/2$ disjoint lines yields a k-bounded TFNP instance, and therefore our result rules out fully black-box constructions of a hard-on-average distribution of source-or-sink instances with a bounded number of disjoint lines from a one-way function.

In this section we model a one-way function as a sequence $f = \{f_n\}_{n \in \mathbb{N}}$, where for every $n \in \mathbb{N}$ it holds that $f_n : \{0,1\}^n \to \{0,1\}^n$. The following definition tailors the standard notion of a fully black-box construction to the specific primitives under consideration.

Definition 5.1. *A fully black-box construction of a hard-on-average distribution of k-bounded TFNP instances from a one-way function consists of a sequence of polynomial-size oracle-aided circuits $C = \{\mathsf{Gen}_n, C_n\}_{n \in \mathbb{N}}$, an oracle-aided algorithm M that runs in time $T_M(\cdot)$, and functions $\epsilon_{M,1}(\cdot)$ and $\epsilon_{M,2}(\cdot)$, such that the following conditions hold:*

- **Correctness**: *For any function $f = \{f_n\}_{n \in \mathbb{N}}$, for any $n \in \mathbb{N}$, and for any index σ produced by Gen_n^f, there exists at least one and at most $k(n)$ distinct inputs $x \in \{0,1\}^n$ such that $C_n^f(\sigma, x) = 1$.*
- **Black-box proof of security**: *For any function $f = \{f_n\}_{n \in \mathbb{N}}$, for any oracle-aided algorithm $\mathcal{A}$ that runs in time $T_\mathcal{A} = T_\mathcal{A}(n)$, and for any function $\epsilon_\mathcal{A}(\cdot)$, if*

$$\Pr\left[\mathcal{A}^f\left(1^n, \sigma\right) = x \text{ s.t. } C_n^f(\sigma, x) = 1\right] \geq \epsilon_\mathcal{A}(n)$$

for infinitely many values of $n \in \mathbb{N}$, where the probability is taken over the choice of $\sigma \leftarrow \mathsf{Gen}_n^f()$ and over the internal randomness of $\mathcal{A}$, then

$$\Pr\left[M^{\mathcal{A}, f}\left(f_n(x)\right) \in f_n^{-1}\left(f_n(x)\right)\right] \geq \epsilon_{M,1}\left(T_\mathcal{A}(n)/\epsilon_\mathcal{A}(n)\right) \cdot \epsilon_{M,2}'(n)$$

for infinitely many values of $n \in \mathbb{N}$, where the probability is taken over the choice of $x \leftarrow \{0,1\}^n$ and over the internal randomness of M.

We note that, as in Definitions 3.1 and 4.1, we split the security loss in the above definition to an adversary-dependent security loss and an adversary-independent security loss, as this allows us to capture constructions where one of these losses is super-polynomial whereas the other is polynomial. Equipped with the above definition we prove the following theorem in the full version of this paper [33]:

Theorem 5.2. *Let $(C, M, T_M, \epsilon_{M,1}, \epsilon_{M,2})$ be a fully black-box construction of a hard-on-average distribution of k-bounded TFNP instances from a one-way function. Then, at least one of the following properties holds:*

1. $T_M(n) \geq 2^{\zeta n}$ *for some constant $\zeta > 0$ (i.e., the reduction runs in exponential time).*

2. $k(T_M(n)) \geq 2^{n/8}$ *(i.e., the number of solutions, as a function of the reduction's running time, is exponential).*

3. $\epsilon_{M,1}(k(n) \cdot n^c) \cdot \epsilon_{M,2}(n) \leq 2^{-n/2}$ *for some constant $c > 1$ (i.e., the security loss is exponential).*

In particular, Theorem 5.2 rules out standard "polynomial-time polynomial-loss" reductions resulting in at most $2^{n^{o(1)}}$ solutions. That is, if $T_M(n)$, $\epsilon_{M,1}(n)$ and $\epsilon_{M,2}(n)$ are all polynomials in n, then the number $k(n)$ of solutions must be at least sub-exponential in n (i.e., $k(n) \geq 2^{n^{\Theta(1)}}$). In addition, if the number $k(n)$ of solutions is constant, the running time $T_M(\cdot)$ of the reduction is sub-exponential, and the adversary-dependent security loss $\epsilon_{M,1}(\cdot)$ is polynomial (all as in [8]), then the adversary-independent security loss $\epsilon_{M,2}(\cdot)$ must be exponential (thus even ruling out constructions based on one-way functions with *sub-exponential* hardness).

In what follows we first describe the oracle, denoted f, on which we rely for proving Theorem 5.2. Then, we describe the structure of the proof, showing that relative to the oracle f there exists a one-way function, but there are no hard-on-average bounded-TFNP instances. For the remainder of this section we remind the reader that a *q-query algorithm* is an oracle-aided algorithm A such that for any oracle $\mathcal{O}$ and input $x \in \{0,1\}^*$, the computation $A^{\mathcal{O}}(x)$ consists of at most $q(|x|)$ oracle calls to $\mathcal{O}$.

The oracle f. The oracle f is a sequence $\{f_n\}_{n \in \mathbb{N}}$ where for every $n \in \mathbb{N}$ the function $f_n : \{0,1\}^n \to \{0,1\}^n$ is sampled uniformly from the set of all functions mapping n-bit inputs to n-bit outputs.

Part I: f is a one-way function. We prove the following standard claim stating that the oracle f is an exponentially-hard one-way function.

Claim 5.3. *For every $q(n)$-query algorithm M it holds that*

$$\Pr\left[M^f\left(f_n(x)\right) \in f_n^{-1}\left(f_n(x)\right)\right] \leq \frac{2(q(n)+1)}{2^n - q(n)}$$

for all sufficiently large $n \in \mathbb{N}$, where the probability is taken over the choice of $x \leftarrow \{0,1\}^n$, and over the choice of the oracle $f = \{f_n\}_{n \in \mathbb{N}}$ as described above.

Part II: Solving oracle-aided bounded-TFNP instances relative to f. We show that any oracle-aided k-bounded TFNP instance $C = \{C_n\}_{n \in \mathbb{N}}$, where each C_n is a circuit that contains at most $q(n)$ oracle gates, can always be solved by an algorithm that issues roughly $k(n) \cdot q(n)^2$ oracle queries. We prove the following claim:

Claim 5.4. *Let $C = \{\mathsf{Gen}_n, C_n\}_{n \in \mathbb{N}}$ be an oracle-aided $k(n)$-bounded TFNP instance, where Gen_n and C_n are circuits that contain at most $q(n)$ oracle gates each for every $n \in \mathbb{N}$. If C satisfies the correctness requirement stated in Definition 5.1, then there exists an $O(k(n) \cdot q(n)^2)$-query algorithm $\mathcal{A}$ such that*

$$\Pr\left[\mathcal{A}^f\left(1^n, \sigma\right) = x \text{ s.t. } C_n^f(\sigma, x) = 1\right] = 1$$

for all $n \in \mathbb{N}$, where the probability is taken over the choice of the oracle $f = \{f_n\}_{n \in \mathbb{N}}$ as described above and over the choice of $\sigma \leftarrow \mathsf{Gen}_n^f()$. Moreover, the algorithm $\mathcal{A}$ can be implemented in time $k(n) \cdot q(n)^2 \cdot \mathsf{poly}(n)$ given access to a PSPACE-complete oracle.

Our proof of Claim 5.4, which is provided in the full version of this paper [33], is obtained by further generalizing our extension of Rudich's classic proof technique [34]. As discussed in Sect. 4, by extending and refining Rudich's proof technique once again, we show that his approach allows to rule out even constructions of bounded-TFNP instances.

6 Public-Key Cryptography Does Not Imply Bounded-TFNP Hardness

In this section we generalize the result proved in Sect. 5 from considering a one-way function as the underlying building block to considering a collection of injective trapdoor functions as the underlying building block (thus proving, in particular, Theorem 1.4 and Corollary 1.5). Specifically, we prove that there is no fully black-box construction of a hard-on-average distribution of TFNP instances having a bounded number of solutions from a collection of injective trapdoor functions. Our result is obtained by presenting a distribution of oracles relative to which the following two properties hold:

1. There exists a collection of injective trapdoor functions.
2. There are no hard-on-average distributions of TFNP instances having a bounded number of solutions. Specifically, our result will apply to any subexponential number of solutions, exactly as in Sect. 5.

From the technical perspective, instead of considering an oracle $f = \{f_n\}_{n \in \mathbb{N}}$ where for every $n \in \mathbb{N}$ the function $f_n : \{0,1\}^n \rightarrow \{0,1\}^n$ is sampled uniformly, we consider a more structured oracle, $\mathcal{O}_{\mathsf{TDF}}$, corresponding to a collection of injective trapdoor functions. Proving that the oracle $\mathcal{O}_{\mathsf{TDF}}$ is indeed hard to invert is quite standard (based, for example, on the approach of Haitner et al. [23]). However, showing that relative to the oracle $\mathcal{O}_{\mathsf{TDF}}$ we can solve bounded-TFNP instances is significantly more challenging than the corresponding proof relative to the oracle f.

We say that $\tau = \{(\mathsf{KG}_n, \mathsf{F}_n, \mathsf{F}_n^{-1})\}_{n \in \mathbb{N}}$ is a collection of injective trapdoor functions if for every $n \in \mathbb{N}$ and for every pair $(\mathsf{td}, \mathsf{pk})$ produced by $\mathsf{KG}_n()$, the function $\mathsf{F}_n(\mathsf{pk}, \cdot) : \{0,1\}^n \rightarrow \{0,1\}^m$ is injective (for some $m \geq n$) and the function $\mathsf{F}_n^{-1}(\mathsf{td}, \cdot)$ computes it inverse whenever an inverse exists (i.e., it outputs $\perp$ on all values y that are not in the image of the function $\mathsf{F}_n(\mathsf{pk}, \cdot)$) – see Sect. 2.2 for more details. The following definition tailors the standard notion of a fully black-box construction to the specific primitives under consideration.

Definition 6.1. *A fully black-box construction of a hard-on-average distribution of k-bounded TFNP instances from a collection of injective trapdoor functions consists of a sequence of polynomial-size oracle-aided circuits $C = \{\mathsf{Gen}_n,$*

$C_n\}_{n\in\mathbb{N}}$, an oracle-aided algorithm M that runs in time $T_M(\cdot)$, and functions $\epsilon_{M,1}(\cdot)$ and $\epsilon_{M,2}(\cdot)$, such that the following conditions hold:

- **Correctness**: For any collection τ of injective trapdoor functions, for any $n \in \mathbb{N}$, and for any index σ produced by Gen_n^τ, there exists at least one and at most $k(n)$ distinct inputs $x \in \{0,1\}^n$ such that $C_n^\tau(\sigma, x) = 1$.
- **Black-box proof of security**: For any collection $\tau = \big\{(\mathsf{KG}_n, \mathsf{F}_n, \mathsf{F}_n^{-1})\big\}_{n\in\mathbb{N}}$ of injective trapdoor functions, for any oracle-aided algorithm $\mathcal{A}$ that runs in time $T_\mathcal{A} = T_\mathcal{A}(n)$, and for any function $\epsilon_\mathcal{A}(\cdot)$, if

$$\Pr\left[\mathcal{A}^\tau\left(1^n, \sigma\right) = x \text{ s.t. } C_n^\tau(\sigma, x) = 1\right] \geq \epsilon_\mathcal{A}(n)$$

for infinitely many values of $n \in \mathbb{N}$, where the probability is taken over the choice of $\sigma \leftarrow \mathsf{Gen}_n^\tau()$ and $x \leftarrow \{0,1\}^n$, and over the internal randomness of $\mathcal{A}$, then

$$\Pr\left[M^{\mathcal{A},\tau}\left(\mathsf{pk}, \mathsf{F}_n(\mathsf{pk}, x)\right) = x\right] \geq \epsilon_{M,1}\left(T_\mathcal{A}(n)/\epsilon_\mathcal{A}(n)\right) \cdot \epsilon_{M,2}(n)$$

for infinitely many values of $n \in \mathbb{N}$, where the probability is taken over the choice of $(\mathsf{td}, \mathsf{pk}) \leftarrow \mathsf{KG}_n()$, $x \leftarrow \{0,1\}^n$, and over the internal randomness of M.

We note that, as in Definitions 3.1, 4.1 and 5.1, we split the security loss in the above definition to an adversary-dependent security loss and an adversary-independent security loss, as this allows us to capture constructions where one of these losses is super-polynomial whereas the other is polynomial. Equipped with the above definition we prove the following theorem in the full version of this paper [33] (generalizing Theorem 5.2):

Theorem 6.2. *Let $(C, M, T_M, \epsilon_{M,1}, \epsilon_{M,2})$ be a fully black-box construction of a hard-on-average distribution of k-bounded TFNP instances from a collection of injective trapdoor functions. Then, at least one of the following properties holds:*

1. *$T_M(n) \geq 2^{\zeta n}$ for some constant $\zeta > 0$ (i.e., the reduction runs in exponential time).*
2. *$k(T_M(n)) \geq 2^{n/8}$ (i.e., the number of solutions, as a function of the reduction's running time, is exponential).*
3. *$\epsilon_{M,1}(k(n) \cdot n^c) \cdot \epsilon_{M,2}(n) \leq 2^{-n/2}$ for some constant $c > 1$ (i.e., the security loss is exponential).*

In particular, and similarly to Theorem 5.2, Theorem 6.2 rules out standard "polynomial-time polynomial-loss" reductions resulting in at most $2^{n^{o(1)}}$ solutions. That is, if $T_M(n)$, $\epsilon_{M,1}(n)$ and $\epsilon_{M,2}(n)$ are all polynomials in n, then the number $k(n)$ of solutions must be at least sub-exponential in n (i.e., $k(n) \geq 2^{n^{\Theta(1)}}$). In addition, if the number $k(n)$ of solutions is constant, the running time $T_M(\cdot)$ of the reduction is sub-exponential, and the adversary-dependent security loss $\epsilon_{M,1}(\cdot)$ is polynomial (all as in [8]), then the adversary-independent security loss $\epsilon_{M,2}(\cdot)$ must be exponential (thus even ruling out constructions based on one-way functions with *sub-exponential* hardness). Given our claims in the remainder of this section, the proof of Theorem 6.2 is derived in a nearly identical to proof of 5.2, and is therefore omitted.

In what follows we first describe the oracle, denoted $\mathcal{O}_{\mathsf{TDF}}$, on which we rely for proving Theorem 6.2. Then, we describe the structure of the proof, and explain the main challenges in generalizing our proof from Sect. 5.

The oracle $\mathcal{O}_{\mathsf{TDF}}$. The oracle $\mathcal{O}_{\mathsf{TDF}}$ is a sequence of the form $\{(\mathsf{G}_n, \mathsf{F}_n, \mathsf{F}_n^{-1})\}_{n \in \mathbb{N}}$ that is sampled via the following process for every $n \in \mathbb{N}$:

- The function $\mathsf{G}_n : \{0,1\}^n \to \{0,1\}^{2n}$ is sampled uniformly from the set of all functions mapping n-bit inputs to n-bit outputs.
- For every $\mathsf{pk} \in \{0,1\}^{2n}$ the function $\mathsf{F}_n(\mathsf{pk}, \cdot) : \{0,1\}^n \to \{0,1\}^{2n}$ is sampled uniformly from the set of all *injective* functions mapping n-bit inputs to $2n$-bit outputs.
- For every $\mathsf{td} \in \{0,1\}^n$ and $y \in \{0,1\}^{2n}$ we set

$$\mathsf{F}_n^{-1}(\mathsf{td}, y) = \begin{cases} x & \text{if } \mathsf{F}_n(\mathsf{G}_n(\mathsf{td}), x) = y \\ \bot & \text{if no such } x \text{ exists} \end{cases}.$$

Part I: $\mathcal{O}_{\mathsf{TDF}}$ is a hard-to-invert collection of injective trapdoor functions. We show that the oracle $\mathcal{O}_{\mathsf{TDF}}$ naturally defines a hard-on-average collection of injective trapdoor functions. Specifically, the key-generation algorithm on input 1^n samples $\mathsf{td} \leftarrow \{0,1\}^n$ uniformly at random, and computes $\mathsf{pk} = \mathsf{G}_n(\mathsf{td})$ (where F_n and F_n^{-1} are used as the evaluation and inversion algorithms). We prove the following claim stating that collection of injective trapdoor functions is exponentially secure.

Claim 6.3. *For every $q(n)$-query algorithm M it holds that*

$$\Pr\left[M^{\mathcal{O}_{\mathsf{TDF}}}\left(\mathsf{G}_n(\mathsf{td}), \mathsf{F}_n(\mathsf{G}_n(\mathsf{td}), x)\right) = x\right] \leq \frac{4(q(n)+1)}{2^n - q(n)}$$

for all sufficiently large $n \in \mathbb{N}$, where the probability is taken over the choice of $\mathsf{td} \leftarrow \{0,1\}^n$, $x \leftarrow \{0,1\}^n$, *and the oracle* $\mathcal{O}_{\mathsf{TDF}} = \{(\mathsf{G}_n, \mathsf{F}_n, \mathsf{F}_n^{-1})\}_{n \in \mathbb{N}}$.

The proof of Claim 6.3, which is provided in the full version of this paper [33], is based on the observation that the inversion oracle F_n^{-1} is not quite useful. Specifically, the function G_n itself is uniformly chosen and thus hard to invert, and therefore any algorithm M that is given as input $(\mathsf{pk}, \mathsf{F}_n(\mathsf{pk}, x))$ should not be able to find the trapdoor td corresponding to $\mathsf{pk} = \mathsf{G}_n(\mathsf{td})$. Combining this with the fact that the function $\mathsf{F}_n(\mathsf{pk}, \cdot)$ is uniformly chosen and *length doubling*, such an algorithm M should not be able to find any y in its image, unless y was obtained as the result of a previous query (and, in this case, its inverse is already known). Therefore, the task of computing x given $(\mathsf{pk}, \mathsf{F}_n(\mathsf{pk}, x))$ essentially reduces to that of inverting a uniformly-sampled injective function.

Part II: Solving oracle-aided bounded-TFNP instances relative to $\mathcal{O}_{\mathsf{TDF}}$. We show that any oracle-aided k-bounded TFNP instance $C = \{\mathsf{Gen}_n,$

$C_n\}_{n\in\mathbb{N}}$, where Gen_n and C_n contain at most $q(n)$ oracle gates, and the input to each such gate is of length at most $q(n)$ bits, can always be solved with constant probability by an algorithm that issues roughly $k(n)^3 \cdot q(n)^9$ oracle queries. We prove the following claim:

Claim 6.4. *Let* $C = \{\mathsf{Gen}_n, C_n\}_{n\in\mathbb{N}}$ *be an oracle-aided k-bounded TFNP instance, where for every $n \in \mathbb{N}$ it holds that Gen_n and C_n are circuits that contain at most $q(n)$ oracle gates, and the input to each such gate is of length at most $q(n)$ bits. If C satisfies the correctness requirement stated in Definition 6.1, then there exists a $O(q(n)^9 \cdot k(n)^3)$-query algorithm $\mathcal{A}$ such that*

$$\Pr\left[\mathcal{A}^{\mathcal{O}_{\mathsf{TDF}}}\left(1^n, \sigma\right) = x \ s.t. \ C_n^{\mathcal{O}_{\mathsf{TDF}}}(\sigma, x) = 1\right] \geq \frac{1}{2}$$

for all $n \in \mathbb{N}$, where the probability is taken over the choice of the oracle $\mathcal{O}_{\mathsf{TDF}} = \{(\mathsf{G}_n, \mathsf{F}_n, \mathsf{F}_n^{-1})\}_{n\in\mathbb{N}}$ as described above and over the choice of $\sigma \leftarrow \mathsf{Gen}_n^{\mathcal{O}_{\mathsf{TDF}}}()$. Moreover, the algorithm $\mathcal{A}$ can be implemented in time $q(n)^9 \cdot k(n)^3 \cdot \mathsf{poly}(n)$ given access to a PSPACE-complete oracle.

The proof of Claim 6.4, which is provided in the full version of this paper [33], generalizes the proof of Claim 5.4 (which holds relative to the oracle f defined in Sect. 5). Recall that for the proof of Claim 5.4 we introduced an adversary that runs for $q + 1$ iterations, with the goal of discovering a new oracle query from the computation $C_n^f(\sigma, x^*)$ in each iteration where x^* is any fixed solution of the instance $C_n^f(\sigma, \cdot)$. This approach is based on the observation if no progress is made then there exists an oracle g' for which the instance $C_n^{g'}(\sigma, \cdot)$ has too many solutions. The oracle oracle g' can be constructed by "pasting together" partial information on the actual oracle f with full information on an additional oracle g that is partially-consistent with f.

When dealing with the oracle $\mathcal{O}_{\mathsf{TDF}}$, which is clearly more structured than just a single random function f, this argument becomes much more subtle. One may hope to follow a similar iteration-based approach and argue that if no progress is made then there exists an oracle $\mathcal{O}'_{\mathsf{TDF}}$ for which the instance $C_n^{\mathcal{O}'_{\mathsf{TDF}}}(\sigma, \cdot)$ has too many solutions. However, "pasting together" partial information on the actual oracle $\mathcal{O}_{\mathsf{TDF}}$ with full information on an additional injective trapdoor function oracle that is partially-consistent with $\mathcal{O}_{\mathsf{TDF}}$ may completely fail, as the resulting oracle may not turn out injective at all.

Our main observation is that although pasting together the two oracles may not always work (as in Sect. 5), it does work with high probability over the choice of the oracle $\mathcal{O}_{\mathsf{TDF}}$. By closely examining the way the two oracles are combined, we show that if the resulting oracle is not a valid collection of injective trapdoor functions, then one of the following "bad" events must have occurred:

- The adversary was able to "guess" an element pk for which there exists td such that $\mathsf{pk} = \mathsf{G}_n(\mathsf{td})$ without previously querying G_n with td.
- The adversary was able to "guess" a public key pk and an element y for which there exists an input x such that $y = \mathsf{F}_n(\mathsf{pk}, x)$ without previously querying F_n with (pk, x).

We show that the probability of each of these two events is small, as we choose both G_n and all functions $F_n(\mathsf{pk}, \cdot)$ to be length increasing and uniformly distributed.

Acknowledgments. We thank Nir Bitansky, Tim Roughgarden, Omer Paneth, and the TCC reviewers for their insightful comments and suggestions.

Alon Rosen is supported by ISF grant no. 1255/12, NSF-BSF Cyber Security and Privacy grant no. 2014/632, and by the ERC under the EU's Seventh Framework Programme (FP/2007-2013) ERC Grant Agreement no. 307952.

Gil Segev and Ido Shahaf are supported by the European Union's 7th Framework Program (FP7) via a Marie Curie Career Integration Grant (Grant No. 618094), by the European Union's Horizon 2020 Framework Program (H2020) via an ERC Grant (Grant No. 714253), by the Israel Science Foundation (Grant No. 483/13), by the Israeli Centers of Research Excellence (I-CORE) Program (Center No. 4/11), by the US-Israel Binational Science Foundation (Grant No. 2014632), and by a Google Faculty Research Award.

References

1. Abbot, T., Kane, D., Valiant, P.: On algorithms for Nash equilibria (2004). http://web.mit.edu/tabbott/Public/final.pdf
2. Asharov, G., Segev, G.: Limits on the power of indistinguishability obfuscation and functional encryption. In: Proceedings of the 56th Annual IEEE Symposium on Foundations of Computer Science, pp. 191–209 (2015)
3. Asharov, G., Segev, G.: On constructing one-way permutations from indistinguishability obfuscation. In: Kushilevitz, E., Malkin, T. (eds.) TCC 2016. LNCS, vol. 9563, pp. 512–541. Springer, Heidelberg (2016). doi:10.1007/978-3-662-49099-0_19
4. Barak, B., Goldreich, O., Impagliazzo, R., Rudich, S., Sahai, A., Vadhan, S., Yang, K.: On the (im)possibility of obfuscating programs. In: Kilian, J. (ed.) CRYPTO 2001. LNCS, vol. 2139, pp. 1–18. Springer, Heidelberg (2001). doi:10.1007/3-540-44647-8_1
5. Barak, B., Goldreich, O., Impagliazzo, R., Rudich, S., Sahai, A., Vadhan, S.P., Yang, K.: On the (im)possibility of obfuscating programs. J. ACM **59**(2), 6 (2012)
6. Barak, B., Mahmoody-Ghidary, M.: Merkle puzzles are optimal - an $O(n^2)$-query attack on any key exchange from a random oracle. In: Advances in Cryptology - CRYPTO 2009, pp. 374–390 (2009)
7. Beame, P., Cook, S.A., Edmonds, J., Impagliazzo, R., Pitassi, T.: The relative complexity of NP search problems. In: Proceedings of the 27th Annual ACM Symposium on Theory of Computing, pp. 303–314 (1995)
8. Bitansky, N., Paneth, O., Rosen, A.: On the cryptographic hardness of finding a Nash equilibrium. In: Proceedings of the 56th Annual IEEE Symposium on Foundations of Computer Science, pp. 1480–1498 (2015)
9. Bitansky, N., Paneth, O., Wichs, D.: Perfect structure on the edge of chaos. In: Kushilevitz, E., Malkin, T. (eds.) TCC 2016. LNCS, vol. 9562, pp. 474–502. Springer, Heidelberg (2016). doi:10.1007/978-3-662-49096-9_20
10. Brakerski, Z., Gentry, C., Halevi, S., Lepoint, T., Sahai, A., Tibouchi, M.: Cryptanalysis of the quadratic zero-testing of GGH. Cryptology ePrint Archive, Report 2015/845 (2015)

11. Chen, X., Deng, X., Teng, S.: Settling the complexity of computing two-player Nash equilibria. J. ACM **56**(3), 1–57 (2009)
12. Cheon, J.H., Fouque, P.-A., Lee, C., Minaud, B., Ryu, H.: Cryptanalysis of the new CLT multilinear map over the integers. Cryptology ePrint Archive, Report 2016/135 (2016)
13. Cheon, J.H., Han, K., Lee, C., Ryu, H., Stehlé, D.: Cryptanalysis of the multilinear map over the integers. In: Oswald, E., Fischlin, M. (eds.) EUROCRYPT 2015. LNCS, vol. 9056, pp. 3–12. Springer, Heidelberg (2015). doi:10.1007/978-3-662-46800-5_1
14. Cheon, J.H., Jeong, J., Lee, C.: An algorithm for NTRU problems and cryptanalysis of the GGH multilinear map without an encoding of zero. Cryptology ePrint Archive, Report 2016/139 (2016)
15. Cheon, J.H., Lee, C., Ryu, H.: Cryptanalysis of the new CLT multilinear maps. Cryptology ePrint Archive, Report 2015/934 (2015)
16. Cook, S.A., Impagliazzo, R., Yamakami, T.: A tight relationship between generic oracles and type-2 complexity theory. Inf. Comput. **137**(2), 159–170 (1997)
17. Coron, J., Gentry, C., Halevi, S., Lepoint, T., Maji, H.K., Miles, E., Raykova, M., Sahai, A., Tibouchi, M.: Zeroizing without low-level zeroes: new MMAP attacks and their limitations. In: Advances in Cryptology - CRYPTO 2015, pp. 247–266 (2015)
18. Daskalakis, C., Goldberg, P.W., Papadimitriou, C.H.: The complexity of computing a Nash equilibrium. SIAM J. Comput. **39**(1), 195–259 (2009)
19. Garg, S., Gentry, C., Halevi, S., Raykova, M., Sahai, A., Waters, B.: Candidate indistinguishability obfuscation and functional encryption for all circuits. In: Proceedings of the 54th Annual IEEE Symposium on Foundations of Computer Science, pp. 40–49 (2013)
20. Garg, S., Pandey, O., Srinivasan, A.: Revisiting the cryptographic hardness of finding a Nash equilibrium. In: Robshaw, M., Katz, J. (eds.) CRYPTO 2016. LNCS, vol. 9815, pp. 579–604. Springer, Heidelberg (2016). doi:10.1007/978-3-662-53008-5_20
21. Goldreich, O.: On security preserving reductions - revised terminology. Cryptology ePrint Archive, Report 2000/001 (2000)
22. Goldreich, O.: Foundations of Cryptography – Volume 1: Basic Techniques. Cambridge University Press, Cambridge (2001)
23. Haitner, I., Hoch, J.J., Reingold, O., Segev, G.: Finding collisions in interactive protocols - tight lower bounds on the round and communication complexities of statistically hiding commitments. SIAM J. Comput. **44**(1), 193–242 (2015)
24. Hirsch, M.D., Papadimitriou, C.H., Vavasis, S.A.: Exponential lower bounds for finding brouwer fix points. J. Complex. **5**(4), 379–416 (1989)
25. Hu, Y., Jia, H.: Cryptanalysis of GGH map. Cryptology ePrint Archive, Report 2015/301 (2015)
26. Hubácek, P., Naor, M., Yogev, E.: The journey from NP to TFNP hardness. In: Proceedings of the 8th Innovations in Theoretical Computer Science Conference (2017)
27. Impagliazzo, R., Rudich, S.: Limits on the provable consequences of one-way permutations. In: Proceedings of the 21st Annual ACM Symposium on Theory of Computing, pp. 44–61 (1989)
28. Luby, M.: Pseudorandomness and Cryptographic Applications. Princeton University Press, Princeton (1996)

29. Miles, E., Sahai, A., Zhandry, M.: Annihilation attacks for multilinear maps: cryptanalysis of indistinguishability obfuscation over GGH13. Cryptology ePrint Archive, Report 2016/147 (2016)
30. Minaud, B., Fouque, P.-A.: Cryptanalysis of the new multilinear map over the integers. Cryptology ePrint Archive, Report 2015/941 (2015)
31. Papadimitriou, C.H.: On the complexity of the parity argument and other inefficient proofs of existence. J. Comput. Syst. Sci. **48**(3), 498–532 (1994)
32. Reingold, O., Trevisan, L., Vadhan, S.: Notions of reducibility between cryptographic primitives. In: Naor, M. (ed.) TCC 2004. LNCS, vol. 2951, pp. 1–20. Springer, Heidelberg (2004). doi:10.1007/978-3-540-24638-1_1
33. Rosen, A., Segev, G., Shahaf, I.: Can PPAD hardness be based on standard cryptographic assumptions? Cryptology ePrint Archive, Report 2016/375 (2016)
34. Rudich, S.: Limits on the provable consequences of one-way functions. Ph.D. thesis, EECS Department, University of California, Berkeley (1988)
35. Sahai, A., Waters, B.: How to use indistinguishability obfuscation: deniable encryption, and more. In: Proceedings of the 46th Annual ACM Symposium on Theory of Computing, pp. 475–484 (2014)
36. Savani, R., von Stengel, B.: Exponentially many steps for finding a Nash equilibrium in a bimatrix game. In: Proceedings of the 45th Annual IEEE Symposium on Foundations of Computer Science, pp. 258–267 (2004)
37. Simon, D.R.: Finding collisions on a one-way street: can secure hash functions be based on general assumptions? In: Nyberg, K. (ed.) EUROCRYPT 1998. LNCS, vol. 1403, pp. 334–345. Springer, Heidelberg (1998). doi:10.1007/BFb0054137

Author Index

Printed in the United States
By Bookmasters